THE COMPLETE WORKS

OF

MENNO SIMON,

TRANSLATED FROM THE ORIGINAL

DUTCH OR HOLLAND,

Containing Renunciation of Popery, Foundation and Plain Instruction, The True Christian Faith, Concerning the New Birth, Cross of Christ, Pleasing Meditation on the Twenty-fifth Psalm, The Spiritual Resurrection, Excommunication, The Education of Children, Reply to Gellius Faber, A Supplication to Christians, Apology, Reply to John A'Lasco, The Triune, Eternal and True God, Father, Son and Holy Ghost, Christian Baptism, Reason Why, A Confession, Reply to Zylis, and Lemmekes, Replication, The Incarnation, Reply to Martin Micron, Jesus, the True Scriptural David, Letters, &c.

FIRST PART.

"The mouth of the righteous speaketh wisdom, and his tongue talketh of Judgment; the Law of his God is in his heart; none of his steps shall slide." Ps. 37: 30, 31.

"Remember them which have the rule over you, who have spoken unto you the word of God; whose faith follow, considering the end of their conversation." Heb. 13: 7

Published in 1871 by John F. Funk and Brother, Elkhart, Indiana

Published in 1983 by Pathway Publishers Aylmer, Ontario and Lagrange, Indiana

Reprinted in 1983 by Pathway Publishers
Printed in the United States of America

Second Printing, 1995

PUBLISHERS' PREFACE.

The writings of a good man, when read with an unbiased mind, and with a sincere desire to be profited and instructed, are always beneficial to those who read them; for "of the abundance of the heart the mouth speaketh," and "a good man, out of the good treasure of the heart bringeth forth good things."

Such writings may be the means of doing much good among men, especially in these times of worldly conformity, in which there is such a great opposition to the cross of Christ; in which men love ease and pleasure, and make many devices to avoid those self-denying principles of the religion of Jesus, and hope to gain the crown of life in some other way than that in which he himself walked, and pointed out to all his true followers; in which mankind are so much given over to the pursuit of the perishable things of this world, to honor, wealth and power, and are so deeply sunk in sin and unrighteousness; in which error and deception are so prevalent that on every side we hear the cry, "Lo, here is Christ," and "Lo, he is there," so that sometimes it seems almost impossible, for those who are not firmly established in the faith, to maintain themselves unmoved, and remain unshaken in the midst of this "crooked and perverse generation."

We believe that these works of the zealous and pious Menno, in which he protests so powerfully against the prevailing corruptions of the times, both in the church and in the ordinary walks of life; in high and in low places, or wherever found, and advocates with such uncompromising firmness and devotion, the imperative necessity of a true and sincere change of heart, through the regenerating power of the Holy Ghost, a new life, a pious and holy walk, which delights in good works, follows the footsteps of Jesus in love, humility, and meekness; is a light in the world, and labors for the glory of God and the salvation of *all men*, are well adapted to promote vital, christian piety, to strengthen and confirm the faith of believers, to encourage and cheer the weary pilgrim on his journey Zionward; to instruct and teach us clearer views of duty; to set before us the true character of the truly penitent child of God, what he must do and how he must live to become an heir of the kingdom above; to show what the church, and what all believers should be; to warn the impenitent; to expose erroneous views; to teach sinners the way of life, and admonish them to turn from their evil ways, to flee from the wrath to come, and seek the Lord while he may be found; and thus believing, we have felt that these writings should be placed before the public in English, so that all who understand this language may have the opportunity to read and examine them for themselves.

These works were originally written in the Dutch language, only a portion of which have been previously translated into the English and German languages. Hence the greater portion of the book will be entirely new to most of the readers of the present day. And inasmuch as the church, bearing the name of Menno, has now so extended itself that it has become a body of considerable importance, and many of the members are much better versed in the English language than in the German, it is meet that the complete works should be published in the English language, so that those professing the same faith with Menno, may enjoy the benefit of his labors even at this distant day.

For the foregoing reasons we have undertaken the arduous and laborious task of translating from the original Holland or

Dutch language the entire work, including all his writings, as far as known, with the exception of such of them as he himself rejects and of which he makes mention in his article on the Ban or Excommunication.

In the translation, we have followed the edition of his works, published in the Dutch language by John Van Veen, in Amsterdam, in Holland, in 1681.

The first part of the writings of Menno Simon, with the exception of the "Account of the severe persecutions of Menno Simon," &c., and several letters in the latter part of the volume, were formerly translated into the German language and published in several editions; and from the German translation, they were again translated into the English language, by I. Daniel Rupp, and published by Elias Barr & Co., in Lancaster, Pennsylvania, in 1863. This translation has been followed in part in the present work, though the whole of it was diligently compared with the original Dutch language, revised and corrected.

The work has required a great deal of time, care, labor and expense. The original work being written in very old style language, on which account many passages were difficult to be understood, but the translators have worked faithfully, and by comparing such passages with different editions of the work, and using such other means as they could command, we feel assured that we can offer to our readers a reasonably correct translation of the works of Menno.

We have found a few places where neither the English nor the German editions formerly published were entirely correct, and this will account for some differences which the reader may observe by comparing the different translations, and there may still, possibly, be some passages which could be greatly improved, but without boasting of anything that we have, humbly, in the fear of the Lord, sought to accomplish, we believe that, as the result of our labor, we are enabled to present to the reader, a book which gives a very correct expression of the writings of Menno, in the English language.

And if by the publication of this work we may be instrumental in doing good to the souls of others; if thereby the cause of Christ shall be advanced and the faith of believers confirmed; if thereby a single soul may be saved, and God glorified, then we shall feel that our labor has not been in vain.

May God bless the work; may it be the means of doing much good; yea, through it, may many souls be converted, and brought from the darkness of sin and error to the glorious light of the Gospel of Truth. May God be glorified and honored and mankind humbled and brought to Jesus. This is the prayer and sincere desire of your humble servants,

THE PUBLISHERS.

THE CONVERSION

OF

MENNO SIMON,

AND HIS

RENUNCIATION

OF THE

CHURCH OF ROME,

WHEREIN IS BRIEFLY AND PLAINLY NARRATED HOW, AND FOR WHAT CAUSE, HE RENOUNCED POPERY; ALSO HIS SUBSEQUENT CALLING TO THE PREACHING OF THE GOSPEL.

WRITTEN BY HIMSELF,

AND ORIGINALLY PUBLISHED IN THE DUTCH LANGUAGE

A. D. 1554.

TO THE READER.

BELOVED READER, We are falsely accused, by our opponents, of following the teachings of Munster, concerning the king, the sword, rebellion, retaliation, polygamy and other abominations. But my kind readers, know ye that I, never in my life, accepted any of the foregoing doctrines; but on the contrary, I have opposed them for more than seventeen years, and to the best of my abilities, have warned all mankind against this abominable error. I have also, through the word of God, led some on the right way. Never in my life have I seen Munster, nor have I been in the communion of that sect. I also hope, through God's grace, neither to eat nor drink with such (if such there are), as the scripture teaches me; unless they confess their error with all their heart, bring forth fruits meet for repentance, and follow the Gospel in the right manner.

MENNO SIMON.

Menno Simon's Renunciation

OF THE

CHURCH OF ROME.

MY READER,

I write to you the truth in Christ, and lie not. In the year 1524, being then in my twenty-eighth year, I undertook the duties of a priest in my father's village, called Pingjum, in Friesland. Two other persons of about my age, also officiated in the same station. The one was my pastor, and was well learned in part; the other succeeded me; both had read the scriptures partially; but I had not touched them during my life, for I feared, if I should read them they would mislead me. Behold! such a stupid preacher was I, for nearly two years.

In the first year thereafter a thought occurred to me, as often as I handled the bread and wine in the mass, that they were not the flesh and blood of the Lord. I thought that it was the suggestion of the devil, that he might lead me off from my faith. I confessed it often—sighed and prayed, yet I could not be freed from this thought.

Those two aforementioned young men and myself spent our time daily in playing, drinking, and all manner of frivolous diversions, alas! as it is the fashion and way of such useless people; and when we were to treat a little of scripture, I could not speak a word with them without being scoffed at; for I did not know what I asserted. Thus concealed was the word of God to my understanding.

At length I resolved that I would examine the New Testament attentively. I had not proceeded far therein, ere I discovered that we were deceived. My conscience, which was troubled on account of the sacramental bread, aforementioned, was soon greatly relieved, without any human aid or advice; though I was encouraged by Luther in the belief, that human authority cannot bind to eternal death.

Through the illumination and grace of the Lord, I continued daily to examine the scriptures, and was soon considered by some, though undeservedly, as being an evangelical preacher. Every one sought my company, the world loved me and had my affections, yet it was said that I preached the word of God, and was a fine man.

Afterwards it happened, before I had ever heard of the existence of brethren, that a God-fearing, pious man, named Sicke Snyder, was beheaded at Leeuwarden, for being rebaptized. It sounded strange to me, to hear a second baptism spoken of. I examined the scriptures assiduously and meditated on them earnestly, but could find nothing in them concerning infant baptism. After I had discovered this, I conversed with my pastor on the subject; and after much discussion, he had to admit, that there was no scriptural foundation for infant baptism. Notwithstanding all this, I dared not trust my own understanding, but consulted several ancient authors. They taught me that children were to be washed by baptism from their original sin. I compared this doctrine with the scriptures and found that it made baptism take the place of the blood of Christ.

Afterwards, desiring to know the grounds for infant baptism, I went and consulted Luther. He taught me that children were to be baptized on account of their own faith. I perceived that this also was not in accordance with the word of God.

Next I consulted Bucer. He taught that infants were to be baptized, that their baptism would cause those who had their training, to be more careful in bringing them up in the way of the Lord. I perceived that this doctrine, too, was without foundation.

I then consulted Bullinger. He directed me to the covenant and circumcision. This I found incapable of being substantiated by scripture.

Having thus observed that authors varied greatly among themselves, each following his own opinion, I became convinced that we were deceived in relation to infant baptism.

Shortly after, I went to the village in which I was born, called Witmarsum. Covetousness and a desire to obtain a great name, were the inducements which led me to that place. There I spoke much concerning the word of the Lord, without spirituality or love, as all hypocrites do, and by this means I made disciples of my own stamp, such as vain boasters and light-minded babblers, who, alas! like myself, cared but little about these matters. Although I had now acquired considerable knowledge of the scriptures, yet I wasted that knowledge through the lusts of my youth in an impure, sensual, unprofitable life, without any fruit, and sought nothing but gain, ease, favor of men, splendor, reputation and honor, as all generally do who embark in the same ship.

Thus, my reader, I obtained a knowledge of baptism and the Lord's supper, through the illumination of the Holy Ghost, through much reading of the scriptures, and meditating upon them, and through the gracious favor and gift of God, but not by means of the service of misleading sects, as it is reported of me. I hope that I write the truth and do not seek vain glory; though some, doubtless, may have contributed to my assistance in the pursuit of truth, yet will I, for this, render thanks to the Lord forever.

Meanwhile it happened, when I had resided there about a year, that quite a number broke in upon baptism; but whence the first beginners came, or where they resided, or who they properly were, is to this hour unknown to me, neither have I ever seen them.

Afterwards the sect of Munster made inroads, by whom many pious hearts in our quarter, were led into error. My soul was much troubled, for I perceived, that though they were zealous, they erred in doctrine. I exerted my feeble efforts, as far as I was able, in opposing them by preaching and exhortations. I conferred twice with one of their leaders, once in private, and again in public; but my admonitions availed nothing, because I did that myself which I well knew was not right.

The report spread far abroad, that I could readily silence these persons. All looked to me. I saw that I was the leader and defender of the impenitent, who all depended upon me. This pained my heart; I sighed and prayed, Lord help me, lest I make myself partaker of other men's sins. My soul was troubled and I reflected upon the result of my doings, namely, that if I should gain the whole world, and live a thousand years, and at last have to endure the wrath of God, what would I have gained?

Afterwards, the poor straying flock, who wandered as sheep without a shepherd, after many severe edicts and slaughters, assembled near my place of residence, called Oude Klooster, and, alas! through the ungodly doctrines of Munster, and in opposition to the Spirit, the word and the example of Christ, drew the sword to defend themselves, which the Lord commanded Peter to put up in the sheath.

After this had transpired, the blood of the slain, although it was shed in error, grieved me so sorely that I could not endure it. I could find no rest in my soul. I reflected upon my carnal, sinful life, my hypocritical doctrine and idolatry, in which I continued daily under the appearance of godliness. I saw that these zealous children willingly gave their lives and their estates, though they were in error, for their doctrine and faith. And I was one of those who had discovered some of their abominations, and yet I myself remained satisfied with my unrestrained life and known defilements. I wished only to live comfortably and without the cross of Christ.

Thus reflecting upon these things my soul was so grieved that I could no longer endure it. I thought to myself—I, miserable man, what shall I do? If I continue in this way, and live not agreeably to the word of the Lord, according to the knowledge of the truth which I have obtained; if I do not rebuke to the best of my limited ability the hypocrisy, the impenitent, carnal life, the perverted baptism, the Lord's supper and the false worship of God, which the learned teach; if I, through bodily fear, do not show them the true foundation of the truth, neither use all my powers to direct the wandering flock, who would gladly do their duty if they knew it, to the true pastures of Christ—Oh, how shall their shed blood, though shed in error, rise against me at the judgment of the Almighty, and pronounce sentence against my poor, miserable soul.

My heart trembled in my body. I prayed to God with sighs and tears, that he would give to me, a troubled sinner, the gift of his grace, and create a clean heart within me; that through the merits of the crimson blood of Christ, He would graciously forgive my unclean walk and unprofitable life, and bestow upon me, wisdom, Spirit, candor and fortitude, that I might preach his exalted and adorable name and holy word unperverted, and make manifest his truth to his praise.

I began in the name of the Lord to preach publicly, from the pulpit, the word of true repentance; to direct the people into the narrow path, and through the power of the scripture to reprove all sin and ungodliness, all idolatry and false worship, and to present the true worship, also baptism and the Lord's Supper, according to the doctrine of Christ, to the extent that I had at that time received grace from God.

I also faithfully warned every one in relation to the abominations of Munster, concerning *kings, polygamy, dominion, the sword*, &c., until after the expiration of about nine months, when the gracious Lord granted me his fatherly Spirit, aid and power; then I voluntarily renounced all my worldly honor and reputation, my unchristian conduct, masses, infant baptism, and my unprofitable life, and at once willingly submitted to distress and poverty, and the cross of Christ. In my weakness I feared God; I sought out the pious, and though they were few in number, I found some who were zealous and maintained the truth. I conversed with the erring, and through the aid and power of God, with his word, reclaimed some from the snares of damnation, and gained them to Christ, while the hardened and rebellious, I commended to the Lord. Behold, thus, my reader, the God of mercy, through the benign influence of his abounding grace, exerted upon me, in my heart, a miserable sinner, produced in me a new mind, humbled me in his fear, taught me to know myself in part, turned me from the way of death, and graciously called me into the narrow path of life, to the communion of his saints. To him be praise forever more, Amen.

About one year thereafter, while I was secretly exercising myself in the word of God by reading and writing, it happened that six, seven or eight persons came to me, who were of one heart and one soul with myself, in their faith and life, and as far as man can judge, were unblamable, and according to the testimony of the scriptures, separated from the world and subdued to the cross. They sincerely abhorred not only the sect of Munster, but the anathemas and abominations of all other worldly sects. For the sake of those pious souls who were of the same mind and spirit both with them and with me, they with much solicitude kindly requested me, to reflect on the great sufferings and necessity of the poor, oppressed souls (for the hunger was very great and the faithful stewards were very few), and apply to advantage the talents which I had unmeritedly received from the Lord.

When I heard this my heart was greatly troubled. Trouble and fear were on every side; for on the one hand I was sensible of my limited talents, my great ignorance, my weak nature, the timidity of my flesh, the unbounded wickedness, perversity and tyranny of the world, the powerful sects, the subtlety of different minds, and the heavy cross that would oppress me, should I comply with their solicitations, and on the other hand, the miserable, starving condition and necessity of these God-fearing, pious children, for I saw plainly that they erred as innocent sheep which have no shepherd.

At last, after much prayer, I placed myself and these circumstances before the Lord and his church, in order that we might pray earnestly to the Lord for a season; should it accord with his acceptable and holy will that I could or might labor to his praise, that he would give me such a mind and heart as would enable me to say with Paul, "Woe is me, if I preach not the Gospel," and if not, that he might provide a way to prohibit the same, for Christ says, "That if two of you shall agree on earth as touching anything that they shall ask, it shall be done for them of my Father which is in heaven. For where two or three are gathered together in my name, there am I in the midst of them," Matt. 18: 19, 20.

Thus, my reader, behold, I was not called to serve among the followers of Munster, nor of any other seditious sect (as it is falsely reported concerning me), but I have been called, unworthily, to this office by a people who were ready to receive Christ and his word, led a penitent life in the fear of God, served their neighbors in love, bore the cross, sought the welfare and salvation of all men, loved righteousness and truth, and abhorred wickedness and unrighteousness, which shows pointedly that they were not such perverted persons as they are slanderously reported to have been. But they were true Christians, though unknown to the world, if in anywise we believe that Christ's word is true, and his unblamable, holy life and example infallible.

Thus have I, a miserable sinner, been enlightened of the Lord, converted to a new mind, fled from Babel, entered into Jerusalem, and finally, though unworthily, called to this high and arduous service.

When the persons before mentioned, did not desist from their supplications, and my own conscience in some degree made me uneasy (although in weakness), because I saw the great hunger and need, already referred to, I surrendered myself, soul and body, to the Lord and committed myself to his grace, and commenced in due time, according to the contents of his holy word, to teach, and to baptize, to labor in the vineyard of the Lord with my limited talents, to build up his holy city and temple, and to repair the dilapidated walls. The great and mighty God has made known and revealed the word of true repentance, the word of his grace and power, together with the salutary use of his holy sacraments, through our humble service, doctrine and unlearned writings, together with the careful service, labor and help of our faithful brethren, in many towns and countries, to such an extent, and made the condition of his churches so glorious and bestowed upon them such a subduing power that many exalted and proud hearts not only became humble; the unclean, pure; the drunken, sober; the avaricious, benevolent; the ferocious, mild, and the ungodly, pious; but they also faithfully yielded their possessions and blood, bodies and lives, for the blessed testimony they had, as may yet daily be seen. These are not the fruits and evidences of false doctrines, in which God is not a co-worker. Neither could they endure so long under such grievous misery and oppressive crosses, were it not the power and word of the Almighty which sustains them. Yea, more, the Lord endued them with such grace and wisdom, as Christ has promised to all his children in their trials, so that all the worldly-wise and renowned teachers, together with the blood-guilty, daring tyrants, who, O God, boast that they are Christians, were vanquished and abashed by these invincible champions and pious witnesses of Christ. Those ferocious persons knew of no other weapons or refuge to which to resort than those of banishing, seizing, punishing, burning, murdering, and destroying, even as has always been the custom of the old serpent, from the beginning, and as may yet, alas! be daily witnessed in many places of our Netherlands.

Behold this is our calling, our doctrine and fruits of our labor; on account of which we are so grievously slandered, and so malevolently persecuted; whether or not all the prophets, apostles, and faithful servants of God, have endured similar sufferings on account of their faithfulness, we willingly leave all the pious to judge.

But as much as regards my poor, weak and imperfect life, I freely confess that I am a poor, wretched sinner, conceived in sin, of sinful seed, and sinfully brought forth. I can say with David, that my sins are ever before me. My thoughts, words and actions convince me. I see with holy Paul, "That in me (that is in my flesh), dwelleth no good thing," Rom. 7: 18. Nevertheless, I must be allowed to boast this much in my weakness, if this wicked, desolate world would hear our doctrine (not ours, but the doctrine of Christ), with patience, and, in the true fear of God follow it submissively, this would undoubtedly, be a more christian-like and better world than, alas, it now is.

I thank God, who has made me willing with holy Paul, to hate the evil and follow the good; and willingly would I with my own blood, reclaim this wicked world from ungodly and evil works, and gain it to Christ. Through the grace of God, it is my desire to fear the Lord with all my heart; to love, seek and serve him, to do right before him, and be an unblamable pious Christian.

I hope through the mercy and assistance of the Lord, that no one upon earth may have reason to accuse me of leading an avaricious and luxurious life. Money and affluence, I have not; neither do I desire them, although alas, some from a perverted heart, say that I eat more roasted than they do seethed; and drink more wine than they do beer. My Lord and Master, Jesus Christ, was also called a winebibber, and a glutton. I trust that through the grace of the Lord, I am innocent in this matter, and stand acquitted before God.

He who purchased me with the blood of his love, and called me, who am unworthy, to his service, knows me, and knows that I seek not wealth, nor possessions, nor luxury, nor ease, but only the praise of the Lord, my salvation, and the salvation of many souls. For this I, my poor, feeble wife and children have for eighteen years endured extreme anxiety, oppression, affliction, misery and persecution, and at the peril of my life, have been compelled everywhere to live in fear and seclusion; yea, when ministers repose on easy beds and downy pillows, we generally have to hide ourselves in secluded corners; when they at weddings and feasts, pipe and beat the tambour, and vaunt loudly, we must look out, when the dogs bark, lest the captors be at hand. Whilst they are saluted as doctors, lords and teachers by every one, we have to hear that we are ana-baptists, hedge preachers, deceivers and heretics, and must be saluted in the name of the devil. In short, whilst they are gloriously rewarded for their services with large incomes and easy times, our recompense and portion must be fire, sword and death.

Behold, my faithful readers, in such fear, poverty, misery and danger of death, have I, wretched man, performed to this hour, without change, the service of the Lord, and I hope through his grace to continue therein to his glory, as long as I remain in this earthly tabernacle. What I and my faithful co-workers have sought or could have sought in performing these our arduous and dangerous duties, is apparent to all the well-disposed, who may readily judge from the works and their fruits.

I will here humbly entreat the reader for Jesus' sake, to accept in love, this my confession in relation to my illumination, conversion and calling, and to meditate thereon. I have made it out of urgent necessity, for the information of the pious reader, because I was slandered by the clergy, and am accused, without foundation of truth, of being called and ordained to this service by a seditious and heretical sect. He that feareth God let him read and judge.

MENNO SIMON.

AN ACCOUNT

OF THE

SEVERE PERSECUTIONS OF MENNO SIMON, AND A DESCRIPTION OF THE PLACE WHERE HE LAST PREACHED THE GOSPEL, DIED AND WAS BURIED.

"All that will live godly in Christ Jesus," says Paul, "shall suffer persecution," 2 Tim. 3:12. These words, although often confirmed, through the inconsiderate wickedness of this world, we find particularly confirmed in the example of our author Menno Simon. For, after he had been persecuted in many ways and sought for by his opponents, they, in order that their design might be accomplished with certainty, issued a decree in which it was stated that whosoever should shelter, or in any manner conceal Menno Simon or any of his followers, should suffer death; which decree was enforced in the year A. D. 1539 in the case of Tjaert Reyndertz,* a peasant living near Harlingen (prov. Friesland, Neth.), who, because he secretly harbored Menno Simon in his house, in his great danger and distress, was a few days after, taken to Leeuwarden (in the same province), and as an ungodly criminal put on the wheel, though even his enemies acknowledged that he was a pious man.

Besides this, another decree was issued in the year A. D. 1543, throughout West Friesland, by which a general pardon, the favor of the Emperor, freedom of the country, and besides, one hundred Carl guilders ** was promised to any criminal, even murderer, who would deliver Menno into the hands of the executioner; and, in order that their purpose might be more readily accomplished, his name, person, clothing and stature were described, and this description posted upon the church-doors; so that he could not even find a hut of straw where he could quietly rest with his wife and little children, for any length of time. Menno himself relates that in 1546, at a certain place, where they yet boasted of being evangelical christians, four dwellings were, at once, confiscated, because the owner had rented one of them for a short time to his sick wife and little children, though the neighbors were not aware of it. This severe persecution compelled Menno to remove to a place situated between Hamburg and Lubeck, six and a half or seven miles from Hamburg, three miles from Lubeck, and nearly a mile from Oldeslo, which formerly was a large forest of oaks, but which is now an open field, generally called Woeste Veldt, belonging to the nobleman and estate of Van Vriesenburg; which nobleman was at that time a very cruel person, on which account he was generally shunned and feared. But having spent much of his youth in the Netherlands, and having often witnessed the death of martyrs, he was very compassionate towards them, being conversant with their doctrines. He clandestinely gave them liberty to dwell there, and assiduously and faithfully assisted them; although he was requested by the king's order not to permit them to live there; therefore he announced to them, through one of his servants, that they should leave

---

* See Martyr's Mirror, English edition, published by D. Miller, Lampeter Square, Pa., 1837, Page 382.

** Forty Dollars.

before sun-down, at the risk of punishment, yet, he sent a faithful servant after the first, to tell them the cause of this announcement, and to inform them that the men should either absent or conceal themselves for a week or two. In the mean while he succeeded in quieting this excitement, through one of the courtiers. After this the exiles came hither from every side, until there was quite a little community there, who lived in comparative quiet. Each family had to pay one dollar a year for this protection, and were taxed no further. This may well be considered a special dispensation of God's providence, that the exiles were fostered and protected by a very cruel person, who was feared by all around him. For which reason Menno considered it expedient, as it was said, to remove to that place.

Menno Simon died about thirty years after he left the church of Rome. During this time he taught and proclaimed the gospel, purified of Roman idolatry and superstition. His last exhortation was given on his death-bed, while the hand of death seemed already to rest upon him, showing his unquenchable zeal. He, however, partially recovered and was better for several days, but on the day of the anniversary of his renunciation of popery, he suddenly became worse, though well taken care of, and the next day, being Friday the 13th of January, 1561, he calmly fell asleep in Jesus, in the sixty sixth year of his age, and was buried in his own garden, which according to Hoornbeck, was also customary with the primitive Christians under the persecutions of the pagans.

———o———

NOTE 1.— Although the "Martyrs' Mirror," page 59, and T. J. van Braght in his "Bloody Theatre" and others, write that Menno Simon died on the 13th of January 1559, yet we are led to think that he died in 1561, for the following reasons:

The old biography of Menno Simon mentions 1561 as the year of his death, which statement we deem correct; also on the 23rd of January 1559, he wrote a tract (see his Reply to Zylis and Lemmekes in this book), and sent it to the German teachers, Zylis and Lemmekes. Now, if he died on the 13th of January 1559, he must have written this ten days after his death.

NOTE 2.—The reader should know that although some old biographies mention 1505 as the year of his birth, yet we will take 1496; for, the "Martyrs' Mirror," "The Bloody Theatre," "The Decline of Tyrants" and "Annals," all mention that he died in his sixty sixth year. If Menno, then, died in 1561, he necessarily was born in 1496, or else he died in the fifty sixth year of his age.

A FOUNDATION

AND

Plain Instruction

OF THE

Saving Doctrine of Our Lord Jesus Christ,

BRIEFLY COMPILED FROM THE WORD OF GOD.

TOGETHER WITH OTHER INSTRUCTIVE TREATISES,

BY

MENNO SIMON.

TRANSLATED FROM THE DUTCH INTO THE ENGLISH LANGUAGE.

"For other foundation can no man lay than that is laid, which is Jesus Christ." 1. Cor. 3: 11.

———•·•———

ELKHART, INDIANA:
PUBLISHED BY JOHN F. FUNK AND BROTHER.
1871.

TO THE READER.

PIOUS, BELOVED READER, Since I perceive that our work, called, "THE FOUNDATION OF CHRISTIAN DOCTRINE," which I published a few years ago, has been, through the grace of God, to whom be eternal praise and thanks, productive of much good to some; and God's holy word which was obscured for such a long time, has been again a little explained, through our limited talents, and as many well disposed children, requested and entreated me, diligently to revise and correct such parts as were obscured through the negligence of the printer, and which deprived the reader of the sense, I was prevailed on, and did so. In some places I made additions; explained the obscure parts, corrected those that were defective, and omitted redundancies; the style and language I improved, in order to be better suited to aid the kind reader, and to make known and acceptable to many, the despised truth.

Not my reader, that I changed the original doctrines and contents; by no means! I have not changed, but as appears to me, improved its form, and given it more force and distinctness. Those who fear God may judge. The former, as well as this, is God's word; and all that the first teaches, this teaches also. May the Almighty, Merciful Father grant that through his grace our little work, so lightly esteemed, may produce much fruit in many thousands, Amen.

MENNO SIMON.

PREFACE.

NOTE.—*The following Preface shows to whom this book is addressed, and was written at the time when the errors of Munster yet prevailed.*

To those in authority and all others, of whatever condition, class or calling they be, Menno Simon wishes the illumination of the Spirit, and the pure knowledge of the kingdom of God, from our heavenly Father, and his Son Jesus Christ, our Lord, who has loved us and washed us from our sins with his blood. To him be praise, honor, glory, and thanksgiving forever, Amen.

Dear Sirs, Friends and Brethren, since we learn from the scriptures, and from experience find, that the prediction of the prophets, Christ and of the apostles, concerning the terrible oppression, misery, want, persecution, danger, anxiety, and false doctrine, in these latter times is being accomplished to its full measure, Matt. 24; Mark 13; Luke 21; 1 Tim. 4; 2 Tim. 3; 2 Pet. 2; Jude 1, and this so powerfully, that unless the merciful Father graciously shortens these days no flesh will be saved.

Therefore, we poor miserable men entreat and admonish every one, and that through the mercy of the Lord, for once candidly to read our doctrine and faith, lay it well to heart and understand it correctly, that you might know what kind of doctrine we inculcate, what kind of faith we maintain, what kind of life we lead, and how we are disposed, on account of which we have to hear and suffer so much, endure imprisonment, exile, be robbed, derided, defamed and slain as poor, innocent sheep. In order that you may sincerely lament and weep over your former bloody deeds, before God, and with greater circumspection guard and preserve yourselves from such things, and henceforth be found a more pious, sincere, yea, a more God-fearing magistracy, Ex. 18: 23; Deut. 1: 17; not afflictors and destroyers, but fathers and guardians of all miserable and wretched; not exterminators, but defenders of righteousness; not persecutors but followers of Christ and his word. Therefore, anoint your eyes with eye-salve, that you may see and understand which is the right way, the truth and the life; the way which is so strait and narrow and found of so few; the truth which is known to none, except those who are taught of the Spirit of the Lord, illuminated and drawn by the Father; the life which is to know God the Father as the only true God, and Jesus Christ whom he sent; that you may see him whom you fiercely pierced, and that you may with holy Paul, with your whole hearts, humble yourselves before the Lord with much fasting and weeping; clothe yourselves in sack-cloth; rend your hearts and not your garments, that you may find grace in his sight. For he is long-suffering, gracious and merciful, and pardons the iniquity of all who sincerely repent and seek his grace. Be no longer like Jeroboam, Ahab and Manasseh, but like David, Hezekiah and Josiah; that you need not on account of the office entrusted to you stand confounded in the great and dreadful day of the Lord, in that day which shall burn as an oven; and all who have dealt unrighteously and used violence upon the earth, shall be burnt up as dry straw and stubble, Mal. 4.

Therefore, we most humbly entreat you, for the sake of the merits of Christ, that you would thoroughly ponder and reflect upon our faith, doctrine and undertaking; and not esteem us to be worse than you do thieves and murderers, whom you do not condemn without having certain knowledge of their case. Our doings are not thievish, nor have we to do with perishable possessions, but with God and his word, our bodies and souls, eternal life or eternal death. Therefore do not look upon the usages and customs of the fathers, nor upon the worldly wise and the learned, for it is deeply hidden from their eyes. They were always those who, from the beginning, thrust from them the wisdom of God through their own wisdom and have trampled it under foot; for the wisdom of God, which we teach, is that wisdom which none may understand, except those who are desirous of living and walking according to the will of God; it is that wisdom, which is not to be brought from afar nor taught in colleges. It must come from above and be learned through the Holy Ghost; as Paul says, Rom. 10: 6—9. "Say not in thine heart, who shall ascend into heaven? (That is, to bring Christ down from above). Or, who shall descend into the deep? (That is, to bring up Christ again from the dead). But, what saith it? The word is nigh thee, even in thy mouth, and in thy heart; that is, the word of faith which we preach; that if thou shalt confess with thy mouth the Lord Jesus, and shalt believe in thine heart that God hath raised him from the dead, thou shalt be saved." Therefore, look to God's word, to the testimony and example of the holy prophets, the Lord Jesus Christ and his apostles. Let these be your doctors and teachers, and not the ambitious, mercenary preachers of this world; then you will soon perceive, whether we are within or without the truth. May the almighty and eternal God give you such hearts and minds. To him be honor, praise and gratitude, dominion, power and majesty for ever, Amen.

Seeing then, beloved, that satan can transform himself into an angel of light, 2 Cor. 11, and thus sow tares among the Lord's wheat, such as the sword, polygamy, secular kingdom, and kings and other like errors on account of which the innocent have to suffer much; hence we are prompted to publish this our faith and doctrine; and we desire for Jesus' sake that we might obtain so much grace, that they would not treat and judge us except according to the word of God, as is reasonable and just. But should we not obtain so much grace, we have to commend it to the Lord, who is the only helper of every one in need. We will, nevertheless, through the grace of God, abide in the word of the Lord; and comfort ourselves with the scriptures, which say, "Thus saith the LORD that created thee, O Jacob, and he that formed thee, O Israel, fear not; for I have redeemed thee, I have called thee by thy name; thou art mine. When thou passest through the waters, I will be with thee; and through the rivers, they shall not overflow thee; when thou walkest through the fire, thou shalt not be burned; neither shall the flame kindle upon thee; for I am the Lord thy God, the Holy one of Israel, thy Saviour," Isa. 43: 1, 3. Again: "Fear ye not the reproach of men, neither be ye afraid of their revilings; for the moth shall eat them up like a garment and the worm shall eat them like wool." "I, even I, am he that comforteth you: who art thou that shouldst be afraid of a man that shall die, and the son of man which shall be made as grass?" Isa. 51: 7, 8 and 12. Christ also says: "Fear not them which kill the body, but are not able to kill the soul; but rather fear him which is able to destroy both soul and body in hell." "Whosoever therefore shall confess me before men, him will I confess also before my Father which is in heaven; but whosoever shall deny me before men, him will I also deny before my Father which is in heaven," Matt. 10: 28, 32, 33. "With the heart," saith Paul, "man believeth unto righteousness; and with the mouth confession is made unto salvation," Rom. 10: 10.

Since then the scriptures urge us so much, both to believe and to confess, and so kindly comfort us against the raging and raving of men, therefore, we also desire to abide by the same until death. And hereby testify before you in Christ Jesus, that we neither have, nor know any other foundation, faith or doctrine, than that which may be plainly read, heard, and understood in the following, from the word of God, Amen.

MENNO SIMON.

THE DAY OF GRACE.

In the first place we teach, what Jesus, the teacher from heaven, the Oracle and Word of the Most High God himself taught, John 3: 2, that now is the time of grace, a time to awaken from the sleep of our abominable sins, Rom. 13: 11, and obtain an upright, converted, renewed, contrite and penitent heart, and sincerely lament before God, our past profligate and dissolute course of life, and in the fear of God, to crucify and mortify our depraved, sinful flesh, temper and nature, and arise with Christ into a new, righteous, and penitent life and conduct, Eph. 4: 22; Gal. 5: 24. Even as Christ says, "The time is fulfilled, and the kingdom of God is at hand: repent ye and believe the Gospel," Mark. 1: 15.

The time is fulfilled, that is, the promised day of grace approaches; the time for the appearing of the promised seed; the time of redemption, the time of that offering by which all things were to be reconciled in heaven and upon earth, Gen. 3: 15; Col. 1: 19; the time for the consummation of all the literal and figurative transactions into a new, spiritual life and an abiding truth; the time for which the fathers, Jacob, Moses, Isaiah, David, Daniel, &c., with all the patriarchs and prophets hoped, and which they desired with many tears, and through faith saw from afar, and drew comfort and hope therefrom, Heb. 11: 23; yea, it was to them such a great and pleasing consolation, that good old Simeon desired to live no longer, when he beheld the time and saw the Redeemer. He said, "Lord, now lettest thou thy servant depart in peace, according to thy word, for mine eyes have seen thy salvation, which thou hast prepared before the face of all people," Luke 2: 29—31.

The time is fulfilled, the predictions of the prophets and promises of the fathers appear in their full power; the sworn oath is accomplished; Israel has received its King David, its Prince and Chief who has arisen as a mighty one to prepare his way, Ps. 2: 7; Is. 9: 5; Jer. 30: 9; his going forth is from the heavens; the Anointed, who was the desire of all nations, has come, girded about his loins with the sword of the Spirit and valiant for battle, Mic. 5; Hag. 2; Is. 24.

He has declared the gospel of the kingdom, the word of his Father; he taught and left unto his followers, an example of pure love, and an unblemished life, Matt. 4: 17; Jn. 7: 14, 15; conquered the mighty, destroyed the power of the devil, bore our sins, abolished death, reconciled the Father, acquired for all the chosen children of God, grace, favor, mercy, eternal life, dominion and peace, Heb. 2; 1. Pet. 2; 1. Cor. 15, and has been ordained by his Eternal and Almighty Father as an omnipotent King over the holy Mount Zion, as the head of the Church, a Provider and Dispenser of heavenly blessings; yea, an Almighty Ruler over all in heaven and on earth, Is. 2; Eph. 2; and this is what Christ here declares, "The time is fulfilled, and the kingdom of God is at hand," Mark. 1: 15.

Out of compassion and a sincere heart, I exhort you with the apostle Paul, that you take heed to this day of grace, and be obedient to the word of God, which says, "I have heard thee in a time accepted, and in the day of salvation have I succored thee; behold, now is the accepted time; behold, now is the day of salvation," and with Paul let us "give no offence in any thing, that the ministry be not blamed; but in all things approving ourselves as the ministers of God, in much patience, in afflictions, in necessities, in distresses, in stripes, in imprisonments, in tumults (understand this in relation to things which befall us), in labors, in watchings, in fastings; by pureness, by knowledge, by long-suffering, by kindness, by the

Holy Ghost, by love unfeigned, by the word of truth, by the power of God, by the armor of righteousness on the right hand and on the left, by honor, and dishonor; by evil report, and good report; as deceivers, and yet true; as unknown, and yet well known; as dying, and behold, we live; as chastened and not killed; as sorrowful, yet always rejoicing; as poor, yet making many rich; as having nothing, and yet possessing all things," 2 Cor. 6: 2—10. Oh, my beloved Sirs, Friends and Brethren, my mouth is open unto you, and my heart is enlarged towards you; for your sakes I am much grieved that you are so careless, and do not observe the people by whom these plain and intelligible scriptures were written; that you so entirely despise the word of the Lord, and suffer this precious time of grace, which God gives us all for improvement, to pass away so shamefully, and regard nothing more than to live with the whole heart, according to the impure and wicked lusts of your flesh, bowing the knees before dumb idols. Alas! it is time to awake! Remember that the angel has sworn, Rev. 10: 6, by the eternal and living God, who created heaven and earth, that after this time, there shall be time no longer. From the scriptures we cannot otherwise conclude, but that this is the last watch of the year, the last proclamation of the holy gospel, the last invitation to the marriage of the Lamb, which is to be celebrated, promulgated and sanctified before the great and terrible day of the Lord. Hereby we may learn and determine that the summer will pass away and the winter approach. Those, who, like the foolish virgins, neglect to prepare their lamps, will come too late, knock in vain and be excluded, Matt. 25: 11. Therefore comfort not one another with idle comfort and vain hope, as some do who think that the word should be taught and observed whilst they reject the cross. I mean those who know the word of the Lord, but do not live according to it. Oh, no! it is the word of the cross and will, in my opinion, remain so to the last, for it must be sustained with much suffering, and sealed with blood. The Lamb is slain from the foundation of the world, Rev. 13: 8; yea, he did not only suffer in his body, but also through the cross and death entered into that glory, which he, for a time, had left for our sakes, Luke 24; Jn. 11: 25. If Christ then had to suffer such torture, anguish, misery and pain, how shall his servants, children and members expect peace and freedom from suffering while in the flesh? "If they have called the Master of the house Beelzebub, how much more shall they call them of his household?" Matt. 10: 25. "All that will live godly in Christ Jesus," says Paul, "shall suffer persecution," 2 Tim. 3: 12.

Christ also says, "Ye shall be hated of all men for my name's sake," Matt. 10: 22.

Therefore banish the pernicious thought, that you may hope for another time, from your hearts, and be not deceived by your vain hopes, for I have known some who waited for a more convenient season, but did not live to realize their hopes. Had the apostles and fathers thus waited, the gospel of the kingdom would not at this day have been preached, and the word of the Lord would have remained unknown.

Alas! were you christians and the people of God as you boast yourselves to be, you should be able to say with Paul, "Who shall separate us from the love of Christ?" Rom. 8: 35. For then the flesh, the devil, sin, hell and death would all be subdued; there would then be no desire to remain long in this depraved, wicked, sanguinary world; neither would ye then boast of anything save the cross of Christ, Gal. 6: 16, and like Paul, with the whole heart desire to be delivered from this body and dwell with Christ, Phil. 1: 23.

I sincerely desire that you may awake, and not hope nor wait for a more acceptable time. If however the merciful Father will give us liberty and peace, we will gladly receive them with all thankfulness, from his gracious hands; but if he will not, his great name shall, notwithstanding, be praised forever.

We have all enjoyed the acceptable time of grace, for now is the day of salvation, Is. 49: 8. Let us therefore not be like ungrateful, disobedient, blood-thirsty Jerusalem, who with such perverted minds rejected the divine peace, the heavenly grace and merciful calling; but let us awake, with sober hearts, and give ear to the inviting voice, and in this accepted time arise from the deep slumber of our abominable and offensive sins, for the Lord is at hand. "The night is far spent, the day is at hand; let us therefore cast off the works of darkness, and let us put on the armor of light, let us walk honestly, as in the day; not in rioting and drunkenness, not in chambering and wantonness, not in strife and envying; but put ye on the Lord Jesus Christ, and make not provision for the flesh, to fulfil the lusts thereof," Rom. 13: 12—14. Let every one be vigilant, and improve the time which God has graciously given for repentance. *Ecce nunc tempus acceptum, ecce nunc dies salutis.* "Behold, now is the accepted time, behold, now is the day of salvation," 2 Cor. 6: 2.

SINCERE AND TRUE REPENTANCE.

In the second place we exhort you in the language of Christ, "Repent ye, and believe the Gospel," Mark. 1: 15. Oh, thou faithful word of grace! Oh, thou faithful word of divine love! thou art read in books, sung in hymns, preached with the mouth, with life and death and proclaimed in many countries, but in thy power they desire thee not;* yea more, all those who rightly teach and receive thee, are made a prey for the whole world. Alas, beloved Sirs, it will avail us nothing to be called christians, and boast of the Lord's blood, death, merits, grace and Gospel, as long as we are not converted from this wicked, impious and shameful life. It is in vain that we are called christians; that Christ died; that we were born in the day of grace, and baptized with water, if we do not walk according to his law, counsel, admonition, will and command and are not obedient to his word.

Therefore awake, and behold the doings of the world. On every hand you see nothing but sensuality, wine-bibbing, infernal pride, lying, fraud, avarice, hatred, strife, adultery, fornication, war, murder, hypocrisy, open blasphemy, idolatry, and false worship, Hos. 4: 11; Mic. 6: 14; Gal. 5: 19 —21; in short, nothing but a powerful persecution of all that God teaches, commands and enjoins. Who can relate the terrible and alarming condition of the world at the present time? yet they (the wicked) want to call themselves the holy christian church. Oh, no! they who do such things, saith Paul, shall not inherit the kingdom of God, 1. Cor. 6: 9, 10; Gal. 5: 19; Eph. 5: 5. Oh, ye men awake and see for yourselves, for thus saith the word of the Lord, Verily, verily, I say unto you, except ye be born from above ye shall not see the kingdom of God, Jn. 3: 3. Also, "Verily, verily, I say unto thee, except a man be born of water and of the Spirit, he cannot enter into the kingdom of God," Jn. 3: 5, and again, "Verily, I say unto you, except ye be converted, and become as little children, ye shall not enter into the kingdom of heaven," Matt. 18: 3. What does it profit to speak much of Christ and his word, if we do not believe him, and obey his commandments? Again, I say, awake and banish the accursed unbelief with all unrighteousness from your hearts, and live a pious, penitent life, according to the scriptures; for Christ says, "Except ye repent, ye shall all likewise perish," Luke 13: 5. Here do not understand such repentance as is taught and practiced by an erring world, which consists only in an outward appearance and human righteousness, such as hypocritical fastings, pilgrimages, praying and reading Pater Nosters and Ava Marias, hearing frequent masses, auricular confessions, and the like hypocrisies which Christ and his apostles did in no wise teach and command. Hence it cannot be a propitiatory sacrifice, but rather will be a provocation, and tend to excite the divine displeasure. Such doctrines are unavailing

---

*There are multitudes in the world who profess to believe in the word of God, but by their works deny the power thereof.

and fruitless commands of men, the accursed and enchanted wine of the Babylonian whoredom, which those who have dwelt upon the earth, through the just anger of God, have drunk for so many ages, Rev. 17: 2. But we speak of a repentance possessed of power and works, as John the Baptist teaches, saying, "Bring forth therefore fruits meet for repentance, and think not to say within yourselves, we have Abraham to our father," Matt. 3: 8. "And now also the axe is laid unto the root of the trees; every tree, therefore, which bringeth not forth good fruit is hewn down and cast into the fire," Luke 3: 9.

Behold, dear reader, the repentance we teach, is to die unto sin, and all ungodly works, and live no longer according to the lusts of the flesh, even as David did, 2 Sam. 13: 12; 18: 1. When he was reproved by the prophet on account of his adultery, and for numbering the people, he wept bitterly, called upon God, forsook the evil, and committed these sinful abominations no more. Peter sinned very grievously but once, and no more. Matthew, after being called by the Saviour, did not again return to his ways of life. Zaccheus and the sinful woman did not again return to their impure works of darkness. Zaccheus made restitution to those whom he had defrauded, and gave half of his goods to the poor and distressed. The woman wept very bitterly, and washed the feet of the Lord with her tears, and wiped them with the hair of her head; she anointed them with precious ointment, and sat humbly at his feet, to listen to his blessed words.

These are the precious fruits of that repentance, which is acceptable to the Lord; therefore, it was said to David, that the Lord had put away his sins from him; to Peter it was proclaimed, that the Lord had arisen from the dead; Matthew was called to be an apostle; Zaccheus was told that he had become a son of Abraham, and Mary, that she had "chosen that good part which shall not be taken away from her," Luke 10: 42. To the adulterous woman, Christ said, "Go, and sin no more," Jn. 8: 11.

Such a repentance we teach, and no other, namely, that no one can glory in the grace of God, the forgiveness of sins, the merits of Christ, and count himself pious, unless he has truly repented. It is not enough that we say, we are Abraham's children, that is, that we are called christians and esteemed as such, but we must do the works of Abraham, that is, we must walk as all true children of God are commanded by his word, as John writes, "If we say, we have fellowship with him (God) and walk in darkness, we lie, and do not the truth; but if we walk in the light, as he is in the light, we have fellowship one with another, and the blood of Jesus Christ, his Son, cleanseth us from all sins," 1 Jn. 1: 6, 7.

I ask all my readers, if they ever have read in the scriptures, that an impenitent, obdurate man, who fears not God nor his word, who is earthly minded, sensual, devilish, and lives according to his lusts, can be called a child of God and a joint heir of Christ?* I believe you will be constrained to answer, no. But he that with all his heart, ceases from evil and learns to do well, to him the grace of the Lord is proclaimed throughout the whole scriptures, as the prophet says, "Wash ye, make you clean; put away the evil of your doings from before mine eyes, cease to do evil; learn to do well; seek judgment, relieve the oppressed, judge the fatherless, plead for the widow. Come now, and let us reason together, saith the Lord. Though your sins be as scarlet, they shall be as white as snow; though they be red like crimson, they shall be as wool," Isa. 1: 16—18. Again, "If the wicked will turn from all his sins that he hath committed, and keep all my statutes, and do that which is lawful and right, he shall surely live, he shall not die; all his transgressions that he hath committed, they shall not be mentioned unto him," Ezek. 18: 21, 22. And further, read and search the whole scriptures, the true instructions and testimonies of the holy prophets, evangelists and apostles, and you will find it clearly set forth, how this godly repentance is to be earnestly received and practiced, and that without it no one can receive grace, enter into the kingdom of heaven, or ever hope for it.**

* The impenitent are without grace.
** These remarks apply to those who have ears to hear and hearts to understand, and not to infants that are incapable of understanding.

In short, as far as in us lies, we teach repentance from the word of the Lord, in order that we may subdue those carnal lusts which war against the soul, 1 Peter 2: 11, crucify the flesh with the affections and lusts, Gal. 5: 24, refrain from conformity to this world, Rom. 12: 2, cast off the works of darkness and put on the armor of light, Rom. 13: 12; that we "love not the world, neither the things that are in the world," 1. Jn. 2: 15; "put off the old man with his deeds, and put on the new man, which is renewed in knowledge after the image of Him that created him," Col. 3: 9, 10; yea, cast off the old Adam with his whole nature and deceitful lusts, such as pride, avarice, unchastity, hatred, envyings, gluttony, drinking, idolatry, and put on the new man, which, after God, is created in righteousness and true holiness, whose fruits are faith, love, hope, righteousness, peace, and joy, in the Holy Ghost, Eph. 4: 22; Rom. 14: 17; Gal. 5: 16; be patient in suffering, merciful, compassionate, chaste, sincerely hating and rebuking all sin, and entertaining a sincere love and zeal for God and his word.* I repeat it, that this repentance, which we teach, must be sincere, fruitful and acceptable to the Lord, according to the instructions of his word. He that receives this repentance in sincerity, and abides therein unto the end, may rejoice and thank God, for the end thereof is eternal life. But he that rejects it and does not desire it, let him take warning that the end thereof is eternal death.

Beloved Sirs, Friends and Brethren, do for once truly and sincerely lay it to heart, what it is, and what the consequences will be, willfully to transgress the commands of the Lord and haughtily sin against the word of God. Adam and Eve did but once eat of the fruit of which the Lord had forbidden them, therefore, for Adam's sake the earth was cursed. In the sweat of his face he was doomed to eat his bread all the days of his life. Eve and her daughters must bring forth in pain, and be in subjection to their husbands. They were driven from Paradise, and with all their race, doomed to return to dust, from whence they were taken. Here also there was no forgiveness nor consolation of grace to be obtained. But the Eternal Word, God's Eternal Son must needs come from high heaven, assume human nature, suffer hunger, temptation, misery; the cross and death, as the scriptures teach.* Oh, beloved Sirs, if this single transgression was so great before God, what will become of those who so proudly, all their days, despise the holy word, covenant, will and commandment of the Lord, who do not confess their sins and transgressions, though they are full of iniquity from the crown of their heads to the soles of their feet. Cain was cursed and became a vagabond upon the earth as long as he lived, because he so enviously slew his innocent brother Abel. Alas! what will become of those, who, at the present day without compassion or justice, persecute, plunder and murder the pious Abelites, who with fervent hearts seek Christ and eternal life?

The ancient world was drowned in the waters of the flood, because the sons of God looked upon the daughters of men, that they were fair, and took to themselves wives of all which they chose, and also because they would not be reproved of the Spirit of God, for every imagination and thought of their hearts were evil continually. Reflect upon the lusts with which the marriages of the world at the present time are contracted, yea, like dumb beasts; how the Holy Ghost is reviled, slandered and grieved, and how they all walk in their perverted ways which lead to hell, yea, to eternal damnation and death.

Sodom and Gomorrah, with the surrounding cities, on account of their pride, wantonness, cruelty, and abominable crimes, were burned up with the fire of the furious wrath of God, and cast into the abyss of hell. Alas, alas, what will befall those miserable men in the great and terrible day when the Lord will appear in his glory, whose pride, excess, debauchery, pomp, tyranny, bloodthirstiness, adultery, fornication, and papal abominations, no heart can conceive, no tongue express, no pen describe! Rom. 1: 24.

Koran, Dathan and Abiram, though they were of the seed of Abraham, and some of

---

*Such are the fruits of true repentance.

*Thus Christ came into the world to redeem mankind.

them were born of Levi, yet because they revolted against Moses and Aaron, and sought to enter into the sacerdotal office, without being called, they and all their company, were swallowed up by the earth alive, Num. 16: 32. Consider what will ultimately happen to our Korites, whom God never acknowledged, much less were sent by him, and whose office, calling and service are not from God and his word, but as the scriptures teach, from the bottomless pit, the dragon and the beast, Rev. 9: 1; 13: 4; 20: 1—3, who mislead so many poor, miserable souls with their seducing doctrines, Babylonian sorceries and hypocritical lives, and not only despise, but also rail, persecute, crucify and kill Christ, the righteous Moses and Aaron. If Moses, the faithful servant of God, could not enter the promised land because he once doubted the word of the Lord, how much less shall this unbelieving, perverted and obdurate generation enter the eternal land of promise and glory, that not only disbelieve and despise the word of the Lord, the acceptable gospel of Jesus Christ, but also bitterly hate and persecute it, trample the blood of Christ under foot, stop their ears against the truth, and refuse to be taught by any means, either with the truth, the unblamable lives of the saints, or the innocent blood of the witnesses of Jesus, which has been shed, and in many countries flowed like water.

O, ye miserable men, who are so entirely depraved and miserable before God, take heed to the word of the Lord, cleanse your bloody hands, and your impure and unbelieving hearts, and no longer despise the grace of God with your vain boastings, and say not Abraham is your father, Jn. 8: 39; that you are the children of God; that Christ died for you, or that you will also confide in his mercy. "Trust ye not in lying words," says Jeremiah, the prophet; say not, here is the temple of the Lord, the temple of the Lord, the temple of the Lord, for it avails nothing, that Christ died, and that we are called by his name, if we do not possess a sincere, regenerating, vigorous faith in Jesus Christ, pure, unfeigned love, willing obedience, and a pious and irreproachable life. God's mercy, we read, is to his saints, and he hath care for his elect, but the hope of the wicked is vain, Wis. 3: 9; 5: 15. "The eyes of the Lord are upon the righteous, and his ears are open unto their cry," Ps. 34: 15. "Ye are my friends," says Christ, "if ye do whatsoever I command you," John 15: 14. Therefore, we pray and exhort you again to reform; he is still the same unchangeable God, Mal. 3: 6. He is a strict, jealous and rigid punisher of all wickedness; yea, a righteous judge of all ungodliness and of every evil work. He visits the iniquities of the fathers upon the children unto the third and fourth generations of them that hate him, Ex. 20: 5. On the other hand, he is compassionate, kind, and merciful unto all that do righteously, and fear his name, to many thousands who love him and keep his commandments.

O reader, reader, beloved reader, it is a fearful thing to fall into the hands of the living God! The time is fulfilled, now is the accepted time, now is the day of salvation. The kingdom of heaven is at hand; would you inherit and enter into it, you must repent, not only in appearance, as the hypocrites do, but as sincere penitents, with all your hearts, and all your powers, and bring forth good fruit. If not, you must be cut off and cast into the fire of his fierce wrath, John 15: 6; Luke 3: 9. *Imo nisi resipuerite, omnes similiter, peritites,* i. e., "Except ye repent, ye shall all likewise perish," Luke 13: 3.

FAITH.

In the third place, we teach with Christ and say, "Believe the gospel," Mark. 1: 15. That gospel is the glad tidings and promulgation of the favor and grace of God toward us, and the forgiveness of our sins through Christ Jesus. The believer, by faith, receives this gospel through the Holy Ghost, and does not look upon his former righteousness or unrighteousness, but hopes against hope, Rom. 4: 18, and with the whole heart depends upon the grace, word and promises of the Lord; since he well knows that God is true, and that his promises are sure, Ps. 33: 4; Rom. 3: 4; 1 Cor. 1: 9; thereby the heart is renewed, converted, justified, made pious, peaceable and joyous, Rom. 14: 17; Gal. 5: 22; he is born a child of God, John 1: 13, approaches, with full confidence, the throne of grace, Heb. 4: 11, and thus becomes a joint heir of Christ and a possessor of everlasting life, Rom. 8: 14; 1 Tim. 1: 16. Such then awaken in time; they hear and believe the word of the Lord; they weep over their past unworthy lives and conduct; they desire help and advice for their sick souls. To such, Christ, who is a comforter for all troubled hearts, says, "Believe the gospel;" that is, fear not; rejoice and be comforted; I will not punish nor chastise you, but will heal you, comfort you, and give you life, Is. 41: 10. A bruised reed I will not break, and smoking flax I will not quench, Matt. 12: 20; "I will seek that which was lost, and bring again that which was driven away, and will bind up that which was broken, and will strengthen that which was sick," Ezek. 34: 16; for I am not come to call the righteous, but sinners to repentance, Matt. 9: 13; Mark. 2: 17; Lu. 5: 32; according to the good pleasure of my heavenly Father, I came into the world, and by the power of the Holy Ghost, I became a visible, tangible and dying man; in all points like unto you, yet without sin, Heb. 4: 15; I was born of Mary, the spotless virgin; I came down from heaven, proceeded from the mouth of the Most High; I am the first born of every creature, the first and the last; the beginning and the end, Rev. 22: 13; the Son of the Almighty God, Luke 1: 32, anointed with the Holy Ghost to preach the gospel to the poor, and to bind up the broken hearted, to proclaim liberty to the captives, to give sight to the blind, to open the prison to them that are bound, and to proclaim the acceptable year of the Lord, Is. 61: 1, 2; Luke 4: 18. Believe the gospel. I am the Lamb that was offered for you all. I take away the sins of the whole world. My Father has made me unto you "wisdom, righteousness, sanctification, and redemption," 1 Cor. 1: 30; Rom. 6: 10. Whosoever believeth on me shall not be ashamed; yea, all that believe that I am he, shall have eternal life, Rom. 10: 11; John 3: 16.

Behold, beloved Sirs, Friends, and Brethren, all who believe this are those of whom the scriptures say, "To them gave he power to become the sons of God, even to them that believe on his name, which were born, not of blood, nor of the will of the flesh, nor of the will of man, but of God," Jn. 1: 12, 13. These are they who are justified by faith, and have peace with God, through our Lord Jesus Christ, by whom also we have access by faith into this grace wherein we stand, and rejoice in hope of the glory of God, Rom. 5: 1, 2, and this, as Paul says, is all of grace and love, all have sinned and come short of the glory of God; being justified freely by his grace, through the redemption that is in Christ Jesus, whom God has set forth to be a propitiation, through faith in his blood, &c., Rom. 3: 23—25. There is none, that of himself, can rejoice in, or boast of this faith;* it is the gift of God, Eph. 2: 8. All who receive faith from God, receive a tree full of all manner of good and delicious fruit; happy are they who receive this gift of God, for it is more precious than gold, silver or precious stones; it is incomparable, he that obtains it, obtains Christ Jesus, forgiveness of sins, a new mind and eternal life, for the true faith, which is acceptable to God, cannot be dead; it must bring forth fruit, and thus manifest its nature; it works continually in love; walks willingly in righteousness; mortifies flesh and blood; crucifies the lusts and desires; rejoices in the cross of Christ; renews and regenerates, quickeneth, makes free and gives peace in Christ Jesus. Behold, such a faith, I say, is the gift of God, Eph. 2: 8, by which the righteous, according to the scriptures, are to live as did Abel, Enoch, Noah, Abraham, Moses, Rahab and all the saints. Every good tree bringeth forth good fruit after its kind, Matt. 7: 17; every tree which bringeth not forth good fruit, although in its full foliage, must be accursed and consumed with fire, Matt. 3: 10. Thus also a fruitless, powerless faith, such as is possessed by the world, and does not work by love, be it ever so learned, wise, eloquent, plausible and

---

* Salvation is the gift of God.

miraculous, still, it is in the sight of God unclean, dead and accursed, 1 Cor. 13: 2.

Therefore, we exhort you, with Christ Jesus, "Believe the gospel;" that is, believe the joyful news, the message of divine grace through Jesus Christ; leave off sinning, manifest repentance for your past lives, submit to the word and will of the Lord; then you will become heirs and joint-heirs, citizens and children of the new and heavenly Jerusalem, made free from your enemies, hell, sin, death and the devil, and walk according to the Spirit, and not according to the flesh, Rom. 8: 6. *Quid credit filio dei habet vitan aeternam*, i. e., He that believeth on the Son of God hath everlasting life, John 3: 36.

A SUPPLICATION TO THE MAGISTRACY.

We poor, wretched men, deprived of all human assistance and consolation, who like innocent sheep without a shepherd, have become a prey to the roaring lions of the forest, and devouring beasts of the field; a spectacle and reproach to the whole world, have to suffer daily, under the oppressive sword of lords and princes; have to hear and endure, the inhuman revilings and abuse of the learned, the abominable lying and scoffing of the common people; we humbly entreat the imperial majesty, kings, lords, princes, authorities and officers, every one in his calling, dignity and honor, and all our beloved and gracious rulers, through the deep and bloody wounds of our blessed Lord Jesus Christ, that you would but once lay aside all displeasure and evil opinions concerning us, and with sincere pity reflect upon the inhuman and severe trials, misery, necessities, crosses and martyrizations of your distressed and innocent servants; for the great God before whom we stand, who is the Searcher of all hearts, and before whose eyes all things are open and revealed; who knows that we seek nothing else upon this earth than that we, with a good conscience, may live according to his holy commandments, ordinances, word and will; but if there are some pernicious sects, as alas! in our day there have been, they will, no doubt, in due time become manifest.

Do therefore condescend so much as to peruse our writings diligently and meditate upon them with a God-fearing and impartial heart, so that you may know with certainty why we are not deterred from our doctrine, faith and practice, by coercion, poverty, misery persecution and death; that you may thus more thoroughly examine the truth and be no longer guilty of innocent blood. Be pleased to show some natural candor, and human charity towards your poor servants. Think not in your hearts, that we poor, forsaken men, after the flesh, are wood or stone; but we are with you descended from one father, Adam, and from one mother, Eve, and are created by the same God, having a common entrance into this world, are clothed with the same nature, desiring rest and peace, concerned for wives and children as well as you, and naturally, as all other creatures on earth, fearful of death.

Therefore, humble yourselves in the name of Jesus, that your poor souls may be saved. Examine I say, our doctrine and instructions, and you will find through the grace of God, that they are the pure and unadulterated doctrines of Christ, the holy word, the word of eternal peace, the word of eternal truth, the word of divine grace, the word of our salvation, the unconquerable word, against which the gates of hell shall never prevail, Matt. 16: 18; they are the two-edged sword that proceeded out of the mouth of the Lord, Rev. 1: 16, the sword of the spirit by which all must be judged, that dwell upon the earth, Eph. 6: 17.

O, ye beloved sirs, put the sword into the sheath; for as true as the Lord liveth, you do not fight against flesh and blood, but against Him, whose eyes are a flame of fire, who judgeth and maketh war in righteousness; who is crowned with many crowns, whose name no one knoweth but himself; who is clothed with a vesture dipped in blood; whose name is called the Word of God; who rules the nations with a rod of iron; who treads the winepress of the fierceness and wrath of almighty God; who hath on his vesture and on his thigh a name written, KING OF KINGS, AND LORD OF LORDS, Rev. 19: 11—16.

O, ye highly renowned lords and princes, it is against this Being that you are in this manner contending with your counsel and sword. Remember what the great prophet of the Lord, Zechariah, said concerning the children of God, who, in this world are ever subject to suffering, "He that toucheth you, toucheth the apple of mine eye," Zech. 2: 8. It is a fearful abomination, and bitter enmity, thus miserably to murder, destroy and exterminate those, who with such warm hearts, seek the Lord and eternal life, and who would not molest any one upon the earth. "Precious in the sight of the Lord," David says, "is the death of his saints," Ps. 116: 15. It is Jesus of Nazareth whom ye persecute, Acts 9: 5, and not us; therefore awake, forbear, fear God and his word, for we shall all be called to appear before one Judge, before whom neither power, exaltation, comeliness, fine speech nor talents will avail. Judgment will there be passed in righteousness upon all flesh, impartially and without respect to persons; the oppressed will then receive justice, and the crucified Jesus with his elect, released from the power of death, and the hands of tyrants, will enter into his promised inheritance, kingdom and glory.

Seeing then that you deal so unjustly and tyranically, according to the evil intentions of your hearts, without the sanction of scripture and mercy, with the helpless and God-fearing, how can you expect any grace and mercy in the day of the Lord? when we shall all have to stand before the impartial judgment seat, where every one will be rewarded according to his deeds, 2 Cor. 5: 10.

We desire not such favors as the evil-doers of this world; for we have not sinned in this our doctrine, faith and practice, although we have to suffer so much; but we, only with the word of the Lord, as the scriptures direct us, resist the anti-christian doctrines, ordinances and life. We resist neither the emperor, the king, nor any authority to which they are called of God; but we are ready to obey till death, in all things which are not contrary to God and his word, and well know what the scriptures teach and enjoin concerning this matter, Rom. 13: 1—8. But we desire so much mercy, that under your gracious protection we may live, teach, labor, and serve the Lord, according to the dictates of our consciences, so that to you and many with you, the gospel of Christ may be rightly preached, and the gate of life opened. Alas! if the learned had the word of God, and we had it not, how gladly would we be taught by them. But since we have it, and they do not, therefore we pray, for Jesus' sake, do not urge us to leave Christ and join anti-christ; to go from truth to error; from life to certain death.

Oh, ye renowned lords and princes, who are appointed of God, to be heads and rulers, consider well and believe on the word of the Lord; for if you will not desist from unrighteousness, fear God and do right, it would be better for you if you had never been born. The innocent blood of Abel calls unto heaven, and will be strictly demanded at your hands at the last day. Again we say, awake, fear God's word; for God, the Lord himself, will rule in heaven, in his kingdom, that is, in the hearts of men. He will permit none to detract from his glory, or become exalted above him. Lucifer, the fair angel of God, desired to exalt himself to the Most High, and was cast out of heaven into the abyss of hell; and is retained in chains of darkness till the judgement of the last day, Isa. 14: 12—15; Rev. 12: 7—9; Pet. 2: 4.

Beloved Sirs, receive it in love, and be not offended, for the truth must be made known. Your pride has arisen to heaven; look to Christ and his word, his example and his life; judge impartially, and you will find this to be true. The Almighty, eternal Father, through his eternal Wisdom, Christ Jesus, has instituted and commanded all things in his kingdom, that is, in his church, relating to doctrines, sacraments and life, according to his divine counsel, will and wisdom. But you, through the counsel and instigation of the learned, by your inhuman, and cruel mandates, have changed, destroyed and corrupted these, as if the almighty and eternal word should yield to your command and authority; and as though the divine ordinances of the Son of God might be changed into a more suitable form, and to a better purpose through the wisdom of men. O presumption of all presumption! O folly of all follies! Why exalt thyself, O earth and dust! Acknowledge Christ Jesus, your chief Lord, who, of God, is made to you a Prince and Judge. "The heaven, even the heavens are the Lord's," saith David, "but the earth hath he given to the children of men," Ps. 115: 16. I have no doubt, that if any were to rise up against the emperor or king, and enter into his kingdom and government, he would not be borne with patiently, nor go unpunished; how much less then, will a poor, fleshly mortal go unpunished, who rises up against the Almighty Emperor, and King, Christ Jesus, to dethrone him from the seat of his divine majesty, and to rob him of his sceptre, and the crown of his glory, as though Christ Jesus, the eternal wisdom of God, was unreasonable and unfit for the heavenly government. Reflect what became of those haughty and proud hearts from the beginning, who desired to place their seats unto the throne of God.

Therefore, humble yourselves under the mighty hand of God, as Peter teaches. Take as an example, the great and prosperous king Nebuchadnezzar, and observe how grievously God punished him, on account of his pride; and how, after being punished, he turned to wisdom, feared the Almighty, highly praised his wonderful and glorious works, and his great and adorable name.

Beloved Sirs, awake, and mend your ways, for it does not become the creature to rise up against the Creator. Christ *alone* will be the head of his church, the Teacher in his school; and he *alone*, the King who will judge his kingdom; not with the doctrines and commands of men, nor with slaying and murdering, but with his Holy Spirit, power, grace and word.

Therefore, we pray you, O ye great ones of the earth, whom we, through the mercy of God, acknowledge in all temporal things, as our gracious lords, that you would receive the eternal, Almighty King, Christ Jesus, as the only Savior, Lord and sovereign of our poor souls, even as he was ordained by his Father; and that you would attend to the duties of your office and temporal government, to which you have been called; for we with all our hearts, desire to render unto "Cæsar, the things which are Cæsar's; and unto God the things which are God's," Matt. 22: 21. Be pleased also to consider this, our doctrine and instruction, concerning baptism, the Lord's supper, and the shunning of Babylonian deeds; and compare them well with the word of the Lord. We hope, through the grace of God, that you will find, in truth, that we believe and teach nothing but that which the true oracle of the Lord has commanded us, and the holy apostles have taught and confirmed; to this end, may the great Lord grant you his grace, Amen.

CONCERNING BAPTISM.

Christ, after his resurrection, commanded his apostles, saying, "Go ye therefore, and teach all nations, baptizing them in the name of the Father, and of the Son, and of the Holy Ghost; teaching them to observe all things whatsoever I have commanded you; and, lo, I am with you alway, even unto the end of the world, Amen," Matt. 28: 19, 20.

Here we have the Lord's command concerning baptism, when and how, after the ordinance of God, it shall be administered and received; namely, that the gospel must first be preached, and then those baptized who believe therein, as Christ says, "Go ye into all the world, and preach the gospel to every creature; he that believeth and is baptized shall be saved, but he that believeth not, shall be damned," Mark. 16: 15. Thus has the Lord commanded and ordered; therefore, let no other be taught, or practiced forever. The word of God abideth forever. Young children are without understanding and cannot be taught, therefore, baptism cannot be administered to them without perverting the ordinance of the Lord; misusing his exalted name, and doing violence to his holy word. In the New Testament there are no ordinances enjoined upon infants, for it treats, both in doctrines and sacraments, with those who have ears to hear, and hearts to understand, Matt. 13: 16. Even as Christ commanded, so the holy apostles also taught and practiced, as may be plainly perceived in many parts of the New Testament. Thus Peter said, "Repent, and be baptized every one of you in the name of Jesus Christ for the remission of sins, and ye shall receive the gift of the Holy Ghost," Acts 2: 38. Again, Philip said to the eunuch, "If thou believest with all thine heart, thou mayest," Acts 8: 37. Here, faith did not follow baptism, but baptism followed faith, Mark 16: 16.

Christ has thus commanded baptism, and received it himself, according to the following manner: When the time had come, and the hour had approached, in which he would fulfill the commission enjoined upon him, preach the word, and make known his Father's holy name, he came to John, to the Jordan, and desired to be baptized of him, that he might fulfill all righteousness. He prepared to meet temptation, misery, the cross and death, and as a willing, obedient child, resigned himself to the will of his Almighty Father; he himself saith, "I came down from heaven, not to do mine own will, but the will of Him that send me," Jn. 6: 38. He was baptized of John, attested to by the Holy Ghost, and acknowledged by the Father, as a beloved Son, Matt. 3: 17; 17: 5.

Behold, thus Christ commands, and was himself baptized; thus the apostles taught, and practiced. Who will rise up against the Lord, and say, it shall not be so? Who will teach and instruct wisdom? Who will accuse the apostles and evangelists with falsehood? It would be entirely unbecoming for a child to command and judge his father, or a servant, his master, and it is much more unbecoming for the creature to exalt himself above his Creator. But now it is manifest that the whole world, with its unprofitable doctrines, and commandments of men; with its anti-christian customs, long standing usages, its tyrannical, murdering sword, judges over Christ and his word. The truths of Christ are esteemed lies; his wisdom, foolishness; his light, darkness, and his gospel, perverted and false. In short, Christ must be silent and suffer.

Now it may probably be said, that this was necessary in the beginning of the gospel, because at that time, there were no believers whose children might be baptized; but now, if the parents are believers, then are the children also to be baptized, even as Abraham, when he believed, circumcised his children, Gen. 17: 23. O no! this does not follow.

Although Abraham believed God, only one-half of his seed was circumcised, namely, the male children, and not the female, though he was the father of the female, as well as of the male children, of which, by the grace of God, more shall be said in the replication.

In the beginning the gospel was to be preached, and faith followed hearing, and baptism followed faith; this is incontrovertable, for so the Scriptures teach, Rom. 10: 17. But that the children of believers should be baptized because Abraham's children were circumcised, can in no wise be sustained by Scripture; but if it could be established, though it cannot, there would then be but few children baptized, for the number of true believers, it is to be lamented, is very small, as any one may see.

They are not all christians who are so called. But those only who have the Spirit of Christ, are true christians, though I know not where many are to be found. Yea, what more shall we say? All who with Abel bring an acceptable offering; those who are born with Isaac of the free woman, and with Jacob have the birthright, and have obtained the paternal blessing, must be slain by bloodthirsty Cain, mocked by Ishmael, and hated by Esau, even as we hear and see on all sides. May God effect a change for the better.

Behold, this is the word and will of the

Lord, that all who hear and believe the word of God, shall be baptized (as above stated), thereby to profess their faith, and declare that they will henceforth not live according to their own will, but according to the will of God. That for the testimony of Jesus they are prepared to forsake their homes, chattels, lands and lives, and to suffer hunger, affliction, oppression, persecution, the cross and death; yea, they desire to bury the flesh with its lusts, and arise with Christ to newness of life, even as Paul says, "Know ye not that so many of us as were baptized into Jesus Christ, were baptized into his death? Therefore we are buried with him by baptism into death; that like as Christ was raised up from the dead by the glory of the Father, even so we also should walk in newness of life," Col. 2: 11, 12; Rom. 6: 3, 4.

Beloved Reader, take heed to the word of the Lord, for this also Paul teaches, who received not his gospel of men, but of the Lord himself; even as Christ died and was buried, so also ought we to die unto our sins, and be buried with Christ in baptism; we are not to do this after we have been baptized, but we must commence and do all this before hand. "For if we have been planted together in the likeness of his death, we shall be also in the likeness of his resurrection. Knowing this, that our old man is crucified with him, that the body of sin might be destroyed, that henceforth we should not serve sin; for he that is dead is freed from sin," Rom. 6: 5—7; for even as Christ died, hath taken away sin, and liveth unto God, so every true christian dieth unto sin, and liveth unto God.

Think not that we teach, that christians are to die unto sin, in such a manner, as to become insensible to sin. Not by any means; but they die unto sin, so as to be no longer obedient to their impure lusts, as Paul says, "Let not sin therefore reign in your mortal body, that ye should obey it in the lusts thereof," Rom. 6: 12; also, John says, "Whosoever is born of God doth not commit sin; for his seed remaineth in him; and he cannot sin,* because he is born of God," 1 Jn. 3: 9; 5: 18.

---

*According to the Holland, "He has *no desire* to sin."

For as the death of our Lord would not have profited us, had he not risen from the power of death to the praise of his Father, neither will it avail us anything to bury our sins in baptism, if we do not arise with Christ Jesus from the power of sin, unto a new life, to the praise of the Lord. "For in that he (Christ) died, he died unto sin once," says Paul, "but in that he liveth, he liveth unto God; likewise, reckon yourselves to be dead indeed unto sin, but alive unto God, through Jesus Christ." And, "As ye have yielded your members servants to uncleanness and iniquity, unto iniquity; even so now yield your members, servants to righteousness and holiness." For being made free from sin, ye became the servants of righteousness, and have your fruit unto holiness, and the end everlasting life, Rom. 6: 10, 11, 18, 19, 22.

Here observe, intelligent reader; you who desire to know the truth, and seek the salvation of your soul, what the great and holy apostle Paul has taught you. If you believe his word, doctrine and testimony to be true, you will no doubt readily perceive, from these instructions, and from many other passages in the Scriptures, that baptism is no more applicable to infants, than circumcision was to the females of the Israelites; for we are no more commanded to baptize infants than Israel was to circumcise female children. It is also impossible for little children to die to sin, as long as they have not been made alive to it; neither can they rise to a new life, as long as they are not born of God through faith, and by the Spirit of God led into righteousness. Therefore beware, for the intent of baptism is to bury sin, and to rise with Christ into a new life, which can by no means, be the case with infants; therefore, consider well what the word of the Lord teaches you on this subject.

Again, Paul calls baptism "the washing of regeneration." O Lord, how lamentably thy Holy Word is abused. Is it not greatly to be lamented, that men are attempting, notwithstanding these plain passages, to maintain their idolatrous invention of infant baptism, and set forth that infants are regenerated thereby, as if regeneration was simply a pressing into the water? O no, regeneration is not such a work of hypocrisy, but is an inward change, which converts a man by the power of God, through faith, from evil to good, from carnality to spirituality, from unrighteousness to righteousness, out of Adam into Christ, which can in no wise take place with infants. The regenerated live by the power of the new life; they crucify the flesh with its evil lusts; they put off the old Adam with his deeds; they avoid every appearance of evil; they are taught, governed and influenced by the Holy Ghost, Rom. 1: 17.

Behold this is true regeneration with its fruits, of which the Scriptures speak, and comes through faith in the word of God, without which no one, who has arrived to the years of understanding, can be saved; as Christ says, "Verily, Verily, I say unto thee, except a man be born again, he cannot see the kingdom of God," Jn. 3: 3. Yea, it is all in vain, if one were even baptized of Peter, or Paul, or Christ himself, if he were not baptized from above with the Holy Ghost and with fire, Matt. 3: 11, as Paul says, "In Christ Jesus neither circumcision availeth anything, nor uncircumcision, but a new creature," Gal. 5: 6; 2 Cor. 5: 17. All who are thus born of God, changed and renewed in the inner man, and translated from Adam into Christ, are ready to obey the word of the Lord, and say with holy Paul, "Lord, what wilt thou have me to do?" They deny themselves with all their minds and hearts; they submit to the word and ordinances of the Lord, without dislike or opposition; they receive baptism according to the command of the Lord, Matt. 28: 19. They become and manifest themselves as fruitful branches of Christ, the true Vine, and joint heirs in the church of the Lord, John 15: 5. They receive forgiveness of their sins, and the gift of the Holy Ghost; they put on Christ; enter the ark of safety, and are secured from the dreadful flood of wrath, which, like a net, will come upon all them that dwell upon the earth. This, however, is not effected by the power of the water or the sign, but by the power of the divine word, received through faith; for where there is no faith, which through love worketh obedience (we again speak of those who have come to the years of understanding), there is no promise. "He that believeth not the Son, shall not see life; but the wrath of God abideth on him," Jn. 3: 36.

The Lord commanded Moses that he should stretch forth his hand, and with the rod smite the sea, and the waters should be divided. Moses believed the word of the Lord; stretched forth his hand and smote the sea with his rod; the waters were divided and Israel was redeemed; not by the rod and the stroke, but by the power of the divine word received by Moses, through a sincere and living faith. Had Moses not believed the word of God, and through disobedience not smote the sea, undoubtedly affrighted and oppressed Israel would have fared ill. He also received a command in the wilderness to erect a brazen serpent, so that when Israel looked thereon, they might be healed of the bite of the serpents. Moses believed the word of the Lord, and erected a serpent; Israel looked upon it and was healed, not through the virtue of the image, but through the power of the divine word, received by them through faith. In the same manner salvation is ascribed to scriptural baptism, Mark. 16: 16; the forgiveness of sins, Acts 2: 38; the putting on of Christ, Gal. 3: 27, and incorporation into his church; not on account of the water, or the administered sign (else the kingdom of God would depend upon the elements and signs), but on account of the power and truth of the divine promise, which we receive by obedience through faith. For all those who teach reliance upon words, the elements and works, with Aaron, make a golden calf, and suffer a people without understanding to commit idolatry and abominations therewith, for in Christ, faith alone availeth, which worketh by love, the new creature, and the keeping of the commandments of God.

Beloved sirs, friends, and brethren, awake and delay not, render the Most High his due praise and honor, and give ear to his holy word, for those who maintain that the baptism of children that are incapable of understanding, is a washing of regeneration, do violence to the word of God; resist the Holy Ghost; make Christ a liar, and his holy apostles false witnesses; for Christ and his apostles teach that regeneration comes through faith from God and his word, which word is not to be taught to those who are unable to hear or understand,* but to those who have the ability, both to hear and understand; this is incontrovertible.

The holy apostle Peter also explains the same and says, that "even baptism doth also now save us; not the putting away of the filth of the flesh, but the answer of a good conscience toward God (or the covenant of a good conscience toward God), by the resurrection of Jesus Christ," 1 Pet. 3: 21.

Here Peter teaches us how the inward baptism saves us, by which the inner man is washed, and not the outward baptism by which the flesh is washed; for only this inward baptism, as already stated, is of value in the sight of God, while outward baptism follows only as an evidence of obedience which is of faith; for could outward baptism save without the inner washing, the whole Scriptures which speak of the new man, would be spoken to no purpose. The kingdom of heaven would be bound to elementary water; the blood of Christ would be shed in vain, and no one that is baptized could be lost. No, no! outward baptism avails nothing so long as we are not inwardly renewed, regenerated, and baptized of God, with the heavenly fire and the Holy Ghost. But when we receive this baptism from above, we will be constrained through the Spirit and word of God, by a good conscience, which we thereby obtain, to believe sincerely in the merits of the death of the Lord, and in the power and benefits of his resurrection; and henceforth, because we are inwardly cleansed by faith, and the spiritual strength which we have received, we submissively covenant with the Lord, through the outward sign of baptism, which is enjoined on all the believers in Christ, even as the Lord has covenanted with us in his grace, through his word, that we will no longer live according to the evil, unclean lusts of the flesh, but walk according to the witness of a good conscience before him.

Though these words of Peter are very plain, the learned are not ashamed to force them into a very different signification, by means of their plausible comments and their much boasted reason (probably that they may retain the favor of the world, and live in opulence without cross or affliction), and teach, that baptism is a sign of grace ; which according to my limited understanding, can in no wise be established. Our sign of grace is Christ Jesus alone, through whom God's abundant love is freely dispensed and declared unto us. By signs he was gloriously prefigured to the ancient patriarchs, as by the coats of skin to Adam and Eve; by the rainbow to Noah, by circumcision to Abraham, by which sign they were assured of the divine covenant. But we are assured of God, of his divine grace, and his eternal peace, by this one sign only, which is Christ Jesus. The seal in our consciences is the Holy Ghost, but baptism is a sign of obedience, commanded of Christ, by which we testify, when we receive it; that we believe the word of the Lord, that we are sorry for, and repent of our former life and conduct; that we desire to rise with Christ unto a new life; and that we believe in the forgiveness of sin through Jesus Christ. Not, my beloved, that we believe in the remission of sins through baptism; by no means; because by baptism we cannot obtain faith and repentance, neither do we receive the forgiveness of sins, nor peace, nor liberty of conscience, but we testify thereby that we have repented, received pardon and faith in Christ, as before said. With the fathers it was not thus, for they, through the signs, received assurance and comfort that the promise would be true and sure. We have this assurance in Christ Jesus alone, in whom all the figurative signs were completed; so that we have in this only true sign, Christ, that which the fathers had in many figurative signs. In short, had we forgiveness of sins and peace of conscience, through outward ceremonies and elements, then the REALITY would be superceded, and his merits made of no effect.

Behold, this is the only and true foundation of baptism maintained by the Scriptures, and none other. This we teach and practice though all the gates of hell rise against us; for we know it is the revealed word of the Lord, and his divine ordinance, from which we dare not take away, nor add

---

* This has reference to infants, that are incapable of understanding.

thereto, lest we be found disobedient and false before God (who alone is the Lord and God of our consciences), for, "every word of the Lord is pure; he is a shield unto them that put their trust in him," Prov. 30: 5.

Oh God, what are the learned and highly learned masters of this world doing, who are so earnestly engaged in derogating from God's word and wisdom, and ingeniously urging their own vain reason and wisdom; they will not prosper; God will not give his honor to another, for he is the Lord; that is his name, and beside him there is no other, Isa. 42: 8. Conquering, he will conquer them. He will turn wisdom to folly and their reason to disgrace, for he "knoweth the thoughts of the wise, that they are vain," 1 Cor. 3: 20.

Luther writes, that children should be baptized on account of their own faith, and adds, "If children had no faith, then their baptism would be blaspheming the sacrament," &c. It appears to me, to be a great error in this learned man, through whose writings at first the Lord effected much good, that he maintained that children, without knowledge and understanding, had faith, while the Scriptures teach so plainly, that they know not good from evil, that they cannot discern right from wrong, and he (Luther) says that faith is dormant and concealed in children even as in a believing person who is asleep, till they arrive at the years of understanding. If Luther writes this as his sincere opinion, he writes much in vain concerning faith and its power, but if he writes to please men, may God have mercy upon him, for I know of a truth it is only human reason and the invention of men; but it shall not make void the word and ordinance of the Lord. We do not read in Scripture that the Apostles baptized a single believer while asleep. They baptized those who were awake, and not the slumbering. Why then do they baptize their children before that sleeping faith awakes and is confessed by them?

Bucer does not thus support this doctrine, but he maintains infant baptism differently, namely, not that children have faith, but that they, by baptism may be added to the church of the Lord, and instructed in his word. He admits that infant baptism is not expressly commanded, nevertheless he maintains that it is right. O Lord! how lamentably they do err, who court the favor and honor of men, and seek not the favor and honor of God. Since infant baptism is not expressly commanded of God, as he acknowledges, it cannot be acceptable to the Lord, *Et per consequence*, i. e., and by consequence, no promise can follow. Therefore, the reader should know, that true christians ought not to be governed in this matter, by the opinions and traditions of men, but by the word and the ordinances of God. For we have but one Lord and Master of our conscience, Christ Jesus, whose word, will, command and ordinance, it becomes us, as his willing disciples, to follow, even as the bride rejoices greatly to hear the bridegroom's voice, John 3: 29.

Since we have not a single command in the Scriptures that infants are to be baptized, or that the apostles did practice it; we modestly confess, with a good conscience, that infant baptism is but human invention; a selfish notion; a perversion of the ordinance of Christ; a manifest abomination, standing in the holy place, where it ought, properly, not to be, Matt. 24: 15.

Beloved sirs, how little the word of the Lord is regarded, which says, Ye shall not do after that which is right in your own eyes, but observe whatsoever I command you, Deut. 12: 8. Did not the Father testify from heaven and declare, "This is my beloved son, in whom I am well pleased; hear ye him?" Matt. 17: 5. Does not the whole Scripture direct us to Christ? Are we not baptized in his name that we should hear his voice, and be obedient to his word? Do you not boast to be the apostolic church? Why do you then depart from Christ and adhere to anti-christ; from the apostolic doctrine and practice to the doctrine and practice of the learned? Do observe how severely and frequently God punished men for the self-formed opinions which they maintained as works of holiness and divine worship.

Nadab and Abihu, because they offered strange fire before the Lord, were suddenly destroyed by fire, before the altar, through the wrath of God.

Saul had mercy on Agag, the king of the

Amalekites, and prompted by his good intentions, spared the best sheep and oxen, to sacrifice unto the Lord, contrary to the word of the prophet. That seeming act of mercy and laudable zeal was punished as the sin of witchcraft and idolatry, because he acted according to his own judgment, and not according to the word of the prophet. He was reproved by the prophet, smitten with a pestilence, his kingdom taken from him, and given to a more faithful one, 1 Sam. 15: 23.

Manasseh, the king of the Jews, and others in Israel, made their children pass through fire. They built temples and altars in all the high places, also in cities and countries, with good intentions; for they were desirous thereby to honor the Almighty and eternal God, as may be plainly seen, 2 Kings 21: 3—6. This glorious and holy choice was so offensive before God, that Jeremiah refused to intercede for the people. Israel was desolated, Jerusalem and the temple burnt; and the people with the holy vessels were carried into a foreign land, 2 Kings 25: 9; 2 Chron. 36: 12. Therefore, saith God by the prophet, Obey my voice, and I will be your God, and ye shall be my people; and walk ye in all the ways that I have commanded you; not those of your own choice; that it may be well with you, Jer. 7: 23.

What advice then, my beloved friends, shall be given in relation to such wilful deceivers, who so presumptuously do violence to the expressed word of the Lord, and so shamefully belie the Almighty, the Most High God, and teach that it is the word of God; though such things he never proposed, much less commanded, and never will.

How awful it is thus to sin against God, and so lamentably to pervert his holy and precious word! Yea, they shall be severely punished of the Lord with heavy judgments, they shall not escape the ire of his fierce wrath, if they do not repent and reform; for God is an enemy to all liars. They have neither part nor lot in his kingdom; but their portion is eternal destruction, in the lake of fire, 2 Thes. 2: 8; Rev. 20: 10; 19: 20.

In the second place, it is evident, that infant baptism is an accursed, abominable and idolatrous institution; for all those who are baptized in infancy, are called christians and are accounted partakers of the Lord's grace, merits, death and blood, and are called his people, although the whole course of their lives, is entirely heathenish, wild and dissolute; yea, they indulge in nothing but gluttony, drinking, gaming, whoring, cursing and swearing, as though the water in baptism could make and preserve them christians. O no! Paul declares, "He that hath not the Spirit of Christ, is none of his," Rom. 8: 9. Yea, the helpless, innocent children, though baptized with the blood of the Lord, and having the sure promise of the kingdom of God, if not baptized, with this baptism, must be buried without the grave yard as accursed. What infamy!—what blindness! We will say nothing of godfathers, of crossing, breathing upon, sprinkling with salt water, anointing, spitting upon, and their abominable exorcism, all of which is nothing else than open blasphemy, and not commanded of God. What abominable, detestable idolatry these things are.

In the third place, we are informed by historians, ancient, and modern, and also in the decrees, that baptism was changed both as to its mode and time of administering. In the beginning of the holy church, persons were baptized in common water on their first profession, upon their own faith, according to the Scriptures. Afterwards a change was made; they were examined seven times before being baptized; after that, they were baptized at two stated periods; namely, at Easter and Whitsuntide. Higinius, the tenth pope, instituted godfathers, in the year A. D. 146. Finally, Luther tells us, that in the year A. D. 407, Pope Innocent confirmed infant baptism by a decree, and it is to be feared that it will not be abrogated, but at the expense of much innocent blood of the saints and children of God; even as the prophets, in their days reproved the accursed abominations and idolatry of the kings, priests and people, not by admonition only, but also with their blood, as we read in both sacred and profane history.

If infant baptism was commanded of God, in his word, why did Innocent add his decree? How can baptism as practiced by the world, be right, since it has been so frequently changed? We entreat you, for Jesus' sake, to reflect that Christ Jesus and not the learned, is King and Lord of his Church; and rules over it with his sceptre, Spirit and word, Matt. 11: 27. As it is said, He is made unto us Wisdom, and none can instruct him; he appeared, in order that he might testify to the truth. They that love the truth, hear his voice; believe his word, and not that of the learned; for his word is truth; but the word of the learned, in this respect, is seduction; for Christ commands that believers should be baptized; but in relation to infants, that are without understanding, he gave no command. But the learned say, he that has not his children baptized, and is himself baptized upon his faith, as Christ commanded, is a fanatic, ana-baptist and heretic.

We have here given you the principal reasons why we oppose infant baptism, not only in doctrine, but also to the sacrifice of our lives and possessions. For we well know, by the grace of God, that there is not one word in the Scriptures in its support. We tell you the truth and lie not. Is there one under the canopy of heaven who can show us, by divine truth, that Jesus Christ, the Son of Almighty God, the Eternal Wisdom and Truth, whom alone we acknowledge as the Lawgiver, and Teacher of the New Testament, has given a single command that children should be baptized; or that his holy apostles ever so taught, or practiced?

What need then to urge this upon us by tyranny and punishment? Only show it to us in the word of God, and the difficulty is removed. For God, who is omniscient, knows, that in our weakness, we humbly seek to walk according to the divine ordinances, word and will, for which we, poor miserable men, are shamefully reviled, banished, robbed and slain by every one in many countries, like innocent sheep; but the Lord be eternally praised! We are esteemed as unworthy of heaven or earth, even as Christ said, "They shall deliver you up to be afflicted, and shall kill you; and ye shall be hated of all nations for my name's sake," Matt. 24: 9.

It is our determination, in this matter as in all other matters of conscience, in view of the wrath of Almighty God, that we will not be influenced by lords and princes, nor by doctors and teachers of schools, nor by the influence of the fathers, and long established customs, for in this matter, neither emperors, nor kings, nor doctors, nor licentiates, nor councils, nor proscriptions against the word of God, will avail. We dare not be bound to any person, power, wisdom or times, but we must be governed alone, by the expressed and positive commands of Christ, and the pure doctrines and practices of his holy apostles, as remarked above; for if we do so, we neither deceive any one in this matter, nor are we deceived. Alas! woe to him, woe to him, who departs from this foundation, or is compelled to do so, either through the infirmities of the flesh or tyranny, or by false doctrine; and will not testify of the word of his Lord until death, unto this wicked and sinful generation, both in word and deed, Matt. 10: 38; 16: 24.

Observe, all of you who persecute the word of the Lord and his people, this is our instruction, doctrine and belief concerning baptism, according to the instruction of the words of Christ, namely, we must first hear the word of God, believe it, and then upon our faith be baptized; we are not seditious or contentious; we do not approve of polygamy; neither do we seek nor wait for any kingdom upon earth.

O no! no! to God be eternal praise; we well know what the word of the Lord teaches us and testifies to, on this subject. The word of the Lord commands us that we, with a sincere heart, desire to die to sin, to bury our sins with Christ, and with him to rise to a new life, even as baptism is a figure thereof.

That we seek to walk humbly and uprightly in Christ Jesus, in the covenant of his grace, and his eternal peace, and with an approved conscience before God, even as the mouth of the Lord has commanded; as he has testified by his example, and as we are taught by the pure doctrines and practices of the apostles, 1 Pet. 3: 21.

COUNTER ARGUMENTS WITH THEIR REPLICATIONS.

Having briefly noticed the Lord's command, and the apostolic doctrine, practices and signification of baptism; that it is and will be the true baptism to the end of time, we will also, now, through the grace of God, as a duty, refer and reply to some scriptural passages of which the learned wrongfully make use, to make void the ordinance of the Lord, and place in its stead their own.

In the first place, they teach that we are all the children of wrath, and sinful; born of the sinful seed of Adam, and therefore, say they, children are to be baptized, in order to be purified and washed from original sin, &c.

To this we reply thus: With the word of the Lord, we believe and confess that we all come from, and are born of unclean seed; that we through the first Adam, who was of the earth, became wholly depraved, and children of death and of hell, Rom. 5: 12. Nevertheless, as we fell, and became sinners in Adam, we also believe and confess, that through Christ, the second and heavenly Adam, we were restored to grace and justified. For he appeared upon earth, that in and through him we might have life. Through him only we glory to have obtained grace, favor and the forgiveness of our sins with God our Father; and not through baptism, whether we are children or believers; for if redemption, and the washing away of original sin, were through baptism, and not by the blood of Christ alone, then would the sweet smelling sacrifice, which is of eternal worth, have been in vain, and without effect, or, there would be two remedies for our sins. Alas, no! the Scriptures speak but of one, which is Christ with his merits, death and blood, 1 Pet. 1: 19. Therefore, he who seeks the remission of his sins through baptism, rejects the blood of the Lord and makes water his idol. Therefore, let every one be careful lest he ascribe the honor and glory due to Christ, to the outward ceremonies and creature elements.

It is true, Peter says, "Repent and be baptized every one of you in the name of Jesus Christ, for the remission of sins." But this is not to be understood, that we receive the remission of our sins through baptism. O no! for if it be so, then Christ and his merits must fall. But we receive the remission of our sins, in baptism, as follows: The Lord commanded his gospel to be preached to every creature, so that all who believe and are baptized, may be saved. Where there is faith, which is called the gift of God, by Paul, there also are the power and the fruits of faith. Where there is an active, fruitful faith, there also is the promise; but where such a faith does not exist (we speak of adults), there also is no promise. For he that hears the word of the Lord, and believes it with the heart, manifests his fruit, and faithfully observes all things the Lord commanded him; for the Scriptures teach, the just shall live by faith, Heb. 10: 38. Then the remission of his sins is preached to him, as Peter teaches and instructs.

Had Noah and Lot not believed the word of the Lord, they would have fared ill. Had Abraham not believed, he would not have obtained such glorious promises; but they believed, and did right, and became heirs of righteousness, Heb. 11: 8.

Had Moses and Israel not believed the word of the Lord and been disobedient, how could they have been succored in the sea and in the wilderness? But they believed, and according to his promise, were protected by the mighty hand of the Lord. But those who provoked him, and believed not his gracious word, and the great miracles, fell in the wilderness, and entered not the promised land.

There was also reconciliation connected with the sacrifices of the Old Testament, not on account of the worth of the smoking offerings upon the altars; for it was not possible, says Paul, that the blood of bulls and goats should take away sin, Heb. 10: 4. Before it was offered, it was all the Lord's, and the cattle upon a thousand hills, were his, says David, Ps. 50: 10. But because the righteous believed the word of divine promise as true, and walked in obedience

CONCERNING BAPTISM.

to his command, so now also is the remission of sins preached through baptism; not on account of the water, or the ceremonies performed, for Christ, I repeat, is the only source of grace; but, because the righteous receive the promises of the Lord by faith, and obediently follow his word and will.

This direction does not extend to infants. For in all the Scriptures, there is not a single command given to baptize them. Therefore, it is not required of them as a sign of obedience. Since, then, infant baptism is performed without the command of God, it cannot be a ceremony of God, but a pernicious superstition of men, and evidently idolatry; therefore, the promise of God cannot rest upon such abominations. It seems to me, it is high time to awaken, and to give heed to the Scriptures. For Jesus' sake, sin is not imputed to infants that are innocent, and incapable of understanding. Life is promised, not through any one ceremony, but out of pure grace, through the blood of the Lord, as he himself says, "Suffer the little children to come unto me and forbid them not; for of such is the kingdom of God," Mark. 10: 14. But concerning baptism he did not command them any thing.

According to my opinion, it is a great error, which some entertain, that the children of the Jews were acceptable to Christ on account of circumcision; and that ours are acceptable to him on account of baptism. O blasphemy and infamy! In every instance, Christ, the only medium of divine grace must be set aside, and grace must be attributed to the lifeless rites and elements. Here I would ask all Pedo-baptists, how they are going to prove that these blessed children were all circumcised, and that there were not among them female children? If they were acceptable on account of their circumcision, as they pretend, then, why were not adults who were circumcised, acceptable?

Although they were circumcised, he commanded that adults should be baptized upon their faith; but concerning infants he gave no such command. He took them into his arms, laid his hands upon them and blessed them; promised them the kingdom, and dismissed them; but did not baptize them.

Thus did the wisdom of God himself; but the world would be his teacher. Christ does not command that infants should be baptized, but believers; but the world commands that we should baptize children and not believers.* Yea more, if any one is baptized upon his faith, because the Lord has so commanded; and for conscience' sake has not his children baptized, because God does not command it, his name, alas! is reproached by all, and he is subjected to torture, misery and death; and this is not to be attributed so much to the rulers, as to those who are esteemed teachers and preachers, for what the rulers do, they generally do by the counsel and instigation of the learned. By their fruits, they show who is their father, for they do his works. It seems to me they always have been, and ever will be those, who, with their false doctrines, revengeful spirits, and hard hearts, shed the blood of the righteous, Rev. 17: 6; 18: 24. Alas! such persecution is so disgraceful, that it is almost a shame to mention it. For as clear as the sun shines on this world, and is seen by every one, so manifest is the inhuman, raving tyranny of the learned against the Lamb and his chosen. God grant that the eyes of these blind, perverted, blood-thirsty teachers, with all their tyranny, may be opened, that they may become satisfied and weary of their false doctrine and the shedding of innocent blood, Amen.

In the second place, they teach that the children of Israel under the Old Testament, were admitted into God's covenant and church through circumcision; but now, our children are admitted through baptism. To this, in accordance with Scripture, we reply, No. Whoever reads the Scriptures understandingly, will clearly perceive, that Abraham was in covenant with the Lord, many years before he was circumcised. And that the children were circumcised on the eighth

---

* Menno means to say that Christ commands, that those who have come to years of understanding, who have the ability to receive the truth and believe it, should be baptized, and not infants who can neither receive nor understand the truth, and therefore are incapable of believing.

day, although they had been in the covenant before. For it is evident, that we do not become the children of God through any outward rites, but through the paternal and gracious choice, through Christ Jesus. But an outward sign was required of Abraham as a seal of obedience and faith. And likewise of his seed, that they should circumcise the male children on the eighth day; no sooner nor later, and not the female children. Had the covenant depended upon the sign, and not upon the assurance of grace, what would have become of the female children, and the males that died uncircumcised before the eighth day?

Beloved reader, give heed to the word of God. Although the women and female children were not circumcised, they had the promise in common, in the promised seed, the holy land, the kingdom and glory. They were no less the seed of Abraham and subject to the covenant of God, and the things signified by the sign thereof, than the circumcised men and male children. From which it is evident, that the children of Israel were not in the Lord's covenant, on account of circumcision, as Pedo-baptists assert, but through the divine choice of grace.

And even as Abraham and the children of Israel, the female as well as the male children, were in the covenant not through the sign, but through the divine choice, so also are our children in the covenant of God, although not baptized. The word of Paul is incontrovertible. He (God) has chosen us in him, before the foundation of the world, and has ordained us his children through Jesus Christ, Eph. 1: 4.

Again, Children are entitled to the kingdom of heaven, and are under the promise of the grace of God, through Christ; as has been said; and therefore we truly believe, that they are blessed, holy and pure, acceptable to God; are under the covenant, and in his church, but by no means, through any external sign; for there is not a word in all the Scriptures whereby to maintain, that children should be admitted into the covenant and the church by such a sign. Besides, it is very evident that they cannot be taught or admonished by word, or sacrament, as long as they are without the ability to hear and understand.

Therefore, are the signs not to be used for any other purpose than that for which they were instituted and commanded of the Lord. Since Christ has ordained and commanded to baptize believers; and has not said a word about infant baptism, we believe and teach that the baptism of believers is of God and his word, and infant baptism of the dragon and the beast.

All the rites ordained of God, both of the Old and New Testament, are ordained to exercise our faith and to show our obedience. Therefore we should not use and change them at our pleasure; but we must use them as the Lord himself has ordained and commanded, if we would escape being punished by the fierce wrath of God, as were Nadab and Abihu, Lev. 10: 2.

Since Christ has commanded that believers should be baptized, and not infants, and the holy apostles taught and practiced thus, in accordance with the instructions and commands of Christ, as may be seen in many places of the New Testament, all reasonable-minded men must admit, that infant baptism, although alas, practiced by nearly the whole world, and maintained by tyranny, is nothing less than a ceremony of anti-christ, open blasphemy, an enchanting sin, a molten calf; yea, abomination and idolatry.

We also well know how they apply circumcision as a figure of baptism, and adduce the saying of Paul in proof thereof, namely, "In whom also ye are circumcised with the circumcision made without hands, &c., Col. 2: 11. He that will attempt to prove, by this passage that infant baptism is right, does violence to holy Paul, and falsely perverts his testimony. For he does not teach that external circumcision is a figure of baptism, but alludes to inward circumcision. For even as actual circumcision of the foreskin was performed with a knife of stone, so also must our inbred and carnal nature be cut off with that spiritual knife of stone, and circumcised with a circumcision made without hands. The stone is Christ. The knife is the word of God, 1 Cor. 10: 4; Heb. 4: 12. It is with this circumcision that believers, not children, are circumcised, as Paul evidently intends to teach by this scripture, "Ye are circumcised with the circumcision made without hands, in putting off the body of the sins of the flesh by the circumcision of Christ, buried with him in baptism, wherein also ye are risen with him through the faith of the operation of God," Col. 2: 11. It appears to me, that these words plainly show that Paul spoke not in relation to the baptism of infants; but in regard to the inner circumcision of the believers. Read also what we said above concerning Romans 6.

In the third place, they say that children are regenerated, put on Christ, and receive the Holy Ghost in baptism.

To this we reply: To be regenerated, to put on Christ, and to receive the Holy Ghost, is one and the same thing; and according to its power, inseparable. Have you the one, you have the other also. But that does not at all concern infants; for regeneration takes place through faith, through the word of God, and is a change of heart, or of the inward man, as above said. To put on Christ, is to be transplanted into Christ, and to be like-minded with him. To receive the Holy Ghost, is to be a partaker of his gifts and power, to be taught, assured and influenced by him, as the Scriptures teach. This cannot take place with infants; for they have no ears to hear the word of the Lord, and no understanding to comprehend it; for through the word and the hearing of the word all this is accomplished.

Here it may be asked, whether God is not powerful enough to work faith in children; because John the baptist, yet unborn, leaped for joy in his mother's womb.

We reply to this, that we are not speaking of the power of God; he made aged and barren Sarah fruitful, and caused Balaam's ass to speak. But it does not follow that all old, barren women will become fruitful, and that all asses are to speak. He does not at all times do all that he can, or has power to do; we speak only of the precept of the Scriptures, what they teach and command us concerning this matter.

Because infants do not understand, they cannot believe, and because they do not believe, they cannot be born again. Reason teaches us that they cannot understand the word of God. That they do not believe and are not regenerated, is evident from their actions. Whether they are baptized or not, their inbred nature is prone to evil from their youth. They know no difference between Christ and satan; between good and evil; between life and death. Whereby then shall we know their faith, regeneration, or that they possess Christ and his Spirit? The regenerating word must first be heard and believed with a sincere heart, before regeneration, the putting on of Christ and the influences of the Holy Ghost follow.

Behold, thus we are taught by the word of the Lord. He that does, therefore, not desire the palatable bread of the divine word, upon which our souls have to live, may satisfy himself with the husks that the swine eat, Luke 15: 16; we cannot forbid him. I trust that the gracious Father will protect and preserve us forever, through his great mercy, from their anti-christian doctrines and Pharisaical leaven.

In the fourth place, they say that although infants are not so washed from original sin in baptism, that there are no remains of it, still, for the sake of baptism it shall not be imputed to them as sin.

To this we reply: Thus to teach and believe, is open blasphemy against Christ and his blood. I have proved more than once by the word of the Lord, that Christ is the only remedy for our sins, and that there is forever none other, Isa. 43: 25; Matt. 1: 21; Acts 4: 12. If men will not believe the word of God, there is no human help for them. But the way or manner in which believers receive the remission of sins, in baptism, is fully explained above, and he that reads it understandingly, will give the Lord Jesus the praise due him, and not ascribe the remission of his sins to rites and elements.

In the fifth place, they say that Christ has cleansed and sanctified his church with the washing of water by the word. Children, they say, belong to the church, therefore they must be cleansed with the washing of water by the word, Eph. 5: 26.

To this we reply: Paul does not speak of infants, but of those who hear and believe the word of the Lord, and thus by faith, are sanctified and cleansed in their hearts; for such are cleansed by the washing of water, as the mouth of the Lord has commanded.

Since infants have not this pure, sanctifying faith, nor the means thereto (that is, the understanding), and are not commanded in Scripture to be baptized; how can they then be cleansed with the washing of water by the word, having no faith in the word, and no washing of water by the word? Therefore, all pedo-baptists should know, that their infant baptism does neither cleanse nor sanctify, but that it is idolatry *in toto*, without promise, pernicious, and contrary to the word of the Lord.

We have before shown, that the remission of sins, or reconciliation was connected with, and consequent upon the Jewish offerings, if performed according to the instructions of Moses. But when not thus performed, they did not obtain reconciliation, but made themselves the more guilty, as Saul, Uzziah, Nadab, Abihu and others. In like manner is the church sanctified and cleansed, with the washing of water, by the word, if it is done in every respect according to the instruction of the word. But if it is not done so, we are not cleansed but much more commit sin.

And although infants have neither faith nor baptism, think not therefore that they are damned. Oh no! they are blessed; for they have the Lord's own promise of the kingdom of God; not through any elements, ceremonies and external rites, but only by grace, through Jesus Christ, Matt. 19: 13—15. And therefore, we do truly believe, that they are under grace, acceptable to God, pure, holy, heirs of God and eternal life, and on account of this promise, all sincere, christian believers, may assuredly rejoice and comfort themselves in the salvation of their children.

In the sixth place, they say that infants are to be baptized on account of the promise made them, as above stated; although Christ did not baptize the children brought to him, nor had them baptized; but they say that he had infant baptism taught and practiced after his death.

To this we reply: This is a false doctrine, and has not the word of God to sanction it; yea, it cannot be supported by a single word in the Scriptures. We rejoice with all our heart, that they have this promise; **the Scriptures**, however, do not teach that they should, therefore, be baptized; and that they were not baptized before Christ's death, gives us greater assurance of this still, and that for this reason: We certainly know, that he taught no other word, no other doctrine, no other baptism, nor did he give another Spirit, or another promise, nor did he instruct others to teach differently after his death, than he did before that event. That he commanded his holy apostles, after his death and ascension, to teach and practice infant baptism, can never be proved by the word of the Lord.

Oh Human Nature! thou art not ashamed to charge lies upon Jesus Christ and his apostles, and to practice infant baptism under the semblance of the divine word, as if the Lord had taught it, although he never did. How much you are like those who say, "The Lord saith it; albeit, I have not spoken," Ezek. 13: 7; thus saith the Lord.

As often as the question is put to us, Why shall infants not be baptized, since they are in the church of God, and partakers of his grace, covenant and promise? We answer: Because the Lord neither taught nor commanded it.

In the seventh place they say, The Scriptures inform us that the apostles baptized whole families, from which we may readily conclude, that there were infants among them.

To this in the first place, we reply: Since they endeavor to maintain their position with uncertain conjectures, they acknowledge by their own arguments, that they have no scriptural authority for this doctrine.

In the second place, we answer: In things of such importance, we dare not build upon uncertain suppositions, but upon the sure word, which is a lamp to our feet and a light to our path, Ps. 119: 105.

In the third place, we answer: Four families are mentioned in the Scriptures, as having been baptized; namely, That of Cornelius, of the Jailor, of Lydia and of Stephanas, Acts 10: 48; 16: 15, 33; 1 Cor. 1: 16, and the Scriptures plainly show that three of these were all believers; namely, the family of Cornelius, of the Jailor, and that of Stephanas. But touching the family of Lydia, although the Scriptures say nothing defi-

CONCERNING BAPTISM.

nitely concerning it, the reader should know that it is not usual in Scripture, nor the common custom of the world, to call the family by the woman's name, as long as the husband is living. Since then, Luke mentions the family by the name of the woman, reason teaches us, that Lydia was at that time either a widow or a virgin. Of the probability as to whether there were infants in her house or not, we shall let the pious reader judge.

In the fourth place, we answer: The word *household*, or *houses*, does not include the minor children as mentioned in the Scripture; for Paul speaks of vain talkers who subvert whole houses. Now it is incontrovertible that an infant cannot be subverted by any false doctrine. Therefore, by the word *house* or *houses*, no others can be understood than *those* who have ears to hear, and hearts to understand.

In the last place, they appeal to Origen and Augustine, and say that these assert, that they have received infant baptism from the apostles.

To this we answer and inquire, Can Origen and Augustine prove this by the Scriptures? Have they done so? We desire to know; if not, then must we hear and believe Christ and his apostles, and not Augustine and Origen.

That this is not the case may readily be seen from Cyprian, because he neither enjoined nor condemned infant baptism, if those who for many years past have been preachers at Norlingen, have rightly informed me in their church records, and not deceived me in the meaning of the word *Liberum*.

Cyprian also was a Greek, as well as Origen, and lived twenty-five years after him. If then infant baptism was the doctrine of the apostles and practiced by them, as Origen and Augustine assert, it must first be proved by the Scriptures, and in that case Cyprian must have committed a great sin to leave the observance of the doctrines and practices of the apostles at liberty. For any thing that is apostolic, dare not be changed by any man. The word of Paul is indisputable, "Though we, or an angel from heaven, preach any other gospel unto you than that which we have preached unto you, let him be accursed," Gal. 1: 8. Else we would be constrained to acknowledge, that the twelve apostles with their doctrine, were not the twelve foundations and twelve gates of the new Jerusalem, Rev. 21: 12.

If infant baptism is apostolic, why does Tertullian write and say, "They who are to be baptized, confess for a considerable time in the church, before the bishop, that they renounce the devil, his pomp and angels. After that they are," &c.

Revanus annotates on this passage and says: That it was the custom of old, that adults (grown persons) be baptized by the washing of regeneration.

That infant baptism was not apostolic may be distinctly seen from the insipid remarks of Athanasius, as Rufinus plainly shows; see *Eusebius*, 10 *Libro Ecc. His., Cap.* 14.

Remember also how the early writers contended about infant baptism. Had it been apostolic, and found in the gospel, why should they have thus wrangled.

Read also Erasmus Rotterod, *in sua concion, i. e., in his public orations*, Sebastus Frank's Chronicle, Ulrich Zuingli, in his book of Articles, Martin Cellarius, *de immensis operi, Dei, i. e., Concerning the immense works of God*, and you will find, that infant baptism is not the doctrine and practice of the apostles.

Behold, beloved reader, I admonish and advise you, if you seek God with all your heart, and do not wish to be deceived; depend not upon men and their doctrine, no matter however old, holy and excellent they may be esteemed; for the divines, both ancient and modern are opposed to each other; but put your trust, alone in Christ and his word, in the sure instruction and practice of his holy apostles, and you will through the grace of God, be perfectly safe from all false doctrines and the power of the devil; and may walk with a free and pious mind before God.

AN ADMONITION ADDRESSED TO THE SCORNERS OF THE WORD CONCERNING BAPTISM.

We well know, beloved reader, that there are many unprofitable talkers, who teach from the letters of the Scriptures, that infants should not be baptized, but only christian believers; nevertheless they say: Why my beloved, what can water avail us? We have been once baptized in the name of God. Had we only the new life, it would suffice us. O dear Lord! thus is thy precious word every where esteemed of this vicious world as fables of Æsop; as if Omnipotent Majesty, the Eternal Wisdom and Truth had taught and commanded some things to no purpose. No, my good reader, no; his name is the Sovereign Lord; his word is his will; his command is eternal life. All things which he has taught and commanded us, he will undoubtedly have us to observe; if we do not, woe to us. Christ says, "Ye are my friends if ye do whatsoever I command you," John 15: 14. "My counsel," says the prophet, "shall stand, and I will do all my pleasure," Isa. 46: 10. Therefore, O Creature, do not longer fight against God. Give ear to him and obey his voice, for it is his divine counsel, word and will. Who are you, that you would contend with God? Christ's sheep hear his voice. True christians believe and obey. Are you a sincere christian, born of God? Then why do you dread baptism; which is among the least that God commanded you? It has always been a difficult and important command to love your enemy; to do good to those who hate you; to pray in spirit and in truth, for those who persecute you; to crucify your wicked and ungodly flesh, with its impure lusts and desires; to subdue your arrogant pride; your avariciousness; your offensive unchastity; your bloody hatred; your eating and drinking to excess; to renounce your accursed idolatry; to desist from your envious revilings; to curb your slanderous tongue; to govern your heart, and flesh; to love and fear with all your heart, your Lord and God, your Creator and Redeemer; and in all things to submit to his holy word, and serve your neighbor in sincere and unfeigned love, with all your powers, with all your possessions, with your counsel, with your labor, yea, if required with your death and blood; with a sincere heart to suffer misery, disdain, and the oppressive cross of Christ for the Lord's word; and to confess Christ Jesus before lords and princes, in prison and bonds, by words and deeds, unto death.

We think that these, and the like commands, are more painful and difficult to perverse flesh, which is naturally so prone to follow its own way, than to have a hand full of water applied; and a sincere christian must at all times be ready to do all this; if not, he is not born of God; for the regenerated are of one mind with Christ Jesus.

All who, by the grace of God, have been translated from Adam into Christ, and become partakers of the divine nature, and are baptized of God, with the Spirit and fire of heavenly love, will not contend so deridingly with the Lord, and say: My beloved, what can water avail? But they say with trembling Paul, "Lord, what wilt Thou have me to do?" And with the penitents on the day of Pentecost, "Men and brethren, what shall we do?" They will renounce their own wisdom, and willingly obey the word of the Lord, for they are influenced by his Spirit, and through faith, with willing, obedient hearts perform all things commanded them of the Lord.

But as long as their minds are not renewed, and they are not of the same mind with Christ; are not washed in the inner man with clean water, from the living fountain of God, they may well say, What can water avail us? For as long as they are earthly and sensually minded, the whole ocean would not cleanse them.

My faithful reader, think not that we put great stress upon the elements and rites. I tell you the truth in Christ, and lie not. If any one were to come to me, even the emperor, or the king, and would desire to be baptized, still walking in the unclean, ungodly lusts of the flesh, and were he not unblamable, penitent and regenerated, I hope by the grace of God, I would rather die than to baptize such an impenitent and sensual man. For where there is no renewing, regenerating faith, leading to obedience, there is no baptism.* Even as Philip said to the Eunuch, "If thou believest with all thy heart, thou mayest." But nevertheless, you ought to know, should the subject for baptism come with a hypocritical heart, under semblance of faith, that his hypocrisy would not be imputed to the baptizer as a sin, but to the dissembler; for no man knows the heart of man, save the spirit of man which is in him, 1 Cor. 2: 11.

It appears to me, that you may readily conclude from the language which we have used that we desire no other water, than that which the word of the Lord has commanded. For since we believe that Christ is the true Messiah, to whom the law and the prophets pointed, whom all the righteous fathers and patriarchs desired; that he came from heaven and testified to the truth, and that his command is eternal life, we must, therefore, hear his voice and obey his word; if not, we actually show that we do not believe, but that we reject his counsel and word, and are ungrateful towards him, for his love.

I know well, that many of you will say, We were once baptized in the name of God, and with that we are satisfied. To which we reply: If you fear God with all your heart, and acknowledge that his word and ordinances are just and good, you must decide that you are not baptized in the name of God, but contrary to it. It is true that the adorable, exalted name of God was pronounced over you, but not otherwise than it is pronounced over church-bells, churches, altars, consecrated water, tapers and palms. All anti-christian idolatry and abominations, alas, are performed under the semblance of the divine name; although they are not done by virtue *of*, but *against* his name, for they are done contrary to his word and will.

My dear reader, reflect well upon these words and judge them by the word of God, and you will find that the baptism which you have received is without the command of God's word; that it originated through self-righteousness, and was invented by man, and therefore it must be accursed of God, who alone will reign and rule in his church. Would you rejoice in the promise and be partakers of the church of Christ, you must believe the word of the Lord, be obedient to, and follow his counsel, will and ordinances. But if you refuse, and follow your own, and not the Lord's counsel and will, you cannot comfort yourselves with any scriptural promise, for "he that believeth not," says Christ, "is condemned already."

Therefore, do no longer comfort yourselves with such vain comfort, and say, We have been once baptized; for at heart you are yet entirely unbelieving; yea, rebellious and unclean. Your whole life is earthly and carnal, your baptism anti-christian, and without the sanction of the word of God. Therefore, awaken, repent, believe in Christ, seek, fear and love God with all your heart, then the word of the Lord and his unction will teach you what is proper for you to do or not to do, in this matter. And say not, as some do, I will renounce the church and idolatry; I will serve my neighbor, &c.; but I do not wish to be baptized.

O you blind men! Do you think that the Lord is pleased with your staying away from the church, or with your alms, or any thing of the kind, if you reject his counsel and word? No! no!! He desires your obedience, but not sacrifice. He desires the whole heart, the entire man. With him, neither church nor alms will avail, neither words nor deeds, as long as you do not manifest a new heart and life. "For in Christ Jesus," says Paul, "neither circumcision availeth anything, nor uncircumcision, but faith which worketh by love, a new creature, and the keeping of the commandments of God," Gal. 5: 6; 6: 15; 1 Cor. 7: 19.

And whosoever is renewed in Christ and born of God, he liveth no more, as Paul says, but Christ Jesus liveth in him. In all his ways he conforms to the word of the Lord, for that powerful, active faith constrains him to all obedience, and to every good work. But where this new life is not,

---

* There can be no scriptural baptism administered.

there fair words may indeed be, but in truth, there is only unbelief, disobedience, wantonness, presumption, and perverseness.

I hereby entreat and admonish you, beloved reader, not to be so obstinate against the Lord, and say, What can water avail us? But do reflect that Christ Jesus himself was baptized, Matt. 3: 13, although he was without sin, neither was guile found in his mouth, 1 Pet. 2: 22; yea, who was himself righteousness, the way, the truth, and the life. Tell us then, what could water avail Christ, who was all in all things? The disciples also at Ephesus were re-baptized of Paul, because they knew nothing of the Holy Ghost, although they had been baptized with the baptism of John. If Christ himself was baptized, who was without sin, and others were re-baptized of Paul, who had been baptized with the baptism of John, which was also from heaven, Why do you then despise the Lord's baptism, you who are poor, miserable sinners, who were baptized without knowledge and faith, with the baptism of the dragon and the beast?

Cyprian, the Martyr, with his entire council in Africa, resolved that those who were baptized of heretics, should be re-baptized with the christian baptism, and this for the reason, that they maintained that the baptism of heretics could not be the baptism of Christ. Reflect a little, kind reader, who they were that baptized you; by whom they were sent; what kind of faith they had; what kind of lives they led; with what doctrine and practices you were baptized. If you will seriously reflect thereon, I hope by the grace of God, if you desire true peace and liberty of conscience, you will soon be aware that you never knew either the external or internal baptism, much less received it.

Behold, beloved reader, here you have the true foundation and scriptural instructions of the baptism of Christ, and an explanation of the baptism of anti-christ.

Pray the Lord, the Most High, for a sound and clear understanding, that you may sincerely know the right and blessed truth, believe, and in the fear of the Lord, faithfully observe it. Cease from all useless disputing and gainsaying; for whosoever will dispute and gainsay with the determination to remain in the broad way, will ruin his soul, never walk with a good and sure conscience before God, and always find occasion to dispute and wrangle.

Therefore, do examine, believe, and obey the word of God with a sincere and devout heart, and be not deceived by being led into the appearance of godliness, by fair speeches, and you will certainly obtain the sure doctrine of the saving truth, and the consoling promise of grace. The Lord Jesus Christ grant you his grace, Amen.

THE LORD'S HOLY SUPPER.

You know, beloved sirs, friends and brethren, that every where much is written, preached and said concerning the Lord's Supper. But with what knowledge, with what faith, love, peace, unity, and after what manner and ordinance they celebrate it, is plainly evident. It is true, the Lord commanded, in the New Testament, the breaking of bread, or the last Supper, but not in the manner in which you celebrate it. Your Lord's Supper is common to all, no matter who, or what they are; to the avaricious, proud, gay, drunkards, haters, idolators, debauchees, adulterers, whoremongers, and rogues. It is also celebrated, as may be seen, with abominable pomp and splendor, with hypocrisy and idolatry; and besides, it is dispensed by such ministers who only seek worldly honor, ease and the satisfaction of the cravings of their flesh and bodies.

Since so many of you are so zealous about the Lord's Supper, but not according to the Scripture, as you shall hear; for your table may more properly be called the devil's table than the Lord's table, 1 Cor. 10: 21,

I desire for Jesus' sake, that you would in the true fear of God, reflect to whom, why and wherefore the Lord instituted, ordained and left, this his last Supper, to his church, so that it may prove to you a living and an affecting sign; that it might bring to your minds, and set forth the Lord's great and abundant kindness, true peace, the love and union of his church, the communion of his flesh and blood; and that you may die to unrighteousness, and every ungodly work; live to righteousness and godliness; renounce the devil's table; and that you may sit down at the Lord's holy table, in the church of Christ, with true faith, a pious, penitent and regenerated life, and with unfeigned, brotherly love.

Thus saith Paul, "I have received of the Lord that which also I delivered unto you, that the Lord Jesus, the same night in which he was betrayed, took bread; and when he had given thanks, he brake it and said, Take, eat; this is my body, which is broken for you; this do in remembrance of me. After the same manner he took the cup, when he had supped, saying, This cup is the New Testament in my blood, this do ye, as oft as ye drink it, in remembrance of me." 1 Cor. 11: 23—25.

Here you have Paul's explanation of the words of the Holy Supper, instituted by Jesus Christ, Luke 22: 19, 20, concerning which words, the learned have disputed much; and alas, some of them, through their idolatrous misunderstanding (if we may call it such, and not pride), have disputed at the expense of much innocent blood; and what holy Paul says concerning them, is fulfilled, "Professing themselves to be wise, they became fools," Rom. 1: 22. For they disputed most about the sign, which avails little, but the thing signified for which the sign was instituted, which avails much, they touch not. In my opinion, they also pay little attention as to what the qualification of the guests or communicants should be, in order to sit with Christ at his table, and to celebrate this Holy Sacrament.

There is not a single word commanded in the Scriptures, that should give cause for dispute concerning the visible and tangible sign, or what it signifies. The spiritual, judge all things spiritually. For whatever that may be in substance, it can be handled, seen and tasted. But this we should most consider, that we in our weakness ought to follow, and as much as possible conform ourselves to the signification, that is, that which is set forth, represented and taught by this sign to all true christian believers.

On this account, we will not trouble the well meaning and pious reader, with jarring, fruitless disputing, concerning the outward sign, as the learned do; but we only desire, by the help and grace of the Lord, by the power of the divine word, to point out correctly, for whom, and why Christ Jesus left and ordained this Supper; so that we may not esteem the visible sign above the reality, and depart from the truth to images.

To come to a right, profitable and christian understanding of the Lord's Holy Supper, what it is, to whom, why, and wherefore it was enjoined, four things in particular should be observed and well considered.

In the first place, we must take heed that we do not, as some, who make the visible, perishable bread and wine, the Lord's real flesh and blood. To believe this, is contrary to nature, reason and Scripture; yea, it is open blasphemy of the Son of God, abomination and idolatry. But as Israel had to hold the passover annually, at the appointed time according to the command of Moses, to commemorate that the Almighty God, the God of Abraham, of Isaac and Jacob, did graciously preserve his people from the punishment and plagues, when he slew the first born of the Egyptians; and by his strong hand and outstretched arm, so gloriously and wonderfully led them out, and redeemed them from the iron furnace of Egypt and the dread tyranny and dominion of Pharaoh, according to the word of his promise, and hence the *paschal lamb* is called the *Lord's passah*, that is, *passover*; the sign for the reality; for the *lamb* was not the *passover* although so called, but it only typified the *passover*, as said. So in the Holy Supper, the *bread* is called the *body*, and the *wine* the *blood* of the Lord, Matt. 26: 26—28. I say the sign is put for the *reality*,* not that

---

* Reality, the thing signified or typified.

it actually is the real flesh and blood of Christ; for with that he ascended into heaven, and sitteth at the right hand of his Father, immortal, and unchangeable, in eternal majesty and glory; but it is an admonishing type and memorial that Jesus Christ the Son of God has redeemed us from the power of the devil, from the dominion of hell and eternal death, by offering up an immaculate sacrifice, his innocent flesh and blood, and has triumphantly led us into the kingdom of his grace, as he himself says, "This do in remembrance of me," Luke 22: 19.

In the second place, it is to be observed, that there is no greater evidence of love, than that one suffers death for another, as Christ says, "Greater love hath no man than this, that a man lay down his life for his friends," John 15: 13. Since this holy sign is only a memorial of the Lord's death, and since death is the greatest evidence of love, as said, we are therefore reminded, when we are at the Lord's table, to eat his bread and to drink his cup, that we not only earnestly show forth and remember his death, but also all the glorious fruits of divine love, manifested towards us, in Christ; namely, that God, in the beginning, made man after his image, incorruptible, placed him in Paradise, and made all creatures subject to him. When he was beguiled of the serpent, he was cheered and comforted with the promise of a coming Conqueror and Savior, Jesus Christ. God sent Moses and the prophets, who sedulously practiced the law, and pointed to the promised Christ and his kingdom. Christ Jesus, according to the promise of the Scriptures, finally appeared in this world, a true man, born of the Virgin Mary, and in much misery, affliction and labor, preached the saving and gracious word to the house of Israel; sought the lost sheep, and brought them to their true Shepherd; appeased and reconciled us before the Father, through his painful death and precious blood, Rom. 8: 3. As he himself says, "For God so loved the world, that he gave his only begotten Son, that whosoever believeth in him, should not perish, but have everlasting life," John 3: 16.

Oh, wonderful, unsearchable and incomprehensible love of God! He did not send into this unfriendly world an angel, a patriarch, or a prophet, but his eternal ALMIGHTY WORD, his ETERNAL WISDOM, the brightness of his glory, in the form of sinful flesh, and "made him to be sin for us, who knew no sin; that we might be made the righteousness of God in him," 2 Cor. 5: 21.

My good reader, do not understand this as if Christ had been a sinner; by no means. The Scriptures acquit him of all sin. He was the spotless lamb. He knew not sin, neither was guile found in his mouth. But Paul calls him *sin*, according to the Hebrew manner of expression; that is, an offering for sin, as the prophet says, "He was wounded for our transgressions, he was bruised for our iniquities; the chastisement of our peace was upon him; and with his stripes were we healed, Isa. 53: 5. He gave his life as an offering for sin.

Behold, worthy reader, all those who sincerely believe in this glorious love of God, this abundant, great blessing of grace in Christ Jesus, manifested toward us, are more and more renewed through such a faith; their hearts overflow with joy and peace; they break forth with joyful hearts, in all manner of thanksgiving; they praise and glorify God with all their hearts, because they, with a good conscience have received the Spirit; they believe and know that the Father loved us, so that he gave us poor, wretched sinners, his own and Eternal Son, with his merits, as a gift and an eternal ransom, as Paul says, The grace and love of God, our Savior, appeared not on account of the works of righteousness, which we have done, but according to his mercy he saved us, by the washing of regeneration, and the renewing of the Holy Ghost; which he shed on us abundantly, through Jesus Christ our Savior, "That being justified by his grace, we should be made heirs according to the hope of eternal life," Tit. 3: 7.

Here it is proper to observe, how the Righteous died for the unrighteous, when we were yet sinners and enemies; how the spotless Lamb was prepared for us, in the fire of affliction, suffered upon the cross, and was offered an eternal propitiation for our sins; how the Creator of all things was bruised for our sakes, and he, who was above all the children of men, became the most unworthy, and was counted with evil doers; how the Innocent bore the sins of the whole world, blotted out all our transgressions, and redeemed us with his crimson blood, as the Scriptures declare, "I restored that which I took not away," Ps. 69: 4. In short, how that Jesus Christ through his obedience, delivered Adam and all his seed from the consequences of disobedience, and by his painful death, again restored life.

The apostle Paul acknowledged this great and glorious work of divine love, broke forth and said, "Who shall separate us from the love of Christ? Shall tribulation, or distress, or persecution, or famine, or nakedness, or peril, or sword, as it is written, For thy sake we are killed all the day long; we are accounted as sheep for the slaughter. Nay, in all these things we are more than conquerors through him that loved us. For I am persuaded, that neither death, nor life, nor angels, nor principalities, nor powers, nor things present, nor things to come, nor height, nor depth, nor any other creature, shall be able to separate us from the love of God, which is in Christ Jesus our Lord," Rom. 8: 35—39.

And this is what John says, Let us love him for he first loved us. Nature teaches us to love those who love us. And this is the first fruit of the Holy Sacrament, if rightly celebrated.

In the third place we have to observe, that by the Lord's Supper we are reminded of, and admonished to christian unity, love, and peace, after which all true christians should seek and strive. "For we being many," says Paul, "are one bread, and one body; for we are all partakers of that one bread," 1 Cor. 10: 17.

Like as natural bread is made of many grains, broken by the mill, and kneaded together with water, and baked by the heat of the fire; so is the church of Christ made up of many true believers, broken in their hearts, with the hammer of the divine word, and are baptized with the water of the Holy Ghost, and with the fire of pure, unfeigned love, into one body, 1 Cor. 12: 13. And as the natural body is in harmony and peace with all its members, and as each member naturally discharges its duty to promote the good of the whole body; thus it also becomes the true and living members of the body of Christ, to be in harmony, of one heart, one mind and one soul; not quarrelsome and unpeaceable, not spiteful and envious, not cruel and hateful, not malicious, not obstinate or rancorous, one toward another, like the ambitious, covetous, and the proud of this world; but in all things, one toward another, be long suffering, friendly, peaceable, ever ready in true christian love to serve his neighbor in all things possible; by exhortation; by reproof, by comforting, by assisting, by counseling, with deed and with possessions, yea, with bitter and hard labor, with body and life. Ready to forgive one another, as Christ forgives and serves us with his word, life and death, as Paul says, "Put on, therefore, as the elect of God, holy and beloved, bowels of mercies, kindness, humbleness of mind, meekness, longsuffering; forbearing one another, and forgiving one another, if any man have a quarrel against any; even as Christ forgave you, so also do ye; and above all things, put on charity, which is the bond of perfectness; and let the peace of God rule in your hearts, to the which also ye are called in one body; and be thankful," Col. 3: 12—15.

And again; as in the natural body, the more honorable members, such as the eye, the ear, the mouth, &c., do not despise the less honorable members, on account of their inferiority; and as the inferior members do not envy the superior members, on account of their superiority, but as every member in its place, is peaceable, and contributes to the good of the whole body, be its functions high or low; so it is also in the church of the Lord. Paul says, Some he appointed apostles; some prophets; some evangelists; some pastors and teachers. Let every one be mindful that he boasts not of what he is, has, or possesses, for it is all the grace and gift of God. Let every one attend to his duty, "for the perfecting of the saints, for the work of the ministry, for the edifying of the body of Christ; till we all come in the unity of the faith, and of the knowledge of the Son of God, unto a perfect man, unto the measure of the stature of the fullness of Christ," Eph. 4: 12, 13.

This is also set forth in the Holy Supper;

but how the world, calling themselves christians, live up to this, is shown by their fruits and actions.

In the fourth place, we have to observe, that the Holy Supper is the communion of the body and blood of Christ, as Paul says, "The cup of blessing which we bless, is it not the communion of the blood of Christ? The bread which we break, is it not the communion of the body of Christ?" 1 Cor. 10: 16.

Since then it is a communion, as said, we would fraternally exhort all of you, that you would earnestly examine yourselves, whether you have been made partakers of Christ? Whether you are flesh of his flesh, and bone of his bone? Whether you are in Christ, and Christ in you? For all who would worthily eat of this bread, and drink of this cup, must be changed in the inner man, and converted and renewed in their minds, through the power of the divine word and the operation of faith; become new creatures, born of God, and translated from Adam into Christ; be of a christian disposition, long suffering, peaceable, merciful, affectionate, truly humble, and obedient to the word of the Lord. The proud, ambitious, selfish and carnal heart must be circumcised; the evil eye must be plucked out; the ear that delights to hear evil, must be closed; the unprofitable, backbiting tongue must be bridled; the unclean, bloody hand must be cleansed; the impure, unchaste flesh must be restrained, &c.; they must lead a crusade against the world, the flesh and the devil; their loins must be girded about with truth; having on the breast-plate of righteousness; their feet shod with the preparation of the gospel of peace. They must be armed with the shield of faith; with the helmet of salvation, and the sword of the Spirit. They must be led by the Spirit of God, that they may become sincere christians; and strive with all their powers, that they, in their weakness, may be like-minded with Christ Jesus, Rom. 8: 14.

When Christ instituted and celebrated the Holy Supper with his beloved disciples, he said, With desire I have desired to eat this passover with you before I suffer. Then he took the bread, and brake it, and said, Take, **eat, this is my body which is broken for you.** Likewise also the wine, This cup is the New Testament in my blood, &c.; this do in remembrance of me, 1 Cor. 11: 24, 25, as if he had said, Behold, dear children, so far has that love which I have had for you and the whole human family, and ever shall have for you, constrained me, that I left the glory of my Father, came into this world of affliction, and am as a poor, miserable servant, to serve you, for I beheld that you all belonged to satan, and there was none to redeem you; that you had all gone astray, like erring sheep, and there was none who cared for you; that you were a prey to devouring wolves, and there was none to ransom you; that you were wounded with death, and there was none that could heal you. Therefore, did I come from heaven, and became a poor, weak, and dying man, in all things like unto you, sin excepted. In my great love I zealously sought you, and I found you helpless, loathsome, and miserable, yea, half dead, the services of my love I have so cordially manifested toward you; your sores I bound up; your blood I wiped off; I poured wine and oil into your putrid wounds; set you free from the jaws of the bears and lions of the pit; I laid you upon my shoulders, and led you into the tabernacles of peace; your nakedness I covered; had compassion on you in your misery; I fulfilled the law for you; your sins I took away; I proclaimed to you the peace, the grace and favor of my Father; I made known to you his good will; I pointed out the way of truth; and I have powerfully testified to you, by my unheard-of signs and great miracles, that I am the true Messiah, the promised Prince and Savior.

Behold, beloved children, so long have I been with you, taught my Father's word, admonished, reproved and comforted in his name; but now my hour is at hand; this night I shall be betrayed. All that the prophet said of me has come to an end. But since I can serve you no longer with my doctrine and life, I will, at last, serve you with my painful sufferings, body, blood, cross, and death.

And this is the reason why I called you to this Supper, so that I might institute a memorial for you in the use of bread and wine, that you might occasionally come together after my death, and commemorate the gracious favors of my ardent love, so abundantly manifested towards you; and especially, that I loved you so dearly, that I offered my body; and shed my blood for you. Greater love hath no man than this, that a man lay down his life for his friends. I have by my death obtained for you everlasting reconciliation, grace, mercy, favor and peace with my Father, as I told you, namely, "Even as the Son of man came not to be ministered unto, but to minister, and to give his life a ransom for many," Matt. 20: 28.

Beloved reader, take notice of the word of the Lord and this institution. For where this Holy Supper is celebrated with such faith, love, devotion, peace, harmony, and so much sincerity of heart, there Jesus Christ is present with his grace, Spirit, and promise, and with the merits of his sufferings, misery, flesh, blood, cross and death; as he himself says, "Where two or three are gathered together in my name, there am I in the midst of them," Matt. 18: 20. But where the pure knowledge of Christ, living faith, the new life, christian love, peace and harmony do not exist, there is not the Lord's Supper, but a despising and mocking of the blood and death of Christ, a consolation of the impenitent, a seducing hypocrisy, and open blasphemy and idolatry; as, alas! we know and see by the world.

Oh! delightful assembly and christian banquet, commanded and ordained of the Lord himself, where there are no carnal pleasures to gratify the flesh and appetites, but where are set forth, sought for, and desired by all true christian believers, the glorious and holy mysteries, by the visible signs of bread and wine.

Oh! delightful assembly and christian banquet, where there is no unseasonable, slanderous mockery, and where no trivial songs are sung; but where the pious christian life, peace, and harmony among all the brethren; besides the joyful word of divine grace, his gracious kindness, favor, love, service, tears, prayers, cross and death are set forth, and taught with cordial thanksgiving and devout joy.

Oh! delightful assembly and christian banquet, to which the impenitent and proud despisers, according to Scripture, are not invited; such as whore-mongers, rogues, adulterers, debauchees, the giddy, robbers, liars, defrauders, tyrants, shedders of blood, idolators, slanderers, &c., for such are not the people of the Lord; but those, who are born of God, the true christians, who have buried their sins, and walk with Christ in a new and godly life; those who crucify their flesh; who are led by the Holy Spirit; who sincerely believe in God; who seek, fear, and love him, and in their weakness, willingly serve and obey him; such are members of his body; flesh of his flesh, and bone of his bone.

Oh! delightful assembly and christian banquet, where neither gluttonous eating and drinking is practiced, nor the impious vanity of piping and drumming is heard; but where the hungry consciences are filled with the heavenly bread of the divine word, and with the wine of the Holy Ghost; and where the peaceful, joyful souls are singing melodies before the Lord.

Awaken, O you, who sit in darkness and walk in the region and shadow of death. Awaken, I say, and observe that the supper, which you have held to the present, is not the supper of Christ, but of anti-christ; not the table of the Lord, but the table of the devil. For it is generally dispensed only by open deceivers, and worshippers of idols; and received by a people who are as yet entirely obstinate and carnally minded, disbelieving and rebellious against the word of God. And moreover, they believe it to be the real body and blood of the Lord, and celebrate it with such unbecoming, heathenish pomp and splendor. O! abomination and idolatry!!

Beloved reader, I bear witness to the truth in Christ and lie not, that the Holy Supper of Christ is not to be dispensed by a deceiver, nor to be received by an impenitent and obstinate sinner. It does not require such a gorgeous and splendid array, as that in which the world is wont to celebrate it; neither golden vessels, nor hypocritical semblance of confessions, absolution, bowing, and smiting upon the breast, &c., but it must be celebrated with a broken heart, true penitence, a humble mind, with unfeigned, ardent love, with peace and joy in the Holy

Ghost. Again I say, awaken, and reflect upon what I write. God's work is not imitating a dead letter; it is not trifling; nor is it the sounding of many bells and organs, and of singing; but it is a heavenly power, a living, moving of the Holy Ghost, which warms the heart and mind of the believers; pervades, comforts, anoints, encourages, awakens and enlivens them; makes them joyful and happy in God. For this is the true nature and power of the Lord's word, if it be rightly preached, and of his Holy Sacraments, if rightly used.

It is, therefore, high time, to take heed to the word of the Lord; for all who are earthly and carnally minded, are not born of God and his word; are obstinately averse to the Lord's word; love not their neighbors, nor are ready to help them; and are not in the communion of God, therefore they cannot be members of his body, or guests at his table. For Paul says, To be carnally minded, is death. Christ says, Those who are not born from above, cannot see the kingdom of God. Samuel says, Disobedience is as iniquity and idolatry. John says, He that loveth not his brother (neighbor), abideth in death. Again, He that loveth not, knows not God, for God is love. In short, without love, all preaching, all faith, baptizing, celebrating the Lord's Supper, prophesying and suffering are vain.

We do, therefore, admonish all those desiring to celebrate this Supper, that they would rightly learn to know what the true Supper is, what it signifies, how and wherefore it is to be used, and who are to be partakers of it. And then also to examine themselves well, as Paul teaches, before they eat of this bread and drink of this cup; that they do not comfort themselves with the visible sign, and err in regard to the reality represented by the signs; for they who know not Christ and his righteousness, believe not him and his word, and walk not according thereto; but according to the superstitious doctrines and commands of men, and partake of the Lord's table, eat and drink damnation to themselves.

All who have received the word of the Lord through faith, acknowledged it to be true, and have again transgressed it, and have not continued to walk in the acknowledged truth, but are walking again in the broad way, have returned to the love of the world, and are rejecting Christ and his word, and depending upon the seducing doctrines, the interpretations and false promises of the learned; such have no part at the Lord's table, for they are without God, as John says, "Whosoever transgresseth, and abideth not in the doctrine of Christ, hath not God," 2 John 1: 9.

All who walk in the pride of their hearts, despise their neighbor on account of poverty, distress and affliction, and know not that they themselves are poor mortals, seed of Adam, food for worms, and a wilting flower; yea, dust and earth, whether they are emperor, king, rich, or learned, and all who thus sit at the Lord's table with a proud heart, eat and drink damnation themselves.

All who boast of the Lord's Spirit, name, covenant, word, knowledge, merits, grace, blood and death, yet reject his holy counsel, doctrine, command, ordinance and his unblamable example, despise and grieve his Holy Spirit, hate, defraud and speak falsely against their neighbor, and sit at the Lord's table, eat and drink damnation to themselves.

All who love houses, lands, possessions, friends, children, the world, favor, ease of the body, honor and this life, more than they do Christ and his word, and attend the Lord's table, eat and drink damnation to themselves. Christ says, He that loveth any thing more than me, is not worthy of me, and cannot be my disciple, Matt. 10: 37; Luke 14: 26.

And this is the sum of the whole matter, that all those who would sit at the Lord's table, with the disciples and guests of Christ, whether rich or poor, high or low, must be sound in the faith, and unblamable in conduct and life. None are excepted; neither emperor nor king, prince nor earl, knight or nobleman. Yea, as long as they err in doctrine and faith, and are in their lives carnal and blamable, they are by no means to be permitted, with the pious to partake of the communion of the Holy Supper; for they are not in Christ, and therefore must remain without, till they are truly converted to Christ; walk in the ways of the Lord, are of one spirit and one faith with Christ and his church. For the Lord's Supper is a communion of the flesh and blood of Christ, which is not to be given to the ungodly and obdurate, but to the sincere, penitent, christian believers, as a pledge of reconciliation.

If any one has a good appearance before men, and is inwardly proud, avaricious, carnal and without the Spirit of God, he is not judged of the church, but of the Lord himself, the Searcher and Trier of men's hearts and reins, as the Scripture says. We do, therefore, admonish all those who would go to the Lord's table; to examine themselves before they partake of it; for all who eat unworthily of this bread, and drink of this wine, eat and drink damnation to themselves, 1 Cor. 11: 29.

Thus, beloved sirs, friends and brethren, does the Holy Supper instruct and admonish us: First, The bread, as the body of Christ, which he offered for us, and the cup, the blood of Christ which he shed in great love, for the remission of our sins.

In the second place, we are admonished to union, love, and peace, which must be among all true christians, according to the spirit, doctrine and example of Christ; for Paul says, "We being many are one bread, and one body," &c.

In the third place, we are admonished to a pious and unblamable life, to true regeneration, which is of God; to all righteousness, thanksgiving, peace and joy in the Holy Ghost. For it is a communion of the blood and body of Christ, of which no one is a partaker, nor can be, unless he becomes a humble, peaceable, pious christian, dead unto sin, and born of God according to his word; one who is in Christ, and Christ in him; flesh of his flesh, and bone of his bone, is a true partaker of the body and blood of Christ; as Paul says, "We are made partakers of Christ, if we hold the beginning of our confidence steadfast unto the end," Heb. 3: 14.

Behold, beloved readers, here you have the true instructions concerning the Lord's Holy Supper, with its significations, fruit, power, nature, and the guests, as the mouth of the Lord has ordained, and the holy apostles have left and taught us; and with what knowledge, faith, love, unity, peace, piety, and according to what usage and ordinance it should be celebrated in the church of God.

Herewith compare the supper of the world, and you will learn to know which is the true one; what an abomination anti-christ has made of it, what enchantments he practiced with it, and how we poor sinners, with all our forefathers, have, as idolatrous Israel of old, for hundreds of years, offered incense unto the brazen serpent, and danced before the golden calf. O! my faithful reader, fear God, with sincerity examine the Scriptures, and believe the truth.

THE CORRUPTION OF THE HOLY SUPPER.

The Scriptures teach that we have no other offerings for sin than the body of the Lord, as before said. But since the enemies of Christ have possessed the cathedral for so many years, they have, as the Scriptures teach, altered the laws of the Most High, and instead thereof, instituted their abomination of desolation, and corrupted the Holy Supper with their councils, violence and false doctrine, till, alas! it retains but the shadow, and the mere name, and this they did to destroy and corrupt the true, eternal offering of Christ, which alone avails with God, and changed it into a daily offering for sin, as we may plainly read in the canons of the mass; which undoubtedly is an abomination of abominations; for thereby, Jesus Christ, the all-sufficient and eternal offering, is entirely renounced and made of no effect, as the Propitiator and Mediator of the New Testament. He is thrust from the throne of his Majesty; his merits, cross, blood, and death are rejected; yea, all the types and shadows of Moses, all the predictions of the prophets; the promise of angels, and the whole New Testament, are thereby denied; though all harmoniously point to the one and eternal offering of Christ; and instead of it, they have ordained an unholy, blind, seductive and carnal idolatry, with a piece of bread! Beloved reader, here put no other construction upon these words; for what I write is the truth.

They have brought it so far with this ungodly seduction, that they have arrogated to themselves all power in heaven, upon earth, and in hell; they therefore break the bread into *three* pieces. With the *first*, they reconcile God; with the *second*, they intercede for the world; and with the *third*, as they pretend, they pray for the souls in purgatory.

Through this accursed infamy they rose so high in honor, that they are above all the potentates of earth, whom they made their own servants. By their hypocritical service and enchanting idolatry, they have hoarded money, goods, gold, silver, land, rents, cloisters, cities, principalities and the dominions of this world; because every one loved this splendid service as a holy and divine work; honored and feared their exalted and pompous names as the messengers of God.

By this ingenious and subtle magic, the Roman anti-christ has gained such respect and authority, that even the imperial majesty, the highest sovereignty on earth, whom we are commanded of God to respect and fear, had to humble himself and kiss his feet; yea, what is still worse, Frederick Barbarossa, a great and renowned emperor, could not be reconciled with Pope Alexander III., until he humbled himself at Venice, before the church, and suffered the Pope to tread upon him with his feet!

Behold, thus *anti-christ* has enchanted the whole world with his offering. The gracious Father be eternally praised, that he has, through his paternal grace delivered us, his poor children, from this enchanting offering, and given us to know the only and eternal offering of his Son, Jesus Christ, who, according to the order of Melchizedek, is ordained an eternal High Priest over the house of God; who, in the days of his flesh, offered up prayers and supplications with strong crying and tears, unto him that was able to save from death, and was heard, because he honored God. This one, I say, offered an acceptable offering, a sweet smelling sacrifice, of eternal worth, whereby he appeases the Father's wrath, reconciles the human race, opened heaven, closed hell; made peace between heaven and earth; and sits now, and henceforth, at the right hand of his Father, till his enemies be made his foot-stool; yea, with this one offering, he has perfected forever all those who are sanctified. This cannot be gainsayed, whether by emperor or king, doctor or teacher, angel or devil. His word stands firm and immovable. He has with one offering, I say with *one* offering, perfected for ever those who are sanctified.

O my beloved reader! I mean all those who are yet without the Spirit of Christ and his word, Take heed what the word of the Lord teaches you, and observe the true doctrine of Christ, the true teachers, the true sacraments, the true church, and the true christian life, which is of God, so that you may once learn to know what kind of pastors feed you; what kind of baptism and supper you practice; by what kind of offering you are reconciled; what kind of lives you lead, and of whose body you are members.

O how long, says Solomon, will you simple ones love simplicity? And you scorners delight in scorning? How long will you remain under the heavy bondage of sin? How long will you remain in the communion of the devil, and suffer yourselves to be dragged down to the abyss of hell by the cords of unbelief? Awake, and ransom your poor souls! Come out from among them. Flee from all false doctrine; avoid every appearance of evil; believe in Christ Jesus; repent and lead an unblamable life; follow Christ with a sincere heart; enter into the house and covenant of his everlasting peace, into the communion of his flesh and blood. Take upon you his easy yoke, and light burden, and you will find rest for your souls; you may then of a truth say, that you are christians; that you have obtained the remission of your sins, by the grace of God, through the merits of Christ; and that you are joint heirs of the eternal kingdom. May God grant unto you all his grace and mercy, Amen.

In the second place, they made the bread,

in the Holy Supper, into the real flesh, and the wine into the real blood of Christ, and understood the words of Christ literally: Take, eat, this is my body, &c., and did not observe that Christ, John 6, does fully instruct us, how we are to eat his flesh and drink his blood; and says, that it would profit nothing really to eat his flesh, and to drink his blood, for this could not be done, because he was about ascending to heaven where he was before; we are therefore not literally to understand this eating his flesh, and drinking his blood; but spiritually, as he himself says, "The words that I speak unto you, they are spirit, and they are life." All those who thus understand this from the Scriptures, are by many, reproached as accursed heretics and profaners of the sacrament, and must suffer for it by water, fire and the sword.

O dear Lord! is this not an ungodly error, and great blindness, to teach and to believe, that a piece of bread, and a drink of wine should be changed into the real and essential flesh and blood of the Son of God, whereby we may be delivered from hell, the devil, sin and death, and are made children of grace? O, horrible heresy!

O miserable, blind people, believe the words of Christ, when he says, that it profiteth nothing to eat his visible and real flesh; and that his words are spirit and life, John 6: 63; believe that he ascended up to heaven and sitteth at the right hand of his Father; therefore he cannot be eaten nor confined in the body by any one, nor can he be consumed by age, fire, or worms, as may be plainly seen, is the case with the visible bread and wine.

But where the Lord's church, the beloved disciples of Christ, have met in Christ's name to partake of the Holy Supper in true faith, love and obedience, there the outward perishable man eats and drinks perishable bread and wine; and the inner, the imperishable spiritual man eats (in a spiritual sense) the imperishable body and blood of Christ, which can not be eaten nor consumed, as above said. Like is profited by like; this is incontrovertible. The visible man is nourished upon visible food, and the invisible man is fed upon invisible bread, as we may plainly learn from the word of the Lord.

Therefore, all who are in Christ and with believing, penitent hearts, rely upon the pure offering of the body and blood of Christ, and know that it is the only ablution and reconciliation for their sins, the only and eternal medium of grace; eat the true flesh and drink the true blood of Christ, not with their mouths, but *spiritually*, by faith, as said before.

The reader may readily observe from these words, that the bread is no flesh, and that the wine is no blood; for were they flesh and blood, as the idolators pretend and teach the poor people, one of two consequences must follow; either the perishable bread and wine are changed into the imperishable and heavenly Son of God; or the Son of God must be changed into bread and and wine. This is incontrovertible.

O dear Lord! they are more ignorant than the heathens ever were; true, the heathens worshipped and honored the sun, moon and stars, which have their influence upon things below. They worshipped the ox, the dragon, serpents, fire, and other creatures; some of which had living breath within them. They also worshipped images of wood, stone, gold and silver, made by skilful workmen, who cast, carved and decorated them in the likeness of man. But those who are called by the name of Christ, pray to, worship, and adore a piece of bread, and a mouthful of wine, as the real flesh and blood of Christ, who came from heaven for our salvation; became man, and was made an offering upon the cross for our sins. O intolerable abomination and infamy! that the praise of God, the glory of Jesus Christ is converted and changed into such a feeble idol, which can neither avenge, speak, hear, see, stand nor walk; which worms eat and time consumes; and must be locked up, preserved, assisted, and carried about by the hands of men, like the idols at Babylon, of which Baruch writes.

O my faithful reader, learn rightly to know Christ Jesus. He is not like the fabulous Proteus,* *now* like the everlasting Almighty Son of the eternal, Omnipotent God, and *then* a perishable creature, bread and

---

*Proteus could according to poetic fables, change himself into different shapes.

wine. Oh no! he is unchangeable through all eternity. Neither can he be confined in any house, church nor chamber, in silver or golden vessels; for, according to his eternal, divine Being, heaven is his throne and the earth his footstool, and after his holy humanity, he ascended into heaven and sits at the right hand of his Father. He is the eternal and Almighty Power, Brightness, Word, Truth, Wisdom, and image of God. He has all power in heaven above and on earth below, all things are under him; at his name every knee shall bow, and every tongue confess to him, that he is the Lord, to the honor and glory of his Father, and he will not appear again in the flesh, but he will come in the clouds of heaven, to judge the goats and sheep.

Therefore I say again, He cannot be eaten, nor can he be digested in the body of man. Augustine plainly acknowledges this; when he says, "Why do you make ready to eat? only believe, and you have eaten him."

Beloved reader, we well know, that Augustine did not write this of the natural eating of the Holy Supper; but of the spiritual eating, which is by faith; and with that view, we adduced it, so that the god-fearing reader might see the difference between outward and inward eating, and not mistake the one for the other; for the external use of the sign is nothing but a false appearance and hypocrisy, if the thing which is invisibly represented, is not connected with it. That this is the case with infant baptism and the world's supper, may be readily proved from the Scriptures; but where the mystery is connected with the sign, for which purpose it is ordained, there is the baptism of Christ, and his Supper, as the Scriptures teach. But this is hidden from the world. They acknowledge that the Scriptures teach a Supper, but what it actually is, what it prefigures, and who are to partake of it, they know not, so completely has the Babylonian whore deceived and bewitched them in this matter.

The Holy Supper, as taught by Christ and his apostles, reproves all idolatry; foreign mediums of reconciliation; hatred, discord, and unrighteousness; for it directs alone to the one offering of Christ which was made by his flesh and blood, once for all, as related; it represents christian peace, harmony, brotherly love, and a pious, unblamable life, as already said; therefore they desire not this Supper, and have forsaken the Lord's word and ordinances, and have turned away from the Creator to the creature, and from the true Reality, to the perishable signs; yea, they call the disgraceful and sinful mass, the sacrifice of the Lord; and the bread and wine his real flesh and blood; for this is the custom and manner of the ungodly, because they know not the true God, the God of heaven and earth, and believe not his holy and inestimable word; but hate the true service and are opposed thereto. In God's stead they have a visible and tangible creature; and maintain a service of their own choice. So did Israel with the golden calf; with Baal and Moloch; and Antioch with his Maosim (god of forces); the Babylonians with their Bel; the Egyptians with their Isis, &c. From this source, originates all disgraceful idolatry, which is practiced with this abomination, such as carrying about the bread, exalting it, praying thereto, offering of incense, and on every occasion seeking to pay it Divine honor and Divine service; to maintain which there is not a tittle nor a letter, nor an inference, in all the Scriptures. Yea, alas! many esteem it so highly, that they say this is the one who reconciled us upon the cross. Even as Israel said to the calf, "These be thy gods, O Israel, which brought thee up out of the land of Egypt," Exod. 32: 4.

Beside this, the use of the cup is withheld from the people in the Roman church. If it were the Lord's Supper, as they pretend, they would, in every respect, use it according to the ordinance of the Lord. But this custom shows that it is not the Supper of Christ, but a deluding seduction of antichrist.

Therefore, be wise and sober, you who name yourselves after the name of Christ. Spew out the wine of Babylonian whoredom which you have drank. You have danced and burned incense long enough to the golden calf. Give the Almighty the praise and honor due him; lest it happen to you as it did to faithless, disobedient, and idolatrous Israel. Although the Lord God graciously redeemed them from the power and tyranny of Pharaoh, yet they had to suffer punishment on account of their unfaithfulness and obstinacy, and were destroyed in the wilderness. And so it is also in vain that we are redeemed by the blood of the Lord from the dominion and power of the devil, if we do not repent, but remain idolatrous, and believe not in Jesus, and in our weakness are not obedient nor live according to his word.

In the third place they teach, that this bread is dispensed for the remission of sins. My faithful reader, take notice of what I write. Where Jesus Christ, his word and Spirit are not known and acknowledged, there is nothing but unbelief, idolatry, error, and an uncertain, wavering conscience, as may be seen.

They all seek some remedy for their sins, but the true remedy, Christ, they do not acknowledge; hence they have contrived so many remedies, that we can neither describe nor relate all of them; such as absolution, holy water, fastings, confessions, masses, pilgrimages, infant baptism, bread and wine, &c.

I know not to whom to compare this generation, other than to a sick and wounded person, who has entrusted himself under the care of an unskilful physician, who can give him no suitable medicines, and apply no healing plasters; he spends his money in vain; he suffers pain and affliction, and is getting worse instead of better. A skilful, experienced physician is recommended to him, who, prompted by pure love and mercy would visit him without money and without price, bind up his wounds, and gladly cure him; but the sick man will not receive such a good and well-disposed physician. Who then could feel for such a man, because he would rather perish than get well?

So it is with this perverse generation. They feel and are sensible, at times, that they are failing and sick, but they seek medicine and counsel of those who sicken them still more with their poison; and are not healed of their wounds and cured of their diseases. They refuse the skilful, the heavenly Chirurgeon and Physician, Jesus Christ, recommended by all the patriarchs, prophets, apostles and by angels; yea, appointed by the Father himself, him they will not have who would willingly visit all so deadly wounded; he offers his services without money and without price; he has a well scented, healing salve, good to heal our wounds, it is his powerful word to instruct; and his crimson blood, to reconcile, as was said. But they desire him not; they turn him away with violence, false doctrine, reproach, lying, treason, rebellion, persecution, and murder; as has been fully shown. O dear Lord! What counsel shall be given to this disobedient, perverse, and blind people?

My worthy reader, we testify the truth in Christ; beware, believe, obey, hope and seek, where and what you will; we are assured that you will find in the word of God, no other remedy for your sins, than the one we have pointed out to you, which is Jesus Christ; else the Scriptures must be false.

Thus says Isaiah, "I, even I, am he that blotteth out thy transgressions for mine own sake, and will not remember thy sins," Isa. 43: 25.

"The Lord hath laid on him the iniquity of us all," Isa. 53: 6.

The angel said to Joseph, "Thou shalt call his name Jesus, for he shall save his people from their sins," Matt. 1: 21.

"This is my blood of the New Testament, which is shed for many, for the remission of sins," Matt. 26: 27.

"Behold the lamb of God, which taketh away the sin of the world," John 1: 29

"For he hath made him to be sin for us, who knew no sin; that we might be made the righteousness of God in him," 2 Cor. 5: 21.

"Who, his own self bare our sins in his own body on the tree," 1 Pet. 2: 24.

"The blood of Jesus Christ his Son cleanseth us from all sin," 1 John 1: 7.

"He loved us, and washed us from our sins in his own blood," Rev. 1: 5.

My good readers, look well to yourselves, and be not deceived; if there were any other remedy for sin than the one pointed out, as related, we might then with propriety say, that these and other passages, have not rightly directed us, and holy Paul also erred not a little, when he says, "There is one God, and one Mediator between God and man, the man Christ Jesus, who gave himself a ransom for all, to be testified in due time," 1 Tim. 2: 5, 6.

All those, then, who seek other remedies for their sins, however glorious and holy they may appear, than the only remedy provided by God, deny the Lord's death, which he died for us, and his innocent blood which he shed for us; and they are those of whom the Lord complains and says, through his prophet Jeremiah, My people have committed two evils; they have forsaken me, the Fountain of living waters, and have hewn them out cisterns, that can hold no water, Jer. 2: 13.

All false doctrine goes to deny the true throne of grace, Jesus Christ, who alone is our righteousness, acceptable to God; and all false doctrine goes to the erection of strange Baals to be worshipped instead of Christ, as said before.

Behold, beloved sirs, friends and brethren, here you have the salutary truth and the only ground of the Lord's Supper plainly and briefly set before you, what it is, for whom it is ordained, and what it teaches, and represents to us with its mysteries and significations.

You have also a view of the anti-christian supper, with its dreadful abominations, whereby the Lord's Supper is destroyed, and the kingdom of anti-christ is fortified, and is placed in the stead of God's throne, whereby, alas! so many hundreds of thousands of poor souls were and are yet daily deceived; on account of which so many pious hearts are so slanderously spoken of and reproached by the learned, and so dreadfully murdered and slain in some cities, because they renounced this abominable idolatry.

Place these two beside each other; weigh them well by the spirit, word and ordinances of the Lord, and you will find, if you do at all believe that the word of God is true, to what abomination and frightful idolatry the world has come, and that we have, according to our feeble abilities, plainly explained to you the immovable foundation of truth out of the word of God.

Praise the Most High, all of you who fear the Lord, that he has manifested his unbounded love and grace toward us poor sinners, in this dreadful time of unbelief; that he let shine out of darkness, the clear light of the holy gospel, and the true knowledge of his son Jesus Christ, which was concealed for several centuries in this dark Egypt, under the thick clouds of the anti-christian abominations, 2 Cor. 4: 6. Therefore, let us be vigilant thereto, and diligently walk therein, so that thick darkness may not again cover us, as the prophet says, Jer. 13: 16.

O my dear reader, rightly learn to know Jesus Christ, who has ordained this Holy Supper and the breaking of bread for his disciples and all christians. Believe the glorious and unspeakable gifts of his grace. Fear, love, honor, and serve him; walk in godly union, love and peace with your neighbor, even as this Supper, with its representation, testifies and admonishes; die to your wicked flesh, crucify its unclean lusts; in all things lead a life according to the spirit, word, and example of the Lord, so shall your Supper redound to his praise, and your souls shall have life everlasting.

SHUNNING BABYLON.

We further teach and admonish from the word of God, that all true children of God, who are regenerated from the incorruptible living seed of the divine word, who have separated themselves, according to the Scriptures, from the idolatrous generation, and yielded to the yoke and cross of Christ, and who are able to judge between true and false doctrines, between Christ and antichrist, must shun, according to Scripture, all seducing and idolatrous preachers with their doctrines, sacraments and worship. They must avoid all, of every doctrine, faith, sect, creed and name, who are not found in the pure doctrine of Christ, and in the scriptural usage of his sacraments, because they have neither calling, doctrine, nor life, according to the word of God, but are sent by anti-christ, and ordained in his employment and service. And

Because they not only fail to observe and acknowledge the pure doctrine of Christ, and the established usages of the apostolic church, in relation to the holy sacraments, but because they also have changed them into vain confusion, abominable and open idolatry, as has been stated.

Because they have deceitfully mingled the light froth of man's doctrine, with the fair, precious gold of the divine word; and the pure wine, with the unclean waters of their foolish wisdom.

Because they so shamefully censure, abuse, assail, and would willingly root out and burn the city of God, the city of righteousness and eternal peace; the lovely Jerusalem with its sacred temple, the house of prayer, and rule therein with their spiritual money-changers, Pharisaic commands, and enchanting traffic.

Because like Belshazzar, they, in their Babylonian idolatries and drunkenness, so miserably misuse and degrade the precious vessels and utensils of the Lord, the precious souls whom he has consecrated with his crimson blood, and by whom the *true* service of the Lord should be performed, Rev. 1: 5; Dan. 5: 3.

Because like Herod, they mock Christ, the eternal Wisdom of God, as a fool arrayed in a fool's garment; and his holy apostles, the witnesses of his eternal truth, they regard as useless talkers and liars, and thrust them out with scorn.

In short, they preach and lay before the poor people, lies for truth; darkness for light; death for life, and anti-christ for Christ.

Therefore it is unfit that the bride of Christ, who stands prepared to hear only the bridegroom's voice, the dear children of God who have their feet washed and their garments cleansed in the blood of the Lamb, John 3: 29; who are established upon the immoveable foundations of the apostles and prophets, upon the precious corner stone, Christ Jesus, should again hear the strange voice and doctrines of anti-christ, again defile their garments, and in faith, doctrines, worship, and life accord with anti-christ. They who do so, if they repent not, are condemned by the Scriptures and adjudged to death.

This we teach according to our limited talents, with all earnestness, as much as in us is, not out of contempt, as the Lord knows, nor yet out of obstinancy, caprice, or party stubbornness, as the world ascribes to us. Oh no! God preserve all his own from party spirit. But we so preach out of the true fear of the Lord and the great distress and burden of our consciences. God's pressing word, and love for your poor souls, urge us, as may, through the grace of God, be seen with more clearness hereafter.

SENDING PREACHERS.

According to the Scriptures, the calling and sending of true preachers were performed in two ways; some were called by God alone, without any human instrumentality, as was the case with the prophets and apostles. Others were called through the medium of the pious, as may be seen from Acts 1: 23—26; 1 Tim. 3: 7. We hope no one will be so ignorant, who is otherwise of a candid and rational mind, but that he will know that the whole Scriptures, both of the Old and New Testaments, were written for our instruction, admonition and correction; and that they are the true sceptre and rule by which the Lord's kingdom, house, church and congregation must be governed and adjusted, 2 Cor. 3: 16. Every thing contrary to Scripture, whether it be in doctrines, faith, sacraments, worship or conduct, should be measured by this infallible rule, and demolished by this just and divine sceptre, without any respect to persons, and brought to nothing. Therefore would we, your willing servants and associates, of like mortal nature with you, each one in the office and station to which he is called, humbly admonish you, in all love, that you would reflect on the salvation of your immortal souls, and would rightly examine the *sending* or *calling*, the doctrine and conduct of the bishops, pastors and preachers of your churches. Examine them by the aid of the spirit of the Lord, and by the doctrines and customs of the apostles, because you have persecuted and destroyed so many pious, godly christians, by the idols' houses of the ungodly, which are supported by the bloody havoc-cries of the learned. Yea, we doubt not, but that if you follow our advice with a sincere heart, you will soon perceive, that we, miserable men, do nothing more in this matter, than the word of God teaches and enjoins; and that your preachers are not the servants of Christ, but hirelings, hypocrites, deceivers and mockers, concerning whom the Scriptures warn us, on every side, and represent them under many evil names, John 10: 12; Matt. 3: 4.

Candid reader! let this be to you a true and unwavering rule, that all who rightly preach Christ and his word, and thereby bring forth obedient children to the Lord, must have been called through one of the aforementioned means. They must have been brought into the vineyard of the Lord, through the true and unfeigned love of God and man, through the power of the Holy Ghost. They must improve the talent of grace which they have received from God, they must rebuke sin, and teach faith and righteousness, without any respect of person, they must set forth the word and praise of the Lord ; they must faithfully perform the work and service of the Lord and bring the gathered sheaves into his barn and the acquired wealth into his treasury. Such a shepherd was the faithful Moses; for when the Lord informed him that Israel had made a molten calf, he hastened from the mountain, and when he heard the tumult and saw the multitude playing, and dancing, a provoked zeal burned in his heart, so that he cast down and brake the stone tables which the Lord had written with his own finger. He cared neither for life nor death, but rushed forth among the idolatrous people, and rebuked them by his word and by the sword, because they gave to a molten creature the honor of Almighty God, who with such love gloriously effected their deliverance from Egypt, Exod. 32: 7.

When Zacharias, the son of Barachias, a man full of the Holy Ghost, saw the false worship of the people, he hazarded his life, and stood forth for the honor of the Lord. He rebuked his brethren, erring Israel, and said, "Why transgress ye the commandments of the Lord, that ye cannot prosper?" 2 Chron. 24: 20.

Also the worthy prophet Jeremiah was burdened with much suffering and cares. He was much troubled on account of his faithful services, and had determined in his heart to prophesy no more in the name of the Lord; but when he saw that the people were ungodly and neither acted nor spoke aright, he said, "God's word was in my heart as a burning fire shut up in my bones, and I was weary with forbearing and I could not stay," Jer. 20: 9.

Again, also holy Paul says, "Wo is unto me, if I preach not the gospel! For if I do this thing willingly, I have a reward; but if against my will, a dispensation of the gospel is committed unto me," 1 Cor. 9: 16.

Behold, my good reader, all who by such a power are touched in their hearts, who are moved by the Holy Ghost, who are pressed by love to God and man, and urged by the Lord himself, or by his spotless christian church; or are called to the service of the Lord by an unblamable, truly believing, christian church, to rightly teach in the house of God; that is, the church of Jesus Christ, with sound doctrine, and by a pious and unblamable conduct, admonish, rebuke, reprove and comfort them in paternal love; to set forth and administer the Lord's holy baptism and Supper, in a right manner; to repel diligently, with God's word, all deluding and false teachers; and to exclude all evil members from the communion of the godly, &c. To such, the word of Christ is, As my Father hath sent me, even so send I you; without such a sending, no one can ever rightly preach the gospel, as Paul says,

SENDING PREACHERS.

"How shall they preach except they be sent?"

Yes, it was with this sending and calling that all the prophets, apostles and servants of God came forth. They assumed not the honor to themselves, as do the preachers of this world; but like Aaron, they were called by God, or, as has been said, by the spotless church. They were brought by the spirit of God, with pious hearts, into his service; they had always esteemed themselves unfit to serve the people of God, or stand forth in such a high and responsible station.

When Moses was called of the Lord, that he might lead out the people, he refused from his heart, he excused himself and declined, because he was of a slow tongue; he desired not the office to which the Lord had chosen him, yea, he resisted so long that the Lord was angry, Exod. 4: 10—15.

Isaiah was confounded because he was to preach the word of the Lord. He lamented that he was of unclean lips till the angel purged them with a coal from off the holy altar, Isa. 6: 6.

Jeremiah was called and prepared from his birth of God, to be a prophet; he said, Ah Lord God! I am not fit to preach, for I am but a child, Jer. 1: 6.

Peter was asked by the Lord three times, if he loved him, before he gave him charge of his sheep, John 21: 15.

Paul was called from heaven, and appointed by the Lord himself in the service of the Gospel; for the Lord chose him as suitable for the ministry, Acts 9: 3.

Matthias was chosen through the zealous prayers of the church, and the lots of the apostles, to be an apostle in the place of Judas, Acts 1: 26.

All who are not sent of God, nor by an unblamable christian church, conformably to the regulations of Christ and the apostles are not called, as above said. Such are not called by the Holy Ghost; by the pure, unfeigned love of God and their brethren; and with a correct knowledge and zeal for the divine word; but they enter upon it with a temporal, sensual life, seeking man's favor, praise, money and profit. They will never gather fruit in the vineyard of the Lord, though they may be learned in language, eloquent and esteemed as great and excellent men. But all that they attempt is lost labor. They will rise too early, or go out too late, their calling is powerless, their service is vain, their labor without fruit, yea, it is nothing but sowing by the way, and beating against the wind; for no one can serve in this high and holy office, conformably to God's will, except those whom the Lord of the vineyard has made worthy and fit, by the spirit of his grace.

Since then, this sending is the true sending and calling, which is taught in the Scriptures, as has been observed, we faithfully counsel the reader, that in the pure fear of God, he would mark what kind of people their teachers are; of whom, in what way, and to what they are called. For it is manifest that some of them are useless, haughty, lustful men; some are avaricious, usurers, liars, deceivers, others again are drunkards, gamblers, licentious, open seducers, idolaters,&c., concerning whom it stands written, If they repent not, they shall not inherit the kingdom of God, 1 Cor. 6: 9, 10. Some also, are idle profligates, young and haughty, wholly unlearned in the Scriptures; and were anointed and shaven by anti-christ, when they obtain a little knowledge of the Latin tongue, like as if the qualifications for the ministry and for the care of our souls, were not to be founded upon godliness and the gifts of grace, but upon language; Oh no, my reader, no, their foundation must be sought for more deeply.

Besides this, those so chosen, desire nothing but a sensual, corrupt, carnal life, dishonest, filthy lucre and benefices, which heretofore anti-christ and his servants have collected together and multiplied by means of sorcery, theft and robbery.*

They are only called by carnal love, favor and faction; one has a son, another a brother, a third a favored friend, a fourth is made willing by money and gifts.

They are also with a similar spirit installed and established in their office; to wit, with eating, drinking, gormandizing and luxury; with pompous greeting, choir letters, appellations, presentations, investitures, and such like anti-christian titles.

---
* That is what the priests seek.

But by whom are they thus called? By the church? No. Christ's church knows no such callings, customs, practices and teachers, but they are called by the assemblies of the impenitent, the haughty, avaricious, fornicators, gamblers, drunkards and idolaters, who neither know God nor his word, but who abuse, persecute and hate all christian truth, and walk after the lusts of the flesh.*

Again, to what are they called? That they may preach the pure word of God? That they may go before the poor people, with doctrines and conduct consistent with the commands of Scripture? O no; but that they may teach the doctrines and commandments of men; that they may withstand the holy truth, and betray the pious and godly, who refrain from the broadway, into the hands of the blood-thirsty; and in this manner assiduously serve and support the dominion of hell.

My beloved reader, why shall I complain so much; it is yet much worse than I can write. One blind man calls another; one idolater another; one ungodly man, another. It is, as the prophet said, deceivers, liars, drunkards, and gluttons are good prophets for this people, Mich. 2: 11.

O sensual preachers! You who with Korah, Dathan and Abiram ran uncalled, particularly you who know that your calling and conduct are not of the word and Spirit of God, judge your hearts by the word of the Lord, fear his rigid punishment and severe sentence, and reflect how the aforementioned persons, for the same reason, were fearfully destroyed by the Lord before all Israel, Num. 16: 32.

It suits perverted fleshly ease to live in voluptuousness here upon earth, with fattened bodies, with gloves on the hands, with ostentatious show, to be greeted by men as doctor, lord and master. But when the messenger of death shall knock at the door of your souls and say, "give an account," you will no longer remain as stewards and hirelings; then you must appear before the throne of the eternal Majesty, and the poor miserable souls which you have led out of the true way of Christ, with your lying mouths, your unbelieving, blind hearts, sensual, corrupt bodies, false and deceiving doctrine, idolatries, sorceries, and ungodly wanton lives. O where will you conceal yourselves from the wrath of God? Then shall you cry, O ye mountains fall upon us, and ye hills cover us, Rev. 6: 16. O then you will know what kind of calling you had; what kind of life you led, that you served no other God than your belly, the devil, and your selfish evil flesh, that you came uncalled, that you have sought nothing but the milk, wool and flesh of the sheep, and that one blind man has led another, till both have fallen into the abyss of the eternal wrath of Almighty God, and the torments of hell.

O precious souls awake and fear God, for the hour draws near that your momentary laugh will be changed into an everlasting weeping; these short lived joys to eternal pain, and this easy, carnal life to death and endless wo. Jude says, "Wo unto them! for they have gone in the way of Cain, and ran greedily after the error of Balaam for reward, and perished in the gainsaying of Core." Again, to them "is reserved the blackness of darkness for ever," Jude 1: 11, 13.

Behold, beloved sirs, friends and brethren, we openly declare that the sending and calling of your preachers are neither of God nor his word, but are from anti-christ, the dragon and the beast; that they are not called to preach the word of the Lord, by the Spirit of God, and the church, but they are called and urged by their lusts with the priests of Jeroboam, to worship the golden calf, 2 Chron. 13: 8, 9. They enter not in by the right door, therefore, the Scriptures testify that they are thieves and robbers, John 10: 8.

Since then, we have been saved out of the mouths of the lions and bears of the pit, and out of the snares of concealed thieves and robbers, through the great Shepherd of the sheep, the High Priest of our souls, Christ Jesus, and are now upon the chosen and fruitful mountain of Israel, and the green luxuriant pastures of the holy word (the Lord be eternally thanked), our hungering consciences have been fed with the food of eternal life, it must ever be a condemnable folly to forsake such a true shep-

---

* Observe by whom the priests are chosen.

herd, and such precious pastures, and again enter upon the barren and waste deserts, under the false shepherd who does nothing else but rob and deprive God of his glory, and ruin and murder our poor miserable souls, John 10: 10.

This I have said particularly in relation to the *Popish priests*. What the calling and sending of the Lutherans and Zuinglians is, by what spirit they are moved, what they seek, and what fruits of repentance they show by their doctrines and sacraments, we willingly leave all the godly to judge.

THE DOCTRINE OF THE PREACHERS.

As I have presented to the reader, the first part in relation to the sending and calling of a true preacher, according to the word of God, I will now, through the grace of God, present in like manner the second part, relating to the doctrine; for there is but little difference between their calling and their doctrine, as the calling is, even so, most commonly, is the doctrine.

Where the spirit of God urges or moves to preach, there will the word be incorruptibly taught in the power of God; and upright children of the spirit will thereby be born. But where flesh and blood calls, there will a carnal doctrine be taught and carnal disciples will be made, for that like produces like is incontrovertible. I deem it unnecessary here to prove this with much scripture, for their actions bear testimony.

The Scriptures plainly show how a preacher rightly called by the word of God is to rightly teach that word without perverting glosses, without any mingling of leaven; as Peter says, "If any man speak, let him speak as the oracles of God," 1 Peter 4: 11. They are the children of the Holy Ghost who speak the word of the Spirit, as Christ said, "It is not ye that speak, but the Spirit of your Father which speaketh in you," Matt. 10: 20. "For he whom God hath sent speaketh the words of God," John 3: 34. To preach the word salutarily and unblamably, is one of the highest and greatest commands enjoined by Christ. He said, "Go ye in all the world, and preach the gospel to every creature," Mark 16: 15.

The Gospel, the word of God, preached unmingled, in the power of the spirit, is the only right, true seed from which are born the truly believing and obedient children of God. If the church of Christ brings forth children from the doctrine of man, and not from God's word, she is not faithful unto Christ, and her children are not of his seed.

Therefore may nothing else be preached in Christ's kingdom and house, the church, except her King and husband's own commands and words, according to which she and all her servants must conform.

This command and word (I say), Christ commanded all true messengers and preachers to observe, as he spoke; *Preach the gospel.* He does not say, preach the doctrines and commands of man; preach councils and customs; preach glossy ordinances and opinions of the learned, but he says, "Preach the gospel," and "teach them to observe all things whatsoever I have commanded you," Matt. 28: 20.

My faithful reader, observe that all the true servants of God, both of the Old and New Testaments, taught nothing but God's word, as may be seen and read in many places in the Scriptures.

Moses was found faithful of God in all his house. He regulated and taught nothing which God had not before commanded him, Num. 12: 7; Heb. 3: 2.

Isaiah, and all of the other prophets, testified in many places what kind of doctrine they taught, and from whom they had received it; and said, Thus saith the Lord your God, who brought you out of the land of Egypt; thus spake the Lord of Hosts, Again the mouth of the Lord has spoken it. Paul dare not speak of any thing which

Christ had not wrought through him, Rom. 15: 18. Yea, Christ himself did not teach *his* word, but the word of his father, he said, My doctrine is not mine, but is of him who sent me, "All things that I have heard of my Father, I have made known unto you," John 7: 16; 15: 15. Since then the true messengers of God, taught nothing but the word of the Lord, which is the only doctrine from which our souls can obtain eternal life, as the Lord said, Deut. 8: 3. So it is easily here to mark and judge what kind of teachers they are who direct the poor uncultivated people to legends, histories, fables, holydays, images, holy water, tapers, palms, confessions, pilgrimages, masses, matins and vespers; who teach of purgatory, vigils, times, bulls, offerings, and satisfaction for souls and sins, who also make a piece of bread and a drink of wine, to be the essential body and blood of Christ; who teach and say that when they have but spoken these words, *Hoc est corpus meum* (*this is my body*), the Lord, willing or not willing, must descend unto their idolatrous hands, even though the Heavens should rend assunder, and the earth crumble down, O blasphemy!

O dear Lord! my heart trembles in my body, that I must relate and mention such terrible abominations. But because the simple plain people, who do not guard themselves against such seducers; who, conscientiously, are bound hand and foot, and are blindly rushed into eternal death, and the abyss of hell, by these useless men, therefore I cannot remain silent, but must disclose this, through undissembled love to God and your souls. Who knows but God may give grace that you may be prevailed upon to hear, your eyes opened to see, and your hearts to understand, that you may be freed from the snares of the devil, whereby you are taken.

Yes, my dear reader, they have made lords, princes, and the world drunk by their cup, Rev. 17: 2, and have completely bewitched them, so that all who turn from their shame, and would not pervert the honor of their Savior, by a piece of bread, all who shun false teachers, and desire the salutary administration of the Lord's Supper, as above said, will be upbraided by all men, as profaners of the holy Sacrament, and they must suffer and be banished, as degraded and accursed heretics.

O blind leader! you, who during your life have not rightly understood one sentence of the word of the Lord, nor have received one ray from his spirit, but have trodden the kingdom of God with your feet, and have thrust it from you with your horns, Ezek. 34: 21. How truly are you associates of those of whom it stands written, that they say, "We have made a covenant with death, and with hell are we at agreement; when the overflowing scourge shall pass through, it shall not come unto us; for we have made lies our refuge, and under falsehood have we hid ourselves," Isa. 28: 15; again, "Wo unto them that call evil good, and good evil; that put darkness for light, and light for darkness," Isa. 5: 20. "Wo unto you, for ye shut up the kingdom of Heaven against men," said Christ, Matt. 23: 13, and make the poor souls err from the way. Yet again, Wo unto you!

However, I am not much astonished that such persons teach such shameful doctrine, since they have neither known Christ nor his word, but they hold and teach all things as they were taught from youth up, out of the old usages, and the papistical laws. But that which grieves me most, is, that those also who now are aware in part of the hidden whoredom of the Babylonian woman, and have put from them some of her abominations, yet cling to human sophistry, so that they can neither be moved nor taught, with the powerful word of God, with the unblamable lives, the candid professions, or the innocent blood of so many godly saints. Nevertheless, some of you, have, at times, to yield to the truth with stopped mouths and subdued hearts, but still ye cease not to upbraid, defame, and belie, with envious tongues and slanderous lips, the bright, clear truth of Christ, and the pious children of God, before your carnal, blind churches which are of like calling with yourselves. This also your writers do as may be seen and heard every where. Besides, I fear that they are not less guilty than the papists in moving the lords, princes and ruling powers, by commissions, complaints, revilings, outcries, and writings, to persecute the Lamb of God, and his chosen, Rev. 17: 6; and to cause an uproar, when their deceiving leaven, particularly the calf worship of their infant baptism, and their unfounded supper, is rejected. Let each one behold for himself and learn to know them rightly. I know of a truth that they are without the Spirit, the sending, or the word of Christ; for I am sensible how malicious they generally are toward those who are rightly led, who fear the Lord with all their heart and who would gladly become christians. In their doctrines and deeds they seek, not less than the papists, friendship of man, honor, pomp, bounties, fine houses, and an easy licentious life.

O my beloved reader, these are not the teachers who lead many to righteousness, and who shall shine, as the light of heaven and as the stars, now and in eternity, Dan. 12: 13. For I know not where a single congregation shall be found which they have led with their doctrines and conduct to repenting lives, and to the worship of God. Their great clamor is against the pope and his cardinals, bishops, priests and monks. Moreover, all those who gladly seek the best for their poor souls, must be upbraided by them, as profaners of the sacraments, anabaptists, fanatics, and heretics, who through the word of God, reprove their deceiving doctrines, idolatrous sacraments, and idle lives.

Yea, when they can find but one (though cut off), who was before united with the people of God, but who has now fallen into some vice, they judge and sentence *all* the godly by this *one*; Behold! say they, what manner of people they are. They seek nothing so much as to find cause of censure; therefore, they look upon Judas, but not upon Peter, Andrew and John; they do not regard what manner of people they are themselves, nor what kind of disciples they have.

Besides, it is nothing but the grace, favor, mercy, and the love of God, that they teach and preach to their covetous, proud, gorgeous, impure, drunken, and impenitent church, not observing that such as they are, cannot inherit the kingdom of God, as the whole Scriptures testify; they also strengthen the hands of the wicked, so that no one repents of his wickedness, as the prophet lamented.

O ye useless unprofitable teachers, who are believed to bear the vessels of the Lord, these my words are to you! Why do you declaim so much of faith and love, whose fruit you so greatly hate and dislike? If you have the fear and unfeigned love of God, let them appear and be made manifest through your words. Say, beloved preachers! Where is your christian humility, your godly, christian zeal, pleasure, peace and joy in Christ Jesus?

Where is your mercy which you shew? where are the naked whom you have clothed, the hungry whom you have fed, and the needy whom you have entertained? Matt. 25: 41—43. Where are the lost whom you have again sought, the wounded whom you have bound up, and the sick whom you have healed? Ezek. 34: 4. Where is your unblamable, pious life which is from God? That which you preach, perform and do, is for the most part idle hypocrisy.

Some of you approve in some degree, of a pious, christian life, preach also much of Christ, of his merits, spirit and grace, and are yourselves, manifestly those who lead a gross, carnal life, who crucify Christ anew, grieve his spirit, and despise his grace, as may be seen.

O preachers, preachers! how aptly has the Holy Ghost likened you to dry wells and empty clouds from which no water can be obtained, and to unfruitful trees from which no fruit can be taken, 2 Pet. 2: 17; Jude 1: 12. I know not to what you may be more suitably compared, than to a woman who lives in all manner of shame and wantonness, and yet talks much about modesty, decency and virtue: Should not her words be regarded as mockery? Might it not be said, why do you talk of modesty and chastity, since you are full of all manner of immodesty and shame?

We are well aware that you have demolished some of the little idols of Babylon, such as the Roman ablution, the invocation of departed saints, vile purification, abstaining from meats, and the like self-righteousness, idolatry, and other superstitions, but, alas, the horrible blasphemy and abominations are still retained; such as accursed unbelief, obstinacy, earthly-mindedness, unscriptural infant baptism, the idolatrous supper, and the impenitent, old life which is of the flesh.

Therefore, we testify with the truth and declare that you are not ambassadors of God nor teachers of Christ. For it is plain that you reject the word and ordinances of the Lord, and run of yourselves, Jer. 8: 6, and have pastured yourselves under the name and appearance of the evangelical shepherds of the Lord, and have led to destruction so many hundreds of thousands of souls, through your wanton doctrine, idolatrous sacraments, and carnal lives.

But the teachers who are sent of God, and who have been rightly called, teach the word of God in purity, abide in its holy ordinances, and live (after their weakness) unblamably, for they are born of God, and are taught and moved by his Holy Spirit, they seek neither gold, nor possessions, neither an easy life nor earthly applause, they wait upon their enjoined duties with all earnestness, they fear God from the heart, seek their neighbor with fidelity; they are armed with the weapons of righteousness, on the right hand and on the left, Rom. 6: 7. They deal without respect to persons. The powerful, sharp sword of the divine word, cuts out of their mouth; it is a shining lantern in their hands; they are taught in righteousness, are full of all spiritual wisdom; they divide the good from the evil; the holy from the unholy, and the clean from the unclean. In short, they shine in doctrine and conduct, even as from the beginning till the present time, it has been written and remarked of all true prophets, apostles and servants of God.

O dear Lord, how lovely are those pastors and teachers who seek nothing else but the extension of the kingdom of God; who rightly preach the word of repentance and grace, that they may win many souls; and for this end, they expose their reputation, houses, property, persons and lives.

These are they, who, with Christ, the chief shepherd, gather together and feed his lambs; but the others are those who scatter and destroy them. They are prophets, but **not of God**; they preach, but not out of the Lord's mouth. They strengthen the hands of the ungodly. They destroy the souls who should have eternal life, and encourage those who must forever die; and this they do for handfuls of barley and pieces of bread. They preach to the people peace when there is no peace. Therefore, shall they stand in shame, who follow such abominations, although they yet are not ashamed and yet forbear to blush, Ezek. 13: 16.

Behold, dear reader, since they so shamefully deprive Christ of his honor and gain, and scatter his sheep, and, with the sword of their deceiving doctrines, destroy the poor souls who are so greatly loved by the Lord, for whom he so earnestly seeks, and whom he so dearly purchased. Since they so enviously war against the word and ordinances of the Lord, we say and teach with Christ, "Let them alone; they be blind leaders of the blind." Guard yourselves against such false prophets; for though they come in the appearance of sheep, they are nevertheless, inwardly ravening wolves. They are the strangers whose voice Christ's sheep know not. They are those of whom Paul warns us and says, "Now I beseech you, brethren, mark them which cause divisions and offences contrary to the doctrine which you have learned; and avoid them; for they that are such serve not our Lord Jesus Christ, but their own belly; and by good words and fair speeches deceive the hearts of the simple," Rom. 16: 17, 18.

Again, John says, "Whosoever transgresseth, and abideth not in the doctrine of Christ, hath not God. If there come any unto you, and bring not this doctrine, receive him not into your house, neither bid him God speed, for he that biddeth him God speed, is partaker of his evil deeds," 2 John 1: 9, 10, 11.

The word of God, abundantly exhorts us that we should leave such and beware of them; shun their voice and retreat from them, and not take them into our houses, as has been said. If we are Christ's sheep and the children of the Holy Spirit; so must we even hear Christ's voice, and follow after and obey the monitions of the Holy Ghost. Reflect how sincerely holy Paul admonished the Philippians, that they should guard against strife, evil doers, and the concision.

He taught the true servants of God that they should shun those, who failed no further (as it appears) than that they out of zeal, without knowledge, held fast to the circumcision which they had received from their fathers, and would not admit that it should be abolished through Christ, for this he sharply reproves them. How much more earnestly it becomes us to beware of them, who deceive the whole world, who upbraid and persecute the godly, and crucify all truth, against all false teachers and blasphemers of God, who urge, institute and practice all manner of idolatrous and abominable doctrine.

THE CONDUCT OF PREACHERS.

As you have just heard the ground of the calling and doctrines of the preachers, we will proceed, and through the grace of God point out by the Scriptures how the *true* apostles, bishops, teachers and pastors, in the church of Christ, should conduct themselves in their deportment and lives; it is not enough that a man appears to speak much of the word of the Lord, but what he says must also be maintained by a devout and unblamable conduct, as the Scriptures teach.

Thus says Paul, "But I keep under my body, and bring it into subjection; lest that by any means, when I have preached to others, I myself should be a cast-away," 1 Cor. 9: 27. If it becomes the hearers and disciples to lead an unblamable life, how much more does it become teachers, because they rule the hearers and are their overseers; as Paul says, "Remember them which have the rule over you, who have spoken unto you the word of God; whose faith follow, considering the end of their conversation," Heb. 13: 7.

He also admonishes Timothy thereto, and says, "Let no man despise thy youth; but be thou an example of the believers, in word, in conversation, in charity, in spirit, in faith, in purity," 1 Tim. 4: 12. In all things shewing thyself a pattern of good works; in doctrine, shewing uncorruptness, gravity, sincerity, &c., Tit. 2: 7. For it is undoubtedly proper, if any one teaches and reproves others, that he first himself be rightly taught and unblamable, as Paul teaches, "If a man desire the office of a bishop he desireth a good work. A bishop then must be blameless, the husband of one wife vigilant, sober, of good behavior, given to hospitality, apt to teach; not given to wine, no striker, not greedy of filthy lucre; but patient, not a brawler, not covetous; one that ruleth well his own house, having his children in subjection with all gravity; for if a man know not how to rule his own house, how shall he take care of the church of God? Not a novice, lest being lifted up with pride, he fall into the condemnation of the devil. Moreover, he must have a good report of them which are without; lest he fall into reproach and the snare of the devil, he must be sober, just, holy, temperate; holding fast the faithful word, as he hath been taught, that he may be able by sound doctrine, both to exhort and to convince the gainsayers; even so must their wives be grave, not slanderers, sober, faithful in all things," 1 Tim. 3: 1—11; Titus 1: 8, 9.

Behold dear reader, it is requisite that every preacher and teacher, who would rightly govern and rule in the church of God, be thus qualified; for if any one were to reprove and teach others, and is himself not blameless and is ignorant; he will justly have to hear; Why do you teach others and teach not yourself first! Thou teachest a man should not steal, and thou dost steal. Thou sayest a man should not commit adultery, and thou dost. Thou adhorrest idols, yet thou committest sacrilege. Thou boastest of the law of God; and dishonorest God by breaking the law, Rom. 2: 21—23.

All those thus called, who are in doctrine sound, and unblamable in life, may teach, exhort, reprove, root up, and build in the name of the Lord; their labors will not be fruitless, as may be seen, in the case of Moses, Samuel, Elias, Elisha, Isaiah, Jeremiah, Peter, Paul, John, and with all the true prophets, apostles and servants of God, who preached the word unblamably in the power of the Spirit.

Their doctrine cuts like a sharp edged sword, for it has power, it is fruitful, has spirit and energy, as the prophet says, "As the rain cometh down, and the snow from heaven, and returneth not thither, but watereth the earth, and maketh it bring forth and bud, that it may give seed to the sower, and bread to the eater, so shall my word be, that goeth forth out of my mouth; it shall not return unto me void, but it shall accomplish that which I please, and it shall prosper in the thing whereto I sent it," Isa. 55: 10, 11.

Yea, all those who enter the vineyard of the Lord with such a sending or calling, and with such a spirit, doctrine and conduct, as said, are the shepherds of whom it is written, "I will give you pastors according to mine heart, which shall feed you with knowledge and understanding," Jer. 3: 15.

They are the teachers who turn many to righteousness; and they shall shine as the brightness of the firmament, as the stars forever, Dan. 12: 3.

They are the spiritual streams, and the rivers of the paradise of Christ, which issue from the fountains of the paradise of God, to irrigate and fertilize the whole country, Gen. 2: 10—14.

They are the spiritual posts and pillars in the court of the tabernacle of Moses with hangings of fine twined linen, Exod. 27: 9.

They are the three score valiant men, of the valiant of Israel, who are around Solomon's bed; they all hold swords; being expert in war; every man with his sword upon his thigh, because of fear in the night, Cant. 3: 7, 8.

They are the seven horns or trumpets, of the golden years, before whose sounds, teaching and preaching, the walls of Jericho fell, that is, all false doctrine, all powers and dominions raised up against the true Joshua, Jesus Christ, and his people, are brought low, Josh. 6: 10.

They are the beautiful messengers of peace, who preach the gospel of grace, favor, mercy, love, and peace, and bring glad tidings of good things, to us, poor, miserable, troubled sinners, Isaiah 52: 7; Rom. 10: 15.

They are seven mighty mountains, whereupon grow roses and lilies, whose sweet scent refreshes with joy all who fear the Lord, 2 Esd. 2: 19.

They are the splendid crown of twelve stars of the woman, pregnant and in travail, Rev. 12: 1, 2.

They are the walls of the new and heavenly Jerusalem, based upon the twelve foundations, that is upon the ground and doctrine of the twelve apostles, Rev. 21: 14.

See, worthy reader, with such and similar glorious images and parables, are all the pious pastors and teachers honored in the Scriptures, whom the Holy Ghost has ordained as bishops and overseers in his church, congregation and house.

These may say with holy Paul, Follow us as we are the followers of Christ, "for our exhortation was not of deceit, nor of uncleanness, nor in guile, but as we were allowed of God to be put in trust with the gospel, even so we speak; not as pleasing men, but God, who trieth our hearts; for neither at any time, used we flattering words, as you know, nor a cloak of covetousness; God is witness. Nor of men sought we glory," 2 Thess. 2: 3—6.

I repeat it, These are they who gather with Christ what has been scattered, bind up the wounded, and heal the sick, for they are influenced by the Spirit of the Lord and urged by unfeigned love. They are vigilant, and assiduous in the discharge of entrusted duties. They fight daily with the weapon of obedience. They tear down, break and destroy all that which is against the word of God, not by external power, with sword and spear, but by the preaching of the holy word, in power and spirit, with the word of the Lord. They till, sow, water and plant. They cut down what is ripe. They gather their grain and sheaves, and carry them into the Lord's barn, and their fruits will abide unto eternal life.

Since the Scriptures require such teachers,

as before-mentioned, it is then indispensable, that we weigh the conduct of your preachers in the balance, and determine their actions, by the plummet of the divine word, before your own eyes, that you may discover how much they are wanting in their conduct of the pattern of the true bishops, preachers and pastors, spoken of by Paul to Timothy and Titus, in all their lives and actions; and that they are the very reverse, who, without spirit, word, work or truth, but in semblance only, are so called of the world.

It is manifest, beloved reader, that they have changed the meek office of a true bishop, preacher and pastor, which is an office of christian service, and if rightly attended to, is an office full of labor, poverty, trouble, care, reproach, misery, tribulation, cross and affliction, into ungodly gorgeousness and princely glory, that they may be greatly respected and feared, of those whose names are not written in heaven, to this end they appear in splendid robes; are dressed in shining garbs, Rev. 13: 8; are called by pompous names, and use in their services crosses, ointments, caps, togas, unclean purifications, and have cloisters, chapels, bells, organs, music, masses, offerings, &c., of which there is not a word to be found in the Scriptures. Under these splendid trappings may plainly be seen the slily, croaching wolf, the earthly, sensual mind, the antichristian seductions and bloody abominations; for they seek nothing but the favor of men, honor, splendor, venery, idleness, self, gold, silver, gluttony, &c., and suffer themselves to be called spiritual doctors, teachers, lords, abbots, guardians, fathers and priors.

Alas! how vastly they do differ from the prophets and apostles in their office, services, examples, usages, lives, and in all they did; who entered the vineyard of the Lord without purse, without money, or much clothing; who were made a spectacle to the whole world; and for Christ's sake were killed all the day long, and accounted as sheep for the slaughter; as may be seen from the Scriptures.

But these have their chests and coffers full, they are waxed rich through the abundance of the Babylonian sorcery, and have become princes on earth, Rev. 18: 15. In all things they are blamable, violating female chastity, which is carried on to such an unblushing degree, that it cannot be expressed; they are unchaste, unmerciful, malicious, scorners, unfriendly, unrighteous, liars, drunkards, and full of inordinate desires. Their tables are full of uncleanness, as Isaiah the prophet says. Their hearts are full of avarice, and they are malicious towards those who will not contribute to their support. They even prepare war against them, as Micah teaches; are full of adultery; sit with harlots in their houses; beget children illegitimately. They are unbelieving, refractory, proud, ambitious; obey not the word of the Lord; are bound with the cords of the devil, and there are many who have not known the truth, are a scandal and disgrace to the world. Their dreadful, abominable fruits make this manifest to all. They fight against Christ and his word; hate all the pious; speak reproachfully of all those who seek, love, and fear the Lord with all their hearts. In short, it is impossible to relate all their abominable crimes, lewdness, ungodly deeds, private and public vices, infamy and abominations.

O dear Lord! how much more have they become the reverse of the upright and true bishops, overseers and pastors, although this proud generation boast that they can bring Christ down from heaven, reconcile God, forgive sins, and that they are the true pillars, heads and eyes of the church.

Although I have written this especially of the Roman priests, the reader should know, that I cannot acquit those in any wise, who boast of the word; for with the exception of adultery and fornication, and a few of the abuses of the bread, which are not found with them, they seek and desire, in the common walks of life, unreasonable gain; they idolize baptism and the Holy Supper, and oppress, backbite and slander the pious, about the same as the others do.

Therefore, I fear all who preach for money, and flatter the world, are the spiritual sorcerers of Egypt, 2 Tim. 3: 8, priests of the groves, servants of Baal, and prophets of Jezebel, destroyers of the Lord's vineyard, Jer. 12: 10, defilers of the land, Jer. 23: 11, blind watchmen and dumb dogs, spoilers of the good pastures, they trouble the clear waters, are devourers of souls, Ezek. 22: 27, false prophets and ravening wolves, devourers of widows' houses, thieves and murderers, enemies of the cross of Christ, whose end is destruction, whose God is their belly, and whose glory is in their shame, who mind earthly things, Phil. 3: 18, 19, false teachers, founders of sects, cursed children, wandering stars, withered trees, without fruit, twice dead, plucked up by the roots; foaming out their own shame, to whom is reserved the blackness of darkness forever, Jude 13; anti-christs, locusts that rose from the bottomless pit, came to hurt those who have not the seal of God in their foreheads, Rev. 9: 4. In short, if they will not repent, they are already condemned according to the Scriptures, Tit. 3: 11; Rev. 21: 8.

Not that I would judge any one, my good reader, I well know that it is written, Judge not, that ye be not judged; condemn not and ye shall not be condemned; but they are judged of him, who says, "The word that I have spoken, the same shall judge him in the last day," John 12: 48.

Who do such and the like things, says Paul, shall not inherit the kingdom of God. But if any one shall do the works whereof Paul speaks, he will not be judged of me, nor by any other man, but by the word of the Lord. Therefore we entreat you to measure the conduct of your preachers with the Scriptures, and you will find, by whom they are judged.

O miserable preachers, whose blindness we may well lament; how much better would it be for you never to have been born. For if you have finished your short, perishable, voluptuous and idle life; and have not repented, as above stated, your portion will be God's eternal wrath, punishment and judgment in the torments, the pains and burnings of hell; woe and death shall be your end, as the Scriptures threaten, Phil. 3: 19.

The reason is, because you reject Christ, and despise his word, which is everlasting food for the soul, upon which we must eternally subsist. You despise his word because it reproves your vain and frivolous conduct, showing that you are indeed sensual; of the world, and of the devil, as is evident; and that you so miserably deceive poor souls; and so cruelly hate, belie, reproach and betray all those who sincerely seek the salvation of their souls; take their property, deprive them of honor, and life, who in great love admonish, by the word of God, your deceiving teachers, and reprove their ungodly deeds with all discretion, Deut. 8: 3; Matt. 4: 4.

O Balaam, Balaam, how long will you so unmercifully kick and cuff the poor ass which has to suffer all the opprobium, scorn, and disgrace, for the sake of his master's testimony? And never kindly listen how he answers you in a human voice, and reproves your great folly and error? That he is driven by an angel with a naked sword, namely, by the Spirit and word of the Lord, that he can longer carry (endure) you in your ungodly deeds.

Well now! seed of Cain, Korah and Balaam, prepare for defence; lie, cheat, censure, blaspheme, hate, root up, disgrace, and murder as much as in you lies; allege all the councils, authors, and learned teachers who have been for centuries; appeal to all the lords and princes, emperors, kings and the mighty of the earth. Use all the power, art and cunning that you can command, it will avail you nothing; the Lamb will conquer and gain the victory, the people of God will triumph, not with tangible weapons, but in patience with the Spirit and Word of God. Jerusalem and the temple must be built up, although the Azotus and Sanballat may attempt to hinder it, not with inanimate stones, which are now tread upon in every street with your unclean feet, Neh. 4: 6; although all the gates of hell may resist, Babel must be destroyed and laid waste. The ten kings *will* and *must* perform their services. You will gnaw your tongues for pain, bitterly cry and weep on account of the torments of Babel, and say, Alas! alas! that great city, that was clothed in fine linen, and purple, and scarlet, and decked with gold, and precious stones, and pearls! For in one hour so great riches is come to nought; for her sins rose up to heaven, and the Lord remembered her wickedness, Rev. 18: 16.

The gospel *will* and *must* be heard; lies

must be exposed, and your blind folly made known to all men; although I and my brethren may be called off by death before this takes place, yet it will undoubtedly happen at the appointed time, which the Holy Ghost so plainly foretold and taught through the worthy disciple, John.

O stiffnecked, and evil generation, how long will you resist the Holy Ghost? How long will you revile the truth, and prefer lies? How long will your hands drip with the blood of the innocent? Reform your wicked lives, fear God with all your hearts, renounce all your glossy, sensual and carnal doctrine, come forward with us, treat us according to the word of God, that the gospel may be rightly preached, and maintained by a pious and blameless life. O, if you would do this, no innocent blood would be shed, and the truth would be made known.

But we are afraid it will be as the prophet said, "The wicked shall do wickedly, and none of the wicked shall understand; but the wise shall understand," Dan. 12: 10. For it is the custom of all the sects, who are out of Christ and his word, to defend their foundations, faith and actions with the sword. The Romans, the Arians, the Circumcellions, the Lutherans, the Zuinglians, and the Munsterites, are our witnesses; but Christ's people suffer and forbear.

Is it not a grievous error, that these poor people want to be called Christians, and are guilty of such abominable things, such as exterminating, robbing, apprehending, burning, torturing, murdering, &c., under pretences, as if the kingdom of Christ, the glory of the Lord, the word and truth of God, were to be defended and maintained with such horrible disgrace?

Alas, no! you miserable men, no. All who are moved by the spirit of Christ know of no sword but the word of the Lord; their weapons are powerful, fervent prayer, a long-suffering and patient heart, strong, immoveable faith, a living hope, and an unblamable life, whereby the gospel of the kingdom, the word of peace, is to be promulgated, and to be defended against the gates of hell.

Beloved reader, if you have the fear of God, then learn rightly to know your bishops, prophets, pastors and teachers, and remember what is written, "Come out from among them, and be ye separate, saith the Lord, and touch not the unclean thing; and I will receive you, and I will be a Father unto you, and ye shall be my sons and daughters, saith the Lord Almighty," 2 Cor. 6: 17, 18; and again, "Come out of her, my people, that ye be not partakers of her sins, and that ye receive not of her plagues," Rev. 18: 4. Consider that the mouth of the Lord said, "Beware of false prophets, which come to you in sheep's clothing, but inwardly they are ravening wolves: ye shall know them by their fruits. Do men gather grapes of thorns, or figs of thistles?" Matt. 7: 15, 16. They are the salt which has lost its savor, and is henceforth good for nothing, but to be cast out and to be trodden under foot of men, as the Lord says, Matt. 5: 13.

In short, they are those of whom Paul warned and said, "This know also, that in the last days perilous times shall come; for men shall be lovers of their ownselves, covetous, boasters, proud, blasphemers, disobedient to parents, unthankful, unholy, without natural affection, truce-breakers, false accusers, incontinent, fierce, despisers of those that are good, traitors, heady, highminded, lovers of pleasure more than lovers of God; having a form of godliness, but denying the power thereof; from such turn away," 2 Tim. 3: 1—5.

Again, thus you see that your preachers are such persons as described, and that the Scriptures abundantly admonish and command that we shall forsake them, fear them, avoid and flee from them, &c. And this is the reason why we openly teach *not* to hear their seducing doctrines, *not* to use their sacraments, and to have nothing to do with their false worship.

Rather say, What godliness can Israel bring from Assyria, Egypt, or from Babylon?

How can the true service be found with the priests of Baal? How can you be taught in divine things to righteousness, by those who are ignorant thereof themselves?

How can you learn Christ from antichrist; and the word of God from false prophets?

How can you be blessed by the cursed, and be rightly led by the blind?

How will you draw water from dry fountains, and gather fruit from withered trees? 2 Pet. 2: 17.

How can you be partakers of the Lord's table and of the table of devils?

How can you drink both of the Lord's cup and the devil's cup, and be in the communion of Christ and of anti-christ? 2 Cor. 10: 21.

You cannot serve two masters who are opposed to each other; you must love the one and hate the other, or else you will hold to the one and despise the other. You must be for Christ or against him, you will gather with him, or destroy in opposition to him, Matt. 6: 24.

Since we, by the grace of God, so plainly see how your preachers are sent, see their doctrine and lives, how they go without being called, falsify the word of God, lead a wanton, sensual life, deceive the poor people; and being so abundantly admonished by the Scriptures, that we should forsake, avoid, and shun such preachers, because they are so diametrically opposed to Christ and his word, and we desire to be obedient to the voice of our shepherd in this matter as it becomes all the pious of Christ, for the kingdom is promised to the obedient, as the Scriptures say, "Not every one that saith unto me, Lord, Lord, shall enter into the kingdom of heaven; but he that doeth the will of my Father," Matt. 7: 21.

And we also, agreeably to the contents of God's word, have departed from their doctrine, sacraments and service, and this we testify both by word and deed, with possessions and blood, before lords and princes, in cities and in the country, before you, and the world as an admonition, doctrine and instruction, so that you all, both teachers and hearers, might awaken, to reflect on the truth, repent and come out from the kingdom and fellowship of anti-christ, and enter the kingdom and communion of Christ; and thus extricate your poor souls from the snares of unbelief, that you may be rescued, preserved and eternally saved.

For we will sooner endure, in our mortal bodies, misery, poverty, tribulation, hunger, thirst, heat, cold, bonds and death, and adhere to the word of the Lord, than lead secure easy lives with the world, and for the sake of a short and temporal life, ruin our souls.

We think with holy Peter, that we should rather obey God than man; and with virtuous Susanna, it is better to fall into the hands of man, than into the hands of God. All who fear the Lord may read and judge.

COUNTER ARGUMENTS

OF

BABYLON AND ITS BUILDERS, WITH THEIR REPLICATIONS.

Beloved reader, although we have clearly shown you the difference between true and false preachers, and why we should not hear them, we hope that the god-fearing, who acknowledge the word of the Lord to be true, might fully comprehend this GROUND AND TRUTH; still we find some among those preachers, who partly know that their cause cannot stand the test of the Scripture.

Nevertheless, not being born of God, nor fearing him but seeking unlawful gain, the world and ease, they have garbled a variety of scriptural passages, by which they persuade the simple, those who dread the cross of Christ, that it is lawful to hear their doctrine and attend upon their church services, and this they do in order to live at ease and enjoy good times.

In the first place, they say that Christ said, "The Scribes and Pharisees sit in Moses' seat: all, therefore, whatsoever they bid you observe, that observe and do; but do not ye after their works," Matt. 23: 3. From which they conclude, that, as the Scribes and Pharisees were sitting in the seat of Moses, and mingling leaven with the unleavened lump, of which Christ warned his disciples, saying, all therefore whatsoever they bid you observe, that observe and do, they also now sit in Christ's seat, although they are in their doctrine and lives not upright and free from guilt; that therefore we are to hear them, so far as they preach the word of God, but not to do after their works.

To which we reply: First we ask them whether they and the Pharisees are one or not? If they answer yes, they must then be their own judges, and decide that they are of those who crucified Christ, stoned Stephen, beat the apostles, persecuted the saints, and they are of those who are threatened with eternal woe; they may well then be afraid and fear the Lord and his judgments. If they answer no, then they can prove nothing with this passage.

Secondly, we reply: If they adduce this passage, *quasi argumentum assimili*, i. e. as it were an argument of similitude, and remark that to sit in Moses' seat, is to rightly preach and attend to Moses' law with its ceremonies. This did the Scribes and Pharisees, they left the law and ceremonies entire and altered nothing therein, although they practiced some superstition with it, as may be seen from Matt. 15: 3. For had they altered the law and ceremony, they would not have been sitting in Moses' seat.

But even as the Scribes and Pharisees did sit in Moses' seat, these will then also have to show that they sit in Christ's seat, that is, they must prove that they preach Christ's gospel, baptism, supper, separation; preach and practice all things correctly, or the *argumentum assimili* cannot stand. If this is the case, we may then ask counsel of the Scriptures; why they suffer the traditions of men to be added thereto? But we well know that the Scriptures are silent on this subject.

Thirdly, we reply: So long as the Scribes and Pharisees were sitting in Moses' seat, and practiced the ceremonies and taught the law which pointed to Christ, as before related; so long did Christ direct his disciples and the people, at that time, to them; for the law was not fully accomplished; the perfect sacrifice, which was to abolish all typical sacrifices, was not yet offered; the veil of the temple was not yet rent, the figures and shadows were not yet changed into the new and abiding reality. After it had all been accomplished according to the Scriptures, and all things made new in Christ, he did not then send out the Scribes and Pharisees with Moses' law, but his disciples with his own doctrine; and said, "Go ye into all the world and preach the gospel to every creature," Mark 16: 15, "teaching them to observe all things whatsoever I have commanded you," Matt. 28: 20.

Since then all things are new in and through Christ; and as the people of Moses were directed to his preachers, by Christ before his death, to those who sat in Moses' seat and rightly taught the law, and ceremonies; in like manner, in the new Testament, are we, after the death of Christ, directed to those preachers who sit in Christ's seat, teaching his words unblamably, and using his sacraments as the Scriptures teach.

But the Scriptures abundantly warn us of those who adulterate Christ's doctrine, misuse his sacraments, seduce the people, lead dissolute and wanton lives; such we are to shun, avoid and abandon, not to admit them into our houses, for they sit in anti-christ's, and not in Christ's seat, as said, Matt. 7: 15.

Secondly, they adduce what Paul says, "Quench not the spirit; despise not prophesyings; prove all things; hold fast that which is good, abstain from all appearance of evil," 1 Thess. 5: 19—22.

I answer: Paul himself explains, according to our opinion, of what spirit and prophecy he thus spake. For if it were the opinion of the apostle that we should repair to houses where this open seduction and idolatry are carried on, and there prove their spirit and doctrines, Paul would then have contradicted himself, when he says, that we shall separate, shun and flee from them; for we know of a certainty that they do corrupt the word and sacraments of the Lord, and seek nothing but a good living, and are without the spirit and doctrine of Christ.

O no; Paul did not write this of such preachers as the Scribes and Pharisees were, neither of the idolatrous priests of Egypt and Babylon (understand well what I mean): but he said this touching the prophets, pastors and teachers in the Church of Christ, that we are not to quench their spirit, but prove their doctrine, and hold fast to that which is good. And if they taught any thing not in accordance with the Scriptures and the true faith, to avoid it. If any man prophesy, let him prophesy according to the proportion of faith, Rom. 12: 6, and this is to what John exhorts his disciples, "Beloved, believe not every spirit, but try the spirits, whether they are of God," 1 John 4: 1. And this passage, Abstain from all appearance of evil, may be understood as not properly referring to what is just mentioned.

My good reader, we have proved your preachers so well, both as to their spirit and doctrine, that we may with a clear conscience say, that they are not of God and his word, but of the bottomless pit, of the dragon and of the beast. Say, dear reader, how shall we acknowledge those as teachers who so wantonly fight against the word of God? What communion has light with darkness? What concord has Christ with Belial? 1 Cor. 6: 14. The greater part of their teaching and action is delusion and hypocrisy. My reader, do not pervert these words, for what I write is the truth, and I can prove it to the whole world, from their doctrines, lives and sacraments.

Thirdly, they ask, Why will we not hear them; for the wise men of the East gave heed to what Herod said?

Answer: To adduce this passage seems to me to be so puerile, that it is by no means worthy of reply. For Herod did nothing else than by the instruction of the scribes, point out to the wise men the town in which the king of the Jews should be born, and he did it with a blood-thirsty heart, as the following act shows; he sent them to Bethlehem and said, "Go and search diligently for the young child, and when you have found him, bring me word again, that I may come and worship him also," Matt. 2: 8.

Herod was afraid when he heard that the Jews had a king born, lest he might lose his kingdom and glory; he therefore spoke, out of pure hypocrisy and slyness, with the wise men, for he was desirous of the child's death, to prevent its becoming a king. But when he saw that he failed in his hypocrisy, he became very much enraged, and showed his fierce, tyrannical, ungodly disposition; he sent forth and slew all the children that were in Bethlehem, and in all the coasts thereof, from two years old and under, that by the slaying of all the innocent children he might also destroy the born king, as may be seen from Matt. 2: 16.

O my good reader, how justly they do appeal to this hypocritical, lying, ambitious and tyrannical Herod; for the greater part of them are of the same spirit and disposition. They are so much pained that Christ is born again through his word. They practice hypocrisy like Herod; they lie, and say that they are sincere; but they fear their unlawful gain, their rich and lazy life, lest Christ should rule, as Herod feared, lest he should lose his kingdom. And they are ready to destroy the pious, as Herod was determined upon the blood of Christ, as you have heard.

Since then they are manifestly hypocritical liars, and earthly-minded, and also intent upon blood, as may be seen in some places; therefore we will also take for an example in this matter the wise, who, being admonished by a heavenly inspiration, did not return to Herod, and, through the grace of God faithfully observe the Lord's inspiration, counsel, doctrine and admonition, and turn to those who point out Christ in full power and practice, and teach in the truth, according to the spirit.

Fourthly, some of them say, Although the devil should preach the word of God, why should we not hear him?

In the first place I reply to these vain, slanderous calumniators, that it would be well for them to learn rightly to distinguish between the spirit and disposition of the devil, and the spirit and nature of Christ, before they would utter such unseasonable, blasphemous words before the poor people.

The devil was a liar from the beginning, and will undoubtedly always be. Since then he is a liar, and lying his nature, disposition and work, as the Lord says, how can he then sincerely and rightly teach and preach the word of God, which is truth, and is diametrically opposed to his lying disposition and nature, and though he did teach the truth correctly, and give Christ his praise, still he does so with a false heart; for he is a devil and the truth is not in him.

He confessed Christ, rightly and according to the contents of his word, when he said, Thou art Christ, the holy one of God; thou art Christ, the Son of God. However, Christ did not desire his confession, but reproved him and said, Hold your peace, and come out of him, for his confession was made with a diabolical heart, as said.

Secondly, I say, If any one would hear the voice of the devil, he need not go far; alas! he can hear him every where. All who speak lies, speak of the devil. In the beginning he spoke through the serpent; in Israel through the false prophets, and now through his preachers, in order to deceive the people of the world, and divert them from the truth, that they never can be saved.

Since then, that from the beginning he has been, and still is a lying spirit, an adversary of God, a falsifier of the Scriptures, and a murderer of souls, and will eternally be such, who can neither teach nor endure any thing good, because he is by nature unclean, a liar, and a deceiver, always the enemy of every thing that is good, we will therefore stop our ears, through God's grace, and not hear such blasphemous speaking; turn our backs upon the devil, with all his lying preachers, as the Scriptures teach; and we will sincerely believe the Scriptures, which direct us to Christ to hear him. Christ directs us to his disciples, and they direct us to such teachers who are blameless in doctrine and life, as related. May the merciful and gracious Lord eternally preserve all the pious hearts against this Herodian generation, and against the devil's preachers, Amen.

Fifthly, some also say that we may hear them, if we suffer ourselves not to be deceived by them.

I answer: The reader should observe how the people of God ever were, from the days of Abraham, separated from the world; and especially since the days of Moses, they have had their own particular preachers, teachers, ceremonies, ordinances and services, as may be abundantly read and seen in all the books of Moses.

Secondly, that Israel was commanded by God, that if a false prophet were to rise up among them, and though he were to do wonders and signs, he should die, Deut. 13: 4.

Thirdly, Israel was not allowed to teach or to receive any doctrine or worship from any strange nations circumjacent to them, but to keep closely to the law and testimonies.

Fourthly, where there arose some ungodly kings, such as Jeroboam, Ahab, Manasseh and many others, who loved their own righteousness and idolatry more than the word and right worship of the Lord; and when the false prophets multiplied, who turned the people from the Lord and his law, then also did the Lord raise up true prophets such as Isaiah, Jeremiah, &c., to reprove the disobedient, idolatrous kings and false prophets, and to warn the people faithfully of them, and said, "Hearken not unto the words of the prophets that prophesy unto you; they make you vain; they speak a vision of their own heart, and not out of the mouth of the Lord," Jer. 23: 16. These prophets all gloriously pointed to Christ, to his kingdom and reign.

Fifthly, that Christ, as well as Moses, ordained and appointed in his kingdom, community, or church, prophets, preachers, teachers, ceremonies and ordinances, which are to be observed by all true christians for ever.

Sixthly, the holy apostles teach, advise, and admonish us, that we are to separate ourselves from those, in doctrine and in worship, be they baptized or not, who agree not with the spirit, doctrine, regulations and examples of Christ.

Seventhly, that the whole world with their spirit, doctrine, sacrament, worship and conduct, are far from Christ's spirit, word, sacrament, worship and example; and, alas! are nothing but a new Sodom, Egypt and Babel, Rev. 11: 8.

Eighthly, that all those who acknowledge God's word, and are partakers of his Spirit, are called on to let their lights shine out of darkness and give light to the world, that they reprove all ungodliness by word, deed, life and death, confess the Lord's holy name, word and will, and confirm it by a pious and unblamable life, according to the Scriptures.

Ninthly, that "whoso shall offend one of these little ones which believe in me (Christ), it were better for him that a mill-stone were hanged about his neck, and that he were drowned in the depth of the sea," Matt. 18: 6.

Tenthly, that we reflect well, why or for what reason we are not to hear such preachers. If we do hear them, and desire to be taught of them, then we seek the truth among lies, and life among the dead. But if we will not be taught of them, but use our liberty, as they call it, we must confess that such hearing is no hearing, but trifling and hypocrisy, by which we despise the spirit, doctrine, ordinances, counsel, admonition, community and church of Christ; and strengthen the seducing abominations, idolatry, and kingdom of anti-christ, and conform to the world in all appearance of evil, act the hypocrite, grieve and vex many a pious child of God, cause strife among the pious, and esteem lightly the innocent blood which is shed in many places on this account.

Behold, my readers, all who fear the Lord, and rightly examine and judge *these ten articles*, here briefly stated, by the Spirit and word of the Lord, will not halt here, but they will faithfully take heed to the counsel and admonition of the Holy Ghost; reprove the world both by works and doctrine; avoid every appearance of evil, and walk unblamably in the house of the Lord.

But touching the false worship, the light-minded comfort one another, and say, children may be baptized; for the child is clean; the water is clean; to wash and to bathe is also clean, &c. We may also receive the supper of the Lord at the hands of these preachers, although it is in idolatrous houses; christians have no idols any more, they only use bread and wine as such, which is pure to the pure; Paul says, To the pure all things are pure. They appeal to the case of Naaman, the Captain of the king of Assyria; and to the house of Rimmon, and say, We care not for the idolatry of the priests, but we worship Him who made heaven and earth.

I answer: Can a single passage be adduced from the Scriptures, that uncleanness, sin, falsifying the ordinances of God, idolatry, disobedience to the word, and hypocrisy are all pure to the pure, that is, to the true believers; then we might consider a little on it. But we know certainly, that not a single passage can be advanced.

O my reader, if the men of God had thus understood the Scriptures, as these poor people do, the three valiant young men would have by no means suffered themselves to be cast into the fiery furnace. The upright Eleazer, the God-fearing pious mother with her seven sons, the holy prophets, apostles and pious witnesses of God, would have saved their lives, would have escaped the cruel tortures and pains, and said, To the pure all things are pure, we will cheerfully comply.

O no! my good reader, no: the clean are not to touch the unclean. Touch not the unclean thing, says the Spirit of God through Isaiah and Paul, that is, what the Scriptures forbid. He that washed himself, after the touching of a dead body, if he touch it again, what availeth his washing? Is it not folly for any man to wash his clothes, and afterwards tread them into the mire again? The Scriptures plainly teach, that "the just shall live by faith," and that a "good tree brings forth good fruit." We certainly know that an humble, lowly-minded soul will never magnificently array itself in gold, pearls or other costly apparel; that those who fear the Lord, will be honest, chaste, sober; they will not talk, drink, sing and dance with dishonorable women; for the knowledge, fear and love of God and his word forbid them; and should one do so, we would know that his light is darkness, and his conduct not agreeable to the Scriptures. And so it is unbecoming to those who boast of the word, and would reprove seduction, the idolatry and abominations of preachers by the Scriptures, and yet associate with them in their doctrine, sacraments, false service, for words without actions profit nothing. "Have no fellowship with the unfruitful works of darkness, but rather reprove them," Eph. 5: 11.

It is true, that to the pure all things are pure, which are not contrary to the Spirit and word of God. For none are called pure in the Scriptures, except those who conform to the Spirit and word of the Lord. All who agree with the word, to them all lawful, pure things, are pure, such as eating, drinking, clothing, houses, manors, land, gold, silver, wives, children, goods, food, to wake, to sleep, to speak, to be silent, and all things which God has given us as necessaries; because they are pure, they will also use all lawful, pure things purely; namely, in the fear of God, with thanksgiving and moderation, to the praise of God and to the service of their fellow man; to which end, these things were given of God, for the use of men.

All things prohibited of God, such as hypocrisy, unfruitful works, conformity to the world, living in affluence and splendor, and living in idolatry, are by all means, impure to the pure, to the faithful, obedient children of God; and the pure can never use things impurely through all eternity, according to the will of God; for the Spirit of God and his word forbid them.

Adam was allowed of God to eat of all the vegetables and fruits of the earth, for his subsistence, except of the tree of knowledge of good and evil; for if he should eat thereof, he must die. All the fruits and creatures allowed of God, were pure to pure Adam, but one tree was impure to him through the command of God; he ate thereof, and he, with all his seed, fell under the power of death.

And even as all things are pure to the pure, and are for the good of the pious, so also to the impure all things are impure, and to the evil all things are evil; because they are impure, they use all the creatures of God impurely. They eat and drink to excess; they dress gorgeously; and indulge in lewdness; they raise their children to idleness; they avariciously hoard gold, silver, houses and lands, and there is nothing they use purely according to the will of God; for they are impure, sensual, disobedient to the word, and are earthly-minded, as the Scriptures say.

Further; it is also an abominable calumny and slanderous seduction, what some pretend and say; outward idolatry cannot defile and make impure, if not sanctioned by the heart.

My good reader, if that were true all the passages would have been spoken to no purpose, which say; neither be ye idolators as were some of them; have no fellowship with the unfruitful works of darkness; avoid all appearance of evil, &c., then would also the offence of the cross have been ended. No, no, it becomes a true christian to be wholly pious, to glorify God, both in body and spirit.

Aaron, a high priest called of God, a type of the Lord Jesus, when he was constrained of the people to make gods for them which should go before them, he was overcome through the weakness of the flesh, that he yielded to the idolaters, and made them a golden calf. Aaron did not worship it in his heart; for he well knew it was not the God who led them through the red sea, but that it was a creature made of gold. Nevertheless this guilt was charged to Aaron, for Moses said, "What did this people unto thee, that thou hast brought so great a sin upon them?" Ex. 32: 21; yea, the Lord would have destroyed him had not Moses interceded for him, Deut. 9: 20.

We would, that all founders of sects and erring spirits, whose rejection of the cross, ease, carnal minds and hypocrisy, is cloaked under the semblance of the word of God, would reflect well upon the history of Aaron; I trust they would no longer conceal their nudity and disgrace with fig-leaves; but would clothe themselves with the true coat of skins, with Jesus Christ, made of God; for they comfort and encourage the poor, rude people in their idolatry and faith, by their ungodly dealings, which they call liberty, grieve the pious unto death, discourage and offend the poor, wavering souls of whom it is written, "Whoso shall offend one of these little ones, which believe in me, it were better for him, that a millstone were hanged about his neck, and that he were drowned in the depth of the sea," Matt. 18: 6.

What christian liberty is, and how it is to be used according to the will of God, is fully explained in Rom. 14.

Say, beloved, how can we include in christian liberty, that which is so openly committed against so many passages in the Scriptures against brotherly love, and contrary to all the examples of so many saints, as said?

O, were they pure in heart, who introduce such subtle arguments, and would they but love Christ supremely over every thing, how soon they would then know that that which they maintain is contrary to the spirit and word of God. But I fear they are those concerning whom it is written, "There is a generation that are pure in their own eyes, and yet are not washed from their filthiness," Prov. 30: 12.

Touching Naaman, we have to notice attentively the following passages.

First, that Naaman was neither a Jew, nor a proselyte, but a foreigner, who was not included in the doctrine, ceremonies, ordinances and righteousness of Israel, although he would no longer serve idols, and would serve and offer to God, he had not yet received the sign, viz., circumcision.

Secondly, that he was the servant of his master, upon whom the king depended; and therefore had to attend to the service of his master when the king worshiped in the house of Rimmon, and would worship none other than the true God who had cleansed him.

Thirdly, that we cannot conclude with certainty from the answer of the prophet, how far he did, or did not comply.

Fourthly, that the house of Rimmon, and the service thereof, and our temple with its services, are not the same; for in the house of Rimmon the name of God, the laws, the ordinances and ceremonies, were not abused, for they were not known there. But what abuses, disgrace, scoffings, abomination and blasphemy, are carried on in our temples under the name of Christ, all rational men may determine by the Scriptures.

But if any one says, Why do you concern yourselves about the doings of the priests? Worship God as Naaman did, this sounds to us thus, "Behold your pious father will be often slanderously mocked, insulted, reviled and much abused; let such things not move you, or confound you, but be unconcerned and contented. Submit quietly, but in your heart honor your father, &c." Say, beloved, what rational and upright child could bear to see his father thus assaulted, and yet keep his silence?

Since then, we see with unclouded eyes, how miserably they treat our eternal Father, who loved us so greatly, in their houses of abomination; and how they behave towards his son, Jesus Christ, who bought us with such a precious price. Again: How they quench his Holy Spirit, hate his will, his word, and abuse his sacraments, reject his ordinances and commands, revile and reproach his children, deceive poor souls, and rob Christ of his glory; and with all this, they desire us to unite with such open enemies of God; to act the hypocrite with them, to listen to their ungodly seductions and abominations; if we should, we would be very ungrateful children, and without love. This is incontrovertibly true.

No; such is not the way of pious christians; but as Christ defends his church, is not ashamed of her, and enlightens her by his Holy Spirit and word, comforts her in all her distresses, strengthens her in sufferings and endows her with power and wisdom, before lords and princes, wise and learned, and before the whole world, that all have to be silent and ashamed in presence of a poor, humble christian; and in the day of judgment acknowledge her before his Father, and will bestow upon her the eternal kingdom; and so do the spirit and love of Christ also demand of us, that we confess before men his divine honor, word, will, ordinances and commands, and besides, we are to testify it by our works, possessions, blood, life and death, and not clandestinely frequent such houses of abomination, where his great and adorable name is so miserably dishonored and slandered; and where we hear not the truth, nor learn any piety. For it is nothing but hypocrisy which they teach; although they disguise it with the word of the Lord, as may be evidently observed by their works.

All, teachers and hearers, run, says the prophet, like a frantic heifer, they all hate reproof and instruction, and live imprudently according to their own lusts. They desire not God's word, therefore, I fear the scourge is ready, and the avenging sword of the Lord is drawn; that soon one ungodly man will eat another, so that many of them will be destroyed, for these foolish people will be punished.

Fifthly, we have to observe, that in the New Testament we are only directed to the Spirit, word, counsel, admonition and usages of Christ; what he allows us we may do, but what he forbids we dare not do; it becomes all true Christians to conform thereto, and not according to such doubtful histories and obscure passages, from which we can draw no sure ground, and which teach the very reverse of what the Lord's apostles publicly taught.

Here I would faithfully admonish the sincere reader, that he would not suffer himself to be deceived with such words; but at all times to keep and abide in the unchangeable and sure ground, which the faithful witnesses of Christ, the holy apostles have left us, which they taught us plainly in their writings; for the deceivers seek but to confound the wavering, and to be free from the cross of Christ.

But, say they, We esteem it to be better to do so sometimes, in order that we may administer to our wives and children, and serve the poor, than that we should wholly abandon the preachers, and thereby make all our possessions a prey.

To which we reply, in the first place: The first command teaches, "Thou shalt love the Lord thy God with all thy heart, and with all thy soul, and with all thy mind." Where the name of the Lord is profaned, and where his word is violated, there it behooves you in all love, to reprove such things with an unblamable life, by the word of God, and to defend the praise of God, as much as in you is; reflect upon what the Lord says, Whosoever loves father, mother, brother, sister, wife, children, possessions and life more than me, cannot be my disciple, Luke 14:26.

Secondly, that all who believe that God made heaven and earth, and sustained Israel forty days with bread from heaven, and water from the rock, sent Elias his necessary food by a raven; who gives the birds in the air, the fishes in the water, and the reptiles upon earth, their food; they will not doubt the goodness, power and promise of their Lord Jesus Christ, who says, "Seek ye first the kingdom of God, and his righteousness, and all these things shall be added unto you," Matt. 6:33, for if the countenance of his grace is in this matter over those who reject him, how much more over those who fear him and keep his commandments.

Thirdly, that the Almighty, bountiful God, God Almighty, who is all-sufficient to support the poor and needy without any idolatry, hypocrisy and service of the devil; because he has no delight in such offerings and gifts of unrighteousness; as the prophet says, Behold, to obey is better than sacrifice, and to hearken, than the fat of rams; for rebellion is as the sin of witchcraft, and stubbornness is as iniquity and idolatry, 1 Sam. 15:22, 23.

All, therefore, who say that they do this on account of their wives and children, and for the sake of the poor, ought to know that they love their wives and children more than God, and lessen the arm and power of God, and lie unto the Lord; they should know that they only cover and adorn their indolence, their dislike of the cross, their unbelief, earthly-mindedness and hypocrisy under such pretense. Let every one take heed to himself and fear God, who has eyes like flaming fire, which penetrate heaven and earth, and cannot be blinded by fair words.

Again, they further pretend that Paul purified himself according to the custom of the Jews, and Timothy was circumcised. This is quite different, for these were things which God had commanded, although they ended in Christ. The reason why Paul consented thereto was, that he might preach the word with more freedom to the Jews, as he says, "Unto the Jews I became as a Jew, that I might gain the Jews; to them that are under the law, as under the law, that I might gain them that are under the law," 1 Cor. 9:20.

And since these works did not originate with anti-christ, but from God, with which Paul would not offend the weak Jews; as explained; how can we then show by them, that we are at liberty to hear false preaching, receive the baptism and enjoy the supper of anti-christ; and to take part with the world in open idolatry and blasphemy? Although this may not be done with the heart, it is at least so in appearance. Or we must consider the works of the law, which were of God, to be as unclean and ungodly as the works and abominations of darkness, which are of the devil; and esteem the renunciation of the cross of Christ as highly as the zeal with which Paul undertook to teach the Jews the Gospel of Christ.

O my faithful reader, if you would not lose your poor soul, do not then dishonor Christ, rightly seek his praise, obey his Spirit, doctrine, counsel, admonition and example, and you will never be made ashamed; you will soon discover that the purification of Paul, and circumcision of Timothy, are different from the doings, abominations, idolatry and blasphemy of anti-christ, which have been practiced from time to time, in the name of Christ, even to the present day. May the gracious, merciful God grant that you may all come to the knowledge, and walk in his truth, Amen.

Lastly, they say, That we are yet prisoners in Babel, and that we may therefore do in semblance the works of Babel; and assert the sayings of Baruch, "Ye shall see in Babylon gods of silver, and of gold, and of wood, borne upon shoulders, which cause the nations to fear; beware, therefore, that ye in no wise be like to strangers, neither be ye afraid of them, when ye see the multitude before them and behind them, worshiping them; but say in your hearts, O Lord, we must worship thee," Bar. 6: 4, 5.

Answer: Here we have first to observe, what is shown by the Babylonian captivity; when the Israelites did not serve God aright in their own country, they were scattered according to the prediction of Moses, by the righteous and gracious judgment of God, among the heathen nations, and were led captive under the dominion of Babylon. So it is with those who boast themselves as being the spiritual Israel; because they became unfaithful to the Lord, and rejected his word, and turned their ears to preachers of lies, the Babylonian king, anti-christ, has taken advantage of them and deprived them of the true doctrine, ceremonies and services, and led them captive under his dominion, and has bound them miserably with the cords of error and idolatrous abominations.

But all those who are again enlightened by the Spirit and word of the Lord, born of God, and die unto the old man, sin; forsake all human misleadings, and rightly use the holy sacraments of the Lord, his ordinances and divine services, they are freed from spiritual Babylon, that is, from sin, hell, death, devil, from the doctrines and commands of men, from all idolatry and abominations, as Paul says, There is, therefore, now no condemnation to them which are in Christ Jesus, who walk not after the flesh, but after the Spirit; for the law of the Spirit of life in Christ Jesus, hath made me free from the law of sin and death, Rom. 8: 1, 2.

All, then, who say that they are yet captives of Babylon, testify that they have not been set at liberty by the Cyrus (Jesus Christ), from their sins, and have not come from Chaldea to Jerusalem, Isa. 24: 28; Ezra 1: 1—4.

Secondly, that Israel is not commanded here to conform themselves to the gentiles; but when they saw them carry their idols, even as we may see on the days of papistical processions and abominations, although we are not in their temple, then they should worship God only, and give him the honor; for if God had commanded them to conform in all things to the Babylonian idolatry, and only serve the Lord with their heart secretly, then Shadrach, Meshach and Abednego acted foolishly in refusing to worship the great golden idol, on account of which they hazarded their lives. O no! the miraculous work, shown of God to them, testifies that they acted rightly. All, then, I say, who teach that true believers are not released from Babylon, do thereby deny the merits, death and blood of Christ, deny faith with its power, and the Holy Ghost with his liberty, and despise wholly the innocent blood of the free witnesses of the free children of God, which is shed so abundantly.

Let every one see well to what he believes and teaches; for I fear that both the shedder of blood, and the despiser are alike guilty. My good reader, examine the Scriptures well, and you will find, that to the free children of God here upon earth, there is no liberty promised as to the flesh, for Christ says, "Ye shall be hated of all nations for my name's sake," Matt. 24: 9. Again, "If any man will come after me, let him deny himself, and take up his cross and follow me," Matt. 16: 24. Again, "Whosoever killeth you will think that he doeth God service," John 16: 2. "All that will live godly in

Christ Jesus," says Paul, "must suffer persecution," 2 Tim. 3: 12. And "through much tribulation we must enter into the kingdom of God," Acts 14: 22. For the liberty of the spirit is to be maintained with much misery, tribulation, persecutions, bonds, fear and death. "The disciple is not above his master, nor the servant above his lord; it is enough for the disciple that he be as his master, and the servant as his lord," Matt. 10: 24.

Behold, beloved sirs, friends and brethren, here you have the leading parts, and chief articles of a CHRISTIAN GROUND AND FOUNDATION, with a plain instruction and exposition of the anti-christian abominations and Babylonian acts, whereby the true apostolic foundation, for a long time, was corrupted and razed to the ground; and we have contrasted light with darkness, truth with falsehood, that the whole truth by our seeking, doctrine and belief, undertaking and weak attempts, may be made manifest.

And I hope by the grace of God, that you will readily receive it, if you are at all honestly disposed, read it with a sincere heart, fear God, and acknowledge Christ as the true head; and see that we are grounded upon the only eternal corner stone, that we walk in the right way, although in weakness and to have the plain truth, and that there is no other ground or way, and truth to be found in the Scriptures, that can stand before God, other than this, which we have pointed out, and which we on every occasion maintain and defend in so much tribulation.

I have served you all with this small gift, as I received it from my God. I gladly would that I could serve you longer with great and abundant grace, to the praise of the Lord. Therefore, have I renounced praise, honor, ease, and forsaken all, and willingly submitted to the pressing cross of my Lord Jesus Christ, which ofttimes weighs very heavily on my weak flesh. I seek neither gold nor silver (the Lord knows this), but am ready, with faithful Moses, to suffer affliction with the people of God, rather than to enjoy the pleasures of sin for a season; and I esteem the reproach of Christ greater riches than the treasures in Egypt, for I know what the Scriptures have promised us, and this is my only joy and desire of my heart, that I may extend the borders of the kingdom of God, publish the truth, reprove sin, teach righteousness, feed the hungry with the word of the Lord, lead the stray sheep into the right path, and win many souls to the Lord through his Spirit, power and grace, and so act in my weakness, as he taught me who purchased me, a miserable sinner, with his crimson blood, and gave me this mind, by the gospel of his grace, namely, Jesus Christ, to him be praise and glory, and the eternal kingdom, Amen.

A CHRISTIAN

AND

AFFECTIONATE EXHORTATION TO ALL IN AUTHORITY.

Also to the learned, to the common people, to sects and to the bride of Christ, that it not a little scorched by the heat of the sun every where.

We have shown you in the preface, faithful reader, why or wherefore we published these our writings, to wit: on account of the abominable deceptions, and the manifold dangers at this time, for there are to be found so many schisms, communities, churches and sects, who are all called after the name of the Lord; such as *Romans* or *papists*, *Lutherans*, *Zwinglians*, erring sects, and the christians who are upbraided as anabaptists. Even as in former times among the Jews, were the Chasidim, Zadikin, Essenes, Sadducees, Pharisees, &c., which sacred and profane history mention. Each boasts to be the Church of Christ, and to have the word of the Lord, although the greater part of them not only live inconsistently with the Spirit, word and example of Christ, but they very enviously upbraid and slander, and are inimically opposed to it; and it is just as it was in the beginning, that the pious every where have to suffer much from the impious; as Abel had to suffer of Cain; Isaac of Ishmael; Jacob of Esau, &c., although created by the same God, by nature have one common origin, boast all of one Christ; and in the day of judgment, find the same judge. Anti-christ rules through hypocrisy and lies, with power and sword; but Christ reigns patiently with his word and spirit. He uses no other sword nor sabre. O man! man! Look upon the irrational savage creatures, and learn wisdom. Roaring lions, frightful bears, and all devouring wolves agree among themselves with their respective species; but you, poor, helpless worms; you, who are created after God's own image, and are called rational beings, born without tusks, claws and horns, born with an unsound, feeble nature, senseless, speechless and powerless, yea, neither able to walk nor stand, and have to depend entirely upon maternal aid, which teaches you that you are to be peaceable and not contentious; but when you attain your understanding and manhood, you are so very unsettled, tyrannical, revengeful, bloodthirsty and unmerciful, so much so that it cannot be fully conceived, related or described. Your open works bear testimony to this, notwithstanding you boast yourselves to be christians. O no! my faithful reader, no! Christ teaches, "Peace I leave you, my peace I give unto you," John 14: 27. Paul says, "Let the peace of God rule in your hearts, to which also ye are called in one body, and be ye thankful," Col. 3: 15. Again, "The Son of man is not come to destroy men's lives, but to save them," Luke 9: 56.

Since there are so many of you who treat the children of God so inhumanly, as we see, we have compiled summarily our *acts, principles, faith and doctrine*, from the word of God, and have published them; so that every slanderous evil speaker and bloody persecutor, may therefrom learn what our undertaking properly is, what we seek and do, and upon what ground the city of God must be built, and which of all the aforementioned congregations or churches is the right and true church of Christ. Even as there was but one Adam and one Eve; one Noah and one ark, one Isaac and one Rebecca, so there is but one church of Christ, which is the body, the city, the temple, the house and bride of Christ, having but one gospel, one faith, one baptism, one supper, and one service; walking in the same way and leading a pious, unblamable life, as the Scriptures teach.

All who have not the pure, uncorrupted word of God, the true, living faith, with the Lord's holy baptism and Supper, in power and Spirit, and walk the broad road of the flesh, are not the community and church of Christ. Here neither name nor boasting avails; we must be in Christ, and Christ in us; we must be moved by his Spirit, and in every respect abide in his holy word, otherwise we have no God.

The children of Israel were not saved, although they were of the seed of Abraham, because they walked not in the way of Abraham. Much less we, though we are called after the name of Christ, if we seek not his promise with all our souls, and not sincerely hear and follow, and be obedient to his holy will.

Since it is well known to all the pious, that we and our forefathers, for many centuries, were under the heavy burden, and in the service of Egypt, deceived by the false prophets, never heard the book of the law, the holy city and temple lay waste, and were under the tyranny and dominion of Babylon, as heard above. The merciful Father had compassion on the pressing misery and tribulation of his people, and raised up to us the true Moses, Zerubbabel, Christ Jesus, through his word and Spirit; now then, it becomes you, O you highly renowned lords and princes, since you and we boast of the same Christ, gospel, redemption and kingdom, that you no longer obstruct by your mandates and powers, the journeying of the people of God to the eternal promised land; but you should favor them more, and prosper their journey by your gracious permission; that you may hear and read with the venerable and pious Josiah, with a broken, meek heart, in the true fear of God, the lost book of the law of Christ, which has been lost for a long time. Rend your hearts and not your garments; for you are not only led off from the true path, but you are so much bewitched by the man of sin, that you persecute the innocent, pious hearts, who in no wise injure you or any one upon earth.

That you would, with king Cyrus, release the poor captive children from the land of Chaldea, who cry and weep at the rivers of Babylon, that they may again possess the spiritual land of Canaan, and build up the spiritual Jerusalem, the altar and the temple in their ancient city, and establish the spiritual priesthood, and practice the spiritual offering and divine service according to the instructions of the word of God, that they may no longer hear and observe the Babylonian laws, namely, the teachings of men and their commandments; but the law of Israel, God's word and righteousness. Some of you, though alas few! are so far taught, through the grace and word of God, that I trust, you know, that neither usages nor councils, neither learning nor sword, nor mandate, can bend or break the word of the Most High, the word of truth, the word of the heavenly witness, the gospel of the kingdom, for other foundation cannot be laid to all eternity, than that which is laid, which is Christ Jesus, 1 Cor. 3: 11.

Therefore, wisdom cries, "Turn you at my reproof; behold I will pour out my Spirit unto you, I will make known my words unto you," Prov. 1: 23.

Love righteousness ye rulers of the land.

"Be wise, now, therefore, O ye kings; be instructed, ye judges of the earth, serve the Lord with fear, and rejoice with trembling," Ps. 2: 10, for the king that honors wisdom shall rule forever.

Do, therefore, with a meek heart, and in the fear of God, examine these our faithful instructions, and judge by the Spirit and word of Christ, as much as in you is; compare them with the doctrine and lives of the apostles, with the piety, love, customs, actions, misery, cross and sufferings of the primitive church; I hope, by the grace of God, you may plainly comprehend that our doctrine is the infallible doctrine and ground of the Scriptures. Read this OUR FOUNDATION, together with other books, appended to this, viz: *the book concerning faith and its power; concerning regeneration or the new creature; of the cross, sufferings and persecution of the saints; of excommunication, ban or exclusion, and other tracts, published from time to time*, and you will then find, by the grace of God, that this doctrine is the pure gospel, which the Lord taught by his own mouth, and which his holy apostles preached through the whole world, and by the power of the Spirit testified thereto with life and death. Ours is no new doctrine, as the preachers without truth, pretend and persuade you; but it is the old doctrine, which was preached and practiced in the church, for more than fifteen hundred years, whereby the church was, is, and shall be borne, till the end.

O you high-renowned lords and princes, turn to the truth of God, and receive reproof, and wisdom; for through wisdom, kings reign, and princes decree justice; observe how far your spirit, faith and lives differ from the Lord's Spirit, word and life.

Think you, dear sirs, that you are born to live merely in splendor and magnificence, and to lead a vain, sensual life? That you may freely continue in your licentious and pernicious lusts, and still be Christians? O no, "If any man have not the Spirit of Christ, he is none of his," Rom. 8: 9.

Solomon says, "As a roaring lion, and a raging bear; so is a wicked ruler over the poor people. The prince that wanteth understanding is also a great oppressor," Prov. 28: 15. The poet also well knew this, when he says, *Quic quid delirant reges, plectantur Achivi*, i. e., The mischief which kings do, the common people have to pay or atone for; but a wise king disperseth the ungodly.

Therefore, beloved sirs, see well to it; this is that to which you are called, namely: that you are to chastise and punish, in the true fear of God, with all equitable and just discretion, the open evil doers; such as thieves, murderers, sodomites, adulterers, debauchers, menslayers, the violent, fornicators, sorcerers, robbers, &c., that you give each his portion, execute judgment and righteousness, and deliver the spoiled out of the hand of the oppressor, that you are to prevent, by proper means (understand without tyranny and bloodshed), open deceivers, who so miserably lead poor, helpless souls, by hundreds of thousands into destruction, whether they are priests, monks, preachers, baptized or unbaptized; so that they will no longer derogate from the almighty majesty of God, our only and eternal Savior, Christ Jesus, the Holy Ghost, together with the word of grace; nor introduce those ridiculous abuses and idolatry, under semblance of truth, as has been done to this time; and by this means, in all love and earnestness, enlarge, assist and protect, without violence, blood or sword, the kingdom of God, by your gracious permission, wise counsel, pious, unblamable life.

Behold, beloved lords, this is your calling and your incumbent duty; do not domineer so maliciously over the children of God and his word, as alas, many of you evidently do, and as it is customary.

Such rulers were Moses, Joshua, David, Hezekiah, Josaphat, Josiah, Zerubbabel, &c., they faithfully discharged their enjoined duties, conformed to the word of God, protected their subjects with solicitous concern, obeyed the commands of the Lord, abolished the false prophets and the priests of Baal, with their altars, groves and idolatry, and faithfully kept their people and country, to observe the ordinances of the Lord, his laws and divine service as commanded by Moses; they feared God, and had the book of the law to which they conformed, and by which they judged the people; and always remembered the Lord their God, who set them over his people as potentates and rulers.

They feared God with all their hearts, praised his name, and humbled themselves with all their strength, as David did, when he was girded with a linen ephod, and danced before the ark of the Lord, yea that he was even despised of his wife Michal; but he said, I will play before the Lord, who chose me, and I will be yet more vile than this, in my own sight.

O you highly renowned, noble lords, believe Christ's word, fear the wrath of God, love righteousness, do justice to widows and orphans, judge rightly between man and man, fear no man's highness; despise no man's littleness, hate all avarice, chastise with discretion, suffer the word of God to be taught in liberty, prevent none to walk in the ways of truth; yield to his sceptre who called you to this high charge, and your throne shall be established for ever.

Now as the sceptre of Christ is an upright sceptre, and teaches, judges and corrects every one, without respect to person, I, a poor and unlearned being must lay aside my diffidence, and grow bold in love, whereby I would desire to save your poor souls, and with Samuel reprove Saul, with Abdia reprimand Jeroboam, with Elias chide Ahab, with Isaiah reprehend Hezekiah, with Nathan and Gad rebuke David for their misdeeds and transgressions, and thus proclaim my Lord's Spirit, word and will, who knows but there might be some one that will regard the fidelity and love of his poor minister; hear his well-meaning voice and christian exhortation, and depart from an ungodly and evil way; thus some of the aforementioned kings heard the reproving word of the mouths of the prophets with fear, and reformed, and meekly received the word.

And were it even so, that my faithful service and love, should be rewarded with death, as I have reason to suspect it may happen, because haughty and proud flesh is unwilling to be reproved, but uses at all times its evil nature, however, nothing worse can happen me, than did the pious Isaiah of Manasseh; Zechariah of Joaz; Urijah of Jehoiakim, Abimelech and other priests of Saul; John of Herod; Christ of Pilate and of the Scribes; and as it happened to all the apostles and pious witnesses of the whole world.

I do not esteem my life to be better and dearer than the beloved men of God did their lives. I can only be deprived of perishable and mortal flesh, which must once die, and return to dust, though I should live to be as old as Methuselah; not a hair can fall from my head without the will of my heavenly father; if I lose my life for the sake of Christ and his testimony, and on account of my sincere love for my neighbor, I certainly know, that I will save it in life eternal, therefore, I cannot conceal the truth; but I must testify and reveal it without hypocrisy in the true fear of God, to my beloved lords.

Beloved, noble lords, learn rightly to know yourselves, whence you are, what you are, and what you will be. All of you, one as well as another, be he emperor or king, are from the same seed that we poor and unregarded are, and you came into this sorrowful world as we did, and you are no more than vapor, frail flesh, a withering flower, dust and ashes, as we all are. To-day you are kings and triumph in great and high honor, to-morrow you are laid low, and must be food for serpents and worms.

O Sirs, my beloved sirs, humble yourselves; righteous is he who will examine your case, and mighty is he, who will pass judgment upon you; his name is the RULING LORD; he is the Almighty, the holy, the terrible, the high adorable and omnipotent God, who created heaven and earth, and who has in the hands of his strength all majesty, power and dominion. Learn to know him; learn to fear him. Awaken, look out, the time is not far off, when you will hear, "*Give an account of thy stewardship; for thou mayest be no longer steward,*" Luke 16 : 2.

Therefore, do not hear those who seek fat prebends and a lazy life, they deceive you, they teach you according to the lust of your hearts; they flatter you for the sake of unlawful gain, they preach to you wanton deception according to their own opinion, and not out of the mouth of the Lord; they fatten their bodies, and have fine times, from the fatness of your poor souls (beloved sirs, understand rightly what I mean), although they boast much of the gospel; hear them, who are not like the wind-shaken reed, those, who with John and Elias, are not so much frightened by the wilderness of misery, who suffer daily for the truth's sake, love gold and wood alike, who esteem all things alike, both praise and reproach, riches and poverty, life and death, who seek only the honor of Christ, and the salvation of their beloved brethren, and preach nothing but the pure, unmixed word of God, and seal it, with spirit, power and work, as it is commanded of Christ, and as it is proclaimed and taught through the whole world by his holy apostles.

I repeat it, hearken not, follow not, and believe not the multitude of the learned, who suffer themselves to be called doctors, lords and masters, for they are sensual and bloodthirsty, but seek and follow the faithful in Christ, who are called the curse and filth of the earth, among these you will find Christ's Spirit, truth, power, works and life. You will also, through the grace of God, find how far you and your spirit, faith, baptism, supper, conduct, church and actions are outside of Christ's Spirit, doctrine, commands, prohibition, ordinance and usage.

Say, O you kings and rulers of the land, Where is your faith and love, with their pious nature? Where is the fear of your God? Your lamp and light? Your humble heart, dead unto sin? And your unblamable, godly life, which is out of God? Is it not all world and carnality which you seek and follow? We generally find in your houses and courts nothing but extravagance, pomp and showy clothing, hardness and presumptuousness of heart, insatiable avarice, hatred, envy, backbiting, betraying, whoredom, debauchery, gambling gaming, eating, drinking, dancing, swearing, stabbing, housebreaking, &c. This is your chivalric custom and court conduct during the whole course of your lives; and you never once reflect on the misery, tribulation, humility, love and righteousness in which the Lord of lords, and King of kings, lived before you, what he taught the children of men, and what pattern or example he left them; the affliction and misery of the wretched reach not your ears; the sweat of the poor we find on your houses, and the innocent blood on your hands; you receive gifts and presents to pervert judgment, and you take counsel together against the Lord and his anointed. The prophets of Jezebel, and the priests of Baal, sensualists and flatterers, are much respected with you, they set upon soft cushions, and live well. But those who with Micah, preach to you adversity and truth, must expect imprisonment, bonds, and death, and are deserving of all disgrace; yea, it has come so far (may God make it better) that where four or five, ten or twenty have met in the name of the Lord, to speak of the word of the Lord, and to do his work, in whose midst Christ is, who fear the Lord with all their heart, and lead an unblamable life before all the world, that if they be apprehended, and complaint brought against them, they must then be devoured by fire, or be destroyed by the sword, or sink into the depths of the waters.

But they who have met in the name of Baal, a meeting of all manner of mischief, who exceed Sodom and Gomorrah far in wickedness, where all manner of inhuman things are carried on between man and man; and between woman and woman; as it is in Spain, in Italy, and in the cloisters, in public brothel-houses, theatres, fencing-schools, and the accursed drunken taverns, where many live in open disgrace, and act so shamefully against God's word. Such live unmolested and at peace.

I do not mention the public assemblies of all manner of idolatry, where the most high, blessed and precious name of God is so miserably blasphemed, the blood of Christ despised, the Holy Ghost grieved, the truth disgraced, lies commended, and poor souls deceived. The blind, ignorant people are not only directed to the holy water, bread, wine and the mass, but also to the dumb idols, of wood and stone, as alas! it may be so extensively witnessed.

O my beloved lords, what are you doing? Where is the sword of righteousness which was given to you, of which you boast? You have to acknowledge that you leave it in the scabbard, and in its stead you have drawn the sword of unrighteousness. Yes, beloved sirs, things are so (God better it), that the prophets write and call with propriety, "Thy princes are rebellious, and companions of thieves; every one loveth gifts, and followeth after rewards; they judge not the fatherless, neither doth the cause of the widow come unto them; therefore saith the Lord, the Lord of hosts, the Mighty One of Israel, Ah! I will ease me of mine adversaries, and avenge me of mine enemies," Isa. 1: 23, 24.

"Behold, the princes of Israel, every one is wise in thee to their power to shed blood. In thee have they set light by father and mother; in the midst of thee have they dealt by oppression with the stranger; in thee have they vexed the fatherless and the widow;" they are like the devouring wolves to shed blood and destroy souls for the sake of their avarice, "Behold, therefore," says the Lord, "I have smitten mine hand at thy dishonest gain which thou hast made, and at thy blood which hath been in the midst of thee," Ezek. 22: 6, 7, 13.

"Woe to them that devise iniquity and work evil upon their beds! when the morning is light, they practice it, because it is in the power of their hand. And they covet fields, and take them by violence; and houses, and take them away; so they oppress a man and his house, even a man and his heritage. Therefore, thus saith the Lord; behold against this family do I devise an evil, from which ye shall not remove your necks; neither shall ye go haughtily; for this time is evil," Micah 2: 1—3.

"Hear, O heads of Jacob, and ye princes of the house of Israel; Is it not for you to know judgment who hate the good and love the evil? Who pluck off their skin from off them, and their flesh from off their bones; who also eat the flesh of my people, and flay their skin from off them, and they break their bones and chop them in pieces, as for the pot, and as flesh within the caldron. Then shall they cry unto the Lord, but he will not hear them, he will even hide his face from them at that time, as they have behaved themselves ill in their doings," Micah 3: 1—4.

"Woe to her that is filthy and polluted to the oppressing city! she obeyed not the voice; she received not correction; she trusted not in the Lord; she drew not near to her God. Her princes within her are roaring lions; her judges are evening wolves; they gnaw not the bones till the morrow; her prophets are light and treacherous persons; her priests have polluted the sanctuary, they have done violence to the law, the just Lord is in the midst thereof; he will not do iniquity; every morning doth he bring his judgment to light, he faileth not; but the unjust knoweth no shame. I have cut off the nations; their towers are desolate; I made their streets waste, that none passeth by," Zeph. 3: 1—6.

There are but few of you, I fear there is scarcely one, who seeks the Lord with all his heart, fears, loves, and serves him; therefore, will also the fury of God be poured out upon you like water, and the sword of his wrath will come upon you, as may be seen daily in many places; God better it.

The wise man says, "Power is given you of the Lord, and sovereignty from the Highest, who shall try your works and search out your counsels; because being ministers of his kingdom, ye have not judged aright, nor kept the law, nor walked after the counsel of God; horribly and speedily shall he come upon you; for a sharp judgment shall be to them that are in high places. For mercy will soon pardon the meanest; but mighty men shall be mightily tormented. For he who is Lord over all shall fear no man's person, neither shall he stand in awe of any man's greatness; for he hath made the small and great, and careth for all alike. But a sore trial shall come upon the mighty," Wis. 6: 3—8.

Therefore, beloved lords, take heed that you rightly execute your responsible and dangerous office according to the will of God; for, alas! I fear that many of you, as yet, have paid but little attention to this matter, and hence it is that anti-christ rises up with his wickedness, and Christ is rejected with his righteousness; lay to heart what is written, "Keep thee far from a false matter; and the innocent and righteous slay thou not; for I will not justify the wicked," says the Lord, Exod. 23: 7.

Here I well know that we have to hear of Munster, dominions, polygamy, sword, theft, murder and of the like abominations and disgrace, which, you always assert, result from baptism; and under this pretext you reprove every thing the mouth of the Lord commanded, and what the holy apostles taught and practiced, and for this purpose you cite some seditious sects and factions, that the cry of the learned and your blood-shedding may be sanctioned.

No, my beloved sirs, it will not acquit you in the day of the righteousness of God. I tell you the truth in Christ; notice the rightly baptized disciples of Christ, who are baptized inwardly with Spirit and fire, and externally with water, who are baptized according to the word of God; know of no weapons other than patience, hope, quiet, and God's word. Paul says, "The weapons of our warfare are not carnal, but mighty through God to the pulling down of strong holds; casting down imaginations, and every high thing that exalteth itself against the knowledge of God, and bringeth into captivity every thought to the obedience of Christ," 2 Cor. 10: 4, 5. Our weapons are not weapons with which cities and countries are desolated; walls and gates broken down and human blood shed in torrents like water, but they are weapons with which the spiritual kingdom of the devil is destroyed, and the ungodly passions are annihilated, and the flinty hearts are broken, that have never been sprinkled with the heavenly dew of the holy word. We have and know no other weapons besides, the Lord knows, even if we should be torn into a thousand pieces, and as many false witnesses were to rise against us, as there are spears of grass in the fields, and grains of sand upon the sea shore.

Again, Christ is our fortress; patience our defence; the word of God our sword; and our victory is a candid, firm, unfeigned faith in Jesus Christ. We let those take spears and swords, who, alas, regard human blood and swine's blood alike. He that is wise let him judge what I mean.

We acknowledge, beloved sirs, that some of the false prophets were baptized externally in appearance, with us, with the same baptism; even as thieves, murderers, highway robbers, sorcerers and the like, were baptized with you; but they were not of us· for had they been of us, as John says, they would no doubt have continued with us.

Christ says, "There shall arise false Christs, and false prophets, and shall shew great signs and wonders; insomuch that if it were possible, they shall deceive the very elect; behold, I have told you before," Matt. 24: 24.

This warning of Christ was not given to the ungodly, obdurate despisers, for they are already entangled in the snares of unrighteousness, but is given to the contrite of heart and to the willing souls, so that they may learn to know the Spirit, and not suffer themselves to be led into error; "For the devil, as a roaring lion, walketh about, seeking whom he may devour," 1 Peter 5: 8.

The craftiness and artifice of the devil, who assumes the appearance of an angel of light, are not known by some, therefore, so many have stumbled and erred, and were led into crooked paths by the deceivers; but this was not through baptism; for the elementary water can neither teach, nor pervert, but it was done through false prophets, of which, I say, we have been so faithfully warned by the mouth of the Lord.

Beloved sirs, fear God, judge rightly; the truth of God can never be changed into seduction and error, through the lies of the devil. O no! the word of our God shall stand forever.

Should the devout angels be unjustly judged, for the sake of Lucifer's arrogance and be punished with his punishment? Or should all the apostles be traitors, for Judas' sake? By no means. Every one shall bear his own burden. "The son shall not bear the iniquity of the father, neither shall the father bear the iniquity of the son. The soul that sinneth *it* shall die," Ezek. 18: 20.

Should we reproach the doctrine of Christ and his apostles, because the father of lies has resuscitated, in the name of Christ, the practice of circumcision as essential to *salvation*? That the dead will not rise in the day of judgment? That Philetus and Hymenius asserted that the resurrection of the dead has already taken place? That some pretended that the great day of the Lord was at hand?

How could the apostle help it, that the Nicolaitans had their wives common, as Eusebius relates? That the Ebionites denied the deity of Christ, and taught that Christ began only to exist in Mary? And that the Corinthians maintained, that the world was created by angels; that Christ was no more than a mere man, and had not yet risen, but shall rise with us in future, and that he would reign one thousand years in the flesh with his saints?

All these sects arose in the days of the apostles, nevertheless the gospel of Christ remained the true gospel, the doctrines of the apostles, the true doctrine.

The Scriptures teach that we are to flee from, and avoid such leaders of sects and heretics; and we hope to obey willingly the injunction all the days of our lives.

Therefore, my beloved sirs, pass an impartial and rational judgment in this matter, as before God, who will judge you in the great day; this we ask of you for Jesus' sake; for we seek nothing else upon earth (the Lord knows), than the true foundation of the truth, the praise of Christ, the obedience of his word, and that with a good conscience, as we testify to the whole world, with our writings, word, possessions, blood, life and death.

We also write the truth in Christ and lie not, that spiritually, we acknowledge no king, neither in heaven above nor upon earth beneath, than the only, eternal and true king, spiritual David, Christ Jesus, who is Lord of lords, and King of kings.

And if there is one who will declare himself king in the kingdom and dominion of Christ, as did John von Leyden, of Munster, he shall not go unpunished with Adonijah, 1 Kings 1, for the true Solomon, Christ Jesus himself, must possess the kingdom, and sit eternally upon the throne of David.

But, according to the flesh, we teach and exhort to be obedient to the emperor, king, lords and princes, yea, to all in authority, in all their transactions and civil regulations, so far as they are not contrary to the word of God, Rom. 13: 1—3.

We teach and confess that we know of no sword, nor commotion in the kingdom or church of Christ, other than the sharp sword of the Spirit, God's word, as is abundantly shown in our writings, which is sharper and more piercing than any two-edged sword, and it proceeds from the mouth of the Lord, whereby we make the father at variance against the son, and the son against the father, the mother against the daughter, and the daughter against the mother, and daughter-in-law against the mother-in-law. But the sword of worldly policy we leave with those to whom it is committed. Let every one be careful and not take the sword, lest he shall perish with the sword, Matt. 26: 52.

We acknowledge, teach, and approve of no other matrimony than that one, which Christ and his apostles publicly and plainly taught in the New Testament, namely, one man and one woman, Matt. 19: 4, and that they may not be divorced except in case of adultery, Matt. 5: 32, for the two are one flesh, but if the unbelieving depart, a sister or brother is not under bondage in that case, 1 Cor. 7: 15.

We acknowledge, teach and seek no other kingdom than that of Christ, which shall endure for ever, in which there is no pomp, splendor, gold, silver, meat and drink, but righteousness, peace and joy in the Holy Ghost; we confess with Christ, that our kingdom is not of this world; we brought nothing into this world, therefore, it is evident we can not take any thing out of it, as the Scriptures say, 1 Tim. 6: 7.

We know of no murdering, much less do we teach or permit it; for we truly believe that a murderer has neither lot nor part in the kingdom of God, Gal. 5: 21. O beloved sirs, how should we desire the blood of any man, since we have to die daily for man's sake? The Lord who created us knows that we seek nothing, but that we might instruct, and be a pattern to all the world, with our doctrine, life, blood and death, that they might reflect, awaken, repent and be saved, for this is the nature of pure love to pray for persecutors, to render good for evil, to love the enemy, to heap coals of fire upon the head; and let him avenge who judges rightly, Rom. 12: 20.

We know of no theft, much less do we teach or permit it, but we are ready before God and man, with all our hearts, to bestow our possessions, gold, and all that we have, however little it may be, and in addition thereto our sweat and labor, to meet the necessities of the poor, as the Spirit and word of the Lord, and true brotherly love teach us. We well know that theft is expressly forbidden in the Scriptures, Eph. 4: 28, and that it will be punished by death* according to the laws of the land, and if not repented of, with eternal death according to the word of God.

The Almighty merciful Lord, through his paternal grace, Spirit and power, will undoubtedly keep and preserve, inoffensive to the end of the world, all the pious, god-fearing, and faithful who acknowledge him, and are sincere, from all such terrible errors and ungodly abominations.

And should it be the case, that one remained among us who uses violence (which is quite unknown to me), and would do that which is from the devil, my beloved sirs, know you that such an one was not of us from the beginning, and will for ever not be of us, except he be thoroughly converted, repent sincerely, and become one with the Spirit, doctrine and example of Christ, as the Scriptures teach. May the gracious Lord grant that they may awaken, overcome their drowsiness, learn to know their works, see their nakedness, and be extricated from the snares of the devil, by which the poor, miserable people are so lamentably led captive at his will.

Therefore, beloved lords, beware that you be not, in judging faith, like the reckless and senseless, who persist without any knowledge of the matter, in their own opinion and wantonness, like irrational creatures, upbraid the good, and praise the evil, persecute and condemn what they understand not. Again, I say, be not like those blood-thirsty, raging and malicious men; but examine the Scriptures with trembling, with Solomon pray for wisdom, look to the Spirit, word, doings and example of Christ, and pass an impartial righteous sentence, according to the truth, as it is enjoined upon, and commanded unto all the princes and judges in the Scriptures, as is heard.

O beloved sirs, take heed. If our faith, doctrine, sacraments, transactions and doings are not of God, as we are every where slandered, then are we the most miserable of all men upon earth; if whilst we are to be every one's deceiver, heretic, anabaptist, knave, footstool and prey; have to endure the stocks, gallows, wheels, sword, water, fire, and all manner of misery; our poor souls must nevertheless be the property of

---

* In some countries theft was formerly punished by death.

the devil, and brands of hell, although in our weakness we so cordially seek the Lord, and are so sincere, as may be seen. O no! my beloved sirs, no; the Spirit, doctrine and life of Christ will not deceive us; for his word is truth, and his commands eternal life. The promises of God stand sure and immovable; and they will not fail to the pious.

Therefore, we pray and admonish you, yea, we counsel and desire that you would contrast our seeking with your seeking; our spirit with your spirit; our doctrine with the doctrine of the learned; our conduct with your conduct; our poverty with your riches; our rejection and reproach with your seeking of honor; our affliction and tribulation with your voluptuousness and luxurious living; our patience with your tyranny; our hard bonds and reproachful death, with your ungracious fury and unmerciful fierceness. I speak of the guilty; if you should then find that your doctrine, faith, life, seeking and doings are more in accordance with the Spirit, word and life of the Lord, and are better than ours, then instruct us with a paternal spirit; we will willingly hear it, and be obedient, for we do desire to obey the truth unto death.

But if you can not reprove us by the Scriptures, and see that our doctrine is the best, it would then be heathenish, ungodly and tyrannical, to force us out of life into death, thrust us from heaven into hell, by the sword and violence; this you will have to acknowledge and confess. But I am afraid, so much discretion will not be manifested to us wretched children, that the matter be weighed in the balance of the holy word, and determined by the plummet of Christ. But the upbraiding, betraying and tumult of the priests and your unmerciful edicts must be our scriptures; and your rackers, hangmen, wrath, torturing, water, stocks, fire and sword, O God, of which we, grieved children, hear in many places, must be our instructors, which we at last must pay with our possessions and blood. Beloved lords, with christian discretion, love and friendship, reflect upon this how it agrees with the Spirit, doctrine and life of Christ? We well know that all bloody preachers who teach and advise such things, and all the rulers who practice and uphold the same, are not the disciples of Christ; the hour in which you shall have to render accounts, when you depart this life, will teach you this truth. It can never be, says Cyprian, that such lion-like fury and lupine ferocity should dwell in the heart of a Christian. O how good it would be for some of you, yea, how good it would be if you had never been born; for there are so many of you who neither regard law nor gospel, heaven nor hell, God nor the devil; but the evil flesh will follow its propensity.

Think you, beloved sirs, that the Almighty God and Lord, who holds the heavens and the earth in the hollow of his hand, who kills and makes alive, the ruling Lord over all, who upholds all by the word of his power, who creates and destroys, the consuming fire, before whose presence the hills melted like wax, Ps. 97: 5, that he will yield and give away to sensual minds and earthly hearts? No! no, before him the great and small are alike; the rich and the poor; the strong and the weak; the learned and unlearned; the wise and the foolish, are all alike. He is no respecter of persons, all who fear him not, and conform not to his counsel, doctrine, Spirit and example, be he emperor, king, doctor, or licentiate, he must suffer eternal punishment and be under his judgment and wrath.

Beloved sirs, fear God, do right, learn wisdom and truth, cleanse your hands, which are wet and imbrued in innocent blood, and reflect how the righteous God will punish in due time, all unrighteousness, malice and violence; and how severely he ever did, and will avenge and require the innocent blood, torture and death of his saints, of those blood-thirsty tyrants.

The blood-thirsty Cain had to be an accursed vagabond and exile in the land all the days of his life, because he so miserably murdered his innocent brother Abel.

The unmerciful, arrogant murderer, Pharaoh, with his whole host, was destroyed in the Red sea, by the righteous judgment of God, on account of his tyranny and cruelty, which he exercised towards the children of Jacob, God's people.

Joash was slain by his own servants to

avenge the innocent blood of Zachariah, whom he slew between the temple and the altar, 2 Kings 12; 2 Chron. 24: 20—22.

Manasseh was led captive on account of his great abomination and idolatry which he practiced; and on account of the innocent blood with which he filled Jerusalem, 2 Chron. 33: 1—18.

Ahab was shot through with an arrow, and his blood was licked up by the dogs at the waters of Samaria, 1 Kings 22: 34—38, and his wife Jezebel was thrust out of the window, and was trodden under foot of horses, and her flesh was eaten of dogs, 2 Kings 9: 33, to punish her for her ungodly deed, and the blood of Naboth, according to the word of the Lord, which he spake by Elijah, the Tishbite.

Sennacherib must leave Jerusalem with disgrace, on account of his slanderously pompous words, by which he blasphemed the Most High. The angel of the Lord slew, in one night, one hundred and eighty-five thousand men in his camp, and he was thrust through with the sword by his own children, in the temple of his idol, Nisroch, 2 Kings 19: 35, 37.

Nebuchadnezzar, on account of his pride, was rejected by the people, for the space of seven times, or years, his dwelling was with the irrational creatures, he ate grass like oxen, his body was wet with the dew of heaven, till his hairs were grown like eagles' feathers, and his nails like birds' claws, Dan. 4: 32, 33.

Belshazzar caroused with his mighty men, princes, wives and concubines; they were merry, drank out of the holy vessels which Nebuchadnezzar, his father, had plundered out of the temple at Jerusalem; and being in full glee and joy, praising their gods of gold, silver, brass, iron, and of stone, the impenitent and obdurate tyrant was punished of God without mercy, that he, the same night was deprived of his dominion, nation, body and life, Dan. 5: 23, 30.

Antiochus, the Great, a king and prince of all wickedness, a tyrant of tyrants was punished of God with such a plague, that worms crept from his bowels when yet alive, and pieces of flesh fell from his body, and the stench was so intolerable, that no one could endure it, yea, he himself could not abide his own smell. The righteous wrath of God laid hold upon this ungodly miscreant, and he had thus, under unheard of pain and sufferings, to end his proud, bloodthirsty, unrighteous life, and depart from this world, 2 Macc. 9: 9—12.

Herod, arrayed in his royal attire, seated upon his throne, through the flattering applause of his people, on account of his eloquence and wisdom, exalted himself against God, in his heart, and in that very hour he was smitten by the angel of the Lord, was eaten of worms, and, according to the writings of Eusebius, departed this life in such a way that all the proud, haughty tyrants may look at themselves in the case of Herod, as in a mirror, and fear.

In short, as it happened to Pilate, Nero, Domitian, Maximinius, Diocletian, and generally to all malicious, blood-thirsty tyrants, and what kind of death they generally died, who rose up against Christ and his saints, may be read both in sacred and profane history.

What kind of death and with what conscience some of these blood-guilty of our day, departed this life, I will not write for certain reasons; I will nevertheless say this much, that neither emperor nor edicts, upon which they relied all the days of their lives, could neither quiet nor pacify them in the hour of their death, but ofttimes were troubled in their hearts, and with lamentations, painfully bewailed the innocent blood, which they shed in the emperor's name, and said, O we poor, miserable men, what will become of us?

O God, what counsel? Beloved sirs, what counsel shall be given you? How will your poor souls fare, in the day, "In the which the heavens shall pass away with a great noise and the elements shall melt with fervent heat, the earth also, and the works that are therein shall be burnt up?" 2 Peter 3: 10, when we must all appear before the judgment seat, and stand before the impartial judge? when every one shall be rewarded according to his works? he that keepeth Israel shall neither slumber nor sleep, "For yet a little while, and he that shall come will come, and will not tarry," Heb. 10: 37.

Therefore, desist from touching the apple of the Lord's eye; for he that touches his saints, touches the apple of his eye. Take pity on your own souls, which must suffer for it with eternal death, if you do not turn to God with all your heart, and no longer shed the blood of the innocent; for they daily call to him, "How long, O Lord, holy and true, dost thou not judge and avenge our blood on them that dwell on the earth?" Rev. 6: 10, they call, I say, and their cries are entered into the ears of the Lord of Sabaoth, avenging he will avenge, and the blood of his servants he will require at your hands.

Do not excuse yourselves, beloved sirs, and judges, that you are the servants of the emperor; this will not acquit you in the day of vengeance. It availed Pilate nothing that he crucified Christ in the name of the emperor. Serve the emperor in imperial matters, so far as Scripture permits, and serve God in divine matters, then you may claim his grace and call yourselves after his name.

Do not interfere with the right and kingdom of Christ; for he alone is the Ruler of the conscience, and beside him there is none other, let him be your emperor, and his holy word your edict, in this matter; and you will soon be satiated with raging and murder. You must heed God before the emperor, and obey God's word before the word of the emperor, if not, then you are the judges of whom it is written in Micah, They all lie in wait for blood; they hunt every man his brother with a net. "That they may do evil with both hands earnestly, the prince asketh, and the judge asketh for a reward; and the great man he uttereth his mischievous desire: so they wrap it up. The best of them is as a brier; the most upright is sharper than a thorn hedge; the day of thy watchmen and thy visitation cometh; now shall be their perplexity," Micah 7: 2—4.

Therefore, fight no longer against the lamb and his chosen, it will be hard for you to kick against the pricks.

But you will, with all scoffers, say in your hearts, when is the promise of his coming? O beloved sirs, do pay attention, we have known so many who have made as ostentatious a display as you, in silk and velvet, with gold and silver, and sat in exalted seats, and passed sentence upon innocent blood, but now they are no more; we inquire for their places, and they are not to be found.

The day will usher in as lightning, and the hour shall come upon them like a tempest; beware and reform. We see that the tree buds, that the summer is nigh at hand, and our Redeemer is hastening, who redeems all the troubled souls from their afflictions, and he will recompense all proud scoffers according to their demerits.

Yea, the day is coming, and is not far off, when "the righteous man shall stand in great boldness before the face of such as have afflicted him, and made no account of his labors; when they see it, they shall be troubled with terrible fear, and shall be amazed at the strangeness of his salvation, so far beyond all that they looked for, and they, repenting and groaning for anguish of spirit, shall say within themselves, This was he, whom we had sometimes in derision, and a proverb of reproach; we fools accounted his life madness, and his end to be without honor; how is he numbered among the children of God, and his lot is among the saints! Therefore have we erred from the way of truth, and the light of righteousness hath not shined unto us, and the sun of righteousness rose not upon us. We wearied ourselves in the way of wickedness and destruction; yea, we have gone through deserts, where there lay no way; but as for the way of the Lord, we have not known it. What hath pride profited us? or what good hath riches with our vaunting brought us? All those things are passed away like a shadow, and as a post that hasteth by," Wis. 5: 1—9.

Then will the terrible, intolerable judgment pass upon all who know not God, and that obey not the gospel of our Lord Jesus Christ, who shall be punished with everlasting destruction from the presence of the Lord and from the glory of his power, when he shall come to be glorified in his saints, and to be adored by all them that believe. Then the wicked will hear, "Depart from me ye cursed, into everlasting fire, prepared for the devil and his angels," Matt. 25: 41.

Then shall your laughter be changed into weeping, your joy into sorrow, your sumptuous, temporal lives into everlasting death, your luxury into everlasting woe, your pride into dust and worms, your violence into suffering, your pomp into stench, and your cruel and unmerciful tyranny be retributed with unquenchable hell-fire.

My beloved sirs, with him nothing will be concealed or forgotten. He is the judge that searches the hearts and tries the reins, who penetrates the heights of heaven and the depth of the abyss, and the length of the earth, who will not only judge and punish evil works, and every idle word, but also every unclean, carnal thought.

O dear Lord! O Lord of lords! where then will be the emperor and his edicts, the false prophets, and their deceiving doctrine? Then they will howl and weep, and cry in anguish of soul, O ye mountains fall upon us, ye rocks hide us from the face of him that sitteth upon the throne, and from the wrath of the Lamb. Then, there you will see, that it was nought but lies and wind with which you comforted yourselves, as said, Rev. 6:16.

Beloved lords, awaken! It is yet to-day; do not boast because you are of the royal family, and are called gracious lords, for it is but smoke, dust and pride; but boast and rejoice when you are born of God, when you become a "chosen generation, a royal priesthood, a holy nation, a peculiar people; that ye should show forth the praises of him who hath called you out of darkness into his marvellous light," 1 Pet. 2:9.

Boast not that you are mighty upon earth, and have great power, but boast rather that you rule your land in the true fear of God, with virtue, wisdom and righteousness, to the praise of the Lord.

Boast not that you can subdue lords, princes, cities and countries; but boast if you subdue your earthly mind and can overcome carnal temptations by the power of faith, and die to ungodliness, and triumph through Christ, and be taken in the kingdom of glory, with all the pious soldiers of God, and receive the promised crown at the hand of the Lord, for if you be such kings, then you are not only kings according to the flesh, but also according to the Spirit; those who love the prince of all kings, who are cleansed of sin by his blood, who have made God and his father their kings and priests, those reign and conquer with all the children of God, the world, flesh, blood, sin, death, devil, false doctrine, and the infernal gates; they rejoice not because their names are enrolled in the register of the kings of this world; but they rejoice because their names are written in the book of life, in heaven.

O you high-renowned noble lords and princes, O that you would in all love and meekness receive this simple, plain, but true instruction of your poor servant, and not despise it, whereby I have so fully, and with a good heart, admonished all your worthy highnesses.

Look not upon my weakness nor to my little understanding, but look to the Spirit, word and example of Christ, which I have recommended and taught in sincerity of heart to you and to all men, according to my weak abilities.

Do sincerely repent, so that you stand before God; wail and weep with David; put on sackcloth and raiments of hair; scatter ashes upon your heads; humble yourselves with the king of Nineveh; confess your faults with Manasseh; die unto your ambitious flesh and pride; fear the Lord, your God, with all your powers; judge in all wisdom with fear and trembling; help the oppressed; grieve not the distressed; promote the just cause of the widows and orphans; protect the good; punish the evil in a christian manner; discharge the duties of your offices properly; seek the kingdom and country that will endure forever; and reflect that you, however highly esteemed, upon earth are only pilgrims and sojourners in a strange land.

Obey, believe, fear, love, serve and follow your Lord and Savior, Jesus Christ, for he it is before whom every knee shall bow; he is the eternal word, wisdom, truth and Son of God. Seek his honor and praise in all your thoughts, words and actions, and you shall reign in eternity.

APPEAL TO THE LEARNED.

Herewith I will leave all the lords and princes, with all the magistracy and rulers, and those sent by them, in the hands of the Lord, and address myself to you, O you learned, you, who think that you have the keys of heaven, and are the eyes and the light of the people; I will speak with you, as with those whose salvation I seek with all my heart, because I see with open eyes, that both you and your disciples run voluntarily into the eternal destruction of your souls, and nevertheless boast that you are the sent teachers, and your churches the churches of Christ, and would cordially and brotherly admonish you, one and all, Romans, Lutherans and Zuinglians, concerning the following articles.

That you would notice, in the first place, that your ministry and services are not of God and his word, but are from the bottomless pit, for it is evident that you blaspheme and persecute the word, ordinances and commands of Christ, and teach and enforce the word, ordinances and commands of antichrist; that you profane the temple of God, build and honor temples of stone, break the living images in which the Spirit of God dwells; make and dress images of gold, silver and wood; that you hate a pious, blameless life; encourage and defend, by your dissolute examples, a disorderly, passionate life of the flesh. Say, my beloved, Where is there a single letter in the Scriptures concerning all your doings and worship, such as of masses, infant baptism, auricular confession, &c.? Is not, in truth, the greater part of what you do and transact, all deception, hypocrisy, blasphemy, abomination and idolatry? Whence do you derive your offices and services, and of whom are they? I would advise you, in true love, that you would reflect upon them according to the Scriptures, and in the true fear of God.

Secondly, consider what you are properly seeking through this your office and service. You and I, heretofore, stood in the same calling, office and service; I candidly confess that in all my studies, from my youth, in preaching and singing, I sought only a vain, lazy, good living, praise and favor of men, yea, solely the gratification of my carnal desires, till the gracious and great Lord bestowed me upon the gift of his gracious Spirit, and opened the understanding of my heart, that I acknowledged with the preacher Solomon, that all my seeking, life and doings were vanity, and that the end thereof was certain death and hell.

But that you continue so to seek is too palpable to be denied. For if there were no prebends and cloisters, but few preachers, priests and monks would be found. This I certainly know. So long as these exist, the world shall never be in want of deceivers and hypocrites.

Say, beloved, what else is your whole seeking and doing, than world, carnality, gluttony, and a voluptuous life? Who can scrutinize and fully describe your earthly mind and sensual life? Some of you make an ostentatious display in ermine, in silk and velvet, others live in full revelry, others are avaricious and hoard; some violate virgins and maids, others pollute the bed of their neighbor, others' chastity is like the chastity of Sodom; all your doctrine is deceiving, your sacraments are enchanting, your piety is principally ungodliness, and your divine service is an open abomination and idolatry; some of you neither fear God nor the devil; you blaspheme the name of God, his holy word you falsify, his children and servants you persecute, and, in reliance upon his grace, you do all manner of evil; if you can only lead a life free from care, and enjoy fine times, then all is well done. Say, beloved, is it not so? Worthy men, is it not so? This is your chief seeking and striving, among great and small, this you must acknowledge and confess; for the fruit is manifest to all the world, and it cannot be any longer concealed.

O men, men! beware! If any one could enter into life, on this broad way which you teach, and in which you walk, and keep his soul in God, we might truly lament and say, that the prophets, apostles, and all the witnesses of God, and also Christ Jesus himself, did not act wisely, and that they have not dealt rightly towards us, that they passed their lives with so much anguish, suffering, tribulation and pain in this sorrowful vale of tears, and directed us, miserable, weak children into such a way.

O no, my beloved, no; truth will eternally be truth; if you are not converted to a better and christian mind; if you die not to your deception, and also to your vain, carnal life, repent, and become in your dispositions like innocent, little children, you cannot enter the kingdom of heaven, "For to be carnally minded," says Paul, "is death."

Teach, call, hope, boast in any way you choose, if you desire to be saved, you must walk in the ways of the Lord, hear his word, and be obedient thereto; for nothing avails in heaven and upon earth, whereby you can be saved, neither baptism nor the Lord's Supper, neither eloquence nor erudition, neither councils nor long standing usages, neither emperors nor edicts, neither Christ with his grace, merits, blood and death, if we are not born of God (understand it right, those who have ears to hear, and minds to understand), believe his word sincerely, walk in the light, and do right, as John says, "This, then, is the message which we have heard of him, and declare unto you, that God is light, and in him is no darkness at all; if we say that we have fellowship with him, and walk in darkness, we lie, and do not the truth; but if we walk in the light, as he is in the light, we have fellowship one with another, and the blood of Jesus Christ, his Son, cleanseth us from all sin," 1 John 1: 5—7.

O transgressors, transgressors, examine your hearts, give heed to my words and learn wisdom, you who live in voluptuousness and sit at ease, who say in your hearts, It is we, besides us there is none other; what we command shall be heard, and what we speak must be valid upon earth; we cannot go astray in the Scriptures, and in counsel we cannot err, and we can teach nothing unlawful. Ah! alas! your boasted wisdom leads you astray, and the pride of your hearts causes you to stumble; return, your path is slippery, and your way leads to the abyss of hell.

Beloved men, learn to know what God's own and eternal Son, Christ Jesus, sought upon earth, what he taught, and what example he left you; his seeking was his Father's praise, and the salvation of our poor souls; his doctrine was his father's word, and his precedence a sure way to the kingdom of God. "Who being in the form of God," says Paul, "thought it not robbery to be equal with God, but made himself of no reputation, and took upon him the form of a servant," Phil. 2: 6, 7; and came poor and miserable into this sorrowful world; there was no room in the inn when he was born; he had not whereon to lay his head; nor in his death had he wherewith to quench his thirst, although it is he through whom the almighty, all-bountiful Father grants to all his created beings, residence, clothing, meat and drink, as Paul says, "For ye knew the grace of our Lord Jesus Christ, that, though he was rich, yet for your sakes he became poor, that ye through his poverty might be rich," 2 Cor. 8: 9.

If you have any fear of God, and would not lead your own, and the souls of your poor people wilfully to death, then contrast your seeking with the seeking of Christ, your doctrine with the doctrine of Christ, your spirit with the Spirit of Christ, and your life with the life of Christ, then you may truly find whether you are in or out of Christ, who is your God, what Lord you serve, and of whose spirit and kingdom you are.

Thirdly, observe what fruits and usefulness your office and services bring forth; for what is your doctrine other than a useless, feeble sowing in the wind, which has neither spirit nor power; your sacraments are an encouragement to the impenitent, and your lives examples of wickedness. Where are the avaricious whom you have meliorated, the drunkards you have made temperate, the polluted you have made pure, the haughty whom you have humbled? How will you teach others, being yourselves untaught, and beget Christ an acceptable church, and are yourselves the servants of anti-christ, and the children of Belial? You and your disciples, therefore, must ever confess, both high and low, men and women, that you are all dead bodies, and have not the Spirit of God; for with you we do not find contrite hearts, true knowledge of Christ, true love, an earnest desire after the kingdom of God, dying to earthly things, true humility, righteousness, friendliness, mercy, chastity, obedience, wisdom, truth and peace; but every where we find hateful, envious, obdurate, malicious hearts, an aversion and despising of the divine word, lust and love of this world, haughtiness, pride, pomp, lies, knavery, disgrace, adultery, whoredom, robbery, burning, slaying, cursing, swearing, and all manner of malice.

Behold, you withered trees, and careless shepherds, these are the fruits you bring forth, and the sheep you pasture, these are the churches and disciples you comfort with the blood of the Lord, preach to them grace and peace, and to whom you dispense baptism and the Lord's Supper. If I write not the truth, reprove me.

O beloved sirs, so entirely have you lost every christian virtue, and understanding, besides, the light, and the Scriptures; you hold captive in ungodliness under the power of hell, the poor, ignorant people, whole kingdoms, cities and countries; yea, the whole wide world, and that, O God! for such small hire, namely, for one hand full of barley and one piece of bread, as the prophet says, O, that my words might be a lie, and not the truth; sunshine is clear, but still clearer is the truth which I write.

And this is not enough for you, O you men, that you so miserably deceive the poor wretched souls; and besides this, you also rebuke, defame, belie, and betray all those who seek and fear God with all their hearts, rebuke all unrighteousness with doctrine and life, and so willingly walk in Christ. You deprive them of their possessions and lives that you may be greatly honored among the people, and be not evil spoken of in your doings, that you be not hindered in your unlawful gain; and that you may enjoy an easy and voluptuous life to the end of your days.

O how rightly you are depicted by the wisdom of God, which says, "Woe unto you, scribes and pharisees, hypocrites! for ye shut up the kingdom of heaven against men; for ye neither go in yourselves (mark), neither suffer ye them that are entering to go in," Matt. 23: 13.

What I think, I write, and dissemble not. I fear, worthy sirs, that there are many of you so ungodly, and so far determined upon unlawful gain, indolent life, and the praise of men, that you would rather see all the god-fearing put to the stake, than lose a guilder of your rents, or to hear a harsh word from the magistracy, for the sake of the truth.

O you, with wanton looks, when will you be ashamed? You diamonds! when will you be softened, and you Moors, when will you become white? I think never more; for how can you do any thing good, because you have learned evil, and are used to it from your infancy?

Alas! my soul must grieve and painfully mourn for your sakes, that you have erred so lamentably, and besides this, you cover all your disgrace under the word and name of Christ, and do not observe, O you men, that you, together with all the false prophets, are promised in the Scriptures, and threatened by the Spirit of the Lord, every where with nothing but punishment, wrath, damnation and blackness of darkness, the flaming lake and eternal gnashing of teeth, weeping, wailing, fire, woe and death.

The hour is near at hand when we shall hear, "Give an account," &c. Alas, would it then be due to us, when the day is at hand, to walk a thousand years on burning coals and in red hot armor (flames), then we might even rejoice and be of good cheer; but now it is hidden from your eyes, through your haughtiness, avarice and momentary luxury.

Perhaps I would be smitten on the cheek by some of you, and with Micaiah, be compelled to hear from Zedekiah, "Which way went the Spirit of the Lord from me to speak unto thee?" 2 Chron. 18: 23. O my beloved, fear God and understand the truth. You direct the poor dissolute souls to the subtlety and philosophy of the learned, to the many councils, to customs and usages of long standing, to imperial edicts, to the doctrines and commandments of men, which are nothing but quicksands, which cannot save the house from the tempest, but I do not so, but, with Moses, the prophets, apostles, angels, and the Father himself, I direct you to Christ Jesus, to whom all the emperors, kings, councils, usages and the learned, will have to yield; for his word is truth, and his commands are eternal life. To him every knee shall bow, of things in heaven and things in earth, and things under the earth; all who reject him, reject the Father that sent him, Phil. 2: 10.

This I teach you; I direct you to his Spirit, word, life, command, prohibition, ordinances and usages, as to a sure and immovable foundation, laid in Zion, to a plain and safe way, prepared of God, who, according to his sure promises, will lead all the truly penitent and Christian believers into eternal life.

Beloved men, observe, there were four hundred false prophets in the days of Ahab, king of Israel, who unanimously prophesied prosperity and felicity, that he should advance, for God would give the enemies of the king into his hands; while there was but one Micaiah, who spoke the real truth and predicted adversity in the name of the Lord, 2 Chron. 18: 6, 7.

And there were also four hundred and fifty prophets of Baal, and four hundred prophets of the groves, all of whom did eat at Jezebel's table; there was only one Elijah, a man of God, and a prophet of the Lord, who was zealous for the law of his God, and defended his praise, 1 Kings 18.

Joash, with all the princes, priests and common people, were unanimous in their groves and their false worship, which they had chosen after the death of Jehoiada, the high priest, and there was but one Zechariah, who reproved the ungodly abominations, and threatened them with the wrath and punishment of his God, 2 Chron. 24.

Even as those renowned and worthy men of God, though they were few, reproved, with pure, divine ardor, in the power of the Spirit, and faithfully admonished by the law of God with their great and glorious talents, all the disobedient and idolatrous kings, princes, priests and the common people, without respect to persons; and on account thereof suffered disgrace, misery, tribulation, bonds and death, as we may abundantly read and see in the Scriptures and in history; I do also here, with my small talents, for similar views and reasons, openly testify to the truth, because I see, that you all hypocritically flatter lords and princes, and caress the world, and because there is, alas, nobody who opposes this ungodliness with the word of the Lord, nor reproves the wickedness of the world; I must, on this account, hear and bear much, as did the above mentioned although I mean it so well, and have such true grounds.

O worthy men, deliberate! reflect on the matter. Consider the end; contemplate the consequence. You console yourselves with the invention of men; but we put our trust in the word and truth of God; you seek the world, we seek heaven; you place your affections upon the present, we upon the future; you depend upon the emperor and temporal powers; we depend on Christ and his promises, till we all shall appear before him, who will come in the clouds of heaven, to requite all flesh; then you will see what you sought, what office you conducted, what fruits you brought forth, for what hire you served, whose word you preached, whose counsel you rejected, and whom, O men, you have so enviously pierced.

Hereby I will commend you to the Lord, you learned and preachers; and entreat for God's sake (to the good of all your souls), that you accept this my faithful warning with gratitude and love, written to you, with a sincere and Christian intention; read it with an understanding heart; reflect upon it, and examine it with fear and trembling. I certainly know that you will find nothing in it but kindness, love, zeal, and a sure foundation of the only and invincible truth.

And though some of you may think that I reprove too severely, you ought to know that I have not done so without the instruction, counsel and doctrine of the holy prophets, Christ and the apostles. I have given no name without the word of God. Let him that is innocent thank God and rejoice; he that is guilty, is not reproved by me, but by the Spirit and word of God.

O, ye whom I desire as friends, fear God and his judgment; reform your earthly carnal life; abandon all your deceptions, blindness, seducements and abominations, in which you have hitherto been involved; seek the right truth with all your powers; pray to God for wisdom; warn every one; deal and act unblamably; then you will not be of that number of shepherds called by such dreadful names in the Scriptures, and you will not be partakers of that displeasure, punishment and wrath, but you will inherit grace, mercy and life, as the prophet says, "But if the wicked will turn from his sins that he hath committed, and keep all my statutes, and do that which is lawful and right, he shall surely live, he shall not die; all his transgressions that he hath committed, they shall not be mentioned unto him," Ezek. 18: 21, 22. The gracious and merciful Lord, grant you all his grace, knowledge, Spirit, wisdom, light and truth, that you may sincerely awaken, repent, and be eternally saved, Amen.

APPEAL TO THE COMMON PEOPLE.

Give ear, ye people; you who trust in lies, and boast that you are Christians; tear your bands asunder, and suffer yourselves to be led no longer as asses bound and under a heavy burden of sin, by these aforementioned drivers, for they deceive you; they preach to you according to their own opinion, and not out of the mouth of the Lord; they comfort you in your wicked ways; they call and cry only mercy and peace, though it is displeasure and judgment, as the prophet says. The priests and prophets teach a false worship, and comfort my people in their calamity, that they shall esteem it lightly, saying, "Peace, peace, when there is no peace;" they are the blind leaders, who lead you and themselves into the pit, and the blind watchmen who watch not over the city of God. Thieves and murderers, who slay your poor souls with the sword of their false doctrine, and steal from you the word and kingdom of the Lord; greedy shepherds who seek your wool, milk and flesh, and not your souls. In short, they are those who wholly desolate the kingdom of Christ, and promulgate in high honor the kingdom of anti-christ through the whole world, and who always comfort and defend you, poor children, in your dissolute abominations, your obdurate, blind life, so that, alas! there is none who is sincerely converted to the Lord, laments his sins, and says, What do I?

O, worthy children and brethren, my heart in my body quakes and fears, when I reflect that such a numberless multitude of men are born in vain and to no purpose; who will have eternally to endure the wrath and judgment of the Lord, if they repent not, and shall never find grace.

Beloved children, take heed, for thus Christ Jesus teaches you, I tell you of a truth, "Except ye be converted and become as little children, ye shall not enter into the kingdom of heaven," Matt. 18: 3. O, dear Lord, this is spoken by God's eternal truth, which cannot lie, and how ungodly you ignorant people live, and how far you are from the innocence of children, your fruits testify; for you despise God and his word; you hate all righteousness and truth, many of you live as the irrational creatures, others quarrel, curse, swear, are covetous, practice usury, lie, cheat, injure and defraud one another; fidelity and piety are seldom found among you, faithlessness, and knavery, alas, every where; eating to excess, gambling, gaming, drinking and carousing are pastimes amongst you; to pollute women and defile virgins is called courting and loving. To take the advantage of, and defraud one another, is called understanding and wisdom; you are valiant at beer and mighty at wine; unrighteousness and destruction are in all your ways, the poor and weak you oppress, and you revile the afflicted, the god-fearing and pious; you think and practice nothing but evil, you are without understanding, says the prophet, as a frantic heifer. Pomp and splendor you call the fashion and custom of the country. The one lies in wait for the other's honor, property, and life, and seeks his destruction, as the prophet says, your faith is hypocrisy, your worship idolatry, your whole life is world and flesh, as may be seen, and then you say, he that walks in simplicity, walks right, as if ignorance, blindness, despising the truth, and godliness, were a pious, humble and plain life. Dear children, be ashamed of your offensive wantonness and accursed folly.

Do you suppose that Christ is a liar, and his word a fable? O no! his sentence stands immovable, and shall never be altered; if you live in pride, avarice, voluptuousness, unchastity and in carnal lusts, believe not Christ and his word, continue to be earthly-minded, and are not born of God, you must die eternally, or the Spirit of God is not true, but false.

Say, beloved, why extol the apostles and prophets, while you revile their doctrine as heresy, and their lives as madness? Why suffer yourselves to be called christians, while you hate and oppose Christ's word and example?

Say you, we are without understanding, untaught, and know not the Scriptures? I then again reply: The word is plain and needs no comment, namely, "Thou shalt love the Lord thy God with all thy heart, and with all thy soul, and with all thy strength, and thy neighbor as thyself," Matt. 22: 37, 39. Again, You shall give bread to the hungry and entertain the needy, Isa. 58: 7.

If you live according to the flesh, you shall die; for, to be carnally minded is death; the avaricious, drunkards, and the proud, shall not inherit the kingdom of God; for he will judge adulterers and fornicators, Rom. 8; 1 Cor. 6, and many like passages. All who do not understand such passages, we must confess and acknowledge, are more like irrational creatures then men, more like blocks than christians.

O my children, my beloved children, do not deceive your own souls; seek wisdom and understanding, even as you do your daily food, that you may find great riches; for the kingdom of heaven suffers violence. Strive, says Christ, to enter in at the strait gate; ask and you shall receive; seek and you shall find; knock and it shall be opened unto you. The Almighty, great God is not satisfied with a bare name, but he desires a true, sincere faith, unfeigned, ardent love, a new, converted heart, true humility, mercy, chastity, patience, righteousness and peace; he desires the whole man, heart, professions and actions. He who delights in the word of the Lord, speaks the truth from the heart, crucifies his flesh, and will give his goods and blood for the word of the Lord, if it be required.

Behold, dear children, this is the way in which we will all have to walk, if we desire to be saved; therefore, awaken and learn wisdom. Hear the inviting voice of God, open unto him, and meet him, that he complain not of you, as he did formerly through his prophets, of obdurate and stiff-necked Judea and Jerusalem. "I have nourished," says he, "and brought up children, and they have rebelled against me; the ox knoweth his owner, and the ass his master's crib; but Israel doth not know, my people doth not consider. Ah, sinful nation, a people laden with iniquity, a seed of evil-doers, children that are corrupters! They have forsaken the Lord, they have provoked the Holy One of Israel unto anger, they are gone away backward," Isa. 1: 4.

Jeremiah says, "Every one turned to his course, as the horse rusheth into the battle; yea, the stork in the heaven knoweth her appointed times; and the turtle and the crane, and the swallow observe the time of their coming; but my people know not the judgment of the Lord," Jer. 8: 6, 7.

Remember, dear children, how greatly Jesus Christ took to heart the obstinacy and blindness of the Jews; when he said, "Jerusalem, Jerusalem, how often would I have gathered thy children together, even as a hen gathereth her chickens under her wings, and ye would not," he wept and said, "If thou hadst known, even thou, at least in this thy day, the things which belong unto thy peace, but now they are hid from thine eyes," Luke 19: 42.

"Wherefore lay apart all filthiness and superfluity of naughtiness, and receive with meekness the ingrafted word, which is able to save your souls," James 1: 21. Seek God with a full heart, repent sincerely, cleanse yourselves inwardly before the Lord, let go world, flesh, false doctrine, and every thing contrary to the honor, will, and word of God; hear, believe and follow Jesus Christ, the only, and true shepherd of your souls, who sought you in such great love, and purchased you with such a precious price, then you may, of a truth, boast that you are the people of God, and the church of Christ. To him, the Lord and Savior Jesus Christ, be praise and the eternal kingdom, Amen.

APPEAL TO CORRUPT SECTS.

Christ said, "False christs and false prophets shall rise, and shall show signs and wonders, to seduce, if it were possible, even the elect. But take ye heed, behold, I have foretold you all things," Mark 13: 22, 23. O, you backsliding, erring children! Mind, had you taken to heart this faithful warning of our Lord and Savior, Christ; had you acknowledged his Spirit, doctrine, and holy life as a perfect Spirit, doctrine and life, and acknowledged him as the true Prophet, promised in Scripture; and had you received him as the true and living Son of God; you would never have been led so far from his ways, nor would such frightful errors have taken place. But, O Lord! I fear that some of you are so far enchanted, that you will nevermore come to Christ, the true Shepherd; for you, through a perverted and obscure understanding of the Scriptures, defend, as just and right, the abominable works of ungodliness, which are not only contrary to the Spirit, word and will of Christ, but also contrary to reasonable modesty, nature, and reason.

Is it not a grievous error, that you suffer yourselves to be so sorely bewitched by such worthless persons, and so lamentably misled from one unclean sect to another; first to that of Munster, next to Battenberg, now Davidists; from Beelzebub to Lucifer, and from Belial to Behemoth? Ever learning, but never able to come to the knowledge of the real truth. You suffer yourselves to be led about by every wind of doctrine. You choose out a way for yourselves, as do also the priests and monks; you hold not to the head, Christ, from which all the body, fitly joined together, cometh unto a perfect man, unto the measure of the stature of the fullness of Christ.

I fear that your sins will be punished; for you are earthly, and carnal minded, whereby you thrust from you the pure knowledge of Christ, and hate his cross; and against all admonition of Scriptures, against the undeceiving example of Christ and his saints, you conform yourselves in the splendor, pomp, eating, drinking, folly, hypocrisy, and false worship, of this proud, useless, vain and idolatrous world, which you should, by right, instruct and admonish by a pious, humble, sober, and godly walk.

O, you backsliding children! consider how grievously you disgrace the holy Moses, who teaches and speaks to you out of the mouth of God. He says, "I will raise them up a prophet from among their brethren, like unto thee, and will put my words in his mouth; and he shall speak unto them all that I shall command him. And it shall come to pass, that whosoever will not hearken unto my words which he shall speak in my name, I will require it of him," Deut. 18: 18, 19. This is repeated by Peter and Stephen in Acts 3: 23; and 7: 37.

What do you do with all the great prophets of God, as David, Isaiah, Jeremiah and Ezekiel, who, in so many places, with such plain words, through the inspiration of the Holy Spirit, direct us to Christ and his word? They must either testify to lies, or your prophets must be deceivers and false teachers. This is incontrovertible.

Did not holy Paul say, "But though we,

or an angel from heaven, preach any other gospel unto you than that which we have preached unto you, let him be accursed," Gal. 1: 8. That your prophets, with their king, dominion, polygamy, sword, &c., do not agree with Paul and the doctrine and gospel of the apostles, you are all forced to acknowledge and admit, whence it forcibly follows, that they, with their doctrine and conduct, are cursed and anathematized.

Say, my beloved, what do you do with the revealed and infallible word and testimony of the Almighty Father, which he himself has testified of his Son, and said? "This is my beloved Son, in whom I am well pleased; hear ye him," Matt. 17: 5. *Him shall you hear;* but since you reject his Spirit, word and example, you follow and hear those who, with their spirit, doctrine and conduct, are from the bottomless pit, yea, manifestly anti-christs and false prophets.

Know you not, that the Son of God has himself commanded us that we should observe all that he has enjoined, and that he will be with us until the end of the world?

Will you then say, that the doctrine of Christ and his apostles was imperfect, and that your teachers bring forth the perfect instruction? I answer, that to teach and believe this, is the most horrible blasphemy, the most mocking perversity, that can be uttered against the Most High; for you thereby declare that Christ is not the true Son of God, the perfect Teacher, and the true image of righteousness. You deny the whole Scripture, you reject the testimony of Moses and all the prophets, who pointed to the only and true Christ, as has been shown; you disparage the word of the Father, and reject Christ Jesus, with his Spirit, word, kingdom and spiritual government; you put your trust and hopes in lying, mortal flesh, and upon earthly, carnal things, which, as the Scriptures teach, must be dispersed like dust before the wind. Examine the Scriptures in the fear of the Lord, and reflect, if such is not a gross blasphemy against the Almighty.

Say, you deceived children, where is there a syllable in the whole doctrine of Christ and the apostles (according to which Spirit, doctrine, conduct and example all Scripture must be understood), by which you can prove and establish one of all your erring articles?

If you would appeal to the literal understanding and transactions of Moses and the prophets, then must you also become Jews, receive circumcision, literally possess the land of Canaan, again erect the Jewish kingdom, build the city and temple, and according to the law, offer sacrifices, attend to the worship of God, and declare that Christ, the promised Savior, has not yet come, who has changed the literal and figurative ceremonies into new, spiritual and abiding substances.

You miserable, erring sheep, observe, I have before remarked to the magistrates, that the kingdom of Christ is not of this visible, perishing world, but that it is an eternal, spiritual and abiding kingdom, where there are no eating and drinking, but righteousness, peace and joy in the Holy Ghost. There no king reigns, but the true King of Zion, Christ Jesus. He is the King of righteousness, the King of peace, the King of kings, who has all power in heaven above, and on earth beneath; before whom every knee shall bow, and every tongue confess. The true king David in Spirit, who, through his righteousness, merits and crimson blood, has ransomed the sheep from the mouths of the savage lions and bears of the pit, has slain the great and terrible Goliah, and obtained for the spiritual Israel of God, eternal welfare and peace. Neither the King nor his servants bear any sword but the sword of the Spirit, piercing even to the dividing asunder of soul and spirit, the word of God, with which he brings forth, builds, extends and governs his kingdom, guards and defends it under the pressing cross, in all trials and temptations, from the gates of hell, onsets and powers, and not with iron or steel, as the rude, vindictive world does; for his kingdom and dominion is spirit, and not letter, as has been shown.

Again, under this kingdom, and under this King, no other wedlock must be tolerated, except between *one* man and *one* woman, as God had in the beginning established in the union of Adam and Eve; and Christ has further said, that these two are one flesh, and that they shall not separate, save for the cause of fornication, Matt. 5: 32.

This is not a kingdom in which a display is made of gold, silver, pearls, silk, velvet and costly finery, as is done by the proud wicked world, and which also your leaders teach and give you liberty to do under this deception, viz., that it is harmless if you do not desire and serve them from your heart. Thus might satan approve his haughtiness, and make pure and good the desire of his eyes. In the kingdom of all humility (I say), the outward adorning of the body is not desired and sought with power, but the inward adorning of the spirit, with zeal, diligence, and a broken, contrite heart.

Here is known no lying, eating, drinking, or hypocrisy; here none conforms himself to a drunken, luxurious, idle and idolatrous world, nor lays from him the cross of Christ, as you do, but all are upright and godly in heart and deed. They speak the truth from the heart. They lead a circumspect, temperate life; shun all idolatry and false doctrine from within and without; abstain from all appearance of evil; perform the true worship of the heart; abide firmly in the word and ordinances of Christ; lead an unblamable life before the whole world, and testify of Jesus Christ with the mouth, works, possessions and blood, as the divine honor requires it.

Here that confession is unknown to which some of you pretend, here we confess only to the true God before whom we have sinned, and to our neighbor against whom we have trespassed.

Here modesty, rectitude, and honesty are taught and practiced, but not immodesty, disgrace and uncleanness. I think you understand well what I mean.

In short, here the Spirit, word, will, commands, prohibitions, ordinances, customs, and examples of Christ are taught. To which all Scriptures refer us, and not the opinions of false prophets, high sounding words, enchanting appearances, boasting, dreams, and lying miracles, against which, the Spirit of God, and the Scriptures everywhere warn and counsel us.

Dear children, reform yourselves. Every one who teaches you otherwise, than is testified by the word of the Lord, even though he were one who could dry up the bottom of the sea, and hurl the stars down from heaven, let him be abandoned, and let his doctrine be regarded as deceiving and erroneous, for, to all eternity there may no other foundation be laid, than that which is laid, Christ Jesus. He is the corner stone and foundation in Zion, on whom all the building fitly framed together (according to his will, Spirit and word), groweth into a holy temple unto the Lord.

O ye backsliding children, hear the word of God and make haste, for your way is in darkness, and your path leads to death. Embrace the truth and learn wisdom, for your comforters have destroyed you and rendered uneven the way in which you must go. Munster and Amsterdam may well be to you an eternal warning and example. When a prophet, said Moses, speaks in the name of the Lord, if the thing follow not, nor come to pass, that is not the thing which the Lord hath spoken.

O dear Lord! How many innocent hearts have they ruined? How many poor souls have they deceived? What gross shame have they cast upon the word of the Lord? What great abominations have some of them committed under the appearance of good? How have they made the poor, blind magistrates, who are, alas, destitute of a correct understanding of the holy word, to be guilty of innocent blood?

I think it is time you should see and learn to know your lying faithless, and deceiving prophets. They are the foxes which destroy the vineyard of the Lord. These are the thieves and murderers of your souls; false prophets who deny the Lord that bought them; who have directed you, poor erring sheep, by their own lying visions, dreams, and thoughts of their hearts, and have led you against all the Scriptures upon a false and loose foundation.

How like unto those you have become, of whom Eusebius writes, that they walked according to the lusts of their hearts, as the prophets foretold; who denied Paul and the New Testament, and carried with them a book, which they boasted, fell from heaven as a present to them.

So it is with you, O ye entranced (bear with me, for it is the truth which I write).

The prophets you read according to the Jewish understanding. You say the doctrine of Christ and the apostles is at the present time fulfilled; and pretend that there is now another dispensation, &c., and observe not that you thereby deny the Son of God, and gainsay the whole Scriptures; you comfort yourselves with mere lies, as also did disobedient Israel in their time.

Oh dear Lord! How long shall these sore plagues endure? how long shall the name of the Lord through you be blasphemed, and his holy word through you be disgraced? Is it not a grievous error (man phrenzy), that Christ, the Son of the living God, who, brought forth in eternal righteousness, has reconciled heaven and earth by the blood of his cross, with his word of truth, and with the counsels of eternal life, is rejected from your hearts, which he so dearly bought, and which should, so properly be the dwelling place of Christ; and poor, sinful flesh, and mortal man descended from Adam, full of all unrighteousness, haughty speeches, lies and open deception is received by you and adopted in stead.

Oh, beloved children, what are you doing? Are you so thoroughly enchanted that you have lost all reason, intelligence, the Scriptures, and everything, so that you cannot see at all? then may God be merciful unto you. Good children, observe that a letter of the law of Moses could not be changed till the new Moses, Christ Jesus, came, who was promised through the law and the prophets. If then the letter of the law was so strong, effective and firm, and in its time unchangeable, although given only through a servant, and sealed by perishable blood, how much more powerful, effectual, firm, and unchangeable is the free law of the Spirit, which was given through the Son himself, and confirmed by the blood of the eternal covenant.

All who taught anything contrary to the word of Moses, were false prophets, for nothing was to be taken from, nor added thereto, but all appeals were to the law and the testimony, Deut. 4: 2. All the prophets of the present day are false who teach contrary to the Spirit, word, commands, prohibitions, ordinances and example of Christ, even though such should exhibit themselves in appearance, as holier than John, more zealous than Elias, and more miraculous than Moses.

They persuade you that the doctrine of the apostles is imperfect, but that *they* now teach that which is perfect. This is a deception above all deceptions, as above said, for thereby the creature is honored more than the Creator. Paul does not refer to any better doctrine or perfection other than that which is shown by the doctrine of the apostles, which will abide in everlasting clearness, according to the infallible promise of God, and which we shall receive in the resurrection of the righteous, when all doctrine shall receive an end. This is true, otherwise Paul is at variance with himself, and the true reality is not to be found in Christ.

Again, will you say, then, with the Jews and Scribes, that Elias will come before the great and terrible day, and thus wait for something new?

First, I answer with Christ's own words, that "all the prophets and the law prophesied until John, and if ye will receive it, this is Elias, which was for to come," Matt. 11: 13, 14.

Secondly, Even though Elias himself were to come, he dare not teach any thing against the foundation and doctrine of Christ and the apostles, but he must, if he would preach aright, teach and preach conformably to the same, for, by the Spirit, word, actions and example of Christ, all must be judged, and receive the last sentence, otherwise the whole Scriptures are false.

Therefore, one of two things must follow, either that we are not to look for an Elias any more, since John was the Elias who was to come; or if an Elias should come yet, he must propose and teach us nothing but the foundation and word of Christ, according to the Scriptures; for Christ is the man who sits upon David's throne, and shall reign forever in the kingdom, house, and congregation of Jacob.

I would then, herewith sincerely admonish you all to weigh and prove all spirit, doctrine, faith, and conduct, with the Spirit, doctrine and conduct of Christ, and that ye be temperate. All spirits which accord therewith, are from God, but those which are contrary, are from him, who from the beginning has turned Adam and his race aside from God, and has led them by lies onward to death.

If you will not hear, but will ever turn your ears to lies, and believe the deceiving creature more than the infallible Creator; if you set your feet upon slippery places; if you neither fear nor regard Scripture admonitions, nor the power and punishments of God, but reject and set aside all as idle and useless, and suffer yourselves always to be comforted with falsehoods, visions, dreams, splendid delusions, false interpretations and continue, without the cross, on the broad way, then will the righteous Lord send to you mockers and deceivers, and by his righteous judgment suffer you to be led from one ungodly course to another, as may already be seen.

You shall be satiated with lies, vanity, folly and hypocrisy. You will reap the fruits of your wantonness, and at last, with all false prophets and lying wonder workers, you shall hear the words, "I know you not whence ye are; depart from me, all ye workers of iniquity," Luke 13: 27.

Be ye then eternally warned and faithfully admonished of God. Beware, the day approaches, repent, reform. The word of God is true. Is there any one among you who fears God, let him reflect on what I here write; search the Scriptures and believe the truth, for God hates all liars. Eternal woe and gnashing of teeth will be the portion and reward of the hypocrite; "Whosoever transgresseth and abideth not in the doctrine of Christ, hath not God," 2 John 1: 9.

O ye miserable, enchanted children! turn again. If ye knew what it was to forsake the living fountain of Christ, and dig for yourselves dry wells which can neither yield nor hold water, Jer. 2, how soon would you turn your back on the false prophets and their hypocritical lives, surrender yourselves to the true Shepherd of your souls, Christ Jesus, and follow and obey his sure counsel, teaching, admonition, ordinance, and holy example (although in weakness); but alas, enchanting blindness has obscured your understanding. The beloved, merciful Lord grant you eyes to see and hearts to understand; this is our sincere wish, Amen.

TO THE BRIDE, KINGDOM, STATE,

AND

CHURCH OF THE LORD, GRACE AND PEACE.

Thus spake the Bridegroom, Christ Jesus, through Solomon to his bride, the church, "Rise up, my love, my fair one, and come away, for lo, the winter is past, the rain is over and gone, the flowers appear on the earth; the time of the singing of birds is come, and the voice of the turtle is heard in our land; the fig tree putteth forth her green figs, and the vines with the tender grape give a good smell. Arise, my love, my fair one, and come away," Cant. 2: 10 13.

Chosen, true children, you, who with me, are called to the like grace, inheritance and kingdom, and are named after the Lord's name, hear the voice of Christ, your king; hear the voice of your bridegroom, ah, thou bride of God, thou friend of the Lord, arise, and adorn thyself to honor thy king and bridegroom. Though thou art pure, purify thyself yet more; though thou art holy, hallow thyself yet more, and though thou art right, rectify thyself yet more; adorn thyself with the white silken robe of righteousness; hang about thy neck the golden chain of all piety; gird thyself with the fair girdle of brotherly love; put on the wedding ring of true faith; gird thyself with precious fair gold of the divine word. Adorn thyself with the pearls of all modesty; wash thyself with the clear waters of grace, and anoint thyself with the oil of the Holy Ghost. Wash thy feet in the clear, limped river of Almighty God; let your whole body be pure and clear, for thy friend hates all wrinkles and spots; so will he have pleasure in thy beauty and will praise thee and say, "How fair is thy love, my sister, my spouse! How much better is thy love than wine, and the smell of thine ointments, than all spices. Thy lips, O my spouse, drop as the honey-comb; honey and milk are under thy tongue," Cant. 4: 10, 11.

Rejoice, O thou bride of the Lord! for your beloved is fairer than all the children of men, "The chiefest among ten thousand, his head is as the most fine gold, his locks are bushy and as black as a raven. His eyes are as the eyes of doves, by the rivers of waters, washed with milk and fitly set. His cheeks are as a bed of spices, as sweet flowers; his lips, like lilies, dropping sweet smelling myrrh. His hands are as gold rings set with the beryl; his belly is as bright ivory, overlaid with sapphires. His legs are as pillars of marble, set upon sockets of fine gold. His countenance is as Lebanon, excellent as the cedars; his mouth is most sweet, yea, he is altogether lovely," Cant. 5: 10—16. Cry out and say, "Hearken, O daughter, and consider and incline thine ear; forget also thine own people, and thy father's house, so shall the king greatly desire thy beauty," Ps. 45: 10, 11.

Draw near, O thou queen, O thou well-prepared and fairest of all woman; bow thy neck with Esther, under his powerful sceptre; hear his word and fear his judgment; acknowledge his great love, for he has greatly humbled himself towards us. "Thy birth and thy nativity is of the land of Canaan; thy father was an Amorite, and thy mother a Hittite, and as for thy nativity, in the day thou wast born, thy navel was not cut, neither wast thou washed in water to supple thee; thou wast not salted at all, nor swaddled at all," Ezek. 16: 3, 4. Thou wast polluted in thy blood, behold so despised were your souls, as the prophet lamented. But he has pitied thee, promised thee life, nourished thee and clothed thy shame, purified thee from thy uncleanness, wiped off thy blood, anointed thee with balsam, clothed thee with spiritual clothes; he has adorned thee with bracelets, ear-rings, and a beautiful crown, and has taken thee for his bride, and made an everlasting covenant with thee; he has fed thee with oil, honey and wheaten bread; he has led thee to the chamber of his love, and kissed thee with the mouth of his peace.

How lovely and gracious a bridegroom and king is he, who has chosen his miserable, impure, unesteemed, yea, unchaste servant, to such an exalted station, and has called her to be such a glorious queen, and has spared no labor, pains nor costs, till he has made her the fairest, purest, most worthy and precious among women.

Arise, make haste, adorn and dress yourselves, extol and praise him who has created you, and called you to such a high honor through the word of his grace.

The winter is past, the rain is over and gone, the flowers appear on the earth, and the voice of the turtle dove is heard in our land; there is nothing more which can harm or hinder, for hell, sin, the devil, death, the world, flesh, fire and sword, are already overcome by all the children of God, through Christ! All they know is Christ Jesus, their seeking is the pure apostolic doctrine and the pious, unblamable life, which is from God.

Praise be to the Most High, who has silenced the falsehoods, for the truth sounds in every street. Anti-christ sinks to shame, and Christ rises to higher honor, yea, the unfruitful, cold winter has disappeared, and the fruitful pleasant spring has come, the lovely fair flowers shoot forth and vegetate, in every place; the voice of the turtle dove is heard. The wholesome, holy word, the word of repentance, the word of grace and eternal peace, is testified with word, writings, life and death, in many countries.

"The fig tree putteth forth her green figs, and the vines with the tender grape, give a good smell; arise, my love, my fair one, and come away," Cant. 2: 13. Faith assumes verdure, love blooms, the sun softens, and the truth is published and testified to, which remained fruitless for so many years; although you must, for a short time, bear the heat of the sun, yet you so well know that the kingdom of glory, in eternal joy, is promised and prepared for you.

Rejoice and watch; thou art black but comely, thou art as the tents of Kedar, as the curtains of Solomon. "Awake, O north wind, and come, thou south; blow upon my garden, that the spices thereof may flow out," Cant. 4: 16. Fear not, little flock, for it is the Father's good pleasure to give you the kingdom, not the perishing kingdom of Assyria, Media, Macedonia, nor of Rome, but the kingdom of the saints, the kingdom of the great King, the kingdom of David, the kingdom of grace and eternal peace, which shall never more perish, but shall abide and stand forever, therefore, hear him and be obedient, that you be not thrust out with the haughty, disobedient Vashti, but with the pious Esther, live in endless glory, before the true Ahasuerus, Christ, and abide with him forever.

Arise, thou daughter of Zion, and observe what is promised thee. O Jerusalem, although thou, as a comfortless one, sittest for a while, and must bear all manner of storms and hail, but your helper will arrive in time, who brings forth thy righteousness as the morning, and is thy shelter from the wind and storm. For He who loved thee has said, "Behold, I will lay thy stones with fair colors, and lay thy foundations with sapphires, and I will make thy windows of agates and thy gates of carbuncles and all thy borders of pleasant stones, and all thy children shall be taught of the Lord; and great shall be the peace of thy children. In righteousness shalt thou be established; thou shalt be far from oppression," Isa. 54: 11—14.

Behold, thy wall stands firmly upon twelve foundations, thy gates are of pearls, the city is of pure gold, the river of living waters, proceeding from the throne of God and the lamb, is in the midst of your way, and the tree of life is on either side, and its leaves serve to heal the nation. Happy and holy is he who has part in this city.

Therefore, so purify yourselves, you who seek the Lord, circumcise the foreskin of your hearts, for the holy city may be inhabited by no uncircumcised person, the golden streets are trodden by no unclean feet; the unclean, drink not of the pure waters; the fruit of life shall never be eaten by any of the ungodly, "For without are dogs, and sorcerers, and whoremongers, and murderers, and idolaters, and whosoever loveth and maketh a lie," Rev. 22: 15.

Be ye all minded like Christ Jesus. Be earnest to hold the union of the Spirit through the covenant of peace; ye are all one temple, house, city, mountain, body and church in Christ Jesus.

Place your candle upon a candlestick, build your city upon a high mountain; live unblamably, behave in all things consistent with Christianity, fear God in all your ways, praise him in all your works; for great is the grace which has appeared. Prove yourselves in all things, as those who are born of God; shun all false doctrine; repay not evil with evil, but return the evil with good; pray without ceasing; in patience possess your souls; judge all your thoughts, words, and lives, after the thoughts, words, and life of Christ, so shall you in eternity never more be deceived.

Walk worthily after the calling whereby ye are called. Let the tyrannical, blaspheming, upbraiding, and furious, hate the Lord and his word, they persecute you not, but Christ Jesus, to whom they are inimical, they will be judged in their time, and, if they do not repent, will be repaid again in their own bosoms.

Strive and wrestle valiantly, in order that the crown be not taken from you. Fly to the mountain of the covert of Christ Jesus. Gird yourselves with the weapons of righteousness, declare God's word with freedom, neither shrink nor give way. God is your conductor; be faithful unto death, so shall you inherit the crown of life.

Whosoever overcomes, will be clothed with white clothing, and his name shall not be erased from the book of life. Although we appear to the unwise, to die and depart from the right way, our souls are, nevertheless, in hope and peace, Wis. 3: 2.

"It is a faithful saying," says Paul, "for if we be dead with him (Christ), we shall also live with him; if we suffer, we shall also reign with him; if we deny him, he will also deny us," 2 Tim. 2: 11, 12. Therefore, fear your God from the heart, watch and pray and commend to him your affairs, as Jeremiah did. He has chosen you to be his loving bride, children, and members; called you to the kingdom of his grace, and the inheritance of his glory, and has bought you with the immaculate blood of Christ Jesus.

Peace be with you, the Spirit, power and grace of our Lord Jesus Christ, be with all my fellow laborers, believers, brethren and sisters, till eternal life, Amen.

CONCLUSION OF THIS BOOK.

Behold, dear sirs, friends and brethren, here we have briefly pointed out and declared upon what foundation and Scriptures we are built, what we seek and have in view, and how we rebuke, with the word of the Lord, all abominable sects and ungodliness of the whole world, both with the greatest and the smallest, without any respect of persons, and we point out to every one, the wholesome, pure truth. The god-fearing may read and judge. But this I have not done in order that the cross of Christ may be avoided, in no wise, for I know and am persuaded, that the lamb with the wolf, the dove with the kite, and Christ with Belial, can never be at peace, the truth must be hated; and were it so, that Christ himself should speak from heaven, still would neither Scripture nor godliness, neither Christ nor apostle, neither prophet nor saints, neither lives nor property, be regarded by men. All those, who rebuke, in pure, upright zeal, the haughty, avaricious, proud, idolatrous, bloodthirsty world, and who seek their happiness and eternal welfare, with all the heart, must suffer and be oppressed.

You must (said Christ), be hated of all men for my name's sake. Through much tribulation you must enter into the kingdom of God. Christ himself so suffered and then entered into his glory.

Therefore, I have done this, that the precious, pure truth, might be revealed; that here and there some might be won; the right way pointed out to the blind; the hungry fed with the word of God; the erring directed to Christ, the shepherd; the ignorant taught; the kingdom of God extended; and his holy name magnified and praised, this, together with our innocence, shall be a witness on the day of judgment to all bloodthirsty tyrants, and all deceivers, false prophets, and all hardened and impenitent, that to them the truth had been testified. But will ye not hear, then be your sins upon you; I have declared unto you according to my small gifts, God's Spirit, word, foundation, ordinance and will, and have pointed out to you righteousness. Whoever has ears to hear, let him hear, and whoever has understanding, let him understand.

I testify my Savior openly; I acknowledge him, and dissemble not. If you repent not and be not born of God, in your spirit, belief, life and worship, and become not one with Christ, then is the sentence of your condemnation on your poor souls already finished and prepared.

All, who teach you otherwise than we have here taught and testified to you, from the Scriptures, deceive you. This is the narrow way through which we all must walk, and must enter the strait gate, if we would be happy. Here is excepted, neither emperor nor king, duke nor count, knight nor nobleman, doctor nor licentiate, rich nor poor, man nor woman. Whoever boasts that he is a christian, the same must walk as Christ walked. "If any man have not the Spirit of Christ he is none of his." "Whosoever transgresseth and abideth not in the doctrine of Christ, hath not God," 2 John 1: 9. "He that committeth sin is of the devil," 1 John 3: 8. Here neither baptism, Lord's Supper, confession, nor absolution will avail anything. These and other Scriptures stand immoveable, and judge all those who live out of the Spirit and word of Christ, and whose thoughts are upon earthly and carnal things; they shall never be overthrown, perverted nor weakened, by angel or devil.

Will you say, with refractory Israel, we will not hear the word which you have preached to us in the name of the Lord? but we will do as our forefathers, our kings and princes have done from former years till the present time. So I answer with holy Jeremiah and say, Although you have pleasure in lies, and do such abominations, so hath the Lord taken your wickedness to heart, and has sent you one hard punishment after another, as hunger, pestilence, storms, grief, misery and the consuming, devouring sword, that your land is turned to a waste, to amazement and a curse, as one evidently may see in many places, because you perform strange worship; despise the Lord, your God; cast his word aside; shed innocent blood; walk according to your wantonness; sin against God, and walk not according to his law, ordinance and commands, as the mouth of the Lord has commanded you.

Again, as the unprofitable and rebellious world are warned and rebuked against their will, the prophets, and the true servants of God, are judged and destroyed by the princes and magistracy, as seditious mutinists, and are persecuted by the priests and common people as deceivers and heretics. Therefore, we have made up our minds to both teach and suffer, expecting that we will fare no better in this matter than they did, but we say with Ezekiel, That when this shall come to pass, then shall you find that the undissembled, pure word of the Lord, had been taught to you.

The merciful, gracious father, through his loving Son, Christ Jesus, our Lord, grant to you all, the gift and grace of his Holy Spirit, that you may hear and read these our christian labors and service of true love, with such hearts, that you may strive for, confess, believe, and follow after the genuine truth, with all your soul, and be eternally saved, Amen.

Dear, worthy lords, grant to your poor servants, that we may fear the Lord from the heart, and preach the word of God, and do right. This we pray you for Jesus' sake. O Lord! Father of all grace, open the eyes of the blind, that they may see thy way, word, truth and will, and walk therein with faithful hearts, Amen.

MENNO SIMON.

THE TRUE CHRISTIAN FAITH,

WHICH CONVERTS, CHANGES,
MAKES PIOUS, SINCERE, NEW, PEACEFUL, JOYFUL AND BLESSED
THE HUMAN HEART;

WITH ITS NATURAL PROPERTIES, NATURE, OPERATIONS AND POWERS.

CAREFULLY REVISED, AND MORE FORMALLY PRESENTED, IN THE YEAR 1556.

BY

MENNO SIMON.

"He that believeth in me (said Christ) though he were dead, yet shall he live. And whosoever liveth and believeth in me shall never die," John 11: 25, 26.

"For other foundation can no man lay than that is laid, which is Jesus Christ," 1 Cor. 3: 11.

ELKHART, INDIANA:
PUBLISHED BY JOHN F. FUNK AND BROTHER.
1871.

THE TRUE CHRISTIAN FAITH.

We wish all the chosen children of God, our beloved brethren and sisters in Christ Jesus, an increase of faith, grace, peace and spiritual joy, perfect righteousness and eternal life, all which is of God, our heavenly Father, through Jesus Christ, his only begotten Son, our Lord, who loved us, and washed us from our sins in his blood. To him be praise, honor, glory, kingdom, power and majesty, from eternity to eternity, Amen.

CHOSEN, beloved children, brothers and sisters in Christ Jesus, although, O God! we are so unwisely prevented by this irrational, blind world, from preaching the true gospel of our Lord and Savior Jesus Christ to every one, verbally; and, although the cruel, bloody tyranny, encouraged by our useless, wicked priests and preachers, is used so unrestrainedly against Christ and his word (for these poor children seek and love dross more than gold, chaff more than wheat, lies more than truth, and darkness more than light), yet shall God's only invincible truth, which always triumphs, through the Holy Ghost, in the true children of God, bear its crown; notwithstanding that it is stung so miserably in the heel by the conquered serpent and his seed, the proud despisers, liars and blood-shedders, that it can scarcely stand in obedience to its Lord Jesus Christ. Notwithstanding their raving, this envious, bloody seed and serpent must, with bruised head, and quite powerless, remain under its sway, for through the power of the Spirit, and the gospel truth in Christ Jesus he is wholly overcome.

Since then, this old, crooked serpent, which was from the beginning, proudly and falsely opposed to God, and was a cruel murderer, is put under the feet of Christ and his church, and has endured and seen his lying seed destroyed and trampled under foot, through the revealed truth, therefore, does he gnash his teeth in furious rage, and breathe out his accursed, infernal breath of heresy through his prophets and preachers. He casts out of his mouth the terrible streams of tyranny through the rulers and the mighty of the earth, after the glorious church (woman), pregnant with the word of the Lord, with a view to exterminate and destroy her seed. But God be eternally praised, who has protected her against the red dragon, and has prepared her a place in the wilderness.

Since, then, for reasons assigned, I cannot teach publicly, nevertheless, I will serve you by writing, as long as the Lord will permit me, and I live. I will serve you with my small talents, which the gracious Father has granted me through his Son, Christ Jesus, out of the abundant treasury of his heavenly riches. I say with Paul, Not with the wisdom of man, not with words of wisdom to serve you, for I possess and know them not. I let those seek them who are eager after them. My boasting is, with Paul, only to know Christ, and him crucified; for to know him is eternal life. Therefore God cannot endow us with better wisdom than with this, although it is foolishness to the world; for truth is more precious than gold and silver; than all pearls and precious stones; there is nothing under heaven to be compared to her. Her ways are ways of pleasantness, and all her paths are peace; she is a tree of life to them that lay hold upon her; and happy is every one that retaineth her.

Yes, beloved brothers, every one who is thus rightly taught of God, in this wisdom (for she is the wisdom of the saints), may glory, by the grace given him, over all graduated doctors, theologists, jurists, orators and poets, although he could neither write nor speak, and were he the most helpless upon earth. But all those who are not instructed in this wisdom from God, though they were as glorious as Solomon, as victorious as Alexander, as rich as Crœsus, as strong as Hercules, as learned as Plato, as subtle as Aristotle, as eloquent as Demosthenes and Cicero, and as well skilled in languages as Mithridates; yea, so greatly experienced that his like were not to be found from the beginning, nevertheless, he is a fool in the eyes of the Lord; this must be confessed and acknowledged.

With this wisdom, I say, so much as the gracious Father, the Giver of every perfect gift, has given me through his Son, Jesus Christ, I desire to serve not only our brothers and sisters, but the whole world, with all my heart, that all the hungry and thirsty souls may be clothed from above, and be satisfied with this celestial wisdom, who desire to live according to the will of the Lord; those souls which he created to his honor, and purchased with the blood of his Son, that they may learn to know God through his Son and word, in spirit, who says, "Let not the wise man glory in his wisdom, neither let the mighty man glory in his might, let not the rich man glory in his riches; but let him that glorieth, glory in this, that he understandeth and knoweth me, that I am the LORD, which exercise loving kindness, judgment and righteousness, in the earth; for in these things I delight, saith the LORD," Jer. 9: 23, 24.

O, dear children, you who are born of the word of the Lord through the Spirit, reflect rightly upon these things in your hearts, how incomprehensibly great the heavenly bounty and grace are, which have appeared to us, through Christ, and have been given us of the Father, that he has so graciously bestowed upon us, grievous sinners, in our most abominable blindness, the glorious and divine gift of his wisdom; yea, when we knew neither God nor Christ, were strangers to the life that is out of God, children of wrath and of eternal death, knew not the word of peace, and strayed like sheep who knew no shepherd; that he has so graciously bestowed upon us this great treasure, the true knowledge of the kingdom of God; the treasure which lies buried in the field he discovered to us by his Spirit, and made known to us the mystery of his good will, and the true regenerating signification of his holy gospel, which cannot be taught in colleges, cannot be purchased, is not to be brought from foreign lands, nor can it be merited by any thing; that he has opened to us with the key of his word and Spirit, the saving truth, and has closed it to all emperors, kings, lords, princes, the wise and the learned, before the whole world; that he redeemed us from the power of darkness, and, according to his will and good pleasure, led us into the kingdom of his dear Son; yea, that he has made us kings and priests, that we are to be a chosen and holy people; a people to serve him in love, and to be his own, that we are to publish his power and virtue, because he has called us out of darkness to his marvelous light, as Peter says. O great grace and love!

Most beloved brothers, always rejoice in the Lord. Again, I say, with Paul, rejoice, that the great King, Jesus Christ, who has all power in heaven and on earth, that he has manifested such grace towards you, that he has called you, poor, unesteemed children, to such high honor, you who are the reproach and disgrace of the whole world, that he has made you kings and priests; Kings, I say, who have been anointed with the oil of grace, through the Holy Ghost, crowned with the crown of honor, clothed with the garment of righteousness, and governed by Christ, your King; not with the weapons of death, such as fire-arms, spears, swords, horses, riders and servants, as the kings of this world do, but with the invincible and eternal sceptre of the power of God, namely, with the sharp-edged sword of the holy word, which will victoriously triumph by virtue of your unconquerable faith, over gold, silver, cities, countries, lords, princes, flesh, blood, banners, banishment, swords, stakes, water, fire, hunger, thirst, naked-

FAITH.

ness, hell, sin, law, fear, devil and death; you will be perfect in life and death, and secure from all your enemies, both visible and invisible, who would deprive and rob you of the promised kingdom, through the advice and seed of the old serpent. The dominion and government of the spiritual king are spiritual, therefore, they cannot be fatally hurt or conquered by tyranny, false doctrine, or evil lusts; for they can do all things through Christ, who strengthens them, who also is their helper and redeemer, whose shield and sword is their glory.

Again, you are also priests anointed of God, not with the external oil of Aaron and his sons, nor with the perishable blood of oxen and sheep; nor with the splendid garments of gold, silk and precious stones, as the law required; but anointed, sprinkled and affected with the oil of the Holy Ghost, with the blood of Christ, and clothed with the garment of righteousness, ordained and called of God, not to slay the creatures daily, and offer them upon altars, in outward temples of stone, as Moses commanded the priests in the law; but you are to slay human beings, all your lives, with the sword of the divine word (understand *spiritually*), together with your own refractory flesh and blood, that is, that you teach and reprove them, and yourselves, with the Spirit and word of the Lord, that you and they die to your unrighteousness and evil lusts, destroy them, and thus offer in your spiritual house or temple, not made with hands, upon the only and eternal altar of our reconciliation, Jesus Christ.

Besides, you are not such priests, who of their own righteousness offer bread and wine for the sins and transgressions of the common people, and for the souls of the deceased, neither are you to sing nor read mass, nor worship the golden, silver, wooden and stone images, nor serve nor burn incense to them as the poor, ignorant priests of the world do; but you are holy priests, who purify and sanctify your own bodies daily, and in time of need voluntarily offer them as a sweet smelling sacrifice, for the truth's sake, together with your ardent prayers and joyful thanksgiving, out of a believing, converted, pure heart; for such offerings are well pleasing to the Lord.

Would to God, that all who are called priests, were changed into such priests; ah! how much innocent blood would be spared, how gloriously the truth would be spread, and what a noble Christian world this would be!

Say, beloved brothers, who can fully comprehend *this* grace, or relate these benefits? Again, formerly, we all strayed as lost sheep, which have no shepherd; we walked according to the lusts of our evil flesh, even as they all do, who know not the way of the Father; we were unbelievers in divine things, blind and without understanding, full of bruises and putrifying sores from the sole of the foot to the crown of the head, and by nature, children of wrath like others. But blessed be the Lord, now we are washed, now we are sanctified, now we are justified in the name of our Lord Jesus Christ, through the Spirit of our God, 1 Cor. 6: 11; in short, we are converted to the true Shepherd and preserver of our souls, Jesus Christ, who pastures us in the rich pastures of his truth, feeds us with the bread of his word, sustains us with the tree of life, and refreshes us with the water of his Spirit. Who can comprehend and relate this grace?

Besides this, when we were yet ungodly and enemies, he did not punish us as he did the angels that sinned, nor like the first depraved world, nor like Sodom and Gomorrah, nor like those who worshipped the calf, nor like those in the day of provocation, nor like the seditious and adulterers, nor like those in the wilderness, who acted contrary to his will and word, for he destroyed all of them; but he saved us through his great mercy, led us by his right hand, drew us by his goodness, renewed us by his word, begat us by the Holy Ghost, and enlightened us by the clear light of his truth; that we by his grace renounced the world, flesh, devil and all manner of evil, willingly entered upon the path of peace and submitted to the easy yoke of his gospel. It appears to me, this may properly be called grace.

Most beloved children, take heed: Since then, the gracious Father has dealt so marvelously with us according to his great mercy, and manifested his love toward us without our merits, it is right and becoming that we also love, fear, praise and honor such a benevolent Lord and merciful Father, with all our powers serve him, and be obedient to him in all our weakness.

Since then, he has manifested, toward us afflicted sinners, such unspeakable love and grace, as said, which love and grace cannot be rightly seen and understood, with the blind eyes and the ignorant reason of the flesh, but must be seen and understood with the inward eyes of the mind, and through the unction of the Holy Ghost; that is, with a sincere, sure, immoveable, confident, vigorous, unfeigned and pure faith; such as the Scriptures teach.

Such an unfeigned faith being required as mentioned, and clearly finding in the word of the Lord, that all dealing and aim of true christianity, concerning the new birth or creature, true repentance, dying unto sin, a new life, true righteousness, obedience, salvation and eternal life, lie in a sincere, active faith, according to all Scripture, as may be seen and read in many passages; therefore have I, through the grace of the Lord, undertaken to prove to all lovers of eternal truth, by divine testimony from the word of the Lord, which is the true doctrine that avails before God, and has the promise in the Scriptures; namely, which has energy, power, work, and effect, agreeing with the gospel of Christ and the doctrines of the apostles, in order that all those who see, read or hear our writings, may thoroughly and understandingly know that the stubborn, fruitless faith of this world is vain and dead, and is eternally banished and accursed of God; and its fruits vain hypocrisy, commands of men, idolatry, and false service. It regenerates none, it is earthly and carnally minded, hating and persecuting the truth; for this faith knows neither Christ nor his word, as may be evidently seen through the whole world. God knows of no other faith than that which has power and fruit, regenerates the heart, converts and renews, as the Scriptures say, "The just shall live by faith," Hab. 2: 4.

It is all in vain to boast of faith where the godly, new fruits and works of faith are not.

I therefore, exhort all my god-fearing readers in the Lord, and entreat all, that they would impress those things on their souls, and write them on the tablets of their hearts, that our holy and christian faith is not a dead or superannuated speculation, as the world thinks, nor is it only verbal boasting, as we find it among the great and tolerated sects; but it is an active gift and power of God, a living, heavenly inspiration in a melted, open heart, or conscience which firmly believes and lays hold upon, and acknowledges the whole word of God (the threatening law, as well as the consoling gospel), to be right and true, whereby the heart is pierced and moved through the Holy Ghost with a peculiar, regenerative, renewing, vivifying power, and it first produces the fear of God, for it knows the judgment and wrath of the Lord, over all transgressions and sins which are committed against his will and word. The heart dreads, fears, and is astonished before God, and therefore, dares not do, counsel, or permit anything which it acknowledges through the word, in the Spirit, that God, the righteous judge, hates and forbids in his holy word.

This faith also produces the love of God whereby we love him; for it acknowledges from the testimony of the holy Scriptures, rightly understood, in Spirit, the unsearchably great riches of grace, wherewith our merciful, good Father, through Christ, has so graciously endowed us. Therefore it loves in return its loving God, awakened by the manifest beneficence of the aforesaid grace, and is thus voluntarily urged, through the active power of love (resulting from such unfeigned faith), to obedience of all the commands of God, even as Christ says, "If a man love me, he will keep my words," John 14: 23.

Behold, this is the faith with which we have to deal in the following writings. It is the only faith which has the promise in Scripture of salvation and eternal life, through Christ, the only and first begotten Son of God. To him be praise, honor and glory, from eternity to eternity, Amen.

We see that if any one wishes to build a good house, or high and permanent tower, that first a solid foundation is laid, so that it will sustain the heavy superstructure; that the work, commenced at such great expense, be not ruinously and shamefully demolished and abandoned. Thus it must be with all true christians; they must have, in their hearts, such a sure and solid foundation that they may stand unshaken in the building of their faith, against all the raging tempests, rains and floods, which will try them not a little, so that they may successfully accomplish, by the help of the Lord, their undertaken work and building; so that they may not again depart from the right road, to the everlasting shame and injury of their poor souls. Paul says, "If any man draw back, my soul shall have no pleasure in him," Heb. 10: 38.

Faithful brethren, take heed: This precious, and only well adapted corner-stone, ground and foundation in Zion, prepared for us by the Father, upon which we have to build the edifice of our faith, is Jesus Christ. All who are founded upon this ground, will not be consumed by the fire of tribulation; for they are living stones in the temple of the Lord, they are like gold, silver and precious stones, and can never be prevailed against by the gates of hell, such as false doctrine, flesh, blood, world, sin, devil, water, fire, sword, or by any other means, if ever so sorely tried; for they are founded upon Christ, confirmed in the faith and assured in the word through the Holy Ghost that they are not to be turned away from the pure and wholesome doctrine of Christ by all the furious and bloody Neros under the heavens, with all their cruel tyranny; they are not to be diverted from an unblamable and pious life, which is of God, as we have seen in many places for more than twenty years past; for they are as immoveable as Mount Zion, as firm pillars, brave soldiers, and as pious, valiant witnesses of Christ; they have fought till death, and do daily fight for the word and truth of the Lord (God be eternally praised). I speak of those who have the Spirit and word of the Lord.

Yea, that stone lies firm in their hearts, and is so sealed by faith in them, that in their greatest need they regard neither father nor mother, wife nor child, money nor possessions, life nor death; for they are so constrained by veneration to God in their hearts, because Christ says, "Whosoever therefore shall confess me before men, him will I confess also before my Father which is in heaven; but whosoever shall deny me before men, him will I also deny before my Father which is in heaven," Matt. 10: 32, 33; that they are not allowed to speak a false word, even to escape the hands of the bloodthirsty and the dangers of death; as may be seen.

But I fear, yea, indeed it is found to be the case, that the greater part of all those who call these poor innocent sheep, accursed heretics; who betray, catch, banish, take their lives and possessions, are not ashamed, nor tremble before their God who hates all lies, to use, for the sake of a stiver, yea for nay, and nay for yea, and yet dare boast of Christ and call themselves after his name. If they are such liars and so unfaithful in small things, what they would do in greater things where life and possessions come into requisition, as is the case with these poor sheep, may be easily imagined.

O reader, reflect. If the old, crooked serpent, with all his deception, falsehood and lies, lived in the christian hearts, as is the case with their persecutors, their goods would not be plundered, and their blood would not be shed. And they would not only conceal the truth, but they would with all the children of the devil hate and oppose it. All who are born of the truth, hate lies. Again, all who are born of lies, hate the truth. If they hate the truth, how can they speak it? especially when life and possessions are at stake. If our rulers and judges wish to be assured of this difference, let them call some of their evil doers before the judgment seat, who are guilty of death, and examine them in relation to things whereof they are accused; but without punishing them, what does it avail, though they would freely confess their guilt, for which they are to die, as these innocent children do in their faith? Yea, what is more, let your most high-renowned monks, in their profession, caps, &c., your most accomplished priests in their terms and masses, be as severely tested as you do these, in their faith; then we will see what will become of all their professions, caps, terms and masses. But the common proverb is: The wolf escapes, but the lamb has to suffer.

Since then, I say, all those who are born of the truth, and have Christ and his truth, and his Spirit, dwelling in their hearts, in such during their lives, and in death, we find nothing but the simple, plain truth of Christ, by which they are born unto righteousness, and are converted; yet it is manifest, that however piously, and unblamably they live, our lying, adulterous, lewd, idolatrous, drunken priests and monks (who openly rob God of his glory, and maliciously murder those whom Christ purchased with his precious blood, belie them before the whole world, betray and bring them to the stocks and posts, and all this for no other reason than that they are urged through the manifest truth, through their strong faith and through the Spirit and fear of the Lord, to renounce their leaven, vain, false doctrine and idolatrous sacraments, and with all their hearts, to live according to the will of God. O Lord! thus they live with those who seek and fear Thee with all their hearts.

Say, beloved lords, when shall this cruel, disgraceful murdering, bloody seed, be prevented by you from continuing in their Judas like conduct? When will you turn your backs to their deceiving lies, and turn your faces to Christ? When shall the innocent blood be wiped from your deadly and avenging sword, and again be put into the sheath? When will you hear and fear God, more than you do lords and princes? When shall the abominations of anti-christ be rooted out of your heart, and instead thereof, the doctrine of Christ be planted therein? When will you be satisfied with pious and unblamable lives, and be satiated with the blood of innocent saints? When shall Christ Jesus, with his word, Spirit and life, through faith, be conceived in you, and in deed be born in you? I fear *never*. For you are earthly and carnally minded, the eyes of your understanding are darkened, that you desire the world rather than heaven; lies rather than truth; sin rather than righteousness; the honor and praise of man rather than that of God.

Yes, beloved lords, why say so much? With you it is the same as with the priests and preachers, who, through the instruction of Scripture, know the truth in part; but since they love their cross-fleeing body more than God, they preach and teach only so far as the mandates and resolutions of the princes permit and suffer, so that they do not incur the displeasure of the world, and be deprived of their worldly honor, and their easy life. It is the same case with you, my dear lords. Though many of you well know that the teaching, ceremonies, divine service and life of your priests and preachers are untrue, deceiving, idolatrous, false and carnal, and that ours are the doctrine and ceremonies of the Lord, according to Scripture. Yet, in order to retain the friendship of the emperor, and your incomes I mean you who are guilty of blood, Christ Jesus with his innocent lambs must, without any mercy, if the mandates are enforced, as the ringleaders of all rogues and thieves, who are deserving of all torture and shame, be caught, banished, robbed and doomed to death. And then you say: The emperor's mandates judge you.

Beloved lords beware; the hour is fast approaching, that the Almighty, the great, and terrible God, the impartial, righteous Judge, will judge and sentence all our doings; then you will see too late, whom you have persecuted and pierced. Therefore, awaken in time, fear God, remember him, and reform, while it is yet called to-day.

I entreat you, my reader, be not displeased that I have digressed so far; for it was not done without a cause. But now, we will continue in the name of the Lord, in the thing we have undertaken, and treat and teach as much of it, as the merciful Father will grant us grace and aid thereto, that we may modestly show to all the godfearing, who seek the truth from their hearts, the difference between faith and unbelief; the fruits of faith and of unbelief, and that they may grow in the true christian faith, until the gracious Father, out of the abundance of his glory, makes them strong in the inner man, by power, through the Spirit, and till Christ dwell in their hearts, through faith, that they may be rooted and grounded in love, may be able to comprehend, with all saints, what is the breadth and length and depth and heighth, and to know the abundant love of Christ, which passes knowledge, and be filled with all the fullness of God. And besides, that they may know that it is all hatred and lying which the scribes teach and cast up, touching our faith concerning the sword, sedition, polygamy, &c. I speak of that, which I and my beloved brothers preach and teach, verbally or by writing, publicly or privately, to all the well disposed.

Cordially beloved brothers, when we can, with spiritual eyes, rightly see into the impure, abominable doctrine of faith, with all the abominable unbelief and blind evil life, resulting from such abominable doctrine of those, who boast themselves to be christians, then we may with propriety be astonished, yea, grieved to death at their great blindness and grievous errors. For however inhuman and rude, it must be called the holy christian faith.

THE PAPISTIC BELIEF.

It is true, the papists teach and believe, that Jesus Christ is the Son of God, that he offered up his flesh, and shed his blood for us, but if we would enjoy them, and be partakers thereof, we must adhere to and obey the pope and his church, hear mass, receive the holy water, perform pilgrimages, call upon the mother of the Lord, and the departed saints, confess at least twice a year, receive papistic absolution, have our children baptized, and commemorate the holy days. The priests must vow chastity; the bread in the mass, must be called the flesh, and the wine, the blood of Christ; besides all their other idolatry and abominations, which are daily practiced by them.

And all this is called, by these poor, ignorant people, the most holy christian faith, and the institution of the holy christian church. Although it is nothing but mere human opinion, self-chosen righteousness, seductive hypocrisy, manifest deception of the soul, ungodly, indecent bodily nourishment and gain of lazy priests, an accursed abomination, an incensing of God, a disgraceful blasphemy, an unworthy despising of the blood of Christ, a self-devised undertaking, and a disobedient contumacy to the divine word. In short, a false, offensive, divine worship, and open idolatry, of which Jesus Christ (to whom the Father points us) has not left or commanded us a single letter of all these things.

It does not suffice that they practice such abominations; they not only also despise as vain and useless all true fruits of faith, commanded of God himself, the sincere, pure love and fear of God, the love and service of our neighbor, the true sacraments and divine service, &c., but they also revile them as damnable and heretical, and exterminate and persecute them. I think this may properly be called a sect.

THE LUTHERAN BELIEF.

The Lutherans teach and believe, that we are saved by faith alone, without any regard to works. They maintain this doctrine as firmly as though works were not at all necessary; yea, that *faith* is of such a nature that no work can be suffered or allowed beside it. And, therefore, had the highly important, zealous, and earnest epistle of James (because he reproves such a frivolous, vain doctrine and faith), to be esteemed and considered as straw. O presumption! Is the doctrine straw, then must also the chosen apostle, the faithful servant and witness of Christ, who wrote and taught it, have been a man of straw; this is as clear as the meridian sun. For the doctrine shows the character of the man.

Let every one take heed, how, and what he teaches; for with this same doctrine they have led the reckless and ignorant, great and small, citizens and the common people, into such a fruitless, wild life, and have so much unbridled them, that we would scarcely find such an ungodly and abominable life among the Turks and Tartars, as we see among them. Their open deeds bear testimony; for the excessive eating and drinking; the superfluous pomp and splendor, the whoring, lying, cheating, cursing, swearing by the wounds, sacraments and sufferings of the Lord, the shedding of blood, fighting, &c., which exist among many of them, and, alas, have neither measure nor bounds. In many carnal things, both the teachers and disciples are the same, as may be seen. I well know, what I write, and what I have heard and seen, I testify, and I know that I testify the truth.

If any one can simply say with them, Ah! what dishonest knaves and villains these desperate priests and monks are! They wish them the venereal or some other disease; the ungodly pope with his shorn crew, say they, have deceived us long enough with purgatory, confession and fasting; we now eat as we have hunger; fish or flesh, as we desire; for every creature of God is good, says Paul, and is not to be rejected. But what follows they do not want to understand or know; namely, to (live as) the believing, who know the truth and enjoy it with thanksgiving. They further say, How shamefully they have deceived us poor people, they have robbed us of the blood of the Lord, and directed us to their mummery and to their enchanting works. God be praised, we now know that all our works avail nothing, for the blood and death of Christ alone must blot out, and pay for our sins. They begin to sing a *psalm: Der Strick ist entzwei und wir sind frei,* &c., i. e. The cord is cut asunder and we are at liberty, while the smell of beer and wine issues from their drunken mouths and noses. Any one who can but read this *distich,* if he live ever so carnally, is a good evangelical man, and a fine brother. And should some one come, who would, in true and sincere love, admonish or reprove them, and direct them to Jesus Christ, to his doctrine, sacraments and unblamable example, and show that it does not become a christian to carouse and drink, and to revile and curse, &c., he must from that hour hear, that he is a legalist (*Werkheiliger*), one who would take heaven by storm, or a factionist, a fanatic or hypocrite, a defamer of the sacrament, or an anabaptist.

Behold! thus God, the righteous Lord, suffers these to err and go astray in their hearts, who rely upon the precious death and the most holy flesh and blood of our Lord Jesus Christ, the Son of God, together with his saving and reverent word, in their sensual lusts and wantonness, and make it an occasion of their unclean and sinful flesh. It appears to me this may also truly be called, a liberal and free sect.

THE BELIEF OF THE ENGLISH OR ZUINGLIANS.

The English, or Zuinglians believe and confess that there are two sons in Christ Jesus, the one is God's son, without mother, and *impassive;* and the other is the son of Mary, or the son of man, without father, and *passive.* And in this *passive* son of Mary, the *impassive* Son of God dwelt; so that the son of Mary, who was crucified, and died for us, was not the son of God. This was acknowledged by one of their principal teachers, called Martin Micron, also by one Harman Von Ronsen (if I recollect his name rightly), before me, two or three times in a large assembly, in the year 1554.

Further, the said Micron, when I questioned him in relation to the *aura seminis* of the woman, concerning which we had not a few words, acknowledged and said: I have to confess that a woman has no seminal functions but an afflux of catamenial fluid to the uterus. See, before God, it is the truth that I write. He also wrote in a book, printed in England; these words, touching the coagulating of the fluids in the uterus. If the fluids thus changed, as the book says, and as he confesses, that a woman has only catamenial fluids in the uterus, as said; then, it is evident, that they believe (if they agree with him) that their Savior is not God's first and only begotten Son, but the mere result of a vitiated state of the uterine fluids.

John A'Lasco also writes, that Christ partook of no other flesh than that which was subject to sin and death, in order that he might be tempted. He states in the same book, "If he is holy, why was he sentenced in the Father's judgment, for the sake of sin?" This I cannot otherwise understand, before God, than that he believes, that the man, Christ Jesus, was a sinful Christ and guilty of death. Read his defence made against me, of the Incarnation; there you will find his ground.

O God, watch over all true hearts, that they may never believe such intolerably great abominations. It makes me shudder, and I am astonished in my heart, yea, I am ashamed in my soul, that I must make mention thereof; for it is too offensive. But since they defame and slander us daily before all men, both verbally and by writing, what a very detestable foundation and doctrine we have of Christ (since we confess, with the Scripture, that he was the first and only begotten Son of God, who died for us), and they present these abominable things to the poor, simple people, as said, and deceive them so miserably thereby; for this reason, am I constrained in my conscience, to the honor of God, and to the warning of all godfearing souls, to notice this and present it to the reader, whose mind is held captive by them, to reflect upon; for I know not how we could believe more cruelly and abominably of Christ, teach, feel, think or speak of, than to say, It was not the Son of God who died for us, but it was the result of a vitiated catemenial fluid; a man of sin and death, &c.

And though they may gainsay and deny this, and say that I wrote this gratuitously concerning them, it is true; it happened repeatedly, and before many pious hearts; they may deny it, but it will be found true in the day of the righteous judgment, before the eyes of the Eternal and great majesty, as I have written it. O abominable sect!

THE TRUE CHRISTIAN BELIEF.

We teach and believe, and this by virtue and power of the whole Scriptures, that the whole Christ Jesus from above and below, inwardly and outwardly, visibly and invisibly, is God's first and only begotten Son, the incomprehensible, eternal Word, by which all things are created, the first born of every creature; that he became a true man in Mary, the immaculate virgin, through the almighty, eternal Father, eternal Spirit and power, beyond the comprehension and knowledge of men; sent and given unto us out of pure mercy and grace, from the Father; the express image of the invisible God, and the brightness of his glory. We teach and believe that the first and only begotten Son of God, Jesus Christ, is our only and eternal Messiah, prophet, teacher and high priest, who has fulfilled the required and commanded law for all his believers, inasmuch as they could not fulfil it on account of the weakness of their flesh; who taught us the good will and pleasure of his Father, and went before us as an unblamable pattern, and freely offered himself upon the cross for our sins, as a sweet-smelling sacrifice to the Father. Through whom we all, who sincerely believe this, have received the forgiveness of our sins, grace, favor, mercy, liberty, peace, life eternal, a reconciled Father and free access to God, in the Spirit; and this all through his merits, righteousness, intercesion and blood, and not through our own works. Behold this is the true summary of our belief concerning Christ, our Savior, the Son of God.

All who can believe this, as certain and true, are sealed, through the word of God, in their spirit, are inwardly changed, receive the fear and love of God, and bring forth, out of their faith, righteousness, fruit, power, an unblamable life and a new being; as Paul says, "With the heart, man believeth unto righteousness." Through faith, says Peter, God purifies our hearts. And thus follow the fruits of righteousness out of an upright, unfeigned, pious, Christian faith. Observe this well.

All those who sincerely believe the righteous judgment of God and his eternal wrath over all sin and wickedness, and do not doubt in spirit, look at the fallen angels; they look at the first, depraved world, at Sodom and Gomorrah, and upon disobedient, refractory Israel. They take particular notice how God humbled his innocent Son, who knew no sin, and in whose mouth guile was not found; how he was humbled, and made the most miserable among men for the sake of our sins. Yea, that he was so beaten and tortured, that while extended on the cross, he piteously complained to his Father saying, "My God, my God, why hast thou forsaken me?" Matt. 27: 45.

All who truly believe this, will certainly flee from all unrighteousness, as they would from the fangs of a serpent; they turn away from all sins, and dread them more than a burning fire, or a piercing sword, for their whole mind and conscience testify to them, that if they knowingly and willfully sin against the law and word of God, and do not receive Christ in a pure and good conscience, live according to the flesh, and despise the inviting voice of God that they will fall under the dreadful, eternal sentence and wrath of God.

This the pious and aged Eleazar believed, who was well versed in the law, 2 Macc. 6: 18, and the god-fearing, virtuous mother, with her seven sons, 2 Macc. 7: 1, the three faithful young men in the fiery furnace, the beloved Daniel, and the fair, virtuous Susanna, the honorable pattern of all pious women, Daniel 13. They would rather endure for a season the wrath and fury of tyrants, than sin, and thus bring upon themselves the eternal anger and wrath of God. The righteous, say the Scriptures, live by faith. For the true evangelical faith, which makes the heart sincere and pious before God, moves, changes, urges and constrains a man, so that he will always hate the evil, and willingly do the things which are right and just; even as it is unnecessary to admonish or warn a man of understanding not to cut his own throat, or drink poison, or thrust himself from a high tower, or run into deep water; for he well knows if he did so, he could not escape death. It is also unnecessary that we should admonish, or warn those, who sincerely believe that the wages of sin is death, that drunkards, liars, fornicators, whoremongers, adulterers, avaricious, idolators, blasphemers of God, envious, blood-shedders, perjurers, thieves and the like sinners, shall not inherit the kingdom of Christ, that they shall not get drunk, nor commit fornication, &c. The divine fear, which is of such a faith, warns, exhorts, reproves, urges and deters them, so that they will never more consent to such carnal, ungodly works, much less do them. For their faith, which is sealed of the Spirit through the word, teaches them that the end thereof is death.

We must thus believe with the heart, as Paul says; that is, we must so adhere to the word to receive and impress it upon our hearts, that we may never turn or be diverted from it, but that faith be more and more rooted in our hearts, that, through the virtue thereof, we may fear God with all our powers, and do sincere penance. Sincere, unfeigned fears drive out sin, for it is impossible to be justified without the fear of God.

Here observe, what an excellent, pleasing fruit of faith the fear of the Lord is; it is the only power which expels the sins of believers, buries; slays, destroys and makes sin nought, this is the first part of true repentance, as we are taught and admonished by the baptism of believers. "The fear of the Lord is the beginning of wisdom; a good understanding have all they that do his commandments; his praise endureth for ever," Ps. 111: 10.

Further, All who comprehend with a sincere, unwavering, believing heart, the great solicitude and ardent care of God for us (here I speak of him according to the manner of man), and his unbounded kindness, mercy and love, as paternally manifested toward us through Christ Jesus, that he did not spare his eternal Son, by whom he created the heavens and the earth, the seas and the fullness thereof, his incomprehensible, eternal Word, power and wisdom, but for our sakes, gave him over, humbled him, suffered him to endure hunger, and thirst, was derided, taken, mocked, his holy face spit upon, scourged, crowned with a crown of thorns, condemned, crucified and slain, that we, through his sickness and stripes, might be healed, through his poverty, might become rich, through his being despised, obtain glory ; through his cursing, obtain blessing; through his punishment, receive grace; through his blood, the remission of sin; through his offering, be reconciled, and through his death, might obtain eternal life. He also created every living creature for our use, and made them subject to us. He serves and provides us with winter and summer, heat and cold, night and day, rain and dearth; to us he sent his holy apostles with his holy word, endowed us with his Spirit, enlightens, governs, admonishes, reproves and comforts us; he has given us the necessary shelter and food to supply our wants, and in the midst of a perverted lion-like generation, he has kept and preserved us by his grace, &c. I say, again, he who believes this with all his heart, apprehends and lays hold of it, can never be prevented, neither by angel nor devil, neither by life nor death; but must love this gracious Father, from his inmost heart, who has manifested so great love and mercy towards us grievous sinners; yea, praise, honor, thank, serve, and be obedient to him, all the days of his life.

For this is the greatest delight and joy of believers, that they in their weakness may walk and live according to the will and word of the Lord, and where the unfeigned, pure love of God dwells, there without fail, must also be the voluntary, ready service of that love, namely, the keeping of his commands. Solomon says, "They that put their trust in him shall understand the truth, and such as be faithful in love shall abide with him," Wis. 3: 9. And this is what Paul says, "In Jesus Christ neither circumcision availeth any thing, nor uncircumcision; but faith, which worketh by love," Gal. 5: 6.

That love is of such an effective power and nature, may be very plainly seen in natural love; we need not admonish rational parents, to provide their children with necessary food and clothing, for natural love will admonish them thereto. And thus with man and wife, who sincerely love each other with conjugal love; they think it no displeasure willingly to serve each other and be fellow helpers, as it becomes them, being one flesh. And so is also the nature and property of holy, divine love, for all those who by faith are one with the Father and his Son, Christ Jesus, in love and spirit, through the true and genuine knowledge of the aforementioned favor, need not be admonished that they should serve the Lord, seek the kingdom of God, use baptism and the Lord's Supper, according to the ordinance of the Scriptures, constrain heart and tongue, reflect upon the law and will of God with all earnestness, hear Christ and follow him, and that they should not love gold and silver, money and possessions, wife and children, life and death above Christ and his word. For the effectual nature of the ardent love of God, which is of a pure heart, good conscience, unfeigned faith urges and constrains, moves and operates so much in their hearts, that they stand prepared with body, soul, possession and blood, to do what he commanded them, and not do that which he prohibited; as we may see (God be praised) in great plainness and power, and hear daily of many pious hearts.

And it is hereby evident, if we would love God and walk in obedience to his commands, we should believe, have a special regard to his favors, and with the heart adhere closely to the word of his promise, as said; for that love which is sincere, is a very precious fruit, it is a branch and plant of faith from which the other part of true repentance flows, namely, the unblamable new life, represented to us by baptism, as related above, of the fear of the Lord; without which love, all eloquence, all tongues, all knowledge and understanding, all boastings of faith, learning, miracles, prophesying, alms, persecution, cross and suffering, are vain before God; yea, unfruitful and dead.

Every one that loveth is born of God, and knoweth him, for God is love, such a one does all things according to the nature and word of the Lord, for it is the fulfilling of the law, obedience to his commands, the bond of perfection and peace, and it is prefigured by the splendid girdle of Aaron and his sons.

Love, says Solomon, is as strong as death; jealousy is as cruel as the grave; the coals thereof are coals of fire, which have a most vehement flame; many waters cannot quench love, yea, so firm and strong and ardent is love that it surpasses every thing, conquers and consumes what is opposed to Christ and his word, be it world or flesh, tyrant or devil, sin or death, or whatever we may think of or name; and this is all through the power and Spirit of Jesus Christ from whom it originates.

Moses preceded with fear, then came Christ with love. First the terrific law, and afterwards the consoling gospel; first wrath in the feelings of our consciences, afterwards grace; first uneasiness of pain, then peace; first tribulation, then joy. In short, first the letter which killeth, then the Spirit which quickeneth.

Behold, my reader, such a faith as mentioned, is the true christian faith, which praises, honors, magnifies and extols God the Father and his Son Jesus Christ, through filial fear and fruitful love, for by it we know the good will of the Father towards us through Christ; by it, I say, we know that all the promises to the fathers, the waiting of the patriarchs, the whole figurative law, and all the predictions of the prophets, are fulfilled *in* Christ, *with* Christ, and *through* Christ. That Christ is our king, Prince, Lord, Messiah, the promised David,* the Lion of the tribe of Judah, the strong Giant, the Mighty God, the Everlasting Father, the Prince of peace, God's almighty, incomprehensible, eternal Word and Wisdom, the first born of every creature, the Light of the world, the Sun of righteousness, the true Vine, the Well of life, the true Door and Shepherd of the sheep, the true Foundation, and the precious Corner-stone in Zion, the right Way, the Truth and Life, the promised Prophet, our Master and Teacher, our Redeemer, Savior, Friend and Bridegroom. In short, our only and eternal Mediator, Advocate, High-priest, Propitiator and Intercessor, our Head and Brother. And since we know all this by faith, therefore, I say, we also observe his word rightly, hear his voice, and implicitly follow his example, and counsel, and depart from ungodliness; the heart is changed, the mind is renewed, and with Moses we rely upon the future promises, as though they were in sight, and patiently wait for them with pious Abraham, till he, with all the chosen, shall in reality inherit them. "Now faith," says Paul, "is the substance of things hoped for, the evidence of things not seen," Heb. 11: 1. He says, further, But hope that is seen is not hope. God, says Christ himself, is a Spirit; his word, grace, and the promise of the New Testament; his kingdom and government are spiritual; and thus we have to believe all things through an upright, pure, and sure faith, with a candid heart, and judge and see with spiritual eyes; but we may well say with Paul, " All men have not faith," 2 Thess. 3: 2.

Therefore, all those who stop their ears to the threatening, punishing and death-dealing law, and will not fear God, reject, and desire not the gracious gospel of Christ, shut their eyes to the light of righteousness, and will neither see nor walk the true way, harden their hearts, and will not acknowledge the just judgment of the wrath and displeasure of God, his mercy and favor and his unbounded grace, are unbelievers; for they reject Christ Jesus, run haughtily into perverse ways; they choose to themselves a righteousness and means of salvation contrary to the word of God; the wisdom of the Lord they esteem foolishness; his truth as lies; his gospel as delusion; the virtuous, christian life as madness; and the true use of his sacraments, as heresy. Open idolatry, commands of men, superstition and offensively ornamented lies, are their greatest consolation and true worship; their belly is their God; they love the world more than heaven; all their delight is in covetousness, avarice, pride, pomp, gold, silver, money and possessions; in buying and selling, they cheat and deal treacherously; their common life is drinking, gambling, cursing, swearing, hatred, strife and fighting; they follow the flesh in its lusts; they defame and seek

---

* Jer. 23: 5; Rev. 5: 5; Isa. 9: 5; John 1: 1; Col. 1: 15; John 12: 35; John 15: 1; 10: 2; 1 Cor. 3: 11; Isa. 28: 16; John 14: 6; Deut. 18: 18; John 3: 2; 15: 5; Tit. 2: 12; John 3: 29; 1 Tim. 2: 5; Eph. 1: 22.

FAITH.

the calamity of their neighbor, his dishonor, disgrace and shame. In short, they say, with the fool, in their hearts, "There is no God," Ps. 14: 1.

Although they boast of God with the mouth, praise his name with their lips, bow their knees outwardly before him, and say that they are redeemed with the death and blood of Christ; it is nevertheless vain hypocrisy, for they do it only from habit, and feignedly, and not inwardly through faith, in power and truth. They are those of whom it is written, "They profess that they know God, but in works they deny him; being abominable and disobedient, and unto every good work reprobate," Tit. 1: 16. And this, because they do not believe Christ and his word, their end is death, as he says, "He that believeth not shall be damned," yea, is already condemned.

It is true what Paul says, "Without faith it is impossible to please him (God); for he that cometh to God, must believe that he is, and that he is a rewarder of them that diligently seek him," Heb. 11: 6. O for an open heart! For profound understanding! Yea, if we rightly examine these words, we have reason to be astonished at the wisdom and understanding of Paul. For if we rightly reflect upon the matter, we must ever confess before the Lord, who tries our reins and hearts, that we never believed it with the heart, that God is, and hence, we have led a vain, ungodly life. For it cannot be otherwise; if any one believes with all his heart, that God is, he will also believe that his word is true, that the wages of sin is death, that all things are open to his eyes, and that there is nothing concealed before him. That we must give an account of all our thoughts, words and deeds, before his judgment seat in the day of his coming. Believing all this, we then begin to be astonished before such an omniscient and righteous Judge, yea, to fear and tremble greatly.

In the second place, all who believe with the heart, that God is, they also believe that he is true, and therefore, none can be saved contrary to his word; for he is the God of truth, and in him there are no lies. His uttered word abides, it can neither be bent nor broken; those who thus believe, begin to fear his righteous judgment; they cast behind them all their false patchwork, all false promises, all the bolsters and cushions of the false prophets, and they seek the Lord who has bought them. They are abased in their own eyes; for the heart is humbled. They sigh, weep, pray, lament, knock, and call at the throne of grace, till they are heard and encouraged by the word of his peace, comforted with the promise of his grace, and anointed with the Holy Ghost.

In the third place, all who believe that God is, also believe that he is gracious and merciful, that he has bestowed and sent us his only Son, that he taught us the right way, fulfilled the law for us, reconciled us to the Father, and redeemed us by his blood and bitter death; has conquered hell, the devil, sin and death, and obtained for us grace, favor, mercy, and eternal life, &c., and therefore, the sorrowful, afflicted hearts, which saw through the terrible, threatening law, nothing but the wrath of God and eternal death are again revived. They become candid, peaceable, and joyful in the Holy Ghost, are of a joyful disposition, and are thus made to belong to their Head and Savior, are united and made one with Him, ingrafted through the Spirit of God and pure, unfeigned love, that they are of one heart, one soul and spirit with him; they think, speak and live in their weakness as he has taught and commanded them in his word. They renounce and avoid all false doctrine, unbelief, false sacraments, and all idolatry; put off the spotted garment of sin, which is the evil perverted life, and is of the flesh. They seek the doctrines and sacraments commanded them of Christ; that divine service which is taught in the Scriptures, and that pious and unblamable life which is from God. For by faith they are changed in the inner man, converted and renewed, because they have a sealed, and assured conscience, which bears witness to them that God is, that he is righteous and true, gracious and of abundant mercy. And therefore they desire, seek and do nothing, either inwardly or outwardly, but that which they know, through the word, that Christ Jesus, with his holy apostles has commanded and taught them.

Behold, my brethren, here you have now

the true properties and nature of a true christian faith, and what a great mystery, signification, spirit and power are contained summarily in these words, *He must believe that God is.* "Whosoever believeth in him should not perish, but have eternal life," John 3: 15; "He that believeth and is baptized shall be saved," Mark 16: 16; "Whosoever believeth on him shall not be ashamed," Rom. 10, and the like passages. For it will always be the case where there is a true, christian faith, there also will be a dying to sin, a new creature, true repentance, a sincere, regenerated and unblamable christian. One does no longer live according to the lusts of sin, but according to the will of him who purchased us with his blood, drew us by his Spirit, and regenerated us by his word, namely, Christ Jesus.

But where there is only nominal faith, and no righteousness, or change, or new and penitent life, there is nothing but unbelief, hypocrisy and lies. No matter how much we may speak, or dispute about the Scriptures, this rule will remain firm, and can never be broken. "*If ye live after the flesh, ye shall die,*" Rom. 8: 13. All therefore, who live in pomp and splendor, in excessive eating and drinking, adultery, fornication, avarice, hatred, envy, lasciviousness, defrauding and such sins; all who defame the Lord's holy and high name, word, will, and also his community, slander and traduce their neighbor; deprive him of his honor, name, welfare, body and goods; and all who curse and swear by the Lord's sufferings, wounds, sacraments, cross and death, are unbelieving heathens, and not believing christians. This is as clear as the light of day, for their fruits testify before the whole world, that they are not the true olive tree and vine from which we may pluck or gather the true, ripe fruits; for, that they comfort themselves with the doctrines and commands of men, use a strange baptism, Lord's supper and divine worship, which Christ has not taught; seek the remission of sins by foreign means; such as holy waters, masses, auricular confessions, pilgrimages, &c., walk in a perverted, crooked path, believe not Christ and his word, all must confess who have only natural discernment and understanding. All who acknowledge Christ to be the Son of God, and his word as the truth, acknowledge that his commands are eternal life, and that they seek no other worship, word, sacraments, or means of reconciliation, nor another way of life than that which Christ, God's own Son, presented and taught them by the word of his truth.

Hence it is evident, that where sincere and true faith is, which avails before God, which is a gift from him, and comes from hearing the holy word, through the blossoming tree of life, full of all manner of precious fruits of righteousness, such as the fear and love of God, mercy, friendship, chastity, temperance, humility, candor, truth, peace and joy in the Holy Ghost, &c., there is a sincere, evangelical, pious faith; there also are the sincere, gospel fruits of an evangelical nature.

I say gospel fruit, for the strange fruit, such as infant baptism, masses, matins, vespers, caps, palms, crosses, chapels, altars, bells, &c., know not the gospel, for they are neither commanded of God, nor of Jesus Christ, his Son, nor by the apostles and prophets, therefore, are they abominations and not believing fruits, even as the golden calf was with Israel, the worship of Baal, the high places, altars and churches, and the crime of making their children pass through the fire.

The true evangelical faith looks upon, and has respect to the doctrine, ceremonies, commands, prohibitions, and unblamable examples of Christ alone, and strives to conform thereto with all its powers, even as fire in its nature can produce nothing but combustion and flame; the sun, nothing but light and heat; the water causes moisture, and a good tree brings good fruit after its natural properties; and thus upright, evangelical faith produces true evangelical fruit, and that, after its true, good, evangelical nature; yea, even as an honest, virtuous bride, by the virtue and the nature of natural love, is ever ready to hear and obey the voice of her bridegroom; and from a sincere, pious disposition, favor and love which she has for and towards him, will ever so conduct herself, before her most faithful friend and beloved husband, whom she respects and loves with all her heart, that for his sake she voluntarily endures what ever may befall her; even also it is with a sincere, regenerated believer, who has been joined to Christ, by grace through faith; he has become one with Christ through this ardent love, that he is ever willing and prepared to do his bidding and will, to endure all things for the sake of the holy name of Jesus, in evil as well as in good report. Eager to endure all things that may befall him at any time, be it joy or tribulation, satiation or hunger, refreshing or thirst, honor or dishonor, in good or bad report, in prison or at liberty, in exile or at home, ease or discomfort, life or death. Such a soul partakes of her bridegroom's nature and disposition, is pious in heart and thought; true in words and well seasoned; all her ways are righteousness, devoutness; wise as the serpent; harmless as the dove; a genuinely pious disposition, fidelity, zeal, peace, fervent prayer, an unblamable conduct, a sincere, pure, brotherly love, and a voluntary obedience to Christ and his holy word; for the righteous live by faith, as we shall incontrovertibly and plainly show, by the grace of God, in the following examples, recorded and testified to in the holy Scriptures, Amen.

NOAH'S FAITH.

The holy Scriptures testify concerning Noah, the son of Lamech, that he found grace before the Lord, because he was a righteous man, unwavering and perfect in his generation. Peter calls him a preacher of righteousness. High and glorious is the testimony, which is given in the Scriptures concerning this man.

When all the world was depraved before God, and the face of all the earth was full of wickedness, the sons of God saw the daughters of men that they were fair, and they took them wives of all whom they chose, and would not suffer themselves to be reproved by the Spirit of God; then spake the Lord, I will yet give them respite for a hundred and twenty years; he also gave Noah a command, that he should make a ship or ark, by which he and his house might be saved from the coming flood, for God the Lord was about to destroy the whole world with water. Noah believed the word of the Lord with all his heart, and kept it in his mind, as if he saw it before him with his eyes. He commenced building as he had been commanded, for he believed with his whole heart, that the threatened punishment would come. And when the appointed year was completed, and the disobedient, wicked world repented not, the word of the Lord must be accomplished. Noah went into the ark with all clean and unclean creatures as the Lord commanded him. The same day that he entered the ark, the fountains of the great deep were broken up, and the windows of heaven were opened, and it rained forty days and forty nights, till all the high mountains upon the face of the whole earth were covered; fifteen cubits upward did the waters prevail; and all creatures upon the earth that had in them the breath of life, as men, birds, beasts and worms were destroyed. Noah and his family, together with the animals which were with him in the ark, were preserved in the ark by the power and grace of Almighty God, in whom Noah trusted with all his heart.

Through faith, saith Paul, Noah honored God, and prepared the ark for the salvation of his house, according to the divine command which was not yet seen, through which he condemned the world, and became an inheriter of the righteousness which is by faith.

Oh! lovely example, O glorious pattern of a sure and firm faith. For, as he believed his God, so was he upright and unwavering. He believed the threatened punishment firmly, as if he saw it before his eyes, and therefore he labored so many years, and, through the eternal Spirit of Christ, he warned the unbelieving, disobedient spirits, or men led captive by sin, to repent and reform. He feared the word of the Lord, and doubted not that it would happen as the Lord had spoken. He well knew that the word of the Lord was powerful, as the prophet said, "O Lord, thou spakest from the beginning of the creation, and saidst thus, Let heaven and earth be made; and thy word was a perfect work," 2 Esdras 6: 38.

And when he had preached and built forty, eighty or a hundred years (the Scriptures do not say how long he built and taught), he did not become weak in faith by long delay, for he well knew that the punishment of God would come upon the unconverted, because he had formerly so told him, and that he, and his would be preserved through the mercy and grace of him who promised, for he is the God of truth, and no lie is found in him.

The Lord God warned the pious Noah, and said, "The end of all flesh is come before me, for the earth is filled with violence through them, and behold, I will destroy them with the earth," Gen. 6: 13. So also hath he through his own blessed Son, through his holy prophets and apostles, with his holy word, truthfully warned us and said, If you repent not, be not born of God, believe not in Christ, walk not in his commandments, reform not your wicked lives, but serve strange Gods, be haughty, proud, ambitious, lustful, blood-thirsty, malicious, unjust, idle, earthly, fleshly, and devilish, you will die in your sins, and shall not enter into the kingdom of heaven, shall be condemned, shall be cast into the fiery pool, must inherit eternal woe and pain, with all the accursed, and with devils, and have no part nor communion in the kingdom of Christ, to all eternity.

My readers, take heed, if we, with the upright and godly Noah, observe the faithful warnings of Christ and his Holy Spirit, and believe with the whole heart; believe the word of God to be true and immutable, the threatened punishment will come in its time, even though it should be delayed a thousand years; yet, I advise that every one watch, for all who die in their sins, receive their punishment, for the time of grace is then expired; then we would undoubtedly fear and tremble to the inmost of our souls, at the wrath and punishment, threatened in the Scriptures to all the impenitent which will be eternal in its duration; we would pray to God for grace, would clothe ourselves in sackcloth and mourning garments, would truly repent, reform the wicked life, follow after righteousness, and with our new and spiritual Noah, Christ Jesus, enter into the new and spiritual ark, which is his church; ever being careful and fearful that the deluge of the coming wrath of God, will not unexpectedly overtake us with all the unbelieving and impenitent, who acknowledge neither God nor Christ, neither Spirit nor word, as it overtook the corrupt antediluvian world as mentioned; yea, we would sincerely watch for the coming of the Lord, and give heed to the time of grace, preserve our wedding garment, and have oil in our lamps, that our house be not unseasonably broken through, and we with the guest, who had not on a wedding garment, be cast forth from the Lord's wedding, into outer darkness and abide eternally without.

Because alas, we do not believe the threats, punishments, wrath and judgments of the Lord, and have little regard for the examples of Scripture, therefore, we say with the mockers, Beloved, where is the promise of his coming? All things abide as they were from the beginning since the fathers fell asleep. It will, I fear, happen with us as it did with the unbelievers and disobedient who were overtaken with sudden destruction in the time of Noah and Lot, as one may plainly see and read concerning the coming of the Lord, Matt. 24; Luke 17; because we do not believe the threats, judgments, and wrath of the Lord, but disregard them, therefore do we lead such a reckless, unbridled life, follow the lusts of the flesh, eat, drink, build, sow, reap and marry without any fear or care, and avariciously hoard up gold, silver and possessions, and haughtily say in our hearts there is peace and liberty, till swift destruction shall overtake us.

Again, let every one look well and watch. The messenger, with his peremptory summons is already at the door, who will say, Render an account; thou mayest be no longer steward. But could we, with the unwavering and pious Noah, firmly believe the coming eternal wrath and punishment, also the promises through Christ, to all true children of God, we would, undoubtedly, not be found so inattentive, drowsy and indifferent, but with full earnestness without delay, rise from our abominable sin, separate ourselves from our grievous errors, and shun wickedness as we would a hungry, roaring lion, or a blood-thirsty enemy; we should also watch with open eyes all our days, lest the Master of the house overtake us when we sleep and regard us not. Let us not strike our fellow servants; neither eat nor drink with gormandizers, that he may not give us our portion and lot with the hypocrites. Concerning this watching, read Matt. 24; Mark 13: 37.

ABRAHAM'S FAITH AND OBEDIENCE.

Abraham, the highly renowned patriarch, who had not his equal in honor, as Sirach writes, believed God and trusted upon his word with the whole heart, and thus manifested obedience and power as the result of his faith. The Lord commanded him and said, "Get thee out of thy country, and from thy kindred, and from thy father's house, unto a land that I will shew thee, and I will make of thee a great nation, and I will bless thee, and make thy name great, and thou shalt be a blessing, and I will bless them that bless thee, and curse him that curseth thee, and in thee shall all families of the earth be blessed," Gen. 12: 1—3. When he heard the command, he believed his God and consulted not the ease of his body nor his natural reason, but renounced both, and did not strive nor dispute with God, in whom he trusted and by whose command he went forth; he did not desire to know before hand into what land he should go. He believed his God with his whole heart, he was obedient and went forth at that hour, together with Sarai, his wife, not knowing where he should go. He reposed firmly and surely upon the promise of God, who would not deceive nor betray him, for he well knew that he was a God who was true and firm in all his words, and that he would bring him into such a country as he had promised him.

Behold, how upright and perfect, how plain, obedient, and full of confidence is true, christian faith, as may be seen in this patriarch. Compare your faith and its fruits with Abraham's faith and its fruits, and I presume you will find that you have never yet become his faithful seed and children; for it is manifest that you are stubborn and unbelieving, so fleshly and earthly minded that you would not give a clay house, a poor bed, a cow or a horse, nor would you endure a hard word for the sake of the word of the Lord, and his testimony; and I doubt whether you would forsake father or mother, or the land of your birth, for the sake of your faith, and like Abraham, travel with wife and children to an unknown land. Cursed unbelief keeps off the whole world from the truth; for many of you say, We well know that you have the truth, but what does it avail? We are poor and full of years, we cannot longer labor or earn; we have a house full of children and cannot earn our bread in other lands; we fear, also, that the Lord may not have such a care for us as he had for Abraham; others, say we, have much wealth, we are young in years, and may live long, yet father and mother hinder us. The wife says, my husband opposes me; the husband says, my wife is against me, and the like unbelieving fleshly excuses and cares. They never take to heart, nor understand, that Christ has richly promised you, that if you abide by his word, you shall receive all the necessaries of the earth, as food, clothing, and shelter. "I have been young, and now I am old; yet have I not seen the righteous forsaken, nor his seed begging bread," Ps. 37: 25.

Faithful readers, observe, if we had a firm faith and a sure confidence, like this godly man, and dare trust from the heart upon the living God, O how little should we trouble ourselves with such heathenish cares, concerning dwelling, eating, drinking, and clothing, for we well know, that Christ,

God's own Son, has promised that if we seek the kingdom of heaven, and his righteousness, and turn our hearts to some honest labor, he will not forsake us to all eternity, but will supply all our necessities, for he cares for us.

Secondly, observe his faith, when a message came to Abraham, that Lot, his brother's son, was taken to Sodom by Chedorlaomer, the king of Elam, and his confederate kings, Abraham rose up with three hundred and eighteen of his servants and followed after the aforementioned kings; he overtook them in the night and slew them and re-took all their goods, together with Lot, the prisoners and their wives, Gen. 14: 16.

Here the faithful patriarch manifested his love, the result of faith, and feared not the power of the four kings. He trusted in the living God, he sought not his own safety, nor the safety of his servants, but willingly risked all, in order that he might rescue his oppressed kinsman from the hands of his enemies, as an example for all the spiritual children of Abraham, that they should so love their brethren who are born of the incorruptible seed of the holy divine word, and not only assist them with money and goods, but also in an evangelical manner, risk and give their lives for them in time of need. I say in an evangelical manner; for the aid of the sword is forbidden to all true christians. According to the New Testament, all true believers should meekly suffer, and not fight and combat with swords and firearms. But if we wish to save or gain our neighbor's soul, by the help of the Spirit and word of our Lord, or if we see our brethren in need or peril, and persecuted for the sake of the word of the Lord, then we should not close our doors to them, but receive them in our houses, share with them our food, aid, comfort and assist them in their tribulations, &c. In such cases, we should risk our lives for our brethren, even if we knew beforehand that it would be at the cost of our lives. This example we have of Christ, who for our sakes, did not spare himself, but willingly yielded his life, that we through him, might live.

In the third place, observe, that to Abraham the promise was given, that his seed should be as numerous as the stars of heaven; that they should be strangers in another land that was not theirs, and that they should be oppressed and compelled to serve four hundred years, &c. When this promise was made he believed; he believed this, and his belief was reckoned to him for righteousness. He waited with patience, and it was fulfilled in its time; he murmured not, nor disputed with God, because his seed should suffer so greatly for so many years. An admonition to all true christians that they should cleave to the word of the Lord, with all the heart, and should hold firmly to his promise; for God cannot forget or break his word; heaven and earth shall pass away, but his word shall stand and abide forever. All who shall trust in it, to them it shall be reckoned as righteousness, as it was to Abraham. Through faith he saw the promise from afar; he saw it, and comforted himself therewith. In like manner also with us, the promise of the future, eternal life, is given through Christ, and we are informed that for his name's sake, we must suffer much from this perverted and wicked generation. This promise is seen from afar, and all who sincerely believe it and comfort themselves therewith, will doubtlessly receive it in due time, however hard and long they may be persecuted and tormented by the evil Egyptian race. For, although the children of Abraham were grieved with much sorrow and pain for some hundreds of years, yet did the Lord, according to his promise, lead them forth victoriously, and gave them the land of promise; and thus it will be with us if we doubt not the promises, but receive them with a firm faith, as Abraham did, and through faith walk in all the commandments of God, possess our souls in patience and honor, fear, love, thank and serve the Lord. How lamentably soever, we are here persecuted, oppressed, smitten, robbed and murdered by the hellish Pharaoh, and his fierce, unmerciful servants, or burned at the stake, or drowned in the water, yet shall the day of our salvation arrive, and all our tears shall be wiped from our eyes, and we shall be arrayed in the white silken robes of righteousness, and with Abraham, Isaac and Jacob, follow the Lamb, and sit down in the kingdom of God and possess the precious, pleasant land of

FAITH.

eternal peace. Praise God, ye who suffer for Christ's sake and raise your heads, for the time is near when you shall hear, Come ye blessed, and ye shall rejoice with him forever.

In the fourth place, observe, that Abraham received a command from God, that he and also his male children of eight days old, should be circumcised, with all his servants, those who were born in his house, and those who were bought, and this should be a covenant sign between God and him. He was not disobedient to God, nor yet displeased with him, neither did he complain nor murmur against him on account of the great pain and smarting he should suffer in his old age, by performing such a dishonorable and ridiculous ceremony, whereby he could neither praise God, nor help or serve his neighbor, but he heard and believed the word of the Lord, and humbly and submissively followed it without delay. He well knew, that unless he would believe the word of God, he could obtain no grace, no blessing, no promise, for only the obedient obtain the promise.

Here again the simple, plain submission, and willing obedience of Abraham's faith, are made manifest by its fruits; for if he had followed flesh and blood, and reasoned with himself, he undoubtedly would not have obeyed, but he would have entered into argument with God, and said, No, Lord, it shall not be so, for this sign will profit me nothing, for Thou art not praised thereby nor my neighbor served. All the heathen who know not thy great name will mock at it as foolishness, from the very nature of the ceremony. O no! He spake not against the Lord, but he believed and acted, and it was reckoned to him for righteousness, and he was called the friend of God.

This is for the encouragement of all the pious, that they should believe, and submissively follow the word of the Lord, however heretical and ridiculous it may appear to them, not murmuring against the Lord why he so commanded it; but it is enough that they know that he has commanded, and in what manner he has commanded.

Again, it shames all haughty despisers and unbelieving mockers, who so presumptuously open their blasphemous, wicked mouths against Christ, and say, What can baptism profit us, or why does God demand so much water? It is enough, if we are inwardly pious men, regard the commands of love, and lead a pious, virtuous life, and such like hypocritical words; for these poor miserable hypocrites know not when the inward man, of which they boast, has become upright through faith and pious in God, through the grace, word, and Spirit of the Lord, that he dare not depart one hair's breadth from the word and ways of the Lord, but does willingly all things whatsoever the Lord has commanded him, let it be what it will.

It is very manifest that Christ Jesus has commanded water baptism, upon the confession of our faith, and that he received it himself, Matt. 3: 16. The holy apostles did not teach nor practice otherwise; their signification and effect were not otherwise, and so many glorious promises depend thereon, as may plainly be seen and read, Mark 16: 15 (understand me rightly), not by virtue of the wrought sign itself, but that we receive Christ, in whom the Father gave the promise through faith, and are ready to live according to his word. Say, beloved, how shall one obtain the accompanying promise if he does not do what is commanded? But what does it avail all who believe not the Lord's word, who would rather have money, goods, body and life, than Christ? They are earthly and fleshly minded, they strive against Christ, disobey the Scriptures, dispute and say, What can water benefit us? But if they believed the word of the Lord from the heart, as Abraham did, and were new and changed men in Christ Jesus, through the power of the same faith, they would love their enemies, do good for evil, pray for those by whom they are persecuted, be ready to forsake possessions and all that they have and are for the glory of the Lord, and for the necessary service of their neighbor. They would not reject the cross of the Lord, but flesh and blood would be mortified; they would fear God and his judgments, and love him, for his kindness; they would undoubtedly not murmur and dispute, but stand prepared, like Abraham, to seal their faith by its fruits; they would receive the commanded baptism, surrender themselves to all obedience, and according to their weakness, walk as the Lord commands, teaches and enjoins upon all true Christians.

Since they believe not Christ and his word, they neither fear nor love him; therefore they reject, upbraid and blaspheme his holy doctrine, Spirit, commandments, prohibitions, ordinances and usages as deceiving heresy, and obedience to him as an open abomination. O reader, beware! God, the Lord, is a God who adheres to his word; he brought calamity upon Adam and Eve and their posterity on account of the forbidden fruit. For a small transgression Uzzah was punished with death, 2 Sam. 6: 7. On account of one transgression, the faithful Moses was not permitted to enter the promised land. Whoever received not the bloody sign of circumcision, was to be cut off from among the people. Therefore, it must be plainly understood, that his word and will must be obeyed, otherwise we cannot be saved, for he is the God who has made heaven and earth and the fullness thereof; the Almighty, terrible God, who lives forever in his majesty and glory; the Lord and Ruler over all. Woe to him who speaks against him and despises his word and will. The works of such an one testify that he believes not in Christ, and whosoever believeth not, as Christ himself declares, is condemned already. Therefore, it is all in vain to excuse ourselves or seek evasion. How any one who is so unbelieving and rebellious, that he refuses God a handful of water, can conform himself to love his enemies, mortify the flesh to the service of his neighbor, and to take up the cross of Christ, I will leave the serious reader to reflect upon, in the fear of God.

I know for certain, that all their disputation, pretentions and evasions are nothing but fig leaves, and their lives, nothing but hypocrisy.

In the fifth place observe, when the Lord had spoken to Abraham, that at the end of the year he would return, and that Sarah, his wife, should have a son, whom he should call Isaac, and that he would make his eternal covenant with him and his seed after him; though he was nearly a hundred years old, and Sarah ninety, nevertheless, he doubted not. He did not think upon, or regard his own frailty and the barrenness of Sarah, but firm and strong in faith, he trusted upon the promise of his God, and praised him for his grace; for he knew that God was able to perform that which he had promised. Therefore, from this same Abraham, because he believed the word of the Lord, descended as many as the sand which is upon the sea shore or the stars of heaven, Gen. 22: 17.

Behold, most beloved, how an upright, unfeigned, christian faith regards God as almighty and true; it knows that he can and will do all that he has promised, and therefore, Abraham looked not upon the frailty and age of himself and Sarah. He doubted not the promised words, but believed without wavering, for he knew well, that the same God who created heaven and earth, and the fullness thereof through his word, who stretched the heavens abroad, and to the stormy, raging sea set an established bound, whose word sustains the earth in the midst of the water, who rules all with the word of his strength, and gives life to the dead, could undoubtedly, when he chose, render that fruitful, which before was barren.

Since then, such a promise was given to him of God, he doubted not, but hoped for that, which in nature, was not to be expected. Through faith in God, he received that which was promised to him, namely his son Isaac, through the aged and barren Sarah; so in like manner it is spiritually with us; if we believe, with the whole heart, the promised word of grace, which is the gospel of peace, whereby the redemption from our sins, through the blood of the Lord, is made known; so will also our dead conscience flourish and live; we shall receive the spiritual Isaac, Christ Jesus, with the eternal blessing, and bring forth fruit. Christ said, My mother and my brethren are those, who hear the word and will of God, and do accordingly; but whosoever believeth not this Isaac, receives not Christ, but the wrath of God abides upon him.

In the sixth place observe, how severely the Lord tried the faith of Abraham, when he said, "Take now thy son, thine only son, Isaac, whom thou lovest, and get thee into the land of Moriah, and offer him there for a burnt offering upon one of the mountains which I will tell thee of," Gen. 22: 2. Abraham heard the word of the Lord and was obedient. He took his son with him and went to the place, which the Lord had commanded him; and when he came there, Isaac said, Father, behold here is fire and wood, but where is the lamb that shall be offered? Abraham answered his son, and said, "My son, God will provide himself a lamb for a burnt-offering."

O my most beloved, reflect! Observe the conduct and conversation of Abraham and his son Isaac. I suppose reason will teach you how full of trouble and grief the mind of the father was on account of his beloved son, for Abraham was flesh and blood as we are. That son, who was born to him in his old age, through the promise and gift of God, his only son born of a free woman, the desire, the joy and the peace of his heart, the staff of his age, through whom he received the comforting promise, must be slain and burned with fire.

How hard and sorely he was tried, yet did he not oppose God with a single word, nor contend and say, Why hast thou given me a son since he must die? Neither did he reprove the Lord, by saying, that he had falsified his promise, for it was through Isaac that the promise was made, but he confided in his God with his whole heart; he laid aside all reasoning and wisdom, and followed not sense nor flesh. He spared not his beloved son for the Lord's sake. He loved his God far above his child, and therefore he refused not to offer him willingly as a burnt offering to Him from whom he received him. He bound him and lifted him upon the wood, and raised his hand and knife to slay him; he believed that God could again raise him from the dead. He was about to obey the command which he had received, when an angel spake from Heaven, saying, "Lay not thine hand upon the lad, neither do thou any thing unto him, for now I know that thou fearest God; seeing thou hast not withheld thy son, thine only son from me," Gen. 22: 12. And thus the obedient, faithful Abraham received his son as a type of the resurrection. The word of James is true, "Abraham believed God, and it was imputed unto him for righteousness, and he was called the friend of God," James 2: 23.

Beloved children, we must always stand confounded before God, when we compare our little, weak faith and its fruit with the faith of Abraham. He refused not to travel in an unknown country, as soon as he was commanded. He was a man full of peace, and sought not his own interest. He released Lot out of the hands of his enemies. He believed the promise concerning the promised land and seed. He murmured not on account of the long time nor of the oppression of his seed. He suffered himself to be circumcised in advanced age. He believed the Lord's promise concerning Isaac, and taught all his servants and children, that they should follow the way of the Lord, and do that which was right. He was willing to offer Isaac as the Lord had commanded him. This may truly be called faith.

So entirely was this pious man dead to himself, that he denied all his lusts, his will and mind, and loved his God alone. He trusted, feared, loved and honored his God, with all his soul and heart, and walked according to his commandments, as is evidenced by his fruits, as may be observed and understood from many passages of Scripture. But what kind of faith our false, boasting christians possess, who suffer themselves to think that they are the seed of Abraham, I will let their fruits be the judge; for they covet and hoard, curse and swear, lie and cheat; they are haughty and proud, eat and drink intemperately, commit fornication and adultery, fight, rob, steal, take usury, and are full of idolatry and wickedness. Those who have a little light refuse to remove from one village to another, or from one city to another, for the word and truth of the Lord; they seek their own interests, and esteem brotherly love but lightly; they are earthly minded, and flee from the cross of Christ; they regard not the promise and goodness of the Lord; they fear not his coming judgment, and punishment; they love the creature more than the Creator; his name be blessed forever, Amen.

In short, I know not what it is, in which they do not serve themselves, nor act contrary to the command of God. They boast notwithstanding, that they are the children of Abraham, and have his promise. Ah no! my friends, your prophets have led you astray, and your false hopes deceive you; as true as the Lord lives, if you believe not his word, from the whole heart, nor through the power of the same faith, walk in his ways, bring not forth the christian fruits of righteousness, and do not follow the footsteps of this pious patriarch; you are not his seed and children, neither have you his faith nor his promise. But all who receive Christ in their hearts, through faith, and adhere strictly to his word and obey it, are the spiritual children of Abraham, and fellow heirs of his promise, for they are reckoned his seed.

FAITH AND FIDELITY OF MOSES.

Moses, a servant and messenger of God, was also found faithful, vigorous, living and active in his faith. He was called of the Lord, that he should lead Israel out of Egypt. He did not exalt himself to the high station of a prince, but humbled himself before God with all his heart, and said, Send, Lord, whom thou wilt, but what am I, that I should go to Pharaoh and lead forth Israel? Besides, I am not eloquent, neither heretofore, nor since thou hast spoken unto thy servant, but am of a slow tongue. He refused so long, that the Lord was angry. With fear and trembling, he at last took upon himself the commanded duty, and surrendered himself to his God, in whom he trusted.

He went willingly before the fierce Pharaoh, and showed great wonders and power before him and all his servants. He ransomed the people, through the out-stretched arm and strong hand of God. He divided the Red Sea and passed with Israel, unharmed, through the deep, Exod. 14: 21, 22. He received the tables of stone on which were written the commandments of the Lord. He caused bread to rain from heaven, and water to flow from the flinty rock. He prepared the tents and the ark of the testimony, as he was directed upon the mountains. He ordained the figurative priesthood, with all the duties, offerings, sanctifications, apparel, &c., according to the command of the Lord.

He went with the people, pitched the tents, and took them up again at the command of the Lord. He gave them the commands and statutes of the Lord. He stood as a faithful mediator between God and the people, when they had sinned, and he turned the wrath from Israel. He punished idolaters, whoremongers and the rebellious. He slew Sihon, king of the Amorites, and Og, king of Bashan. The Lord was with him in all his ways.

By faith, says Paul, "He refused to be called the son of Pharaoh's daughter, choosing rather to suffer affliction with the people of God, than to enjoy the pleasures of sin for a season, esteeming the reproach of Christ greater riches than the treasure in Egypt, for he had respect unto the recompense of the reward; by faith he forsook Egypt, not fearing the wrath of the king, for he endured, as seeing him who is invisible. Through faith he kept the passover, and the sprinkling of blood, lest he that destroyed the first born should touch them," Heb. 11: 24—28.

Kind reader, respect the word of the Lord, for when we look spiritually upon such holy examples and contrast them with the insupportable pride, haughtiness, avarice, idolatry, disobedience and unfaithfulness of the prince of the world, and with the blind, mad unbelief of the common people, then we must acknowledge that they are far from the obedience and active faith of Moses. Yea, they are unbelieving heathens, and not Christians.

Moses believed his God and acted rightly in all his transactions. He was kind, and solicitous for the welfare of the people under his care, as he was commanded. He was the meekest of men; served neither for gift nor reward, but obeyed the voice and word of the Lord; was faithful in all his house, and faithfully prosecuted his duties in the fear of the Lord. He faithfully commanded out of the mouth of God, and in upright love, faithfully admonished the people, that they and their descendants, from generation to generation, should hear and be obedient to the voice of the Lord God of their fathers, and should follow no other customs, commandments, righteousness or worship, than that which he had taught or commanded them, till the new prophet, the teacher of righteousness, the blessed seed of Abraham, Christ Jesus, should come.

But if we would go to our rulers, princes, lords, bishops, priests, monks and preachers, and all those who boast of the name and faith of Christ; if we would rightly measure their faith and obedience with the word of the Lord, which is the true standard, and should find some who sincerely seek Christ from the heart, fear, love, believe and trust him; who teach and practice rightly the ordinances, commands, sacraments and true worship of God; who conform their whole lives both inwardly and outwardly, according to the word and example of the Lord; and who, in love, execute the service which is enjoined on them, as this faithful Moses has done in all his transactions, I fear they are so few that we should have to go far and search long to find them, and if there are still some, they must be, alas, given as a prey to the bloodthirsty, and bear the cross of the Lord.

I testify to you the truth in Christ, and lie not. All who hear not the voice of Christ, believe not his holy word, follow not his pure unblamable life, from the whole heart, in all humility, patience, meekness, obedience and love; have not the working and living faith of Moses, but are, after the contents of his doctrines, already judged. O, reader, beware! neither money, name, nor boasting will avail you, but power and deeds, if you wish to be saved, and not be condemned.

THE FAITH OF CALEB AND JOSHUA.

Joshua and Caleb, through faith, passed over Jordan and entered the promised land. When Moses sent out the twelve spies to view and explore the country, he said, "Get you up this way southward, and go up into the mountain, and see the land what it is, and the people that dwelleth therein, whether they be strong or weak, few or many; and what the land is that they dwell in, whether it be good or bad, and what cities they be that they dwell in, whether in tents or in strong holds, and what the land is, whether it be fat or lean, whether there be wood therein or not; and be ye of good courage, and bring of the fruit of the land. Now the time was the time of the first-ripe grapes," Num. 13: 17—20.

They went up and viewed the land, even as Moses had commanded them by the mouth of the Lord, and after forty days they came to Moses and Aaron, and to the whole congregation in the wilderness of Paran to Kadesh, carrying with them grapes, pomegranates and figs, saying, "We came unto the land whither thou sentest us, and surely it floweth with milk and honey, and this is the fruit of it. Moreover, we saw the children of Anak there. And Caleb stilled the people before Moses, and said, Let us go up at once and possess it; for we are well able to overcome it. But the men that went up with him said, we be not able to go up against the people, for they are stronger than we. And they brought up an evil report of the land which they had searched unto the children of Israel, saying, The land through which we have gone to search it, is a land that eateth up the inhabitants thereof, and all the people that we saw in it are men of great stature; and there we saw the giants, the sons of Anak, which come of the giants; and we were in our own sight as grasshoppers, and so we were in their sight," Num. 13: 27—33.

"And all the congregation lifted up their voice and cried; and the people wept that night, and all the children of Israel murmured against Moses and against Aaron; and the whole congregation said unto them, Would to God that we had died in the land of Egypt, or would to God we had died in the wilderness, and wherefore hath the Lord brought us unto this land, to fall by the sword, that our wives and our children should be a prey? Were it not better for us to return into Egypt? And they said one to another, Let us make a captain, and let us return into Egypt. Then Moses and Aaron fell on their faces before all the assembly of the congregation of the children of Israel. And Joshua and Caleb rent their clothes; and they spake unto all the company of the children of Israel, saying, the land which we passed through to search it, is an exceeding good land. If the Lord delight in us, then he will bring us into this land and give it us; a land which floweth with milk and honey. Only rebel not ye against the Lord, neither fear ye the people of the land, for they are bread for us; their defence is departed from them, and the Lord is with us; fear them not. But all the congregation bade, stone them with stones," Num. 14: 1—10.

Behold, dear reader, it is because these two faithful men believed the word and promise of God, with all their hearts, that they trusted firmly in his Almighty power, paternal mercy and great works, as if they had already obtained them. They saw the heinous unbelief and heard the bitter murmuring of their brethren, that they thereby detracted from the Almighty Majesty, as if he were not able to fulfil his promises unto them, and that he had deceived them by his enticing words, therefore, they were very sorrowful and sad, and rent their clothes, as has been said. And therefore they were the only two persons of six hundred thousand, that came with Moses out of Egypt, who entered into the promised land. All the rest died in the wilderness during the time of forty years, and they did not reach the promised land, because they did not believe on the Almighty God, the God of their fathers, Abraham, Isaac and Jacob, who with such unheard-of signs and wonders, led them through the Red Sea, and so graciously upheld and guarded them in the wilderness.

Thus, alas, it is with some at the present day. They have spied the pleasant land, have seen and tasted its precious fruits, have been enlightened by the word of the Lord, have tasted the heavenly gifts, have partaken of the Holy Ghost, have tasted of the sweet word of God, and the power of the world to come, and have beheld the grace of the Lord, but since they do not consult God, but their own sinful, disobedient, evil flesh, which always seeks its own pleasure, and will not willingly bear the cross of the Lord. They behold with carnal eyes, and see that so many powerful tyrants and fenced cities are arrayed against them, that they have to pass a howling wilderness, and must ascend many high mountains; that they must give as a prey, honor, money, possessions, wife, children, body and life; hence they murmur against Moses and Aaron, and seek to stone Joshua and Caleb. They cause their poor teachers and leaders, who with true love direct to the word and examples of Christ, and preach the pure truth, such intolerable suffering. They backbite and defame them beyond measure, and choose for themselves, here and there a captain, false prophet or teacher, who, with fair words and under the appearance of good, lead them back to Egypt. They prefer temporal to eternal things, they fear perishing man more than the immortal, eternal God, the Lord and Creator of the world. With unbelieving, carnal Israel, they say in their hearts, We are not strong enough to go up against this great and strong people, and are not able to obey the doctrine, ordinances and example of Christ, for all the world is against us, all lords and princes persecute us, the preachers and priests upbraid and defame us, and we must become a by-word and a derision to all the world. We are much too weak to bear such great misery, therefore they want to transfer it to the Lord. Thus you think and err, for your unbelieving, carnal hearts have so blinded you, that you know not the righteous judgment of God, you hope not that a holy life shall be rewarded, and esteem not the honor of an unblamable soul.

Dear reader, take warning, for as true as the Lord lives, I tell you, that all those who thus cast aside the word of the Lord, again become unbelieving in God, and become so earthly and carnal-minded that they fear those whom they ought not to fear; and fear not those whom they should fear; who think more of the perishable creatures, such as home, lands, gold, silver, wife, children, body and life, than of the everlasting God and his eternal kingdom, and have a greater desire to enjoy in peace, for a season, the dark Egypt of this ungodly world, than to inherit the pleasant fruitful land, in endless peace with God; such shall all fall in the wilderness, and unless they repent, shall never enter into his rest, Heb. 4: 1.

But those who, with Joshua and Caleb, hold firmly to the word of the Lord; who firmly believe on Christ, as the Scriptures direct; who are firmly assured in their hearts by the Holy Ghost, that God will not fail in a single word, but that he will fulfill, in its time, all that he has promised; who are not prevailed on by the gates of hell; who suffer not themselves to be deceived by the subtle lies and philosophy of the learned; who are not frightened by the tyranny of the blood-thirsty; who are not vanquished by carnal lusts; nor enchanted by the fine appearance of false prophets, but walk humbly in the King's highway; who follow Christ, their Shepherd and Leader, and judge all their ways by his Spirit, word, and unblamable example; who turn not aside, neither to the right hand, nor to the left; behold they are those who will victoriously enter the spiritual, promised land, the eternal rest and peace, God's eternal kingdom and glory, with all the saints and believers, and through grace, eternally inherit it with Christ, as Joshua and Caleb inherited the figurative land through faith, and with their children inherit it. O children believe. "All things," says Christ, "are possible to him that believeth," Mark 9: 23.

THE BELIEF OF THE PIOUS KING JOSIAH.

Josiah, an illustrious and pious king in all his works, did that which was pleasing to the Lord, and walked in all the ways of his father David, and departed not therefrom, neither to the right hand nor to the left. And when he was yet a child he began to seek the God of David, his father. And in the eighteenth year of his age he sent Shaphan, his scribe, to Hilkiah the high priest, that money might be given to those who worked at the house of the Lord. And Hilkiah said to Shaphan, I have found the book of the Law in the house of the Lord, and Hilkiah gave the book to Shaphan and he brought it to the king. And when the king heard the words of the law, which were written in the book, he rent his clothes, as one who feared his God. He believed the word of the Lord, and feared the coming wrath which he threatened in the book which was found. He then commanded Hilkiah, Ahikam, Achbor, and Shaphan saying, "Go ye, inquire of the Lord for me, and for the people, and for all Judah, concerning the words of this book that is found, for great is the wrath of the Lord that is kindled against us, because our fathers have not hearkened unto the words of this book, to do according unto all that which is written concerning us," 2 Kings 22: 13.

So they went to Huldah, a prophetess, the wife of Shallum, and asked her as Josiah had commanded them; the woman answered them, "Thus saith the Lord God of Israel, Tell the men who hath sent you unto me, Thus saith the Lord, behold, I will bring evil upon this place, and upon the inhabitants thereof even all the words of the book which the king of Judah hath read, because they have forsaken me, and have burned incense unto other gods, that they might provoke me to anger, with all the works of their hands; therefore, my wrath shall be kindled against this place and shall not be quenched. But to the king of Judah, which sent you to inquire of the Lord, thus shall ye say to him, Thus saith the Lord God of Israel, as touching the words which thou hast heard, because thine heart was tender, and thou hast humbled thyself before the Lord, when thou heardest what I spake against this place and against the inhabitants thereof, that they should become a desolation and a curse, and hast rent thy clothes and wept before me, I also have heard thee, saith the Lord. Behold, therefore, I will gather thee unto thy fathers, and thou shalt be gathered into thy grave in peace, and thine eyes shall not see all the evil which I will bring upon this place, and they brought the king word again.

"When now the king heard these words, he sent and gathered unto him all the elders of Judah and Jerusalem. And the king went up into the house of the Lord, and all the men of Judah and all the inhabitants of Jerusalem with him, and the priests and the prophets, and all the people both small and great, and he read in their ears all the words of the book of the covenant, which was found in the house of the Lord. And the king stood by a pillar, and made a covenant before the Lord to walk after the Lord and to keep his commandments, and his testimonies, and his statutes with all their heart, and all their soul to perform the words of this covenant that were written in this book. And all the people stood to the covenant," 2 Kings 22: 15—20 and 23: 1—3. And Josiah caused all who were to be found in Israel to serve the Lord, and they departed not from him as long as Josiah lived.

Here, dear reader, observe what kind of faith Josiah had, and what the fruits thereof were. He heard the word of the Lord, and believed it. He rent his clothes, inquired of the Lord and renewed the covenant because he heard what God had commanded in the same book; that they should not do according to their own thoughts; that they should not follow after strange Gods, nor the abominations of the Canaanites and the other heathens which were dispersed before them, but they should serve the Lord alone and cleave to him, and keep his commands as he directed them. He was strong in the Lord, resolved in a manly spirit, and acted valiantly in all his doings, for he believed and trusted God with all his strength; and with earnest zeal, he tore down all that his forefathers and former kings, out of their own imaginings and choice, had brought in and established as holy service.

He burned all the vessels of Baal and tore down all the groves, high places and altars, in the land of Judea and Samaria. He defiled Topheth, which is in the valley of the children of Hinnom. He destroyed the horses of the sun, and burned the chariots of the sun with fire. He broke down the altar of Bethel and offered the idolatrous priests and the dead bones thereupon, as the man of God had proclaimed aforetime. He destroyed all that was opposed to the law of God. He kept the passover of the Lord as it was written in the book of the covenant, in such a glorious manner as no judge or king had kept it before. He also put away all sooth-sayers and wizards, images, idols, and all the abominations, that were spied in the land of Judah and in Jerusalem, that they might perform the words of the law which were written in the book that Hilkiah, the High priest found in the house of the Lord, and like unto him there was no king that turned to the Lord with all his heart and all his soul, and with all his might, according to all the law of Moses; neither after him arose there any like him, 2 Kings 23: 24, 25.

Hear now, O ye great princes and kings, and all those who suffer themselves to think that they are faithful lords and christian princes, to you is my admonition! Have you any fear of God? Any love to Christ or his blessed word? Or is there yet any sincerity of nature with you, who have understanding? Then know that you are not gods from heaven; but poor dying men of the impure guilty seed of Adam. Humble yourselves under the Almighty hand of God, and compare Josiah with his faith and works with your faith and works, in order that you may learn to know how far you are from the Spirit and word of Christ, and that you bear nothing else than a mere, idle, vain, empty name.

Whilst Josiah was yet a child, and young in years, he feared God, and manifested a mature mind and understanding in all his works; but you, my dear lords, fear neither God nor the devil. Cursed unbelief is your mother, and unrighteousness, your sister. In divine things you are blind, deaf and dumb; yea, during your whole lives, you are as destitute of understanding as children.

Josiah was eight years old when he was made king, and in the eighth year of his reign, he began to seek the God of his father David; but your seeking, from the cradle on, is solely pomp and splendor, haughtiness of heart, wantonness, riding, sporting, killing, enlargement of your dominions, increase of patronage and treasure, fighting, warring, taxing and usury; to afflict the destitute and poor; to domineer one over another, and to live, with all your might, openly, according to the lusts of the flesh. The open deed testifies that I write the truth.

Josiah began, in the twelfth year of his reign, to purify Judah and Jerusalem from the high places, groves, idolatry and molten images, but you build them in every city, village, street and alley; upon every high mountain and in every deep valley, and whoever would admonish you with the Spirit and word of Christ, must be a heretic and must tread the press of affliction.

Josiah was solicitous for the house of the Lord, and appointed and paid artificers to labor thereat. But you break down, and by your vindictive mandates, tyranny and the sword, oppose the house and dwelling of Christ, which is his church, which he has sanctified by his Spirit, cleansed by his blood, and adorned by the word, ordinances and sacraments of his Father. You prevent it from being rebuilt in its apostolic clearness, and from becoming perfect in its doctrines, sacraments and conduct, according to the command of Christ and his holy word.

Josiah expelled all soothsayers and wizards. He offered the idolatrous priests upon their idolatrous altars, and burned the dead bones, &c., but the bones of the man of God from Judah, and of the prophets of Samaria, he burned not. But you sustain and cherish, as shepherds of the flocks of Christ and keepers of your souls, false prophets and deceiving priests; the greater part of whom are open drunkards, libertines and idolaters, full of all unrighteousness, covetous in heart, whose belly is their god, blind watchmen, and dumb dogs, who dishonor God, and destroy poor miserable souls. You have them in preference in your courts and give them the highest seats at your tables. They are honored with high names and great titles, and are greeted by every one as doctors, lords and masters. You present them splendid dwellings, great rents and possessions, and say, They who serve the gospel must live by the gospel; although they do nothing but place soft pillows and cushions under you, and preach according to the itching of your ears. But the true, pious teachers and faithful servants of Christ, who sincerely seek your salvation and that of the whole world, who direct you to Christ, who rightly use his sacraments and ordinances, who desire to lead you and all men on the right way, and who walk unblamably, they must without mercy or christian modesty be persecuted by you, sentenced to fire and water, and must bear mockery and shame before all the world.

Josiah made a covenant with the Lord, and with all the elders, priests, prophets and common people, that they should serve the Lord as long as they lived, &c. But you have made your covenant with antichrist and with all your preachers, priests, monks, judges and rulers, that the perverted, broad way should be pursued, the doctrines and institutions of men should be taught, followed and observed, instead of the true service of God; to the people, doctrine, commands, Spirit, Supper, life and separation of Christ, you give no place, and whoever acts or speaks contrary to your abominations, must lose his possessions or his life.

Josiah heard the word of the Lord and became contrite in heart; he rent his clothes and wept before the Lord; he feared the coming wrath, because they and their forefathers had rejected the word of God. But you, my dear lords, are so hardened and blinded, so bound by your sins, and lusts of the flesh, through cursed unbelief; so enchanted by the false prophets, that we cannot, in the least, move your impenitent, hardened hearts, neither by the threatening law of the Lord, nor by his fierce wrath, and terrible judgement; neither by the devouring flames of hell and eternal death, nor by the peaceful gospel of grace; neither by the precious blood of Christ, nor by the pious, unblamable life of all the saints, who with their simple *yea* and *nay*, are daily murdered, before your eyes as innocent sheep, on account of their faith and piety. It is time that you awake, and take notice how you and we, with our forefathers, have so abundantly merited the righteous punishment and wrath of God. May the merciful Lord grant you eyes that you may see.

Josiah turned to the Lord with his whole heart, soul and might, but you dare proudly disregard the God who has created you, deny the Lord who has purchased you, and turn yourselves to dumb idols, to wood, stone, gold and silver images, to water, bread and wine, to the unprofitable doctrines and commandments of men, yea, to open abominations and idolatry, not observing that it stands written, "Idolaters shall have their part in the lake which burneth with fire and brimstone," Rev. 21: 8.

Behold, dear sirs, the above is true; it is manifest by your pride, whoredom, carnal life, and by the ruins of burnt countries and cities, the great number of churches, cloisters, priests and monks, matins, vespers, and every other false worship.

Besides, when we, on account of the multitude of our sins, are visited with pestilence, famine, war, and other dangerous evils and plagues, your only remedies, to appease the wrath of God, and quench the burning fire of his anger, are idolatrous masses, processions, as they are called, dead bones, images, crosses, banners. They, the papists I mean, bear these strange abominations, and follow after them with uncovered heads, folded hands, and burning waxcandles, &c. Therefore, you turn not aside the fierce wrath, but augment it more and more, for the Lord will not give his divine honor to works of man's choice nor to any creature, neither does he accept any such masses, processions, crosses, images and abominations, nor regards them in his mind, as the prophet said.

Beloved sirs, repent. The statute book of Christ is entirely lost to you. Christ and his truth, sacraments, Spirit and life, you have never known nor possessed in the least degree. You serve strange gods, you hear, follow and use the doctrine, sacraments, ordinances and commands of anti-christ; you lead an unclean, ungodly and carnal life. O sirs, take warning! your sins have arisen to heaven.

Although it is so little regarded by you, God grant it may be otherwise, yet this book of Christ, by the grace of God, has been found again by some. The pure, unadulterated truth has come to light, through the pure, unmingled gospel, and is daily read in your ears, and explained before your eyes with a godly, virtuous life, with an open confession, and above all, with much of the property and blood of the saints; yet your hearts continue so stony and hard that they cannot be converted or moved, neither by grace nor wrath; neither by adversity nor prosperity, as we have said. Behold thus has the blindness of Sodom, the darkness of Egypt, the hardening of Pharaoh, through the righteous judgment of God, come upon our kings, princes, lords and rulers.

Dear sirs, awake! and make haste, the trumpet is sounded, prepare yourselves! Your mortal sickness and cankering, filthy wounds are shown to you. I counsel you to suffer yourselves to be helped. You possess neither Christ nor his word. Your controversy is against the Lamb and his chosen. Your way is in darkness, and leads to the abyss of hell. The wrath of the Lord has gone forth over you and your land, for you live more carnally and evil than can be imagined or described.

O my dear sirs! reform, repent, so that you may stand before God; cleanse your hands and hearts before the Lord; change your pride, into humility, and your mirth, and joy into sorrow; rend your hardened hearts, and your garments; hear and seek Christ, and not anti-christ; implicitly obey Christ's Spirit, doctrine, sacraments, commands and infallible example, and not the vain doctrines and commandments of men, for they corrupt and profit not.

Put away from among you, all offence,

abominations and idolatry, masses, altars, infant baptism, the idolatrous bread, or supper (I mean such as is used by the world), images, confessions, the wanton sodomy, unchastity of the papistic priests and monks; destroy and root up all accursed heathen disgrace; such as brothels, every species of gambling, open houses of drunkenness, together with idolatrous temples, high places, groves, churches and cloisters, which were so numerously built contrary to the Scriptures by our forefathers, through blindness and ignorance.

We call on all, poor, deceiving teachers and false sects, great and small, who are against the Spirit, ordinances, word and life of Christ, sincerely to repent, and help us to resist, not by violence, tyranny or sword; as, alas! it is the custom with you, but by the Spirit of Christ, with doctrine, exhortation and the like virtuous services and mild means, so that they may turn from evil, and hear and follow Christ.

Permit all faithful messengers and servants of God to preach Christ, to use his sacraments and ordinances according to the Scriptures, lead a penitent and unblamable life, and gather unto Christ a glorious church, that they may, through the Spirit and grace of God, according to the Scriptures, win and bring unto Christ an unspotted, pure virgin.

Again I say, reform; you have erred and mocked God too long, and worshipped antichrist instead of Christ too long; walked too long in the perverse and broad way of death. Awaken! it is yet to-day; behold, the true book of the law; the saving, pure gospel of Christ which was hid for so many centuries by the abominations of anti-christ, is found.

Hear and read attentively, believe and observe it faithfully; it is the word of the Lord God, which Jesus Christ, the first and only begotten Son of the Almighty Father, brought from heaven and taught us. Bow to his righteous sceptre, fear, love, serve, honor and follow him with all your heart, with all your soul and with all your powers, as did the pious Josiah. For the Lord our God, is Lord of lords, and God of gods, a mighty, and a terrible God, which regardeth not persons, nor taketh reward.

Yes, beloved lords, Can you thus convert yourselves with all your hearts? Can you change your hearts and humble yourselves before God? Deny yourselves, seek and follow Christ and his righteousness? Renounce the world and flesh with all its lusts, as you have heard? Then you will become, true, spiritual kings, and priests; then you will possess your souls in peace, gain the victory and conquest over all the deadly enemies of your souls; you will live and die in grace; then you may in truth, without any hypocrisy, be called christian kings and believing princes. The testimony of Peter to all christians, I say to *all* christians, is true, "Ye are a chosen generation, a holy nation, a peculiar people," 1 Pet. 2: 9.

But if you refuse this and remain what you are now, preferring perishing, temporal pleasures, joys and glory, to the imperishable, eternal joy and glory; I desire then that you would reflect upon what Sirach says, "Why are earth and ashes proud? He that is to-day a king, to-morrow shall die," Sir. 10: 9. Yea, what are they all, who are of Adam, but dust and ashes, a passing wind, a vapor, poor, miserable, mortal flesh, food for worms, yea men, and not God. O, Sirs, take warning, awake and reform yourselves! God is Lord, who will judge you. Once more, take warning.

Behold, my kind reader, here you have before you a few examples of true faith, as Noah and Abraham, before the giving of the law, and Moses, Joshua, Caleb and Josiah, under the law, cited from Scripture, wherefrom you may learn how simple and plain, unfeigned, open and obedient, yea, how full of all kind of virtues and fruits a true faith has been from the beginning, as may be seen in Abel, Enoch, Isaac, Jacob, Joseph, Jephthah, Baruch, Gideon, Sampson, Rahab, Samuel, David, Ezekiel, Elias, Helias and others. Now I will, by the grace of God, present you with a few examples from the New Testament, whereby you may very clearly learn what an indescribably great power, fruit, spirit, life and energy, a true, evangelical, christian faith in its true nature always includes. So that you will not, through a false notion, conform to this ignorant, unbelieving world, who boast and pretend that their fruitless, dead opinion and historical knowledge of Christ, is a sincere, evangelical faith.

THE FAITH OF THE CENTURION OF CAPERNAUM.

At the time when the Lord Jesus entered Capernaum, the servant of a centurion lay sick, whom he loved much. When he heard that Jesus was there, he had the consent of some of the elders of the Jews, and sent them with a request to Jesus, that he would come to him and restore his sick servant, and Jesus went with them. And not being far from the house of the centurion, he sent some of his friends to him, who said, Lord trouble not thyself; for I am not worthy that thou shouldst enter under my roof (here notice his humility), and I did not think myself worthy personally to call and see thee; but speak the word, and my child shall be healed. He acknowledged that all must bow to Christ and his word, and said, I also am a man under authority, having soldiers under me, and I say unto one, Go, and he goeth; and to another come, and he cometh; and to my servant do this, and he doeth it. As if he would say to Christ, Behold, Lord, I am but a man, and have to serve the councils at Rome, nevertheless, I have so much power over my servants, that they must obey what I command them; but thou, Lord, art such a Lord that all the mighty have to bow to thee, all that is in heaven above and on earth beneath, must yield to thee. If thou but command sickness and death, they will have to obey thee, and leave my child. And again, if thou command health and life, they will have to return again. Therefore, it is not necessary that thou shouldst come into the house of thy unworthy servant; Lord, only speak the word, and my child will again be restored. When Jesus heard these words, he was quite astonished, and said to the people that followed, Verily, I say unto you, I have not found so great faith, no, not in Israel, Matt. 8.

Behold, faithful reader, here you have the centurion as a living example, by which you may learn how a true christian faith humbles itself before God, and doubts not his power, and how kindly and graciously *he* deals with *his* poor servants, be they male or female. The centurion was moved with compassion towards his poor servant, and had great concern for him, that he spared no pains to trouble the elders of the Jews to send to Christ and entreat him to come and heal his sick servant. This is to the disgrace and shame of all false christians, and especially to many rich, some of whom are more severe on the poor servants and hirelings, and have less feeling for them, than they (with your leave) have for their domestic animals; for as soon as the servants sicken, so that they cannot perform all manner of drudgery, they are unmercifully turned out of doors, and sent to this or that asylum, or to their parents and friends, who sometimes, scarcely have a mouthful of bread or a bed in their houses. Others again have to get a substitute in their place, while sick, and pay him out of their own earned pittance; and if they in health even do fulfil their engagements with hard and severe labor, still, some of these unmerciful, blood thirsty, treat these innocent ones, who have to watch when they sleep, labor when they rest, run when they command, stand when they sit, in such a manner, as to take the greater portion of their earnings, or scandalize them; now, say they, a spoon is lost; anon a dish is broken; in short, they always speak evil of them and can never be pleased. Yea, some of them would feed them upon water or straw, and pay them with the whip and chaff, even as they do their laboring oxen and horses, if they were not afraid and ashamed of men, for they would not be ashamed before God, alas, whom they know not. O woe, unto such heathenish tyranny and unmerciful cruelty!

The centurion calls his servant *his child*,

by which he manifests his paternal love and humility towards his poor servant. Though he was lord, and held in high honor, nevertheless, he did not exalt himself above his poor servant, for he well knew that one God created both of them, that they were born of one seed, and had one origin. But what conduct such heathen christians manifest towards their oppressed servants, their actions, alas, openly show!

How lamentably some of the poor children are despised by some of them. How many disgraceful words have some of them to hear, and how many sore stripes to endure. Their scolding and rash words, continue from morning till night; some of them make their girls prostitutes; yea, what shall I say more. These poor children are regarded by them, and especially by the rich, as the poor, despised donkey, by the magnificent, fat horse, and the filthy pebbles by the beautiful pearls. Ah! reader, it is all much worse than I can describe; it is indeed time that they would look into these things, and reflect more deeply upon love.

The centurion humbled himself before the Lord with all his heart, esteeming himself not worthy that Christ should come under his roof. But our haughty, proud heathens strut about with puffed up hearts and extended necks, high-minded, idle, and daring; one boasts of his family, another of his wealth, a third of his wisdom, a fourth of his skill and beauty, &c. But the innocent and meek Christ says, Learn of me; for I am meek and lowly in heart, and falsely boast that they have his name, word, death and blood, yet know it not.

The centurion believed, that Christ was mighty and able, by his word, to do all that he desired; but this miserably benighted people esteem it not more than they do Lucian and Æsopian fables. Hence it is, that they lead such an impenitent, carnal life, and use such idolatrous sacraments and false worship, and have departed so far from the true King's highway, still they would be the true, apostolic, and believing church of Christ; but even as Christ testified to the centurion, that he had not found such faith in Israel; so we might, on the other hand, testify and say of this people, that such a heedless, cruel, haughty, proud, and unmerciful unbelief is unknown among the heathen, and is not to be found with them, who never heard of the word of Christ. Behold, thus does the righteous Lord let those err and fall into blindness of heart, who so little regard his most holy word, hate and thrust his fatherly grace, goodness, Spirit, knowledge and faith from them.

But it is not so with you, my most beloved. Take this sincere, pious centurion as an example; imitate him in his faith, love, humility and virtues, and be as solicitous for your servants, as he was for his servants; teach, admonish and reprove them with a paternal spirit, as often as they err; set them an unblamable example, in all righteousness and piety; have compassion with their severe labor; comfort them in their poverty; comfort them and grieve them not; supply them with their necessary wants, food and their earned hire, and do not curtail them; protect them in all honorable things; rebuke them not without cause, lest they become timid; do not drive them away from you, but let them unmolestedly serve out their time as agreed, lest the name of the Lord be blasphemed; be at all times friendly towards them, and if they are weak and sick, assist and minister unto them; get others to serve in their place, without detriment to them, till the Lord take them hence, or restore them to health; sympathize with them, and be merciful; assist them in all their need; lift not your hearts above them, nor despise them, for they are your brethren according to the flesh. In short, be you so minded in love towards them as Christ Jesus is towards us. At all times remember that we also have a Lord in heaven, before whose judgment-seat we must all appear and render on account of all our works.

But if they are wanton and obstinate, and will not hear your word and command, nor follow your admonition and counsel; would rule and not serve; waste their time and not labor industriously; are unfaithful, rebellious and troublesome; roguishly ruin your family and children, &c.; then agree with them and bring the matter, touching their wages, before two or three witnesses, so that the blame may not rest upon you, and the word of the Lord be not blasphemed. In such case then, let them be dismissed, that your good conscience be not disturbed on their account, and your house and children be not depraved. Yea, my brethren, you should do to your poor hirelings, even as you desire that it should be done to you, being called with them. This the law and the prophets teach.

THE FAITH OF ZACCHEUS, THE PUBLICAN.

Luke says that "Jesus entered and passed through Jericho; and behold, there was a man, named Zaccheus, which was the chief among the publicans, and he was rich; and he sought to see Jesus, who he was, and could not for the press, because he was little of stature; and he ran before, and climbed up into a sycamore tree (or as some say, into a wild fig tree), to see him; for he was to pass that way; and when Jesus came to the place, he looked up, and saw him, and said to him, Zaccheus, make haste, and come down; for to-day I must abide at thy house, and he made haste, and came down, and received him joyfully, and said unto the Lord, Behold, Lord, the half of my goods I give to the poor; and if I have taken any thing from any man by false accusation, I restore him four fold; and Jesus said unto him, This day is salvation come to this house, forasmuch as he is also a son of Abraham," Luke 19: 1—9.

Paul says, For whatsoever things were written aforetime were written for our instruction; and though we know Zaccheus' faith, fruit, mercy, love and true conversion, it avails us nothing, if we do not practice and come up to his faith, with its contrite, pious fruits. I therefore entreat all my readers, who live openly in sin; all the wealthy, avaricious, unrighteous merchants and grocers, all financiers and bankers, all who love money; judges, lawyers, advocates, preachers, priests and monks, all drunken landlords, together with all those who deal in unlawful gain; I entreat all by the love of our Lord and Savior, Jesus Christ, that they would well consider, with an understanding heart, this history and narrative touching Zaccheus, in order that they may learn therefrom, that they do not yet possess the right, true faith and that christianity which avails with God; and that they have nothing but a fruitless, vain boasting of Christ and of faith.

Zaccheus was chief of the publicans, and he received Christ joyfully in his house and heart. He believed and was renewed; he reformed his life, and departed from his former evil ways. That our open transgressors do not yet reform their old, ungodly lives, and that they do not desire Christ and his faith, however much they may boast, is as clear as the light of day.

Zaccheus was rich, and one half of his wealth he gave to the poor. But our rich people seek more and more, how they may increase their money and possessions, build their houses splendidly, and add farm to farm. They do not defend the cause of the poor and needy; are unmerciful, proud, avaricious and wanton; do not remember what is written concerning them, "Go to now, ye rich men, weep and howl for your miseries that shall come upon you; your riches are corrupted, and your garments are moth-eaten; your gold and silver is cankered, and the rust of them shall be a witness against you, and shall eat your flesh as it were fire," James 5: 1—3. Neither do you reflect on what David says, "I have seen the wicked in great power, and spreading himself like the green bay-tree; yet he passed away, and lo, he was not: Yea, I sought him, but he could not be found," Ps. 37: 35, 36. Ah! what a hard saying which the Lord uttered, "Woe unto you that are rich, for ye have received your consolation," Luke 6: 24, and "It is easier for a camel to go through the eye of a needle, than for a rich man to enter into the kingdom of God," Matt. 19: 24.

Zaccheus said to the Lord, "If I have taken any thing from any man by false accusation, I restore him four fold," but our miserably avaricious, never cease from defrauding their neighbor. For the whole, broad world, both man and woman, are so greedy after unlawful, shameful gain, that it cannot be imagined nor related.

Lords and princes daily invent new devices and practices, that they may increase their dominions, interests, tolls and rents. They tax, shave, grasp and rob without any mercy or bounds; they draw the very marrow from the bones of the poor, and show by their actions, that they are companions of those of whom it is written, "Thy princes are rebellious, and companions of thieves," Isa. 1: 23. O that he knew Christ, would repent, cease to do evil, and would reflect more on love.

Judges, lawyers and advocates also seek all artifice to get unlawful gain; with few exceptions they all serve for gifts and money, for if they did not expect profit or gain, I am persuaded that burgomasters and judges would be few in the whole empire. For the sake of gain, they sit and judge, and they often encourage causes for the sake of a fee. Some of them pervert law and right for the sake of a gift, and do not reflect on what Jehoshaphat said to the judges, "Take heed what ye do; for ye judge not for man, but for the Lord, who is with you in the judgment; wherefore now let the fear of the Lord be upon you; take heed and do it; for there is no iniquity with the LORD our God, nor respect of persons, nor taking of gifts," 2 Chron. 19: 6, 7.

Captains, knights, servants and such like bloody men, are ready to serve for the sake of gain, and swear with uplifted fingers that they will destroy cities and countries, take citizens and inhabitants, kill them and take their possessions from them, although they never harmed them, nor gave them any provocation. O God! what execrated, ungodly abominations and traffic. And still it must be said, that they protect the country and people, and that they assist in administering justice!

Priests, monks and preachers are equally bent upon unlawful gain. They are not shocked to make God's only and first begotten Son, his eternal, Almighty Word and Wisdom, the one and only everlasting foundation of heaven and earth, Jesus Christ, with his holy apostles, to be open, false witnesses, heretics, and deceivers; for Christ says, "He that believeth and is baptized, shall be saved," Mark 16: 16. But they say, He that believeth and is baptized, is a heretic, and shall be damned. Christ says, "But if thou wilt enter into life, keep the commandments," Matt. 19: 17. But they say, None can keep God's commandments.

Paul says, If ye live according to the flesh ye shall die; again, The unrighteous, drunkards, the avaricious, the haughty, the unchaste and the like, shall not inherit the kingdom of God. But they say, We are poor sinners; who can always live as the Scriptures teach? Christ died for sinners, and the like consolations, whereby they deny Christ and his word, and thus encourage the whole world, rich and poor, small and great, in their hardened and wicked life, that there are, alas, few who truly repent, or seek after God. They preach what the ignorant blind world desires, that they may quietly enjoy the reward of Balaam (their cloisters and stipends, I mean), that they may lead an epicurian life without care; for they, poor creatures, know not that they are those of whom it is written, "Woe unto them! for they have gone in the way of Cain, and ran greedily after the error of Balaam for reward, and perished in the gainsaying of Core," Jude 1: 11, accursed people, 2 Pet. 2. O God, that they would beware!

The unrighteous merchants and grocers (I say the *unrighteous*, for I do not mean those who are righteous and pious), together with all those who deal avariciously and penuriously, are so bent upon accursed gain, that they exclude God from their hearts. They censure what they should properly praise, and praise what they should censure; they lie and swear; use many vain words; adulterate their merchandise to cheat the people, and to take what is not their own; they sell, lend and trust the needy at exorbitant gain and usury, never seriously reflecting nor taking to heart, that it stands written, "That no man go beyond and defraud his brother in any matter," 1 Thess. 4: 6.

I would that they might more seriously lay to heart the doctrine of Sirach, "A merchant shall hardly keep himself from doing wrong; and a huckster shall not be freed from sin; many have sinned for a small matter, and he that seeketh for abundance will turn his eyes away; as a nail sticketh fast between the joinings of the stones, so doth sin stick close between buying and selling. Unless a man hold himself diligently in the fear of the Lord, his house shall soon be overthrown," Eccl. 26: 29; 27: 1—3.

This I write as a warning to the god-fearing merchants and grocers, so that they will not imitate the ungodly, lest they be overcome by avarice, but be circumspect in dealing and beware of dangers.

Some are made thieves, some murderers, others jugglers, necromancers, some are whoremongers, others gamblers, others are betrayers, others become executioners and tormentors, and also some persecutors and slayers of the pious, &c., and all this for the sake of accursed gain, whereby they openly testify (because they walk in such a way and are so bent upon unlawful gain), that they are of the devil and not of God, that they have not the faith and word of Christ, but in every respect are inimical and opposed thereto.

Yes, kind reader, the whole world is so contaminated and involved in this accursed avarice, fraud, false practices and unbecoming gain, in this false traffic and merchandise, with this finance, usury, and self-interest, that I scarcely know how it could be worse; yet they are still the priest's and preacher's christians, and are said to earn their bread honestly, and to do justice to all.

Ah! my reader, how different all this is from the faith, disposition and converted life of Zaccheus. For if they had the mind, faith and power of Zaccheus, which we must have, if we would ever be saved, it is my opinion that few lords and princes would continue in their violence and wanton lives; few riders (knights) and servants in their ungodly service and deeds of blood; few judges, lawyers and advocates in their courts and offices; few rich persons in the unlawful use of their riches; few merchants and grocers in their usurious and dangerous trade; and few preachers, priests and monks would continue in their incomes, stipends and cloisters. There would soon be a different state of things; because it cannot be, but that the righteous live by faith. Yea, they would, with joyful heart, say with Zaccheus, The poor we willingly serve with our goods, and if we have defrauded any one, we will gladly satisfy him.

All who, like Zaccheus, rightly receive Jesus Christ in the house of their consciences; rightly receive the word of Christ as he did, and be also truly born through the word; are rightly influenced by the Spirit of Christ; and are of the same mind with him, it is impossible that they could defraud any one even of a farthing; for we see that the disposition and usage of all true believers is to injure none on earth; but, as much as in them is, assist all; to defraud none, but to do justice to all. As Paul says, "Let him that stole, steal no more; but rather let him labor, working with his hands the thing which is good; that he may have to give to him that needeth," Eph. 4: 28.

But why say much? For my part I do not know where to find the mighty and the rich; in what courts we can find judges, lawyers and advocates; and in what cities and countries, merchants and grocers; or what cloisters and churches we can look for preachers, priests and monks, who rightly believe and follow Christ; who, being regenerated, penitent and pious, desist from all improper practices, fraud, craftiness, robbery, and unlawful gain, and say with Zaccheus, Those whom we have defrauded we will repay fourfold. The prophet complains that every one from the least even unto the greatest, is given to covetousness, Jer. 8: 10.

Since then they are determined upon accursed, abominable avarice, and unlawful gain, and deal so rudely and plainly contrary to love, and none any where repent, hence, it is evident that they are not in the church of Christ, for the church of Christ is called his body and bride in the Scripture. If the church be his body, she must then be flesh of his flesh, and bone of his bone; and if she be his bride, she must be of his generation, be righteous, holy, meek, chaste, true, lovely, merciful; yea, hear and be obedient to his voice; therefore, Christ cannot admit of any other members in his church but those who are of one heart, spirit and soul with him, partakers of his Spirit; who are dead to all unrighteousness, bury the old evil life of sin, walk by faith, unblamably in love, receive the truth joyfully, willingly serve their neighbor, as did this believing, regenerated and renewed Zaccheus.

He desired to see Christ, and received him with joy; he believed his word, and abandoned his ungodly life; he ministered to the poor, and reconciled those whom he had defrauded. In short, he proved himself to be a pious, sincere, regenerated child of God in all his actions; therefore he heard the peaceable, joyful word of divine grace, "This day is salvation come to this house, forasmuch as he also is a son of Abraham," Luke 19: 9.

Behold, worthy reader, those who believe, are penitent and renewed as Zaccheus was, and walk in love, belong to the church and body of the Lord, as Christ himself says, "By this shall all men know that ye are my disciples, if ye have love one to another." They are the living stones of the Lord's temple, and the true citizens of Jerusalem; in which neither sorcerers, nor whoremongers, nor murderers, nor idolaters, nor whosoever loveth and maketh a lie, have part. Yea, as long as Zaccheus was such a one, he was without; for such, says Paul, have neither lot nor part in the kingdom of God and of Christ.

But as soon as he believed the word of the Lord, through faith he repented and turned himself to love; from that hour he was entitled to citizenship, with Christ himself; the path of life was opened to him, peace declared, salvation bestowed, and he was acknowledged and received as a joint-heir of grace, and a child of God, as the Lord says, This day is salvation come to this house, &c. For as Christ is holy, so must also his children, brethren, members, church and bride be holy; for it is written, Be ye holy, for I am holy.

THE MURDERER'S FAITH.

The evangelists teach that there were two malefactors crucified with Christ; the one on the right hand, and the other on the left. "One of the malefactors which were hanged, railed on him, saying, If thou be Christ, save thyself and us? but the other answering rebuked him, saying, Dost not thou fear God, seeing thou art in the same condemnation? And we, indeed justly; for we receive the due reward of our deeds; but this man hath done nothing amiss; and he said unto Jesus, Lord, remember me when thou comest into thy kingdom. And Jesus said unto him, Verily I say unto thee, To-day shalt thou be with me in Paradise," Luke 23: 39—43.

Good reader, observe particularly what I write. When we critically view the confession of this evil doer, we are astonished at the great power, the good nature, the abundance of fruit, spiritual vision, energetic love and the free confession of his faith. It is evident that he had been an abandoned, ungodly reprobate, who neither knew nor feared God, but maliciously committed all manner of sins, robbed his neighbor of his goods and shed his blood. Matthew and Mark call him a murderer, and Luke calls him a malefactor. This appears to be the case as he testifies himself, that he had to die for crimes which he had committed.

Notwithstanding all this, as soon as this malefactor, extended on the cross between Jerusalem and Mount Calvary, heard in his last distress, the word of God from the mouth of the Lord, it wrought in him so powerfully, that his heart within him was touched and changed, which led him to seek, from that moment, the salvation of his fellow-men and rebuked his reviling companion, saying, Fearest thou not God? He confessed his own sins and his maliciousness, saying, We are receiving according to our merits and works; and he acknowledged the condemned Jesus (who was cursed to die on the cross as one of the most abandoned malefactors, by the chief priests, pharisees and scribes, and denied of the people and condemned to death), to be innocent, righteous, pure and without sin, saying, This one has done no evil. Besides this, he also sought grace and mercy of God, although it appeared to human understanding that he was denied all mercy, and every favor both by God and man. For he was at this time the most rejected and despised of all men, as the prophet laments, Isa. 53: 6, and the thief applied to none other, in heaven or upon earth, than to this poor, innocent, calumniated, banished and crucified Jesus; in full confidence drawing near to him, as the throne of divine grace, that he might obtain the remission of his sins, saying, "Lord remember me when thou comest into thy kingdom."

I think, this may justly be called, a true, christian faith, and a truly worthy fruit of penitence and repentance; and it was nothing else to the Lord, but a refreshing of his thirsty soul, as a molifying of his deep wounds, as a consolation of his sore distress, and as a comfort in his painful sufferings and cruel death, so that he in the same hour, heard the consoling, joyful word of divine grace and eternal peace, from Jesus, namely, Fear not, all thy sins which thou didst commit in thy ignorance are covered, they shall never more be remembered, either by me or my Father. I pledge my innocent blood as security; therefore, be of good cheer, what thou didst desire, thou hast already obtained, "To-day shalt thou be with me in Paradise."

Behold my reader, here you have, in the malefactor mentioned, a fair example of a sincere, christian faith, with its properties, disposition, nature, power and fruits. With this same murderer, many vain despisers comfort and flatter themselves in their sinful and impenitent lives, think and say to themselves, God is merciful; he knows that we are the children of Adam, if we do not live as the Scriptures teach, and as they would have us live, yet we hope, by the grace of God to be saved, as was the murderer. These poor creatures know not that the thief will be a sore condemnation to them; because they hear the word of the Lord so often, and believe it not, neither are they obedient thereto. Ah reader! do not thus mock God; I fear many will fail in their hopes in this matter.

Again, I say that all wilful despisers, who thus say and think in their hearts, must be eternally convicted by this thief, and shall stand confounded, for as soon as he heard the gospel of grace, he received it in a pure conscience, through faith, and became penitent, regenerated and pious. And these hear it from year to year, see daily so many fair fruits, and that it is so gloriously testified by possessions and blood; nevertheless, they remain unbelievers and are hardened in sin; for they reject the inviting grace, they resist the operating Spirit, they contemn the preached word, they trample under foot the proffered gift, and say, where are the Scriptures, whereby we may comfort such unreasonable, shameful scorners, or promise and proclaim to them the grace and peace of the Lord?

I fear they are the sterile, unfruitful earth, of which Paul speaks, which drinketh in the rain of the holy, divine word, that cometh oft upon it, and nevertheless, bears only thorns and thistles; are rejected and nigh unto cursing, which are to be burned. They are those of whom Solomon laments and says, "How long, ye simple ones, will ye love simplicity? and the scorners delight in their scorning, and fools hate knowledge? Because I have called, and ye refused; I have stretched out my hand and no man regarded; but ye have set at naught all my counsel, and would none of my reproof, I, also will laugh at your calamity; I will mock when your fear cometh and when distress and anguish cometh upon you, then shall they call upon me, but I will not answer," Prov. 1: 22—28. But because they do not look for light, he will turn it into the shadow of death, and make it gross darkness.

The murderer believed as soon as he heard. O! that they would do so; and think upon what David said, "To-day, if ye will hear his voice, harden not your hearts as in the provocation," Heb. 3: 15.

The murderer heard but *once* and *believed*, and these hear it so often, and yet they believe not. He heard and was changed; but these hear and continue the same, and harden their hearts yet more and more.

He reproved his reviling companion, and admonished him, that he should fear God; but these blaspheme and revile all the faithful who do so; and love those who hate the truth. He unreservedly confessed his sins and wickedness, without fear; but these, no matter however avaricious, drunken, proud, unchaste, unclean, envious and idolatrous they are, do not confess their transgressions and sins, and when called to repent and reform, they say, Yea, what have we done?

He acknowledged that Christ's kingdom was not earthly, for he said, *When thou comest into thy kingdom;* but these have all their pleasures in gold and silver, in eating and drinking, in splendor and wantonness, and in the perishable, visible riches of the world; they do not regard the invisible, eternal riches, which Christ out of grace, has bestowed upon all his believers, and merited them by the shedding of his precious blood.

He confessed the poor, condemned, crucified Jesus before all the rulers, priests, Pharisees and before the people, and acknowledge him as his Savior and Lord; but these, alas! deny his Almighty Majesty, his heavenly origin and glory, and do not regard his judgment, Spirit, word, ordinances, commands, sacraments and promises, although he has seated himself as a triumphant and conquering prince, at the right hand of the Father, and has received all power, both in heaven and upon earth, in eternal glory of the Father.

He sought mercy, favor and the forgiveness of his sins, of Christ; but these seek it of their preachers, priests and monks, through masses, confessions, absolution, bread and wine, holy water and the like superstitions and abominations.

He heard, because he believed on Christ, the pleasing words, *To-day thou shalt be with me in Paradise;* but these shall hear, because they believe not on Christ, the dreadful, intolerable and awful sentence, *Depart from me ye cursed into everlasting fire.* Their faith was unlike, as will also be their reward. Let all mockers take this to heart.

And thus, take notice, finally this penitent sinner will rise up against those who have comforted themselves with him in their sins, and criminate and condemn them before the face of his Majesty. For they having so often heard the sweet melody of the divine word, and never were grateful, nor ever learned or believed it with open and renewed hearts; but the murderer heard it but once, and immediately believed. Ah! dear children, beware and seek Christ while he may be found, and call on him while he is yet near, lest his anger go forth, and the fire of his fierce wrath consume you.

Think you, O perverted scorners! that you can receive or reject faith, repentance, sorrow for sin, and the grace of God, at pleasure? O no! Holy Paul says, "Even as they did not like to retain God in their knowledge, God gave them over to a reprobate mind," Rom. 1: 28. That sentence shall be passed upon all proud scorners. Children beware!

Notice this parable, There is a very rich potentate, emperor or king, whom I, through great ignorance, hated all my days; he had compassion upon me, and because I am such a poor man, he, through his faithful servants, tendered me not only his favor and friendship, but also a great sum of gold, many precious stones and gems, and all this out of love and compassion; and I am so ungrateful, that I will not only not give meat and drink to the faithful servants of this kind prince, who loves me dearly, for these great favors; but I turn them with ignominy and disgrace, out of doors, throw mud and stones at them, put them into prison and bonds, deprive them of property and life, take the proffered gifts, place them in a closet, and trample them under foot, &c., and inform the prince, That I do not now desire his presents, but if he will, in the course of one or ten years offer them again, then I will perhaps, make up my mind and receive them and tender my thanks for the favors. Now, I will allow you all to judge, whether it would be right that such a prince should again offer his favor, since I treated him and his servants so perfidiously? Or whether he should not much more turn his favor into displeasure, and his love into wrath toward me, for my presumptuous tyranny, haughty rejection of his favors, and severely punish me? I think, you would award me his punishment and not his grace.

Thus it is with you, O you scorners! The

merciful Lord, whose riches and grace are immense, has graciously pitied us in these abominable, last days, and had compassion on our great blindness and deadly poverty, although we hated his holy will from our infancy, and through his faithful servants freely offered us his beloved Son with his holy word, Spirit, merits, ordinances and example, tendered us his grace, peace and eternal life, kingdom, inheritance, joy and glory, together with the remission of our sins; he dug about us and fostered us, barren trees, for many years. He calls and teaches daily, through his chosen, who willingly sacrifice possession and life as a testimony; he puts at variance the father against the son, and the son against the father; the mother against the daughter, and the daughter against the mother; the members of the family against one another, and friend against friend, &c. Some he suffers to be driven about in strange countries, in tribulation, in sorrow, in misery, in fear, in want, in vexation, in deserts, in mountains, in dens and in caves of the earth. He gives signs in the sun, moon, and the stars in heaven; in earthquakes, war, pestilence, new diseases, famine, and unheard of wonders upon the earth. As a hen gathers her chickens, he would gather us under the wings of his love; and as a faithful shepherd of his sheep, he would bring us to the right fold of his grace; bring us into the chamber of his covenant, and kiss us with the lips of his peace; wash us from all our uncleanness, and make us his bride; redeem us from the dominion of hell and death, and lead us into the kingdom of heaven, and of eternal life. In short, he would release us from the power of darkness and the devil, and receive us and make us holy as his chosen children and heirs.

But, alas, in relation to you, it is altogether vain; as already said, his proffered grace and word you reject; you persecute and kill his faithful servants and ministers; you defame and blaspheme the unblamable, pious life, together with the confession of the saints; you scoff at his great signs, wonders and reproofs, and your faces are like those of the lecherous, and your hearts as diamonds; you are neither ashamed, nor will you be converted; you say with perverted scorners, Depart from us, for we desire not the knowledge of thy ways. What is the Almighty, that we should serve him? And what profit should we have, if we pray to him? Job 21: 14, 15.

Since then, you are so ungrateful to your God, yea, are altogether vain and insulting towards him, who has shown to us, from the beginning, such great mercy, that you entirely reject and disregard his paternal admonitions, chastisings, doctrines, commands, obedience to his holy word, and the innocent blood of his saints, together with all his great powers and miracles; yea, you consider them as mere deception and heresy; that you do not regard the day of grace; that you inconsiderately trample under foot Christ and his holy Spirit, gospel, regenerations, faith, sacraments, death and blood, together with all his other spiritual riches and heavenly gifts; and that you do not fear, seek, love, honor thank nor serve the Almighty, immortal, only and eternal God; and still hope that you will be saved with the murderer, then I tell and warn you in sincere love, while it is yet to-day, that your hopes will not be realized, for when you think to find him, he will then hide himself from you; he will turn his fierce countenance upon you, as the Scriptures say, "Then shall they call upon me, but I will not answer; they shall seek me early, but they shall not find me," Prov. 1: 28.

I therefore entreat and exhort my readers in general; to hear while you have ears, and see while you have eyes; understand while you have hearts; awaken and watch while you have time and space, lest your ears, eyes, hearts, and opportunities be taken from you, and you become deaf, blind, impenitent, hardened and perverted.

Friends, beware! now it is to-day, yesterday is past; to-morrow is not promised us. Short is the time; behold, the judge is at the door, therefore delay not, to turn unto the Lord, and defer it not from day to day; for his wrath will soon overtake you. Late repentance, says Augustine, is seldom true; but if true, it never is too late. Repent while you enjoy health, says he, that you may be certain.

Therefore, do as did the thief or murderer, for, as soon as he heard, he believed.

Do you also thus hear, and thus believe, for the eyes of the Lord are upon the faithful. The Savior says, those who hunger and thirst after righteousness, shall be filled; those who seek, shall find; those who ask, shall receive; those who knock, to them it shall be opened. But if you refuse, when he seeks to bestow his grace upon you, he will also refuse when you seek him, and would fain obtain his grace. "They that despise me," saith the Lord, "shall be lightly esteemed," 1 Sam. 2: 30.

Therefore, seek while it is day, that you may find; ask, that you may receive; hear, that you may believe; believe, that you may do; and do, that you may live; for, from hearing, cometh faith; out of faith, doctrine; on obedience, the fulfilment of the promise depends.

For this reason all things are imputed to faith in the Scriptures; such as true repentance, regeneration, sanctification of the heart; the righteousness which avails before God; the blessing of salvation and everlasting life; for faith is the source and cause of all good, as is fully related.

Seeing, then, that this is the true and proper ground of the Scriptures, as we have briefly explained, you will then have to confess that all wilful scorners are put to shame in their doings, by the thief, and that he will be their accuser in the day of the Lord, as the Lord says of the Ninevites, and of the Queen of the South.

All who hear and believe the word of Christ, and are turned by the power of faith with all their hearts to Christ, acknowledge Christ openly, by an unblamable, pious life, before all the world, confidently seek his grace and mercy, &c.; to them he is a glorious comforter, a precious balm and liniment in their troubled and wounded consciences, by which they may see and know God's unbounded favor, mercy and love, towards all truly penitent sinners, if they have sinned ever so long and heinously, that they by faith may satisfy their souls with him, and not doubt the grace of God on account of their sinful lives in which they formerly walked; for the Lord did not withhold his grace, nor did he say, No, thief, your sins are too great and numerous, and you also have sinned too long. But as soon as he saw his new heart, and heard him confessing, he bestowed his grace upon the poor, distressed sinner, and forgave him all his sins, and said, *To-day thou shalt be with me in Paradise; for he that believeth on me has eternal life.* The prophet also says, If the righteous turn from his unrighteousness and does righteously, I will not remember his unrighteousness which he did.

FAITH OF THE SINFUL WOMAN.

Luke says, "One of the Pharisees desired Jesus that he would eat with him, and he went into the Pharisee's house, and sat down to meat; and behold, a woman of the city, which was a sinner, when she knew that Jesus sat at meat in the Pharisee's house, brought an alabaster box of ointment, and stood at his feet, behind him, weeping, and began to wash his feet with tears, and did wipe them with the hairs of her head, and kissed his feet, and anointed them with the ointment," Luke 7: 36—38.

Here we again learn to know, in the case of this sinner, what kind of a heart, disposition, fruit and life, a sincere, true Christian faith produces. She was possessed of seven devils (if she was the woman called Mary Magdalene, whom the evangelists mention), and as it appears, lived according to the inclinations of her flesh, for she is called a sinner in the Scriptures, so long as the Lord had not called her out of darkness into light, from lies unto truth. As soon as she heard his word, she with eagerness received it in a sincere and renewed heart, by which she, who was a great sinner, became a penitent and pious woman. Her unrighteous, carnal heart was so warmed and touched, that her eyes streamed with tears, that she wet the feet of the Savior therewith. Her hair she used as a towel to wipe his feet; her avarice was quelled; she anointed his head and feet with precious ointment, which might have been sold for three hundred pence; her proud heart was humbled; she did not seek the highest seat at the table, but she sat mournfully at the feet of the Lord, and heard his blessed word.

When the Pharisee saw this, he murmured; Christ said to him, "Simon, seest thou this woman? I entered into thine house, thou gavest me no water for my feet; but she hath washed my feet with tears, and wiped them with the hairs of her head. Thou gavest me no kiss, but this woman, since the time I came in, hath not ceased to kiss my feet. My head with oil thou didst not anoint; but this woman hath anointed my feet with ointment. Wherefore I say unto thee, her sins, which are many, are forgiven; for she loved much, but to whom little is forgiven the same loveth little. And he said unto her, Thy sins are forgiven; *** thy faith hath saved thee; go in peace," Luke 7: 44—48, 50.

Beloved reader, take notice that all the proud, haughty, avaricious, carnal and adulterous, who call themselves Christians, but who are by no means such, testify by their disposition, heart, mind and walk that they hate and are inimical to Christ, are shamed and reproved by this regenerated, penitent sinner, in all their actions; for through her faith she changed her proud, haughty and obdurate heart into an humble, contrite and broken one.

They say that they believe, and yet there are no limits nor bounds to their accursed wantonness, foolish pomp, show of silks, velvet, costly clothes, gold-rings, chains, silver belts, pins, buttons, curiously adorned shirts, handkerchiefs, collars, veils, aprons, velvet shoes, slippers and such like foolish finery; never regarding that the enlightened apostles, Peter and Paul have, in plain and express words forbidden this to all christian women. If this is forbidden to women how much more then should men abstain from it, who are the leaders and heads of their women. Notwithstanding all this they still want to be called the christian church.

Every one makes an ostentatious display; yea, sometimes goes beyond his ability to pay. One is desirous to excel another in foppery, or at least to be equal with him. And does not reflect that it is written, "Love not the world, neither the things that are in the world. If any man love the world, the love of the Father is not in him; for all that is in the world, the lust of the flesh, and the lust of the eyes, and the pride of life is not of the Father, but is of the world; and the world passeth away, and the lust thereof; but he that doeth the will of God abideth for ever," 1 John 2: 15—17.

Again, I say, this sinful woman believed, and from that moment she was freed from disgraceful sins, for the unclean devil was cast out, as you have heard. But what abominable, disgraceful unchastity, adultery and fornication is practiced among many men and women (who boast that they believe), in many cities and countries, is best known to him before whose eyes all things are open; and, alas, not wholly concealed before men. It is manifest that the world is full of lasciviousness, adulterers, fornicators, sodomites, buggerers, bastards and illegitimate children, and, alas, it has come so far, that they live at peace and liberty, notwithstanding that God commanded through Moses, that both the adulterer and adulteress should die, Deut. 22: 22; that there should be neither whores nor whoremongers in Israel, and the illegitimate children even to the tenth generation were not to be admitted into the congregation of the Lord. And further, It was the express command and ordinance of God, that if any one in Israel had intercourse with a virgin, who was not betrothed or engaged, he was compelled to marry her, if her father consented, and was not to put her away all his days, because he humbled her, Exod. 22: 16.

Ah! reader, reflect upon what the last command contains. They all boast, however lascivious they are, that they are spiritual Israelites, that they have the truth, and are baptized in the name of Christ, and yet they are not ashamed to reduce their poor, weak sisters, who are comprised with them in the same faith, baptism, holy Supper and worship, to poor, deluded and degraded strumpets, against all Scripture and christian love; although God's own word,

FAITH.

and the quoted command tell them, that if they have lain with them, they should marry them and never forsake them. If they would more seriously reflect upon these things, many a disgraced one would be saved of her shame, whereas now, many a child is so unmercifully disgraced and many a girl and virgin bereaved of her honor and virtue.

I write you the truth in Christ, you may believe it if you will, that if you are a christian or would be one, and have seduced but one poor child with your subtle attempts and pretences, and if you would not lose your soul, you will have to marry her and not forsake her, nor cast her from you; for you have humbled her, as heard. Behold, this is the Lord's own word and law. All, therefore, who knowingly despise this law of God, and reject the disgraced and marry another, will have to confess before God that the *first one* is his wife, and not the *last one*. O, you violators of female chastity, reflect upon these things and learn wisdom.

Would you say that this command has reference only to Israel and not to the christian, I would then ask you in the first place, Whether you consider yourself to be a christian or not? If you say *no*, do then all you can, and look for the judgment threatened to all out of Christ. But if you say *yes*, then the matter is already decided, that she must be your wife. For a christian must not live with a sister, in such a manner as to make her a prostitute. O no! the Scriptures teach, that christians are members of Christ, and not whores and profligates. I hope this blunt language will be understood.

In the second place I ask, Which of the two people should be the more holy and virtuous, the literal or the spiritual? If you say the literal, then you have exalted Moses with his people and service above Christ, which thing is evidently opposed to all Scripture. But if you say the spiritual, then the matter is again decided that she must be your wife; then the literal must not make his sister to be a prostitute, much less the spiritual, which is the Lord's own body, brother, sister, generation and bride.

In the third place, I ask, Whether the command, Thou shalt love thy neighbor as thyself, is not given to the christians as well as to Israel? If you say *no* you have denied the whole New Testament, which teaches and earnestly insists upon the love of our neighbor. But if you say *yes*, then I say for the third time, that she must be your legitimate wife. Because you did, contrary to the command of love, so abominably disgrace and humble her, therefore, the Scriptures teach that you are to restore her to honor, and that you shall take her to be your wife. Let every one see to it, the commands of love will ever remain. Blessed are they who take heed to them and observe them in fear.

In the fourth place I ask, Whether there is any one who, with a good conscience, can transgress and break the command of God? If you say *yes*, then you deny the Scriptures, which teach, that we shall walk in the ways of the Lord and keep his commandments. But if you say *no*, then I tell you the fourth time, that she is, and must be your wife; for it is the command of God, firmly based upon love, that if you have lain with a virgin, you should marry her and never forsake her, as heard.

Behold, my reader, here you are more than plainly taught what the word of the Lord teaches in regard to this matter. And if you continue so ungodly as to transgress the command of the Lord by disgracing one, and marrying another, you may read the consequences in 1 Cor. 6: 9, 10, unless you sincerely repent.

This I write by no means, to encourage him who has, in days gone by, ignorantly done so, to leave the wife whom he afterward married, and take in her stead the disgraced one; not at all, for I doubt not but that the merciful Father will graciously overlook the errors of those who have ignorantly done so, and who will henceforth fear, and willingly obey his commands. But I write this, that every one should guard himself against such disgrace, and reflect more profoundly upon the command of the Lord and of love, and observe how Christ is so wholly neglected by the world; for, alas, they are generally influenced by their accursed lusts, whether they are lords, princes, priests, monks, noble or ignoble, citizens or peasants; with few exceptions, they are so much inflamed, that they follow this unbecoming, devilish disgrace of accursed lechery, like the dog pursues the hare. They are, says Jeremiah 5: 8, as fed horses in the morning, every one neighed after his neighbor's wife. There is nothing that can deter or prevent them from this accursed abomination, neither natural honor, nor Moses, with all his threatenings, neither the prophets, nor Christ Jesus himself, nor the apostles, neither heaven nor the angels; yea, neither hell nor devil; neither life nor death; if they can only satisfy their unchaste, disgraceful lust, then all is well with them.

They are wholly bent upon this; some they seduce with fair words, others by false promises and gifts, some by giving them wine to drink; by dancing, and songs of levity, some by courteous flattery, by amorous tenderness, and the like artifice; yea, some deceive by their affected sighings and weepings, so that they can only accomplish their ungodly designs, and gratify their lusts, then all is right, and they rejoice. But they do thereby incense Almighty God, transgress his holy word, disgrace their neighbor, do violence to the law of love, defile the marriage bed, violate virgins, have illegitimate children and destroy their poor souls eternally; about all this they care nothing. They say, this is our portion and our lot and nothing else.

I, therefore, say with Moses, Cursed be they of God, who do works of iniquity; and all the people shall say, Amen. And with Job, That hell will consume them, as drought and heat consume the snow-waters; with Paul, That God will judge them; and with John, Their part is in the lake which burneth with fire and brimstone, which is the eternal (second) death. Ah! that these poor people would take heed, believe and observe the words of the Lord.

In the second place, I write this; that every one might awaken, sincerely repent, and weep over his past disgraceful conduct before God, lest he cast him off eternally; but be gracious to him for the sake of the blood of his Son; and no more defile the bed of his neighbor, nor disgrace virgins, but live in all honor, each with his own wife; that the unmarried keep free from lechery, and if he cannot restrain himself, let him seek a pious wife in the fear of God; and he that has transgressed, and has not taken another, that he honor the disgraced one, and according to christian love and the word of God, extricate her from her degraded state; thus teaching their children, and children's children, from generation to generation, even as Tobias did his Son, saying, Beware of all whoredom, my son, and take not a strange woman, but keep to your own wife.

"Know ye not," says Paul, "that your bodies are the members of Christ? Shall I then take the members of Christ and make them the members of a harlot? God forbid," 1 Cor. 6: 15. Again, he says, "For this is the will of God, even your sanctification, that ye should abstain from fornication; that every one of you should know how to possess his vessel (body) in sanctification and honor; not in the lust of concupiscence, even as the gentiles which know not God, for God has not called us unto uncleanness, but unto holiness," 1 Thes. 4: 3—7. Yes, good reader, true believers have to lead an honorable and chaste life; that not as much as adultery, lechery, and unchastity be privately or openly mentioned among them; if any one among them, only mention it, it is an abomination, for thus it becomes the saints to live.

As we find many wicked men who shamefully seduce poor, simple hearts; so on the other hand we find impudent women and girls, who are often the first cause that such disgrace is sought and sometimes practiced upon them. Although many are not guilty of the deed, nevertheless they are not guiltless, that they make so free with other men and associates in open triflings, singing, dancing, drinking, kissing, courting, flirting, and the like vanity and abominations, whereby they kindle the fire of base passions, which continue till consumed, as may be seen.

O how properly Sirach admonishes us, when he says, "Meet not with an harlot, lest thou fall into her snares; use not much the company of a woman that is a singer, lest thou be taken with her attempts; gaze not on a maid, that thou fall not by those things that are precious in her; give not thy soul unto harlots, that thou lose not thine

FAITH.

inheritance; look not round about thee in the streets of the city, neither wander thou in the solitary places thereof; turn away thine eye from a beautiful woman, and look not upon another's beauty; for many have been deceived by the beauty of a woman; for herewith love is kindled as a fire. Sit not at all with another man's wife, nor sit down with her in thine arms, and spend not thy money with her at the wine; lest thine heart incline unto her, and so through thy desire, thou fall into destruction," Sir. 9: 3—9.

Were it now so, that the aforementioned married and unmarried women were true believers, even as was the sinful woman, they would then also fear the Lord, they would abandon all vanity and ungodly actions, and lay snares for none, nor give any occasion for evil; yea, would walk honorably and modestly; avoid all manner of pride and superfluity, and make, or desire no other clothes than those necessary and comfortable for their daily labor. They would not frequent the idolatrous temple and idle banquets, for which occasions this pompous show is generally gotten up.

The sinful woman adorned her soul and not her outward appearance, for she believed; but these adorn their bodies, and not their souls, for they believe not.

The sinful woman sighed and wept, was afraid of the wrath and judgment of the Lord, for she saw that she had done wrong, and sinned; but these laugh and sing, dance and prance about, and do not see their enormous misdeeds, and great sins, and therefore, they do not fear the wrath and judgment of the Lord.

She was compassionate and merciful; anointed the head and the feet of the Lord, and found the true worship; but these are unmerciful and cruel, and know of no other worship than to go to the chapel to receive holy water; to offer tapers and wax-candles to blind blocks and images; to offer masses and vespers; to call upon the departed saints for help; to confess once or twice a year to their idolatrous, drunken, lascivious priests; to receive their bread of abomination and absolution, and the like superstitions and delusions.

The sinful woman sought the company of the righteous; but these seek the company of the unrighteous. They visit each other to talk all manner of foolishness; to injure their neighbor's reputation; to defame and backbite; to speak disgracefully of one another, speak of costly furniture, houses, goods and handsome companions, men and fine clothing. In short, their works openly show that they have not the faith of the sinful woman, and belong not to the congregation of the righteous.

The sinful woman sat at the feet of Jesus and heard his holy word; but these hear teachers, who can tickle their ears, and preach to please them. In short, why need I say much? it is, O God! so corrupted, that we find the whole world filled with foolish men and women, I mean spiritually, deaf ears, unenlightened hearts; the blind are leading the blind, and they will all fall into the pit of eternal death, unless they are again enlightened, if we believe it to be true what the mouth of the Lord has taught us; for their doctrine, sacraments, and worship are altogether false; their unbelief, and carnality prevail every where.

Behold, reader, here take notice, how vastly this sinful woman differs after conversion in her faith and conduct, from the faith and conduct of the world. They are like the sinful woman before her conversion, but not after conversion. Whether such are believers, I will let the sensible reader to reflect upon with the Spirit and word of the Lord.

I know of a certainty, that a proud, haughty, avaricious, selfish, unchaste, lecherous, wrangling, envious, disobedient, idolatrous, false, lying, unfaithful, thievish, defaming, backbiting, blood-thirsty, unmerciful and revengeful man, whosoever he may be, is no christian, even if he was baptized one hundred times, and attended the Lord's Supper daily; for it is not the sacraments, or the signs, such as *baptism* and the *Lord's Supper*, but a sincere, christian faith, with its unblamable, pious fruits, represented by the sacraments, that makes a true christian and has the promise of life.

Here, neither masses, holy water, holy days, rosaries, auricular confession nor absolution, avail; only a believing, contrite, broken heart, spirit and mind, a penitent, changed, new heart, a pious life, dead unto sin, according to the truth will avail. Such was the confession and repentance of the sinful woman, and she also heard immediately, *Thy sins are forgiven, thy faith hath saved thee, go in peace.*

But the abominable, auricular confession which is so highly esteemed by the world, is nothing but hypocrisy, human righteousness and superstition, open delusion of unbelievers, a false hope of the impenitent sinner, and a subtle invention of gain by the avaricious priests, whereby they set aside true confession and repentance, and comfort and encourage the world in their reckless, ungodly life.

But if you would rightly confess and repent, and receive true absolution of God, then approach him with a believing, penitent and regenerated heart, with a sorrowing, broken, distressed mind, leave off sinning, do justice to your neighbor, love, aid, serve, reprove and comfort him, and if you have sinned against him, or deceived him, acknowledge it to him and reconcile him. Behold, this is the only true confession and penance, which is taught in the word of God. The Lord grant that you may rightly understand, and perform this confession and repentance.

I, therefore, entreat and desire all women, through the mercy of the Lord, to take this sinful, sorrowing woman as a pattern and follow her faith, humble yourselves before the Lord, and reprove your avarice, pride, obscenity and all manner of evil. Let all your thoughts be pure, and let your words be circumspect and seasoned. And whatsoever you do, that do in the name and fear of the Lord Jesus, and do not adorn yourselves with gold, silver, costly pearls, and embroidered hair; but dress yourselves in such apparel, as becomes women professing godliness, and which is serviceable. Be obedient to your husbands in all reasonable things, so that those who do not believe may be gained by your upright, pious conversation without the word, as Peter says.

Remain within your houses and gates, except you have something of importance to do, such as attending to your temporal concerns, to administer to the needy, to hear the word of the Lord, or to attend upon his holy sacraments, &c. Attend faithfully to your charge, to your children, house and domestics, and to all that is commanded you, and walk in all things like the sinful woman did after her conversion; that you may be true daughters of Sarah, believing women, sisters of Christ, and joint heirs of a future life, 1 Pet. 3: 6; then you shall hear the gracious words, *Thy sins are forgiven, thy faith hath saved thee, go in peace.*

FAITH OF THE WOMAN OF CANAAN.

Matthew writes that Jesus was in the land of Gennesaret, and says, "Then Jesus went thence and departed into the coasts of Tyre and Sidon, and behold, a woman of Canaan came out of the same coasts, and cried unto him, saying, Have mercy on me, O Lord, thou son of David; my daughter is grievously vexed with a devil; but he answered her not a word. And his disciples came and besought him, saying, Send her away, for she crieth after us; but he answered and said, I am not sent but unto the lost sheep of the house of Israel. Then she came and worshipped him, saying, Lord help me. But he answered and said, It is not meet to take the children's bread and to cast it to the dogs; and she said, Truth, Lord; yet the dogs eat of the crumbs which fall from their masters' table. Then Jesus answered and said to her, *O woman, great is thy faith; be it unto thee even as thou wilt.* And her daughter was made whole from that very hour," Matt. 15: 21—28.

Here you again have a fine example and pattern of a sincere, christian faith; for when this woman perceived how powerfully Jesus preached grace, and hearing besides that he could do what he desired, that he manifested love and mercy, and that he sent none away comfortless, she unhesitatingly

FAITH.

approached him, not doubting his grace, mercy, love and power, although she was not heard at the first or second request. She was importunate both in her faith and prayer, with such a desire that she might partake of the spiritual crumb of his mercy, and obtain relief for her poor daughter. Yea, she manifested such a faith, constancy, humility and piety, that the Lord said to her, "*O woman, great is thy foith; be it unto thee even as thou wilt.*"

Faithful reader, observe; were we with spiritual eyes rightly to look upon this woman's faith and fruits, we would be aptly taught of her, especially in two particulars.

For, as soon as she heard that the Lord taught pure mercy, grace, repentance and reformation, preached the kingdom of God, raised the dead, made the blind see, the deaf hear, the cripples walk, the leprous clean, healed the sick, and cast out unclean spirits; that he reproved the scribes, pharisees and the common people, for their unbelief, perverseness, blind hypocrisy and carnal lives, and testified that he was the prophet and Messiah, promised in the law and the prophets, whereby his fame spread abroad through all Judea and the adjacent countries; hearing all this, her tender heart and mind were so turned to him, through such testimonies, miracles, doctrines and deeds of love, that she did not doubt his mercy, power, goodness and grace; she therefore, went to him with a sincere desire, in sure and true faith, trusting with all her heart, that he would not deny her humble prayer, but that he would graciously hear and grant it; and she also obtained what she desired.

She heard and believed; she saw and confessed. But these insane people imagine that they are christians, but are, according to my understanding, greater disbelievers, blinder, more hardened and worse than Turks, Tartars, or any of the heathens. Their works testify that I write the truth; and they cannot be moved to hear, or obey the truth by godly means and services; neither by doctrine nor exhortation, neither by the unblamable lives nor the innocent blood of saints, which is daily shed before their eyes, as has been mentioned before, when treating of the *faith of the murderer.*

The movement and doctrine of the holy divine word, we have had in Germany a number of years, and have it yet daily more abundantly, in such power and clearness, that they may plainly see that it is the finger and work of the Lord. For the haughty are humbled, the avaricious are made kind, the drunkards become sober, the unchaste made pure, &c., and dare not indulge in a single thought, or word, or act contrary to the will, word and Spirit of the Lord, and they receive it with such an affection, that they do not fear to forsake father, mother, husband, wife, children and possessions, nay willingly suffer death on account of it. For many of them are burned, drowned, killed with the sword, apprehended, exiled, and their property confiscated; yet all this avails nothing with these obdurate people. If it is but reported (when an innocent sheep has been slaughtered), that he was an anabaptist, it is sufficient; they never inquire what he professed and what scriptural grounds he had; what his conduct and life were, whether he injured any one, or not. Neither do they reflect, that it must be a special power and work which restrains one wholly from drunkenness, lasciviousness, pomp and pride, from all vanity, abominable lying, carnal life and from all idolatry; and constrains him to all sobriety, chastity, meekness, piety, truth, and the true worship, on account of which, we have to hear all manner of disgrace, and to endure persecution and misery, and so often endure the loss of life, as you may see.

If a thief is led to the gallows or a murderer is broken upon the wheel, or if a malefactor is punished with death every one inquires what he has done. He is not sentenced by the judges as long as they do not understand fully the ground and truth of his evil deed; but if an innocent, contrite christian, whom the gracious Lord has rescued from the evil, ungodly ways of sin, and placed in the way of his peace, is accused by the priests and preachers, and placed before the judges they deem him unworthy of an impartial examination, in relation to what reasons or Scriptures move him that he will not hear his priests and preachers, nor have his children baptized, nor attend their service, nor longer eat and drink with them, and serve the devil. Nor do they desire to know why he reformed his life and received the baptism of Christ, or what urges him that he willingly suffers or even would die for his faith. They only ask, *Is he baptized?* If he answers in the affirmative, the sentence is fixed, that he must die.

All who see or hear such miracles of Almighty God that such poor, unlearned men, yea, sometimes, poor, feeble women, or girls, are so fortified in God that they fear neither judge nor executioner; that neither fire nor water, neither halter nor sword, neither life nor death can deter them from their faith. These persecutors do not inquire what they did, whether they are traitors to their country or city, whether they have taken the property of others, or disgraced some one's daughter or wife; or whether they did any thing, not in accordance with the word of God, with common honesty and natural probity? O no! So much discretion and love are not to be found. If they only have the word of the Lord, and believe it and fully obey his commands and ordinances, and gladly regulate their poor, weak lives by the truth; then they are called rebels by the lords; heretics by the learned; and are adjudged by the common people as well deserving such cruel punishments and disgraceful death. Behold, thus has the murderous, blood-thirsty devil deceived the whole world, through his priests and preachers; yea, that I fear, scarcely one is to be found among a hundred thousand, who will lay to heart such a strong faith, obedience, frankness, power, great suffering and ignominious death, so that he would once reflect upon his abominable unbelief, disgraceful wickedness and presumptuous, carnal life, or doubt the doctrine of his teachers, sacraments, their lives and worship. How truly did the prophet say, "The righteous perisheth and no man layeth it to heart," Isa. 57: 1. There cannot be found beneath the wide canopy of heaven, a more hardened unbelief, more perverse, scornful, obdurate wickedness, more accursed madness, more execrated ungodliness, or a worse state of things than that which is related.

If there is a report of war and warriors, the whole land is in dismay, great and small, citizens and peasants; defensive armor is provided; they watch and make ready for defense as much as possible. Or if they hear of famine or pestilence, then all tremble, who have come to years of understanding. And, if on the contrary, there is a time of tranquillity, peace, prosperity and weal, then all who hear it, rejoice. But *now*, the trumpets of the Lord Jesus Christ are blowing, and the drums are beating; warning us to tender love, through all his apostles and prophets, to shun the crafty wiles and subtle assaults of satan, and that all who follow and are obedient to him, must die. However, but few are to be found who put on the armor of God; but few who are guarding against the secret encroachments of satan, and preparing to resist him. Both men and women, voluntarily run into his hands and eagerly do the things which delight him; and those who do not, have to await great tribulation and much misery.

Besides, it is manifest that the abominable pestilence of false doctrine will destroy the whole world. The bread of life, which is provided for all the spiritual hungry, is very scarce, in consequence of the envious cry and false writings of the serpent-like preachers; and alas, there are few who weep and sigh on this account.

The eternal grace, mercy, favor, glory, kingdom and joy of Christ are offered unto us. But our ears have waxed dull, our hearts become hardened, and our perverted wickedness, desire them not. But this pious woman did not so; she heard, believed, saw his miracles and confessed his power; and therefore, prayed with confidence and obtained what she desired for she believed Christ with all her heart and doubted not his grace.

In the second place, she admonishes all pious parents, that they should be solicitous for the salvation of their children, because she so faithfully entreated for her demoniac daughter, not desisting till she was heard. For it cannot be otherwise, that if I am a true christian, all my work before God and my neighbor, are works of love, for God (by whose word a christian is born), says John, *is love.* That the Father and those who are born of him, are alike, of one mind and heart, is as clear as day-light.

If I seek the praise of the Lord with all my heart, and desire the salvation of my neighbors, many of whom I have never seen; how much more should I desire the salvation of my children, whom God gave me, who are out of my loins, and are naturally my flesh and blood? So that the mighty Lord may be praised and be eternally honored by them.

What I write, I consider unquestionably true; I write it from a true testimony of my own conscience, as before Almighty God, before whom I am, that all true, believing parents are thus minded towards their children, that they would far sooner see them set in a dungeon for the sake of the word of the Lord and his testimony, than be with the deceiving priests, in their idolatrous churches, or with drunken, erroneous interpreters in taverns, or in company with scorners, who despise the name of the Lord, and hate his holy word.

Sooner far would they see them, for the sake of the truth of the Lord, bound hands and feet, and dragged before lords and princes, than to see them marry rich persons, who fear not God, neither walk in the ways of the Lord, but pass away time in splendor, with music, in excessive drinking, dancing and singing; sooner far would they see them scourged from head to feet, for the sake of the glory and holy name of the Lord, than to see them adorn themselves with silks, velvets, gold, silver, costly, striped and fashionable clothes, and the like vanity, pomp and haughtiness. Yea, far sooner would they see them exiled, burned at the stake, drowned, or placed on the wheel, for righteousness' sake, than see them live out of God, in all earthly and carnal lusts, than to be emperors and kings, and then be damned.

Woe to all, yea woe to all those who are not solicitous for the salvation of their children. If I so love their bodies that I overlook their sins; if I do not punish the transgressions of the young with the rod, and reprove the aged with words; if I do not teach them the ways of the Lord; if I do not set them an unblamable example; if I do not direct them at all times to Christ and his word, ordinances, commands and example, and do not seek their salvation with all my heart and soul, then I will not escape my punishment, for in the day of the Lord, their souls, blood, damnation and death will be required at my hands, as a dumb and blind watchman.

Christianity plainly teaches us that all christian parents should be as sharp, saturating salt, a shining light, and as unblamable, faithful teachers in their houses. The high priest, Eli, was punished because he did not zealously reprove his children.

If I see my neighbor's ox or ass go astray, I must bring him to the owner, or keep him safe, as Moses teaches. If it becomes me thus to do with another's animal, how much more solicitous should I be for the souls of my children, who are so readily misled by the youthful flesh, in which no good dwells.

If I see my neighbor's ox or ass, fallen in a pit, or meet him on the way lying under the weight of a burden, I must not leave him till he is extricated, how much more should I be solicitous for my children, whom I have before me, that they lie not under the burden of their sins; and if they are not earnestly reproved and instructed in grace, they will fall into the infernal abyss of eternal death.

Again, if I see my neighbor's house on fire, and his goods perishing, it is reasonable that I should exert myself to put out the fire, and if possible, to save the goods; but it is much more reasonable, that I extinguish the fire of base desires in my child, with the water of the divine word, and preserve, as much as is in my power, the heavenly goods.

The Holy Scriptures teach, that God purifies the heart by faith; that faith comes by hearing; and by faith we are justified. Therefore, let every one take heed, who truly loves his children, that he rightly and purely instruct them, as soon as they can hear and understand the word of the Lord; that he lead them in the ways of truth, and that he zealously watch over all their doings, that they may from youth, learn to know the Lord, their God, fear, love, honor, thank and serve him; so that the inborn nature of sin may not rule in them nor conquer them, to the everlasting shame of their poor souls.

Moses taught Israel saying, "These words,

which I command thee this day, shall be in thine heart, and thou shalt teach them diligently unto thy children, and shalt talk of them when thou sittest in thine house, and when thou walkest by the way, and when thou liest down, and when thou risest up, and thou shalt bind them for a sign upon thine hand, and they shall be as frontlets between thine eyes, and thou shalt write them upon the posts of thy house and on thy gates;" "that your days may be multiplied, and the days of your children, in the land which the Lord sware unto your fathers to give them, as the days of heaven upon the earth," Deut. 6: 6—9; 11: 21.

In another place he says, "And it shall be when thy son asketh thee in time to come, saying, what is this? That thou shalt say unto him, By strength of hand, the LORD brought us out from Egypt, from the house of bondage," Exod. 13: 14.

Joshua commanded Israel, according to the command of the Lord, and said unto the twelve men, "Pass over before the ark of the LORD your God into the midst of Jordan, and take you up every man of you a stone upon his shoulder, according unto the number of the tribes of the children of Israel, that this may be a sign among you, that when your children ask their fathers in time to come, saying, What mean ye by these stones? Then, ye shall answer them, That the waters of Jordan were cut off before the ark of the covenant of the LORD; when it passed over Jordan, the waters of Jordan were cut off; and these stones shall be for a memorial unto the children of Israel forever," Joshua 4: 5—7.

Behold, dear reader, thus the Israelites were obliged to teach their children from youth, and to acquaint them with all the blessings and miracles of the Lord, which had been bestowed on them and their fathers, so that they might fear, love and serve the Lord all their days, and thus receive the blessing, and escape the curse which was included in the law.

In like manner with us, if we rightly confess Christ, we believe his word, and we and our children desire to obtain the happy fields and pleasant land, and eternally inherit the grace which he has promised his children; therefore, let us not neglect it, but lay it well to heart, that we teach our children rightly in the word, and instruct them in relation to his righteous judgments, so that they will learn to fear the Lord with all their heart, and turn from evil.

Let us also keep before them God's unbounded mercy, love, and services of his grace, so that they may love him and walk in his statutes. Let us imprint on their hearts, Jesus Christ, our only and eternal Savior, with his Holy Spirit, word and example, so that they may rightly know him and follow in his footsteps; and let us set them an example in all wisdom, righteousness and truth; with a pious and virtuous life, so that they may, through such discreet admonition and unblamable example of their pious parents, be instructed in the kingdom of God and trained to all manner of good.

For all who have such a faith as this woman had, and see that the end of sin is death, will not cease to sigh and lament to God, that he would, in mercy, assist their poor children to so resist the impure spirit of the devil that he may not lead them captive at his evil will, to the eternal shame and disgrace of their poor souls.

But that they may, from their youth, rightly learn to know the immortal, eternal God and Father, through Jesus Christ his beloved Son, and in truth serve and submit to his cross; and recount all the mighty works and miracles of the Lord our God, the great mercy, grace, favor and love of the Almighty Father, his blessed word, will, ordinance and life, with all the merits, power and fruit of the death and blood of Christ his blessed Son; also the munificence, wisdom, truth and the gifts of his eternal and Holy Spirit, this to their children, and children's children, and all their descendants, till the Lord Jesus Christ appear in the glorious majesty of his heavenly Father in the clouds of heaven, to the final judging, and where every one will be rewarded according to his works, be they good or evil, 2 Cor. 5: 10.

Behold, worthy reader, thus it behooves true christians to teach, admonish, reprove, and correct their children, to set them an example in all righteousness, raise them in the fear of the Lord, be solicitous for their poor souls, lest they through their negligence, depart from the true path, die in their sins and finally perish in their unbelief.

The Lord spoke of Abraham and said, "Shall I hide from Abraham that thing which I do; seeing that Abraham shall surely become a great and mighty nation, and all the nations of the earth shall be blessed in him? For I know him, that he will command his children and his household after him, and they shall keep the way of the Lord to do justice and judgment," Gen. 18: 17—19.

Pious Tobit taught his son and said, My son, obey thy father, serve the Lord in truth and be just, and this teach to thy children, that they give alms, always fear God, love him, and confide in him with all their heart.

And when they attain the age of maturity, and have not the power to refrain (but he that has, him I would advise with Paul, that he use it to the Lord), let them not marry to those out of Christ and his church, be they noble, rich, or handsome, as do the proud, avaricious and unchaste of this world; but let them marry those who fear, love, seek, honor, follow and serve the Lord with the whole heart; be they noble or ignoble, rich or poor, comely or uncomely, for they are holy and children of saints, and therefore, it is of the Lord, and must be done in his name.

Let every one beware and do right, lest the wrath and fearful judgments of God be inflicted upon him on account of his lewdness and evil desires, even as the judgments, in the days of Noah and Lot, were inflicted, Gen. 6.

But, alas! how few there are who take this to heart, and sincerely seek the salvation of their children. If they can but provide for them temporally, then their desires are gratified. The priests' ordinances, and church services alone are their faith, hope, and the foundation of their salvation; they neither know nor seek any other.

Their whole life from beginning to end is contrary to the word of Christ. For as soon as they are born they are carried to the idolatrous, false bath (baptism); the holy name of the Lord is mispronounced over them; they are raised in all vanity and blindness, in pomp and splendor, in open idolatry and false worship, and in the ignorant, unrestrained life of the world.

In and out of their houses they hear and see nothing but unrighteousness, malice, lying, defrauding, cursing, swearing, infidelity, avarice, quarreling, fighting, intoxication, whoring, and all manner of disgrace. They never learn to know Christ and his word, but they hate the truth and persecute righteousness. In short, they show by their actions that they are full of the evil, unclean spirit, and are led by his will, as may be seen.

For as your spirit is, so must also your fruits be. Is the Spirit of Christ in you, which is holy and pure, then are also your whole life and fruit pure and holy. Again, if the spirit of the evil one is in you, then all your ways and fruits will be evil and impure. This is incontrovertible.

Therefore, says Paul, "As many as are led by the Spirit of God, they are the sons of God." Again, those who are led by the spirit of the evil one, are the sons of the devil. Dear reader, reflect well upon this. Yea, if these poor people had but a spark of the Spirit of the Lord, they would a thousand times sooner be seethed in boiling oil, and burned with fire, then hear and see such foolishness, ungodliness and wantonness in their children, much less would they teach them or set them an example in such things. For it is incontrovertible, according to the power of the Scriptures, if they do not be partakers of Christ, that their end will be eternal death.

Therefore, all you who fear the Lord, love your children with divine love, seek their salvation with all your hearts, even as Abraham, Tobit, and the Maccabean mother did. If they transgress, reprove them sharply; if they err, exhort them parentally; if they are child-like, bear them patiently; if they are of good understanding, instruct them christian-like; dedicate them to the Lord from youth; watch over their souls as long as they are under your care; so that you will not lose your salvation on their account; pray without ceasing, like this pious woman did, that the Lord may grant them his grace, that they may resist the devil, subdue their natural depravity by the Spirit and help of the Lord, and walk from their youth up before God and his church, in all righteousness, truth and wisdom, in a firm and sure faith, in unfeigned love and living hope, in an honorable and holy life, unblamable and without offence, abound in the fruits of faith, unto eternal life, Amen.

In addition to all the aforementioned examples, the diligent reader may also, with a pious and good conscience (mind) seriously reflect upon the faith of the immaculate, glorious mother Mary, of Matthew, of the aged Simeon and Hannah; also of the blind man (Luke 1; Matt. 9; Luke 2: 15, 18; Mark 10), and such like more; and I trust that he will, by the help and grace of God, fully understand how simple, plain, unfeigned, pious, righteous, forbearing, ardent, peaceable, joyous, merciful, amiable, ameliorating, modest, moral, humble, zealous, unblamable and pious a true, regenerating, christian faith is inwardly in power, before God, and outwardly in fruits, before one's neighbor.

Yea, even as a good, fruitful tree, of its own accord, without any compulsion, always brings forth its own good fruits, so also a true christian faith must bring forth its own good fruits. For it is infallible, the righteous must live by faith.

If Abraham, Isaac, Jacob, Moses, Joshua and Samuel, with all the patriarchs and prophets believed the word of the Lord, which was declared to them by angels, or were found so faithful therein, how much more should we believe and be faithful to that word which the Prince of angels, God's only begotten Son, the true witness and Teacher of righteousness, Christ Jesus, who came from the high heavens, from his Father's bosom, brought down and taught on earth.

It will not suffice to say, That Jesus Christ is the Son of God, that he fulfilled the law for us, that he paid for our sins with his blood, and made reconciliation with the Father, by his offering and death; neither will it suffice to only believe that his gospel is true, his word is right, the wages of sin is death, and that grace is eternal life; but the heart must rightly comprehend it, and the mind must be resolved upon it, otherwise it will not justify. Paul says, "With the heart man believeth unto righteousness," Rom. 10: 10.

All who believe with their whole hearts, that Christ Jesus is the righteous Branch of David, the righteous, wise King; the true, promised Prophet; the right Way and Truth, and our only Propitiator, Intercessor, Mediator and High Priest, Jer. 22: 5, also believe that all his words are immutable and true; and his offering sufficient and perfect; they, therefore, obey his word, walk in his commands, bow to his sceptre and pacify their consciences by his grace, reconciliation, merits, offering, promises, death and blood. They believe and acknowledge, if they neglect his word and will, and presumptuously transgress his commands, and live according to the flesh, that God will require it at their hands and punish them eternally, with the fire of his wrath, through his righteous judgment. For if those who wilfully transgressed the Mosaic law, were to die without mercy, upon the testimony of two or three witnesses, how much sorer then will those be punished, who trample under foot the Son of God; who esteem the pure blood of the New Testament as impure, and profane the Holy Spirit of grace? Heb. 10: 28.

Yes, kind reader, if we truly believed, and acknowledged it from the inmost of our souls, it would so move our hearts, and enkindle them with the fear and love of the Lord, that although all the tyrants that ever were, would rise in all their dread torture, and blood shedding, and stand before us, they would not in the least deter or hinder us from the word and way of the Lord. Besides, all our impure, carnal thoughts, unseasoned words, and useless, ungodly works would soon die, as Sirach says, "The fear of the Lord driveth away sins," Eccl. 1: 21; and it is impossible, without the fear of the Lord, to become right.

Seeing then, it is very evident, that a sincere, christian faith acknowledges God in his righteousness, and therefore fears his judgment, and thus through fear buries sin and dies to it, as more than once related, and that nevertheless, you live in all avarice, unchastity, drunkenness, wrath, lewdness, blindness, idolatry, and all manner of wickedness, tell us, beloved, where is then your faith and word of God of which you boast so much? Do you not know that it is written, "If ye live after the flesh ye shall die?" Or do you think that you can trifle with God as with a man? Be not deceived, says Paul, God will not be mocked.

Ah! reader, take heed, I tell you the truth in Christ, Beware! if you do not repent with all your heart and seek God, through Christ, do not hear, believe and fear him, but remain earthly and carnal, and walk after the lusts of your flesh, your sentence already pronounced, will be *death*. As Christ himself says, I judge no man, but the word that I have spoken, the same shall judge him in the last day.

I, therefore, faithfully admonish you, as before God, even as I do mine own soul, divest yourselves immediately of false doctrine, of all unbelief, idolatry and earthly, disgraceful lives, in which, alas! you have hitherto walked, lest the wrath of God overtake you in the sleep of your sins.

Awaken! He is still merciful, seek and receive the true doctrine, true faith, true sacraments, the true service, and lead a godly life, as the Scriptures teach, "Then shall thy light break forth as the morning, and thine health shall spring forth speedily, and thy righteousness shall go before thee; the glory of the LORD shall be thy reward," Isa. 58: 8.

Further, I say, If you truly believed and rightly understood that you became, through Adam's disobedience, children of the devil, of wrath, and of eternal death, subjected to the righteous curse and judgment of God, and that now all obstacles and all your sins are taken away and reconciled through the precious blood of Christ; so that you are called from wrath into grace, from cursings to blessings, and out of death to life (not to mention the favors which are daily shown you), then your hearts would sprout forth as the sweet-scented, blooming violet, full of pure love; yea, flow as the living fountain, from which flow forth the refreshing sweet waters of righteousness, and you would, with holy Paul, say, from the bottom of your soul, Who shall separate us from the love of Christ? Since it can never be, if I am in the bonds of perfection with him, and love him with a pure heart, a good conscience and unfeigned faith, that anything then can turn me away or separate me from him. For it is my own desire and highest joy, that I hear and speak of his word, and in my weakness, walk as he commanded and taught through his Son, should it even cost money and possessions, flesh or blood, his will be done.

Behold, dear reader, since then it is manifest in the Holy Scriptures, that the true Christian faith through the fear of God, dies to sin, and through love does the things of righteousness, though in weakness, I therefore let you judge whether those believe from the heart, who with the mouth say, that the blood of Christ is the propitiatory sacrifice of their sin, and nevertheless seek and follow up all kinds of idolatry, such as infant baptism, holy water, absolution, auricular confession, masses, gold, silver, and wooden images, wafers, stone churches, and the drunken adultery of the priests. Ah! how well it would be for them to reflect.

I say, As true as the Lord lives, there will eternally be found no other remedy for our sins, whether in heaven or upon earth; neither works, merits nor sacraments, even though they are used according to the Scriptures; neither cross, tribulation, angels, men, nor any other means will avail, but alone the immaculate, crimson blood of the Lamb (Christ), which was, out of pure grace, mercy and love, shed for the remission of our sins, Mark 14: 24.

Hence, it is incontrovertible, that all those who use such strange, idolatrous means for sin, belong not to the believing, grateful church of Christ. Therefore, I will present you with a few passages from the gospel and writings of the apostles, and set them before your eyes as a clear mirror, in which you may view yourselves, and see whether you are believing Christians.

Thus teaches the word of the Lord, "Verily, verily, I say unto thee, Except a man be born again, he cannot see the kingdom of God." And again, "Verily I say unto you, Except ye be converted, and become as little children, ye shall not enter into the kingdom of heaven."

Prove yourselves with this; if you are born of the pure seed of the holy word, then the nature of the seed must be in you; and if you have become like little children, then there are no more pride, unchastity, avarice, hatred and envy in you; for the innocent children know nothing of such sins. But if you continue to live in old Adam, and not in Christ, and walk after the base, impure desires of your flesh, then you practically prove that you are not born of God, and have not his faith.

The word of the Lord teaches again, "Go into all the world and preach the gospel to every creature; he that believeth and is baptized shall be saved." Here, prove yourselves again, He that believes and is rightly baptized, truly repents, circumcises his heart, dies to sin, rises in Christ to a new life, &c. But if you remain impenitent, your hearts uncircumcised, not dead to sin, but live out of Christ and his word, then is the deed your witness, that you are disbelievers and have not the baptism of Christ. Again does the word of the Lord teach, "If thou wilt enter life keep the commandments." For in Christ, says Paul, neither circumcision nor uncircumcision availeth, but the keeping of the commands of God. And this is his command, "Thou shalt love the Lord thy God with all thy heart, and with all thy soul, and with all thy mind, and with all thy strength, and thou shalt love thy neighbor as thyself," Mark 12: 30.

Hereby, prove yourselves again, If you love God, you will keep his commandments, you will do to your neighbor as you would have him do to you; but if you despise his word, do not follow his ordinances in doctrine, baptism, Holy Supper, and separation, and if you do not walk according to his holy, godly commands; also belie, cheat and betray your neighbor; if you take your neighbor's life, disgrace his wife, daughters or servants, and treat him perfidiously; if you mislead the poor, blind souls from the true way and obedience of the Lord, be it through persecution or false doctrine, and thus bereave them of the eternal kingdom, and lead them to hell, then it is more than clear, that you hate the command of the Lord and have not his faith.

Again, the word of the Lord teaches, "Enter ye in at the strait gate; for wide is the gate, and broad is the way, that leadeth to destruction, and many there be which go in thereat; because strait is the gate, and narrow is the way, which leadeth unto life; and few there be that find it," Matt. 7: 13. At another place it is written, "If any man will come after me, let him deny himself, and take up his cross and follow me." He that loves father and mother, man or wife, son or daughter, more than me, is not worthy of me.

Here prove yourselves again, Have you such a spirit, such frankness and faith, that you, in time of need, are ready to forsake father, mother and your all, for the sake of God's word and his testimony; to take upon yourself the cross of Christ; to deny yourself in all things; to enter, with Christ, upon the way of suffering, and thus enter, with the poor small flock, at the narrow, strait gate; then may the Lord strengthen you. But if you live unto yourselves, reject the cross of Christ, and love father, mother, wife, children, property or life more than Christ; walk on the broad way with the multitude and enter the wide gate, then the mouth of the Lord gives testimony that you are disbelievers and that your end is damnation.

Again, says the word of the Lord, "And they that are Christ's have crucified the flesh with the affections and lusts," Gal. 5: 24. For those who live after the flesh, such as adulterers, whoremongers, incontinent, avaricious, drunkards, gamblers, thieves, hateful, haughty, defamers, blood-thirsty, idolaters, shall die.

Prove yourselves again, If your lusts do not reign in you, if you do not walk in any of these and such like carnal ways, which have been mentioned, but if you can smother them and trample them under foot, through faith, then thank God, fight piously, watch and pray. But if you satiate your lusts, and walk in the impure ways of your flesh, then reform yourselves; for then it is evident that you are not, penitent, believing christians, but impenitent, carnal heathens.

Again, The word of the Lord teaches, "Therefore, take no thought, saying, What shall we eat? or what shall we drink? or, wherewithal shall we be clothed? For after all these things do the gentiles seek; but seek ye first the kingdom of God, and his righteousness; and all these things shall be added unto you," Matt. 6: 31.

Here prove yourselves again, If you believe

that the strong and mighty God, who nourished Israel forty years with bread from heaven and with water from the rock, and kept their clothes from being worn out, and fed Elias by a raven, will not forsake you in your distress, but will provide for you by his grace; this is a true evidence that you have the word of the Lord. But if, through your cares, you are induced or constrained, that you neglect the kingdom of God and his righteousness, seek temporal, more than eternal things, and are so much concerned as if God had more concern for the flowers and fowls than for you and your children, boast not that you believe the promise and word of the Lord.

Again, the word of the Lord teaches, "For God so loved the world, that he gave his only begotten Son, that whosoever believeth in him should not perish, but have everlasting life. For God sent not his Son into the world to condemn the world, but that the world through him might be saved. He that believeth on him is not condemned; but he that believeth not is condemned already, because he hath not believed in the name of the only begotten Son of God," John 3: 16—18.

Here prove yourselves the seventh time. If you sincerely believe these words of Christ with the whole heart, that the Almighty, Eternal Father so loved you and the whole human family, that he sent his incomprehensible, Almighty, eternal Word, Wisdom, Truth and Son, by whom he created the heavens, earth, the sea and the fulness thereof, and his eternal glory, into this vale of misery; that he let him become a poor, grieved, miserable man; that he let him, for the sake of all our sins, suffer hunger and thirst; permitted him to be slandered, apprehended, crowned with thorns, scourged, crucified and killed; then it cannot fail that your old carnal mind must become a regenerated, spiritual mind; your thoughts must become chaste and pure; your words must become discreet and well seasoned and your whole life pious and unblamable.

Instantly you should awaken, walk in the right way, keep aloof from all abomination and idolatry, forsake false prophets, preachers and priests; and seek the true teachers, sacraments and divine service; for a true, sincere, Christian faith cannot be idle; but it changes, renews, purifies, sanctifies and justifies more and more; it makes joyous and glad, for by faith it knows that hell, devil, sin and death, are conquered through Christ, and that grace, mercy, and redemption from sin, and eternal life, are acquired through him. In full confidence, the possessor of true christian faith approaches the Father, in the name of Christ, receives the Holy Ghost, becomes partaker of the divine nature, and is renewed after the image of him, who created him, lives by the virtue of Christ, which is in him; all his ways are righteousness, godliness, honesty, chastity, truth, wisdom, goodness, benevolence, light, love and joy.

He sanctifies his body and heart as a habitation and temple of Christ and the Holy Ghost; hates all that is against God and his word; honors, praises and thanks God with a sincere heart; and there is nothing to deter him, neither judgment, wrath, hell, devil, sin nor eternal death. For he knows that Christ is his Intercessor, Mediator and Propitiator. He acknowledges with holy Paul, that "There is, therefore, now no condemnation to them which are in Christ Jesus, who walk not after the flesh, but after the Spirit," Rom. 8: 1. The Spirit of the Lord assures him that he is a child of God, and a joint heir of Christ; he, therefore, wholly dedicates himself to his Lord and Savior, Jesus Christ, who called him through grace, drew him by his Spirit, enlightened him by his word, and purchased him with his blood.

Behold, this is the nature of living faith, which has such an urgent, cogent power, spirit, fear, energy and life; which avails with God and has the promise in the Scriptures. Happy he who has such a faith and will salutarily retain it to the end. I repeat it, prove yourselves, whether you are in the faith; in Christ or out of Christ; penitent or impenitent. For in the mirror presented, you may view the whole face of your conscience and life, if you but believe that the word of the Lord is true and right. Here notice how the true, christian faith, through grace, is the only living fountain, whence flows, not only the penitent, new life, but also obedience to the evangelical ceremonies, such as baptism and the Lord's Supper will have to come and follow, not as those compelled through the law, for the rod of the oppressor is broken, but voluntarily, through the free will and submissive spirit of love, which is of a christian nature, and is ready to all good works and obedience of the holy divine word.

For all the truly regenerated and spiritual conform in all things to the word and ordinances of the Lord; not because they think to merit the propitiation of their sins and eternal life; by no means; in this matter they depend upon nothing except the true promise of the merciful Father, graciously given to all believers, through the blood and merits of Christ, which blood is, and ever will be the only eternal medium of our reconciliation, and not works, baptism or Lord's supper, as said above.

For if our reconciliation depended upon works and ceremonies, then it would not be grace, and the merits and fruits of the blood of Christ would be void. O no! it is grace, and will be grace to all eternity; all that the merciful father is doing or has done for us grievous sinners, through his beloved Son and Holy Spirit, is grace. Hence it is that they hear the voice of the Lord, believe his word, and therefore they should willingly observe and perform (although in weakness), the representation of both signs, under water, and bread and wine, set forth in obedience. For a truly believing christian is thus minded, that he will not do otherwise than that which the word of the Lord enjoins and teaches; for he knows, that all presumption and disobedience, are like sins of witchcraft, and the end thereof is death.

Yes, good reader, the true christian belief, as the Scriptures require, is so lively, active and powerful with all those, who have rightly received it through the grace of the Lord, that they do not fear to forsake father, mother, wife, children, money and possessions for the word and testimony of the Lord; to suffer all manner of scorn, disgrace, fatigue, hardship and prison, and finally to have their poor, weak bodies, which are so fearful of suffering, burned at the stake, as may be frequently seen in the pious children and witnesses of Christ Jesus, especially in these our Netherlands.

Alas! how many did I know before, and know the greater part of them now, both men and women, men and maid-servants (would to God that they be increased to many hundred thousands), who, from the inmost of their souls, seek Christ and his word, and lead, in all meekness, a pious, unblamable life before God and man; sincere and holy in doctrine, full of the fear and love of God, ready to help one another, merciful, compassionate, meek, sober, chaste, neither refractory nor seditious; but quiet and peaceable, obedient to the magistracy in all things not contrary to God; and who have, nevertheless, for a number of years, not slept in their beds, and even do not now; for they are so much hated by the world, that they have been persecuted, betrayed, taken, exiled and slain like highwaymen, thieves and murderers, and that without mercy; and for no other reason, than that they, out of true fear of God, dare not take part in the abominable, carnal life, and with the accursed, disgraceful idolatry of this blind world; neither dare they hear nor acknowledge the unchaste, drunken, lecherous priests and deceiving blind preachers, as the true apostles and teachers of God; they dare not receive the bread with the avaricious, envious, proud, drunkards, whores and rogues, from their hands, nor carry their children to the anti-christian washing and baptism, but seek such preachers and teachers, and also such a baptism, supper, church and life, which are in accordance with the Scriptures, and may stand according to the word of the Lord.

Behold, before God, I write the truth, indeed they are such a people, if I otherwise know them rightly, hypocrites excepted, who, in the flesh, weep more than they laugh, mourn more than they are joyful, rather give than receive; who are ready not only to sacrifice possessions, and their all, but also body and life for the praise of the Lord, and to the necessary service of their neighbor, according to the command of the Scripture, as much as in them is. No matter how much the poor children are harassed, they are still so much strengthened in God, that they can neither be moved nor deterred. They possess their souls with patience, waiting for the joy which is promised. Truly

FAITH.

said Christ, "Ye will be hated of all men for my name's sake," Matt. 24: 9.

Since then it is evident from all this, that the true evangelical faith is of such a nature, as said, and is the only means and tree, which, through the grace of God, bears and propagates all manner of good fruit; therefore, it is considered, in Scripture, the most precious, and greatest work, and all things are ascribed to faith, such as miracles, and the power to become the children of God, and be justified; be blessed and saved; purified and sanctified; and have eternal life, as we have related when treating of the Malefactor's faith.

Not, dear reader, that we believe that faith merits this on account of its worth; by no means; but because the pleasure of God, through his word, has given his promise through true faith; then it must also by virtue of that word follow faith. For the Scriptures plainly teach, that all things, visible and invisible, must hear, yield, serve and follow the powerful word of God, as when he said, Let there be heaven and earth. Heaven and earth sprang into existence at these words. For God's word, says Esdras, is his perfect work. God also says to Israel, If thou shalt hearken diligently unto the voice of the LORD thy God, all these blessings shall come upon thee; but if thou wilt not hearken, the curse shall be upon thee; and it also happened, as it was told Israel, "For God," says Balaam, "is not a man that he should lie; neither the son of man, that he should repent." For these reasons the promise must follow true faith, or else it cannot be denied that God, who is a God of truth, must be untrue and faithless. O no! all that he wills must be done; what he promises must be fulfilled, and not otherwise than he has promised, for he alone is true, and we are all liars," Rom. 3. Paul says, "If we believe not, yet he abideth faithful; he cannot deny himself."

Since then faith so firmly acknowledges that God cannot break his promise, but must keep it, because he is the truth and cannot lie, therefore, does he make his children free, joyful, and glad in spirit; though they are confined in prisons and bonds, have to suffer by water and fire, in chains and at the stake; for they are assured in the spirit, through faith, that God will not withdraw his promise, but will fulfill it in due time; for they believe on Christ in whom the promises are sealed, and through him also acknowledge his grace, word and will; notwithstanding that they, in former times, lived so ungodly, and walked according to the flesh.

They hope with faithful Abraham, where nothing is to be hoped, and wait for things invisible, as though they saw them, and with full confidence adhere to the assurance, truth, faithfulness and power of the heavenly promise, which is made to us by the infallible, true mouth of our Lord Jesus Christ, the Son of God, without any previous work or merit, through the gracious choice and will of his merciful Father in his true word. And this regenerating, justifying, converting, penitent, active and confident faith, which comes from the Father of light, by hearing his holy word, is the only faith that avails with God, and which has the assurance of the promise of grace in the word, through the Holy Ghost; besides this, the Holy Scriptures know of no other faith.

Before now, I have read in some books, which they have written, that there is but *one* good work which saves us, namely, FAITH, and but *one* sin which will damn us, namely, UNBELIEF. This I will leave as it is, and not find fault with it; for where there is a sincere, true *faith*, there are also all manner of sincere, good fruits. On the other hand, where there is *unbelief*, there are also all manner of evil fruits; therefore, is salvation properly ascribed to *faith*, and damnation to *unbelief*.

Faithful reader, pay attention. Since we plainly perceive that the whole world, Papists, Lutherans, Zuinglians, Davidists, libertines, &c., walk the broad road of sin, and lead a carnal, vain life, and do not abide by the pure, salutary, perfect, doctrine, sacrament and unblamable, pure example of Christ; therefore they are themselves witnesses, that they reject the corner stone, Jesus Christ, and believe not his word and truth, though a few of them write much of faith and speak of the Scriptures. Say, beloved, did you ever read in the Scriptures, or did you ever hear, that a truly believing, regenerated christian, after repentance and conversion, remained proud, avaricious, unchaste, greedy, hateful, tyrannical and idolatrous, and continued to live after the base desires of the flesh? You must say, *no!* If you speak of Peter and David, you must observe how short or how long a time their fall lasted, and what penance they did. Turn yourselves to the east or west, south or north, and you will find ungodly, vain, pompous, foolish actions and conduct, with all those who boast of faith, so that we shall have to say with Christ and John, They are, with few exceptions, of the devil and not of God. For the devil, from the beginning, was proud and haughty, so are they; he was a liar, so are they; he was a falsifier of the word of the Lord, so are they; he was disputatious against God, so are they; in short, he is a revengeful murderer, an abominable, blood-thirsty tyrant, so are many of them. The way in which they use those who seek Christ sincerely and believe, fear, follow, serve and call on him, has been more than once fully related.

Yea, alas, they are so wrathful and enraged at them, that they will scarcely call them by their right names, but they call them anabaptists, fanatics, rioters, factionists, hedge preachers, deceivers, heretics, new monks, knaves and miscreants, although they seek the kingdom of God and his righteousness with all their hearts, which God knows, who tries the reins and hearts of men, and wish no evil to any one upon earth.

This they all do through the ignorant, defaming of the envious, inhuman, lying, crying and writing of their learned priests and preachers, who ever since the blasphemous beast of anti-christ ascended his kingdom and glory, have always been the true cause of the tyrannical shedding of innocent blood in the past and present; for they are those who instigate the magistracy to murder, and the thoughtless, reckless people to defame and blaspheme, and, I fear, that they will continue to be the cause till the end.

Nevertheless, the chosen are to awaken, repent and obey the voice of the Lord; for idolatrous, blood-thirsty, confused Babel shall sink, and be desolated; and fair Jerusalem, the city of peace, shall increase, and through the power of Almighty God must be built up in glory. Of this all rejoice, who are called to the marriage of the Lamb, and whose names are written in the BOOK of LIFE with God. Here is the understanding, wisdom, faith and patience of the saints; let him that has understanding, observe, that the word of the Lord is true. Blessed are they who are ready to meet the coming of the Lamb.

Behold, such a faithless, impenitent, tyrannical, idolatrous, refractory, disobedient, blind, carnal people they are, who imagine that they are the believing church, and the lawful bride of Christ. These poor children do not observe that all under heaven is spoiled, even as the prophet complains that "there is no truth, nor mercy, nor knowledge of God in the land; by swearing, and lying, and killing, and stealing, and committing adultery, they break out, and blood toucheth blood," Hos. 4: 1, 2. The world, says John, lieth in wickedness. If we come to the lords and princes, there we find such pride, arrogance, pomp and wantonness, such banqueting, eating and drinking to excess, with some, such adultery and whoredom, and such unreasonable, blind idolatry, and with many, such unmerciful, raging tyranny that they are in truth more like proud Nebuchadnezzar, drunken Belshazzar, and Nabal, and blood thirsty, vain Antioch, Nero, and Maximinus, than christian, believing lords and kind princes. If we come to the judges and rulers, to each in his station, with some we find only violence and injustice, with some nothing but avarice, astonishing practices; they steal honestly and rob honorably; pass sentence for gain and gifts; honor the high and despise the poor, do not justice to the poor widow, orphan and the oppressed stranger, execute their office and power with rigor, and not fraternally; serve princes and not God, as the prophet Micah laments, What the prince desires, the judge does, so that he will again reward him. Alas! where shall we find one, who loves God with all the heart, hates avarice, seeks the truth, who will defend the godfearing, and do him justice?

If we come to the priests or monks, there we find such insatiable avarice, that they offer and sell prayers, psalms, matins, vespers, masses, sermons, baptism, Lord's Supper, absolution, and all their church services, together with their own souls; take rents and gold from the deceased, will go six or ten miles, from one place to another for a guilder; where they find the most milk, wool and meat, there they prefer to be among the sheep; like to be flattered and honored by the world; suffer themselves to be called doctors, lords, masters, abbots, provosts, priors, fathers, guardians, commanders and presidents; like to wear long garments; seek to be greeted at the market, and take the first seats at the table and in the church, as Christ said of the scribes and pharisees, Mark 12: 39. Besides, the greater part of them live in such whoredom and sodomy that the angels are astonished and blush; they defile one woman after another, also one virgin after another; they defraud and corrupt the whole world, both temporally and spiritually; they have all their joy in a temporal, carnal life; study by day and by night, how they may pamper their proud, idle, lazy flesh; eat and drink, saying, as it is written, "Come ye, say they, I will fetch wine, and we will fill ourselves with strong drink; and to-morrow shall be as this day, and much more abundant," Isa. 56: 12. They betray the faithful, pious hearts, who with all their powers seek Christ and eternal life; they warn every one of the truth and its followers, and cry, Hear us, we are your teachers and pastors, we will pledge our souls for you in the judgment of God; and thus encourage the malicious, lest they be converted from their wickedness. Promising liberty to others, and are themselves servants of corruption. I do not know how they could make it worse; nevertheless, those unblushing, abominable men, who according to the law of Moses, would have been stoned, and who according to the Scriptures must be eternally cursed and condemned, unless they repent, alas, are called the pastors and teachers of this poor, rude people. Behold, thus the world is corrupted.

If we come to the preachers, who boast of the word, we will find, that some are open liars, others drunken sots, some usurers, some wanton and gay, some defamers and slanderers, others persecutors and betrayers of the innocent; how some of them live, how they came to get their wives, and what kind of wives they have, this I will commit to the Lord and to themselves. They teach secretly that there are *two sons* in Christ, the Son of God, and the son of Mary, and that he who died for our sins, was not the Son of God; they also teach and practice a baptism which is not commanded in the Scriptures, and a supper, in which they consider the *bread* the *body*, and the *wine* the *blood* of Christ; they have, and hold no other BAN, than the gallows, and the wheel; lead an unconcerned, easy life; they live of mere flattery, deceit and the booty of antichrist, and preach just as much as the worldly, carnal magistracy desire to hear; promise peace to the poor impenitent, although there is no peace.

If we come to the common people, we find such an unbecoming, carnal, blind, uncircumcised horde, that we are astonished; they know neither God nor his word. If nature teaches anything reasonable, that is all their piety; but of the Spirit, word, ordinances, will and life they indeed know but very little. In short, it has come so far in the world, that we may lament and say with the holy prophet, "Run ye to and fro through the streets of Jerusalem, and see now, and know, and seek in the broad places thereof, if ye can find a man, if there be any that executeth judgment, that seeketh the truth," Jer. 5: 1.

Not one stone has remained upon another; all is desolated which Christ and his faithful messengers taught us of faith, love, baptism, Supper, reconciliation, sin, repentance, regeneration, separation, teachers, deacons and of true, divine service, nevertheless, they are called the church of Christ by their blind priests and preachers, even as if Christ and the Father were to be satisfied with names, bread, wine and water. O no! the chosen of God are the church of Christ, his saints and beloved, who washed their clothes in the blood of the Lamb, who are born of God, influenced by the Spirit of Christ; who are in Christ and he in them, who hear and believe his word, who follow him in their weakness, in his commandments, walk in his footsteps with all patience and humility, hate the evil, and love the good, earnestly desiring to apprehend Christ as they are apprehended of him, for all who are in

Christ, are new creatures, flesh of his flesh, bone of his bone, and members of his body. How you and the rest of mankind conform to this, I will leave you and all reasonable readers to reflect upon, in the fear of God, both according to your understanding, and according to the Scriptures.

Since, then, all things are desolated through the righteous wrath and judgment of God, because (as Paul says) they delighted in unrighteousness and lies, by the false prophets and ravening wolves, so that nothing salutary has remained according to the true sense and ground of Christ and his holy apostles, and since we find nothing in the whole world, among all the great sects, only vain boastings, mere names, false doctrine, false sacraments, vain unbelief and an impenitent, carnal life, and this under the name and semblance of Christ and his holy church, therefore, I am constrained, by true, christian love, to make known the power and ground of the holy Scriptures, according to my small gift, given me of God, and through this to show which is the *true, christian faith*, having the promise; namely, the faith which changes man from evil into good, to a divine nature, both inwardly and outwardly, and makes him, as said, holy, righteous, obedient, new, pious, peaceable and joyful; in order that all good, pious hearts, who desire to walk in the right way, but who are hindered therefrom by their blind priests and preachers, may read or hear this my faithful EXPOSITION and INSTRUCTION, and that they may thereby be instructed in the truth; that the indifferent and drowsy may be awakened, and that all hypocrites may be ashamed, and reform; and that all those who love God sincerely, may be more instructed and taught in the faith, if they do by any means acknowledge this as the sure FOUNDATION of God, as it is, and will be, for ever. Lord, grant that many may read and understand it, and thus receive and obey it, that they may sincerely repent and be saved, Amen.

And since I do it out of a sincere heart, and labor not with any other view, of which the great God, the Searcher of the hearts and reins of men is my witness, than that I may teach repentance to the ignorant, rude world, which knows not Christ, lead them to Christ and his doctrine, sacraments and example, that many might be saved; and as we plainly see there are many profligates who have reformed their sinful, carnal lives, and commenced an upright, penitent, pious life in the fear of the Lord; then it is gross ingratitude, yea, hardened, ungodly tyranny, to hate me and my faithful co-workers so enviously, and recompense us so shamefully, who manifest such great fidelity and love towards them in our manifold sufferings and trials.

But thus they treated all the prophets and faithful servants of God from the beginning, who preached to them the word and will of the Lord with great fidelity, reproved their sins, sought their salvation till death, with all their powers, with many tears, watchings, prayers, labors, cares and sorrows; therefore, it is not strange, and no wonder, that they will treat us so; for Christ says, "For so persecuted they the prophets, which were before you," Matt. 5: 12.

I hereby entreat and desire, through the mercy of our Lord Jesus Christ, all my readers and hearers in general, of whatever name, office, station and condition, that you be pleased neither to defame nor to reject my labor, as long as you have not read it impartially, heard it rightly and understood it. Therefore, separate the doctrine, sacraments and life of Christ, from the doctrine, sacraments and life of the priests and preachers; separate faith and unbelief, spirit and flesh, righteousness and unrighteousness. Seek after the truth, strive zealously for your salvation, believe that God is true, that he will reward the good and punish the evil, that his word is, and will for ever remain truth. Fear his judgment, love his bounties; then you shall know, by the grace of the Lord, that the aforementioned is the true Christian faith, which avails before God, and has the promise in the Scriptures, as we have so abundantly testified and shown to you by the word of God, and with such strong and incontrovertible reasons, Scriptures and examples, without deceit and fraud, as it were before, in Christ Jesus.

May the Almighty, eternal, merciful God and Father, through his beloved Son, Jesus Christ, lead you all, one with another, into

FAITH.

his holy, divine knowledge and evangelical truth, and make your faith so fruitful and active, that you may, with sincere, new hearts, patiently submit to his cross in every trial and affliction, and that you may walk, with unfeigned love, be peaceable and joyful in spirit, as the unblamable, pious children of God, before the Lord and his church all the days of your lives, and ultimately obtain the promise of grace, the end of your faith, and the salvation of your souls, Amen.

TO THE CHRISTIAN READER.

CONCLUSION.

Beloved reader, here you have my FOUNDATION AND DOCTRINE OF FAITH, with its *properties, power, operation and fruits*. I therefore entreat you all, if you appreciate Christ and your own salvation, suppress your perverted minds, be not enraged and embittered, should you find any thing contrary to the usages of our forefathers, standing usages, or philosophic writings and the cry of the learned; but first prove it rightly, and scrutinize it well with Christ and the word, spirit, life and example, of his holy apostles, whether it is not the true content, meaning, doctrine and sense of the whole Scriptures; if so, you will have to give up the unscriptural usage, and the deceptive cry of the learned, and hold only to the word of the Lord, if you would be saved. Let, therefore, your heart be impartial, and your judgment sincere after truth; for the Almighty God and Lord, before whom every knee shall bow and every tongue confess, will not and cannot yield to any of the learned, or to long-standing usages or customs; for he is Lord, and we are his servants. We must follow *him*, and not he follow us. Reader, lay it to heart.

Likewise, if you find that we preach our doctrine rightly, respect not the dignity of any man, fear no man's tyranny, nor yield to the learned, but that we in true, sincere love, faithfully teach, admonish and reprove all who do amiss, without respect of persons, with the Holy Spirit, word, example and ordinance of the Lord, in all things not right; then, I entreat you again, that you would be pleased not to attribute this to spiritual pride, but to well-meant frankness and christian simplicity. I desire that you would all walk rightly, so that you may be saved, on account of which I have to endure not a little tribulation. I refuse not to become as a fool before all the world, so that I may make many wise in Christ, and with the Holy Spirit and powerful word of the Lord, lead them to wisdom and to the saints; and I well know that Christ and his apostles, and the prophets, were guilty of the same foolishness, and were of the same mind with me in this matter.

If I reprove, they reprove more; If I threaten with the wrath of the Lord, they do so much more. Were they on that account carnal and proud? Far from it, Yes, my reader, had not the dark smoke of men-pleasing-preachers, the accursed, false doctrine of the dreadful, abominable locusts out of the abyss, risen up; but had sincere reproving, the true, pure doctrine, the scriptural usage of the holy sacraments, and the separating of the impenitent, without respect to person, continued in the world, never would the pleasing sun have lost his splendor, nor would the church have lapsed into such a grieved and deadly condition; therefore, I esteem it with Paul, to be unimportant, to be judged of men in this matter. For I know that I mean it well, do right and reprove only with the truth, so that they may be converted.

May the true heavenly Light, Jesus Christ, be eternally blessed, and enlighten all dark, benighted hearts with the clear and lucid ray of his Holy Ghost and eternal truth, that they may view, in unfeigned, pure faith, the eternal brightness of Christ, to the praise and honor of his great name, and to the salvation of many souls, Amen.

A

Fundamental Doctrine

FROM THE

WORD OF THE LORD,

EXHORTING ALL, WHO ARE CALLED AFTER THE NAME OF CHRIST, TO THE HEAVENLY BIRTH AND THE NEW CREATURE, WITHOUT WHICH, NONE WHO HAVE COME TO THE YEARS OF UNDERSTANDING, ARE OR CAN BE A TRUE CHRISTIAN.

DILIGENTLY REVISED AND ENLARGED

BY

MENNO SIMON.

A. D., 1556.

"In Christ Jesus neither circumcision availeth anything, nor uncircumcision, but a new creature," Gal. 6: 15.

"For other foundation can no man lay than that is laid, which is Jesus Christ," 1 Cor. 3: 11.

ELKHART, INDIANA:
PUBLISHED BY JOHN F. FUNK AND BROTHER.
1871.

A FUNDAMENTAL DOCTRINE

FROM THE

WORD OF THE LORD, OF THE NEW BIRTH.

Hear my words, all people, and understand them, all you who imagine that you are Christians, and presumptuously boast of the grace, merits, flesh, blood, cross, kingdom and death of the Lord, notwithstanding we find among you neither Christian faith, brotherly love, repentance, the right use of the sacraments of Christ, the pure doctrine, nor the unblamable, godly life, which is out of God, to which the Scriptures admonish us; neither the true, divine service, evangelical disposition, nor obedience; but throughout, nothing else than abominable, dark unbelief, a lewd, carnal life, false doctrine, false, self-devised sacraments, a devilish heart and mind, an accursed, heathenish idolatry under the name of Christ, blind, blood-thirsty tyranny, envious and furious revengefulness against all the children of God; yea, open obstinacy, disobedience and rejection of the words of Christ and of his Holy Ghost, as may be very plainly perceived and seen throughout the world.

In order that you may comfort yourselves no longer with lying and vain hopes, contrary to all Scriptures, to your eternal damnation, and not glory in vain, in the aforementioned riches and glory of the children of God, namely of the kingdom, grace, merits, flesh, blood, cross, death and promises of Christ, &c., which do not yet pertain to you, because you are yet altogether earthly, carnally and devilishly minded, reject Christ, and do not keep to his Spirit, word and example, without which no one can be a christian; therefore I have undertaken through the merciful grace of the Lord, as much as is in my power, to inform you, briefly, by the infallible, powerful, saving word of the holy gospel of Christ, and out of the pure doctrine of his holy apostles, in this my epistle, who they are, or who they are not, that are endowed through the grace of God, and to whom pertain the aforementioned gifts, merits and promises of Christ.

Tell me, most beloved, where or when did you read in the Scriptures, which is the true witness of the Holy Ghost and the plummet of our consciences, that the unbelieving, disobedient, carnal adulterer, whoremonger, drunkard, avaricious, idolatrous or pompous had a single promise of the kingdom of Christ and his church, yea, part or communion in his merits, death and blood? I tell you the truth, nowhere do we read it in the Scriptures, nor ever will we; but thus it is written by Paul, "For if ye live after the flesh ye shall die." Adulterers, whoremongers, buggerers, effeminate, unclean, idolators, drunkards, proud, avaricious, betrayers of the innocent, and bloodshedders, thieves, murderers, backbiters, perjurers, sorcerers, liars, unmerciful, the disobedient to God and Christ (if they repent not) will not inherit the kingdom of God, yea, their portion will be in the fiery lake which burns with fire and brimstone, which is the second death, Rom. 8: 13; 1 Cor. 6: 10; Eph. 5: 5.

Behold, worthy reader, this is God's irrevocable sentence and judgment upon all who live after the flesh, whoever they be, emperor or king, duke or earl, knight or squire, noble or ignoble, priest or monk, learned or unlearned, rich or poor, male or female, bond or free. All, who live after the flesh, must forever remain under the just sentence and eternal wrath of God, otherwise the whole Scriptures are untrue.

Therefore, are the poor, ignorant people comforted in vain with masses, matins, vespers, confessions, pilgrimages and holy water, and what is more, with Christ's grace, death and blood. The word stands firm, "For if ye live after the flesh ye shall die; for to be carnally minded is death." Therefore, I advise and entreat you all in general, to hear Christ Jesus, who is sent to us as a witness of the truth from heaven; for thus says he, "Verily I say unto you, Except ye be converted and become as little children, ye shall not enter into the kingdom of heaven." At another place, "Verily, verily, I say unto thee, Except a man be born again, he cannot see the kingdom of God." Again, "Verily, verily, I say unto thee, Except a man be born of water and of the Spirit, he cannot enter into the kingdom of God."

Faithful reader, take heed; these words are not invented or instituted of man, nor are they the resolution of any council; but they are the infallible, precious words, which the Son of God, Christ Jesus, brought to us from the mouth of his Father, and declared unto pious Nicodemus, the scribe, with a double affirmation. That word is powerful and clear, and has not only reference to Nicodemus, but to all the children of Adam, who have come to the years of maturity. But alas, it is so obscured by the offensive, leavenous mire of human commands, statutes and glossaries, that scarcely one or two is found in a thousand, who have the true sense and understanding of the heavenly birth, much less have they the active nature, power, properties and fruits of it. Yea, they have brought it so far, through their philosophy, wisdom and self-chosen holiness, that the eternal Wisdom of God, Christ Jesus, eternally blessed, is banished as a poor, senseless fool, out of the house of his honor, which is his church, with his Holy Ghost, word, baptism, Supper, divine worship, separation and unblamable example; and the man of sin, the son of perdition, is placed in his stead, with his abominable doctrine, idolatrous infant baptism and supper, with his unclean purifications and promises, with his churches, convents, priests, monks, masses, matins, vespers, holy water, images, pilgrimages, purgatory, vigils, confessions, absolutions, &c.; all of which in short, are nothing but the doctrines and commands of men, raised up contrary to the Scriptures, an accursed idolatry and abomination, an open denial of the Lord's death and offering, a despising of the New Testament, or of the covenant which was sealed by the innocent blood of the Lamb, a destroying and desolation of the saving ordinances of Christ, of *doctrine, baptism, Supper, life and separation*, abundantly testified in the Scriptures, which ordinance he taught in this world with incontrovertible clearness and power according to the command of his Father, and left it to his children in his word, and none other can be established eternally that will stand before him.

In short, writers and the learned have corrupted every thing so much through their councils, decrees and statutes, with all the tyranny and violence of the great, that there is scarcely an article entire, of all that Christ and his holy apostles taught. All the aforementioned abominations, together with the ungodly, carnal life of the whole world, I call on as witnesses, nevertheless they would be called the holy christian church; and he that admonishes them in sincere, pure love, with the Spirit and word of the Lord, must be an accursed anabaptist and heretic. I tell you again, They want to be the christian church, and it is evident from all their actions, that they are not christians; but carnal, proud, avaricious, lascivious, lewd, drunken, idolatrous, blind heathens; and what is worse, some of them are unmerciful, murderous, ferocious, revengeful and bloodthirsty fiends; many of their works are done according to the will of the devil. We may with propriety complain of this matter; for the righteous judgment is come upon them, that they are unconvertible and that little of a salutary kind remains with them.

O! how miserably is the fair vineyard desolated, and how lamentably are its branches withered, its walls are broken down, the destroying foxes have destroyed the grapes, the clouds are dry and give no rain; there is neither pruner nor knife at hand; and if there is one he must be devoured by the dragon, or slain by the apocalyptical woman, drunk with blood. O merciful, gracious Father, how long will this great misery endure? Our rulers are like voracious lions and bears. Our fathers are our betrayers. Our leaders, our deceivers. And those who feign to be our pastors, are thieves and murderers of our souls. Well may we sigh and lament from the inmost of our hearts; for our house is left unto us desolate. For that which was heretofore the church and kingdom of Christ, is now, alas! the church and kingdom of anti-christ, and for no other reason than because they ungratefully rejected the word of grace, and will not have the ruling Lord Jesus Christ, to rule over them with the righteous sceptre of his holy word and Spirit; nevertheless, this poor, blind people hope to obtain the grace and promises of God through their infant baptism, masses, confession and the like superstitious ceremonies and idolatries, which they call the true, divine service, and use it as a remedy for their sins. Ah! no, most beloved, no; for, says Solomon, "The hope of the ungodly is like dust, that is blown away with the wind." I have said it once, and repeat it, and that from the mouth of the Lord, who can neither lie nor deceive, "Except ye be converted, and become as little children, ye shall not enter into the kingdom of heaven." And "Except a man be born again, he cannot see the kingdom of God," Matt. 18: 3; John 3: 3.

My beloved reader, take heed to the word of the Lord, and once learn to know the true God. I warn you faithfully to take heed; he will not save you, nor pardon your sins, nor show you his mercy and grace, except according to his word, namely, If you repent, if you believe, if you are born of him, if you do what he has commanded, and walk even as he walked. For if he could save unjustified, carnal man, without regeneration, faith and repentance, he did not teach us the truth; but he is the truth, and there is no lie in him. Therefore, I tell you again, that you cannot be reconciled with all your masses, matins, vespers, ceremonies, sacraments, councils, statutes and commands under the whole heavens, together with all the popes and their adherents from the beginning; for I warn you, they are abominations and not reconciliations. Christ says, "In vain do they honor me," because they teach commandments of men. But if you, by any means, wish to be saved, your earthly, carnal, ungodly life, must be reformed; for the Scriptures teach nothing but true repentance and reformation, and present to us admonitions, threatenings, reprovings, miracles, examples, ceremonies and sacraments; and if you do not repent, there is nothing in heaven or on earth that can save you; for without true repentance, we are comforted in vain. The prophet says, "O my people, they which lead thee cause thee to err, and destroy the way of thy paths," Isa. 3: 12. We must be born from above, must be changed and renewed in our hearts, transplanted from the unrighteous and evil nature of Adam, into the true and good nature of Christ, or we can never be saved by any means, whether human or divine. Wherever true repentance and the new creature are not (I speak of adults), man must be eternally lost; this is incontrovertibly clear. Upon this every one may confidently rely, who does not wish to deceive his soul.

That regeneration of which we write, from which comes the penitent, pious life having the promise, comes alone from the word of the Lord, if it be rightly taught, and if rightly understood and received in the heart by faith through the Holy Ghost. The first birth of man, is out of the first, earthly Adam, and therefore its nature is earthly and Adamic, that is, carnal-minded, unbelieving, disobedient and blind in divine things, deaf and foolish, whose end, if not renewed by the word, will be damnation and eternal death. Would you, therefore, have your inbred, evil nature reformed, and be free from eternal death and damnation, so that you may obtain, with all true christians, what is promised them, you must be born again. For the regenerated are in grace, and have the promise, as you have heard. They, therefore, lead a penitent and new life, for they are renewed in Christ, and have received a new heart and spirit. Before, they were earthly, carnally minded, but now, heavenly, spiritually; before, unrighteous, now righteous; before, evil, now good. And live no longer after the old, depraved nature of the first, earthly Adam, but after the new, sincere nature of the new and heavenly Adam, Christ Jesus; as Paul says, "Nevertheless, I live; yet not I, but Christ liveth in me." Their poor, weak life they renew daily, more and more, and that after the image of him who created them; their minds are after the mind of Christ, they gladly walk as he walked; crucify and mortify their flesh with its evil lusts; bury their sin with baptism in the Lord's death, and rise with him to a new life; circumcise their hearts with the word of the Lord, and are baptized with the Holy Ghost in the spotless, holy body of Christ, as obedient members and fellow-heirs of his church, according to the true ordinance and word of the Lord. They put on Christ and manifest his Spirit, nature and power in all their fruits; fear God with all the heart, and seek, in all their thoughts, words and works, nothing but the praise of God and the salvation of their beloved brethren. They know not hatred and vengeance, for they love those who hate them; do good to those who despitefully use them, and pray for those who persecute them; hate and resist avarice, pride, unchastity, pomp, drunkenness, fornication, adultery, hatred, envy, backbiting, lying, defrauding, quarreling, bloodshedding and idolatry, all impure, carnal works, and forsake the world with all its lusts; meditate upon the law of the Lord by day and by night; rejoice at the good, and are grieved at the evil; evil they do not repay with evil, but with good; they seek not *self*, nor their own good, but what is good for their neighbors, both as to body and soul; feed the hungry, and give drink to the thirsty; entertain the needy, release prisoners, visit the sick, comfort the faint-hearted, admonish the erring, and are ready after their master's example, to give their lives for their brethren. Again, their thoughts are pure and chaste, their words are true and seasoned with salt; with them *yea* is *yea*, and *nay* is *nay*, and their works are done in the fear of the Lord; their hearts are heavenly and new; their minds, peaceful and joyful; they seek righteousness with all their powers. In short, they are so assured in their faith through the Spirit and word of God, that they will valiantly overcome, by virtue of their faith, all bloodthirsty, cruel tyrants, with all their tortures, punishment, exiling, plunder, stocks, stakes, executioners, tormentors and counsel; and out of a pure zeal, with an innocent, pure, simple *yea* and *nay* are willing to die. The glory of Christ, the sweetness of the word, and the salvation of souls are dearer to them than any thing under heaven.

Behold, worthy reader, all those who are born of God with Christ, who thus conform their weak life to the gospel, are thus converted, and follow the example of Christ, hear and believe his holy word, follow his commands, which he, in plain words commanded us in the holy Scriptures, form the holy, christian church which has the promise; the true children of God, brothers and sisters of Christ; for they are born with him of one Father, and of the new Eve, the pure, chaste bride. They are flesh of Christ's flesh, and bone of his bone, the spiritual house of Israel, the spiritual city, Jerusalem, temple and Mount Zion, the spiritual ark of the Lord, in which are hidden the true bread of heaven, Christ Jesus and his blessed word, the green, blossoming rod of faith, and the spiritual tables of stone, with the commands of the Lord written thereon; they are the spiritual seed of Abraham, children of the promise, confederates of the covenant of God, and partakers of the heavenly blessings.

These regenerated have a spiritual king over them, who rules them by the unbroken sceptre of his mouth, namely, with his Holy Spirit and Word, he clothes them with the garment of righteousness, of pure white silk; he refreshes them with the living water of his Holy Spirit, and feeds them with the bread of life. His name is Christ Jesus. They are the children of peace, who have beaten their swords into plough-shares, and their spears into pruning hooks, and know of no war; and give to Cæsar the things that are Cæsar's, and to God the things that are God's, Isa. 2: 4; Matt. 22: 21. Their sword is the sword of the Spirit, which they hold in a good conscience through the Holy Ghost. Their marriage is that of one man and one women, according to the ordinance of God. Their kingdom is the kingdom of grace, here in hope, and after this in eternal life, Eph. 6: 17; Matt. 19: 5; 25: 1.

Their citizenship is in heaven; and they use the creatures below, such as eating, drinking, clothing and dwelling with thanksgiving, and that to the necessary wants of their own lives, and to the free service of their neighbor, according to the word of the Lord, Isa. 58: 7. Their doctrine is the unadulterated word of God, testified through Moses and the prophets, through Christ and the apostles, upon which they build their faith, and save their souls; and every thing that is contrary thereto, they consider accursed. They use and administer their baptism on the confession of their faith, according to the command of the Lord, and the doctrines and usages of the apostles, Mark 16: 16.

The Lord's Supper they celebrate in remembrance of the favors and death of their Lord, and in reminding one another of true and brotherly love.

The *ban* extends to all the proud scorners, great and small, rich and poor, without any respect to person, who heard and obeyed the word for a season, but have fallen off again, and in the house of the Lord, teach or live offensively, till they again sincerely repent.

They sigh and lament daily over their poor, displeasing, evil flesh, over the manifold errors and faults of their weak lives. They war inwardly and outwardly without ceasing. They seek and call the Most High; fight and struggle against the devil, world and flesh during their lives, press on towards the prize of the high calling that they may obtain it. And they prove by their actions that they believe the word of the Lord; that they know and have Christ in power; that they are born of God and have him as their Father.

Behold, worthy reader, as I said before, so I say again. These are the christians who have the promise, and are assured by the Spirit of God, to whom are given and bestowed Christ Jesus, with all his merits, righteousness, intercessions, word, cross, suffering, flesh, blood, death, resurrection, kingdom, and all his possessions, and this all without merit; given out of pure grace from God. But what kind of doctrine, faith, life, regeneration, baptism, supper, ban and divine service, sectarian churches have, of whatever name; and what kind of reward is promised them in the Scriptures, I will let the reasonable, meditate upon, with the aid of the Spirit and word of the Lord.

Here I would call on all the high and mighty lords, princes and rulers, all under the canopy of heaven, also on all the popes, cardinals, bishops, the wise and learned, who from the beginning perverted and darkened the Scriptures, to show us one single word in the whole Bible, I say in the *Bible* (for we do not regard human fables and lies), that an unbelieving, refractory, carnal man, without true repentance and regeneration, ever *was* or ever *will* be saved, simply because he boasts of faith and the death of Christ, or heard the masses and service of the priests, as the whole world does; if so, they shall have gained the point. But this never has been from the beginning, and never will be to the end of time; if such vile men could be saved without repentance and regeneration, by hearing masses, and confessing, as they, poor children, without the warrant of the Scripture, hope, then we might of a truth say, that the aforementioned means were stronger (though they are idolatrous), than the word of the Lord; for the word knows no mass, but says, "Except ye repent, ye shall all likewise perish," Luke 13: 3. Then would also Moses and the prophets, Christ and his apostles, have been false witnesses, and have miserably deceived us poor sheep, because they directed us upon such a narrow path.

Ah no! friends, no! Beware, I tell you, God will not deceive you. For he says through the prophet Malachi 3: 6, "I am the LORD, I change not." All that he has testified to us in his holy word through his prophets, through Christ and his apostles, is his eternal, immutable will; on this we may all rely if we wish not to deceive our souls. In short, all is in vain to counsel and advise. True repentance and the birth from above, must take place; we must believe Christ and his word, and we must abide by his Spirit, ordinance and example willingly, or eternal misery must be our portion. This is incontrovertible.

Therefore, I admonish and entreat you, as those whom my soul loves, repent! repent!! delay not; "The axe is laid unto the root of the trees; therefore, every tree which bringeth not forth good fruit is hewn down, and cast into the fire," Matt. 3: 10. Watch over your poor souls, that have been bought with a precious price, and be no longer comforted with open lies, nor be fed upon chaff; for behold, I tell you, there is nothing under heaven that can, or will stand before God, but the new creature, "and faith which works by love," "and the keeping of the commandments."

My faithful reader, do not only believe me, but believe the word, to which, by the grace of God, I directed you with my small talents; for as true as the Lord liveth, all who teach otherwise than we have shown from the word of the Lord, whosoever they be, are prophets who deceive you, who place pillows under your arms, and cushions under your heads; who whitewash the wall with delusions, and speak peace to the wicked, but not out of the mouth of the Lord. For as certain as it is that the penitent and regenerated are the true christians, who have obtained God's truth, the true light, pardon of their sins, and the sure promise of eternal life, so certain also it is, that the sensual and impenitent are false christians, and have serpentine lies, darkness, propensity for sin, and the certain promise of eternal death. That this is the truth, will be found so in eternity before Almighty God; of this his word is to me a true witness; and I am confidently assured of it through his grace.

Now, perhaps, some may answer: Our belief is, that Christ is the Son of God, that his word is truth, and that he purchased us with his death and blood, and that we were regenerated in baptism, and received the Holy Ghost, therefore, we are the true church and congregation of Christ.

We reply: If your faith is as you say, why do you not do the things which he has commanded you in his word? His command is, REFORM. BE YE CONVERTED. KEEP THE COMMANDMENTS. Now it is evident that you are becoming worse daily; that *unrighteousness* is your father, and *wickedness*, your mother, and the express command of the Lord is foolishness and derision to you. Since you will not do as he commands, or would have you do, but act as you choose, it proves sufficiently that you do not believe that Jesus Christ is the Son of God, although you say so. Nor do you believe that his word is truth; for faith and its fruits are inseparable, this you will all have to confess by the grace of God. O, you poor, blind men! be silent and blush, let Christ Jesus with his Spirit and word be your teacher and example, your way and your mirror. Do you think it will do only to acknowledge Christ according to the flesh? Or if you but say that you believe on him and are baptized; that you are christians, and that you are purchased with the blood and death of Christ? Ah no! I have told you often, and tell you again, you must be born of God; in your life you must be so converted and changed that you become new creatures in Christ, that Christ be in you, and you in Christ, or you can never be christians, for, "If any man be in Christ he is a new creature," 2 Cor. 5: 17.

If you believe rightly in Christ, as you boast, then manifest it by your lives that you believe; for "The just shall live by faith," as the Scriptures say. That this is all true has been fully testified and shown by the works of Abel, Enoch, Noah, Abraham, Isaac, Jacob, Joseph, Moses, Joshua, Caleb, Samuel, David, Matthias, Zaccheus, Magdalene, Paul, and all the pious children of God, who were from the beginning and to this day. But how you conduct yourselves in your faith, and how you are minded, may be plainly seen by your excessive lies, fraud, avarice, hoarding, cursing, swearing, pride and wantonness; for your hearts burn in unrighteousness; you fear neither God nor his word; nevertheless, you boast that you believe on Christ, have his word, and that you are christians, &c. I repeat it; *Reform*, or hold your peace and be ashamed.

Further, you imagine that you were regenerated in your baptism and received the Holy Ghost. Faithful reader, remember, that if it even had been so unto you as you say, you will have to acknowledge that your regeneration then took place without hearing the word, without the faith and knowledge of Christ, and without all knowledge and understanding; and besides, that the aforementioned birth and the received Spirit are altogether without operation, wisdom, power and fruit; yea, are vain and dead in you. That you live neither after the Spirit nor in the power of the new birth, is evident from your gross avarice, drunkenness, pride, and idolatrous, carnal lives; of which all those baptized among you are my witnesses. Yea, my friends, if you were born of God in your baptism, and had received the Holy Ghost, as your comforters persuade and assure you, then it could not be otherwise than that the new, spiritual life and its fruits would also be manifest, as it was the case with the saints from the beginning, and is yet; for it is clear, that the regenerated do not presumptuously live in sin, but through faith, in true repentance, by baptism, are buried into the death of Christ, and also arise with him to a new life, and those who have the Spirit of the Lord, bring forth also the fruits of the Spirit. That you do not bury your sins, but serve them in full power, and also bring not forth the fruits of the Spirit, is daily testified by your vain, carnal and abominable lives. My friends, out of true love I warn, admonish and entreat you, to awaken and observe what the word of the Lord teaches; for the Spirit of the Lord will not dwell in a wicked soul, nor in a body subjected to sin.

In the second place, I say, If you are rightly baptized according to the word of the Lord, as you imagine, then you have put on Christ, and live no longer after Adam's inbred, evil nature, but after the regenerated, good nature of Christ. But since this is not the case with you, and you are yet altogether carnal and earthly, as is evident from all your fruits, therefore it is clear that you are not regenerated, baptized christians, but impenitent, carnal pagans, for your works are chiefly done after a heathen will, as we may see and hear. Once more, I say, awaken and hear what the word of the Lord says, "If Christ be in you, the body is dead because of sin; but the Spirit is life because of righteousness," Rom. 8: 10.

In the third place, I tell you, if you are rightly baptized according to the word of the Lord, then you are members and joint heirs of the body of Christ, and have the evidence of a good conscience before God. Inasmuch as a body is never divided in itself, nor hates its members, or does them harm, but one member serves and assists another; and since it is evident, and is indeed found to be so with you, that you unmercifully persecute, murder and exterminate the chosen members of Christ, who are of your own flesh and blood, whom he purchased by his death, regenerated by his word, endued with his Spirit, and has chosen as his own peculiar people; and besides a regenerated, new and good conscience, seek no help nor comfort of human institutions, but solely adhere with a pure faith to the grace, righteousness, prayer, merits, death and blood of the Lord; and you depend upon, and comfort yourselves with, the masses, confession, absolution, holy water, bread, wine, oil and vigils of the priests and monks; so the works themselves testify that you are not serviceable members of the beforementioned body, but are much more destroyers and defilers; that you have not a firm, joyful, peaceable and good conscience, but a wavering, damning, restless and evil conscience before God. For we see that all these above-named superstitions and false worship, which all regenerated, pious and good consciences esteem as mere abominations, are your chief support and comfort, because you neither have Christ nor know him. My friends, beware, you are miserably deceived by your comforters. The spirit of prophesy says, "And unto the angel of the church in Smyrna write; These things, saith the first and the last, which was dead and is alive; I know the blasphemy of them which say they are Jews, and are not; but are the synagogue of satan," Rev. 2: 8, 9. Well may it be said at the present time to all the great and specious sects; I know the great defamations, and see the wicked lives of those who say they are regenerated, baptized christians, and are not, but are satan's synagogue; for I see not how they could do worse.

But if we come to the rulers and potentates, there we find nothing but haughtiness and pride, splendor, dancing, whoring, pleasure riding, sporting, stabbing, killing, warring, destroying cities and countries, and living according to the lusts of the flesh.

If we come to the subordinate officers, and judges, there we find insatiable avarice, treachery and roguery, cunning devices to defraud the helpless and God-fearing (the good and pious I do not mean); they seek gifts and presents; the right of the righteous they pervert, and willingly accept of gifts to shed innocent blood; they persecute the truth; they reject what is right and good; the fear of God is not before their eyes.

If we come to the divines whether preachers, priests or monks, there we find such an idle, lazy, wanton and carnal life, such a corrupted, anti-christian doctrine and understanding of the Scriptures; such hatred, envy, defaming, betraying, lying and uproar against all the pious, that I would be ashamed to mention it before the virtuous and honest. The common people run, as a frantic heifer, as the prophet laments, Hos. 4. They lie, cheat, curse and swear by the wounds and sacraments of the Lord, by his judgment, hand, power, suffering, death and blood. I am ashamed that I have to think of these scandalous abominations. They gamble, drink and quarrel. In short, neither their superfluous, wicked lives, nor their great folly can be prevented; yet it must be said, that the mentioned lords, judges, learned and common people, are the truly regenerated church and baptized congregation of Christ. May the merciful Lord graciously preserve all his chosen children from such a regeneration, baptism and church, in all eternity.

I testify to you the truth in Christ Jesus, take heed, if you will; Jesus Christ did not endure from the beginning such openly impenitent, carnal sinners in his holy city, kingdom and church, and he will never endure them, this you may believe.

O Almighty God and Lord, how miserably thy holy and paternal will, and thy adorably great name are derided, and how little is thy saving, precious word esteemed; yea, what an abominable, idolatrous, carnal, revengeful and blood-thirsty devil is made of thy beloved Son; for they cover all their abominations, sins and disgraces with his blessed, holy name, word, death and blood.

Be ashamed, O you heedless, perverted men, be ashamed, I say, before God and his angels that you are so rebellious and refractory; that you live so rudely, and yet dare say that you are the rightly regenerated congregation and baptized church of Christ. Oft have I told you, and tell you again, that all who are born of God, rightly baptized with the Spirit, fire and water, as the Scriptures teach, are of a heavenly and divine mind; their sins they bury, lead a penitent, pious, virtuous life according to the word of the Lord. They show the nature and power of Christ which dwells in them by word and work; they bring forth the fruits of the Spirit, and subdue the works of the flesh; they are useful members of the body of Christ, and labor according to the gift received. In short, they are fruitful branches of the true vine, and their fruits abide to eternal life, John 15.

But since it is manifest in you, that you show the reverse in all your fruits, and we do see in your whole lives, that it is but world and flesh with you, therefore, it is clear, that your boasting of the new birth, spirit, baptism, congregation and church is not the truth; but vanity, lies and falsehood.

The holy Scriptures and our common belief, teach us that the holy, christian church is an assembly of the righteous, and a congregation of saints; and he that can see but partially into the Scriptures, must confess that your church and assembly are a church and assembly of the unrighteous, lascivious, impenitent, sensual and sodomites; yea, of the blood-thirsty wolves, lions, bears, basalisks, serpents, and fiery, flying dragons.

Ah, friends, lift your heads, and open your eyes! O ye bewitched! look over the whole world, what life they lead who have received the same baptism with you; who practice the same sacraments and worship, who indulge in the same boasting of the death and blood of the Lord, and say that they are the church and people of Christ. For it is clearer than mid-day, that many of you are so insane, so influenced by the spirit of the devil, that you hate, envy, bite and devour one another; so that you wholly destroy principalities, cities, castles and citadels with your accursed fightings and uproar; human blood you shed like water; deprive the poor citizen and peasant (those of your own faith) of body and possessions by burning, robbing, plundering, catching, imposition, torturing, nay even those who have never harmed you, or given you a rash word. In truth, I know not, how the infernal Behemoth could be more devilish and cruel than you or your members, who imagine that they are the church of Christ. God preserve us! You disgrace families, you persecute the pious and god-fearing; you encourage open brothels, tippling houses, boxing schools, gaming boards, and the like disgraces, idolatrous houses and images, with all false service and the like, without measure and bounds. I will not touch upon your intolerable, blasphemous cursing and swearing, lying, defrauding, drunkenness, whoring, pomp, splendor, &c. What more shall I say, I will forbear; for it strikes me that none can be found under the broad canopy of heaven, who can minutely relate the gross abominations, wicked acts, abuses and scandals of your fellow-believers in infant baptism; a righteous person must be astounded at those great sins. O dear Lord, strengthen us! Yea, whosoever does not rightly understand that you are not born from above, but are baptized contrary to all Scripture, and that all your boasting of the forgiveness of sins, of the mercy, grace, merits, flesh, blood, cross, death, church, kingdom and eternal promise of God is vain, and without the Scriptures, and must be, we may say, an irrational man.

Ah, readers! How little you think upon the word of the Lord, which is so highly recommended to you; and how little you regard your poor souls, which are bought with such a precious price, and are eternally to live with God in heaven, or to be dying forever with the devil in hell. Think you, my friends, that the Lord is a dreamer, or his word a fable? Ah, no! not a letter will fall to the ground of all that he spoke. It is high time that you would reflect that God's promise of grace is not given to the unregenerated and impenitent, but to the regenerated and penitent. Let every one take warning and trust no longer in lies, believing that he is baptized and regenerated, nor trust to long standing usages, nor upon papistic decretals, nor imperial mandates, nor upon the wisdom and glossaries of the learned, nor upon the good opinion of any man, council, institution or wisdom. God says through the prophet, "My counsel shall stand, and I will do all my pleasure." The word of God is eternal. Neither princes, nor power, nor the commands of men with all their imperial edicts are to constitute faith, neither can a soul be saved by them. Only the heavenly counsel we must hear and follow, that which Jesus Christ, God's first and only begotten Son himself brought from heaven, and taught from the mouth of his Father, and confirmed by signs and wonders, and finally sealed it with his crimson blood. This counsel stands, and can never be changed or prevailed against by the gates of hell. By this counsel we are, in common, taught that we must hear Christ, believe in him, follow his footsteps, repent, be born from above, become as little children, not in understanding, but in malice, be of the same mind with Christ, walk as he did, deny ourselves, take up his cross and follow him; and that if we love father, mother, children or life more than him, we are not worthy of him, nor are we his disciples. Again, that adulterers, whoremongers, murderers, drunkards, idolaters and the like sinners shall not inherit the kingdom of God. That we love not the world and the things therein, nor conform to the world; that we, through faith, are to die unto our evil flesh, and conquer the devil; that we are to lead an upright, unblamable, pious life through faith in all things, act according to the will of the Lord. Again, that we are to baptize upon faith and not without it, celebrate the Lord's Holy Supper in a sincerely, penitent communion, I mean so far as man can judge. That we practice exclusion or the ban according to the Scriptures. That we are to fear, serve and love the Lord with all the heart, and walk in his commands, and that we are to assist, comfort and serve our neighbor as much as in us is, and the like doctrine and instruction.

Behold, worthy reader, here you have in part the immutable, eternal counsel of God, which was sealed in the councils of his Majesty, and besides this, he recognizes no other. Blessed are they who receive this with a firm faith, and conform thereto according to their abilities, in all weakness; that is, live according to the Spirit, word, ordinance, command, prohibition and unblamable example of Christ. On the contrary, cursed are they who despise, reject, curse, hate, defame, mock, persecute, destroy, and cast it from them, and comfort themselves with human power, institutions and fables. For they deny the Lord who bought them, and reject the gospel of peace; believe not that Jesus Christ is their Messiah, Savior, High Priest and Prophet. Ah! how well for them if they had never been born. May the Lord mercifully grant them converted and renewed hearts, that they may repent and be eternally saved, if it be possible.

I will now close the matter and direct the well-meaning reader to the Scriptures; since the whole word, with few exceptions, is built upon human doctrine, lies, invented fables, perverted glossaries, vain idolatry and false service, by which the people of the world comfort themselves and boast of what they neither have nor are; therefore have I briefly, according to my few talents, in sincere, faithful love, shown you in this epistle, who, according to the unadulterated word, are the truly regenerated and baptized christians that have the promise, or who are not such; so that all who truly hunger and thirst, and who are zealous for God, may be rightly satisfied with the truth unto eternal salvation; and no longer follow deceit to their eternal condemnation. Yea, that all who stand before the eyes of the Lord, with their poor, miserable souls, may be benefited, become whole and be saved. The Lord strengthen you, believe God's infallible word, reform your sinful lives, pray with confidence and be obedient to the gospel of Christ, that you may receive the eternal promise to your eternal joy and salvation with all the saints, which God the merciful Father has promised to all his beloved children through Christ Jesus. Grace be with all who seek Christ and eternal life with all the heart, Amen. If you will suffer Jesus Christ, with his eternal Spirit and word to be judge, then you will learn that the sure Foundation of truth has been shown.

AN EXHORTATION

TO THE

DISPERSED AND UNKNOWN CHILDREN OF GOD.

To all the chosen children of God, dispersed here and there, to the sanctified in Christ Jesus, unknown to me in the flesh, my beloved brethren and fellow believers in the faith, to you be the kingdom and portion of the grace and peace of Christ.

Sincerely beloved brethren and sisters in Christ Jesus, I inform you with great joy, that some praiseworthy brethren have written and informed me that the merciful, faithful Father has endued you with the heavenly gift of his divine knowledge, and enlightened you with his Holy Spirit, that your faith works by love, your hope is lively, and your union among each other, is christian-like, that your peace is pleasant, and that the church of the Lord is increased and extended daily in great power and glory, through the grace of God. For which I thank his paternal kindness with joyful heart, and I pray his grace inasmuch as he has called you to the fellowship of his beloved Son, and to the imperishable, eternal kingdom of his glory through his holy gospel that he may now and henceforth preserve you with the great power of his divine arm, in your faith, love, doctrine, truth and life, without any offence till the end. Faithful is he who has called you, and he will undoubtedly do it, if you only continue to be ardent in prayer, and unwavering in your undertaking, never become sleepy nor slothful, nor at last return again, as did refractory, disobedient Israel to the flesh pots of Egypt. May the Lord eternally and graciously preserve us. Since, then you are called to such a high and glorious grace, as related, and we undoubtedly know our weak, vile flesh, and the sinful nature which we possess from Adam which makes our whole heart and life unclean, and besides we learn from the Scriptures, that our opponent, the devil, goes about like a roaring lion, having rest neither day nor night, but always seeking that he might devour us; therefore I exhort you as my fellow-combatants, against the evil flesh, and the tents of death, that you may strictly watch inwardly and outwardly over yourselves, that you circumcise, teach, purify and sanctify your hearts with the Spirit of God; exhort and reprove one another; curb your thoughts; subdue and extinguish your impure evil lusts, in the fear of the Lord; for blessed are the pure in heart; walk worthy of the Lord and his gospel to which you have come. Whatever God has commanded, do it without murmuring; act so that none may truthfully complain of you; be sincere children of God, unblamable in this crooked and perverse generation, and shine as beautiful, clear, torch-lights in the midst of a dark night in this evil world.

Take the Lord Jesus Christ as an example, and follow his footsteps; walk as he walked, for therefore did Moses and all the prophets preach; to that end did the Son of God come down from heaven; he sent out the holy apostles, and instituted baptism and the Lord's Supper as the mouth of the Lord commanded, that we may thereby be admonished to awaken, to repent and lead an unblamable, pious life in all righteousness. "Be ye holy; for I am holy," says the Lord; Peter says, "But ye are a chosen generation, a royal priesthood, a holy nation, a peculiar people; that ye should show forth the praises of him who hath called you out of darkness into his marvelous light," 1 Peter 1: 16; 2: 9. You are guests called to the table of the Lord, and have come to the marriage of the Lamb; ye are his chosen friends and bride, therefore, hear his voice willingly, and whatever is pleasing to him, do cheerfully. Adorn yourselves with the shining garment of white linen; be faithful unto death, and beware of all strange gods; dedicate yourselves wholly unto the Lord, that he may be your Lord and bridegroom, and teach, reprove, govern and lead you with his Holy Spirit and word, and have his perfect work in you; for you are in his grace, and through his grace you are accepted of him; espoused unto him, bought with his precious blood, reconciled to the Father, sanctified as priests and kings, and made heirs of his eternal kingdom. Therefore it is proper and right that we should be grateful to such a kind Lord, for such gifts; hear him, lay his word to heart and do what is well pleasing to him.

Beloved children; fear not, but be comforted in the Lord; for he is such a faithful, pious King, to whom you have sworn and bowed your knees, that not the least of his promises shall fail you; he will be our shield and great reward, therefore, doubt nor stagger not; for it is but a small thing that we endure the heat of the sun, tribulation, fear, sorrow, temptation, robbing, persecution, prison and death for a short time. The messenger is now at the door, who shall say to us, "Come ye blessed of my Father, inherit the kingdom prepared for you;" thus will our mourning and temporary pain be changed into ceaseless joy; these tyrants, with their bloody mandates, will come to an end, and all our persecutors, avengers, executioners and torturers will cease; we will follow the Lamb, adorned in white garments, with palms in our hands and crowns upon our heads; neither torment nor pain, nor pangs of death will harm us; but we will forever exalt, praise and thank, in inexpressible joy and glory, the Lamb who sits upon the throne.

Behold, my children, all the truly believing, pious hearts comfort themselves with this approaching change, whereby they possess their souls with patience; well knowing that great is their reward in heaven, and that on the other hand, all the ungodly shall have their portion in the eternal, unquenchable fire, under the intolerable, dreadful sentence of God, in the abyss of hell, if they do not be converted and repent with all their hearts. Woe! woe! to these wretched people, for it was an evil day in which they were born!!—My children be cheerful in Christ, and despair not, for so long as we desire God sincerely, seek, fear, love, honor and serve him, and with an upright, pure zeal walk in the truth, neither world, flesh, tyranny, devil, sin, hell, nor death shall hinder us; but the victory, which is gained by a firm faith in the blood of Christ, will, through the grace of God, be on our side, and this through the Spirit of Christ which abides in us. David says, "By my God I have leaped over a wall," Ps. 18: 29. Paul says, "I can do all things through Christ, which strengtheneth me." Christ says, "Be of good cheer I have overcome the world;" and thus will they overcome, who will abide in Christ, as we may not only see in the prophets and apostles, but also in many pious hearts at the present day, in great power and clearness.

I have nothing particular any more to write; therefore, beware that you walk wisely and circumspectly; preserve your wedding garment; have oil at all times in your lamps, lest the Lord meet you in an undue time, find you unprepared and in nudity, and close the door on you, or cast you into outer darkness.

With unfeigned, true, brotherly love, and out of a pure heart, love each other sincerely, as those who are regenerated not of corrupt but of incorruptible seed, out of the word of the living God, which will abide forever; for love is of God and of a divine nature, and does right before God and man, is long-suffering, compassionate, peaceable, and gives offence to none. In short, it is unblamable and brings forth christian fruit; it is the spiritual girdle of Aaron and his sons; the girdle of perfection and the fair bond of peace. O how completely happy is he, who is girded with this bond, for he is born of God, he is in God and God is in him; yea, where this love is, there we find the true, sincere and pious christian. Therefore, take care of this bond, for if you lose it, you will lose Christ Jesus and eternal life.

Beware of false doctrine, of all discord, strife and dissention, and without wavering, adhere to the Spirit, word and example of Christ if you would not be deceived; for every spirit which is not satisfied with the Spirit, word and example of Christ, and will not conform thereto, in his weakness, he is not of God, but is the spirit of antichrist, which would rob you again and all the pious of the precious light of revealed truth, which graciously appeared to us, poor children, in these abominable days, and would again lead you on the crooked paths of death, under the semblance of the Scriptures.

My children in Christ, be you warned. Out of true brotherly love, I write to you. The merciful, gracious God grant that you may read, hear, and understand it, with such hearts, that it may bring much fruit among you, and that your fruits may abide in eternal life. Pray for your poor, unknown brother, who loves you, in truth. He that continues to be perfect to the end, shall be saved. The saving power and fruits of the crimson blood of Christ, be with you, and with all my chosen brothers and sisters to eternity, Amen.

A Consoling Admonition

CONCERNING THE

SUFFERINGS, OPPRESSIONS

AND

Persecutions of the Saints,

FOR THE

WORD OF GOD AND HIS TESTIMONY.

BY

MENNO SIMON.

"Blessed are ye when men shall revile you, and persecute you, and shall say all manner of evil against you, falsely, for my sake. Rejoice and be exceeding glad, for great is your reward in heaven; for so persecuted they the prophets which were before you," Matt. 5: 15.

"For other foundation can no man lay than that is laid, which is Jesus Christ," 1 Cor. 3: 11.

ELKHART, INDIANA:
PUBLISHED BY JOHN F. FUNK AND BROTHER.
1871.

PREFACE.

I, MENNO SIMON, sincerely desire that all the true children of God may obtain grace and peace, a perfect understanding of the Lord, a firm mind in all temptations, from God our heavenly Father, through his Son, Jesus Christ our Lord, in the power of his Holy Spirit, to our edification and salvation, Amen.

Beloved brethren and sisters in the Lord, since the all-merciful God and Father, through his boundless grace and goodness, has again, in these last times of unbelief, abominations and idolatry, in this terrible, wanton, ruthless, perverted and bloodthirsty world, revealed before the eyes of the consciences of some, his blessed, only, and eternal Son, Jesus Christ, who was unknown for so many centuries; since he has again opened the book of the divine declarations and eternal truth, which had been closed for many centuries; since some of those who lay dead, not for four days only, as Lazarus did, according to the flesh, but for twenty or thirty years, yea, who all their lives slumbered in the spiritual death of sin and all ungodliness, have awakened from the foul grave of unbelief and unrighteousness, and have been called to a new, unblamable life; and since through the preaching of his word, in the power of his Holy Spirit, he continues to call the poor, miserable, starving sheep out of the hands of the faithless shepherds, and out of the clutches of the ravening wolves; since he leads them out of the dry, unfruitful pastures of man's doctrine and commands, to the green, fat pastures upon the mount of Israel, and places them under the power and protection of their only and eternal shepherd, Jesus Christ, who, through his precious, crimson blood has purified and purchased them for his own; therefore, the gates of hell foam and rage. Herod with the whole city is above measure frightened and enraged, because he has heard of the wise men, who are taught of God, that the King of the Jews is born. The great dragon, the old, crooked serpent, who was cast from heaven, whose head and power has been bruised and broken by the promised seed of the woman, is overcome by the blood of the Lamb, and, on account of the word of his testimony, burns with anger. He knows well that his time is short, and therefore he carries on his works and tyranny, through his children and servants, the unbelievers, with great wrath and fierceness, against those who have been sprinkled with the blood of the Lamb. Annas and Caiaphas, with all the scribes, counsel to slay Christ. Judas and all false apostles and teachers betray and deliver him up. Herod, with all his lords and princes, scorn and mock him. The people cry out, crucify him! crucify him!! Pilate, and all those who bear the sword, sentence him to stocks, fire, sword and water. The servants seize, spit upon, scourge, crown and crucify him. The centurion pierces his side, the others mock, blaspheme and upbraid him. Who is there that does not persecute, crucify and dishonor with heart, word or deed, the poor, innocent, peaceful, defenceless Lamb? Yea, in the ungodly Cain, has the bloody, murderous tyranny taken its origin, and has fully shown its artfulness, properties, fruit and nature to the pious, godly Abel.

Inasmuch, then, as the Lamb and its chosen members, from the beginning, have been persecuted and slain by the malice of the creatures of the conquered serpent, and inasmuch (according to Scriptures) as this persecution will not cease so long as there are righteous and unrighteous people on earth; and as in our days, especially, the cross of Christ, on every hand (as it was in the days of our ancestors), is laid upon all God-fearing children, who are inwardly born again from the powerful seed of the holy word; therefore I cannot neglect to admonish my beloved brethren and sisters, fellow-believers and fellow-sufferers with the word of the Lord, concerning the suffering, cross and persecution of the saints, which is abundantly related in the Scriptures, and was abundantly visited upon our fathers, both of the Old and New Testaments, and also upon many pious witnesses of our own days; that they may, according to the example of our fathers, fearlessly and valiantly continue the undertaken contest, in all constancy, patience, strength, courage and valor, through the power of their faith in Christ Jesus; and that they may thus receive the promised crown. For this purpose may the Father of every good and perfect gift, through his beloved Son Jesus Christ, our Lord, grant us the riches of his grace, in the power of his Holy Spirit, Amen.

THE CROSS OF CHRIST.

"Blessed are they (said Christ) which are persecuted for righteousness' sake; for theirs is the kingdom of heaven."

I know well, worthy brethren and sisters in the Lord, that the true laborers and servants of the Lord, have each one planted and watered according to the gifts which they have received; they have caused you to be born again of the living word of the holy gospel of Jesus Christ, and that they have built in a godly manner upon Christ, the firm and immoveable corner stone; have taught you the word, will and ordinances of God according to his good pleasure; have united you in love as a willing, obedient, pure bride to your bridegroom, Christ Jesus. That they have in full earnestness, shown you the narrow, scornful way; have preached the cross, and have pointed out and admonished you in regard to the pains and costs of this godly building, for it can never be otherwise, as you well know, than that all who would hear, follow and enter through the right door, Christ Jesus, and would walk upon the highway to eternal life in the light of Christ, must first deny themselves, and all they are, with the whole heart. They must, in all misery, ignominy and trouble, take upon themselves the pressing cross, and must follow the rejected, outcast, bleeding and crucified Christ, as he himself said, "If any man will come after me, let him deny himself, and take up his cross and follow me." Yes all who do not stand prepared to take up this grievous life of the cross and trouble, and hate not father and mother, son, daughter, husband and wife, houses, land, money, goods and life, cannot be Christ's disciples.

My faithful brethren this is a true and sure word; for the eternal truth, Christ Jesus, has in many places of the Scriptures, been pointed out and testified in great clearness; "Behold," he says, "I send you forth as sheep in the midst of wolves; be ye therefore, wise as serpents, and harmless as doves. But beware of men; for they will deliver you up to the councils, and they will scourge you in their synagogues, and ye shall be brought before governors and kings for my sake, for a testimony against them and the gentiles," Matt. 10: 16—18.

Again, "The brother shall deliver up the brother to death, and the father the child; and the children shall rise up against their parents, and shall cause them to be put to death, and ye shall be hated of all men for my name's sake," Matt. 10: 21, 22.

Again, "The disciple is not above his master, nor the servant above his lord. It is enough for the disciple that he be as his master and the servant as his lord. If they have called the master of the house, Beelzebub, how much more shall they call them of his household," Matt. 10: 24, 25.

Again, "He that loveth father or mother more than me, is not worthy of me, and he that loveth son or daughter more than me, is not worthy of me. And he that taketh not his cross and followeth after me, is not worthy of me. He that findeth his life shall lose it, and he that loseth his life for my sake shall find it," Matt. 10: 37—39.

Again, "Then shall they deliver you up to be afflicted, and shall kill you; and ye shall be hated of all nations for my name's sake," Matt. 24: 9.

Again, "They shall put you out of the synagogues; yea, the time cometh that whosoever killeth you, will think that he doeth God service," John 16: 2.

Again, "We must through much tribulation enter into the kingdom of God." "All that will live godly in Christ Jesus, shall suffer persecution." "If we be dead with him, we shall also live with him; if we suffer, we shall also reign with him," Acts 14: 22; 2 Tim. 3: 12; 2: 11, 12.

Yea, the whole Scriptures abound with exhortations, examples and histories of the troubles sorrows, miseries, proscriptions, upbraidings, reproachings, deceivings, imprisonments, plunderings, ignominious death and crosses of the saints.

Since then, from the beginning of the world, true righteousness, devotion and piety, are thus miserably hated, persecuted, and cast out, as it has been abundantly shown in the case of the pious fathers, and as may be seen and found in these last times, as we have said, I deem it necessary to show from the word of the Lord, to our youthful, weak, and untried brethren and sisters, who such persons are, that persecute us, and inflict upon us this trouble and sorrow; wherefore they do so, wherewith they maintain their tyranny and bloody deeds for right; what profit we receive from the cross, and what is promised to those, who, through the power of faith, overcome all temptations and extremities, and maintain the conflict through Christ Jesus, in order that they, through such counsels, may be ready and prepared for all trials. That they may put on the breast-plate of righteousness, the helmet of salvation, with the shield of faith, and be girded with the sharp, piercing sword of the Spirit in all humility, meekness and patience, with ardent prayers and sighs to the Lord, in order that when any swift, unseen uproar, shall arise against us, it shall not fall upon us unawares, that an unexpected storm shall not cast down our house, the heat of the sun shall not scorch the growing plant, the heat and power of the fire shall not consume the erected works, and that we be not drawn off and frightened to a deadly apostasy by their threats, uproar and tyranny. Therefore, my beloved, read and understand in all love, for the Lord knows that out of pure love, I have written this for the benefit of my dear brethren, according to my received gifts, Eph. 6; 1 Thess. 5.

In the first place, dear brethren, I esteem it to be very necessary that all the godly, and strivers under the cross of Christ, who seek for encouragement in their crosses and sufferings, which they endure for the sake of the testimony of God and their consciences, to consider carefully and earnestly, who and what they are that so madly persecute, oppress and afflict them; of what disposition and nature they are; upon what way they walk, and of what father, according to the Spirit, they are born. All who carefully observe them, and try them by the Scriptures, will find, according to my opinion, that they are not Christians, but are an unbelieving, fleshly, earthly, wanton, blind, hardened, lying, idolatrous, perverted, malicious, revengeful, unmerciful and murderous people. A people, who by their actions and fruits, show that they neither know Christ nor his Father, although they so highly praise his holy name with the mouth, and extol it with their lips; who tread in slippery, crooked and perverted paths; who display not Christian love and peace; who bathe their hearts and hands in blood; their disposition is to seize and kill. They are children and co-partners of him, who from the beginning was a murderer and a liar, of whom the whole Scriptures testify, that they shall forever bear, the intolerable curse and malediction of the righteous judgment of God, and the devouring flames of hell, unless they awake from the deep, deadly sleep of their sins, sincerely repent, believe the joyous Gospel of Jesus Christ, and put on Christ, and thus show by their whole lives and actions, that they seek their God with all their might, fear and love him, be they emperors, kings, doctors, licentiates, citizens, peasants, man or woman, For with God, says Paul, there is no respect of persons, but whosoever committeth sin, he shall bear it.

Worthy and faithful brethren in the Lord, observe what a blind, naked, poor, miserable and unwise people, in divine things they are, who so bitterly persecute and destroy you without mercy, on account of your faith. Therefore, it becomes all the true and chosen children of God, however severely they may be dealt with, and belied by these people, not to be angry with them, but sincerely to pity them, and sigh sorely over their poor souls, with all meekness and ardency, after the example of Christ and Stephen, to pray for their raging, cursed folly and blindness, for they know not what they do. Who knows but God may give them eyes and hearts, that they may see and know their blindness and unbelief; see what an impure life they lead, what kind of people they persecute, and whom they have pierced.

O my beloved brethren! observe and consider well upon your own former life; we have all, in former times, served one Lord, were attired in the same habit, as has been said. But what we now are, we are not of ourselves, but of God, by grace through Christ Jesus. The mighty God, who lives forever, according to his great mercy, has called us out of our accursed darkness into his marvellous light, his ears are not stopped, nor his hand shortened; he can undoubtedly hear and help them as he helped us. If they never repent, but continue with impenitent, perverted hearts, in all ungodliness, blood, wantonness and tyranny, till they die, we know what the Scriptures testify concerning them; that they shall not inherit the kingdom of heaven; but their part shall be in the fiery lake which burns with fire and brimstone, and the fire will be everlasting, Rev. 21: 8.

Every one, then, who reflects that his persecutors are so wholly blind and destitute of understanding, concerning what the Spirit directs, as above said, and that their lot shall be like that of the angels of the bottomless pit, the intolerable wrath of God, death and hell, which shall last forever, and the sufferings which we have to endure from them for the testimony of Jesus, are but temporary and momentary, will through grace, by this means, preserve his heart pure from all wrath, malice and retaliation towards them, and will ardently pray for them; he will commend his affairs to God in all humility, long-suffering, and peace, will preserve his spirit unbroken, amid prisons, fire and water.

Again, I deem it a soft and mild salve, and a cooling to our miseries and grief, if we but reflect upon the reason why our persecutors so malevolently hate us, and so relentlessly destroy our name, property, reputation, welfare and lives, which is, because the grace of God, through Christ, has enlightened us; because we have believed the preached Gospel, and have ceased from our blind, ruthless life and deadly works; because we desire, in our weakness, to follow in the fear and love of God, after the righteousness of faith which is required of God, and in obedience to the holy word; because we acknowledge the ever blessed Jesus alone for our Redeemer, Mediator, Intercessor, spiritual King, Example, Shepherd, infallible Teacher and Master; because we judge and prove all spirits, doctrines, councils, ordinances, statutes and ceremonies as far as regards spirit and faith, with the Spirit, doctrine, ordinances, commands and ceremonies of Christ, and thus esteem the commands and ceremonies of men, which are contrary to the commands and ceremonies of God, not only as vain and useless, but also as accursed and idolatrous, according to the Scriptures; because we regard and honor God more than man, we hold in exaltation his high, holy, true and precious word; because we, according to the Scriptures, listen not to the unclean, unsound, idolatrous, deceiving and blood-thirsty preachers; because we admonish and set an example in all love, as far as we are able, to the whole world, with the word and sacraments of God, and with humble, meek lives, though in weakness, according to our abilities; and we rebuke and shame (though always for their good), their deceiving doctrine, idolatrous sacrament and their wanton, earthly, fleshly life. In short, because we, in good faith, point them to the sure and infallible truth of God, to the true light and to the high-way of eternal life, and thus warn and alarm them, as much as we can, with doctrine and life, against eternal death, in hell and the wrath of God.

Behold, my faithful brethren, it is for the reasons here enumerated, that the world lies, writes, calls, preaches, and is so malicious towards all the pious; they burn with such inhuman rage, as may be seen, that the ravening, fierce wolves and roaring lions, when compared with them, cease to be wolves and lions, but seem to be like tame deer, or innocent lambs. They are so moved by the inflamed, blood-thirsty spirit of their father, that they regard neither the law of God and Christ, which is love, nor reason and discretion, nor the inwardly written law of nature, by which one honest man should reasonably, according to the good pleasure of God, meet, bear, admonish and serve another in all love. Yea, oft times the natural father delivers the son up to death, and the son his father; the mother the daughter, and the daughter her mother; and one brother delivers another on account of his faith, as said.

Behold, thus haughtily and maliciously, they assume, without any awe or fear, the umpire of God and the office of the Holy Ghost. They banish Christ Jesus, the head of all princes and powers, who has all might in heaven and upon earth, from the throne of his divine majesty; and judge also with their iron sword, after their own, blind opinions, and carnal desires, the chosen, godfearing, pious hearts, enlightened in God, through Jesus Christ, over whom no literal sword may ever judge, for they are spiritual, and from their inmost soul are zealous for God and his holy word, even till death.

Behold, so malicious and haughty is human reason, and so revengeful and envious is satanic hatred, that they do not fear to strive against the Most High, and pierce Christ Jesus with their murderous, deadly sword, and persecute with all their power, the Holy Spirit, gifts, word and truth of God, and all that he commands and will have us to do.

O that God would grant that the blind watchmen of this world, I mean the preachers and theologians, may sound their horns to a right tone and at a proper time, or that they would let them hang on the walls, in order that they may not therewith, tyrannically call out the deadly, murder cry, nor longer deceive the carnal, blind world, nor instigate the rulers and magistracy to the destruction and murdering of the saints, like hounds pursuing the roe; that God would grant that the poor, common people would sicken of their leaven and husks; yea, of their spiritual stealing and murdering; also that all rulers and magistrates would tear the bridle from their mouths, and cast their instigators from their backs, and not suffer themselves to be thus driven like dumb beasts, and then, according to my opinion, it will be well for their poor souls before God. Still, I fear that the lying, murderous serpent, will continue its envious bitings; and the striving woman, the new Eve and her children must endure, to the end, in all patience and long-suffering, its daily bites and stings in the heel.

Since I have here pointed out to you, in a few words, the spirit and nature of those who destroy you and seek your property, life, and the principal, urging reasons which impel them to do so; I will now present to my brethren, some histories and examples from the holy Scriptures, for the comfort and encouragement of all miserable, afflicted, and troubled hearts who suffer oppression, and misery in the flesh for righteousness' sake, in which histories and examples these things may be clearly found and traced.

In the first place, Eve, the mother of us all, brought forth her two sons, Cain and Abel. Abel was a keeper of sheep, but Cain was a tiller of the ground. In process of time it came to pass, says Moses, That Cain brought an offering to the Lord from the fruits of the field, and Abel brought one from the first of his flock. The Lord regarded Abel and his sacrifice but he looked not upon Cain and his gift, therefore, Cain was very wroth, and his countenance fell through great wrath, even as the ungodly always are envious of the pious, because the Lord regards the pious and loves their sacrifices. Cain spoke deceitfully to his pious, humble brother Abel, who knew not the malicious, bloody heart of his brother, saying, Let us go out, and when they were in the field, Cain's hot, envious spirit could no longer be restrained, and his blood-thirsty, revengeful spirit could not be hid. That which lays concealed in the heart must break out in the actions; he arose against his innocent brother and in his fierce wrath slew him. Why did he do this? Because Cain was of the evil one and his works were evil, and his brother's works were righteous.

It seems to me, dear brethren, that this is a fair example and a good reference; for the righteous always have been offscourings and a prey to the unrighteous, and so will they continue to be as the Scriptures sufficiently testify, and as daily experience plainly teaches.

Again, God blessed the patriarch Isaac, and gave him two sons. The elder was

Esau, and the younger, Jacob. Esau was a husband-man and hunter, and had great pleasure in the chase. Once as he came home much fatigued, he sold his birthright to Jacob, his brother, for some food, Gen. 25: 33.

After this it came to pass, that Jacob, through the artifice and craft of his mother, obtained the blessing of his father Isaac, by assuming the name and appearance of Esau. This was the intention and will of God, to remember the literal synagogue and the church of Christ, according to his word to Rebecca, while she was yet pregnant; namely, "Two nations are in thy womb, and two manner of people shall be separated from thy bowels; and the one people shall be stronger than the other people; and the elder shall serve the younger," Gen. 25: 23.

When Esau was now aware of this, he wept bitterly and said, Rightly is he called Jacob, for he has supplanted me twice. Esau sought the blessing, but did not obtain it, for God willed it otherwise, as said above.

Esau became very angry with his brother Jacob, on account of the blessing with which his father had blessed him. His malicious, bitter fierceness broke forth, and he said, "The days of mourning for my father are at hand; then will I slay my brother." Then had the blessed Jacob to flee from his dear father and mother before his wrathful brother. He fled to a distant country, and became a servant for twenty years in the house of Laban, who did not deal with him according to equity and love. He dared not again enter the land of his birth, till the Lord said unto him, "Return unto the land of thy fathers, and to thy kindred; and I will be with thee," Gen. 31: 3.

My dear brethren, observe; as the patriarch Jacob, on account of his external birthright and blessing, was hated and persecuted by his carnal, fierce brother, Esau, thus also it is at the present day, with all those who, after the Spirit, are called after the name of Jacob, namely, true Christians, that in the power of the Holy Ghost, through the medium of faith, tread upon the devil, world, flesh, and blood; they obtain the birthrights which are written in heaven, and are blessed through our true Isaac, Christ Jesus, with spiritual blessings in heavenly things, to eternal glory. They are maliciously hated and persecuted to death by their carnal and licentious brethren; must flee from one land to another, from one city to another, with great misery, hunger and distress; in prison, in bonds, with hunger, stripes, water, fire and sword, all the days of their lives, as may be seen.

Thus tyrannizes the fleshly Esau over the spiritual Jacob, on account of the spiritual birthright and blessing, although they are both born of the same father, Adam, from one mother Eve, and are created after the image of God.

Thirdly, Saul, the first king of Israel, on account of his thoughts and disobedience, was rejected of the Lord; and David, the son of Jesse, the Bethlehemite, according to the command of God, was taken from the sheep, and anointed by Samuel in his stead, yet he did not assume the government during the life of Saul. The Lord was with David, and strengthened his hands. He did great works in the name of the Lord; he released the stolen sheep out of the mouth of the lion and bear; he slew the terrible, great Goliath; he subdued two hundred of the uncircumcised Philistines. He acted in all things prudently, right and valiantly; for the Lord was with him. When Saul returned from the slaughter of the Philistines, the women of all the cities of Israel came to meet the king, singing and rejoicing with all manner of stringed instruments, and tambours, speaking joyfully one to another, Saul hath slain his thousands, but David his tens of thousands. This enraged Saul sorely, and he said, They have given David ten thousand and me but a thousand! what else does he want but the kingdom. From that day forth David had no favor with Saul, for Saul sought his life secretly and openly, with great assiduity and craft; although Saul well knew the piety of David and that the Lord was with him; yet his heart burned with such ill-will, envy, revenge and blood-thirstiness, that when David escaped, the good Abimelech and the priests of the Lord were put to death and the whole city, Nob, was laid in ruins for David's sake, 2 Sam. 22.

He regarded neither the piety, kindness, fidelity nor well-doing of David towards him and all Israel, nor the grace, works and will of God, but became unmindful and drunken in his wrath and envy, so that the enemies and betrayers of David, as Doeg, the Edomite and the Ziphites were highly regarded and honored by him, but the peacemakers, and those who advised for good, as his son Jonathan, were hated by him, and held in suspicion. In short, David must take to flight, and for some years fly from one land to another, from one wilderness to another, and from one mountain to another, till Saul was overcome by the Philistines upon Mount Gilboa, when, through vain despair and impatience he thrust the sword, which he had borne against the righteous and innocent, into his heart, and thus took his own life.

Thus the Almighty Lord and Potentate of all things, punishes the haughty, bloodthirsty tyrants, each one in his time, who bear the sword of their office against God and his chosen, as may be seen of Saul, of Pharaoh, Antiochus, Ahab, Jezebel, Herod and others. On the other hand he can guard his chosen, and help them out of all difficulties, how hard soever they may be pressed. This he has shown in the deliverance of Israel when he led them through the Red Sea, and in preserving David, Helias, Elisha, Daniel in the Lion's den, and the three young men in the fiery furnace, and in many other instances.

Here again we have a clear example in the case of Saul and David, how the proud, reckless, self-willed and carnal princes every where, although they wish to be called christian princes, and gracious lords, act and behave towards the true David, Christ Jesus, and all his saints, whom he has anointed with the oil of the Holy Spirit; who have power from above, with him, in and through him to overcome the fearful, infernal bear, lion and Goliath, hell, sin, death, devil, malediction and wrath of God. They can have peace nowhere, with this evil disposed Saul, howsoever innocent, godfearing, and pious they may be. Neither innocence nor piety, praying nor tears, word nor Christ, avail. As in the case of David, every thing must be perverted and construed for the worst. This has ever been the case, and according to my opinion, will remain so to the end.

Still my brethren, fear ye not, for all your persecutors and enemies become old like a garment, how mighty, glorious and great they may be esteemed. "All flesh is grass, and all the goodliness thereof is as the flower of the field." But ye shall flourish and increase in God, and your fruit shall never more decay, for the kingdom of Jerusalem is given to you, and the glorious Lord will have honor in you, though Saul rages, and will give to you the eternal kingdom, which he has prepared and set apart everlastingly for you, and all the chosen, Isa. 40: 6.

Fourthly, Jeremiah, the son of Hilkiah, a priest of the priests of Anathoth, was sanctified from his mother's womb, and was chosen of God to be a prophet and a seer from his youth. He rebuked Judah and Benjamin on account of their disobedience, stubbornness, transgressions, false worship, idolatry and bloodshed, with the mouth and law of God. He taught repentance and reformation, prophesied of the promised Messiah, whom he called the Branch and Root of David. He preached the coming punishment and wrath of God, namely, the captivity and destruction of the kings, the destruction of the city and temple, and the captivity of the people for seventy years.

And these, his prophecies, faithful warnings, visions and rebukes from the mouth of the Lord, became to him as sharp, piercing thorns; they cast his word and admonitions aside, and would not hear them. The pious prophet and true servant of God must be regarded as their betrayer, a factionist and heretic. The word of the Lord was to him as a daily mockery. He was oft-times imprisoned and scourged, and thrown into a foul pit. They counselled concerning his death. He was so pressed with the cross, that he once resolved in his heart, to preach no more in the name of the Lord, yea, he cursed the day of his birth, and the man who brought the message to his father, that a man child was born. Thus the worthy man of God, had to bear the heavy cross for many years, for the sake of the word and truth of the Lord, Jer. 20. He had to yield his ear to all reproaches, and his back to scourging, till the floods of trouble burst upon the hardened, rebellious, unbelieving people, but alas! they saw too late, that Jeremiah was a right messenger, and a true prophet of God. Besides all this he had to close his life in Egypt, being stoned to death, as a reward for his ardent love and difficult, bitter work.

My dear brethren in the Lord, here I will end the narratives from the Old Testament, for time will not suffice to relate all. The pious Joseph was grievously hated by his brethren, and by them was cast into a pit and again drawn out, and sold to the Ishmaelites, and was complained against as a perfidious adulterer, by the unchaste wife of his lord. Though he was innocent, yet he must suffer his lord's wrath, imprisonment and bonds. Also the high-renowned, evangelical prophet, Isaiah, under the bloody and idolatrous tyrant, Manasseh, was sawn asunder, as the historian mentions. The spiritual prophet, Ezekiel, was stoned by those who remained of Dan and Gad. Urijah of Kirjath-jearim, was slain with the sword by Jehoiakim the king of Judah. Zacharias the son of Barachias, was stoned between the temple and the altar. The great, wonder-doing prophet Elijah, must retreat before the blood-thirsty, idolatrous Jezebel; the three youths, Shadrach, Meshach and Abed-nego, were cast into the glowing furnace, and Daniel into the lion's den. The venerable, pious, old Eleazar, and his worthy, pious wife, with their seven sons, were so inhumanly and barbarously treated by the terrible Antiochus, were murdered, martyred and destroyed.

Behold brethren, every christian should beware that this is the only reward and crown of this world, with which they reward and honor all true servants of God, who present to them in pure love, the kingdom, word, and will of God; who call to repentance and reformation; who have rendered many kindnesses, services and favors; direct to salvation, righteousness, truth, piety and love; who are the golden candlesticks in the tabernacle of the Lord, and flourish and blossom as the fruitful olive tree in the house of God. All who reflect on these and similar histories and narratives of the pious men of God, will undoubtedly not despond, but in all their miseries, crosses and sufferings will stand, through the grace of God, and abide unwavering to the end.

Since I have now presented some histories out of the holy Scriptures, by which it is plainly seen that true righteousness every where, has suffered, and has been destroyed, under the law as before the law; therefore, I will now, through the grace of God, present some examples out of the New Testament, by which all may learn, and acknowledge with Paul, that, "All that live godly in Christ Jesus shall suffer persecution," 2 Tim. 3: 12.

First, John the Baptist, a man sent of God, as the Evangelist testifies; a burning and shining light, as Christ says, and of whom Isaiah had prophesied a long time before, saying, "The voice of one crying in the wilderness, Prepare ye the way of the Lord, make his paths straight," Matt. 3: 3, whom Malachi called the messenger of the Lord, whose birth, greatness, holiness, office, doctrines and works were announced, by Gabriel, the heavenly messenger, to Zacharias, his father. John was filled with the Holy Ghost from his mother's womb. He preached repentance to all Judea, pointed out CHRIST, the Savior of the world, and said, "Behold the Lamb of God, which taketh away the sin of the world!" Of him the Son of God himself gave testimony, that he was no wavering reed, that he was not clothed in soft raiment, that he was greater than a prophet, that he was the promised Elias, that he came in the way of righteousness, and among all that were born of women, there had not arisen a greater than he; he was also held by the people as a prophet, yet did they say, "He hath a devil," yea, Herod, the king, cast him forth as a profligate vagrant, and after some days, this holy man of God was beheaded by the executioner, as a shameful transgressor, on account of his rebuking Herod's incest, and besides, it was given to a vain, haughty, dancing maid, and an unchaste, adulterous woman, to be shown and presented to the drunken, useless and ungodly guests of Herod, in a charger, as a present and banquet dessert.

O Lord! how lamentably and grievously the righteous are destroyed on account of their piety, by this abominable, bloody, murderous world, and no one takes it to heart. Yea, they are so dealt with, that it appears before the eyes of the unwise, as if the godly were an offence and an abomination, and were banished and cursed of God, and that they might neither hope for, nor find, to all eternity, comfort or grace from God. O no! the Lord be blessed; although their lives may appear to the foolish world to be but idle phrensy, and their end to be without honor, yet do we know that they are the people and children of the Lord, and the apple of his eye, that their blood and death are dear to him; that after a little suffering and trouble they shall be recompensed with good; that theirs is the kingdom of heaven; that they will not be touched with the pains of eternal death, Wis. 3, but their precious souls shall be in eternal rest and peace. Yes, my brethren, every christian may trust and rejoice in the Lord in all his trials and in all his need.

Again, Stephen, the crowned of God, a man full of faith, power and the Holy Ghost, who did great signs and wonders among the people, as Luke writes, was endued of God with such wisdom and spirit, according to the promises of Christ, that also his enemies, namely, the Libertines, Cyrenians, Alexandrians, &c., were silent, and stood abashed before him. As they saw this, the spirit of their fathers displayed itself as it had done from the beginning; consuming envy must use its artifices; Stephen must lead the way; they have rejected justice and equity; the men of Belial they employed to belie the pious Stephen, and say, We have heard him speak blasphemous words against Moses and against God; and that Jesus of Nazareth shall destroy this place, and shall change the customs which Moses delivered unto us; thus have the lies of the serpent overcome justice. They counsel to exterminate the saints. His own enemies saw his countenance, as the countenance of an angel of God. He spake the word of the Lord without fear, rebuked the false trust in the law and the temple, and testified of Jesus Christ in great power, of whom Moses and all the prophets prophesied. At length he grew very warm and ardent in his speech to the multitude, because they had ungratefully rejected the merciful visitation of God in his proffered race. O ye stiff-necked! he said, and you uncircumcised in heart and ears, ye do always resist the Holy Ghost; as your fathers did, so also do ye. Which of the prophets have not your fathers persecuted? They have slain them which shewed before of the coming of the just One, of whom you have been now the betrayers and murderers; who have received the law through the dispositions of angels, and have not kept it; and when they heard these reproving and sharp words, they could no longer endure it, for they were cut to the heart, and gnashed their teeth at him. But Stephen, being full of the Holy Ghost, looked up steadfastly into heaven and saw the glory of God, and Jesus standing on the right hand of God, and said, "I see the heavens opened and the Son of man standing on the right hand of God," Acts 7: 51–56. Then they called aloud and stopped their ears, and as if they could not longer endure the blasphemous words with which the wicked heretic (as they considered him), boasted and with which he gave such honor to Christ; they rushed upon him with one accord and with great vehemence and wrath, cast him out of the city, and stoned him, but Saul kept the witnesses' clothing. Stephen called out, Lord Jesus receive my spirit. He kneeled down and cried with a loud voice, after the example of his master on the cross, "Lord lay not this sin to their charge, for they know not what they do," Acts 7. Thus the pious martyr fell asleep in the Lord, and received the crown of life which God has promised to all those who fear, love and seek him from the heart, with all sincerity.

O! god-fearing reader, observe and learn to know by such examples, that all those who believe the word of the Lord with true hearts, who become partakers of the Holy Ghost, who are clothed with power from on high, out of whose mouth flow grace and wisdom, who shame the world, rebuke sin, and with Stephen, must be cast out of the city and stoned.

Dear brethren, pray ardently and prepare yourselves. Through much misery and trouble you must enter into the kingdom of heaven. Here is the patience and faith of the saints. O my brethren, watch.

Again, Paul, a servant of God, and an apostle of Jesus Christ, a chosen vessel, a champion of the holy word, an apostle and teacher of the Gentiles, who was not called by men, but of God himself, from heaven to the service of the gospel, was powerful and zealous in his teaching, and unblamable in his life. He labored more than all the other apostles, cast out devils in the name of the Lord, awakened the dead Eutychus again to life, restored health to the sick, shook off the serpent without receiving injury; as a true prophet, he foretold many things which were to come to pass in the last times, was taken up into the third heaven and to the paradise of God, and saw such vision, of which no man might with propriety speak. He was an infallible leader in all righteousness, holiness, piety and virtue, who sought and loved not himself, but God and his neighbor from the whole heart; he had nothing by which to justify himself; he regarded all gain as loss, that he might win Christ alone; yes, he dare not speak of any thing, but what Christ had wrought through him. It availed not how holy, unblamable, zealous, high called, powerful or how devout he was; yet he must, with Simon, the Cyrenian, help to bear the cross of Christ; for as soon as he was called from heaven, taught and baptized by Ananias, and had left off his tyranny, and preached Christ in Damascus, he was let down over the wall in a basket to escape the snares of the blood-thirsty.

He was often imprisoned; thrice scourged with rods, stoned once, in Ephesus he was cast to wild beasts, and at last, after inconceivable and innumerable pains and journeys from one land to another, after enduring much from nakedness, cold, heat, thirst, hunger, labor, watchings, dangers and anguish, he was seized by the Jews at Jerusalem, and scourged; they accused him before the judges, swore to take his life, secured him in Cesarea, and after his appeal to Cæsar, he arrived with much danger and shipwreck at Rome, he was brought before the emperor, and at last, under Nero, the most blood-thirsty of tyrants, was put to death by the sword. He offered up his soul and surrendered his life.

In like manner were the apostles imprisoned and scourged in Jerusalem; the church was dispersed and persecuted, and James was put to death with the sword under Herod. All who desire to become acquainted with other narratives besides those here noticed, from the Holy Scriptures, can read the church history by Eusebius, there will they find similar inhuman abominations, tyranny, unmercifulness and envious falsehoods against the innocent. Besides they will find such extraordinarily strange inventions to torture, martyr, kill, root out and murder christians, that a natural man, to say nothing of a spiritual one, must in his heart, be awe-stricken and sickened.*

My most beloved brethren in Christ Jesus, be of good cheer and trust ye in the Lord, you who willingly submit to the cross of Christ. You may see and observe from the Scriptures, in the above examples from the Old and New Testaments, how all pious men and children of God, the righteous and prophets, apostles and true witnesses of Christ, yea, Christ himself, as we shall yet hear, have gone through this lonesome wilderness, through this narrow, ignominious and bloody way of misery, crosses and sufferings, to the true, promised land, and to eternal glory.

Yea, this is, and remains the only narrow and straight way, and door through which we must all enter, neither can we ever desire in any other way to enter with the saints

---

* As a further illustration of this subject the following extracts from Eusebius and others, concerning the humility and meekness of the believing Martyrs of that day (Eus. B. V. C. 3), is given.

"They followed Christ Jesus in all humility, although they were oft made martyrs.

"However they did not call themselves MARTYRS nor consented that others should call them such; but when even one of us called them MARTYRS they reproved us severely, saying, That this name properly belonged to Christ, who alone was the true and faithful Martyr and witness of the truth, the first born of the dead and the RESTORER of eternal life. Or that this name could only appropriately be given to those, who after laying off a testimony had departed this life and gone to God. But we (say they), as humble, poor people, wish alone to adhere undeviatingly to the confession, and therefore, they entreated the other brethren with tears, that they would pray to God that they might obtain the witness of a MARTYR (full confession), and they were so humble, though in truth they were MARTYRS, still they avoided the honor of the name. But among the heathens they acted with all constancy, showed great magnanimity, by

into eternal life, rest and peace, as Christ himself said, Whosoever will follow after me must deny himself, take up his cross, and follow me; therefore, dear brethren, you who have sought, feared and loved the Lord, must suffer and bear much from this wicked and idolatrous race. Fear not those who take your earthly goods from you; for Christ and heaven they cannot take from you, or those who kill the body, for they cannot kill your soul, but fear him who has power to cast both soul and body eternally into hell. Yes, my brethren, would you be the people and disciples of the Lord, you must also bear the cross of Christ; this is, without doubt, the truth.

Again, we have set forth to the kind reader, several excellent histories out of the Scriptures, in which are represented the tyrannical mind, the envious heart, the wolfish rage, the murdering deeds of this miserable, brutal, murderous and blood-thirsty world, against the righteous. We shall now, through the grace of God, notice for a short time, not only how the servants, of whom we have spoken, suffered but also how the Lord and Prince himself had to endure much, to again enter into his glory.

The apostles abundantly testify that the Lamb of God, the ever blessed Christ Jesus, the true Head of all true believers, had not only suffered from the beginning, as above said, but that he must suffer in the flesh in these last times, although he was the conqueror of the serpent, was promised to Adam and Eve; a blessing and benediction to all people, the true Shiloh, Messiah and Emmanuel, the true plant of David, the Lord who justifies us, the Prince of Peace, and the true Son of the Almighty and living God, whom all the righteous and true prophets desired.

When he had now become man, according to the promise of the fathers, he preached repentance and regeneration in the full power of the Spirit, in all love, righteousness, peace, humility and obedience; the rigid, terrible judgment of God over the impeni-

---

scorning the offered insults, and through patience, suffered. For among the brethren they were meek, among persecutors brave, a terror to the refractory, subject to Christ, opposing the devil; they humble themselves under the mighty hand of God, by which they are now exalted; they favored all, they accused none, relieved all, bound none; prayed for those who persecuted them, as did Stephen, saying, "Lord, lay not this sin to their charge." The devil opposed them powerfully, because they, out of great love in Christ Jesus, restored the fallen, whom the devil would fain have devoured. They entreated God to give them grace and constancy, lest they might depart from the church and become a prey to the devil.

"They preferred peace before every thing else, and commanded us to maintain peace. They were martyred without cause and were conscious that they made no discord among the brethren and no grief to the church; but they admonished assiduously, that we should, by all means, maintain and preserve peace, and cherish love, which is the bond of union.

"These things we mentioned for the benefit of the reader, because they have been recommended by worthy and beloved men. And on account of those who deal so haughtily with the brethren, and when the pious err through weakness, they have no compassion upon them, as if Christ should have no mercy on them. We will further relate what we found in the beforementioned book. There was one among the number apprehended for Christ's sake, called Alcibiades, who led a strict, zealous life, he would use no sustenance except bread and water; and as he was determined to live thus abstemious in prison, it was made known to Allalas, that Alcibiades did wrong, because he would not rightly use the creatures of God, lest he might cause others to take offence thereat. But when Alcibiades was informed of the matter, he then enjoyed all things with thanksgiving, for there was a spirit which taught him and persuaded him to obey.

"Afterwards, Montanus, Alcibiades and Theodotius were regarded by many in the land of Phrygia as prophets, for in those days many favors were granted to some of the churches through the gift of the Holy Ghost, so that they believed that the gift of prophecy was imparted. And when great contention arose among the brethren, the churches in France again issued their sentence, with all discipline, reverence and the true exposition of the faith, and brought forward the epistles of the martyrs, who among them ended their lives, which they wrote in their prisons to the brethren in Asia and Phrygia.

The whole Bible, especially the 11th chapter of the epistle to the Hebrews, speaks of the great crosses, tribulation, the martyrdom and deaths of the believers. Here we read of inhuman, cruel torturings, such as was neither heard before nor since. Boiling water and oil were poured upon their naked bodies; they were placed upon red hot gridirons and roasted there; their members were pierced through with sharp pointed instruments, they were scourged, and red hot irons were applied to their limbs; sharp thorns were thrust into their posterior and privates; other indignities were offered not to be mentioned; hot pitch was thrown into their faces; their eyes were bored out with pointed irons; they were beaten from head to foot with clubs; they were dragged through the streets by their feet; they were tent; and also the eternal kingdom, grace, mercy, the sincere favor and love of his heavenly father over the penitent. He was himself that Word, fulfilling all righteousness, blessed of God forever, the infallible Example, the eternal Wisdom, Love and Truth, the brightness of the divine glory, the express image of his Father, after whom the first man was created, understand according to the inner man, the eternal power of God, the Almighty Word of God, through whom all things were created, are governed, and in whom all things stand. He knew no sin, neither was guile found in his mouth; he is the true light of eternal life, and by the darkness, which is in the world, he is hated, blasphemed, rejected, despised, and trampled upon as the most degraded of men. The King of kings, the Lord of lords, became poorer than the foxes or the birds; for he had not where to rest his blessed head. On the day of his birth, there was no room in the inn; the manger was his couch. Even shortly after his birth, his parents had to fly with him to the land of Egypt.

Although in the time of his ministry he made the blind see, the deaf hear, the dumb speak, the leprous clean, the palsied and feeble, sound, cast out devils, restored the dead, twice he fed thousands with a few loaves and fishes, and showed to them the works and service of pure love, and although none could rebuke him in his word or his life, yet, their blood-thirsty, envious hearts were so enraged at him, that they desired that the wicked murderer, Barabbas, who was sentenced to death by the law, should live, and that the eternal Life himself, the Creator and Upholder of all creatures, should die. His pure, heavenly body, the seat of all virtue, is scourged and abused, the glorious countenance and head of all honor is disfigured with blood, spit and thorns. They also mocked him with a ludicrous garment, so that even the heathen judge, Pilate, pitying, said, "Behold the man!" Yea, worthy brethren, it avails nothing, no pain, torture, nor misery was enough; they would not be satisfied, till he was taken away and condemned to the most shameful death, extended upon the cross, his hands and feet nailed

suspended and their flesh torn from them with pincers, that their bodies were all raw; then vinegar, salt and lime were mixed and poured upon them; they were then rolled about upon thorns, potsherds, broken glass and other sharp instruments, then the tortured body was placed upon a gridiron, and roasted lingeringly to protract the pain, rolling the mangled body backward and forward upon the gridiron till the ghost was given up.

"They were cast before beasts of prey, such as lions, bears, and leopards; and before infuriated bulls; and after repeated torments, were again cast into prison, and after a short time tortured anew, which was repeated often, as we read of Maturo, Sanato, Allalo and others; and above all the amiable Blandina, whom they tortured six different ways; she may properly be called the pattern of martyrs. Others died in prison on account of their excruciating pains; some were starved to death; some women they hung up by the feet and suffocated with offensive smoke; flayed them, led them about on camels, and tore them to pieces with tongs; cast them into privies; their bones were broken, and they were cast into clefts of rocks; their heads were bruised so much till the brain ran down upon the earth; cut off their sinews and veins, then thrust them down precipices; they were first severely tortured, butchered like swine and then cast into the sea; their abdomen cut open and barley strewn in, and in this condition left to be devoured by hogs; yea, some of the tyrants, for fierce anger ate pieces of their livers; they watched day and night, lest their remains would be taken and buried!

They were smeared over with honey and lard, and suspended in baskets in the air for the flies, wasps and bees to eat; women and virgins were stripped stark naked, and while thus exposed, suspended by one leg, forcing the head down and leaving them in this position for one day; they cut off their breasts, horrible! horrible to relate!! melted lead they poured into their secrets; forced red hot spears in! applied red hot iron; sturdy trees they bent down and tied each leg fast to a tree, and then let them spring up again, and thus tore the women; took sharp splinters of pine wood, forced them under the nails of their hands, and then set them on fire; melted lead they poured down their backs. Twenty sharp pointed pieces were forced under the nails of one Benjamin, of Persia; this was not enough; they forced a sharp rugged tube into his urethra—and this was repeatedly done; after this a rod full of thorns was taken and forced into his posterior, till the valiant man gave up the ghost. It is impossible, nay, incredible, with a few words to describe the unheard of cruelties and tortures which were practiced; besides these, other modes of torturing were invented, and he that succeeded in inventing the most cruel mode was highly honored. The number that were slain like beasts, was so great that even the executioners became fatigued and their swords became dull.

"One king in Persia, as history relates, had sixteen thousand slain. But the more the christians were opposed the more their numbers increased, so powerfully did Christ reign in them, that the heathen themselves said, *The christian blood is a true seed, &c.*"

to the wood, and his side pierced with a spear. He was crucified as a prince and leader of the vicious, and reckoned among murderers. Thus they requited him for his incomprehensibly great love and beneficence, and in his great, bitter thirst, in the last hour of his sufferings, he could not obtain a drop of water, but they gave him vinegar and gall. In short, they treated him so that he cried, while extended upon the cross, with a loud voice to his Father, "My God, my God, why hast thou forsaken me?" He also laments through the prophet, "I am a worm and no man, a reproach of men and despised of the people." He might well sigh and lament with Jeremiah or Jerusalem, and say, "All ye who pass, behold and see if there be any sorrow like unto my sorrow." Thus he, who was eternally rich, for our sakes became poor; the eternal Glory was dishonored, eternal Righteousness, persecuted, eternal Truth, blasphemed, eternal Happiness, rejected, eternal Blessing, cursed, and the eternal Life was made to suffer a shameful death.

Most beloved brethren in the Lord, observe well, if the laborers have not spared their Lord's Son, but have cast him out of the vineyard and have slain him, how much more shall they destroy the servants. "If they have called the Master of the house Beelzebub, how much more shall they call them of his household?" Matt. 10: 25. Christ said, "If they have persecuted me, they will also persecute you." And further, "If the world hate you, ye know that it hated me before it hated you," for the disciple is not greater than his master, nor the servant than his lord; but it is enough for the disciple to be like his master, and the servant to be like his lord; and other like passages may be found in Scripture.

I hope, worthy brethren, that from these examples, the pious may have learned and fully understood, what kind of a people it always has been, from what father they are born, and by what spirit they are moved, who from the beginning till the present day, have rejected and persecuted Christ, the lovely, peaceful, innocent and obedient Lamb and his saints; who have plundered, belied, imprisoned, tortured, crucified, stoned, beheaded, drowned, roasted, strangled, slain and murdered them; and, according to my understanding of the word of the Lord, this tyranny shall not cease till the rejected, murdered and crucified Christ Jesus, and all his saints shall appear in the clouds as an almighty Potentate, Conqueror and glorious King, before all the tribes and people, at the last judgment.

Inasmuch as the fearful tyranny of this blind world, always has been and is yet practiced upon the children of God, and as said, will probably always be practiced; and since, no other way leads, nor can lead through the narrow door to life, than this only, stony and thorny way of the cross (I mean according to the flesh; for according to the spirit it is broad and easy), as the Scriptures testify; therefore, have your feet shod with the gospel of peace, with the precious promises of God, with the pure knowledge of Christ, with the denial of yourselves, with the patience and faith of the saints and with the sure hope of the kingdom of God; that the hard stones and the sharp, stinging thorns of persecution, through which all the pious are tempted, do not terrify you and lead you upon the broad, easy way of the flesh. Lay aside all obstacles and besetting sins, the cursed works of darkness, avarice, unnecessary cares, love of home, goods, gold, silver, pomp and splendor; all things which are perishable, drunkenness, superfluity, idolatry, vanity, carnal and improper words, and all manner of wickedness, that you may not be overcome and thus led off the only, narrow high-way, upon crooked and dark by-ways. As, alas, may be frequently seen in our days.

Therefore, my dear brethren and sisters in the Lord, take the crucified Jesus as your example, and also all the righteous apostles and prophets of God, and learn through them, how they all entered at this strait gate and forsook their all. They prepared their hearts and were endued and drawn of God, that they knew, sought, loved and desired nothing else than eternal, heavenly blessings, the unchangeable things, God and eternal life. Thus they were grounded in ardent love, and became firm and immovable, so that they could not be affrighted from the love of Christ, neither by life nor death, angel, prince, potentate, hunger, sword, martyrdom, pain nor ease. Their thoughts, words, acts, sufferings, life and death, were Christ's. They sought not their kingdom and rest upon earth, for they were spiritually, heavenly-minded. All their fruit was righteousness, light and truth. Their whole lives were pure love, chastity, humility, obedience and peace. The perishable, wicked world with all its evil works, was to them an offence and abomination. They loved their God with all their soul, and therefore, they rebuked all that was against his holy will, honor and word. They loved their neighbors as themselves, and therefore, they admonished and rebuked them in love, served them, pointed out and taught them God's pure will, word and truth, and sought their salvation with all their power, with great loss of life, goods and reputation, therefore has the foolish, envious, unthankful world, which swims in blood, so grievously hated, persecuted and rewarded them with death.

My dear brethren, it was not only the prophets, apostles and those of former times, to whom those things happened, which the Scriptures relate, but we have in these times witnessed the like with our own eyes. How many pious children of God have we known in the space of a few years, and we yet know some, the Lord be praised, who sought Jesus Christ and the eternal, unchangeable life, and continue so to seek, who fear God from their inmost soul, whose hearts burn with the word and love of the Lord, out of their mouths flowed power, spirit and wisdom. Their whole life was repentance and piety, they hated, shunned and rebuked all ungodliness. None could reprove their conduct with the word of God; they were opposed to the idle, fleshly, ungodly life of this world, as they yet are, and by the grace of God will continue to be. They listen not to the deceiving prophets, confide not their precious souls to the care of the spiritual thieves and murderers, neither serve nor honor wooden, stone and silver gods, and do not use the unscriptural, earthly sacraments, &c. In short, because they heard, believed, feared, served and loved the true and living God, therefore, did the lying serpent open its mouth and spew out so many false, slanderous, yea, inhuman lies, into the face of the pious, and has, from the seat of its pestilences, defamed and depicted them in such horrible colors and shape, through their blind disciples, that they have become the curse and offense of the whole world; that all the people close their mouths and noses, and flee from them in horror; yes, every one, who can slander and defame the poor, god-fearing christians, is the favorite preacher and esteemed teacher of the world.

No lie is so gross and disgraceful, that they dare not bring it against the godly. At one time they accuse and upbraid us, as though we wished to invade cities and countries; they say, That we will injure the whole world; now we are adulterers, again, thieves and murderers; now, we say there is no repentance left to the sinner; again, we have rejected Christ and the Testament. In short, whosoever does not defame and upbraid the godly, is not considered by the world as a christian! O Lord, how pure and free are all the saints in heart and conscience before God, from all these and such like lies and slanders.

All these unchristian, infernal lies are not enough for the world, but they who know Christ, and would gladly live after his word, must endure something harder; they must meet with severer persecution, as we may witness with our own eyes, for how many pious children of God, have they within a few years deprived of their homes and possessions, for the testimony of God and their conscience sake; how many have they betrayed, driven out of city and country, and put them to the stocks and torture; the poor orphans and children are left naked in the streets; some they have hanged, some they punished with inhuman tyranny, afterwards choked them with cords on stocks and pillars; some they roasted and burned alive; some with their own reeking bowels in their hands, powerfully confessed the word of God; some they slew with the sword and gave them as food to the fowls of the air; some they cast to the wild beasts, some have their houses torn down, some have been cast into the muddy bogs, some have had their feet cut off, one of whom I have seen and conversed with; others wander about here and there, in hunger, affliction, mountains, deserts, holes and caves of the earth, as Paul says. They must fly with their wives and little children, from one country to another, from one city to another. They are hated, abused, slandered and belied by all men, and spoken against in the pulpit and the councils; they have deprived them of food, driven them forth in the cold winter, and point at them with the finger of scorn, yea, whoever can wrong a poor, oppressed christian, supposes he has done God some service, as Christ says in John 16: 2.

Observe, dear brethren, how far the whole world is from God and his word, how swift their feet are to shed blood, how maliciously they hate the light, and how bitterly they persecute, defame and destroy the eternal, saving truth, the immaculate gospel of Jesus Christ, the pious, godly life of the saints. This is not only done by the papists and Turks, but also by those who boast of the holy word; who at first preached much concerning faith, that it was the gift of God, and that it must not be forced with the iron sword, but with the word, into the hearts of men, for it is a willing assent of the heart.

But the learned, within the last few years, have suppressed this doctrine, and as it appears to me, have effaced it from their books, for lately they draw unto their carnal doctrine, lords, princes, cities and countries; they preach the contrary from that which they did formerly, as is evident from their writings. By their seditious writings and preachings they deliver into the hands of executioners, many pious hearts, who gainsay, reprove and admonish them, by the clear word of God, and point out to them the true ground of the gospel, which is powerful, active faith, which works by love, a penitent, new life, obedience to God and Christ, and the true, evangelical ordinances of baptism, Lord's Supper and *Separation*, as Christ himself instituted and commanded, and his holy apostles practiced and taught.

Yea, all who do this out of pure love, must be accursed as anabaptists, factionists, deceivers and heretics, all the pious may expect this, nevertheless all of them, lords, princes, preachers, scribes and common people, be they Papists, Lutherans, or Zuinglians, wish to be called the christian community and holy church; and never take notice of their ungodly, impure and impenitent lives, that they are altogether earthly, carnal, and contrary to the word of God. There are some, whose hands are stained and reeking with the blood of christians, and all their doings are diametrically opposed to the Spirit, word, and example of Christ. O! that these poor, blind, hardened ones would lay this well to heart, and examine well the nature and spirit of true christianity. They would be ashamed before God, and sincerely lament that they so miserably abuse his glorious name, blessed word, divine grace, and his crimson, precious blood, of which they vainly boast, and thus make the name of Christ as a cover to all their wickedness and disgrace.

For a truly believing christian is one that is born of God according to the Spirit, has become a new creature in Christ, crucified his flesh with its lusts, and hates all ungodliness and sin. All his fruits are righteousness, patience, truth, obedience, humility, chastity, love, and peace; he is influenced by the Spirit of the Lord, and his delight is in his law; he meditates thereon by day and by night, all his words are seasoned by grace, he sincerely strives for the life which is from God, and fears him with all his soul. In short, according to the grace received, he is of one mind with Christ.

Could these miserable people only see that a christian is thus minded, as related, that he is such an amiable and peaceable creature and child of God; and if they had the grace, they also would be thus minded. If they were christians as they boast, they would then hate none, but would be hated, would belie none, but would be belied, would prejudge none, but be prejudged, would betray none, but be betrayed, would rob none, but be robbed, would not murder, but be murdered, would not devour the lamb, but be torn of wolves, not ensnare the dove, but be taken by the falconer and devoured.

If our persecutors are christians, as they imagine, Why are they then not of God and born of his word? Why are they yet the old, accursed creature, and live according to the lusts of the flesh? Why are they influenced by the spirit of the devil? Why have they fixed their thoughts and affections upon perishable and temporal things, and are concerned therewith day and night? Why are they guilty of talking of all manner of unchastity, vanity, lying, cursing and swearing? Why do they not fear God and his word? Why are they like the old, deceitful serpent, and obedient to him? Why are they still like terrible, ravenous beasts and birds of prey, instead of innocent lambs and doves, as the Scriptures teach?

Ah! dear brethren, let them boast as they will, Christ Jesus does not know such wicked and blood-thirsty christians. He only knows those having his Spirit, who sincerely believe and are obedient to him; are flesh of his flesh, and bone of his bone; are meek, humble, pious, holy and pure of heart; confess Christ Jesus in word and deed before this wicked world; deny themselves and take up the cross and follow him, and say with holy Paul, "Who shall separate us from the love of God?" They glory in nothing but in the cross of our Lord Jesus Christ, by which they are dead to the world and the world unto them. All who are thus minded, are the anointed of God, saints and christians, and not the impenitent, carnal, blood-thirsty boasters. Every one may be mindful that this is true, else the whole Scriptures are false.

It appears to me, dear brethren, that the pious reader may fully understand from what has been said, what kind of people these are, who so shamefully tread you with their feet; strike, belie, and deprive you of life and property, and also the reason why they do so, namely, on account of your infallible testimony of God and your consciences. Even as all from the beginning, who sought, feared and loved God, walked according to his divine word and will, reproved and admonished the confused and erring world, for their good, and were ever considered as off-scourings and heretics.

We will now proceed in the name of the Lord, and show with few words, what a feeble and unbecoming excuse our persecutors advance, which before God is as stubble and sulphur before fire, whereby they think to excuse themselves, that they are doing right to slander and molest the pious; all sinners seek some excuse, and no matter how disgracefully soever any one conducts himself, he wishes not to be considered as wicked, but as a righteous, pious and true christian!

In the first place, our persecutors accuse us as seditious, even as those of Munster are, and that we are not obedient to the magistracy.

To which we reply, in the first place: That the Munsterites were seditious, and in many things acted contrary to the word of God. But we do not agree with them. We are wholly opposed to these seditious abominations, such as resisting the king, seeking earthly power, taking up the sword, polygamy, acting the hypocrite with the world and the like guilt and disapprove of them; we neither eat, drink, nor have any communion with those who do such things, according to the doctrine of Christ and Paul, unless they renounce their errors and become sound in the saving doctrine of Christ.

As the Papists and Lutherans are not a little divided, so we are more divided in our views, from the Munsterites and other sects which sprang from them. That this is the truth, we have shown by our writings, life, and oral testimony, before lords, princes and the whole world; and it has been testified by the blood of many pious christians, which flowed like water, in many countries, for many years, to the present time.

But we cannot help that the world will not believe this. Nevertheless, we testify that our hearts and consciences are pure and free before God, of all sedition, hatred, vengeance and thirst for blood; and we strive earnestly to live as much as possible, in peace with all men, according to the doctrine of Paul, and if it be not possible for us to keep peace with them, still we do not desire to avenge ourselves, but we will commit it to him, who says, "To me belongeth vengeance and recompense," Deut. 32 : 35. And we commit to him alone all our concerns, as Jeremiah and all the pious did from the beginning.

In the second place, we reply: Why do they so indiscreetly accuse us of such sedition, since we are wholly innocent and clear, and since they pay no attention to their own bloody, murdering uproar, which they, alas!

commit without bounds? O Lord! how many principalities, cities and countries, have they destroyed, how many houses have they fired, how many hundred thousand have they murdered, how many poor peasants, who were peaceable, and innocent of sedition, have they robbed of their possessions and destroyed their goods? How many women and virgins have they disgraced? What brutal and inhuman tyranny did they commit and continue daily to practice? all this they do not notice, yea, it must be said, all is right and well done. Ah! how well does this accord with the doctrine, nature and Spirit of Christ, or with the disposition of innocent children, whom christians must resemble, in malice, or with defenceless lambs and innocent doves, to which the Scriptures direct us. If the temporal magistracy have not the disposition and Spirit of Christ, then all must acknowledge that they are not christians.

I am well aware, that these tyrants, who boast themselves christians, justify their abominable warring, uproar and shedding of blood, by referring us to Moses, Joshua, &c., but do not reflect that Moses and his successors, with their iron sword, have served their day, and that Christ has *now* given us a new command *and* another sword. I do not speak of the sword of the judge, for that is quite different; but I speak respecting war and sedition. They do not reflect, that they bear the sword of war, contrary to the gospel, against their own brethren, namely, their brethren in the faith, who have received the same baptism, and have broken the same bread with them, and are thus members of the same body. Again, what a strange, bloody uproar the Lutherans have made for several years, to introduce their doctrine, I will leave to them to reflect upon; yet have we, although innocently, to be called the seditious heretics and they, the pious, peaceable christians! Behold, thus lamentably is their understanding of this world darkened. Well then, let them deal with us as they think proper, the merciful, gracious Father will preserve us from such abominable disturbances as the Munsterites have caused, and which, alas! are yet in vogue among the supposed christians; for we have, by the manifest grace of God, beaten our "swords into plough shares, and our spears into pruning hooks;" and we shall sit under the true Vine, Christ, under the Prince of eternal peace, and will never take part in bloody wars.

In the third place, we reply: That we know and use no other sword than that which Christ himself brought down from heaven, and which the apostles used with power and Spirit; which proceeds from the mouth of the Lord, the sword of the Spirit, which is "sharper than any two-edged sword, piercing even to the dividing assunder of soul and spirit, and of the joints and marrow, and is a discerner of the thoughts and intents of the heart." With this sword and no other, we desire to destroy the kingdom of the devil, reprove all wickedness, preach righteousness, raise the father against the son, the son against the father, the mother against the daughter, and the daughter against the mother, &c. In such a way, even as Jesus Christ, the holy apostles and the prophets did in this world. I do not here mean the prophets, Elias and Samuel, understand me rightly, who also used the sword; but I mean the prophets Isaiah, Jeremiah, Zecharias, Amos, &c., who only reproved with doctrine, and not otherwise.

That is the sword we bear; and we will lay it down for none, neither for emperor, king, nor other authorities. Peter says, "We ought to obey God rather than men." We must serve, to his praise, him who committed us, whether we chance to live or die, as it may please God.

That the world is now ascribing to us this uproar as a reward for the pure love which we have manifested toward them, we must endure, as did our forefathers. "Art thou not he," said Ahab to Elijah, "that troubleth Israel?" The prophet answered, "I have not troubled Israel; but thou and thy father's house." Jeremiah, on account of his faithful warning and salutary admonition, was regarded by them as a mutineer, rebel and heretic; Christ Jesus was crucified; Paul and the apostles were cast into prison as deceivers and rebellious, and finally had to suffer martyrdom. If the world could pass a true sentence, they would well perceive, that Christ and his followers were not tumultuous towards the world, but the world towards them; and also, that we do not rise against any one, but that the whole world are in uproar, tyranny and raving against us, as may be seen.

Again, that we are opposed to the magistracy in the things to which they are ordained of God, is not true; understand me, in lawful things, such as giving toll, tribute, paying taxes, &c. But that they are to rule and lord over our consciences, contrary to the Spirit of Christ, as they please, to this we do not consent, but we will sacrifice possessions and life, rather than knowingly sin against Jesus Christ and his holy word, for any man's sake, whether he be emperor or king.

That we are right in this respect, the Scriptures abundantly testify; and therefore, with pious Susanna, we wish rather to obey God than man, and thus fall into the hands of men, rather than into the hands of God. May the gracious Father, through his blessed Son, Jesus Christ, grant to this deaf, blind world, ears to hear, and eyes to see, that they may be converted and be eternally saved.

In the second place we are, without cause, maliciously accused that we are stubborn, selfish and unconverted persons, who will by no means suffer ourselves to be taught or instructed.

To which we reply, first: If this accusation even were true, it is still very unbecoming for our persecutors to exterminate or harm us, because they would be, or boast themselves christians, for the punishment of the wicked will be eternal, as the Scriptures testify.

All men, says Paul, have not faith, but it is a gift of God. Now if it is a gift, it may not be enforced by worldly power, nor sword, but it must by means of the pure doctrine of the holy word, in conjunction with the ardent prayer of humility, be apprehended, by the grace of God, through the influence of the Holy Ghost. Moreover, it is not the will of the Householder, that the tares be rooted up, until the time of harvest; as is clearly evinced in the Scriptural parable.

Now, if our persecutors were christians, as they suppose, and if they considered the word of the Lord as true, Why do they not hear and follow the word and commandment of Christ? Why do they root up the tares before the time? Why are they not afraid, lest they root up the good wheat, and not the tares? Why do they arrogate to themselves the duty of the angels, who, at the proper time, shall bind the tares in bundles, and cast them into the furnace of everlasting fire?

Since, by our belief or unbelief, unbelief it must ever be, if their assertions are true, we injure no man upon earth; therefore, justice demands that they should commit us with our belief or unbelief to the Lord alone, and his judgment, who, in the fullness of time, will judge all things in righteousness, and that they should not, like savage pagans, pursue us with the sword of destruction. The true disposition of a pious and sincere christian, is to lead poor, wandering sinners to repentance, and not to destroy them, as these men do. In regard to all those who envince a contrary spirit, it is an easy matter for any intelligent christian, to show from the Scriptures of what father they are children.

Again, we reply: That we are prepared, in every way, even unto death, for the reception of all sound doctrine, admonition, instruction, and chastening, in righteousness; we spare no labor, pains, nor expense, if we can only obtain faithful stewards to dispense bread to us in proper season; for our souls hunger after the living bread, and our spirits thirst for the living water. All who are rightly qualified to break the former, and pour out the latter, we desire to hear with devotedness of heart, and to live in obedience to their doctrine.

But we will have nothing to do with the leaven of the Pharisees and Sadducees, the lies and deceivings of false prophets, the stealing and outrages of thieves and murderers, let what may happen by divine permission. Thank God, we have tasted the heavenly bread, hence, we have become heartily tired of the leaven and husks of the learned; we have drank the pure water, the impure we leave for them; we have received the truth and rejected lies; the light hath shined upon us, there is no more place for darkness. In short, we have found Christ, the true Messiah, his saving word, his pure ordinance, and his holy, and unblamable life, according to the gift of grace within us, and as a consequence, have turned away from anti-christ, with the confident hope, that we will never more observe, or make use of his ordinance of infant baptism, and idolatrous supper, nor ever be reconciled to his odious, carnal, ungodly life.

If in this matter we do wrong, and transgress in the presence of God and his church, as they imagine, then the fathers and the Scriptures must have miserably betrayed us. But no; the word of God is truth, and the truth shall abide forever, even though the whole world be offended.

And because we dare not again take part in their false doctrine, pretended sacraments, idolatry, false worship, and in their shameful, wicked, and ungodly life; because by the Spirit of God, the evidence of the Scriptures, and by the witness of our own consciences we have turned away from such; therefore, must we be called stubborn, selfish, obstinate, and, alas! must be to all men heretics, spoils and derision.

I hope, beloved brethren, that such absurd accusations may never dismay the hearts of the pious, nor render them faint, inasmuch as they are entirely destitute of foundation; whilst we, on the contrary, have the whole Scripture, together with prophets, apostles, saints, nay, Christ Jesus himself; all of whom in truth and righteousness, remained steadfast and immovable, even unto death, in their opposition to all false doctrine, torture and tyranny, and did not, in a single point, agree with their ungodly deeds or consent to them, neither in heart, speech, nor behavior.

Ought we then to reject the heavenly light, and embrace the darkness of condemnation? Forsake eternal truth, and everlasting life? Follow after lies, and pursue death, for the sake of a little perishable wealth, and the enjoyment of temporal life for half an hour? If so, it would be better for us that we had never been born. From a contingency so dreadful, it is our firm hope, that God, by his boundless love, will ever preserve and protect us.

In the third place we answer: That we sincerely detest and abhor such teaching and conversion, as our persecutors would make use of, in order to instruct and convert us; for their end is death, according to the testimony of the whole Scriptures; the reason is, that their doctrine is false and deceptive, their sacraments are idolatrous, and contrary to the word of God; their worship is sheer idolatry, and their whole life is earthly, carnal, and contrary to the word of God; as may be seen, James 3: 15, yea, they are a people of whom we may justly testify as they do of us, namely, This is a stiff-necked, seditious, unconverted people, whose hearts are harder than diamond, a people who know not their God, as the prophet speaks of Israel, saying, "The ox knoweth his owner, and the ass his master's crib; but Israel doth not know, my people doth not consider," Isa. 1: 3.

Ah, sinful nation, a people laden with iniquity, a seed of evil-doers, children that are corrupters! They have forsaken the Lord, they have provoked the Holy One of Israel unto anger, they are gone away backward, "They hold fast deceit, they refuse to return. I hearkened and heard, but they spake not aright; no man repented him of his wickedness, saying, What have I done? Every one turned to his course, as the horse rusheth into the battle; yea, the stork in the heaven knoweth her appointed times; and the turtle, and the crane, and the swallow, observe the time of their coming; but my people know not the judgment of the Lord," Jer. 8: 5—7. And more passages of a similar nature.

Like John the Baptist, one might well rebuke them, and say, Bring forth fruits meet for repentance, and say not that you are christians, as the Pharisees said they had Abraham for their father; for such perverse, carnal christians, God knoweth not. The axe is laid unto the root of the tree, therefore, every tree that bringeth not forth good fruit is hewn down and cast into the fire. Paul says, Neither drunkards, covetous, envious, proud, idolaters, adulterers nor fornicators shall inherit the kingdom of God; hence, in the spirit of commiseration, we may aptly say to our persecutors, who are still such, Reform, for alas! lords, princes, rulers, learned, unlearned, citizens, countrymen, man and woman, all, on every hand, have become degenerate, walking in the accursed fruits of profanity and ungodliness; they reject God and his word; they grieve the Holy Spirit; they persecute the righteous and pious; the fear and love of God are an abomination to them; yet to such as walk in the way of truth, die unto flesh and blood, are heavenly and spiritually minded, with sincerity of heart seek Christ Jesus and the imperishable everlasting life; they say, Reform, be instructed, and use similar expressions, just as if we had the lies, and they the truth; although according to the gift imparted to us, we love and seek the Lord sincerely; but what they do, I leave to any intelligent christian to decide.

Moreover, even they themselves demonstrate, that the fruits and ardent charity of our members far exceed that of theirs, nevertheless, we have to be looked upon, as deceived, selfish, obstinate, and unconverted heretics, while they consider themselves the real, spiritually anointed christians, the truly legitimate children of God.

Now, dear brethren, judge by this how puerile and nonsensical is the excuse of the world, with regard to their tyrannical proceedings, and how indiscreetly and childishly, we are accused by them. O! it is our heart's desire, that all our persecutors may receive grace unto repentance from the Lord; for it is high time that they awake, and turn unto him.

Again, our persecutors bring in an excuse, saying it is right that we should be persecuted, for by us many men are deplorably misled, and brought to destruction.

To this we reply: That if the case is examined, and sentence passed upon it, according to the flesh, it does appear that many are miserably deceived by us, for all those who follow our doctrine, faith, life, and confession, in obedience and power, must bring into jeopardy all which they have received from God; character, reputation, land, house, gold, silver, father, mother, sister, brother, husband, wife, son, daughter, yea, life itself. The finger of scorn will generally be pointed at them; they shall be trampled under foot, hated of all men, slandered and calumniated, betrayed, and delivered up unto death; gallows, racks, offensive pools, stocks and swords, as also hunger, thirst, want, toil, affliction, distress, anxiety, nakedness, sorrow, buffeting, bonds and imprisonment, must be their portion and recompense here upon earth; no man may administer unto, or befriend them, but at the risk of person and property; the father may not receive and assist the son, nor the son the father. In short, they are looked upon by the world as unworthy of heaven, or earth; moreover, they show all pomp, splendor, gluttony, intoxication, carnal life, &c., which the world delight in, and make use of, as much as their means will allow; besides they teach humility, soberness, and an humble, despised life, in the fear of the Lord, which the world hates and rejects. It is, therefore, no wonder, in my opinion, that the erring, blind world who neither have the Holy Spirit nor know it, as Christ says, who seek, understand, and judge earthly things alone, should regard, consider, and detest such a life, as the result of imposture and deception.

But those, who are taught of God, who have risen with Christ to newness of life, are made partakers of the Holy Spirit, are spiritually-minded, look upon, and judge all things by the Spirit, they do not consider it as imposture and deception, but esteem it above all gold, silver, knowledge, wisdom, riches, honor, parade, ostentation; nay, above all that is named under heaven; for they know from their hearts, that this is the only doctrine that leadeth to immortality and eternal life; they look not at the things which are transitory, but at things which are imperishable. They provide and prepare a treasure and inheritance that abideth in heaven, but earthly treasure they esteem not; seek the wisdom which is eternal, being therefore regarded by the whole world as fools; adorn themselves with the inner garment of righteousness, despising the outer moth-eaten garment of pride; strive for that kingdom and crown of glory which will abide forever, and the earthly kingdom with its glory, they leave to such as take delight in them.

Hence, dearly beloved, it is absolutely necessary to judge all things spiritually; for the world is come to such a state that the pure doctrine of Jesus Christ and his Holy apostles, is esteemed heresy; to preach

Christ Jesus, his Spirit and life, his unadulterated word, will and ordinance, and to turn the people from ungodliness to piety, is considered as imposition and deception. Behold, how blind and ignorant, in divine things, are our persecutors who so miserably oppress, persecute and destroy us for the sake of the truth. Yea, my brethren, here is the patience, and faith of the saints; all, who in their hearts experience this (as here related), will possess their souls in patience, let the opposition be ever so great, and will pray for their enemies with all the ardor of the power that is in them.

In the fourth place, our persecutors accuse us with great bitterness, because we separate ourselves from their doctrine, sacraments, church service, and from a carnal life, and in such things we dare have nothing to do with them; they say that, in this thing, we condemn them, and banish them to hell.

To this we reply, in the first place: The reason why we can never, by word or deed, consent to their preachers, sacraments, church service, and impure, carnal life nor allow them, is that they are openly opposed to God and his word; the preachers serve when they are not sent; their doctrine is false, deceptive and contrary to the saving doctrine of truth; their life is in every respect, blamable; they preach for filthy lucre's sake; they act the hypocrite for the world, to flatter the desires thereof; the foundation of their faith and religion, is emperor, king, prince and potentate; what they command, they teach; and what they forbid, that they leave untouched. Their infant baptism is unfounded in Scripture; their supper is idolatrous and impure, and by the impure, administered and received; their church-service is contrary to the doctrine of the apostles; and for the most part so carnal and ungodly is the ordinary tenor of their life, that every child of God must be exceedingly amazed and astonished at it.

Seeing then that their doctrine, sacrament, church service and life, are in fact, so palpably opposed to the word of God, how could we again intermingle and enter into familiarity with them in such heinous abominations? That we separate ourselves from them, is the express word and will of God. For, says Paul, "What fellowship hath righteousness with unrighteousness? What communion hath light with darkness? And what concord hath Christ with Belial? Or what part hath he that believeth with an infidel? And what agreement hath the temple of God with idols? For ye are the temple of the living God; as God hath said, I will dwell in them, and walk in them; and I will be their God, and they shall be my people. Wherefore come out from among them, and be ye separate, saith the Lord, and touch not the unclean thing; and I will receive you, and will be a Father unto you, and ye shall be my sons and daughters, saith the Lord Almighty," 2 Cor. 6: 14—18.

These words of Paul are plain and intelligible, and it is, therefore, utterly impossible, that those who have, through the beneficence of God, received from on high, the true Light, Christ Jesus, unfeigned righteousness, pure, effective faith, have become a fit and worthy temple of the Lord, are under the influence of the Holy Spirit, are chosen and adopted as the children of God, that such should again have fellowship with darkness, Belial, unrighteousness, infidels and idolaters; for while you, through the grace of God, are convinced that their doctrine, sacraments, church-service and life, are fundamentally false, if you have a true zeal for God; count all things but dross, that with Paul, you may win Christ, according to Scripture; abhor that which is evil, and cleave to that which is good; have washed your robes in the blood of the Lamb, and have conformed in all your thoughts, words and actions, to the touchstone of the holy word, and example of Christ, how then can you again have communion with them, and say amen to their abominations? We cannot serve two masters at once; we cannot at the same time hold communion with Christ, and the devil; we cannot be the children and servants of God, and also of satan; if we love that which is good, we must abhor that which is evil; if we embrace the truth, we must forsake lies; and such passages and Scriptures there are many.

Now, forasmuch as we thus separate ourselves from them, and testify by word and deed, even unto death, that their works are evil; therefore they are filled with the most inhuman rancor and indignation, and say from the heart, as all the ungodly have done from the beginning, "Let us lie in wait for the righteous; because he is not for our turn, and he is clean contrary to our doings; he upbraideth us with our offending the law, and objecteth to our infamy, the transgressions of our education," &c. He exposeth our secret designs and cunning devices. "He is grievous unto us even to behold; for his life is not like other men's, his ways are of another fashion. We are esteemed of him as counterfeits; he abstaineth from our ways as from filthiness; he pronounceth the end of the just to be blessed." "Let us condemn him with a shameful death," Wis. 2: 12, 15, 16, 20.

Here, my dearly beloved brethren, the Holy Spirit has given a faithful delineation of our persecutors; for our actual confession, that is to say, our separation from them is the sole reason why the blind, blood-thirsty world, frantic with rage, tyrannizes over us with so much cruelty; and why we must bear and suffer so much; as Peter also says. They think it more strange that you run not with them to the same excess of riot, speaking evil of you. Nay, for this reason, Isaiah, Jeremiah, Zechariah, Shadrach, Meshach, and Abed-nego, Daniel, Eleazar, the mother with the seven sons, Christ Jesus and all the pious had to die and bear the cross; because they earnestly reproved the world in its doctrine, ceremonies and conduct, and opposed them unto death.

This is, even unto this day, the only and principal reason, and in reality there is no other, notwithstanding our persecutors allege many, as we have shown, why we must be considered by the world as anabaptists, heretics, knaves, deceivers and movers of sedition, and be regarded as fit subjects for persecution. But, thank God, we know the reason of our suffering; we know also that he who called us to this grace, and in whom we put our trust, will successfully plead our cause, and will faithfully stand by and deliver his poor, oppressed children, in every time of need, to the advancement of his eternal praise and everlasting glory.

Although our persecutors assert that our separation from them is the result of pure obstinacy and caprice, yet their declaration is false and unjust, in the presence of God who knoweth the hearts of all men; because our separation has no other foundation nor design than this, that we desired, in our weakness, to observe with all our heart the word of God, and keep his commandments; and that we might, in real charity, and in fact, show to the whole world that they lie in wickedness, and are strangers to God and his word, to the end that they may, in due time, awake and turn from iniquity. For how can they in truth, teach others generosity, chastity, humility, and every virtue, if they themselves are abandoned to avarice, lewdness and pride, and addicted to every vice? It would be the height of folly for a person to point out the right way to others, warning them of robbers and murderers, while he would take a winding, unfrequented road and voluntarily offer himself an easy prey to thieves and robbers. My brethren may reflect upon what I mean.

It is not sufficent for a sincere christian merely to speak the truth; but he must also demonstrate in power and in deed, that which he speaks, conforming himself thereunto, or he shall hear, with the Pharisees, You say, and do not; and also as Paul, in writing to the Romans, says of the Jews, "Thou that preachest a man should not steal, dost thou steal? Thou that sayest a man should not commit adultery, dost thou commit adultery? Thou that abhorrest idols, dost thou commit sacrilege? Thou that makest thy boast of the law, through breaking the law, dishonorest thou God?" Rom. 2: 21—23.

In short, a christian teaches and acts; professes and practices; believes and obeys; directs and advances; his heart, word and deed are in unison; if not he is a hypocrite, and no christian; as, alas! there are numbers in our day, who boast highly of knowledge and wisdom, though in power they are vain and unfruitful.

Again, we reply: That our persecutors do violently and unjustly accuse us of condemning them to hell. Ah no! far be it from us to condemn any man under heaven before his time, let him be ever so wicked. For we are well aware that the Scriptures say,

"Condemn not, and ye shall be not condemned." There is one who, in the fullness of time, will judge every man according to his works, namely, he to whom the Father has committed all judgment; whosoever usurps his judgment shall not go unpunished. Moreover, we know not the measure of grace the sinner may be made partaker of before death; therefore we are clear and innocent before God, of condemning others. Nevertheless, we are permitted to judge and speak by the word of God, as follows: If a miser does not abandon his avaricious principles; a whoremonger, his lewdness; a drunkard, his intoxication; an idolater, his worshipping of strange gods, and by a pious, penitent life, turn to the true and living God with sorrow and anguish of heart, in the operative faith of Jesus Christ, he is no christian, nor shall he inherit the kingdom of God; if sentence is thus passed, it is not we that judge, but the Scriptures; as Christ says, "He that rejecteth me, and receiveth not my words, hath one that judgeth him; the word that I have spoken, the same shall judge him in the last day," John 12: 48. We are well assured that God neither does, nor can save any man contrary to his word; for he is truth, and cannot lie. Where there is no faith, no newness of mind, there is no repentance, nor sorrow of heart, &c.; upon such, alas! Christ Jesus has already passed sentence, saying, "If ye believe not that I am he, ye shall die in your sins;" "Except ye repent ye shall all likewise perish," and more similar expressions.

Brethren, we therefore judge no man with our word before the time, as you well know; but we commit that unto Jesus Christ and his word, who will judge them in due season; we do not condemn them by our separation, as they complain; but we teach and admonish them by word and work, with all dilligence and fidelity, that they might cease from evil, follow that which is good, do righteousness, seek and fear God in a good conscience, lest they die in sin and unbelief, and abide forever the wrath and judgement of God. Nevertheless, the pure charity and faithful service of the pious are ascribed to bad motives, and construed to their disgrace.

In the fifth place, many cover their tyranny and shedding of blood with a thin fig-leaf, and say, We judge you not, but the emperor's mandate judges you.

To this we reply: If our persecutors are christians, and have the knowledge of Christ, as they suppose, we earnestly desire in the spirit of humanity, for God's sake, that they would draw a comparison between the emperor and Christ, and observe with attention, whether the emperor and Christ are of one spirit; whether he walks as Christ taught his disciples; also, that they would compare the mandate of the emperor, with the gospel of Christ. If they discover that the emperor does not agree with Christ in spirit and life; and that his mandate, after which they frame their conduct, is contrary to the gospel, then they must acknowledge that the emperor is no christian, and that his mandate is proscribed and accursed in the presence of God.

It is the most lamentable blindness that they fear and honor the poor, earthly emperor more than Christ Jesus, and his bloodthirsty, malicious mandate, than the gospel of love. Yet they desire to be considered christians. O! that the emperor and his subjects were christians! This is our most earnest desire. Then would be spared a great deal of innocent blood, which is now spilled like water, contrary to all Scripture and charity.

Say now, all who are guilty of innocent blood, and who palliate your conduct with the mandate of the emperor, Where have you read a single passage in the whole life of Christ, which authorizes men to shed blood and punish with the sword for the sake of faith? Where have the apostles once taught or countenanced such a practice? Should not the cause of the Spirit (understand faith) be reserved unto the judgment of the Spirit? Why do you and the emperor place yourselves in God's stead, judging things which you understand not, neither are they commanded you? Do you not consider what befell Pharaoh, Antiochus, Herod, and many others, because they feared not the Most High, and vented their wrath against his people? Consider, O you tyrants and blood-thirsty! that the emperor is not the head of Christ, but that Christ is the head of the emperor; that the emperor shall not judge and govern Christ, but Christ, the emperor. Dear men, how can you be so arrogant and so rebellious against him who created you? Do you consider the Scriptures as mockery and as destitute of truth? Or do you hope that your life will remain forever, and that it will never run out? Stand in awe of Him who locks up the heavens and the earth in the palm of his hand, who sends forth the lightning, gives wings to the tempest, and shakes the foundations of the mountains, who rules all things with the power of his word, at whose name every knee shall bow, of things in heaven and things in earth, and things under the earth, and to whom every toungue shall confess that he is the Lord. As soon as he calls, you must appear at his tribunal (his summons is peremptory), no matter who you are, where you be, or what your pretentions; there will be no equivocation, no counsel, no excuse; when he calls, you must be there to give an account; you may be no longer steward; yet a little while, and the wicked shall not be; though his throne is exalted unto heaven, and his dominion extends to the ends of the earth, yet in a short time, he shall be sought, and shall not be found.

Therefore, beloved brethren and children in the Lord, be of good cheer, and full of consolation in Christ Jesus; for all who persecute you shall be as grass; and all their power and glory as the flower of the field; therefore, be not afraid of perishable, mortal man, but fear the Lord who has chosen you; for all the children of men shall wither as the grass, vanish as the mist, and wax old as a garment; but you shall abide forever, as the Scripture testifies, and your souls shall enjoy everlasting life.

Yes, beloved brothers, the longed-for day of your visitation is at hand, in which you shall stand with great power against those who have afflicted you, and exacted your sweat and toil, nay, your blood and life; then shall all our persecutors be as ashes under the soles of our feet; and know, but too late, that emperor, king, duke, prince, crown, sceptre, majesty, power, sword and mandate, are but earth, dust, wind and smoke.

With this day, all afflicted and oppressed Christians, who now labor under the cross of Christ, console themselves, in the firm hope of a future life, and commit all tyrants with their heathenish mandates unto God and his judgments; they remain firmly attached unto Christ Jesus and his holy word, and conform thereunto, their whole doctrine, faith, sacraments and life, never paying respect to any other doctrine or mandate; even as the Father commanded from heaven, and as Christ Jesus with his holy apostles taught in all clearness, leaving it as a legacy unto all pious, god-fearing children.

I suppose, beloved brethren, it is sufficiently evident that the apology of tyrants, in which they aver the justice and right of the outrageous murders, is perfectly futile and barbarous; and that their accusation against us has no foundation or truth; is diametrically opposed to Christ and his word, nay, contrary to the principles of love and equity. May the Father of mercies grant unto all, who suffer for his truth's sake, a sound understanding of his word and truth, and a freedom of mind in all temptations, Amen.

We will now, by the grace of God, show, in a few words, how greatly it serves for our good, that our flesh is afflicted and tempted with many crosses and tribulations here upon earth.

Beloved brethren, when we consider the weakness of our sinful nature, and how prone we all are to evil from our youth; that in our flesh dwelleth no good thing, and that we have drank iniquity and ungodliness like water, as Eliphas, the Temanite, said to Job. And have, at all times, although we seek and fear God, an affection for the things of time and sense. The gracious God and Father, who, through his eternal love, is always greatly concerned for his children, has prepared, and left in his house, an excellent remedy therefor, namely, the oppressive cross of Christ; so that we, who in unbounded mercy are received, through Christ Jesus, to the glory of the Father, believing in pureness of heart on Christ Jesus, and love him in our weakness, may, through the aforesaid cross, that is, through much affliction, oppression, anxiety, apprehension, bonds, robbery &c., forsake all the transitory delights and enjoyments of earth, die unto the world and the flesh, love God alone, set our affection on things above, where Christ sitteth on the right hand of God, as Peter also says, "Forasmuch, then as Christ hath suffered for us in the flesh, arm yourselves likewise with the same mind; for he that hath suffered in the flesh, hath ceased from sin; that he no longer should live the rest of his time in the flesh, to the lusts of men, but to the will of God," 1 Pet. 4: 1, 2.

It appears to me utterly impossible, beloved brethren, that they, who voluntarily submit to the word and will of God; who are willing and prepared to support the word in all things, on which account they are constantly persecuted, afflicted, slandered, imprisoned, robbed and put to death, should turn again and set their affection upon carnal pleasures, and the vain and sinful desires of the world. For, of what value are money and possessions to us, if we but believe, that we have in heaven a better treasure; that temporal riches can neither render us happy, nor afford us relief, and that we know not how soon they may be taken from us by robbers? Or, why should we gratify the lusts of the flesh, when we look for, and expect nothing else every instant, than to be apprehended by the officers, and be treated by the executioners after this manner; be racked, tortured, drowned, burned and assassinated? Moreover, how can the world afford us any enjoyment, seeing we are looked upon by the whole world as deceivers, heretics, scorners and fools?

Forasmuch as eternal Wisdom recognizes an extreme weakness, and since earthly ease, peace, and prosperity have so great a tendency to ruin and undo us before our God, and to render us careless, refractory, lukewarm and drowsy, he has appointed his cross as an awakening rod for the use of all his followers, by which, as a faithful Father, he restrains, awakes and excites the children of his love; as Solomon says, "My son, despise not the chastening of the Lord; neither be weary of his correction; for whom the Lord loveth he correcteth even as a father the son in whom he delighteth," Prov. 3: 11, 12. "If ye endure chastening, God dealeth with you as with sons; For what son is he whom the father chasteneth not. But if ye be without chastisement, whereof all are partakers, then ye are bastards, and not sons. Furthermore, we have had fathers of our flesh which corrected us, and we gave them reverence; Shall we not much rather be in subjection unto the Father of spirits, and live? For they verily for a few days chastened us after their own pleasure; but he, for our profit, that we might be partakers of his holiness," Heb. 12: 7, 10.

Behold, brethren, these words of the apostle are, beyond measure, gracious, and replete with consolation unto all those who have to bear the cross of Christ; for as a well-disposed and faithful earthly father who loves his children, desiring to teach and instruct them that which is best, does sometimes, out of pure paternal love, sharply admonish, chasten and punish them with stripes, for the good of his dear children, not regarding the pain inflicted in the flesh, in order that they may not disregard their father's will, command and voice, but that they may gladly obey it and learn and practice modesty, piety and obedience; so does our heavenly Father ofttimes chasten his elect children with his paternal rod, that they may hear and obey him in his holy word, will and commandment; practice piety and every moral virtue; fear God with sincerity of heart; unite not, nor familiarize themselves with the world; live no longer unto flesh and blood; and hereby, as obedient and chastened children of God, be finally made partakers of the promised kingdom and inheritance.

But if they refuse the rod of chastisement, reject the cross of Christ, and become, in consequence of their Father's kind chastening, the longer, the more abandoned and refractory; despise their Father's will and word; deal and act according to their own inclination, then they must at last be cast off and be considered as infamous bastards, and not as legitimate children.

Therefore, holy brethren, refuse not the rod and correction of your kind Father, for its tendency is extremely beneficial, namely, that you lay aside every weight and the sins which so easily beset you, and in all things, without exception, fear, love, and obey your Father. Thus, is this rod of the cross of Christ pure love and benevolence, and not indignation and wrath; as may be perceived and evinced by the Spirit of God, and not by the dictates of the flesh.

For a similar reason did God ofttimes permit his people, Israel, to be chastised by the Philistines, Assyrians, Chaldeans, &c., when they forgot and rebelled against their God, in order that by such scourges and punishments, they might again seek their God, hear his law, cease from evil, and act uprightly in all things. Notwithstanding, the paternal punishment was for the most part lost upon Israel, as the Prophet says. He hath often reproved, but what did it avail? The rod amendeth not the wicked children, saith the Lord God.

"Behold, famine and plague, tribulation and anguish, are sent as scourges for amendment. But for all these things they shall not turn from their wickedness, nor be always mindful of thy scourges," 2 Esdras 16: 19, 20.

Again, "Thou hast stricken them, but they have not grieved; thou hast consumed them, but they have refused to receive correction; they have made their faces harder than a rock; they have refused to return," Jer. 5: 3.

The above cited words of the prophet show plainly why the Israelites were so often punished and stricken of the Lord, namely, that they might turn themselves from iniquity. Yet all in vain, as the prophets lament and declare in the above words.

Beloved brethren, let this serve you as an admonition, that you be not like circumstanced with disobedient and hard-hearted Israel, but that you willingly submit yourselves to the chastening of your merciful Father, reflecting upon that which is written, "When we are judged, we are chastened of the Lord, that we should not be condemned with the world," 1 Cor. 11: 32.

Therefore, dearly beloved brethren and sisters in the Lord, reject not the chastening and instruction of your affectionate Father, but receive, with abundant joy, the exhortation of his sincere affection, giving thanks, that through his paternal favor he has chosen you in Christ Jesus, as the children of his love, taught and called you by the word of his power, enlightened you with the Holy Spirit, that through the salutary influence of the cross of Christ, you may restore to health your poor, weak, mortal flesh, which is subject to so many loathsome, infectious diseases of concupiscence, and wean it entirely from the pleasures and enjoyments of the world; that you may be made partakers of the cross of Christ, and rendered conformable unto his death, and, by this means, attain unto the resurrection of the dead; as Paul, in a cetain place instructs, saying, "We are troubled on every side, yet not distressed; we are perplexed, but not in despair; persecuted, but not forsaken; cast down, but not destroyed; always bearing about in the body the dying of the Lord Jesus, that the life also of Jesus might be made manifest in our body," 2 Cor. 4: 8, 10. But we who live, surrender ourselves daily unto death for Jesus' sake, that the life also of Jesus might be made manifest in our mortal flesh.

Behold, for this reason, he teaches, admonishes, rebukes, threatens and chastises that we should deny ungodliness and worldly lusts; die entirely unto the world, flesh and the devil; seek our treasure, portion and inheritance in heaven, alone Love and believe the true, living and eternal God, looking in patience for that blessed hope, and the glorious appearing of our Lord and Savior Jesus Christ, who gave himself for us, that he might redeem us from all iniquity, and purify unto himself a peculiar people, serving him in righteousness and godliness all the days of our life.

And for the same reason James says, "My brethren, count it all joy when ye fall into divers temptations; knowing this, that the trying of your faith worketh patience. But let patience have her perfect work, that ye may be perfect and entire, wanting nothing," James 1: 2, 4, for as gold, in passing through the fire, is severed from the dross and becomes more and more refined, so the susceptible man of God is subdued, purified, and refined, in the fiery furnace of affliction, that he may enhance the everlasting praise and glory of Christ and the Father, and may out of a pure heart, without hinderance, fear, love, honor, thank, and serve the same eternal God.

And this is the word that is written in the

book of Wisdom, namely, "Having been a little chastised, they shall be greatly rewarded; for God proved them, and found them worthy for himself. As gold in the furnace hath he tried them, and received them as burnt offering. And in the time of their visitation, they shall shine, and run to and fro like sparks among the stubble. They shall judge the nations, and have dominion over the people, and their Lord shall reign forever," Wis. 3: 5, 8.

Beloved brethren, be you, therefore, full of consolation in the Lord, and bear willingly your tribulation as pious soldiers of Christ, that you may please him who hath called and chosen you as soldiers. Paul says, "If a man also strives for masteries, yet is he not crowned, except he strive lawfully." Conduct yourselves, therefore, valiantly in the strife, and you shall gain favor in the eyes of your King; but if you become intimidated, throw down your arms, and forsake the combat, you shall receive no crown; for Christ says, "He that endureth to the end, shall be saved."

I fear that some may be found among our young and inexperienced brethren, who suffer themselves to be perplexed by the fleeting thought. Wherefore doth the way of the wicked prosper? And why do the righteous suffer much tribulation? Yea, it appears in the eyes of the imprudent as if the ungodly were born to prosper; for they grow and increase like a blossoming branch. They marry and are given in marriage; they sow, plant, and gather the grain into barns; they hoard money in their chests; their dwellings are magnificent and filled with costly things; they deck themselves with gold and silver, with silk and velvet; they nourish their hearts as in a day of slaughter; their fields and meadows flourish luxuriantly; their cattle are healthy and prolific; their children are merry, gay and vigorous in their sight; they play upon the organ, the tambour, the viol and the lute; they sing and leap for joy, and say to their souls, Rejoice, and be gay while life endures.

Their preachers confirm and console them, and their worship is a pleasure exceeding all pleasures. In short, it would appear as if they were loved and blessed of God with a peculiar love, and that the righteous are accursed and hated of God with a peculiar hatred; for they are like a slender shrub in a barren soil; like a poor affrighted owl that is persecuted by all other birds; like a pelican of the wilderness; and as a sparrow alone under the housetop, Ps. 102. All who look upon them, mock them; all who know them, despise them. There is no kingdom, principality, city, nor country, large enough to endure and tolerate a poor, rejected Christian. All who abuse, slander, and injure them, think they do God service.

Brethren, were we to speak, or judge after the manner of men, we would doubtless complain with holy Jeremiah, Jer. 12: 1, and say, "Righteous art thou, O Lord, when I plead with thee; yet, let me talk with thee of thy judgments. Wherefore doth the way of the wicked prosper? Wherefore are all they happy that deal very treacherously?" Again, "Wherefore lookest thou upon them that deal treacherously, and holdest thy tongue when the wicked devoureth the man that is more righteous than he?" Hab. 1: 13, and Esdras, Are they of Babylon better than they of Sion? Asaph's feet were almost gone, his steps had well nigh slipped, when he saw the prosperity of the wicked, and observed the opposition and tribulation of the righteous, Ps. 73.

I counsel and admonish all who have to contend with such thoughts, that they direct their hearts and eyes unto the word of the Lord, and observe with attention that which is written concerning the end and issue of both, and first of the ungodly. Job says 21: 13, "They spend their days in wealth, and in a moment go down to the grave." Again, "Fret not thyself," says David, Ps. 37: 1, 2, "because of evil doers, neither be thou envious against the workers of iniquity; for they shall soon be cut down like the grass, and wither as the green herb." Again, "If ye live after the flesh," says Paul, "ye shall die;" "To be carnally minded is death," and many similar passages.

But respecting the end of the righteous, it is written, "The souls of the righteous are in the hand of God, and there shall no torment touch them. In the sight of the unwise they seemed to die, and their departure is taken for misery, and their going from us to be utter destruction; but they are in peace," Wis. 3: 1—3. "Many are the afflictions of the righteous, but the Lord delivereth him out of them all," Ps. 34: 19. Again, "Blessed are ye when men shall revile you, and persecute you, and shall say all manner of evil against you falsely, for my sake. Rejoice, and be exceeding glad; for great is your reward in heaven," Matt. 5: 11, 12. Again, "Seeing it is a righteous thing with God, to recompense tribulation to them that trouble you; and to you who are troubled, rest with us, when the Lord Jesus shall be revealed from heaven with his mighty angels in flaming fire, taking vengeance on them that know not God, and that obey not the Gospel of our Lord Jesus Christ; who shall be punished with everlasting destruction from the presence of the Lord, and from the glory of his power, when he shall come to be glorified in his saints, and to be admired in all them that believe," 2 Thes. 1: 6—10; yea, all who truly read, believe, and understand the Scriptures, and have a correct perception of the vast dissimilarity in end and issue of both, will not envy them their short-lived prosperity, joy, and felicity, but will, by the grace of God, be prepared for, and find consolation in their own cross, tribulation and affliction.

Moreover, brethren, we are well aware that the cross appears to the flesh as grievous, harsh, and severe, and is not, in this life, looked upon as productive of joy, but much rather of sorrow; yet, since it contains within itself, a source of profit and delight, in that it adds to the piety of the pious, separates them from the world and the flesh, makes them revere God and his word, as mentioned above; and that it is also the Father's holy will that by it the sincere be approved, and the pretender exposed in his hypocrisy; therefore, all the true children of God are prepared through love, to do the will of the Father, rejoicing in it; as Paul says, Gal. 6: 14, "God forbid that I should glory, save in the cross of our Lord Jesus Christ, by whom the world is crucified unto me, and I unto the world." Again, The apostles "departed from the presence of the council, rejoicing that they were counted worthy to suffer shame for his name," Acts 5: 41.

For, inasmuch as we well know that the cross is a sting and vexation to our poor, weak flesh, as we may also find in the case of Job, Jeremiah, Elijah, and others; yea Jesus Christ himself, earnestly desired, that if it were possible, the cup might be removed from him, nay, in excess of agony he trembled, quaked, and sweat as it were great drops of blood, so that an angel appeared unto him from heaven strengthening him, therefore our best counsel is, that in faith and humility of heart, we fly for refuge to our God, as all sincere bearers of the cross have done from the beginning, and seek, in full confidence, his grace, aid, assistance and consolation; For whom does he forsake, that trusts in him? And who hath called upon him, that he did not hear? He is our God and Father, our Lord and King, our helper and protector, our strength and fortress, our consolation and refuge in the time of need; he is the horn of our salvation and our shadow at noonday. By my God, says David, have I leaped over a wall. If God is for us who can be against us? We can do all things through Christ, who strengthens us. To him commit thy cause; he worketh in his saints that which is pleasing in his sight. Some he has rescued from the hands of tyrants, some he has preserved in the midst of fire; for others he has stopped the mouths of fierce and ravening lions; he has released some from prison and confinement, others have trampled the fear of death under their feet, and through the strength of their faith, have triumphantly and victoriously conquered hunger, thirst, shame, derision, nakedness, stripes, imprisonment, anguish, and, in addition, the gallows, rack, massacre, torture, water, fire, life, death, &c.; for they were actuated by the constraining, effective influence of divine love, which converts the bitter into sweet, and the horrible into that which is greatly to be desired. "Love," says Solomon, "is strong as death;" many waters cannot quench love, neither can the floods drown it; all who possess it, ought to say with Paul, "Who shall separate us from the love of God? Shall tribulation, or distress, or persecution, or famine, or nakedness, or peril, or sword? As it is written, For thy sake we are killed all the day long; we are accounted as sheep for the slaughter. Nay, in all these things we are more than conquerors through him that loved us; for I am persuaded, that neither death, nor life, &c., shall be able to separate us from the love of God, which is in Christ Jesus our Lord," Rom. 8: 35—39.

Therefore, beloved brethren, bearers of the cross of the Lord, acknowledge your God; fear, love, believe, confide, and serve him, and that in the fullness of pureness of heart, according to the example of all saints, and of Christ Jesus, and the Father of mercies and of truth, in the excellency of his love, will not forsake you, but will care for you as the apple of his eye, will faithfully support you, in every misfortune and extremity, will extend his hand, and guard and preserve you, in life or in death, as is pleasing in his sight, to the enhancement of his glory, and to the salvation of your own souls, for he is so kind and faithful, that he will not suffer you to be tempted above that you are able to endure, but will in his boundless mercy graciously make a way for you to escape, if you only remain steadfast in the belief of his word, and consider him as your faithful Father.

Dear brethren, if in your trials and temptations, you exhibit such evidence as here related; drinking with patience the cup of the Lord; bearing witness of Christ Jesus and his holy, inestimable word, in action, and conversation; suffering yourselves, in perfect constancy, to be led as meek lambs to the slaughter, for his testimony's sake; then will the name of the Lord be sanctified, and exalted with praise and abundant glory; the hope of the righteous shall be revealed; the kingdom of heaven, spread abroad; the word of God acknowledged; and your poor, weak brethren and companions in the Lord, edified and confirmed by this your plain dealing.

Yea, my brethren, in the manner here related, we are informed and instructed, even unto this day, by the offering and blood of Abel; by the faith and obedience of Abraham, Isaac, and Jacob; the chastity of Joseph; the patience of Job and Tobit; the excellent and manly confession of Eleazer; the mother and her seven sons; the candor, constancy, and piety of all the pious before us; the pure, unspotted love, humility, peace, righteousness, and voluntary offering of Jesus Christ, that according to the promise of God, he was sent from heaven, in everlasting love, by God our heavenly Father, and descended upon earth as an infallible teacher, and as an eternal example of all good.

My dearly beloved brethren and sisters in Christ Jesus, dispersed abroad in every land, for whom, out of pure, christian love and duty, I have composed and written this exhortation; I will now draw to a conclusion, and I entreat you, in all humility, that you consider well, in the first place, the nature of the people who so malevolently persecute you, spoiling your property, and destroying your lives.

Secondly, why they persecute and injure you. Thirdly, that all saints, as also Christ Jesus himself, have suffered and all the pious must suffer persecution; as may be seen. Fourthly, how futile all their arguments are, with which they try to excuse themselves of their bloody deeds, accusing us, as though they did right, and we justly merited every kind of punishment and disgrace.

Fifthly, how profitable and advantageous to us the cross of Christ is, which, for the sake of the word of the Lord, we must take up and bear daily; how we should desire to hear, believe and obey Christ Jesus. Now, if you consider with discretion, according to the Scriptures, and reflect, in purity of heart, upon these five points, I have not the least doubt that this exercise will afford you invincible strength, and an invulnerable armor and shield against all tribulation, persecution and distress.

Finally, I beseech and exhort you to consider with earnest diligence that which is promised to all the conquering soldiers of Christ Jesus in the world to come, namely, the eternal, incorruptible kingdom, the crown of glory, and the life that will remain forever. Therefore, O thou people of God! equip thyself and make ready for battle, not with external weapons and armor, as the blood-thirsty barbarous world, but with the firmness of confidence, the tranquillity of patience, and the vehement ardor of prayer.

THE CROSS OF CHRIST.

There is no alternative, the combat of the cross must be maintained, and the wine-press of afliction must be trodden. O thou bride and sister of Christ, prepare thyself; the thorny crown must pierce thy head; and the nails transfix thy hands and feet; thy person must be scourged, and thy face spit upon. Gird thyself round about, and be prepared; for thou must go forth with thy Lord and Bridegroom without the city, bearing his reproach. On Golgotha thou must offer up thy sacrifice. Awake and pray, for thine enemies are more numerous than the hairs of thy head, or the sand of the sea. Though their hearts, hands, feet, and swords are exceedingly red, and stained with blood, be not dismayed; for God is thy leader. Thy life on earth is an incessant warfare. Strive valiantly, and thou shalt receive the promised crown.

"To him that overcometh will I give to eat of the tree of life, which is in the midst of the paradise of God," and of the hidden and heavenly manna.

Him that overcometh will God make a pillar in his temple, and will write upon him his name and the name of the new Jerusalem.

He that overcometh shall not be hurt by the second death. He that overcometh, the same shall be clothed in white raiment; and his name shall not be blotted out of the book of life, but Christ Jesus will confess his name before his heavenly Father, and before his angels.

He that overcometh shall sit with Christ in his throne, even as Christ overcame, and has sat down with his Father on his throne, Rev. 3.

O thou soldier of God, prepare thyself and fear not! The wine-press thou must tread; thou must go the narrow way, and enter in through the strait gate unto eternal life.

The Lord is thy strength, thy refuge and consolation; he is with thee in prisons and bonds; he flies with thee to foreign lands; he is with thee in fire and in water; he will never leave thee, nor forsake thee; yea, he will come quickly, and his great reward shall be with him.

"Blessed are they which are persecuted for righteousness' sake; for theirs is the kingdom of heaven."

Be not grieved that thou art black; thou art still comely and pleasing to the King.

As a rose, thou must grow among thorns, and be stung with the prickles. Rejoice for the King delighteth in thy comeliness.

Though in his first appearance he was offered as an innocent Lamb, and opened not his mouth, yet the time shall come when he will appear in judgment as a triumphant Prince and a victorious King. Then will our persecutors look upon him whom they pierced: then will they cry aloud and exclaim, Ye mountains fall upon us, hide us ye hills. But you shall leap and dance in excessive joy like calves of the stall, Matt. 4. Joy and exultation will never forsake you; for your King, Bridegroom and Redeemer, Christ Jesus, will remain with you forever. "God shall wipe away all tears from their eyes; and there shall be no more death, neither sorrow, nor crying, neither shall there be any more pain," Rev. 21: 4.

Praise, thanksgiving, and glory to God, shall flow from your mouth in an eternal stream. I repeat it, Strive, the crown of glory is prepared, shrink not, neither draw back; "For yet a little while, and he that shall come, will come, and will not tarry. The just shall live by faith: but if any man draw back, my soul shall have no pleasure in him," Heb. 10: 37, 38.

Take heed and watch, lest the fire of the cross consume you as wood, hay and stubble, and the rains and storms of persecution overthrow the house. Let not the heat of the sun wither the cross, lest like the dog you turn again to that which you have ejected. Let not your garments and your feet, which you have washed, become unclean, lest seven worse spirits enter you, and so the last error be worse than the first.

Therefore, beloved brethren and sisters in the Lord, fear God with all your heart, and with all your souls, and seek him with all your powers. Watch night and day; knock before the throne of his mercy, that with his paternal hand he may support you under every affliction, succor you in trouble and distress, and graciously preserve you in his way, word and truth; that you may not dash your feet against a stone, and so failing in your profession and your life, be overcome and disgraced; but that you may preserve the treasure, intrusted to your care, pure and untarnished against that day, and thus obtain, with all saints, the promised land, inheritance, kingdom, life and crown. May the Father of mercies and of love, grant this unto you and us through his blessed Son, Jesus Christ, in the power of his eternal Holy Spirit, to his praise, and everlasting glory, Amen.

A PLEASING MEDITATION

AND

Devout Contemplation,

TOGETHER WITH

CHRISTIAN DOCTRINES FOR A TROUBLED AND ANXIOUS CONSCIENCE, WHICH IS OPPOSED BY THE WORLD, FLESH, HELL, DEATH AND THE DEVIL.

ON THE TWENTY-FIFTH PSALM,

CALLED IN LATIN

Ad te levavi annimam meam,

EXPLAINED BY WAY OF SUPPLICATION.

BY

MENNO SIMON.

"Blessed are ye when men shall revile you, and persecute you, and shall say all manner of evil against you, falsely, for my sake. Rejoice and be exceeding glad, for great is your reward in heaven; for so persecuted they the prophets which were before you," Matt. 5: 11, 12.

"In my distress I cried unto the Lord, and he heard me. Deliver my soul, O Lord, from lying lips, and from a deceitful tongue," Psalm 120: 1, 2.

"For other foundation can no man lay than that is laid, which is Jesus Christ," 1 Cor. 3: 11.

ELKHART, INDIANA:
PUBLISHED BY JOHN F. FUNK AND BROTHER.
1871.

PREFACE.

It is evident, dear reader, that I am clandestinely, slandered and belied by the envious; therefore have I, briefly and prayingly sought to express the feelings of my heart, grounds, spirit, faith, doctrine, object, &c., after the tenor of the twenty fourth psalm according to the Latin, and the twenty fifth, according to the Hebrew; not in words of human wisdom, nor in great logic and rhetoric, but in a plain narration as dictated by my heart, to show the different dispositions of a true and of a false christian, together with all the grounds and hope of my faith; what I maintain concerning Christ Jesus, his doctrine, baptism, Holy Supper, ordinances, commands and prohibitions; my disposition towards lords, princes and all who are, as yet in the darkness, of unbelief and know not the light of truth; to show that I seek, and by the grace of God shall seek nothing upon earth but the unadulterated word of our Lord Jesus Christ; and this according to Scripture.

If I do err in some things, which I hope, by the grace of God, is not the case, I pray every one, for the Lord's sake, that I may not be put to shame; if any one has more powerful writings and convincing truth, that he through brotherly exhortation and instruction would assist me, I desire with my heart to accept of it, if he is right. Deal with me as the Spirit and word of Christ teach; if any one can convince me of an error by the Scriptures, and if I will not renounce it, but continue obstinate to the word of God and brotherly admonition, then practice upon me the tyranny of Nero, Diocletian, or Maxeritius, as an obdurate and ungodly heretic; for this I stand prepared, although this would be contrary to the usages and doctrines of the first church; for it is evident, that they persecuted not on account of faith, much less did they kill them, but the erring and heretical they faithfully admonished, and those who would not return were then excommunicated.

Afterwards, in the time of Arius, they exiled them. Ultimately the bloody tyranny of anti-christ generally prevailed. All had to suffer who did not agree with the Pope in his abominations. It is yet the case, which alas! may be plainly seen in many places.

Many who have neither seen nor heard me, call me a deceiving heretic. This must be all endured. I am no better than the pious fathers, who had to hear and suffer; nevertheless, I feel disposed to give my life, if it would induce the world rightly to understand my seeking, faith and doctrine; for I assuredly know that I have the word of God. My reader, pervert not what I write. I desire nothing else, before God, who created me, than to deal plainly, with a living voice, before every one, as one willing to be overcome by the Spirit of Christ, or to overcome; for my desire is that I and many with me be saved; hence, it is unnecessary to use the sword against me; If I have not the truth, I desire with all my heart to be instructed in it; but if I have, you then do not persecute me, but him, who is the truth, Christ Jesus.

Again, I say, with the Spirit and word of Christ, I desire to overcome, or to be overcome; in this I appeal to all the world. But it is in vain, the truth they will reject, and maintain and defend lies with the sword; for it is the true disposition and manner of anti-christ to defame, slander, apprehend, torture, burn and murder, contrary to the Spirit and word of God. But the Lord will see and judge it.

I would, therefore, faithfully admonish the reader, to zealously and earnestly strive after the kingdom of God, and examine this *Psalm* with assiduity; every word of it, with a submissive, humble heart; I hope he will find, through the grace of God, that it is replete with consolation in persecution, and that it clearly points out the difference between a believer and an unbeliever.

May God, the Father of our Lord Jesus Christ, grant the reader a zealous, ardent heart, a sincere, active faith, unfeigned, christian love, and obedience to his holy word, through Christ Jesus, his beloved Son our Lord, to him be everlasting praise, Amen.

THE TWENTY-FIFTH PSALM

EXPLAINED BY WAY OF SUPPLICATION.

Verse 1. UNTO THEE, O LORD, *do I lift up my soul, O my God, I trust in thee; let me not be ashamed.* O Lord, thou that bearest rule, Lord of heaven and earth, I call thee Lord, though I am not worthy to be called thy servant; for from my youth I did not serve thee, but thine enemy, the devil; him I served diligently; nevertheless, I do not doubt thy grace; for I find in the word of thy truth that thou art a bountiful, rich Lord to all those who call upon thee. Therefore, I call unto thee, O Lord hear me, hear me, O Lord! With full confidence and assurance, I lift up, not my head or my hands as the hypocrites do in the synagogues, but my soul. I lifted up my heart, not to Abraham, for he never knew us, nor to Israel, for he never had knowledge of us, but alone to thee, for thou art our Lord and Father, thou art our Redeemer, this is thy name, from days of yore. Hence it is, dear Lord, that I trust in thee, for I truly know that thou art a faithful God over all who trust in thee. If I am in darkness, thou art my light; am I in prison, thou art with me; am I forsaken, thou art my comfort; am I in death, thou art my life; if they curse me, thou dost bless; if they grieve me, thou dost comfort; if they will slay me, thou wilt raise me up; and if I walk in the dark valley, thou wilt ever be with me. It is right, O Lord, that I lift up my grieved and miserable soul to thee, trust in thy promise, and am not ashamed.

2. *Let not mine enemies triumph over me; yea, let none that wait on thee be ashamed.* O Lord of hosts, Lord of lords, my flesh is weak; my misery and necessities are great; nevertheless, I fear not the sensual scoffing of my enemies; but I fear greatly, lest I deny thy adorable and revered name, and depart from thy truth, and that they rejoice over my weakness and the transgression of thy will, and mock me and say, Where is thy God now? Where is thy Christ? And that thy divine honor be thus reproached through me. O Lord, preserve me; keep me, O Lord! for my enemies are strong and many; yea, more numerous than the hairs of my head, and the spears of grass in the fields; my unclean flesh is never at rest; satan encompasseth me as a roaring lion, that he may devour me; the blood-thirsty, revengeful world is determined upon my life; they also hate, persecute, burn and murder those who seek thy praise. Wretched man, I know not whither to go, misery, tribulation, fear and dread are on every side; strife within, and persecution without. I say with king Jehoshaphat, If I know not whither to go, I lift my eyes unto thee, and depend only on thy grace and mercy, as Abraham in Gerar, Jacob in Mesopotamia, Joseph in Egypt, Moses in Media, Israel in the wilderness, David in the mountains, Hezekiah in Jerusalem, the young men in the fiery furnace, Daniel in the lion's den; yea, all the pious fathers trusted in thee, and were not made ashamed.

3. *Let them be ashamed which transgress without cause.* O Lord, thou that bearest rule, even as thy merciful grace is over all who fear thee, so also is thy fierce wrath over all who despise thee; who walk after their lusts, and dare to say with all fools, "There is no God;" we have made a covenant with death, and with hell an agreement; God knoweth not what we do; thick clouds are a covering to him that he seeth not the works of men; we will eat and drink,

for to-morrow we die; for our life is short and full of trouble, and there is no consolation when we have gone hence; we will live in affluence, while we yet can and use the creatures as we desire; we will oppress the poor, defraud the righteous; we will condemn him with the most disgraceful death. O, dear Lord, thus does the world err, and live every where in the lusts of the flesh, lust of the eyes, and in the pride of life; it is mere deceit, unrighteousness and tyranny, wherever we turn. Few are they who fear thy name. Paul says, "To be carnally minded is death;" sentence is already passed; if we live according to the flesh we must die, so teach the Scriptures; if we do not repent there is nothing more certain than fierce anger. Therefore, dear Lord, threaten thou, reprove, admonish and teach, perhaps they may yet repent, know the truth and be saved; they are the works of thy hands, created after thine image, and dearly bought; let them not be confounded like Cain, Sodom, Pharaoh and Antiochus with all those who have transgressed without a cause.

4. *Shew me thy ways*, O Lord; *teach me thy paths.* O Lord of hosts, I know through the word of thy grace that there is but one way which leadeth to life, which is strait and narrow for the flesh, beset with thorns and dangers all around, and is found by few, and still fewer walk therein; it is like a treasure hid in a field which none can find but he to whom it is shown by the Spirit. Dear Lord, there is no way but thou alone; all who walk through thee will find the gates of life. There is another way which seems very pleasant to the flesh, which appears soft, smooth and broad, strown with roses, pleasant and agreeable to the eye, but its end leads to death. On this way the whole world walks, unconcerned and without fear, and prefers things perishable to imperishable, evil to good, and darkness to the light of the world. They all walk on the perverse, broad and crooked way; they become faint in the way of unrighteousness, and know not the way of the Lord. It is true, the way of error seems right in the eyes of fools, but I know through thy Spirit and word that it is the certain road to the abyss of hell. Therefore, I entreat thee, dear Lord, be merciful to me a poor sinner; show me thy path, and teach me thy way; for thy way is the right way, godly, pleasant, humble, chaste, full of peace and of all good, and will lead my soul to eternal life.

5. *Lead me in thy truth and teach me; for thou art the God of my salvation; on thee do I wait all the day.* O Lord! Lord! "My tears," says David, "have been my meat day and night." My heart within me quakes, my strength forsakes me, and the light of my eyes is dim, and this on account of the innumerable dangers and snares which beset my soul. I am in constant fear lest I be led from the way of truth by misapprehension or through the deceit of satan. O Lord, the subtlety of the learned is great; satan uses his wiles artfully; some teach but the doctrine and commandments of men which are fruitless and corrupt trees. Some cry only grace, spirit and Christ, and daily trample on thy grace, grieve thy Holy Spirit, and crucify thy Son with their vain, carnal life, as is evident. Some who had before escaped Babylon, Egypt and Sodom, and taken upon them the yoke and cross of Christ, are again devoured by satan, and so deceived by the false prophets, as if they had never known thy word and will. Yea, seven spirits, alas! worse than the former, entered them, although they cloak themselves under thy word and ordinances, and pretend that it was thy pleasure, word and will; although thou never didst think of it, much less didst thou desire it; on account of which I am much grieved and full of sorrow of heart, well knowing that thy true word is no deceiving lie, as they teach, but it is the truth which thy infallible mouth taught here upon earth and in this grievous world. All who are of the truth hear thy voice, as the voice of their only Shepherd, and the true Bridegroom; but from the voice of a stranger they flee, always fearing lest they might be deceived. O Lord, remember thy afflicted and poor servant; thou art a Searcher of all hearts, thou knowest me that I seek nothing but thy will. Therefore, dear Lord, direct me to thy truth, and teach me; for thou art the God of my salvation; besides thee I acknowledge none other; thou only art my hope, my comfort, shield, defense and fortress upon which I depend with

confidence, and wait upon it in fear, misery, tribulation and need.

6. *Remember*, O LORD, *thy tender mercies, and thy loving kindnesses, for they have been ever of old.* O Lord of hosts, when I am buoyed up in the waters of thy grace, I find that I cannot fathom or measure them, for thy mercies are greater than all thy works. Who is it, dear Lord, that ever came to thee with a pious heart that thou didst reject? Who ever sought thee and found thee not? Who did ever desire help of thee and did not obtain it? Who ever prayed for thy grace and did not receive it? And who ever called upon thee that thou didst not hear? Yea, dear Lord, how many didst thou accept in grace, who, according to thy strict justice, merited otherwise. Adam departed from thee and believed the counsel of the serpent; he broke thy covenant and was found a child of death before thee; thy paternal kindness did not reject him, but thou didst seek him graciously, thou didst call and reprove him, and his nudity thou didst cover with coats of skin, and so graciously comfort him with the promised seed. Paul, thy chosen vessel, raved like a roaring lion and a devouring wolf in thy holy mountain, nevertheless, thy grace shone around him in his blindness and illuminated him; thou calledst him from heaven, and didst choose him as an holy apostle and as a servant of thy house. I also, dear Lord, the greatest of all sinners, and the least among all the saints, am called thy child or servant, for I have sinned against heaven and before thee; although I did resist thy precious word and thy holy will, with all my powers, before this with open eyes; and with full understanding I disputed, taught and lived after the ease of the flesh, and sought my own praise more than thy righteousness, honor, word and truth; nevertheless, thy paternal grace did not forsake me, a wretched sinner; but received me in love, converted me to another mind, led me with thy right hand and taught me by thy Holy Spirit, till I voluntarily fought against the world, flesh and the devil; renounced all my pleasure, peace, glory, lust and the ease of the flesh, and willingly submitted to the pressing cross of our Lord Jesus Christ, that I may inherit the promised kingdom with all the valiant of God and the disciples of Christ. Again, I say, Thy mercies are greater than all thy works; therefore, dear Lord assist me, stand by me, comfort me, a poor sinner; my soul is in great distress, and the dangers of hell surround me; help Lord, and preserve me, and be not angry; remember, O Lord, thy great mercies, of which all are made partakers who have graciously waited upon thy holy name, and remember, O Lord, thy tender mercies, and thy loving kindness, for they have been of old.

7. *Remember not the sins of my youth, nor my transgressions; according to thy mercy remember thou me, for thy goodness' sake*, O LORD. O Lord, thou that bearest rule, "I was shapen in iniquity and in sin did my mother conceive me," I am of sinful flesh; Adam's corrupt seed has been sown in my heart, from whence so much misery has grown up. I, a miserable sinner, did not know my infirmities, so long as they were not manifested to me by the Spirit. I thought I was a christian; but when I saw rightly, I found myself, without thy word, altogether earthly, and carnal; my light was darkness, my truth was lies, my righteousness sin, my worship open idolatry, and my life, certain death. O dear Lord, I knew myself not till I viewed myself in thy word; then I learned to know, with Paul, my blindness, nakedness, uncleanness, depraved nature, and that nothing good dwelt in my flesh. I was full of wounds, and bruises and putrifying sores from the sole of the foot even to the head. Ah, alas! my gold was dross; my wheat, chaff; all my services were deceit and lies. I walked before thee in the flesh; my thoughts were carnal, my words and works without the fear of God; my watching and sleeping were unclean; my prayer hypocrisy. In short, I did nothing without sin. O Lord, remember not the sins of my youth, so often committed knowingly and unknowingly, nor my daily transgressions, of which I am guilty in my great weakness, but remember me according to thy great goodness, I am blind, enlighten thou me; naked I am, clothe thou me; I am wounded, heal thou me; dead I am, raise me up. I know of no light, medicine, or life except thee; accept of me graciously, grant

me thy mercy, favor and faith, fullness, and thy good will, O Lord.

8. *Good and upright is the Lord; therefore, will he teach sinners in the way.* O Lord of hosts, although I have walked so unrighteously before thee from my youth, that I am ashamed to lift my eyes to thee in heaven, nevertheless, I appear at thy throne of grace; for I know that thou art merciful and kind, and desirest not the death of the sinner, but that he repent and live. Thou didst send forth thy faithful servant, Moses, who gave Israel the law by the disposition of angels, also thy servants and prophets who preached the way of repentance, and broke the bread of life for the people; sin they reproved earnestly; proclaimed thy grace far abroad, and taught the truth; thy sharp piercing word was in their mouth, their light shone as the golden lights; they were as flowering olive trees, as a sweet smell of costly perfumery, yea, as the fair mountain strown with roses and lilies; nevertheless, they did not desire them, but thrust them out furiously, derided, persecuted, and delivered them unto death; still the wells of thy mercy flowed; thou didst send thy beloved Son, the dear pledge of thy grace, who preached thy word, fulfilled thy righteousness, accomplished thy will, bore our sins, blotted them out with his blood, and brought about reconciliation; conquered the devil, hell, sin and death, and obtained grace, mercy, favor and peace for all who truly believe on him; his command is eternal life; he sent out his messengers, ministers and apostles of peace, who spread this grace abroad through the whole world; who shone as bright, burning torches before all, that they might lead me and all erring sinners into the true way. O Lord, not unto me, but unto thee be praise and honor; their words I love, their usages I observe; thy Son, Christ Jesus, whom they preached to me, I believe; I seek his will and way; thy abundant, great love I acknowledge, not through me, but through thee, for thou art good, and I am evil; thou art true, and I am deceitful; thou art righteous, and I am unrighteous; instruct me, dear Lord, teach me in the right way; foster me for I am of thy pasture; take me into thy care, under the shadow of thy wings; protect me, for I am greatly tormented; I am poor, wretched, and grieved unto death.

9. *The meek will he guide in judgment, and the meek will he teach his way.* O Lord, thou that bearest rule, thy divine grace has shone around me, thy word has taught me, thy Holy Spirit has influenced me till I forsook the course of the ungodly, the way of sinners, the seat of scorners. I was ungodly, and carried the banner of unrighteousness for many years; I was a chief one in all manner of folly; idle words, vanity, gambling, drinking, eating to excess were my daily pastime; the fear of God was not before my eyes; besides, I was a lord and a prince in Babel; every one sought me; the world loved me and had my affections. I had the first place at feasts and in synagogues; I had the preference among all men; I was respected of the aged, and every one revered me; when I spoke, they were silent; when I nodded, they came; when I bid them depart, they went; what I desired, they did; my words prevailed in all things; the desire of my heart was granted; but as soon as I, with Solomon, saw that all was vanity, and with Paul, esteemed all as nothing, I renounced the ungodliness of this world, sought thee and thy kingdom which will abide in eternity. I have found everywhere the counterpart and reverse; before, I was honored, now I am dishonored; before, all was love, now hatred; before, I had friends, now they are my enemies; before, I was considered wise, now a fool; before, pious, now wicked; before, a christian, now a heretic; yea, I have become an abomination and evil-doer to all. O Lord, comfort me, preserve thy troubled servant; for I am exceedingly poor and wretched, my sins rise up against me, the whole world hates and mocks me; lords and princes persecute me, the learned curse and slander me, my dearest friends forsake me, and those who were near to me, stand aloof; who will have mercy on me and receive me? Miserable am I, dear Lord; have mercy on me and receive me with honor; for there is none that can preserve me, but thou; therefore, I entreat thee, Lord, vouchsafe thine ear to supplication; lead me by the right hand, lead me in the right way lest I stumble upon the dark mountains. I see that the children of men do neither teach

nor do right; deceit and hypocrisy are in all flesh; the deceiving sects are great and many; every one avers his as if it were built upon a rock, yet they have not thy truth. Therefore, dear Lord, teach me thy truth and cast me not off from thy presence, for I am miserable; I am in the midst of lions and bears, which seek to destroy my soul, and thrust me from the way of truth. O Lord, strengthen me, keep me in thy way for I assuredly know that it is the infallible truth and the sure way of peace.

10. ALL *the paths of the* LORD *are mercy and truth unto such as keep his covenant and his testimonies.* O Lord of hosts, they all boast of thy grace and favor, although they, in all their works, prove themselves children of wrath; they lie, cheat, eat, drink, are guilty of adultery and fornication, they covet and hoard, curse and swear without bounds, and all this they cloak with thy grace and the blood of Christ; every one sings lustily; the mercy of the Lord is great; Christ died for our sins; our doings are unjust, sinful and fruitless. It is true, dear Lord, in the true sense of the word, that they have no lot in thee, their hope is vain, their labor is without fruit, and their works, useless; yea, their hope is like thistle-down before the winds; they will have no part in thy kingdom, for they are still impenitent, and believe not thy truth. Alas! they know not that thy mercy is forever over those who fear thee and keep thy covenant. Thy goodness, says David, is extended to the saints; thine eyes are upon the righteous, and thine ears are open to their cries; but thy face is against them that do evil, to cut off the remembrance of them from the earth. I am thy friend if I do what thou hast commanded. It is true, dear Lord, that Christ was given to us, and died for us, yet not for such a purpose that we are to live according to our wicked lusts, and sinful will, but according to thy good will, word and command. Lord, I know that thou art no less righteous than good, that thou hatest the evil, and lovest the good; to the good thou art kind, but to the wicked thou wilt in due time appear as a righteous Judge. What did the pure blood of the eternal covenant demand of Cain and Judah, because they despised thy grace and excluded themselves from the merits of thy Son? What does it profit Pilate, Herod, Annas, and Caiaphas to have seen thy fountain of grace, Jesus Christ; nay, touched him, and yet condemned to the accursed death of the cross, the immaculate Lamb, the King of glory! But they who keep thy covenant and preserve thy testimony like Abel, Enoch, Noah, Abraham, Isaac and Jacob did, to them thy ways are peace and joy; yea, altogether mercy, kindness and truth.

11. *For thy name's sake*, O LORD, *pardon mine iniquity; for it is great.* O Lord, Lord! I pray thee with holy David, rebuke me not in thine anger, neither chasten me in thy hot displeasure; for my loins are filled with a loathsome disease, and there is no soundness in my flesh; my sins have borne me down; there is no peace in my bones. From the bottom of my heart I humble myself with beloved Daniel. O dear Lord! O thou great and terrible God! I have sinned, and done unjustly, before thee I have been ungodly, I wandered from thee, and walked not in thy commands and statutes; thy preferred grace I rejected; thy holy word I thrust from me; thy beloved Son I crucified, I grieved thy Holy Spirit, I acted unjustly in all my doings. O Lord, the multitude of my sins frighten me; there is no evil but what I am guilty of. I was as envious as Cain; proud and unchaste as Sodom; unmerciful as Pharaoh; refractory as Korah; lascivious as Simri; disobedient as Saul; idolatrous as Jeroboam; hypocritical as Joab; haughty as Nebuchadnezzar; covetous as Balaam; drunken as Nabal; insolent as Sennacherib; blasphemous as Rabsaces; blood-thirsty as Herod; lying as Ananias. Yea, I say with king Manasseh, That my sins are more numerous than the sands of the sea shore and the stars in the heavens; they trouble by day and by night; nothing good dwells in my flesh. All that I seek is unrighteousness and sin; that which I would not that I seek and do; I, miserable man, know not whither to go; if I go into myself, I find great faults, impure desires, a vessel of sins; if I go to my neighbor, he has nothing to give me, so that here nothing else avails, but thy word. The wages of sin, says Paul, is death; but thy

grace is eternal life. This grace I seek and desire; for this is the only ointment which can heal my soul; the sinful woman availed herself of this, Luke 7, as soon as she was sensible of her wants; David availed himself of this when he disgraced Bathsheba, the wife of Uriah, and slew him; great was his distress, he saw his wickedness and said, "I have sinned against the Lord." He desired balm; "O God!" said he, "according unto the multitude of thy tender mercies blot out my transgressions, wash me thoroughly from mine iniquity, and cleanse me from my sin," Ps. 51: 1, 2. In the same hour he heard the gracious word of the prophet, "The Lord also hath put away thy sin." His troubled heart was quieted; he praised his name, proclaimed his mercy, and exalted his grace above all his works. O Lord! O dear Lord! I a grieved sinner, have the same disease, I desire the same balm, and I desire help from thee; I seek only comfort with thee, O Lord, for thy holy name's sake. Help me, that I may eternally praise thee. Wash me from all my sins, and be merciful to me in all my transgressions, for they are great.

12. *What man is he that feareth the* LORD? *Him shall he teach in the way that he shall choose.* O Lord, thou that bearest rule, thy path is the path of peace; blessed is he that walketh therein; for we find mercy, love, righteousness, humility, obedience and patience in her ways. She clothes the naked, feeds the hungry, gives drink to the thirsty, entertains the needy, reproves, threatens, comforts and admonishes; is sober, honest, chaste and upright in all her ways; none takes offense at her; her goings forth are to eternal life, but few there are that find her. Yea, I fear dear Lord, that there are scarcely ten of a thousand that find her, scarcely five who cherish her; it continues as it was from the beginning, when there were but four upon earth; of whom the Scriptures testify that two were disobedient, and a third one slew his brother. There were eight righteous when the world was drowned, and one of them mocked his father. In Sodom and Gomorrah, with the adjacent country, there were four righteous persons, one looked back and was changed into a pillar of salt. About six hundred thousand valiant men left Egypt, of whom but two entered the promised land; not, dear Lord, that all were damned who died on the way, but they did not, on account of their unbelief, inherit the promised Canaan. Thus also, dear Lord, is the eternal land promised us, if we walk the way which thou hast chosen for us. But now they walk the crooked way of death; and even as those did not inherit the temporal, so will also these not inherit the eternal Canaan. O Lord, well may I sigh and say, Where is he who fears the Lord? Where is he, who has understanding? Where is he, who seeks God? "They are all gone out of the way, they are together become unprofitable; there is none that doeth good, no, not one. Their throat is an open sepulcher; with their tongues they have used deceit; the poison of asps is under their lips; their feet are swift to shed blood, destruction and misery are in their ways, and the way of peace they have not known; there is no fear of God before their eyes," Rom. 3: 12—18; all that is among them is infidelity and lies; they despise and blaspheme thy righteousness, yet they sing and speak much of thy truth, and glory in thy great name, although there is not one ripe grape on their vine, nor any good fruit to be found with them. But those who fear thee, O Lord, depart from all iniquity; For thy fear, says Sirach, dispels sin, and is the beginning of wisdom. Thine eyes are upon those who fear thee, thy Holy Spirit leads them, thy gracious hand preserves them; they will not fear nor tremble; for thou art their protector and shelter against intense heat; thou didst pardon their sins; rescue them; thou dost enlighten them, makest glad their souls, givest them grace, blessing and peace. He that fears thee, walks uprightly in all his ways, for thou teachest him in the way that thou hast chosen.

13. *His soul shall dwell at ease; and his seed shall inherit the earth.* O Lord, thou Lord of hosts! those who acknowledge thee shall be blessed in the paradise of their God, upon Mount Zion, in the heavenly Jerusalem, in the church of the living God, in the assembly of the righteous whose names are written in heaven. They are released from hell, sin, the devil and death, and

they serve before thee in peace and joy of heart through life. They repose without fear, for thou art their strength and shield. They rest under the shadow of thy wings, for they are thine. They fear not, for thou warmest them with the beams of thy love; they hunger not, for thou feedest them with the bread of life; they thirst not, for thou givest them to drink of the waters of thy Holy Spirit; they want not, for thou art their treasure and their kingdom. They dwell in the house of thy peace, in the tabernacles of righteousness, and in sure peace. They have pleasure in thy law, and speak of thy word day and night, amongst all the people. They wash their souls in the clear waters of thy truth. They view their consciences in the clear mirror of thy wisdom; their thoughts are upright, their words are words of grace, seasoned with salt. Their works are faithful and true. The light of their piety shines around them; what they seek they find; what they desire they obtain; their souls dwell in the fullness of thy goodness; the dew of thy grace has besprinkled them; the soil of their consciences bears wine and oil without measure, and although they must endure, in their flesh for a time, much misery, suffering and trouble, yet they know well that the way of the cross is the way of life. They are not ashamed of the way of the cross and the weapons of the Lord. They patiently go with Christ to the conflict, and contend valiantly, till they have reached the boundary of life, and have received the crown. Nothing can hinder them, since they have become partakers of thy Spirit, and have tasted of thy sweetness. They neither waver nor turn aside; their house stands firmly upon a rock; they are as the pillars of the holy temple; they have eaten of thy hidden manna. O Lord, to thee be praise! Thy fear abides continually before their eyes. They walk in thy way, therefore, shall their souls be blessed, and their seed, if born of the Holy Spirit and word, will enjoy the land of everlasting life, wherein thou, and thy chosen shall reign in endless glory.

14. *The secret of the Lord is with them that fear him, and he will show them his covenant.* O Lord, Lord, the thoughts of my heart terrify me, and my heart trembles within me; because, with Ezra, I perceive that so many are born in vain. What shall I say, dear Lord? Shall I say that thou hast ordained the wicked to wickedness, as some have said? Be that far from me; I know, O Lord, that thou art eternally good, and that nothing wicked can be found in thee. We are the works of thy hand, created in Christ Jesus to good works, that we should walk therein. Water, fire, life and death, hast thou left to our choice. Thou willest not the death of the sinner, but that he should repent and live. Thou art the eternal light, therefore hatest thou all darkness; thou desirest not that any should perish, but that all repent, come to the knowledge of thy truth, and be happy. O dear Lord, so grievously have they blasphemed thine unspeakably great goodness, eternal mercy, and almighty Majesty, that they, O gracious God, Creator of all things, have made thee to be as a cruel devil, by saying that thou art the source of all evil, thou who art the Father of days and of lights. It is plain that evil cannot flow from good, light from darkness, nor life from death; yet must their stubborn hearts and carnal minds be attributed to thy will, in order that they may continue upon the broad way, and have a cover for their sins; and this, because they do not acknowledge thy divine goodness, nor their own inbred wickedness. O Lord God, thou hast loved us with an eternal love, thou hast chosen us before the foundation of the world, that we should be unblamable, and holy before thee in love, not regarding what we find written by the faithful Paul concerning Esau, Pharaoh and Israel; he hath done all for us, for the best, in order that we should give the honor to thy name, and not to ourselves. What have we miserable sinners, of which we may boast? What have we that we have not received from thee? All that we have is of thy fullness. For this, all who know thy word thank thee. O dear Lord, the mystery of thy holy word is not revealed to the rich, the honorable, or the wise, but to the poor, simple children. Yea, Father, said Christ, such was thy good pleasure. Isaiah says, Thou wilt look upon the miserable, and those who are of a broken spirit, and who fear thy word. Therefore, dear Lord, we

miserable sinners pray thee to lead us in thy truth; to teach us thy mysteries; to enable us rightly to know the power of thy covenant, that thou art ours, and we are thine; that covenant which thou hast made with us in Christ, without any merit on our part. For thy mystery will be found with those who fear thee and those to whom thou hast made known thy covenant.

15. *Mine eyes are ever toward the Lord, for he shall pluck my feet out of the net.* O Lord! thou who bearest rule! I say with the prophet, If thou shouldst mark iniquity, who could stand? I, a miserable, great sinner, have, with the full lust of my heart, turned to all folly, to gold, silver, pride, haughtiness, to strange and forbidden flesh. I have turned mine eyes to open idolatry, to wood and stone, and have served them many years, upon high mountains and under green trees, as the prophet said, My idolatry was according to the number of my days. I have bowed my knee before the graven and molten images, and said, Save me, for thou art my God. I sought sight from the blind, life from the death, and help from those who could not preserve themselves from dust, corruption, thieves and worms. Yes, I have said to a weak, perishable creature, that grew out of the earth, was broken in a mill, baked by the fire, chewed with my teeth, and consumed by my stomach, to a mouthful of bread: Thou hast released me; as Israel said to the golden calf, "These be thy gods, O Israel, which brought thee up out of the land of Egypt," Ex. 22: 4. O God! thus have I, a miserable sinner, courted the whore of Babylon for many years, for I supposed that she was modest, honest and chaste; a queen of righteousness, who was glorious, holy and acceptable before thine eyes, for I saw her adorned with purple and scarlet, with gold and precious stones, and pearls, a golden cup in her hand, powerful over all kings upon earth. Therefore, I knew not that she was so very loathsome and polluted; that there was in such a splendid cup so much abomination; that she was such an unblushing, impudent whore and murderess; that deceived the world, persecuted the chosen, and drank the blood of the saints. But now I have seen her abominations, and I quake, because I left thee, the living Well, so long, and comforted myself with useless pools, that can give no water; that I gave thy honor to images and other creatures; and worshipped the creature more than the Creator, who is blessed forever. This happened, in part, through the deceitfulness of my eyes, because I was bewitched in my heart, by the goodly appearance of the woman. But now, dear Lord, my eyes are constantly directed unto thee, till thou hearest me; they are directed to thy mercy seat, till I obtain grace and mercy from thee, for thou alone art he, who can help me in the time of my temptation, and pluck my feet out of the net of sin.

16. *Turn thee unto me, and have mercy upon me; for I am desolate and afflicted.* O Lord of hosts, my sins and transgressions I do not hide from thee, but unreservedly acknowledge that I spent my former days after the will of the heathen, and walked with them in all manner of ungodly lusts, pride, wantonness, in eating and drinking, and in abominable, blind idolatry. I did all that pleased my wicked flesh, I was a child of wrath, even as others; thy holy name I held in derision; thy word was as a fable to me; in reliance upon thy grace, I did all manner of evil; I was as a white-washed sepulcher; outwardly in behavior, I was moral, chaste and mild, there was none that reproved my conduct, but inwardly I was full of dead men's bones, stench and worms; my platter was clean on the outside, but within, was full of rapine and lust. What I did privately is a scandal to mention, all my thoughts were unclean, vain, proud, ambitious and ungodly; my heart was full of disaffection, hatred, envy, vengeance and dislike; my thoughts were bent upon all manner of wickedness; I sinned without bounds; I neither feared God, devil, law, gospel, heaven nor hell; there was nothing that could deter me; I neither regarded thee nor thy word; my course was onward to all wickedness; I sought nothing but the friendship and love of this world. I did not commit adultery, fornication, and such like other abominable sins, before men, only because I feared to lose their favor and my reputation, and not because I feared thee; yet, my vanity, merriment, drunkenness, sinful lusts, open sins,

weakness, pride and idolatry were called the true worship; yea, all my transactions, private and public, were not concealed before thine eyes. Thus did I, a grieved sinner, spend my days, and did not, O God of grace, acknowledge thee as my God, Creator and Redeemer, till thy Holy Spirit taught me, through thy word, made known to me thy will, and gave me a partial knowledge of thy mysteries; now I know how dishonorably I have walked before thee, not otherwise than if I had spit in thy face, treated thee with indignity and derided thee as foolish. O Lord, have mercy upon me; for I am desolate and afflicted; my sins are great and many; my conscience troubles me; my thoughts cause me to quake; my heart laments and sighs, because I sin so heinously before thee; my sins have separated me from thee, hid thy countenance from me, and excited thy wrath. I have become a prey and brand of the burning pool, although the longer, the more I was grieved, the more I was consoled by thy word, for it teaches me concerning thy mercy, grace and favor, and the remission of my sins, through Christ, thy beloved Son, our Lord, not regarding that I neither knew nor feared thee. This promise pacifies and gladdens me; it leads me, with the sinful woman, to thy blessed feet, with full confidence and clear conscience, well knowing that thou wilt not cast off from thee thy returning son, although I have spent thy paternal inheritance and possessions dishonorably, with harlots and rogues, in a strange country, devoured it in my unrighteousness. My God, turn the pleasing countenance of thy peace unto me, I have sinned before heaven and in thy sight; lay thy hand of grace upon me; have mercy upon me, a poor sinner; for I am desolate and afflicted.

17. *The troubles of my heart are enlarged; O bring thou me out of my distresses.* O Lord, Lord, my heart weeps and sighs, my conscience quakes and trembles, my soul is as a grieved mother deprived of her only child, and cannot be comforted, since I, an ungodly sinner, neither sincerely sought, acknowledged nor appreciated thy godly love and paternal kindness. I have lived more disgracefully than the irrational creatures, for they, in eating, drinking and other things do not go beyond their instinct, and do not transgress the laws of nature; but I have lived more uselessly, sinfully, intemperately and unrighteously against the laws of nature, than my ungodly flesh naturally desired; I was conscious that the desires of my flesh were death; thy Spirit warned me of my evil doing; yet, my flesh suppressed all warning. I was in all things a servant of sin, and sworn unto unrighteousness. I drank down sin as water; my delight was in all manner of folly; the outstretched arm of thy grace, I saw not; thy calling voice, I heard not; thy inviting love, I regarded not. In short, I hated thy knowledge, and thy fear I cast behind me; and this is not all, dear Lord, that I acted so lamentably in my ignorance, but I daily find, that my righteousness is as filthy rags; when I think that I am going, I am falling; when I stand, I am down, and that when I am something, I am nothing. Therefore, O Lord, preserve me, for the fear of my heart is very great; yea, greater than I can express it; I often am as a woman in travail, my countenance is changed pale; my hands are upon my loins on account of the trouble of my heart; the dangers of hell surround me, the fatness and marrow of my bones are dried up; for here neither money nor possessions, neither flesh nor blood avail, but my soul is at stake, eternal life or eternal death is the issue; I, therefore, pray, Forsake me not, dear Lord, but open the eyes of thy mercy and behold my great burden, stand by me and deliver me from all my distress.

18. *Look upon mine affliction and my pain; and forgive all my sins.* O Lord, thou that bearest rule, if the righteous call upon thee, thou receivest them; thou art nigh to those who are of a broken heart; thou dost comfort those who are of a contrite spirit; the offering that is acceptable to thee is a contrite spirit; a broken heart thou dost not despise. Thou didst send forth thy beloved Son, anointed with thy Holy Spirit, to preach the gospel to the poor, to heal the broken hearted, to preach deliverance to the captives, and recovery of sight to the blind; to set at liberty them that are bruised, to proclaim the acceptable year of the Lord, Luke 4: 18; to comfort all that

mourn; to appoint unto them that mourn in Zion, to give unto them beauty for ashes; the oil of joy for mourning; the garment of praise for the spirit of heaviness. He preached ransom to all who are heavy laden, and with faithful hearts come to him; he invites all the thirsty to the waters of life; he bore all our sins upon the cross in his own body; and our debt he blotted out by his blood, even as Moses did before, through types and shadows, when he sprinkled unclean Israel with the blood of oxen and rams, and with the ashes of the heifer; under the law nearly all things were purified by the shedding of blood, Num. 19; Heb. 9. If the figurative blood had such virtue, that it could purify the flesh to sanctification, how much more shall the blood of the beloved Son, who offered himself unspotted through the eternal Spirit, purify our consciences from dead works. O ever living God, through the merits of thy Son, and through the riches of thy grace we receive the remission of our sins; yea, through his blood thou didst reconcile all upon earth and in heaven above. I, therefore, dear Lord, confess that I have or know of no remedy for my sins, for neither works nor merits, neither baptism nor the Lord's Supper can avail, although all sincere christians use both as signs of thy word, and hold them in respect; but alone the precious blood of thy beloved Son, which is bestowed upon me, and who has graciously redeemed me, a poor sinner, through mere grace and love, from my former walk; therefore, O God of truth, with whom there is no lie, remember the words of thy prophet, which he spake in thy name, namely, "If the wicked will turn from all his sins, that he hath committed, and keep all my statutes, and do that which is lawful and right, he shall surely live, he shall not die; all his transgressions that he hath committed, they shall not be mentioned unto him," Ezek. 18: 21, 22. O my God, look not upon me, but upon the eternal Melchisedec, Christ Jesus, whom thou hast appointed high priest over thy house, upon the blessed King of thy righteousness, who has no beginning nor end of days, and is a high priest for ever; who did not honor himself, but is ordained of thee, as Aaron, who in the days of his flesh, offered up prayer and supplications, with strong crying and tears, unto him that was able to save him from death, and was heard in that he feared; for his sake hear me, for his sake accept me, for his sake be merciful to me, console thy afflicted servant. I have no comfort neither in heaven above nor upon earth, but in thee alone, have mercy upon me in my great distress; my unclean, sinful flesh afflicts me; my wicked nature wages war against me, and besides, for thy word's sake, I have become an abomination, an outcast and a fable to all men. All who hear of me shake their heads at me; without and within I have no peace. I say again, my sins combat me, my soul is in tribulation and pain; therefore, dear Lord, I pray thee not for gold and silver, for they can profit me nothing in the day of vengeance, neither for long life, for they are always perverse, but this I desire alone of thee, from my whole heart, that thou wouldst look upon me, a miserable sinner, with the gracious eyes of thy mercy; in my affliction and pain, comfort me with thy Holy Spirit, and forgive all my sins.

19. *Consider mine enemies, for they are many and they hate me* WITH CRUEL *hatred*. O Lord of hosts, when I was of the world, I spake and did as the world, and the world hated me not; but as soon as I had eaten the book that was shown to me, although it was in my mouth sweet as honey, yet it made my belly bitter, for there was written therein lamentations, and mourning, and woe, Ezek. 2: 10. While I served the world I received my reward; all men spake well of me, even as the fathers did of the false prophets. But now, that I love the world with a godly love, have sought from my heart their welfare and happiness, rebuked, admonished, and instructed them with thy word, pointing out to them Jesus Christ and him crucified, they have become unto me as a grievous cross, and as the gall of bitterness; so fiendlike is their hatred, that not only I myself, but all those who love me, showing me favor and mercy, must, in some places look for imprisonment and death. O blessed Lord! I am more despicable in their eyes than a notorious thief and murderer; I am like a lost sheep in the wilderness of the world, chased, tormented, and pursued unto death by ravenous wolves. Am I not

THE TWENTY-FIFTH PSALM.

like a person without hope, forsaken and comfortless like a ship in the depth of the ocean, destitute of mast, sail, and helm, tossed about by every wave and every tempest? My flesh had almost said, I am betrayed because I find the unrighteous, froward nation enjoying riches, honor and prosperity, and reposing in quietude and peace, while the godly must endure so much hunger, thirst, affliction, and violence; their habitation is insecure, they must toil and labor for their bread; they are accursed, defamed, persecuted and hated of all men, as the filth of the world, and as an abomination. O blessed Lord! mine enemies are many and great, their heart roars like the furious lion, their words are as deadly arrows, their tongues are always against me; at one time I am reviled by them as a false seducer, at another reproached as an accursed heretic, although by thy grace I possess nought but unyielding truth. Thus am I their mortal enemy, because I instruct them in the way of righteousness. O Lord! I am not ashamed of my doctrine before thee and thine angels, much less before this rebellious world; for I know assuredly that I teach thy word; I have taught, throughout, a true repentance, a dying unto our sinful flesh, and the new life that cometh from God. I have taught a true, sincere faith in thee, and in thy beloved Son, that it might be made powerful through love. I have taught Jesus Christ and him crucified, very God and very man, who, in an incomprehensible, inexpressible, and indescribable manner, was born of thee from all eternity, thy eternal Word and Wisdom, the brightness of thy glory, and the express image of thy person, and that in fullness of time, through the power of thy Holy Spirit, he became, in the womb of the unspotted virgin, Mary, real flesh and blood, a visible, tangible, and mortal man, like unto Adam and his posterity in all things, yet without sin; born of the seed or lineage of Abraham and David, dead and buried, arose again, ascended into heaven, and thus became before thee our only, and eternal Advocate, Mediator, Intercessor, and Redeemer. If all the prophets, apostles, and evangelists have not taught this with the greatest clearness from the beginning, I will gladly bear my shame and reproof. I have taught no other baptism, no other supper, no other ordinance than that sanctioned by the unerring word of our Lord Jesus Christ, and the declared example and usages of his holy apostles, to say nothing of the superabundant evidence of the historians and learned of both the primitive and the present church. Since then, I substantiate my doctrine by the evidence of thy plain, ineffable word, and by the ordinance of thy Son, who can reprove me, and show with the argument of truth that I am an imposter? Does not the whole Scripture teach, that Christ is the truth, and shall abide forever? Is not the apostolic church, the true christian church? We know that all human doctrines are chaff and froth, and that anti-christ has spoiled and corrupted the doctrine of Christ; why then do they hate me, because out of pure zeal I teach and propound the doctrine of Christ and his apostles unadulterated? No one however, hates the opposers of antichrist but such as are his members. Had I not the word of Christ, how cheerfully would I be taught it, for I seek it with fear and trembling; in this I can not be deceived. I have by grace, through the influence of thy Holy Spirit, believed and accepted thy holy truth as the sure word of thy pleasure; it will, also, never deceive me. Let them write and vociferate, threaten, and dispute, boast, extirpate, persecute and destroy, as they please, still thy word will triumph and the Lamb will gain the victory. Yea, I rest assured, that with this my doctrine, which is thy word, I shall, at the coming of Christ, judge and condemn, not only men, but also angels. And though I and my beloved brethren were totally extirpated, and taken from the earth, yet thy word would remain eternal truth. We are no better than our co-workers who preceded us. Yet the time will arrive when they shall exalt thy power, and look, perhaps too late, upon him whom they have pierced. O Lord! with that cruel hatred they hate me! Whom have I slandered in a single expression? Whom have I curtailed a pennies worth? Whose gold, silver, or cattle, have I desired? I have loved them with a pure love, even unto death; thy word and will have I taught them, and with earnest diligence have I shown them, by thy grace, the way that leadeth to felicity, therefore my enemies are many, and hate me with cruel hatred.

20. *O keep my soul, and deliver me; let me not be ashamed, for I put my trust in thee.* O Lord, Lord! the word of Paul fills me with terror, where he says, "Let him that thinketh he standeth take heed lest he fall," "For if a man think himself to be something when he is nothing, he deceiveth himself," for the flesh, destitute of thy Spirit, is perfectly blind in divine things, ignorant, entirely false and unjust, nay, sin and death, as I have remarked publicly in speaking of David and Peter, for though David was a great prophet, a man after thine own heart, faithful in all thy ways, yet when thy Spirit departed from him, where were his chastity, love, humility, and the fear of his God? did he not become an open adulterer, murderer, and boaster of his own glory, until thy Spirit again enlightened him by the word of the prophet, and he acknowledged the deadly sin he had committed, how foolishly he had acted before thee? In like manner as regards Peter; he acknowledged Christ, thy beloved Son, not by flesh and blood, but by the Spirit of thy grace, was called by Christ a stone and a rock, was ready to go with Christ into prison and to death; the trial came, thy Spirit forsook him for a season; he could not bear the trifling expression of a maid, he denied Christ, and swore that he knew him not; but as soon as Christ looked upon him, and thy Spirit returned, he acknowledged his fall, wept bitterly, and afterwards publicly preached the name of Jesus among all nations, paying no regard to his having been strictly forbidden to do so, by imprisonment, stripes and menacing words. He frankly answered, "We ought to obey God rather than men." I beseech Thee, therefore, blessed Lord, that thou wilt keep my soul, which is bought with so dear a price, lest I turn from thy truth; for though I may now think with Peter, that I could give my life for Thee, and with Paul, that neither tribulation, nor distress, nor persecution, nor famine, nor nakedness, nor peril, nor sword, nor life, nor death, nor any other creature, shall be able to separate me from thy love, yet I do not sufficiently know myself. All my trust is in Thee; I have not yet resisted unto blood, although I have drank a little of the cup of thy affliction, yet I have not tasted the dregs; for when prisons and bonds are suffered, when life and death, fire and sword are threatened, then will the gold be separated from the wood, silver from the straw, and pearls from the stubble. Forsake me not, therefore, gracious Lord, for trees of deepest root are torn up from the earth by the violence of the storm, and the lofty, firm mountains are rent asunder by the force of the earthquake. Had not Job and Jeremiah, men of thy love, well nigh lost all patience in temptation, and murmured against thy will? Suffer me not, therefore, gracious Lord, to be tempted above what I am able to bear, for thou art true and faithful, lest my soul be ashamed. I pray not for my flesh, being well aware that I must once suffer and die; but this alone I desire, that thou strengthen me in my warfare; assist and preserve me, make a way for me to escape in temptation; deliver me, and let me not be ashamed; for I put my trust in Thee.

21. *Let integrity and uprightness preserve me; for I wait on thee.* O Lord of hosts! O God, when the husbandman had sown good seed in his field, his enemy came while he slept and sowed tares among the wheat, so that when the sons of God came to present themselves before the Lord, satan came also among them, Job 1; wherever Jesus is, there will the devil be found near at hand, as alas, I have observed in my short time; thy saving word, thy gracious gospel, which is the proper food of my soul, imparting to it the power of eternal life, which has been trampled upon for so many years by anti-christ as an idle tale, and a useless fabrication, is again received, believed, and acknowledged, in power, by some through the influence of thy compassionate favor; the hellish lion or behemoth roars, now in excessive rage; walks about seeking to devour them, has no rest, nor repose, knowing well that his kingdom and dominion must decline and be destroyed thereby; makes use of all his cunning and subtlety, and transforms himself into an angel of light; those whom he has lost through thy word he has allured again by false doctrine into his snare and net, and has changed the pure, salutary sense of the

Scriptures, by means of false prophets and unskilful teachers, into a meaning entirely carnal, and completely calculated to mislead; has authorized the sword and destructive weapons, and excited a vindictive spirit against the whole world; moreover he has instituted open adultery under cover of the custom of the Jewish fathers; also established a literal king and kingdom, together with many other abuses, at which a sincere christian is astonished and confounded. But all which thou hast not planted shall come to nought. O Lord! preserve me pure and upright in thy truth, that I may neither believe, nor teach anything that is not in conformity with thy holy will and word, with true faith, sincere love, real baptism and supper, a blameless life, a scriptural separation from such as cause offence in doctrine and in life. Preserve me, gracious Lord, from all error and heresy; preserve me as thou hast done heretofore in thy mercy; grant that I and my beloved brethren may seek, love, and fear thee with all our hearts, render obedience to the magistracy in all things not contrary to the word of God; for this, says Paul, is good, and acceptable in thy sight; preserve us from the wiles of the devil who would fain teach us of another king after the spirit, beside the true King of Zion, Jesus Christ, who rules over thy holy mountain with the iron sceptre of thy word, is King of kings and Lord of lords, is set at thy own right hand in the heavenly places, far above all principality and power, and might, and dominion, and every name that is named, not only in this world, but also in that which is to come; under whose feet all things are put, who hath all power in heaven and on earth, before whom every knee must bow, and every tongue confess that he is Lord, to the glory of thy great name. O gracious Lord, let integrity and uprightness preserve me under thy cross, that I may not deny thee, and thy holy word, in the time of temptation, nor conceal thy divine truth and will under the mask of hypocrisy, lies, and obscure equivocal expressions, so that at the appearance of thy dear Son, my Lord Jesus Christ, I may receive with all saints, the promised kingdom, inheritance, and reward which, with firm assurance and perfect confidence, we daily hope, and expect, as the consequence of thy gracious promise.

22. *Redeem Israel, O God, out of all his troubles.* O LORD of hosts, now, that I have confessed my sins before thee, prayed for my transgressions, praised thy mercy, and desired thy grace, I must, with David, beseech thee, in behalf of my brethren; for I observe Israel scattered abroad and going astray, like sheep without a shepherd, and the pleasant vineyard of the Lord is laid waste, and trodden down of all men; the chosen seed of Abraham, the house of Jacob, has again become a proper slave or bondservant in the grievous service of Pharaoh in Egypt; the royal line of Judah is carried away into Babylon, together with the holy vessels, which are so lamentably abused by Belshazzar, and his concubines. Jerusalem, the personification of peace, which was likened to a dove, is changed into a barbarous gormandizer of innocent blood, and a rapacious lioness; she that was princess among the nations, the city of the great king is become destitute of kings, citizens and walls waste and solitary; the temple of the Lord, the house of prayer, in which the true worship ought to be performed, has become a notorious nest of robbers, a den of lions, bears, wolves, basilisks, dragons and serpents, a house of all idolaters; nay, the unchaste bed of the adulteress Jezebel. The bride of Christ, the glorious Church, who was clothed in variegated raiment, and decked with divine ornaments, in honor of the king, is changed completely into a disgraceful harlot. The ark of the Lord, the glory of Israel, is seized by the Philistines, and taken into the temple of Dagon. Why make a long lamentation? Judea is changed to Babylon, Canaan to Egypt, and Palestine to Sodom, and the King of glory, Christ Jesus, blessed forever, is daily esteemed as a simpleton, and despised as a fool; his holy apostles, the beloved witnesses of thy truth, must as liars, give way with their doctrine to all men; his knit or wrought garment, which the Scriptures were unwilling should be rent or divided, is torn into four or five pieces; anti-christ exercises authority and dominion in all countries by the preaching of lies; and with violence, is thy word proscribed and rejected; if I travel east, west,

north or south, I find in all places, nothing but vain obstinacy, perversion, blindness, avarice, pride, wantonness, rioting, drunkenness, pomp and splendor, strife, envying and ungodliness. I find (I repeat), violence, false doctrine and an impure, deceptive employment of thy sacraments, throughout the world; I find the influence of tyrants triumphing in the courts of all princes; that the learned speak like the beast, are ambitious, avaricious, gluttonous, earthly and carnally minded, and teach according to the lusts and desires of men; there are scarcely any who seek for truth, and if there are, they must bear thy cross; therefore are my cheeks wet with tears day and night; my soul findeth no comfort; neither bread nor drink is sweet to my taste. Like the prophet Micah, I may well go naked; make a wailing like the dragons, and mourning as the owls; for the wound of Israel is incurable. In sorrow, I may well lament with Esdras, and say, "Our sanctuary is laid waste, our altar broken down, our temple destroyed; our psaltery is laid on the ground, our song is put to silence, our rejoicing is at an end; the light of our candlestick is put out, the ark of our covenant is spoiled, our holy things are defiled, and the name that is called upon us is almost profaned; our children are put to shame, our priests are burnt, our Levites are gone into captivity, our virgins are defiled, and our wives ravished; our righteous men carried away, our little ones destroyed, our young men are brought in bondage, and our strong men are become weak; and which is the greatest of all, the seal of Sion hath now lost her honor; for she is delivered into the hands of them that hate us," 2 Esd. 10: 21—23. Redeem Israel, O God, out of his troubles! look with the eye of thy mercy, upon our great misery and distress, release us from the iron furnance of Egypt, bring us out of the land of the Chaldees, let the holy city be builded again upon her own heap, having walls and gates; repair and rebuild thy fallen temple, the stones of which are trampled upon in every street. Gather together thy wandering sheep, receive thy returning bride, who has behaved so perversely with strange lovers. O God of Israel, create in us a pure heart, that longeth for thy blessed word and will. Send forth faithful laborers into thy harvest, who cut and gather the grain in due season; perfect the builders who lay for us a good foundation, that in the last days thy house may be established, and appear above all the hills, that many people may go thither and say, "Come ye, and let us go up to the mountain of the Lord, to the house of the God of Jacob; and he will teach us of his ways, and we will walk in his paths," Isa. 2: 3; that we may walk before Thee, in peace and liberty of conscience, all the days of our lives, under a good government and blameless teachers, with a christian baptism, true Supper, godly life, and a just separation; that thou mayest in power be eternally honored and praised in us, as in thy beloved children, through thy dear Son, Jesus Christ, our Lord, to whom with thee, O Father, and thy Holy Spirit, be praise and everlasting dominion, Amen.

A

Plain Instruction

FROM THE WORD OF GOD, CONCERNING THE

SPIRITUAL RESURRECTION,

AND

NEW OR HEAVENLY BIRTH.

BY

MENNO SIMON.

"Blessed and holy is he that hath part in the first resurrection: on such the second death hath no power," Rev. 20: 6.

"For other foundation can no man lay than that is laid, which is Jesus Christ," 1 Cor. 3: 11.

ELKHART, INDIANA:
PUBLISHED BY JOHN F. FUNK AND BROTHER.
1871.

THE SPIRITUAL RESURRECTION.

"Awake thou that sleepest, and arise from the dead, and Christ shall give thee light," Eph. 5: 14.

The Scriptures point out to us two resurrections: namely, a bodily resurrection from the dead at the last day, and a spiritual resurrection from sin and death, to a new life and a change of heart.

That a man should die spiritually unto sin, be spiritually buried and rise again to a life of righteousness in God, is plainly taught in various parts of the Scriptures.

Paul also exhorted to the same effect, "Put off, concerning the former conversation, the old man, which is corrupt according to the deceitful lusts; and be renewed in the spirit of your mind, and that ye put on the new man, which, after God, is created in righteousness and true holiness,"Eph. 4: 22—24. "Put off the old man with his deeds, and put on the new man which is renewed in knowledge, after the image of him that created him," Col. 3: 9, 10. Mortify your earthly, &c. Before a resurrection from the dead can take place, the death of the body is necessary, and before death, sickness, pain and tribulation must precede, which have a tendency to make death still more bitter to the flesh. Likewise in a spiritual sense, there can be no resurrection from sin and death, unless this body of sin be first destroyed and buried, and has sensibly endured pain and the burden of sin, that is sorrowfulness of heart, remorse and a sincere repentance on account of sin, as is evidently shown in the Scriptures. David says, "O Lord, rebuke me not in thy wrath; neither chasten me in thy hot displeasure. For thine arrows stick fast in me, and thy hand presseth me sore. There is no soundness in my flesh, because of thine anger; neither is there any rest in my bones, because of my sin. For mine iniquities are gone over my head; as a heavy burden they are too heavy for me. My wounds stink and are corrupt, because of my foolishness. I am troubled, I am bowed down greatly, I go mourning all the day long. For my loins are filled with a loathsome disease, and there is no soundness in my flesh. I am feeble and sore broken; I have roared by reason of the disquietness of my heart. O Lord, all my desire is before thee; and my groaning is not hid from thee. My heart panteth; my strength faileth me; as for the light of mine eyes, it also is gone from me," Ps. 38: 1—10.

Endure sorrow and distress, according to James 4: 9, "Be afflicted and mourn and weep; let your laughter be turned to mourning, and your joy to heaviness." Paul says, "Ye were made sorry after a godly manner," to repentance, "For godly sorrow worketh repentance to salvation, not to be repented of; but the sorrow of the world worketh death;" seeing that ye sorrowed after a godly sort, what carefulness it wrought in you, what clearing of yourselves, yea what indignation, what fear, vehement desire, and revenge.

Behold, thus we have to die with Christ unto sin, if we would be made alive with him; for none can rejoice with Christ, unless he first suffer with him; for this is a sure word. Paul says, "If we be dead with him, we shall also live with him, if we suffer, we shall also reign with him," 2 Cor. 2: 11.

This resurrection includes the new creature, the spiritual birth and sanctification, without which none shall see the Lord, this Paul testifies in a few words, saying, "In Christ Jesus neither circumcision availeth any thing, nor uncircumcision, but a new creature." Again, "If any man be in Christ he is a new creature; old things are passed away; behold, all things are become new," and this is the first resurrection; "For, if we have been planted together in the likeness of his death," that is, through mortifying the sinful nature of earthly Adam, with all his members or wicked lusts; we shall be also in the likeness of his resurrection," and know that our old man is crucified with him, that the sinful body is destroyed, and keep the true sabbath in Christ, by putting off the sinful body in the flesh, circumcised with the circumcision of Christ, which is done without hands, buried through baptism, in which we have also risen with him through faith, which is the operation of God; we cease from all works of the flesh, are led by the Spirit, bring forth the fruits of the Spirit, henceforth, we do not serve sin; let it suffice that we have spent our former days after the manner of the gentiles, when we walked in vanity, wantonness, drunkenness, eating and drinking, and in abominable idolatry, and that we spend the remainder of our days not after the lusts of men, but live according to the will of God, that we may say with Paul, "I am crucified with Christ; nevertheless, I live; yet not I, but Christ liveth in me; and the life which I now live in the flesh, I live by the faith of the Son of God, who loved me, and gave himself for me," Gal. 2: 20; therefore, "He died for all, that they which live, should not henceforth live unto themselves, but unto him which died for them, and rose again," 2 Cor. 5: 15.

To have a more correct knowledge of this resurrection and regeneration, we must bear in mind that all creatures, bring forth after their kind, and every creature partakes of the properties, propensities and dispositions of that which brought it forth, as Christ says, "That which is born of flesh, is flesh," and cannot see eternal life; and "that which is born of Spirit, is spirit," life and peace, which is eternal life; that which is born of flesh, out of the earth through corruptible seed, is carnally-minded, that is, earthly, and speaks of earthly things, is desirous after earthly and perishable things; all his thoughts, feelings and desires are directed towards earthly, temporal, or visible things, such things as those of which it is born, or from which it proceeds. That which is born of flesh and blood, is flesh and blood, and is carnally-minded, "Because the carnal mind is enmity against God, for it is not subject to the law of God, neither indeed can be." Therefore, those who are carnal cannot please God; for such are altogether deaf, blind and ignorant in divine things. A carnal man cannot apprehend or comprehend divine things, for by nature he has not that discernment; but on the contrary his mind is depraved; God is not in his mind. A carnal man cannot understand spiritual things, for he is by nature a child of the devil, and is not spiritually-minded, hence, he comprehends nothing spiritual; for by nature he is a stranger to God; has nothing of a divine nature dwelling in him, nor has communion with God, but is much rather at enmity with him; he is unmerciful, unjust, unclean, not peaceable, impatient, disobedient, without understanding and unhappy. So are all men by nature according to their birth and origin after the flesh. This is the first or old Adam, and is comprised in the Scriptures in a single word, ungodly, that is, without God, a stranger and destitute of the divine nature.

This is the nature and property of the earthly and devilish seed; for as the seed is, so is the fruit; for "whatsoever a man soweth, that shall he also reap; for he that soweth to his flesh, shall of the flesh reap corruption," and bring forth fruit unto death; he sins like his father, of and through whose seed he is born, for he is the father of lies and sinned from the beginning, and did not abide in the truth; he, therefore, that sins, is of the devil, for sin is not of God, but of the devil, and he that sins has not seen God, nor known him; and we know that the son of God was made manifest to take away sins and destroy the works of the devil, and through his death deprive him of power, who had the power of death, that is, the devil, and deliver them, who through fear of death were all their life-time subject to bondage. For by the sin of one man all were made sinners. He that sins is the servant of sin; and does the will and works of him whose servant he is, and whose spirit leads him; for every one is a servant to him whom he serves, whether of sin unto death, or of obe-

THE SPIRITUAL RESURRECTION.

dience unto righteousness; for he that does unjustly shall receive according to his works. To them Paul speaks, that they should awaken from the sleep of sin and death, so that the second death shall have no power over them; saying, "Awake thou that sleepest, and arise from the dead, and Christ shall give thee light," Eph. 5: 14.

On the other hand, all those who are born and renewed from above out of God, through the living word, are also of the mind and disposition, and have the same propensity for good, as he has of whom they are born and begotten. What the nature of God or Christ is, we may readily learn from the sacred Scriptures; for Christ has expressly portrayed himself in his word; namely, his human nature, which he would have us understand, and follow; not according to his divine nature; for he is the true image of the invisible God, the brightness of his glory, and the express image of his person, who dwells in ineffable light whom none can approach or see, but that we follow him and conform unto him in his life and walk upon earth, as exemplified in words and works; that we, thereby, may become partakers of his nature in the Spirit. In the Scriptures Christ is every where represented to us as being humble, meek, merciful, just, holy, wise, spiritual, long suffering, patient, peaceable, lovely, obedient, and good, as the perfection of all things; for in him there is sincerity. Behold, this is the image of God, or Christ in the Spirit, whose example we should follow till we become like it in nature, and evince it by our walk; all the regenerated children of God are thus minded, for they partake of the nature of him who has begotten them; and are as the others, comprised in one word, namely, Godly, or godly persons, having communion with him, are of one mind and disposition with him, and have the image of God in them, as the Scriptures, both of the Old and New Testaments, abundantly show, especially in the epistle of Paul to the Colossians, where he says, "Put off the old man with his deeds," and, "put on the new man, which is renewed in knowledge after the image of him that created him;" "Put on, therefore, as the elect of God, holy and beloved, bowels of mercies, kindness, humbleness of mind, meekness, long suffering, forbearing one another, and forgiving one another, if any man have a quarrel against any, even as Christ forgave you, so also do ye; and above all these things put on charity, which is the bond of perfectness; and let the peace of God rule in your hearts to the which also ye are called in one body; and be ye thankful," Col. 3: 9—15. "My little children, of whom I travail in birth again until Christ be formed in you," "Let this mind be in you, which was also in Christ Jesus," for Christ is the image of God to whom we must conform. "For whom he did foreknow, he also did predestinate to be conformed to the image of his Son." Those, therefore, who have conformed to the image of Christ Jesus, are the truly regenerated children of God, and have put off the old man, and put on the new which is created after God, in true righteousness and holiness.

When these have conformed to the image of God, have been born of God, and afterwards continue in God, they will not commit sin, for the seed of God remains in them; and they have overcome the world, are crucified to the world, and the world unto them; have mortified their flesh, and buried their sinful body with Christ in baptism, with their lusts and desires, and no longer serve sin unto unrighteousness, but much more righteousness unto salvation; for they have put on Christ, and are purified through the Holy Ghost, in their consciences, from dead works to serve the living God; bringing forth through the Spirit the fruits of the Spirit, whose end is eternal life. For since they, as above said, have renounced the devil, flesh, and the world, and have quitted the service of sin, they have, as faithful servants, voluntarily obligated themselves to God with David, to live, henceforth, according to his blessed will all their days. On the other hand the devil and his adherents, the world and flesh, being very envious, are waging war against them, and are their deadly enemies. The regenerated have now become enemies of sin and the devil, and have taken the field against all their enemies, with their Prince of life and faith, under the banner of the red cross, armed with the armor of God, and surrounded with angels of the Lord, always watching with great solicitude, lest they be overcome by their enemies, who never slumber, but go about like roaring lions seeking whom they may devour; and although they receive occasionally a wound, and are overtaken by their enemies, still their souls remain uninjured, and this wound is not unto death; for they have the unction of God. They have the true Samaritan and the true physician with them, who binds up and heals their wounds; for he has compassion over our weakness and sickness. Through his stripes and wounds we are made whole. Nor are they so thoroughly overcome that they will cast aside their weapons, and surrender themselves again, to become servants of sin, and to be ruled by it; but being encouraged anew of the Lord, and in the strength of his power, they persevere valiantly in battle, till they, through him, by whom they can do all things, have gloriously conquered their enemy, and say to him, "O death, where is thy sting? O grave, where is thy victory?" And with Paul say, Thanks be to God, who giveth us the victory, through our Lord Jesus Christ. "The Lord," says Jeremiah, "is with me as a mighty, terrible one, therefore my persecutors shall stumble, and they shall not prevail," and say with David, "Blessed be the Lord, my strength, which teacheth my hands to war and my fingers to fight," and they are not moved till they have broken their enemies to pieces. "Blessed be the Lord who hath not given us as a prey in their teeth; our soul is escaped, as a bird out of the snare of the fowler: the snare is broken, and we are escaped" from our enemies, and out of the hand of those who hate us. The Lord is a rewarder of them that diligently seek, love and serve him; as it is written, "Behold the Lord cometh, and his reward is with him;" yea, his reward and the gift of God are eternal life, through Jesus Christ our Lord. For, if you serve the Lord Jesus Christ, you will receive the reward of your inheritance, the crown of life, which God has promised those who love him.

As stated above, that every creature has the nature and disposition of that of which it is born, therefore, we will speak a few words concerning the nature, properties and effects of the seed of the divine word, whereby we are begotten in the image of God; for where this seed is sown upon good ground, into the heart of man, there it grows and produces its like in nature and property, it changes and renews the whole man, from the carnal into the spiritual, the earthly into the heavenly, it transforms from death unto life, from unbelief to belief, and makes man happy, for through this seed all nations upon the earth are blessed. Therefore, says James, "Lay apart all filthiness and superfluity of naughtiness, and receive with meekness the engrafted word which is able to save your souls." It is also the pure, unadulterated milk, whereby the young and new born children of God are nurtured, till they attain to a perfect man, unto the measure of the stature of the fullness of Christ, it is also strong food for the perfect and aged in Christ Jesus. In short, this seed of the divine word is spiritual food, whereby the whole inner man is ascertained, so that he perish and faint not in this wilderness and desolate world, as all have to starve and faint who do not daily gather the bread of the divine word to satisfy their starving souls, for "Man shall not live by bread alone, but by every word that proceedeth out of the mouth of God." Therefore, is he blessed who hungers after this heavenly bread, and receives the ingrafted word; for it will bring forth after its nature, in due time, an hundred fold. For, says the Lord, "As the rain cometh down, and the snow from heaven, and returneth not thither, but watereth the earth, and maketh it bring forth and bud, that it may give seed to the sower and bread to the eater, so shall my word be that goeth forth out of my mouth; it shall not return unto me void, but it shall accomplish that which I please," Isa. 55: 10, 11.

Behold, this is the nature, property and effects of the seed of the word of God, by which man is renewed, regenerated, sanctified and saved through this incorruptible seed, namely, the living word of God which abides to eternity; and that he is clothed with the same power from above, filled with the Holy Ghost, and thus united to God, that he may become a partaker of the divine nature, and be made conformable to the image of his Son, who is the first of the regenerated, and those who rose with him from the sleep and death of sin, henceforth serve him not in the oldness of the letter, but in newness of the Spirit.

He that is sincere, and has this nature and disposition in his heart, has put on Christ Jesus, is become like unto him, has the image of God in his heart, and is spiritually minded, is led by the Spirit in his spirit, from whose spiritual body, spiritual fruits are brought forth, as a well springing up unto eternal life. For they are regenerated through the word which was sown in their hearts, begotten of God, and born anew to bring forth fruit of eternal life; they, therefore, as children born of God, are the same as the Father, of one mind and disposition; have the divine nature of their Father, who has begotten them; whose thoughts are heavenly, whose words are truth, well seasoned, whose good works are holy, acceptable to God and man; for they are holy vessels of honor, useful and ready to every good work.

Even as Paul exhorts those who are born of the corruptible seed of flesh and blood, who are earthly, carnal, without understanding and blind in divine things, yea, children of wrath, that they should die unto sin, mortify and bury the lusts and desires of the flesh, and then rise by virtue of the heavenly seed from the sleep and death of sin, and be regenerated, and walk in newness of life, which is the first resurrection, saying, "Awake thou that sleepest, and arise from the dead, and Christ shall give thee light." So does he also admonish all regenerated children of God, who have been changed in mind and disposition, through the eternal saving seed of God, who have been regenerated and are risen, that they should be godly, spiritually and heavenly minded, and strive for and desire heavenly, incorruptible things; and that their heart should be where their treasure is, and their conversation in heaven, as fellow saints of the house of God, telling them, "If then ye be risen with Christ, seek those things which are above, where Christ sitteth on the right hand of God; set your affections on things above, not on things on the earth; for ye are dead, and your life is hid with Christ in God, when Christ, who is our life, shall appear, then shall ye also appear with him in glory," Col. 3: 1—4. Here we have an account how the regenerated children of God who have risen with Christ from the dead, and now live with him, converse upon heavenly things, and appear to the world as not living, for their life is hid in God, as St. John says, "Now are we the sons of God, and it doth not yet appear what we shall be; but we know that, when he shall appear, we shall be like him; for we shall see him as he is," 1 John 3: 2.

With these and the like words the Scriptures admonish the truly regenerated and those who have arisen, that they should take heed to their calling, and continue perfect in a new, godly walk, for if they have been made partakers of Christ, they should persevere to the end, lest they again depart from the living God through the deceitfulness of sin and an evil heart of unbelief; and they should remain steadfast and perfect, as the chosen children of God, and inherit the kingdom of their Father, and reign in eternity and rule over sin, death, devil and hell, and all the enemies of the kingdom, whom they overcome with Christ, as valiant men; therefore, will they also sit with Christ at the table of the Lord, and eat the bread and drink the wine of the kingdom of heaven; even as Christ overcame, and sitteth with his Father in his kingdom which is prepared for them; as a city well fortified; free from all care of their enemies; in full rest, full of life and joy; for they eat of the tree of life which is in the midst of Paradise; which pleasure garden is ever close to the unregenerated, who are still earthly and carnally minded, who still have by nature the vail and partition wall of sin before their hearts.

These are they, who died with Christ unto sin, and have truly risen; they are the new born, to whom the power is given to become the sons of God; were redeemed out of all nations; have on the wedding garments against the marriage of the Lamb; have received the sign TAU in their foreheads by which the servants of God are designated; these are the spiritual bride of Christ, his holy church, his spiritual body, flesh of his flesh, and bone of his bone. They have come to the heavenly Jerusalem, the city of the living God, which came down from heaven; have come to an innumerable company of angels, to the general assembly of the church of the first born which are written in heaven, and to Jesus, the Mediator of the new covenant; they are fellow citizens in the household of God who have put off the corruptible garment, and put on the incorruptible; have acknowledged the name of God, and kept his commandments, and the faith of Jesus; the true sheep of Christ, who hear his voice, and follow no other; the first fruits of his creatures, who have the Spirit and mind of Christ, therefore, they know what the will of the Lord is; yea, the chosen generation, the spiritual and royal priesthood, a holy nation, a peculiar people; who in times past were not a people, but now the people of God, for God had compassion on them; these are the souls who were slain, under the altar, for the word of God.

In short, with them old things have passed away; behold all things have become new; but this is all of God, who has reconciled us unto himself through Jesus Christ; these are they who stand before the throne of God, with palms in their hands, and clothed in white, saying, "Blessing, and glory, and wisdom, and thanksgiving, and honor, and power and might be unto our God forever and ever, Amen," Rev. 7: 12.

This is a short instruction concerning the spiritual resurrection or new birth, and the difference between the natural and spiritual; between the earthly and the heavenly; and how every one is disposed, inclined, and of what mind he is, according to his birth or origin, and that he is of the same disposition, of the same mind and of such a nature as that is of which he is born, that which generated him; for the natural man is not spiritual, neither is that which is born of flesh and blood, the spiritual birth of God from heaven; but like produces like. As the natural man is, so are they, who are naturally born. Such as God is, who is a Spirit and dwells in heaven, such are also they who are spiritually born from heaven, who far exceed those naturally born of flesh.

Here, as in a mirror, one may view and examine himself, and judge of what birth, mind, disposition, nature, life and conduct he is; for here a man, by taking a little pains, can judge and prove himself, for a man's walk, word and actions, and the thoughts of his heart, all show what he is; for man knows himself best, and no one knows what is in man, but the spirit which is in him.

Again: therefore, all those who find on proving themselves, that they are not renewed and regenerated after their first birth, according to the flesh, in mind, understanding, spirit and disposition, but are yet altogether carnally, earthly, worldly and devilishly minded; and from their depraved, inbred nature, are prone and willing to do all manner of evil, should humble themselves before God, with Jeremiah, saying, Let us examine and prove our ways, and let us turn unto the Lord, let us lift our hands and hearts to God in heaven, and say, We have sinned before heaven and in thy sight, and have excited thy wrath; Let us weep and let our eyes run over with water, and say with David, "O come, let us worship and bow down; let us kneel before the Lord our Maker," and entreat him that he would make glad the work of his hands, and renew us whom he created; let us humbly entreat him for his Spirit, which is the great cause of all this, and say, Lord, send forth thy Spirit, and they will be created, and thou wilt renew the face of the earth, and thus they continue in prayer and in their desires to God, till they are clothed with the power of the Spirit from on high, converted and renewed in the spirit of their mind; and with astonishment say, This is the change wrought by the right hand of God, the most High, Ps. 104: 30; 95: 6.

Also let those, who, on examining themselves, find that they are born from above by the grace of God, and that they are new creatures in Christ, and have become a temple of God, take heed to themselves according to the counsel of the Scriptures, in order that, since they are washed, purified, regenerated and sanctified, they do not again defile themselves, and pollute the temple of God; for if any man defile the temple of God, him shall God destroy. They pray in the spirit with assured confidence, to God, their Father, with David, O God strengthen us and confirm in us that which thou didst cause in us! He will then hear in his holy temple, according to his promise, For he is faithful who has begun the good work in you, he will also perform it until the day of Jesus Christ. Peter says, "Give all diligence to add to your faith, virtue; and to virtue, knowledge; and to knowledge, temperance; and to temperance, patience; and to patience, godliness; and to godliness, brotherly kindness; and to brotherly kindness, charity; for if these things be in you, and abound, they make you that ye shall neither be barren nor unfruitful in the knowledge of our Lord Jesus Christ; but he that lacketh these things is blind, and cannot see afar off, and hath forgotten that he was purged from his old sins; wherefore, the rather, brethren, give diligence to make your calling and election sure; for if ye do these things, ye shall never fall; for so an entrance shall be ministered unto you abundantly, into the everlasting kingdom of our Lord and Savior, Jesus Christ," 2 Pet. 1: 5—11.

May the God of all grace, who will gather all his chosen in the last resurrection, into his kingdom, grant us such hearts, minds and dispositions, that we, through true faith, may die unto ourselves, deny and renounce ourselves, that we may have part in the first resurrection spoken of, which resurrection does not take place in the bodily resurrection from the dead, as will be the case in the other resurrection, at the last day, but this resurrection consists alone in dying unto, mortifying and burying the sinful body through putting off, and dying unto the old life, and to rise and be received into a new, divine conduct and pious life, Amen.

CONCLUSION.

HERE, kind reader, you have a brief instruction of the first, or *Spiritual Resurrection from death or the sleep of sin*, also some inducements to awaken and arise, and henceforth to live a new, godly, pious, unblamable life, according to the example of Jesus Christ, as the Scriptures abundantly instruct us, and as is partially related here; for the Father himself, in heaven directs us to Christ, and says, "This is my beloved Son, in whom I am well pleased, hear ye him." He says, Ye shall hear him. Moses also testifies of him, and says, "The Lord, thy God, will raise up unto thee a prophet from the midst of thee, of thy brethren, like unto me; unto him ye shall hearken;" and "every soul which will not hear that Prophet, shall be destroyed from among the people," Deut. 18: 15; Acts 3: 23.

Thus we counsel and admonish all in general, of whatever name, rank, class or condition; that they would be pleased to take good heed to the word of the Lord, which we have here briefly presented, according to our limited gift; I hope, by the grace of God, that you will find nothing in it but the infallible truth of Jesus Christ, for we have not directed you to men, nor to the doctrine, nor commands of men, but alone to Jesus Christ, and to his holy word which he taught and left upon earth, and sealed it with his blood and death, and afterwards had it promulgated throughout the world, by his faithful witnesses and holy apostles.

Besides, we say, that all doctrines, which do not agree with the doctrine of Jesus Christ and his apostles, if ever so fair in appearance, they are accursed. For his word is the truth, and his command is eternal life, therefore, we kindly entreat you, from our inmost souls, that you be pleased to accept and read with an understanding heart, this our *Instruction concerning the Spiritual Resurrection and New Creature*, and compare and prove it with the doctrines of the apostles; if it does not agree with theirs, let it be accursed, "For other foundation can no man lay than that is laid, which is Jesus Christ."

A Fundamental Doctrine,

OR AN ACCOUNT OF

Excommunication, Ban, Exclusion,

OR

SEPARATION FROM THE CHURCH OF CHRIST;

ITS NATURE, POWERS, TO WHOM IT EXTENDS;
ITS REASONS, OBJECTS AND DESIGN, &c.—WHY IT WAS TAUGHT
AND PRACTICED BY THE APOSTLES, AND COMMANDED THAT WE SHOULD PRACTICE IT.
FAITHFULLY COMPILED FROM SACRED SCRIPTURES, FOR THE USE OF ALL
LOVERS OF THE DOCTRINE OF ETERNAL TRUTH, TO PROMOTE
CHRISTIAN PEACE WITHOUT RESPECT TO PARTY.

BY

MENNO SIMON.

"Be of one mind—let nothing be done through strife or vain glory," Phil. 2: 3.

"For other foundation can no man lay than that is laid, which is Jesus Christ," 1 Cor. 3: 11.

ELKHART, INDIANA:
PUBLISHED BY JOHN F. FUNK AND BROTHER.
1871.

PREFACE.

Brethren and sisters in Christ Jesus, it is known, and evident to all the true children of God, who are enlightened by his Holy Spirit, that human reason is so depraved in Adam, that it possesses but little light which can lead to godliness; yea, it has become so unfit, haughty, ignorant and blind that it would even attempt presumptuously to alter, bend, break, gainsay, judge and find fault with the word of the Lord God; it will not yield to any spirit or gift and persists that it is right, and that all it does or says is God's word; whereby the saving truth, and blessed love and peace have often to endure and suffer much injury, infamy and disgrace.

In the second place, it is evident that also the enchanting spirit of anti-christ has made the whole world so drunk with the cup of his abominations; has so rejected the doctrine of Christ and his holy apostles, sacraments, Spirit, life, ordinances, usages, example and the true worship, that but little of a salutary nature is left among men; hence it is difficult to restore what has been destroyed to its true order and proper usage, to which the Lord had ordained it.

In the third place, it is evident that the old master, satan, the arch enemy of God and souls, is always about us, as a roaring lion, and seeks whom he may devour, as Peter says. He assails us in divers ways; now with the unclean, wicked nature of our depraved flesh, and anon with some enchanting, false doctrine and fair words; and again, by persecution, cross and fears; then with liberty and worldly life of the flesh; now with riches and abundance, then again with defects, wants and poverty. In short, he shoots his fiery darts constantly; they fly by day and by night, in secret and in public. He that does not zealously abide in the fear of God cannot withstand the manifold assaults of his temptations. Yea when we think the end is attained, then we are assailed the most violently. Some are led to quarreling and wrangling under the semblance of truth; such are called by Paul, "Men of corrupt minds, and destitute of the truth," whose fruits are abominable envy, disgraceful defamation, slanderous words, unclean, perverted minds, a lamentable destruction of the holy peace of God, a grievous denial of pure, christian love, a hindrance of the saving doctrine, the fruitful mother of faction, and an easy way to ruin, as we have abundantly seen in the days of the revealed truth.

O! brethren, take warning; again I say, beware and watch; for James says that such wisdom is not from above, but it is earthly, sensual, devilish; for the wisdom which is from above, is first pure, then peaceable, gentle and easy to be entreated, full of mercy and good fruits, without partiality and without hypocrisy. Yea, my brethren, where there is no peaceable, friendly, saving and impartial wisdom, there is nothing but forced appearance of good; powerless, impure and sinful prayer; an unsteady, wavering mind; a restless and troubled conscience, full of strife and dissension, no matter how much we may boast of the truth. The Lord grant that we may see this.

In the fourth place, it is evident that the community or church cannot continue in the saving doctrine, an unblamable and pious life without the proper use of the *Excommunication* or *Ban;* even as a city without a good police, or laws and regulations, or a field without any inclosure, and a house without walls and doors, so is also a church which has not the true apostolic *Exclusion* or *Ban;* for without it there would be an opening for all deceiving spirits, for all abominations, and for proud scorners, for all idolatrous and wantonly, perverted sinners; yea, for all lewd debauchees, sodomites, adulterers and knaves, as is the case with all the great sects of the world, which call themselves, though improperly, the church of Christ; according to my opinion it is the distinguished usage, honor and prosperity of a sincere community, if they with christian discretion teach the true apostolic *Separation*, and observe it carefully in love, according to the ordinance of the holy, divine Scriptures; it is more than evident, that if we had not with due zeal insisted upon it, we would be esteemed and called, by every one, the members of the sect of Munster and all other perverted sects. But, thank God, since, in consequence of the proper use of excommunication, it is well known, among several thousand honorable, sincere persons, in different principalities, cities, and countries, that we are guiltless of, and free from all ungodly abominations, and preverted sects, and that we also do make this known, unreservedly, to the whole world, not only by our doctrines and walk, but with our possessions and blood.

Observing that now the bright light of the holy gospel of Christ shines again in refulgent splendor in these vexatious times of all anti-christian abominations; God's own and first begotten Son, Christ Jesus, is gloriously revealed, his good will and pleasure and holy word concerning faith, regeneration, repentance, baptism, the Lord's Supper, and the whole saving doctrine, life and ordinance, have again come to light through much seeking, prayer, reading, teaching and writing; that now all things (God be praised for his grace) proceed according to the true, apostolic rule in the church, whereby the kingdom of Christ rises in honor, and the kingdom of anti-christ is sinking. For this reason the arch enemy of our souls violently opposes and uses his old wiles and arts most subtlely against it. He appears under the cloak of a christian; understand me rightly; he proudly boasts of faith; upbraids, yea, rejects all the Babylonian deeds; is baptized; seats himself with the saints at the Lord's Supper; praises the lives of the pious; hears exhortations; gives alms; receives the poor; washes the saints' feet; says that Christ is the Son of God. In short, in appearance he is an unblamable, regenerated, penitent and true christian. But in the mean time, he watches where he may assail us most easily and injure us the most; he pleasingly approaches the depraved and enchanted souls, some of whom, as is evident, as yet know little about the nature and disposition of the Holy Ghost; he presses them closely, for he knows how skillfully to defend his cause with the letter of the Scriptures; he speaks gently; whatever he does, he does as though out of pure fear of God, and love to the church, with the word and truth of the Lord. He commences as though in the anxiety of a distressed conscience, to argue and dispute, principally concerning the separation which he can not well tolerate and endure; here and there he raises pernicious questions and answers, whereby he so influences and inflames the perverted and enchanted, that some of them, when they cannot stand before the power of the truth, from mere partisan spirit, leave the pleasant Jerusalem of peace and return again to unclean, blind Babel; or build up a sect of their own, as I have, with much sorrow, seen it to be the case two or three times. Behold, this is the pearl which the old deceiver seeks with his ire and wrangling; for whether we stay away from the idolatrous church or not, be baptized or not, it is immaterial to him; if he can only inflame our hearts with hatred and envy one towards another, corrupt our minds, mar our love, destroy our peace; if he can but sow discord, defamation, hatred, lies, enmity and backbiting, which generally arise from such disputes; if he can but do this, then he has accomplished what he sought. Ah! dear brethren, beware, for it is more than clear, that all those who have not the meek, friendly, peaceable and affectionate Spirit of Christ, but are contentious, are not of God. Be this known to you.

Inasmuch then, that we know, that he did from the beginning of the expounded gospel, to the present moment, cause us much pain and sorrow of heart, with his cunning, unfruitful questions of contention, and other pernicious disputations, I do most affectionately and sincerely entreat all who would desire to walk peaceably and quietly in the

PREFACE.

fear of God with a good conscience, before the Lord and his church, that they would all, before God in Christ Jesus, lay this sincerely to heart, how faithfully the Holy Spirit of Christ warns us concerning our unprofitable, foolish questions, answers, disputations, and quarrels, 1 Tim. 6; for the Spirit of Christ is the Spirit of love and peace, and therefore, teaches it to all of his children, and writes it upon the tablets of our hearts with his gracious finger. Ah! do reflect upon what we teach; and that his holy kingdom and word are a word and kingdom of peace, and not of strife; that his messengers and servants, are messengers and servants of peace, in order that you, who call yourselves after his holy name, who alone has graciously called you into his kingdom of peace, through the word of his peace, may escape the snares of the devil, and that you may so conduct yourselves in all your ways after the will and pleasure of Christ, towards all men, and observe his holy word and ordinance, and defend it; that you may promote that true righteousness required of God, such as faith, love, repentance, regeneration, piety and peace with all other fruits of the Holy Ghost; gladden the hearts of all the sorrowful of heart, and the young and tender souls in Christ Jesus, and strengthen, console and encourage them in all their trials, need, temptations, tribulation and fear; so that the most holy city and temple, which lay desolated for so many centuries, may again be rebuilt, and all its usages, ordinances and services restored to primitive order. Yea, that the saving light of the true gospel of Christ may be spread among all nations, kindred and tongues, in its full splendor; and that the accursed, lying and anti-christian darkness may be dispelled.

Then observe that the powerful word of the Lord is more and more miraculously breaking forth, and that, therefore, all true hearts would gladly see and have unanimity in this part of the Ban, whereby they are sometimes so greatly troubled and perplexed, as related, that they might all orderly proceed, observing one rule, according to the Scriptures as it becomes christians; and that I, an unworthy person, the weakest of all the saints, have been severely tried in this part by many, different spirits for twenty-two years, and have endured many an attack, whereby others are not only taught of me, but I am also taught of others, the Giver of all good gifts be praised for all this. And also that I have acquired more knowledge in some things, through length of time, and through many adventitious circumstances, examination and study; therefore, I was fraternally requested and besought, by several, pious hearts who would gladly see all things right, that before the close of my life, I would examine and revise the *Ground and meaning of the true apostolic Ban or Separation*, arrange it formally, and present it for examination to the elders and ministers of the church, and to all those desiring peace, so that if any one, after my departure, as I am now an old, feeble man, might cause any trouble, strife or dissension among the quiet and peaceable, under pretence that he heard this or that from me at any time, or might infer wrong views from some of my writings which have not yet been so fully explained by me *concerning husband and wife*, and of open, offensive, carnal sinners, as it is done here, in order that the brethren may refer them to my *conclusive ground*, after I shall have fallen asleep in God, and made my exit hence. Besides, that the pious, doubtful conscience may thereby be relieved, so that they may attain an assurance of confidence in their minds. To which request, although christian-like and just, I have undertaken to respond with diffidence, because I well know that they are not all brethren and sisters in truth and power who will read, hear and see it, but also others. And where the disposition is not friendly, nor love true, there the understanding is generally partial and the construction unjust, as I, alas, have often experienced in my days. Ah! that some of them would obtain grace. Besides, I know, that the opinions, judgments, affections and minds are different; and that the all-prevailing truth and the fear, Spirit and unction of the Lord, are not possessed by every one in their fullness; therefore, I fear that all will not receive and follow this doctrine as the *True Ground of Truth*. O that we all had the eyes of understanding, those of us who think we see, it would, according to my opinion, soon gain a strong hold with some.

Yet I confidently expect that those, who in the true fear of God sincerely seek union and peace among the pious, and are anxious for the truth, will not despise and upbraid me for this my solicitous and brotherly labor for the edification of holy peace, and explanation of eternal truth, accepted by me in true christian faith; but that they will accept it, and give the praise to God for his grace; for it appears to me, although perhaps I may be in error, almost impossible to hit upon a more certain way according to truth, in which we may stand before God and man, than that which I have impartially, and according to my limited talents, pointed out and explained as before God in Christ Jesus, and which is according to the sacred Scriptures.

I do not serve the stiff-necked, haughty and perverse scorners, neither immovable bigots and wranglers, but those, I serve, who are of an impartial, new, christian mind, who suffer themselves to be instructed, and are under the guidance of the Holy Spirit, and live in the fear of God and in pure love, who have received the Lord's holy word and truth in a pure mind; who implicity follow it through the received unction, and are free from all bitter, party spirit, vain honor, hatred and envy; for with such we find the amiable spirit of peace, sincere and pious disposition, an unleavened, pure heart and conversation, and, therefore, also an upright and pure understanding, and an incorrupt, saving ground and exposition, and they live no more unto their selfish flesh, but unto Christ and their neighbors, resist none, are humble, are opposed to all unscriptural contention and strife, readily acknowledge their short comings wherein they have erred; reconcile their neighbors whom they had grieved, regarding neither honor nor dishonor; heap fiery coals upon the heads of their adversaries; walk unblamably, in order that they may awaken them again unto truth with love, lead them from the way of error, bring them unto Christ, and save them eternally. Behold these are they, I say, whom I serve with my writings; for they have Christ in power with his Spirit, word and love, and thus with him, and in him they have TRUE CHRISTIANITY, which will stand before God, which is a useful, cheering, peaceable and joyful thing. Ah, children, be admonished; learn rightly to know the subtlety of the devil, and beware of discord. May the merciful Father grant unto us the wise Spirit of his grace, Amen.

EXPLANATION

OF THE

TRUE APOSTOLIC SEPARATION OR EXCOMMUNICATION.

1. *What is meant by Separation or Excommunication?* Sincerely faithful children in the Lord, whom I love in truth, Since I have undertaken, in paternal fidelity, this very critical task, for the benefit of you and all the pious generally, I say a critical task, for I am well aware that it has caused much grief among the humble for some time; and I fear that all is not over yet, I, therefore, entreat you all in general, both the afflicted and unafflicted, by the bloody wounds of Jesus, all of you, who with me bow your knees before the Almighty, great God, I exhort you by the righteous judgment, which he will hold at his future coming in the clouds of heaven, in flaming fire, with his mighty angels, that you would be pleased to judge this my work impartially, and with a pure heart of peace; read article after article, nay, every word, with sincere, christian discretion, in impartial, true love, according to the rule and foundation of truth; and, in the first place, well observe what *Excommunication* of the church of Christ is in power, which was left and taught us in the word by the Lord's holy apostles, so that you despise none ignorantly, nor say with scorners, Let them freely excommunicate; their excommunication is not dangerous, and similar unguarded expressions. I tell the truth in Christ, and lie not, that I would sooner suffer myself to be cut into pieces, till the day of judgment, if it were possible, than to suffer myself to be excommunicated, according to the Scriptures, by the servants of the Lord, from his church. O brethren, beware!

All that was cursed in Israel according to the ordinances of the law, whether man or beast, had to die, and the accursed goods had to be burnt with fire. This was a dreadful and severe curse. But in the kingdom and government of Christ, if we rightly view it in its true character; if repentance follow not, it is still more dreadful; it is not now a bodily extermination or the death of our flesh, as Moses' curse or excommunication was, nor is it an exclusion from a temple or synagogue, even as is the excommunication of the Jews or of the world; but it is a true declaration of the eternal death of the soul, made through the sincere servants of Christ, against all offending, carnal sinners, and stubborn wranglers; a delivering over to satan; yea, a common renouncing, excommunicating or separating from the congregation, church, body and kingdom of Christ, and that in the name of Christ, with the binding efficacy of his Holy Ghost and powerful word.

Since, then, this is such a dreadful and severe anathema, as related, then may every one see well to it, that he walk and conduct himself so before God and his church, as not to be eternally smitten with such a curse, either of Christ or his church that he must be an excommunicant out of the holy congregation, body, city, temple, church, kingdom and house of Christ. For all who are out of the congregation and church of Christ, must be in that of anti-christ; this is incontrovertible. And what the award of such will be, if they will not repent, may be plainly read in Rom. 1: 32; 6: 23; Gal. 5:

21; Rev. 21: 8. Ah! children, beware; be careful with all your powers; watch assiduously; pray fervently and be prepared; for God's judgments are terrible; "It is a fearful thing to fall into the hands of the living God," Heb. 10: 31.

2. *Over whom this Apostolic Excommunication is to be used.* We find in many places of the holy Scriptures, that the truly believing church is the spiritual body, bride, camp, city and temple of Jesus Christ, our only spiritual Head, Bridegroom, King and High Priest, prefigured by the literal Eve, Rebecca, and the camp, city and temple of Israel. In the political dominion of Israel, no leper, none that had an issue, nor those who were defiled by the dead, were suffered to come into camp as long as they were not healed and purified according to the law; none were allowed to ease themselves within the camp; neither an uncircumcised, nor an unclean person, was allowed to eat of the passover; all those (here observe well Israel's Ban) had to die without mercy, on the testimony of two or three witnesses, who despised the word of the Lord and set aside his commandments; those who were guilty of abomination in Israel, and served strange gods. For, says Moses, they were to be a holy people to the Lord. Num. 5: 2; Ex. 12: 48; Deut. 17: 6; Ex. 19: 6.

And thus it is in the Christian dispensation; for his church is a congregation of saints, or an assembly of the righteous, even as the Nicean fathers some centuries ago, did confess with us; and, as Adam had but one Eve, who was flesh of his flesh and bone of his bone, Isaac but one Rebecca, who was of his own family, and Christ but one body, which was heavenly and from heaven, and was perfect and holy in all its members; thus has he also, spiritually, but one Eve, but one new Rebecca, who is his spiritual body, spouse, church and bride, namely, the believers, the regenerated, meek, merciful, dead to sin, righteous, peaceable, amiable and obedient children in his kingdom and house of peace; pure, chaste virgins in the Spirit, holy souls, who are of his divine family, and holy flesh of his flesh, and bone of his bone.

From which, according to the doctrine of the holy apostles, it is evident that the obstinate disturber or sectary who causes, contrary to the doctrine of godliness, offence and discord, and those who do not abide in the doctrine of Christ, who lead an offensive life, or the over-curious, inquisitive and lazy, who live at the expense of others, shall not be suffered in the holy house, camp, city, temple, church and body of Christ, which is the church; but that we, with one accord, should exclude and shun them, according to Scripture, to *our* salvation, and *their* reformation. Faithful children, be you warned. Terrible is the word which John utters, "Whosoever transgresseth, and abideth not in the doctrine of Christ, hath not God," 2 John 1: 9. And in another place, "He that committeth sin, is of the devil," 1 John 3: 8.

3. *The reason why this Excommunication is commanded in the Scriptures.* John teaches and says, That God is love. Since, then, as God is love, so does he also manifest the nature, of that which he is, namely, love. That this is the truth, may be readily perceived from the creation and preservation of all his creatures; the restoration of Adam and Eve; the preservation of Noah and his sons from the flood with an ark; in blessing Abraham, Isaac and Jacob; in ransoming Israel from Egypt; in sending Moses and the prophets; and more especially in the holy incarnation of our Lord Jesus Christ, the Son of God; in his gracious, efficacious doctrine, miracles, prayers, weeping, cross, blood and death; also, in the effusion of his Holy Spirit, and sending forth his holy apostles.

Since then it is evident that God is love, and will be forever, who in the beginning manifested the glorious fruit of love towards his children, he now likewise does this by his *exclusion or separation*, although it is terrible and severe, and notwithstanding that it has such a terrible consequence with the stubborn and unconverted sinner, as heard; and since he is the wise and omniscient God, who with his flaming eyes sees into the inmost recesses of the hearts and reins of men, who judges their ways and knows us best, who are his feeble creatures and workmanship, what weak vessels we are; yea, who knows that some of us can scarcely withstand a gentle breeze of deception, but suffer ourselves to be led away immediately; or that we are soon polluted with the pernicious, abominable life of the wicked; for this reason he has, through his paternal love and great mercy, given us, his poor, weak children, this means of *Separation*, approved it by the Holy Spirit and word in the beginning, and commanded it to this end, that we should exclude the restless, stubborn wranglers and schismatists, together with the offensive, carnal and lewd, from his holy congregation, church and house of peace; and, according to the Scriptures, avoid and shun them till they repent, in order that they move us not, through fair words, in the confident hope we have in the truth of Christ, for their false doctrine eats as a canker, 2 Tim. 2: 17; nor that the abominable with their impure, carnal life pervert us, nor give us a bad name among those without; this is the *first reason* why the Spirit of the Lord so earnestly commanded and taught Excommunication in his holy word. Whether this *reason* is not a special work of the love of Christ, which is of great usefulness, service, power and fruit to all the pious, I will let all the faithful consider in the fear of God.

The other *reason* is, that all those who again forsake the holy word and true way and go astray in the world, despise the holy covenant, make void their received baptism and the promise of righteousness; again hear the false prophets, love the world, walk the broad way of the flesh, or cause contention, schisms and sects and perverse things among the pious, may be deterred by means of this excommunication, and brought to repentance, seek union and peace, and thus be set free before the Lord and his church, from the satanic snares of their strife, or from their ungodly life. Behold, this is the other reason why the Spirit of the Lord so earnestly recommended and taught excommunication in his holy word. And whether this is not a special work of his love, and of like power, usefulness, service and fruit to the impious, if they will by any means observe it in fear, as the first is to the pious; upon this I will leave the faithful to reflect in the fear of God. Yea, whoever can rightly understand and see, in my opinion, the aforementioned *reasons*, according to the Scriptures, has already found the true ground of the holy excommunication.

Since we know, then, that this our excommunication or separation is commanded us in the Scriptures, for two such highly important reasons, as related, therefore, we have reason enough, if we rightly boast of the Christian name, regularly to teach the evident and direct command, doctrine and ordinance of the Lord and his holy apostles, as a highly useful and good work of great love; and obediently to follow it; and besides, it is also evident, that those sin heinously against the word of the holy apostles, and their great love, and the fidelity and love of the church, and especially against their own souls, who call this useful, divine ordinance, in the perverseness of their sinful flesh, a contentious work of the devil, and thus trample it so shamefully under the unhallowed feet of their impious calumny, into the mire; haughty is that man who would rebuke his God, or gainsay and censure his word. Reflect upon that in which we have instructed you.

4. *The true Apostolic Excommunication has no respect to persons.* Undoubtedly, it is well known to us all, dear brethren, that it is so strongly and earnestly commanded in the Scriptures, nay, it is one of the chief commands, that we are to honor father and mother, and that all had to die according to the law of Moses, who cursed and disobeyed them. And also, that the bond of undefiled, honorable matrimony is so unchangeably bound in the kingdom and government of Christ, that neither a man nor woman can forsake one the other, and take another, understand rightly what Christ says, except it be for fornication, Matt. 19: 9. And Paul also holds the same doctrine, that they shall be bound to each other, and that they are to live in union; that the man has not power over his own body, nor the woman over hers, 1 Cor. 7: 4.

Both these rules, the first in relation to parents, and the second in relation to wedlock, stand fast and unbroken, and can never be altered or infringed by any man, so long as we can, in God and with God, in a good conscience, observe and keep them, as the aforementioned rules require, without transgressing the holy word; but if this cannot be done thus, the spiritual must not, in that case, yield to the carnal, but the carnal must yield to the spiritual; this is incontrovertibly true.

I, therefore, entreat all the pious, for the Lord's sake who are sanctified with us unto Christ Jesus, through the Spirit of peace, and through faith in his precious blood, that they will impartially and spiritually examine these following grounds or reasons, which so urgently engage our attention, with God-fearing and understanding hearts, and learn, that we should unreservedly proclaim this ground with christian discretion, to such of our fellow-believers, whose lot it may be, to be thus situated, from which God preserve them, and that we should inculcate it in faithful love to the salvation of their souls, without giving offence to the young and tender minds. All who fear God, I will let judge what we teach.

The *first reason* is, that we truly know through the Spirit and word of God, that the heavenly espousal, between Christ and our souls, is made by faith, through his innocent death and precious blood, and must be voluntarily kept unbroken, in obedience to the only and eternal bridegroom, and that, therefore, a man shall not, for the sake of father, mother, son, daughter, husband or wife, in life or death, be disobedient to his word, in the smallest matter, or yield in the least; for God, the Lord will, shall and must alone be the God of our consciences, and the only Lord of our souls; and not our father, mother, husband or wife, as we may plainly see from Deut. 13: 6.

The *second reason* is, that the faithful apostles, John and Paul, implicitly teach us, that in the first place, we are to *shun* the apostates, lest they contaminate us with the impure, deceiving doctrine, and with their ungodly, carnal lives; that we do not partake of their unfruitful works, and for the reasons above assigned; and since we plainly see, that none can sooner contaminate and pollute us, than our own fathers, mothers, husbands, wives or children, if they are corrupted, and especially on account of the daily intercourse with, and natural love for them, which of necessity is existing between them; and moreover, since husband and wife are one flesh, I scarcely know, how they will escape the snares of death, if they do not especially observe the holy word and counsel of the Lord in this respect; for now they pray and sigh, and anon they rage and quarrel. Now they slander and defame, then they weep and lament. Ah! children, take warning. Their tears are crocodile's tears, and their tongues are set on fire from hell, as James says. I forbear to mention that some of them run after idolatry and false prophets, violently revile the holy word, sacraments and ordinances of Christ, and highly recommend the abominations of anti-christ, besides, the conduct of some of them is nothing but sheer avarice, pride, wantonness, eating and drinking to excess; and how scandalously some of them live with their poor wives, especially when they are intoxicated, I will leave the Lord to judge. And that any one could live in the midst of such wanton, carnal, ungodly abominations, and not be hurt in his faith, love and unction, and have intercourse with such abominable unclean, adhesive pitch vessels, and not be polluted in his conscience, I will leave all who have an understanding of the holy word, to reflect upon with the unction of the Spirit.

The *third reason* is, because Paul teaches us that we are, in the second place, to avoid the apostate, that he may be led to reflect upon, and to repent of his wicked life or sectarian doctrine, through the shame of such shunning. Knowing then, that this is the *ground* and *object* of the Holy Spirit, in regard to excommunication, as related; therefore it is also proper, and according to the Scriptures, that we, in this matter, implicitly follow his divine counsel, love, doctrine, good will and earnest commands, and obediently follow him and observe *it*, in true love, towards our most beloved father, mother, husband, wife and children, rather than towards others, because, I say, they are our dearest friends; yea, our own flesh and bone, and we cannot by any other salutary means, lead them from evil, and again lead them in the way of the saints. Reflect upon what we teach you.

The *fourth reason* is, because we certainly know that there is but one excommunication in the Scriptures, which does not only extend to the spiritual communion, such as the Lord's Supper, and the hand and kiss of peace; but it extends also to the bodily communion, such as eating, drinking, daily actions and conduct, 1 Cor. 5: 10, 11, and that if the father is to shun the son, or the son the father, the husband his wife, or the wife the husband, only in the spiritual communion, and not in natural communion, in that event there would be two kinds of excommunications in the Scriptures; the one would only extend to the spiritual communion, and the other, both to the spiritual and natural communion; this is clear as daylight. Again, reflect upon what we teach you.

The *fifth reason* is, because pious parents, as well as the church, consent and approve of the excommunication of the apostate children; and the pious children consent that the apostate parents should be excommunicated; and the husband consents that the apostate wife should be excommunicated, and the pious wife, that the apostate husband be excommunicated, and that they be severally dealt with according to the Scriptures; and if they would then afterwards shun them only in spiritual communion, they would make void their own sentence, which they in common with the church pronounced; and thus they would not seek the salvation of their dearest friends with that spiritual love and zeal with which the word and Spirit of the Lord command them, and they would still be in great danger of perdition. In order, unmolestedly to escape this, their excommunication has been commanded, taught and left on record in the word of the Lord, to every man, woman and child, without exception. Again, I say, reflect upon what we teach you.

The *sixth reason* is, because I have known no less than three hundred married persons in my time who did not observe the ordinance, counsel, doctrine, will and command of the Lord and his apostles concerning shunning, and thus run together into perdition. We stand dismayed O God! at the thought that such an evil may in part be ascribed to our silence. We will, therefore, endeavor to so act, in the future, while the care of the church is unworthily entrusted to us, as to prevent, in a measure, all corruption and apostasy, according to apostolic doctrine and counsel; and freely, purely and fully teach and maintain the ordinance of excommunication, as well between parents and children, man and wife, as among others; to all our brethren, if circumstances require it, in order that we, in the first place, clear our own souls, and thus stand acquitted before God and his saints in the great day of Christ; and secondly, So that none can excuse himself and say, It was never told me.

Behold, chosen brethren in the Lord, *these* are the important articles and principal *reasons* which urge us most that we willingly teach this *doctrine*, and put it into practice. Is there now a single individual under the canopy of heaven, learned or unlearned, young or old, without or among us, man or woman, who can truthfully teach us that the espousals of the spirit, made with Christ, through faith, should yield to human wedlock? Or that a husband cannot deceive or corrupt his wife, or a woman her husband? Or that a pious man is not bound according to the Scriptures, to promote the salvation of his unconverted wife, or the wife, of her unconverted husband? Or that there are two excommunications in the Scriptures; that the one only extends to the spiritual church, and the other both to the spiritual and temporal? Or that the pious husband dare not vote with the church to exclude his impenitent wife, or the wife against the husband in excluding him? Or that there is an exception in the whole Scriptures of man or wife, parents or children, in this respect? Or that spiritual love has to yield to conjugal love? If so, then we desire with all the heart to abandon this our doctrine, and acknowledge our error, and with great zeal teach the contrary before the whole world, as is christian-like and right; for we regard neither slander, nor praise, honor, nor disgrace; but we have only regard for the honor of God and Christ, and the eternal salvation of your souls; on account of which, we are considered by many as the off-scourings and filth of the world.

But if this cannot be done, as it never can, then in the first place, my sincere prayer, and fraternal admonition, is to all who might have erroneous views of this matter, that they would not improperly meddle through impure and perverted minds, by slandering the chief stone and the builders; nor that they would persuade any to disobey the word, or keep them in the dangers of apostacy and perdition, lest they make themselves guilty of other men's sins; but that they would give the good will and ordinance of the Lord, due honor and praise in this respect; pluck out the offending eye of their misunderstanding, and pass a sound judgment according to truth; avert sin from the church, and thus observe the incontrovertibly clear word, counsel and command of the Lord, with all the pious, and assist with all deliberation to maintain it.

Secondly, I entreat all who might be at all concerned about the slanders of the irrational, that they would view the matter impartially in a divine light, and consider that not only excommunication is hated by the world but also all the doings of Christ, such as the true evangelical baptism, Lord's Supper, life and the whole divine service; yea, they are considered as an abomination, scandal and disgrace, and they, out of mere hatred of truth, are not ashamed to call all the pious, accursed heretics, anabaptists, ringleaders, whores and knaves; and in many places deprive them of possessions and life, as may be seen, although the pious are so much honored of God, that he acknowledges and adopts them as his chosen children, as his sons and daughters; as the apple of his eye; as his bride and spouse; and endues them with the gift of eternal life. For there is nothing under the canopy of heaven, that they love more than their God, as they fully testify and make known by their actions. And thus it is in this matter. For how can there be a greater love for God, and how can there be found a more praise-worthy confession, than where one is willing and ready, not only to give up his temporal goods, ease, honor and happiness, but also to shun his dearest friends upon earth in full health, out of sincere regard to Christ, in obedience to his eternal and holy truth? No abominable slander nor disgrace becomes the pure knowledge of God nor the unfeigned obedience of his most holy word.

Thirdly, I entreat all dear brethren in general, that they would always consider with wise and sober minds, to what end they bent their shoulders under the pleasing yoke of the living and Almighty God, so that they may act and walk in a becoming manner, in the most holy covenant of grace, before Him and all mankind; and live and walk with their consorts in such piety, love, union and peace; and with such fidelity and care, observe that hereafter in eternity, we have not to hear of excommunication or exclusion; but of sincere, christian piety, delight and divine joy. Reflect upon these things which we teach you.

Fourthly, I entreat all, whose lot it should be at any time, to be afflicted with this sore punishment, that they would wisely examine themselves in the pure fear of God, that they would not seek the solicitous, selfish, lazy and idle flesh above Christ, nor cover it with fig-leaves, lest the wrath of the Lord who hates all lies, hypocrisy and subtle roguery, punish them with blindness and perversion, and assign them their portion with hypocrites; but that they might, by virtue of true faith in Christ Jesus, valiantly overcome themselves, and obediently and fully observe what the Holy Spirit of the love of Christ has commanded and taught by his holy word in this regard. Ah! let us reflect upon this.

Finally, I entreat elders, teachers, ministers and deacons, in the love of Christ, that they would not teach this whole matter carelessly and irrationally; but teach and inculcate it in the full fear of God, and with christian deliberation and paternal solicitude, in a true, apostolic manner; not too hastily, nor too slowly; not too rigidly nor too leniently; lest they seethe a kid in its mother's milk; but that they take of the first green ears of their land, dry them by the heavenly fire of pure, unfeigned love, and beat them into pieces in the mortar of the holy word, and pour upon them the oil of the Holy Ghost, which makes us willingly obedient unto Christ; pour upon them the sweet smelling frankincense of a sincere and firm faith from which all must result, to be a sweet savor to the Lord; and thus bring Him an acceptable meat-offering in his holy temple. Lay to heart, in true love, the ground of my admonition.

5. *That we are to put away from the*

church the openly offensive, carnal sinners, and excommunicated of God, and thus direct them to true repentance with the Scriptures. BEFORE I proceed to explain this article, I would earnestly admonish the reader, that about eighteen years ago, I published an admonition, in which I made no distinction of sin; but through my inexperience, directed them without discrimination, to three different admonitions. I say inexperience; for to the best of my knowledge, I neither heard nor knew at that time, any thing of fornication, adultery, and such like, among the brethren; it appeared to me impossible, that those who entered with us upon the paths of righteousness, should have any desire or will to such gross abominations, and therefore, I did not earnestly reflect upon the matter. See, before God it is the truth which I write.

I likewise wrote a book in 1549, in reply to those who would only extend excommunication to the spiritual church, and who charged us on all sides with slanderous words, that we practiced a rigid, cruel, unmerciful and Pharisaic excommunication.

Finally, I wrote a few words against Gellius Faber; and to this day I have made no particular distinction thereof, in my writings, nor could I have made it. This I acknowledge openly; for my information of it was too limited, so long as the matter was not disputed and did not again present itself to me for reconsideration. But now, having heard the ground of dispute, and having carefully weighed all the circumstances connected with it, in the balance of the holy, divine word, the six following reasons have given me such a powerful assurance in the matter, the Helper of all distressed souls be praised for his grace, that we are to exclude from the holy church of the Lord, all offensively carnal sinners, such as fornicators, adulterers, drunkards, &c.; and that all these ought to be put to open shame and reproof, with their ungodly works, without previously admonishing them, by virtue of the holy, divine word; that they may be led to repentance, I say by virtue of the word, for, in the first place, it is evident, as Paul teaches, that "neither fornicators nor idolators, nor adulterers, nor effeminate, nor abusers of themselves with mankind, nor thieves, nor covetous, nor drunkards, nor revilers, nor extortioners, shall inherit the kingdom of God," 1 Cor. 6: 10, but that their portion will be eternal death in the lake of fire.

Since then, it is clear, that the condemnation of God is already pronounced against them by his eternal Spirit and powerful word, both in heaven and upon the earth; that they have excluded themselves, and by their ungodly works, forsaken the church, that they are not as they were before, flesh of Christ's flesh, and members of his holy body, but have become carnal and devilish; yea, as dogs and swine, and again servants of sin; therefore we would, in fact, declare as void and unjust, the righteous judgment of the great and Almighty God, pronounced by his own Spirit and word, through his holy apostles, against such abominable defilers, if we would still admonish those who are already the children of the devil, hold them as brethren, and salute them with the peace of the Lord, and treat such miserable wretches as the children of God, and joint heirs of Christ, at the mere promise to do better, without any evidence of true repentance. I desire, that we might all impartially, and in the fear of God, reflect how such a great despising of Christ and his righteous judgment, could stand according to the Scriptures.

In the second place, it is evident that all those who are envious of us, are assiduously bent upon finding but a mote in us, because they so despitefully hate us for the truth's sake, in order that they may magnify it into a beam and defame us grossly. If we were to acknowledge such open, offensive disgrace, and receive as brethren such God-forsaken defilers, without evident fruits of sincere repentance, on a mere promise, which is, perhaps, more the result of shame and hypocrisy, than the fear of God, and break with them the peaceable, blessed bread of the Lord's Holy Supper, and thus by actions evince that they are joint members of our church; then we would, undoubtedly, expose the fair bride, honored in Christ, to all the ungodly as a disgrace and scoff to all our enemies. May the gracious Lord preserve us from this, that we may never think of it, much less do so. Take notice of this.

In the third place, it is evident, that with these three admonitions concerning such gross, offensive abominations, we would make many great hypocrites; for I hear that there were some within a few years, who carried on their horrible roguery and infamy in secret, till time and circumstances could no longer conceal them; yea, as I have understood, if some of them had not been detected by great wisdom, they would, I fear, have continued in their old course; but as soon as it was disclosed they began to wail and weep. Who could ever be so blinded, that when he has disgraced his neighbor's wife, daughter or maid, or robbed him of his money, and being seized, spoken to and admonished, that he would not say, I am sorry that I did so. Since then that experience teaches us the longer the more, as heard, therefore it is also proper and consistent with the Scriptures, that we should not foster and countenance such shameless defilers, much less are we to cherish them in their ungodly actions and wicked career with false prophets, but direct them where the Holy Spirit through the Scriptures direct and place them, namely outside of the church; so that we do not derogate from the Lord's sentence, pronounced in his word, against such people, that the community of grace, the unleavened lump of Christ, the anointed King and Priest of God, may continue to be agreeable and dignified; and also, that the transgressors may be brought sincerely to repent before God and the church, and may again present their offering and gift with a clean, pure, new conscience, as the truly sanctified saints of Christ, to the altar of reconciliation in his holy temple. Ah! reflect upon what we teach.

In the fourth place, it is evident that Paul teaches us that we are to shun a heretic, after we have admonished him twice, if he will not amend, Tit. 3: 10. Since then, we are not urged by the Holy Spirit to reprove a man more than once or twice, some of whom are outwardly yet quite pious, and perhaps some of them know no better, but suppose they are in the right, why beloved, are we then to admonish those thrice, who are not ashamed to sin against God's powerful word, but also against the law of nature? Who premeditatedly disgrace their neighbor's wife, daughter or maid? Who frequent riotous taverns and houses of ill fame? Or those who are perfidious in their dealings? In short, all those are sentenced to eternal death, by the Spirit and word of the Lord, if they will not repent as heard.

It would, according to my opinion, be very unbecoming, if we rightly reflect upon it, that we should run after those who are already condemned, to admonish them thrice before separation should take place; and though they regard not the first and second admonition, that we should still hold them as brethren in the church till the third time; and that if they would even then evince that they were sorry, they should remain brethren; if not, that it should then be told them before the church, out of the word of God, that they had no more fellowship with Christ, but are accursed according to the Scriptures. All who are taught of God, I will let judge how such doctrine and conduct could stand the test of the justice and word of the Lord.

In the fifth place, it is evident, so far as I am able to judge, that holy Paul wrote his first epistle to the Corinthians with such a view, as related; for he says, "I have written unto you not to keep company, if any man that is called a brother be a fornicator, or covetous, or an idolater, or a railer, or a drunkard, or an extortioner; with such a one no not to eat," 1 Cor. 5: 11. He does not even mention one admonition, much less two or three; but he says, "A little leaven leaveneth the whole lump," which is undoubtedly true; for facts have more than satisfactorily proven how often the pious, on their account, are considered rather as an offensive savor, who should otherwise be a sweet savor, were it not for those shameful members.

In the sixth place, it is evident, that Paul did not only thus teach this doctrine; but also showed it by an open example to the unclean Corinthian who sat with his stepmother in a very unbecoming manner; for without any previous admonition he judged him according to his ungodly works, and excommunicated him, by the word and Spirit of the Lord, from the church, and delivered him unto satan, into whose hands he had already fallen through his unnatural, detestable incontinency, in order that through this severe sentence and open shame, he might mortify and bury his unclean, shameful flesh, with its carnal lusts, and that his soul might be saved in the day of the Lord, and was not received again before the term of a year or longer, as history informs us, till they saw that he sincerely repented, and feared lest he might be swallowed up with over much sorrow.

And it would, according to my opinion, be proper that we should not so soon again admit such carnal defilers, who have beyond measure defamed the holy word, and brought such great tribulation upon the pious with their ungodly, abominable disgrace, though they may seemingly lament and promise much; but examine more closely the fruits of their repentance for some time; for it is not always repentance, though they say, We have sinned! but repentance is a converted, changed, pious and new heart, a broken and contrite spirit, from which flow the tears of sincerity, a candid confession, a true departure from the evil of our ways, an earnest and sincere hatred of sin, and an unblamable, pious, christian life; this is repentance that will stand before God. I entreat you to learn rightly to know both repentance and sin. Take heed thereto.

Behold, faithful brethren, here you have my most important Scriptures, discourses and reasons which moved me more deeply to reflect upon this matter in the fear of God. I say again, as I did above, in speaking of the separation of husband and wife: If there is one under the canopy of heaven, let him be whomsoever he will, that can convince me with divine truth, that a secret or open fornicator, adulterer, drunkard, &c., is a member of the holy body of the Lord, until he has been admonished two or three times (observe this well); or that the sentence of the Holy Spirit pronounced by Paul, and through many other Scriptures, against such deadly abominations, depends upon the condition of two or three admonitions, or that we have no cause to fear that the pious would be exposed to ridicule and slander if we had no other evidence of repentance than a mere verbal promise; or that we may, by the power of keys, retain those whom God has already excluded by the word of his truth; or that it is consistent with the Scriptures that the church may, with the Holy Spirit and word of Christ, in such cases as mentioned, judge uncertainties, I mean without evident repentance, and retain and salute as brethren the hypocrites as well as the righteous; or that the church may also, truthfully, proclaim the grace, mercy and peace of God and eternal life, by the authority of the Scriptures, to those who are under his displeasure, curse, wrath and sentence of eternal death, on account of their deadly and wicked deeds; or that the abomination or sin which caused them to be excommunicated, does not lead them to death; or that the Spirit of grace through a sincere faith and true repentance, which avail with God, does not assure the transgressor more of the promise than the outward association with the church; if he can convince us of all this, we desire then cordially to follow him, and change and renounce our views.

But if this cannot be done, as it never can be, I therefore entreat all who are concerned, that they would not liken themselves unto vain comforts and false prophets, who strengthen the hands of the wicked, daub the wall with untempered mortar, and teach peace, peace, where there is no peace, Ezek. 13: 10, but that they would leave the sentence of the Lord which proceeded from his divine righteousness, unbroken; and tear the deceptive bolsters and pillows from under the heads of the ungodly, and keep clean and pure the holy vineyard, city, house, temple, body and church of Christ, as much as in them lies, that they may build upon a sure foundation, and direct the impenitent sinners to repentance, as heard. Deal faithfully, reflect upon these things and learn wisdom.

6. *Of secret sinners, who are again inwardly admonished of the Holy Ghost and are sincerely and truly converted.* The full desire of my heart is, that each one would so fear and know God as to say in spirit and truth with David, "Whither shall I go from thy Spirit? Or whither shall I flee from thy presence? If I ascend up into heaven, thou art there; If I make my bed in hell, behold, thou art there; If I take the wings of the morning, and dwell in the uttermost

parts of the sea, even there shall thy hand lead me, and thy right hand shall hold me; if I say, Surely the darkness shall cover me; even the night shall be light about me; yea, the darkness hideth not from thee; but the night shineth as the day; the darkness and the light are both alike to thee; for thou hast possessed my reins; thou hast covered me in my mother's womb," Ps. 139: 7—13. And with Isaiah, "Woe unto them that seek deep to hide their counsel from the Lord, and their works are in the dark, and they say, Who seeth us? And who knoweth us?" Isa. 29: 15. Observe this denunciation, "Woe unto them," &c.

Chosen brethren, take heed; none under the canopy of heaven, can so conceal himself that he cannot be seen by the flaming eyes of the Lord, or not be found by the avenging hand of his wrath in his wickedness. Yea, the least thought is not concealed in our hearts which is not open to the eyes of the Lord. I, therefore, warn all in general, that you with all your powers watch against sin, whether secret or open; if sin is not sincerely repented of, your portion will be eternal death. Let all the impenitent and heedless sinners reflect upon this.

This I write to all beloved brethren as a christian warning, that you may fear the Lord's sentence, both openly and privately, and carefully avoid sin. Though we may not be reproved or seen of men here, still we cannot escape the eyes and punishment of God! Ah! that we all understood this.

However, should it ever happen that any one should sin against God in private, from which may his power preserve us all, and should the spirit of grace, which works repentance, again operate upon his heart, and cause genuine repentance, of this we have not to judge; for it is a matter between him and God. For since it is evident that we do not seek our righteousness and salvation, the remission of our sins, satisfaction, reconciliation and eternal life in or through excommunication, but alone in the righteousness, intercession, merits, death and blood of Christ. There are but two objects and ends why the ban is commanded in the Scriptures, which can have no reference to such an one. Because, in the first place, his sins are private; hence no offence can follow. And secondly, because he is in deep contrition and is penitent in life. Therefore, he has no need then of being brought to repentance. Nor are we any where commanded of Christ to put him to open shame before the church. Reflect upon these things.

7. *What is the true sense of the passage in Matt. 18, where Christ says, "If thy brother shall trespass against thee,"* &c. Our only and eternal High Priest and Teacher Jesus Christ, undoubtedly knew our poor, imperfect and feeble nature, that if we are not watchful, we would often fall into errors towards our neighbor, and therefore does he teach and say, "If thy brother shall trespass against thee, go and tell him his fault between thee and him alone; if he shall hear thee, thou hast gained thy brother; but if he will not hear thee, then take with thee one or two more, that in the mouth of two or three witnesses every word may be established; and if he shall neglect to hear them, tell it unto the church, but if he neglect to hear the church, let him be unto thee as a heathen man and a publican." Whereupon Peter asked him, "How oft shall my brother sin against me, and I forgive him? Till seven times?" Jesus saith unto him, "I say not unto thee, Until seven times; but, Until seventy times seven," Matthew 18: 15—17, 21, 22.

It is evident that these words of Christ teach, in the first place, that if any one should err or sin against his brother through negligence, infirmity, inconsiderateness, inexperience, or ignorance, that he should not, therefore, hate him in his heart; nor conceal or connive at his transgression; but out of true, brotherly love admonish and reprove him, lest his brother fall into greater errors and perish; but by this means reclaim him, and, as Moses says, not make himself guilty for his sins. It is the nature and disposition of christians not to hate any on account of his infirmities, but they seek with all their hearts how they may lead such an one in the true way of love by instructing him; for a true christian knows nothing of hatred.

In the second place, those words teach us that he, who has transgressed, should receive the admonition of his brother, in love

EXCOMMUNICATION.

and be again sincerely reconciled; as he teaches at an other place, and says, "Therefore, if thou bring thy gift to the altar, and there rememberest that thy brother hath aught against thee; leave there thy gift before the altar, and go thy way; first be reconciled to thy brother," Matt. 5: 23, 24. Here it is also the nature and disposition of the anointed, those who are born of the holy seed of divine love, that if they trespass against a brother, they have neither peace nor rest of conscience till they are again fully reconciled in Christ Jesus, and that without hypocrisy. For they are a seed and generation of peace, children of love, who manifest their christianity in full power; and testify by deeds that they know God. But those who do not so, have the words of Jesus to judge them. Although the first transgression may not be of itself a sin unto death; but in the course of time, it would cause the transgressor, if he regard not love, to become estranged and carnal, therefore he should bear such severe punishment on account of his wickedness. For it is evident that he, who despises his brother, rejects the affectionate admonition, acts against christian charity, despises the church of God, rejects the word of the Lord, would rather continue unreproved in his transgression, through his immovable stubbornness; rather walk in the crooked paths of the unrighteous; yea, sooner forsake the kingdom and people of Christ, than subdue his stubborn, proud flesh, and again be reconciled in love, according to the word of the Lord, with his brother against whom he transgressed. Paul rightly observes, "That to be carnally minded is death." Observe this.

In the third place, if the transgressing brother will sincerely receive, the brotherly admonition of his offended brother in love, be humbly reconciled, and afterwards ceases transgressing, then in that case he will no more remember, but sincerely forgive him, although he may have frequently sinned against him. Even as God for Jesus' sake, forgives all of our sins; so must we also forgive our neighbor all his transgressions in Christ, which he has committed against us. And we should not under any circumstances indulge in hatred or vengeance against him, although he should never reform. We have a true example in Christ, and Stephen, his witness. And it is also the nature and disposition of all the anointed, who are born of God, that they possess their souls in peace and patience, to keep pure and uncorrupted their conscience, their prayer unhindered, their love perfect, their faith sound and true, their minds firm and unwavering, no matter how we behave towards them.

From all of which it is more than clear that these three several admonitions of which Christ speaks, first between him and you alone; secondly before witnesses and thirdly, before the church, do not extend to all offensive, carnal sinners, over whom the eternal sentence of death is already pronounced; but it has reference only to the shortcomings between brother and brother, and that for the following seven, *reasons*.

First, he says, "If thy brother trespass against THEE," observe what he says, "AGAINST THEE," not AGAINST GOD; for all the sins he commits against you, you may forgive him, so far as respects *you;* but not as it respects *God*.

Secondly, he says, "Tell him his fault between *thee* and *him* alone." Observe, "between *thee* and *him* alone." And I trust that all who understand the holy word will assent that an open transgression or sin, requires no private admonition, but is to be publicly reproved.

Thirdly, he says, "That in the mouth of two or three witnesses every word may be established." Observe, that he says, "Two or three." And that an open transgression requires no witness, but is itself its own accuser and witness, is clear as the meridian sun.

Fourthly, he says, "Then tell it unto the church," observe, "unto the church." And for us to tell an open, well known disgrace to them, which is already known, is quite useless, to this all must assent who have understanding.

Fifthly, he also says in Luke 17, "And if he trespass against thee seven times in a day." Observe, he says, "Trespass." That now, any christian should commit a deadly sin against his brother, seven times in a day, not to say seventy times seven, is not possible; much less against God.

Sixthly, he says, "And seven times in a day turn again to thee, saying, I repent." Observe, he says, "Turn to thee seven times in a day." My opinion is that if any one were to come to us two or three times in a year, not to say daily, to pillage our chests or purses, or disgrace our wives, daughters or maids, and every time say, Ah, brother I repent, he would soon be told that he is a desperate rogue and an ungodly knave. Again, I say, Observe this.

Seventhly, he says, "Thou shalt forgive him." Observe, he says, "Thou shalt forgive him." And the Scriptures plainly teach that none can forgive sins (these are the ten thousand talents which were owing to the king), but God alone. And that we alone can pay the hundred pence that we owe our brother, as the Lord teaches in the parable with all plainness.

Behold, in this sense the Holy Scripture remains salutary unto us, and proceeds in its proper order when, where one brother trespasses against another, three admonitions are given before excommunication, Matt. 18: 15—18, to a heretic one or two, Tit. 3: 10, and to an open, offensive, sensual sinner, who is already condemned by the word of God, none at all, 1 Cor. 5; 2 Cor. 13.

Do impartially, and in love, reflect upon what the Scriptures say, without hypocrisy.

8. *That we are not to pervert the truth with David's sin, repentance and remission; but have to understand it rightly according to Scripture.* It is evident that abominable, carnal sins, such as fornication, adultery and the like, generally arise from blindness of heart; that they are committed premeditatedly; are the result of unclean, inflamed passions and carnal lusts; notwithstanding the beginning of them may have taken their rise apparently from infirmity. Of this we have a true example in David, although he was a man after God's own heart, and by virtue of his faith slew the giant, Goliath, whom all Israel dreaded, and rescued the lamb from the jaws of lions and bears, yet he was so captivated in his flesh by the sight of his eyes that he sinned greatly; for as soon as he consented, sin was committed, and his heart, which was before a temple of the Holy Ghost, was so blinded and bewitched, that he, without any dread, fell into one deadly sin and wickedness after another; yea, as appears, he never once thought of the Lord who saved him from so many dangers, and called him to such distinguished honor, and endowed him with such a precious spirit. For when it was told him of Bath-sheba, that she was with child to him, he sought to hide his flagrant act; he had Uriah called from the field and pretended as if he wished to consult him in relation to the war, admonished him twice, that he should go into his house; why he did so, is well understood. Afterwards he invited him to a feast, pretending as if he was sincere; so that he might make him drunk, and have him go in unto his wife and cover David's shame. But when he failed in all this, he gave this truly valiant man an ungodly, treacherous letter, that Joab should place him in such a point where the danger of being killed was greatest, so that he might be slain.

Behold, thus you see how one wicked act engendered another when he consented to the lusts of the eyes, and gave place to sin. Yea, he was blinded to such a degree in his inflamed flesh, and was so deeply involved in sin, that, according to the rigor of the law, had he not himself wielded the sceptre, he would have been two-fold guilty of the ban or curse of death; first, because he was an adulterer; secondly, because he was guilty of innocent blood.

He boldly continued in such abominations till the prophet came to him, and through a parable, so wisely reproved him that he pronounced his own sentence as worthy of death. When he heard the word of the prophet who appealed powerfully to his heart, he was moved, sought for grace, and without delay turned to God with a broken heart, and bitterly wept over his great sin, and confessed to the Lord that he had sinned against him; prayed and sighed painfully, and said, "Have mercy upon me, O God! according to thy loving kindness, according unto the multitude of thy tender mercies blot out my transgressions; wash me thoroughly from mine iniquity, and cleanse me from my sin." "Create in me a clean heart, O God; and renew a right spirit within me; cast me not away from thy presence; and take not thy Holy Spirit from me," Ps. 51: 1, 2, 10, 11. On account of which he was again comforted of the prophet, who said unto him, "The Lord also hath put away thy sin; thou shalt not die." Nevertheless, he had to endure a severe punishment on account of it, for, said Nathan, "Therefore the sword shall never depart from thine house; because thou hast despised me;" and the Lord said, "Behold, I will raise up evil against thee out of thine own house, and I will take thy wives before thine eyes, and give them unto thy neighbor, and he shall lie with thy wives in the sight of this sun;" because thou hast despised me. Observe, he says, "Because thou hast despised me," 2 Sam. 12.

And behold, thus the wantonness of David resulted in greatly despising God, and it was a grievous sin unto him. True are the words of James, "Then when lust hath conceived, it bringeth forth sin; and sin, when it hath finished, bringeth forth death," Jas. 1: 15.

Thus it is in the new state of things in Christ; for since we are not to punish the abominable, carnal transgressors with fire, stone or sword, as upright Israel did of old, but only by excommunication, as is well known to all who are taught of God; therefore, it behooves us to consign those with their wicked deeds, where the Scriptures direct them, namely, into death, and to the wrath of God, as holy Nathan did blood-guilty and adulterous David. They will then, under such a dread, severe sentence, which, according to the Scripture is pronounced upon them by exclusion, in true love, by the grace of God, go within their hearts, and are provoked, like penitent David, to true repentance; yea, that we may evidently see by all their words, works, and whole life in truth, that the gracious Father has again received and indued them with his Spirit, and pardoned their sins; then, and not till then, understand well what I say, have we the same word of promise whereby we can again comfort them and proclaim to them the grace of the Lord, namely, "The Lord also hath put away thy sin, thou shalt not die;" "thy sins are forgiven, go and sin no more;" for that a truly penitent person should be left unconsoled of God or man, is impossible. O, reflect on what has been quoted.

Thus it becomes us rightly to divide the Scriptures, that we do not make the sin, repentance and remission of David as an example of encouragement to the rash, blind world, that we do not receive, as brethren, the offensive, carnal sinners, namely, those who are banished of God, at a mere promise to reform; but they should show such repentance that the church may be satisfied of their sincerity. For we must not build upon uncertainties, and comfort in vain, but like Nathan, comfort when we see true repentance, if we would not wish to flatter sinners with lies, and derogate from the judgment of God, as heard.

9. *Of the inconsiderate backsliding, and immediate recovery of Peter.* Dearly beloved brethren, beware; we have shown and explained to you, that the abominable, carnal sins generally arise from the sudden enkindling of the passions, and so it can happen that sins may be committed through infirmities. Of this we have a true example in Peter; for when the Lord said to him, "Simon, Simon, behold satan hath desired to have you, that he may sift you as wheat; but I have prayed for thee, that thy faith fail not; and when thou art converted, strengthen thy brethren." To which he replied with much assurance: "Although all shall be offended, yet will not I." "Lord, I am ready to go with thee, both into prison and to death."

Peter was for venturing all with his Master, as he said; but as soon as he stood alone, he could not endure a single question put to him by a maid; he openly denied Christ, although the evening previous he said that he would die with him. Yea, he was so alarmed and frightened that he began to curse, and to swear that he did not know Christ.

O God! there lay the upright, bold Peter, the firm rock, broken. Although he had been taught of the heavenly Father and honored by Christ, the beloved Son of God, with the promise of the keys of the kingdom of heaven, nevertheless, he could not endure but such a faint blow. Behold, thus man is nothing, poor, miserable, sick and impotent, especially in so great need, if he is not strengthened by the Spirit of God. But what was it? Peter had to learn to know what that man is, who depends upon his own strength, and not in the full fear of God, upon Christ and his grace. Besides he learned how to be compassionate and merciful towards his poor, fallen brother, who would again be heartily converted and rise without hypocrisy from his fall.

It appears to me that this may justly be called an unexpectedly precipitate error in Peter. For he entertained not a single thought before, that he would deny his Lord and Savior. And he also rose in the very hour, went out and wept bitterly, and on the third day he was again comforted with the gospel by the holy angels of the Lord.

Observe, brethren, how Paul teaches, "Brethren, if a man be overtaken" (observe, he says overtaken), "in a fault, ye which are spiritual, restore such a one in the spirit of meekness; considering thyself, lest thou also be tempted," Gal. 6: 3.

Chosen brethren in the Lord, I would then most affectionately entreat you by the words of Paul and the fall of Peter, and admonish you faithfully in Christ Jesus, that you would by all means, discriminate, by the spirit of wisdom, between backsliding and remaining in that condition. For if any one continues in a sin, upon which eternal death depends, he is already condemned by the Scriptures. But if any one falls into it unwarily, of him the prophet says, "Shall they fall and not arise?" And as Paul says, "Restore such a one." It is, therefore, just and right that we be truly circumspect; that we do not depress too much a poor, broken-hearted sinner, who would willingly be restored and rescued from his deplorable condition; but we must, in christian meekness, tender him the hand of charity, lift him up and help him to bear his burden as much as we can, and as far as our consciences and the word of God permit. Ah! take heed, be not too rash in such a case, lest you may also be tempted or overcome, as Paul says. Let holy Peter be an admonition to you, in order that you will not lose yourselves in your proud minds. "For if a man think himself to be something, when he is nothing, he deceiveth himself," Gal. 6: 3. In short, "Let him that thinketh he standeth, take heed lest he fall," 1 Cor. 10: 12. For the snares are more numerous than we are aware; those who would wish to escape them must be dead to sin, regenerated and true christians, be constant in prayer, be circumspect, watch assiduously, and must be led and influenced by the Holy Ghost, else they are already in the snare of death. Ah! let us reflect upon this.

Let every one examine himself fully, whether he has not sinned before God since his conversion, and became a faulty vessel. He that may think he is free, let him cast the first stone. But he that does not find himself altogether free, let him, with Peter, strengthen his weak brother, who, perhaps, has not sinned half so heinously.

Since then, it is manifest, that to *fall*, and to *remain* in that condition, and presumptuously to sin, are different; therefore, will I leave such sins, on account of which the people of the Lord are grieved, if such should be the case, to the spirit, unction, deliberation, fear of God and love of the church, to look into with wisdom and understanding. If they deem it deserving excommunication, let them judge as the Scriptures teach. If they consider it not in that light, but only as a sin, unwarily committed, that they then restore the sinner or transgressor, with a spirit of meekness and love. This is my admonition with the faithful apostle, father, teacher and predecessor, the apostle Paul, to all the pious. These words are full of power and spirit, "Considering thyself, lest thou also be tempted."

10. *How we should understand, according to the Scriptures, the saying of James, "If any of you do err from the truth,"* &c., Jas. 5: 19. In the first place, the rational law of nature teaches us, that if one sees the house or goods of his neighbor on fire, or sees his neighbor sick, or his body, his wife, his children or his cattle needing assistance, he must willingly render him aid, and extend his hand to his neighbor, in time of need.

Again, Moses says, "Thou shalt not see thy brother's ox or his sheep go astray, and hide thyself from them; thou shalt in any case bring them unto thy brother," Deut. 22: 1.

Thirdly, Christ says, "What man of you, having a hundred sheep, if he loose one of them, doth not leave the ninety and nine in the wilderness, and go after that which is lost until he find it," Luke 15: 4.

Observe then, how the law of nature, of Moses and of Christ, teaches us such great love and discretion, not towards men alone, but towards our temporal goods, and to our creatures, so it is proper that we, who are born of the holy seed of love, should seek for the soul of our neighbor, whose feet we see upon the way of sin, which leads to death. Thus James says, "Brethren, if any of you do err from the truth, and one convert him, let him know that he which converteth the sinner from the error of his way, shall save a soul from death, and shall hide a multitude of sins," James 5: 19, 20.

Here we would entreat all pious hearts, for Jesus' sake, that they would make a distinction between those who ignorantly err, and those who willingly go in the way of death, in order that the word of James be not construed so as to become a false comfort and support, to wanton and benighted sinners; for it is clear, that they are already condemned to death by the Scriptures, as we frequently have observed; but when any of our Father's little ones, Christ's sheep err, and begin to turn their ears to false doctrine, which is adorned with fair words, who suffer themselves, through their lusts, to be led from the truth, and begin to set their feet upon the broad way, and bow their hearts, again to covetousness, pride, haughtiness, &c., entertain inordinate desires for the property, wives, daughters, maids or the ungodly, vain company of their neighbors, become old and weak in their faith, dislike the truth and err grievously, and yet suppose that they go upon the right way, such erring ones, we should not suffer to be lost, but should seek them with all our power and might, not with one or two admonitions only, as is done with heretics, Tit. 3, nor but three times, as is the case in a dissension between brother and brother, Matt. 18, but as often as the Lord gives spirit and grace, till they again conform, in all things to the truth, depart from their errors, and enter upon the right way, or till they become as ravening, biting dogs or unclean swine. Yes, my brethren, whoever can, with the truth, reclaim such a poor, erring sinner, lead him from the way of error, and bring him back to the fold of Christ, rescues his soul from death, and covers a multitude of sins, with which, alas, he was already too much stained. From whom? From men, or from God? Not from men, but from God; for it is impossible to hide from men that which they see, and which happens before them; as adultery, fornication, murder, open idolatry, drunkenness, &c. The idolatry of Aaron, with the golden calf, the misconduct of David with Uriah and Bathsheba, and the denial of Peter are examples. For although they repented, and their sins were covered from the sight of God, yet were they manifest to the whole world as admonitions and warnings, and as examples of his grace over all who truly repent; of this covering of sin, David spake, "Blessed is he whose transgression is forgiven, whose sin is covered. Blessed is the man unto whom the Lord imputeth not iniquity," Ps. 32: 1, 2.

I will now leave to the godly for reflection, whether these words of James as here expounded, are not salutary; for those worthy of exclusion would be excluded, the erring be sought, love would exert its full power, the penitent would be rescued from death. Both their open and secret sins would be covered before God, and all would proceed according to the Scriptures. In true love observe what is the mind of the holy word.

11. *How the latter part of the twelfth, and the beginning of the thirteenth chapter of the second epistle to the Corinthians, are to be understood.* We find by Paul's epistle to the Corinthians, that there were many parties and sects among that people. Some boasted that they were of Cephas, others of Paul, and others again, of Apollo. On this account, Paul reproved them in love, and admonished them to be one in Christ. He writes also in the eleventh chapter of the same epistle, "When ye come together in the church, I hear that there be divisions among you, and I partly believe it, for there must be also heresies among you, that they which are approved may be made manifest among you." There were also some among them who said there was no resurrection, 1 Cor. 11: 18, 19; 15: 12; therefore, he also

feared that when he came, he would not find them as he desired, nor that they would find him as they desired; lest more dissension than union, more malice than love, more wrath than meekness, more strife than peace, more whispering than rebuking of wickedness, more pride than humility, more tumult than quiet, should be found among many. Such is commonly the condition where the high and proud of heart, who neither know nor love the peaceful, humble Spirit of Christ, are highly esteemed, and have attained authority over the plain, simple people. Who regard the adornment of words more than spirit and power. This I write in upright, undissembled love, without regard to party. God grant us grace to enable us to perceive it.

Again, we find that there were some impenitent amongst them such as selfish, covetous, contentious, fornicators, incontinent and unchaste. Therefore he feared that when he came, he would have great sorrow on account of those who had already sinned before, and not repented of their lewdness and unchastity. For it is manifest that lewdness at that time was so prevalent among the gentiles, that the holy apostles admonished and counseled the brethren among the heathen, in a common council, as may be seen from Acts 15; Rom. 1; 1 Cor. 5, 6, 7.

It is evident, that, at that time, some were very little concerned about the lewdness and dissensions, which were so prevalent, that the apostolic excommunication was not very rigidly enforced. This may be seen from Paul's own words, and reproving, to wit, "Ye are puffed up," &c., 1 Cor. 5: 2.

Through their heedless disobedience, they permitted the good and evil to exist among them, so that the faithful man of God upbraided them sharply, saying, "This is the third time I am coming to you. In the mouth of two or three witnesses shall every word be established. I told you before, and foretell you, as if I were present, the second time; and being absent now, I write to them which heretofore have sinned, and to all other, that if I come again, I will not spare," 2 Cor. 13: 1, 2. These hard words of Paul testify clearly that in that time, although such wicked persons, as fornicators, unchaste, sectarians, &c., were held in communion, yet they did not regard his writings concerning the Ban; for it is plain if the historian rightly testifies, that some years had passed away before Paul made his last journey to them, and it is against all Scripture and reason to suppose that they, in the mean time, admitted these persons with Paul's consent. It is manifest that he rebuked all iniquity both with word and writing, and directed to the ban, as had been related, yet the foul leaven which was against the holy, divine word, and which disgraced the church, they did not put away. He wrote and expressed his meaning by these words, that all those who oftentimes had sinned and had not repented, and those who sinned more recently, that if he would come the second time, that if he should find one or the other, testified to by two or three witnesses that they have been guilty of ungodliness, that he would not then spare him. Observe this.

It is also manifest that he did not write this rebuke privately to this one or that one, but openly to a whole church, in a common epistle, that the disobedient might be rebuked, as we, unworthily, at times write, and teach the word of the Lord, and there is not a syllable which tells us to admonish such once, twice or thrice, but to reprove them in round terms; that if he came, he would make known to them their merited punishment. His words are firm and immovable, that we shall not eat, or have fellowship with fornicators, idolators, &c. O! reflect upon what the Scriptures say, 1 Cor. 5.

12. *It is our duty to pass the sentence and judgment of Christ without blame, according to the Scriptures, and to make use of his keys in a proper manner.* Chosen brethren in the Lord, forasmuch, then, as I have seen in my day much ignorance and misapprehension displayed by many in regard to this point, some of whom, in my humble opinion, were too rigorous, while others were too lenient and remiss, in consequence of which some of our members have been affected, alas! with no little sorrow. And as I have now faithfully explained the true apostolic excommunication, in pure, unadulterated love without partiality, therefore, I am further impelled by the same love to offer a few remarks upon the keys and their appurtenant

use, inasmuch as they pertain to the excommunication; so that no one, misled by ignorance, may with anti-christ presumptuously place himself in Christ's seat, nor follow and execute his own judgment, design and resolution, but those of Christ, his Lord, and the doctrine, ordinance and commandment of the holy apostles, without any regard to the flesh, party or self-wisdom, lest he should reject him whom God saves by his grace, and retain him, whom he in his righteousness rejects; for, to him alone pertains the right of binding and loosing, as we shall hear more fully in the sequel. Therefore, consider our quotations.

It is to be observed, in the first place, that there are two heavenly keys, namely, the key of binding, and the key of loosing; even as the Lord said to Peter, "I will give unto thee the key of the kingdom of heaven, and whatsoever thou shalt bind on earth, shall be bound in heaven; and whatsoever thou shalt loose on earth, shall be loosed in heaven," Matt. 16: 19. At another time, and after his resurrection from the dead, he spoke in a similar manner to his disciples, "Receive ye the Holy Ghost; whosesoever sins ye remit, they are remitted unto them; and whosesoever sins ye retain, they are retained," John 20: 22, 23.

In the second place, we must observe that the key of binding is nothing else than the word and righteousness of God, the directing, demanding, constraining, terrifying and condemning law of the Lord, by and through which all are locked up under the curse, sin, death, and the wrath of God, who do not by faith receive Christ, the only and eternal means of grace, hear his voice and follow and obey his will.

Again, On the other hand, the key of loosing is the abundantly cheering and delightful word of grace, the pardoning, consoling and unbinding gospel of peace, by and through which all those are delivered from the curse, sin, death and the wrath of God, who, with regenerated, new, converted, voluntary, rejoicing and believing hearts, receive Christ in power and with a firm confidence in his innocent blood and death, fear, love, hear, follow and obey him.

In the third place, it is to be observed that this binding key of Christ is given to his ministers and people for this purpose, namely, that by and through it they shall, in the power of the Spirit, represent unto all earthly, carnal, obdurate and impenitent persons, their great sins, unrighteousness, blindness and wickedness, together with God's righteous wrath, judgment, punishment, hell and everlasting death, and thus render them contrite, dismayed, humble, broken, penitent, dejected and sorrowful of heart before God, and little in their own eyes. Wherefore, it is compared in its power and virtues to the rod of the oppressor, a hard hammer, the north wind, a sorrowful singing, and sharp detergent wine, Isa. 9: 4; Jer. 23: 29; Cant. 4: 16.

Again, On the contrary, the key of loosing is given to the end that with it the ministers and people of God may direct such contrite, troubled, dejected, sorrowful and broken hearts, as beforementioned, which are enabled, by the first key, to feel and see the deep, mortal wounds, their great defects and the profound fascination in which they were held, to the spiritual, brazen serpent; to the throne of grace; to the open fountain of David; to the merciful, compassionate High Priest, our only and eternal Offering of reconciliation, Christ Jesus; and thus heal their dangerous, malignant and deadly abscesses, stripes and the venomous wound of the infernal serpent. It is, therefore, likened in strength and virtue to the cheering olive-branch of Noah's dove; the balm of Gilead; the voice of truth; the south wind; the joyful pipe, and sweet, soothing oil, Gen. 8: 11; Jer. 8: 22; Cant. 4: 16; Luke 10: 34.

In the fourth place, it must be observed that these keys are given to us from heaven, by him who created heaven, earth and the sea with the fullness thereof, the eternal power, word and wisdom of the Almighty Father; the King of all glory, our only and eternal Redeemer, Intercessor, Bridegroom, Prophet and Teacher, Christ Jesus. We may, therefore, with the greatest propriety, be careful in regard to the ban, with fear and trembling, and not be influenced by flesh and blood, hatred or love, favor or disfavor, enmity or friendship, strife, dissension or partiality; but should execute it in the fear of the Lord, as the earnest, heavenly command, word, and will of our Savior, in an upright, clear conscience without respect of persons. For without doubt they are precious keys since they are given us from heaven, as a present from such an illustrious friend. Ah! suffer yourselves to be told.

In the fifth place, it is to be observed that these keys are given to, and bestowed upon none but those who are anointed of the Holy Ghost, even as Christ says, "Receive ye the Holy Ghost," &c. From this it is evident that they must be a believing, true, penitent, sober, chaste, humble, upright, friendly, obedient, devout, peaceful, and spiritual people; observe, a people dead unto sin, a regenerated people, who sit with the apostles in the seat of righteousness, and pronounce with them the righteous judgment of the Lord, against all stiff-necked, ungodly sinners, and teach, admonish, chastise, punish, and, in real power, judge or bind with the word and Spirit of the Lord, the unbelieving, impenitent, earthly-minded, drunken, adulterous, lecherous, unchaste, proud, haughty, unrighteous, perverse, disobedient, quarrelsome, carnal sinners. For it is evident that a carnal man cannot understand the things of the Spirit of God; but they that are spiritual, examine and judge all things aright, yet they themselves are judged of no man. Yes, my brethren, it is utterly impossible for one carnal-minded man, or for one quarrelsome person to teach, instruct or chasten another correctly through the Spirit of Christ, or in the power of his word justly to separate him from his church according to the will of God. For their fruits plainly testify that they are both impenitent, destitute of the Spirit, nature, and disposition of Christ, and subject to death and the curse.

Therefore, fear God, and know how or what you judge. For if one should sentence a ban-deserving person, such as a fornicator, drunkard, or any other carnal transgressor, to excommunication, while he himself was wrathful, avaricious, proud, haughty, uplifted, ambitious, unchaste, lying, quarrelsome, impure, envious or false hearted, and would secretly continue in his wickedness, then, according to Paul, he would sentence his own soul, for he says, "Thou art inexcusable, O man whosoever thou art that judgest: for wherein thou judgest another thou condemnest thyself," Rom. 2: 1.

I therefore, counsel and admonish all the pious generally, who sit in judgment upon a sinner that is to be excommunicated, that they previously examine well their own conscience, heart and mind, and see whether they have the Spirit of Christ, whether they sit in the apostles seat, and also whether they do it out of pure fear of God, in obedience to his word, and out of sincere love to the brethren or out of flesh and blood through hypocrisy, to the will of men. For if they have not the Spirit of Christ, do not sit in the seat of the apostles and carry the keys of heaven, their judgment can not be of God, and will tear down more than build up. It is even in reality nothing but a sore judgment against their own souls. But if they have the Spirit of Christ, sit in the apostles seat and make use of the keys of heaven, their judgment will doubtless be righteous, will agree as the judgment of Christ, and they will not by any means make themselves guilty in passing judgment against the transgressor. Those who are born of Christ, may judge what I advance.

In the sixth place, it is to be observed that these keys must not be made use of, except in the name of Him who committed them to us, and by his power, that is with his Spirit and word, for He alone is the King and Prince of his church, the Shepherd, Teacher and Master of our souls, before whose sceptre we must all bow, and whose voice we must hear, if we would wish to be saved, as has been heard.

Since then he is both the Ruler and the Giver of this, and both the binding and loosing are in his hand, and must therefore be done in his name, with his Spirit and word alone, as related; therefore we may well take heed lest through our profaneness, inclination or foolish purpose, we loose those whom he himself has bound in heaven, or bind those whom he himself has loosed in heaven even as the sin of perdition and the man of sin, together with all his deceiving and impure prophets, O God, have done for many centuries. O, children take heed.

As far as concerns the key of binding of

this evangelic ban, it is clear that when an open fornicator or adulterer is convinced by two or three witnesses, or an abuser of himself, or an idolater, or a drunkard, or envied, or a perverse, self-willed disputer, or an impenitent, froward, lazy, fastidious and idle glutton, or a blasphemer, thief, robber or murderer, is brought before the church, they have the judging word of the Scriptures, by which they may separate and exclude him, and announce to him by the Spirit of Christ, that he is no longer a member of the body of Christ, has no more promise, but that he shall endure everlasting death, and fail of the kingdom of grace. In short that his final part and lot, unless he sincerely repents, shall be the burning lake of fire, hell and the devil. For his works show plainly that he is of the wicked one.

Behold, such are those over whom the first key has power. For the righteous judgment of God, and his firm, binding word, take hold of them, since they again forsake Christ; despise his holy word and covenant; live according to the flesh; stir up strife and dissention; break the bond of love; separate the pious; disquiet those of a gentle, peaceable disposition; introduce and establish offences and slanders, as the evident fact has frequently taught and as is known to many others, alas! as well as to myself. Ah me! what a severe stroke he receives who is bound by the people of God, with this dreadful key; and punished by his righteous Spirit, with this dreadful curse. O Father, grant them thy grace.

The same thing applies to the key of loosing in this use of the ban. For if a poor, proscribed sinner humble himself again before his God, heart broken and penitent, groans and weeps bitterly, experiences heartfelt sorrow for his sins and an earnest longing for the truth, hates perverse paths of the ungodly and walks again in the path of the pious. In short, if he conducts himself so in his whole life, that we cannot perceive any thing in him but that the Spirit of the Lord has again anointed him, and received him into his grace, and would have him included in the number of the Lord's people; they have then the cheering word of promise, by which they may again bring him to the altar of the Lord, sprinkle him with the spiritual hyssop of God, announce to him the grace of Christ, and receive him again as a beloved brother in Christ Jesus and greet him with the salutation of his holy peace. For, says the prophet, "Have I any pleasure at all that the wicked should die? saith the Lord God, and not that he should return from his ways, and live?" Ezek. 18: 23.

Forasmuch as it is manifest and established that Jesus Christ alone has the key of David, who unlocks heaven for the true penitent, unties the knot of unrighteousness and forgives and remits their sins; and again, as it is he who closes heaven against the impenitent, carnal sinners, binds them under his judgment and retains their sins, and we are nothing more than heralds, ministers and messengers in his name, and can make it neither longer nor shorter, narrower nor wider than taught us by his Spirit, and commanded us in his word, as heard, therefore it is evident, that they greatly err, who, in the pride of their ignorance, suffer themselves to think that they have power to retain or remit the sins of any man, or who with perverse, inconsiderate minds dare separate or excommunicate any one out of carnal motives, hatred or bitterness, and not purely and solely through the Spirit and word of Christ; or on the other hand, retain him through natural affection, friendship or partiality, contrary to the word of God and comfort him with uncertainties in his sins, winking at them; for with such, after the example of the false prophets, they strengthen the hands of the ungodly, since they retain them, and appear to adjudge their life, though without true repentance they shall not live. Ah! brethren beware.

I would, therefore, brethren and sisters, in the love of Christ, have you all faithfully admonished in God, that no one attempt, in this weighty, important and spiritual matter, to act higher or lower, severer or milder than the word and Spirit require, whether it be with the binding of the first key in righteousness unto eternal death, or with the loosing of the second key in grace unto eternal life; lest, by passing an unscriptural judgment, he offend against God and his neighbor, and so be constrained to undergo the punishment of his pride, along with the angel of the bottomless pit. Observe this!

Ah! most beloved brethren, to what an amazing extent, in my opinion, is that man taught of God, who is able in this thing so to keep the true, royal highway, that he can properly employ the intrusted keys in devout, heavenly wisdom, and correctly pass and impose his Lord's judgment with a sure, sealed conscience in true, apostolic measure, to the edification of all the pious. Let all who are born of God, who are impartial and pure in heart, reflect, with the unction of their spirit, upon the grounds of my writing and admonition.

CONCLUSION AND EXHORTATION TO ALL THE PIOUS.

BEHOLD, beloved brethren, with much trouble, pains and anxiety, I have now, in the infirmity of my declining years, added another small gift to the treasury of the Lord, not of the price of a dog, nor of the hire of a harlot, which was forbidden to Israel; but of the abundant benediction of my God, namely, from the settled principles of his truth. Though it is not to be compared in value or worth with the gold, silver, metal, silk, or precious stones of the offering, yet, if it be reckoned with the rams' skins, goats' hair, and shittim wood, I have already attained my wish. For my prayer and desire before God and his church is, that the living building of the heavenly tabernacles may advance with the greatest speed to the attainment of their intended splendor and magnificence. For this cause, I have suffered not a little hardship, affliction, sadness, poverty and reproach, so that I hope I may boast in my weakness with all the pious of God, apostles and prophets, yea, with Christ Jesus himself, that the zeal of the Lord's house hath eaten me up.

I would, therefore, earnestly desire all the pious, who, with a pure, unadulterated conscience, have drank the water of love out of the fountain of God, that they do not despise this gift, but that, with candid and discerning minds, they examine, as in the presence of God in Christ Jesus, its nature, principles, vigor, cogency and virtuous tendency; and having thus passed a sound, impartial judgment upon it, that you leave it unbroken in all its parts. For it is my valedictory which I now offer, as I take my leave of you all in this part, of the ban and retire to rest.

In this I have not sought the acquirement of human favor or honor, the indulgence of flesh, or the promotion of party purposes, but I have illustrated the principles of truth, confirmed the holy ordinance of the apostles, rendered due praise to the justice and mercy of God, assigning to each its part, have added nothing new, nor varied in the least from its principles of my plan, except that in consequence of much conversation with the pious, and meditation upon certain writings, as also on account of great dangers, actual occurrences, and heinous abominations, and in order to put a stop in some measure to all offensive, disgraceful actions, I have more deeply considered the excluding sentence of the flagrant, carnal sinner, and, in this way, placed it upon a more certain basis, as may be seen.

As we are well convinced that the depth of satan is to some but partially known and manifest, and as a consequence that he does great injury, by means of his subtle, pernicious wrangling and disputation, as may be seen; therefore, my first earnest request unto all, who are named after the name of Christ, is, that they would reflect soberly, judiciously and discreetly upon the nature, character, heart, mind, Spirit and disposition of Christ, and consider that all which he has commanded, left and taught his followers, is nothing but pure righteousness, truth, patience, love and peace. Also, that they bow their knees before him, and have received the token of his most holy covenant; that they should bury their former sinful life in his death; circumcise their hearts with his sharp word and Spirit; follow him, walk in all his ways, and be one with him in both the inward and the outward man, as taught in Scripture; also, that they reflect upon the high promise, and follow his word and will, in power and in truth. For he is such a God, that he does not take pleasure in outward shadows, ceremonies, types, bread, wine, water, and nominal service, but in spirit, deed and truth.

My second request is, that they would on the other hand, consider the nature, character, heart, spirit, mind, and work of satan, that he is from the beginning a shrewd, cunning deceiver, an impudent, wanton liar, and a revengeful murderer, a malicious envier of the honor and truth of God; a falseifier of his Holy Word, and a deadly enemy of pious souls; seditious, factious, unruly, schismatic, envious, perverse, and destitute of love; incapable of conceiving and bringing forth any thing but hatred, backbiting, lies, deception, jealousy, impurity of heart, vice and shame, and all in semblance of the truth. In *semblance* of the *truth*, I repeat, for although he is the infernal satan, beelzebub, belial, behemoth, leviathan, the angel of the bottomless pit, the prince of darkness, the old serpent, and the very devil himself, yet it is manifest, notwithstanding, that he has the power of transforming himself into an angel of light, as Paul informs us.

There is nothing of an external nature oppressive or vexatious to him, if he can only gain possession of the citadel of our hearts, and expel therefrom, Christ's nature, disposition, Spirit and power; if he can do this he has already won the prize of his craftiness, yea, if a man was even baptized by Peter or Paul himself, had received the bread of the Holy Supper from the hand of the Lord, would nevermore take part in papistic idolatry, yet if he retained but one of the fruits of the devil, whether hatred, or party spirit, envy, bitterness, avarice, revengefulness, pride, unchastity, or any other vice, we must declare with the Scripture that his spirit is devilish, and his life hypocrisy. For it is very evident that the whole man must be regenerated, sincere, unsophisticated, spiritually minded, godly, holy, devout, united and subject to Christ; as James says, "Whosoever shall keep the whole law, and yet offend in one point, he is guilty of all," James 2: 10.

Yes, worthy brethren, those who are so far taught of God, that they are able, well and truly to distinguish between Christ and the devil, in relation to their nature, disposition, doctrine, and works, and thereby perceive that the disposition of Christ is productive of life, and the disposition of the devil is productive of death, shall, and will undoubtedly, separate and depart entirely, from all vain and unprofitable disputation, schism, separation, contention, dissension, sedition, and sectarianism, and also from all deadly abominations, sins, and shameful actions; of this I am fully convinced by the grace of God.

My third request is, that they would all, with candor and sincerity of heart, meditate upon the glorious and illustrious names with which they are honored in the Scriptures, namely, Children of God, saints and beloved of God, chosen of God, regenerated seed and children of Abraham, seed of peace, plants and scions of righteousness, fruitful grafts of Christ, members of the body of Christ, flesh and bone, mothers, sisters, brothers, disciples, guests, friends, sons, daughters, maiden, virgin, bride and spouse of Christ, His holy vineyard, camp, city, Jerusalem, temple, ark, house, abode, chosen people, citizens of heaven, living stones, companions of the saints, apostles and prophets, house-hold of God, kings and priests, doves, sheep, the light of the world and the salt of the earth, &c., to the end that by such meditation, their conduct inwardly and outwardly, privately and publicly, may be such in all their ways, words, and works, before God, in the presence of the church, and before the whole world that they may, by grace, with the pious, walk worthily of all such glorious names, in love, peace and harmony, and by his paternal bounty forever escape the severe curse of excommunication, before mentioned, and not with the goats to the left hand, hear the stern sentence, Depart from me, ye cursed, but with the sheep to the right hand the cheering words, Come ye blessed, and be not numbered in eternity with those who are bound by the ban of the word, in the power from God, and styled in Scripture, a cursed, ungodly race, cursed children, children of wrath, and of the devil, servants of sin and perdition, mockers, revilers, wicked, carnal, perverse, unrighteous, ungodly, stiff-necked sinners, dogs and swine, for whom are reserved the eternal woe, death, fire, lake and torment of hell. O, brethren take heed!

My fourth request is, to all those to whom the charge of the word of the Lord is committed, who are fellow laborers with me in the ministry, that in all their actions, they so conduct themselves before God and his church, that no man can in truth censure or speak evil of them; as sincere ministers of Christ; faithful and true in all things; men full of the Holy Ghost, born of the incorruptible seed of God; encompassed with heavenly light; transplanted into the good disposition of Christ; partakers of his grace; taught and anointed of God; having their minds upon eternal things; hating their own fame, vainglory and impure, carnal lusts; lowly and little in their own eyes; of a meek and gentle spirit; compassionate, merciful, paternal, long-suffering, friendly, humble, chaste, given to hospitality, submissive, mild, courteous and peacful; well versed in the sound doctrine; seeking and acting in accordance with the good nature, disposition, character, heart, mind and example of Christ; confirmed in spirit, blameless shepherds, taking oversight of the flock of God, not by constraint, but willingly; not for filthy lucre's sake, nor for the sake of their own bellies, but of a ready mind; neither as being lords nor rulers, but being examples to the church of Christ, that in consequence of their faithful ministry they may run in fullness of joy upon the mountain of the Lord without fear or shame, and escape unharmed the mouths of fierce, ravenous wolves.

Yes, my brethren, if we could all proceed according to this rule in unity of spirit, unaccompanied by the destructive foxes, how soon would the bride of the lamb, shine forth in costly and variegated apparel, adorned in white and glittering robes, splendid bracelets, ear-rings and neck-laces (understand the beauty and ornament of her virtues), and with the brilliancy of her appearance, excite the admiration of the whole world; whereas now, in consequence of deceitful workers, cunning wranglers and sowers of dissension, she must sit, at times, in rags and tatters, and, oh God! be the scorn and derision of multitudes.

The anguish of my soul is ofttimes so great that I am unable to write; God omnipotent, strengthen me. And this, because I see that the house of the Lord has to endure so many offences, not only from without, but, alas! from within also. O men! men! arm yourselves! for the words of Paul are true, that the ministry of the New Testament is not a ministry of the letter, but of the Spirit. Its duties, therefore, cannot be truly discharged to the glory of God, by the proud, the arrogant, the ambitous, or the self-willed, who wish to perform every thing after their own mind, humor and inclination, for they pull down more than they build up, and do more injury than they do good. This is a necessary consequence, inasmuch as according to the tenor of the doctrine of Paul, this ministration is neither the depth of wisdom nor eloquence, nor a dead letter, with which they are generally replete, but it is God, Spirit, truth, power and life, of which they are entirely destitute. O take heed.

Arm yourselves, I repeat; for true teachers are called in Scripture, the angels of the Lord and valiant soldiers; be therefore manly; keep the commandment of God; hold fast and waver not. They are called watchmen and trumpeters; blow your trumpet to the right sound; watch over the city of God; watch wisely, I say, and neither slumber nor sleep. Spiritual pillars they are styled; O be steadfast in the truth; bear your burden willingly, waver not, neither be faint. Messengers of peace they are called; Ah, brethren live up to, and justify your name, walk in peace, maintain and break it not. They are called bishops and overseers; O take great care of the flock of Christ; take great care of them, I say, and see that you neither destroy nor neglect them. Shepherds they are called; O keep and feed the lambs of Christ, and leave them not to pine away. They are styled teachers; make known the word and truth of Christ; publish it abroad and conceal it not. They are styled spiritual nurses and fathers; O nourish and cherish your young children; vex them not, neither cast them away. They should be as the parent bird to her young; gather together the young and tender ones in Christ, and scatter them not, nor hurt them. They are called the stewards of God; O perfect the mystery of the name; abuse it not, nor disgrace it. They are called the light of the world; shine and glitter in full glory, and conceal not the brightness of your virtue. They are called the salt of the earth; O let the salt penetrate through and through, and be not ill savored. Ministers in Christ's stead; Ah, brethren serve, but rule not; let no man glory in any gift, I beseech you. We are receivers, not givers of grace, not of ourselves, observe; we are servants, and not lords. Ah brethren, bow down and submit. My chosen in love and truth, the joy and delight of my soul, so long as you stand fast in the Lord, abide in the way of peace and are faithful to your brethren. Walk worthy of the vocation unto which you are called; fear your God with all your heart; love the brethren; discharge faithfully the duties of your ministry; he is rich from whom you will receive your reward. Watch and pray. Pray, I say, and that with confidence, and so the Giver of every good and perfect gift, will not withdraw from you his grace, Spirit, love and wisdom. Doubt not, neither be afraid. Let the glorious, typified breastplate of Aaron, Christ Jesus, decorated with its beautiful colors, its twelve pearls, its Urim and Thummim, be bound fast to the breast of your conscience, with the two golden chains of the two testaments, and with the two yellow laces of pure faith and unadulterated love; wash the feet of your affections, purify them in the spiritual laver, Christ Jesus, with the living water of his eternal and Holy Spirit, take of the blood of his unspotted offering, and in a true spirit, put it on the tip of your right ear, in order rightly to understand his word, and upon the thumb of your right hand, and upon the great toe of your right foot, in order to act and walk uprightly before him, and in the presence of his congregation. Have your spiritual mitres, girdles and garments made for glory and for beauty, that, like verdant olive trees and luxuriant vines, and as burning torches and brilliant luminaries, in the firmament of the holy word, you may serve in fullness of glory, with all the faithful servants of Christ, day and night in his holy temple, to the glory of God and to the reformation of Israel; bring forth abundance of fruit, and when he shall appear with all his chosen saints, apostles and prophets, you shall receive in everlasting joy the promised reward. Sweet, gracious, and full of consolation is the word which the Lord utters, "Well done, thou good and faithful servant; thou hast been faithful over a few things, I will make thee ruler over many; enter thou into the joy of thy Lord," Matt. 25: 21. Ah brethren, from our hearts, let us be admonished, that we be faithful to Christ and his church.

Brethren and sisters, I will now in the peace of Christ, commit you all with one accord into the hand of the King of peace, and I do, with Paul, entreat you from my heart. "If there be therefore any consolation in Christ, if any comfort of love, if any fellowship of the Spirit, if any bowels and mercies, fulfill ye my joy, that ye be like minded, having the same love, being of one accord, of one mind, let nothing be done through strife or vain glory; but in lowliness of mind, let each esteem other better than themselves," Phil. 2: 1—3. For you well know by whom and whereunto we are called. Reflect upon this. So that no one may lose himself, on account of the shameful actions, and abominations of another, nor destroy the good works of Christ, disturb the peaceable, grieve the pious, offend the weak, give excuse to the wanton, drive the wavering again to the world, bring reproach upon the word of the Lord and his church, bring revilers into repute, and encourage the blood-thirsty; but that we be careful in all things to finish with joy, our course in Christ Jesus, and magnify his holy name, refresh one another in the peace of Christ, strengthen our sick, weak members, and young brethren, reprove the disorderly, publish abroad the truth of the Lord, and show unto all men, a blameless, christian example. To this end may the eternal God of omnipotence, grant us all, collectively and individually, the active spirit of his grace, with perfect obedience and love in Christ Jesus, our Lord, Amen. Ah, chosen children! God knows this is my final adieu to you all. Love the brethren, and beware of dissension.

A PLEASING
Instruction and Doctrine

HOW ALL PIOUS PARENTS, ACCORDING TO THE SCRIPTURES,

ARE REQUIRED TO

GOVERN, CORRECT AND EDUCATE THEIR CHILDREN,

IN A

PIOUS, VIRTUOUS AND GODLY LIFE.

BY

MENNO SIMON.

"Withold not correction from thy child; for if thou beatest him with the rod, he shall not die. Thou shalt beat him with the rod, and shalt deliver his soul from hell," Prov. 23: 13, 14.

"Correct thy son, and he shall give thee rest." "The rod and reproof give wisdom; but a child left to himself bringeth his mother shame," Prov. 29: 17, 15.

"For other foundation can no man lay than that is laid, which is Jesus Christ," 1 Cor. 3: 11.

ELKHART, INDIANA:
PUBLISHED BY JOHN F. FUNK AND BROTHER.
1871.

"Hast thou children? Instruct them, and bow down their necks from their youth. Hast thou daughters? Have a care of their body, and show not thyself cheerful towards them," Eccl. 7: 23, 24.

"He that maketh too much of his son shall bind up his wounds. Cocker thy son, and he shall make thee afraid; play with him, and he will bring thee to heaviness. Laugh not with him, lest thou have sorrow with him, and lest thou gnash thy teeth in the end. Give him no liberty in his youth, and wink not at his follies. Bow down his neck while he is young, and beat him on the sides while he is a child, lest he wax stubborn, and be disobedient unto thee, and so bring sorrow to thine heart," Eccl. 30: 7—12.

"Chasten thy son while there is hope, and let not thy soul spare for his crying," Prov. 19: 18.

PREFACE.

To THE ELDERS in all churches, and chosen of God in Christ Jesus; my beloved brethren in the Lord, unto you be grace, peace and mercy from God, our father, through the merits of our Lord Jesus Christ, in the power and operation of the Holy Spirit, which he shed on us abundantly, through Jesus Christ, our Savior; that, being justified by his grace, we should be made heirs according to the hope of eternal life. To whom be praise forever and ever, Amen.

My dearly beloved brethren in the Lord, we thank the Lord always for you in all our prayers, and pray without ceasing, unto our kind Father, in the name of his Son, Jesus Christ, that he would strengthen you with the gift of his Holy Spirit, that you may be filled with all knowledge, wisdom, discretion and power, necessary rightly to oversee the church of Christ, and to dispense the word of God to sincere, pious souls, according to your gift and calling, and that you may walk worthy of the vocation whereto you are called and chosen of God and his holy church, as shepherds and teachers, to the end that the saints may be kept firmly united by the common service, to the edification of the body of Christ. Take diligent care of your charge, and display a sincere concern for your flock, at all times earnestly exhort them to love, to good works, like Paul; to the pure fear and love of the Lord; to a godly, unblamable conversation, in all humility, righteousness, love, peace, harmony, mercy, and obedience to the whole word of God. Caution them against all false doctrine, and against the sword of evil tongues; for if a man bridle not his tongue, nor restrain it, his worship is vain and unprofitable. Also, that they take heed in their whole walk and conversation; circumcise their hearts; season their words, and perform all their actions in the fear of the Lord; that they may procure a good name for the gospel of Christ and his holy church; comply with his word and will, and thus attain unto salvation. Beware of all innovations and strange doctrines not contained in the word of Christ and his apostles, nor conformable thereunto. Show forth, at all times, Christ and his word. If any man introduce a doctrine differing from that taught by Christ and his word, let him be excommunicated. "For other foundation can no man lay than that is laid, which is Jesus Christ." He is the precious corner-stone in Zion, which shall abide forever. Hear, believe, trust, follow, hope and abide in him; press diligently after him, conforming yourselves unto his Spirit, word and life, and you shall neither deceive nor be deceived. My dearly beloved brethren in the Lord, I beseech and admonish you, neglect not the ministration of your brotherly love, but attend faithfully thereto. Take heed unto yourselves and to all the flock over which the Holy Ghost has made you overseers, to feed the church of God which he hath purchased with his own blood. Again, all the elders I, who am also an elder, exhort with Peter," Feed the flock of God which is among you, taking the oversight thereof, not by constraint, but willingly." You who teach obedience, be yourselves obedient to the church of Christ, in all things which are good and expedient; as examples for the flock. As Paul directed Titus, saying, "In all things showing thyself a pattern of good works; in doctrine, showing uncorruptness, gravity, sincerity, sound speech that cannot be condemned; that he that is of the contrary part may be ashamed, having no evil thing to say of you." Also, "Watch thou in all things, endure afflictions, do the work of an evangelist, make full proof of thy ministry." Do all in the fear of the Lord faithfully, and with obedient and perfect hearts, for you are made keepers of the charge of the house, for all the service thereof, and for all that shall be done therein. Study, therefore, to show yourselves approved of God, workmen, obedient, blameless, that need not be ashamed, rightly dividing the word of truth. My wish and desire therefore is, that you be earnest in this, so that they who believe in God, may be made zealous to excel in good works, which is good and profitable unto all men; instruct, reprove, rebuke, exhort and console, as occasion may require; and forsake not the fraternal assembling of yourselves together, the meeting and ordinance of the Lord. Strengthen one another kindly with the word of the Lord, that you may increase in faith, love and righteousness, and come unto a perfect man, unto the measure of the stature of the fullness of Christ.

With this, dear brethren, I will commit you to Almighty God, with the earnest desire that you propound unto all the brethren this brief admonition, concerning the education of children, in order that every one may observe and comply with the same in the full sense, in the bringing up, teaching and instruction of his children. The Lord Jesus Christ be with my beloved, yea, dearly beloved brethren throughout eternity, Amen.

THE EDUCATION OF CHILDREN.

UNTO ALL ELDERS and joint-heirs in the faith of Christ, grace be unto you and peace from God, our heavenly Father, through his beloved Son, Christ Jesus, our Lord and Savior, by the power and co-operation of his Holy Spirit, to his everlasting praise and glory, and to our edification and salvation, Amen.

You are aware, beloved brethren and sisters in Christ Jesus, that we all, without exception, inherit from Adam an ill-disposed, evil and sinful flesh; nay, that all our desires from our youth are evil continually, as Moses writes; also, that we find nothing in ourselves, as the treasure of our first birth, but perfect blindness, unrighteousness, sin and death. If now the power of this innate disposition is to be diminished, suppressed and destroyed, it must be accomplished by the pure fear of the Lord, which proceeds from a true faith through the word of the Lord, and from a clear perception of the righteous judgment and terrible wrath of God, which will burn forever against all impenitent sinners. For the fear of the Lord is the beginning of wisdom; it drives out sin and makes upright, pious children, as we learn from Jesus Sirach, Eccl. 12; Prov. 9.

Since, then, the merciful Father of our Lord, Jesus Christ, the great, Almighty Lord, has encompassed us with the light of his grace, and through faith in Jesus Christ, has awakened us from iniquity and ungodliness to a life of righteousness; therefore, let us diligently follow the glorious example of the true love of Matthew, the publican, who was not satisfied with enjoying the heavenly calling and grace himself, but went and invited other publicans and sinners, that they might also be saved and obtain the like spirit, grace and mercy from the Lord, for such is the nature and disposition of Christ, Matt. 9.

Trade, therefore, among yourselves with the talent given you from on high, and sincerely compassionate your unbelieving, blind parents, brothers, sisters, husbands, wives, servants and neighbors; do not conceal from them the gift, grace, word and will of God; for their feet are in the way of death; perhaps they may, at some time or other, extricate themselves from the snares of unrighteousness in which they are bound and entangled, and turn themselves to the Lord with all their hearts. My dear brethren, understand this as regards men of sense and discretion. Brethren in Christ, if we should see any such in danger of being drowned or burned, or in any danger that threatened their lives, and there was a prospect that we could render them assistance, would not our inmost souls be moved with compassion towards them, if haply we might afford them relief? Undoubtedly. And now we see with our own eyes, if we but believe the Lord's word, that they are walking in the shadow of eternal death, are already committed to the grave of hell, and liable to be devoured forever by the eternal, unquenchable fire, unless from their hearts they turn unto Christ and his word, repent, and become regenerated, as the Scriptures teach. Therefore, consider seriously the heartrending misery and wretchedness of their poor souls which must live forever, either in heaven or in hell, and strive diligently and faithfully whether they may not yet, in some way, by your faithful ministry of pure love, and by the direction and instruction of the divine word, be rescued and delivered from everlasting destruction, and be made partakers of eternal salvation. For genuine charity is of such a nature that it is constantly hungering and thirsting after the glory of God and the salvation of all men, even of those who are strangers to us according to the flesh.

Beloved brethren and sisters in Christ Jesus, forasmuch as we are now constrained, by saving charity, with benevolence and sympathy, and know through the unction of the Spirit and word of God, that the nature of man is completely corrupted in Adam, and is opposed from youth, to the word of the Lord, as aforesaid; therefore, let us be particularly vigilant and solicitous with regard to our own children, displaying unto them a greater degree of spiritual love than towards others; for they are the natural offspring of our flesh and blood, a serious and precious charge committed by God to our especial care. Be, therefore, particularly mindful, that you instruct them from their youth in the way of the Lord, that they fear and love God, walk in all modesty and submission; that they be genteel, well-disposed, discreet, honor and obey their father and mother, using reasonable language, not lying, nor clamorous, not stubborn, nor self-willed; for such is not becoming the children of the saints, Deut. 6; Eph. 6. The world desire for their children that which is earthly and perishable, such as money, honor, fame and wealth. From infancy they train them up to vice, pride, haughtiness and idolatry. But with you, who are born of God, this is not the case; for it behooves you to seek something else for your children; namely, that which is heavenly and eternal, and hence it is your duty to bring them up in the nurture and admonition of the Lord, as Paul teaches, Eph. 6: 1—4. Moses commanded Israel to teach their children the law and commandments of the Lord, to talk of them when they sat down in their houses, and when they walked by the way, and when they lay down, and when they rose up. Now, since we are a chosen generation, a royal priesthood, a holy nation, a peculiar people, that we should show forth the praises of him who hath called us out of darkness into his marvellous light, Deut. 6: 7; 1 Pet. 2: 9; therefore it behooves us to show ourselves patterns and examples in all righteousness and blamelessness, and to appear unto the whole world as we are thereunto called; for if we do not keep a strict eye upon our own children, but permit them to follow their evil inclination, corrupt nature and disposition, not correcting and chastising them according to the word of the Lord, we may with the greatest propriety lay our hands upon our mouths, and remain silent. For why should we teach those not of our household, when we take no pains to preserve our own families in the love and fear of God? Paul says, "If any provide not for his own, and specially for those of his own house, he hath denied the faith, and is worse than an infidel," 1 Tim. 5: 8.

My dearly beloved brethren and sisters in Christ Jesus, take heed that you do not ruin your children and train them in vice, through carnal love, and thus give offence; lest in the day of judgment, their souls be required at your hands, and it happen unto you, on account of your children, as it did unto Eli, the high priest, who was chastened by the hand of the Almighty, on account of his sons, 1 Sam. 3: 11—18; but diligently imitate the testimony declared by the angel of the Lord respecting pious Abraham, "I know him," says he, "that he will command his children and his household after him, and they shall keep the way of the Lord, to do justice and judgment," Gen. 18: 19. This is the chief and most important care of the godly, that their children may fear God, do good, and be saved; even as the God-fearing Tobias admonished his son's children, saying, My son hearken unto thy father; serve the Lord in truth, and cleave unto him in equity; be mindful of him, and let not thy will be set to sin or to transgress his commandments; teach this to thy children that they give alms, fear God all their days, and trust in him with their whole hearts.

My beloved brethren and sisters in Christ, who sincerely love the word of the Lord, thus instruct your children from youth up, and daily admonish them with the word of the Lord, setting a good example. Teach and admonish them, I say, in proportion to the development of their understanding; constrain and correct them with discretion and moderation, without anger or bitterness, Col. 3; lest they be discouraged; spare not the rod, if reason and necessity require it, and reflect upon what is written. He that loveth his son causeth him oft to feel the rod that he may have joy of him in the end. He that chastiseth his son shall have joy in him. "He that maketh too much of his son shall bind up his wounds; and his bowels will be troubled at every cry." A horse unbroken becometh headstrong: and a child left to himself will be wilful. "Give him no liberty in his youth, and wink not at his follies," Eccl. 30: 7, 11. Bow down his neck while he is young, lest he wax stubborn, and be disobedient to thee, and so bring sorrow to thine heart. Correct thy son, and keep him from idleness, lest thou be made ashamed on his account, Prov. 29.

Dearly beloved brethren and sisters in the Lord, if all parents, who glory in the name of the Lord, would deeply impress the words of Sirach upon their hearts, and inscribe them on the tablet of their souls, O how virtuous, pious and devout would many children be raised, who now, alas! run wild and unrestrained, honoring neither their parents, nor the church and gospel of Christ. "An evil-nurtured son," says Sirach, "is the dishonor of his father;" again, says he, "Though they multiply, rejoice not in them, except the fear of God be with them; for one that is just, is better than a thousand; and better it is to die without children, than to have them that are ungodly," Sir. 22: 3; 16: 2, 3.

Beloved brethren, consider these words well, and revolve them in your minds. Necessity impels me to write; for some, alas! live such lives with their children, that one is constrained to write and reprove. I write and admonish you again: Take heed, lest the blood and condemnation of your children come upon you. If you love your children with a godly love, teach, admonish and instruct them in God, lest the word, blood and death of the Lord be made unto them of no effect, and his name and church be blasphemed by the unwise, through them.

Beloved brethren in Christ, if you rightly know God and his word, and believe that the end of the righteous is everlasting life, and the end of the wicked eternal death, endeavor to the utmost of your power, to conduct your children in the way of life, and divert them from the way of death, as far as in you lies. Pray to Almighty God for the gift of his grace, that in his great mercy, he may guide and preserve them in the right path, through the directing influence of his Holy Spirit. Watch over their salvation as for your own souls. Teach, instruct, admonish, threaten, correct and chastise them, as circumstances require. Keep them away from naughty, wicked children, among whom they hear and learn nothing but lying, cursing, swearing, fighting and knavery. Have them instructed in reading and writing, bring them up to habits of industry, and let them learn such trades as are suitable, expedient and adapted to their age and constitution. If you do this, you shall live to see much honor and joy of your children. But if you do it not, heaviness of heart shall consume you at last. For a child left to himself, without reproof, is not only the shame of his father, but he bringeth his mother to shame, Prov. 29.

This brief admonition I have written to my beloved, from motives of sincere love, and not without a reason; for in the course of my ministry, I have too frequently observed, how disorderly, improperly, nay, heathenlike, many persons conduct themselves towards their children. The absurd, senseless love of the flesh, has such an influence over some, and they are so blinded by the natural affection for their children, that they can neither perceive nor observe any evil, error or defect in them, notwithstanding they frequently abound in idle tricks and wantonness, are disobedient to father and mother, murmur at them, collect and carry abroad lies, quarrel and fight with other children, and mock people as they pass by, crying and calling after them.

Brethren in Christ, to connive, by reason of a blind, carnal love, at these and similar disgraceful tricks of children, is a love not to be applauded, but much rather to be shunned and avoided; for it is earthly, sensual, devilish. And forasmuch, as we ought to be the salt of the earth, the light of the world, the holy nation, the chosen generation, yea, the bride of Christ, it by no means becomes us, to have, or to bear such sensual love or preposterous affection, in any circumstances, towards our children; but it is our duty, as far as in us lies, diligently and earnestly to instruct and govern our children and household, as well as ourselves, in conformity to the sincerity of godliness, a life of virtue, and the word of God.

With this, I will have delivered and preserved my soul in the presence of the Lord and his church, and I do desire, for the Lord's sake, that this epistle may be taken in good part, and read by the elders, in the hearing of all the brethren, to the end that the innocent may take heed, and be circumspect, and those who are guilty of these mis-steps, errors and failings, may reform, and that without considering me as being officious, in regulating the concerns of their household. Ah no! in the presence of God, I desire nothing in this, but that in all things, you conform yourselves to the Scriptures, and to christian gravity, and that all the concerns of the Lord's church, may be conducted according to the divine will and ordinance. The Searcher of hearts and reins knows that I lie not. I would, therefore, that you also accept and receive it in love; for in sincerity have I written it.

And now, beloved brethren and sisters, I commend you to God, and to the word of his grace, which is able to build you up, and to give you an inheritance among all them which are sanctified.

The very God of peace sanctify you wholly, that your whole spirit, soul, and body be preserved without spot, and blameless, unto the coming of our Lord Jesus Christ. Faithful is he who called you. May the merciful Father, through his beloved Son, Jesus Christ, our Lord, strengthen you all with the precious gift of his Holy Spirit, Amen.

LETTERS WRITTEN BY MENNO SIMON.*

FIRST LETTER.

A Dissuasion to all the brethren and sisters in Christ, living at Amsterdam and there about, not to attend the papal worship; because they do not feed the hungry souls with the bread of the divine word, but with the leaven of human doctrine.

> "Thou shalt rise up before the hoary head, and honor the face of the old man," Lev. 19: 32.
>
> "Look at the example of the old," Sirach 2: 11.
>
> "Whatever you hear and accept, keep that in your heart, and you shall have peace," Laodis. 1: 13.
>
> "For other foundation can no man lay than that is laid, which is Jesus Christ," 1 Cor. 3: 11.

To ALL the true children of God, and partakers of the Promise of the Kingdom of Christ, grace and peace be with you.

My beloved in Christ Jesus, I am troubled at heart for your sakes, inasmuch as I hear that you hunger and thirst after righteousness, and that there are so few carvers, who rightly cut the bread of the divine word for the hungry consciences, and that there are so few shepherds who rightly pasture the sheep of Christ, and that there are so few masons to rightly adjust the living stones in the temple of the Lord; so few watchmen who rightly watch the city, the new Jerusalem, and blow the trumpet; that there are so few fathers to beget the children of God, and so few to nourish and feed these begotten ones, but that every thing is to the contrary. For those who truly serve in that capacity do not deny the bread, nor the children to whom it belongs. And had they the bread by which the soul lives, not so many children would famish, while they distribute the bread once or twice a week (understand, the bread necessary to support the body). Inasmuch as they give the eggs of cockatrices unto the people, therefore observe what the prophet says concerning them, "He that eateth of their eggs dieth," Isa. 59: 5; John 6: 58.

Again, concerning the shepherds who pass themselves for shepherds of Christ, who pasture the sheep for the sake of their own selves, as Ezek. 34: 8 says, For you see how little they care for the sheep; they do not care whether they have pasture or not. If they only get the wool and milk they are satisfied. They pass themselves for shepherds, but they are deceivers; for they are widely different from the shepherds of which we read in Jeremiah. Shepherds after his heart, whom the Holy Spirit has sent; for they have not the love of Christ which Peter had, and therefore Christ has not commanded them to pasture his lambs; if they are not commanded to do so, namely, if they are not sent, how can they then preach, in-

---

* The first two of these letters, in the complete works of Menno Simon, are found at the close of the volume, but as one of those to the brethren in Amsterdam has appeared at the close of both the English and German editions formerly published we give them both, together with two other of Menno's letters a place here.

THE PUBLISHERS.

asmuch, as they are not divine shepherds who lead the sheep into the green pastures of the divine word, but let them famish. They are not the shepherds who lead them to the limpid waters, but they lead them to the stagnant pools which they have clarified with their feet, that is, by their glazings and good opinions, Ezek. 34: 19.

They also pass themselves for joiners who build the Lord's house; but they know not Christ, the corner stone; they never adjusted a stone in the house of the Lord, namely, of the living stones which are built into a spiritual building, which building is the church of God, Heb. 3: 6. For wherever there are two or three stones together, cemented by the cement of love, there they busy themselves to break them down, and to destroy them, as you may see verified in all countries and cities. O, how different are they from those of whom Paul says, "Ye are God's husbandry, ye are God's building," and we are God's laborers, namely, such as should build the house of the Lord according to his word, 1 Cor. 3: 9.

If they, then, be no builders they must be those who break down. They also pretend to be the husbandmen who take care of the vineyard. How they take care of it, and protect it against all wild animals, I will leave every christian to consider for himself. How they seek the profit of the Lord of the vineyard, and how they give him the usury or honor, the Lord of the vineyard knows. He also knows how they scourge, rob, hunt, banish and kill his children, for no other cause than that they neither do nor dare consent to them, inasmuch as they see that they are not the true husbandmen, but destroyers, Matt. 10: 17; 21: 34.

Yet they pass themselves for watchmen. If they are watchmen they are blind watchmen and dumb dogs which cannot bark, Isa. 56: 10. Hosea, the prophet, shows what they watch for, and how they blow the trumpet, Hosea 4. How far they are from the word of the Lord, which says, "Son of man, I have made thee a watchman," Ezek. 3: 17. "Lift up thy voice like a trumpet, and show my people their transgression," Isa. 58: 1.

They want to be fathers who bring forth the children of God and nourish them. But how can they beget children, when they have never rightly conceived. O, how different they are from the fathers of whom Paul speaks, "Ye have not many fathers; for in Christ Jesus I have begotten you through the gospel," 1 Cor. 4: 15; "My little children, of whom I travail in birth again until Christ be formed in you," Gal. 4: 19. Here observe, who are the fathers of the true children. Now show me one child they have begotten, namely, one child which was born of God through the gospel. Paul also says, "I have fed you with milk," 1 Cor. 3: 2, "even as a nurse cherisheth her children," 1 Thess. 2: 7.

Behold, sincerely beloved brethren and sisters in Christ Jesus, you will observe that you have few carvers who cut the sweet bread, but it is leaven which they give you; that they are not shepherds who pasture the sheep, but wolves that destroy them; that they are not builders that build the temple, but they break down that which was built; that they are not husbandmen who protect the vineyard of the Lord, and give him his rent, but they are false husbandmen which scourge, stone, torture and kill the servants, as you, alas, may plainly see; that they are not the watchmen who watch over the city of Jerusalem and warn her of the enemy, but they betray the citizens and kill them; that they are not fathers nor nurses, but they kill that which was begotten and nourished, as Pharaoh, king of Egypt, killed the true Israelites which he could lay hold on. Therefore it is necessary to separate from them and to shun them, as we read in Matt. 7: 15, "Beware of false prophets;" and Paul says, "Beware lest any man spoil you through philosophy and vain deceit, after the tradition of men, after the rudiments of the world, and not after Christ," Col. 2: 8.

The church of Christ is the bride of Christ, and he will not that his bride conceive but of the incorruptible seed, 1 Pet. 1: 23, as Paul says, "I have espoused you to one husband, that I may present you as a chaste virgin to Christ," 2 Cor. 11: 2. Yea, Paul would have the bride or church so pure, that if there were any who caused divisions and offences contrary to the doctrine which they had learned, they should be avoided.

Yea, if they had any in the church that were drunkards, covetous, fornicators, idolatrous or proud, they should avoid them and not eat with them, 1 Cor, 5: 11. How, then, could they suffer such to preach? Yea, if they preached any other gospel than that which was preached unto them, they should be accursed, Gal. 1: 8.

To the Philippians Paul says, "Beware of dogs, beware of evil-workers, beware of the concision," and says, "Brethren, be followers together of me, and mark them which walk so, as ye have us for an example; for many walk, of whom I have told you often, and now tell you even weeping, that they are the enemies of the cross of Christ; whose end is destruction, whose God is their belly, and whose glory is in their shame, who mind earthly things," Phil. 3: 2, 17, 19. Mark to what kind of people he refers.

The apostle would have the bride so pure that no dissension was allowed, no drunkards, covetous, idolaters, nor those that taught any other doctrine than he taught; and Christ himself says to the church, "Beware of false prophets, which come to you in sheep's clothing, but inwardly they are ravening wolves, ye shall know them by their fruits," Matt. 7: 15, therefore I will leave all intelligent christians to judge what those do that say that they are at liberty to do as they do. Shall we, who pretend to uphold the glory of God, grant it as a liberty to go where God is blasphemed, and his ordinances broken? It was commanded Aaron to serve in the priest's office. When Dathan and Abiram would serve as such, why did the earth open its mouth and swallow them, if it was free to them? Num. 16: 32. The children of Aaron, Nadab and Abihu would always let the fire burn on the altar. If it were allowed now, to put strange fire upon it, then why were they burned? Lev. 10: 1, 3.

Read how the worshipers of the calf, the murmurers and the fornicators, all received their punishment, Exodus 32; Numb. 21: 5, 6; 25: 8, 9. Yea the man of God at Bethel, how free was it to him, when God had said unto him that he should not, in that place eat bread nor drink water, when by the lies of the old prophet he did eat and drink contrary to God's command? It was so free that he had to die for it, 1 Kings 13.

There are very many Scriptures upon that point which I will leave for the sake of brevity. But I would that every christian should do as Christ teaches us, saying, "Search the Scriptures," John 5: 39. Those of Berea, searched the Scriptures daily, Acts 17: 11.

If you search the Scripture you will learn from it, that if you would be a member of the holy body of Christ, you must follow the Head and obey him, John 3: 36; 2 Thess. 1: 8.

If he commands you to beware of false prophets, Are you then at liberty either to do so or not? What kind of officers would you be, if the emperor should issue a decree and the subjects disregard it (take it as a liberty), if you did not punish them for not regarding it?

Now, the chief Emperor (Christ), has issued a decree, which decree he has sealed with his blood, and in this decree it reads, that we must be born again, repent, deny ourselves, take upon ourselves the cross, believe on Jesus Christ, and on our faith be baptized, in the name of the Father, and of the Son, and of the Holy Ghost, and to obey his commandments, Matt. 28: 19; to "render unto Cæsar the things which are Cæsar's, and unto God the things that are God's;" to love the Lord with all our heart and with all our strength, and to love our neighbors as ourselves; not to live unto ourselves, but unto him who died for us and rose again; to "beware of false prophets," and to "abstain from all appearance of evil," Matt. 22: 21; Luke 10: 27; 2 Cor. 5: 15; Matt. 7: 15; 1 Thess. 5: 22.

Now say, most beloved, which of these are we at liberty to do or not to do? Are we at liberty to be born again or not? Are we at liberty to deny ourselves, or to believe on Christ, or not? To be baptized, to give unto Cæsar that which is due him, and unto God that which is his, to beware of false prophets, and to abstain from all appearance of evil or not? If we are at liberty to observe these or not, just as we see proper, why does the Lord Jesus then say at the conclusion, And teach them to keep my commandments? Matt. 28: 19. If, now, he has commanded it, he desires it to be obeyed. That which is free is neither commanded nor prohibited, as Paul says in regard to eating and the keeping of certain days, 1 Cor. 10: 28. Yet he commands not to offend the brethren by such liberty.

Now, beloved children, if you confess that Christ Jesus is the Son, in his house, then let him be wise enough to rule; for he has bought this house with his blood, and has delivered the bondmen. Some he has made pastors and teachers, and Paul teaches us how they should be minded. If you go to the papistic teachers, whom you know beforehand as not being sent of Christ, and therefore bear no fruit, are you then obedient unto the voice of the Lord? O, no, Eph. 4: 11; 1 Tim. 3; Rom. 10: 15.

Since the Holy Spirit directs to those that are unblamable, and since you go to those that are blamable both in doctrine and in life, and since Christ has commanded to beware of such, and as you go to hear them, saying, I am at liberty—therefore judge for yourselves whether you are a child of God or not. And, if you say thus you are at liberty, then I ask you, Who gave you this liberty? Paul says, "Ye are not your own, for ye are bought with a price; therefore glorify God in your body and in your spirit, which are God's," 1 Cor. 6: 19. By what means then can you obtain this liberty?

Christ Jesus has also commanded his church to baptize believers on the confession of their faith. If I, now, do not believe, and do not suffer myself to be baptized in accordance with God's word, but suffer my little children to be baptized, without God's word, Am I then, obedient unto the voice of the Lord? Can I then inherit the promise given to the believing?

Christ ordained in his church the Holy Supper, bread and wine, in rememberance of his death; now it is changed into a Roman mercery. Is a christian now allowed to keep the perplexing, papal day-meal, and neglect the Lord's Supper? Judge for yourselves, since Paul says, "Ye cannot be partakers of the Lord's table and of the table of devils," 1 Cor, 10: 21. If we cannot partake of both, then we must neglect one or the other. O, beware of them!

Behold, beloved children, I have here given you some instruction according to the limited talents which the Lord has given me. Judge whether it would be becoming in a married woman to be with another man, if it were but once a year. So, if you be the bride of the Lamb, then you are not allowed to conceive of any body but of Christ, and his holy word. If you be the body of Christ then you must have the Spirit of Christ; if you are baptized into the body by the Spirit, then you must be obedient unto the Head, which is Christ. If you be in the city, the New Jerusalem, whose citizens are of one mind, then you must be obedient unto the King of that great city, namely, unto Christ. If you be the branches, then you must bear fruit like unto that of the stock. If you be the vineyard of the Lord, then beware of the foxes. If you be the temple of the Lord, then you must be submissive unto your High Priest. If you be the ark of the covenant, then the tables of the covenant, which are written with the finger of God, namely, the commandments of God, must be engraven in your hearts, that all men may read that you are an epistle of Christ, 2 Cor, 3: 2, 3.

O, beloved children, that the Lord would grant that we might verbally speak together, we trust that we could satisfy you on all points. Therefore you that fear God, separate from Babel, and go to Jerusalem, and do not suffer yourselves to be ensnared by such light-minded, artful words as, "I am at liberty." The drunkard may drink to excess, the gambler, gamble, the whoremonger indulge in his carnal passions, notwithstanding it is sin; likewise, we are at liberty to hear false doctrine, or to suffer infants to be baptized, yet it is unscriptural, and therefore sin. I herewith commend my beloved children to the Lord. May the rich Word of his grace enlighten you with his pure knowledge and grant that you do his will in all things, that the fallen temple may again be built upon its true foundation and that we may obtain the end of faith, that is, the salvation of souls, Amen.

MENNO SIMON.

November 14.

SECOND LETTER.

Second Epistle of Menno Simon. Being a consolation to his much beloved brethren and sisters in Christ Jesus, at and about Amsterdam, beseeching them to visit one another during the time of pestilence, and not to fear death, because it is but a passage into a better life.

"O man, what! art joyful! what! dust and shadow art thou! Proud, for thy life lies buried in death!"

"For other foundation can no man lay than that is laid, which is Jesus Christ," 1 Cor. 3: 11.

Mercy, grace and peace be unto you. The Lord said unto Martha, "I am the resurrection, and the life; he that believeth in me, though he were dead, yet shall he live; and whosoever liveth and believeth in me, shall never die," John 11: 25. Chosen brethren and sisters in the Lord, whereas I hear that the fire of pestilence is raging about you, therefore I am constrained by the love I bear to you and to all the pious, as I am aware that all flesh is affrighted at death, and that the death of friends is hard to our natural feelings, to write you, who are overshadowed by the heavenly light and called into the communion of Christ, a short epistle of consolation, that you may now, and at all times diligently watch for the coming of the Lord, and prepare your whole life, heart, mind and actions for death. For Paul says, "It is appointed unto men once to die," Heb. 9: 27. Also Sirach says, "All flesh waxeth old as a garment; for the covenant from the beginning is, Thou shalt die," Sir. 14: 17.

If we, with a new, regenerated and penitent soul, firmly adhere to Christ, truly believe his word, faithfully follow his footsteps, are governed by his Holy Spirit, and die unto the old, sinful life, nay, in every manner, die unto the world, flesh, and devil; if we sincerely seek God's kingdom, righteousness, word, will, truth, praise and honor, and walk inoffensively in his ways, then we shall live with, in, and through him forever, John 11: 25, and we shall not be hurt by the second death, Rev. 2: 11, notwithstanding that we were, aforetimes, dead in sins, as all the others, full of covetousness, unchastity, pride, hatred, envy, idolatry, and were, by nature, children of wrath, Eph. 2: 3, for unto the truly penitent and believing it is all forgiven through the death of Christ, it is requited by his blood, and reconciled by the only peace-offering of his innocent, bitter death, so Paul says, "There is, therefore, now no condemnation to them which are in Christ Jesus, who walk not after the flesh, but after the Spirit. For the law of the Spirit of life in Christ Jesus hath made me free from the law of sin and death," Rom. 8: 1, 2. Therefore be of good cheer and grateful; praise him who has delivered you by the power of his word from the dominion of sin and death, and has thus called you to the inheritance of his glory by the Spirit of his grace. Again, I say, give him the praise, and that with a godly, pure conscience and with an unblamable, holy life in faith, wholesome, firm and unblemished in love, living in hope, and fervent in prayer, adorned with the raiment of righteousness, and girded with the beautiful girdle of perfection in the Spirit; having oil in your lamps, sober and awake, so that when the true Head, the glorious King and Bridegroom of our souls comes, he may not find you asleep, and that on account of your not being ready, he does not cast you into eternal darkness, and close the door upon you, and thus give you your part with the hypocrites. I repeat it, be sober, and awake; labor while it is day, lest the dark night overtake you. O, reflect on what is meant! Ps. 117: 1, 2; Rom. 15: 11; Col. 3: 14; 1 Pet. 5: 8; John 12: 35.

Beloved, faithful brethren, be strong in

the Lord, of good cheer, and consoled; for your whole life and death are in the hands of the Lord. Yea, all your hairs are numbered, and without him not one shall drop from your head; he knows the number of your days, nay your life is measured as a hand breath. Therefore fear not, but willingly serve each other in time of need. O, leave not off visiting the sick, for by this you shall be established in love, as Sirach says, chapter 7: 35. "And it is also the nature of true love, to lay down our lives for the brethren," 1 John 3: 16. Reflect on what I tell you; you are aware of one thing, that an obedient, virtuous son, servant, or bride, does not fear the coming of the father, lord or bridegroom, but they long for their coming; "There is no fear in love; but perfect love casteth out fear," 1 John 4: 18. You are also aware that a fatigued laborer is desirous of rest, and an afflicted soul of consolation. And I have no doubt but my beloved children are sealed in God with a good conscience; that he is your Father, and you are his children; that Christ Jesus is your Lord, and you are his servants; that he is your bridegroom and you his bride; and that you, for the sake of his blessed name, will unfeignedly proclaim and teach it to the whole world for doctrine, instruction and reproof, that they may, sincerely repenting, be gained unto God; on account of which you must suffer such excessive misery, trouble, privation and slander from the indolent, wicked generation, as may be noticed on every hand.

Therefore we should reasonably not be afraid of death, which is but a rest from sin and the entrance into a better life, nor be sorrowing about the friends who have fallen asleep in God, as those do who do not expect the reward of the saints; but we should joyfully raise our heads, gird our loins with truth and be joyfully taken up to the heavenly Canaan thus, with our only and eternal (mark, eternal), Joshua, Christ Jesus, to take the promised inheritance, and thus be freed from the laborious, troublesome way of our hard pilgrimage, which we must lead through the rough desert of this wild world so long as we shall be here; and then we shall rest in eternal peace, Eph. 6: 14; Luke 22: 29; Rev. 14: 13.

O, chosen brethren and sisters! how gloriously are they gifted of God, who, in grace, are delivered from the body of sin, and from all perishable things, and are taken up into the holy tabernacles of peace, and called to the eternal, holy sabbath-day!

The old, crooked serpent shall no longer sting them in their heels; yea, no pain nor disease shall touch them, and the last enemy, which is death, is already overcome; their tears are dried up, and their souls are at sure rest and peace in the paradise of grace, in Abraham's bosom, under the altar of God, Rev. 6: 9, on Mount Zion, delivered from their great tribulation, clothed in white robes, worshiping before the throne of God and the Lamb, waiting a little while until the number of their brethren shall be fulfilled, Rev. 6: 11, to be fashioned like unto the glorious body of Christ, Phil. 3: 21, to shine forth as the sun, and thus joyfully enter into the eternal wedding and feast which is prepared in heaven unto all the chosen ones, by the blood and death of Christ.

O, how holy and blessed are they who are called of Christ to this feast, and have come to it, clothed in unspotted, clean garments! O, sing the pleasing and joyous hallelujah in your hearts, and thank him who has given them all this by the Spirit of his love, in eternal grace, and who has chosen you to enjoy the same part with them!

Reflect and be consoled. No more at present, but sincerely fear God, serve him in truth, uphold unity, love and peace; watch and pray; walk unblamably; fight your fight patiently; strive after the good; be friendly to one another; willingly submit to your elders and obey them, and remember them and me in your prayers. May the God of peace, our merciful Father, by his blessed Son, Christ Jesus, bless you now and at all times, unto more righteousness, in perfect love.

Your brother and lover of your souls in truth; at present enjoying tolerable health.

MENNO SIMON.

November 14.

THIRD LETTER.

An Epistle of Menno Simon, to the brethren at Franeker, province of Friesland, Netherlands.

"The love of God is true wisdom,"

"For God so loved the world, that he gave his only begotten Son, that whosoever believeth in him should not perish, but have eternal life," John 3: 16.

With a sorrowing and troubled heart I write to you, because a letter was handed me, signed by five brethren, in good standing, from which I learn that a violent dispute has arisen (God better it) amongst some of you, concerning the ban (excommunication). If I do not misunderstand, one party would that no transgression should be punished with excommunication until the transgressor should have been thrice admonished. I cannot agree with this doctrine. For there are some sins, as for instance, murder, witchcraft, incendiarism, theft and other like criminal deeds, which require summary punishment at the hands of the magistracy. If we were to admonish transgressors thrice, in such cases, before they were punished, then the sweet bread of the church would be changed into sour leaven, before the whole world. Therefore act with discretion, and do not treat criminal matters, especially if they are public, the same as you would other carnal works which are not considered, by the world, as requiring disgraceful punishment.

The other party desires, if I understand the matter right, that all transgressions should be punished with excommunication, without being first admonished at all; and that all penance should be outside of the church. That doctrine is, according to my humble understanding, erroneous and against the word of Christ, Paul and James. For avarice, pride, hatred, discord, defamation and quarreling are carnal things which work death, if not repented of, Gal. 5: 19, 20; James 3: 16; notwithstanding, they are not punished until after having been thrice admonished as the Scriptures command. I wish that it were taken into consideration, that, as "the wages of sin is death," so also, the repenting, converted heart brings forth life, as may be seen in the case of David, Peter, the murderer, Zaccheus and others.

I also understand that these same brethren are of the opinion that if some brother should secretly have transgressed in something or other, and, in sorrow of heart, should complain to one of his brethren that he had thus sinned against God, that then this same brother should tell it unto the church; and if he should fail to do so, that he, then, should be punished with the transgressor. This opinion is not only absurd but it sounds in my ears as a terrible one. For it is, clearly, against all Scriptures and love, Matt. 18; Jas. 5: 19, 20.

Excommunication was, in one respect, instituted for the purpose of repentance. Now, if repentance is shown, namely, the contrite, sorrowing heart, how can excommunication, then, be pronounced against such? O, my brethren, do not put this doctrine in force, for it will lead to sin, and not to reformation.

If we were thus to deal with poor, repenting sinners, whose transgressions were done in secret, how many would we keep from repentance, through shame. God forbid, that I should ever agree with, or act upon such doctrine! Lastly, I understand, they hold, that if any one, in his weakness, transgresses, and openly acknowledges his transgression, that they should consider him, then, as a worldling.

This, again, is an absurd doctrine; for, if the transgression was done through weakness, then, let us not be arrogant and too hard on the poor soul, lest we commit a worse fault.

Not the weak, but the corrupt members are cut off, lest they corrupt the others. Of such unscriptural doctrines and practices I want to be clear. I desire that excommunication be practiced in a sincere, paternal spirit, in faithful love, according to the doctrine of Christ and his apostles, as I have abundantly declared in my writings, for over five years.

My chosen brethren, guard against innovations for which you have no certain, scriptural grounds. Be not too severe nor too lenient. Let a paternal, compassionate, prudent and discreet heart, and the Lord's holy word, actuate you.

Follow this my brotherly admonition in this respect, which has been acted upon for twenty one years. I could give you no other and better advice. I feel constrained to write to you, for the above mentioned reason. I have, in sincerity of heart, served my beloved brethren without any partiality, as becomes us in Christ. I was asked to give my grounds for my doctrine, which I am, at all times, willing and prepared to do; not to the pious only, but also to the whole world, as the word of the Lord commands me to do. I do not teach nor live by the faith of others, but by my own faith. O, that they all were of one mind with me! How paternally and discreetly would excommunication, then, be practiced, without all offense; while, now, it is sometimes practiced so offensively.

I beseech all the pious, for God's sake, to seek peace. And if you have offended each other in the least, purify your hearts and be reconciled in Christ Jesus. Remember that you are the Lord's people, called unto peace, put under the cross, separated from the world and hated unto death. If you be baptized in one spirit, then fulfill my sincere desire, and be of one mind with me in Christ. Build up and destroy not. Instruct one another in love, and do not disrupt so that divine peace be with all the children of God, and remain whole with us unto eternal life.

May the peaceful Spirit of Christ protect you all. May you be sound in doctrine, ardent in love, and without offense in life, to the edification of his church and to the praise of his holy name.

Your unworthy brother and servant,

MENNO SIMON.

November 13th, A. D. 1555.

FOURTH LETTER.

An Epistle of Menno Simon, to the church at Emden, East Friesland, Germany.

"For other foundation can no man lay than that is laid, which is Jesus Christ," 1 Cor. 3: 11.

With a sorrowful heart I make known to the brethren that I receive one letter after another complaining of the excommunication, in regard to husband and wife; which causes great trouble with some, at which I am not at all surprised. For, from the commencement of my service, which is more than twenty years, I have feared this issue, which cannot be settled under such excitement as is, at present, found in the Netherlands. Dietrich Philip, our brother, and I counseled with the elders, in regard to this matter, as far back as 1547 and then it was resolved that we should act, in this matter, according to circumstances; and it was again so resolved at Wismar, two years ago. Therefore we should admonish according to the most definite and plain rules; but if we cannot thus convince, we should not force any one beyond what he conscientiously believes to be right, but bear with him in love and patience. I hope that every pious person is sufficiently instructed in the word of the Lord, to know that if either a husband or a wife commit adultery, theft, witchcraft or any thing else that is criminal, that such criminal misbehavior is summarily punished at the hands of the magistracy; or, to know, that, in case one cannot, undisturbedly live up to his faith, on account of his consort, but is at all times combated with false doctrine, beaten and abused, and thus is sliding back in faith, through the obstacles of such fallen consort, one should abandon such consort if he would stand before God and the church and save his soul. But if he or she can live up to his or her faith, in all things, undisturbedly, and is not combated with false doctrine, then they are conscientiously bound to remain together undisturbedly; for they are one flesh and live together as husband and wife should live.

Since there are many dangers and offenses connected with this matter, to punish with excommunication, the souls thus bound, who otherwise walk unblamably, in every respect, before God; and, since we all are flesh, therefore I pray that the merciful Lord may keep me from consenting to or teaching such doctrine. In view of this, my heart was filled with sorrow, on hearing that a certain length of time was given to Swaantje Rutgers, in which to leave her husband; or that, in case of her failure to leave him, she was to be excommuned and delivered over to satan.

O, my chosen brethren, consider well your actions. What slandering words will you put into the mouths of the slanderers! And what bad reports you will spread of the word of the Lord and his church! How many grieved souls will you afflict! Yea, how many souls will you separate from the truth, and what dangers will beset you! We never dared follow such doctrine, for we fear the consequences. O! that you would desist from it. How would I, afflicted man, be rejoiced at it! My heart shall never consent to such indiscreet action, and say, amen, to such intentions.

I desire to teach, according to my humble talents, a gospel that builds up, and not one that breaks down. One that is acceptable, and not one that is offensive; and I do not intend to encumber the service of God with something besetting, for which I have no scriptural grounds. I can neither teach nor live by the faith of others. I must live by my own faith, as the Spirit of the Lord has taught me, through his word.

Here you have my admonition. The Lord grant that you may follow it in all love, peace and unity. Be not too hard nor yet too lenient. Excommunication is instituted for reformation and not for corruption. O, that all were of one mind with me in this matter. How discreetly would the ban be practiced in this respect. But, as it is, every one follows his own inclinations and imagines it Spirit and Scripture.

O Lord! grant them thy Spirit and wisdom, that they may see and judge rightly, "Endeavoring to keep the unity of the Spirit in the bond of peace," Eph. 4: 3. Beloved brethren, follow my advice, for God's sake; for it will cause many souls to rejoice. The Spirit of wisdom be with you unto eternity, Amen.

Your unworthy brother,

MENNO SIMON.

November the 12th, A. D. 1556.

INDEX.

A

Abraham in covenant with the Lord, ...33
An Admonition to the Scorners of baptism, ...38
All things not pure to the pure, ...70
A Christian and affectionate exhortation to all in authority, ...75
Appeal to the Learned 88
———To the Common people, ...92
———To the Corrupt Sects, ...94
Apparel, costly, avoid, ...96
Admonition to strive for the Crown, ...100
Adultery, Menno's views of, ...145
An Exhortation to the dispersed and unknown children of God, ...176
Afflictions of the flesh beneficial, ...205
A Pleasing Meditation on the Twenty-fifth Psalm, ...213

B

Baptism, ...24
———Not to be administered to infants, 25
———Not a substitute for circumcision, ib
———A washing of regeneration, ...26
———Consists of more than water or the administered sign, ...27
———To be administered to those who can understand, ...28
———Inward and not outward saves, ...ib
———A sign of obedience, ...ib
———Luther on infant, ...29
———Bucer and Luther differ on, ...ib
———Infant, an idolatrous institution, ..30
———Changed as to its mode and time, ib
———Infant confirmed by Pope Innocent, ...ib
———Menno's reasons for opposing infant baptism, ...31
———To be administered to the believing, ...ib
———Counter Arguments, ...32
———No saving ordinance, ...ib
———Infant, no ceremony of God, ...33
———Whole families baptized, ...36
———Origen, Augustine and others on infant baptism, ...37
———Without regeneration of no avail, ..38
———The application of a handful of water, ...ib

Birth, the New, Fundamental doctrine of, from the word of the Lord, ...167
———The fruits of, ...169
———Transforms from death unto life, 234
Ban or Exclusion, ...239

C

Conversion of Menno Simon, ...5
Children in covenant with God, though not baptized, ...34
Circumcision no figure of Baptism, ...ib
Children have the promise without Baptism, ...36
Conduct of Preachers and their qualifications, ...61
Counter Arguments of Babylon and its builders, ...66
Consoling Admonition concerning the sufferings, oppressions and persecutions of the saints, ...179
Cross of Christ, ...183
Children, Education of, ...273

D

Decrees issued against Menno, ...8
Day of grace, ...15
Doctrine of the Preachers, ...57

E

Exhortation to take heed of the of day Grace, ...15
Exhorts to observe the doings of the world, ...17
Erring sects, ...76
Examples from the Scriptures, ...186
Extracts from Eusebius, &c., ...191
Excommunication, ...245
———Meaning of, ...ib
———Who are to be excommunicated, 246
———Reason why commanded in Scripture, ...ib
———Has no respect of persons, ...247
———Carnal sinners to be excommunicated and directed to repentance, ...251
———Of secret sinners, who are again inwardly admonisned of the Holy Ghost and sincerely and

INDEX.

	PAGE.
truly converted,	253
——Matt. 18, explained,	254
——Not to pervert the Truth, &c.,	256
——Backsliding and recovery of Peter,	257
——James 5: 19, explained,	258
——12th and 13th chapters of 2nd Cor., explained,	259
——The Judgment and Keys of Christ used in a proper manner,	260
——Conclusion,	264

F

Faith, ... 20
Foundation, conclusion of, ... 101
Faith, true christian, ... 105
——Unfeigned has energy, ... 108
——Papistic belief, ... 111
——Lutheran, ... ib
——Belief of the English or Zuinglians, ... 112
——True Christian belief, ... 113
——God's ardent care for believers, ... 114
——Noah's, ... 119
——Abraham's, and obedience, ... 121
——And fidelity of Moses, ... 126
——Of Caleb and Joshua, ... 127
——Of the pious King Josiah, ... 129
——Of the Centurion of Capernaum, .. 134
——Of Zaccheus, the Publican, ... 136
——Of the Murderer, ... 139
——Of the Sinful Woman, ... 143
——Of the Woman of Canaan, ... 148
——Conclusion, ... 164
Fornication, Menno's views of, ... 145

G

Gain, unlawful, avoid, ... 137

K

Koran, Dathan and Abiram, ... 19

L

Leading Articles of a Christian Foundation, ... 75
Law of Moses could not be changed until Christ Jesus came, ... 97
Letter to the brethren at Amsterdam, ... 277
——Second, to the brethren at Amsterdam, ... 291
——To the brethren at Franeker, province of Friesland, Netherlands, ... 283
——To the Church of Emden, East Friesland, Germany, ... 284

M

Menno becomes a Priest, ... 3
——Impressions concerning the bread and wine, ... ib
——How he spent his time, ... ib
——Begins to read the Scriptures, ... ib
——Begins to examine the merits of infant baptism, ... ib
——Interview with Luther, Bucer and Bullenger, ... ib
——Returns to Witmarsum, ... ib
——Is deeply grieved over the conduct of the Munsterites, ... ib
——Begins to preach repentance, ... 5
——Receives a call to preach from a number of persons who were of one mind with him, ... ib
——Consents to do so, ... 6
——Confesses his weakness and laments over his persecutions and poverty, ... 7
——Severe persecutions, &c., ... 8
——Removes to Woeste Veldt, ... ib
——Protected by the nobleman van Vriesenburg, ... ib
——Death &c., ... 9
Marrying out of the Lord, consequences of, ... 19
Magistracy, supplication to the, ... 22
Munsterites make inroads and defend themselves with the sword, ... 4

P

Preface, The day of Grace, ... 13
Preachers, sending, ... 53
——Must be called, ... 55
——Result of uncalled, ... 56
——Doctrine of, ... 57
——Scriptures show who are the true, .. ib
——False, likened to dry wells, ... 59
——Conduct of, ... 61
——Not to preach for money, ... 63
——Counter Arguments, &c., ... 66
Preface to the persecutions of the Saints, ... 181
——Twenty-fifth Psalm, ... 214
——Ban or Exclusion, ... 241
——Education of Children, ... 271

R

Repentance, true and sincere, ... 17
——Not to be practiced as the world does, ... ib
——Examples of true, ... 18
——Fruits of, ... ib
——To be practiced by those who can understand, ... ib
——Must be sincere, ... 19
Rulers, blood-thirsty, their end, ... 84, 85
Reconciliation does not depend on works alone, but on grace, ... 158
Resurrection, spiritual, ... 229
——Bodily and spiritual, ... 231
——Conclusion, ... 237

S

Sicke Snyder beheaded, ... 3

INDEX.

	PAGE.
Supper. The Lord's Holy,	40
——Sign used for the reality,	41
——Corruption of,	47
——Bread and Wine not the flesh and blood,	49
Shunning Babylon,	52
Sending Preachers,	53
Salvation ascribed to faith,	159
Sufferings for the Cross of Christ,	195
Shunning, Six reasons for it,	248

T

To the Reader,	2, 12

	PAGE.
The time is fulfilled,	15
The Lord's Holy Supper,	40
To the Bride, Kingdom, State and Church of the Lord,	98
The Twelve Foundations of Zion,	100
The regenerated have a spiritual King,	170
The Cross of Christ a source of delight,	209

W

Weapons, carnal not to be used,	82, 95, 198
Water, A handful,	38, 124
What the priests will do for a guilder,	161

A REPLY TO A PUBLICATION

OF

GELLIUS FABER,

MINISTER AT EMDEN,

WHICH HE PUBLISHED IN THE YEAR 1552 (IF I MISTAKE NOT), TO SLANDER THE PIOUS CHILDREN OF GOD, AND TO EMBITTER THEIR CROSS; TO ENSNARE AND DECEIVE THE THOUGHTLESS, AND TO COMFORT AND ENCOURAGE THEM IN THEIR UNRIGHTEOUSNESS AND CORRUPTION.

BY

MENNO SIMON.

Duo opposita (inquit Philosophus) juxta se posita, magis eluscunt.

(Two facts set opposite to each other, says the philosopher, become the more apparent.)

SECOND PART.

ELKHART, INDIANA:
PUBLISHED BY JOHN F. FUNK AND BROTHER.
1871.

May God, our heavenly Father, through his beloved Son, Jesus Christ, our Lord, graciously grant spiritual enlightenment and salutary understanding to all the pious and unprejudiced readers of this work, of whatever class, who sincerely seek the Lord and his saving truth, Amen.

"For other foundation can no man lay than that is laid, which is Jesus Christ," 1 Cor. 3: 11.

Entered according to Act of Congress, in the year 1871, by

JOHN F. FUNK & BROTHER,

In the office of the Librarian of Congress, at Washington.

PREFACE.

Paul writes to Timothy, and says, "This know also, that in the last days perilous times shall come; for men shall be lovers of their own selves, covetous, boasters, proud, blasphemers, disobedient to parents, unthankful, unholy, without natural affection, truce-breakers, false accusers, incontinent, fierce, despisers of those that are good, traitors, heady, high-minded, lovers of pleasures more than lovers of God; having a form of godliness, but denying the power thereof; from such turn away," 2 Tim. 3: 1—5.

Further he says, "I charge thee therefore before God and the Lord Jesus Christ, who shall judge the quick and the dead at his appearing and his kingdom; preach the word; be instant in season, out of season; reprove, rebuke, exhort, with all long suffering and doctrine, for the time will come when they will not endure sound doctrine; but after their own lusts shall they heap to themselves teachers, having itching ears; and they shall turn away their ears from the truth, and shall be turned unto fables," 2 Tim. 4: 1—4.

Again Daniel says, "There shall be a time of trouble, such as never was since there was a nation," Dan. 12: 1.

Beloved reader, if you will pay close attention to the seeking, teaching and conduct of the preachers of the present day, and to the deplorable condition of the common people, you will be convinced that the teachers of whom Paul speaks are here, in great numbers and that the abominable time has arrived. O reader, take heed! It is such a time now, that if Sodom was flourishing as of old, it would compare as pious and righteous with the present, miserable world. Yet, through the just punishment and wrath of God, Sodom was turned into ashes and suffered the vengeance of eternal fire.

"Behold," says the prophet, "this was the iniquity of thy sister Sodom, Pride, fullness of bread, abundance of idleness, was in her, and in her daughters; neither did she strengthen the hand of the poor and needy; and they were haughty and committed abomination before me; therefore I took them away as I saw good," Ezek. 16: 49, 50.

But now the world lives as if they were merely born to ungodliness and sensuality; and as if God was a dreamer and his word a fable. Say, beloved, is it not so? My kind reader, is it not so? Where is he who sincerely fears God and seeks after the truth? Wherever we turn we see nothing but unrighteousness, idolatry, deceit and despising of God. And all this is decked with the holy name, word, death and blood of Christ; besides, with human weakness and with false freedom, to avoid offence, O Lord! as if Christ were the Redeemer of all the impenitent and Mediator of all perverse sinners. No, my reader, no; this is not the case. Beware! Paul says, "If ye live after the flesh, ye shall die," Rom. 8: 13.

Inasmuch, then, that the world is so corrupted, on every hand, that it has become a double Sodom, nay a confused Babel or benighted Egypt, under the pretense and name of christian churches; and since the great and merciful God has, in these latter days of unrighteousness, again revealed unto some the precious word of his divine grace in a pure, christian understanding, and placed it as a clear light amidst the darkness, wherewith he yet in everlasting love will assemble unto himself, before the dark day, an obedient and willing church through the revelation of his holy word and the enlightenment of his eternal Spirit; and since he has chosen them as his own peculiar people from the assembly of anti-christ, through true repentance and a virtuous walk (although in weakness), under the cross of Christ, together with a salutary use of the sacramental signs according to the ordinance of Christ and his apostles and through a free, unfeigned confession of faith in the precious blood of Christ; therefore all the gates of hell arise and rave, so that, alas, true christians can find but little rest upon earth, as may be seen.

The rulers banish and persecute them; drag them into prisons and dungeons, torture and rob them, and in many places deprive them of their manhood, possessions and even life.

This perverse and reckless people ever call us anabaptists; heap one shameful lie upon another; point at us with the finger of scorn, as if we so behaved that fire and sword were too merciful a punishment for our bodies, and eternal hell-fire too merciful a punishment for our souls.

The preachers and the learned "are corrupt, and speak wickedly concerning oppression; they speak loftily," as the prophet says, Ps. 73: 8, although we testify by so many tribulations that we, in our poor weakness, sincerely desire to fear and follow the Lord, and that we seek and desire peace with all mankind; yet, we are infamously slandered; we are accused, everywhere, before lords and rulers of cities and countries, that we are ungodly sects and anabaptists; that we are seducing the populace; conspire to raise mutiny and rebellion; and are falsely accused of other criminal intentions; that they may thus obscure and obstruct the precious word of God, the word of true repentance; the joyous gospel of grace; the true and powerful faith in Christ Jesus; the pious, unblamable life, required by the Scriptures; and destroy the glorious kingdom of Christ, and his righteousness; lest their cause and unfaithfulness be made manifest to the world; as may be educed from their fruits; and that on the other hand, the corrupt kingdom of antichrist, the kingdom of this world, may be preserved uninterruptedly and maintained without shame unto the end, in falsehood, impenitance, open idolatry, a carnal, easy life and in unrighteousness, according to the desires of the old serpent.

Behold thus works the "prince of the power of the air, the Spirit that now worketh in the children of disobedience," as Paul says, Eph. 2: 2; as may, alas, be plainly seen in the case of Gellius Faber, if we well consider his writings, slanders, bitter, offensive words, his false accusations, his vain boasting and gross garbling, and judge them according to the Spirit and word of the Lord.

Notwithstanding that it is well known to many thousands of honest and reasonable people (as I suppose) that we seek nothing else upon earth but that we may in our weakness, willingly walk in the footsteps of Christ, in obedience to his word; that we may again light the extinguished lamp of truth, may call many unto righteousness, and that we may save our souls by the assistance and grace of the Lord, on which account we, poor ones everywhere, must endure so much tribulation, misery, anxiety, cross and persecution; nevertheless, the above mentioned Gellius, who in this case should be our assistant and fosterer (for he claims to be a servant of the holy word), still increases our anxiety and sore persecution, and the hatred and bitterness against us, by his unscriptural arguments and hostility to our foundation and doctrine, by his covert, malicious complaints to the magistracy, and by his infamous slanders which he publishes, through his writings, to the world, to the dishonor of God and his holy word; to the disgrace of all the pious; to the confirmation of his own condemnation, and to the deceiving of the simple. Therefore, no well-disposed person will think hard of me, that I, by an open reply, in accordance with the Spirit and word of my Lord, defend, to the best of my ability, the honor of God, the salvation of my brethren, the foundation of my faith and the praise of Christ, my Lord, whose service I entered, unworthily, by his grace and calling, according to his divine will.

I trust, too, with the gracious help of God, that I shall be able to do this so powerfully and clearly, with so many plain reasons and Scriptures, that not only the theologians but also all reasonable and impartial readers and hearers will, by the grace of God, clearly understand that he and the preachers of his class, support deceiving lies; and that we, through the grace of God, support the sure foundation of truth. I, herewith, humbly beseech and faithfully admonish all my readers, friends and enemies, that they will attentively read, assiduously examine and judge according to Scripture this my forced reply and defense, not with partiality, not drowsily and spitefully but with care and impartiality. This matter is of like importance to us all, namely, the the praise of God, and of Christ, and the salvation of our poor souls. Let none imagine that he is not accepted.

There is but one road and gate that leads to life, which is a strait road, Matt. 7: 13, also, but one doctrine. If we wish to enter with Christ into the kingdom of his glory, we must all walk the strait way and enter in at the narrow gate and be obedient to his word; of this let every one be aware.

Since, then, it is evident that Gellius, and the learned, base their doctrines, sacraments, &c., mainly upon human wisdom, garbled Scriptures, upon ideas and opinions; and that we base ours upon God's word; that he and his followers walk upon the broad road, and that our followers walk upon the strait road; that he is not persecuted, but does persecute by his writings; and, on the other hand, that we are persecuted and do not retaliate; therefore, all right-minded persons must admit that the truth and the true church is not with them, but with us; for it is an infallible rule as proven by the word of God and the example of all the pious, that where the true church is, there also are and necessarily must be the saving doctrine, true sacraments, unfeigned love, a pious, godly life and the excommunion or separation of the impenitent and perverse, according to the word of God; as may be clearly educed, by the grace of God, from the following replication.

I would, therefore, earnestly pray all the pious, for God's sake, that they would assist me by their ardent prayers to the Most High, that he will bestow upon me, a poor, weak man, together with my beloved brethren and faithful servants in the Lord, the gift of his grace and the power of his wisdom; so that we may silence all opponents, by virtue of true doctrine and an unblamable walk, and thus maintain to the end, the house of our God, in pure, godly zeal and christian love, to the honor and praise of his great name, to whom be praise and the eternal kingdom, Amen.

REPLY TO A PUBLICATION
OF
GELLIUS FABER.

Pure and clear is wisdom; strong and powerful is truth; simple and desirable is righteousness; happy is he who possesses them, for his heart rejoices in the Lord, his mouth speaks what is right, and his feet are upon the way of peace.

In the first place, Gellius adduces the saying of Christ, as a warning to all his readers, where he speaks, "Beware of false prophets, who come to you in sheep's clothing, but inwardly they are ravening wolves," Matt. 7 : 15.

Answer. If the reader can rightly distinguish, according to the Spirit and word of God, between the nature of the sheep and the wolves, and understands what this sheep's clothing means, with which the ravening wolves are covered, then the saying would, undoubtedly, not be applied to us, but to our opponents; for in what kind of clothing he here appears, with which he keeps the simple in darkness and binds their souls to damnation, will be plainly and clearly shown, through the grace of God, to all the pious and godly readers, in the following reply, if they compare it with his writing.

In the second place he adduces Paul and says, "Now I beseech you, brethren, by the name of our Lord Jesus Christ, that ye all speak the same thing and that there be no divisions among you; but that ye be perfectly joined together in the same mind and in the same judgment," 1 Cor. 1 : 10.

Answer. If we well consider this saying, we will find that it admonishes all true christians not to live carnally nor to be sectarian; that the one shall not boast of this and another of that; but points us to the only and true Shepherd and Savior of our souls, Jesus Christ, who was crucified for us and in whose name we were baptized; all of which we, in our weakness, would gladly and earnestly do, by the grace and help of God, as our tribulation, misery, affliction, blood and death abundantly have testified in many different instances.

But Gellius so construes it as to keep his readers from the unity of the Spirit, word, house and body of Christ, and to keep them, through his deceitful doctrine, unscriptural infant-baptism, &c., in the unity of the spirit, word, house and body of anti-christ, and undisturbedly upon the broad way.

In the third place, Gellius has addressed his writing to a nobleman, as is generally customary with the learned; thinking, perhaps, that by this means, their aim will be the easier attained, through the favor and assistance of such high officials; something which the pious testimonies, prophets and teachers of God's truth and word, especially of the New Testament never desired and much less sought.

In the fourth place Gellius gives his two principal reasons why he has published his writing. The first is, he says, Because I see that these anabaptists are daily coming into this country, secretly, from the imperial dominion, where they do and can do the most damage, and not only sow here anew, their pernicious seed by hedge-preaching, but also by publications, writings and private letters, which we must stop and silence lest the unwary be deceived, and that we may yet redeem some of them who have not yet become slanderers, &c.

Answer. These very offensive words, like

anabaptists, secretly coming, hedge-preaching, pernicious seed, &c., alas, plainly show the disposition of the man who penned them. Yes, my readers, Gellius knows as well as I do, what Christ has commanded concerning baptism, and how the holy apostles practiced it. Again, that Paul rebaptized some who were baptized of John (although John's baptism was from Heaven) only, because they were not informed concerning the Holy Ghost; that the worthy martyr Cyprian and the African bishops, together with the council of Nice, did not acknowledge the baptism of heretics, as baptism, on account of their being outside of Christ's church, and without his Spirit and word.

Notwithstanding all this, we must be called anabaptists; never minding that we, in our infancy were baptized, not only without the Spirit, faith, word or divine ordinance, but also without all reason and understanding, with an open, anti-christian baptism, by such as he and the learned of his class themselves call anti-christians, apostates, heretics and deceivers who neither rightly understand God nor his word; who practice open idolatry; who bend their knees before wood and stone; who put their trust in idle doctrines and commands of men; who unrestrainedly walk according to the lusts of the flesh, and who worship and honor a creature of God, namely, a piece of bread, as the only and eternal Son of God.

Although we have before us as a pattern, Christ's plain word and the salutary doctrine and open practice of the apostles, besides, Paul and both the councils, as heard; yet, alas, there are no bounds to offensive words, such as anabaptists, &c., which Gellius uses against us.

We may not retaliate, Rom. 12: 19, else we might call them infant-baptists with more propriety than they call us anabaptists; for we have the whole Scriptures on our side, but they have not one word nor one example. But his saying that we do and can do most damage in the imperial dominion, shows, alas, his stupidity and blindness.

All Scriptures teach us that idolaters and carnally-minded shall die, and he well knows that in these countries, their (the world's), worship is nothing less than open idolatry and gross abomination and that their life, as a general thing, is nothing but a reckless, impenitent and carnal life, as is the case at Emden and everywhere. Yet he dares to write that there they do most damage. And this he does for no other reason than because they (the pious) storm the kingdom of hell with the Lord's Spirit, word and power; rebuke open idolatry; teach the true worship; rightly confess Christ; and because they point out the true way to this perverse, impenitent and carnal generation. If this is damaging, as Gellius calls it, then the Scriptures which speak so over-much of an unblamable, pious life, have badly deceived us; this you must admit. O, what a wrong judgment.

Behold, thus does the god of this world blind such rebellious and contentious spirits, who so recklessly contend against the word of God and who do not obey the truth, but obey unrighteousness, Rom. 2: 8, that they become so obdurate and perverse that they call the glorious gain in Christ, attained through his grace, Spirit and power, a loss; and call good, evil, and evil, good; woe unto such, Isaiah 5: 20.

I would further say, that he also says, in other places that we are the only ones who obstruct them in their doctrine of impenitence and offensiveness, by our doctrine (which is not ours but the sound doctrine of Christ), and by our humble and unblamable walk which results from our doctrine through faith; and that we are thus the cause of their not being so highly esteemed as before and that they cannot continue in their ways, as they would like to do; therefore, perhaps, he complains that we do most *damage there*. But we say, It is because they serve the world under the semblance of the gospel, only from carnal motives; and flatter the rulers that they may aggrandize themselves with the property, church and cloister, which was intended (though wrongfully), as a sacrifice to the honor of God and that they may maintain the gospel of Christ by force of arms; because they flatter the people with the idea that Christ remitted our sins; that faith alone, avails; that they are poor, weak sinners who cannot keep the commandments of God, and other like idle consolations; so that every body lives according to the lusts of his flesh, singing and crying, "The cord is loosed and we are free," and turn the grace of God into unrighteousness, as Jude says, 1: 4; because they live in the old state of sinfulness, without any fear of God, as if they never in their lives heard one syllable of the word of the Lord, and as if God would not punish ungodliness and unrighteousness; therefore the just Lord who righteously judges all things, again takes from them the knowledge which they may have had, because of their ingratitude (for they only teach and proclaim the gospel of his grace according to the lusts of the flesh) and give it to those who will bring forth fruit, as Christ spoke to the Pharisee, Matt. 21: 43.

Again, to the unreasonable and offensive word "secretly enter," I reply: Moses and Christ, the apostles and prophets, as also, natural reason unanimously teach us that we should receive, comfort, help, assist and serve the miserable, afflicted and needy stranger; and it is a fact well known to Gellius that these poor children whom he afflicts, have fled in unfeigned fear of their God to a foreign country for protection, with their weak women and little children, to escape the bloody tyrannical sword; not on account of crime or roguery, but on account of the testimony of God and their consciences; even as the pursued doves flee from the bird of prey; and that we, through the grace of God place ourselves under the protection of this or that merciful and kind-hearted ruler; and although they, for the sake of divine truth, are bereft of their native country, possessions and earthly comforts, yet they can, through God's grace, reasonably support themselves, as is promised in Scripture. If he were, in fact, what he boasts to be, namely, a preacher of the holy word, then his inmost soul would be moved to compassion towards these afflicted orphans and innocent hearts; he would be kind to them and assist them as much as is in his power; he would intercede for them before the magistracy, since he may observe in them such a moving spirit and ardent zeal, that they stake their possessions and blood to the praise of their God, as may be openly witnessed. But, now, this misery and sore affliction namely, the flight from the gaping lion's mouth and from fire and sword, into more merciful countries, must be called by him "secretly entering." O, Lord!

What kind of a preacher and christian he is; how he acts according to love; and how he walks according to the word of the Lord in this respect, all reasonable persons who are not more than half blind may judge from these, his writings together with his daily cries of the same kind. To the slanderous sentence "sowing pernicious seed," I reply: Every seed bringeth forth fruit after its own kind, Gen. 1: 11.

My dear reader take heed to what I write. God's word, on every hand, requires a pure heart, a new mind and a penitent, christian life, dead unto sin. John the Baptist says, "Bring forth therefore fruits meet for repentance," Jesus says, "Repent, for the kingdom of heaven is at hand," Matt. 3: 8; 4: 17. Again, I am come to call sinners to repentance, Matt. 9: 13, and many other Scriptures of the kind might be adduced.

Inasmuch, then, that the Scriptures, on every hand, require of us true repentance, and that also the sacramental signs, as baptism and Holy Supper signify, represent and teach to all true christian believers a penitent, unblamable life; and since, according to the tenor of the Scriptures, no one can be a true christian without true repentance and that every kind of seed brings forth fruit after its own kind, as already said, namely, lies, children of lies, and truth, children of truth; and since it is a fact well known to many reasonable persons that God has, through us and our fellow-servants, in his great power and infinite grace, turned unto the true and living God, many a proud, avaricious, unchaste, cruel, lying, carnal and idolatrous heart and has so humbled, moved, renewed and changed them that they would rather die than act hypocritically, or willingly speak or countenance any falsehood against the well being of their neighbors, as is testified in our Netherlands by the precious blood of so many pious saints. And since the fruits of Gellius' seed, that is, his followers, remain so entirely impenitent in their lives and unchanged in their hearts that they live in pomp and splendor, go attired in silk and velvet and are decked with gold and silver; live in all manner of unrighteousness, avarice, carousing, hatred and envy; in short, live according to the lusts of the flesh, and would, for the sake of a penny, falsely swear by the Lord or by their soul, &c.; therefore we will let all reasonable and intelligent persons judge who of us bring forth bad fruits, Gellius and his followers, or we and and our followers. Whoever sincerely seeks and loves the truth, read and ponder.

O, dear Lord! thus thy holy and precious word, the word of thy grace, the word of thy love, by the power and grace of which we will live eternally with thee, is called by this man and by others also, deceit and pernicious seed; and their open lies, obvious error and unreasonable adulteration of Scripture, of which more will be said hereafter, is called the true doctrine of Christ and the holy word of God. If it be wilful slander and perverseness, then, alas, it is too bad. But if it be ignorant blindness or misconception, then, the gracious Father grant them eyes to see. This is my sincere wish, as the Lord knows.

Again, he writes, "that we sow anew our pernicious seed, not only by hedge-preaching, but also by publications, letters &c. To this I reply with holy David: We believe, therefore we speak, and must suffer tribulation. For since God, the merciful Father, has given us, poor creatures, the Spirit of faith and bestowed upon us the Spirit of his love from on high, through his Son Jesus Christ, and has besprinkled our hearts with the heavenly dew of his love, has opened unto us the seven seals of the book of his knowledge; has disclosed unto us the mystery of his divine word and pleasure; has awakened us from the dead and given us life, a new heart, mind and disposition, and has nourished us with the bread of life, so that we, through his grace, have found the beautiful pearl, the precious treasure and eternal peace, which we could not possibly acquire through the deceiving doctrine, subtle sophistry and false consolations of the learned; therefore we would teach, proclaim and imprint on the hearts of all mankind, to the best of our ability, this manifest grace of his great love toward us, that they may enjoy with us the same joy and renewal of spirit, and know and taste with all saints how sweet, good and kind the Lord is to whom we have turned.

We preach, therefore, as much as is in our power, both day and night, in houses and in the open air, in forests and in wildernesses, hither and thither, in this and in foreign lands, in prisons and in dungeons, in water and in fire, on the scaffold and on the wheel, before lords and princes, orally and by writings at the risk of possessions and blood, life and death; as we have done these many years; and are not ashamed of the gospel of the glory of Christ, Rom. 1:16; for we are a living fruit, and strongly feel the moving power in our hearts, as may be seen in many instances by the commendable submissiveness and willing sacrifices of our faithful brethren and joint-heirs in Christ Jesus.

We would save all mankind from the jaws of hell; deliver them from the chains of their sins, and by the gracious help of God, win them to Christ by the gospel of his peace; for this is the true nature of the love which is of God.

He then accuses us of preaching at night, and says in another place "That we secretly enter into cities and towns, from fear of the cross; that we sit with closed doors to treat with the simple; not to convert them to true christianity but to convert them to anabaptism," &c. To which I reply in the first place: It is true that we sometimes have to serve the Lord and preach his word at night (in the dead of night), but I fear that Gellius and the learned are the principal cause of this. For they have so embittered and still embitter all lords, princes, rulers and magistrates against us by their fiendish, unmerited upbraiding, slandering and defaming that we cannot, alas, so much move them, with Scripture, supplications, tears, misery, tribulation, loss of possessions, blood or life, that we can safely go about, verbally to defend the word of God, before these open enemies of the cross of Christ and of wholesome truth; but we must (understand, we teachers) everywhere conceal ourselves in shops and retired places to escape the persecutors and blood-thirsty, if we do not wish to be, at once, torn up and devoured by the terrible beasts which arise from the sea.

Beloved readers, observe well what I write. Gellius accuses us of "preaching at night." It was in the year 1543, if my memory serves me right, that a decree was read throughout West Friesland, "That criminals and even manslayers were promised pardon, imperial grace, freedom of country (in those times banishing was in vogue), and besides one hundred carl-guilders, if they would betray me and deliver me into the hands of the executioner."

About the year 1539, a husbandman, who was a very pious man, named Tjaert Reyndertz, was seized in my stead, because, out of pity and compassion, he concealed me in his house while I was hotly pursued; and was a few days thereafter, put on the wheel, after a free confession of faith, as a valiant soldier of Christ, after the example of his Lord; although his enemies, even, acknowledged that he was an unblamable, pious man.

Also, in 1546, at a place where they boasted of the word, four houses were at once confiscated, because the owner had rented one of them for a short time, to my sick wife and little ones; although the neighbors were not aware of their presence.

What decrees have been issued against some of us, and what rewards have been offered for our apprehension, in different dominions and cities; what imperial mandates and Roman condemnations have been resolved against us; and how we are treated on every hand, is well known to Gellius and to the preachers of his class. That they are the very cause and the authors of these things, I unreservedly write and testify without fear. Behold, thus they hate all those who rightly teach God's word.

Notwithstanding this, Gellius and others are not ashamed to say, "That we, out of fear of the cross, secretly enter cities and towns, sit with closed doors," &c., as if we were stones, and blocks of wood, which neither do nor can fear any deathly evils; while he and his, well know that the chosen men of God, Abraham, Isaac, Jacob, Moses, and Aaron, besides the prophets and apostles, nay, even Christ himself, so feared to die that they sometimes took to flight.

In the second place, I say, that so long as I, poor weak man, have served the pious with my small talent, I have taught more, by far, in day-time than at night. The Lord is my witness that I write the truth Yet we must be upbraided by these perverse people as night and hedge-preachers, as if the word of God could not be taught any where but in their houses of abomination (who know not the Scriptures), and as if God was not a God of the night as well as of the day. O, perverseness.

Say, reader, was not the night pure unto faithful Moses, and all Israel to eat the passover? Exodus 12 : 3—8. Did Christ think it wrong to exhort Nicodemus at night? John 3: 2. Did he not partake, with his disciples, of the Holy Supper, at night, just before his suffering, Matt. 26: 26; Luke 22: 19; 1 Cor. 11: 23. Did not the church assemble at night, when Peter was delivered from the hands of the tyrant by the aid of an angel, out of fear of Herod and the Jews? Acts 12: 7. Did not holy Paul at night preach the word in an upper chamber at Troas, and break the Lord's bread with the disciples, just before his leaving? Acts 20: 7. Did not the saints of the primitive church sometimes meet at night to break the Lord's bread and drink the holy cup? for which they were suspicioned and had to hear and bear many hard names. Does not Hilarius write, that the apostles met in halls and retired places, and that they traveled through many countries and nations, by water and by land, against the prohibitions and decrees of the rulers.

Behold, my readers, whether that which was allowable and free to Moses, Israel, Christ, the apostles and to the primitive churches, namely, the service and preaching of the word of God at night, is free to us or not, especially in these critical times of tyranny, we will let the intelligent reader judge according to Scripture, in the fear of his God.

O Lord! thus they (the world) seek causes, encumbrances and complaints to offend thy poor children more and more and to burden them with the cross, that they may persecute and kill them, in semblance of justice; for they are an obstacle to their works and a smarting to their eyes.

In the third place I say, that I have heretofore twice offered publicly to treat with them on Scripture, under safe conduct, before twenty or thirty witnesses or before a full meeting. But what kind of answer I received, their message, which I yet possess, testifies. Afterwards, in the memorable times of bishop Herman, Elector of Ceulen, at their own request, I offered this same thing again to the learned men of Bon, but my offer was rejected, on account of these kind gentlemen being dissuaded by John A'Lasco and A. H.; by their accusing me of three falsehoods, such as I never thought of and much less said or advised, and which I, for good reasons will not now touch upon, for all of which I have the testimony of a manuscript of a preacher, named Henricus. But what their intentions were, in regard to this matter, I will leave to him who knows all things. Also, the preachers of Wesel, in the land of Kleef, pretended that they would furnish me safe conduct and treat with me, &c.; but when I signified my willingness, in writing, I received an answer that they would let the executioner treat with me; and other tyrannical and unchristian words.

I will yet speak of what I asked in my "Foundation;" in the "Preface to the Twenty-fifth Psalm," many years ago; also in my "Excuse," in the "Supplication to the Magistracy," and also in my "Message to the Learned and Preachers of the German Nations," who boast of the word, concerning a free Treatise on Scripture, published in the year 1552. And I am still willing and prepared, at all times, so long as breath remains in me, or my intellect does not fail me, and so long as I can sit on a wagon or lay in a ship, to appear before Gellius, or anybody else, verbally to defend the foundation of our faith and to testify to the truth of Jesus Christ, if I can do so in safety, in good, christian faith and in sincerity of heart, to the praise of our God, to the extension of his church, to the promulgation of his holy word and to the salvation of our neighbors. This is the main desire of my heart, that I may preach and promulgate his great, adorable name, teach his word, seek his gain and honor and exalt and defend his praise, to the best of my humble ability.

Since it is manifest that the world is, unjustly, so embittered against us, that we are, alas, not suffered to be heard or seen; and that many an innocent, pious sheep, who is not a teacher, is sent hither and thither to be slaughtered by the sword, water or fire, without any mercy; and that we, miserable teachers, are not allowed to live in safety, any where under the broad canopy of heaven, not even in a pig-sty (so to speak), if known; but that we, through open mandates, are already judged before we are delivered, and condemned before we are seized; something which never, as far as we know, transpired since the apostolic times; therefore, I pray all my readers, for God's sake, that they will, in the fear of God, thoughtfully consider what gross injustice Gellius and his followers have done us, by the use of such wrong and bitter words, as *night-preaching*, *hedge-preaching*, *conspiracy*, *secretly entering*, &c., when we neither can nor dare do otherwise, as is well known. Besides, we have on our side Moses and Christ, the apostles and also the example of the primitive church; who served the Lord at night as well as in day time, as has been already heard; and we are also prepared, at all times, to render an account of our faith and to defend the truth; if we can do so in good, christian faith, without deceit and shedding of blood, as has been already said.

I say further: It is by far more praiseworthy to teach the genuine, saving truth, at night, in a secret corner, when we can not openly meet in day-time, than to proclaim, in day-time, deceiving lies and a powerless doctrine of impenitence, from the pulpit; as has, alas, been openly done these many years before the whole world; this must be acknowledged and admitted; for the disorderly state of affairs and the impenitent life of this generation testify to it.

At his saying, that we should be stopped and silenced, lest we deceive the unwary (single) as he calls them, I reply: A better and surer way than the one we have by the grace of God, nobody can point out; of this we are convinced from the inmost of our soul. For we acknowledge and feel that we have the word of God. Nevertheless, we will always freely accept, and willingly follow the instruction of any pious person, who can, in the fear of God, convince us by the Spirit, word, example, commands, ordinances, prohibitions and usages of the Lord, and not by tyranny and violence, and point out any thing that would be more useful and better; to greater honor to God, or more to the edification of his church, than we have followed and confessed during several years of manifest truth, and to which we have unwaveringly testified in so exceedingly much anxiety, misery, tribulation and persecution. For all things in Christ's church that shall avail and stand before his throne must be judged by the Spirit, word, example, commands, ordinances, prohibitions and usages of the Lord. I trust that those who seek and sincerely fear the Lord, will agree with me in this respect.

But with this writing of Gellius he will, surely, not convince us; for it is full of brawling, profanity, defamation, false accusations, tyranny, sophistry, wrong explanations and false doctrines (if I am wrong, rebuke me); so that it does not silence the pious, as was his intention, but makes them still more active; and it will be the cause of strengthening salutary doctrine and truth, and thus be the cause of his loss where he intended to make gain. For I trust, when both our writings are compared one with another, that, through the grace of God, a glorious, clear light will be thrown on the church of Christ; while it will expose to the plain and humble whom he intends, by it, to dissuade from our doctrine what his own nature, works, writings and fruits are, and, by comparing them to Christ's plain word, Spirit, example, ordinances and usages prove to them how earthly and carnal-minded he and his are; how he exercises his profession; what he seeks; what are the fruits of his doctrine; what sacraments he uses; what ban he practices, and what kind of church he holds to, &c.

I would, therefore, faithfully admonish and pray him, not to undertake more than he can accomplish; and not to kick against the pricks, Acts 9: 5, for it will not avail him. But he should remember that many a learned man (not that I esteem learning, if at all opposed to Christ), in past times as well as at present, has industriously tried it, as he now does; but what has been accomplished by it, the fruits openly testify. For some of them have become such zealots against us that they have made themselves guilty of innocent blood; they have grossly offended and condemned to the judgment of the devil, so many pious and faithful hearts, who, through fear and love of their God, dared not walk with them on the broad road; have, besides, written and contended so much for the unity of their churches, that they have brought the poor, reckless people to such a disorderly and wild state, that they, generally speaking, lead such a fruitless, impenitent life that it seems as if never prophetic or apostolic doctrine had been taught, and as if never Christ nor the holy Spirit had appeared on earth.

Had they, now, wisely, obediently and humbly comprehended, listened to and followed the word and ordinance of the Lord, the usage and example of the apostles; had they sincerely feared their God; had they not acted hypocritically with lords and princes, and the world in general; but taught the doctrine in true zeal without any respect of persons or favors; had they faithfully, unto death, rebuked the sins of all mankind, of high and low station alike, with doctrine and with life; had they unwaveringly served God and obediently proclaimed the gospel, in such a manner as to have assembled and built up unto the Lord a truly, penitent people, that is, a true church, according to the example of the apostles; had they not sought their own gain and ease; and had they also not abused and slandered the pious and godly, by their crying and writing; then the precious word, Christ's glorious gospel of grace never would have been profaned so lightmindedly; nor would this poor, unwary people have been degenerated into this wild and reckless state, as, alas, may now be witnessed in all parts of the world.

Thus, I fear, it will be with Gellius; for of what use his preaching and church-service have been these many years, toward bringing about a pious, penitent life in the fear of God, I will let the world judge by his disciples, who are the fruit of his seed.

O, that he would take heed, and not break God's holy and precious word; that he would not slander the pious and godly, who testify to it with their heart, mouth, life and death; that he would learn to know his own envious, impure and bitter heart; his deceiving, inconsistent and infamous doctrine, and his selfish, ambitious flesh; and would humble himself under the mighty hand of God, as the Scriptures teach us to do, for then he might yet be saved. But as it is, I fear that his brawling, slandering and condemning of all the pious; together with his seeking after improper gain, favor and honor of men and the desire of an easy, careless life, will so entirely close his heart and bewilder his senses, that he will not acknowledge or desire the glorious brightness of Christ, nor the wisdom which is of God. God grant that my apprehension be not realized, and that he may yet receive grace; this is my sincere wish toward him and all of our opponents, Amen.

Gellius says further, that he has published his writing for the purpose of redeeming some of our followers, who have not yet become slanderers; and he says also, that some have been redeemed through their faithful services, who now, with united hearts and spirits adore, praise and thank their Lord and God, at the public meetings of the church of God and Christ (these are his words), because they have been delivered from death and damnation, and now feel a delight in Christ, and penitence and peace in their hearts.

Answer. If we, in true, christian zeal and unfeigned love, rebuke or reprove their false doctrine, deceiving, unscriptural sacraments and their reckless, carnal life, with the Spirit, word and life of Christ, and point them to the glorious example of the prophets, of the apostles, of Christ and of all the true servants of God, he calls us slanderers. From this it may be observed that our work of love is ever interpreted to the contrary. For if we write or speak mournfully, it is called sighing and groaning, if we reprove sharply, it is called brawling and slandering. If we pipe, they dance not; if we mourn, they lament not, as Christ says, Matt. 11: 17. It is wrongly spoken, whatever we say to the perverse. Although they commit abomination, yet they are not ashamed, neither do they blush, Jeremiah 8: 12.

If the reproof of open sin, in true, christian love, according to the word of God, is slander, as Gellius calls it, then all the saints of God, the apostles and prophets, as also Jesus Christ himself were slanderers; this is incontrovertible; for they called the false prophets and preachers, false teachers, deceivers, dumb dogs, blind guides, hypocrites, thieves, murderers, wolves, cunning devisers, enemies of the cross, servants of their bellies, children of damnation, dry clouds, dead trees, locusts, &c., before the whole world. But no. To openly reprove deceit, transgressions, blasphemy of God or his word and sin in general is not slandering, as Gellius, through perverseness of heart, pronounces it against the innocent; but it is the fruit of the faithful love of those who would oppose evil and do good unto all. I will leave it to the judgment of all pious and reasonable persons, if he is not a profaner of the church, a brawler and a slanderer, and guilty of innocent blood, who calls the church of God a conspiracy; the regenerated children of God, apostatical anabaptists; the salutary doctrine of Christ, sectarianism and fanaticism; who slanders and condemns the baptism which Christ commanded, and the apostles taught and practiced, as being a heresy; and falsely maintains and practices on the poor, ignorant people, the baptism of anti-christ, with many high-sounding words and phrases? Who promises grace and peace to the proud, obdurate, avaricious, carnal and impenitent boaster, whom all Scriptures judge unto death; because he can, in appearance talk of the Scriptures, although without Spirit, power or change of heart; who, without just cause, maliciously slander, falsely suspicions, and unjustly condemns, the poor orphans and afflicted christians who sincerely seek and fear the Lord; and thus delivers them to the magistracy to be put in dungeons, and to the executioner to be killed.

But as to his boasting, that some of our brethren have again associated with them, and thus others may be yet redeemed by his writing, &c. I answer, in the first place: Christ says, "Wide is the gate and broad is the way that leadeth to destruction, and many there be which go in thereat; because strait is the gate, and narrow is the way which leadeth unto life, and few there be that find it," Matt. 7: 13, 14. My readers, observe that all who wish to leave the broad way and enter upon the narrow one, must enter in at the strait gate, must forsake themselves, take up the cross and follow Christ Jesus; must become regenerated christians, dead unto sin; must crucify their flesh and subdue their lusts; must give up, through the power of faith all visible and perishable things, as gold, silver, home and goods, nay, wife and children; together with all they are and have, for the victory of Christ, if circumstances and the honor of Christ require it; they must be prepared to endure disgrace, hunger, misery, pillage, persecution, bonds and death, for the sake of the testimony of God and their consciences, and must adhere to the word of God, by watching and praying; for all those who are yet laden with the burden of unrighteousness and an evil conscience, as with avarice, ungodly desires, the works of the flesh, &c.; or who feel at all doubtful concerning the word and promises of the Lord cannot enter in at the narrow way and strait gate. Let every one be aware of this.

In the second place I say, that the edification and faith of the true christians is tempted in many and various ways, as both Scriptures and experience clearly teach and testify. Now they are tempted by flesh and blood, which never is at rest, then by the lust of the world, and the lust of the eyes, which invitingly tempt the selfish flesh in which no good thing dwelleth, Rom. 7: 18. Again, by the cross and tribulation, which often press heavily; and lastly, by the flattering preaching of peace and the easy doctrine of the preachers who lustily cry, Peace, peace, as the prophet says, Jer. 8: 11, by means of which they console the timid in their faithlessness and disobedience to God, and make an easy way for those who would enjoy the world according to the lusts of the flesh. It is as Peter says, "While they promise them liberty, they themselves are the servants of corruption," 2 Peter 2: 19. For this reason, some of the seed which is sown by the way side, is picked up by the fowls of the air; some is sown on stony places, where there is not much earth, and although it springs up in a short time; yet it can not stand the scorching sun of persecution, and some is choked by the thistles and thorns, and brings forth no ripe ears, Matt. 13: 4—7.

Behold, the proper reason why some timid, light-minded, carnal, corrupt and selfish spirits have again associated themselves with them, is, Because the way was too narrow and the gate too strait for them, and they could not withstand the storming of the flesh. The smiles of the world were too inviting, and the tyranny too oppressive. The thousand wiles of Satan, by which all the pious alike are tempted, succeeded; because, alas, they preferred earthly to heavenly things, and therefore we could no longer live in unity of spirit and peace with them. For they would not be thus subjected, as the prophet laments, Jer. 2: 17; but would follow their own inclinations in every respect, and walk, without the cross, on the broad way of the flesh, with the world. But by the writings and services of Gellius, they were, surely, not redeemed, as he boasts they were.

Behold, these people of whom he so loudly boasts, were such (we regret to have to say it) as, with Demas, 2 Tim. 4: 10, loved the present world, and who so lived with us for some time that we, according to the divine word, dare no longer eat and drink with them. They are not regenerated as Gellius claims, but they are degenerated in their faith and act hypocritically, with earthly-minded hearts under the feint of prayer; they have not forsaken the broad way which leads to death but the narrow way which leads to life; they do not delight in Christ but have forsaken him; they have found rest for their flesh but not for their souls, through repentance, as Gellius pretends. For facts prove whose cause is right, theirs or ours; whose actions are hypocritical, and whose are not, while our actions sacrifice possessions, blood and even life for their cause; but what theirs do, is well known.

This, then, is my conclusion as to his first reason given, why he published his writing; namely, As the angel of darkness can transform himself into an angel of light; as Paul says, 2 Cor. 11: 14; can feign love and make great promises; can feign true confession of Christ and can use Scriptures masterly, so also, can his servants do, as may be seen by this. For Gellius says he published his writing that he might redeem some and save others from deceit; to silence the anabaptists, as he calls them; to root out the pernicious weeds; to serve the church of Christ; to keep the weak of the Netherlands in the right understanding of evangelical doctrine and the right use of the holy sacraments, &c. But if we rightly consider it, and judge it by the Spirit, word and example of Christ; by the usage of the holy apostles and primitive apostolic churches, we find it to be nothing but an institution of the flesh; an encouragement to the impenitent; an inducement to the broad way; a defence of the churches of anti-christ; a confusing and blind-folding of the simple; a covert instigation to persecution of the pious; a destroying of the church of Christ; a dextrous encumbering of the godly; an unreasonable, envious defamation of the saints; an adulteration of the holy word; yea, an open encouragement to unrighteousness, impenitence and carnal liberty.

Behold, this is the effect, fruit and aim of his writing; although he adorns and covers it under the semblance of good intentions and love. If I should at any time yet meet with him, and not be able to verify these assertions, by their fruits and by virtue of the Scriptures, then I will be willing to recant them and bear my shame; for I trust that I, through the grace of God, know of what I write.

An other reason, says Gellius, why he published his writing is, because a nobleman to whom he addressed it, offered to bear the expenses of printing it, &c.

Answer. Zeal is a good thing and highly commendable, if in a good cause to the service and glory of God. But let every one well consider how, why and wherefore he is zealous; lest he make himself guilty of innocent blood, which is the most abominable sin next to sinning against the Holy Ghost.

If his honor has done this in sincere zeal and with good intentions, as Paul did before his conversion, and meant it to be to the honor of God and to the salvation of his neighbors, then I hope that God will give him more light and make truth more manifest to him. But if he has done it for the sake of an idle name or fame, or for the sake of carnal profit and satisfaction, something which the learned can very adroitly portray to such high persons; or, if he contends against the people of God with a bitter zeal, which I trust is not the case, as does Gellius and the preachers, generally, then his action has become such a gross sin and great blindness that I fear he will never be brought to confess Christ.

I would therefore cordially admonish his honor, and beseech him in christian love that he no more burden himself with the sin of others; for he and every-body else will have burden enough of his own, at the day of judgment. All misleading of the miserable souls; all unbelief and idolatry; all lightmindedness and liberty of the flesh; together with all uproar and tyranny which are apt to be the result of his writing will be required, in the day of Christ, at his hands as well as at the hands of the preachers, if not repented of, because he assists and supports them in their abomination with his advice and assistance, with money and material.

Therefore, in my opinion, his honor would have better first considered the matter well and laid out these expenses to the support, assistance, consolation, nourishment and clothing of the needy, especially in these hard times; and not for the purpose of deceiving many unwary hearts and of putting more encumbrances and persecution on the pious.

Again, that Gellius has published his writing under the permission of the said nobleman, has an appearance as if he was one of those who honor and esteem a person according to the measure of his usefulness. But for what reason he has done so; what his seeking and how his heart is, in this matter, I will leave to the Lord who knows all things.

Experience sufficiently teaches of what disposition the rich are, namely, proudhearted, ambitious and covetous of honor. God's wisdom did not say without a cause, Verily, "I say unto you, It is easier for a camel to go through the eye of a needle, than for a rich man to enter into the kingdom of God," Matt. 19: 24. James also says, "Go to now, ye rich men, weep and howl for your miseries that shall come upon you. Your riches are corrupted and your garments are moth-eaten; your gold and silver is cankered; and the rust of them shall be a witness against you, and shall eat your flesh as it were fire," &c., James 5: 1—3. Again, Paul says, "For ye see your calling, brethren, how that not many wise men after the flesh, not many mighty, not many noble, are called," &c., 1 Cor. 1: 26.

Since, then, the mouth of the Lord, as also his faithful servants, James and Paul, have so plainly expressed the dangers of the rich and of those of high standing; since experience teaches how proud-hearted they are, as may be educed from their high titles, houses, shields, medals, clothes, servants, horses and dogs; and since Christ says, "Verily I say unto you, Except ye be converted, and become as little children, ye shall not enter into the kingdom of heaven," Matt. 18: 3; therefore it would be more in accordance with evangelical righteousness, if Gellius, instead, would industriously teach such proud hearts and high persons, the humility of Christ, so that they may learn to forsake themselves; may learn to know themselves, of what they are born, what they are and what they will be; that they may die unto their excessive pomp, splendor, superfluity and ungodliness; may fear God in all sincerity, and walk in his ways; that they may faithfully serve their neighbors, with their abundance, in true humility of heart, and not continually enkindle the fire of pride, fleshly security and light-mindedness, by his flattery or by high-sounding and supplicating phrases; for the inborn ambitious nature of the flesh of Adam's children is, alas, already too apt to crave such things without being encouraged by flattery and smooth words.

I would, therefore, faithfully admonish all to fear God, to strive after truth and to love their neighbors; for the time is coming, and is near at hand that we all shall hear, each one at his time, "Give an account of thy stewardship, for thou mayest be no longer steward," Luke 16: 2. I do not dedicate this my reply and defense to this or that one, as is the custom of the learned, but dedicate it, in christian humility, "To the pious Reader," and desire to subject it to the judgment of all the godly and pious.

If any one under the broad canopy of heaven can teach me with plainer Scriptures or with more powerful truths, whether he be learned or unlearned, man or woman, I will gladly accept of such instruction and obey them. But, by the grace of God, we are convinced that we are on the sure and true way which Christ has prepared for us. Blessed are we if we walk in it and enter in at the strait gate. Let all of understanding minds, who, in true zeal and in the fear of God, seek the praise of their Lord, read and judge that which now follows.

OF THE MISSION OR CALLING OF THE PREACHERS.

GELLIUS complains very much of a bitter and sneering epistle of the anabaptists, as he calls them, in which they are said to have given five particular reasons, as I understand from his writing, why they cannot conscienciously accept the preachers as true and unblamable, and cannot use their sacraments as true and Scriptural ordinances, &c. Of which the vocation of their preachers is the first reason. Gellius assiduously tries to maintain that their calling is christian-like and according to Scripture and says that ours is sectarian and not according to Scripture.

Answer. How bitter and sneering the said epistle may have been, I do not know, for I have never seen it. But I presume it was not so bitter as Gellius complains that it was; that it was a reproof of his corruption, his deceiving and unscriptural sacraments; something which he ever, maliciously, calls brawling and sneering.

Since I did not read the epistle myself, as said, therefore I will not undertake to defend every word of it; but will undertake a defence, by virtue of my ministry of the divine word, and because I have been disgracefully treated in regard to it, so far as concerns the five articles in which the preachers are reproved or accused, whose vocation Gellius maintains as evangalical and right. And I trust that, with the gracious assistance of God, I will be enabled to defend these articles with such power and clearness of Scripture, that all impartial, reasonable readers, on comparing our writings, will, by the grace of God, behold, as in a mirror, that he and all the worldly preachers are not the called preachers and teachers of the church of Christ, to whom the Scriptures point; but that they are the open preachers and teachers of the world, or of the church of anti-christ against whom the Scriptures on every hand warn us, and in many places terrifies us against them. He that hath ears, let him hear what the word of the Lord teaches.

Gellius points out a difference between the calling or sending of the prophets of Christ and the apostles and between the calling of the bishops, pastors and other servants of the church, and says, "That the sending of the prophets of Christ and the apostles was done without any means of man, solely of God; but that the sending of the bishops and pastors is done of God by means of man."

Answer. We do not contradict this, but agree with him in this respect. But we contradict that the calling of which they boast is done in accordance with the apostolic doctrine and usage; and would say that we should well observe these five, following points or articles, according to the Scriptures; namely, Of whom they are called; what they are that are called; to what purpose they are called; what fruit the called bring forth; and what the proper desire and seeking of the called is.

In the first place, we must observe that the calling which was done in the primitive, apostolic church, by means of man, was not done of the world but of the true christians and obedient disciples of the Lord and his word. For Luke writes, Acts 14: 23, "And when they had ordained them elders in every church, and had prayed with fasting, they commended them to the Lord, on whom they believed." Paul also says to Titus, "For this cause left I thee in Crete, that thou shouldst set in order the things that are wanting and ordain elders in every city, as I have apointed thee," Tit. 1: 5, &c. Read also 1 Tim. 3: 12.

Since the preachers, then, boast of a calling of God, by means of man, as said, therefore I would ask without all artifice, Who is the Paul or Barnabas, or Timothy or Titus that has called and ordained Gellius and his like preachers to the service? If they answer, the magistracy; then I would ask in the second place, If the magistracy, who assumes this matter, have the spirit, calling, ministry, ordinance and power of Paul, Barnabas, Titus and Timothy? If they answer in the affirmative, then I would like to see their grounds proven according to Scripture. If they say, because they are part of the church, as Gellius seems to have it, then I would ask in the third place, Whether they are actuated by the Spirit of God? Whether they have crucified the flesh with its lusts, and in their weakness, walk innocently and christianly according to Christ's example and teaching, with his followers? Whether they have become new creatures? Whether they are in Christ and Christ in them? &c. If they say, God knows, and not we, then I would ask in the fourth place, Are you such trees, then, that we cannot judge your fruits, and such lights that we cannot see its refulgence? My reader, ponder well on these questions.

Scriptures plainly testify that there is no christian but who is in Christ and has his Spirit, Rom. 8: 9. It is evident that the magistracy does not conform themselves to the example and Spirit of the Lord, as may, alas, be perceived on every hand by their fruits. For they live in every respect according to the lusts of the flesh; seek vain honor, treasure, pompous living, &c.; they are earthly, and not heavenly-minded; therefore we should consult the word of the Lord whether such people are competent to ordain preachers, pastors and servants for the church of Christ, while their fruits testify that they are yet without Christ's Spirit, kingdom, church and word themselves, as said.

If they should say that they are not called of the magistracy, but of the church, then I would ask in the fifth place, Whether the church which has called them is flesh of Christ's flesh and bone of his bone? Eph. 5: 30, that is, a church which sincerely seeks and fears God; that walks in obedience to his word; loves and serves his neighbor; controls his ungodly lusts; strives after truth with all his heart; leads an unblamable, pious life, and who is prepared for the sake, of the will and word of the Lord, to sacrifice and abandon, money, goods, blood and life, nay, father, mother, life, husband, wife, children and every thing else, if the honor of God requires it? If they answer no, which is the true answer, then it is already proven that they are not the church and people of the Lord; for the church of Christ must be in unity of spirit with Christ, as has already been heard. If, then, they are not of Christ's church, how can they call preachers unto the church of Christ, as Paul, Barnabas, Timothy and Titus, and the primitive church have done? If on the contrary they answer Yes, then I say again, their open unrighteousness, slander, godlessness, avarice, pomp, drunkenness, superfluity, unchastity, hatred, envy, unmercifulness, violence, &c., testify before the whole world that the answer is not the true one.

Inasmuch as it is manifest that both the magistracy and the subjects are directly contrary to the Spirit and word of Jesus Christ, to his walk and actions; and have not a syllable which in this respect agrees with the spirit and actions of Paul, Barnabas, Timothy, Titus, or of the primitive church; therefore I am very much surprised that he can be so imprudent and inconsiderate, or so very bold as to boast, in these times of grace in which the truth has become so manifest, that he and the preachers of his character were called and ordained of God by the means of man, as were the elders of the primitive church, by Paul, Barnabas, Timothy and Titus.

O, that God would grant that he would once consider and not compare the faithful men and dear servants of God, together with the zealous, regenerated communities and pious children of the primitive churches to this impenitent, reckless and bad world who wish to be considered the true church; and would no more blind the poor unwary hearts who little regard the holy word, with such a semblance and quotation of the Scriptures; for it would be of infinite value to his poor, miserable soul, at the time of his dissolution.

I would now leave it to the reflection of all intelligent readers, how the calling, of which the preachers boast, can stand the test of the Scriptures, while those of whom they boast that called them, are found to be not only no regenerated, pious christians, but besides, open despisers and impenitent contenders against God and his word, as may, alas, be seen, on every hand, by their actions.

In the second place we should observe of what disposition, doctrine and conduct the called servants of the word should be, according to the testimony of the Scriptures; namely, "Blameless, the husband of one wife, vigilant, sober, of good behavior, given to hospitality, apt to teach; not given to wine, no striker, not greedy of filthy lucre; but patient, not a brawler, not covetous; one that ruleth well his own house, having his children in subjection with all gravity;" not a novice; he must be holy, just, temperate, &c. "Holding fast the faithful word as he hath been taught; that he may be able, by sound doctrine, both to exhort and to convince the gainsayers." "Moreover he must have a good report of them which are without; lest he fall into reproach and the snare of the devil," &c. "Even so must their wives be grave, not slanderers, sober, faithful in all things," 1 Tim. 3; Tit. 1.

My reader, observe, this is not my word but the word of the Holy Ghost, which gives a true pattern of a true preacher, bishop, pastor, teacher and servant who will, in the church of Christ, bring forth fruit which will remain, John 15.

The Holy Spirit points us to such teachers, to obey and follow them. Paul says, "Obey them that have the rule over you, and submit yourselves; for they watch for your souls, as they that must give account; that they may do it with joy and not with grief," Heb. 13: 17. In another place he says, "We beseech you, brethren, to know them which labor among you, and are over you in the Lord and admonish you, and to esteem them very highly in love for their work's sake, and be at peace among yourselves," 1 Thess. 5: 12, 13.

Such teachers are compared in the Scriptures, to the oxen that tread out the corn, which shall not be muzzled. They are the elders worthy of double honor, and the faithful laborers, worthy of their hire, Deut. 25: 4; Matt. 10: 10. But how Gellius and all the preachers of the German nations, whom he esteems as faithful servants, conform to this I will leave the impartial reader to judge according to the word of the Lord.

Faithful reader, consider well that which I write. They boast that they are called in accordance with Scriptures, as you may hear; although it is obvious and palpable that they lead a life as the one portrayed by Peter and Jude. Many of them are so fallen in the fullness of Bacchus that they, alas, live night and day as swine in full rest; their tables are full of vomit and filthiness, so that there is no place clean, as the prophet says, Isa. 28: 8; they fearlessly walk after their own lusts, as Jude says; and they esteem as joy the temporal, lusty life, says Peter; they are spots and blemishes, sporting themselves with their own deceivings while they feast with you.

Some of them, also, are open fornicators and adulterers. How their wives, as a general thing, conform themselves to Scriptures, may be educed from their fruits. Others are so avaricious that they have become open usurers. They are so intent upon perishable lucre, money and possessions that I dare truthfully say that they, through the easy doctrine of their gospel, have become lords upon earth; yet, most of them are loved of the world and highly esteemed by the ignorant. Their pomp, laziness, ease-seeking, vanity, light-mindedness, pride, &c., baffle all description to say nothing of their tyranny, lying, brawling, slandering, betraying and uproaring against all who seek and fear the Lord.

Reader, it is as I write. O, how willingly would I be silent and close, if the honor of God and his word, and the love for your souls did not compel me to do so; but as it is I am forced to touch upon their abominable shame. Their abominations are so gross and terrible that my soul shrinks back at the thought of them, therefore, imagine how, if I shall treat and write of them. How their actions and behavior agree with the description of Paul, who teaches us that they shall be unblamable, have but one wife, not given to wine, not avaricious, nor covetous of filthy lucre; that they shall be temperate, modest and amiable; have a good report of those that are without; this I will leave to all pious hearts to judge in the fear of God, according to the Scriptures. Behold, my reader, since it is manifest that they are quite contrary to the word of the Lord, in their walk; therefore it is, in fact, nothing but vain hypocrisy, to call such unfruitful, offensive actions, evangelical edification and such a void mockery, a calling.

But Gellius tries to clear himself of this, and lays the blame on those who, according to his writing, lead an unchristian life after the lusts of their flesh, against the ordinance of the apostles, saying, that they cannot weaken the cause of the pious, by their unrighteousness; I would, in the first place, say, Since he complains of them so much, in his book, and says, that they would better be pastors of swine than pastors of the sheep of Christ; and wishes that they would be ex-officiated, &c.; and since these constitute the majority of them, as may be openly seen; therefore Gellius should admit, that, according to the Scriptures, we should not follow such, nor partake of their sacraments, even, if they were the true sacraments; for he himself admits that they are useless people and wishes them ex-officiated.

In the second place I say, Since Gellius acknowledges that they are unfit for their offices; and since he and they are of one church, calling and service, why does he suffer them to remain in their offices, and why does he not, by virtue of his calling, excommunicate them with the advice and consent of his church? Since they are a hindrance to the community and a reproach and disgrace to Gellius and his brother-preachers, whom I would were themselves pious and unblamable.

If he says that the magistracy are to blame, he then admits, that those magistrates are not true servants and members of Christ, who admit such offensive people, as adulterers, wine-bibbers, covetous, &c., as are met with on every hand, to be preachers, while they ruin the souls of the poor miserable people by their wicked offensive life, to say nothing of their doctrine; whom they might debar with a single word, without blood-shed. And what is more, Gellius himself is a faithless shepherd, and dumb watchman. And the magistracy, which is his elector and companion in church-service, have a contempt for God and slander his word.

In the third place I would say, It would be well for Gellius to first learn to know from the Scriptures the nature of Christ and his church together with the true church-servants, pastors and preachers; to rightly judge all things by the Spirit, word and example of the Lord; and to thoroughly search himself, his brother preachers and his church before contending so maliciously against the pious and accuse them before the whole world, without cause. I would further say, Since (if I understand him aright) he admits that we should not hear the adulterers, wine-bibbers, strikers, &c., nor partake of their sacraments (something which was intended, probably, to make his cause have a good appearance); therefore we are forced to view in a Scriptural light, how he, according to Paul's doctrine, can stand as a pastor of the church and as a servant of Christ.

Paul says, A bishop must be blameless; this applies also to a true preacher, pastor and teacher; and it is obvious that Gellius is not unblamable, but blamable in many respects; that he is a friend of the world, who seeks to please the world, contrary to the word of God and the example of Christ, the apostles and of the prophets, otherwise he would have suffered persecution, 2 Tim. 3:12, and not have exercised his service at ease, for so long a time, as is testified by the example of Christ, the apostles and by all the true witnesses.

Again, that he is a hireling who has been hired as a servant at certain wages and a stipend, contrary to the example of Christ and the example of all the true messengers who have been sent by him. He is not only not persecuted for the sake of the testimony of Jesus but he himself persecutes the godly, pious hearts who have neither injured or harmed him nor any body else. He persecutes them wilfully by his instigation, advice and writings; contrary to the example of Christ and all the chosen, as may, alas, be seen by his writings here cited. Besides this, his doctrine is wrong and deceiving. He is an upbraider, condemner, defamer and backbiter of the innocent who sincerely fear God and are zealous for his word; yea, who would seal it with their blood, something which he does not. This assertion is, alas, made good by his writing in which he, without just cause, accuses and condemns the god-fearing, pious hearts before the whole world as being apostates, anabaptists, conspirers, contrabands, sowers of pernicious seed, excommuned sects, servants of the devil and tools; and thus makes them the objects of suspicion, although they sincerely seek the Lord and daily sacrifice possessions and blood for the sake of his holy word.

Besides, he is a supporter and defender of the kingdom of anti-christ, a falsifier of the Scriptures, an abuser of the sacraments, a strengthener of the impenitent, a liar, &c., as will be plainly shown, by the grace of God, each in its turn.

In the third place it should be observed for what purpose the true preachers are called, namely, that they should teach the word of the Lord; rightly use his sacraments; lead and rule in the church of God; gather together with Christ and not scatter; console the afflicted; admonish those not ordained; seek what is lost; bind up what is bruised; separate those that are incurable, without any respect of person, and should assiduously watch over the vineyard, house and city of God, as the Scriptures teach, Matt. 28:19; 12:30; Mark 16:15.

Behold, my reader, these are the proper reasons why the Holy Ghost has ordained in the house of the Lord bishops, pastors and teachers, according to the precept of Paul saying, "He gave some apostles, and some prophets, and some evangelists, and some pastors and teachers; for the perfecting of the saints, for the work of the ministry, for the edifying of the body of Christ; till we all come in the unity of the faith, and of the knowledge of the Son of God, unto a perfect man, unto the measure of the stature of the fullness of Christ," Eph. 4:11—13.

But for what purpose Gellius and all the preachers of the world are called, may be educed from their doctrine and work; namely, to preach to suit the magistracy and the world. Again, to offer to the two golden calves of Dan and Bethel (understand what I mean); to keep the church of anti-christ, without penance and regeneration in unity and peace of the flesh, on the perverted and crooked road of darkness and death, under the name and semblance of the word, contrary to the Spirit, doctrine and example of Christ; to console the wilful, reckless world, who wish to be called the church of Christ, without regeneration and obedience, in their impenitent and ungodly nature, with the death, blood, baptism and Supper of the Lord; to violently oppose Christ Jesus and his word and Spirit, so that the world may live on in their original state and unrighteousness unrebuked; that the preachers may continue in their improper gain and careless life; and that the ignorant people, both rich and poor may live on in the lusts of their flesh, pomp, splendor, drinking, carousing, in avariciousness and hoarding, in short, may continue in the broad and easy way of the flesh, unreproved.

This is made too manifest to be denied, by deeds which speak for themselves; yet their cause is artfully adorned with the Scriptures; they talk much; boast loudly of the grace and favor of God; they use baptism and supper under the appearace of truth, as if they were the church of Jesus Christ; although, in fact, they are nothing but a selfish, refractory, impenitent, earthly and sensual people, as is obvious by their fruits. If I do not write the truth, reprove me.

Since, then, it is clearer than day-light that they are not called to uphold the church of Christ, which is of God and a divine nature, with salutary doctrines, Scriptural sacraments, an unblamable life; earnest reproving, without favor or respect of persons; with faithful admonition and separation, if necessary; but are, under false pretenses of the name and church of Christ; they are servants of the world; receive their reward from it; honor and love it; speak of it, and please it, and whom it seeks and loves to hear, for they are of the world, as John says, 1 John 4: 5.

Therefore it is, in the third place, an incontrovertible evidence, that they, alas, are no called servants of the church of Christ, as they falsely pretend, but are the servants and supporters of the kingdom of anti-christ, as may be unmistakingly learned from their doctrine, walk and fruits if we closely examine them.

In the fourth place we should observe what kind of fruits they bring forth, for Christ says, "I have chosen you and ordained you, that ye should go and bring forth fruit, and that your fruit should remain," John 15: 16. We confess with holy Isaiah, as does also Gellius, that the doctrine of the holy gospel, if preached in the power of the Spirit, according to the Spirit of Christ, cannot fail to bring forth fruit. "For as the rain cometh down, and the snow from heaven, and returneth not thither, but watereth the earth, and maketh it bring forth and bud," so, also, is the word that goeth forth out of the mouth of the Lord, Isaiah 55: 10.

But Gellius and we should well consider that the sowers should, by the power of true faith and the co-operation of the Holy Spirit, be changed into the Spirit and nature of Christ, and should then teach or present to the people the pure, unadulterated seed, which is the word, without all abuse, leaven and hypocrisy, for where there are such sowers, there it will bud and bring forth. The word of the prophet, which the mouth of the Lord has spoken is true and firm. But where there are not such sowers there they arise too early or start out too late; labor and pains will be in vain; for God works not unto repentance but through those who are of his Spirit.

Inasmuch, then, that the word with true preaching does not remain fruitless as we have seen, and since we clearly see that the seed of the preachers of the world brings forth no fruit unto repentance, but alone hypocrisy, therefore it is an indisputable fact that they have not the word of the Lord in power; but that they are artful workers and not true preachers, or else the word of the prophet must be false, which says, "If they had stood in my counsel, and had caused my people to hear my words, then they should have turned them from their evil way, and from the evil of their doings," Jer. 23: 22.

Since then, that preachers are known by their fruits, and that Gellius and his like preachers have preached their doctrine and sacraments so many years to the whole world (which they may continue to do without fear, while they are not opposing the impenitent in their hypocrisy and uncontrolled life, but rather console and encourage them), and yet do not convert a miser nor usurer to liberality; do not bring forth their disciples further than that they profess in name and appearance; remain unchanged in their heart, hate and oppose true righteousness, walk upon the broad way, and earnestly strive after the world, flesh, money and possessions. The pompous remain pompous; the proud remain proud; and liars continue in their falsehood, as is manifest; therefore this their fruitless preaching, vain doctrine and church-service fully prove that their calling is not of God and his word, but of the son of the abyss, anti-christ and of the world, however much they adorn and boast of their cause. The word of God is and will remain true, Isaiah 55: 11.

Gellius then refers us to his fruits, and says, Is not the preaching of the truth and the light of the holy gospel, which we assiduously preach and promulgate both by teaching and writing a good fruit and glorious testimony that our calling is of God and not of the devil; by which the kingdom of the devil is destroyed and by which the papistical abominations, idolatry, masses, absolutions, vigils, &c., have become a deadly stench?

Answer. If they did not mix the dross with the silver and water with wine, that is, if they would preach the truth, without falsehood, and the light without darkness in the power of the Spirit, and would testify it before the whole world by a pious and unblamable life, then we would agree with them that it is a glorious light and a noble fruit. But while they practice wrong and pervert truth into lies, the true apostolic baptism into the baptism of heretics, the church of Christ into pernicious sectarianism and conspiracy, &c., and on the other hand pervert lies to truth, the anti-christian to christian baptism and the reckless, wild world to the Lord's church, &c., we say that their doctrine is deceiving, offensive and wrong, and is not the true doctrine, as Gellius boasts and pretends.

Yea, my reader, they so preach the word of the Lord that unrighteousness and abuse yet remain in full sway; they so teach the truth, that in many respects, false doctrine, lying and deceiving is not yet weakened nor destroyed; they so use and practice divine service that the high places are honored and idolatry is not avoided; they so preach the christian church, that the church of anti-christ remains in full power, as is openly manifested to the whole world both by their work and their tyranny.

In short, it is manifest that they so preach and promulgate the gospel that no repentance follows but that every one, alas, remains as he is; yea, what is worse, that the people are not only not regenerated but are daily growing more wicked. Neither encomiums, reasoning nor artful demonstrations will avail here, for their fruit testifies that their doctrine is faithless and false, as said before, Jer. 23.

The serpent spoke the truth when he said, "God doth know that in the day ye eat thereof, then your eyes shall be opened; and ye shall be as gods, knowing good and evil," Gen. 3: 5. But that which he promised before was a lie, namely, "Ye shall not surely die." Adam and Eve were thereby deceived. Thus, also, do those who teach the serpent's word. They so teach the impenitent, carnal people, concerning the death of the Lord, by their unscriptural sacraments of impenitance, and so console them in their reckless, Adamic nature and life, by false promises (although they do some times speak the truth, as did the serpent, produce Scriptures, partly reprove sin and praise virtue) that there is no body to be found who truly feels sorry for his sins, who sincerely repents of his wickedness, saying, "What have I done," Jer. 8: 6. Behold, says the prophet, so they practice falsehood and strengthen the wicked that none repent of their wickedness.

That some of them have thus weakened the papistical abominations, for this they and we give praises to the Lord. But what does it avail if they renounce the pope and they themselves step in his stead? It is true that many branches of the tree of anti-christ are hewn off, but the roots and body still remain. And although he destroyed some high places, yet they walk in the ways of Jeroboam and have not come to Jerusalem for the purpose of truly worshiping.

Yea, kind reader, had the learned firmly

trusted the living God, faithfully adhered to his word, and had they not acted hypocritically with the world and had they themselves, in power and deeds faithfully practiced, without fear of the cross and the disfavor of the magistracy, what they have, in some of their writings, pointed out, O, what a noble and clear light would have shone on the world, which now, alas, has become such a pernicious darkness and destruction, and a broad way, through the fear of the cross, through hypocrisy, selfishness, desire of ease, ambition and favor of men.

In the second place he says, Is the whole Bible, translated (into the German language) by the memorable D. Martinus, a despisable fruit? Are the songs or hymns composed by Luther and many others a contemptible fruit? Is, also, the constancy, which exists in these times of peril and danger of body and possessions, as it did in the beginning of the gospel, not a noble and genuine fruit of our calling? But such fruits are of no account in their sight or else they will not see them; although they are the surest and the best fruits, &c. The fruits of the outward life and dealings with men, although often mere hypocrisy, only avail in their sight.

Answer. The deceased translators, authors and composers we will leave undisturbed, for they have already found their Lord and Judge; but we will turn to the living, with whom we have to speak. His saying, that writing, translating and composing are the surest and best fruits, is, in my opinion, a very senseless assertion, for such things can be done through learning and skill in languages, without regeneration and change of heart, as he himself well knows. Yea, as the Bible or the Scriptures are read by the greater part of the world, with impure, carnal hearts, so, also, they can, undoubtedly, be translated, through the knowledge and skill of languages, from one language into another, with a carnal, unregenerated and impious heart.

And as hymns are generally sung in God's houses or temples, carelessly, and are light-mindedly sung, here and there, in the streets and in riotous taverns; so, also, can they be composed by a light-minded heart without spirit or regeneration? These are, therefore, not the surest and best fruits, as Gellius pretends to say, for they do not remain. But whatever some, in by-gone times may have written, in true zeal, which is Scripture or conformable to Scripture and useful to the regeneration of the pious, we should, reasonably, praise and esteem.

However, the surest and best fruits are, to so preach the word of God in power, that many may be born of him and be led to sincerely fear and love him; to cordially serve their neighbors; to die unto flesh and blood; to believe on Jesus Christ with all the heart, and tremble at his word; that they may do nothing contrary to it; may truly worship God and conform their whole life or walk according to his Spirit, word and example, for such fruits remain.

I would further say, He boasts of the danger and constancy (as he calls it) of some of their number; now, in these times of war, which he calls a time of trial, because, (if we understand him aright), they can no longer uphold and protect their cause by force of arms; and consider it a noble fruit, although they have, perhaps, not been tempted unto death as we daily are; and therefore he so indiscreetly condemns and profanes our cause, which the Lord knows we have maintained and will maintain in spite of sword or any other deadly weapon, something which cannot be truthfully refuted. We have patiently walked according to the example of Christ; sacrificed our possessions and blood which might have been saved by a single, hypocritical word; and at all times, for our invincible constancy, we suffer with fire, water and sword; being defenceless, and without any resistance "we are killed all the day long; we are accounted as sheep for the slaughter," Rom. 8: 36.

But we give praise to God, that some of them have sacrificed their blood for the sake of the testimony which they had, and with James count them happy; yea, that they are joint-heirs in the sufferings of Jesus Christ; for their deeds have proven that they sought God and were faithful as far as they were enlightened. But what will that avail them, while they close their hearts to the light of truth; contend against the Spirit, word and will of God; preach lies, pervert and abuse the sacraments, and console and encourage the wild, wicked world in their impenitent, reckless life? Something which the faithful heroes have not done, for they were faithful in every thing which they acknowledged as the truth. If they had acknowledged more they would, doubtlessly, have died for the sake thereof as well as for that which they did, at the time, acknowledge.

If our opponents are of the same spirit then they may boast. But their fruits openly testify that that they are, alas, very different.

Again, he writes, that the fruits of an outward life, alone, avail in our sight, &c. Do not our sore oppression, trials, great tribulation, misery, possessions and blood; besides, our open and frank confession, openly testify that he makes this assertion without all truth. Yea, that he openly slanders and wrongs us? *O malitiosam calumniam ac perversitatem*, (O malicious calumny and perversity).

My kind reader, observe that all Scriptures and the power of true faith constrain us zealously to teach an upright, pious, godly and penitent life; for Jesus Christ says, "Let your light so shine before men, that they may see your good works." Paul, also teaches, "That ye may approve things that are excellent; that ye may be sincere and without offence till the day of Christ." That we might walk worthy of the Lord and his gospel. Peter says, "Having your conversation honest among the Gentiles;" and John says, That we should walk even as Christ walked, Matt. 5: 6; Phil. 1: 10; Col. 1: 10; 1 Pet. 2: 12; 1 John 2: 6.

Since Scripture, on every hand, enjoin upon us a pious life, as has been heard; therefore it is reasonable and just, if we believe the word of God, that we zealously follow, in our weakness, that which the Spirit of the Lord has so clearly taught and enjoined in his holy word.

But his assertion, that such fruits, only, avail in our sight comes, alas, from an impure heart. For, I presume, he well knows, that we plainly teach that we cannot be saved by outward works, however great and glorious they may appear or that we can thus entirely please God; for they are ever mixed with imperfection and weakness and, therefore, through the corruption of the flesh we cannot acquire the righteousness required in the commandments; therefore we point, alone, to Christ Jesus who is our only and eternal Righteousness, Reconciliation and Propitiator with the Father, and do not at all trust in our works. My reader, I write the truth in Christ Jesus, and lie not.

O, that Gellius would quit his unguarded talk, and speak no more than that which is true, for a liar is a disgrace and shall not inherit the kingdom of God; and that he could once feel what a true, christian faith is, what it requires in its nature and what it produces in power; he would then know what it is that brings forth such a pious, penitent and unblamable life which he has in times gone by, so disgracefully slandered and upbraided as devilish fruits, hypocrisy and a new mockery; and, as appears, would yet upbraid, if it was not for the experience of many and the great quantity of innocent blood which has been shed.

Behold, dear reader, now you can see how they adorn and deck their abominable hypocrisy and fruitless, impenitent church-service with writing, translating, singing, &c., although generally alone without repentance and regeneration, as heard; and how they basely construe and explain the sincere, pious fruits of true faith which are taught and represented by all the Scriptures, ceremonies and sacraments; that they may daub the wall with untempered mortar and console the poor, miserable people in their disregard of the word of the Lord. But when the Lord's hurricane, flood and great hailstones shall come with a great noise, then they will break down the wall that they have daubed with untempered mortar and bring it to the ground so that the foundation thereof shall be discovered, &c., Ezekiel 13: 13, 14.

In the third place, Gellius writes that the office of a preacher consists of two parts, namely, in rooting out, destroying and opposing; also in sowing and building, &c., and boasts that their fruits, especially as regards the first part, cannot be denied in many kingdoms and principalities; and that the Lord Jesus Christ (as he says), has, through their services, planted sincere repentance and such true christian faith in many hearts, that the small community at Emden, in sure expectation of a reward in heaven. willingly supports several hundreds of poor people by their alms, &c.

Answer. We admit that the first part of a preacher's office consists in rooting out, destroying and opposing, and the other of sowing and building up, and this is a proof for us that they are not the preachers to serve in such capacity. Although they have renounced, in different cities and countries, (for which we praise the Lord), some abuses and idolatries, which were so gross that they might be plainly noticed, without Scriptures, to be abominations; yet, the root of all deceit remains untouched, namely, the false doctrine and unscriptural sacraments, with which they console the world and encourage them in their impenitence and natural state or Adamic heart which is the source of all unrighteousness, as may, alas, be seen on every hand by the fruits.

If, then, they are the true preachers as they pretend to be, let them execute the first part, namely, To break in pieces with the hammer of the divine word the proud, obdurate hearts, the impure, avaricious hearts, the blood-guilty, tyrannical hearts, &c., of whom it is written that they are worthy of death; to humble them by the eternal judgment and punishment of Almighty God; to discover to them their ungodly and corrupt nature and flesh, by virtue of the commands; that they may learn to know themselves, see their shame and thus, with sorrowing and repenting hearts, in the fear of the coming wrath and eternal punishment of the just and great God, sincerely and tremblingly repent and die unto their sins, crucify their flesh, smother their lusts, and walk before their God with broken and humbled hearts. Behold this is the true and principal rooting out, destroying and opposing to which Scriptures say, the true preachers are called.

Then let such moved and humbled hearts, such penitent and sighing sinners, who are, with Peter and Magdalene, heart broken, bitterly weep, and with David confess their guilt; then point them to the only and eternal seat of grace, Christ Jesus; teach them the eternal mercy, love, favor and grace of God, according to the Scriptures; console them with the gospel of peace; carefully anoint their wounds, caused by the sharp and smarting wine, with the oil of the joyful promises of Christ, that they may thus, through faith arise with Christ from the death of their abominable sins into the new life of all virtue; that they may, in true faith and in pure, unfeigned love, ever walk without all offence, according to the example of Christ and all the pious; and give thanks to the Lord for his manifest love. Behold, thus sow and build, all true preachers who are called of the Spirit of the Lord and are fit for his service.

Dear reader, observe; Since Gellius and the preachers, then, are not such destroyers and builders, rooters and planters, as their deeds testify; but destroy that which is good and build up that which is bad; that they root out truth with their offensive doctrine and plant falsehood with their false sacraments and easy life; therefore our assertion is incontrovertible, that they are not the servants of Christ nor his true messengers.

He writes, "that the Lord, through their service, has planted true repentance and such a true christian faith in many hearts, that the small congregation at Emden were comforted in expectation of a heavenly reward."

Answer. If this were true indeed, as he writes, it should be attested by the fruits and manifested by the works. Paul says, "The kingdom of God is not in word, but in power," 1 Cor. 4: 20. Let nobody falsely boast; we will be judged of one before whom nothing is hidden. Nobody knows what true, christian faith and and true repentance are, but he who has truly received them and felt their power. If God, then, plants repentance in so many hearts, as Gellius pretends, why is he and his like preachers, yet so impenitent, so inimical and refractory to truth, and so offensive and blamable in wholesome doctrine? If those of whom he speaks are of the same mind with him, which we trust they are not, then he has not written the truth; this is too plain to be denied.

Those hearts in which God has planted true repentance and an ardent, true, christian faith cannot, especially in these times of manifest truth, long be hidden, nor remain without the cross promised by the Holy Scriptures, if, even, their own preachers and relations are to persecute them. For if they would testify their faith by a frank confession, by a pious life and by works, which are the fruits of true and ardent faith, they would soon find that they have to bear the cross with Christ, their Lord. However much Gellius may garble it in his writings, the word of Christ is and remains the word of the cross; all who accept the word in power and in truth must be prepared for the cross; this, both Scriptures and experience abundantly teach us.

This had necessarily to be said, lest we be consoled with a false boasting and idea, and lest the word of the Lord, spoken to the false prophets, be applied to us; saying, Ye promise life to those souls to whom you should not promise it, "By your lying to my people that hear your lies," Ezekiel 13: 19.

Notwithstanding, many are suffered in their churches who wantonly live in pomp, splendor, carousing, avarice and according to the lusts of the flesh, which service a true and faithful preacher, through which God works, does not allow, if the evangelical Scriptures and apostolic ordinances and doctrine shall avail and are true.

But, as to the alms and support of the poor, I would say, that it is a good and praise-worthy work, and cordially approve of it. Also, that many pious, gentile philosophers, as Aristotle, Plato, &c., have considered it as right and just. But we contradict that sincere and true repentance, or the true seed and foundation of sincere love, which is a fruit of true faith, consists therein; for we may give in hypocrisy, as well as in love, as may be seen by the Scribes and Pharisees, by the open heathens and daily, yet, by the papists.

Paul also agrees with this, saying, "And though I bestow all my goods to feed the poor, and though I give my body to be burned, and have not charity, it profiteth me nothing," 1 Cor. 13: 3. Therefore, let every one take heed for what purpose and with what heart he bestows his alms. For the love which is of God and of a divine nature hates all boasting and hypocrisy, neither does it know them; of this I am convinced.

If Gellius points to the support and service of the poor, which I deem praiseworthy, as a fruit of true repentance, then I would ask in the first place, Whether he finds a lack of alms with our church; although they are exiled to foreign countries and live in poverty and misery and are partly robbed of their possessions?

In the second place I would say, that while he wants to boast of true repentance, he should first commence with the repentance of such faith as brings forth the love and fear of God, and not with the alms for the poor. For the Lord's own mouth speaks, That love is the keeping of his commandments; yea that it is the greatest commandment, Deut. 6: 5.

Yea, my reader, if he and his could fully comprehend sincere, true repentance and true christian faith, which he thinks has been planted in their hearts, O, how cordially would they fear their God, love and thank him for his favors and loving-kindness, and how willingly would they follow and obey his holy word! But how they do love and thank him for his loving-kindness and how they obey and follow his word, their actions and fruits, alas, too plainly testify.

If they love God, and if a true, living faith and genuine repentance has been implanted in their hearts, as he boasts, why do they, then, yet walk after the manner of the Gentiles in pomp and splendor, in the lusts of their eyes, embellishment of their bodies and houses, in avariciousness, carousing, &c.? and why do they not heed the words of Paul? namely, "If ye live after the flesh, ye shall die," Rom. 8: 13.

If they love their neighbors, as the Scriptures command and true repentance brings forth, why are they, then, so usurious, avaricious and perfidious amongst themselves? Why do they litigate? Hatred, envy, lying, deceit, backbiting and defamation still prevail amongst his followers; besides they curse, swear, brawl, fight, war, destroy, rob and some of them are fornicators, perjurers, &c.; to say nothing about their disgraceful upbraiding, profaning and defaming of all those who seek and fear the Lord. What sort of repentance and faith it is, of which he so loudly boasts, you may consider in the fear of God.

O, my kind reader, it never fails that where true faith is, there, also, is the righteousness of faith; where there is unfeigned, christian love, there also is obedience to the holy word, and where there is true, sincere repentance there also is an unblamable life, according to the truth; this is incontrovertible.

Is it not a false assertion to say that the giving of alms shows true repentance; since we do not know whether it is done in sincerity of heart or in hypocrisy and vanity, while he can plainly see that those who give alms generally are merely of the world and flesh, yea, without regeneration and repentance?

It would be well if he could take to heart what stands written: The alms (gifts) of the ungodly do not please the Most High; and sins are not remitted by much offering; he who offers of the possessions of the poor, does, even as if he slaughtered the Son, in the sight of the Father. But to keep God's commandments, is a pleasing offer and to do according to the command, this is an offer which avails. "To depart from wickedness is a thing pleasing to the Lord; and to forsake unrighteousness is a propitiation." Again, "To obey is better than sacrifice, and to hearken, than the fat of rams," Eccl. 35: 3; 1 Sam. 15: 22.

I would further say that it is my fixed opinion that the beforementioned alms, of which he boasts, are not the two mites or pennies of the widow's necessaries; but only a small crumb of their abundance, riches and wealth. This I frankly assert, and I have not the least doubt that if they would apply, to the support of the poor, their silk, damask and the superabundance of clothes in which they go splendidly attired, the ornaments of their houses, the golden and silver rosaries, the useless, costly ornaments, gold rings, chains, silvered and gilt swords, besides, the booty of the persecuted which may be found in the houses of some, then the poor would not, in the least, suffer from want.

O, my reader, yet by him, this must be called true repentance and a highly boastful work. If such boasting of outward works was heard from our side, how soon would we hear that we are work-saints, and that we want to be saved by our own merits.

O, Lord! O dear Lord!! thus the ignorant people are deceived and consoled in their impenitent, reckless life with their own works and merits. I think that such preachers may justly be called peace-preachers, bolsterers and false daubers of the Spirit of the Lord, since they praise such a carnal people as penitent and happy according to the prophetic word, while they are still quite earthly and carnally-minded; as their daily walk openly testifies before the whole world.

My faithful reader, observe the word of the Lord, and take heed; for it is not always a true christian faith nor sincere repentance which the children of the world, who are prone to walk upon the broad way, sometimes teach and represent as true faith and sincere repentance. But this is true faith; which cordially accepts all the words of God, the threatening commands as well as the consoling gospel, and trusts in them as the sure and true word of God, &c. From such faith, which Paul calls a gift of God, springs the fear of God which drives out sin, and the true love which gladdens, enlivens and cheers the heart and leads it into the obedience of the word.

Where there is such a faith which brings forth a new, converted and changed mind; which makes us dead unto sin and leads us into a new life; changes us from Adam to Christ; puts off the old man with all his works and puts on the new man with his works and thus conforms all his thoughts, words and works to the Spirit, word and ways of the Lord, behold, there is true repentance to which the holy prophets, John the baptist, Christ Jesus, together with all the apostles and pious servants have so earnestly pointed us and so faithfully admonished us.

All those who would rightly preach this faith and this genuine repentance, and would thereby bring forth fruits, must themselves first, truly believe and sincerely repent; this is too obvious to be denied; and that Gellius and his like preachers do not yet, in power and truth, believe and sincerely repent, I will leave to be judged by their own writings and fruits, both here on earth and before the throne of God and Christ.

Gellius further writes, and says, If it were true that many of our audience turn the preaching of the holy gospel to lasciviousness, as in Jude 4, and that our preaching avails but little, although many pious, penitent hearts incontrovertibly prove the contrary, then the old lamentation of the prophet Isaiah were but verified, that says, Who hath believed our report, &c.? He also points to the saying of Christ, namely, If they have kept my word they will also keep your word; with which he doubtlessly means to say, as the world has not kept my doctrine, therefore they will not keep your doctrine.

He also, refers to the four kinds of seed and four kinds of earth, Matt. 13: 8, 19, 23.

Answer. God has never, from the beginning, preached repentance through the impenitent. The mouth and wisdom of God say, "Do men gather grapes of thorns, or figs of thistles," Matt. 7: 16.

Since, it is clear that Gellius and his like preachers remain so earthly and carnally-minded, and are driven by such an unmerciful, tyrannical and slandering spirit, which is, properly, the inborn spirit, nature and fruit of the old serpent; how, then, can they rightly preach the penitent, pious life and the fruitful, merciful, amiable spirit, nature and disposition of Christ, which they not only not acknowledge, but upbraid as hypocrisy and which they sincerely hate in all the pious?

In the second place, I say, that the preaching of peace and the making of cushions of the learned, as they do, will bring forth but few truly repentant persons. For although the world is so wicked and wild that we should reasonably be terrified at their very great wickedness, yet they are so comforted and consoled by their preachers, with their infant baptism, supper, alms and with the merits, grace, death and blood of the Lord, that they presume themselves to be the Lord's chosen holy church and people.

In the third place I would say, because he speaks doubtfully, saying, If it *were* true that many of his audience turn the preaching of the word to lasciviousness, and little fruit was brought forth by it, something which he however does not admit, &c., the reader should well mark how assiduously they defend the world and the church of anti-christ, saying, If it *were* true, &c. Yet the whole German nation has degenerated to such a wild and reckless freedom, by the preaching of their free gospel that if we reasonably admonish and reprove them for their open unchastity, carousing, pomp and splendor, cursing and swearing, lascivious and foul words, we must immediately hear that we are conspirators, vagabonds, fanatics, heaven-stormers, anabaptists and other indecent, disgraceful slanders.

But in regard to the complaint of Isaiah and the saying of Christ, If they have kept my saying, &c., John 15: 20, with which he wishes to cover and adorn his unscriptural practices and doctrine of impenitence, I would ask him: If Christ and the apostles have received those who lived after the lusts of their flesh, such as drunkards, railers, extortioners, avaricious, fornicators, adulterers, &c., as their disciples, so long as they had not sincerely repented?

If he answers in the affirmative, then he speaks contrary to all Scripture. For Paul says, That we shall not eat with such, if he does call himself a brother, 1 Cor. 5: 11, and that they shall not inherit the kingdom of God, 1 Cor. 6: 11. If he answers in the negative, then I would again ask, Why they receive them as disciples while they are not disciples of Christ, but are, according to his own words, of the world?

If he answers that they do not receive them, then I would ask him why they baptize their children before they let them partake of the supper? And whether it would not be better if he would separate them, according to the Scriptures from the communion of those whom he esteems pious? If he answers that he does not know of such, which he can by no means, truthfully say, then I would, lastly ask, if he does not know a tree by its fruits; if he cannot see a light that shines in darkness, as all true christian lights are called in the Scriptures, nor a city which is built upon a high mountain? Matt. 5: 14.

Since Gellius and all the preachers, receive and suffer such impenitent persons, whom he himself calls of the world, as heard, in the communion of their churches, against the practice of Christ and of the apostles, therefore they must thereby acknowledge that Christ's church is of the world or the world of Christ's church; that they, contrary to the apostolic doctrine, ordinance and example, dispense the sacraments also to the world, which according to the Scriptures properly belong to the penitent alone, who have placed themselves in the church of the Lord, in obedience to the word; that they, thereby, include the penitent (if such there be) in the communion of the impenitent; and that they are open flatterers and enemies of the cross of Christ, Phil. 3: 18, who act hypocritically with the higher class and flatter the world, lest they lose their favors; and thus openly and faithlessly transgress the Lord's word and ordinance, for the sake of their bellies and reject it as powerless and discouraging.

Again, as to his reference to the Lord's parable, I would say, That I would have him take a better view of it and not console himself herewith; for it has reference to the true preachers and disciples who have been put to the trial of the cross of Christ, in obedience to the word, and not to the cross-fleeing preachers and the world, as may be learned not alone from the Scriptures but also from experience.

For some reject the received and manifest truth, and the sown seed is devoured of the fowls of the air and does not bring forth fruit. Some are withered by the scorching sun of the cross, oppression and misery, which proves them wood, hay and stubble, 1 Cor. 3: 12.

Others are smothered by the cares of this world, and by deceitful riches and the lusts of the flesh, so that the received knowledge dies in them, and the lusts and love of this world prevail, which in our times, as well as in the times of the primitive church, is too often the case with those who, with Demas, alas, again grasp the love of the world.

But the last receive it in a sincere, pious heart, and meekly bring forth fruit with patience; although they are much tempted by all kinds of trials, anxiety, oppression and deadly perils, yet they are, by the gracious help of God, so armed with a true faith, love, hope, and patience or long-suffering; are so confirmed in God, that neither the fire of tribulation can consume them (for they are gold, silver and precious stones), nor sword and pain can frighten or deter them from the ways of the Lord, Rom. 8: 38.

That the beforementioned parable has reference to such christians and not to the world and its preachers, is too clear to be controverted or denied. And Gellius and his like preachers of the world remain defenders of unrighteousness, comforters of the impenitent and servants of the kingdom of anti-christ, who not only pitifully deceive their own souls but also those of their church, and support and defend them in their gross abominations and impenitent carnal lives, by their perversion of Scriptures and useless consolations, to their eternal destruction.

In the fifth place it should be observed, what the preachers' desire and seeking should be. The Scriptures teach that Moses and Jeremiah, Exod. 4: 10, reluctantly accepted of the service when they, Jer. 1: 6, were called and sent of God, as Jeremiah laments when the cross bore heavily upon him, Exod. 4: 10; Jer. 1: 6; Jer. 20: 8.

All that the prophets, apostles and faithful servants of God ever sought and desired was nothing else than that they might proclaim the name of their God and might point their neighbors to the way of peace. They did not seek money, gold, honor and an easy life, but they executed their office to which they were appointed, and which was, alas, not weighed by the heedless people, under many sore trials, miseries, anxieties, tribulations, beatings, poverty, oppression and tortures, and at the risk of life even, as sacred and profane histories, in many instances, teach. But why the preachers of the world have hitherto refused and yet refuse the service, and what they seek thereby, experience and the Holy Spirit plainly teach us, saying, that they *promise* death to the pious and life to the wicked, for the sake of a hand-ful of barley or a piece of bread; that they seek the fat and the wool, milk and flesh; that they eat but do not feed the Lord's sheep, Ezekiel 34: 3; that they preach peace for their bellies' sake (that is, if well paid), and war if not well fed, &c.

Facts testify openly that it is true that they do not seek the salvation of souls, but a careless, easy life; for we never saw in all our life that the preachers lived where there were no rents or liens. That, also, Gellius does not seek the salvation of his sheep, but the rents, he has testified when he left Norden, where he was called by the same calling, and moved to Emden where the annual income was greater; something which the paters, in times gone-by, esteemed as unjust in their concilions and decrees, and punished with excommunication.

If he sought the salvation of their souls, and not the rents, as becomes a good and faithful shepherd, according to the example of Jesus Christ and of all faithful servants, why, then, did he make void his first calling, which was, according to his assertion, divine, and leave the first sheep who were no less delivered through the death of the Lord, and bought with his precious blood, than the last, of which he now has the charge. O, hypocrisy and feigning!

Again, Gellius says in regard to the sustenance of the preachers, That they have little care as to how the community, of whom the magistracy are a part, provides them the necessaries of life, while it is certain that if they serve the gospel, as he says, they shall also live of the gospel; and cites Matt. 10: 10; Luke 10: 7.

Answer. If Gellius and the preachers were such servants as are referred to in these Scriptures, then it is plain, that the sustenance of the gospel was promised them. But if any-body goes into the service and uselessly destroys and ruins the Lord's goods, if faithless, seeks his own self in all things and does the things which are contrary to the will and honor of the Lord, should such a faithless servant receive the reward which is reasonably due to the faithful, assiduous laborer? I think you will answer in the negative; and that he should rather receive the displeasure and punishment of the Lord. For he speaks, "When the Lord therefore of the vineyard cometh, what will he do unto those husbandmen? They say unto him, He will miserably destroy those wicked men, and will let out his vineyard unto other husbandmen, which shall render him the fruits in their seasons," Matt. 21: 40, 41.

We acknowledge that sustenance has been promised, by Scriptures, to the true and faithful servants. But, since Gellius and his like preachers are unfaithful servants who destroy the Lord's goods, steal his gain, scatter his sheep and do not gather them together; who, alas, fearlessly lead to hell his precious treasure, namely the poor miserable souls, in great numbers, as those truly regenerated can scripturally judge by the testimony of their open deeds; therefore their sustenance is not the sustenance of true preachers, but an unreasonable, shameful gain; an unbecoming livelihood and the reward of the deceived souls; this, all of sound understanding must acknowledge and admit.

O, my faithful reader, remember, so long as the world donates such splendid houses and large incomes to their preachers, the false prophets and deceivers will be numerous.

They pretend to vindicate by Scripture all heresy, deceit, idolatry, pomp, hypocrisy, tyranny and drunkenness, together with their unreasonable and shameful service of the flesh and world, and make the ignorant and blind world believe that it is right.

But I openly testify, I testify it unreservedly that the preachers of the world, to take them all in all, are Balaamites, who love the reward of unrighteousness, and serve for the sake of a handful of barley and a piece of bread, whereby they profane the name of God, Ezekiel 13: 19. "Prophets which eat at Jezebel's table," 1 Kings 18: 20, servants and defenders of Maaz, 1 Chron. 2: 27, who are honored with great rewards of Antioch, that is, anti-christ; Ahabites, who, for the sake of an acre, stone the pious Naboth, 1 Kings 21, that is, who advise and instigate the world by their speeches, writings, backbiting, complaints and permission to the killing of many an innocent, pious child of God.

Again, they are priests of Jeroboam, who, contrary to the example of Christ Jesus and his holy apostles, hire themselves, for an annual stipend, to an unevangelical service of impenitence, which is practiced, in all respects, without power, spirit, repentance and regeneration, as may openly be seen; their service is vain labor and mockery, besides, an unbecoming speculation.

O, how distinctly has the Holy Ghost portrayed them before our eyes, if we would but see, saying, "And through covetousness shall they, with feigned words, make merchandise of you." Again, "Having men's persons in admiration because of advantage," 2 Peter 2: 3; Jude 16, and other like sayings; For that they have sought unreasonable gain and an easy life, from youth, and yet seek it, is so obvious, that it cannot, at all, be denied.

Besides, their liens and properties have

been obtained from anti-christ, through artful dealings, enchanting roguery and clerical robbery, and are yet, daily, thus obtained from those who walk upon the broad way without repentance, and who find, alas, no pleasure in the Lord's holy word.

They act hypocritically and flatter the magistrates and those of high-standing; they console the impenitent and persecute the pious; they adulterate the plain word, sacraments and ordinances of Jesus Christ, by which the church should be gathered and maintained in Him; they preach to suit and please the world, that they may receive, under the semblance of the gospel, the blood-reward of the poor and miserable souls, for which they assiduously strive; that they may peaceably possess it and turn it to the advantage of easy times. Yet they console themselves with the idea that they serve the gospel and therefore should live of the gospel. Behold, thus they give a scriptural shape to all kinds of false doctrines and works, and thus they give a fine appearance to hypocrisy.

My faithful reader, I warn you in sincere love, take heed. Again, I say unto you, The true and faithful servants of Jesus did not have such annual stipends, rents and property attached to the apostolic churches; but the greater part earned their livelihood by their own labor; yet served the church of Christ, and, in all love and humility, walked before them with true doctrines and an unblamable life. They have diligently watched over the Lord's house, city and vineyard; opposed all evil and deceiving spirits with the word of the Lord; admonished the disorderly, consoled the afflicted, reproved the transgressors, excommunicated the disobedient and refractory; served reasonably, left the world to the world, and have patiently borne its cross; and what necessaries they needed they received, not of the world, but at the hands of their pious disciples, in humility, without avariciousness or on desire of shameful gain. Scriptures allow this much, as said above, for they rightly pastured the Lord's sheep, they faithfully planted the vineyard, assiduously tilled the land, and stored the sheaves and fruits in the Lord's barn, as the example of the prophets and apostles points out and the Spirit and word of the Lord command, and enjoin upon all faithful servants.

I will conclude my remarks in regard to the calling of the preachers, and would yet say, Since the Scriptures teach that the servants of the holy word are called either of the Lord himself, or by means of the pious, as has been heard; that they shall be unblamable; able rightly to rule the Lord's church, bring forth permanent fruits, destroy and build up; that they shall not seek unreasonable gain, but sincerely seek the honor and praise of God and the salvation of their neighbors, &c.; and since we plainly see and palpably feel that they, alas, are altogether called of such as we would wish had the Spirit of Christ; moreover that they are blamable in all things, for they are of an unmerciful, tyrannical disposition, and of an earthly, carnal life; pervert the gospel, and do not teach it in power and true repentance; wrongly use the sacraments without power, spirit and repentance, and dispense it to those who are not disciples of Jesus Christ; they deceive the people; do not bring forth permanent fruits, plant that which is evil and root out that which is good; they do not seek the honor and praise of God but their own profit and gain, the favor of the world and an easy, careless life, I will let their doctrines, sacraments, fruits and life testify to this; therefore I say without any reservation that they are *not* the called preachers and servants of the church of Christ, whom we shall, according to the Scriptures, obey, accept and follow, as they pretend we should, but that they are preachers for the sake of gain and servants of anti-christ, against whom we are, on every hand, warned by the word of God; not to hear or follow them nor their doctrine but to flee from and *avoid* them as deceivers, false prophets, wicked men and faithless servants.

Yea, my reader, what can they say about their calling, preaching and church-service? It is, briefly stated, not possible, according to the sure promises and prophecies of Christ Jesus and the prophets, that a true and faithful preacher, witness or teacher, especially in these evil times and in this wicked and tyrannical world, can faithfully teach and proclaim, without respect of persons, the pure gospel of Jesus Christ, without being exiled, proscribed or killed; much less enjoy life at ease and liberty, as they do, without persecution, yea, receive annual stipends of the world and be highly honored and loved by them.

Peruse all the Holy Scriptures and see if you can find that Christ Jesus, with his holy apostles, true witnesses and followers fared as they do and received as they do; whether persecution, cross, tribulation, anxiety, prison and death were not, generally, their lot and part. Besides experience, yet daily, teaches this abundantly.

If, then, the preachers acted rightly, if they were walking according to the example of Christ and his apostles; if their teachings and dealings were right, as they pretend them to be, then all the Holy Scriptures must be wrong, the word of the cross be fulfilled and Christ and his prophecies must be false, this is incontrovertible. Therefore, all their boasting and artful citations concerning their calling, office, doctrine and church-service, together with their defense are, in fact, wrong, futile, hypocritical, unjust and without truth. "For all seek their own, not the things which are Jesus Christ's," Phil. 2: 21; their own ease and not the salvation of their neighbors; they are enemies of the cross; they serve their own bellies, Rom. 16. If they would rightly reprove all the ungodliness, idolatry, abuse, pride, pomp, splendor, hypocrisy and unfaithfulness of this world, without respect of persons with the same earnestness, assiduity, heart and mind, &c., as did Christ with his holy apostles and true witnesses, and in other respects would not act so freely; if they would hate all unrighteousness of the world as Christ Jesus and his apostles hated it, then they would not long remain at ease in their comfortable houses; they would not have such incomes and they would be little regarded by this reckless, wild world. Of this I am convinced.

But they do differently; they make the garment to fit the man (as the saying is), and they so teach and act that the world may suffer them and love them and that they may be the friends of the world, so that they may be at ease, not be persecuted and enjoy good times; this is something which is generally well understood, and a sure proof that their sending or calling together with their doctrine and church-service is in every particular without the ordinance, Spirit and word of God, as said before.

Herewith, Gellius' article on the calling has been replied to. I would earnestly beseech him and all the preachers to reflect in the fear of God for before the flaming eyes of the Lord, which search heaven and earth, nothing wrong will be hidden, however artfully it may be covered before man's eyes, and however much it may be decked and adorned with smooth words.

Next, Gellius denies our calling, and says, Before we can agree with the preachers or teachers who claim that they bring forth fruit, they must first be rightly called of a church of God, and not from a collection who have been deceived by false prophets; and then come boldly forward and preach; or they must show by facts (as he says) that Christ has done wrong, and that he should have rather preached secretly to avoid the cross (as he says we do) than in public, &c.

Answer. The sending or calling of Moses, of Christ, of Paul, of the apostles and prophets was also denied by the perverse. Moses had to hear that he had killed the Lord's people and that he had led them into the wilderness that they might perish through want and misery. Christ Jesus was called a wine-bibber, blasphemer and one possessed of the devil, Matt. 11: 19. Paul was called a rebel and an apostate Jew, &c. Behold, thus in their times the sending of the faithful servants of the Lord, nay, the the Lord and Messiah himself was despised, although testified by many miracles. How much more, then, shall we be despised, who are such weak and insignificant instruments, and live in seven fold worse and more wicked times than those in which they lived.

Inasmuch, then, as we are accused by our opponents, the learned, that we are not called of a church of God, but of false prophets, or of a false church, therefore I would briefly admonish the reader, to weigh well with the Scriptures who, how and what the church of God is; that it is not a collection of proud, avaricious, extortionate, vain persons, drunkards and impenitent, as the church of the world is, of whom the learned are called but a collection or congregation of saints, as the Holy Scriptures and the Nicene symbol clearly teach and represent, namely, of those who, through true faith, are regenerated of God unto Christ Jesus and are of a divine nature, who will gladly conform their lives according to the Spirit, word and example of the Lord, are actuated by his Spirit and are willing and prepared patiently to bear the cross of their Lord Jesus Christ.

Behold dear reader, such were they whom the apostles and faithful servants won unto Christ Jesus, and added to his church with his Spirit and word, nor does Scripture acknowledge any others. From such and of such they have, with fasting and prayer, chosen and called unto the service of the Lord the pious and unblamable pastors and teachers; and not of the world, as has been heard.

Since, then, the preachers of the world and their congregations, are not the church of Christ but are such preachers and churches as shown, by their spirit, words and deeds that they are of the world; and since the merciful, great Lord in these latter days of abominations, graciously gathers together, by his Spirit and word, many faithful hearts from the different unscriptural sects, both great and small, and from different nations and tongues, in one faith; and places them as an admonition to sincere repentance, with their doctrine, life, goods and blood, before the whole world, yea, as a light upon a candlestick ; therefore these must be the Lord's church and people; or else the word of God, which is and remains true, must be wrong and false. And some from these and of these are chosen with fasting and prayer and ordained to the service of the Lord by the laying on of hands according to the example and doctrine of the apostolic churches; now, all of sound mind may judge and weigh, according to Scripture whether such a calling or choosing is not consistent with Scripture and according to the usage of the primitive churches; and whether it cannot stand before the Lord and his church as divine, holy and just.

Further, it is a fact well known to me, that the preachers tell the simple, and which Gellius' writing, if carefully read, also insinuates that I should have received my faith, doctrine and calling of a deceiving, refractory and corrupted sect, by the secession of whom the Lord intends to purge his church. For this reason I am necessarily forced to explain my actions briefly, which I, under different circumstances, would, for the sake of modesty, remain silent; namely, how I first came to the knowledge of my Lord and Savior, Jesus Christ; and how I afterward, unworthily, became one of his servants; and I hereby beseech all my readers, for God's sake to consider well this my narration, and that they will not think hard of it, nor consider it as vain boasting that I here tell it; for the honor of my God and the love for his church urge me to do so. Let all judge me as they will He who has created me and has hitherto graciously delivered me from my enemies, knows me; he knows what I seek in this life and what my greatest desire is.*

Again, that Gellius wants us to preach publicly, has been sufficiently replied to above, as I trust, in treating of night preaching. Yet I would propound these three questions.

In the first place, Whether a person would not be guilty of blood, if he would persuade somebody by artful words or force him into a deep water or by such means get him to take poison, if he knew beforehand that death would be the consequence?

In the second place, Since he boasts to be a called preacher and preaches in public, I would ask, Why he is not moved to love and compassion for his own country? Why he does not, amongst the papists, openly proclaim his faith, sacraments and doctrines, contrary to the emperor's decree, tyranny, persecution and ill-will as he would have us to do?

Thirdly, since he will admit, as I suppose, and must admit, if he judge according to the Scriptures, that the avaricious, proud, haughty, drunkards, vain, extortioners, liars, unrighteous, &c., can not inherit the kingdom of God, and that they therefore are not christians; I would ask him, Why it is that he does not lay aside the fear of

---

* Here follows in the original works of Menno Simon his renunciation of the Church of Rome. See First part, Page 4.

the cross (of which he blames us) and separate, without all respect of person, the impenitent of his church, from the communion of his sacraments, according to the doctrine and ordinance of the Holy Ghost, since it is God's express word and ordinance? He would have us preach publicly, notwithstanding that he well knows that we can no more do so without the loss of life, than to go on the water without sinking, or to take poison without dying. For he and the learned have brought about such a state of affairs, by their disgraceful slanders and preaching, that we are, alas, already judged before we are caught. Besides he advises the magistracy to stop our doings; and he well knows how he treated a certain person, about ten years ago, who would gladly proclaim to the people the testimony he had, in sincerity of heart, and that he refused me a discussion of Scripture twice, as has been heard. Yet he says, if we are true teachers we should preach in public; while he himself, for the sake of a livelihood and the fear of the cross does not preach his doctrine (whatever it amounts to) in his own place but has moved to another and more safe place, and there, although he can freely practice his doctrine and sacraments, he neglects separation, scriptural reproof and the ordinances of God from the fear of the cross. Now the reasonable reader may educe from all this what kind of a christian, not to mention preacher, he is; since he would have us, miserable ones, to do that which he himself dares not do nor touch, as you may see.

If Gellius could take these three questions to heart and would consider them in a scriptural light and in the fear of God, he would be ashamed all his life that he so indiscreetly attacks us, against all love, reason, intelligence and the Scriptures and that he, under such a semblance, so tyrannically strives after the ruin, blood and death of the pious.

But in answer to this writing that the prophetic and apostolic doctrine and sacraments should not be taught and dispensed in secret, retired corners and shops, but in public, I would say, We admit that Christ Jesus, generally preached in public, however with such discretion that he sometimes avoided the raving, mad people, after they had resolved upon his death, until the time of his suffering had arrived (which time was known to him beforehand), and the prophecies were fulfilled, Luke 21:32.

Also, that although Jesus Christ sent his disciples to preach the gospel to all people, to Gentiles as well as Jews, he did not command them, nor would he, that they should serve and dispense his sacraments, namely, baptism and Supper to the enemies of his word, Matt. 28:19; Mark 16:15. Therefore it is obvious that he accuses us of this without any truth or foundation of the Scriptures. He does not only accuse and reprove us but also Christ Jesus, God's eternal word and wisdom himself; for he has celebrated his Holy Supper, at night in a secret place, with a separate people; he also accuses and reproves Paul and the primitive, apostolic church, who oft held their brotherly meetings at night, in retired places, as has been sufficiently adduced above. Observe how openly he speaks against God's word.

He writes further, that our calling is not testified by any thing, further than that we not only fill the hearts of many with a mad and irreconcilable hatred of all church ordinances and true servants of the church, however pious they be, but also inspire them with a contentious, envious spirit.

Answer. If animosity and bitterness of heart had not so entirely blinded him, and if but a small spark of a true, christian spirit were in him, then he would soon acknowledge the precious fruits of true repentance. But as it is, he has become so blinded, that, alas, he calls the glorious fruits of the Holy Spirit, the fruits of the devil and new monkery; and the burdensome, pressing cross of so many pious saints, the cross of evil-doers or heretics. Which is in my opinion an abominable sin and gross slander.

The Pharisees said, "This fellow doth not cast out devils, but by Beelzebub, the prince of devils," Matt. 12:24, although they strongly felt in their hearts that it was the finger and power of God. Christ said that it was blaspheming against the Holy Ghost, Luke 12:10. But what Gellius does against us I will leave to the Lord.

God knows that I wish that I might deliver him and all the preachers from their sore damnation, even at the cost of my own life. Behold, thus I hate him and all those who seek my life; although we must hear so much evil spoken against us; and I trust that all who fear the word of the Lord, will be of one mind with me in this regard. Notwithstanding this, he writes that we fill many hearts with anger and irreconcilable hatred against them, &c. By no means. And this for no other reason than that we in sincere and faithful love, earnestly reprove the hypocritical deceivers, whom he calls the true and pious servants of the church, and the unscriptural infant baptism, together with all abuses, which he calls church ordinances not only by the Spirit and word of the Lord, but also by our possessions and blood, and because we point them to Christ Jesus and him crucified, to his Spirit, word, ordinances and to the doctrine and usage of his holy apostles.

I truly believe that a spiteful, envious person has no part in God's city. And if we, who are daily killed for our love, are yet spiteful and envious, then much suffering is in vain. I trust that I write the truth when I say that I am more terrified at hatred and envy than at fire and sword. Yet we must hear that we are spiteful. Behold, thus good is ever turned to evil and our love to hatred. What sentence the Scriptures pronounce against such may be seen in Isaiah 5.

He also accuses us That we are not unanimous but quarrel amongst ourselves in regard to many articles of christian religion; namely, in regard to obedience to the laws; to the justification of man; to the Godhead of Christ and his becoming man, and in regard to the powers of the magistracy, &c.

Answer. I trust that I can write with a clear conscience that we, who are grains of one loaf, are also of one mind in Christ Jesus. But as in the times of the apostles, false teachers arose in the apostolic church who started and taught false doctrines and who were, after faithful admonition, separated from the communion of their church, if they did not repent, as may be learned from many Scriptures; so also it is in our times. Satan is ever at work. Paul says, "There must be also heresies among you, that they which are approved may be made manifest among you," 1 Cor. 11:19. And if such be deaf unto truth, reject admonition and start perverse sects, then we may no longer receive them as brethren, as the Scriptures teach us. So long as we continue to do this in obedience to the holy word and in the true fear of God, we are convinced from the inmost of our hearts, that we will be clear of all sectarianism as also of blasphemy and perversity; although we must innocently hear such charges from the world.

Since it is a fact well known to Gellius and his fellow-preachers that peace-breakers and sectarians are not allowed in our communion at all, but are unanimously separated from us, according to apostolic doctrine and usage, Rom. 16:17; Tit. 3:10, therefore it is very wrong in him to call so many pious persons contentious, and cause them to be of such bad report with the world, without truth; while they hate discord and strife and seek nothing but that they may humbly follow the crucified Jesus, in the peace of their hearts.

If he should say that he accounts them as of us because they have received the same baptism with us, then I would say again that Peter, Simon, Paul and &c., were also one. Then all papists, Lutherans and Zuinglians besides all thieves, murderous wizards, buggerers fornicators and rogues are one; for they have received one baptism; this is incontrovertible.

Again, in regard to his accusation that we dispute among ourselves in regard to obedience to the laws; the justification of man; the power of the magistracy &c. I would say, that I trust I can testify before the Lord and his church with a clear conscience, that I never but once to my knowledge, disputed, or as Gellius calls it quarreled with any one in regard to the justification of man, and this one has already run to ruin. Nor have I ever discussed the questions of obedience to the laws or the power of the magistracy other than by way of brotherly instruction. What our confession and grounds are concerning the before-mentioned articles, may be clearly educed from our writings.

O, dear Lord, that Gellius would once consider his own words when he writes that the calling of the pious should not be nullified on account of the impious, and would have sufficient fear of God in him to feel concerned about the lies, violence and injustice which he unreasonably practices on us. For what else does he but wilfully defame the pious, perhaps against his own sentiments, that he may oppose the word, may uphold his cause by making ours false and suspicious, lest his pharisaical faithlessness be made manifest. Yea, he writes as if he would say, Judas was a traitor and thief, therefore all the other apostles are traitors and thieves. Again, Simon was a rogue, therefore all the members of the apostolic communities were rogues, &c. For he well knows that we do not, may not suffer heretics, peace-breakers &c. in the communion of the peaceful and pious, as already heard.

O, that he would leave off slandering the peaceable and could rightly see into the angry quarreling, bitter hatred, division, rupture and brawlings of all those who uphold infant baptism; could see how dreadfully they are divided amongst themselves; that they are so inflamed by envious zeal one against another that they not only slander and adjudge each other to hell by calling each other fanatics, profaners of the sacraments and anti-christians, but that they also take up the sword against each other, as is the way of sectarians; that they utterly destroy countries and inhabitants, cities and towns, against the meek nature, doctrine and example of Christ Jesus and his apostles.

Besides their learned men are so divided amongst themselves that we can scarcely find five or six in one country who agree in doctrine. One includes every thing in the providence and predestination of God, *Quasi necessarium* (as an implied necessity). Another disputes it; the third includes Christ's flesh and blood in the bread and wine; the fourth understands it spiritually; the fifth baptizes the children on their own faith; the sixth on the strength of the covenant with Abraham and its promise; the seventh says that faith is no obstacle to persecution; the eighth denies it; the ninth believes in faith without fruits or work; the tenth says, that faith through love shall be active; the eleventh says, that the sacraments may be dispensed to the impenitent and perverse; the twelfth denies it; and other like differences exist among them.

Notwithstanding they call the godly, pious hearts and peaceable children of God, who are zealous for God and his righteousness, as much as is in their power, and who do not countenance quarreling, a contentious sect and ungodly, deceiving conspirators, while they, on the contrary, are peaceable, teachers of one mind; besides they call the impenitent, wicked world the church and people of the Lord.

Behold, so manifestly the Lord "will destroy the wisdom of the wise, and will bring to nothing the understanding of the prudent", 1 Cor. 1:18, yea, that to them Christ Jesus is Belial, and Belial Christ Jesus; light, darkness and darkness, light, 2 Cor. 6; that they, alas consider the doctrine, life, power, confession, and the sacrifice of possession and life of the chosen as nothing; but that they judge every thing perversely, unfavorably and with partiality, according to the flesh, and thus construe every thing to offensiveness; that they seek all kinds of excuses to offend the pious, to blaspheme truth and to uphold unrighteousness, that nobody be converted, repent and sincerely seek and follow the word of the Lord. O, Lord! grant that this may be made manifest unto them.

He further writes: "Nor is it a desirable fruit, but a shameful disgrace that they, contrary to the example of Christ, and the apostles constitute themselves a church, desecrate the Lord's Sabbath, leave the open assembly and service, hate and upbraid the servants, and not only not examine the solicitous labors and prophecies of the servants but also boldly despise them, contrary to the command of the Holy Ghost and the doctrine of the command of the Sabbath."

Answer. Observe, reader, how adroitly they can adorn lies, and how frightfully they can suppress and despise truth under cover of virtue. All the evangelical Scriptures teach us that the church of Christ was and is, in doctrine, life and worship, a people separated from the world. It also was in the times of the Old Testament, 2 Cor. 6:17; 1 Peter 2:9, 10; Exod. 19:12.

Since the church always was and shall be a separate people, as has been heard, and since it is as clear as the meridian sun, that for centuries no difference has been made between the church and the world, but that they have been indiscriminately blended together in baptism, Supper, life and worship, which is so plainly contrary to all Scripture, therefore we feel ourselves constrained by the Spirit and word of God, and not of our own account, to gather together, to the praise of Jesus Christ and to the salvation of our neighbors, and not unto us, but unto the Lord a pious and penitent church or community from all untrue and deceiving sects of the whole world, not contrary to the doctrine and example of Christ Jesus and the apostles, as Gellius falsely accuses us, but according to the Spirit, doctrine and example of Jesus Christ, manifested unto us; yea, gather them *patiently* under the cross of misery, in spite of all the violence and gates of hell, and not by force of arms and persecution as is the custom of the world, but separate them from it, as the Scriptures teach, that they may be an admonition, example and reproach to the impenitent world as has already been heard.

They keep and sanctify the Sabbath which is not the literal, but the spiritual Sabbath, which never ends with true christians, not by wearing fine clothes, not by carousing, vanity and idleness, as the reckless world do, but by the true fear of God, by a clear conscience and unblamable life, in love to God and their neighbors; for that is the true religion, Heb. 12:1, and in the fear of their God they do not attend the public Sabbath and holiday gatherings which are, alas, not consecrated to Christ, but to anti-christ in all manner of vanity and hypocrisy, in pomp and splendor; nor do they take part in their idle church-service which tends to nothing but deceiving that they may thereby attend the gathering of the saints and the true service, convince the erring, and thus make manifest, truth and the true doctrine, to the reformation and salvation of all mankind.

They do not hate and envy the open deceivers and false preachers who so miserably deceive the poor people, as Gellius accuses us, but earnestly reprove them in love according to God's Spirit and word, that they may repent and be converted, as the Scriptures teach us.

In short, they do not despise the solicitous labors and the prophecies of the true and faithful servants of Christ, nor the precious gifts of the Holy Spirit, against the commands of the Holy Spirit and the doctrine of the command of the Sabbath, as he very wrongly complains we do, but they shun, at the risk of possessions and life, according to the advice, doctrine and admonition of the Holy Spirit, and the doctrine of the Sabbath, the false labors, and the powerless, impenitent and hired prophecies of the anti-christian servants, who do not serve Christ and the church, as they boast, but serve their bellies and the world; and they dare not hear and follow them because their doctrine and fruits show that they are those whom the Scriptures and divine truth forbid us to follow.

Their priests, says the Lord, "teach for hire, and the prophets divine for money." They rely upon the Lord, and say, Is not the Lord amongst us? No evil can betide us; therefore "Zion shall be plowed like a field, and Jerusalem shall become heaps," Mic. 3:12; Jer. 26:18. It is also manifest that Gellius and his like preachers have done the same thing of which he accuses us, for they, long before we did, have separated themselves from the papists into a separate church, as is known to all mankind to be incontrovertible. But we are sorry to say that our separation from them was caused by themselves. For if we would have found them to be right we would have remained with them; but as it is, we have, alas, to leave them at the cost of life and possessions, as may be seen.

Behold, my kind reader, here you have before you, my brief reply to the main articles concerning the calling of preachers, which Gellius so respectfully brought forward to the defense of his cause and to the detriment of ours.

I have no doubt but that you, by the grace of God, will find a clear difference, explanation and foundation, if you compare his writing with ours and judge according to the word of the Lord by the manifest fruits on both sides; and this is the summary of my writings, that nobody can be a truly called preacher and God-pleasing servant in the Lord's house and church, without having the Holy Spirit which worketh in all true christians; without regeneration which transforms the heart from earthly to heavenly things, through faith; nor without unfeigned love, which seeks nothing but the praise of God and the salvation of his neighbor, nor without the salutary, precious word which cuts and cleaves without respect of person; nor without the pious, unblamable life which is of God.

CONCERNING BAPTISM.

I deem it unnecessary to write much concerning the baptism of the believing, in this place; why we teach that it shall be received and practiced at the confession of faith; for we have explained this matter before, by so many plain Scriptures and reasons, to the intelligent reader, that he can plainly see and palpably feel the foundation and truth.

Therefore I will refer to the main articles and arguments with which Gellius undertakes to defend his infant baptism as apostolic and christian, and will rebut them with the Scriptures; and I trust to be enabled, by the grace of God, to do this with such clearness and power that all attentive, intelligent readers may fully perceive that he can stand before the holy ordinance, word and truth of the Lord, with his infant baptism, as little as he can with his calling.

Before I enter upon the examination of the matter, I would, not without cause, first relate to the kind reader, that some years ago, I had a discussion with John A'Lasco, Gellius and Herman; and, as we had a lengthy reasoning concerning baptism, and they admitted that all the Scriptures which I adduced, relating to the matter, were spoken by the ancient or believing, we at last got on the subject of infant baptism, which, according to their opinion was also right, although not Scriptural. At last, after having had a lengthy discussion and after they had made many unscriptural assertions, I propounded two questions and prayed them for God's sake to answer them Scripturally. The first question was, Has a ceremony any promise, which is practiced without the command of God? They answered that it had not. Then I asked them, in the second place, Is not such a ceremony, which is practiced without the command of God, idolatry? They answered that it was.

When I heard them answer these questions thus unreservedly, I said, Well, dear men, what will become of your infant baptism? They all three simultaneously answer: Yea, dear Menno, if you would ask of us for the command, then show us first where it is commanded that we should baptize the believing. When I heard this I was much alarmed, for I perceived that, in fact, they meant nothing but party and carnality. I pointed them to the sixteenth chapter of Mark, where the Lord speaks, "Go ye into all the world, and preach the gospel to every creature. He that believeth, and is baptized shall be saved," Mark 16: 15, 16.

But this was no command to them. Then I referred them to Matthew 28: 19, where the Lord says, "Go ye therefore, and teach all nations baptizing them (or as the Greek text has it: Make all nations disciples, and baptize them), in the name of the Father, and of the Son, and of the Holy Ghost."

This did not avail with them, for it reads, they said, "baptizing" and not "baptize them;" although, alas, they well knew that the surest translation is the Greek text in the imperative mode, namely, baptize them; something which I had till then never noticed so particularly.

Behold, they contended so wilfully against the plain word and truth of God, that they openly denied it to be a command; while they had many times read (also according to the Lutheran translation) that the Lord had commanded it in an express command, saying, "And baptize them."*

---
* German Translation

When I perceived that they wanted to find an excuse by means of the use of the participle, I proposed the following, If I command my servant and say, Go and plow the ground, sowing it with wheat; as the Lord said, "Go and teach all nations, baptizing them," &c., have I not, I now ask, commanded my servant to plow the land and to sow it with wheat, although I use the participle sowing, the same as baptizing was used. They answered that this was using philosophy and not the Scriptures. Behold my reader, thus boldly they sought to deny the truth.

Seeing that they, although convinced, obstinately persevered in falsehood and would not receive the powerful and plain truth, as did the Pharisees, I was much grieved and said, Men! men!! Since I find it to be a fact that you, in perversity of heart, reject God's truth, and delight in falsehood, I will be silent and not speak another word with you concerning this matter; for, alas, it is all in vain! Reader, in the day of the appearance of Jesus Christ, before his impartial and eternal judgment, it will be found true as I here write.

Behold, so dishonestly do they deal with God's precious and eternal truth, that they *then* pretended that there was no command to baptize the believing, and *now* they have an abundance of commands to baptize the unconscious children. O, God! thus they mock with the souls of men, and they know not how much to garble, bend and break the sure foundation of truth, that they may remain on the broad road, without the cross, that they may please the world and that they may lead a careless life according to the lusts of the flesh.

Gellius first says in regard to this matter, That we blasphemously speak against the holy church, because we say that the children cannot believe, cannot repent and cannot obey the word of the Lord, while they (as he says) constitute a great part of the church, and that they are referred to in plain and clear words by the prophet Joel, in the preaching of repentence, &c.

Answer. His commencement is unscriptural and his end will be unscriptural. Observe, the word of God shall be our judge. Say, beloved, is it not a great blindness in him to undertake to include unconscious children in the preaching of repentance? and a little further on admits himself that they cannot, in their feeble understanding, understand the doctrine, which is a doctrine of penitence. If they cannot understand the doctrine how can they then believe; if they do not believe how can they then repent, and if they do not repent how can they be included in the preaching of repentance? If they, then, have neither doctrine, faith nor repentance, which he admits they have not, on account of their feeble understanding, and which is not necessary for them to have, while they are God's own and while sin has not become alive in them to bring forth fruit, therefore all of sound judgment must admit he reproves himself and acknowledges that he wrongfully accuses us, when he says, that we speak blasphemously against the holy church, because we say that the unconscious children cannot repent, believe nor obey; for he admits that they, in the feebleness of their understanding, cannot understand the doctrine, from which faith, repentence and obedience originate, as has been already said.

In the second place he writes, That there is one church and one faith, both under the Old and New Testaments, from the time of Adam to the end of the world; and that from the time of Abraham, under the Old Testament, preaching and circumcision was commanded for the purpose of the gathering, edification, growth and extension of the church, and under the New Testament, preaching and baptism, without regard to the age of persons.

Answer. I understand it that all those who, from the time of Adam to the present time, and also hereafter, had, have and shall have the Spirit, mind and nature of Jesus Christ, and who did, do and shall walk as obedient children by virtue of such a spirit, in truth, were, are and shall be the Lord's church, kingdom and people. But we would have reasonably expected that Gellius would have added that each in his times had a peculiar doctrine, ordinance and usage. That from the time of Adam to Abraham no ceremony was practiced on the children because the Lord had not commanded it; and that circumcision was commanded from Abraham to the time of Christ. But now we have Christ, the promised prophet, Deut. 18: 15; Acts 7: 37, to whom all the Scriptures pointed that we should obey and follow him. He is the eternal Word and Wisdom of God; all that abide in his doctrine, walk in the truth, for his word is truth, and his command is eternal life. What ordinance this wise counsellor has commanded us concerning the children, under the New Testament; what he has commanded us and what he has not, concerning them, all pious, faithful hearts may learn from his holy word.

But what he says in regard to them, that in the New Testament no regard is made as to age, but that we should preach to all and baptize them, is in my opinion so directly contrary to Scripture, common sense and his own words, that he should reasonably be ashamed of the assertion. For how can we teach a little, unconscious child repentance according to the word of God? Christ commanded that we should preach the gospel to those who have understanding, and those who believe are to be baptized. Nor has he left in his gospel any other command, ordinance or example concerning this matter.

Besides, he acknowledges that the children, on account of their feeble understanding, cannot understand the doctrine, as already heard. Yet he writes, in the face of this plain ordinance of the Almighty God, and his own confession, that in the New Testament, teaching and baptizing are commanded, without respect to age.

Behold, thus grossly err all who reject the word of the Lord. Is this not violently rejecting Christ and accepting anti-christ, and is it not plainly wrong? I must admit that I have never read a word in the Scriptures with such misunderstanding.

In the third place Gellius writes, That the church should give the seal of the covenant of grace to children according to the command of God because they are participants in the covenant or promise of God, and in the sanctity of the church and in eternal life; for the covenant is not altered and God is no less gracious to our children, who are born under the promise, than to the children of Israel who were born according to the flesh; for it is written, I will be thy God and thy children's after thee; and that therefore, in the gathering of the churches, under the Old and New Testaments the same command obtains, both as regards the preaching, and the use of the holy sacraments.

Answer. Gellius does even as all the false prophets have done who miserably deceived the people, and pretended that the Lord of lords said so, although the Lord had not spoken it, as Scripture informs us, Jer. 23: 17; Ezek. 13: 7.

Say, reader, is it not an intrepid deed and a condemnable boldness, that he dares publish to the whole world that God has commanded it; since eternal Wisdom has neither commanded it by word nor deed? Peruse the whole New Testament from beginning to end, and if a word can be found that the mouth of the Lord has commanded it, or that the apostles have anywhere taught or practiced it, then we will, by the grace of God, unanimously admit that he is right.

Inasmuch, as it is clear that nothing has been mentioned concerning it in all the Holy Scriptures, as has been said, and that he, in the face of this, dares write that they do it according to the command of God, then the pious reader may imagine how abominably he sins against his God, especially since truth is manifest, and how lamentably he deceives the poor souls by open falsehood when he writes that God commanded it; since the Holy Spirit, I say, has not expressed it in a single word, nor manifested it unto the church of God by word or practice of the true witnesses of Christ.

His assertion that the command is not altered, is so diametrically opposed to truth, that we may well wonder at it. The Scriptures clearly testify that God promised Abraham the multiplying of his seed, and the land of Canaan as an eternal inheritance, and commanded him that he should circumcise himself, his son Ishmael, &c.; also all male children of the age of eight days; for it was a covenant in the flesh, Gen. 17.

And thus was commanded to Abraham, at the promise of the multiplication of his seed and the possession of the land of Canaan, the blood-sign of the circumcision of the foreskin, on the eighth day of their age, of all the male children and not the female children. But to us the blood-sign of circumcision is not commanded, but baptism in the water. Now, observe the first difference. Not on the eighth day, but when we, through the spirit, in faith, are born of God, and have become followers of Abraham. Observe the second distinction. Not alone the males, but both males and females, who through the preaching of the holy word, have died unto the old life and have arisen with Christ in newness of life; who are pricked in their hearts; who circumcise their hearts and minds; who put on Christ, and who have the testimony of a clear conscience, before God, Rom. 6; Acts 2: 37; Col. 2; 11; Gal. 3: 27; 1 Pet, 3: 21. Observe the third difference. Not to possess a literal kingdom and land, and to become a great people upon earth, as was promised to Abraham and his seed; but to bear all manner of anxiety, affliction, tribulation and misery upon earth, for the sake of the testimony of the word of God; to turn the heart away from all visible and perishable things; to die unto pomp, splendor, the world and flesh, and thus to walk in our weakness as Christ has walked in his perfection, &c.

Behold, reader, how openly he adulterates the Scriptures, and how grossly he perverts the truth when he writes that the command is unchanged, and that the gathering of the churches under the Old and New Testaments are the same, and that no different commands are given, both as regards preaching and the use of the sacraments; for it is all changed and renewed as may be clearly educed from the foregoing references. I will leave to your reflections if such a thing may not be called perverting truth into falsehood.

Again, from his saying that the church is no less gracious to our children than to the children of Israel, born in the flesh, I understand him to say, If God will not have our children baptized, that he is less gracious to them than he was to the children of the circumcision; by which he openly testifies that he couples the kingdom, grace and promise of God with that sign.

If God is only gracious to such children as have received, or may receive that outward sign, then it must necessarily follow that God has been ungracious to, and displeased with all the children before the law of circumcision; besides to all children who died before the eighth day, and during the forty years they passed in the wilderness, together with all the maids and women, because they were not circumcised; then he must also be displeased with all the children under the New Testament, for they are not commanded to be baptized.

O no, to children belongs the kingdom of God. Not by virtue of any sign, but alone by grace through Christ Jesus, Matt. 19: 14. And as to his calling infant-baptism a sealing of the covenant of grace, I would reply, If he can show me a place in all the New Testament where the baptism of the believing is called a sealing of the covenant of grace, then I will admit that he is right. But I know to a certainty, that he cannot do so. If the baptism of the *believing*, which is ordained of God himself, is not called such, how can infant baptism, then be called such, which is not ordained of God, but is merely self-chosen fiction invented of man?

If he should allude to the circumcision, I would say that they are two distinct and different signs, and that the first has no relation whatever to the second; for these following reasons: Firstly, because all the signs, before and under the law, given to the patriarchs, as the coats of skins to Adam; the rain-bow to Noah; the circumcision to Abraham; the yearly offering of the high priests, &c., Gen. 3: 21; 9: 16; 17: 10, 11; Lev. 16, all, unitedly pointed to Christ who has now appeared, and in whom all the preceding signs are fulfilled; and we now have no sealing or assurance through outward signs and symbols, but through the true Sign of all signs, Christ Jesus, as he himself says, "As Moses lifted up the serpent in the wilderness, even so must the Son of Man be lifted up, that whosoever believeth in him should not perish, but have eternal life; for God so loved the world that he gave his only-begotten son," John 3: 14 —16. Secondly, because we, now, are not a people according to the letter, as was Israel, but are a people according to the spirit; who, before they receive the sign, are turned to God through the preaching of repentance; who die unto the old sinful life; who receive the light of grace in their hearts; who accept the true Sign of peace, Christ Jesus, through faith; arise with him into a new life and are thus sealed in their hearts, through the promise of the Holy Ghost and the eternal covenant and the grace of God. For if we were not sealed in our hearts before the sign, then we could not truly repent before the sign; nor could we burden ourselves with disesteem, disgrace, anxiety, tribulation and misery which are connected with the cross.

But by the sign, which we accept in obedience to the holy word, we testify that we, through Christ, the true Sign, given us by the Father, and made known to us through the word, have peace with God, and that we are assured of the spirit of his grace.

Behold, my reader, here you may now observe that the signs of the New Testament do not seal or assure us, as the learned teach the poor people; but that our only, eternal surety, is Christ Jesus; that the sealing of our hearts is the Holy Spirit; and that the signs or sacraments are nothing more than that they are given to the penitent, sealed and assured christians, for the purpose of admonishing and reminding us that we should walk in continual repentance; that we should practice our faith, and that we should eternally give praise to the Lord for his inexpressibly great kindness and grace, through Jesus Christ.

All who teach differently, and point you to water, bread and wine as a sealing or assurance, as Gellius does, points you away from the true Being, to the signs; from Christ to Moses again; give you a vain hope and a false surety and cause you to remain impenitent and without Christ all your lifetime; for you console yourself so much with the signs, that you remain without the signified truth, as may, alas, be plainly seen by the whole world.

For however drunken, covetous, pompous vain and given to lies they may be, they still boast themselves christians. They are so consoled with this ungodly sealing of the idolatrous water (I say ungodly sealing because it is so directly contrary to the word of God) and with the bread and wine of the preachers, that they all walk upon the broad road, and remain without the word of God.

Behold, this is the proper fruit and effect of the sealing of Gellius, which he so highly praises and so artfully teaches. But, as regards the saying: I will be your God and your seed's after you, from which they conclude that as the children of Abraham were circumcised with him on account of the promise; that also our children should be baptized on account of the same promise, I would reply, Firstly, God promised Abraham to be his God and his children's God. In this promise the females were included as well as the males; this must be admitted. Notwithstanding, Israel did not circumcise the females but only the males, although the females were included in the promise; and that because God had so ordained it. From which it may be safely educed that the male children of the seed of Abraham were not circumcised for the sake of the promise but for the sake of the ordinance which was commanded to Abraham and his seed. For if it had been done for the sake of the promise, and not for the sake of the ordinance, then the females should also have been circumcised, as joint participants and joint heirs of the same promise. This is incontrovertible.

In the second place I would say, That if Israel had followed the doctrine of Gellius, and some other preachers, in respect to this matter, then they would also have circumcised the females, notwithstanding they were not commanded to do so; for they were joint heirs of the covenant of grace, as our children whom they want to have baptized, are joint heirs of the promise.

If they should answer, that the ordinance referred to the males and not to the females, although the females were joint heirs of the covenant of grace, then I would reply that their cause is already lost. For as the command of circumcision at that time, had only reference to the males and not to the females, although the females were joint heirs of the promise, so also does now the ordinance of baptism have reference to the believing and penitent, and not to the unconscious children, although they are joint heirs of the promise, as heard.

They further say, If infant baptism is not commanded neither is it prohibited. To this I reply: The circumcision of the females was neither ordained nor prohibited, even as infant baptism is neither ordained nor prohibited, yet they did not circumcise the females, and that because they were not commanded to do so. Therefore, all who blame us because we do not baptize our children, who are joint heirs of the promise and are not prohibited from being baptized, also blame Israel because they did not circumcise their female children, who were joint heirs of the promise and were not prohibited from being circumcised.

Thirdly, I would say, since I observe that Gellius only includes the children of believing, and not of unbelieving parents in the baptism, and since he well knows that the proud, avaricious, pompous, envious, blood-guilty, whoring and idolatrous are not believers, nor, according to Scripture, joint heirs of the promise, therefore I cannot stop wondering at his inattention, that he, against his own belief and doctrine, yet baptizes the children of such parents, whom he must acknowledge, as being without God and Christ, and therefore having no promise. If he says that he does not know the faith of others, then I would say again, that he then acknowledges, in the first place, that his infant baptism has an unstable foundation, if we, according to his own words, are to baptize them on account of the promise to the parents, while he does not know whether the parents believe or not; and, in the second place, that such parents are not fruitful trees nor shining lights.

But what shall we say! If Gellius were to tell all his pompous, drunken, usurious, and unrighteous members, without respect to person, that they are without Christ and have no promise, and would not baptize their children, he would not long remain a preacher at Emden, nor enjoy his easy, careless life in peace.

He further writes, That Paul testifies that baptism has taken the place of circumcision, has the same signification and is called the circumcision of Christ.

Answer. In this instance Paul himself rebukes him, that he has mistaken his word; for he says, "Beware, lest any man spoil you through philosophy and vain deceit, after the tradition of men, after the rudiments of the world, and not after Christ, for in him dwelleth all the fullness of the God-head bodily; and ye are complete in him, which is the head of all principality and power; in whom also ye are circumcised with the circumcision made without hands, in putting off the body of the sins of the flesh by the circumcision of Christ. Buried with him in baptism, wherein also ye are risen with him through the faith of the operation of God, who hath raised him from the dead; and you, being dead in your sins, and in the uncircumcision of your flesh, hath he quickened together with him, having forgiven you all trespasses," Col. 2: 8—13.

My faithful reader, observe the word of the Lord; the doctrine of the New Testament, and his sacraments treat of none but those who have ears to hear and hearts to understand. For it is a service of the Spirit, and not of the letter, as Paul says, 2 Cor. 3: 6.

Inasmuch as the preachers ever point the poor, simple people to the elementary water, bread and wine, and teach that baptism is our seal which assures us that we are heirs of the covenant of grace; that God operates through his sacraments, &c., and, since we find, however, that neither the sealing, surety nor power are found in their hearts, as the fruits testify, but that they are led by the preachers to a false profession, vain hope and an unstable surety, under the semblance of the gospel; therefore I would faithfully admonish all my readers and hearers with these words adduced from Paul, not to be at all deceived by such high-sounding, smooth words of the philosophy and artful fictions of men, nor by the hypocrisy and worldly institutions of the learned, but to follow after the perfect Institutor, Christ Jesus, in whom is embodied the perfection of the God-head, truth, light, power, righteousness, &c., and who therefore does not point to uncertain, deceitful, dark and unrighteous ways, but in him all true christians are perfect and full of his grace, Spirit, love and power.

He is the head of all principalities before whom every knee shall bow, and whom all tongues shall confess that he is the Lord, and that besides him there is no other, Isaiah 45: 23; Phil. 2: 10. Therefore his word shall avail, and his command shall stand, and not that which the world adds to his kingdom or church, in which all regenerated children, who are of his Spirit, are not now circumcised unto Christ, with hands, as was the case with literal Israel, but the impure foreskins of their hearts are circumcised with the Lord's word, Spirit and power, that they may become in spirit a new, regenerated Israel and people of God, by dying unto their sinful flesh, and by smothering the old man through the circumcision of Christ, which purifies and changes their hearts through his word and Spirit. For the penitent are buried with him in baptism, die unto the old sinful life, and arise in the new life of righteousness and virtue, by means of faith, through which God operates by the preaching of his powerful word, and the inspiration of his Holy Spirit. The faithful God and Father who has resurrected his Son from the dead, has also bestowed his power upon us, poor sinners, and has graciously resurrected us, who were dead in so many gross sins and tresspasses, into a new life with him; has called us from darkness unto light, and has placed us with him in a celestial being, in Christ, Eph. 2: 1; 1 Pet. 3, &c.

Behold, dear reader, this is the proper ground and meaning of the words of Paul, by which Gellius tries to show, that baptism has taken the place of circumcision and is called the circumcision of Christ.

Judge now, if you fear God, whether you find a word in the writings of Paul, that has reference to unconscious infants. That this saying of Paul has reference to the believing and penitent, and not to unconscious children, all reasonable, to say nothing of spiritual persons, must acknowledge and admit. Notwithstanding, he writes that this saying implies that baptism has taken the place of circumcision and is called Christ's circumcision. He does, or will not observe that the circumcision of Jesus Christ to which Paul alludes, is done without hands, and that he daily serves with his hands the infant baptism which he calls the circumcision of Jesus. Behold, thus lamentably does he satisfy Paul, and thus violently break the word of God.

If he seeks an evasion to adorn his cause, and say, that God works through his sacraments invisibly in the heart, which the sign represents, then the deceit will be more distinct. For how shall God operate through a sign which is an abomination before Him? I say an abomination, because he has not commanded it, and because neither doctrine, confession, faith nor repentance precede it, which these signs represent, in the New Testament. Then, also, the sign and the signification must be one and the same, which never was nor ever will be the case unless the letter becomes spirit. This is incontrovertible. Yea, my reader, how the baptized children are circumcised with the circumcision of Christ Jesus in the foreskin of their hearts, which is the circumcision of the New Testament, the deeds and the fruits of the world, alas, plainly show.

In the fourth place he writes, As in the Scriptures, which testify that women are participants in the merits of Christ, and are disciples, a command is implied that the Holy Supper shall be dispensed to them, so, also, a command is implied in the Scriptures, which testify that children are of the church of Christ and of the Kingdom of God, that they should be baptized.

Answer. The words of Gellius prove clearly that women are participants of the Lord's Supper; for he acknowledges that they are disciples. If they are disciples, as they are in fact, then it is manifest that they hear the word of God, believe, repent, suffer themselves to be baptized, and that they are gifted of God in power with the representation of the Holy Supper, and that they are participants of his mystery no less than the men. Since they are believing and penitent disciples, as heard, therefore it is reasonable and right that they should partake of the sign, whereby this mystery of faith and of the holy gospel are represented to the believing, and admonished to the repenting. As we cannot deny but that the believing, repenting women understand and realize the representation of the Holy Supper—namely, the remembrance of the offering of the flesh and blood of Christ, the love of God and one's neighbors, &c., for which purpose it was instituted by the Lord, therefore they should have a place at the Lord's table, as believing, penitent disciples and guests. Now, Gellius, to make his infant baptism of effect, must prove and show to us by works, Scriptures and truth, that little, unconscious children realize the effect of holy baptism, namely, faith, repentance, obedience to the word, a clear and peaceable conscience, &c., for which purpose the sign of baptism was instituted of the Lord, as the believing, penitent women realize the signification of the Holy Supper. But if he cannot prove this, then it is sufficiently plain that this, his assertion and argument are not according to the Scriptures, but that it is deceitful, false, and contrary to God's word.

He further says, If such a command to baptize children is not sufficient, as the one he has adduced from the Scriptures, then he wants us to point him out a prohibition (as he says), or sufficiently prove that God wills that we shall not baptize children.

In the first place, I reply: Gellius herewith openly betrays that his reference to the command of infant baptism can, in his own opinion not stand, according to the Scriptures. For he turns from the doctrine of commands and wants us to point out a prohibition, never observing that if one wants to partake of anything (that is a ceremony), he must first adduce and point out the command of the institution.

If he wants to make good the infant baptism which he teaches and practices, then he must prove that it is commanded, and not ask us to point out or show where it is prohibited.

We practice baptism in a manner as the mouth of the Lord has commanded, for we know that it stands written, "What things soever I command you, observe to do it; thou shalt not add thereto nor diminish from it," Deut. 12: 32; Prov. 30: 6. Yea, my reader, I would say to Gellius and the learned that if they can find an instance in all the Scriptures where the pious and faithful servants of God have changed a word of the commands, and ceremonies, and practiced them differently than God had commanded them, then we will further reflect upon the matter. But we know it to a certainty that it cannot be done.

The Lord commanded Israel that they should circumcise their male children on the eighth day; there was no command that they should not do it on the fifth, or on any other day. Yet they never circumcised a female; nor did they circumcise on any other day but the eighth. For the ordinance and command of the Lord was on the eighth day, to the male children, and not on the seventh or ninth; nor to the female children as has been heard.

If they, now, had circumcised the females, or if they had circumcised the males before, or after the eighth day, although it was not expressly forbidden, they would have committed an abomination, as did Nadab and Abihu with the strange fire, and circumcised without God's word; by the grace of God, no man can Scripturally convince me to the contrary.

It was also commanded Israel that they should eat the Passover in remembrance of their deliverance and departure out of Egypt, on the fourteenth day of the first month, in the evening; it had to be a male lamb, without blemish, of the first year, &c., Ex. 12: 5. Israel did just according to the command, and never offered a female lamb, but in every instance a male, although the Lord had not expressly prohibited the offering of a female lamb, for if they had offered a female, they would have offered contrary to the command, which stipulated that it should be a male.

In the second place, I would say that I would refer to the testimony of the Almighty and great God, who says, "This is my beloved Son in whom I am well pleased, hear ye him," Matt. 17: 5. If Gellius, now, can point to a single word of divine truth and unadulterated testimony of the Holy Scriptures, that this Son of God, Christ Jesus, the Father's eternal Truth and Wisdom, has taught or commanded one word of infant baptism, or that his holy apostles and missionaries have taught or practiced it, then I will recall my doctrine, willingly submit to dungeons and bonds, confess my guilt, repent and stand before the whole world conquered and abashed; this I promise in sincerity of heart.

But, if he cannot do so, as he never can, and still professes that infant baptism is apostolic and right, whereby he forsakes the ordinance of Christ and the apostles doctrine and usage; consoles the people in their impenitence—then it is manifest that he is a deceiver of the poor souls and an adulterer of the holy word, who would be wiser than the Son of God himself; for he says that it is a sealing of the covenant of grace, an embodiment into the church of

Christ, &c. And the great Lord has not at all commanded that he should reprove the Holy Spirit which has not manifested unto us in the Scriptures this doctrine and usage; nor the apostles that they did not at all disclose unto the pious such an important matter, as he says, and that they have not given a word in all their writings, in testimony thereof, and thus manifested it unto their descendants.

In the third place I would refer Gellius, and all his preachers, to Luther, who writes very clearly that we should renounce not only that which is contrary to the word of the Lord, but also that which is beside it, and advises every body, although, alas, he himself did not follow the advice, to follow certainties and not uncertainties; for the Scriptures admit of no addition nor diminishing, by which he has caused quite a rupture in popery. If the Scriptures admit of no additions, and we find nowhere a word in Scripture commanding infant baptism, as Luther himself admits, then I would leave it to the impartial judgment of all who have understanding, whether infant baptism is not prohibited.

In the fifth place, Gellius writes, They say that the children have no ears to hear; and cannot distinguish between good and evil. But it does not follow from this, he says, that the sacrament of the embodiment into the church should not be practiced upon children; for the children of the ancient church had no such ears that they could hear, and they could as little distinguish between good and evil, as our children can.

Answer. If Gellius will show us the command, ordinance or usage of the Lord, that we shall take them in by such sign, then we will consider the matter further. But he cannot do so.

We say with holy Paul, "Blessed be the God and Father of our Lord Jesus Christ, who has blessed us with all spiritual blessings in heavenly places in Christ, according as he hath chosen us in him before the foundation of the world, that we should be holy, and without blame before him in love; having predestinated us unto the adoption of children by Jesus Christ to himself, according to the good pleasure of his will, to the praise of the glory of his grace," &c., Eph. 1: 3—6.

My faithful reader, understand well what these words of Paul mean. This paternal adoption unto membership; this great favor, love and grace through Christ Jesus; this holy, unblamable life in love, of which Paul speaks, is taught by the gospel. All who rightly believe this, and who are, through faith, truly converted, changed, renewed and born of God, and have the Holy Spirit, are children of the covenant, are graciously accepted of God, and are blessed with all spiritual blessings in heavenly places in Christ; even before they have the sign of baptism.

Behold, thus we are, by God's choice through faith in Christ Jesus, and through the inspiring power and renewing of the Holy Spirit, embodied into the body of Christ, which is the true church, and become flesh of his flesh and bone of his bone; and not through any outward sign.

But this rule does not apply to unconscious children; for they have no ears to hear nor hearts to understand. They are, however, in grace, children of the kingdom, participants in the promise; not through any outward sign, I say, but in the adoption of Grace through the reconciliation, mediation and merits of the death and blood of Christ, as the Scriptures teach. The New Testament treats with those of understanding minds, and its sacraments belong to the penitent. Let this be to you a sure and eternal reference and doctrine.

All those who give a different meaning to the signs of the New Testament, by their philosophy, and teach you that they should be dispensed before faith, deceive you, however much they may adorn it with choice words, such as, sealing, sign of grace, embodiment, &c., for it is in fact, nothing but human wisdom, deceiving of souls and hypocrisy. If the children under the old covenant were incorporated by circumcision, and the children under the new covenant are incorporated through baptism, as he says they are, then we are forced to conclude that the children which died before the eighth day and those who were left in the wilderness, besides, all the females, were not in the Israelitic church, and consequently had no share in the grace, covenant nor promise.

The same would also apply to our children which are hindered from baptism, through death. O, abomination and blasphemy! If that is not attaching God's selection, grace, favor, love, kingdom, covenant and salvation, to the element, water, and to works, I will leave to the judgment of all the godly and pious.

In the sixth place he writes, and says, We have ever received, in return for our assiduity and clear, convincing explanation of the Scriptures, yea, for our solicitous care, to again gain them, nothing but anathemas. For what else do we hear from them than that we are wolves, blood-hounds, deceivers, &c., who run their own course and bring forth no fruit?

Answer. All those who rightly seek our salvation, who rightly teach the word of the Lord, and who walk before us with an unblamable life, understand, according to the doctrine, Spirit, and example of Christ Jesus, are not reproved by us, nor by the Scriptures; but we sincerely thank and love them and will by the grace of God, never despise their fraternal assiduity and paternal solicitude, but will, in sincere love and very thankfully, accept them, and as much as we, in our weakness, are able to do, follow them. But we are not to blame that Gellius and the preachers are called deceivers, false prophets, ravening wolves, men guilty of blood, &c., by the Scriptures, but they themselves, are the cause; because they so lamentably adulterate the Scriptures, reject Christ Jesus and his Spirit, word and walk; because they preach according to their own pleasure, seek improper gain; because they teach and walk to suit the world, destroy the poor sheep by their false doctrine and deceiving practices; and because they upbraid, blaspheme, belie, betray the pious, faithful hearts and thus deliver them to the sword of the magistracy and executioner, as may, alas, be too clearly witnessed at many different places.

Yea, reader, if he cannot bear to be called by such hard names, of which he is guilty, according to the Scriptures, then he should reasonably consider how shamefully he accuses, in his writings and conversations, the poor, miserable souls who are quite innocent, as being ungodly heretics, apostles of the devil, deceived conspirators, hedge-preachers, sneaks, adulterators, &c., and how he, by his rebellious, fiendish, bloody doctrine, deprives the innocent of their property, welfare, honor, blood and life; and instigates the unmerciful cruel tyrants to robbery, imprisoning, banishing and murder. My faithful reader, reflect, and see if I do not write the truth.

In the seventh place he writes, The example of the apostles shows that it is a command; for the Holy Spirit testifies that the apostles baptized whole families; no children are excepted, which, surely, would have been excepted if it were wrong to baptize them.

To this I reply, in the first place, that Gellius hereby testifies that there is no command for infant baptism; for he here founds his doctrine and faith upon presumption and not upon imperative words, according to which all things should be judged that are to be a pleasure in the sight of the Lord. In the second place I would say, that the Holy Spirit has testified in plain words, that the three families of which the Scriptures make mention in particular, to have been baptized, were all believing persons as may be plainly understood from reading Acts 10: 16.

But as to the house of Lydia, it is plain that she at that time had no husband; for the house is called after her name, which is neither the custom of the world nor of the Scriptures, if the husband is alive. Since the New Testament, then, makes mention of but four households in particular, to have been baptized, and three of them were believing, and the fourth, as appears, had no husband, as has been heard, how much then should we rely on it, that there were little children in these households, both nature and the Scriptures teach us.

He further writes, That it cannot be gainsayed that the children, all through, the Scriptures, are always included in the household, for a household or family includes both young and old; therefore also children should be baptized because the Scriptures mention that whole households were baptized, which includes children.

I reply: If Gellius proves to us, by the testimony of God's word, that the unconscious children have faith, then we would gladly include them in the believing, baptized households and allow them to be baptized. But as he cannot possibly do so, we would faithfully admonish him and all the preachers to take heed, how and what they say concerning this matter; for all they philosophize and teach about it, is mere deceit. Besides, I would yet ask, if we can also cause unbelief in small children by false doctrine, or, if we can teach them faith, through God's word? If he answer in the affirmative, then his answer is contrary to all the Scriptures, common sense, and contrary to his own words; for he admits, that they, through their feeble understanding, can not comprehend the word. But if he answer in the negative, then he admits, himself, that his including both old and young in one household, is contrary to Paul. For Paul says, that the vain talkers and deceivers subvert whole houses, Tit. 1: 10, something which cannot be done to little children, on account of their not having sufficient understanding, as he himself admits. He also says that we too boldly exclude the children, which the Holy Spirit has not excepted, &c. To this I reply: The Holy Spirit has commanded and ordained that we should teach the understanding, and baptize the believing, and this ordinance we follow. Therefore, it is not boldness, but obedience to do as the mouth of the Lord has commanded us. But whether the preachers are not boldly opposing the Holy Spirit, who reject his doctrine, advice and ordinance as heretical and sectarian, and institute instead a doctrine and ordinance to suit their own taste, of which we find not a single word in the Scriptures, I will leave all the pious to judge according to the word of the Lord.

As to his reference to Tertullius, Cyprian, Origenes and Augustinus, I would reply: If these writers can support their assertions by the word and ordinance of God, then we will admit that they are right. If they cannot do so, then it is a doctrine of men, and condemned by the Scriptures, Gal. 1: 8. In the second place I say, Rhenanus annotates on Tertullius that it was customary with the ancients to baptize adults with the bap- of regeneration.

Cyprian left infant baptism optional.

Erasmus writes that the ancients have disputed much concerning infant baptism, and never came to a conclusion.

Zuinglius writes, Although we are aware that the ancients baptized children, yet it was not practiced so commonly as it is in our times. They were openly instructed in faith; and when they verbally confessed their faith which was imprinted in their hearts, they were allowed to be baptized. This doctrine (he says) I wish to have again resuscitated, Lib. Art. 18.

Bucer writes that the ancients generally baptized adults and not children.

Oecolampadius writes, I, in my weakness, cannot yet find Scriptures which command infant baptism.

Luther admits that they have no express command to baptize children.

What Martin Cellarius and others write, concerning this matter, is too lengthy to be here reproduced.

Since it is plain that few children were baptized of the ancients, as the above mentioned Rhenanus, Zuingli and Bucer show; that Cyprian left infant baptism optional, and the others acknowledge that there is no express command for it; how can Gellius, then truthfully write that they received infant baptism from the apostles; that it is an incorporation into the church, and a sealing of the covenant of grace?

Yea, my reader, if infant baptism has the virtues which Gellius ascribes to it, then our ancestors grossly sinned to have baptized so few children; and also because they left optional that which (he says) the apostles practiced and taught to be an incorporation into the church, a sign of grace and a sealing of the covenant of grace.

In the third place I answer, If we consider the confession and doctrine of the learned in regard to infant baptism, we find it to be such a Babel that we are forced to acknowledge that it is not of God. For some of the ancients (not the apostles) as appears, baptized some children, but not a considerable number. Some said they had received it from the apostles; others, again, denied it. Some have, and some still baptize them to wash off hereditary sin; others because they are children of the covenant. Some baptize them for the sake of the faith of the church; others, again, for the sake of the faith of their parents. Some on the strength of the faith of the patriarchs; others on the strength of their own faith; and again, others that better care shall be taken of their education. Behold, thus the defenders of infant baptism are divided among themselves.

Inasmuch, then, as they do not teach

one doctrine and are not of one mind in regard to infant baptism, therefore it is manifestly proven that they baptize them without the word of God. For if their cause had a foundation in Scripture, then they would baptize to the same purpose or end, according to the same ordinance, rule and doctrine. This is incontrovertible.

In the eighth place he writes "that it is not prohibited at all, in Scripture, nor testified that infant baptism is wrong. And that the Lord Jesus Christ testifies that it is not his word and will, but the will of his Father who is in heaven."

Answer. Peruse all the Scriptures—Moses and the prophets, Christ Jesus and the apostles, and diligently meditate upon them, and you will find different instances that God was not only displeased at unbidden ceremonies and worship, but that he has often severely punished such. O, dear Lord, what blind reasoning! If they can, with a clear conscience do so because it is not expressly forbidden that infants shall be baptized, then they may as well accept holy water, candles, palms, clocks, confession before a priest, masses, the building of convents, altars, the becoming of monks, pilgrimages and the praying for the departed souls, &c., as just and right; for there is not a word to be found in the Scriptures which expressly prohibits these works; or which says: You shall not do these things.

If he should say that the circumstances of Scripture and its fruits testify that they are contrary to the word of God; then I would again say: Still clearer do the circumstances of the Scriptures and the fruits testify that infant baptism is contrary to God's word. For the mouth of the Lord has not commanded so at all. All those who practice it, misuse the name and ordinance of God, and act hypocritically, and those that receive it, console themselves, when they come to years of understanding, that they are baptized children, although their whole walk is manifestly, for the greater part, quite impenitent, ungodly, earthly and carnal.

In the second place I answer: Christ Jesus has testified and said, "Go ye into all the world and preach the gospel to every creature. He that believeth and is baptized, shall be saved," Mark 16: 15, 16. Behold this is the express, eternal and unchangeable ordinance of the Lord, which he has commanded and left for his church to follow. Also have the apostles so taught and practiced it.

If now the unconscious children have faith, that is, if they are penitent, Rom. 6; have circumcised the foreskin of their hearts by the circumcision of Christ, Col. 2: 11; if they have a clear conscience before the Lord, if they have a new mind, which are all the result of faith, and which are represented by baptism—then baptism can not be refused them. But while it is plain that they have not one of the beforementioned qualities, therefore we say that infant baptism is a self-chosen superstition, an abuse of the glorious and holy name of God, an adulteration of the ordinance of Christ, a vain, hypocritical consolation to the impenitent, a sacrament of the church of anti-christ, nay, an open deceit, blasphemy and idolatry. Notwithstanding all this, this thoughtless man writes that it is the word and will of the Father, and then uses the eternal Father and his beloved Son and Holy Spirit, together with the chosen, holy apostles, as a cover for his deceitful abomination and wicked blasphemy. O Lord!

In the ninth place he writes: "That they have the promise, that God, the Father, Son and Holy Ghost, a true and living God, is powerful in his command and works; and will, through his power, sanctify the children of the church and bestow on them his Spirit."

Answer. If he could prove that infant baptism was commanded by the word of God, by apostolic doctrine and usage, or by the example of Christ, as he pretends that it was, then we would gladly admit it to be a holy rite, and pleasing to God, and that it would be a blessed, admonishing, useful, fruitful and powerful thing, for God commands nothing in vain. But since it cannot be proven that it was commanded, and since baptism cannot apply to little children, because the signs of the New Testament are applied to the penitent, therefore we say again, that it is not a God-pleasing ceremony, but according to all Scripture, a wicked blasphemy and abomination, as has already been heard. And how powerfully God works through such abominations, may be plainly seen in the cases of Nadab, Abihu, Jeroboam, Uzza and others.

The pious reader should also know that the children of the churches are not sanctified by means of ceremonies, words and water, but solely through the grace, favor, merits, blood and death of the Lord, and by no other work nor means, at all. But as to his writing that God bestows upon the baptized children his Spirit, we would say that we would have him consider more deeply and learn to know what the work of the Spirit is, before he teaches such doctrine.

Is it not deeply to be regretted that such people dare take upon themselves the care of souls, while they have not yet learned what is the nature, fruit and power of the Holy Spirit? For wherever the Holy Spirit is, there also must be its fruits; this is incontrovertible. And what fruits we find in children when they begin to become of understanding minds, we may, alas, educe from their words, works and life.

I would further say, that if the Spirit is bestowed upon children, through baptism, as he says, and since the Scriptures teach that the Holy Spirit is given to the believing, then it must follow therefrom, since the children do not believe, that the Holy Spirit is not given them through faith, but that it is given through the merits of the ceremony of baptism, which the preachers practice. And what is worse, such a spirit, which in every respect is without knowledge, intelligence, inspiration, power, fruit and work, as may be seen. O, great blindness and error!

In the tenth place he writes: "The Lord Jesus Christ commanded that the children should be brought to him (which the anabaptists do not at all) and that he embraced them, laid his hands upon them and blessed them, that is, baptized them with the Holy Spirit; and all this, done by Christ, is not powerless."

Answer. Here I would ask Gellius, and all who practice infant baptism, Firstly, If all the believers brought their children to Christ when he was preaching? If they answer in the affirmative, then they ought to be ashamed; for they can not prove their assertion by the Scriptures. But if they answer in the negative, then they acknowledge that they in the first place, are wrong to teach and practice that children should be brought to him, that is (according to their understanding), to baptize them.

In the second place I ask, whether in any part of Scripture *bringing to Christ* is called baptism? If they answer in the affirmative, then they can not produce proof. If they answer in the negative then they admit that they, in the second place, adulterate the word of God, by explaining and construing bringing to Christ to mean baptizing.

In the third place I ask, whether Christ baptized the children, brought to him, with water? If they answer in the affirmative, then I would answer with John, that Christ, himself, did not baptize, John 3: 5. But if they answer in the negative, then they acknowledge, in the third place, that it is a false doctrine to try to defend infant baptism on the strength of this bringing to him.

In the fourth place I would ask, because he says that Christ baptized the children with the Holy Spirit. If, then, baptizing with the Spirit is the same thing as baptizing with water? If they answer in the affirmative, then Spirit must be letter, or letter, Spirit. But if they answer in the negative, then they, themselves, pronounce sentence against infant baptism; that Christ's action with the children does not teach nor imply it.

In the fifth place I would ask, How we are to understand this bringing to him—in a carnal, or spiritual way? If they answer in a carnal way, then I would say, that it cannot now be the case, since Christ, in body, is taken from us and removed hence, where we cannot approach in the body, 1 Tim. 6: 16. But if they answer, in a spiritual way, then I would again ask why Gellius so shamefully abuses the pious, whom he calls anabaptists, by writing that they do not at all bring their children to Christ (something which could not have been written in purity of heart), while many of them are so solicitously caring for the salvation of their children by teaching, admonishing and punishing them, and by having a constant solicitude for them, as God's word and the love of their children command and teach all christian parents to do.

O, that God would grant that Gellius and his followers would more deeply consider this spiritual bringing to Christ, as I trust that many of ours do, by the grace of God; and that they would abandon this unscriptural infant baptism, of which they make so much ado. This, in my opinion, would be a very desirable thing. For, as a general thing, they abandon their children, from the cradle on, to the wiles of the devil, by educating them in ignorance, blindness, pomp, splendor, vanity and idolatry, as their fruits plainly show to all of understanding minds. Behold, my reader, from these questions and answers you may conclude whether Gellius and the learned can stand on the strength of the saying, "Suffer the little children to come unto me," with their doctrine and practice of infant baptism, which they practice so indiscriminately, and about which they make so much ado?

Observe, too, that Gellius, by his writing that we do not bring our children to Christ, at all, not only judges and disgraces us, but also Christ Jesus, because he has not commanded us such bringing to him; he also judges the holy apostles who have not testified nor taught us a word in regard to this matter neither by word nor practice in the whole Scriptures.

In the eleventh place he writes: Since Luke testifies that John the baptist was sanctified in his mother's womb, and leaped in the presence of Christ (which, he says, doubtlessly, was caused by a spiritual movement), and as also Jacob, &c, therefore it is manifest that God also works in the children of the church according to their measure, through his Holy Spirit, and that infant baptism is a command and has the promise.

Answer. If these particular miracles of God, which were wrought in the case of John and of Jacob, are to be a common rule, then these following miracles were also common rules, namely, that Sarah and Elizabeth, two barren women, conceived in their old age, and that Balaam's ass spoke; Num. 22: 28; and, therefore, all aged, barren women should conceive, and all asses speak. O no. That such miracles of God were no common rule things, may be educed from the floating of iron at Helizeum; from the passage of the Israelites through the Red Sea, and from the standing still of the sun and moon, 2 Kings 6: 6; Ex. 14: 21; Joshua 10: 13.

I would further say, if, according to the doctrine of Gellius, it follows from the case of John, that all the children of the church, or of the believing members, have the Holy Spirit, then the greater part of his fellow-believers of the German nation (whom alone, he esteemed as faithful servants, and who, with him, are of the same calling, office and service) are greatly contemned in their doctrine, faith and usage; for he writes that the children of the holy church have the Holy Spirit, and they believe and teach that they have the evil spirit, for, before they baptize them, they say, Depart thou evil spirit, and give room to the Holy Spirit.

Behold, thus it is generally with all who teach and practice this shameful doctrine. And, although they are unanimous in the practice, yet they are so divided in opinion as to the grounds of this doctrine, that we are forced to say that it is nothing but a vain mask and infernal mockery. Notwithstanding he writes that infant baptism is commanded, and that it has the promise; while he well knows that he cannot advance one plain word from all the Holy Scriptures, to show that the wisdom of God has commanded it, or that the apostles have taught or practiced it; or, moreover, that its signification, penitence, regeneration, &c., can apply to children. To say nothing of the author mentioning that the primitive, incorrupt church did not practice it, as has been heard

Is not this adulterating the word of God, breaking the Scriptures, perverting truth into lies, stealing the honor and praise of God, killing souls and defending the church of anti-christ? I say again, as I did before, I have never read a word in the Scriptures with such misunderstanding.

In the twelfth place he writes: "That, according to Matthew, baptism was not first instituted by Christ. For it was before commanded of John and practiced by the disciples of Jesus Christ; so that we are not obliged to follow one rule."

Answer. Let every one take heed, and observe what the word of the Lord teaches. Gellius, alas, is not at all ashamed to deny the plain word of God, and writes: "That we are not obliged to follow one certain rule in regard to baptism; that Christ did not command to baptize the believing persons alone; nor that his heavenly Father did, when he commanded John that he should baptize; and that it was not Christ's meaning that such and such persons should be baptized." Behold, thus the Lord's holy word is perverted.

Inasmuch as Gellius so degrades his Lord's mouth, and so lamentably adulterates his word, therefore I will place the words of Christ, according to Matthew and Mark, before the reader, that he may see what rule and law he has made concerning baptism, and what command he has given. Christ says, "All power is given unto me in heaven and in earth. Go ye, therefore, and teach all nations, baptizing them (understand, whom you make disciples, by your doctrine) in the name of the Father, and of the Son, and of the Holy Ghost, teaching them to observe all things whatsoever I have commanded you," Matt. 28. Again, "Go ye into all the world, and preach the gospel to every creature. He that believeth (namely, the gospel) and is baptized, shall be saved; but he that believeth not shall be damned," Mark 16: 15, 16. Behold, this is the word and ordinance of the Lord, how and when we are to baptize. I think these words are too plain to admit of perversion by fine words and accuteness—*preach the gospel* and baptize *those that believe*.

But that John taught and practiced baptism before Christ, is evidence for us and not against us, for he practiced upon those who confessed their sins, Matt. 3: 6, and not upon unconscious children, as the disobedient, offensive preachers do.

Since John did not baptize any but the penitent, before Christ; since Christ commanded it at the confession of faith, the apostles taught and practiced it so, and, also the primitive church, as heard, therefore, the reasonable reader may reflect, in the fear of God, how miserably and lamentably the poor souls are deceived by these degenerated men who so boldly adulterate the pointed, plain words of Christ concerning baptism, and his pleasing, salutary ordinance, and thus destroy it and found it upon an unstable foundation and wrong meaning.

But his writing, "That the apostles were commanded to gather unto Christ a church, from all nations, and to teach them, not that which Moses, but that which Christ had taught," we admit. Yet through no other command nor ordinance than that they should preach the gospel, make disciples through the doctrine, baptize these disciples, and thus to gather unto the Lord a peculiar people, who should walk in Christ Jesus in righteousness, truth and obedience, as the regenerated children of God, and give eternal praises to his great and glorious name. And with such a people, who walk in his fear, love, word, ordinances and commands, he will be, always to the end of the world. But of infant baptism not a word is mentioned.

In the thirteenth place, he writes, "That the apostles, some of whom were baptized of John, and those who came to him from the cities and from Jerusalem were indiscriminately baptized of John, and could not have had much knowledge of Christ, or a true, strong, sincere faith in him."

Answer. If I understand him aright, he would conclude from this, that, as the baptized disciples were not, before baptism, thoroughly fitted in the doctrine, faith and repentance, but had to exercise themselves in continual penitence, and to die unto sin, as baptism represents, that also the children, although they have no faith before baptism, will, after baptism, when they become of understanding minds, study the doctrine, repent, die unto sin, and walk in newness of life.

To which opinion (if this be his opinion) I would reply: The prophets prophesied of John, Isa. 40: 3; Mal. 3: 1. His birth was made known by an angel; Christ testified of him, that he was the second Elias, a shining light, not clothed in soft raiment and not like the waving reed; that he was the greatest of all children born of woman, &c. From which it may be safely educed that he was no light-minded nor reckless preacher, but that he earnestly and valiantly executed his office, according to the pleasure of God, and that he rightly practiced the commanded baptism according to the ordinance. And, although his disciples were not so thoroughly instructed in all things, yet he did not baptize any but those who confessed their sins, as said, Matt. 3, Acts 19.

But, as to his explanation of the words: "If thou believest with all thine heart," which Philip spoke to the Ethiopian, that they mean to believe without deceit and hypocrisy which he rightly asked of the Ethiopian; and of Luke, to leave an example to all servants of the church, how those of mature years should be baptized, he has rightly pointed out, since he also had arrived to years of maturity. We say, that this is right. We would also state what we desire of all baptizers, is: That they first examine well the faith and foundation of those who wish to be baptized, before they baptize them, that they, in their work and service, may not prove hypocrites.

I think that this is a plain example that the servants of the church should not ask the confession of faith from others, but from those, themselves, who wish to be baptized, as also Otto Brunsu. says concerning this: He says not (he writes), If you do believe or answer for your child, it is then permitted to be baptized.

Since Gellius refers us to the disciples and to those baptized of John, and, as appears, would thereby demonstrate that baptism does not require true faith, and that it makes no difference whether faith comes before or after; and, since we, also, are called anabaptists by him, therefore I in my weakness, would ask him, If the command of Christ and the example of the eunuch are not sufficient to show that faith should precede baptism, and that baptism requires true faith, and why Paul re-baptized the disciples of John, who had before been baptized with the baptism of John, while John's baptism was not of men, but from heaven? Matt. 21: 25. He cannot, scripturally, answer it otherwise, than that it was done because they had never known that there was a Holy Ghost. Inasmuch, then, as these disciples were once baptized in their years of maturity, with divine baptism, and lacked nothing but that they did not have an understanding of the Holy Ghost, and were, on that account, re-baptized of Paul—therefore Gellius should consider whether or not true, christian baptism requires true faith, and whether he does not wrong us by contemptuously calling us anabaptists because we re-baptize those who were not baptized with a divine baptism, as were the disciples of John, but with an anti-christian baptism, without any knowledge, faith, command or word, as the reckless, ignorant world, in part, can judge and see.

If we, then, are anabaptists because we re-baptize those who received a baptism instituted of man and which was practiced upon those who had no knowledge whatever, how much, then, was Paul an anabaptist since he re-baptized those who were of understanding minds and baptized with a baptism which was from heaven and ordained of God.

In the second place I would ask, since he calls us anabaptists, as has been heard, Why he still adheres to Cyprian, together with both the Concilions—the African and the Nicene? which unanimously resolved: "That heretics have no baptism, and that therefore those, who have been baptized of heretics, should be baptized with the true baptism." If he says that it is according to the Scriptures and right, then he admits that he was not baptized with the right baptism, and that we are right in re-baptizing those who have been baptized of such who are not alone by Scripture, but also by Luther, Zuingli and the learned, pronounced anti-christian servants and the root of all heresy, before the whole world, as we may on every hand see in their writings.

But if he pronounce it offensive and sectarian, then he thereby testifies, in the first place, that the church, or at least a great part of it, was at that time offensive and sectarian.

In the second place, That he couples God's Spirit, word, work, ordinance and command with the anti-christian and heretical service and works.

In the third place, That he is an anti-christian and heretic himself, since he was baptized with an anti-christian and heretical baptism, and that he yet defends it as the true baptism.

O, my reader, that Gellius had but half an understanding of the word of God, and could but see a little of the truth, he would, all his life-time lament to God that he has so lamentably profaned the Lord's express command and ordinance, given through John, Christ and the apostles; that he has so inimically slandered the pious, and that he passes such a thoughtless and ungodly sentence, by his writings that he not only pronounces us, but also Cyprian, all the African bishops, the Nicene Fathers, besides also, holy Paul himself open anabaptists, nay, heretics.

In the fourteenth place he writes, "That it is with baptism as it was with circumcision. As God commenced circumcision with Abraham, upon preceding instruction,—and, for the purpose of the sealing of the promise, it was practiced upon Abraham's seed and children—so John, the baptist and the apostles commenced baptism with those of mature years, and it was gradually practiced upon the children, since it could not be otherwise on account of circumcision."

Answer. That it is with baptism as it was with circumcision before, namely, in this respect; that it was commenced on previous instruction—is our ground and doctrine; for Christ Jesus has so ordained it and his holy apostles have so taught and practiced it. But that it should, by the command of Christ and by the teaching and practice of the apostles, gradually have been practiced upon the children, is mere conjecture and not Scripture.

For if it were so, then the apostles did wrongly that they did not, according to the manner of circumcision, commanded of God, baptize both the believing and the children (something which they did not do), as Abraham circumcised himself and his house together with the males of eight days old after him, according to the command of God, and did not gradually institute circumcision, as Gellius maintains, and would make us believe, that the apostles should have done with baptism.

But that he writes that this should have been done on account of circumcision is conjecture and not Scripture; for as the apostles and also John served on the believing ones of the Jews the sign of baptism, why not, then, on their children, if God had so ordained and commanded it, as Gellius pretends he did?

No, no, the command of the Lord concerning circumcision expressly applied, first to Abraham and his household, and then directly to the males of eight days old, Gen. 17: 14; but this is not so with regard to baptism, for it applies only to the believing and not to the unconscious children, Matt. 28; Mark 16. Therefore baptism was not gradually practiced upon the children, as Gellius pretends; but it was afterward instituted without the word, ordinance and command of God, by disobedient and self-conceited men, who, alas, have considered a wrought ceremony above the Lord's command and its representation, as is generally the case with the learned and worldly-minded.

Again, as to his writing "that the promise is sealed by baptism, and that it is given not only to the aged, but also to the children"—the reader should observe that the promise of the grace of God, and of the eternal covenant, is not sealed, now any more, by the perishable blood of oxen and rams, nor by visible water and ceremonies, but solely by the precious blood of Christ on the cross. Blessed is he, who believes it, and cordially accepts it. This promise is made to the unbaptized children, no less than to the baptized believing, so long as they are clothed with childish innocence, and continue in simplicity. But when they come to maturity and accept the dispensed gospel of grace through faith, then the Scriptures teach us that we should baptize them, Matt. 28: 19; Mark 16: 15. But if they reject grace, and lead an easy, impenitent life, neither Christ's blood nor death will avail them; much less will word and water avail them. For, "he that believeth not" (the Scripture means those of understanding minds) "is condemned already," John 3: 18.

In the fifteenth place he writes, "They err abominably, because they conclude, from the Scriptures and examples which have reference to those of mature years, to a certainty, that it is an ordinance of God that the children should not be baptized, notwithstanding that there is not a tittle in the whole New Testament which forbids it. And therefore they are no less wrong than I should be if I would not feed my children that cannot labor, because Paul says, he that does not labor shall not eat, which is incontrovertibly spoken in regard to those of mature years, and not to children.

Answer. In my opinion, Gellius wilfully intends to uphold the things contrary to Christ and truth, that he may execute the office of an anti-christian preacher, according to the pleasure of the world. For, when he *should* write that we act rightly according to the Scriptures, and that there is not a tittle in the New Testament that children should be baptized—he writes that we err abominably, and that there is not a tittle that forbids infant baptism, &c.

Inasmuch as he so willfully and violently contends against the Lord and his truth, and since he in various ways seeks to give his cause a fine appearance by the use of many borrowed words, lies, conjectures and perversion of the Scriptures, and says that we err abominably, &c., therefore I would briefly state: That if he can at any time prove to us by the unadulterated, divine Scriptures and truth, that John the Baptist practiced infant baptism any where; or that it was commanded of Christ and taught and practiced by the apostles; or, that it was, through the ordinance of the Lord, gradually practiced upon children, as he writes it was; or, that bringing to him is called ed baptism and baptism bringing to him, in the Scriptures; or, that Christ and the apostles have baptized the children that were brought to them; or, that Christ baptized them with a spirit that was powerful in works (the Spirit of God is never idle); or, that small children have faith, or that they are penitent, that they bury their sins and are circumcised through faith and thereby arise with Christ in newness of life; or, that circumcision is called baptism, and baptism circumcision; or, that they have the answer of a good conscience; or, that baptism, anywhere in the Scriptures, is called a sign of the covenant of grace, a sealing of the promise, and an incorporation into the church, or that unconscious children speak with tongues as the believing members of the house of Cornelius did, of whom Peter says, "Can any man forbid water, that these should not be baptized, which have received the Holy Ghost as well as we?" Acts 10: 47, or, that the true, primitive church practiced it by the apostolic doctrine, usage or command; or, that God is powerful through works which he has not ordained, then we will lay aside our pen, repent and confess before the whole world that our cause is mere deceit, and nothing but falsehood, in this respect.

But if he cannot do so, as it is impossible for him to do, then I would faithfully admonish and fraternally beseech him to consider earnestly and thoroughly how shamefully he reflects on God, the Father, Son and Holy Spirit, John the Baptist and the apostles, in this matter of infant baptism; how lamentably he adulterates the plain Scriptures and deceives the poor souls; what gross falsehoods he teaches the poor people; how deceitfully he teaches the accursed abomination and passes it for a holy, glorious work; and also, how unjustly he accuses us of abominably erring, we, who clearly have on our side Christ's plain word, the apostolic doctrine and usage, the signification of baptism, and the usage of the true, primitive churches; while he cannot show by a single word of all the Scriptures, that his infant baptism has any foundation in the ordinance and command of God. My faithful reader, beware; fear God; act justly; search the Scriptures; shun falsehood and follow the truth.

Again, by undertaking to draw the saying of Paul, "That if any would not work, neither should he eat," into his argument, he contradicts himself, and is unworthy of a reply. For, as Paul thereby commands the idlers and busy-bodies to earn their own bread by honorable labor, lest they become an offense, and troublesome to others, and since such cannot apply to children, therefore such labor was not thereby commanded them. Neither does Paul say, he who does not work, &c., as Gellius writes; but he says, "If any would not work, neither should he eat." So, too, baptism is not commanded to be practiced on unconscious children, but it is commanded in the Scriptures to be practiced upon those who believe the word of the Lord, lead a penitent life and who have a sound understanding and comprehension of baptism, as has been said several times.

In the sixteenth place he writes, "That in Christ Jesus no respect of persons or time is made. For the glory of the kingdom of Christ is not limited to any cities, times or persons; so, neither to any age nor generation."

Answer. Herewith, if I understand it, he would assert that, although, according to his assertion, baptism has taken the place of circumcision, and the males only were circumcised in Israel, that notwithstanding this, both males and females are to be baptized, now, be they believers' children, and born of believing parents or not. If that is his meaning and foundation, then he should know that as the grace, favor, love, covenant and promise of God under the New Testament, extended to both men and women, so, also did it extend to all under the Old Testament. For, if God had coupled his covenant of grace and all to signs, whether it be circumcision or baptism, and if those alone were in the church who had received the sign, then the Israelitic women and maids, and also the children of the primitive churches, were in a bad situation; since the first, according to the Scriptures, were not circumcised, and the latter, according to the ancient authors, were not baptized, as has been already said.

No, reader, no. Abraham and all his seed, I mean both men and women, young and old, were the Lord's people and church. But the males only, were circumcised, and not the females, the male children of eight days old, and not the female children, according to the ordinance of God; yet, they all, both men and women, were members of the church under the covenant of God, and were children of the promise, although, I repeat it, the males only were circumcised, and not the females.

So it is under the New Testament. The gospel is preached, and all who believe it and are baptized, shall be saved; be they males or females. They are members of the church of Christ under God's covenant and grace; they are joint heirs of the kingdom of God, and children of eternal life; also the children, although they are not baptized, Mark 16:16; Acts 5:14; 1 Cor. 12:13; Rom. 8:14.

For, as God would have his ceremonies under the Old Testament, such as circumcision, the passover, sin-offering, burnt-offering, &c., practiced just as he ordained and commanded them through Moses, in the same manner he will have his signs, under the New Testament, such as baptism and Supper, practiced in no other way than he has commanded and ordained through his Son.

For he says, "This is my beloved Son in whom I am well pleased; hear ye him." If, now, this Son had ordained infant baptism, then we should practice it, if we would be his disciples; but since he has not done so, we pronounce it, according to the Scriptures, accursed, as said, Gal. 1:8.

I further say, If they, now, place the children of both believing and unbelieving parents, on the same foundation, which, according to my opinion would not be contrary to the Scriptures, then they must recall their doctrine whereby they, before, applied the grace and covenant of God, with many words, to the children of believing parents, and admit that their doctrine in regard to Abraham and his seed, whereby they make baptism take the place of circumcision, has no similarity to, nor connection with it, at all; for it was not commanded of Abraham to circumcise all the children round about him, who were not his seed, but only those which were of his seed, as may be learned from Genesis 17.

In the seventeenth place he writes, Would to God that they could once rightly understand the 5th chapter, of Paul's letter to the Ephesians, wherein he describes the church, saying, Christ loved the church, and gave himself for it, that he might sanctify and cleanse it with the washing of water in the word, or as Erasmus says, through the word. Then he goes on and says, This incontrovertibly includes the children along with their parents, that is, the believers and their seed, nay, the whole church. How should they, then, be excluded from the word, while it reads, He has cleansed the church with the washing of water by the word?

Answer. I trust that we, through the grace and enlightenment of the Lord, in our weakness, do not misunderstand these words of Paul, but that we do rightly understand the meaning. We offer Gellius and all the learned, the use of all the Scriptures, besides all reason and experience, if they can show one tittle in the Holy Scriptures to prove that reason and experience teach, that we can teach little children the word of God, from which originates the true cleansing of the heart, or that the Scriptures of the New Testament any where apply the word and sacraments to them; if they can, then we will admit that they are cleansed by baptism through the word, or in the word. But, if they can not do so, then it is already proven that these words of Paul are not written in regard to little children.

It is true, Christ has so loved his church, that he has given himself for her, and has sanctified her through the power and merits of his innocent blood, and cleansed her by water, which is a sign of a new and penitent life, but not otherwise than in the word, or through the word, which, preached in the power of the Spirit, and accepted in true faith, is followed by the ordained baptism as commanded.

Christ said, "Ye are clean through the word which I have spoken unto you," John 15: 3; not, my reader, that they were clean on account that it was outwardly spoken unto them, but because they believed that which was spoken unto them. For God does not cleanse the hearts through any literal water, word or ceremony, but through faith in the word; otherwise all who outwardly hear the word and receive the outward sign of the water, would be holy and clean; this is incontrovertible.

In the eighteenth place, He advances an argument and syllogism. Whatever pertains to the church, also pertains to the members of the church. Baptism pertains to the whole church, both old and young—therefore baptism pertains to all the members of the church.

Answer. In my opinion it were better for Gellius, since he boasts himself a preacher of the holy word, to leave his logic to the wise of the world, who, alas, seek their own praise and honor more than they do God's; and satisfy himself with the true doctrine, foundation and truth of Christ, and with the unpretentious, plain testimony of Matthew, the publican, and of Peter and John, the fishermen, &c., that he does not deceive the unlearned by such accute reasoning and lead them off the true way.

As to his major proposition (as he calls it), I would say, that if Gellius had applied it to grace, reconciliation, promise, eternal life, &c., which were bestowed upon the whole church, young as well as old, for Christ's sake, and not upon the ordinance of the church, then he would have been right; but as it is, he will have to admit that it is wrong, and contrary to the word of God. For, as regards the ordinances of which he speaks, in which baptism is included, I would say, that all the members of the church are not of one and the same calling, service and work, and are not under one and the same ordinance; for the Lord has ordained apostles, prophets, evangelists, pastors and servants, in his church, and all are not, on that account, apostles, prophets, evangelists, pastors and servants. Thus it is with the ordinances of baptism and the Holy Supper, in his church; not that we should therefore serve them to the unconscious children, but only to the believing and penitent, according to the Scriptures.

As to his minor proposition, I would say, our doctrine, belief, foundation and confession is, that our unconscious children, so long as they live in their innocence, are, through the merits, death and blood of Christ, in grace, and joint heirs of the promise, as has already been heard. The doctrine of the New Testament, which is a doctrine of the Spirit, does not include them with those who are ruled and governed by the word and sacraments of God, and who are properly called the church of Christ in Scripture.

That the children should be counted into the church on account of the promise, we consent to, but we controvert that they should be included in the ordinances of the church; for this is contrary to all Scripture and common sense, as we will prove by Christ's own words. He also openly reproves Christ and the apostles, together with the Holy Spirit. For he writes, "Baptism pertains to both young and old;" while they have not left us a single example, nor one word in all the Scriptures whereby it is taught or commanded, as may be seen.

Since both his major and minor propositions are not consistent with the word and command of God, as shown, how then, his conclusion, that baptism pertains to all the members of the church, can be consistent with the word and ordinance of God is sufficiently clear to the kind reader.

I would further say, that if this, his syllogism, is right and true, namely, Whatever pertains to the church, must pertain to all the members of the church, &c., which, however, is not so, then it would also be true that as doctrine, faith, knowledge of Christ, true repentance, a regenerated, new life, the circumcision of the heart, a clear conscience, baptism, Lord's Supper, the love of one's neighbor, a living hope, ardent thankfulness, &c., pertain to the church

—therefore they pertain to all the members, both young and old.

If he denies this first proposition of mine, then he denies his own, for it is like his. If he denies, besides, the second, because children, on account of their weak understanding, as he admits, cannot understand the word, and that they, therefore, cannot repent nor be admitted to the Supper, &c., then he testifies that the children do not belong to the church which is governed by the Lord's word and sacraments; and that his syllogism, wherewith he includes all the members of the church, both young and old, in one and the same ordinance, is wrong and false, nay, contrary to God's word. This is my answer to the argument of Gellius and his fellows. How they can stand with this, according to the Scriptures, you may reflect upon in the fear of your God.

In the nineteenth place, he makes a long discourse in regard to the child which was, according to Mark and Luke, called to Christ; and will thereby prove and teach that children believe, or if they do not believe, that they are accounted as believing, be they of whatever age they may. He further writes that a child of two, three or four years old may be corrupted by bad examples; and that we are too timorous because we dare not baptize those whom Christ accounts as believing (as he says).

Answer. If Gellius and the learned had received but a little understanding of the nature, power and properties of true faith, they would be ashamed all their lifetime to have such a poor idea of that precious faith which is a power and gift of God. Moses says that the children have no knowledge of good and evil. The wise man says, that they have no understanding. Paul says, "Brethren, be not children in understanding," 1 Cor. 14: 20, and yet Gellius dares write that they believe; as if faith were but a dead thing that has no motive power or work.

O no, true faith, which avails before God, is a living and saving power which is, through the preaching of the holy word, bestowed of God upon the heart; that moves, changes and regenerates it to newness of mind; that smothers all ungodliness; that destroys all pride, ambition and selfishness; that in malice, makes us like children, &c. Behold, such is the faith which the Scriptures teach us, and not a vain, dead and unfruitful conjecture, as the world pretends it to be. And that such faith is not to be found in children of two, three or four years old, both the Scriptures and common sense teach us.

O, dear Lord! what great blindness, that this thoughtless man does not observe that he and his like preachers, some of whom have grown already gray, who daily read the Scriptures after their manner, are yet so unbelieving that they dare, for the sake of a piece of bread, adulterate the plain word of God, lead the poor, miserable souls to hell, in great numbers, upbraid, slander and hate all the pious, and innocently heap upon them slanderous lies and disgraces, incite the magistracy to tyranny and blood, and that they delight in pomp, splendor, the lusts of the flesh, avarice, &c., which is such clear proof that they are not alone unbelieving, but that they are also quite earthly and carnally-minded; and yet they assert that a child of two or three years of age has faith. O, folly and error!

The reason that Christ called unto himself the child, and placed it in the midst of his disciples, was because the disciples were casting about as to who would be the greatest. He set the child as an example to them, and said, "Verily I say unto you, Except ye be converted, and become as little children, ye shall not enter into the kingdom of heaven." And that we must inherit the kingdom of God, as a child (in malice, understand), as Mark and Luke write. Paul says, "In malice be ye children." Christ says, "Whosoever therefore shall humble himself as this little child, the same is greatest in the kingdom of heaven; and whoso shall receive one such little child in my name, receiveth me. But whoso shall offend one of these little ones which believe in me, it were better for him that a mill-stone were hanged about his neck, and that he were drowned in the depth of the sea," Matt. 18: 4—6. Behold, Christ himself explains to what children we should apply this.

As to his writing that children are accounted believing, is merely a conjecture and opinion which cannot be substantiated by a single word of the Scriptures. Again, as to his assertion that a child, two, three or four years old may be offended, I would say, first, If we were to apply, as Gellius does, this saying, "Whoso shall offend one of these little ones which believe on me," &c., to young children (to which I, on my part, do not consent), then the whole world might well be astounded at these words, from the inmost of their souls. For how they educate their young children, and with what ungodly, offensive life they walk before them, their disgraceful ill-manners and roguery, alas, teach us, both in city and country. O, reader, that the world would take to heart the salvation of their children, and not, from the cradle on, lead them in the way to hell, by their doctrine and example; what a blessed thing it would be for their souls at the day of judgment!

Second, If the preachers and magistrates would rightly understand this saying of Christ, and believed it just and true, then, in my opinion, the offensive, deceiving doctrine would soon be at an end, and the tyrannical sword be put into the sheath, by which, now, alas, hundreds of thousands of souls, are offended to everlasting destruction, and consigned to the kingdom of the devil. O, Lord! "Woe unto the world because of offences," says Christ, God's mouth and wisdom.

To his writing that we are too timorous, because we dare not baptize children, I would say this, that the Scriptures teach us not to do that which we see proper, but that which is commanded us, Deut. 4: 2; 12: 32.

Nadab and Abihu, the sons of Aaron, offered strange fire before the Lord, which he commanded them not, And there went out a fire from the Lord and devoured them, Lev. 10: 1, 2.

Jeroboam was chosen king of the ten revolted tribes of Israel, worshipped in a manner not commanded of God, and therefore he was told by the prophet that God would take away the remnant of his house, as a man taketh away dung, till it be all gone, 1 Kings 14: 10.

Uzziah was smitten for life because he burned incense upon the altar of incense, to which the Lord had not called him, 2 Chron. 26: 16.

Luther writes in his preface to Isaiah and says, "God will not be told how he is to be served. He will teach and lead us. His word should be our guide; for without his word it is all idolatry and vain falsehood, however fine and pleasing it may appear." Again, in the 3rd chapter of Daniel, "Worship without God's word is ever idolatry."

I would further say, All those who seek God, and sincerely fear him, obey his ordinance and word.

Israel never circumcised a female, nor offered a ewe for the passover; for God ordained that the males should be circumsised on the eighth day, and that rams should be offered, Gen. 17: 11; Exod. 12: 5, as heard before.

Since we clearly learn from the Holy Scriptures that Moses and the prophets and besides, the Father, himself, unanimously point to Jesus, who is Wisdom and Truth, to obey him; and since we surely know, by the grace of God, that he is the true Prophet and perfect Teacher, whose word is truth, and whose command is eternal life, and since he has not commanded us a single word of infant baptism, nor his true witnesses, the holy apostles have taught it or left an example, and since we also find that the signification is not applicable to children, and besides, that the Scriptures do not admit of strange worship, self-chosen ceremonies, nor addition, nor subtraction, and that God has several times punished such self-chosen righteousness and worship, as heard; and further, that the primitive church did not practice infant baptism, as has been often heard, therefore we are so timorous, that we dare not baptize our little children; for these cases to which we have referred, together with the unfeigned love of salutary, divine truth, the sincere fear of our God, and the power of our faith, although in weakness, prevent us.

O, reader, would God grant that our opponents could rightly understand what frightful abominations they commit on every hand with their infant baptism, and how they practice it to the dishonor of God and corruption of their neighbors, then, I trust, this matter would soon be reformed, and by the help of God, be changed to a scriptural usage.

In the first place, they falsify God and the Holy Scriptures by their infant baptism; for they assert that it is God's ordinance, while there is not a single word or example to be found in all the Scriptures, that teaches infant baptism.

In the second place, they thereby destroy the true church of Christ, and establish an anti-christian one which bears the name and semblance of the christian church; although it hates and despises its doctrine, spirit, ordinances and usages, taught by the Scriptures.

In the third place, they thereby console the world in their unrighteousness; for however ungodly, adulterous, perjurious, covetous, pompous, envious, blood-thirsty, greedy, drunken, carnal, idolatrous and hypocritical they be, yet they boast that they are baptized christians.

In the fourth place, they hate and persecute all those, who, out of pure, godly zeal, avoid this deceitful abomination, reprove their damnable worship, and point them to Jesus and his word alone. Nay, they are called their apostate anabaptists, apostles of the devil, deceived heretics, off-scourings and booty.

In the fifth place, although they, and their authors, in the past, have condemned unto hell the institutions and commands of men, and have written one volume after another against it, yet they, alas, altogether adhere, to this abhorrible abomination, because they want to avoid the cross, and gain the favor of the world; they act hypocritically in all things, and do the things which are pleasing to the world; they heap one abominable error upon another; hang crosses upon the child's breast and forehead; they conjure and ask the parents if they believe, &c., drive out devils, and commit other disgraceful acts; so that we are forced to say that all the infant baptizers are hypocrites of all hypocrites, and that infant baptism is an open incorporation into the church of anti-christ, the beginning of all deceit, and an accursed blasphemy and enchantment, which is not only contrary to the plain word and ordinance of the Lord, but also against all reason, nature and common sense. For who that has read the word of the Lord at all, does not know, that a cross made with the fingers cannot help or save a child? That the innocent creature, the unconscious child, which is cleansed by the blood of the Lord, is not possessed of the devil, and that one cannot insure the faith of others, since it is a gift of God?

Say, kind reader, What worse mockery and hypocrisy could be imagined, than to ask of one in the name of another: Do you believe? Do you renounce Satan, &c.? and on an affirmative answer, to baptize an unconscious child that knows nothing of neither yes nor no, of God nor devil, of truth nor falsehood, of life nor death? O blasphemy and shame!

O, Lord! O, dear Lord!! how long shall this gross deceit and vile abomination be practiced! I think it were high time that the world should take heed, and learn to know such open deceivers and their doctrine, baptism, supper, life and fruits, and that they would pay more attention to the ordinance, will, word, ways and works of the Lord.

In the twentieth place, he accuses us of a false security, as he calls it, because we, or ours, say that we are assured in our hearts that they err, and that we are right, &c.

Answer. The Lord speaks through Moses, "Whosoever will not hearken unto my words which he" (that is Christ) "shall speak in my name, I will require it of him," Deut. 18: 19.

The Father says, "This is my beloved Son, in whom I am well pleased; hear ye him," Matt. 17: 5.

Christ says, "Teach them to observe all things whatsoever I have commanded you," Matt. 28: 29.

Paul says, "Though we, or an angel from heaven, preach any other gospel unto you than that which we have preached unto you, let him be accursed," Gal. 1:8.

John says, "Whosoever transgresseth, and abideth not in the doctrine of Christ, has not God. He that abideth in the doctrine of Christ, he hath both the Father and the Son," 2 John 1: 9, and other like sayings.

Since all the Scriptures point us to the Spirit, gospel, command, ordinance, usage and example of Christ; and since we, in our worship, do not follow conjectures, our own desires, false explanations and doctrines of men, as we are accused of, Christ's plain word and command, the doctrine and usage of the holy apostles, and of the true, primitive church; and, as they (our opponents) are no more commanded to baptize children than Israel was to circumcise females, or that they should found churches, altars and places of worship on hills, or in dales, or that they should offer their children as burnt-offerings, or that the papists should baptize bells as they are accustomed to, and since they call and persecute the baptism ordained of Christ, as the baptism of heretics, and esteem and practice infant baptism, which was instituted through hypocrisy, as a christian baptism, and since they, besides, boast that they do right by not abandoning this practice; therefore I would gladly leave it to the judgment of all reasonable and impartial readers, who of us are the Sanherib, Holofernes, Pharisaical, and deceiving sects, mentioned as trusting in false security.

He further writes, What else has deceived the anabaptists in the past, that they took up the sword, than just such security. They imagined that they, as the people of God, were marked with the sign, Tau; should subdue the whole world, and hang us preachers, who they said knew better, to our own door-posts?

Answer. Reader, observe, What else does he hereby say than, Beloved lords, will you yet be merciful unto such an offensive people and wicked heretics? Persecute, imprison, banish and destroy them. They are deserving of it. You may consider and judge whether the Holy Spirit, in the Revelation does not call this the sting of scorpions, Rev. 9: 10. Further on he says that our church was originated by me; something which, as will be hereafter shown, I do not admit. He knows very well that I never was found in the company of the rebellious; but that I reproved their doctrines and abominations with the word of the Lord, as much as I ever did those of the preachers. Notwithstanding, he accuses us of these ungodly practices and wicked deeds; that he may thereby make us, who are innocent, suspicioned of all the world, and deliver us unto the sword of the magistracy. I will leave it to the consideration of all the pious and good-fearing, if this is not seeking the blood of the innocent.

O, that he would have sufficient discretion not to mix the innocent with the guilty. For what else does he seek than to change Simon Peter into Simon Magus, and John and James into Judas?

If I should say, I have known some infant baptists which were open perjurers and thieves, therefore Gellius and all the infant baptists are perjurers and thieves. Would not that be wrong? O, faithful reader, how justly has holy David portrayed such slanderers, saying, The wicked murder the innocent in secret places; his eyes are privily set against the poor. He lieth in wait secretly, as a lion in his den; he lieth in wait to catch the poor, &c., Ps. 10: 8, 9. For, by such murderous cries, it is caused, that in different places, the pious and faithful hearts —men and women, youths and virgins, the gray-headed, the lame and halt are pitilessly and mercilessly imprisoned and robbed, their children sent abroad in the world, homeless and penniless, as the most wicked upon earth. Some are thrown into boiling oil; others are hanged, racked, drowned, strangled, burned, beheaded or tortured by some other heathenish and tyrannical means. Behold, such are, alas, the consequences of the deceiving and false writings of such blood-thirsty preachers, in some countries.

Would to God, that he and his preachers, together with all the papists and monks, who are guilty of innocent blood, may find mercy and grace before the eyes of the great and Almighty God, in the day when the fearful sound of the last trumpet shall sound, and that the innocent blood of which they are guilty, be not counted against them. This is my sincere wish and prayer. But if they continue in their present minds, and do not turn from ungodliness, then, says the Spirit of God, the fiery pool will be their reward and part, Rev. 19: 21.

Further, I would say, Just as we hate and reprove (understand this in a gospel-like way) the bitter and inimical heart, and the bloody and fiendish crying and writing of Gellius and all the contentious—so, also, do we hate and reprove those that take up the sword, steal, rob, or in any manner

REPLY TO GELLIUS FABER.

wrong any one on earth, be he friend or foe.

In this we should pay no respect as to persons, be it father, brother, emperor, king, neighbor, friend, great or small, baptized or not baptized. All those who shed human blood against the word of God, who act contrary to love, who wrong, offend or afflict their neighbor, can not be our brethren, for they plainly show that they are not christians.

We must ever hear that the rebellious and their aiders at Munster, have, in the past, alas, taken up the sword, contrary to God's word, as if we were one with them in that abomination; although we are quite innocent in the matter. But they do not see that they arm whole countries and corrupt them; that they destroy one principality after another, that they use all manner of violence, and thus cause affliction, misery and sorrow, every where. Yea, this is, alas, called doing right.

Since it is manifest that not only France, Italy, Spain and Burgundy, but also all the German nations, and the rest of the world who boast of the word are guilty of the same deeds, as regards fighting, warring, robbing and shedding blood; why do they, then, reprove the crimes of the rebellious, while they are so far from being innocent, yea, have done the same criminal deeds as those they reprove? Paul says, "Therefore thou art inexcusable, O man, whosoever thou art, that judgest; for wherein thou judgest another, thou condemnest thyself; for thou that judgest, doest the same things," Rom. 2: 1.

In the last place he writes, Our eyes have seen better than the eyes of the anabaptists in regard to wilful sinning, because they have made many doubtful and caused some to recede, &c.

Answer. If he aims this at us, then he should know that he has written more than he should have done. For I can say with a clear conscience, that I never was troubled concerning this matter by the brethren, and that the doctrine has not been broached among us in my time.

I have ever taught that all sins which are repented of are pardoned in the blood of the Lord, be they what they may. David's adultery and shedding of innocent blood, is to me a sure testimony. Yet everybody should take heed that he sincerely fears God, acts rightly, and that he does not wilfully sin against his God, that he does not pervert falsehood into truth, nor truth into falsehood, as did the scribes. For who knows but that he who wilfully sins against his God, will never truly repent and receive grace? Christ says, "Whosoever committeth sin, is the servant of sin," John 8: 34.

I fear that if his imperial highness were to present to me many costly gifts, and I should ungratefully squander them, or trample upon them, or cast them from me, his imperial highness would, undoubtedly, severely punish me for such ingratitude, and would probably not again offer me such favors and costly presents.

Therefore, take heed that you do not wilfully despise and adulterate your Lord's word, nor walk according to the pleasure of a carnal mind; lest the manifest grace at once be withheld from you, and you are led into perverse ways. *Qui timet Deum, recedit a malo*, he that fears God, shuns evil.

As Gellius exerts himself to adulterate, by his false doctrine, the word of the Lord, to render of no avail his precious blood, and to harden and console the impenitent, reckless world in their wild and wicked ways, under an appearance of the holy word; so he also exerts himself, in my opinion, to root out the salutary, pure truth from earth, and to deliver the pious and godly children into the hands of the executioner, by all manner of false defamations and criminal accusations. If I am wrong rebuke me.

If the name, "grasping kite," is not more applicable to him than a gathering hen, by which name he would like to be called, I will leave to himself and the Lord.

But the Lord, who is the shield and surety of all the oppressed, defends them against the ungodly. He destroys the liars. He abhors the bloody and deceitful; "There is no faithfulness in their mouth; their inward part is very wickedness; their throat is an open sepulchre; they flatter with their tongue," Psalm 5: 9.

Therefore they shall not stand before the storm; their light shall be extinguished, and their glory shall vanish. For the Lord is strong, who shall judge them, and he will require the poor, deceived souls, and the innocent blood at their hands, and he will give them their reward.

Behold, dear reader, from this you may see that the doctrine and confession of the preachers in regard to infant baptism, can not stand, according to the Scriptures; that it is not founded upon the Lord's command, nor upon the doctrine or practice of the holy apostles, as is the baptism of the believing, but merely upon logic, opinion, conjecture, falsehood, borrowed names and custom. If you be of reasonable mind, then let the infallible and true word of the Lord, and your impartial heart judge between us and the learned.

I would hereby, for God's sake, beseech all readers not to think hard of it that I reprove falsehood, according to the Scriptures; defend truth with truth, point out the right way, seek the salvation of your souls, controvert the false prophets, expose their deceiving, secret snares and defend the Lord's praise. He who seeks the Lord in sincerity of heart, read and judge.

THE LORD'S SUPPER.

WE will very briefly review and reply to the treatise of Gellius on the sacrament called the Lord's Supper, because we have published our foundation and belief of this matter, and referred to many Scriptures, in the past. Whosoever finds a delight in the truth, may read them and reflect on them in the fear of God. Yet we would, in our weakness, remind the pious reader, before we commence our reply to Gellius' publication, that it is written, "For we, being many, are one bread and one body; for we are all partakers of that one bread," 1 Cor. 10: 17. Since we learn from the Scriptures that the Holy Supper was instituted of the Lord as a sign and testimony, not to the world but to the church of God, that all of us who are one bread are members of one body, namely, of the body of Christ; and since we plainly see that both the dispensers and partakers of the worldly supper, are not true members of the Lord's body, because the dispensers are all hirelings, thieves of the honor of God, and murderers of our souls, who retain the thoughtless, reckless people in all manner of unrighteousness, blindness, and in an unbridled, carnal life, by their promises, philosophy and logic; who deceive all the world and hate, upbraid, belie, apprehend, banish and exterminate the pious, who renounce evil, follow the word of the Lord, and ever eat of his bread; and because the partakers, generally, are an impenitent, light-minded and vain people, nay, worldlings, part of whom not only little regard the Spirit, word and knowledge of the Lord, but trample it under foot, as may be seen—therefore we abstain from their supper; for the sincere fear in our hearts, caused by the word of God, prevents us from partaking of it with such dispensers and partakers, lest we also partake of their deceiving actions and abominable abuse, and, at the day of Christ, receive the same reward with them.

He boasts a great deal of his admonition, yet all his admonition is nothing but vain boasting, without all power; for how can he and his like preachers rightly teach Christ, and admonish others, while they are yet filled from the top of their heads to the soles of their feet, with all manner of unrighteousness, blindness and disgrace?

They would do well to reflect upon the words of Sirach, and rightly learn to know themselves, because many of them are as yet such useless people, that they are more fit to be herders of swine than to be shepherds of the sheep of Christ, as he writes. And because Gellius is not only an adulterer of the Scriptures and deceiver of souls, but also a very cruel, profane and defaming man, as may be very clearly educed from his writings.

He writes that they admonish them in the first place, what should be the qualifications of the partakers, according to the doctrine of the law, and especially of the holy gospel.

Answer. Wherever the law is preached rightly and taken to heart, through faith and manifested in Spirit and power, there we find a subdued mind, a penitent, humble heart, and a conscience which trembles before the word and true fear of God, and which allays and disperses sin, as Sirach says.

This is the real intention and object of the law: To reveal unto us the will of God, to discover unto us sin, to threaten us with the wrath and punishment of the Lord, to proclaim death and to point us to Christ, that we may, before the eyes of God, be humbled in heart, die unto sin, and seek and find the only and eternal medicine and remedy for our souls, Jesus Christ.

In the same manner it is in regard to the gospel. Wherever it is preached in true zeal, according to the pleasure of God, and unblamably in the power of the Spirit, so that it penetrates the hearts of the hearers, there we find a converted, changed and new mind, which joyfully and gratefully gives praises to his God for his inexpressibly great love towards us, miserable sinners, in Christ Jesus, and thus enters into newness of life willingly and freely, by the power of a true faith and a new birth.

If Gellius would knock at the innermost heart of his followers, and of himself, with the hammer of the law, and zealously enkindle in them the fire of the holy gospel, so that they would, in true repentance, change their unclean, obdurate hearts, and abandon their heathenish pomp and splendor in their houses, and clothes, their vain show of gold and silver, their extravagance, avariciousness, drinking and carousing, and would enter with Christ into newness of life, then I would admit that that which he has written here concerning the Lord's Supper, did well compare with their walk. But as it is, he consoles the poor with an empty purse, only, and acts in a manner entirely contrary to that in which he should. For the signs of the New Testament are in themselves quite powerless, vain and useless, if the signification, namely, the new, penitent life, is not there, as has been said above in treating of baptism.

He further writes, that they, in the second and third place, admonish them (their hearers) that it is not enough to know and understand the doctrine, but that it should be, also, manifested in their walk, yea, at the risk of body and life, that they should be prepared for the cross and temptation, that they should patiently and obediently bear it, and follow their bridegroom, for the devil dislikes such confession and therefore hates and persecutes them.

Answer. Caiaphas said unto the Pharisees and Scribes, "It is expedient for us that one man should die for the people, and that the whole nation perish not," John 11: 50.

His intentions sounded right, yet his cruel, blood-thirsty heart did not perceive that it was he, who, through bitter zeal, sought the life of the king of all glory.

We do not controvert but that Gellius and his fellow preachers sometimes talk of a pious life, according to the Scriptures, and admonish their hearers of the cross; but how they love true righteousness, which true doctrine brings forth, and how they treat the confessors thereof, may, alas, be educed from their indiscreet and disgraceful writing and crying.

Since he writes that he thus admonishes them, as heard, and that it is plainly manifest that he not only hates the true righteousness, power, fruit and obedience which true preaching brings forth, but also crucifies it, I fear, by his indiscreet and disgraceful writing, therefore, the godly, pious reader may consider if he is not like unto the Scribes and Pharisees, in this respect, who, although they understood the law, yet so hated righteousness, that they, by their connivance and advice, crucified him who was promised in the law, the Fulfiller, Christ Jesus.

Dear reader, understand what I write. Outward preaching, hearing, baptism and Supper do not at all avail before God; but before him avail teaching and believing, faith and works, outwardly baptism and Supper, according to the letter, and inwardly according to the Spirit and truth. Behold, this is what God's word and ordinance teach us.

So long as such impenitent, carnal people are the dispensers, and such vain, pompous, covetous, extortionate, carousing and drinking people the partakers, so long, I say, it is not the true Supper of the Lord, but it is a supper of the impenitent, an encouragement to the unrighteous, and an enchanting mockery, however much it may be adorned and decked, before men, with high-sounding words and praises; for outside of the church of Christ, which is a gathering of the penitent, there is neither baptism nor Holy Supper. Again understand that which I write, Neither water, bread nor wine avail in Christ without true repentance, if they were, even, served by the apostles themselves; before him avail, alone, a new creature, a converted, changed and broken heart, a sincere fear and love of God, unfeigned love of one's neighbors, a sober, humble, peaceable and converted life, according to the word and example of the Lord. Where there is such a new being, lo, there is true baptism, and the true Supper. But to be baptized outwardly and partake of the Supper, according to the letter, and not inwardly before God in Spirit and truth, I repeat, is nothing more nor less than a shadow, vain mockery of God's work, nay, hypocrisy and deceit.

Is it not a lamentable blindness, that these poor, misled people attach so much value to the outward, visible sign, and do not observe that they are, with all their heart inimical to the invisible signification, for which the visible sign was commanded in the Scriptures? as if God had a special pleasure in the mere elements, water, bread and wine, and not in the proper signification, which is represented and admonished thereby.

O no, reader, we can not please nor serve God with mere water, bread and wine; for by his hand, it was all created. But we can serve and please him with the signification of his baptism and Supper, namely, that we thereby testify our faith and obedience, that we will walk in continual and eternal penance, that we will remember his inexpressibly great love and blessings, that we are thereby admonished that he has offered for us his spotless, pure body, and that he has shed his precious blood for the reconciliation of our souls, in his ardent love for us; that we will ever walk with him in unity of the Spirit, and follow him; that we will love, assist, console, reprove, bear, admonish and serve each other as members of one body; and that we will prove ourselves unto death, as the newly born children of God in all righteousness, holiness and truth. Behold, dear reader, for this purpose the signs of the New Testament were instituted. If Gellius and his like preachers were to use the Holy Supper in such heart and spirit; if the signification, fruit, spirit and power, although in weakness, were found in them and their disciples, as it is represented and taught by the sign, then we would, by the grace of God, soon meet, and not dispute about the use of the sign. But so long as they walk on the broad road, practice and uphold infant baptism, defame the baptism of the believing, do not separate their disciples and church from the world, and teach an unblamable doctrine and life, so long we cannot unite with them in doctrine and sacraments, whether this is attended by prosperity or adversity, as God pleases. For we know to a certainty, that the Lord's invincible, strong truth is on our side, and the damnable, weak falsehood on theirs.

My faithful reader, reflect upon what I write. Our separation from the doctrine and sacraments of the preachers is principally for two reasons. In the first place, because we can plainly see, from the Scriptures and by their actions, and are assured, that they are not pastors but deceivers. All the Scriptures teach us that we shall not hear, but shun such preachers. For if we are afraid of thieves, murderers and wolves, according to the flesh, how much more should we fear those who so miserably devour our poor souls, who retain us in darkness, deprive us of the light of Christ, and fearlessly lead us to the frightful, indissoluble darkness of everlasting and infernal torment, for the sake of a meal of bread. For God's sake, dear reader, do not think hard of me. Behold, before God it is true what I write.

The second reason is, that we may, by such shunning, testify to you and all others, by open deeds, that you are outside of the Spirit, word, kingdom and church of Christ, that you walk upon the wrong way and that you are miserably deceived by your preachers—so that you may yet awaken in time, depart from evil, walk in truth and be eternally saved.

If you are of reasonable minds, then consider well what we hereby seek, and think not that we are so thoroughly deprived of reason that we walk this narrow way, through contentiousness and partizanism. O, how gladly would we save our weak bodies, our wives and small children, our possessions and lives, and live peaceably with the world, if we were not constrained by the love of God, and the eternal salvation of your souls and our own. But, as it is, we should, for the two mentioned reasons, sacrifice all to robbery, and, if the case require, to death, in sincere, genuine love. For, as a general thing, truth is maintained dearly; and sincere, faithful love crowned with a crown of thorns. O, Lord!

In the last place he writes, "From this, every pious christian may educe, how unreasonably these people, who accuse us of enmity, contention and discord, and who quarrel about the articles of faith among themselves, and thus sow enmity, contention and discord, as said, Yea, who never thoroughly searched our doctrine, and who have scarcely seen us partake of the Supper, notwithstanding, they reprove us of our Holy Supper, and leave the assembly of Christ's church."

Answer. To this I would reply in the first place: The unrighteousness which shuts us out from the kingdom, church, body and Supper of Christ, is not merely included in enmity, contention and discord, but also in all other kinds of works of the flesh, such as, pomp, splendor, avariciousness, drinking and carousing.

Although enmity and discord are, by the use of their supper, partially appeased among some of them, as he writes, yet all the other abominable sins and unrighteousness remain untouched as may be very plainly and publicly seen by their fruits. The heathens, too, conclude peace among themselves, when they are at variance with each other, yet they are not the right grains of the Lord's bread, and the true members of his body. Let every one of sound mind reflect upon what I say.

In the second place I say, He can not with truth substantiate his accusation against us, that enmity, contention and discord exist among us.

But as he and his fellows berate our christian doctrine and faith, our sacraments and actions before the whole world, cause much trouble and affliction; and we, by the grace of God, do not treat them inimically, but patiently bear with them, teach, reprove and admonish them; maintain truth with truth; and in sincerity of heart, show and point out to them the right way, at the risk of blood and life, for which they so hate us, so also, some raise up among us, as was the case in the times of the apostles, who would rather follow their own opinion than the Scriptures; who again return to the broad road, seek honor and a name, and therefore make unscriptural pretensions. With such we entreat and reason, admonish and reprove them, as the Scriptures teach us, and I trust we do this reasonably and in love. If they suffer themselves to be taught, change their ways and strive after peace, then we thank the Lord for his blessing. But in case they despise fraternal admonition, remain obdurate in their ways and cause contention and discord, then they cannot be our fellows and brethren, until they acknowledge their faults, and return to the Lord's people in peace, 1 Tim. 6:5; 2 Tim. 2:17; Tit. 3:11. If this should be called causing contention, enmity and discord about the articles of faith, or whether it should be called purification of the house of the Lord, all the right-minded may judge, both by their common sense and the Scriptures.

In the third place I say, the reason why we do not hear their doctrine, and do not see their partaking of the supper, as he complains, is, because we have for a long time witnessed by their fruits, that their doctrine is vain and powerless, and their sacraments are not according to the word. For of what spirit both their preachers and disciples are, may, firstly, be educed from the dishonest, infamous, bitter, false, spiteful and incentive writings of the preachers, and, secondly, from the abominable show of clothes, the extravagance about their houses, and from the superfluous, carnal life of the best of their disciples. What does their fine appearance, their ornamental logic avail, while they, in fact, forsake the Scriptures and the signification, fruit and power of the holy sacraments, nay, hate and persecute it? If I do not write the truth, reprove me.

In the fourth place I would say, Gellius accuses us that we forsake the church of Christ. But I say that we, according to the teaching of the word and ordinance of God, and to the example of the holy apostles, forsake the world and their false prophets, and that we, through the Spirit and grace of God, rid the church of Christ from snares, faithfully admonish her members, and in our weakness, establish and edify them, according to the command of the holy word, Isaiah 52: 11; 2 Cor. 6: 17; Acts 2: 40; Rev. 18: 4. What shall this poor man say and boast of the church of Christ, while she is yet quite unknown to him? I voluntarily make this offer: If they allow me a discourse with them under safe conduct, either privately before witnesses, or publicly, before a full assembly, and if I cannot prove or maintain, by the power of the truth that the preachers, in general, are deceivers and not pastors, and that their pompous, avaricious, extortionate swearing and cursing disciples, are of the world and are not christians, then I will publicly acknowledge before all the world, that we not only have forsaken the church of Christ, but also lamentably destroy her and cause many a pious heart much misery, affliction and trouble, in vain.

But, as we can substantiate these assertions by the power of the truth, why, then, must we yet hear so many evil words? It were, indeed, high time that the preachers would quit their deceiving, that they and their disciples, who, where and what they be, would awaken, that they would tremble at the wrath and punishment of God, would repent, conform themselves to the Spirit, word and example of the Lord, and establish a true christian church, in accordance to the command of the Scriptures, and that they disclaimed and abjured their borrowed names and false boastings, as evangelical teachers, faithful shepherds, soul-savers, and preachers of the holy word, which they, to the dishonor of God, merely claim in appearance.

Behold, reader, I write to you the truth and lie not. I seek nothing, before my God, but that I may gain Gellius and all the preachers, wherever they may be, to Christ, by the Spirit and word of God; or that I may be vanquished of them and stand abashed before all the world, as an open deceiver. If they, now, be of christian disposition, and preachers of the holy word who are desirous of unity, as they pretend to be, then let them agree to what I desire they should, namely, a free discussion of the grounds and doctrines of both sides; that thereby the pure, saving truth of Christ may be maintained, and the impure, damnable falsehood of anti-christ be destroyed.

But in case they refuse this, as they have before twice refused me, and continue their infamous defamation and upbraiding as they have ever done before, and accuse us with all manner of accusations before the common people, that we forsake the church of Christ; that we are a misled, deceived people, and that we pervert good into evil; what else can we then do but leave them to the Lord and his judgment; and willingly submit to the cross, as we have done, possess our souls in patience, admonish those of unperverted heart, as much as possible, minutely consider what kind of preachers and pastors they have, what great injustice they do us, poor miserable ones; how scornfully they reject truth, and maintain falsehood, since we, in all humility and true love, invite them to this free, christian discussion of the Scriptures, to the praise of Almighty God, and his eternal truth, and to the beneficial refreshment of all the oppressed and afflicted souls. But they refuse us this, and besides, slander and defame us by their infamous publications without discretion, and without all foundation and truth, and thus, disgracefully accuse us before the whole world, and cause many pious, innocent children to be deprived of their possessions, honor and lives, even, as may, alas, be witnessed in many different localities of the Netherlands.

EXCOMMUNICATION, BAN OR SEPARATION.

Before I commence a reply to Gellius' excuse why they do not practice Excommunication, Ban or Separation in their church, I would briefly refer the kind reader to different passages of the Scriptures to show that the Excommunication, Ban or Separation was not always practiced in the same manner, nor according to the same ordinance, by the Lord's people. The ban of Moses was punishment with death, Deut. 13; Lev. 16; Numb. 31; Josh. 7. This ban was in force until the Roman dominion. At that time a change was made; for, under the Roman scepter, they were not allowed to put the law in force, in regard to capital punishment as before. But they separated those who disobeyed the law; that is, they ejected them from their synagogues and assemblies, shunned their daily intercourse, neither ate nor drank with them, as may be learned from many of the Scriptures of the apostles, Luke 15: 2; Matt. 18: 17; 1 Cor. 5: 11; 2 Thess. 3: 6—14.

To this shunning, rule and usage, the doctrine and example of Christ Jesus, and the holy apostles unanimously point us; and these two following benefits are derived from them.

In the first place, that we be not deceived by the erroneous doctrine of false spirits, and weakened by their carnal, vain life, 2 John 1: 10. "Know ye not," says Paul, "that a little leaven leaveneth the whole lump? Purge out, therefore, the old leaven," &c., 1 Cor. 5: 6, 7.

Yea, my reader, wherever this excommunication, ban or separation is zealously and earnestly taught and maintained in the fear of God, without respect of persons, there, doubtlessly, the church of the Lord will be maintained unprofaned, in salutary, pure doctrine, and in an offensive life. But where this is neglected, we find nothing but vanity and worldliness, as may be plainly observed by all the churches and sects which are not of us.

Reader, observe, so long as the literal Israel, in this respect, followed the ordinance of the Lord, and punished those deserving of the ban, according to the word of the Lord, they remained upright and pious; but when they neglected it, inclined their ears to falsehood, and gave way to false prophets, they deviated from the way of life, and degenerated into all kinds of wickedness and idolatry, as the prophetical Scriptures, on every hand, complain and testify.

It was also the case with the primitive church; for so long as the pastors and teachers strictly required a godly, pious life, served baptism and Supper to the penitent alone, and rightly practiced separation, according to the Scriptures, they remained the church and community of Christ. But as soon as they commenced to seek an easy, careless life, and to shun the cross of Christ, they laid aside the rod, preached peace to the people; gradually abandoned the ban; and thus established an anti-christian church, a Babel or worldly church, as may, alas, be noticed, to look back over the last several centuries. Yea, my reader, if we had not until now strictly maintained this means ordained of God, then, we and ours, at this day, would have been a reproach and curse to the world, while, now, I trust, they, in their weakness, will be, by the grace of God, an example and a light to many men; although the world will not acknowledge it. In short, a church without ban or separation, is like a vineyard without an enclosure and trenches, or a city without walls; for the enemies have free ingress into it to sow and plant their pernicious tares unhindered.

In the second place, that the wicked, by a reasonable admonition, and separation from the pious, may, at heart, become ashamed, humble themselves and sincerely repent before God and the church. Therefore, Paul delivered the Corinthian unto Satan for the destruction of the flesh, that the spirit might be saved in the day of the Lord Jesus, 1 Cor. 5: 5. He also thus delivered Hymeneus and Alexander, that they might no longer blaspheme, 1 Tim. 1: 20. At another place he writes, "If any man obey not our word by this epistle, note that man, and have no company with him, that he may be ashamed; yet count him not as an enemy, but admonish him as a brother," 2 Thess. 3: 14, 15.

Behold, reader, here you have it briefly stated of whom, how, and to what purpose, the ban or separation is ordained in the house and church of the Lord. Judge, now, if you fear God, if it is not an especially noble and necessary institution of pure love, which is ordained of the God of love to a service of love, although the unenlightened and refractory judge and consider it as enmity. For its ultimate design and fruit is, that the church may remain sound in doctrine, and unblamable in life; and that the erring, either in doctrine or life, may be converted, and again return to the pasture and flock of the Lord. But how far, yea, how very far, are all the preachers and churches of the world from this God-pleasing ordinance and very necessary practice.

His first excuse that separation is not practiced in their church is, That the papistical abomination has so abominably destroyed the ordinance of the churches and the right usage of the ban, by their abuse, that it cannot be immediately re-established.

Answer. If we diligently search the writings of the historians and compare the actions of the church; to which they refer, with the Scriptures, then, I think, that we surely find that there was not among all the German nations, a true, apostolic, christian church which stood right in doctrine, sacraments, ordinances and life; but that they were all founded upon the papistic foundation and abominations, and remained so, these many years.

Since, then, the church is not founded by the apostles upon the foundation of Christ, but is founded of the Pope, upon his own foundation, and is in every respect a papistical, and not a christian church, and since it is palpable that it has at this hour, neither teachers, communion, life nor sacraments conformable to the ordinance, doctrine and example of Christ, therefore he can not practice the ban until he separates himself, because he is an adulterer of the Scriptures and deceiver of souls, and then all the church, because they are generally impenitent in life and outside of the command, ordinance and word of Christ in doctrine, as may be plainly noticed. *Cogita quae dico, Qui male facit, non videt Deum*, 3 John 11. Remember that it is spoken, "He that doeth evil hath not seen God."

In the second place he writes, "We admit that in many churches negligence is found, which we cannot commend; which is caused in some places by the punishment of all open transgressions by the magistracy, so diligently that the pastors esteem it unnecessary to put the ban in force."

Answer. In my opinion it is high time that the preachers would quit their trifling with the souls of men; that they would unreservedly acknowledge that they are not the church of the Lord, but a poor, erring and worldly flock; and then would earnestly commence to learn to know themselves and next, to preach rightly the word of sincere repentance, in the power of the Spirit. All those who would accept it in sincerity of heart and truly repent, should serve the sacraments of the Lord, according to the ordinance of God, and those who would stubbornly reject it, should, by virtue of the holy word, be excommunicated, without respect of persons; *then* they might gather a church unto Christ, and rightly practice the ordinance of the Lord, according to the Scriptures.

But so long as they baptize unconscious children, esteem all those who are baptized as christians, dispense the bread to the impenitent, and admit all the avaricious, extortionate, pompous, drinking and carousing, in the communion of their churches, the world will be their church, and their church the world. In such a state of affairs they may preach and admonish all their life-time about separation, and the true church ordinances, but never establish them, since it is evident that all their doctrines and sacraments are nothing but a vapor, vain and powerless, for they are not the rightly called preachers, their sacraments are not the true sacraments and their disciples are not the Lord's church and people.

Say, beloved, how shall a house be built without workmen, timber, iron, stone and mortar? *Qui sanicordis est, cogitet quae dico.* He who is of sound mind, may ponder on what I say.

I would further say, that if Gellius rightly understood Christ and his word, he would be ashamed all his life-time; and for these two reasons:

Firstly, because he undertakes to excuse the neglect of the pastors, by saying that the magistracy punish open trasgressions, as if therefore it were not necessary. I think that hundreds of pastors can be found in Germany, who never in their life knew that the avaricious, drunken, adulterous, &c., should be excommunicated; nay, what is worse. that the greater part of them are themselves guilty of such infamous doings.

In my opinion it is as clear as day-light that his covering up and decking this ignorance, nay, negligence and disgrace, with the excuse that the magistracy punish the transgressors is nothing less than to willfully defend falsehood and oppose truth.

Secondly, because he complains that the magistracy do not grant authority or hearing to the pastors. Say, kind reader, where, in all the days of your life, did you read in the apostolic Scriptures, that Christ or the apostles requested the authority of the magistracy to punish those who would not hear their doctrine or obey their words? Yea, reader, I know to a certainty, that wherever the magistracy is to maintain the ban by the force of the sword, there are not the true knowledge, Spirit, word and church of Christ. If this is not rightly called by the papists, *Invocare brochium seculare*, that is invoking the assistance of the world, I will leave to the judgment of the discreet reader.

Also, observe here his hypocrisy and his pernicious flattery of those in high standing; for where do we find, alas, more ungodliness than among those in authority? Notwithstanding, he wants the ban to be maintained by them, as if they were the true and faithful members of the church of Christ and children of his community; and never observes that if the pastors would rightly judge, according to the holy word, the magistrates, next to the preachers themselves, would be the first who should be, according to the Scriptures, separated and excluded from the communion of the pious.

Since he, in this instance, so openly wheedles the magistrates and those of high standing, and thus flatters them, against all the Scriptures, therefore I cannot neglect to admonish all magistrates and subordinates, and in faithful love to warn them, to consider how miserably they are deceived by the preachers. Beloved lords, observe. You all boast that you are christians and have the word of God, while it is manifest that so many of the lords and princes, daily shed human blood like water, by their ungodly warring and tumult; that they rob many innocent people of their homes and property, that they cause many afflicted orphans and helpless children to be made; and that many of them drink and carouse day and night; abuse the creatures of God above measure, namely, wine, beer, victuals, clothes, &c., all of whom are deserving of excommunication and can not stand the test of the Scriptures, as, I presume, many of the learned and preachers themselves, well know; yet they connive at such, desire their authority and assistance; they act hypocritically with them, they talk so as to please them, do not separate and punish them, however wickedly they behave; dispense to them the bread and wine as if they were members of the body of the Lord and brethren of his church. By this they so comfort and encourage them in their wickedness, that they never stop to inquire into the fear and ways of the Lord; for it is all peace, peace, whatever they preach, as the prophet complains, Jer. 8: 8; Ezek 13: 22. Beloved lords, take heed; they lead you straightway to the abyss of hell; therefore, beware. I tell you the truth in Christ Jesus, they deceive you. Again, I say, beware, they deceive you.

On the other hand, they hate and upbraid above measure, all those who seek the Lord sincerely, who strive after his holy word, in their infirmity, and who would gladly, in their weakness, lead a pious, godly life, in the fear of the Lord; because they point them to Christ; and in true, godly zeal, and brotherly love, reprove and admonish them, to their own good, of their false doctrine, false sacraments, hypocrisy and indifferent life, according to the teachings of the Scriptures. Nay, we are called apostles of the devil, apostates, anabaptists, conspirators and heretics, by them.

Behold, thus they connive at and flatter

those of high standing, although they, generally, are upon the broad way; and thus they shamefully upbraid the innocent who never harmed them, and who would gladly lead a pious life. Yet they boast that they are preachers of the gospel and teach the word of God.

In the third place he writes: The disrespect to the servants of the church, has, everywhere, become so prevalent, through the doings of these devilish conspirators and heretics, that few churches submit themselves, in unity of spirit, to their pastors, which is necessary.

Answer. That the disrespect to the preachers has become so prevalent, is caused by nothing else but their own, exceeding wickedness, deceit, avarice, blasphemy and shamelessness, as the prophet says, "Behold, I will corrupt your seed, and spread dung upon your faces, &c." "Ye are departed out of the way; ye have caused many to stumble at the law; ye have corrupted the covenant of Levi, saith the Lord of hosts; Therefore have I also made you contemptible and base before all the people, according as ye have not kept my ways, but have been partial in the law," Mal. 2: 3, 8, 9.

Yea, dear reader, they have become so sinful, and have so trafficked with the souls of men, that the just and great God could no longer endure it; he therefore graciously inspired some pious hearts with the Spirit of his divine knowledge, in his great love, and has discovered unto them the decked, babylonian woman, the preachers and their churches, with all their fornication, abominations and blood-guiltiness, and thus made manifest their inhuman disgrace. And these, on account of their warning, all, in unfeigned love, against the deadly, enchanting poison of her cup, by doctrine, life, example, blood and possessions, by which they seek nothing but the praise of God and the salvation of their neighbors, are called devilish conspirators and heretics. O, Lord! O! never heard of blasphemy! O disgrace of all disgrace!

Ah, my reader, my faithful reader, if we could reason with them, how soon would it be shown who are the devilish conspirators and heretics! But what does it avail? The Scribes and Pharisees sat upon exalted seats, but Christ had not whereon to lay his head. Besides, he had to hear, that he was possessed of the devil, and wrought his miracles in the name of Beelzebub.

Is it not a perverse, lamentable hypocrisy, that this man undertakes to blame us for their not practicing the ban, while it is known and manifest to the whole world, that the greater part of the preachers are such an indifferent, blind and carnal people, that they neither acknowledge God nor his word, and seek nothing else than that they may satiate their carnal appetites and continue in their careless easy life? What kind of christians their churches or disciples are, what knowledge they have, and how they fear God, may, alas, be educed from their words and works, in city and country.

In the fourth place he writes, It is a fact well known to the whole community (he refers to the community at Emden) that we have for several years, assiduously labored to again establish the christian ordinance of the ban.

Answer. The world acknowledges no ban, but when such a transgression has been committed, that the executioner bans them with the sword, noose or fire, for the sake of their evil-doing. Or, if one sincerely repents and returns to God, abolishes the wicked, sinful life, in true fear, and puts on the new life of true repentance, that they, along with the papists, often deprive such an one of honor, possessions and life, or exile him and thus drive him into the mouth of the gaping lions.

But that they should, according to the Scriptures, shun the misers, drunkards, fornicators, &c.; that they should neither eat nor drink with them, they do not know, since they are, as a general thing, unchanged at heart, earthly-minded and full of all manner of avarice, pomp, extravagance and carnal works.

Therefore I say again, they will admonish all their life time, concerning the ban, but never establish it according to the word of God; for how can one avaricious person shun the other, one drunkard the other and one deceiver the other, according to the Scriptures, and separate him from the communion of the church, while they are altogether earthly-minded and without the communion, Spirit and word of the Lord, as has been heard.

In the fifth place he writes, "The example of the anabaptists frightens us, who so practice the ban with discord, hatred and irreconcilable anger one against the other, that it tends more to the destruction than to the edification and gathering of the church, among them."

Answer. All that I read and see of him, is a benighted vision, wrong judgment, wheedling of those of high standing, upbraiding and slandering the pious, excusing perverseness and adulteration of the Scriptures.

O, how little does he, as appears, fear God; for here he undertakes to cover up his fleeing from the cross and his disobedience, by citing the example of others. Reader, remember that the word of God should teach and govern us; that some refractory persons take offense at us, we cannot prevent. We act as the word of God has commanded us.

All those who once enter into the obedience of the word, and afterwards live or teach contrary to it, can not be permitted to continue with us as brethren and sisters, if they will not hear our admonitions. In this case, neither greatness nor littleness, riches nor poverty avail. With God there is no respect of persons; they must all bow to the Spirit, word and scepter of Jesus, or else they cannot remain our brethren.

Since it is manifest that the Spirit of the Lord becomes extinct in such as seek the broad road, and are desirous of the freedom of the flesh, of money and possessions; and that they offend the pious by their light-mindedness or self-conceit, therefore, they should, though reluctantly, be separated from the intercourse of the godly, when there are no hopes left of their reformation. If they take offense at this, because they hate to bear this shame, which is visited upon them in love, for no other purpose than for their reformation, and therefore slander and upbraid us, as, also the preachers do because we dare not hear their teaching, and partake of their sacraments, we cannot help this; nor can we prevent that some of them become Davidists* and Epicurians† (as

* Davidists are the followers of David George, a sect of quiet mystics in the sixteenth century, who were accused of very erroneous sentiments.

† Followers of Epicurus, an ancient Greek philosopher.—Webster's Royal Octavo Dict.

Gellius calls them), in spite of all our faithful admonitions, assiduity, labor and brotherly service.

The fact is, the seed did not fall on the right kind of soil, but by the wayside, on rocky ground and amongst thorns, Matt. 13: 5.

I repeat it. We have applied to them the faithful service of our brotherly love, from our inmost hearts; admonished and entreated them, and have patiently borne with some for one or two years, still waiting on their reformation, and in truth have not hastily separated them, as he accuses us, without all foundation. Since we follow and practice the ordinance of the Lord, in this respect, if he feared the Lord, he should reasonably commend our action, because we do rightly, follow the commands of God, at the risk of possessions and life, and because we act according to the Scriptures, without all respect to persons; and he would acknowledge the truth, and confess that not our example frightens them, but the fear of the cross. For if they would justly act and treat with kings, dukes, lords and princes, and also with their drunkards, misers, vain-showers, &c., then it would be quite a different thing with them; this I dare unreservedly say, and could prove it by facts.

In the sixth place he writes, "If they think that they do much good by their banning, toward the edification of the church, then let them point out from the several hundreds which they have banned, not ten, but only five, whom they have banned in love, and reformed through their brotherly love, or whom they have brought to order and saved by their banning."

Answer. He seeks all kinds of causes to blaspheme the word and work of God, that he may give some appearance of reality to his cross-fleeing and hypocrisy. Inasmuch, as he says that separation tends more to destruction than edification, therefore the reader should know that we daily find, by experience, that the following benefits are derived from separation, among us: Firstly, that we thereby obey God's word. Secondly, that we thereby rid the community from false doctrine, discord, and offensiveness, as has been said. Thirdly, that the disobedient are thereby, daily admonished to reflect, repent and return. Fourthly, that we thereby testify that we do not consent to, nor unite with the Munsterites, and other rebellious sects. Fifthly, that we thereby admonish all preachers and their churches, that they are without the ordinance and word of God, in this respect. Sixthly, that thereby the whole world may learn from us that the advice, doctrine, ordinance and command of God should be maintained and obeyed.

Behold, dear reader, these are the fruits which true separation, daily brings forth, by the grace of God. But these, the preachers, alas, do not regard. If it were true that few are reformed thereby, as he imputes, they must still admit that these beforementioned results are obtained thereby.

Reader, take notice that however we may act, it is of no avail with the perverse; for if we had disregarded this means and divine ordinance, as the preachers do, and had left every body to follow his own mind, from which the great Lord ever preserve us, how loudly would they cry that we were rebels and Arians*. But while we separate them, according to the Scriptures, from the communion of the church, it is called a destructive means and a hasty ban. Behold, thus they seek, on every hand, to destroy truth and uphold falsehood.

In the seventh place he writes, "It is better not to use the ban, than to abuse it, to the destruction of the church.

Answer. If it were true as he asserts, then, still a good thing should not be abandoned for the sake of some. If the ban is a means of destroying and rupturing the church of Christ, then Christ and the apostles have very much deceived us in this regard, to have taught us this ordinance, openly, both by word and example, as may be read in the Scriptures. But what does it avail? He might briefly state his point thus: We do not separate and ban, for we are, as a general thing, all led by an erroneous spirit, and members of the body of anti-christ.

In the eighth place he writes, "None have proved a greater obstacle to us in re-establishing the ban, than the anabaptists, who have caused a disturbance in the edification of the church, of Christ, and in its right course; who have brought the servants into disrepute, and have, under semblance of truth, drawn many zealous hearts from the church (on whom it was to be practiced) and led them into falsehood."

Answer. If I had not learned to know Gellius from his other writings, this excuse of his, in regard to the ban, would more than clearly teach me what kind of a man he is. O, dear Lord? It is nothing but hypocrisy, falsehood and deceit, whatever he says! He writes that we obstruct the ban; yet, if he would confess the truth, he would be forced to admit, that we do not obstruct him, but his own unbelief, carnal-mind and his cross-fleeing flesh, as said before.

He writes that we have disturbed the edification of the church, while it is manifest that we point out to all the churches of the world, by doctrine and life, by the periling of possessions and blood, the right way to a true worship and ordinance, and that they are those who, with all their strength, disturb the course of the edification of the church of Christ, by their light-minded doctrine, false sacraments, and vain life.

He writes that we have brought the servants into disrepute, because we reprove them, in unfeigned love, and point them by doctrine and life to Christ's example, Spirit and word, while he acknowledges above, that some are more fit to be herders of swine than shepherds of the sheep of Christ.

He writes that we have, in semblance of truth, drawn many zealous hearts from the church, and led them into many errors; while the facts show that we do not separate them from the church but from the world, and that we lead them, by the hand and help of God, into eternal truth.

I would further say, Their doctrine has been preached for over thirty years, in Germany, and there are whole kingdoms, principalities and cities where not a single anabaptist, as he calls them, is to be found. Who is it that obstructs the pastors there in re-establishing the ban? In all the time that they have preached and taught their doctrine, they have never yet banned an adulterer, drunkard, miser, &c., and excluded such an one from the communion of

---

* Arians, followers of Arius, a presbyter of the church of Alexandria, about 315, who maintained that the Son of God was totally and essentially distinct from the Father; that he was the first and noblest of those beings whom God had created—but inferior to the Father in nature and dignity: also, that the Holy Ghost was not God, but created by the power of the Son.—*Buck's Theol. Dic.*

their churches; notwithstanding he writes that we obstruct and hinder them. O, dear Lord! thus are the pious everywhere evil spoken of, although they seek God sincerely, and would gladly see a christian church, true in doctrine, sacraments, ordinances and life.

In the ninth place he writes, "For two reasons we could not so soon establish it (he means the ban) as the anabaptists did. Firstly, because our gatherings are open and consist of many hundreds, whom we cannot all know; while their gatherings are secret and consist of but few. Secondly, because we do not establish sects, as they do, which is a work of the flesh, and befriended of the devil; but we establish an eternal church unto Christ, which is beguiled and robbed by the devil."

Answer. Above he has partly acknowledged that many of their hearers are of the world. Here he writes that their gatherings consist of many hundreds, and that they gather an abiding church; yet they never came to the point that they separate their disciples and church from the world, and conform to the divine ordinance. The reason is because they are of the world.

But to his writing that their assembly is large and kept in public, and that ours is small, I would, with the word of the Lord, reply in this manner, "Wide is the gate, and broad is the way, that leadeth to destruction, and many there be which go in thereat; because strait is the gate, and narrow is the way which leadeth unto life and few there be that find it," Matt. 7: 13, 14.

Yea, my reader, if you attentively read the Scriptures you will find that the number of the chosen ones ever was small and the number of the unrighteous was always great. The pure and true gospel of Jesus Christ, the true knowledge of eternal truth, never was so appreciated by the world that the true believers can be counted by many thousands in any country or city. Christ Jesus and his eternal truth must ever abide with few, in retired places; but anti-christ and his falsehood can go abroad undisturbedly and in public, and count his followers by thousands.

Again, by his writing that they cannot know all on account of their great numbers, he testifies that brotherly love is very scarce with them; for where is there a christian pastor who does not know his sheep? and where is the christian brother who does not know his neighbor? If the preachers do not know all, on account of their great numbers, still one brother should know the other; they should teach, admonish, comfort and reprove each other; they should seek each other's salvation; for this the word and unction of God teach us.

Reader, observe. He pretends "that they cannot possibly know all;" and I, who am most of the time, keeping myself in retired places, could point them out in great numbers. Let him, once travel through city and country where they boast of the word, and let him take a close observation, and he will find out how they dare heap one falsehood upon another, and one ungodly act upon another; how they dare swear by the Lord's sacred flesh, blood, death, wounds and sacrament, and how they are decked with different, vain ornaments. Let him take a view of the taverns, fencing-schools, the houses of ill-repute, &c., of which there is no lack in Germany; let him examine the courts of kings and princes; and into the ways of the nobility, and I presume he will find thousands doubly deserving of separation. But an earthly mind and perverse heart has, alas, little regard for the ordinance and word of the Lord.

Again, to his assertion that they do not establish sects, as he says we do, and that it is a carnal work, I would reply thus: I do sincerely wish that Gellius and all the Papists, Lutherans, Zuinglians, Davidists, &c., could appreciate this matter, for it is written of heresies and heretics, that they shall not inherit the kingdom of God.

It is a small matter to us to be called heretics by the world; for the children of God, in the apostolic times, were also called the same. Notwithstanding, we, in our humility, would say this in regard to this matter, that we point to Christ Jesus, God's eternal Wisdom, Truth and Son; for he is the One on whom to rely, and we unreservedly refer to his doctrine, ordinance and usage. If any one under the whole canopy of heaven, can convince us with the infallible truth that we are wrong and act contrary to his word, then we will gladly hear it and obey the truth.

But in case they cannot do so, they must

confess that we are the apostolic christian church, and that they are the deceiving, carnal sects.

But that sectarians are raised amonst us, and not amongst them, is also a strong proof that we are the church, and that they are not. For Paul says, "There must be also heresies among you, that they which are approved may be made manifest among you," 1 Cor. 11: 19. John says, "They went out from us, but they were not of us," 1 John 2: 19.

Say, beloved, why should Satan beguile these with heresies, who are already heretics and his adherents? But those that turn to the Lord, such he beguiles and seeks to devour them, Gen. 3: 15; 1 Pet. 5: 8.

In the tenth place he writes, If they only said that we do not teach the ban, it might insult us and many teachers and churches, and they might almost be disgraced thereby. But they say that we neither have, hold to, nor practice it.

Answer. In my opinion it would be well for him not to ridicule these things, but to closely observe the word of the Lord. Before God, the literal teaching does not avail; but before him, avails action in power and truth. If they should say that this would cause a disturbance, then I would ask what kind of protectors and shepherds they are, if they neglect the will and word of God on account of the disturbance of the world. Let all the right minded judge this according to the Scriptures, Matt. 10.

In the last place he writes, But, admit it to be true that this failure exists in all of our churches, although the contrary is true of many of them, for in the German church in London, England, one is banned; and it is not altogether neglected here in Emden. Would the church on that account lose its name and henceforth, as they say, be no longer the church of Christ? Then, truly our body, to which the church is likened, would lose the name of body on account of some blemish or wound.

Answer. I think this is *posuimus mendacium spem nostram*, to make lies our refuge. For he says, the contrary is true of many churches; yet he can point to only one, of the many kingdoms, principalities, cities and towns, who is banned, namely, at London, England. I have never, in all my life time heard of a more ridiculous assertion. How manifestly does the great Lord turn their wisdom to foolishness and their understanding to nothing, 1 Cor. 1. Yet the blind, ignorant world does not see it.

Reader, reflect, and see if these are not the mockers of which Peter and Jude prophesy, 2 Pet. 3: 3; Jude 8. The whole German nation or people, nay, all countries, are so replete with ungodliness, abominations and wickedness that we should stand dumb-founded. Yea, that the righteous, who fear the Lord, are as scarce as the grapes of a vintage which has been diligently gleaned, and in which few are left to pluck and use, as the prophet laments, Mich. 7: 1; and out of so many hundreds of thousands, he points to one who was banned at London, that it may be said that they practice the ban, and thus that they thus may give a semblance to their disobedience.

I think that they act so awkwardly, that the whole world must see that it is nothing but hypocrisy, falsehood and deceit. O, Lord, how long will this mockery be endured! But to his writing that if the church should lose her name on account of an error, that then, also, our bodies would lose its name on account of a blemish or wound, I would reply: If this was the only error in their church, then there would yet be hopes of a reformation; but their failures and short-comings are so numerous, that they would better be compared to a dead body, than to a body that has but one blemish or wound, as he pretends to say.

I think that in this instance the cunning of the fox which destroys God's vineyard (which he, in his writing imputes to us) is plainly discernable here. For how cunningly they flee from one latibulo (hiding-place) to another, lest they be caught, may, alas, be clearly educed from this frivolous excuse of the ban.

CONCERNING THE CHURCH, AND AN INSTRUCTIVE COMPARISON HOW WE MAY DISTINGUISH BETWEEN THE CHURCH OF CHRIST, AND THE CHURCH OF ANTI-CHRIST.

GELLIUS complains that we destroy and leave the church of God, and that we are devilish sects and conspirators; and, on the contrary boasts that they gather an abiding church. Therefore, in my opinion, it is necessary, in the first place, to compare the churches with the requirements of the Scriptures, that the pious reader may know the difference, and see which and what the Church of Christ is, and also what the church of anti-christ is; how long they both have existed; of whom they are; of whom they are brought forth; to what purpose they are begotten; of what disposition or nature they both are; what their fruits are; and by what signs they may be known, lest he be deceived by the preachers, and mistake the church of Christ for a heresy and conspiracy, and the church of anti-christ for the church of Christ.

In the first place, it should be taken into consideration, that the community of God, or the church of Christ, is an assembly of the pious, and a community of the saints, as is represented by the Nicene symbol; who, from the beginning have firmly trusted and believed in the promised seed of the woman, which is the promised Prophet, Messiah, Shilo, King, Prince, Emmanuel and Christ; who accept his word in sincerity of heart, follow his example, are led by his Spirit, and who trust in his promise in the Scriptures, Deut. 18:18; Gen. 49:10; Jer. 23:5; 33:15; Isaiah 7:14.

Such are now, generally called christians or the church of Christ, because they are born of Christ's word by means of faith, by his Spirit, and are flesh of his flesh and bone of his bone, as the children of Jacob, on account of their natural birth, were called the house of Israel, Rom. 9:7—9.

On the contrary it should be observed that the church of anti-christ is a gathering of the ungodly, and a community of the impenitent, who reject the aforementioned seed, Christ, and his word, and oppose his will, and for that reason are called the anti-christian community or church, because they, through the spirit and artifices of anti-christ, although in semblance of the word, and in the name of Christ, teach, believe, act, and establish a strange worship, contrary to the Spirit, word, example and ordinance of Christ.

In the second place, it should be observed that the church of the pious is from the beginning; yet, it had not always the same ordinance; nor was it always called by one name in the Scriptures. For, before their departure from Egypt, they had no particular, written law; yet they feared the great and powerful God, faithfully served Him, offered burnt-offerings, and walked in his ways, as may be seen in the case of Abel, Noah, Abraham, Isaac, Jacob and others; they were, at that time, called God's children. Afterwards, Abraham was commanded to circumcise himself and his household, and all the males after him, on the eighth day after their birth, Gen. 17:10. About four hundred years after that, Moses gave the law; and from that time they were generally called the people of God, or the house of Jacob and Israel. At last Christ Jesus, the Messiah of all the world appeared, to which all the Scriptures point. All those who hear him, believe his word and follow him, are now called christians, or the church of Christ, as heard, Isaiah 58:2, 4; Jer. 23:5.

Although at different times she was under different ordinances and usages, and, although the church is called by different names, as said, yet all, before, under and after the law, who, in sincere, true fear of God, walked, and continue to walk according to the word and will of God, and trust in Christ, are one community, church and body, and will ever remain so; for they are all saved by Christ, accepted of God, and gifted with the Spirit of his grace. It should also be observed that the church of the ungodly, which is the church of anti-christ, commenced first with the ungodly, who were inspired with the spirit of the devil, which is envious of all good things; and will be unto the end. For the anti-church has generally existed, from the beginning, side by side with the christian church, and is the most numerous; and till the deluge, it is spoken of, in the Scriptures as the "children of men," Gen. 6: 2; John 8: 44. But from the flood until the circumcision of Abraham they are called Gentiles. After the time of the circumcision they are called Gentiles or uncircumcised, Gen. 17: 11; Rom. 15: 9.

They did not know the true and living God, but they worshipped and served the handiwork of men, wood, stone, silver and golden gods, besides, dragons, serpents, oxen, fire, the sun, moon, &c., until the apostles preached the gospel unto all the world, and gathered a church unto Christ, Matt. 28: 19; Mark 16: 15; Rom. 10: 17; Col. 1: 23, which church has been in the meantime so destroyed by anti-christ, that the greatest number have degenerated into open Gentiles and idolaters, although, in appearance they call themselves christians; for they bend their knees to rods and blocks, and require the assistance of the artificer. Others, and these are the best minded of them, seek consolation and their salvation in wrought ceremonies, water, bread, wine, and absolutions; so that we are forced to say that they are the church of the impenitent, and the church of anti-christ.

In the third place, it should be observed that the christian church is of God, as Paul says, "For both he that sanctifieth, and they who are sanctified, are all of one," Heb. 2: 11. For as Christ Jesus, who is the true Savior, is of God, nay, God's only begotten and firstborn Son, so also are all those who, in sincerity of heart, believe his word, and are actuated by his Spirit. John says, "But as many as received him, to them gave he power to become the sons of God, even to them that believe on his name; which were born, not of blood, nor of the will of the flesh, nor of the will of man, but of God," John 1: 12, 13.

Again, "Every one that loveth, is born of God," 1 John 4: 7. On the other hand it should be observed that the church of anti-christ is of the evil one, as the Lord said unto the Pharisees, "Ye are of your father, the devil, and the lusts of your father ye will do. He was a murderer from the beginning, and abode not in the truth, because there is no truth in him. When he speaketh a lie, he speaketh of his own; for he is a liar, and the father of it," John 8: 44. "He that committeth sin, is of the devil; for the devil sinneth from the beginning," 1 John 3: 8.

Reader, observe. By these words the spirit of truth has already judged all liars, blood-shedders, avaricious, perjurers, adulterers, drunkards, pompous, idolators together with all the unrighteous that they are of the devil; that is, that they are the devil's community. Nevertheless they boast that they are the church of Christ, as also the Pharisees boasted that they were Abraham's seed and children, John 8: 39—44.

In the fourth place it should be observed that the church of Christ is begotten of sincere, pious preachers and christians, who are actuated by the Spirit of Christ; and who are, as Moses, Samuel, Isaiah, Jeremiah, Peter, Paul, John, &c., unblamable in doctrine and life; who, in pure and faithful love, seek the salvation of their neighbors, and who can, in sincerity, say with Paul, "Be ye followers of me, even as I also am of Christ," 1 Cor. 11: 1; who preach the word in the power of the Spirit; who are shining lights before all men; and who with all their strength strive with their received talent, and may make a great gain to the treasure of the Lord, Phil. 2: 15; Matt. 5; 16. For it was God's way and will from the beginning, to proclaim the doctrine of repentance through pious and unblamable servants, as has been sufficiently shown above under the head of the "Calling of the Preachers."

On the other hand it should be observed that the church of anti-christ is brought forth by faithless preachers, who are actuated by the spirit of anti-christ; who with Korah, Dathan and Abiram seek the applause of the people, Num. 16: 2, who with Balaam seek inordinate gain, Num. 22: 24; and who with the prophets of Jezebel seek choice victuals. Who, with Hananiah flatter the people, Jer. 28: 11; who, with the false prophets preach Peace, Ezek. 13: 16; who are earthly and carnally minded, and seek nothing but world, ease, honor, belly and gain, Phil. 3: 19; Rom. 16: 17.

O, reader, how the greatest and highest esteemed preachers of our day, whose names have become wide spread, seek the poor, naked and crucified Christ Jesus, and the souls of men with their gospel, may, alas, be educed from the accursed, ungodly pomp and splendor about their houses, and from the vain and curious ornaments, chains, rings, silk and satin, of their women and children. Notwithstanding their doctrine is called the evangelical theology, and they, the servants of the holy word.

In the fifth place, it should be observed that the church of Christ is begotten by the Spirit and word of Christ. For as an honorable woman can bring forth no legitimate children but from the seed of her lawful husband, so, also, the bride of Christ, namely, the church, can bring forth no true christians but from the legitimate seed of Christ, that is, from the unadulterated word, rightly preached through the Holy Spirit, and conceived in the heart of the hearers. Paul says, "In Christ Jesus I have begotten you through the gospel," 1 Cor. 4: 15; James says, "Of his own will begat he us with the word of truth," Jas. 1: 18; also read Rom. 10; 1 Pet. 1.

On the other hand the church of antichrist is begotten of deceiving doctrine, through the spirit of error. Paul says, "Now the Spirit speaketh expressly, that in the latter times some shall depart from the faith, giving heed to seducing spirits, and doctrines of devils; speaking lies in hypocrisy," 1 Tim. 4: 1. Yea, reader, what else has the church of Christ abolished, and the church of anti-christ re-established, but the false doctrines of the learned, the many inconsistent concilions, decrees, statutes, doctrines and commands of men? What else blinds the German nation, to-day, and what else retains them in their ungodliness, but the lightminded doctrine of the preachers, the ungodly, infant baptism, the unscriptural, idolatrous supper, and the neglect of the Lord's ordinance (separation), as it was practiced by the apostles?

The prophets on every hand complained that Israel inclined their ears to false preachers, Isaiah 30: 9; Jer. 8: 8; 14: 14.

Christ Jesus, and his holy apostles faithfully warn in many Scriptures against false prophets; for they deceive you, says Christ; they serve their bellies and not the Lord Christ, says Paul; they promise others liberty and are themselves servants of corruption, says Peter. They turn the grace of God unto lasciviousness, Jude 4, and they are of anti-christ, Matt. 7: 15; 16: 9; 2 Pet. 2: 19. O reader, reflect diligently on what I write.

In the sixth place it should be observed that the church of Christ is begotten for the purpose of hearing the Lord, to fear, love, serve, praise, honor and thank God sincerely, as Moses says, "And now, Israel, what doth the Lord thy God require of thee, but to fear the Lord thy God, to walk in all his ways, and to love him, and to serve the Lord thy God with all thy heart and with all thy soul; to keep the commandments of the Lord, and his statutes," Deut. 10: 12.

Again, "Ye shall walk after the Lord your God, and fear him, and keep his commandments, and obey his voice, and ye shall serve him, and cleave unto him," Deut. 13: 4. Peter says, "Ye are a chosen generation, a royal priesthood, a holy nation, a peculiar people; that ye should show forth the praises of him who hath called you out of darkness into his marvelous light," 1 Peter 2: 9.

Behold, the church of Christ is begotten that his great miracles, his Almighty Majesty, his inextinguishable love, and his adorable, high and holy name may be eternally glorified.

But the church of anti-christ despises, hates and reviles God, as the prophet says, They transgress my covenant, as Adam did, by which they despise me. Yea, all who reject the Lord's will, word, advice, admonition, chastening, grace and love, hate him and will not be ruled by him They do not his will, but their own; they say in their hearts: Depart from us, we will know nothing of thy ways; who is this Most High, that we should serve him? Behold, thus they boldly despise the Almighty, eternal God, who is the Creator, Messiah and Lord of all the world. May the dear Lord grant them eyes that they may see their great faults, and hearts to realize them; this is my sincere wish for them, Amen.

In the seventh place it should be observed that the church of Christ in her weakness, is disposed and minded as Christ; for Paul says, "If any man be in Christ, he is a new creature," 2 Cor. 5: 17; he is led by the Spirit, and acknowledges through this Spirit that he abides in God and God in him; he partakes of the divine nature. Yea, dear reader, the true church hates that which Christ hates, and loves that which he loves; for she is his Bride, flesh of his flesh, and "made to drink into one Spirit." Therefore she can not be otherwise minded than Christ is minded, for she is begotten of his word and abides in him and he in, over, and through her, 1 John 4: 12; John 15: 4—7.

Compare this with the church of antichrist, and you will find that it is of like nature as her father of whom she is begotten, namely, proud, envious, murderous, false, disobedient, self-conceited, earthly and carnally minded, selfish, avaricious, bold, proud, pompous, superfluous, impure, and altogether opposed to Christ. For all things that Christ prohibits, they do; and that which he commands, they despise; whatever he hates, they love, and whatever he loves, they hate; notwithstanding they boast that they gather an abiding church, as has been heard, 1 Cor. 8 : 6 ; 1 John 3 : 24; 4 : 13. He that hath ears let him hear, and judge whether or not I speak the truth.

In the eighth place it should be observed that the church of Christ brings forth the fruits of Christ, as he says, "I am the vine, ye are the branches. He that abideth in me, and I in him, the same bringeth forth much fruit," John 15: 5.

Every tree bears after its own kind; all who are born of God, and partake of the divine nature, fear, love, serve and praise God with all their heart; walk unblamably; fraternally teach, admonish, reprove, uphold, and comfort their neighbor; daily die unto the flesh and its lusts ; conform their ways according to the word of the Lord and continually lament over their being such poor, weak and frail sinners, Matt. 7 : 17.

They strive to become conformable unto the death of the Lord that they may arise from the death of their sins, and that they may attain unto a perfect being in Christ. Not, my reader, that they have already attained or become perfect. By no means; but they strive, with Paul, to follow after, if that they may apprehend that for which also I am apprehended of Christ Jesus, Phil. 3: 12.

On the other hand look at the fruits of the church of anti-christ. Their preachers falsely teach, boldly deceive, and live an easy, superfluous life. The magistracy behave as if they were born for no purpose but to make war and tumults; to torture, murder, destroy cities and countries; to make vain show, drink, carouse, and to live in all manner of lasciviousness, yea, many act so that they, alas, would better be called *Leones rugientes* (roaring lions) and *lupi ves pertini* (howling wolves) than *humani* (human beings) and reasonable persons to say nothing of christians.

The common people drink, carouse, curse, swear, grasp, tear, lie, and cheat. In short, we find such behavior on every hand, as if God was a chimera, and his word a fable. Behold, such are the fruits of those who boldly boast that they are the church of Christ. Oh! would to God that they could see what Christ Jesus, after whom they call themselves, and his holy apostles, have taught them in plain words, and what example they left them, that they might yet be saved. For as it is they only play with the letter, cry and boast; but, alas, no spirit, work, power and fruits are apparent.

THE SIGNS BY WHICH BOTH CHURCHES MAY BE KNOWN.

Although I think, kind reader, that the difference between both churches may be fully perceived in the foregoing comparison, yet I will, for the sake of greater clearness, briefly present the following signs by which the one church may be known from the other, that truth may be the more fully testified and manifested.

The first sign by which to distinguish the church of Christ is the salutary and unadulterated doctrine of his holy and divine word. God commanded Israel to abide by the doctrine of the law and not to deviate therefrom, neither to the right hand nor to the left, Deut. 5: 32. Isaiah admonished them to conform themselves to the law and its testimony, or they would not receive light, Isaiah 8: 20. Christ commanded his disciples, saying, "Go ye into all the world, and preach the gospel to every creature," and "teach them to observe all things whatsoever I have commanded you." The prophets testify on every hand that they spoke the word of God, Thus speaketh the Lord of hosts, they say; again, the mouth of the Lord says; again, thus speaketh the Lord God who has led you out of the land of Egypt, and other like testimonies. Paul also says, "But though we, or an angel from heaven, preach any other gospel unto you, than that which we have preached unto you, let him be accursed," Gal. 1: 8. In short, where the church of Christ is, there his word is preached purely and rightly; but where the church of anti-christ is, there the word of God is adulterated; there we are pointed to an earthly and unclean Christ and to means of salvation which are strange to the Scriptures; there we are taught a broad and easy way; there the great are flattered, truth perverted into falsehood; there easy things are taught, such as the poor, ignorant people will gladly hear. In short, there they are consoled in their unhappy state, that they may underrate it, and say, "Peace, peace, when there is no peace," Jer. 8: 11. They promise life to the impenitent, while the Scriptures say, that they shall not inherit the kingdom of God, 1 Cor. 6: 10; Gal. 5 : 21.

The second sign is the right and Scriptural use of the sacraments of Christ, namely, the baptism of those who, by faith, are born of God, sincerely repent, who bury their sins in Christ's death, and arise with him in newness of life; who circumcise the foreskin of their hearts with the circumcision of Christ, which is done without hands; who put on Christ, and have a clear conscience, Tit. 3: 5; Rom. 5: 4; Col. 3: 11; 1 Pet. 3: 21. Again, the dispensing of the Lord's Holy Supper to the penitent, who are flesh of Christ's flesh, who seek grace, reconciliation and the remission of their sins in the merits of the death and blood of the Lord, who walk with their brethren in love, peace and unity, who are led by the Spirit of the Lord, into all truth and righteousness, and who prove, by their fruits, that they are the church and people of Christ.

Where baptism is practiced without the command and word of Christ, as those do who not only baptize without faith, but also without reason and consciousness; where the power and representation of baptism, namely, dying unto sin, the new life, the circumcision of the heart, &c., are not only not upheld, but also quite hated by those of mature age; and where the bread and wine are dispensed to the avaricious, pompous and impenitent; where salvation is sought in mere elements, words and ceremonies, and where a life is led contrary to all love, there is the church of anti-christ; this all intelligent persons must admit. For it is manifest that they reject Christ, the Son of God, his word and ordinance, and place in its stead their own ordinance and works, and thus establish an abomination and idolatry.

The third sign is obedience to the holy word, or the pious, christian life which is of God. The Lord says, "Ye shall be holy, for I, the Lord your God, am holy," Lev. 19: 1. Christ says, "Ye are the light of the world." Paul says, "Be blameless and harmless, the sons of God, without rebuke, in the midst of a crooked and perverse nation, among whom ye shine as lights in the world," Phil. 2: 15. John says, "He that saith he abideth in him, ought himself also so to walk, even as he walked," 1 John 2: 6.

But how holy the church of anti-christ is, how her light shines, how unblamably and purely they walk, and how their life conforms to Christ's life, may, alas, be educed from their words and works, on every hand.

The fourth sign is the sincere and unfeigned love of one's neighbor, for Christ says, "By this shall all men know that ye are my disciples, if ye have love one to another," John 13: 35. Yea, reader, wherever sincere, brotherly love is found without hypocrisy with its fruits, there we find the church of Christ. John says, "Let us love one another; for love is of God; and every one that loveth is born of God, and knoweth God. He that loveth not, knoweth not God; for God is love," 1 John 4: 7, 8.

But whether the church of anti-christ is not there where brotherly love is rejected, where they hate, defame, strike and beat each other, where every one seeks his own interest, where they treat each other deceitfully and faithlessly, curse, swear and slander, where they defile their neighbors' maidens, daughters and wives, deprive each other of honor, possessions and life, commit all manner of recklessness, abominations and malice against each other, as may, alas, be seen on every hand, all intelligent persons may judge according to the Scriptures.

The fifth sign is, that the name, will, word and ordinance of Christ, are unreservedly confessed, in spite of all the cruelty, tyranny, uproar, fire, sword and violence of the world, and that they are upheld unto the end. Christ says, "Whosoever therefore shall confess me before men, him will I confess also before my Father which is in heaven," Matt. 10: 32. "Whosoever therefore shall be ashamed of me, and of my words, in this adulterous and sinful generation, of him also shall the Son of man be ashamed, when he cometh in the glory of his Father, with the holy angels," Mark 8: 38. Paul, also, says, "For with the heart man believeth unto righteousness; and with the mouth confession is made unto salvation," Rom. 10: 10.

But what kind of a church is found, where they are papistic, when with the papists; Lutheran, when with the Lutherans, &c., now build up, and anon demolish and act the hypocrite to suit the magistracy, every one may judge who is enlightened by the truth, and taught of the Holy Spirit.

The sixth sign is the pressing cross of Christ, which is taken up for the sake of his testimony and word. Christ says unto his disciples, "Ye shall be hated of all nations for my name's sake," Matt. 24: 9. "All that will live godly in Christ Jesus, shall suffer persecution," 2 Tim. 3: 12. Sirach says, "My son if thou come to serve the Lord, prepare thy soul for temptation. Set thy heart aright, and constantly endure, and make not haste in time of trouble. Cleave unto him, and depart not away, that thou mayest be increased at thy last end. Whatsoever is brought upon thee, take cheerfully, and be patient when thou art changed to a low estate. For gold is tried in the fire, and acceptable men in the furnace of adversity," Eccl. 1: 5. Also read, Matt. 5: 10; 10: 23; 16: 24; Mark 13: 13; Luke 6: 22; John 16: 2; Acts 14: 18; 2 Tim. 2; Heb. 11: 37; 12: 2.

That this very cross is a sure sign of its being the church of Christ, has been testified not only in olden times by the Scriptures, but also by the example of Jesus Christ, of the holy apostles and prophets, by the primitive and unadulterated church; and also, by the present pious, faithful children, especially in these our Netherlands.

On the other hand, the ungodly, heathenish, lying, hating, envying, upbraiding, blaspheming, and the unmerciful apprehending, exiling, robbing and murdering, as may be witnessed in different localities, are plain signs of the church of antichrist. For John saw that the Babylonian "woman was drunken with the blood of the saints, and with the blood of the martyrs of Jesus," Rev. 17: 6. He also saw that to the beast which arose from the sea, a mouth was given, speaking great things and blasphemy against God and his holy name, and his tabernacle or church, and them that dwell in heaven. And it was given unto him to make war with the saints, and to overcome them, Rev. 13: 5, 6, 7. Yea, dear reader, this is the proper way and work of the church of anti-christ, To hate, persecute and put to the sword those whom she cannot enchant with the golden cup of her abominations.

O Lord! O, dear Lord! grant that the wrathful dragon devour not entirely thy poor, small number; grant that we, by thy grace, may, in patience, conquer by the sword of thy mouth; and may leave an abiding seed, which shall keep thy commandments, preserve thy testimony, and which shall eternally praise thy great and glorious name. Amen, dear Lord, Amen.

Herewith I will abbreviate the doctrine of the churches, and conclude this subject with the following questions and answers, which, I trust, by the grace of God, will enlighten the diligent reader considerably.

Quest. What is the church of Christ?
Ans. A community of saints.
Q. With whom did she originate?
A. With Adam and Eve.
Q. Of whom is she?
A. Of God, through Christ.
Q. Of what kind of servants is she begotten?
A. Of those who are unblamable in doctrine and life.
Q. Whereby do they beget her?
A. By the Spirit and word of God.
Q. For what purpose do they beget her?
A. That she shall serve, thank and praise God.
Q. Of what mind is she?
A. Of Christ's mind, in weakness.
Q. What kind of fruits does she bring forth?
A. Fruits which are conformable to the word of God.
Q. What is the church of anti-christ?
A. A community of the unrighteous.
Q. With whom did she originate?
A. With the first ungodly.
Q. Of whom is she?
A. Of the evil one, through anti-christ.
Q. Of what kind of servants is she begotten?
A. Of such as are blamable in doctrine and life.
Q. Whereby do they beget her?
A. By the spirit and doctrine of anti-christ.
Q. For what purpose do they beget her?
A. That she may despise, forsake and hate God.
Q. Of what mind is she?
A. Of an earthly, carnal, and devilish mind.
Q. What fruits does she bring forth?
A. Fruits contrary to the gospel.

THE TRUE SIGNS BY WHICH THE CHURCH OF CHRIST MAY BE KNOWN.

I. By an unadulterated, pure doctrine, Deut. 4; 6; 5; 12; Isaiah 8: 5; Matt. 28: 20; Mark 16: 15; John 8: 52; Gal. 1.
II. By a scriptural use of the sacramental signs, Matt. 28 : 19 ; Mark 16 ; Rom. 6: 4; Col. 2: 12; 1 Cor. 12: 13; Tit. 3: 5; 1 Pet. 3; Matt. 26: 25; Mark 14: 22; Luke 22: 19; 1 Cor. 11: 22, 23.
III. By obedience to the word, Matt. 7; Luke 11 : 28; John 7 : 18; 15 : 10; Jas. 1: 22.
IV. By unfeigned, brotherly love, John 13: 34; Rom. 13: 8; 1 Cor. 13: 1; 1 John 3: 18; 4: 7, 8.
V. An unreserved confession of God and Christ, Matt. 10: 32; Mark 8: 29; Rom. 10: 9; 1 Tim. 6: 13.
VI. By oppression and tribulation for the sake of the Lord's word, Matt. 5 : 10; 10: 39; 16: 24; 24: 9; Luke 6: 28; John 15: 20; 2 Tim. 2: 9; 3: 12; 1 Pet. 1: 6; 3: 14; 4: 13; 5: 10; 1 John 3: 13

THE TRUE SIGNS BY WHICH THE CHURCH OF ANTI-CHRIST MAY BE KNOWN.

I. By a light-minded, easy and false doctrine, Matt. 7: 16; 15: 9; 16: 4; Rom. 16: 26; 1 Tim. 4: 2; 2 Tim. 2: 16, 17.
II. By an unscriptural use of the sacramental signs, as infant baptism and dispensation of the supper to the impenitent, 1 Cor. 11: 19, 20.
III. By disobedience to the word, Prov. 1; Tit. 1: 15, 16; Matt. 7: 26; 25: 26.
IV. By hatred of the brethren, 1 John 3: 15.
V. By hypocrisy and denial of the name of God and Christ, Matt. 10: 33; Mark 8: 38; Luke 9: 26.
VI. By tyranny and persecution against the godly, John 15: 20; 16; Rev. 12: 13.

Behold, dear reader, we have here shown you the foundation of both churches; what they are, of whom they are, and by whom they are begotten; of what mind they are, what kind of fruits they bring forth, and by what signs they may be known.

Whoever does not willfully err, to him a plain way is hereby pointed out. If you, then, would be a true member of the church of Christ, you must be born of the word of God; be of a christian mind; bring forth christian fruits; walk according to his word, ordinance and command; die unto the flesh and the world; lead an unblamable life in the fear of God; serve and love your neighbors with all your heart; confess the name and glory of Christ, and be prepared for all manner of tribulation, misery and persecution for the sake of the word of God and its testimony, John 3: 3, 4; 15: 4; 8: 31; 1 Pet. 1: 23; Phil. 2: 15; Rom. 8: 14.

But if you refuse this and remain unchanged in your natural state, lead an impenitent, easy life, lay aside the word and ordinance of the Lord, act the hypocrite with the world, and refuse the cross, then you cannot be a member of the church of Christ; or else the word of God must be false and fallible; for on every hand the Scriptures teach faith, love, the fear of God, repentance, obedience, dying unto the flesh, self-denial, a new life, and the cross. Therefore, sincerely fear God, deny yourself, search the Scriptures, follow the truth, and take heed lest you be deceived and eternally lose your soul for the sake of temporal life and its enjoyments, Mark 1: 15; 8: 36; John 1: 3; 13: 14; Luke 13: 24; 9: 25; Rom. 6: 8; Col. 3: 9; Gal. 6: 1; Matt. 16: 25.

Having given a scriptural explanation of the difference between the two churches, I will now turn to Gellius' argument by which he would prove their church to be the christian, and ours the heretical and conspirator's church. This, I trust to be enabled to show by the word of the Lord, so that the impartial reader must clearly see that he (Gellius) strives, with all his power, to suppress the salutary and plain word of God, together with his church, and to excuse and uphold as well as he can the deciving serpent and his church.

In the first place he writes: "The saints at Corinth and of the church of Galatia, whom Paul reproves on account of their abominable sins, still continued to hear the word of God, and to receive the sacraments from their bishops and pastors."

Answer. If Gellius and the preachers would conform their doctrine and life to the Scriptures; would rightly serve out their sacraments, would separate their church from the world, according to the Scriptures, then we might talk of listening to the preachers. But so long as the preachers remain deceivers, use their sacraments contrary to the word of God, and their disciples are of the world; so long as they practice neither ban nor punishment as the Scriptures require, it is, in my opinion, of no use to say much in regard to this, for it is manifest that they are without Christ and his word.

Reader, understand this matter rightly. Paul did not bear with the ungodly state of affairs in the beforementioned churches, as the preachers of the present day, do; but he rebuked them, in severe terms, especially those of Corinth, and pointed the obedient to the separation, if they, at his coming again, had not reformed themselves, 2 Cor. 12: 13.

Gellius should, reasonably, also do this and should not console the poor, reckless people with the idea that other people, in the past, have also sinned; for this is surely what Sirach calls, excusing with the example of other people; neither can it help his cause; for, in the first place, these churches were rightly built, but afterwards some of them were misled by false prophets and heretics, and led into byways. Some of them, as appears, have again given themselves to an easy, carnal life, as is generally the case with those who turn their backs upon the truth, delight in new doctrines, discord and disputation, as experience, alas, has sufficiently taught me for these last, several years, Jude 19; 2 Pet. 3: 3.

Paul calls the disturbers at Corinth, contentious and heretics; and those of Galatia he calls deceivers; he desires and commands that they be separated from the church, lest the whole lump be leavened by this leaven, 1 Cor. 5: 6; Gal. 5: 9.

Since the beforementioned churches, being rightly established, in the first place, and being afterwards made contentious by the heretics and carnal who arose among them, were reproved of Paul, because they suffered such contentious persons, with their open abominations, to remain in the church; how, then, can Gellius make good their cause by their example, while he and his preachers never were the true preachers, and their churches never were separated from the world, and therefore were not the church of Christ, as heard?

In the second place, he writes: Zachariah, Elizabeth, Joseph, Mary, Simeon and Anna, together with other saints, heard the word of God in the church of the Jews, among whom were the murderers of Christ; and, the disciples of the prophets did not separate the murderers of the prophets from the church."

Answer. These words of Gellius show that the Jewish synagogue, although many pious persons were among them, as Zachariah, Elizabeth, &c., was not the christian or apostolic church, and that they had not the ordinances of Christ and his holy apostles, nor used them; for it can never be shown that the apostolic church, so long as she remained the apostolic church, were persecutors and murderers of the pious, or that she suffered such, as was at that time the case with the Jewish synagogue. Therefore he answers and judges himself, for he does not claim that their church is the Jewish synagogue in which such abominations were found, but he claims that they are the christian church, which never thought of such things, much less practiced them.

Again, we should not follow the before-mentioned church in such abominable abuses and sins, but should be thereby admonished how we should, according to the doctrine of Paul, treat such, which ever arise among the pious; and that we should not, on account of such, mistrust the promises of the Lord, as if we were not the church of Christ; for we are thereby taught that, in the church of Christ, which is ever beguiled by her opponents, offenses, blasphemies and heresies will arise; that, however, we should separate such whenever the case requires it, after proper admonition; whereby she openly testifies before God and man, that she is clear of such offenses and deceivings. This the worldly church does not do; they suffer and retain them as members, against the word and command of God, against the ordinance of the Holy Spirit, and against the example or usage of the holy apostles; notwithstanding they well know that the institution and command of the Lord does not admit it, yet they willfully do this. Therefore they can not be Christ's church and community so long as they continue to do so; or else the express word of God must be fallible and false. O, reader, reflect upon this matter.

But from his writing that the disciples of the prophets did not separate them from the church, among whom were the murderers of the prophets, I understand him to say that their church still remains the church of Christ, notwithstanding numbers of wicked and ungodly persons are found among them, and suffered to remain among them, directly contrary to the evangelical Scriptures and the usage of the apostolic church. O, no, reader, beware, this cannot be. So long as the transgressors and willful despisers are unknown to the church, she is innocent; but when they are known and not excluded, after proper admonition, but suffered to remain in the communion of the church, then, in my opinion, she ceases to be the church of Christ. For she transgresses willfully, and does not abide in the doctrine of Christ; she despises the word and ordinance of God, because she will not bear the cross of Christ to the praise of God and to the service of their neighbors, and, because she does not want to lose the favor of men, and makes herself guilty of the sins of others, therefore she, according to John, has not God in power and in truth, 2 John 1:1; 1 Tim. 5:22; Deut. 17:2; Lev. 19:17; Matt. 18:15.

In the third place he writes, "That they are plainly the church of God and Christ who publicly assemble, keep the word, accept and preach it; who with open confession and in the holy, divine name, dispense and partake of the sacraments, and who banish the offensive criminals and obdurate sinners."

Answer. If to meet publicly, although in all manner of vanity, pomp and splendor, to preach as the world likes it, to baptize infants, to break the bread with the impenitent, feignedly to pray, and exterminate thieves and murderers with the sword, constitutes the church of Christ, then, also, all the papists, together with the Arians, monks, &c., were Christ's church; for they all have done these things publicly. This is incontrovertible. Oh no, no! But where they meet in the name of Christ, where the unadulterated word of God is preached, be it in secret or public, where the baptism and Holy Supper are served in accordance with the ordinance of the Lord, where not merely the criminals, who are judged by the law of the emperor, but also drunkards, whores and adulterers, avaricious and extortioners, are excluded from the communion of the pious, according to the doctrine and example of the apostles. Behold such is the visible church which is attested by the Scriptures.

In the fourth place he writes, "That they, invisible to the eyes of man, which cannot search the heart, but only before the eyes and judgment of God, are the true church of Christ and of God, which are found in the visible church. that is, among the number of the elect; since God, through the preaching of his holy gospel and through the use of his holy sacraments, powerfully works in them, and whereby many are again born unto life everlasting, who are only known to Him who knows his people, and who searches the hearts of men. These are the true bride of Christ."

Answer. In part I admit this to be right, however with this understanding; that the visible church, in which the invisible (as he calls them) should be included, must be salutary in doctrine, sacraments and ordinances, and unblamable in life before the world, so far as man, who is able to judge only that which is visible, can see.

Since it is as clear as day that Gellius and his like preachers are blamable in every thing, because they adulterate the word of God, abuse the sacraments, flatter the world, upbraid the pious, do not separate their church from the world, and none of their disciples reprove such open transgressions and abuses, but every one is satisfied with his doctrines and sacraments, follows and maintains them; therefore they all act the hypocrite, walk upon the broad way, hate the cross of Christ and lay it upon others. Notwithstanding all this, that the invisible church should still be among them, I cannot admit; and for this reason; for I know to a certainty that it never fails, that where the true church of Christ is, there she will be made manifest among this wicked and perverse generation by words and work, for she can as little be hidden as a city upon a hill, or a candle upon a candle-stick, Matt. 5; 14; Phil. 2; 15.

In the fifth place he writes, "That the churches at Rome, Corinth, Ephesus, &c.; and also the strangers here and there in Ponto, Galatia, Cappadocia, Asia, and Bithynia, are called, by Paul and Peter, saints and chosen. For the church, he writes, is called after the better part of its members, and is called the church of God or of Christ, holy, pure, and unblamable."

Answer. Think not, kind reader, that all those who lived at Rome, Corinth, Ephesus, Ponto, Galatia, Cappadocia and Bithynia, are called the church of Christ, of Paul and Peter, as all those who live in Meissen, Duringen and the German countries are called the church of Christ by the preachers. By no means. But they meant the small number, who, begotten by the word of the divine power, separated themselves from the world, and with open confession willingly placed themselves under Christ and his covenant. If I should write, the chosen children and saints of God at Antwerp, Ghent, Leeuwarden, and the strangers in the German countries, here and there, I would not mean all those that live at those places mentioned. By no means. For *they* also live there, who persecute and trouble the chosen children of God; but I would refer to those who confess Christ Jesus, through true faith and are obedient to his holy word.

Behold, reader, if the preachers, in the same manner, would separate their church from the world, would preach the word of God in purity, would use the sacraments in accordance with the Scriptures, and would strive with their churches, after a pious and christian life, then he might truthfully boast that the chosen, which he calls the invisible church, are included in their church, as he pretends they are.

In the sixth place he writes, "If they should say, your church is not believing, holy and unblamable, then I would refer them, first, to the Jewish church, from which we may learn that they, at the time of Elias, Jeremiah, Daniel and all the prophets, of John the Baptist, of Christ and the apostles, were not all holy; this the Scriptures of the prophets and of the apostles sufficiently teach us. But that they, notwithstanding both people and magistrates were for the most part wicked, were called the church of God and of Christ, and were thus called on account of some pious persons, to whom God sent his prophets."

Answer. If the preachers would rightly discharge the duties of their office, as Elias, Jeremiah and the prophets did; and if some were found in their church who follow the word of the Lord, as in the time of the prophets, then this might help the case of Gellius. But they are not such as Elias, Jeremiah and Daniel, nor the teachers who are led by the Spirit of Christ; but are such preachers and teachers as were reproved of Jeremiah, as may be seen in many of his Scriptures; such as were destroyed by Elias, and against whom we are faithfully warned of Christ and his apostles not to hear them, Jer. 8: 14; 23: 27; Matt. 7: 15; John 10: 3.

I would further say, Israel was the literal people, and had the promise of the fathers, on account of their birth after the flesh. The law was given them that they should serve God, and walk according to his commandments; when they transgressed the law and did not observe that which God had commanded them, they yet remained the literal people; and God, ever mindful of the covenant made with Abraham, Isaac and Jacob, has awakened his faithful servants, the prophet, and often sent them to reprove them earnestly, out of the word of the Lord, to point them again to the law, and boldly threaten them with punishment for their sins, Gen. 15: 17, 18; Deut. 5: 32. This is not the case with us at present; for we are not the literal race, brought forth from the loins of Abraham and Isaac, but are begotten of the word of God, through the Spirit. If we again forsake this birth which is of God, do not abide in the word of Christ, and again enter into the broad way, then we do not remain his church and community, 2 John 1: 9. Behold, reader, it being manifest that Gellius and the preachers of his class, together with their churches, never were the spiritual people, because they, as appears, are not born of God in truth but are earthly and carnally minded, live according to the lusts of the flesh, did not enter in at the right gate, teach an impure doctrine, and use strange sacraments, whereby no abiding church can be gathered unto Christ, as has been heard; and, besides, they act altogether contrary to the Spirit, word and will of Christ, nay, hate and despise them; how then can they be likened in the fall, unto Israel, who were the people and church, on account of the patriarchs, while this people and church never were the church of Christ in Spirit, as has been heard?

Lastly I would say, All the Scriptures, both of the Old and New Testaments, on every hand, point us to Christ Jesus, that we shall hear him, Matt. 17: 5; Mark 9: 7; Deut. 18: 15. Whosoever does not hear him, it will be required of him. Therefore take heed. As I have said before, although all the pious, from the beginning, were the community, church or body, yet at different periods they have had different doctrines, ordinances and worship.

Moses gave the law and Israel had to obey it, until Christ appeared, who was promised. We are now directed to his Spirit, word and ordinances. If it can be proven to us by his word, that his Spirit suffered drunkards, avaricious, pompous, adulterers, blasphemers, tyrants and murderers (understand, such as do not repent), in the communion of the apostolic churches; and also that his Spirit ordained open deceivers and worldly minded persons to be bishops and pastors, then I will admit that they are the church of Christ; but if they cannot do so, as it is impossible for them to do, then they must confess that their church, which is full of such people—aye full, is not the church of Christ, as they boast it to be; but that it is a disorderly, refractory and disobedient people, nay, that it is the church of antichrist, and of the world; and that their pretensions in this respect are nothing but open seduction, falsehood and deceit. Reader, observe, I testify this unto you in Christ; believe it if you will; I write the truth unto you.

In the seventh place he writes, "In the second place I refer them to the church of the Corinthians, whom Paul, in the first place, reproves on account of their dissensions," saying, "I, brethren, could not speak unto you as unto spiritual but as unto carnal," 1 Cor. 3: 1.

Answer. Heretofore I have said that this church was first rightly taught of Paul, and won unto Christ; but, being deceived by philosophers, who despised the doctrine of the cross, and by false apostles, they became divided; for which they were reproved and fraternally instructed of Paul, and admonished to separate the unfaithful and carnally minded; for the Scriptures command and instruct us to do this, namely, that such should first be admonished, and if they do not repent, that they should be unanimously separated from the communion of the church. Judge now, what Gellius can substantiate hereby; since he and his, never having been separated from the world, are not the church of Christ. Yea he, good fellow, does nothing more nor less than that he hereby manifests his cross-fleeing and open disobedience, and that he covers up and defends the abominable transgressions of his disciples, however gross they be, with the precedents of others.

In the eighth place he writes, "In the third place I refer them to the parable of Christ, of John the baptist, and of Paul. Christ likens the church unto a field in which the tares grow with the wheat until the harvest. Again, she is likened unto a net in which both good and bad fish are caught. Again, unto the virgins, of whom five were wise and five were foolish. Moreover, unto a royal wedding, where the good and evil are gathered together, one of whom is found by the king, to be without a wedding garment."

Answer. This first parable is explained by Christ himself, saying, "He that soweth the good seed is the Son of man; The field is the world" (understand it rightly, Christ says, It is the world, and not the church, as Gellius claims); "the good seed are the children of the kingdom; but the tares are the children of the wicked one; the enemy that sowed them is the devil; the harvest is the end of the world; and the reapers are the angels," Matt. 13: 37—39.

Reader, understand it rightly. Christ, the Son of man, sows his seed (God's word), through his Spirit, in the world; all who hear, believe and obey it, are called the children of the kingdom. In the same manner the opponent sows his tares (false doctrine), in the world, and all that hear and follow him are called the children of evil. Now, both wheat and tares grow together in the same field, namely, in the world. The husbandman does not want the tares to be plucked out before their time, that is, he will not have them destroyed by rooting them up, but wants them left until the harvest, lest the wheat be destroyed with the tares, Matt. 13: 29, 30.

O, reader, if the preachers rightly understood this parable and feared God, they would not cry so loudly against us, who, alas, are every where called *tares, heretics* and *conspirators,* "Down with the heretics;" even if we were heretics, from which God save us. Oh! what noble wheat they destroy! But what does it avail? Satan must rebel and murder; for it is his nature and work, as the Scriptures teach, Gen. 3: 4; John 8.

Some of the other parables, as of the net in which good and bad fishes are caught; of the wise and foolish virgins and their lamps; of the wedding of the king's son and the guests, and of the threshing floor with wheat and chaff, although the Lord spoke them in allusion to the church, yet they were not spoken for the purpose that the church should knowingly and willfully accept and suffer open transgressors, drunkards, carousers, defilers of women, avaricious, robbers, gamblers, and usurers, in their communion; because, then, Christ and Paul would differ in doctrine; for Paul says that we should avoid and shun such. But they were spoken because many intermix with the christians, in semblance only, and place themselves under the word and sacraments, who, in fact, are no christians, but are hypocrites and enemies before their God; and these are likened unto the refuse fish; unto the foolish virgins who had no oil in their lamps; unto the guest without a wedding garment, and unto the chaff, which will be cast out by the angels, at the day of Christ. For they pretend that they fear God and seek Christ; they receive baptism and the Lord's Supper, and outwardly act in semblance, but, in fact, no faith, repentance, true fear and love of God; no Spirit, power, fruit nor work is found in them.

But, as to the two kinds of laborers in the vineyard, Matt. 2: 28, 29, and as to those called to the great supper, Luke 14: 16, the reader should know, that they have a different meaning and cannot conform to his sentiments. Whosoever loves truth, may examine them, and judge by the Holy Scriptures what their proper meaning is. Again, as to his citation of the vessels to dishonor, I will let Paul's words explain them. He says, "If a man therefore purge himself from these, he shall be a vessel unto honor, sanctified and meet for the Master's use, and prepared unto every good work," 2 Tim. 2: 21.

Behold, dear reader, here you may observe how miserably he perverts the word of the Lord, that they may, apparently, be the church of Christ, although they knowingly and willfully admit open transgressors to the communion of their church, against the Scriptures. But the flaming eyes of the Lord, which search every thing, cannot be blinded by such sophistry.

In the ninth place he writes, "The church, now being perplexed by such evils as these which she has to suffer unto the day of judgment, as some of these parables imply; nay, that it never was her lot to be entirely rid of evil ones and hypocrites, however strictly she used the ban, therefore they are wrong, and grossly sin by condemning us, and saying that we are false teachers, and not the church of God, as was the church of the patriarchs, prophets and Moses; and by maliciously and wrongfully calling our church, which is founded by our faithful service upon the true foundation, according to the example of all the messengers of God, and which is daily increased and built up, upon the chosen cornerstone, an unbelieving, unholy and blamable church, against all the Scriptures, and thereby not only bringing our church into disrepute, but also all the churches of the German countries, nay of all the christian world, which have and must have a different doctrine from their church, which they call holy, pure, unblamable and spotless on account of their dreadful ban."

Answer. If he should have said that the church is troubled with such evils, and that she must suffer them, in such a manner as to mean that the true church must suffer the enmity, rebellion, violence and tyranny of the wicked, and ungodly actions of the perverse, then he would have written the truth. But since his meaning is, that since the church ever has hypocrites among her number, that therefore the evil ones, that is, open despisers and transgressors should be tolerated; therefore he writes contrary to the word of God; for Paul says, "Therefore put away from among yourselves that wicked person," that is, separate from the communion of your church him who is wicked, 1 Cor. 5: 13.

Again, to his writing, "that we grossly sin by saying that they are not the church of God," and to his boasting "that they build their church upon the corner stone," I would say that his boasting is false; for their light-minded doctrine, false sacraments, reckless life and his indiscreet writing, alas, prove too plainly, that they do not build their church upon the true cornerstone; it being manifest that they, on every hand are at fault, adulterate the word of God, abuse the sacraments, practice no separation, and for the greater part, both teachers and hearers walk upon perverse ways; whether we therefore sin, because in faithful love we admonish them for their own good, and in humility show them that they, under such a state of affairs, are not, neither can be the church of God, the reader may judge. We know to a certainty that where there is no pure doctrine, no pure sacraments, no pious, christian life, no true, brotherly love, and no right minded confession, that there is no christian church; let them boast ever so much.

Again, in regard to his complaint, "That we not only call *them*, but *all* the churches of the German countries, nay, of the whole christian world, unbelieving, unholy and condemn them, the reader should know that we condemn no one; for he, Jesus Christ, to whom the Father has given it, will do that. Yet we say, and teach it verbally and by writing, that all those who are not born of God and his word, are not actuated by the Spirit of Christ, are not changed into his nature and disposition, however high and fine an appearance and name they may assume. In this case, neither emperor, king, doctor, licentiate, pope nor Luther will avail. All who would be in the church of Christ, must be in Christ, must be of his mind, and walk as he walked, or else Christ Jesus, John, Paul and all the Scriptures must be false; this is too clear to be denied, John 5: 22; 1 John 2: 6; Rom. 8: 14; Phil. 2: 5.

Since he accuses us that we condemn all the churches of the German countries, and of the whole christian world, as he boasts, therefore I would answer with a few plain words: If the German churches and the beforementioned world were born of God, were of Christ's mind, walked as he walked then the accusation of Gellius would be right, since we do not acknowledge them to be true churches. But as they prove by deeds that they are without Christ, walk and act against his word and will; as they are quite earthly and carnally minded, therefore, they are not judged of men, but of the word of the Lord, for Christ says, "The word that I have spoken, the same shall judge him in the last day," John 12: 48.

Further, by his writing that the said churches have and must have a different doctrine, he judges himself that they are not the church of Christ. For Christ will, that his church should keep and follow his word, ordinances and commands, whether it be to the joy or to the pain of the flesh.

Behold, dear reader, since it is doubly plain that the Scriptures teach, both by words and examples, that open transgressors should be excluded from the communion of the church; and since the preachers, who fear men more than God, and serve their bellies more than the praise of the Lord, neglect this on account of the cross, which might result from such action, therefore their public actions testify that they are not the bride and sheep of Christ; for they do not hear his voice, neither do they follow his doctrines and commands, 2 Thess. 3: 6; John 10: 26.

Again, to his writing that we consider our church holy, pure and unblamable, on account of the cruel ban, this is my simple reply: We do not at all boast but of the grace of our God through Christ Jesus. Our frailty is great, our stumblings are many, and we feel with Paul, that nothing good dwells in our flesh. Notwithstanding all true members of the church of Christ strive after the unblamable, holy being, which is in him; they conform their walk to the word of the Lord; they follow his commands and ordinances; and separate those who are separated by the Scriptures, which he, alas, calls a fearful ban. O, Lord.

O God! Thus the precious word is esteemed as unworthy by this thoughtless man. For, by this abominable, unseasoned blasphemy, not only we, but also the Son of the Almighty and living God, together with the Spirit of eternal wisdom, by whom this ban was commanded, and also all the apostles and the primitive church, who so diligently taught and earnestly practiced it, are adjudged fools. If the ordinance is foolishness, then the Institutor, and all who teach and practice it, must be fools; this cannot well be denied.

Observe, reader, if this may not be called hating the word and will of God, despising his commands, and speaking blasphemies against the Most High, you may reflect upon, and judge by the Scriptures. O, reader, awaken. Beware, and learn to know your preachers, and of what spirit they are the children.

In the tenth place he writes, "Thus they are given to a wrong understanding, prejudge without knowledge, and leave the church from motives of spiritual pride and fancy of righteousness, more than from motives of sincere righteousness; they have no other reason to leave the church, than that they, according to the manner of the Pharisees, would justify themselves by despising others."

Answer. I fear that it would weary the reader to reply to all his false accusations minutely. Yet I would say, in regard to this, If I could speak with Gellius before the public, I have no doubt but many, through the grace of God, would begin to see that it is not us who have a wrong understanding, but them; that they prejudge us, indiscreetly; remain outside of the church of Christ, from motives of pride; and not only despise us, according to the manner of the Pharisees, but also often deprive us of possessions and life, as may be witnessed in different localities. But we must suffer, bear, and console ourselves with the saying, "Blessed are ye, when men shall revile you, and persecute you, and shall say all manner of evil against you falsely, for my sake. Rejoice, and be exceeding glad; for great is your reward in heaven; for so persecuted they the prophets which were before you," Matt. 5: 11, 12.

In the eleventh place he writes, "They will probably say that if we would be the church of Christ, we must verify the saying of Christ;" "The gates of hell shall not prevail against it;" and ask where our church has existed, inviolated by the devil, anti-christ and heresies. He further writes, "Since the church, which is not limited to certain boundaries, but is scattered over the whole world, has this article of faith," "I believe in the holy, christian church, the communion of saints," "and that she will endure unto the end of the world, therefore we are forced to acknowledge, that God, true to his promise, saves his church, and has always saved her, although the old serpent, the devil, deceives her by the lusts of the flesh, the pomp of the world and by many sects; and, although she is combatted, persecuted and disturbed, by the potentates of the world, until she, inattentive to her cause, drowsy in her prayer, indifferent to the will of God, and ungrateful for the word of God, or, until found apostatical of Christ, so enrages God that he takes from her the light of his word, and lets her fall into weighty errors, and adhere to idolatry, adultery, whoredom, and other sins and disgraces and follow after them, so that the church in such case, almost destroyed and ruined, scarcely is worthy of the name."

Answer. I would beseech the diligent reader earnestly to observe how the words of Gellius sound, which I have here cited at length. He admits that the church, deceived and enchanted by the devil, the lusts of the flesh, the pomp, sects and potentates of the world, has become drowsy, inattentive, ungrateful, and an apostate of Christ, has enraged God, and fallen into all manner of wickedness and sins; yet he claims that she remains the church of Christ, as if the church was inherited by one generation from another, and did not consist in faith, Spirit and power. I would not know what poorer excuse he could find. Therefore observe that which I write, and let it be unto you a certain rule, namely, where the Spirit, word, sacraments and life of Christ are found, that there the Nicene article comes in, "I believe in the holy christian church, the communion of saints, &c. On the other hand, where the Spirit, word, sacraments and life of Christ are not to be found, but where the spirit, doctrine, sacraments and life of anti-christ are followed, there, also, is the church of anti-christ, and not the church of Christ, although we might say a thousand times, "I believe in the holy christian church." For without, or against the Spirit, word, sacraments and life of Christ, there can never be a christian church, however much we may pervert the truth. The word stands immutable. "Whosoever transgresseth, and abideth not in the doctrine of Christ, hath not God," 2 John, 9.

In the twelfth place he writes, "Because God, in his grace, has made an eternal covenant with his church, and has promised her that the gates of hell, although they may rend and weaken her, shall not thoroughly prevail against her, therefore he will, at all times, preserve a shadow of the evangelical doctrine and of his sacraments, upon which the church shall be upheld; and he will also preserve some members upon the true foundation, who will grow up amidst the thistles, thorns, wolves, bears and lions, and deliver them as in a violent hurricane, from the elements, as Noah was saved from the deluge."

Answer. Where they conform themselves to the Spirit, word, sacraments, ordinances, commands, prohibitions, usage and example of Christ, there the holy christian church is found, as has been heard, and there is also the promise that the gates of hell will not prevail against her. For although she grows as a rose amongst thorns, as he expresses himself, keeps herself amongst wolves, bears and lions, and as a ship cast about by wind and waves, she must suffer much tribulation, yet she cannot be capsized, that is, she cannot be turned from Christ (understand this to be the true christian church); for she is built upon a rock, Matt. 7: 24.

That this is the truth, the Scriptures and their examples teach us on every hand; and we also have found it so by facts, within the last few years. For, however fiercely the lions, bears and wolves have roared, raved and torn, for the last few years, by their frightful mandates, apprehending, torturing and murdering; and, although the waves often roll up to the clouds, yet the manifested truth remains with the humble and pious children; and however sharply the thistles and thorns may sting, yet this noble and beautiful rose daily grows, and, praise be to God, increases in size and strength, whereby it is made manifest unto many reasonable persons, that God's promise to the church stands firm, and it is the miracle and power of the Most High; for neither death, nor life, nor angels, nor principalities, nor powers, nor things present, nor things to come, nor height, nor depth, nor any other creature shall be able to separate them from the love of God, which is in Christ Jesus our Lord, Rom. 8: 38, 39.

Yet this thoughtless man thinks that they are the true, christian church, and does not observe that the beforementioned thistles, thorns, wolves, bears and lions, by which the true church has been so much troubled, and still continues to be, are members of the very church which he claims were and yet are the true church of Christ. For they, during the last few centuries, have used one sacrament, and, unseparated, were greeted as the children of grace, and were admitted and accepted in the communion of these churches.

He, besides, also consoles the poor people that the Lord has, at all times, preserved a shadow of the evangelical doctrine and of his sacraments upon which to support his church; as if God was well pleased with such a dead shadow of false preaching and of infant baptism; and, as if the church of Christ, the bride of God and of the Lamb, could be supported by adulterated doctrines and unscriptural sacraments. O, dear Lord! How long shall such errors yet endure? Who cannot understand such palpable deceit? He must have an extremely obdurate and perverse heart, or he must be a very ignorant and blunt man, I think.

In the thirteenth place he produces two arguments whereby he means to prove that their church is the general church (as he calls it) wherewith God has so dealt. And in the first place writes, "in which church anti-christ was seated; for, according to the prophecies of Paul, he had placed himself therein and exalted himself above God; and asserts that it is the true church to which God has given the promise, although she was dreadfully stained and miserably torn up. In our church the anti-christ has been seated, and placed himself as a God, and has exalted himself above all that is of God and religion—therefore our church is the true church and temple of God, to which the promise of God is given." "This argument he proves with these words: "The first proposition is true; for Paul calls the church in which the anti-christ would place himself, the temple of God; the other is also too clear to be denied, from the prophecies of Paul and the teachings of experience. For in the churches which baptize infants, he and all the violent tyrants have exercised their power and violence, and trampled under foot all religion and worship. If both propositions now are true, then it follows, also, that the conclusion is true; and shows the anabaptists, in what a fearful condition they are, since they have left us and our church."

Answer. By the side of this I will place my syllogism: Where true religion and worship, as required of the Scriptures, are trampled under foot, there is not the church of Christ. Anti-christ has, Gellius testifies, trampled under foot the true religion and worship required by the Scriptures, in the church of which Gellius speaks; therefore, the beforementioned church is not the church of Christ. All Scriptures teach that my first proposition is true; for Moses says, "Whosoever will not hearken unto my words which he" (meaning Christ) "shall speak in my name, I will require it of him," Deut 18: 19. Christ says, "If ye continue" (mark, "continue"), "in my word, then are ye my disciples indeed," John 8: 31. Again, Paul says, "If any man preach any other gospel unto you than that ye have received, let him be accursed," Gal. 1: 9. John, also, says, "Whosoever transgresseth, and abideth not in the doctrine of Christ, hath not God," 2 John 1: 9.

My second proposition, Gellius admits to be true; for he says, that anti-christ has trampled religion and worship under his feet, as heard.

Since, then, that the first proposition can be substantiated by the Scriptures, and the second is acknowledged by Gellius to be right, therefore, my conclusion must also be right, namely, that the church to which he refers, is not the church of Christ. For she does not accept the word of Christ, but a strange gospel; and does not abide in the pure doctrine of his holy apostles; therefore they have not God in power, and are not the disciples of Christ; or else the cited sayings must be wrong and false.

As regards the first proposition of Gellius, Paul testifies in plain words, that it is false, for he says, "That day shall not come, except there come a falling away first, and that man of sin be revealed, the son of perdition," 2 Thess. 2: 3. Here Paul teaches in tolerably plain words that the falling away of faith would first come as was also the case here, 2 Thess. 2: 3.

Since Paul openly testifies by the Spirit of God, that the falling away would come before the day of the Lord, and also shows through whom it would come, namely, through the man of sin (son of perdition); and since it is clearly visible that this son of perdition has placed himself in the temple of God, that is, in the hearts of man, or rather, in the stead of God in the beforementioned church, and has quite demolished and destroyed it, and through deceit has changed it, under the semblance of the name of Christ, from the doctrine and ordinances of God to his own doctrine and ordinances, therefore, I would leave the attentive reader to judge if this church, which is quite demolished and destroyed by him, can be called God's temple. If he judge that it cannot be so called, then he judges rightly; otherwise many passages of the Scriptures would be fallible and false; and, as a consequence, God and the devil, Christ and anti-christ must have been seated in one temple, and reigned in one church. But, if they deny this, then I would again say that

Luther and the learned have done wrong in bringing about such a disturbance, tribulation and misery in the world by their doctrine and change, since they, according to Gellius, still remained the church of Christ, although the anti-christ had quite destroyed and demolished the true religion. Reader, reflect upon this, and judge whether I write the truth or not.

In his second proposition he judges himself; for he writes, that anti-christ was seated in their church, which baptizes children; has placed himself therein as a God; trampled under foot the true religion and worship; he also acknowledges, above, under the head of the separation, that the papists are no christians; for he says, "that those who leave us would sooner become papists than christians again." Kind reader, observe closely what I write. Since it is manifest that the Roman anti-christ has, for a number of years, reigned in peace in their church; has given them to drink from his cup of abominations; has destroyed the true religion, and re-instated his abominations; and since he himself admits that the papists are no christians, therefore, it is certain and plain that their church was not, as he claims, the general christian church and temple of God, to which the promise of God was given. For it cannot be that they can be the disciples of anti-christ and then yet remain the christian church and temple.

Now consider, if the pious, whom he calls anabaptists, are so much out of way, by renouncing all the anti-christian abominations, false, condemned sects and churches; and, if they place themselves in such a frightful position, as he sighingly complains, by humbly submitting themselves to the only, eternal Messiah, Christ Jesus, and by placing themselves as an example of all obedience and virtue, in their weakness, before all the world.

His second argument is this: "In and with all churches which teach the doctrine and faith of Christ Jesus; are not altogether fallen away; do not altogether reject and profane Christ and his holy gospel and which do not altogether trample upon the use of the holy sacraments and neglect them, as under the reign of Mahomet, there still remains the name of the holy church. In and with our church, which has the infant baptism as an apostolic ordinance, the doctrine and faith of Jesus Christ, as taught by the apostles, never was altogether fallen away, as it was with the Turks; although abominably adulterated and weakened by anti-christ; therefore, the name of the church remains with our community and has true members in it."

Answer. If his first proposition was consistent and right, then it would also be consistent and right to say, The doctrine and faith never were entirely fallen away with the Arians, Circumcellians, Munsterians and other sects; the gospel was not altogether rejected and profaned, and the sacraments altogether trampled upon by them, therefore, the name of the church remains with them, and true members of the church are found among them. We are, therefore, also wrongfully called "devilish heretics, conspirers, and apostate anabaptists," by him, for we so highly prize the gospel and the sacraments of our Lord Jesus Christ, that we daily sacrifice our possessions and blood for their sake, as may be seen.

If he should say that the beforementioned sects did not act and teach in accordance with the Scriptures, and that they therefore were not in the communion of the christian church; then he judges himself still more markedly. For the papistic church to which he refers, did not do this; if they did rightly act and teach, then he very unjustly says that they are not christians, as has been heard that he did.

Again, by his writing, "There still remains the name of the holy church," he openly testifies that his assertion is without all foundation in the Scriptures; for he does not refer to the unadulterated doctrine, to the salutary use of the holy sacraments, nor to the pious, unblamable life, which should ever be found in the church of Christ; as if the name could keep the church in God and could bind it to the promise, without the Spirit, word, sacraments, faith and obedience of Christ. No, no, reader, no. "I know," says the First and the Last, "the blasphemy of them which say they are Jews, and are not, but are the synagogue of Satan," Rev. 2: 9. If the name alone constituted the true church, then all the raving tyrants, enemies of christian truth, all murderers, perjurers, whoremongers, avaricious, pompous and unrighteous, would be members of the church of Christ, for they call themselves after the name of Christ. This is incontrovertible.

As to his second proposition, I would say in the first place, Since he says that their church has infant baptism, as an apostolic ordinance, that he thereby heaps open falsehood upon the holy apostles, the upright, pious testifiers of eternal truth; for he never can prove by a single word in the Scriptures, that they taught or practiced infant baptism, as has been sufficiently shown, above.

In the second place I would say, That the church to which he refers, was not only adulterated and weakened, as he calls it, but has become so estranged from God, that she has worshipped, honored and served wood, stone, gold, and silver gods, and, besides bread and wine; as has, alas, been seen these many years, in all the temples and houses of worship, throughout Europe; and, as may yet, daily, be seen in many kingdoms, cities and towns. Yet, Gellius asserts that their church ever was the church of Christ. I have never heard more inconsistent reasoning. Therefore, dear reader, beware, and do not listen to the smooth talk of the learned, for they deceive you. But hearken unto him who says, "I am the light of the world; he that followeth me shall not walk in darkness, but shall have the light of life," John 8: 12, and then you will never be deceived.

Reader, understand what I mean; we do not dispute about whether or not there are some of the chosen one's of God, in the beforementioned churches; for this we, at all times, humbly leave to the just and gracious judgment of God, hoping there may be many thousands who are unknown to us, as they were to holy Elias; but our dispute is, in regard to what kind of Spirit, doctrine, sacraments, ordinances and life, Christ has commanded us to gather unto him an abiding church, and how we should maintain it in his ways.

Behold, reader, these are his most important arguments with which to maintain his assertion, "that their church is the true one," namely, because they sprang from the papists, and practice infant baptism. Just hear how strangely he writes. In my opinion, he pens all that comes in his mind, if it has but a little semblance, that it may tickle the ears of the thoughtless people, and console them in their impenitent, easy life. If these adduced assertions of his were true, then it could not be otherwise than that hitherto the church of Christ must have been the church of anti-christ, or that of anti-christ must have been the church of Christ; also, Christ and anti-christ must have both reigned in one church; infant baptism must have been called apostolic, without the Scriptures, and the mere name constitutes the church of Christ; this, by the grace of God, no one can successfully rebut; let him garble and twist the matter as adroitly as he pleases.

CONCERNING SOME ACCUSATIONS AGAINST US.

In the first place Gellius accuses us, saying, "They (he means us), falsely, adorn and deck themselves with the sanctity of the church. For, since the Holy Spirit, which sanctifies the church both by the remission of sin, and dying unto the old man with all his lusts, and also by the nullifying of the sins in the flesh, is given through faith, therefore I cannot see how they can receive the Holy Spirit, together with true sanctification, and be the true, holy church, while they so bitterly contend among themselves about the divinity of the Holy Spirit (which, besides other evidence, sufficiently proves his divinity by the work of sanctification), as well as about many other articles of faith."

Answer. Zuinglius formerly taught that the will of God actuated a thief to steal, a murderer to kill, and that their punishment was also brought about by the will of God; which, in my opinion, is an abomination of abominations. Now, if I conclude that because Zuinglius taught so, all preachers teach it, it would be a wrong conclusion. Athanasius could not prevent Arius from teaching that the Holy Spirit was a creature of the creature of Christ.

Reader, understand my meaning. I never have thought that God's Holy and eternal Spirit was not God, with God and in God; yet, he would accuse us, who are not guilty, of denying the sanctification, grace, fruit and power of the Holy Spirit, because some, who have been separated from us, have erred in this respect, and probably still err; although he plainly sees and palpably feels the sanctification and power of the Holy Spirit in us, namely, that it smothers the old man with his lusts, and destroys the sins of the flesh; something which he calls the sanctification of the Holy Spirit, as has been heard. Behold, thus he upbraids and accuses the guiltless. Whether this is not the Parisaic, envious and disgraceful spirit, which explains away the good intentions of Christ and his disciples, and thereby inflamed the thoughtless populace against them, I will leave to his own reflection.

In the second place he accuses us, saying, "They have an obdurate faith; one half of which is founded upon the merits of Christ, and the other upon their own merits. For Obbe Philips, who has a great many followers (as he says) does plainly assert that the justification of man is not brought about by faith alone, but by faith, love and good works."

Answer. I would humbly ask Gellius this question: Does it follow that because Obbe Philips formerly taught this doctrine, Menno and the others also teach it? If he answer in the affirmative, then I would say that he does us an injustice, as, alas, he often does. For our doctrine and publications abundantly testify that we and the church of God are not thus minded, but that we seek justification alone in the righteous and crucified Christ Jesus.

But if he answer in the negative, then I wish he would have the kindness and virtue in him to make a difference and not mix the innocent with the guilty; and I also wish that he would say no more than the truth; for he writes that the beforementioned "Obbe Philips has a considerable number of followers," and I make the assertion that he cannot find more than six or ten who believe as he does.

In the third place he accuses us, saying, "How can *they* be a holy church who disagree among themselves about the head of the church; do not suffer him to be the true God, and thereby resuscitate the old Arian heresy."

Answer. We may well sincerely thank the Most High, that he so manifests unto us his paternal grace and great mercy, that even our most adroit and acute opponents cannot accuse us but by such puerile, and, for the greater part, false reasoning. If he would consult natural honor, not to mention love and truth, as much as he, alas, consults bitter and envious feeling, how loth would he be to think that which he now is not ashamed to publish in writing, indiscriminately saying that we resuscitate the old Arian heresy, while he and his like, well know that such have no part in the communion of our churches, so long as they do not renounce such errors, as heard.

O dear Lord, how long will such bitter and envious accusations and false backbitings continue? Would to God that the magistrates would have a little fear of the Lord, and consider what they are doing, and that they would hear and compare the different parties, so that they would once learn whom and for what purpose they persecute, and what kind of people and teachers they are whom they daily maintain and encourage in their injustice and abominations, by their violence.

In the fourth place he accuses us, saying, "If they are the true, holy church, the spiritual bride of Christ, pure, holy, and unblamable, then let them prove the unity of the Spirit, especially concerning the twelve articles of faith, which are the foundation of the church; then the one should not be Mennonite, the other Adam Pastorite, the third Obbeite, the fourth Dirkite, &c. For although they may ban one another as much as they please, it still is evidently true that they are all anabaptists and enemies to infant baptism, and thus still continue to conspire and fanaticize against the churches of Christ."

Answer. I trust that we, by the grace of God, are so wedded to our Lord and Bridegroom, Christ Jesus, that we are prepared to sacrifice our lives for the sake of hearing his holy voice. We do not boast of our holiness and piety, as Gellius accuses us, but of our great weakness. I also trust that we, who are grains of one loaf, agree in not only the twelve articles (as he counts them), but in all the articles of the Scriptures, as regeneration, repentance, baptism, Holy Supper, separation, &c., which we, along with Isaiah, Peter and Paul, Isaiah 28: 16; 1 Peter 2: 6; Eph. 2: 20, accept as the only foundation of the churches, as preached by

Christ's own, blessed mouth, and left and taught us in clear and plain words; and not only the twelve articles as he does.

Neither are we so divided as he says; for Dirk (Dietrich Philip) and we are of the same mind, and I trust, through the grace of God, we will ever remain so. But that Obbe has become a Demas, and that Adam Pastor has separated from us, is not our fault. Such things, also, often happened in the apostolic times. God reclaim them at his will; they have taken their leave, and are, alas, no more counted among us, so long as they do not repent.

His writing "that we still conspire and contend against the church of Christ," and other like bitter and resenting words, show that he is so actuated by the spirit of envy, that he cannot write or speak a discreet and reasonable word about us; but he must call us fanatics, conspirators, hedge preachers and sneaks; and he never observes how different of opinion, and how divided in doctrine the baptizers of infants are, who claim to be the true church; and into how many different sects they are divided. One party is papistic; the other Lutheran; the third Zuinglian; the fourth Calvinistic, &c.; and, although they violently quarrel among themselves, disgrace, condemn and ruin each other, as much as they please, yet it is still evidently true that they baptize their children, are unfriendly to the baptism of Christ, continue to conspire against the truth, and persecute it and the church of Christ. O, reader, that the world would once learn to know who are the fanatics and conspirators; then we might hope for the better, but as it is, it is hidden from their eyes.

In the fifth place he accuses us, saying, "If they are the holy church, then, let them hearken unto the voice of Christ; which says that the word of the holy gospel and its sacraments should not be preached and dispensed in secret nooks and corners, but in public."

Answer. If we are not the true church of Christ, but if Gellius and his like are that church, as he pretends, and would yet have us publicly proclaim our doctrine, why has he then twice refused a public discussion with me, under safe conduct, to which I have invited him, while he well knows that I have to endure so much for the sake of my doctrine and faith? It would be reasonable, if we err in some things, from which God preserve us, that he should go with me before the public, vanquish and convince me of our errors, for God knows that I am willing to be vanquished if I can be convinced by stronger Scriptures and more powerful truths; that he might thus receive the applause of his fellows (which he, in my opinion, very much strives after), and, besides save my soul and the souls of many others.

If he is a true preacher, and a member of the true church of Christ, why does he, then, desire us to go before the public, while he well knows that I could not do so without the loss of blood and life? I freely offer myself, if he can show one plain passage in the Scriptures, that the apostles and prophets have publicly taught at such places where they knew that the people had resolved upon their death, as, alas, they have every where resolved upon our death, and, by the grace of God, we will do the same.

I know to a certainty that he can find no such examples nor Scriptures in the Bible. Yea, dear reader, if he would be straightforward in assigning the reason why he ever desires us to go and preach in public, he would confess that he seeks nothing by his hypocritical and artful pretension, other than to make our cause suspicious with the people, that his cause shall make a good appearance, and that he is very desirous and thirsty after the blood of the innocent, while he, I say, against all reason, love, and Scriptures, desires us publicly to proclaim our doctrine, well knowing that in all Germany, not a place can be found where this could be done without imprisonment, violence, or rebellion. If he, now, were in the truth, as he would like to be considered, namely, an upright, unblamable preacher, how loth would he be to think of such gross disgrace, which he now, alas, dares loudly proclaim both by speaking and writing. David says, "The Lord will abhor the bloody and deceitful man," Ps. 5:6.

In the sixth place he accuses us, saying, "As they want to be the true church of Christ, they would do well to look back to the origin of their church and see how it agrees with the origin and age of the true church. That their church is not of the origin and times of Adam, Abraham, or David, is proven by their wrong opinion and abominable error in regard to the incarnation of Christ, whereby they make him neither God nor man, and rob us of our Messiah. Also, above, under the head of the Calling, he writes, It is an abominable fruit that they have resuscitated, and again introduced into the world such a disgraceful error in regard to the incarnation of Christ. For if Christ was not of our flesh (of which he was not, unless he received it from the woman), then the law was not fulfilled in our flesh; then the righteousness of God is not yet acquitted, which without the ransom would not leave us unpunished.

Answer. The learned ever slander us and complain because we, with the angel Gabriel, Luke 1: 32; with John the Baptist, John 1: 15—36; with Peter, Matt. 16: 16; with Martha, John 11:27; with the apostles, Matt. 14: 33, and with the eternal Father himself, acknowledge Christ, both according to his divinity and humanity, as the true and only begotten Son of God; and we dare not teach and believe more nor otherwise than the word of the Lord teaches us of him. I would therefore beseech all readers and hearers to consider well the following brief answers and references. I trust that, by the grace of God, I will be able to explain the matter so clearly in a few words, that the reader will plainly see that they not only rob us of Christ, the doctrine, sacraments, Spirit, life, ordinances and usage of our Savior, but also rob him of his most holy origin, glory, honor and person; and, that they, by their deceiving comments and reasoning, render Christ a divided, impure and inconsistent Christ, both according to nature and the Scriptures. Whosoever has ears to hear let him hear, and whosoever has a mind to understand let him understand.

THE CONFESSION OF THE LEARNED CONCERNING CHRIST.

The Confession of the Learned concerning Christ, is, "That the eternal word, the second person in the Godhead (these are their words), the eternal Son of God, has taken unto himself the nature of our flesh. Yea, that the whole man, Christ, who was sacrificed, and who died for us, is the natural seed of the woman, of Abraham, and of David. The seed of the woman (they say) according to the ordinance of God, Gen. 3, with which seed, namely, Mary's flesh and blood, the beforementioned divine person, the eternal Word and eternal Son, has united himself; and thus became one person and Christ. Or that the whole person, Christ Jesus, with body and soul, is the natural fruit of the flesh and blood of Mary, in which the eternal Word dwelt. The man, Christ Jesus, died, but the Word remains whole and intact."

Answer. It seems very strange to me that the learned never cease to upbraid us by their indiscreet words, and cause us more and more tribulation, by the bloodthirsty; we, who have plainly and incontrovertibly on our side, the firm and immutable foundation of the holy apostles and prophets, nay, also the blessed word and testimony of Christ; while they have neither common reason nor the Scriptures on their side, as may be seen. For, that all the following weighty and intolerable improprieties and abominable errors result from their confession, is as clear as day.

First, A divided Christ; of which one half must have been heavenly and the other earthly; as some, even dare boldly assert that the person of Christ consisted of two principal parts, namely, God and man.

Secondly, An impure and sinful Christ, for the defense says: *Christum non alterius ullius carnis participem factum esse, quana quae and peccato (ut tentaretur) and morti simul obnoxia esset,* &c., that is, Christ partook of no other flesh but of sin, that he might be tempted and subject to death. At another place the defense says, in regard to Christ: *Si sanctus (inquit) quomodo sub peccatum in Patris judicio condemnatur?* that is, If Christ is holy, why is he then judged in the judgment of the Father because of sins? this agrees perfectly with the writing of Gellius; that the righteousness of God would not leave us unpunished, without the ransom.

Reader, observe, How could they speak more blasphemously of the most holy manhood of Christ, nay, of the Son of the Almighty and eternal God, than they thereby do? For if Christ was flesh of our sinful and death-guilty flesh, and if he was thus tempted of his own flesh, then the sin, of which he was tempted, must have dwelt in his flesh, and then he died for the sake of duty, and not for the sake of grace; this is too clear to be refuted. Nor could it be otherwise, if we assert that Christ's flesh was of Adam's sinful flesh.

Again, If his holy, precious flesh was such a ransom as Gellius claims, how could the righteousness of God be fulfilled and acquitted thereby, according to the holy will of God? If this may not be rightly called, preaching an impure and sinful Christ, and robbing our most holy Savior and Messiah (something of which they accuse us), I will leave all right-minded and reasonable people to reflect upon in a scriptural light.

Thirdly, Two persons in Christ, namely, the one the second person in the Godhead, and the other the man of Mary's flesh, in which human person the divine person dwelt. Which error is not alone controverted by us, but also by Luther, saying, "Beware, beware (I say) of the *Alleosi;* it is the devil's mask; for it will ultimately establish such a Christ as I would not be called after; namely, that Christ henceforth is no more, and that his suffering avails no more than the suffering of a common saint. For, if I should believe that alone human feeling suffered for me, then that Christ would be a poor Savior; he would stand in need of a Savior himself. In short, it is unspeakable what the devil seeks and intends by this *Alleosi.* We say, God is man and man is God; we cry against them that they divide the person of Christ, as if it were two persons."

For, if the *Alleosi* shall stand, as Zuingli teaches it, Christ must be two persons, one divine, the other human. This he says, "Reader, observe, to what kind of Christ they teach and point us.

Fourthly, Two sons in Christ; of which the first is the Son of God without a mother; the second, the son of Mary, without a father; in which son of Mary, the Son of God should have been embodied, and thus have been united, as they claim. Just behold what a monstrosity they produce!

Fifthly, The person, Christ Jesus, then was neither the first nor only begotten Son, but the third son of God in order, who was not born, but created of God; and would be, as Pomer says, the accepted son of God, *Quod & Bonosianorum five Monosolitarum hæresis est.* I say He would be the third in order. For the first is the Word; the second, the first Adam, Luke 3 : 38, and the third, the man of Mary's flesh, who should have been accepted as a son of God, as heard.

Sixthly, Then we are not redeemed and delivered through God's first and only begotten Son, but through Mary's son, created of Adam's impure and sinful flesh, as also the defense and his followers dare assert, in the face of all the Scriptures, saying, that the nature imbodied in the loins of Adam, which committed the transgression also, according to the righteousness of God will requite and remit the same.

Seventhly, If we are thus delivered through Adam's flesh, as they claim, then we should not only give thanks to the Father for his Word, but also to Adam's flesh, through which our deliverance is caused; this, all right-minded persons must admit.

Eighthly, If the man Christ was a creature of Adam's flesh, and we were delivered through him, as the learned claim; and since God speaks through the prophet, That he will not give his glory to another, Isaiah 48 : 11; and since it is manifest that we should honor our Redeemer, Christ, no less than we honor the Father, therefore it must follow that God either did not speak truly through his prophets, or else they were all idolaters because they gave divine homage to a creature of Adam's flesh; something which is so strictly forbidden in the Scriptures, and which often was severely punished of God. Behold, reader, such an inconsistent, impure and divided Christ he is to which the learned point and teach you by their sophistry and garbled Scriptures A christ composed of two persons and two sons; of which one person and son should have dwelt in the other; and of which one person and son should have suffered and the other not; and the one that suffered should have been the son of Mary and not of God. I think this may well be called forsaking the Lord who has bought them, and preaching a strange christ whom the Scriptures never knew.

O, reader, dear reader, how lamentably the deceitfulness of the old serpent robs us, through the reasoning of the learned, of this noble, exalted and precious Messiah, and points us to an impure, sinful, earthly and created being; never minding that the Holy Spirit openly testifies that the Word of God was made flesh, John 1, and that this same incarnated Word is our Emmanuel, and our God, Matt. 1: 25; the Lord who justifies us, Jer. 23; the first and only begotten, John 1; God's own Son, Rom. 8; descended from heaven, John 3: 13; the living bread from heaven which was not his invisible godhead, as the learned say, but his visible flesh, as he himself testifies, John 6: 51; come forth from God, John 16: 30; the first and last, Rev. 1: 11; who humbled himself and did not assume the form of a great emperor or king, but of an humble servant; came down to the level of man; assumed the form of man; obeyed his Father unto death, nay, unto the death of the cross; truly God and man, man and God. God at all times, of God and in God; God's eternal word, who, in due time, according to the promise made to the patriarchs, became a miserable, suffering and mortal man in Mary, the pure virgin, who was of the seed of Abraham, and married to a man of the house of David, named Joseph (upon which Joseph, the evangelists base their genealogy); not divided, as the learned teach, but an undivided, only Christ and Son of God; pure and spotless; planted in her of the seed and Word of his Father, by the Holy Spirit of God; conceived of her through faith; fed and nourished in her virgin body and in due time became man, as Isaac was brought forth of Sarah, and John of Elisabeth; born of her according to the promise; obedient to the law; a light to the world; a preacher of grace; an example of righteousness; and at last, not on account of his own sins, for he knew not sin, but for our sins, he was innocently condemned to death, nailed to the cross, died, buried, arose, and ascended to his Father in heaven, where he dwelt before; and there he is our only and eternal Mediator, Advocate, Intercessor, Expiator and High Priest, with God, his Father, Mark 16; Acts 1; John 6; 16; and thus the Almighty and eternal God, our merciful, heavenly Father, alone receives the honor and praises, through this his Christ, our eternal Messiah, his first and only begotten Son and eternal word; and not through the impure and sinful flesh of Adam, as the learned teach.

Observe, reader, which of these confessions is the most powerful and has the strongest foundation in the Scriptures; and in which of the two the greater love of God, and higher honor to Christ is perceptible. Whether God had taken a man of the seed or flesh of Adam, as the learned teach, or whether he had given his eternal word, power, wisdom, nay, the heart of his own body, (to make a common expression), in death, for us, as all the Scriptures teach us that he did.

O what an inestimable word is this, "God so loved the world that he gave his only begotten Son, &c., John 3: 16. Again, "In this was manifested the love of God towards us, because that God sent his only begotten Son into the world," and again, "Herein is love, not that we loved God, but that he loved us, and sent his Son to be the propitiation for our sins," 1 John 4: 9, 10. Mark, he has sent his *Son* and not a man of the seed of Adam who had no father. Paul says, "He spared not his own Son," Rom. 8: 32, and other explicit sayings.

[☞ Here, in the original works of Menno Simon, follows a brief argument, in reference to the incarnation of our Lord, which the publishers have deemed proper to omit, for the reason that they felt that the book would be more edifying to the general reader without it.]

In the seventh place, he accuses us, saying, "That, secondly, their church has not existed since the time of Abraham; and that she is, therefore, not the true church, is clearly visible from the fact that they, in disobedience to the will of God, refuse the seal of the eternal covenant to the children of the church, which has, since the time of Abraham, been practiced and maintained in the churches."

Answer. Abraham was commanded of God that he should leave the land of his fathers, and of his kinsmen, and that he should leave his father's house, and remove to a land which the Lord would show him. Abraham believed in the Lord, and departed as the Lord had commanded him, Gen. 12: 4—6.

Again, the Lord commanded him that he should offer Isaac, whom he loved, his only begotten of the free woman, as a burnt offering. Abraham believed in God; he was obedient, and prepared to do whatever God commanded, Gen. 22; Rom. 8: 32.

In the same manner he was commanded to circumcise himself, his son Ishmael (Isaac was not yet born) and every man child of his household, and all the males after him, at the eighth day after their birth. Abraham believed in God, and did as the Lord commanded him.

Behold, thus Abraham believed in the Lord; and he counted it to him for righteousness, Gen. 15: 6; Rom. 4: 3. In the same manner God has spoken unto us in the New Testament, not only by angels and prophets, as he did unto Abraham and the patriarchs, but also by his Son, which Son has thus commanded, namely, That the gospel should be preached to all the world; to the Gentiles as well as to the Jews; and whosoever believes it should be baptized, Mark 16; even as it was commanded Abraham to circumcise all males, Gen. 17: 10—13.

This command we have received from the mouth of Christ, therefore we believe in it, even as Abraham believed in his time. We believe it, I say, and do accordingly; we teach those of understanding minds, and baptize those that believe, not in disobedience, as Gellius says, but in obedience to the clear, plain and express ordinance and command of Christ, God's own Son.

Dear reader, observe. The Lord, Christ, thanked his Father, and said, "This is life eternal, that they might know thee, the only true God, and Jesus Christ, whom thou hast sent," John 17: 3. At another place he says, "If ye continue in my word, then are ye my disciples indeed." Mark, he says, "If ye continue," John 8: 31. And, while the merciful and affectionate Father, through his great kindness, has discovered unto us the glorious knowledge, and the wonderful, deep mystery of his beloved Son, and, besides has given us such a fruit through his Spirit, that we dare not willfully and knowingly deviate one hair's breadth from his holy word, ordinance and command, as is testified and shown by our tribulation, misery and deprivation, to the whole world, yet, alas, according to the judgment of Gellius, and of the learned, we are not the believing church, nor the disciples of Christ, as may be seen by their writings.

Behold, thus the righteous judgment of the Almighty and great God is passed upon the wise and learned of this world, that the clear and plain signs, by which the true disciples and church of Christ may, and must be known, are esteemed an abomination and error—that they who have received light from above, through grace, are not accounted christians, by them as has been related.

In the eighth place he accuses us, and says, "They must admit that their church has existed but sixteen or seventeen years, that is, since the time Menno Simon commenced preaching. For they do not want to be counted at all, of the Munsterites, Amsterdamites, and Oude Kloosterites, among whom Menno lost a brother, lest they be called seditious or the seed of sedition."

Answer. We point to Christ Jesus our only and eternal Prophet and Messiah, sent of the Father, who is the only true Cornerstone in Zion, the true Teacher, Law-giver, Commander, Intercessor and Head of his church, together with all his angels, apostles and prophets, through whom he, in former times, spoke, and also his Spirit, word, ordinances, commands, prohibitions, usage and example—and if Gellius, or any other person under the canopy of heaven, be he learned or not, can convince us by divine truth that we teach or maintain any thing contrary to his word and ordinances, then I, for myself, sincerely desire to correct the wrong, and to follow that which is right. This he knows who has purchased me; for I want to be saved. But if they can not do this by the truth, but only in appearance of truth, and thus blaspheme it, as all the perverse do, and have to leave our testimony unbroken, then it is sufficiently proven that our hated, despised, and small church is the true, prophetic, apostolic, and christian church, which was begun with the first righteous who walked according to the will of God; and not with me, as Gellius, alas, maliciously says.

Secondly, I would say, since he has accused us, at different times, of the errors and sedition of the Munsterites, of which we are clear and ever have been, before God and man, therefore, I would beseech him to take a view of his own infant baptist church, of which he is a teacher and head, and see how abominably they have, for years, rebelled amongst each other; how they have afflicted countries and nations with their accursed, ungodly wars, and have given the blood of innumerable human beings, together with their poor souls, to the prince of hell, and have placed them as an offering upon his altar; of which, alas, the learned, by their seditious writings, together with the priests, monks, and preachers, were the principal cause, which is as clear as day to many reasonable persons.

Thirdly, I would say, that in my opinion, he here so indiscreetly alludes to the error of my poor brother, for one of these two reasons: Either, that he thereby would make me suspicioned with the reader, that I, formerly, also was of the same feeling with my brother, or, that he would thereby injure my reputation. For my brother is no longer subject to the punishment of man which he once suffered in the flesh, but alone to the judgment of God. It seems that Gellius can not master this envy and bitterness of his heart; for nobody can be corrected or taught righteousness by such a course.

If he did so for the first reason, namely, to make me suspicioned, then all those who formerly heard me, when yet of the papal church, and all who have ever heard me until this hour, and also my published writings, will be my testimony, that he wrongfully suspicions me; for I never thought of such a thing, much less taught it.

But, if he did so for the second reason, namely, to blemish my reputation, then he should know that I and mine, I trust, never harmed him nor his in the least; and also, that my poor brother, to whom he so cruelly alludes, did no greater wrong than that he erroneously, alas, defended his faith by force of arms, and retaliated the violence committed against him, as all the learned, preachers, priests, monks and all the world do. I presume that I have merited this cruel allusion by nothing less than by my faithful love, because I have, in sincerity of heart, pointed him and all the preachers to the divine truth of the word, and because I have admonished them to their own well-being. And how this allusion, which cannot have been made but in envy, agrees with honorableness, and with the fear of God, all reasonable readers may judge by the Scriptures and the common *rules* of decency. May the kind Lord grant that he may rightly learn the heart from which this unmerited allusion comes, that he may purge it and sincerely repent; this is my revenge and punishment which I invoke on him.

In the ninth place he accuses us, and says, "That we cannot prove that infant baptism is an anti-christian abomination; nor show from the anti-christian ordinance who was the institutor thereof. It can also be proven, he says, that infant baptism was practiced ever since the apostolic times; long before the violence of anti-christ, which was yet unknown, or, at least, very weak, at the time of Augustine."

Answer. We teach and practice such a baptism as was commanded by Jesus Christ, God's own Son; as was taught by his faithful witnesses, the apostles, in clear and explicit terms, and as was transmitted to us by their practice; which is the baptism of the believing, Matt. 28: 19; Mark 16: 15; Acts 2: 38; 8: 36; 10: 48; 16: 33; 19: 5; Rom. 6: 3; Col. 2: 12; 1 Cor. 12: 13; Tit. 3: 5; 1 Pet. 3: 21. Whosoever, now, will teach and practice any other baptism, must show by the Scriptures where it is commanded. But if they can not do this, as is impossible to do, then it is already proven that it is not Christ's baptism, but that of anti-christ, however finely it may be ornamented with learned words; this is too clear to be denied.

But, as to his assertion, that the violence of anti-christ was yet unknown at the time of Augustine, or that it was at least feeble, is too absurd to admit of an answer. Whoever will, may read history, and he will find in great clearness, that anti-christ was, at the time of Augustine, in full honor and that he reigned with his doctrine, in the hearts of men.

In the tenth place he accuses us, and says, "If they

were the true messengers of God, who are to purge and deliver the church of Christ from such abominable, anti-christian errors, they should not be a separated sect; for the prophets, and all the faithful servants of God, by whom God has often purged his church, did not separate themselves from the church and establish a church of their own, but they remained with the church and bestowed their faithful labor upon the church, at the peril of their lives."

Answer. Whatever Gellius does, it seems that he must slander. I say again, take Christ Jesus and all his prophets, apostles, Spirit, word, ordinance and life, and if he can thereby convince us, that in any article we are at fault and contrary to their teaching (his slandering amounts to nothing), or that we do not conform thereto, or, that, in our weakness, we do not agree therewith— I will give up that we are a separated sect. But if he can not do so, as it is impossible for him, and yet calls us a separated sect, he shows thereby that he is no better judge of the church of Christ, than Tertullus was when before Felix, and the Jews at Rome, before Paul.

I would further say, that if he can prove to us that the faithful prophets intermingled with the worshippers of the calf of Jeroboam; with the servants of Baal, and the abominations of Israel, which they so zealously reproved; and remained united with those who disobeyed the law; and, also, that the holy apostles admitted the Pharisees and Scribes, together with other refractory persons, in the communion of their churches—then we admit that he has a good cause to reprove us, and to write as he does. If they did not do so, (and they have not), but, on the contrary, reproved, by the power of the Spirit, the abominations that crept in from time to time, according to the pure word and ordinance of God, at the peril of their lives, then he must admit, that he accuses us without cause, since we do not otherwise than according to the example of the holy apostles and prophets, reprove all false doctrine, unrighteousness and abominations with the pure, apostolic teaching, Spirit, ordinance, and word of our Lord Jesus Christ (without which no true church of Christ can exist); avoid that which is wrong, and, faithfully, in love and purity, teach and promulgate the salutary, christian truth, verbally and by writing, to all the hungry hearts, at the peril of life and possessions.

Lastly, I would say, Since he calls us an excluded sect, because we do not unite with them, why have he and his followers seceded from the Papistic and Lutheran churches? If he answer: Because of their abominations. Then I would again say, that we do it for the same reason. For they forsake the Son of the true and living God, and point us to an earthly creature of the unclean and sinful flesh of Adam as being our Savior; besides, they do not follow the command and ordinance of God in regard to baptism, Holy Supper, and separation. We will never, at any risk, desire to be of one church with those who seek their reconciliation and salvation in the sinful flesh of Adam, who reject God's testimony of his Son and his ordinance; but we desire to be of one church and body with those who give the praise to God through his word; with those who confess the whole Christ as the only, and first begotten Son of God, and who abide unchangeably in his holy ordinances, example, Spirit and word. Let those of understanding minds understand that which the word of the Lord teaches, John 10.

In the eleventh place he accuses us, saying, "From this it follows that the calling of their doctrine is wrong, and that their whole church, service, and walk, cannot aid to salvation, but can only lead to the corruption and destruction of the true churches; and therefore they do not suffer as innocent and harmless christians, but as busy-bodies in other men's matter (he refers to 1 Pet. 4), except that they want to suffer for such a cause of which they must be doubtful themselves, and for which no martyr ever suffered."

Answer. As the Spirit of Christ, and of unfeigned love, accepts all good and godly actions as right and godly, so, also, the spirit of anti-christ, and of bitter envy explains every thing that is right and godly, as wrong and ungodly. For it is testified to with possessions and life that we dare not willfully and knowingly deviate one hair's breadth from the word and example of the Lord, but judge every thing according to the doctrines and usages of the apostles, so far as the Lord gives grace. We, in our weakness, would gladly conform our lives to the requirements of the Scriptures, and gladly seek the praise of God and the salvation of our neighbors, at the peril of possessions and life. Notwithstanding this, he dares write that the calling of our doctrine is wrong, that our walk and actions are not conducive to salvation; that we cause all manner of corruption and disorder, and that we do not suffer as christians, but as evil-doers, who are busybodies in other men's matters. Behold, thus all good offices of the godly, are ever explained to the reverse.

O, reader, beloved reader, that the poor, ignorant world would sincerely accept this, our despised doctrine, which is not of us but of Christ, and that they would faithfully obey it; for then they might change their deadly swords into plow shares and their spears into pruning hooks; they would level their gates and walls, dismiss their executioners and hangmen, for all those who accept our doctrine, in its power, by the grace of God, will not desire to injure any one upon earth, not even their most bitter enemies, much less wrong or harm them by works and actions; for they are the children of the Most High, who sincerely loves all that is good, and, in their weakness, avoid that which is evil, nay, hate it and are inimical thereto. Yet we must hear that we suffer for the sake of wrong-doing, as has been heard.

But in regard to his assertion "that we suffer for a cause of which we must be doubtful ourselves, and for which no martyr ever suffered," he should know that if we at all doubted our faith, we would not so deeply impress the seal with our possessions and blood, as we do; for a house built upon the sand cannot withstand such torrents of water and wind-storms as visit us daily, Matt. 7: 25.

Neither do we suffer on account of an uncertain cause as he says, but for the sake of the name of our Lord Jesus Christ; for the sake of his holy, precious word and ordinances; for the sake of the sincere confession of God and Christ; for the sake of obedience to the Scriptures, for the sake of which all have suffered, from the beginning, who have rightly suffered according to the will of God, as may be plainly and clearly educed from profane and sacred history.

In the twelfth place he accuses us, saying, "That they are the church and Israel, is false, since they stain the true church of Christ by many errors which they daily produce and bring forward as from the abyss of hell; destroy the true sheep of Christ; unreasonably adorn themselves with the sanctity of the church; cause strife and dissension concerning the articles of faith; are carnal, sneak about and preach in secret, and do not agree with the elders of the churches, as said before."

Answer. If the spirit of truth had been the writer in this case, the game would have, doubtlessly, been reversed, and this accusation laid on our opponents; for they still maintain and uphold some gross errors which were formerly brought forward by anti-christ from the abyss of hell (to use his own expression), both by doctrine and force; and thereby cause the godly much affliction and tribulation, cause many a pious child to be deprived of possessions and life, adulterate truth, preach falsehood, are carnally minded, and in fact deny that the man, Christ Jesus, is God's only and first begotten Son, while we, with our small, despised number shun and forsake all the anti-christian abominations and errors, build up the church of Christ and again place it upon the true foundation, again publish and proclaim the clear and plain truth, to many, both verbally and by writing, at the peril of life and the displeasure of the world, confess the whole Christ, as the true, only and first begotten Son of God, as did the angel to Mary, John the Baptist, Peter, Martha, and the Father from high heavens himself, and rightly use his ordinances of baptism, Supper and separation, as all those did from the beginning who rightly knew God, and acted according to his will.

Behold, reader, these are the most important accusations charged against us by him; and that they, for the most part are artful fabrications, false explanations, false suspicions, false accusations and partial charges, whereby he obstructs the course of divine truth, maintains falsehood, insults the godly, and consoles the impenitent in their easy life, is fully proven in this our replication.

In the last place he writes of us, saying, "Experience fully teaches that their teachers and prophets are not the teachers and prophets of God. And that they are not the people of God, I have, perhaps, already proven too powerfully. From which, then, it is clear that our magistracy are right not to let them proceed in their wicked course, but to stop them; and they might, in pastoral and paternal faithfulness or solicitude for the church of Christ, speak and act a little harder towards them, lest the church be quite destroyed. But then we would be their persecutors and blood-hounds."

Answer. Jeremiah, Micah, Elias, Christ Jesus and Paul could not be called the true prophets and servants of God; nor can we. But the great Lord shall, in due time, make it manifest who are the faithful prophets and servants of God and who are not.

Again, to his saying that we are not the people of God, we answer with holy Paul that it is a very small thing that we should be judged by the judgment of men; and especially of such men who are so diametrically opposed to the ordinance, will and word of God, as may be seen in the case of Gellius, by his writing. Yea, kind reader, if he and his like preachers acknowledged us to be the people of God, they would thereby testify that they are are not; something which an ambitious, carnal person, who seeks reputation and fame, never will do.

Again, in regard to his approval of the magistracy hindering our course, which he calls wicked, I would say that the longer and the more he writes, the more indiscreet and offensive he becomes, and the more he manifests his blindness. If he be a preacher called of the Spirit of God, then let him show a single word in all the New Testament, whereby he can prove that Christ or the apostles have ever called on the magistracy to defend and protect the true church against the attack of the wicked, as, alas, he calls us. No, no. Christ Jesus and his powerful word and Holy Spirit is the protector and defender of his church; and not the emperor, king, or any worldly potentate. The kingdom of the Spirit must be protected and defended by the sword of the Spirit, and not by the sword of the world. This is too clear to be controverted, according to the doctrine and example of Christ and his apostles.

I would further say, If the magistracy rightly understood Christ and his kingdom, they would, in my opinion, rather choose death, than to meddle with their worldly power and sword in spiritual matters, which are not subject to the judgment of man, but to the judgment of the great and Almighty God alone. But they are taught by their pastors that they should proscribe, imprison, torture and slay those who are not obedient to their doctrine, as may, alas, be seen in many different cities and countries.

In short, kind reader, if the merciful Lord did not, in his great love, temper the hearts of some of the magistrates, but would let them proceed according to the fiendish instigation and blood-preaching of the learned, no pious person could endure. But some are yet found, who, notwithstanding the crying and writing of the learned, suffer and bear with the miserable, and, for a time, show them mercy, for which we will forever give praise to God, the Most High, and for which we feel very grateful and thankful to such kind and discreet regents.

But, to his writing that in paternal and pastoral solicitude and faithfulness they might use harsher means against us, I would say this: If he had entered in at the right door with Christ, who is the Prince and Head of all true pastors, and if he could taste in his heart, of the friendly and amiable Spirit, nature and disposition of Christ, he would not at all think of such a resolution against the blood of others, much less advocate and invoke it. This I know to a certainty, for the Spirit of Christ is not thus natured, John 10: 2; 1 Pet. 2: 3.

Reader, observe that he, in this instance, does not write plainly that the magistracy should put us to the sword; this e does, because he does not want to be called a blood-hound or persecutor; nevertheless he makes it understood that if they should do so, he would call it a praiseworthy thing. Whoever is not quite destitute of understanding, well understands what he hints at in this instance. O, a doctrine of blood!

O, that he could comprehend the force of the word which the Lord says, "Ye are of your father, the devil, and the lusts of your father ye will do. He was a murderer from the beginning," John 8 : 44. For, since he encourages the blood-thirsty by such writing, and I have myself heard from his own mouth that it is right to persecute and kill one on account of his faith (understand, such faith as they think to be heretical), he, therefore, has thereby burdened the innocent blood on his soul. I say innocent blood, for neither he nor anybody else upon the face of the earth, can, by the grace God, convince us by the force of truth, that we act or do aught against Christ or his word; or that we deserve the punishment and sword of the magistracy.

He should further know that this blood-doctrine of his, is not only contrary to Jesus Christ, God's own Son, and that of his servant, Paul, but also contrary to the doctrine of Luther, see his book, "*De Sublimiori mundi potestate.*" Besides contrary to the doctrine of Hieronimus, Augustine, Theophilactus, Anselmus, Remigius and others, who unanimously agree that the heretics should not be killed, but admonished and convinced, and if they do not repent after admonition, that they should, according to the word of God, be separated from the communion of the church, and shunned.

Besides, this stone thrown by him might light upon his own head. For what greater and more terrible heresy, deception and blasphemy can be imagined than to assert that the pure and holy flesh of Christ, is a ransom for sin, to adulterate so sadly his ordinance and the apostle's clear and plain doctrine of baptism; to neglect Exclusion as required by the word of God; to slander the pious, and to console and encourage the impenitent and carnal minded by garbling the Scriptures, as he has constantly done in his writings from beginning to end.

If we were thus to resolve against those who are wrong in doctrine or faith, as he says we should, then we would have to commence with him, because he is a defender of such great errors, as may be plainly seen by comparing both our writings.

May the merciful, dear Lord permit him and all our opponents to see the right foundation of truth; understanding hearts to understand it rightly, and a willing, free and new mind to believe and follow it with sincerity, Amen.

CONCLUSION.

HERE, dear reader, you have my forced answer to the unseasoned, blasphemous writing of Gellius, which he has published and printed, A. D. 1552, against the unadulterated truth of God and his scattered church; whereby he so lamentably adulterates the salutary doctrine of Christ, and so miserably accuses the innocent, pious hearts, before the whole world, that I could not neglect to do so, by virtue of my office, to which I was unworthily ordained of God, through the pious. I had to controvert him with the word of the Lord, and publish it through the press, as he in the first place has done against us, to the praise of God and his truth, to the justification of the innocent, and to the instruction of the humble.

Whoever seeks and strives after truth may find it; for it has been shown with great clearness; but whoever despises it, does not despise us, but Christ Jesus, who has taught it unto his church through his holy apostles, and who has bequeathed it to us by the testimony of the Scriptures through his Holy Spirit.

I hereby offer myself to you and to the whole world, if these writings are not sufficient for you, to let me have safe conduct to an open and free discussion with Gellius and the learned; and if I cannot maintain my doctrine and faith by virtue of the Scriptures, and if I cannot prove their doctrine and faith as deceiving, then I will not refuse to acknowledge my fault before the whole world, to retract my doctrine and to consign myself and my writings to the fire. But if I can substantiate my doctrine, then I desire and ask nothing more than that they acknowledge their fault, discontinue to deceive the people, repent, teach the truth to the people and flee from falsehood. Herewith I commend you to God; he will guide your feet upon the way of peace, and lead you all in the unadulterated, pure knowledge of his eternal, saving truth, Amen. The grace of our Lord Jesus Christ be with all who sincerely seek and fear him, Amen.

MENNO SIMON.

A VERY HUMBLE SUPPLICATION

OF THE

POOR, DESPISED CHRISTIANS,

TO ALL THE PIOUS, KIND AND REASONABLE MAGISTRATES; CONCERNING THE ABOMINABLE CHARGES, UPBRAIDINGS, BACK-BITINGS AND CLAMOR OF THE LEARNED, WHEREBY THEY ARE, ON EVERY HAND, SLANDERED AND TROUBLED, AS MAY BE HEARD AND SEEN.

BY

MENNO SIMON.

"If a stranger sojourn with thee in your land, ye shall not vex him," "He shall be unto you as one born among you, and thou shalt love him as thyself," Levit. 19 : 33, 34.

ELKHART, INDIANA:
PUBLISHED BY JOHN F. FUNK AND BROTHER.
1871.

To all the pious, kind and reasonable magistrates, lords, princes, regents and commanders, we, poor, despised and scattered children wish eternal happiness, a happy reign, and every blessing of God our heavenly Father, through Jesus Christ our Lord and Savior, Amen.

"Amend your ways and your doings;" "For if ye thoroughly amend your ways and your doings; if ye thoroughly execute judgment between a man and his neighbor; if ye oppress not the stranger, the fatherless, and the widow, and shed not innocent blood in this place, neither walk after other gods to your hurt, then will I cause you to dwell in this place, in the land that I gave to your fathers, for ever and ever," Jer. 7 : 3, 5—7.

"Is it not to deal thy bread to the hungry, and that thou bring the poor that are cast out, to thy house? when thou seest the naked, that thou cover him; and that thou hide not thyself from thine own flesh? Then shall thy light break forth as the morning," Isaiah 58 : 7, 8.

A VERY HUMBLE SUPPLICATION
OF THE POOR, DESPISED CHRISTIANS.

It is well known to many persons, noble, honorable and kind lords, that many are more diligent and zealous to execute the law of Theodosius (although this law was formerly forced from the good emperor by the blood thirsty bishops), the mandate of Charles the fifth, and the decree of the Roman empire, passed against those whom they call anabaptists (issued in our times), than they are, to have the word of God obeyed; never minding that these laws and decrees were made, not on account of baptism itself, but on account of the ungodly errors and abominations which were committed by the doctrine and doings of the baptized; for, if the beforementioned law, mandate and decree were issued on account of baptism, and not on account of the crimes committed at different times by those that were baptized, then were also Christ Jesus, the apostles, Cyprian the Martyr, all the African bishops, the Nicene concilion, and besides the great apostle, Paul, thereby adjudged as public criminals. This is incontrovertible.

Since we are opposed to the Donatists, Circumcelliones, Munsterites, and to the errors, abuses and abominations of all uproarious sects, committed in our times (on account of which, formerly the law of Theodosius was passed, and in our times the imperial mandate and the condemnation of the empire, were issued); also were opposed to them from the beginning of our doctrine and faith; and, since we, before God and his angels, seek nothing upon earth but that we may, humbly and obediently follow the express and clear word, Spirit, example, command, prohibition, usage and ordinance of the Lord, according to which we should judge every thing pertaining to the kingdom and church of Christ, if we would please God, as is testified and shown on every hand, by our tribulation, oppression, misery, anxiety and blood—therefore it is, before God and man, unchristian, nay, manifestly wrong and detestable, to impose the same penalty and punishment on us that is imposed on the Circumcelliones, on account of the baptism, alone, which we have maintained in conformity with the word of God, with the apostolic doctrine and usage, and against all human philosophy and inventions. To treat us, I say, the same as they did the Circumcelliones, who, according to history, committed such detestable, cruel tyrannies, and also the same as they treated the Munsterites, who, contrary to the word of God, to all the evangelical Scriptures, and, also, contrary to sound policy, established a new kingdom, rebellion, polygamy, and such like things; all of which we unflinchingly oppose and reprove, as may be seen by our open actions and doings.

We would, therefore, in the first place, for the sake of Christ humbly beseech your Excellencies, and honorable Wisdom, to consider, in pity and paternal solicitude, how lamentably your miserable subjects, who are created, with you, of one God, and were purchased with the same treasure, and who will at last appear with you before the same judgment, are, without their faults, belied, derided and slandered of the whole world, and especially of the preachers; and how, in many places, they are pitilessly and unmercifully destroyed as the worst criminals upon earth, and are given as food to the fowls of the air; how they are (as our predecessor, Christ), with the criminals, put to the stake and on the wheel; and how many of us, with our wives and little children, are driven from our country and possessions, must roam in foreign countries, naked and destitute; and all this for no other reason, God knows, than that we do not agree with the inordinate way of living of this world, and do not commune with the preachers who oppose the word of the Lord by their doctrine, sacraments and life; that we rightly use baptism and the Lord's Supper, shun all idolatry, self-righteousness and abuses, according to the Scriptures; and that we would gladly, in our weakness, fear the Lord, and follow in righteousness.

We beseech your Excellencies and Honors to consider, in the fear of God, what he requires of you, namely, That you shall rightly judge between man and man, without all respect of persons, and that you shall deliver the oppressed from the hands of the oppressor, The Lord says, "Execute judgment between a man and his neighbor;" "Oppress not the stranger, the fatherless, and the widow, and shed not innocent blood." Consider this; that your despised servants and miserable subjects, who fled from the roaring lions, may, in peace and quiet, serve the Lord, and earn their bread according to the Scriptures, under your paternal care and merciful protection, Jer. 7: 6, 7; 22: 17; Isaiah 59.

Secondly, we desire that your Excellencies and Honors would weigh, with the infallible word of God, with the living example of Christ, and with the pious, unblamable life of the saints, how a true christian should be disposed according to the Scriptures. If reading, singing, water, bread, wine, name and boasting, would constitute true christianity, then there would be a great number of christians. But no, beloved lords, no. The word of God knows no christians but those who are born anew in Christ of the living seed of God, through the pure doctrine of Jesus Christ, which, being preached in the power of the Spirit, is accepted in true faith, by the grace of God and through the operation of the Holy Spirit; who, by virtue of this birth, bury the old sinful life, and arise with Christ in newness of life; who, in their weakness, gladly obey the holy will, word, example, ordinances and commands of the Lord, and who sincerely die unto every thing contrary thereto; who diligently combat all licentious, vain thoughts, and besetting sins which flow from the inherited Adamic nature; and who daily sigh and mourn before the Lord, on account of their human weakness, errors and short comings, with an humble, broken heart; who are prepared to take upon themselves the cross of Christ, and to forsake father, mother, husband, wife, children, possessions and self, for the sake of the testimony of his holy word, when the honor and praise of God require it. In short, they are minded as Christ Jesus; are in Christ and Christ in them; they are led by his Spirit; and they abide immutably in the word of the Lord, through true faith, firm confidence, and a living hope, in all temptations and perils, Rom. 6: 4; Col. 2: 12; Gal. 3: 27; 2 Tim. 3; Matt. 10: 38; Luke 14: 27; Phil. 2: 3.

Inasmuch as it is found in fact that our faithful brethren and sisters in Christ Jesus, the beloved companions in tribulation, and in the kingdom and patience of Jesus Christ, Rev. 1: 9, so sincerely fear and love the Lord, their God, that they would rather give their reputation and money, goods, flesh and blood, and every thing of which human nature is desirous, as a prey to the blood-thirsty, than willfully and knowingly to speak a false word or to act hypocritically, contrary to the word of God; therefore we would beseech your Excellencies and Honors to consider whether they are such pernicious and dangerous people as, alas, they are called by many, and adjudged by all. Yea, dear lords, all their pleasure is in the word of the Lord. Their mouths flow with wisdom, their love smells like the precious ointment on the head of Aaron, their prayers are as the noble incense before the ark of God; their life enlightens as the golden candlesticks in the temple of the Lord, and they seek nothing on this earth, but, that they may serve the whole world unto righteousness, both with body and spirit, and that they may deliver many from the destruction of their souls, and win them unto Christ, through the grace, Spirit, power and word of the Lord; and, that they may thus, with the gracious help of God, improve the short time of their earthly existence, in Christ Jesus, to the praise of God, and to the service of their neighbors, and be eternally saved, Jer. 17: 8; John 1: 8; Ps. 133: 2.

If this is heresy and devilish deceit, as the preachers cry, then the Son of God, Christ Jesus, together with all the prophets, apostles and testimonies of God, were open heretics; and then all the Scriptures which teach nothing but reformation, and point us to Christ, are nothing but deceit; this can not be denied; for they, in their weakness, conform in all their doings, to the word, Spirit, life, command, prohibitions, ordinances and usages of the Lord, as their open actions testify before all the world, Isa. 1: 17; Luke 9: 35; Deut. 18: 15.

Since, then, they and we walk in unity of spirit, and, before God, seek nothing in Christ Jesus, but that we, in our weakness, would gladly follow Christ, as has been said, and we also trust, by the grace of the Lord, that your excellencies will never perceive anything else in your poor servants (we write of those who are united with us in faith and life), therefore, we beseech your Excellencies and Honors, again, for Christ's sake, to discard all prejudice against us miserable orphans, to believe us to be sincere in our profession, and never think that we have any other intentions, if we should become as numerous as the spears of grass upon the fields, or as the sands on the sea shore (something which will never be verified, since the way is narrow and the gate is strait); for Christ, whose name we bear, has taught so with his own mouth; his holy apostles have preached it unto all the world, and have testified it with the holy gospel, and have promulgated it at the peril of life, Matt. 7: 13; Mark 16: 15; Rom. 10: 18.

Thirdly, we desire that your Excellencies and Honors would earnestly consider how the Scriptures are being verified in regard to those who boast themselves christians; how mortally the sword of wrath cuts on every side, and how the hand of divine punishment is laid upon us; great and many are our sins; great and severe is the punishment of the Lord; the fire of wrath is enkindled; unless the Lord in his grace, quench it, it will devour both the green and dry trees, according to the word of the prophet. The prophecy of Christ concerning the latter days; also, of Daniel and of the apostles, are fast fulfilling. The flesh-consuming sword of the Lord glitters everywhere, and his bloody darts are flying in every country; one kingdom has risen against another; one principality against another; one city against another, and one neighbor and friend against another. Some are put to the sword, some are imprisoned; cities and villages are leveled and destroyed; the poor, despised people who are, in part, innocent, are exhausted, profaned, taxed, burned and ruined, without mercy; numbers are rendered adulterers and rogues; one pestilence and epidemic follows another; and one panic another. Storms, hurricanes, misery and tribulation sweep over land and water. In short, the continual severe punishment show that the Lord is angry; notwithstanding the wicked world does not reform, but yet daily degenerates more and more, Deut. 32: 23—35; Ezek. 21: 1—6; Matt. 24: 4.

All of them, in general, boast themselves to be christians, and that they have God's word, although their seeking and doings are quite contrary to Christ and his word. For, if we turn to the magistrates, whom we should reasonably expect to know the ways and judgments of the Lord, as Jeremiah says, we find that they have broken the yoke and rent asunder the bands. If we turn to the preachers, we find there the envy of Cain to all those who fear the Lord, an insatiable love of money, a Balaamitic avarice, a light minded, easy doctrine, idolatrous sacraments, and a lustful, vain, careless life, as may be openly seen. If we turn to the common people, there we find extortion, hoarding, drinking, carousing, lying, cheating, cursing and swearing; some commit adultery and fornication, others are marauders, pillagers, thieves and murderers, nay, they lead, alas, such a life that we may well, in anguish, sigh with Hosea, that "There is no truth, nor mercy, nor knowledge of God in the land; by swearing, and lying, and killing, and stealing, and committing adultery, they break out, and blood toucheth blood," Hosea 4: 1, 2; with Paul, "They are all gone out of the way; they are together become unprofitable," "and the way of peace have they not known," Rom. 3: 12, 17, and, that their sins have reached unto heaven, Rev. 18: 5. O, dear Lord, how long will this dreadfully great blindness, blasphemy, deceit, abomination, bloodthirstiness and recklessness continue!

Noble lords, reform; do works meet for repentance, such as can stand before the Lord; humble yourselves with the king of Nineveh; take off the ungodly, tainted coat of sin; repent in sackcloth and ashes; cry out unto the Lord with a broken heart; rend your hearts and not your garments, as the prophet says; let the pious Josiah be your pattern, who turned himself unto the Lord, with all his heart, and soul and strength, as soon as the law of God was read to him, from the book which was again found, John 3: 7; 2 Kings 22: 11.

Dear lords, seek, fear, and serve God with all your strength; do justice unto the widows, orphans, strangers, and all the forsaken; cleanse your hands of blood, rule your countries in wisdom and peace, and let all your thoughts, words and actions be conformed to the crucified Christ Jesus; follow his footsteps; for "Though your sins be as scarlet they shall be as white as snow; though they be red like crimson, they shall be as wool;" "As I live, saith the Lord God, I have no pleasure in the death of the wicked; but that the wicked turn from his way, and live," Isaiah 1: 18; Ezek. 33: 11; 18: 32.

Inasmuch as those who boast themselves the church, are so estranged from Christ, that they are no more than nominal christians; and, inasmuch as the salt, which is the preachers, has wholly lost its savor, that it does more injury than good, for they flatter more than they reprove, if they can make some earthly gain thereby, and do not seek the praise of the Lord; by which they all, both preacher and hearer, are led upon the broad road which leads to destruction, and since there are, alas, none to stop them in their career, as the prophet complains, and, since we, God knows, would gladly see all men awaken, fear the Lord, sincerely repent and be saved, that thus the fallen city, which is the church, may again be built upon her old foundation, that is, upon the firm foundation of the apostles, and upon the pure doctrine of Christ Jesus, and that such repentance may be verified unto the world by a pious, penitent, christian life, according to the Scriptures; behold, therefore we are so hated of the learned, that by their slanderous crying and clamoring, we are often robbed of our possessions, and our bodies given to the executioner. Some of us, through necessity, are forced to seek refuge in foreign lands, on account of their persecution, as has been said. Therefore we, poor, miserable outcasts, pray your Honors and Excellencies the third time, earnestly to reflect upon this matter, for Christ's sake, and faithfully compare the doings of the preachers and the tenor of the following writing addressed to them, and the matters and things therein set forth, that our apology may be rightly understood, and the truth explained according to the word of the Lord; and that the guilty may no longer be protected in their unrighteousness. Yea, beloved lords, if this was impartially done, in the fear of God, you would soon find, by the grace of God, in great clearness, with whom the truth or falsehood is; and that the doctrine, sacraments and life of the preachers are not in accordance with the Scriptures, but that they are deceitful and contrary to the word of God.

O, beloved, noble lords, we beseech you not to despise our reasonable and christian prayer, but to consider it in love; for it concerns the praise of the Almighty God, his eternal word and truth, and the eternal salvation of all our souls, which are so much desired and so dearly purchased with his precious blood. O, consider the difference, to live eternally with Christ Jesus in the kingdom of heaven, or eternally to die with all the devils in the abyss of hell.

Dear lords, we are in great anxiety and tribulation, and are terrified in two ways. For, if we follow the truth, which we ever intend to do in our weakness, by the grace of God, then we are made a prey to all the world. If we deviate, and again enter into the broad way, from which the merciful Father save us, then we fall into the hands of God and must bear his eternal punishment. The salvation of our souls is worth more than man can comprehend. The sweet-sounding, precious word will once be heard: "Come ye blessed of my Father, inherit the kingdom prepared for you;" and also the fearful word which is threatened to all who are disobedient to Christ, which pierces body and soul, if well realized: "Depart from me, ye cursed, into everlasting fire, prepared for the devil and his angels." Happy they, who are awake at that time, who have their lamps prepared, and saved their wedding garments. Yea, blessed are they who are called to the Lord's Supper.

Dear, noble lords, it is no flattery nor vain display of words; but that which we write, we mean, as our sore persecutions testify.

The merciful, great Lord, Jesus Christ, who is Lord of lords, and King of kings, grant that your Honors may acknowledge the truth, faithfully act in accordance therewith, and that you may rule the people, cities and countries entrusted to your reign, in peace and prosperity, to the praise of your God, and to the salvation of many souls. This is our sincere desire. Amen.

"Blessed are the merciful: for they shall obtain mercy." Be merciful, as your Father is merciful. "Verily, I say unto you, Inasmuch as ye did it not to one of the least of these, ye did it not to me," Matt. 5: 7; 25: 45. The humble and obedient subjects of your Excellencies and Honors, in all things, we can do according to the will of God by his grace.

A LETTER OF CONSOLATION, ADDRESSED TO AN AFFLICTED WIDOW.

Grace and peace be unto you, and kind greeting, sincerely beloved sister in the Lord, whom my soul loves. The merciful Lord having called you to widowhood, my paternal and faithful admonition to you is, as a father to his children, to bear with your lot as becomes holy women, and to serve the Lord, with the pious Hannah in the holy temple, that is, in his church, or a new and upright conscience, with fasting and prayer, night and day; treat, at all times, the needy saints, as the virtuous widow of Sarepta in Zidon, treated the faithful Elijah, at the time of the drouth and panic, when she received him in her house, and fed him with her handful of meal and a little oil; and the meal of the holy, divine word, from the measure of your conscience, and the joyous oil of the Holy Spirit shall not be withheld from you. And, if the new son of your spiritual birth, do sicken a little and lose his breath for a time, through the weakness to which a widow is naturally subject —yet our true Elias, Jesus Christ, will again animate him through his grace, and again restore you to cheerfulness; for, as the Scriptures teach, you receive, love and serve him in his members.

Beloved sister, understand me aright. I speak of the needy saints, and no further. Those who have enough of their own, do not need your aid and services. True christians should not put each other to unnecessary expenses. Faithful sister, walk prudently; fear your God sincerely; crucify your flesh and its lusts; withstand the enemy and all his enchantments; bear every thing piously; do not imprudently cause anybody trouble; diligently attend to your occupation, household and children; carefully shun all unchastity, vain babbling, pomp and splendor; earnestly avoid being led by the temptations of the flesh, that you do not become like the widows who lost their first faith, and followed after the devil, as Paul says; from which may the merciful Father ever save you. Receive in love, this, my brief greeting, written to you in true, paternal affection, and reflect upon it diligently. The saints here, greet you. Greet all pious friends. Pray for me. The eternal, saving power and fruit of the precious blood of Christ, be with my chosen much beloved sister, in eternity, Amen.

Your loving and well wishing brother,

MENNO SIMON.

May 18*th.*

A BRIEF Complaint or Apology

OF THE

DESPISED CHRISTIANS

AND

EXILED STRANGERS,

TO ALL THE THEOLOGIANS AND PREACHERS OF THE GERMAN NATIONS, CONCERNING THE BITTER FALSEHOODS, SLANDERS AND ABUSES WITH WHICH THEY, WITHOUT TRUTH, BURDEN THESE SUFFERING CHRISTIANS AND EXILES, TOGETHER WITH A FRIENDLY REQUEST TO HAVE A FREE DISCUSSION OF THE SCRIPTURES, IN ACCORDANCE WITH THE RULES OF CHRISTIAN LOVE.

BY

MENNO SIMON.

"The servant of the Lord must not strive; but be gentle unto all men, apt to teach, patient," 2 Timothy 2:24.

"For other foundation can no man lay than that is laid, which is Jesus Christ," 1 Corinthians 3:11.

ELKHART, INDIANA:
PUBLISHED BY JOHN F. FUNK AND BROTHER.
1871.

WE, poor and despised christians, who have to endure and suffer so much, on account of the testimony of the word of the Lord, wish to all theologians and preachers of all countries who boast of the gospel, whoever and wherever they are, a new, penitent heart; a true, active faith in Christ Jesus; an unfeigned, ardent love; a salutary doctrine; a sound doctrine according to truth, and a pious, unblamable life, in the fear of the Lord, of God our heavenly Father, in the operation and power of his Holy Spirit, through Christ Jesus, his beloved Son, our Lord and eternal Savior, Amen.

A BRIEF COMPLAINT OR APOLOGY.

It is a fact well known to all, dear men and brethren, how very much the pure, divine truth is disregarded in our Netherlands, caused by the envious crying and clamor of the Papists and Monks; and that the innocent blood is shed like water; on account of which we, miserable children, are forced to flee from the sword of the tyrants, and to seek refuge in foreign lands, with our weak women and little ones, and to earn our bread in tribulation and misery, according to the prophecy of God's word. Many of you, it appears, cry against us, perhaps with good intentions, through misunderstanding, and instigate the magistracy (part of whom should be reasonable and discreet) to persecution, by false accusations, and contrary to all reasonableness and christian love; and you warn every body against us, as being disposed like the Munsterites; that we would take countries and cities, if we had the power; that we are rebels, and use the sword; steal; are polygamists; have our women and possessions in common; will not obey the magistracy; that we murder our children bodily and spiritually; are anabaptists, and profaners of the sacraments, deceivers, and hypocrites; that we boast of being without sin; self-complacent; heaven-stormers; who trust in being saved by our own good works and merits, that we are ungodly heretics and conspirators, new monks, rogues, miscreants and possessed of the devil. In short, we are alas, portrayed by you, in such colors, that all who are not acquainted with our foundation and faith, must shut their mouths and noses at the sight of us, and must have a horror of us; although, before God and his angels, we seek nothing upon earth, but that we, in our weakness, may be cordially united in the Spirit, word and example of the Lord, through his grace, as all the Scriptures teach and imply.

The Almighty, great Lord, who knows all hearts, knows that we are clear, before the Lord and his judgment, of all the beforementioned abominations and slanders, of which we are ever accused by you; also, that we are clear and innocent before all the world. Yea, if any one under the whole canopy of heaven, can prove, by the firm truth, that we, and our adherents, are guilty of one of these capital crimes, or that we were ever guilty thereof, then we will lay our hands upon our mouths and will be bound by life and possessions to the accuser, all our days; with this exception, however, that we do not wish to obey the magistracy, when they command things contrary to the word of God. Is it not a deplorable thing that we are slandered and accused of such inhuman disgraces, while we never even thought of doing them, and much less commit them?

O, dear men and brethren, if you knew what we seek, and how, by the grace of God, we are disposed towards you all, you would not have such hard feelings against us as you have had hitherto; or else you are abandoned to a state of ungodliness and perversity; something which, we trust, is not true of many of you.

Since you are so lamentably mistaken in our intentions, heap one falsehood upon another, and since, alas, we are not allowed at any place, verbally to defend ourselves, therefore we are forced to present a defense in writing, and would humbly pray, and fraternally admonish you all to consider these four things:

First, that you would consider in sincerity of heart, that lies are of the devil, that the lying mouth killeth the soul, that a liar has no part in God's city, that the backbiters are deserving of death, that they shall not abide in the tabernacle of the Lord, and not dwell in his holy hill, Psalm 15: 1.

Secondly, that nearly all of your accusations against us are capital crimes. If we did not fear the Lord, but would strictly ask our rights, according to the law of the world, and retaliate, what would at last become of us; since you publicly accuse us of such accursed abominations, which no man ever can prove against us by the power of the truth.

Thirdly, that this, your action, is directly opposed to all nature, reason, christian love and the word of God; for where was there ever a person of pious nature who did not pity the outcast and sympathize with the afflicted? All the Scriptures teach that ws shall receive, serve, protect and console the afflicted and strangers, in love; and you see plainly how lamentably we poor, pitiable people are every where hated, despised, banished, oppressed, and in some places judged and murdered; yet your hearts are not so much moved as to accost us once with a friendly word, in our sore temptations and tribulations, and to examine our foundation, faith and actions, in a paternal spirit, according to the word of the Lord. But you still cause more enmity against us, that we may find no rest upon earth. You cry, write, falsify, upbraid, clamor, add tribulation to tribulation, drag us to dungeons and prisons, as if you never had read a syllable of the word of the Lord, with understanding minds, nor received a spark of his Holy Spirit. We will leave to your own judgment, if this can be called acting in accordance with unfeigned, christian love, with the doctrine and usage of the apostles, and in accordance with the Spirit, word and example of the Lord.

Say, beloved, where do the Holy Scriptures teach that we shall rule the consciences and faith of others, in the kingdom and church of Christ, by force of the sword, violence, and tyranny of the magistracy— something which is left entirely to the judgment of God? In what instance has Christ and the apostles ever done, recommended or commanded this?

Christ says, "Beware of false prophets;" and Paul commands that we shall shun an heretic after one or two admonitions; John teaches that we shall not greet nor receive the transgressor into our houses, who does not bring the doctrine of Christ, Matt. 7: 15; Tit. 3: 10; 2 John 1: 9; they say not: Down with the heretics, accuse them before the magistrates, imprison, exile and cast them into the fire or water, as the Romans have done for many years, and as many of you would do, you who pretend to preach the word of God.

Fourthly, we would sincerely pray you, for Christ's sake, to consider and examine whether your spirit accords with the Lord's Spirit, and whether your faith accords with his holy word; whether the Spirit of the Lord, and the love of your neighbor constrain you to the service, or whether it is the love of gain and the temporary sustenance of your bodies; whether you preach the pure word of God in sincerity of heart, use his sacraments aright, and whether you lead a pious and unblamable life, as the Scriptures teach; and whether you shun open transgressors, the pompous, drunkards, misers, extortioners, liars, deceivers, contenders, adulterers, fornicators, swearers and unrighteous, and separate them from the communion, without respect to persons, according to the word of the Lord. For we see such living and acting, O, Lord, as if neither prophet, apostle, Christ, nor the word of God was ever upon earth. Nevertheless you men, want to be called the holy christian church, and preachers of sound doctrine, as if Christ did not require more of his church than mere reading, singing, crying, infant baptism, breaking of bread, and calling themselves after his name; and, as if spirit, knowledge, faith, love, repentance, righteousness, works, power and truth were no longer necessary.

No, no, dear men, no. This is required of the church of Christ, to preach his unadulterated word in the power of the Spirit, to believe it sincerely, and to obey it in every particular; to use his holy sacraments, such as baptism and the Holy Supper, according to his own command and ordinance; to seek, fear, love and serve God sincerely; to be born of God; to love, serve, console, help and protect his neighbor; to shun all false doctrines and works of darkness; to die unto carnal lusts, which are contrary to the word of God; to forsake ourselves and the world; to lead a pious, peaceable, chaste, sober and humble life, in righteousnsss, according to the truth. In short, to be of one mind with Christ Jesus. For it is incontrovertible, that where these are, there are also the kingdom and church of Christ. But the deceivers, hateful, liars, slanderers, backbiters, rebellious, bloodthirsty, avaricious, unmerciful, cruel, proud and impenitent, are of the wicked one. The Scriptures teach that their part shall be weeping and gnashing of teeth, eternal death and everlasting fire, prepared for the devil and his angels, John 15: 12; 3: 5; Mark 7: 15; Tit. 3: 5; 2 John 9; Matt. 16: 23; 13: 42.

O men and brethren, if you would take to heart this brief reference, in the sincere fear of God, and would reflect thereon, and judge according to the Spirit of the Lord, you would doubtless find such a great beam in your own eye, that you would not regard the small splinter which may, perhaps, be in your brother's eye (for we are all of Adam's seed). But to know ourselves is understanding, and to conform ourselves in all things to the Lord's word, is a salutary understanding and wisdom.

Inasmuch as we are thus indiscreetly and falsely accused by you, and as you boast to be servants of God who teach his word and works, therefore we would pray you all, for the sake of the blood of Christ, with which we are besprinkled, to consider how you treat us, poor, afflicted ones, that you no more sin by such open falsehoods and tyrannies, as you have hitherto done; but that you may show such a paternal disposition as conforms to the divine operation, and to the christian name; for we testify before him who knows our hearts, before you, and before the whole world, verbally and by writing, by our possessions, and blood, life and death, that we, in our weakness, are prepared and willing to obey the word and will of God, from the innermost of our souls; and we shall ever be prepared as we ever have been from the commencement of our faith and actions, willingly to hear and obey any one who can instruct us in a more powerful spirit and truth, and who can point out a more godly life; but if he can not instruct us for the better, then we ask again, for Christ's sake, to leave us undisturbed in the truth, and not persecute and afflict the pious who walk in it. We hereby give notice to you all, that we are desirous to meet, at any acceptable time and place, with one or two of our members (no matter whether teachers or not), with you before a full assembly, or before twenty or thirty reasonable and pious witnesses, just as you choose, to discuss the following points (for herein we differ), according to the Spirit, word, life, example, command, prohibition, usage and ordinance of God, in sincerity of heart, namely:

Of the right evangelical preachers and teachers—how they should, according to the word of God, be minded and fitted, before they can rightly preach the word of God and serve his sacraments.

Of the doctrine of Christ and his apostles—that it does not change, but must remain unchanged until his coming again.

That Christ is a perfect teacher, and that his offer is a perfect offering.

Of true regeneration; what it is, of whom it is, and what are its natural fruits and disposition.

Of true evangelical faith and love; their proper qualities, power and operation.

Of God's commandments and their keeping.

Of true christian baptism—how it was commanded of the Lord, and how taught and practiced by the apostles.

Of the Lord's Holy Supper—what it is—by whom it was instituted and ordained, and what it implies and represents.

Of the true apostolic Ban or Separation—its proper fruits and usefulness.

Of the pious christian life which is of God.

If you have anything else to discuss, you may present it, and have it criticized according to the word of God.

Behold, dear men and brethren, this is what we would gladly have you accept, if it can be obtained in sincerity of heart, under safe conduct, without any trickery and strategy, according to the rules of christian love, and the word of God, as Origen, Augustin, Hilarius and others have done in their times, with those who were suspected in their doctrine. You can not think hard of us for asking safe conduct and freedom, for it is evident that they cry vindictively and madly against us, on every side.

If you are servants of Christ, and seek the

praise of the Lord and the salvation of your brethren, as Isaiah, Jeremiah, Peter and Paul, did in their times, then you would rejoice; praise the Lord; again restore our respect with the people; and henceforth leave off such slanderous language, as has been mentioned; you would reform your life, accept, and advise and aid in the offered discussion, in christian faith; because we do not propose to have the discussion judged according to human philosophy, wisdom and ideas, as some do, but according to Christ's own Spirit, word, command, prohibition, ordinance, usage and example. But, in case you reject and refuse it, and still continue in your bitterness, falsehoods, slanders, upbraiding, backbiting, and disgrace as you have hitherto done, then we poor, miserable souls, must leave it to the Lord, as has been hitherto done; and possess our souls in patience; suffer ourselves to be punished, and console ourselves with this saying, "Blessed are ye, when men shall revile you, and persecute you, and shall say all manner of evil against you falsely, for my sake. Rejoice, and be exceeding glad; for great is your reward in heaven," Matt. 5: 11, 12. But you must fill the measure of your fathers, and make youselves manifest, that you seek not the sheep, but merely their milk, wool and fat, Ezek. 34: 3. There are but two ways open, namely, You must either cease your false accusations, and slandering, and enter into a discussion with us, or you must acknowledge that you are not the true teachers, and let go your gospel fame and *christian* name.

We would herewith commend you all to the Lord, and desire to say that none should take offense at this; for we have done so for the advancement of the holy word, and for the defense of our respectability, and we would reiterate, that we are, at all times, prepared, and willing for the discussion, on the conditions mentioned.

May the merciful Lord grant you all a sincere, pious heart to love the saving truth of Christ, and to walk in accordance therewith, to the praise of God, and to the salvation of your souls. Amen.

DESCRIPTION OF A TRUE PREACHER.

"A bishop, then, must be blameless, the husband of one wife, vigilant, sober, of good behavior, given to hospitality, apt to teach." He "must be blameless, as the steward of God; not selfwilled, not soon angry, not given to wine, no striker, not given to filthy lucre. But a lover of hospitality, a lover of good men, sober, just, holy, temperate; holding fast the faithful word, as he hath been taught, that he may be able by sound doctrine, both to exhort, and to convince the gainsayers," 1 Tim. 3: 2; Titus 1: 7—9.

By us despised strangers and scattered christians, for the sake of God's word and its testimony. A. D. 1552.

A TREATISE ON,

AND

Scriptural Explanation

OF

EXCOMMUNICATION,

FOR THE BENEFIT OF ALL PIOUS AND GOD FEARING CHILDREN.

BY

MENNO SIMON.

"Evil men understand not judgment; but they that seek the Lord understand all things," Prov. 28 : 5.

"Whoso walketh uprightly shall be saved; but he that is perverse in his ways shall fall at once," Prov. 28 : 18.

"For other foundation can no man lay than that is laid, which is Jesus Christ," 1 Corinthians 3 : 11.

ELKHART, INDIANA:
PUBLISHED BY JOHN F. FUNK AND BROTHER.
1871.

A SCRIPTURAL EXPLANATION
OF EXCOMMUNICATION.

Menno Simon wishes to all fellow-believers, brethren and sisters in Christ Jesus, the grace and peace of God our heavenly Father, through Christ Jesus his beloved Son, our Lord, who loved us and has cleansed us of our sins in his blood. To him be the honor, praise, kingdom, power, and glory, for ever and ever, Amen.

Dear brethren, since I find that, for some time, much strife has been occasioned in regard to the ban, and this so violently and indiscreetly, therefore, I fear brotherly love, christian peace and unity, with some, are more diminished than augmented, as was the case in olden times; and it appears that some, through ambition and self-conceit, are desirous of such corrupting disputation, that they entertain the opinion, in this matter that not the banned ones themselves should be shunned, but only their false doctrine and offensive life, not observing that they have already become entangled in false doctrine; for thereby they nullify the plain ordinance of Christ, "Let him be unto thee as a heathen man and a publican," and also the plain words of the holy apostles, Matt. 18: 17; Rom. 16: 16; 2 Thess. 3: 14; Tit. 3: 10.

Others think that the ban should not be practiced, further than that which pertains to the evangelical usages, as the breaking of bread and the kiss of peace; and garble the plain sayings of the Scriptures, to make their opinions good, namely: Do not keep company with such; with such not eat; "Let him be unto thee as a heathen man and a publican," and other like sayings, 1 Cor. 5: 10; Matt. 18: 17.

Again, there are some who acknowledge the ordinance of Christ, and the doctrine of the holy apostles, in regard to excommunication, as right and just, yet they do not observe it; some, I presume, from being lukewarm, some from motives of carnal love and favor of the apostates, and others on account of being neighbors, or relatives, or perhaps on account of former attachments and favors.

And, since the express ordinance of Christ and his holy apostles, in regard to excommunication, is lamentably weakened, obscured and garbled, by the first mentioned, and visibly transgressed and dishonored by the latter, and thus the door is opened wide to all corruption, and since they thus act against *all* love; First, against the love of God and Christ, for they thereby despise and disobey his holy word, will and ordinance; Secondly, against brotherly love: For by such perverseness and disesteem, they offend and afflict their brethren; Thirdly, against the love of their own souls: For, thereby, they willfully expose themselves to the danger of being corrupted; Fourthly, against the love of those deserving the ban: For they despise the advice of the Holy Spirit, and do not seek to shame them unto repentance; Fifthly, also against common love: For, by communing with the apostates, they make the worldlings suspicious

EXCOMMUNICATION.

that we are one and the same people with the apostates and perverse; and, since the precious word of God and his holy church, is thus blasphemed and profaned by many, on account of their recklessness and disobedience—therefore, in a christian spirit and brotherly love (of which God is my witness), I have endeavored to explain, for the benefit of my beloved brethren and fellow believers in Christ Jesus, the proper grounds of the ban, according to divine truth; how the ban is instituted of Christ; how it was taught and explained by his holy apostles, and what its fruits and benefits are. But this explanation I will leave to the judgment of those who seek and fear God with all their hearts, and who are enlightened and taught by the Spirit of God. Whoever seeks God and the good of his neighbor, will acknowledge that this explanation is in accordance with the foundation, meaning, word and will of God.

Dearly beloved brethren and sisters in Christ Jesus, I, your poor, unworthy servant and co-partner in the faith and tribulation of Christ, trust and pray, for the sake of the precious blood of my Lord Jesus Christ, and, for the sake of love to all, that none willfully, and knowingly contend against Christ Jesus, and against his holy word; nor against his own conscience, for the sake of maintaining his error, so that he may avoid the disapprobation and shame of the world.

I trust that they, as christians, grudge not one against another, but that they seek to win again to Christ their erring brethren. In the same manner, that if the God fearing errs, he is anxious to return again to the right way; if he falls, he is desirous to rise, and if wounded he would be again healed, James 5:19; and if, by the grace of God, he be again delivered from his error and misunderstanding, through the word of the Lord, he is not ashamed, but is exceedingly glad, and praises and thanks his God that he is led from the crooked to the right way, and from his error to a true and sound understanding. He earnestly seeks to deliver and disentangle those whom he has formerly led astray and deceived by his false doctrine and misunderstanding; for true love does not seek *self*, but God and her neighbor. Whosoever has ears to hear, and a mind to understand, let him hear and understand what the word of the Lord teaches us in respect to excommunication, in great clearness.

Christ Jesus says, "Moreover if thy brother shall trespass against thee, go and tell him his fault between thee and him alone; if he shall hear thee, thou hast gained thy brother; but if he will not hear thee, then take with thee one or two more, that in the mouth of two or three witnesses every word may be established. And if he shall neglect to hear them, tell it unto the church; but if he neglect to hear the church, let him be unto thee as a heathen man and a publican. Verily I say unto you, Whatsoever ye shall bind on earth shall be bound in heaven; and whatsoever ye shall loose on earth, shall be loosed in heaven," Matt. 18: 15—18.

Here, faithful brethren, stands the firm foundation of God, as an immovable rock or mountain, at which all will be wounded and hurt, who try to overturn and nullify it, namely: That we shall shun and avoid the apostates, if they take no heed to all the brotherly services and admonitions which have, in faithfulness of heart, been rendered unto them, according to the doctrine of Christ, and the dictates of pure love, if they obstinately continue in their errors, as the Jews shunned and avoided the heathen and publicans, at the time of Christ.

In the first place, the Jews did not admit the uncircumcised heathen to their passover, by command of the Lord, through Moses; nor to their divine service, as appears from the acts of the apostles, for they were strangers to the citizenship of Israel, and Israel was alone the church.

In the second place, they so avoided daily intercourse with them, that they considered it as impure for them to enter their houses, or to eat and drink with them. This also applied to the publicans. As the Jews, then, did not admit such heathen and publicans to their worship, nor to their daily intercourse, but shunned and avoided them, so also, would Christ have us shun and avoid an apostate, unrepenting brother, as was said above. And that this is the proper

EXCOMMUNICATION.

and natural foundation of these words of Christ, as well explained by holy Paul, 1 Cor. 2, of which more will be heard hereafter.

Behold, brethren in the Lord, all who would rightly understand the meaning of the words of Christ, above cited, should know that Christ does not point to the jewish custom, in regard to the heathen and publicans in the time of Moses and of the prophets, but to the custom of his own times; and, he should first, make a distinction between the heathen and publicans, and not consider them as one people; and then well consider, and judge according to the Scriptures, how those two classes were dealt with at the time of Moses and the prophets, before the scepter was taken from them, and they were placed under the yoke of the Romans.

In the first place, it is incontrovertible, that the heathen were not of the seed of Abraham, Isaac and Jacob; that they were uncircumcised, without God and religion, and without law, nay, a people that was no people, as Moses says, Deut. 32: 27. Thus it is, in the second place, incontrovertible that the publicans and sinners were of the Jews. For Luke says, That the publicans came to John, that they might be baptized. Again, That the publicans justified God, and that they were baptized with the baptism of John. Again, All the publicans and sinners came to Jesus to hear him, but the heathen did not come to John and to Christ. Therefore it is manifest that the publicans and sinners were not heathen, but Jews. It is also apparent from the case of the sinful woman and from the publican, Matthew, who was chosen an apostle of the Lord; and no apostles were chosen from the heathen. This is manifestly true, Eph. 2 : 12 ; Luke 3: 2; 7: 29; 15 : 1.

Inasmuch as the Gentiles and Publicans were two distinct people as has been said, and we should turn to the law to ascertain the freedom of the Jews, in regard to the Gentiles, then we must also, in the same manner, ascertain the action of the Jews in regard to the Publicans, after the law; for the one word is as valid as the other, because they are both produced and attested by the mouth of the eternal Wisdom.

We are aware, beloved brethren, that Moses, in his law, allowed a great deal of liberty to the outward Israel; to have intercourse with the Gentile nations, as in buying, trading and usury. But, besides, we also know, that he rigorously judges the willful and open transgressors, by the testimony of two or three witnesses, unto death, without mercy, according to his law, Deut. 17: 6; 2 Cor. 13: 1. If we were to understand the beforementioned words of Christ, Matt. 18, as being of the same nature and rigor as those of the law of Moses, then it would follow, first, from the word *heathen* that we were at liberty to deal with the apostates, as far as regards daily intercourse, as Israel was at liberty to deal with the heathen. And secondly, from the word *publican* it would follow that we should stone and kill the apostates when their apostasy was established by two or three witnesses. But it would not be proper to take too much liberty with them, and to put them to death. Taking life, is also quite inconsistent with the nature and doctrine of Christ, "For the Son of man is not come to destroy men's lives, but to save them," Luke 9: 56.

Let every one take heed; for if he take the word *heathen* alone, and judge that according to the law of Moses, and except the word *publican*, then he does not wrong man, but the Son of God, and disgracefully annuls his holy word and truth. For he says not, Let him be unto thee as a heathen, but "as a heathen man and a publican." Christ says, "Heaven and earth shall pass away, but my words shall not pass away." Therefore it is very advisable not to break the word of Christ Jesus; but to set aside human understanding; to acknowledge the truth; give heed to Christ Jesus; and believe and obey him; for then he will be likened unto the wise builder; if not, his house will fall, and "great will be the fall thereof."

Further, most beloved brethren, we understand that there are some who comprehend these words of Christ, so that we are not bound to shun an apostate and impenitent brother, further than the Gentiles now shun the Gentiles, or fornicators shun adulturers and drunkards, whom they, perhaps, call the publicans. Such, I would earnestly beseech and exhort, first, to consider this matter well, before they accept, believe and teach it as a true foundation; to consider to what class of people Christ was sent from the beginning, and among what class he commenced building and establishing his church. This, Christ sufficiently explains, saying, "I am not sent, but unto the lost sheep of the house of Israel," Matt. 15: 24. Paul, also says, "Now I say that Christ was a minister of the circumcision for the truth of God, to confirm the promises made unto the fathers." Since he then, was, from the beginning, sent unto the Jews, and preached unto them and taught them, and not to the heathen, therefore these words of Christ should not be understood as meaning that we should deal with an apostate as the believing heathen now deal with an unbelieving heathen, but to deal with them as the literal Jews dealt with them at the time of Christ. For Christ, I say, did not preach unto the heathen, but unto the Jews; and therefore he did not point them, by these words, but to the Jewish ban, namely, how they shunned the heathen and open sinners in his times.

In the second place, I pray that every God-fearing heart consider what the word *Gentile* implies; and see if not all fornicators, adulterers, avaricious, unbelievers, perjurers, idolators, murderers and drunkards are included in the word Gentile. Yea, Paul says that they are without Christ, have no God, are dead in sins, and that they are children of wrath, Eph. 2: 11. Since, then, all sinners and Gentiles are expressed in the word "Gentile," for the Gentiles who have not Christ, are also sinners, and without grace, and since Christ here speaks as well of open sinners, as of Gentiles, and, moreover, as every word of Christ has its full weight and measure—therefore, the word of Christ can not be explained as meaning that we should deal with an apostate brother as we would with other Gentiles, who never received nor acknowled the word of the Lord.

In the third place, I hope that no true brother, who is called after the name of the Lord, will knowingly and willfully adulterate the word of the Lord, but that he will give it its due praise and honor, and acknowledge that these publicans and sinners, of whom the evangelists speak, were not of the Gentiles, but of the Jews, as is apparent from Matt. 9: 10; Mark 2: 17. Since it is incontrovertible that the beforementioned publicans and sinners were of the Jews, and were adjudged to death, according to the law; and since Christ points us as well to the publicans, as to the Gentiles, therefore it must follow that it should not be explained as having reference to the times when Israel yet exercised their liberties with the heathen, which liberties were allowed to them, by Moses, in his law; for at that time the transgressors, on proof, were adjudged unto death, according to the law. It would also follow that the lives of the apostates, on proof, should be taken at our hands. O, no, for we know that such a bloody ban is an abomination before God, neither is it known to christians, much less practiced.

If any one should assert that it applies to the present time, that is, of treating an apostate as we now treat a Gentile, and not to the time of Christ, as the Jews then treated a Gentile, he must also re-establish the Jewish people with their law and religion, and their open transgressors, which is impossible. This every one must confess.

Since the word *Gentile* can not be understood as appplicable to the time when the Gentiles were not yet so strictly shunned by the Israelites, for then we should have to adjudge the apostates unto death, according to the word "manifest transgressors;" nor as applicable to the present time, for now we have not the Jewish transgressors—therefore no one can successfully contradict, according to God's truth, otherwise than that it applies to the time of Christ, at which time they did not put transgressors to death, but separated and avoided both the publicans and heathen alike, by means of the same ban.

Having sufficiently proven to the pious and God fearing, by the above mentioned reasons, that Christ spoke those words as applying to his own times, and to no other, we will now show in plain language, first, the proper cause why they so scrupulously avoided the heathen, and, secondly, why they shunned the open transgressors, and did not inflict capital punishment upon them.

It is well known to all readers of the Bible, that the Lord God faithfully warned Israel that they should not make an alliance, nor terms of friendship, with the Canaanites, Hittites, and others; nor to intermarry with them, lest they should be led astray by them, and follow strange Gods, Deut. 7. Joshua says, "Take good heed therefore, unto yourselves, that ye love the Lord your God. Else, if ye do in any wise go back, and cleave unto the remnant of these nations, even these that remain among you, and shall make marriages with them, and go in unto them, and they to you; know for a certainty that the Lord your God will no more drive out any of these nations from before you; but they shall be snares and traps unto you, and scourges in your sides, and thorns in your eyes, until ye perish from off this good land which the Lord your God hath given you," Josh. 23: 11, 13.

Israel, not taking to heart this paternal warning of God, but, contrary thereto, befriended and intermingled with these strange nations, the menace of the Lord God threatened through his faithful servants, Moses and Joshua, was verified. They became quite degenerated by the strange women and idols, with which they intermingled, and were severely scourged and punished of the Lord. Yea, so that the talented Solomon, whose wisdom was far-famed, was so enchanted by the heathen women, that he became unfaithful to the Lord, his God, (who twice appeared unto him), and inclined his heart to strange gods. I think, beloved brethren, this is the just recompense of those who despise the counsel of the Lord.

And they, deceived by the artfulness of the heathen, often sinned against their God, and being, therefore, so often chastised of God, with his just punishment, they, at last, took to heart the warning of God, given through Moses and Joshua, more than they had formerly done; they quit their intercourse with the heathen, altogether, so that they, as appears, also abandoned some liberties, which Moses had allowed them. Yea, so that they considered it as improper to enter into their houses, or to eat with them, as may be plainly observed. And this, for the purpose that they should not, as formerly, be led astray, and turned away from their God. For this reason, the Jews so entirely avoided intercourse with the heathen. If this reason was of weight, every theologian may judge and weigh with the words of God, Num. 33: 35; Judges 3: 13; 1 Kings 11: 1; 3: 12; 9: 2.

Again, the reason why they shunned the public sinners, and did not punish them with death, is this: Because the prophecy of the patriarch Jacob was now verified—that the royal scepter, taken from Judah by Pompey, the great, was now in the hands of the Romans, and that they had officers of their own in Judea, who obeyed their superior; and therefore, the Jews did not punish with death, according to their law, those who willfully transgressed; for they were, at that time, subject to the scepter of the Romans. That this is the truth, the Jews declared before Pilate, when they said, "It is not lawful for us to put any man to death." According to the law they were permitted; nay, it was strictly commanded them; but the lost scepter, now, made it unlawful; for the Roman servants, Herod, Pilate, &c., who, at that time, swayed the scepter in behalf of the Romans, did not want to judge according to the law of the Jews, but according to the rights and statutes of the Romans, in whose name they ruled, and to whom they were bound by oath. When any Jew tresspassed the law of Moses, and not the Roman morals, the beforementioned functionaries did not inflict capital punishment, because the law of Moses required it. And since the Jews were not allowed to punish him according to the law, for the above mentioned reasons, they separated him from their communion, and excommunicated him from their synagogue and shunned him.

Behold, faithful brethren, for the beforementioned reasons, the Jews, at the time of Christ, shunned both the heathen and the jewish publicans. They shunned the heathen, lest they should be led astray and deceived; but the publicans, because, according to the law, were deserving of death, Gen. 49: 10, and yet were not allowed to kill and destroy them on account of the Roman dominion.

Perhaps some will ask, Why then, did they scourge the apostles? Stone Stephen? and why were many saints put to death by Saul? Why was their community destroyed, since they were not allowed capital punishment?

To this I answer: That all this did not transpire without the consent of the Romans, for they, themselves, confessed before Pilate, saying, "It is not lawful for us to put any man to death," John 18: 31. The stoning of Stephen was not done lawfully, but merely in a riot, as Luke declares, saying, *Exclamantes autem voce magna, continuerunt aures suas, and impetum fecerunt unanimiter in eum;* and this the Zurichans have also thus translated into the German: "They cried with a loud voice, and stopped their ears and ran upon him with one accord," as they also intended to do with Christ, and also with Paul, Acts 7: 57; 10: 31; 21: 30; 23: 12; 26: 10; Luke 4: 29. Again, that Saul or Paul destroyed the church, and put to death many of the saints, as he related before Agrippa, we may be sure that he did not do so without the consent of the magistracy; for it is manifest and incontrovertible, that the scepter did not allow them to put any one to death, and, for this reason they said, "It is not lawful for us to put any man to death;" the scepter was taken from them, and came into the hands of the Romans, as has been explained above. If they had been allowed to practice their own law of blood, they would not have delivered Christ unto Pilate; Lucius would not have taken Paul from the tumultuous Jews; Herod would not have imprisoned Peter, nor killed John the baptist, and James; for this would not do, in the worldly adjudication, for one to grasp the jurisdiction of another; such a policy would, doubtlessly, soon fail, Acts 21: 27—40; 24: 7.

We are well aware, beloved brethren, that there are some who call this Jewish shunning, or ban, to which Christ has directed us, a pharisaic leaven, and frankly say, We do not want to be pointed to a leaven, without the Scriptures. Whosoever these may be, we pray them for the Lord's sake, first, to consider well what they say; for, in my opinion, they do not understand their own words. Does not Moses say, "Whosoever does not hearken unto my (God's) words, which he shall speak in my name, I will require it of him," Deut. 18: 19. Does not Jeremiah say, That he "shall execute judgment and justice in the earth?" Does not the Father from high heaven, say, "This is my beloved Son in whom I am well pleased; hear ye him?" Does not Paul say, "In whom (Christ) are hid all the treasures of wisdom and knowledge?" Jer. 23: 5; Matt. 17: 5; Col. 2: 3. I am sure that the word and teaching of Christ is Scripture enough for all the pious. He it is, I say, and not I, who points his believers to the use of the ban. *Tu quis es, qui ex adverso respondes Deo?* That is, Who art thou that wouldst answer God with perverseness?

If there be any brother under the whole canopy of heaven, who can show, by the divine truth, that these words of Christ apply to any other time than to the time of Christ, without violating the Scriptures, then I will gladly hear him, and open my ears to the truth; for I desire not to contend against the truth, which is my testimony, but I desire to uphold it. For, for the sake of truth, I have had to hear and suffer much, these many years; and am yet prepared unto death, by the grace of the Lord, to testify to the truth. But I know, and am convinced, that it can not apply to any other time, without violating the word and Scriptures of Christ, as we have sufficiently shown and proven, to the reader, above, by abundance of reasons and Scriptures.

Secondly, I desire, for God's sake, that my beloved brethren will weigh with the balance of the Scriptures, what leaven is, and what the Scriptures mean by it, before they call this beforementioned ban, to which Christ directs us, a pharisaic leaven. It implies, first, the word and its power, or rather, faith and its power. Secondly, it signifies a corrupting, ungodly being or man. Thirdly, a deceiving, leavened, corrupting doctrine. If the Jewish ban and shunning, to which Christ points us, was a leaven, as some mistakenly assert, then they must show, by virtue of the Scriptures, what leavening and corruption it has caused in the pure word, and in the hearts of the

Jews; for, although God, the Lord permitted some liberties to Israel, through Moses, in their temporal transactions, as said at the beginning, yet he did not expressly command that they should deal with the heathen, but rather warned the Jews against them. They now scrupulously observed the faithful warning of God, being taught them through many perils, and for that reason, probably, they did not make use of the privileges granted them, in regard to dealing with them, lest, by these means, they should be ensnared and corrupted in their hearts by the heathen. Let the spiritual judge, now, whether it can be called leaven, by the Scriptures, since they did not neglect the law and command of God thereby, but, in fact, left it unchanged and whole and were thus shielded against the corrupter.

Sincerely beloved brethren, if we are to esteem as a leaven, this oft mentioned jewish ban, to which Christ directs us, because they, for their consciences' sake, abandoned some of these liberties (for liberties are of a nature that we can enjoy them, or not, at our option; else they would not be liberties), not contrary to the law, but rather in conformity with the faithful warning, advice and admonition of God, contained in the law—then the holy prophet Jeremiah might, for good reasons, have reproved the Rechabites as leaven, because they, on account of the command of their father Jonadab, would not drink wine, plant vineyards, sow the soil, nor build houses, although all this was free to them, according to the law of God; for to them, with Israel, were the possession of the land, and the other blessings promised, Jer. 35: 14. O, no, the Lord did not reckon it as leaven unto them, but it was accounted to their honor to have honored the command of their father, and thereby they obtained the promise of the Lord.

I would further say, that if it is to be called leaven, if we do not partake of our freedom for conscience' sake, or for the sake of the brethren—then freedom cannot be called freedom, and Paul must have been an impure leaven to have taught that we should, if necessary, deny ourselves the liberty, for the sake of the brethren, Rom. 14: 14; 1 Cor. 8: 13; 9: 14; 10: 23.

From all this, it is evident, according to my understanding of the word of the Lord, that it is a frightful blasphemy, unknown to a God-fearing christian, thus to undertake to master and instruct Christ, the eternal Wisdom of God, how he should teach us, and what he should command us; and to call that which he commands us, leaven, although it is a strong and consolatory shield against corruption and deceit; and therefore, not contrary to the law, but in conformity therewith; of this we are convinced, for if it were leaven, contrary to the law, as some say it is, then Christ Jesus would, by no means have approved of it, commanded it and said, "Let him be unto thee as a heathen man and a publican," since he, in other places, has diligently warned his followers against the leaven.

Some, perhaps, will contradict me by saying that the shunning of the heathen by the Jews, that is, not to eat with them, when the victuals were clean, was openly contrary to the express command of the law. For Moses had commanded Israel that they should keep the feast of the weeks, and the feast of the tabernacles, unto the Lord their God, with a tribute of free-will offering of their hands, which they should give unto the Lord, their God, &c., and that they should rejoice before the Lord, their God, they, and their sons, and their daughters, and their man-servants, and their maid-servants, and the Levite that was within their gates, and the stranger, and the fatherless, and the widow, that were among them. To such, I would reply, that these strangers also had to keep the Sabbath; to enjoy the tenths of the third year, the first fruits of the land, the gleanings of the field, olive trees and vineyards with the Levites, the widows and orphans.

The stranger also had, with Israel, an offering for their sins of ignorance; also, the same punishment with Israel; they had to hear the reading of the law every seventh year, in the solemnity of the year of release. Therefore, it follows from these and other like Scriptures, that these beforementioned strangers were citizens among the Israelites, and not uncircumcised heathen. For they were already among the Israelites at the time they yet journeyed in the wilderness.

Moses says, "Ye stand this day, all of you, before the Lord your God; your captains of your tribes, your elders, and your officers, with all the men of Israel; your little ones, your wives, and thy stranger that is in thy camp, from the hewer of thy wood unto the drawer of thy water, that thou shouldest enter into covenant with the Lord thy God, and into his oath, which the Lord thy God maketh with thee this day," Deut. 5: 14; 16: 13, 14; Ex. 20: 10; 23: 12; Deut. 14: 29; 24: 19; Num. 15: 27; Lev. 4: 13; Num. 9: 14; Deut. 29: 10—12.

I think, brethren, that the cited passages sufficiently show and prove that they were called strangers, because they were not of the seed of Israel, and had no part in the distribution of the land; therefore, Moses commanded the Israelites to allow them the right to the tenths of the third year, to the gleanings of the field, of the olive trees and vineyards, and the first fruits of the land, as we have shown and explained from the writings of Moses.

In the second place, it might be asked, why we should shun the apostates, since Christ said, "Let him be unto thee as a heathen man and a publican," and since it is manifest that Christ, himself, did eat with the publicans. To this I reply: What kind of sinners they were, with whom Christ ate, is well explained by the evangelists. For, when the Pharisees murmured, Christ said, "They that be whole need not a physician, but they that are sick; but go ye and learn what that meaneth, I will have mercy, and not sacrifice; for I am not come to call the righteous, but sinners to repentance." What kind of sinners Matthew, the sinful woman, and Zaccheus were, after they had heard Christ is not a mystery, Matt. 9: 12, 13.

Again, Luke says, that all the publicans and sinners came to Christ to hear him, and with such did he eat, and therefore did he say to the murmuring Pharisees, "What man of you, having a hundred sheep, if he lose one of them, doth not leave the ninety and nine," &c., Luke 15: 4.

Again, that he ate with the Samaritans, is no wonder at all, for they received his word and believed on him; but that he should have sought hospitality in a Samaritan city, is not rightly translated, according to the Latin text. Thus it reads in Latin: *Misit nunciosante conspectum suum, and euntes intraverunt in civitatum, Samaritanorum, ut pararent illi and non receperunt eum, quia facies ejus erat euntis Hierosolymam.* Which being translated reads, He "sent messengers before his face, and they went and entered into a village of the Samaritans, to make ready for him, and they did not receive him, because his face was as though he would go to Jerusalem," Luke 9: 52.

What kind of preparation is hereby meant, may, in my opinion, be clearly learned from the case of the seventy, related in Luke 10: 1; whom he sent before his face by two and two, to make preparation for him in all the cities and countries whither he himself would come, not to prepare a place for sojourning, but for the teaching of the kingdom of God. But here they did not receive him. He says not that the master of the house did not receive him, but *they*, that is, the inhabitants of the city, to whom he had sent them to preach, did not receive him; because, as Luke says, he was going to Jerusalem; for the Samaritans and the Jews always have had a severe strife between them in regard to worship and religious matters. Yea, so much so, that the Samaritans were considered by the Jews as being deserving of the ban, John 4: 9; and if it were true, that he desired to find a lodging-place, yet it is apparent that the Samaritans were not Gentiles, but a remnant of the ten tribes of Shalmaneser; for the Samaritan woman said unto Christ, "Art thou greater than our father Jacob?" That Jacob was not the father of the Gentiles, is manifest. She also looked for the Messiah, whom the Gentiles did not know, she said, "I know that the Messiah cometh, which is called Christ," John 4: 25. Again, after Stephen was stoned, Philip came into a Samaritan city and preached Christ unto them; and at that time they could not yet conscientiously preach the gospel unto the Gentiles and go amongst them. From this it may be safely educed that the Samaritans, who claimed the patriarch Jacob to be their father, who looked for the Messiah, and to whom they had already preached the gospel, before they were conscientiously at liberty to go among the Gentiles, were not heathen, but a remnant of the Israelites, as said before; therefore it is no wonder that he requested to sojourn with them. Neither did he say, Let him be unto thee as a Samaritan, but as a "heathen man and a publican."

Behold, dearly beloved brethren, however we turn these words of Christ, they cannot be made to apply to any other time than that of Christ; namely, that, as the Jews at that time dealt with a heathen and publican—so we may also, now treat an apostate who, either through false doctrine, or through an unclean, shameful life, dishonors, rejects and disgraces Christ Jesus and his holy word. I wish, most beloved brethren, that every christian would diligently consider, since we have given our understanding of these words of Christ, whether not also Paul understood these words as meaning the same as we have explained. Yea, he who closely considers this matter, will find that Paul, in his doctrine of separation, has, in every way conformed to this rule of Christ.

Thus Paul says, "It is reported commonly, that there is fornication among you, and such fornication as is not so much as named among the Gentiles, that one should have his father's wife. And ye are puffed up, and have not rather mourned, that he that hath done this deed might be taken away from among you," 1 Cor. 5: 1, 2.

In another place, Paul teaches how Christ loved the church, and gave himself for it; that he might sanctify and cleanse it with the washing of water by the word, that he might present it to himself a glorious church, not having spot, or wrinkle, or any such thing; but that it should be holy and without blemish, Eph. 5: 25. If we admit such open profaners as this fornicator, and, moreover, adulterers, drunkards, contentious, avaricious, upbraiders and idolaters, and do not shun them, then we must ever hear this reproof of Paul, that we are "puffed up" and do not rather mourn to separate such open transgressors from us. O, brethren, brethren! I fear that this admonition of Paul is not sufficiently weighed by some. Paul says further, "For I verily, as absent in body, but present in spirit, have judged already, as though I were present, concerning him that hath so done this deed. In the name of our Lord Jesus Christ, when ye are gathered together, and my spirit, with the power of our Lord Jesus Christ, to deliver such a one unto Satan for the destruction of the flesh, that the spirit may be saved in the day of the Lord Jesus," 1 Cor. 5: 3, 4, 5.

These words of the apostle teach us three things: First, The great love of the faithful servant, Paul, toward his disciples and children; for although he was not present there, yet as present in spirit, he was paternally solicitous for them, and ever taught, admonished and advised them to their own good.

Secondly, In whose name, how, and by whom this separation, shall be practiced, namely, in the name, that is, by virtue of the command and ordinance of our Lord Jesus Christ. For Paul did not undertake to do any thing that he had not first received of Christ, as he says. Yea, if Christ had not first instructed Paul to do so, he would not have dared to command the Thessalonians, in the name of our Lord Jesus Christ, that they should separate themselves from every brother who walked disorderly, and not according to his ordinances. For this may well be called doing things in the name of Christ, when it is done in conformity to his holy word and will.

Again, It shall be practiced by the church; that is, every one shall not separate at his own pleasure; but it should be done by the congregation of God, after proper admonition in love, diligence and faithfulness, with the power of Christ, that is, with the binding or closing key of the Holy Spirit. For if it be practiced without the word and Spirit, without love and brotherly affability, whether it is through bitterness, anger, or a false report, not conformable to the word, for reasons not deserving of the ban,—then it is not a work of God, no medicine to the soul, nor fruit of pure love; but a contention of satan, a corruption and pestilence to the soul, and a manifest fruit of the flesh: In short, a curse, abomination and stench before God. Let every person well weigh these words of Paul, and he will, by the grace of God, find how rigidly this separation is commanded in the Scriptures, and how orderly it should be practiced in the church, with the power of the word and Spirit of Christ.

Thirdly, That we should deliver an unrepenting transgressor unto satan. Not, brethren, that he was not of satan before separation, for as soon as he turned his heart away from the Lord and became ungodly, he became the subject of satan, even as a penitent sinner is a subject of Christ. But now the voice of man, through the church, tells him that he is deprived of the communion of Christ and his church, and that he is now delivered unto satan until he again brings forth true fruits of repentance, before God and his church, that his adulterous, avaricious, refractory and idolatrous flesh may be brought to reflection and become ashamed and repentant by such judgment and shunning of the pious, that he may thus suppress and die unto his flesh, that is, the lusts of his flesh, and that he may by these means be brought to repentance and his soul be saved in the day of the Lord Jesus.

Here the godfearing reader may observe in these words of Paul, the first reason why the Holy Spirit ordained this ban to be practiced in the house of God, namely, for repentance and not for corruption; that, if the transgressor rejects as null and void, all fraternal services and admonitions of faithful love that are shown to him, and remains unrepentant—that, then, according to the advice of the Holy Spirit, the judgment passed upon him, should, with sorrowfulness, be made known unto him in the church and that he is separated from the church that he may thus become ashamed unto repentance.

Again, about this shame, the apostle speaks in another place, "If any man obey not our word by this epistle, note that man and have no company with him, that he may be ashamed," 2 Thess. 3: 14.

Take notice, brethren, that true, evangelical separation is an express fruit of unfeigned love, and not a law of hatred, as some, very wrongly, complain and pretend.

Ah, faithful brethren, if we rightly understood God, if we were enlightened with the Holy Spirit, and loved our neighbors with divine love, how diligently we would be engaged in this matter, to follow the faithful advice of the Holy Spirit, in all reasonableness and love, without respect of persons; no matter whether it concerns father, mother, sister, brother, husband, wife, child, or any relative or friend; for how can we show more spiritual love towards them? But as it is, a great many do not seek that which is of the Spirit, but that which is of the flesh; not their neighbors, but themselves. If they do so through ignorance, then may the merciful Father enlighten them with his Holy Spirit, and guide them into all truth; but if they do so through willful perverseness, then we know that it is written, "To be carnally minded is death," Rom. 8: 6.

In the third place, Paul says, "Your glorying is not good. Know ye not that a little leaven leaveneth the whole lump? Purge out therefore the old leaven, that ye may be a new lump, as ye are unleavened. For even Christ our Passover is sacrificed for us: Therefore let us keep the feast, not with old leaven, neither with the leaven of malice and wickedness, but with the unleavened bread of sincerity and truth," 1 Cor. 5: 6—7.

Again, with these words Paul reproves, first, the Corinthians, and, also, all other churches with them, who glory in being the church of Jesus Christ and the spiritual house of Israel, and yet tolerate such shameful, corrupting leaven, as the Corinthians and the like defilers, in their communion. For how can we glory in the piety of the church and reprove other churches on account of their ungodly doctrine and life, so long as we tolerate the like leaven of doctrine and life among us, without expelling it? If we are unleavened, Why are we not fearful of the leaven? since the apostle tells us that "a little leaven leaveneth the whole lump."

Secondly, He here gives us the outward Israel as an example. For when they kept the passover, they did not keep leavened bread in their houses for seven days. Yea, if it was found in any house the souls thereof had to be rooted out from among Israel. Neither was an uncircumcised or unclean one to eat thereof. Oh, brethren, if the figure and shadow were to be so pure how much more should the reality be pure? For our passover is not a quadruped, but it is the spotless Lamb of God, Christ Jesus. Nor does our passover last seven days, as did the passover of Israel, but it lasts forever, namely, from the offering of Christ until the last day; neither is it kept by unleavened bread, baked of flour, but by the unleavened bread of righteousness and by the word of eternal truth.

Therefore, beloved brethren, let us keep this passover holy and unspotted, to the best of our ability, and let us, in the name of our Lord Jesus Christ, separate from us the corrupting leaven, that is, all those that walk in the foreskin of their hearts, and all impure in life (understand, open, known transgressors), that we may be the holy Israel of God, besprinkled with the blood of the lamb, free from the scourging angel of God, and that we may thus rejoice before the Lord, in sincerity and truth, and celebrate and serve it all the days of our lives.

Further, all the pious may learn from these words of Paul, "Know ye not that a little leaven leaveneth the whole lump?" the second reason, why this separation is so necessary and useful to the house of God, and that it can not stand without it. This has been shown in Israel. Moses, the faithful servant of God, strictly commanded the people of God, that they should, without mercy, destroy from among them the wilful transgressors, when proven by two or three witnesses; also, that if any prophets should arise among them, with signs and miracles to lead them to other gods, they should not hear them, but destroy them. Again, the father should not excuse his child, the husband his wife, &c., but their hand should be the first upon them. Also, they should level and destroy any city which went after other gods, that Israel might hear these things, fear God and no more practice such evil. I think this was a rigid separation which was commanded Israel. If they had stood firm and immutable in this, and had they followed the command, counsel, teachings and admonition of God, according to the Scriptures, and destroyed the false prophets and idolators, they would never have become so estranged from God, and come to such deadly whoring and degeneration (understand this as in the law). For the rejection of the counsel and will of God will never go unpunished, Deut. 13: 5, 7; 17: 11; 19: 15; Heb. 10: 18.

But at present, the Holy Spirit does not teach us to destroy the wicked, as did Israel, but that we should reluctantly separate them from the church, and that in the name of the Lord, by the power of Christ and the Holy Spirit; for a little leaven leaveneth the whole lump. It is a common saying, One scabby sheep mars the whole flock. The lepers were not allowed among the healthy, in Israel; but had to be separated until cured. O, brethren in the Lord! the leprosy of the soul, is a leprosy above all diseases, whether it is in doctrine, or in life. It eats like a cancer, and, as Paul says, "leavens the whole lump." Therefore the Holy Spirit has abundantly taught us to separate such from among us; not to hear the words of the false prophets, for they deceive us; to separate from such who, contrary to apostolic doctrine, cause offense and contention; to shun those who are not pleased with the salutary words and doctrine of our dear Lord Jesus Christ, but are contentious and desirous of quarreling, &c.; to guard against dogs and artful laborers and the selfish; to flee the voice of strangers; to shun an heretic or a master of sects, after having been once or twice admonished; not to greet nor receive in our houses him who does not teach the doctrine of Christ; and to withdraw from every brother who acts disorderly and walks not according to the apostolic doctrine. O, says Paul, that they be cut off who disturb you, Lev. 13: 2; Jer. 23: 16; Titus 3: 10; 2 John 10; 2 Thess. 3: 6.

I think, beloved brethren, the Holy Spirit of God has done well, and fully performed the duties of his office, and his faithful service of divine love toward his chosen people by admonishing, warning, teaching and commanding, in Moses and the prophets, in Christ and the apostles, in regard to the Shunning of heretics and apostates; but, if we through obstinacy or perverseness, still associate with the leprous, against the faithful counsel, teaching and admonition of God and intermingle with them, then we will also be infected with the same disease. It is the recompense of those who know the nature of the disease, and yet neither fear nor avoid it.

Say, most beloved, is it not the greatest foolishness and recklessness willfully and knowingly to run into the hands of the murderer, by opening unto him your house and office; for what else can you expect but stealing, robbing and murdering?

O, that the pious reader would receive the command, teaching, counsel, and admonition, so faithfully given by the Holy Spirit. Shun all heretics (I refer to those who have been of us), and apostates, according to the word of the Lord; whether it is father, mother, wife, child, relative or friend, or whoever will try to turn you from God and his word, and to corrupt you by doctrine or by life. Whosoever loves any thing more than his God, cannot be the disciple of the Lord, Matt. 10: 37; Luke 14: 26. Therefore, believe Christ Jesus, and sincerely fear him in his word, and you will follow his counsel and teaching; but if you be offended thereat, then await your punishment, for, by the grace of God, I know what it is to despise the word and will of God, and what I have felt and seen in this respect.

In the fourth place, Paul says, "I wrote unto you in an epistle not to company with fornicators. Yet not altogether with the fornicators of this world, or with the covetous, or extortioners, or with idolaters; for then must ye needs go out of the world. But now I have written unto you not to keep company, if any man that is called a brother, be a fornicator, or covetous, or an idolater, or a railer, or a drunkard, or an extortioner; with such a one no not to eat," 1 Cor. 5: 9—11.

From these words of the apostle we observe that he had on a former occasion, admonished the Corinthians, in an epistle, that they should shun the fornicators, covetous, &c., but they had *also* understood it as meaning the fornicators of this world. In this epistle, Paul admonishes them that this was not his meaning; for if they should shun such, and not have any dealings with them, they must needs go out of the world. But he meant those who are called brethren, as he shows in plain language, saying, "If any man that is called a brother be a fornicator, or covetous," &c., with such an one do not eat; just as the Jews did not eat with the Gentiles and publicans, at the time of Christ; neither did they keep their company; for Christ and Paul are one and not divided, John 4: 9.

I think, brethren, that this text is so plain and clear that it admits of no controversy; notwithstanding some violate and garble it.

First, they say, "Paul had no authority to burden us with any laws when it was not first taught and commanded him of Christ." To this we answer: Let every one rightly reflect upon, divide and consider the words of Christ, "Let him be unto you as a heathen man and a publican," and he will find, by the grace of God, whether or not Paul first received this doctrine of Christ.

Secondly, they say, "Since Paul makes mention here of the Jewish passover, and adds that we should keep the passover, not in the old leaven," &c., so this passage, and also his sayings, "With such do not company, with such do not eat," must be understood as meaning a spiritual intermingling or communion. To such, we answer: Israel had a passover of seven days, but we have an eternal passover. And, as the Lamb of our passover is eternal, and his offering eternal, so we must now, perpetually sanctify and celebrate it, ever partake of its flesh; ever be sprinkled with its blood, and ever be diligently guarding against the ungodly, corrupting leaven of both doctrine and life. If our feast and passover then, is spiritual and not literal, eternal and not temporal, how can this then be applicable to the Lord's Supper, which eating does not last but for an hour or so?

In the second place, we answer: If these words were spoken of a spiritual communion then it should read in the Greek text, *choinonia*, and in the Latin, *communicatio*, for that signifies a spiritual communion, as Christ communes with us, and the members of Christ commune with Christ; also, community of property. But in the Greek text is a different word, and in Latin it reads: *commisceri sivi commercium habere*, which does not imply a spiritual communion at all, but an outward, temporal communion; and it appears the clearer from these words of Paul that he here speaks of the temporal communion and company, and not of spiritual. For he has prohibited this communion with the apostates and allows the communion with the world, which has no spiritual communion with us, nor can they have. This is incontrovertible. Yea, if the communion or intermingling with the world were prohibited, then we could not make use of the necessaries of life, but we would have to eke out our life in poverty, destitution, tribulation and misery, 1 Cor. 10: 3; Acts 2: 44; 1 Tim. 6: 18; Heb. 13: 16.

Thirdly, we reply: That Paul had reference to common eating, and not to the Lord's Supper; for he calls it in Latin, *cibum capere* (to take food), and not, *panum frangere* (to break bread); and it is manifest that the Lord's Supper is, nowhere in the Scriptures, called *cibum capere*. And if it were spoken in reference to the Supper, as some very mistakenly assert, then it would incontrovertibly follow that we are at liberty to invite the world to the Lord's Supper, to greet them with the kiss of peace and to be one body with them; for this intercourse, unclean and prohibited with an apostate brother, is, according to Paul, clean and allowable with the world. O, no, but as the Jews at that time would not eat a common meal with the heathen and publicans, and Christ having pointed his followers to that usage, so Paul follows the doctrine and command of his Lord and master, Jesus; and says that we shall not eat with such.

I think that it has been sufficiently shown to the pious, that these words of Paul should not be understood as referring to spiritual communion, nor to the Lord's Supper, but only to daily intercourse and common eating. If, now, it is not allowed in outward or carnal communion, it will be less so in inward or spiritual communion.

Dear brethren in the Lord, I would here pray and admonish you all, in humility, to consider well what the proper meaning is of this word *commercium* (intercourse), of which Paul speaks, and how we should understand it, that you may not give too much liberty to the reckless souls, to their own destruction, and that you do not too closely bind the narrow minded, since you have no binding word. For I hear and see, and have, alas, seen too much of it, these many years, that some, on every hand, use no weight nor measure in this matter; and the result is, that there is much dispute and trouble about this separation. May the Lord grant his divine grace to the peace, unity and edification of his holy church. Amen.

Inasmuch as I am an unworthy and humble servant, called into the house of God, and sincerely seek the good of my beloved brethren and co-workers; therefore I will briefly present my views concerning this communion or intermingling, according to my talent, with which I desire to appear before the throne of my Lord Jesus Christ, at the day of judgment, and will leave it to the criticism of God's word, and all theologians. Therefore, my understanding of *commisceri* or *commercium habere*, (that is, to mix with or to commune), of which Paul here speaks, is, that it implies daily communion, company, walk, intercourse, presence, usage, conversation and dealing, and that it does not mean accidental conversation, or necessary dealings, such as dividing a legacy, liquidating debts, and such like incidental dealings, or to be serviceable in times of need; for the word *commercium* does not imply anything so strong. Therefore, in my opinion, some err not a little by attaching the same strength to the phrase "have no company with them," that they attach to "thou shalt not steal, and thou shalt not commit adultery," of which Paul testifies that those who are guilty thereof, shall not inherit the kingdom of heaven. Their argument is, That nay is nay; yea, brethren, if this were the case, who could stand before his God?

Again, if the word *commercium*, which in our language, means an intermingling or communion, is to be explained, that we are not to speak a word with an apostate, not to have any necessary dealings with him; then the word *commercium* would be violated; many a pious child be retarded, many an unscriptural action done, and the faithful Paul would be rejected. For he says, "Yet count him not as an enemy, but admonish him as a brother," 2 Thess. 3: 15. Besides, it would make an evil report of the gospel of Christ.

It is also incontrovertible, that the publicans and some heathen lived in Judea, as, Herod, Pilate, Philip, Sisanius, Testus, &c., before whom they had to appear at times. Again, they also had to pay tribute to the Romans; and, therefore, were obliged sometimes, to speak to them, and had necessary dealings with them; although they diligently shunned their daily company, conversation, intermingling, eating, &c.

Dear brethren, take heed, and do not become masters and despisers of the Holy Spirit, that you do not, through the good opinions of men, make the way narrower nor broader, than the word, Spirit and example of the Lord makes and limits it.

In the fifth place, Paul says, "What have I to do to judge them also that are without? do not ye judge them that are within? But them that are without God judgeth. Therefore put away from among yourselves that wicked person," 1 Cor. 5: 12, 13. Here Paul explains his former words, that he did not apply them, in his first epistle, to those that are without; for God judges them, and not we. We ought to put away from among us the wicked persons, and commend the world to God.

Behold, faithful brethren, how unanimously Christ and Paul agree in the shunning of the apostates. And also, how earnestly Paul has taught and maintained this separation. Yea, that he has six times enjoined to practice this ban, in such a short chapter.

"Ye are puffed up, and have not rather mourned, that he that hath done this deed might be taken away from among you."

"To deliver such an one unto Satan."

"Purge out therefore the old leaven, that ye may be a new lump."

"I wrote unto you in an epistle not to company with fornicators."

"With such an one, no not to eat."

"Therefore put away from among yourselves that wicked person," 1 Cor. 5: 2, 5, 7, 9, 11, 13.

All these are found in one short chapter; besides what he has taught, commanded and admonished in this respect to the Romans, Galatians, Philippians, Thessalonians, Timothy and Titus. John also has explained himself briefly. I do not see how a godfearing heart can have doubts in regard to this matter and how he can contradict it, since there are such good fruits and utility derived from this shunning. But it seems that this vine must have its worms.

Again, the refractory make another objection, and say, "When one is separated from the church it is not necessary any more to shun him, for he is no longer called a brother." To such we reply: That they should, in the first place, consider that if such an one, who has acknowledged the Lord's word and truth, and, for a time, led a pious, evangelical life, and has thus received baptism, becomes apostatized and afterwards sincerely repents, he is not rebaptized; for the Scriptures teach but one baptism. But if those who are of the world repent, they are baptized after repentance; for before, they neither confessed word, penitence, faith, righteousness nor baptism; and therefore it is a different matter. At the day of judgment, it will also be more strictly required of them than of the world, Luke 9: 5; 2 Pet. 2: 20; Matt. 24: 48.

In the second place we say that the world, notwithstanding, esteem them as brethren, and many of them would gladly be greeted as brethren; therefore it is very necessary to shun them, that both the world and they may know and understand that we can not accept such as brethren who are so unclean and blamable in doctrine or in life, lest the word of the Lord and his church be despised by the world, on their account.

In the third place we say, That Israel did not shun their open transgressors, nor the Corinthians their fornicators until they were separated from the church. It is neither a custom nor usage in the Scriptures, to shun anybody so long as he is suffered in the church; and therefore we should not shun any one, before separation; or else we practice a ban neither known nor mentioned in the Scriptures.

In the fourth place we say, That if we commune and associate with an apostate, after separation, then we show in fact that we despise the word, command, counsel, teaching and admonition of God; that we do not seek the reasonable shame of the apostate, which is to lead him to repent; and also, that we do not guard against the corruption of our own souls.

I trust that this is sufficient to appease

every godfearing heart, in regard to the words of Christ, Matt. 18:18, and in regard to the fifth chapter of the first epistle to the Corinthians, and that no more useless garbling, objections and artful excuses be made to turn it to the lusts of the flesh, for they can stand no better than stubble before the fire, and ice before heat. Yea, from these same words of Christ and of Paul it appears clearly how, when, where, with what spirit, of whom, on whom, and for what purpose this ban should be practiced. I think this foundation to be so powerful that it cannot be broken by christian reasonableness nor by divine truth. Let every one fear and love his God with all his heart, and he will, doubtlessly, receive the true knowledge of this matter, and will rightly follow the scriptural and God pleasing usage.

A CLEAR, INCONTROVERTIBLE CONFESSION AND DEMONSTRATION,

FOUNDED ON THE POWER OF THE

HOLY SCRIPTURES,

THAT THE ENTIRE CHRIST JESUS, GOD AND MAN, MAN AND GOD, IS GOD'S OWN, ONLY AND FIRST BEGOTTEN SON; NOT DIVIDED NOR SEPARARATED, BUT AN ONLY, UNDIVIDED PERSON, SON AND CHRIST; GOD'S WORD DULY MANIFESTED IN THE FLESH, TOGETHER WITH A THOROUGH CONFUTATION, REPLY TO, AND SOLUTION OF THE PRINCIPAL POINTS OF THE DEFENSE OF JOHN A'LASCO AGAINST US.

BY

MENNO SIMON.

"I am the living bread which came down from heaven; If any man eat of this bread, he shall live for ever; and the bread that I will give, is my flesh, which I will give for the life of the world," John 6 : 51.

"For other foundation can no man lay than that is laid, which is Jesus Christ," 1 Cor. 3 : 11.

ELKHART, INDIANA:
PUBLISHED BY JOHN F. FUNK AND BROTHER.
1871.

PREFACE.

To the Impartial Reader:—I see and observe, honest reader, that many books, printed in Latin and also written German books, are circulated and read, concerning the incarnation of the Lord, which, in my opinion, so slander our reputation, that those who read or hear them read, shut their noses and mouths at our approach; therefore I feel myself compelled, First, to reply to some accusations of John A'Lasco, wrongfully preferred against me. Secondly, to advance my confession and faith of Christ Jesus, the Son of God; and, Thirdly, to solve and criticise according to divine truth, as far as the grace of God is given me, his principal points with which he refutes our foundation and faith. This I do not for my own sake, for I am well aware that my truths, with him, are lies, and that I will remain, as did all the holy apostles and prophets, the learned heretics and imposters, even if Christ spake in and through me, poor, ignorant creature, with the same power as that with which he spake formerly through the apostles and prophets. But I do this from the pure love of our Lord and Savior, Jesus Christ, and his holy word; from love for my beloved brethren, and also, from a heart inclined towards my opponents, that Christ Jesus the Son of the Almighty and great God, may be made manifest as a true Son of his heavenly Father; that the Scriptures may remain unbroken; and that the afflicted, hungering consciences, which would gladly follow the right, may see and know it and thus thank the Almighty and eternal Father with cheerful hearts, through his first and only begotten Son, Christ Jesus; that, also, the God fearing reader may know through whom he is reconciled with his God; and that we establish our foundation not otherwise than by the clear and positive Scriptures and incontrovertible truth.

Behold, for this reason have I yet undertaken this labor before my death. I, who in my weakness, every day look for the dissolution of this earthly tabernacle with resignation; that I may leave behind me a sure testimony and memento, how honestly or dishonestly, how highly or how triflingly, how greatly or how insignificantly I have esteemed the Lord Jesus Christ, my only and eternal Surety, Consolation, Refuge, Deliverer and Savior, during the period of my service; for I am aware how we are upbraided and slandered.

Therefore have I divided this book in three parts. The first part is a reply to some articles and accusations without regard to the foundation of our actions of which John A'Lasco accuses and blames us, without any truth whatever.

The second part, is my confession of the origin and descent of the flesh of Christ, demonstrated according to the power of the Scriptures.

The third part contains the principal objections, particularly of John A'Lasco to our foundation, which are overwhelmingly answered according to the word of God. I have so divided it, that the reader may not become confused, but may obtain a better and more intelligent understanding and sense of our writings.

I desire and pray all my readers, for the sake of Jesus, whether they are learned or unlearned, favorable or unfavorable, to read my writings with an unprejudiced mind and attentively and intelligently; to read them frequently; to compare them with the Scriptures, and weigh them in the balance of the Scriptures; I pray them to believe the Scriptures, and not the long and many writings, teachings and the colorings of the learned; that they will examine the foundation without bitterness, and believe the surest truth, and follow it in the fear of God, and give him due praise, as becomes all reasonable people, according to the christian name. I doubt not but that all those who read them with due attention, will soon find that the foundation, doctrine and faith of our opponents concerning Christ, the Son of God, is deceiving and erroneous, and that our foundation is the foundation and testimony of the Holy Scriptures; yea, that it is the power and the truth.

I would further pray, that the reader do not think hard of it if I call falsehood, lies; and rebuke evil-doing. I trust, by the grace of God, to do so without any bitter feeling, and with as temperate words as possible; and further, not to become impatient if I sometimes repeat the same words and matter, when necessary; and also that at the end, he will not judge me without consideration and intelligence; and thus become angry with me. For I do nothing more than reasonable purging, according to the truth; nothing more than prove my faith and hope, to be in accordance with the Scriptures, and uphold the honor and praise of my Lord and Savior—something which I am not only called to do verbally, and with my pen, but also with my life-blood, if his glory demand it.

May the beloved Lord, the faithful Son of the true and living God, to whom be all honor and praise, grant all kind and discreet readers a mind desirous to examine diligently, and enlighten the intelligent hearts to understand rightly. Amen.

A CLEAR, INCONTROVERTIBLE CONFESSION, &C.

PART FIRST.

In the first place, John A'Lasco writes, "That I have magnified his name so that I might, on account of the correspondence I had with him, obtain greater honor, more consideration and authority among *ours*" (as he calls them).

Answer. It is true that I called him the noble and highly-learned, &c., in my confession to him and the preachers; but I did this for no other reason than simply to be polite. I did not picture him in such hateful colors as he did me; he calling me a doctor or teacher of anabaptists. Nor have I called him by such high names as he calls himself—Poloniæ Baro. I have not sought through his name what alas, he ascribes to me. I know, thanks be to the Lord, with holy Paul, that I can not be the servant of Christ, if I seek to please men, Gal. 1: 10. If I should become more honored in the name of man, be it a king or emperor, than in Christ, it would not be well with me in the end. For if I seek mine own honor, and not the honor of God, it will not be my honor. But I hope to obtain honor which will remain with me forever; men may judge me as they will, they must confess before their God, in the day of Christ. He who has eyes like a flame of fire, knows what I seek and do, my coming in and my going out, my rising up and my sitting down. If he knew nothing better of me than that which I am judged by man, then I might justly exclaim: Woe unto me, that I was born.

In the second place, he writes, "That I have unjustly attacked his reputation, and profaned their church service."

Answer. I trust that nobody can truthfully show that I have said anything but truth about John A'Lasco or his abettors and followers. But if they feel hurt at the truth, of which he thinks so hard, for this they may blame the truth and not me. I am willing to leave it to the judgment of all reasonable people, whether I wrote justly or unjustly, too much or too little in regard to his doctrine, sacraments, church service, church or community, or that of the preachers of his kind. If their doctrine and church service is of God and his word, why are not their unreasonable and reckless disciples converted from their ungodly ways and doings? For, according to the contents of the Scriptures, it is infallible that the doctrine and service which is of God, has her power and influence, Isaiah 55. But it is too evident from their fruits, that there is nothing threshed from them but chaff. My conscience tells me nothing but that I have done them and their church justice; for I have reproved them, with zeal, of the things which all the prophets, apostles and faithful witnesses of God have diligently done before me, namely: I have reproved their carnal, impenitent lives, as is manifest before all the world. If I have done wrong in this regard, then I may justly accuse Moses and the prophets together with Christ and the apostles, of it, for they have earnestly commanded me, unworthy creature, and all God fearing preachers to do so, for which we, miserable creatures, have to suffer so much in this wild, excited world. He who has created me, knows that I have done so in sincere love to the conversion of their poor souls.

In the third place, he writes, "I have been obliged to deliver our doctrine of your slander, by authority of the divine word, which doctrine you may garble among your followers, by your crying, but which you cannot refute by authority of the Scriptures, notwithstanding your boasting that you do so."

Answer. If it can be called slander to rebuke wrong, according to the Spirit and word of God? Then not only have I slandered, but also Isaiah, Jeremiah, and all the prophets, and also Christ Jesus, together with all his apostles. I have rebuked their cause according to the word of God; and by the grace of God, shown them that they are not the true messengers of God, nor their church, the true one. But it will be hard for John A'Lasco to show that our doctrine, which is not ours, but Christ's doctrine, is wrong, and also that our rebuke according to the Scriptures, is slander; and to prove before his God, who judges all things aright, that his doctrine is right in regard to the incarnation, the baptism of infants, the calling of their preachers, their separation and the unrestrained, reckless life of his church, I fear that we will find plenty of philosophy, invention and coloring, but little scriptural power, foundation, and truth. Yea, kind reader, I am sure that if the violence of the world was ever withstood, as it doubtlessly should be, we would soon find where the victory of the Scriptures would stand.

In the fourth place he says, "If we prove our doctrine by virtue of the divine word, then it will be manifest that we were innocently slandered; and our innocence will be made manifest."

Answer. If he has proven his doctrine and sacraments to be right, by virtue of the divine word, as he boastingly asserts, I will acknowledge that I have unreasonably and wrongfully reproved them in this regard. But it is nothing but consoling the poor people with falsehood, and keeping them on the broad way by fictitious promises. Even if he could prove his doctrine and sacraments, which, however, he can not do, to be in accordance with the Scriptures, then his cause would still not be half way right; for the doctrine and sacraments are useless if the fruitful, active faith, and the pious, unblamable life, are not there; for which purpose the doctrine was promulgated, and the sacraments ordained. And what kind of life is generally led by their followers, and also by the greater part of their preachers themselves, I will leave to the judgment of those who can observe their daily actions and walk, and who have an understanding of the Holy Scriptures.

In the fifth place he says, "If you would have sent your writings to us all, as you promised to do, we might have answered you alone; but you have circulated them first among your own, before sending them to us."

Answer. I do not recollect that I have promised them this; nor can I see why I should have made such a promise, as I had nothing to write but what was my proper faith and foundation; which I desire not only to testify by writing in secret, but also with my life-blood, before the whole world, if only the Lord strengthen and uphold me by his grace.

But, as to his writing that I should have circulated it first amongst ourselves, I would say, that he has said too much; for as soon as I had withdrawn myself from them, I went to a secret place, as I have had to do these many years, for the sake of the testimony of Christ and my conscience, and simply compiled my faith and foundation in writing, and without any delay, after our conversation, sent it to them. However, out of respect, I handed it to M. H. G., he being, at the time, Baliff or Burgomaster (Mayor). The Great Lord is my witness that this is the truth, and since it is a fact as related, how could I have circulated it among ours before it was sent to them, as he accuses me of doing; and, even if I had done as he accuses me, were he and his followers thereby wronged? Since it is not alone my foundation, but the foundation and faith of us all, as is known to many.

But his own reason convinced him that it would seem unreasonable to the reader to write such an infamous, bitter book, without cause, and therefore he must pretend something, so that his writing against the mute Menno, who, on account of the great tyranny, cannot answer before the world, might seem reasonable. But whether it will stand before the impartial Judgment-seat of Christ, will be made manifest in his declaration. May the beloved Lord not reckon it as sin; for I know that I am not guilty.

In the sixth place he writes, "Your followers were the cause, that I must publicly treat with you, for they have steadily circulated the report in West Friesland, and also, in a great part of Holland, that you are at liberty to teach your doctrine in our churches; and that we are certainly conquered, and have nothing wherewith to gainsay."

Answer. I never heard a word of this until I read so in his writing; if some of us have thus boasted, as he writes (which I cannot believe), then it is evident that they have not spoken the truth in that regard, but falsehood; which falsehood is a shameful thing, yea, it is of the devil, and destroys the soul, John 8: 45, 55.

If he has it from hearsay, it was not right in him to listen to such partizans and liars, and to publish it in a book, to the everlasting remembrance of all the world, and the great injury of his neighbors. But if he did it of his own accord, and not from the persuasion of others, which I do not presume he did, then he dishonors his famous name and ruins his soul. For lying, I say, is a shameful thing, and will not find a place in God's city.

Again I say, I do not presume that he wrote this of his own accord, but I imagine that he was too desirous to listen to the liar, too quick to hear, and too hasty to write. Be this as it may, I know that, according to christian reasonableness and love, it does not apply to me; let him adorn it as much as he can. The great Lord will make manifest in due time what each one of us seeks and pretends, yea, maintains, teaches, does and defends.

In the seventh place he accuses me and says, "That I made light of two Latin syllogisms which he communicated to me; that I despised learning and the skill of languages; that I upbraided them as philosophers, and passed myself for simply a theologian, whereby I catch the unlearned and simple, and cause myself great consideration. That, however, my want of excellence is no meanness but rather ignorance. Yea, he has set me forth in such colors that my remembrance, although, alas, not much to my honor, will perhaps be with man as long as the world endures."

Answer. The reason why he applies these epithets to me, is, because I wrote to him and his abettors thus: Let us not controvert these things with subtle syllogisms, nor with sharp, human cavilings, for we do not profess them, but we contradict them alone by the clear, convincing word which cannot be garbled by eloquence, nor broken by human invention. These are my words, A. D. 1543, in my confession written to him and his preachers. Let those of a pious disposition judge now whether I deserve such bitter treatment. But I am aware that I did not earn this crown on account of these words, just mentioned, but for the sake of the poor, despised truth. Reader, do not misunderstand me. Never in my life, have I despised learning and skill in languages, but from my youth, honored and loved them. Although, alas, I never acquired them, yet (thanks be to God), I am not so bereft of my senses, that I should therefore despise or ridicule the knowledge of languages through which the precious word of divine grace came to our knowledge. I wish that all pious minded persons possessed this knowledge, if we would but humbly use it to the praise of our God, and the service of our neighbors, in the pure fear of God.

Is it not a shameful thing that they regard truth so little, and continually try, although unreservedly, to reflect such falsehood upon me. Yea, dear reader, if I would repay evil with evil, as the law of nature teaches me, I would collect some falsehoods, some of which were spoken, and some of which were written against me, of which neither he, nor any other man, can ever convict me. Whether this can be called just and right, I will leave to the judgment of all impartial, reasonable minds.

Would to God that he and all our opponents, would not act differently with me, than I do with them, for I trust they do not desire my blood, or at least the greater part of them. I rebuke and admonish them of all the short-comings which I see, as love for them requires, although they think hard of that. But that I should write falsehoods against them, from this may the Lord save me. For I am well aware from which impure fountain falsehood flows, and what will be the end of it. I am also aware that it is not the seed from which we shall beget God's children, and gather unto Christ a church. I would have them do the same (and not differently), if I should, human-like, fail in some things; that they would admonish and reprove me according to the truth; that they would uphold their truth (if they had any, which, alas, they have not), by force of the Scriptures; and that they would let the seed of the serpent use his falsehood, and the seed of Cain his violence, Gen. 3: 4.

But as to my ignorance, of which he so bitterly accuses me, I am not ashamed to acknowledge before all the world, that I am not only ignorant, but altogether unlearned, and very little versed in the languages. Yea, dear reader, I freely admit, as did Socrates, that I only know one thing, as regards human skill and wisdom, and that is, that I know nothing. But as regards heavenly wisdom, I am so far taught of God, through the grace of the Lord, that I sincerely confess that my Redeemer and Savior, Christ Jesus, is the only and first begotten Son of God; that whosoever believeth in him hath everlasting life; that he that believeth not is condemned; that a liar is of the devil; that "whosoever hateth his brother is a murderer;" that unless ye repent, ye shall all perish; that "the wages of sin is death," John 3: 8; 1 John 3: 15; Luke 13: 5; Rom. 6: 23. And from this unregarded wisdom (eternal praise be to the Lord), I have obtained so much fear in my poor soul, that my earthly, carnal mind is converted into a better; and that I am so sorry that I cannot walk in Christ Jesus, with all my strength, according to the will of God, and be a sincere, unblamable christian; that I cannot bring the whole world from its obdurate, ungodly state, into a new, repentant, christian life, with the Spirit, power, and word of the Lord. For this is my only joy and ardent desire, that we may rightly preach Christ Jesus, according to his holy word; that we may seek, fear, love and serve his holy name. Yea, that we may become the city of the living God, the glorious kingdom, to his honor, and the temple of his Holy Spirit, 2 Cor. 6: 16.

And this same wisdom which produces such power and fruit, I esteem as being the most worthy of all wisdom imaginable; even if taught and restored by an unlearned cart-driver or coal-carrier—yea, it is the only joy and desire of my afflicted heart; the only amelioration of my misery; and will be to the end, by the grace of God, the glorious ornament and crown of my honor. Of this noble, highly learned wisdom and philosophy read in Solomon's proverbs, also Sirach and the Book of Wisdom, and you will find which is its proper virtue, work and power.

Behold, reader, for the sake of this philosophic sweetness, honor, virtue, fruit, love and beauty, which I have not learned of famous doctors nor in high schools, and for the sake of filling my soul with its living power, I have rather chosen to be the ignorant and unlearned fool of the world, that I may be found wise before my God, than to be one of the most famous of the world, and at last be found a fool before the wise God. And this is my short answer and excuse to his charges and bitter upbraidings.

I say again, that in the simplicity of my heart I wrote the words "subtile syllogism," and "sharp cavilings," without, at all, despising science, and that I did not mean thereby to despise or curtail any one. I praise science when justly used to the glory of God. But above all I praise the humble, virtuous science and wisdom which is from above, for it will never perish, but in glorious honor remain with all the pious, into eternal life.

This, now, is the first part of this book, and I would have preferred to remain silent upon these things, if they had not been published to embitter some, to hinder the word, and to the affliction of the God fearing. But as it is, circumstances have rendered it necessary for me to do so. May the beloved Lord grant us his grace. Amen.

OUR CONFESSION.

PART SECOND.

THE reason why we do not admit the foundation, doctrine and faith of the learned, in regard to the incarnation of the Lord, but refute it with the Scriptures and truth, is this: Because we clearly see and palpably feel that they deprive us entirely of Christ, the Son of God, and point us to an earthly, sinful creature, and a man of the impure and sinful flesh of Adam; because their doctrine and pretensions are quite inconsistent with the ordinance of God, and also with nature, the Scriptures and the properties of the names, father, mother and son, and because so many inconsistencies must necessarily be included in Christ, as hereditary sin, condemnation, curse and death; because he would be half man, if the woman, according to their confession, contributed as much to the fruit as does the man; because there would be two persons — one divine and one human, which they call two natures or two parts; because there would be two sons—one the Son of God without mother, and not subject to pain; the other Mary's son without a father, and subject to suffering.

Again, because that if God shall be called a Father of the man, Christ, he must be a creating and not a begetting Father of his Son, and Christ must not be a born, but a created Son of his Father; because he would be the offspring of Adam and his seed, not through the word by which all must stand, but through his own flesh, which was subject to condemnation and death, with which the word clothes him, and in whom (while on earth), it has lived, and because of other gross inconsistencies. Therefore I have deemed it necessary, before I proceed with the confutation and dissection of the controversy, to propose to the reader our faith and confession of Christ the Son of God, according to the wholesome, genuine Scriptures, that he may find and understand that the Lord Jesus Christ is not an unclean, divided Christ of two persons and sons—but an undivided, pure Christ, an only person, yea, God's first begotten and only Son. Let him who is of an understanding mind, and who fears God, read and judge.

In the first place I advance the ordinance of God, Gen. 1:28; 9:1, to which John A'Lasco himself refers me, namely, "Be fruitful and multiply," and prove from this same ordinance that the production of man is brought about from the seed of man, through the woman, 1 Cor. 11:11, as will be enlarged upon hereafter.

To establish this assertion I would first refer to the conception of Sarah, when the Lord spake unto Abraham, saying, I will bless thy wife Sarah, and she shall bear thee a son; and thou shalt call his name Isaac, Gen. 17:19. To understand these words rightly and also Gen. 1, the reader should observe that Sarah, as she herself said, was old and it ceased to be with her after the manner of women, Gen. 18:11. Nevertheless, through faith, she conceived and brought forth unto Abraham a son in her old age.

This blessing of Sarah, according to my humble understanding, was that she was made fruitful by the power of God, according to the promise through the faith of Abraham. Behold, thus Isaac was conceived by Sarah of the seed of his father, and a son was born unto Abraham, according to the ordinance of God, Gen. 1:28; 21:2.

To this add the proverbs of Philon, or rather of the wise Solomon, which reads thus: "I myself also am a mortal man, like to all, and the offspring of him that was first made of the earth," &c., Wisdom 7 : 1.

Again, the Lord said unto Jacob, "Be fruitful and multiply; a nation, and a company of nations shall be of thee; and kings shall come out of thy loins," Gen. 35: 11.

Again, Levi was yet in the loins of his father when Melchisedec met Abraham, Heb. 7: 10. Other clear proofs might also be added.

I now leave the philosophers to philosophize, and the students of nature to argue as much as they please over this matter. God's ordinance, the example of Abraham and Sarah, and the abundant testimony of the Scriptures are sufficient proof for me on this point.

Again, I advance the words of the holy angel Gabriel, when he told Mary that she should conceive and bring forth a son. "Then said Mary unto the angel, How shall this be, seeing I know not a man? And the angel answered and said unto her, The Holy Ghost shall come upon thee, and the power of the Highest shall overshadow thee; therefore also that holy thing which shall be born of thee shall be called the Son of God," Luke 1 : 34, 35. Behold, here is the testimony of a true messenger, that God the Father is a true Father of our Lord, Christ. I think that God's own angel has here reproved the falsehood of those who say that the crucified Christ Jesus has had no father.

Since we find from God's own ordinance and from so many sayings of the Scriptures, that a true child takes its origin from the seed of the father according to God's ordinance, as has been related; and since we are so clearly instructed all through the Scriptures that God the Father is the true Father of his Son, Jesus Christ; therefore we say that we believe and confess, that the eternal Word of God, which is also called the seed, in the Scriptures, came down from heaven, through the overshadowing of the divine power, descended into Mary and miraculously became, above all human understanding, through the working of the Holy Ghost, a true, palpable, passive and mortal but imperishable man, according to the immutable will and gracious promise of the Almighty and heavenly Father; as John, both in his gospel and epistles clearly testifies. A man, I say, like unto us in all things except sin. Not, my reader that he came from the unclean seed and flesh of Adam, and was, through the power of God, preserved from sin, as the learned assert, without the word of God, for that which never knew sin is the seed and origin of his flesh, as John says, "The word was made flesh," John 1 : 14. Besides examine the passages of the Scriptures which testify that Jesus Christ is God's first born and only begotten Son, and you will find how grossly they err who dare say the man Christ has no father, as they do.

Again of Mary, the Lord's mother, we believe and confess that the Almighty, eternal God and Father graciously prepared her virgin body, as he also did that of the aged Sarah, by the power of his Holy Spirit, to receive his precious, eternal Word, through faith, according to the promise of the angel, and that this same word became man; and thus human-like, as Isaac, was nourished and fed on natural food, as a natural fruit, to the certain testimony that he was a true man and no phantasm; in due time, he was born into the world, an undivided and true Son of God and Mary, as a natural child of its father and mother, the *carnalis intercursus* alone excepted, as the Scriptures testify, Luke 8: 10; 1: 27; John 1: 14; 1 John 1: 2; Heb. 2: 14; Phil. 2: 7.

And behold, with such understanding we believe and confess that he is the seed of the woman, of the seed of Abraham and David, who was given of God the Father unto the whole world, through particular favor and grace, for salvation and deliverance, as the highest surety and certain testimony of his divine love, *through* faith, according to the sure word of his promise; and that the above mentioned virgin, ordained of God, conceived, as above stated, the Savior of the whole world, in Nazareth, according to the word of the angel, and was delivered of him at Bethlehem, according to the word of the prophets, Luke 1: 31; Micah 5: 2.

Faithful reader, observe that Matthew

and Luke show that Mary was made fruitful through the Holy Spirit of God, yet they do not particularly point out his genealogy, Mic. 5; Luke 1: 31. In the meantime some sectarians arose in the church, as Cerinthus and Ebion, who, according to history, have instituted gross deceptions.

Finally, John, at the prayer of the bishops of Asia, has written a clear account of the origin of Christ, the Son of God, and that not alone of his eternal divinity, as the learned say, but also of his holy humanity, as may be clearly noticed on all sides, in his writings. And he has, in clear and pointed words, written and incontrovertibly shown, who and what he has been from eternity, saying, "The word was made flesh." He says not; The word was made a man of our, or Mary's flesh, and has installed itself therein, as our opponents say. Besides he shows us whence he came, what he has taught, and what example he left us; what we have received through him, and where he again went to, &c. Whosoever, now, rightly believes the testimony of John, of Christ, the Son of God, has life everlasting through his name, John 1: 14.

But he who does not believe it, and rejects it, is not of God, and has neither Father nor Son, but is an anti-christ and deceiver; and this is our humble and plain confession of Christ, God's Son, as has been heard, 2 John 7, 8, 9.

As I now enlarge upon our doctrine, faith and confession, the reader should know that the Scriptures show on every hand that God, the Almighty Father has created all things through his Word, Jn. 1: 1; Ps. 33: 6; that he rules all things, and upholds and maintains all things thereby, Col. 1: 16, and as it is manifest that Adam was created by this same Word, and that he, through his disobedience was condemned, by the justice of God, to damnation and death, together with all his descendants; and that he of himself and through himself, could not be restored *again*, he being, together with all his seed, corrupted in nature, and condemned by the justice of God; therefore the eternal love of God, if Adam and his seed were not to remain eternally cursed, had to restore Adam and his descendants, by the same Word through which he created him, from his deadly fall, condemnation and curse, that to him alone be the honor, and that through his Word and Son, Christ Jesus, his inexpressibly great love and grace be eternally praised. For if the restoration had been brought about by any other means than the word, we might reasonably give thanks and praise thereto. Behold, with this, our confession, foundation and faith, the whole Scriptures accord, as, by the grace of God, you will clearly see from the quoted Scriptures.

Thus speaks John, "In the beginning was the Word, and the Word was with God and the Word was God," "And the Word was made flesh, and dwelt among us (and we beheld his glory, the glory as of the only begotten of the Father), full of grace and truth," John 1: 1, 14. This testimony we believe to be true; we therefore leave it unbroken, that the whole Christ remain, the Son of God; for we see with open eyes that it accords, and agrees, as far as regards this subject, with all the Scriptures.

We truly believe and doubt not the least, that the Holy Spirit, which seeks to lead us into all truth, did not mean otherwise than he here spoke through this faithful, plain fisherman, John. For if the beloved messenger of the holy peace had not meant it, as he here writes, his writing would not have pacified the churches, which, at that time, were very much troubled about this matter; but it would have still more estranged them than before, and would have pointed us, poor descendants to an obscure and uncertain foundation. Oh no! His testimony is true and plain; and will remain so in eternity. The word has become flesh.

This, our confession, is also authorised by the Lord himself, saying, "I am the living bread which came down from heaven; if any man eat of this bread, he shall live forever; and the bread that I will give is my flesh, which I will give for the life of the world," John 6: 51.

Faithful reader, mark the word of your Lord. Christ says, that his flesh came from heaven, and the learned say that it descended from Adam's flesh. Here they are directly opposite. What now will the God-fearing mind do? If he hold to the testimony and word of Christ, then he must be the deceiver and heretic of the learned. But if he hold to the testimony and word, then he makes Christ a liar. Since we surely know that Christ and the learned are so antagonistic, and since we know to a certainty, that Christ is the undeceiving truth, and that all men are liars, therefore we must not turn from truth to falsehood, but from falsehood to truth. Whatsoever the judgment of man may be, God's word will remain forever, Ps. 116: 11; Rom. 3: 4; Isaiah 40: 8; 1 Peter 1: 25.

Perhaps our opponents will here seek an excuse and say, Christ speaks of his more honorable part, for his divinity is from heaven, and has taken Adam's flesh. I answer: Let them read and believe the word and testimony of Christ, and they will find that they explain it according to their own inclination, and not according to the sense and truth of Christ; for thus he speaks, "I am the living bread which came down from heaven." Mark, he says, "*Came down from heaven*," "and the bread that I will give, is my flesh." Mark again, He does not say, It is my *divinity*, but "my *flesh*, which I will give for the life of the world."

I think that Christ himself, has here sufficiently explained his words, and therefore we do not need the explanation and garbling of the learned. For Christ and John could not have expressed themselves more plainly, in regard to the descending of his holy flesh, than they did in the two mentioned Scriptures. Therefore let every one beware how he garbles. For whosoever falsifies these clear, fundamental evidences, does not falsify the word of a human being but the word of God. Neither does he reject us, but the Son of God, together with his Holy Spirit, and the exalted apostle John, who have left them behind, and taught them in such clear and plain words.

Christ still further declares this our confession, saying, "And now, O Father, glorify thou me with thine own self, with the glory which I had with thee before the world was," John 17: 5.

I think this also is clear evidence that Christ humbled himself, and that he, for our sake, abdicated for a time his divine dominion, right and glory. For, although he was Justice and eternal Blessedness, he did not refuse to become a sacrifice for sin, and a curse for us, Phil. 2: 7; 1 Cor. 1: 29; Gal. 3: 13; 2 Cor. 5: 19.

Yea, kind reader, if he had remained in his first estate, impassive and unchanged, as John A'Lasco and his followers assert; and if he had just surrounded himself with a strange tabernacle of Mary's flesh, then he would not have lost that which he again desired from his Father, while he would have remained, not humbled, but unchanged in his first estate.

But now it is manifest that the eternal, indescribable and inexpressibly glorious word, which from eternity has been with and in the Father in eternal glory and clearness, but in an illegible manner, has in due time left his glory, for a season, for our service, and become a poor, despised, mortal man, and has died a bitter death for us. And thus he again desired his first glory, which he had with his Father before the world began, and which he had, for a time left, for our sakes. This Scripture is too clear to be obscured by acuteness. Therefore believe the word of your Lord, trust in truth and you will not be deceived.

This our confession also accords with holy Paul, for he says, "Now that he ascended, what is it but that he also descended first into the lower parts of the earth? He that descended is the same also that ascended up far above all heavens, that he might fill all things," Eph. 4: 9, 10.

By the side of this plain saying of Paul place also the word and testimony of Christ, which he himself testifies in regard to his descension. For he says, "No man hath ascended up to heaven, but he that came down from heaven, even the Son of man which is in heaven," John 3: 13.

Ponder diligently upon these words of Paul. For if he spoke these words alone in regard to his divinity, and not of his humanity, how would it then accord with the testimony of Christ, just mentioned, who says, "No man has ascended up to heaven, but he that came down from heaven, even the Son of man which is in heaven."

My reader, remember, Christ here calls himself the son of man, and says, "That he came down from heaven." The son of Mary, whom the learned say is of her flesh, did not come down from heaven, but must be of the flesh of Adam, if the foundation of the learned were right. Oh no. But the word *came down from heaven*, is become flesh or man, in the lower parts of the earth, and afterward ascended up far above all heavens where he first was.

Inasmuch then, as Christ not only speaks in this Scripture passage of his divinity, but also of his humanity (since he says The son of man), therefore it is manifest that the man Christ is not originally from earth, but from heaven, for according to his eternal divinity, if that should have been left thus unchanged, as the learned say, he cannot be called the son of man. Again, according to his humanity, he could not be in heaven at the time he spoke these words, if he was of Mary's flesh and not of heaven. Therefore we must accept these Scriptures as regarding the whole Christ, that is, both of his divinity and humanity. From which it forcibly follows that the whole Christ Jesus, God and man, man and God, is from heaven and not of earth, as also John testifies at another place, and says, "He that cometh from above is above all; he that is of the earth is earthly, and speaketh of the earth; he that cometh from heaven is above all," John 3: 31. Again, Christ says, "I came forth from the Father, and am come into the world; again, I leave the world and go to the Father," John 16: 28.

From these it follows (if we will accept the testimony of Christ, John the baptist and Paul, as true) that the Word came down from heaven, became flesh in Mary, dwelt among man, fulfilled the Scriptures, again ascended and sat down at the right hand of his Father, and is adored by all the angels of God. Mark, reader, how the one Scripture exactly fits the other, and how exactly Christ, John and Paul agree. Sure and immutable stands the testimony, that the Word is become flesh.

Paul still further explains our confession, and says, "The first man is of the earth, earthy; the second man is the Lord from heaven. As is the earthy, such are they also that are earthy; and, as is the heavenly, such are they also that are heavenly," 1 Cor. 15: 47. Reader observe. Although Paul properly speaks of the resurrection of the dead, and of its future clearness, yet he testifies by this same Scripture, the coming again, and the difference between the first and the second Adam, when he says, "The first man is of the earth, earthy; the second man is the Lord from heaven." For, as the first man, Adam, is called earthy on account of his being of the earth; so, also, the second man, Christ, is called heavenly because he is from heaven.

If any one should contradict this and say, That Christ here is called heavenly on account of his divinity, you should know that Paul rebukes them with these significant words: The second man, he says "The *second man* is the Lord from heaven." I cannot see how the great witness could express himself more plainly. And since he is, then, such a heavenly Being, and, besides, since he is again glorified of God his heavenly Father, with his eternal glory which he had before the beginning of the world, with God, therefore the holy apostle also calls all his true members, after the resurrection, heavenly. Not that they are from heaven, as Christ is from heaven, but because, by grace, through the power of God, in the resurrection, they will partake of the heavenly glory and of the nature of the angels, as Christ says, "The glory which thou gavest me, I have given them" (his disciples), John 17: 22.

Again, Paul says, "Our conversation is in heaven; from whence also we look for the Savior, the Lord Jesus Christ; who shall change our vile body, that it may be fashioned like unto his glorious body, according to the working, whereby he is able even to subdue all things unto himself," Phil. 3: 20, 21. Read also what Christ says of such, Luke 20; 1 John 3.

For this reason Paul calls them heavenly and says, "As we have borne the image of the earthy, we shall also bear the image of the heavenly," "For this corruptible must put on incorruption and this mortal must put on immortality;" "Then shall the righteous shine forth as the sun in the kingdom of their Father" and as the stars of heaven in brightness forever; yea, when we shall be like unto the Lord, and shall see him face to face, as he is, 1 Cor. 15: 49; Matt. 13: 43; 1 Cor. 13: 12.

Again, at another place the Scriptures say of Christ, I am the First and the Last, and the living One, and I was dead, and behold, I live from eternity to eternity Rev. 1: 8; Isa. 41: 4; 44: 6. In this instance the Holy Spirit brings forward another indissoluble testimony, at which all sharp disputers and famous masters of this world are made ashamed. If they want to pervert this clear and plain Scripture according to their own notion, by their deceitful reasoning, as they do the Scriptures of John 1: 14, and all the Scriptures, then they should know that we do not follow and believe the sophistry of man, but the word of the Lord. If they leave it undisturbed, then their cause is already lost, for the Holy Spirit testifies that the First and the Last, and the living One, died.

That Mary's flesh was not the first and the last all intelligent persons must admit. If then the man Christ had been of Mary's flesh, as the learned say it is, which neither is nor can be the first and last, and if it had thus died, then the Spirit of God, which is the Spirit of truth, would not have spoken rightly. Yea, neither Christ himself, who says, "I am the First and Last," was dead, and behold I am alive.

I would further say, That if the man Christ Jesus was a natural offspring of Mary, and if the eternal Word only lived therein, as our opponents say it did, and if this same man died, and the Word remained unchanged, then Mary's flesh must be the First and Last; this is too plain to be denied.

Since it is evident that Mary's flesh neither is nor can be the First and Last, as has been heard, and since it is true, according to the testimony of the Holy Spirit, that the First and Last has died, therefore I conclude therefrom that the explanation of our opponents, by which they point us to Mary's flesh, is deceitful and false, and that the learned are badly mistaken when they say that the Son of God remained unchanged, and that the son of Mary died. I say again, the word stands immutable, "The Word is become flesh."

Again, with this our confession, foundation and belief, all the prophets who have spoken of Christ, the Son of God, through the Holy Spirit, agree. Micah says, "But thou Bethlehem Ephratah, though thou be little among the thousands of Judah, yet of thee shall he come forth unto me that is to be ruler in Israel; whose goings forth have been from of old, from everlasting," Micah 5: 2. Observe, Isaiah says, "Behold a virgin shall conceive, and bear a son, and shall call his name Immanuel," which signifies God with us, Is. 7: 14; Matt. 1: 23.

He further says, "Unto us a child is born, unto us a son is given, and the government shall be upon his shoulders, and his name shall be called Wonderful, Counselor, The Mighty God, The everlasting Father, The Prince of Peace," Isa. 9: 6.

At another place he says, "Say unto the cities of Judah, Behold your God." Again, Jeremiah says, "Behold, the days come, saith the Lord, that I will raise unto David a righteous Branch, and a King shall reign and prosper, and shall execute judgment and justice in the earth. In his days Judah shall be saved, and Israel shall dwell safely; and this is his name whereby he shall be called, THE LORD OUR RIGHTEOUSNESS," Jer. 23: 5, 6.

My reader, observe, Since the descension of this Prince has thus been from eternity, as has been related, and his name is called, by the Spirit of the Lord, Immanuel, The Mighty God, The everlasting Father, Our Righteousness, &c.; and since the prophets describe him with such significant words, as also the apostles, whence, who, and what he is; therefore I conclude therefrom that the man, Christ Jesus, is not of unclean, sinful flesh, but of the unspotted, pure seed and word of God, his Father, as John says, "The word is become flesh." This, then, is our proper faith and confession of Christ, the Son of God, namely: That we are all created in Adam our father through the ineffable word, and that we, in the same Adam, have become of a sinful nature and subject to death; that we also, by means of this eternal, ineffable word, and not by means of the sinful flesh of Adam, are graciously accepted of God and mercifully called unto life everlasting, as Christ says, that "God so loved the world, that he gave his only begotten Son, that whosoever believeth in him should not perish, but have

OF THE INCARNATION.

everlasting life," Ps. 33 : 6; Rom. 5 : 12; 1 Cor. 15: 3; John 3: 16.

All Scriptures force us that we dare not divide Christ, the Son of God, after the pretensions of the learned; but to confess him as being entirely the true Son of the true and living God. The angel testified of Christ, the Son of Mary, saying, "That holy thing which shall be born of thee, shall be called the Son of God," Luke 1 : 35.

Again, the Father testified, "This is my beloved Son in whom I am well pleased," Matt. 17: 5; Luke 9: 35.

Again, John the Baptist says, "He that sent me to baptize with water, the same said unto me, Upon whom thou shalt see the Spirit descending and remaining on him, the same is he which baptizeth with the Holy Ghost; and I saw it and bare record that this is the Son of God," John 1: 33.

Again, "Nathaniel saith unto him, Rabbi, thou art the Son of God, thou art the King of Israel," John 1: 49.

Again, when Jesus asked his disciples, "Whom say ye that I am? Peter answered and said, Thou art the Christ, the Son of the living God," Matt. 16: 15, 16.

Again, Martha said, "I believe that thou art the Christ, the Son of God, which should come into the world," John 11: 27.

Again, the disciples, together with the others said, Verily, thou art the Son of God.

Again, Christ said to the blind man, "Dost thou believe on the Son of God? He answered and said, Who is he, Lord, that I might believe on him; and Jesus said unto him, Thou hast both seen him and it is he that talketh with thee," John 9: 37.

Again, when the centurion, saw that he so cried out, and gave up the Ghost, he said, "Truly, this man was the Son of God," Mark 15: 39.

Again, Saul was with the disciples at Damascus, and preached Christ in the synagogues, that he is the Son of God, Acts 9 : 20.

Again, John says, "We have seen and do testify that the Father sent the Son to be the Savior of the world. Whosoever shall confess that Jesus is the Son of God, God dwelleth in him, and he in God," 1 John 4: 9. Besides many other clear passages.

Inasmuch as the Scriptures so abundantly testify that also the man Christ is the Son of God, therefore it is manifest that M. M. and those of his mind, do fearfully err when they say, "The man Christ was not the Son of God; he had no Father; but there are two sons in Christ—the one the Son of God without mother, and impassive—and the other the son of mankind, or the son of Mary without father, and he passive," &c. I think this may be called rejecting the Son of God, in the face of all these plain Scriptures, and pointing us to a divided Christ, yea, to an unclean, sinful flesh and creature, guilty of death, whom the Scriptures never knew and still less taught. *O detestibilem blasphemiam* (O detestable blasphemy).

All who can be convinced rightly to believe that the word did not take unto itself a man of Mary's flesh, but that, according to the testimony of John, it is become flesh, have a true understanding of Christ. They will not argue *per Synecdochen, de parte ad totum, neque de toto ad partem*. They will not point to the worthiest part in Christ, nor to the communication or communion of the names; neither will they unite two persons and sons in one person and son, as our opponents do, but they will leave the Scriptures ungarbled in their place, and acknowledge with John the Baptist, John 1: 15; with Matthew 16: 16; with Martha, John 11: 27; and with the whole Scriptures, that Christ Jesus is God's first-begotten and only Son; an only and undivided Christ, God and man, man and God, an only person and Son, who, in his flesh, has fulfilled the handwriting of the law for us, as we could not, in our flesh, on account of our weakness; and is, at last, judged and condemned, as an innocent, spotless Lamb, to die on the cross for our sins and guilt.

Behold, this is our foundation, faith and confession of the most holy incarnation of our Lord Jesus Christ, the Son of God and Mary; on account of which, alas, we are so much upbraided by our opponents, and have to pass for deceivers and heretics; and that for the reason, I say, because we teach and testify with the Scriptures that the Lord, Christ Jesus, is God's own and true Son, as has been heard.

Well, since it is so with them they must

run their course; we cannot prevent it until they are met by the angel of the Lord, and rebuked by the ass, Num. 22; 2 Peter 2. They had, however, better beware, lest they stumble too hard on the Rock of offense, Isaiah 8: 14; Rom. 9: 33. The time to give an account will soon arrive. As for me, I care not how they judge me.

I trust to find my consolation in the Lord who has taken me by the right hand, and who knows all my desires, intentions and doings. He will execute our cause to his honor; for he knows that we do not desire to seek our praise, but his own. Therefore he will protect his own honor. It might doubtlessly happen that through their writing and slandering against us, and through their manifestly erring doctrine, in regard to Christ the Son of God, it might be made manifest to some that they are doubly what they would like to make us. May the great God grant them grace, Amen.

THE CONFUTATION.

PART THIRD.

Before I proceed to the confutation of the arguments of our opponents, I would first faithfully admonish the kind reader that he do not mistake the shining clearness of the eternal God-head, through his high-soaring genius, and not have the audacity to undertake to fathom this ineffable profundity—lest he, when he thinks that he has fathomed it, at once dazzle his eyes and suddenly fall down the precipice. For it is manifest that many smart and acute genii have been mistaken and made fools of themselves by their high-soaring intellect.

The Tritheists held and taught that there were three Gods.

Arius divided the second as being the least of the first substances.

Macedonius said that the third being, namely: The Holy Ghost, was no God; but a servant of God and the Son.

Ætius and Eunomius taught that the Father, Son and Holy Ghost were different things or beings.

The Origenists held that the Son could not see the Father, and the Holy Ghost could not see the Son.

Maximinus feared that the Father was a part of God, and each person was one-third of the trinity.

The Metangismonites said that the second person was in the first, as a small vessel in a larger.

The Allogians said that John uttered a falsehood when he said that God was the Word; because they could not comprehend the mystery of the Word.

The Monarchians as also the Praxeans and Victorians said that the Almighty Father was Jesus Christ, and that he had placed himself at his right hand.

The Sabellians made the person and the names of Christ and of the Father, one; and are called *Patripassians;* for they believed that the Father had suffered. Behold thus, those save who undertake to search things incomprehensible, and who want to soar higher than the Scriptures teach.

Again Erasmus Roterod says, The Word was God. It was Almighty, out of the Almighty, with the Father, not brought forth for that time, but for all time. Thus proceeding from the paternal heart, and never leaving it. He further says, That the Father has begotten unto himself, the Son like unto himself in every respect, from eternity, to eternity. Again he says in *suo ecclesiaste*, Christ is the word of God, Almighty, which, without beginning and without end, ever comes forth from the heart of the Father.

Martin Luther says, The word is that

which God speaks in himself, and which remains in him and is never separated from him. We do not controvert the testimony of Erasmus and of Luther; but we cited them for the reason that it might be observed what diversity of opinion exists.

Philip Mel. says, The word is begotten in thought, and is called the image of God, for that which is thought is the image of the thing thought of. Say, beloved reader, who dare build his conscience upon such foundation and reasoning?

Again, some councils resolved that there were three persons in the Trinity, that is, three real substances, and these same were *Homusii*, that is, of the same nature (co-essential); both of these, namely, the persons and their natures have been suspected.

Behold, thus they follow their own opinions and inclinations, build upon vapor and wind, look at each other, and not at the word of the Lord, confuse the simple minds who are not versed in the Scriptures, proclaim their opinions and not the word; and whoever cannot agree with and follow them, is called a deceiver and heretic, by them; therefore I pray you, for Jesus' sake, not to climb higher in this ineffable Majesty than you have steps, and not to search farther than the word of the Lord has taught, while many a piercing eye has been, and is yet daily dazzled by this adulation. For you can understand as little of the unspeakable beauty and conception, how, and in what manner it was brought about from eternity, as you can form an idea of the indescribable Father himself.

Therefore let not the opinion and flattery of the learned be the foundation upon which you build your faith; but let the undeceiving, plain word of God and the testimony of holy John be a sure foundation whereon to build your faith.

He says, "In the beginning was the Word, and the Word was with God, and the Word was God," "All things were made by him; and without him was not any thing made that was made," John 1: 1, 3.

This same Word, which was from the beginning and which, in the course of time became flesh, is called by Paul the Son, Christ Jesus, and the first begotten of all creatures, Col. 1: 15.

Yea, dear reader, if the learned had left unbroken the testimony of John which he spoke of his eternal divinity; and if they had inclined their intellects to the word of God, there would never have been such dark confusion in the world, in regard to Christ, the Son of God.

Therefore I advise you in faithful love, take heed and beware; for the testimony of John is too clear to be obscured by flattery, and too strong to be broken by philosophy. Whosoever would rather drink the precious, clear wine of divine truth, than the impure waters of human adulation, let him hold to the word of the Lord, and let him abandon the unscriptural, destructive explanations, garblings, opinions and ideas of the learned.

This is sufficient of the eternal and ineffable divinity of Christ. Now, by the grace of God, we will proceed, and maintain by the power of the Scriptures, that those abominably err, who say, The word is not become flesh, but it has taken unto itself our flesh or a man of our flesh, as will be briefly and clearly shown in the following:

In the first place John A' Lasco writes, and says, "Divine justice requires that that which we broke, through our flesh, included in Adam's loins, should be punished in the same flesh. Or, as some say, that the nature which inflicted sin, should be punished for such sin, and that that which incurred death should also destroy it."

Answer. Since he and his followers would uphold their cause with the justice of God, and pretend to say that the inflicter and institutor should suffer punishment, then they should, by right, not use the words "our flesh and nature," but "Adam and Eve," in their writings (for they were the first inflicters and institutors), and not the flesh and nature of their descendants, as may be openly seen, Gen. 3: 6.

The nature of man was first created pure and good; but was corrupted through Adam's disobedience. And as he was thus corrupted in his nature, so all his children were born corrupted; nevertheless, the children were not the inflicters and institutors, but Adam and Eve were. If the justice of God, then, requires the punishment of the inflicter and institutor, it would be but right, according to justice that not any of the children should be punished; for they were not the first that disobeyed; but Adam and Eve should receive the punishment, for they were the first that transgressed.

O, no, Adam and all his seed could not be justified, through the weakness of his flesh. They were guilty above measure, and had not a penny wherewith to pay, but it was liquidated for Christ's sake, who, through his eternal love and mercy (as Adam and his could not be justified in themselves), appearing in the shape and form of sinful man, fulfilled the justice of the Father, and tore to pieces the handwriting of the law, and has effaced and paid for all that which Adam had inflicted and broken by his transgression, by the sacrifice of his precious blood, Rom. 8: 3; Eph. 2: 15.

Since they point to the justice of God, I deem it necessary to treat on this a little further, that the intelligent reader may learn that this assertion of theirs is quite powerless, nay, in every respect without foundation in the Scripture.

It is manifest, kind reader, that Adam and Eve, together with their descendants tempted by the serpent, fell into condemnation and death, by the justice of God, Gen. 3: 6; and that nothing can be born of them but that which is condemned and guilty of death, Rom. 5: 12; 1 Cor. 15.

Since Adam and all his seed, on account of his disobedience, became condemned and guilty of death by the eternal justice of God; and if the Lord Christ, according to his holy humanity, were a natural fruit of the flesh of Adam, as they pretend, then the man Christ must be again condemned and guilty of death, on account of his human birth. This is too clear to admit of denial, or else our opponents must take back their own argument, and acknowledge that God's justice is not eternal.

O, no, the flesh of Christ is holy, pure, spotless, knows no sin, makes pious and saves, is a true bread of souls, as is the word, which, in the latter days, according to the intention and purpose of the Father, became a true, passive man, for the salvation and eternal deliverance of all; and who died an innocent death for us.

It avails in no manner that they say that Mary was blessed, and that her fruit was saved from sin by the power of God. We confess that Mary was blessed, and that the fruit was without sin; but we deny that Mary was without sin in consequence of the blessing; for Paul says, "The Scripture hath concluded all under sin, that the promise by faith of Jesus Christ might be given to them that believe," Gal. 3: 22.

Again, if the man Christ were a flesh of Mary's flesh, then Mary would have been blessed through her own flesh; and Adam would have been reconciled through his own flesh; the justice of God would have been broken, and our condemnation, curse and death be dissolved and requited through flesh, condemned, cursed and guilty of death.

O, no, the Scripture teaches plainly that we have all become sinners in Adam, and that we have all, through sin, fallen under the judgment, wrath, and condemnation of God, and become subject unto death, Rom. 5: 6; 1 Cor. 15: 22. And of Christ it testifies that he is the Lamb without spot; that he has not known sin, and in his mouth no guile is found. Inasmuch then as it is manifest that the Scripture entirely concludes Adam and his descendants in sin, and entirely absolves Christ, therefore the discreet and right minded reader may conclude therefrom, that the holy man, Christ Jesus, is not of the unclean flesh of Adam, but that he is the holy and pure word of God, John 1; and that this saying of the learned, that the justice of God requires, &c., is not the sure testimony and word of God, but merely human flattery and fiction.

Oh, I wish that our opponents would once ponder what the justice of God, in this respect, requires according to the Scripture. I trust they would henceforth not hold so strongly to their foundation as they have hitherto done; neither would they say that if any one does not accept their doctrine he sins against the Holy Ghost; or at least think that they might be mistaken.

In the second place he intimates that we should understand the conception of Mary, of which Matthew and Luke speak, as far as regards the mother, as is naturally due her, according to the ordinance of God, Gen. 1.

Answer. It is surprising to me that a man as learned as he is, reasons so indiscreetly, and dares ascribe the conception of Mary to nature, while it is clearly shown all through the Scriptures that the conception of Mary was brought about by supernatural causes, a particular miracle of the Most High, and a glorious sign of the Lord our God; as Isaiah says, "Therefore the Lord himself shall give you a sign: Behold, a virgin shall conceive, and bear a son, and shall call his name immanuel," Isaiah 7: 14; Matt. 1: 23; Luke 1: 31.

Again, Matthew writes concerning the conception of Mary, thus, "When as his mother Mary was espoused to Joseph, before they came together, she was found with child of the Holy Ghost. Then Joseph, her husband, being a just man, and not willing to make her a public example, was minded to put her away privily; but while he thought on these things, behold, the angel of the Lord appeared unto him in a dream, saying, Joseph, thou son of David, fear not to take unto thee Mary thy wife; for that which is conceived in her is of the Holy Ghost. And she shall bring forth a son, and thou shalt call his name Jesus; for he shall save his people from their sins," Matt. 1: 18—21.

Again the angel said to Mary, "Thou shalt conceive in thy womb, and bring forth a son, and shalt call his name Jesus; he shall be great, and shall be called the Son of the Highest; and the Lord God shall give unto him the throne of his father David; and he shall reign over the house of Jacob for ever; and of his kingdom there shall be no end. Then said Mary unto the angel, How shall this be, seeing I know not a man? And the angel answered and said unto her, The Holy Ghost shall come upon thee, and the power of the Highest shall overshadow thee; therefore also that holy thing which shall be born of thee shall be called the Son of God," Luke 1: 31—35.

From all these it is very evident that the conception of Mary was supernatural and a sign and miracle of the Lord; therefore it is all to no purpose that the learned philosophize it as being caused by nature, for it is irrelevant to the matter.

And if the conception of Mary were ascribed, in part, to nature, in the face of these clear Scriptures, then, still it is apparent from the ordinance of God and of nature, that the material, or origin of the child is of the Father and not of the mother, as has been sufficiently explained above in the confession, and also in my writing against Gellius Faber. Therefore these innovations are nothing but philosophy and human genius, without Scripture, and not worthy of an answer; but I have briefly criticised them, and pray you not to despise my references; but let a trial be given before the accusation, lest you mistake yourselves, as Sirach says.

They further advance that the Scripture speaks of the Savior being promised of the seed of woman, of Abraham and the fruits of the loins of David.

Answer. In the first place I say that he who deduces from these Scriptures that the man Christ was flesh of a woman, nay, the natural seed of Abraham and David, who all descended from the unclean flesh of Adam, must also add the unrighteousness, curse and sin of Adam.

If they should assert that he was free from the unrighteousness, curse and sin of Adam, I again answer: That he was not of the natural seed of Adam; for the seed of Adam was unclean, sinful and accursed—therefore nothing but unclean, sinful and accursed flesh could be begotten therefrom; or else the unclean must beget the clean, the sinful the holy, and the accursed the blessed; and therefore the hereditary uncleanness, curse and condemnation be changed. This is too plain to be controverted.

Yea, reader, if the incarnation of the Lord was, as our opponents say it was, then it would be manifest that Christ Jesus was not so pure in his incarnation as was Adam in the first creation. For if it is asserted, as is true, that Christ was conceived in the virgin Mary, then Adam had no other father on earth but God—wherefore he is also called a Son of God, by Luke. Yet, Adam would, nevertheless have been created of purer nature, and of God; but Christ, if he was of the unclean seed of Adam, must be of less clean nature, that is, of an unclean, human and earthly seed. This is too clear to be controverted.

In the second place I say, If the man Christ were a natural fruit and seed of the impure, sinful flesh of Adam, then he would also be guilty, through the eternal justice of God, of the judgment and death. And if he was guilty, how could he redeem and liquidate ours? Or else we must admit that God's justice was ended; and that the sinful had taken away and atoned for the sinful; the condemned for condemnation, and he that was guilty of death had taken away death.

O, no. No unclean animal was permitted to be offered as an offering of reconciliation in Israel; but it must be without blemish. And if the symbolic had to be entirely clean and without blemish, how much more so should be the true one, whereby the eternal reconciliation is brought about—and whereby all symbolic offerings are fulfilled and finished, Heb. 9: 10; Exodus 12: 5; Deut. 15: 21; Mal. 1: 8.

In the third place I would say, He who asserts that the man Christ is a natural fruit and seed of Adam, Abraham, David and of woman, also asserts thereby that there are two persons in Christ, two sons; the father is no true father, the mother no true mother, and the son no true son, as has been said before.

In the fourth place I say, If the man Christ was of the flesh and blood of Mary, then it is manifest that he was not God's Son, but a *created* creature, since he would not be begotten of the Father, but of the flesh and blood of Mary, according to nature, as has been sufficiently shown.

In the fifth place I say, If the man Christ, were of the flesh and blood of Mary, as they pretend, then it is very evident that the birth of man, according to the ordinance of God, can not be without father and mother; and also that a child does not proceed from the mother, but of the father; and if the man Christ came without a father, from the body of the mother, against the ordinance of God, then a new creation must have taken place in Mary, which creation could not have occurred without the Word. If such a creation did occur, then it is manifest that the one half or part of Christ must be created by the other; Mary's son by God's Son; and that the two, namely, the Creator and the creature, thus became one person and Son. Dear reader, observe what abominations they advance.

In the sixth place I say, As all men have both father and mother, and as each has his generation—the father and the mother—so, also, had Christ Jesus both father and mother. His Father was an incomprehensible Spirit from eternity, and will remain so to eternity; therefore he could have no genealogy on the side of the Father; but the mother, who was the true daughter of Adam, Abraham, Isaac and Jacob, conceived him in her virgin womb through the Holy Ghost, by his Father's word; and she begat a true man in due time. Her genealogy was counted in the Scripture; for when he became incarnate in a human being, he must have a genealogy, of which he was born. And this is the word which Paul speaks, Born of the seed of David according to the flesh, Gen. 22: 18; Ps. 132: 11; Rom. 1: 3; 9: 5; Acts 13: 23. Not that there were two sons in Christ, the one without father, and the other without mother; one the Son of God, and the other the son of man, as our opponents pretend. But he who was God's Son also was the son of man; and he who was the son of man, was also the Son of God. Not two, but an only and undivided Son, as the ordinance of God, and the whole Scriptures teach and imply.

If you cannot understand this, then mark this parable: Charles the Fifth is a son of Austria; he is also a son of Spain; not that he is, therefore, one of two sons—but he is an only and undivided son. On the side of the father he is a son of Austria, and on the side of the mother he is a son of Spain. Thus also, is Christ Jesus a Son of God and a son of man; the Son of God on the side of his Father, and the son of man on the side of his mother. Not one of two sons—but an only and undivided Son. The Son of God and of Mary, as has been shown.

Again, if you are yet in doubt about the fruit of the loins of David, I would first refer you to my "Confession," which I wrote to John A'Lasco and his preachers, A. D. 1543, thereby admonishing you, to observe how the throne and the Kingdom of David, were promised to Christ, by Isaiah and the angel Gabriel; which was, however, not *literally* fulfilled in Christ, but in Solomon, who was a figure and symbol of Christ, as were also Isaac, Moses, Aaron, Joshua and Joseph.

Since the whole Scriptures teach us that his kingdom and throne are not literal but spiritual, therefore we must, in the same manner, judge the fruit and the king who shall sit upon the throne and reign; or else the one word must be understood literally, and the other spiritually. This is too plain to be controverted.

Secondly, observe what Christ asked of the Pharisees in regard to Christ the Son of David, and how he answered them, Matt. 22: 42.

Thirdly, observe that if the man Christ were a natural fruit of the loins of David, all the insolvable, gross inconsistencies would be included in him, which we have partly pointed out above, and upon which we will enlarge if God permits.

Fourthly, observe that all the properties of God are alike perfect in him. And therefore his perfect, eternal love and justice require it, as Christ says, "God so loved the world, that he gave his only begotten Son, that whosoever believeth in him should not perish, but have everlasting life." Yea, says John, therein God's love appeared that he sent his only begotten Son into the world, that we, through him might live; for as he adjudged Adam and all his seed unto death, by his eternal justice, on account of his disobedience, so, also, has he, on account of the obedience of Christ, by his eternal love, promised life to all who believe in him; for as his righteous punishment of the sins of Adam's descendants who reject Christ, lasts forever, thus also his paternal love to forgive sin through Christ, lasts forever to all those who believe in Christ, and accept and obey the word of his grace, John 3: 16.

In the third place, I find that it is said that my foundation is, that Christ was begotten of the Holy Ghost.

Answer. It is very unreasonable that I am ever blamed of things of which I am not guilty. In my first "Confession" I have plainly and clearly shown in Latin letters that I do not believe that Christ was conceived in Mary of the Holy Ghost, but through the Holy Ghost. Yet I must hear that I teach that Christ was begotten of the Holy Ghost.

O, dear Lord, how lamentably I am slandered! What else do they against me than the Scribes did unto Jeremiah, when they counseled about him, and said: Come, and let us devise devices against him, and not regard his reasoning, Jer. 18: 18. Yea, I think that I am born to turn my ear to the slanderer, and my back to the scourger. Nevertheless, I hope, by the grace of the Lord, that the time will come when some of them will yet awaken and acknowledge, in all humility, with penitent hearts that they have not despised me, but the word of God, and that they have scorned his Spirit.

In the fourth place he intimates "That I teach that the Word changes itself into human flesh and blood in the womb of the virgin."

Answer. I presume that it will never be proven by virtue of the truth that I have ever, at any place, said or written so; nevertheless they dare say and write so of us. I have spoken thereof as the high apostle has taught me, that the "Word became flesh." That testimony I leave unbroken; and leave it to the Incomprehensible, to him, who, through his omnipotent power so arranged it for the salvation of us all, how much, and what was changed. Yet, I would, in my simplicity, add (if they explain the testimony of John to which I alluded in unchanged letters, and conclude therefrom: Menno teaches, with John, that the "Word became flesh," therefore his foundation must be that it was changed into flesh, &c.), that they should know that *change* does not always take away the first nature of the substances of which something is wrought.

Adam was a man created of the earth; he was a man of the earth, and remained of earth, as the Lord said, "Dust thou art and unto dust shalt thou return," Gen. 3: 19.

Again, in the resurrection of the dead, all those who have again returned to earth, shall, through the power of God, be resurrected from the earth. It is manifest that at first we were earth, afterward we became flesh of the earth, again we became earth of the flesh, and lastly we became flesh of the earth, out of the first flesh, but in glory and brightness, as the Scriptures testify; and thus the first substance, although changed, of which the thing changed was wrought, remains, as has been heard.

Reader, understand me rightly. I do not present this parable for the purpose of asserting that the Word was changed into flesh and blood, the same as the earth of which Adam was made was changed into human flesh, but I have presented it for the purpose of showing to the reader that, although if the Word was changed in being incarnated, it yet remained the word, John 1: 14; 8: 23; 1 John 1: 2; Rev. 19: 13.

In the fifth place he writes, "The Lord Christ was a Spirit from the beginning, unchangeable, holy and eternal. If he, then, was Spirit and unchangeable, how, then, has he changed his substance or his being, and become flesh."

Answer. If I understand him aright, in Letter E, page five, he says, That he has not yet rightly comprehended my meaning of the phrase "*factum est*," i. e. become. If, now, he has not rightly comprehended me, then I cannot see why he should blame me of such doctrine, unless he cannot understand the testimony of John in any other way, notwithstanding his flattery and corruption; as I have merely testified to the same thing literally and unchanged.

Inasmuch as they verbally and in writing blame me of believing in such change, from the testimony of John (although they never heard such doctrine from my lips, nor read it in my writings), therefore I would pray the reader, for Christ's sake, not to blame me of any thing in regard to the change of the eternal Word than of what I hereby confess and explain in plain words: I believe and confess that there is an Almighty, eternal and incomprehensible God, Father, Word, and Holy Ghost, who has lived in eternal glory and shall live so forever. And that this same Almighty, eternal Father, before all creatures, yea, from the beginning and from eternity, begets of himself this his Almighty, eternal Word, in a divine and therefore incomprehensible manner; and that this, his Almighty, eternal Spirit proceeds or flows from him through the Word or Son; but I do not comprehend it.

I also believe and confess in the same manner, that this Almighty, eternal Father, through his Almighty, eternal Word, which is the Son, has, in the power of his Almighty, eternal Spirit, created heaven and earth with their fullness, and that he, thereby, forever preserves and maintains all things created therein and thereby, but I do not comprehend it.

I further believe and confess that all human nature (at the sound of the last trump), through the power of the Almighty and everlasting God, shall again arise from the earth with a glorified body; and that the children of God, who, here on earth, have walked before him in a firm faith and in meekness, shall receive the glorious, promised kingdom of honor, at the hands of the Lord—that, on the other hand, those who have rejected the Lord and his word shall be eternally tormented with unquenchable, everlasting fire, with the devil and his angels, under the fearful, unbearable judgment of the Almighty and great God; but I do not comprehend it.

Faithful reader, observe, that although I do not comprehend the Almighty, only and eternal God in his eternal, divine being, in the dominion of his glory, in the creation and preservation of his creatures, in the reward of both the good and the evil, and in many of his works, yet I do truly believe it, and for this reason: Because the Scripture teaches so; in like manner I can not comprehend how, or in what manner the incomprehensible, eternal Word became flesh or man in Mary; nevertheless I do truly believe that he became man, because the Scripture teaches so. I know that it is a work that was done by the Lord, and is a miracle before our eyes. Nay, it is such a work that intellect cannot fathom, nor accuteness comprehend. Truly it is said, Who shall tell of his birth?

Inasmuch as I clearly find that it is an exalted and incomprehensible miracle of the Almighty and great God which the Almighty, eternal Father, through the omnipotence of the power of the Holy Ghost, has wrought in Mary; and inasmuch as I know how very perilous and solicitous it is for one to search into the incomprehensible profundity and divine mystery with one's foolish earthly understanding; and to garble the plain testimonies of the Holy Ghost, by deceitfulness and human smartness: Therefore it is that I dare not believe, nor teach more nor less of the holy incarnation than the holy prophets of the Lord, Christ Jesus, and also John, Peter and Paul, teach me on every hand in the Scriptures, with such incontrovertibly clear testimonies; all of which are surer and wiser witnesses to me than all the learned who have been, are, or shall ever be on earth; although, I repeat it, I cannot comprehend the ineffable mystery, with my dull, earthly understanding. Sirach says, Inquire not into the things which you cannot bear; and that which is too great or too exalted for you do not search.

Again, as to the saying of Malachi, "For I am the Lord, I change not," Mal. 3 : 6, and to the question of John A' Lasco, "If He is eternal how could He die?"

Answer. Malachi does not here speak of God's substance or being, but of his intention, counsel, resolution and will. From which I confess that God's intention, counsel, will, purpose, promise and love are eternal and unchangeable and must come to pass as he will and has resolved upon in his wisdom.

Inasmuch as it is manifest that the Almighty, eternal and unchangeable Father rules, and does all things according to his eternal, unchangeable intention, counsel, will and purpose, and as he had, through his eternal, unchangeable love, provided his eternal holy Word, or Son, that he, according to his firm and unchangeable intention, should become the Paschal lamb, as Peter says, Therefore this must happen that the Word, in due time, became flesh, although we cannot comprehend it; for it was the gracious intention, counsel, resolution, providence and will of his Almighty and everlasting Word which will forever stand firm, and which, according to the prophetic word, can never be changed, as has been heard.

Behold, honorable reader, this is my reply to the three questions: If he is a Spirit how could he become flesh? Is he God, how could he change? and if he is Eternal how could he die? as I, before my God, believe and confess. I trust, by the grace of God, to remain firmly therein unto death.

I have not counseled with nature and my intellect in this respect, but with the word of the Lord, which is the true light to my feet, which shows me in plain words that the conqueror, the promised seed of woman from the loins of Abraham, Isaac, Jacob, Judah and of David, born according to the flesh, who is the Blessing, Messiah, Christ, King and Savior of all the world, is not of unclean, sinful flesh, but of the pure seed of his heavenly Father; the word of God conceived of the Holy Ghost, in the virgin Mary, and in her became flesh, as John says. Christ himself also says that he is from above, that he is the bread from heaven, and that he went forth from the Father, John 16. And Paul says that he is the Lord of heaven; descended from above; that he is the Alpha and Omega; our Immanuel, 1 Cor. 15; Eph. 4: 10; Rev. 1: 8; Isa. 7: 14. And, besides, as I plainly see that our opponents dare not advance these and such plain Scriptures, but garble them by their intellect with many exceptions and flatterings; therefore I repeat it, that I turn away from intellect and nature, bind my faith and conscience to the word of the Lord, and truly and firmly believe and trust, that this great miracle of God was thus produced in Mary; although I cannot comprehend it.

Behold, kind reader, whosoever testifies or writes any thing else of me, in regard to the change of the eternal Word, but that which I hereby confess, is a liar and does not testify to the truth. The testimony to which I refer is firm and binding: "The word is become flesh." But how far it was changed he knows who in his eternal love has so arranged it for the salvation and everlasting deliverance of us all, through his Omnipotence. Praise be to God forever, Amen.

Here I will perhaps be asked, if then, the Father is not of divine nature? and whence has Christ derived his humanity? To this I answer: From whence came the abundance of water which flowed from the hard rock? The rock was no water nor watery substance. Was it not produced by the omnipotence of God, to whom nothing is impossible, above all human understanding and comprehension?

Again, how did a virgin conceive otherwise than through the power of God, and the operation of the Holy Spirit, above the comprehension of all philosophers? Nay, above the comprehension of Mary herself, for she said, "How shall this be, seeing I know not a man? and the angel answered and said unto her, The Holy Ghost shall come upon thee, and the power of the Highest shall overshadow thee; therefore also that holy thing which shall be born of thee shall be called the Son of God." He does not say, that holy thing which shall come from thy flesh and blood, as say our opponents.

If they should further say, that if the Word became flesh, and did not take unto itself our flesh, then it did not remain God's Word; as when Lot's wife became a pillar of salt, she did no longer remain man or woman; and when the water became wine it did no longer remain water. I would reply: The Scripture says that Lot's wife became a pillar of salt, and that the water became wine. This the Scripture says, and therefore it is also true. But the Scripture says not that Lot's housewife took unto herself a pillar of salt, and that water took unto itself wine. In the same manner the Scriptures also testify that the Word became flesh; but does not testify, that the Word took unto himself our flesh.

I would further say, that if some Scriptures could be produced to prove that "becoming" is taking unto one's self; or that two persons and sons of different natures and minds can be one person and son; or that there was a true Son from the beginning who had not both father and mother; or that a son can be his father's son, who is not of the father's seed, then we might ponder upon their foundation a little further. But since they never produce such Scriptures, neither are they able to produce them; and since the Scriptures testify that Jesus Christ is the Son of God, therefore the testimony of John remains firm and immutable: "The Word is become flesh," however much philosophers may dispute this.

Lastly I would say, That if the Word did not become flesh, but only took unto himself a man of Mary's flesh, as our opponents assert, and if the same was used as an instrument to suffer for us, then it is manifest that Jesus Christ, a Son of his Father in truth (as John calls him), did not come in the flesh (*corporatus* as Castalion says), for were he to suffer himself, and not another in his stead, then he must come in the flesh, otherwise he could not have suffered. This is too clear to be contradicted. All those who deny this, are deceivers and anti-christs, 2 John 1: 7.

He further writes, "If he is holy why was he condemned for the sake of sin in the judgment of the Father?" At another place he also writes: "Christ partook of no other flesh than that which was subject to sin and death, that he might be tempted."

Answer. If we are to understand his words as they read, then Christ, together with his holy flesh was subject to sin and death; this is incontrovertible. For he says, If he is holy why was he then condemned for sin under the judgment of the Father. Just as if he, was unholy, and guilty of death under the judgment, and deserving of the wrath and punishment of God. But this must be so too if we are to assert that the flesh of Christ was of Mary's flesh. Therefore it is manifest from his words that the sin by which he was tempted dwelt in his flesh; and that thus he did not die, out of grace for us, but as one guilty, for himself. For the wages of sin is death.

O, dear Lord, If the poor Menno was to speak of the Son of God thus blasphemously, and were to include him in sin, O, what an unpleasant, bitter song would be sung about him! But whatever the learned dream and philosophize, must be accepted as right and good.

This, then, is my short reply to his words just cited, namely: Isaiah and Peter testify of him that he did not know sin, and that guile was not found in his mouth. Yea, dear reader, he was holy before his incarnation, holy in his incarnation, and will remain holy forever. For it was needful, that we should have such a high priest, who is holy, innocent and spotless, and who became higher than the heavens; for if he were not innnocent and holy, he could not have requited for our sins and guilt, but must have suffered for his own imperfections and guilt. But now the Scriptures testify that he was bruised for our iniquities and was stricken for our transgression, Is. 53: 5, 8.

In the sixth place he writes and says, "The comparison of the words of Paul, *The form of God* and *the form* of a servant, teaches us that by which God is known to be God, and nothing else, than the immeasurable power and the brightness of his light and glory to which none can aspire; that we must also understand it as that by which a servant is known to be a servant, and that it is nothing else but our human flesh, and that through the disobedience of our first parents it was forfeited under the servitude of sin; nevertheless he writes that we must so understand it that he took upon himself our flesh, but not the servitude thereof," *Hac ille.*

Answer. Here I will leave the reader to choose whether to explain this *form of a servant* as having reference to a servile* form, or, as John A'Lasco thinks, to a sinful form. If it has reference to a servile, and not to a sinful form, then it does not support the assertion that the Word has taken unto himself our flesh. But if it is explained, as John A'Lasco explains it, as having reference to a sinful, and not to a servile condition, then it must necessarily follow that that is also in Christ, on account of which we are called servants, namely, on account of sin, or else the adduced antithetical form is not in place and can not stand, as you will hereafter, by the grace of God, clearly hear and see.

I deny that I misinterpreted the Latin phrase *Exinanivit semetipsum*, as John A'Lasco accuses me of doing; although at one place I wrote, *He has humbled himself*, I trust I have not written it wrongly. At another place I wrote, *The Son, the Word, was humbled*, went beneath himself; was made lower than the angels. But nowhere have I written that he went out from himself, as John A'Lasco wrongfully accuses me. I will leave it to the judgment of all grammarians whether or not I have written correctly.

I think Christ has greatly humbled himself, since he is the Almighty, eternal Word, Wisdom and Power of God, and became such a poor, weak, despised man. He also went much beneath himself, since he was in divine form and became such a despised servant. Yea, reader, that Paul here speaks (Phil. 2: 7, 8), of the servile and not of the sinful condition, we may well deduce from the following Scriptures. "Behold,"

*The words *servile* and *servility* here mean, a condition of servitude as spoken of by Paul in Phil. 2: 7, 8.—*The Publishers.*

says Isaiah, "my servant, whom I uphold; mine Elect, in whom my soul delighteth," Is. 42: 1. Matthew is my witness that the prophet speaks this of Christ; and therefore is he called the servant of his Father, because he has performed the work and service of his Father here on earth, for us poor sinners, as he says, "Even as the Son of man came not to be ministered unto, but to minister, and to give his life a ransom for many," Matt. 20: 28.

Therefore, I repeat it. Paul here speaks of the servile and not of the sinful condition which Christ took upon himself for our salvation. For if he here spoke of the sinful and not of the servile condition, then Christ must also have assumed the form of a servant, that is sin; else the phrase The *form of a servant*, and The *form of God* could not exist together. For as the phrase *form of God* testifies to his true divinity, so also, the *form of a servant* must testify to his true servile form; or it must follow from the argument of John A'Lasco, that, although Christ was in divine form, yet he lacked the divinity, the same as he had the form of a servant but the servility, i. e. sin he had not.

O, no, it is not so. He was in God-form, and was therein truly God; thus he also took upon himself the form of a true servant, and was therein a true servant; as may be deduced from Isaiah, Matthew and the words of Christ. And in this sense the antithesis, the *form of God* and *the form of a servant*, exists, and does not require the exception which John A'Lasco here made. And this is the proper cause and reason why Paul wrote to the Philippians about this, that they should not be contentious one with another, nor seek their own vain, carnal honor, or any thing selfish, but that they should, after the example of Christ, humble themselves one towards another, and walk in love; for although Christ was in the form of God, yea "equal with God, but made himself of no reputation and took upon him the form of a servant," and not the exalted form of a mighty emperor or king. He came to minister unto us and not to be ministered unto, Matt. 20: 28. Yea, "He was in all points tempted like as we are yet without sin," Heb. 4: 15. He sought not his own but that which was ours; and for our sakes "became obedient unto death, even the death of the cross," Phil. 2: 8. Thus the assertion of John A'Lasco, that the Word took unto himself our flesh or a man of our flesh, remains unproven.

But his point that while Christ was here upon earth he still was also in heaven, that his face shone as the sun, that his raiment was white as the light, that he healed the sick, raised the dead, and by his word remitted sin, which power alone belongs to God, does not prove that he received his holy flesh from our sinful flesh; but it rather proves that he still remained God and his word, notwithstanding he, for a time, so humbled himself and went beneath his divine splendor, attributes, right and glory, for our sakes. Whosoever sincerely fears God, let him consider and judge, Matt. 17: 2; Luke 7: 21.

In the seventh place he asserts it as his foundation that the Word did not become flesh, but that he took unto himself our flesh of Mary, and confirms this with the Scripture Heb. 2: 14; which reads thus, "Forasmuch then as the children are partakers of flesh and blood, he also himself likewise took part of the same," and says, "The word was made flesh;" not that he has in any manner changed his first estate, or form, but he has taken unto himself our flesh and has therewith covered his divinity while here upon earth.

Answer. All those who desire a scriptural and correct understanding of the Scriptures quoted, and also of Christ, the Son of God, should well observe that God, the Almighty, eternal Father, the true Creator, who wills and works, is the only source of all good; and that he ineffably before all creatures, begat of himself his Almighty, eternal and ineffable Word, and has, through the same created all things, and thereby governs, maintains and preserves them; and that he in his eternal justice, love, and in all his attributes, together with his ineffable Word and Holy Spirit, is an eternal and perfect God, and beside him there is none other; and that he is eternal and unchangeable in his counsel, purpose, will and conclusion, as was said before, Mal. 3: 6

And, that this Almighty, eternal Father, through his Almighty, eternal Word, in the power of his Almighty, eternal Spirit, has, according to his divine purpose, counsel, will and conclusion, created Adam and Eve, the parents of us all, as righteous, good and pure creatures, unto eternal life, nay, after his own image and likeness, as the Scriptures testify; that he gave unto them the command of life and death, that they might fear, love, praise, thank and serve him, and live according to his will, Gen. 1.

Behold, this is the Creator that created Adam and Eve; it also shows through what he created them, how and for what purpose he created them; what he permitted and what he forbid them to do; what he promised them if they obeyed him, and what he threatened if they should disobey him; and thus the glory of God began to shine, Ps. 33: 5; John 1: 10.

In this piety, holiness and righteousness, Adam and Eve remained so long as they did not deviate from the counsel, word, will and command of God, in which all things have, and must have their being. But man was left in the hands of his counsel, Sirach 15: 14. But through the old serpent, the cunning reptile and envier of the honor of God, and all good, caused the glorious, noble creature of life to be led from the the favor and grace of his Creator into condemnation and death, and obscured the glory of God. He began with Eve, the weaker vessel, to tempt her with the desires of her appetite; for the woman saw, says Moses, that the tree was good for food and pleasant to the eyes. He falsified the word of the Lord, and said, "Ye shall not surely die," and made glorious promises, saying, "In the day ye eat thereof then your eyes shall be opened; and ye shall be as Gods, knowing good and evil."

Adam and Eve disobeyed the command of their God and Creator, by which alone they must live; believed the promise of the serpent; ate, and through the justice of God, fell into the threatened curse, condemnation and death, and thus the deceiving serpent established the kingdom of hell and of death. There, now lay the miserable, accursed Adam and his wife, Eve, in the power of the devil, poisoned "from the sole of the foot even unto the head," both within and without, with his impure, deadly venom, and became subject unto sin and death. According to the justice of God, there was now no way of escape, for Adam and all his descendants; for the word of life was rejected; the holy command of God was transgressed, the venom of the serpent was taken. Alas, all was lost to them! Their eyes were opened, the shame was acknowledged, the gnawing worm was in the disobedient, self-accusing conscience; there was nothing but shaking and trembling, sighing and remorse. They fled before the face of the Lord and knew not where to hide from his wrath; for the justice of God pointed to the word, "For in the day that thou eatest thereof thou shalt surely die."

Here the counsel, purpose, will and conclusion of the Almighty, eternal God were unchanged. He would make manifest his glory and have a man after his own image and likeness.

Inasmuch as this was resolved upon and provided for with God, as has been said; and as with poor Adam, all was lost, as also with all his descendants, for at heart he was full of venom and abashed before his God, therefore should the unchangeable, will, counsel and resolution of the unchangeable God be executed, there must be another who was like the corrupted Adam before his fall; for upon such a man, God's will had resolved; and with Adam all was lost.

Therefore the ineffable, eternal Word, by which Adam and Eve were created, by which all things are and must forever remain; the Almighty power and wisdom of God, must become man, that he might bruise the head of the deceiving serpent, for the salvation of the condemned Adam and all his descendants; that temptation might be overcome; that the holy and unchangeable will of the Father might be fulfilled; that the dominion and power of the devil might be destroyed; and that he might, by his willing obedience and spotless offering, discharge and put away the guilt and deserved death of Adam, by his innocent death.

Behold, this joyous gospel, and these glad tidings of the divine grace, which God declared to the poor, afflicted and fugitive, Adam. He accepted them through faith; consoled himself therewith, and sincerely rejoiced in his grace, Gen. 3: 15; 22: 18; Jer. 23: 6; Luke 1: 28.

And this is the Messiah who, I say, was promised Adam, of a woman, the salvation of all the world; promised to Abraham, Isaac and Jacob; the glorious Branch, Rod, Plant and Fruit of David, symbolized in Solomon, the natural fruit of his loins; who shall sit on his throne and reign in Israel forever. All who believe on him shall receive the mercy, grace and peace of God; but whosoever does not believe on him, on him remaineth the wrath of God, John 3: 36.

From all this it follows that as Adam was created, in the beginning and we in him, through the Word, he and also we are again quickened of God through this same Word, and accepted in grace. John says, "In the beginning was the Word, and the Word was with God; and the Word was God; the same was in the beginning with God. All things were made by him, and without him was not any thing made that was made," &c. "And the Word was made flesh, and dwelt among us, and we beheld his glory, the glory as of the only begotten of the Father, full of grace and truth." Behold, in such plain words testifies the Spirit of God, that both the creation and the restoration of Adam and his seed, was brought about by no other means than through the Word, as has been heard, Matt. 3: 11; John 1; Col. 1: 19.

And to the better explanation of this, and also to learn to understand rightly how entirely sinful, impure, poisoned, powerless, and as nothing we all have become in Adam, I would point you, with Paul, to the law and the Scriptures; they will depict to you the impure, powerless nature and sinfulness of our flesh so plainly, that you are forced to acknowledge that the holy, glorious and spotless Messiah, through whom we all are pacified and reconciled with God, could not be of such impure, sinful and accursed seed and flesh as the learned teach us, and pretend with their philosophic reasoning, without the Scriptures.

Thus speaks Moses, Thou shalt not covet, or thou shalt not desire. Reader, observe: In these few words is properly represented the first righteousness in which Adam was created in the beginning; and which is yet claimed of God according to his righteousness, by his descendants. Ponder diligently on these words of Moses and examine yourself closely, before your God, who tries the hearts and reins, whether or not you sometimes do not, against the law, find such forbidden lusts in your flesh.

If you imagine yourself free from these, you convert God into a liar, 1 John 1: 10; and thereby you also shame all the righteous of God, who were from the beginning; for they have all unanimously complained of their evil-disposed, wicked flesh, and have, alas, too unanimously shown it in their fruits. The Scriptures testify that I speak the truth.

Yea, reader, if any man, born of the sinful flesh of Adam, had completely fulfilled the law, then for such the commanded yearly sin-offering, which was offered by the high priest in the Holy of Holies, was useless and fruitless. Neither would it have been necessary for the Son of the Most high, the eternal word of God to become man; for such a person could have done all this and fulfilled the required righteousness. But as it was, there was neither prophet nor any man of God, born of Adam, so holy, or so pious, but who had to console himself with the promise of God in regard to Christ, also symbolized in the offering, and with the divine grace, through faith.

But if you find that you do not as the law requires, but that you are not alone ever fought by the lusts which dwelt in your flesh, but that you are also often involuntarily conquered thereby, then you must acknowledge that you are already condemned to death by the law of righteousness. For the law says, "Cursed be he that confirmeth not all the words of this law to do them; and all the people shall say, Amen," Deut. 27: 26.

Behold, kind reader, if you would rightly know and acknowledge how miserable, naked, powerless, impotent, unclean, sinful and poisoned all of Adam's seed is become in him, through his transgression, and how his seed is fallen, through the just righteousness of God, into his wrath, judgment, curse, condemnation and death, then, I say, search the law diligently; for it points out to you, First, the obedience to God and righteousness required of you; and also the weakness of your sinful flesh, your impure and evil disposed nature; and that you are already condemned to death, according to the rigor of the above mentioned righteousness, since you, through your inherent, weak nature and evil disposed flesh, do not walk in the required righteousness as God has commanded and required of you in his law, as you will clearly notice by your own unction if you but rightly observe.

Inasmuch as Adam and his seed are so entirely corrupted; as by nature he was created pure and clean, and became wholly impure and evil disposed, and thus fell in the righteous judgment of God; and since every thing is involved in sin; therefore, if this venom was to be weakened in its power; if the corrupted nature of Adam was to be delivered from the curse and judgment of sin; if the righteousness of God was to be appeased; if the power of the devil was to be disturbed; if curse, wrath, condemnation and death were to be taken away; if the hand writing of the law, which required such righteousness of Adam's children, was to be broken to pieces; if the eternal providence, counsel, will and determination of God were to be fulfilled; if his kingdom and glory were to be acknowledged; and if there was to be such a man as the counsel, will, and determination of God required, as has been heard; then the everlasting love of God would require that there should be another man, who, conquering the devil, should disturb his power, fulfill the righteousness of God, promulgate his glory, make a clean sacrifice, and who should thus, out of love and compassion, be innocently accursed and condemned to death; not *of* Adam, but *for* the everlasting salvation of Adam and his seed; that thus the corrupted and condemned Adam, together with his corrupt and condemned seed, should be again accepted in grace, through his name, and be again delivered from their great fall, Gal. 3; Gen. 3: 17; Luke 11: 21; John 14: 30; Col. 1: 14.

It could not, I repeat it, be a man of Adam's flesh; for the corrupted flesh of

THE CONFUTATION.

Adam could not beget fruit which could fulfill this, while it was so thoroughly corrupted and condemned before God; but it must be a man who was free from the deserved curse, condemnation and death of Adam, and also from all his venom, sin and unrighteousness, as has been sufficiently heard.

Observe, my faithful reader, and here learn to know your God in his grace and love. For although the whole Scriptures conclude Adam and Eve, together with all their descendants, entirely under the sin, curse, condemnation and death, according to justice, yet it does not leave in hell the solicitous, afflicted conscience, which has been so far taught and directed by the law, that it feels its wounds and stripes, and acknowledges that it is deserving of eternal death and condemnation; but the Scriptures show in consoling words and symbols, where and of whom to get the healing medicine, namely: of Christ Jesus. For it is he who with all his righteousness, merit, cross, blood and death, was graciously given of God our heavenly Father to the fallen and condemned Adam and his posterity, for their eternal salvation and reconciliation.

I think this may well be called a joyous gospel, and glad tidings to all afflicted and lamenting souls, who having become subject to sin and death under the law, so fearfully tremble at the righteous judgment and wrath of God, that the Almighty, eternal God and Father has so loved us miserable, trifling and condemned sinners who are so far estranged from him and, according to his righteous judgment, are deserving of eternal death, that he sent into this miserable world, his Almighty, eternal and ineffable Word, his only, eternal and beloved Son, the brightness of his glory; and who was like unto Adam before the fall, as a proof and means of his divine grace; and that this One has, through his perfect righteousness, willing obedience and innocent death, led us from the kingdom and dominion of the devil into the kingdom of his divine grace and eternal peace.

Inasmuch as the Scriptures pronounce the first Adam and all his seed to be such an impure, sinful, accursed and condemned Adam, and pronounce Christ, the second Adam, free from all impurity, sin, curse and condemnation, therefore the impartial reader may well deduce therefrom that such a precious, glorious fruit could not be plucked from an elder or thorn bush; but should be begotten from some other source, namely: from him who is the only cause and eternal source of all good things, as has been said.

That the holy and saving flesh of Christ was not of the sinful and condemned flesh of Adam may be plainly observed from the following passages and figures of the Holy Scripture.

Isaiah says, "All we like sheep, have gone astray; we have turned every one to his own way; and the Lord hath laid on him the iniquity of us all." "He hath done violence to no one; neither was any deceit in his mouth. Yet it pleased the Lord to bruise him," Isa. 53: 6, 9, 10.

I must pay, says the Psalmist, in the person of Christ that which I had not taken. He "bare our sins in his own body on the tree," and by his stripes we were healed, 1 Pet. 2: 24.

"For he hath made him to be sin for us, who knew no sin; that we might be made the righteousness of God in him," 2 Cor. 5: 21. Again, we are all sinners and come short of the glory of God; but are made righteous, without merit, by his grace, through the deliverance which is in Christ.

Again, "The Scripture hath concluded all under sin, that the promise by faith of Jesus Christ might be given to them that believe," Gal. 3: 22.

Ye know, says John, that the Son of God "was manifested to take away our sins;" and in him is no sin, 1 John 3: 5. Read also all these Scriptures, Isa. 7: 9 and 40; Jer. 23; Mic. 5; John 1, 3, 5, 6, 8, 9, 10, 11, 14, 16, 17; 1 Cor. 15; Acts, 20; Eph. 4; 1 Tim. 3; 1 John 1, 2, 3, 4, 5; Heb. 1, 2, 3, 7; Rev. 1: 19.

SCRIPTURAL REFERENCES UPON THE FOREGOING SUBJECT.

He is the spiritual tree of life in the midst of the paradise of God, which is not planted by the hands of man, but of God himself, Rev. 2: 7; all those that shall eat the fruits of this tree, with pure hearts, shall live forever; and the leaves of the tree are for the healing of the nations, Rev. 22: 3.

He is the spiritual, brazen serpent, symbolized in the Mosaic serpent, Num. 21: 9, which was erected for us miserable sinners, by the Father, in the wilderness of this world, as a healing sign, which had the venomous form of the venomous serpent, yet had not its venomous nature. All those who believe on him are delivered from the curse, condemnation and death caused by the serpent; but whosoever does not believe on him, on him the wrath of God remains, and he must eternally bear and suffer, according to God's eternal justice, the threatened curse, death and condemnation, John 3: 36.

He is the spiritual mercy seat, which is not, like the ark made of Shittim wood, but of fine, pure gold, from which God graciously hears us and speaks unto us through his Spirit and word, Ex. 25: 10; Rom. 3: 24; Heb. 4: 13. He is the spiritual Paschal Lamb, which is without spot, and in the sprinkling and sanctification of whose blood the chosen Israel of God was ever graciously saved from the destroying angel, and from the wrath of God, in the midst of the cruel, dark Egypt of this world, Ex. 12: 23; Num. 9: 16.

He is the true bread from heaven, which is not made of natural corn or wheat, I mean, of our sinful flesh, but is begotten of the dew of the eternal Word, which is the only and true food for our souls, by which we shall live forever, if we only eat of him through true faith, Ex. 16: 5; Num. 11: 18.

He is the Rock which was torn from the mountain, without hands, that is, without human assistance, which Nebuchadnezzar saw in a dream; and to which Daniel was referred as being the one who should waste and destroy the iron, clay, silver and gold; yea, all the kingdoms of this world; for he has all power in heaven and upon earth; he is a powerful King over all; and to his kingdom there shall be no end, nor pass to other people, Dan. 2: 44.

Behold, kind reader, judge from the above mentioned Scriptures and figures, if you fear God, if such doctrine is based upon the Scriptures, which claims that this righteous, holy, spotless, obedient and saving Messiah was born of the unrighteous, sinful, impure, disobedient and accursed flesh or seed of Adam, and that it took its humanity therefrom. O, no. This pure, clear water, with which all our blemishes were to be washed away, could never be drawn from such an impure, stagnated pool. Let every body reflect what the word of the Lord teaches him.

Now we will, by the grace of the Lord, enlarge upon the Scriptures of Heb. 2, that we may rightly comprehend the foundation and truth thereof; and that, too, that our opponents may not boast that we do not satisfy them; I would first refer you to the first chapter of Hebrews, and have you observe what is said there of Christ.

In the first place it reads, that "God hath in these last days spoken unto us by his Son, whom he hath appointed heir of all things, by whom also he made the worlds."

In the second place it reads, that this same Son is "the brightness of his glory, and the express image of his person."

Thirdly, that he has purged our sins by himself.

Fourthly, that he is the first begotten Son of God, and that all the angels shall worship him.

Fifthly, that he is God, and that his kingdom and throne shall endure forever.

Sixthly, that he laid the foundation of the earth; and the heavens are the work of his hands.

I think that if you earnestly ponder on these Scriptures and rightly observe them, you will soon perceive from whence Christ came, who and what he is. For these plain evidences clearly teach that the world was made by him; that he is the brightness of the glory of God; that he hath purged our sins by himself; that he is the first begotten Son of God, that he is God, and that he has laid the foundations of the earth. This could not be of Mary's flesh, Gen. 1:1; Ps. 33:6; Eph. 3:9; 1:9; Col. 1:16; Heb. 1:2; Ps. 102:26; 1 John 1:7; Col. 1:15.

If they should say that these Scriptures are not spoken in regard to the Son of Mary, but in regard to the Son of God, then they confess thereby a divided Son, two persons, two sons; besides, we are convinced by these very Scriptures that they are spoken of the whole Christ; for he has spoken with us as a man, and we are also cleansed of our sins through his human suffering and death, as the Scripture teaches, 1 John 1:7; 1 Pet. 1:19.

But if they should call to their support the sinecdoche, or commonness of the names, then I would answer in brief, plain, words, that the plain, faithful souls, Peter and John the fishermen, Martha the servant, and the plain Nathaniel, knew nothing at all of such satanic testimony and human cunning; but they have given praise to the visible and tangible Christ, and confessed that he was the Son of God, Matt. 16:15; Jn. 6:69; 11:27.

This is still further declared in the second chapter in these words: "What is man, that thou art mindful of him? or the son of man, that thou visitest him? Thou madest him a little lower than the angels; thou crownedst him with glory and honor," Heb. 2:6, 7.

Here I would faithfully admonish the faithful reader, to observe that both Erasmus and Hieronymus, in their Latin translations, have translated this thus: "Thou madest him a little lower than the angels;" and the Hebrew Psalm also has it: "Thou madest him inferior to God; with praise and honor thou crownedst him," Heb. 2:7; Ps. 8:5.

This agrees with the word of Paul, where he says, "Who being in the form of God, thought it not robbery to be equal with God, but made himself of no reputation, and took upon him the form of a servant," Phil. 2:7. At another place he says, "Though he was rich, yet for your sakes he became poor," 2 Cor. 8:9. This also agrees with the words of Christ, "Now, O Father, glorify thou me with thine own self, with the glory which I had with thee, before the world was," Jn. 17:5. I think these plain Scriptures and clear testimonies prove fully that the teachings of our opponents are unscriptural and erroneous, when they say that the Son of God remained in his first form and estate, and was not bruised for our iniquities.

This same man, who, for our sake, was thus humbled and made less than God and the angels, we see is Christ, who for suffering death was crowned with praise and honor; for as he, for the purpose of obedience, humbled himself to the lowest, for our service, therefore he was again exalted to the highest, by the Father. And thus he was innocently put to death for the sake of Adam and all his posterity, by the grace of God; for Adam and his posterity could not be otherwise delivered from the power of death. For it became *him*, for whom and by whom are all things, who has brought many children unto glory, to make the Prince and Captain of their salvation perfect through suffering, as both the Sanctifier, Christ, and those who are sanctified through him, the regenerated, are all of one, that is, of God, Phil. 2:9; Heb. 2:10.

Thus the sanctified together have one Father with their Sanctifier, as John says, "As many as received him, to them gave he power to become the sons of God, even to them that believe on his name; which were born not of blood, nor of the will of the flesh, nor of the will of man, but of God;" and therefore our Savior "is not ashamed to call them (the sanctified), brethren, saying, I will declare thy name unto my brethren, in the midst of the church will I sing praise unto thee," John 1:12; Heb. 2:11, 12. Yea, dear reader, if the flesh of Christ was of Adam's flesh, and if we were called his brethren on that account, as is the doctrine of the learned, then one brother must beget the other; besides, then all the ungodly, yea, whores and knaves, must also be Christ's brethren and sisters. This is too plain to be controverted.

O, no. Who his brethren are, he has himself plainly declared, Matt. 12:59; Mark 3:35; Luke 8:21. And he not only calls them his brethren, but also, his children, and says, "Behold, I and the children which God hath given me." They are called his children for the reason that he has begotten them unto God his Father, by the word of his grace, through the power of his Holy Spirit, in the besprinkling of his precious blood. At another place he also calls them his mother, bride, flesh and bones; which, according to the flesh, they could not be.

Yea, dear reader, if he had received his flesh from the flesh of his children, as John A'Lasco and his followers claim that he has, then the children must have begotten the father. Christ, the new Adam, would say to his new Eve: I am flesh of thy flesh—and not: "Thou art flesh of my flesh." If you fear God, then reflect and judge, Heb. 2:13; Gen. 2:23.

As the children partake of flesh and blood, so he, in the same manner partook of the same, that he might, through death, take the power from him who had the power of death, that is, the devil, and deliver those who, of necessity, were in servitude all their lives; for he does not accept the seed of angels, but of Abraham; therefore he must become like unto his brethren in all things.

Behold, this is the strongest and most important saying wherewith John A'Lasco (in regard to this subject), disputes the whole Scriptures, divides Christ and makes him into two persons and sons, and, as he thinks, joins together his whole work, arguments, sayings and flatterings. And this is his proper foundation and meaning: "As the children are partakers of flesh and blood, so, also, has the Word, or Son of God received or partaken of this flesh and blood from the flesh and blood of the children; and has thus vanquished hell, sin, death and devil in our flesh, Heb. 2; Phil. 2:7; Hosea 13:14; 1 Cor. 15:54; Col. 2:15; 2 Tim. 1:10.

Inasmuch as he so strenuously insists on the above saying, therefore have I by adducing so many Scriptures, so enlarged upon the inherent, unclean, sinful flesh and nature of the children, and their deserved death and condemnation on the one hand, and the pure, holy flesh and nature of Christ, his undeserved death and judgment on the other, that the reader might thereby rightly understand and comprehend that the Lord Jesus Christ could not be of such unclean flesh and seed of the children, nor partake of such a man; for the flesh of the children is unclean and sinful, but the flesh of Christ is pure and holy.

Since his pure flesh could not be of the unclean flesh of the children, as has been said, and since our opponents so strenuously insist upon it, on account of this Scripture, therefore I will diligently examine it word for word, and, by the grace of God, I will attach to each word its wholesome and right meaning.

First, observe that the word *children* has reference to none other than those who, above, are called Christ's brethren, namely, those who believe in him, and who are born of God by the living power of his Spirit and word, as said.

Secondly, observe what the Scriptural meaning of *having communion* with *flesh* and *blood* is; that it is not simply having flesh and blood, as some have interpreted it; but that it also means, to intermix with flesh and blood, and to do the things which are forbidden of God, through the lusts of our flesh, Rom. 7:7; 3:20.

Thirdly, observe that since the children of God are partakers of sinful flesh and blood and are subject to such human weakness by which they involuntarily ever struggle and fail—therefore they must have such a High Priest who could have compassion with their human failures; as he was tempted in the same manner, although without sin, as said.

Fourthly, observe that the adverb *similiter* (that is, in the same manner), here expresses a true human nature in Christ, it is true, but not a natural conception as John A'Lasco claims and argues; for it is manifest all through the Scriptures that the conception of Mary was supernatural; that it was brought about by the Holy Ghost, through faith, as has been shown above.

Fifthly, observe that the expression "partaking of flesh and blood" means nothing else than *having* flesh and blood; since his children and brethren, also have flesh and blood, as Sebastian Castalion, also, has rendered it, but with such differ-

THE CONFUTATION.

ence that his flesh was holy and knew no sin, and therefore experienced no decay; but the flesh of his brethren and children is sinful, and therefore also subject to decay, 1 Cor. 15: 53; 5: 4.

Sixthly, observe that Paul does not at all times use the words *partaking of flesh and blood*, in the same sense. In one place, 1 Cor. 9:12, he writes, "If others be partakers of this power over you," that is, If others *have* this power over you; again, "He that thresheth in hope should be partaker of his hope," that is should receive that which he hopes to get. Again in the 10th, 17th and 21st of the same epistle, it is used for enjoying.

Inasmuch as the word *partaking* has not, every where in Scripture, one meaning—therefore, wherever it is found, it should not be explained otherwise than according to the true nature and meaning of the Scriptures, or else the whole Scriptures must be broken and garbled for the sake of such a word.

Seventhly, observe that the word *eorundem* (that is, of the same), has reference to the words *flesh* and *blood*, but not to the flesh and blood of the children, for that is unclean, sinful, guilty and condemned; if it had reference to the flesh and blood of the children, as John A'Lasco and M. M. claim, and that the Son of God took unto himself a perfect man, body and soul, of the flesh of the children, then it is incontrovertible that all the following and indissoluble inconsistencies must exist:

In the first place an impure, sinful, accursed, and death-guilty Christ, as is the flesh of the children of whom he should have partaken his flesh; for wherever the flesh of the children is, there, also, is the sin and curse of the children; this cannot be controverted, or else justice must have been changed and the curse taken away and ended by our own flesh. To which M., in the first conversation I had with him, thus replied: "Christ was pure and without sin, and that because Mary did not conceive him of the seed of man." I answered: I must understand, then, that sin is because of the mixture, which is the ordinance of God, and not because of the transgression of Adam. He answered: No, it was because of the justice of God that he became of a corrupted nature. I asked, how? He answered: "Because God had said, That in the day thou eatest thereof thou shalt surely die." I then replied: then God was the cause of the sin of Adam; and the threatened death must not only be punishment of sin, but sin itself. I said, Martin, do observe what reasoning you bring forward.

In the second place it follows that there must be a divided Christ, of whom one half must be of heaven and the other half of earth.

In the third place that there must be two persons in Christ; one divine and one human. To which Martin in our second conversation, thus replied: "There were not two persons in Christ, but one person; for, although the word was one person from eternity, yet it was no person which was conceived in Mary." He further said, "Although each human being is one person, and although the man, Christ, was one man as any other man, yet the man, Christ alone was no person." I am ashamed to touch upon such inconsistent things. Paul justly said, *Ubi disputator seculi hujus?* "Where is the disputer of this world?"

In the fourth place that there are two Sons in Christ—the Son of God without mother, and he impassive; and the son of man without father, and he passive; something which M. M., both in our first and also in our second conversation, several times openly admitted before us all, in plain language. O God, what strange things we hear!

In the fifth place, that not the first begotten and only Son of God, but the fatherless Son of Mary, of the accursed, sinful flesh of Adam, died for us—something which is directly contrary to Christ, John, Paul and the whole Scriptures.

In the sixth place, that the eternal offering of reconciliation, once offered for the sins of the whole world, was not the spotless Lamb, but an unclean, blemished offering which was subject to sin and death, as may also be unmistakably deduced from the writings of A'Lasco, John 3: 16; Rom. 8: 31.

In the seventh place, the angel Gabriel

Peter, and the Lord himself, acknowledge that the man, Christ Jesus, is the Son of God. Thomas acknowledges him as his Lord and God; besides the whole Scriptures teach that he is our Advocate, Reconciler, Mediator, High Priest, Deliverer and Messiah—and if he is yet to be of the unclean sinful flesh and seed of Adam, then it is manifest that a created creature and man of the sinful flesh of Adam, is our Messiah, Deliverer, Reconciliator, Advocate, High Priest, Yea, Lord and God; something which is not alone an abomination and idolatry, but also open blasphemy against God.

* * * * *

In the tenth place, if the eternal Word, by which every thing was created, had partaken of such a carnal son of the flesh of of the children, or of Mary, and had thus united himself into one person and son, then the Creator and the creature, the Son of God without mother, and the son of Mary without father, must have become one, undivided person and son. This is incontrovertible.

In the eleventh place, if the Word has partaken of such flesh as that of Mary, and if it did not become man, then God is not the true Father of Christ, Mary no true mother, and Christ no true son of both his father and mother; besides, the whole Scriptures are denied which testify that Christ is the Son of God.

I think that all these indissoluble inconsistencies, sufficiently show you that John A'Lasco has not given the Scriptural meaning to the word *eorundem*.

Eighthly, observe why Christ, the Prince of our salvation, became man, namely, that he might destroy the prince of death, the devil, by his innocent death, and that he might thus deliver and free his poor, enslaved, timorous brethren and children from the accusing law, from the judgment of sin and the terror of death.

Ninthly, observe that the passage, "He takes* not on him the nature of angels, but he takes* on him the seed of Abraham," should not be understood as having any reference to the taking on of human flesh, as the learned explain it, but to the partaking of grace, by which we are accepted;

*German and Holland translations.

for he uses the word *take* in the present tense and angels in the plural number, and says, "He *takes* not on him the nature of *angels*, but he *takes* on him the seed of Abraham," the children of the promise, Rom. 9:8; the believers, Gal. 3:29; his brethren and children. He accepts them, in grace, to the praise of his Father, Rom. 15:7; prays for their failings and weaknesses, Rom. 8:7; Heb. 5:10. For they can never be freed from the inherent, impure, wicked nature of their sinful flesh, in this life.

Tenthly, observe that a thing which is like unto another, is not necessarily the same thing which it resembles; and, therefore it cannot be maintained by this passage, "Wherefore in all things it behooved him to be made like unto his brethren," that the holy, pure flesh of Christ is of the unclean, sinful flesh of Adam.

Behold, dear reader, if you consider well the explanation of the Scripture, Heb. 2, and weigh it in the balance of the Scriptures, you will very plainly find that this is the meaning of the above mentioned Scripture; that although Christ, the Prince of our salvation, has led us to his glory, and has thus accepted us as brethren and children in faith, yet we are, in our first Adamic birth, so poisoned by the serpent, and so corrupted by nature, that we can nevermore become free of our unclean sinful flesh, so long as we dwell in this tabernacle; but oftentimes (although involuntarily) mix and soil ourselves therewith; and become, therefore, convinced by the hand writing, that we are guilty of death, according to the eternal justice, Rom. 7:7; 3:20; Col. 2:13.

Since we are ensnared by such wicked, sinful, disobedient and death guilty flesh, as all the pious children of God have, from the beginning, dolefully complained of, and could not be entirely freed from the inserted sting of the serpent; therefore it is that our Prince, Savior, Brother and Father, Christ, in his extremely great love, has given himself according to the counsel, purpose, will and determination of his everlasting Father, and in accordance partook of flesh and blood; not of the flesh of the children, for they are sinful and unclean, but as John says, "The Word was made flesh," John

1: 14; Deut. 32: 15; Isa. 64: 4; Job 15: 14; Ps. 143: 2; Gal. 2: 17; 3: 11; 1 John 1: 3; Heb. 2: 14; Phil. 2: 7. Yea, a despised, afflicted, tempted and mortal man; and is thus voluntarily come forward to battle for his associates, sanctified brethren and children; has placed himself heroically in their defense, and has abashed the tempter in his temptation; vanquished him in his power; taken his stronghold; bruised his head; fulfilled and blotted out the hand writing; blotted it out with his precious blood; requited our guilty and deserved death by his innocent and unmerited death, to the fulfilling of the prophetic word, "O death, I will be thy plagues; O grave, I will be thy destruction!" and he has thus delivered and freed his chosen, his saints, his brethren and children from servitude and the penalty of the law; from the judgment of sin, and from the fearful terrors of the threatened death in such a manner that their human weaknesses and involuntary mistakes, for his sake, will no more be counted against them as sin, if they will but walk before him with penitent believing hearts, and will steadily cling to his word with positive, assured consciences, Gen. 49: 10; Isa. 2: 5; Luke 11: 21; Col. 2: 14; Hosea 13: 14; Rom. 8: 2, 3.

Behold, thus Christ, the Son of God, has accepted the seed of Abraham and liberated it, to the praise of his Father; and has therefore appeared in person, and become, in all things, like unto his poor, weak, afflicted brethren in all manner of poverty, misery, affliction, need, fear of death and mortality; that he might thus be a compassionate, merciful and faithful High Priest to reconcile the sins, defects and errors of his saints before God his Father; for, as he has walked with them in the same temptation, battle, misery, anxiety and fear of death, therefore he can also come to the rescue of all those who are tempted of the world, hell, sin, devil and death. This is my reply to the construction which John A'Lasco and his class put upon the Scripture, Heb. 2. If you fear God then read and judge.

In the eighth place he explains the testimony of John and says, "The Word, the Son of God, commenced being of the seed of David, Rom. 1, of the virgin Mary, Matt. 1, flesh, man, Christ, Immanuel," &c. Again, "The Word has accepted our flesh." Again, "The Word, which from the beginning alone was God, is become (that is, it commenced being together) flesh (that is, man), and has dwelt (that is, it has taken its abode) in us (that is, in our flesh) through its participation," as Paul says. These are his words in regard to the Scripture John 1.

O dear reader, what is so clear that it cannot be obscured by human intellect, and what so straight that it can not be bent? If he does it through a misconception he may yet be corrected; but if he does it for other reasons, then it will not be well with his poor soul.

I am surprised that he dares publish such inconsistent explanations, in print, when he well knows that there are to be found so many learned theological men. O, dear Lord! How frightful it is to mix God's clear wine, and the high testimony of the Holy Spirit with such impure water, and thus to corrupt it by earthly wisdom. He has so treated with this plain Scripture, that it would have removed all doubt and given me new courage, if I had had any doubt of my faith and foundation, which, thank God, I have none.

Inasmuch as he so fearfully belittles the wonderful, glorious work of divine grace and love, which the Almighty, eternal Father has so graciously shown us poor, miserable sinners, through his eternal Word and Son; and as he would rather break the holy word and testimony of the Lord, than doubt his own intelligence, therefore I pray every body, for God's sake, not to think hard of me, that I, unlearned man, oppose this and confute his unscriptural explanations with the clear, plain Scriptures and reasoning, and thus lay the foundation of truth.

I trust that no reasonable and impartial person can, in any way, think hard of me, for publicly replying to him, and defending the praise of the Lord, since he has publicly written against me and fearfully violated the word of God, as I understand it.

I would undoubtedly have excused him and not have mentioned his name, if only he and his followers would leave the Scriptures unbroken, and would not so indiscreetly war against the clear, pure truth, both verbally and in writing. But my conscience and the word of God constrain me to protect the praise of my Lord and my faith.

I say First, that he, by his explanation, has broken the testimony of the Holy Ghost, and adulterated the Scriptures; for he writes, "The Word, the Son of God has, of the seed of David, Rom. 1: 3, of a woman, Gal. 4: 4, of the virgin Mary, commenced being flesh, man. In Rom. 1: 3, it reads, "Made of the seed of David according to the flesh;" Gal. 4, born of a woman; and "That which is conceived in her, is of the Holy Ghost," Matt. 1: 20. Inasmuch as he has not left the Scriptures in their natural sense, but has garbled and turned them to his own advantage; and, instead of *born of* and *conceived of* he writes *commenced being*, therefore he shows thereby clearly that he cannot prove his explanation by the Scriptures, but merely decorates it, in semblance, by adducing mutilated Scriptures and palms them off as true.

Secondly, I say that there is not a letter to be found in all the Scriptures that the Word accepted our flesh, which he so oftentimes writes; or that the divine nature miraculously united itself with our human nature; or that the Son of God should have remained unchanged and took on him the son of Mary; or that the Son of God should have bestowed all his Attributes on the son of man, and that one person was made of two, as John Brent says; or that the son of man should be the chosen Son of God, as Pomeranus says; or that the Word, the Son, should have taken on him a perfect man of the flesh of Mary; or that the blood of Mary was concreted in her womb, as the servants of the barbarous churches of London say; or that he put on our flesh; or that he should have dwelt therein; or that he was flesh of our flesh; or that our flesh should sit at the right hand of the Father—therefore I say that they are wrong in all particulars, yea more, that they are anathematized. For they are a strange gospel and new doctrine which is not derived from the Spirit and word of God, but is invented of flesh and blood, Gal. 1: 8.

Thirdly, I say that his explanation is inconsistent in every particular. For he says, The word *commenced being man*, and also, that it dwelt in our flesh. If it *became* man, as it truly did, as the testimony of John, when not adulterated, clearly shows—how could it then, yet dwell in the flesh of man? For to commence being a house and to dwell in a house, are widely different. This all reasonable people must admit.

Fourthly, I say that this explanation of his is inconsistent in itself. For if the word *commenced being man*, then it did not remain unchanged in its first state. But if it remained unchanged, then it did not *commence being man*, but it commenced taking on a man of our flesh and thus it commenced to dwell in one of our flesh, let him turn the matter as he pleases. Therefore I will not let John A'Lasco be the expounder, but will let the faithful and plain John himself explain his own words. He writes, "That which was from the beginning, which we have heard, which we have seen with our eyes, which we have looked upon, and our hands have handled, of the Word of Life, for the life was manifested, and we have seen it," 1 John 1: 1, 2.

Inasmuch as his explanation is inconsistent in itself, and is both contrary to nature and the Scriptures; and inasmuch as John shows me such a plain foundation—therefore I will not establish my foundation and faith on such uncertain, dark and colored flatterings, but I will establish them on the certain, clear and undeceivable testimony of John; for I know that his testimony is true, yea, that it is the unbroken truth and pure word of God.

Fifthly, I say that his explanation of the verb *habitavit*, that is, *has dwelt*, is false, for he says and claims that the Word and our flesh, or the son of Mary, taken on by the Word, are one person and one Christ; and here he claims that the Word, which is the Son of God, has taken its abode in our flesh, and refers to Xenophon. From which one or the other must follow, either that Xenophon and his domicil are one being and thing, the same as the Son of God and the son of Mary (understand, according to his explanation) are one person and Christ—or, if Xenophon and his domicil are two separate things, as they really are, that then, also, the Son of God and the son of Mary, in whom God's Son should have dwelt, according to his explanation, are two separate persons and Christs; for, the one who dwells in a house and the house are two different things, is too self-evident to be denied.

Further I say, that his explanation of the verb *habitavit* is not at all founded in fact. For the evangelist uses the verb *to dwell* in the perfect tense, and says, *Has dwelt*; from which it is evident that John does not here speak of dwelling in our flesh, but of his dwelling *among* men, as all intelligent translators have rendered it. For if he should have spoken it with such a meaning as John A'Lasco explains it, then he would have said *dwell*, in the present tense, or we must acknowledge that the word did not dwell in the man Christ longer than while he walked here on earth, which to my understanding, would be a gross abomination and a great error.

Sixthly, I say that the explanation can not be maintained in any manner; for the whole Scriptures in regard to Christ would contradict themselves. There would be two persons and sons in Christ—a sinful and death-guilty Messiah—the father no true father, the mother no true mother, and the son no true son. The prophets, Gabriel, the angel of the Lord, Christ Jesus, John and Paul, would all be false witnesses, as has been previously heard.

Lastly, I say as before, that John wrote his gospel and testimony of Christ, the Son of God, in a very contentious time. If he had not meant just as he wrote, but if he had written it in such a confused and strange sense as John A'Lasco explains it—then he would not have abated the dispute thereby, but would rather have given new energy thereto.

O no. John has simply, clearly and plainly given his testimony, foundation and faith concerning Christ Jesus, the Son of God, and our only and eternal Messiah, and has testified, without duplicity, that the Word of God, which was from the beginning, became flesh, and that this same incarnated Word has dwelt amongst us. But he did not write a syllable that he accepted *our* flesh, or that he dwelt in a man of the flesh of Mary, as, alas, John A'Lasco, by his human wisdom obscures his simple, plain word and clear testimony, mutilates and controverts it.

Inasmuch as he, in his defense and explanation, has so frightfully broken the Scripture, and has so indiscreetly varied from *the* truth, as you may plainly see from the cited extracts—therefore I felt constrained by the pure love to God and your souls, to discover unto you his great misunderstanding and gross errors; that the glory of the Lord may be maintained and that you may be led to the right, true confession of your God and of his beloved Son Jesus Christ.

But I am grieved to mention his name in such a connection, and that I must publish his errors, although he has given me an ill reputation and hateful name with many by his writing. I commend him to the Lord. Perhaps he thinks that he has thereby done rightly. Whatever I do, I do for conscience' sake, to the glory of my Lord and Savior, Christ; for his glory I love far more than the honor of all creatures—and him I must seek with all my strength, even at the cost of my life.

I am sure that if John A'Lasco seeks the praise of God more than his own; if he loves his neighbor as the Scriptures require, and sincerely seeks after truth, he will not be angry with me, but will love and thank me, for not excusing him in this regard, but faithfully showing him his errors, for maintaining my faith and doctrine according to the truth, for warning my fellow-men against corruption, and most of all for protecting and defending by the word of my Lord, my Lord's glory and great name, as much as is in my power, according to the testimony of the Scripture and my conscience. But if it be considered offensive in me, as I fear it will be, then I must commend it to the Lord who, in his great love, has, to this hour, stood by me in all my needs, with his paternal faithfulness, and who has so graciously succored me in all my temptations. Behold, dear reader, here you may see how far we differ with our opponents in the confession, doctrine and faith of Christ, the Son of God. Now judge, if you fear

God, which of the two parties has the strongest Scriptures and foundation.

If you would have the Scriptures, which they call contradicting in this respect, rightly explained, then you must let go of the foundation of our opponents and cling to ours. For it can never, never be explained by divine truth in the meaning which they attach to them. For every intelligent person who will not wilfully combat the plain truth and reject the Holy Spirit, must acknowledge that from their doctrine it follows that the Lord, Christ, must be an unclean, sinful, accursed, condemned and death guilty Christ; that there are two persons in Christ, the one divine, the other human; two sons—the one the Son of God without mother, the other the son of Mary, or the son of man without father; not God's first begotten and only own Son, but the son of the unclean flesh of Adam, died for us. Besides, all the prophets, Christ, and the apostles must be false witnesses; this is too plain to injure by any writing, or dissipate by flattery.

But whosoever rightly understands our foundation, and confines his reasoning within the limits of the word of God—who believes the testimony of John, to which he testifies in his first chapter, concerning the incarnation, as just and true, and does not injure it; who attributes nothing more to Mary, the mother of our Lord, than what is attributed to a true mother in Gen. 1, and who leaves God, the Father, a true father of his Son, Christ; Mary a true mother, and Christ a true Son, both of his Father and mother; to him all the Scriptures in this respect are plain. He does not require the flattery of any one; for there is not a sentence in all the Scriptures which contradict him; he has an undivided, clean and innocent Christ; the Son of God, and the son of Mary; an only person, of all of which I trust, you have been fully convinced in the foregoing synopsis founded on the power of the Scriptures; and which, by the grace of God, you will see by the following brief collection of references.

The eternal Word of God, by which all things were created, John 1; which is the First and the Last, Rev. 1: 8; which, in due time, in the city of Nazareth, according to the providence of God, 1 Pet. 1: 20, according to the will of God, Eph. 1: 4, according to the promise of God, Gen. 3: 15, through the Holy Ghost, was conceived in the virgin Mary, who knew no man, Luke 1: 27, 28; Matt. 1; Jn. 1: 14. According to which flesh conceived in Mary, through the Holy Ghost, of the eternal Word of the eternal Father, he, in due time, was born of the seed or generation of David, Acts 2: 13; Rom. 1: 4, of a woman, Gen. 3: 15; Gal. 4: 4, of the virgin Mary, Matt. 1: 21; Luke 2: 21, in Bethlehem, an only begotten Son of God, Jn. 3: 16; 4: 9; 5: 13; Rom. 8: 32; according to the promise and the generation of the mother, also, of Abraham, of David and of the seed of the woman, fruit, and son, Gen. 3: 15; Matt. 1: 21; Luke 1: 31; a Savior of the world, Luke 2: 11; the Lord himself from heaven, 1 Cor. 15: 47; the bread which came down from heaven, Jn. 6: 58; Immanuel, Isa. 7: 14; Matt. 1: 23; the mighty Prince, Isa. 9: 6; our God, Isa. 40: 9. The Lord Our Righteousness, Jer. 23: 6; 33: 15.

Behold, faithful reader, here you have our proper foundation, doctrine and confession of Christ, the Son of God; how he is become flesh in Mary, and how he came into the world, as we, before our God, believe and teach our brethren. And we would hereby pray and faithfully admonish every one, gratefully to accept this noble and precious Son of God, with a sincere desire to hear, love, and serve him in gladness of heart, and faithfully follow in his footsteps; walk unblamably in his word and ways; freely promulgate his honor and praise, glorify his holy name, and humbly and obediently bend their hearts before his majesty, since the merciful Father has shown us such great love as to give us, poor, miserable sinners, his only, eternal and beloved Son; for he it is who has victoriously led us poor children, through the merits of his precious blood and bitter death, according to the gracious resolution, counsel, will and purpose of God, his heavenly Father, from the kingdom of hell and from eternal death into the glorious kingdom of his divine honor and eternal peace. Eternal praise be to his illustrious, wonderful, high and glorious name, Amen.

CONCLUSION.

Christ says, "This is eternal life, that they might know thee, the only true God, and Jesus Christ, whom thou hast sent," John 17: 3. At another place he says, "If ye believe not that I am he, ye shall die in your sins," John 8: 24. John also says, "Whosoever shall confess that Jesus is the Son of God, God dwelleth in him, and he in God," 1 John 4: 15. Again, "Who is a liar but he that denieth that Jesus is the Christ? He is anti-christ, that denieth the the Father and the Son. Whosoever denieth the Son, the same hath not the Father," 1 John 2: 22, 23.

O, that our opponents would rightly take to heart these and the like Scriptures, and would learn to know who and what the Son of God is, and from whence he came, then they might yet be delivered from the chains of the deceiver and be led into the light of the true doctrine. But so long as they do not confess Christ it will always be wrangling and disputation, changing falsehood into truth and truth into falsehood. Yea they will be so estranged and blinded that all those who, with the angel Gabriel, with the eternal Father, with John the baptist, with Peter, Paul, Martha, Christ, and with the whole Scriptures, confess Christ Jesus as the true Son of the true and living God, must, alas, be called by them, deceivers and heretics. O, dear Lord, how long will this great abomination continue!

O, that they might yet awaken in time while it is yet to-day, and that they could give just praise unto Christ! Could they see their accursed hypocrisy, idolatry; the lamentable deceit of the poor and miserable people, and the ignorant, reckless life of the wicked world, that they could renounce and quit it, what a blessing it would be to their poor souls! But I fear that so long as the spiritual Antioch complacently stretches the idle life, and Jezebel sets the delicious tables, the accursed Moaz will retain his sway; and that the world will not be in want of false teachers and deceivers.

Kind reader, ponder well what I write. I warn you in faithful love, watch, look and observe well what you believe and what you uphold; for your preachers deceive you. Watch and pray; the day is at hand, yea, at hand, that we must all stand before the impartial judgment seat of our God, who judges without respect of person, and will reward every one according to his works, be he emperor or king, doctor or licentiate, rich or poor, man or woman.

In short, this is my reply to the defence of John A'Lasco. With this I will not only appear on earth, before man, but also, in the day of my Lord Christ. According to the word of his promise, will I, by his grace, appear before the eyes of his majesty.

If you are of reasonable disposition and not blinded by the spirit of the envious partisans, or led away by bitter zeal, then judge between us and our opponents; who of us most glorifies Christ Jesus, the Son of the true and living God; who has most wholesomely adduced the Scriptures; and who has broken and turned them to suit his own professions. But beware of judging according to the flesh; but judge in purity of heart, even as if before your God, according to truth.

From my innermost soul I wish you a true and unfeigned faith, a true confession of God and Christ, the unction and love of God, a pious, penitent, cheerful heart, an unblamable, christian life, and a true understanding and a good judgment, Amen.

Observe: "For God so loved the world, that he gave his only begotten Son, that whosoever believeth in him should not perish, but have everlasting life. For God sent not his Son into the world to condemn the world; but that the world through him might be saved; he that believeth on him is not condemned; but he that believeth not is condemned already; because he hath not believed in the name of the only begotten Son of God," Jn. 3: 16, 17.

MENNO SIMON.

A CONFESSION

OF THE

Triune, Eternal and True

GOD, FATHER, SON, AND HOLY GHOST.

BY

MENNO SIMON.

Originally published in the Dutch Language, A. D. 1597. *Republished in* 1600, *and* 1681.

"For other foundation can no man lay than that is laid, which is Jesus Christ,"
1 Cor. 8 : 11.

ELKHART, INDIANA:
PUBLISHED BY JOHN F. FUNK AND BROTHER.
1871.

PREFACE.

Menno Simon wishes all his beloved brethren and sisters in the Lord, grace and peace, an unbroken, pure and firm faith, unfeigned brotherly love, a sure and living hope, and a God-pleasing, unblamable walk, confession and life, from God our heavenly Father, through his beloved Son, Christ Jesus, in the power of his Holy Ghost, Amen.

WE know, dear brethren and sisters in Christ Jesus, that we are condemned, by the whole world, to water, fire and sword, for the testimony of Christ and our consciences; and that we are the spectacle of, and regarded as the offscouring of all mankind. Besides, we know also that the true Prince of Peace, the blessed Christ Jesus, has summoned and taken us into the mansion of peace through the word of peace; and that he has given and left his followers such a glorious sign by which we shall know them to be his disciples, namely, Love. Therefore it is reasonable and christian-like that we, poor, outcast bearers of the cross, should be united in the perfect bonds of true love, and that we should cling together as the members of one body, "For by one Spirit are we all baptized into one body and made to drink into one Spirit," 1 Cor. 12:13. But now we see plainly how the prince of darkness, who from the beginning was a murderer, seeks, with all diligence, to disturb this same peace in the house of God, to rend this bond in twain, and thus to make odious to many the dear gospel of our Lord Jesus Christ, our cross and confession, and all the christian societies; and thus thoroughly to destroy it, John 8:44. Since his acute attacks are so well known to us, therefore it is necessary ever to be aware, to repent, to seek each other in true christian love, to resuscitate that which has been corrupted, to cure and make healthy that which is diseased, with the oil of the divine word; for during the last four years, alas, christian love and peace have materially decreased with some, on account of much pernicious upbraiding and disputing about the ineffable depths of the divinity of Christ and of the Holy Ghost; also, about angels and devils, and about the ban; and this has always been the case where such disputes were in sway. May the Lord not count it as sin against those who have used the ban. I see this plainly, and as I have been troubled not a little by some about this matter—and since I naturally hate such upbraiding and disputing, for I have these fifteen years never found any use in it, because I love peace and unity, which are in conformity with the word of God, more than my own life. I trust that I speak no lie, for, because of that, my heart is very much troubled, mournful and afflicted, yea, more so than I can write.

Would to God that I could, at the cost of my life-blood, help all afflicted consciences and could lead them to God; for I love nothing more on earth, nor do I seek any thing, before God, than the glory of my Lord Jesus Christ, and the everlasting salvation of my beloved brethren. And therefore I have, at the risk of my poor, diseased body, placed at your disposal and service my firm faith and confession of the eternal, Triune God, Father, Son and Holy Ghost, as taken from the sure word of God; wherewith I will, unwaveringly, live and die before my God, and will appear therewith in his grace, at the day of judgment, trusting hereby to make pleasant and worthy to many, the noble and desirable peace and unity in Christ, and to restore love.

Brethren, there has been enough of disputing, upbraiding, and complaint of one another. I think it is time to discountenance the disturbers of the peace, and to cordially seek scriptural peace and unity. But I desire no peace outside of Christ. I ardently desire and pray all my beloved brethren and sisters in the Lord, to read, hear and understand this my admonishing confession, without any partisan bitterness or spitefulness towards God-fearing, pure hearts, as I have written it in purity of heart, as before God, in Christ Jesus, without hatred or malice. I doubt not but that, if you do this, brethren, I mean the unpeaceable and troubled ones, disquiet, dispute and disunion will far recede from the peace-mountain of the Lord; and peace, love and unity will again install themselves.

I sincerely desire that it may be so read and taken to heart, that the Almighty, eternal Father, with his blessed Son, Christ Jesus, and with the Holy Spirit may remain unchanged in their true, divine being; and that the afflicted, mournful, wavering consciences may find succor, consolation and strength. The beloved Father grant his grace, Amen.

A CONFESSION

OF THE

TRIUNE, ETERNAL, AND TRUE GOD, FATHER, SON, AND HOLY GHOST.

WE believe and confess with the Holy Scriptures, that there is an only, eternal and true God, who is a Spirit. One God, who created heaven and earth, the sea, and all that is therein. Such a God, whom heaven and the heaven of heavens cannot comprehend. Whose throne is heaven and earth his footstool; who measures "the waters in the hollow of his hand;" who spanneth the heavens; who comprehendeth the dust of the earth in a measure, and weigheth the mountains in scales and the hills in a balance; who is as high as heaven, deeper than hell, lower than earth and broader than the sea; "Who only hath immortality, dwelling in the light which no man can approach unto; whom no man hath seen, nor can see;" who is an Almighty, powerful and an over-ruling King, in the heavens above and in the earth beneath; whose strength, hand and power none can withstand. A "God of Gods, and a Lord of Lords;" there is none like unto him, but he is a mighty, holy, terrible, praiseworthy, wonderful, and consuming fire; whose kingdom, power, dominion, majesty and glory is eternal, and shall endure forever, and besides this only, eternal, living, Almighty over-ruling God and Lord we know no other; and since he is a Spirit so great, terrible, and invisible, he is also inexpressible, incomprehensible and indescribable, as may be deduced and understood from the following Scriptures, Deut. 4: 35; 6:4; 7: 6; 10: 17; 32: 39; Jn. 4: 24; 1: 18; Gen. 1: 1; Ps. 33: 6; Col. 1: 16; Isa. 43: 11; 44: 6; 48: 13; 40: 12; Job 11: 8; 1 Tim. 6: 16; Eccl. 1: 7; Matt. 11: 27; Rev. 17: 14; 19: 16; Heb. 12: 29; 1: 8, 10.

This only, eternal, Omnipotent, ineffable, invisible, inexpressible and indescribable God, we believe and confess with the Scriptures, to be the eternal, incomprehensible Father, with his eternal, incomprehensible Son, and with his eternal, incomprehensible Holy Spirit. The Father, we believe and confess to be a true Father, the Son, a true Son, and the Holy Spirit, a true Holy Spirit; not carnal and comprehensible, but spiritual and incomprehensible, for Christ says, "God is a Spirit." Inasmuch as God is such a Spirit, as it is written, therefore we also believe and confess of the divine generation of the heavenly Father, and of his begotten Son, Christ Jesus (brethren, understand my writing well), that they are spiritual and incomprehensible, as is also the Father who begat them; for like begets like. This is incontrovertible, Matt. 3: 17; 28: 18, 19; Mark 1: 7, 11; Luke 3: 16; Jn. 14: 9; 15: 26; 1 Cor. 12: 11. And this same incomprehensible, inexpressible, spiritual, eternal, divine Being, which is begotten of the Father, before every creature, divine and incomprehensible, we believe and confess to be Christ Jesus, the first and only begotten Son of God. "the first-born of every creature," the eternal Wisdom, the power of God, the everlasting Light, the eternal Truth, the everlasting Life, Jn. 14: 6, the eternal Word, Jn. 1: 1. Do not understand this as a literal word; for it is divine and spiritual, and not carnal and literal; for a literal word is but a passing breeze, comprehended in the letter, beginning and ceasing; and then, Christ Jesus, before his incarnation, must have been a literal word. O, no! But he is the eternal, wise, Almighty, holy, true, living and incomprehensible Word, which in the beginning was with God, and was God (mark), by whom all things were made, and without whom not any thing was made that was made, and which will endure forever. And therefore he says, "Before Abraham was I am." Again John the baptist says, "After me cometh one who was before me," John 1: 1, 15; 3: 36; 8: 12; Luke 7: 29, 35; 1 Cor. 1: 9; Heb. 1: 2. Yea he had this glory of the divine being with the Father, before the foundation of the world was laid. He thought it not robbery to be equal with God, his Father; therefore, we confess with John the Baptist, Nathaniel, Martha, and Peter that he is the Son of the living God, Jn. 1 ; 17 ; Phil. 2 ; Matt. 16 : 16 ; Jn. 11: 27; 9: 37; 6: 69.

Dearly beloved brethren understand me rightly. He is the eternal Wisdom, the eternal Power. For, as we believe and confess that the Father was from eternity and will eternally remain; yea, that he is the First and the Last, so we may also freely believe and confess that his wisdom, his power, his light, his truth, his life, his Word, Christ Jesus, has been eternally with him, in him and by him; yea, that he is the Alpha and Omega; or else, we must admit that this begotten, incomprehensible, true, divine being, Christ Jesus (whom the fathers have called a person), through whom the eternal Father has made all things, has had a beginning like a creature; which all true christians admit and look upon as a terrible blasphemy, curse and abomination. The gracious, beloved Father will ever protect and uphold all his beloved children in the right and true confession of his beloved Son Jesus Christ.

Beloved brethren in the Lord, we believe and confess that this same eternal, wise, Almighty, holy, true, living and incomprehensible Word, Christ Jesus, which in the beginning was with God, and which was God, incomprehensible—born of the incomprehensible Father, before every creature, is in the fullness of time, become, according to the unchangeable purpose and true promise of the Father, a true, visible, passive, hungry, thirsty and mortal man, in Mary, the pure virgin, through the operation and overshadowing of the Holy Spirit, and is thus born of her. Yea, that he was like unto us in all things except sin; that he grew up as other men; and at the appointed time was baptized and entered upon his ministerial office, the office of grace and love, which was enjoined upon him from the Father, and which he obediently fulfilled; that he effaced the hand writing, that is, the law, against us; and has at last, through the eternal Spirit of his heavenly Father, offered himself in this his human flesh, nature and weakness, in which, also, he has sighed, wept, and prayed unto the Father, has sweated water and blood, and thus purified our hearts of the deadly works, that we should serve the true and living God; and all who believe on him, have received, through him grace, mercy, remission of sins, and eternal life; and that, by means of his precious blood which he has, in his great love, offered and shed for us poor sinners on the cross, according to the good pleasure of the Father, he is thus become our only and eternal High Priest, Reconciler, Mercy-seat, Mediator, and Advocate, with God his Father. For, as God, the Almighty Father, through his Almighty Word, Christ Jesus, had created Adam and Eve, so he, also, would again thereby restore them and make them pious, when seduced by the serpent, together with all their descendants—that we should give no one the praise of our salvation, neither in heaven nor on earth, but to the only and eternal Father, through Christ Jesus, and that through the enlightenment of the Holy Spirit. This is sufficient of the incarnation, Matt. 1: 16, 25; 5: 4; Mark 15: 37; Luke 2: 7, 40; 22: 67; 23: 46; Jn. 15: 9, 10; 12: 13; 11: 26; Phil. 2: 5, 7; Col. 2: 14, 12; 1: 13, 16; Heb. 3: 2; Eph. 2: 12; 1: 7; Rom. 8: 32; 3: 24, 25; 5: 11, 12; Isa. 53: 12; 1 Pet. 1: 19; Rev. 1: 8; 2 Cor. 5: 14.

Further, beloved brethren, we believe and confess Christ Jesus to be the true God with the Father; and this because of the divine glory, operation and attributes, which are found in such abundance with him, as may be clearly deduced and understood from the following Scriptures. Say, beloved! Is it not the only and true God who has made heaven and earth, and whose kingdom shall endure forever? Doubtlessly, yes. Paul says, "Unto the Son he saith, Thy throne,

O God, is forever and ever; a scepter of righteousness is the scepter of thy kingdom. Thou hast loved righteousness, and hated iniquity; therefore God, even thy God hath anointed thee with the oil of gladness, above thy fellows. And, thou, Lord, in the beginning hast laid the foundation of the earth; and the heavens are the works of thine hands," Heb. 1: 8, 9, 10.

Is it not the only God, who alone is "King of kings, and Lord of lords?" and who reigns in heaven and on earth? Most assuredly. And the Spirit speaks in Rev., that Christ is "King of kings and Lord of lords." Christ himself says, "All power is given unto me in heaven and in earth." Paul says, "That at the name of Jesus every knee should bow, of things in heaven, and things in earth, and things under the earth, and that every tongue should confess that Jesus Christ is Lord," Phil. 2: 10.

Is it not the only God who saith, "I the Lord, the first and with the last; I am he?" Isa. 41: 4. And Christ says, "I am Alpha and Omega; the beginning and the ending, saith the Lord, which is, and which was, and which is to come; the Almighty." And "Fear not; I am the first and the last; I am he that liveth and was dead; and behold, I am alive for evermore," Rev. 1: 8, 17, 18.

Is not this the only God who "trieth the hearts and reins?" Without doubt it is. Christ saith, "All the churches shall know that I am he which searcheth the reins and hearts; and I will give unto every one of you according to your works," Rev. 2: 23.

Is it not the only God, whom alone we should serve and worship? Yes. Christ says, "That all men should honor the Son, even as they honor the Father." Of divine service Paul says, "He that in these things serveth Christ, is acceptable to God," and "Let a man so account of us as of the ministers of Christ," Rom. 14: 18; 1 Cor. 4: 1.

Paul was a servant of Christ, as may be generally seen at the commencement of all his epistles. Of his worship Luke says, that when Christ had ascended to heaven they worshipped him, and returned to Jerusalem. Also Stephen, in his last prayer, says, "Lord Jesus, receive my spirit." Paul also saith, "Let all the angels of God worship him," also the murderer on the cross, "Lord, remember me when thou comest into thy kingdom," Acts 7: 58; Heb. 1: 6; Luke 23: 42; 24: 52. Is it not the only God which is true; and every man a liar? Oh, yes. The prophet says "There was not any deceit in his mouth." Christ himself says, "I am the truth," "To this end was I born, and for this cause came I into the world, that I should bear witness unto the truth," Ps. 116: 11; Rom. 3: 4; Isa. 53: 9; Jn. 14: 6; 18: 37.

Can any one forgive sins and bestow everlasting life except the only and eternal God? O, no! Christ says, "Know that the son of man hath power on earth to forgive sins;" and to the sinful woman, "Thy sins are forgiven." "I give unto them eternal life," Ps. 103: 3; Matt. 9: 6; Luke 7: 48; Jn. 10: 28.

Should we believe in any one but alone on the only God? Not at all. For Christ says, "He that believeth on me hath everlasting life." "Ye believe in God, believe also in me," Jn. 6: 47; 14: 1.

Is it not the only God who is the judge of all the world? who will raise the dead and at the last day sit in judgment? Assuredly, yes. And Christ says, "For as the Father raiseth up the dead, and quickeneth them, even so the Son quickeneth whom he will." "He was ordained of God to be the Judge of quick and dead;" and at his coming he will judge and sentence, Jn. 5: 21; Acts 10: 42; Matt. 25: 31—46.

Behold, beloved brethren, as the throne of Christ is an eternal throne, and as the Scriptures are not ashamed to confess him to be God, and also testify that he founded heaven and earth, that he has all power in heaven and on earth; that he is the first and last; that he searcheth the hearts and reins; whom we should serve and worship; who is truth; who forgives sin, and bestows eternal life; in whom we must believe, and who at the last day will raise us from the dead and judge us, as has been said; so it is incontrovertible that Christ Jesus also with his Father, must be the true God; for God gives his glory to none other; and these are all glories, powers and attributes which belong to no one in heaven nor upon earth, except alone, the only, eternal, and true God; this all taught of God, must fully admit and confess.

Besides, beloved brethren, we believe and confess Christ Jesus, with his heavenly Father, to be truly God; and that because of the plain testimony of the holy prophets, evangelists and apostles, as we may learn from the following Scriptures, and also from some other texts. Isaiah says, "Unto us a child is born, unto us a Son is given; and the government shall be upon his shoulder; and his name shall be called Wonderful, Counsellor, The Mighty God, the everlasting Father, the Prince of peace," Isa. 9:6. Again, "Say unto the cities of Judah, Behold your God! Behold, the Lord God will come with strong hand, and his arm shall rule for him! Behold, his reward is with him and his work before him; he shall feed his flock like a shepherd; he shall gather the lambs with his arm, and carry them in his bosom, and shall gently lead those that are with young," Isa. 40:9—11. Read also Ezek. 34:11.

Jeremiah says, "Behold, the days come, saith the Lord, that I will raise unto David a righteous Branch, and a king shall reign and prosper, and shall execute judgment and justice in the earth. In his days Judah shall be saved, and Israel shall dwell safely; and this is his name whereby he shall be called, THE LORD OUR RIGHTEOUSness," Jer. 23:5, 6; 33:15.

Micah says, "But thou Bethlehem Ephratah, though thou be little among the thousands of Judah, yet out of thee shall he come forth unto me that is to be ruler in Israel; whose goings forth have been from of old, from everlasting," Micah 5:2. Read also Heb. 7:3, 4; Isa. 44:6; Rev. 1:8; 22:13. John says, "In the beginning was the Word, and the Word was with God, and the Word was God," Jn. 1:1. The Lord said unto Thomas, "Reach hither thy finger, and behold my hands; and reach hither thy hand, and thrust it into my side; and be not faithless, but believing. And Thomas answered and said unto him, My Lord, and my God! Jesus saith unto him, Thomas, because thou hast seen me, thou hast believed; blessed are they that have not seen, and yet have believed," Jn. 20:27—29.

Paul says, "Take heed therefore unto yourselves, and to all the flock, over which the Holy Ghost hath made you overseers, to feed the church of God, which he hath purchased with his own blood;" "Whose are the fathers, and of whom, as concerning the flesh, Christ came, who is over all, God blessed for ever." Again, "God was in Christ, reconciling the world unto himself," Acts 20:28; Rom. 9:5; 2 Cor. 5:19. Read also John 14; Col. 22; 1 Tim. 3. Again, "Who being in the form of God, thought it not robbery to be equal with God. But made himself of no reputation, and took upon him the form of a servant," Phil. 2:6.

John says, "We know that the Son of God is come, and hath given us an understanding, that we may know him that is true; and we are in him that is true, even in his Son Jesus Christ. This is the true God and eternal life," 1 Jn. 5:20. Besides, read the whole gospel of John and 1 Cor. 10:15; Eph. 4; Heb. 1:3; 7; 11; 12; 13; and you will, by the grace of God, find a sure and firm foundation.

Behold, faithful brethren, here you have the incomprehensible birth of Christ, his divine glory, operation and power; and a number of precious and plain testimonies of the holy prophets, evangelists and apostles, all of whom with an invincible power, testify and point out, with such clearness, the true, ineffable divinity of our Lord, Jesus Christ. I am convinced and doubt not the least, that a pious, humble, God-fearing conscience will herewith be satisfied, and not search into this incomprehensible depth any further; and if any one desires to search and dispute further, to him I prophesy that he will surely search and dispute all his lifetime, and yet never have a settled mind nor a firm foundation. Therefore, beloved brethren, be warned. Watch and beware.

As we have now pointed out and made known our faith and confession of the true divinity of Jesus Christ; so we will also, now, by the grace of God, set forth in few words, our faith and confession of the Holy Ghost. Let the God fearing judge. We believe and confess the Holy Ghost to be a true, real, or personal Holy Ghost; and that in a divine way—even as the Father is a true Father, and the Son a true Son; which Holy Ghost is a mystery to all mankind, incomprehensible, inexpressible and indescribable (as we have shown above of the Father and the Son); divine with his divine attributes, going forth from the Father through the Son, although he ever remains with God and in God, and is never separated from the being of the Father and the Son. And the reason that we confess him to be such a true and real Holy Spirit, is because we are impelled to this by the Scriptures, for he descended upon Christ at his baptism in the bodily shape of a dove, and appeared unto the apostles as cloven tongues like as of fire; because we are baptized in his name as well as in the name of the Father and of the Son; because the prophets through him, prophesied, performed miracles and works, had dreams and saw visions; for he is a distributer of the gifts of God, and that according to his will. Mark well. He moved Zachariah, the Son of Barachiah, he moved John the Baptist while yet in his mother's womb, and he said to Simeon, "That he should not see death before he had seen the Lord's Christ." "The Holy Ghost said, Separate me Barnabas and Saul." And to Peter, "Behold, three men seek thee." He guides us into all truth; he justifies us; he cleanses, sanctifies, pacifies, consoles, reproves, cheers and assures us; he testifies to our spirit that we are the children of God. This Spirit all receive who believe on Christ; Paul admonishes us, not to grieve him. Whosoever sins against this Spirit (says Christ), unto him it shall not be forgiven. David desired that God might not take from him this Spirit, for all that have not this spirit are not of Christ, Acts 2: 26; Luke 3: 22; John 1: 33; Acts 2: 3; Zach. 7: 12; Jude 14; Joel 2: 29; 2 Cor. 12: 4; Luke 2: 25; Acts 13: 2; 10: 19; Jn. 14: 26; 15: 26; Eph. 4: 30; Rom. 8: 16; Matt. 8: 13; Ps. 51: 11; Rom. 8: 9. Yea, my brethren, from these plain Scriptures, testimonies and references, and a great many other texts which are too lengthy to mention, and which may be found in abundance in the Scriptures and read, we believe the Holy Spirit to be the true, essential Holy Spirit of God, who adorns us with his heavenly and divine gifts, and through his inspirations, according to the good pleasure of the Father, frees us from sin, makes us cheerful, peaceful, pious, satisfies our hearts and minds, and makes them holy in Christ Jesus. And thus we believe and confess before God, before his angels, before all our brethren, and before all the world, that these three names, operations and powers, namely, the Father, Son and Holy Ghost (which the fathers called three persons, by which they meant the three, true, divine beings) are one incomprehensible, indescribable, Almighty, holy, only, eternal and sovereign God, as John says, "There are three that bear record in heaven, the Father, the Word, and the Holy Ghost; and these three are one." Read also Matt. 28: 18; Mark 1: 8; Luke 3: 8; John 14: 16; 15: 26; 1 Cor. 12: 11. And although they are three, yet in Godliness, will, power and operation they are one, and can no more be separated from each other than the sun, brightness and warmth; for the one cannot exist without the other; yet incomprehensible from the incomprehensible Father, even as the brightness and heat of the sun. The one must exist with the other, or else the whole divinity is denied; for all the Father does and has wrought from the beginning, he works through his Son, in the power of his holy and eternal Spirit. This Son does not work without the Father and the Holy Spirit. Neither doeth the Holy Spirit any thing without the Father, and the Son. Therefore the one must remain with the other, or else there must be an imperfect God; for if we deny the divinity of Christ, or the true existence of the Holy Ghost, then we counterfeit and depict unto ourselves a God who is without wisdom, power, light, life, truth, word, and without the Holy Spirit.

Brethren, understand all this in a divine and spiritual sense, and not in a human or carnal manner! Then you will be satisfied with the plain, clear and simple testimony of the prophets, evangelists and apostles, concerning this deep mystery. Let every one see to it with fear and trembling, lest he put his hand in the consuming fire.

Cordially beloved brethren and sisters in Christ Jesus! mark well the following: Since the eternal God is such a great and terrible God, as you have read; since Christ was thus born of the Father as said, and as the attributes of God so richly abound in Christ; and, also, as the prophets, evangelists and apostles so strongly declare, preach and teach him as God; and as the Scriptures so abundantly teach and testify of the Holy Spirit and confess that the eternal Father, with his eternal Son and Holy Spirit, in their divine state, power, glory and sovereignty are ineffable, inexpressible and incomprehensible, as may be plainly understood from the cited Scriptures (for it is all Spirit and God, and therefore beyond human understanding); therefore it is that I pray, admonish and desire all my beloved brethren and fellows in Christ Jesus, with all that men can pray, not to allow and consent to flatterings, innovations nor human explanations, be it by whom it may, concerning this incomprehensible majesty; ever fearing, ye who seek God, with all your powers, that ye do not, by such high-soaring thoughts and human conjecture, mistake the ineffable God who makes all human wisdom, which is contrary to him, foolishness; lest ye, through your vain searching and musing of such unfathomable matters, fall into his hands, and be consumed by the fire of his wrath.

Brethren, I, for myself confess that I would rather die than to believe, and teach unto my brethren, a single word or letter concerning the Father, Son and Holy Ghost (behold, before God I lie not), differing from the express, testifying word of God which so clearly points out and teaches through the prophets, evangelists and apostles.

O, my pious, God fearing, faithful brethren! let us all, one with another, be thus minded; then the desolated cities may be again rebuilt; the strong may remain firm; the wavering be again strengthened; and thus peace, love, and unity be again restored. I know certainly and truly that if any one wants to go further than we here testify and admonish from the word of God, he will fall into error; or mount too high, or deviate from side to side; he will miss the right course and will act no more intelligently than he who would try to pour or confine the river Rhine or Meuse in a quart bottle. But those who abide simply and humbly by the word of God, the testified, prophetical, evangelical and apostolical word, and firmly believe it, although they neither do nor can fully comprehend it, and take heed to all human investigation, disputations, flatterings, explanations, turning and conjecture in these incomprehensible abysses, will, in all temptations, stand firmly, by the grace of God, and walk all their lives before their God with penitent and cheerful minds. I sincerely wish that all the brethren were of like mind with me in this respect; for I have been at enmity with human sophistry and flattery for fifteen years, and I am still; I expect to remain so, and, by the help of God, to take heed not to offer the blood of the Lord with leaven; but I desire, solely, to enter into the sanctuary of God, that is, into his holy church, with the unleavened bread of the unalloyed word of God, overspread with the oil of the Holy Spirit.

O, brethren! were they all, who are called brethren, thus minded with me, how soon then would the sad, afflicted hearts find consolation and cheerfulness, and the divided, restless minds unity and peace. O, Lord Jesus! Have mercy upon thy poor, afflicted sheep, and let every hungry and thirsty soul find thy verdant pastures and limpid waters, Amen.

Beloved brethren and sisters in Christ Jesus! Receive this with the same mind with which I have written it to you; read it plainly to all the brethren, and understand it in a christian manner; and beware, *beware*, yea, BEWARE of all disputation, discord and division. This I desire from my inmost soul, for the Lord's sake. The sincere, evangelical peace be with all my beloved brethren and sisters in Christ Jesus, Amen.

MENNO SIMON.

Sept. 9th, A. D. 1550.

AN EXPLANATION

OF

Christian Baptism

IN THE WATER,

FROM THE WORD OF GOD.

IN WNAT MANNER IT WAS COMMANDED BY CHRIST JESUS, AND HOW IT WAS TAUGHT AND PRACTICED BY HIS HOLY APOSTLES.

BY

MENNO SIMON.

"For other foundation can no man lay than that is laid, which is Jesus Christ," 1 Cor. 3:11.

ELKHART, INDIANA:
PUBLISHED BY JOHN F. FUNK AND BROTHER.
1871.

MENNO SIMON'S SALUTATION.

READ and consider carefully the words which I speak, ye learned, who appear to be distinguished in mind and doctrine above others. I have added this my little German work for the celebration of the rite of Baptism. For I am not well able to promote this cause in Latin, and if able, am unwilling that this, my labor, should perish in the hands of the few, but desire that it may become known to every christian and yield the greater advantage. That there are, in this work, no interpolations of Scripture, nor satires, nor falsehoods, judge for yourselves. Moreover I know it is not the spirit of a christian to lead in any way deceitfully, especially in an affair so serious. Indeed the christian does not know deceit. It becomes the evangelical teacher to set before himself nothing except these most illustrious precepts of the evangelist—such as faith, charity, patience, life, gentleness, peace, mildness, truth, moderation, and finally to so live that no one is able with justice to thrust against him any taint of baseness, that he may teach not only by word, but also by example, following the teachings of Paul who says, "I keep under my body, and bring it into subjection; lest that by any means, when I have preached to others, I myself should be a castaway," 1 Cor. 9: 27. And elsewhere, "Having your conversation honest among the Gentiles; that, whereas they speak against you as evil doers," "they may be ashamed that falsely accuse your good conversation in Christ," 1 Pet. 2: 12; 3: 16. For in the midst of these things it behooves one to repress such ignorance and stupidities, lest that saying of the Savior be turned against us which says, "Cast out first the beam out of thine own eye," Luke 6: 42. For how can I induce others to become christians when I myself am not a christian.

Read therefore, and if any thing be found in this work that has not the flavor of evangelical purity and spirit, I am confounded, not you. For I have written from a sense of pious affection, not that I may injure any one, but for the benefit of all men. Nevertheless, such are my thanks from you for this my kindness toward you, that I know it is not enough except I, with my sanctified Leader, having indeed received Christ as my reward, endure all evil, ignominy and tortures. No wonder. They indeed do not spare me while I seek the truth and declare openly the offered sacrifice, when almost all teachers of righteousness, who were from the beginning, have yielded to death in the same way. This is indeed gratitude, when the world displays its subjection to God. Would that in very truth they were christians who persuade themselves that they are christians. May grace abound with all the diligent through our Lord Jesus Christ, with sincerity.

PREFACE.

Beloved readers, in our first publication of the writings concerning Baptism, we have, with christian truth, satisfied the desire of every pious christian. Yet, there are some light minded, rebellious, contentious and carnal persons who, without cause and Scripture, and in every respect without the fear of God, teach, write, admonish and cry out against us, with partial hearts, saying, "It is heresy and deceit; for it is written and taught adverse to the learned, and against the doctrine of the holy, christian church." Although I had not intended to reply to such perverse, rebellious, disobedient and contentious persons, according to the word of the Lord, Matt. 7, but solely to write to the humble, meek, God-fearing and penitent. For the wise will hear wisdom; will love it and become wiser; but the fool will hear folly, praise it, persist and die in it—yet to such contenders and gainsayers, who speak so hard against the word of God, I would ask two questions; and request them to examine and ponder them well, and return a discreet and becoming reply to me. In the first place: What are properly heretics and deceivers? Secondly, Who are they that admonish and teach against the doctrine of the holy church? If they answer these questions fairly they must themselves pronounce the sentence, that with us *the upright* truth of Jesus Christ is found and not with them; on the contrary, that all manner of heresy, deceit and false doctrine are abundantly taught and practiced by them, and not by us. Which of the two parties, then, are heretics and imposters, I will leave to the judgment of the reader. For *hereticus* means: one who sorts out, one who chooses, one who gleans. *Quia heresis Grece ab electione vocatur, inquit Beda super acta Apostolorum*, one who selects such as will suit his own opinion. If these, then, are truly heretics, who, according to their own meaning, without Scripture, form themselves a faith, then I truly do not know where to find more miserable and more deplorable heretics than those who ever combat, upbraid, betray and persecute us, poor, scattered and rejected christians, as damnable heretics. For there is no worse, or more abominable heresy under heaven than is found among our gainsayers and contenders; while they so shamefully change and garble the word and the perfect ordinance and institution of our beloved Lord Jesus Christ, as to baptize such things which God has neither commanded nor ordained to be baptized, namely: The little, unconscious children and bells; and do not baptize those whom God has commanded to be baptized, namely: Those who believe, while they worship and honor a mouthful of bread and a drink of wine as the Son of God; while they ascribe to themselves, without the word of God, the power over the living and the dead; and while they place in Christ's stead a sinful man, a child of perdition, whose natural pride, pomp, greed, cruelty, uncleanliness and idolatry are beyond description, 2 Thess. 2: 4.

Truly, I do not know how a worse heresy could be invented. Notwithstanding these miserable men cruelly cry against us, *Heretics, heretics, drown them, slay and burn them.* And this for no other reason than that we teach, according to the holy gospel of Jesus Christ, the new life, Baptism on the confession of faith, the Supper as representing both a holy and unblamable church; because we rebuke all false doctrine, idolatry and the accursed carnal life; and point alone to the blessed Christ Jesus, and to no other means of salvation, neither in heaven nor on earth.

PREFACE.

If this is heresy, beloved reader, then, indeed, the true Being is not in Christ; then he is not the true way, the truth, and the life, John 14: 6. Be not frightened by their upbraiding and slandering; for from the beginning it has been the case that the unbelieving, hate, slander and persecute the believing; the wicked, the good; the unrighteous, the righteous; the carnal, the spiritual; the heretics, the christians. It was the case with Cain and Abel, Ishmael and Isaac, Esau and Jacob and with the false prophets and the true prophets; as Christ Jesus has told us before, namely: "Ye will be hated of all nations, for my name's sake," Matt. 24: 9. If they were the true disciples of Christ Jesus as they boast themselves to be, they would persecute, betray or murder no body for the sake of their faith; but with Christ Jesus, they would diligently seek to reclaim that which was lost, Matt. 18: 11, if we were lost, as they claim. If they were the bride of Christ, they would not be spiteful, cruel and blood thirsty, but meek, mild and merciful, yea be thus minded as is the good and faithful bridegroom, Christ Jesus. But they plainly manifest themselves, by their works, not to be the bride of Jesus Christ, but rather to be the bride of him, who, from the beginning was a murderer, that is, the devil, Jn. 8: 44.

If they were the body of Christ, they would not crucify and persecute any one for the sake of the truth of the Lord, but would themselves, with Christ Jesus, and his church, be crucified and persecuted for the sake thereof, Matt. 5: 11; Jn. 16: 1, 2; 2 Tim. 3: 12. For the innocent lamb does not kill, but from the beginning it was killed. Behold, kind readers, what miserable, bloody, tyrannical and murderous heretics our gainsayers, opponents and persecutors are found to be before God, in all their teachings, admonitions, instructions, life and tyranny. But this they do not acknowledge. For it would not do to acknowledge this. If they did, how could they then crucify and persecute the chosen children of God, the children of the kingdom and promise, the brethren and sisters of Jesus Christ, the angels of peace, and the children of the eternal, imperishable life?

But now their minds are so obscured, their eyes are so bedimmed, their ears are so closed up that they cannot understand; for their evil-doing and wickedness have obscured and blinded them. The table of the divine word is to them "a snare, and a trap, and a stumbling block, and a recompense," Rom. 11: 9. The righteous judgment and awful wrath is come upon them, because they so industriously seek falsehood, and so obstinately combat and reject the lovely truth of Jesus Christ.

Christ Jesus says, "Blessed are they which do hunger and thirst after righteousness; for they shall be filled," Matt. 5: 6. But these hunger and thirst after unrighteousness, with which they, according to Paul, are abundantly filled, 2 Thess. 2: 12.

Christ Jesus says, "Every one that asketh receiveth; and he that seeketh, findeth; and to him that knocketh it shall be opened," Luke 11: 9. But these seek diligently, night and day, not after the right way, but after the wrong; hoping yet to find something, either in the word or in our lives, which may be so twisted, bent or applied as to trample upon and nullify, the right, evangelical truth, even as if the eternal Truth, the blessed Jesus had spoken and taught with two tongues; and if they can find any errors in our walk, as there often are (for we are all of the sinful, failing flesh of Adam); then the evangelical truth is all deceit, as if we had no help from God but only human aid. Inasmuch as they so assiduously seek after unrighteousness and delight in falsehood, therefore God smites them with such great blindness that they can neither comprehend nor judge of the teachings of God; yet they desire to clothe their cause, however shameful it is, in the garment of the Scriptures, that they may, under this scriptural, holy appearance, the better deceive the foolish, ignorant populace that desire to be deceived and seduced. And thus they remain, both teacher and disciple, in the service of their perishable flesh which they have chosen as their God, Phil. 3: 18; Rom. 16: 17.

Again, kind reader, they cry and foam with rage against us, saying that we write against all the doctors, and also against the teachings of the holy christian church.

I affectionately and freely admit and acknowledge that we write against the greater part of the doctors or the learned men. For whenever or wherever they write, admonish and teach contrary to the word, ordinances, statutes and institutions of Jesus Christ, we do not consider their famous names and have nothing to do with their human philosophy. But if they teach rightly we do not contradict nor write against them.

I trust, by the most merciful grace of our Lord Jesus Christ, that the oldest, most pious, most upright, truest and most able doctors of the church of Jesus Christ, who were long before all other doctors, are received and believed by me and my beloved brethren, in every word and doctrine. These are, Moses, Isaiah, Jeremiah, David, Christ Jesus, Matthew, Mark, Luke, John, Paul, Peter, James and Jude. If any body can show me a word in all my writing that I have taught or written contrary to the doctrine of these doctors, then I am willing to be abashed, instructed and taught better; but I trust that it can never be truthfully done. If I should write and teach against these pious, unblamable doctors, then my writing and teaching would be against the teachings and admonitions of the christian body, community or holy church.

I acknowledge and know well that I admonish, teach, instruct and write contrary to the instructions and teachings of some communities and churches, in regard to some articles, such as the Papists, Lutherans, and the corrupted sects; but not contrary to the teachings of the holy, christian church. May the merciful Father, whose divine will I industriously seek to obey, save me from teaching, instructing and writing contrary to the doctrine of the holy church; for else woe would be unto my soul forever.

Lest you be ensnared by the word *holy church*, you shall learn and know from the word of God that the holy, christian church is no collection of unbelievers, carnal or willful sinners; notwithstanding they falsely claim to be of Christ Jesus, and think themselves to be the true, christian church. No, kind readers, no. They are not all Abraham's seed who are born of Abraham, "But the children of the promise are counted for the seed," Rom. 9: 8. Thus, also, the holy, christian church must be a spiritual seed, an assembly of the righteous, and a community of the saints; which church is begotten of God, of the living seed of the divine word, and not of the teachings, institutions, and fictions of man. Yea, they are those who are regenerated, renewed and converted; who hear, believe, and fulfill all the commandments and will of God; who "have crucified the flesh with the affections and lusts;" who "are all one in Christ Jesus." "Joint heirs with Christ," and heavenly and spiritually minded with him, Gal. 5: 24; 3: 28; Rom. 8: 17.

These are the holy, christian church, the community of God, the body and the bride of Christ, whom he hath trusted, cleansed and sanctified; but "they that are in the flesh cannot please God." This holy, christian church has a spiritual Prince over her who rules her with the unbroken rod of his divine word; a Master, or Teacher who teaches the commandments of eternal life; and a Bridegroom whose voice she is ever ready to hear, that is, Christ Jesus, 1 Cor. 6: 11; Rom. 8: 8; Ps. 2: 9; Jn. 6: 68; 3: 29.

If, now, I contend against his scepter, trample upon his commandments and teach or write aught against his heavenly doctrine, then I teach and write against the doctrine of the holy, christian church. For this holy, christian church has but one doctrine which is fruitful and godly, which is the limpid, pure and unmixed word of God, the lovely gospel of the grace of our beloved Lord Jesus Christ, Matt. 28: 19; Mark 16: 15; 1 Pet. 1: 25. All teachings and decrees which do not accord with the doctrine of Christ, are but teachings and commandments of men, be they teachings and opinions of doctors, decrees of popes, councils or any thing else; they are doctrines of the devil, and are accursed, Matt. 15: 9; 1 Tim. 4: 1; Gal. 1: 8, 9. Since we write and teach nothing but the pure, heavenly word, and the perfect ordinances of the holy gospel of Jesus Christ and of his apostles; therefore we do not teach and write against the teachings of the holy church, but we sustain them.

Beloved readers, let the light minded run

their course to the end, which is certain death. They will nevermore concede the truth, however powerfully they are vanquished, but they will ever delight in hatred, upbraiding, discord and disputation and never be satisfied, because they will not go into the strait way of the Spirit; taught of Jesus Christ and his holy apostles; notwithstanding they want to be considered the children and the church of God, without obedience. Not so kind readers. Ever remember that there is no holy church of Christ other than the assembly of the righteous, and the church of the saints, which ever acts in harmony with the word and ordinances of the Lord, and to no other doctrine. She neither will nor can accept any other doctrine or ordinances in divine matters, forever.

Because, beloved brethren, the divine ordinance of baptism in the water has thus been destroyed for many centuries, and as a strange baptism has been practiced, contrary to the true doctrine of the holy, christian church, namely, contrary to the word of God, from which evil custom so much false doctrine, disbelief and fruitless, carnal life have resulted—therefore I have again clearly pointed out from the holy gospel, how we should practice the true, scriptural, christian baptism; that the hearts and faith of the wise may be affirmed and assured, and the mouths of the fools may be stopped, and that God may have the glory in his holy word. Read and see if we have not rightly taught and written according to the meaning of Jesus Christ. And because the whole, wide world so shamefully blaspheme and oppose the word of God, and despise his commandments and ceremonies as useless, saying, What good can water do us? never considering that the kingdom of God and the will of God do not consist in external ceremonies, but in the willing obedience to the word of God—therefore we have, in the following writings, so extensively shown from the holy Scriptures, who should be baptized, according to the word of God, namely, the believing, or the regenerated, Mark 16: 16; Jn. 3: 5; Tit. 3: 5.

Besides we have also shown how very weak, useless and groundless all the arguments of the world are, by which they defend infant baptism, that the beforementioned despisers of God may know and understand that they are not baptized according to the evangelical commandment of our beloved Lord Jesus Christ. From which it follows that they are not in obedience to the divine word, and if they are not in the obedience which has the promise (I speak of those of understanding minds), then they cannot inherit nor obtain the promise, so long as they do not believe the word of God, and obediently fulfill it in all respects. Let every one beware, and save his own soul; for our God is a consuming fire.

May the merciful Father, through his blessed Son, Jesus Christ, our Lord, grant you all a true knowledge, and his affectionate grace for your edification, Amen.

CHRISTIAN BAPTISM.

Hear ye, O, illustrious, noble, wise lords and princes! Hear ye all judges of the land, where the sword of God is given to the destruction of the evil doers, to the protection of the good, and to the punishment of the wicked! Hear, ye wise and intelligent, you, who think that you bear the vessels of the Lord! Hear ye, all people, of whatever state, condition, trade or class, who call yourselves christians, and who boast of his bitter death and precious blood! Rom. 13: 1; Tit. 3: 4; 1 Peter 2: 13, 14.

Since we, for the sake of baptism, are so miserably profaned, slandered and persecuted by all mankind, and as we are ever suspicioned by the ungodly sects (who are to you very shameful, perilous and abominable, as may be plainly seen); therefore we say and testify in Christ Jesus, before God, before his holy angels, before you, and before the whole world, that we are solely urged by a God fearing faith which we have in the word of God, to baptize and to be baptized, as the only means; nor will it be found otherwise neither in this life, nor in death, nor in the last judgment of God.

Beloved, we verily seek nothing in this baptism other than to obey our beloved Lord Jesus Christ, who has taught and commanded us this with his own blessed mouth, Matt. 28: 19; Mark 16: 16. Consider, once, we pray you, that we cannot possibly seek carnal profit in this our actions; neither gold, nor silver, nor honor, nor ease, nor long life on earth. For you may plainly see that we are made a prey to the world on account of it. But we are urged solely by the love of God, by an upright, fruitful faith, which faith industriously examines all the words of Christ, giving ourselves in willing obedience to God; knowing to a certainty that if we oppose, and do not obey that which our Lord has commanded, we can never receive nor inherit the heavenly blessing and divine promise. For through obedience every thing is received, as has been mentioned in the preface, Matt. 3: 6; Acts 19: 18; 2: 38; 9: 6; 10: 48; 16: 30.

How could Abraham, Isaac, and Jacob, together with all the beloved fathers and patriarchs, have obtained the consoling promise of God, if they had not done, be it ever so little, that which God had commanded them through his holy word? But they heard the word of God; firmly believed and obeyed it; and therefore they became joint heirs of righteousness, Heb. 11: 8.

On the contrary, however, all those who did not obey God, undoubtedly, must have borne the punishment of the Lord, as did Adam and Eve; Nadab and Abihu; Korah, Dathan and Abiram; as Saul; as the man of God who reproved Jeroboam the king, for his idolatry, and was deceived by the old prophet in Bethel, and other instances, which may be read of in Moses and other scriptural writings, Gen. 3: 17; Lev. 10: 2; Num. 16: 32; 1 Sam. 15: 23.

Since we are so pitiably opposed by all mankind in our doctrine and practice of the christian baptism, and since they do not realize that their opposition tends to eternal death, for they oppose Christ and his word; therefore I will again briefly show them and all persons, from the word of God who shall read, see or hear these my writings, how wonderfully, powerfully, nay, how incontrovertibly this our doctrine and practice are contained and founded on the holy gospel of Jesus Christ, although we have fully shown and proven this before, in our writings on baptism.

Most beloved, there are necessarily three reasons why our faith accepts this baptism under such a heavy cross and anxiety.

First, because of the divine commandment of our beloved Lord Jesus Christ, which can never be broken. Secondly, because of the teaching of the holy apostles. Thirdly, because of the practice of these same apostles. And first of the commandment: After Christ Jesus had risen from the power of death and was going to ascend to his heavenly Father, he thus commanded his disciples, saying, "Go ye therefore, and teach all nations, baptizing them in the name of the Father, and of the Son, and of the Holy Ghost," Matt. 28: 19. Again, at another place, "Go ye into all the world and preach the gospel to every creature, he that believeth and is baptized, shall be saved," Mark 16: 15, 16. While, now, Jesus Christ, the eternal wisdom who cannot err, the eternal truth who cannot lie, has commanded this, namely, that we shall first preach the gospel, from the hearing of which comes faith, Rom. 10, and that we shall baptize those who believe, who will or who can, now, explain this divine commandment otherwise, or make it of more value than the eternal, wise, perfect, blessed Christ Jesus, has made and commanded it?

Brethren, it was not allowed to apply one single word of the Mosaic ceremonies different from what they were contained in the law. For the Almighty God will not that we should follow our own inclinations with regard to the ceremonies which he has commanded us, but alone desires us to observe his good will and pleasure; for that purpose he has commanded them. In the outward ceremonies alone God finds no pleasure; but he has commanded them because he requires of us faithful obedience. His wrath has often come on those who practiced his ceremonies differently from the commandment, as in the case of Nadab and Abihu and many others. For he will, yea, he will that we should not follow our own opinion, but that we should hear, believe and obey his holy voice, Jer. 7: 5—7.

If God would have his ceremonies under the law (which were numerous, and in one respect attended with trouble and expense, and which he commanded not through Christ, his Son, but through his servant Moses), kept thus strictly and unchanged until the time of Christ; how much more so will he have the few ceremonies of the New Testament kept strictly and unchanged, which are but two in number, being baptism and the Supper, which he has commanded, not through his servant but through his only begotten Son, Jesus Christ; and which are neither attended with trouble nor expense.

Consider how troublesome and expensive it was to the Israelites to travel a long distance over hill and dale, to appear two or three times a year before the Lord, at Jerusalem, with their offerings of bullocks, rams, goats and tenths, which they were bound to offer of all their goods, to the Lord. But the christian ceremonies of the New Testament, baptism and Supper, which are commanded us of God, are not at all attended with trouble or expense; although the meaning or representation of these ceremonies to true believers, is attended with great vexation to the flesh. This however is not caused by the ceremonies themselves, but alone through the faith which leads us to these ceremonies, out of love and obedience to the divine word. Most beloved, since the ordinance of Jesus Christ is unchangeable and the only one that is acceptable to the Father; and since he has commanded that we shall first preach the gospel and then baptize those who believe; it follows that all those who baptize and are baptized, without the teaching of the gospel and without faith, baptize and are baptized on their own opinion, without the doctrine and the ordinance of Jesus Christ, and therefore it is idolatry, useless and vain. For had Israel circumcised their females because it was not expressly forbidden, they would yet have circumcised without the ordinance of God, for he had commanded that the males were to be circumcised, Gen. 17: 10. The same it is in this instance. If we baptize the unconscious children, although Scripture has not expressly forbidden it, just as it was not forbidden to circumcise the females, we yet baptize without the ordinance of Jesus Christ; for he commanded to baptize those who should hear and believe his holy gospel, Gen. 17: 10; Matt. 28: 19; Mark 16: 16; Acts 2: 38; 9: 18; 10: 48; 16: 33.

It avails nothing that some say that these

CHRISTIAN BAPTISM.

words of Matthew and Mark extend the holy church to the Gentiles, and that thereby the baptism of infants is not excluded. Beloved reader, it is true by this commandment the holy church is also extended to the Gentiles, to the fulfillment of the prophetic Scriptures which long before had seen this through the Spirit, as Paul proves, Rom. 15. Yet the word stands firmly with regard to both Jews and Gentiles, namely, whosoever believeth and is baptized, shall be saved. Faith is before baptism. For faith is the beginning of all righteousness which avails before God, from which faith, baptism is the result as a sign and token of obedience. If the children, then, have faith, their baptism is not forbidden by the alleged words of Matthew and Mark.

Again, neither does it avail any thing that some allege and say, that the resurrection of the dead was not expressly written in the books of Moses, yet it was implied as Christ Jesus proved to the Sadducees from Exod. 3: 6, namely: I am the God of Abraham, of Isaac and of Jacob. As in these words of Moses the resurrection is not expressed, yet it is implied, as God is no God of the dead but of the living, as Christ teaches, Matt. 22: 32; thus they say, infant baptism is not expressed in the gospel, yet it is implied. To this we reply: That the resurrection of the dead is no outward ceremony which God has commanded us to do; but it is something which God himself will accomplish in us by his Almighty power, therefore it is an invisible consolation in the hearts of all believers, which is comprehended by faith alone. But the baptism of unconscious children is an outward ceremony. If, then, it is an ordinance and word of God which has the promise, it must be plainly expressed in the Scriptures. If not, it cannot be called a ceremony of Christ.

Thirdly, neither does it avail that some allege and say, "Although the believing women have no express word of invitation to the Lord's Supper, neither were they at the celebration of the last Supper of the Lord, yet they are, for good reasons, admitted to the Supper, and it is the same with unconscious children. Although there is no express command for their baptism, neither were they baptized of the Lord nor of his disciples so far as we can learn from the Scriptures; yet they are, for good reasons, admitted to baptism, the same as the believing women are admitted to the Supper."

Kind reader, this is a very crafty argument to deceive the simple and ignorant, for it savors highly of subtlety, but is not at all according to the example of Jesus Christ. Because the Holy Supper represents the death of the Lord Jesus Christ and the love of our neighbors; both of which are known and practiced by the believing women as well as the believing men. If, then, the unconscious children have that which is represented by baptism, namely, death unto sin, the new life, Rom. 6: 4; the new birth, Jn. 3, the putting on of Christ, Gal. 3: 27, the moving, quickening Spirit by which we are baptized into the body of Christ, 1 Cor. 12: 13, and a good conscience, 1 Pet. 3: 16, as have the believing women of what is represented in the Holy Supper, then they should be baptized for the same reason that believing women are admitted to the Supper; but it neither will nor can ever be found in unconscious children.

Fourthly, it avails nothing that some allege from Ecclesiasticus 1: 14, that "To fear the Lord is the beginning of wisdom: and it was created with the faithful in the womb," and will be with the chosen women. If then, they say, "The fear of the Lord is created with the believing in the mother's womb, which fear is a fruit of faith, and as the fruit can not be before the tree, therefore the children from their mother's womb have a fruitful faith; if they have faith, then their baptism cannot be hindered according to the Scriptures." Not so, beloved reader, but judge every thing according to the word of God and his Spirit. For I do not doubt but that you will confess that the faith which avails with God, is a gift of God, from whence all righteousness proceeds, comes by the hearing of the divine word. If, now, it comes by hearing the divine word, as Paul teaches, how will it be found in unconscious children; for it is plain that they can not be taught, admonished or instructed, nay, they are more senseless and helpless at their birth than the irrational creatures; so unconscious that they cannot be taught any thing about carnal things, until their hearing, comprehension and understanding have commenced to develop themselves. If they cannot be made to understand any thing visible, how can they, then, prematurely, that is, before they can comprehend things, be taught and instructed in invisible, celestial matters of the Spirit?

Secondly, you know and acknowledge that where there is a true faith there is the true knowledge of the difference between good and evil; the fear of God, the love of God and also of our neighbor, and the obedience to God and the desire after righteousness. It can not be otherwise than that a good tree bringeth forth good fruit. Faith works all manner of righteousness, as it is written, "The just shall live by faith," and "Faith is the substance of things hoped for, the evidence of things not seen," Matt. 7: 18; Rom. 1: 17; Heb. 11: 1.

Say, dear reader, If faith ever begets good fruits, all manner of righteousness is the substance of things hoped for, the evidence of things not seen—what fruits and righteousness do our little children beget, which are evidence of faith, and what do they hope for, and seek after but eating, drinking, laughter, crying, warmth, play, &c., as has been the nature of children from the beginning. Besides, they often show the growth of the evil, Adamic seed; and as they advance in youth they manifest it still more; but the fruits of faith, or of the new birth they do not show, as may be plainly observed, and if you do not observe it by daily experience, then believe the word of God, which will never deceive you. Thus Moses says, "Your children, which in that day had no knowledge between good and evil," &c., Deut. 1: 39. They had no knowledge between good and evil, as it appears—where, then, is their faith which has the knowledge between good and evil?

Thirdly, you will acknowledge that all righteousness comes by faith as our controverters themselves allege and adduce in their opposition, Rom. 4: 5. Without faith there is no godly righteousness; therefore Paul says to the Hebrews (speaking of those of understanding years), that "Without faith it is impossible to please God," Heb. 11: 6. Inasmuch as the children, then, have no faith by which they can realize what God is and that he is a rewarder of both good and evil, as they plainly show by their fruits—therefore they have not the fear of God, and consequently they have nothing upon which they should be baptized, yet they have the promise of everlasting life, out of pure grace. This is all that the Scriptures accord to them, and all that the word of God says of them, as will be shown below.

Inasmuch, then, as faith must be first and afterwards the righteous fruits which come by faith—such as the fear of God, the love of God, &c., which fruits do not appear in unconscious children, as has been often said; therefore we must presume that Ecclesiasticus does not teach that the fear of God is not in little children immediately after conception; but we are taught here that the fear of God is to the believing in the womb, that it will be given them in due time; because his eyes of fire, those eyes which from the beginning to the end foresaw all things; foresaw when they were yet in their mother's womb, that they in time would hear his holy voice, truly believe, and through faith fear God; and become righteous before him; for true faith cannot be without its fruits, as has been often proven.

If then, faith were in the little, unconscious children from conception, as our opponents say, it would be a fruitless faith, for they do not bring forth fruits; and therefore their preaching in this regard is in vain. For, if that were the case, faith would come by the creation, or conception, of the believing, and not by the preaching of the divine word. Not so, beloved reader. This is a sure, eternal, imperishable and an enduring rule of the divine truth, to fulfill all righteousness, namely: First, the true preaching of the holy gospel of Jesus Christ. Secondly, a desire to hear and understand. Thirdly, to cordially believe this gospel and to fulfill it in fruit. This being the case, it follows that the little, unconscious children have no faith, for they can not understand and learn. If they have no faith, they cannot have the fear of God. Therefore our opponents cannot prove the justice of baptizing little, unconscious children, from this passage of Ecclesiasticus; but they must wait according to God's word until they can understand the holy gospel of grace, and sincerely confess it; then it is time, no matter how young or old they are, to receive christian baptism, as the infallible word of our beloved Lord Jesus Christ has taught and commanded all true believers, in his holy gospel, Matt. 28: 19; Mark 16: 16. If they die before maturity, that is in childhood, before they have come to years of understanding and before they have faith, then they die under the promise of God, and that by no other means than the precious promise of grace, given through Christ Jesus, Luke 18: 16; and if they become of understanding minds and have faith, they should then be baptized. But if they do not accept or believe the word when they shall have arrived at the years of understanding, no matter whether they are baptized or not, they will be damned, as Christ himself teaches, Mark 16: 16.

I know that there are a great many who will ask, "Why I, unlearned man, am not satisfied in regard to this matter with the doctrine of Martin Luther and other renowned doctors, who are versed in the Scriptures and many tongues and sciences —who teach, and particularly Luther, that faith lies dormant in little children the same as in a sleeping believer?"

To this I answer: In the first place, if there were such a dormant faith in little children (which, however, is nothing but invention), then it would not be proper to baptize such children so long as they would not verbally confess it and show it by their fruits. For the holy apostles did not baptize any believers while they were asleep, as we have shown in our former writings.

Secondly, I acknowledge and confess from my inmost heart, before you, and the whole world, that they and many others are well gifted with learning, eloquence, subtlety, languages and science, and that I, poor, ignorant man, am in comparison to them, as a fly is to an elephant; therefore I am heartily ashamed to write and speak against them, with my dull pen and awkward speech. Yet every reader should know that however learned the beforementioned philosophers are, and however ignorant I am, yet our opinions avail the same with God and before him, for, without the command of the holy Scripture, nothing righteous can be done and nothing pleasing to God can be practiced, let him be whosoever he may. The holy Scriptures do not refer us to them nor to any other learned person, but to Christ Jesus, alone. Whenever such highly renowned men, by their subtle acuteness and artful philosophy try to take from us and garble the plain ordinances of Jesus Christ and of his apostles, we must, surely, consider their doctrine, in that respect, as doctrine of men and false; for Christ Jesus is not under them, but above them. Neither has he received his holy doctrine from them, but from his wise Father, Jn. 7: 24; 8: 26; 12: 46; 16: 13.

Since they, by their philosophy, assert that there is a dormant, unfruitful faith in unconscious children, evidently against all Scripture and truth, and that the children should be baptized upon such human phantasy; now, judge for yourselves, you who oppose me, which of the two I would better do—hear the holy word and ordinance of Christ Jesus, to whom the Father, together with all the prophets, have pointed me, or hear the learned, who, against his holy word and ordinance, would have me follow *their* opinion, which they have formed by garbling the Scriptures. Eradicate from your carnal hearts all partisanship and contention so that you can fairly judge of spiritual matters. God grant that all the learned and those that are taught of them, may acknowledge and teach truth, and fulfill it in their works, Amen.

Inasmuch as Christ Jesus has commanded his holy apostles that they should first teach the holy gospel of grace and then baptize those who should believe; we are, for the same reasons, urged by the love of God, to teach this christian baptism according to the word of God, and afterwards obediently receive it, and, by the grace of the Lord, to save it, to the honor of God, both in life and death; notwithstanding all the world opposes us.

TEACHINGS OF THE HOLY APOSTLES CONCERNING BAPTISM IN THE WATER.

Again, we are urged by the pure, chaste teaching of the holy apostles thus diligently to teach and receive this christian baptism: First, because it is written, "Now when they heard this, they were pricked in their heart, and said unto Peter," "Men and brethren what shall we do? Then Peter said unto them, Repent and be baptized, every one of you, in the name of Jesus Christ for the remission of sins, and ye shall receive the gift of the Holy Ghost," Acts 2: 37, 38.

Most beloved, bear in mind, now and all the days of your lives, not only concerning baptism, but concerning all doctrine you may hear, lest you be deceived by false teaching, namely, as all the true prophets of God, who were between Moses and Christ, conformed their teaching to the doctrine of Moses, so the holy apostles, also, conformed their teaching to the doctrine of Christ Jesus, as he had commanded them, saying, "Teaching them to observe all things whatsoever I have commanded you," Matt. 28: 20.

Therefore consider and ponder well that which shall be taught you, by the grace of the Lord, from the word of God, and you will clearly perceive from these words of Peter, how the words of Jesus to Nicodemus, concerning the new birth, should be understood thus, "Verily, verily, I say unto thee, Except a man be born of water and of the Spirit, he can not enter into the kingdom of God," Jn. 3: 5. Beloved brethren, the new birth came to pass through the word of God. When this word was taught on the day of Pentecost, by Peter at Jerusalem, the multitudes heard it from his mouth and from the mouth of the other apostles; their hearts were pierced, for, by faith, they accepted these words, and therefore they said, "Men and brethren, what shall we do? Then Peter said unto them, Repent, and be baptized every one of you, in the name of Jesus Christ for the remission of sins, and ye shall receive the gift of the Holy Ghost." The same as Christ said to Nicodemus, when he first taught of the birth from above, saying, "Verily, verily, I say unto thee, Except a man be born of water and of the Spirit, he cannot enter into the kingdom of God."

Behold, my chosen brethren! how harmonious are both master and disciples in their teachings, namely: First, the birth from above by which we become children of God. Secondly, the water by which the obedience of the children of God is shown. Thirdly, the communion of the Holy Ghost by which we are assured in our hearts of the grace of God, of the remission of sins, and of everlasting life through Christ Jesus our Lord, Jn. 1: 14; 3: 2.

Inasmuch as the holy Peter, who is the apostle of God, a true witness, sent by Jesus Christ with the word of everlasting life, enlightened and taught by the Holy Ghost, has thus taught and commanded us, namely, that we shall suffer ourselves to be baptized upon the confession of faith according to the command of the Lord, Mark 16: 16; in the name of Christ for the remission of sin, therefore we must receive this baptism the same as is commanded us in the Holy Scriptures, or else we cannot obtain remission of sins nor the Holy Ghost. For who has ever received remission of sins, contrary to the word of God? Surely, it is impossible that we can rob God of the remission of sins and of his Holy Ghost. If we, then, desire the remission of our sins and the Holy Ghost, we must do and fulfill all that which God, the Almighty Father has taught and commanded us through Christ Jesus his beloved Son, and through his holy apostles, in all spiritual matters.

Here it avails nothing that some teach and say, contrary to the holy Scripture, "That the little children are born of Adam, with a sinful or wicked nature, and that therefore they should be washed of their inherent guilt and sin, by baptism." To teach and believe thus, my brethren, is first, a fearful idolatry, and abominable blasphemy against the blood of Christ. There is no remedy, in heaven nor on earth, for our sins, whether they are inherent or worldly, but the blood of Christ alone, as we have often shown in our first writings, 1 Pet. 1: 19; 1 Jn. 1: 7; Eph. 1: 7. If we ascribe the remission of sins to baptism and not to the blood of Christ, then we mould a golden calf and place it in the stead of Christ. For if we could be washed or cleansed by baptism, then Christ Jesus and his merits would be of none effect; otherwise we must admit that there are two means for the remission of sin which is not, nor ever can be; first, baptism; second, the blood of Christ. For the most holy and most precious blood of our beloved Lord Jesus Christ must and shall have the praise, as has been so clearly prophesied and testified of all the true prophets and apostles, throughout the Scriptures.

The believing receive remission of sins not *through* baptism, but *in* baptism, in this manner: as they now, sincerely believe the lovely gospel of Jesus Christ which has been preached and taught to them, which is the glad tidings of grace, namely, of the remission of sin, of grace, of peace, of favor, of mercy and of eternal life through Jesus Christ our Lord, so they become of a new mind, deny themselves, bitterly lament their old, corrupted life, and look diligently to the word of the Lord, who has shown them such great love; to fulfill all that which he has taught and commanded them in his holy gospel, trusting firmly in the word of grace, in the remission of their sins through the precious blood and through the merits of our beloved Lord Jesus Christ.

They therefore receive the holy baptism as a token of obedience which proceeds from faith, as proof, before God and his church, that they firmly believe in the remission of their sins through Christ Jesus, as was preached and taught them from the word of God; therefore they receive remission of their sins in baptism, as the lovely promise of grace proclaims and represents; the same as the literal Israelites received remission of their sins by their offerings. For in case that we only sought outward baptism and trusted in the literal practice, and would yet continue in our old, corrupted walk, then indeed, all would be in vain, the same as it was in such case, a vain offering, amongst the ungodly and carnal Israelites. For the Lord of lords so often complained through his holy prophets, that their offering was not pleasing to him, that it was nothing but a corrupt abomination and stench, before his holy eyes; inasmuch that they despised the law, love and the commandments of God, and lived according to the lusts of their flesh, Isa. 66: 4, 5; and other passages.

Secondly, we are not cleansed, in baptism, of our inherited sinful nature which is in our flesh, so that it is entirely destroyed in us, for it remains with us after baptism; but since the merciful Father, from whom are all good and perfect gifts, has graciously given us the most holy faith, so we manifest in the baptism we receive, that we desire to die unto the inherent, sinful nature, and destroy it, so that it will not any longer be master of our mortal bodies, Rom. 6: 12. Although such true believers are often overcome by sin, as John observes, "Whosoever is born of God doth not commit sin; for his seed remaineth in him; and he cannot sin, because he is born of God," 1 Jn. 3: 9.

Brethren, I repeat it, as the Israelites received remission of their sins, through the promise, with which were associated their offerings, when they offered with contrite hearts, not through the offering itself, for then it would be merit, but alone through the word of promise; for it is grace and not merit—so we receive remission of our sins, when we are true believers and are washed and cleansed in baptism, through the promise; not, I say, through the washing of water, for it is not merit, but through the promise, for it is grace, with which promise the Holy Spirit of God has associated the baptism of the believing, in the gospel, as Paul teaches, saying, "Christ also loved the church, and gave himself for it; that he might sanctify and cleanse it with the washing of water by the word, that he might present it to himself a glorious church," Eph. 5: 25—27.

Behold, most beloved, from this it is plain that we are not cleansed by the washing of water, but by the word of the Lord, as the holy Paul clearly teaches us in the beforementioned words. Inasmuch as the little, unconscious children, by reason of their incapability of comprehending and understanding the preaching of the holy gospel, by which, alone, comes faith, Rom. 10: 17; by which faith, alone, God purifies our hearts, Acts 15: 9, and not by the outward baptism, as has been said before, and, inasmuch as the express command and word of God, which associates the promise with baptism, solely refers to those who are begotten of this same word and are thus cleansed in their hearts by faith, it therefore follows incontrovertibly therefrom, that these little children, notwithstanding that they are baptized under a false pretension and false explanation of the divine word, are not cleansed thereby, if they ever were unclean, which however is not the case. Why? Because the promise is not associated with their baptism. Therefore their baptism is not done according to the word; but in every respect contrary to the word. For the word requires faith, and they have no faith. Therefore their baptism is without doubt a baptism of their own choice, without God, without promise, yea, idolatrous, useless and in vain.

Whosoever now wants to oppose this, and does not want to believe the ordinance and word of God, let him take heed to what he does. For by infant baptism he nullifies the command of the Lord; tramples upon his precious blood (for he seeks righteousness in this baptism), and he establishes, contrary to the immutable ordinance of God, and of his own carnal choice, a false baptism which God never commanded. Therefore it neither is his holy will, as has been said above and as will be shown more extensively below.

Again the apostle Peter writes, As Noah, in his day, was saved in the ark from the waters of the deluge, so "even baptism doth also now save us (not the putting away of the filth of the flesh, but the answer of a good conscience toward God), by the resurrection of Jesus Christ," 1 Pet. 3: 21.

By this passage of Peter, the baptism of the *believing* is again clearly affirmed and the baptism of infants nullified. For it is impossible that any one can have a good conscience but those, alone, who believe, and whose hearts are regenerated and converted; who acknowledge the divine word which teaches that God the Almighty Father, whose enemies we were before, Rom. 5: 10, is now again reconciled through Christ Jesus, his beloved Son; that henceforth, through the merits of our beloved Lord, neither hell, devil, past sins, eternal death, nor the wrath of God will hurt or hinder us. All those who truly believe this, shall receive and obtain a joyous mind and good conscience by the resurrection of Jesus Christ as Peter says; because he has so gloriously triumphed over all his enemies, visible and invisible, to our profit; and has again seated himself in heaven, at the right hand of his Father. Such, are first inwardly baptized with the Spirit and fire, according to the word of God, and are thus taught in their hearts by this Spirit, and are led in all divine truth, righteousness, obedience, and evangelical fruits and works. They are inwardly so enkindled with this fire of love, having become conscious, by the word of God, that such great grace, I repeat it, *grace*, has been bestowed on them through Christ Jesus, that they regard neither lords, princes, philosophers, learned men, councils, long usages, women, children, flesh, blood, decrees, nor any other threats; neither life nor death, but remain glad in Spirit, maintain, at the risk of home, not only the outward baptism, but also all the works of love and the fruits of righteousness, which the true mouth of the Lord Jesus Christ has taught and commanded us in his holy gospel, either himself or through his holy apostles.

Behold, beloved brethren, in this manner baptism saves us, as Peter teaches; not the outward literal baptism, but the inward, spiritual baptism, which as obedient children of God, has led us through the power of faith, to the outward literal baptism; for the outward, literal baptism is nothing more than obedience to the divine word, and thus it is a seal or proof of the righteousness from whence the true, fruitful faith comes; the same as was the literal circumcision to the believing and obedient Abraham, Rom. 4: 10, 11.

Since Christ Jesus has commanded that we should baptize the believing, Mark 16: 16—therefore holy Peter followed the commandment in his teachings; and has taught baptism to be a work of faith, namely, the answer of a good conscience toward God, which answer none can experience but those alone who have faith. Inasmuch as there is but one literal baptism taught in Scripture, which baptism shows and is proof of the answer of a good conscience toward God, as Peter teaches, and thus by this Scripture of Peter, infant baptism is prohibited; for they cannot have this consciousness like the believing. Therefore take heed, kind reader, whosoever you are, lest you offend God. For all those who thus lamentably oppose this evangelical baptism of the believing, which baptism is so pointedly commanded of Jesus Christ, and is thus taught and practiced by his holy apostles, either by doctrine, word or sword, must confess and acknowledge that they were hitherto neither right believing, regenerated, obedient, nor inwardly baptized with the Spirit and fire. Again, let every one of you beware and take heed for it does not concern anything temporal, but it concerns your poor, naked souls which have been so dearly bought and delivered by such a precious treasure.

Beloved children in the Lord, however incontrovertibly our cause is confirmed and founded in the word of God, yet some are not ashamed, persistently and continually to write, talk, and slander against us; advising and exciting persecution, slaughter and blood-shed against us; in part I presume from ignorance, partly out of partiality, and because they are enemies of the cross of Christ and because they do not desire the lovely, spiritual life which is of God; and say, "Although infants have not the answer of a good conscience, as the believing have, yet this should be no cause of not administering baptism to them; but they ought to be baptized, that they may the better receive instruction in the word and commandments of God."

Most beloved brethren, when an idolatrous, refractory and disobedient person has not the word of God wherewith to defend his cause, he yet acutely invents something wherewith he can so beautify and adorn his invention and carnal righteousness with a semblance of divinity and holiness, that it seems quite right, just, spiritual, holy, divine and unblamable in the sight of those who are not versed in spiritual matters of faith; and the more so because their unchristian hearts and carnal minds are prone to trust in outward works, yea, through their own choice and opinion, as I understand it. If I write wrongly, then rebuke me according to the word of God; for the greater part of them have always sought righteousness in wrought ceremonies, and not in Christ, as is evident from the fact that, as now, the unintelligent teachers and bishops in the days of the apostles, or soon after, commenced the practice of infant baptism, contrary to the command of God and the doctrine of the holy apostles, as may be readily perceived in the book of Tertullian, called "Corona Milites." He writes that among the ancients almost invariably the adults were baptized with the washing of regeneration. Understand me rightly brethren. Tertullian lived one hundred and eight years after Christ, some say one hundred and forty years. As early as in the days of these ancient writers, the true, evangelical baptism, which was commanded by Christ and taught and practiced by his holy apostles, had become degenerated with many, which baptism he clearly testifies that the ancients almost invariably practiced upon adults. If now, brethren, it were so that the ancients, who were before him, already baptized infants, as it appears, and to which we consent, because he says *almost invariably*; and in another place in the same book, as the Strasburgian philosophers write of him, he says, "That in the same fount or water-bath, both children and adults were baptized." Nevertheless, infant baptism was no apostolic institution nor practice, nor a divine command; for if Christ had commanded it, and the holy apostles had taught and practiced it, then the ancestors of Tertullian would not have baptized some infants, but all the infants of upright, believing parents, indiscriminately.

That it is no divine command nor apostolic institution, was well known and shown by the beloved, aged father, Alexander, bishop of Alexandria, who was a particular opponent of Arrius; for he, so long after the days of the apostles, did not baptize the infants of his church, as may be plainly seen and understood from the Church History of Eusebius, Vol. 10, Chap. 14, translated by Ruffinis, on "The play of Children," by Anthanasius. Therefore the intelligent and learned Erasmus, of Rotterdam, as Sebastian Franck writes of him, who had perused and understood all the noteworthy writers of the world say, That the ancient fathers disputed about infant baptism, but never settled it.

Behold, kind reader, inasmuch as the ancients, from the beginning, were not unanimous in this matter; and inasmuch as they did not all practice infant baptism, as appears from Tertullian and Alexander; and as those who practiced infant baptism have ever sought righteousness therein, as may be seen by their writings—therefore we will not place our foundation upon that which is uncertain, but upon that which is certain, which is Christ's word. Neither will we seek our righteousness in the outward baptism nor in any other works, as does the world, but in Christ Jesus, as all the Scriptures teach us. Herewith we desire to present our cause to the consideration and judgment of all the world and let them tell whether they have ever read in the word of God, I say in the *word of God* or in his gospel, that Christ Jesus and his holy apostles taught two different baptisms in the water, namely, that one baptism should be administered to the believing, which baptism represents death unto sin, a new life, the answer of a good conscience toward God, and the washing of regeneration, Rom. 6: 12; Col. 2: 12; 1 Pet. 3: 21; Tit. 3: 5; and that the other baptism should be administered to infants, which signifies nothing only that they should be outwardly washed with water.

Brethren, judge rightly and do not deceive your souls. We know that they first say "That infants are cleansed of their inherent sins and that therefore their baptism is not in vain." To this we reply with the word of God: That such belief is abominable idolatry; for in this case the blood of Christ avails, and not the outward baptism, as has been shown above.

In the second place they say, "That thereby they are accepted into the covenant of God." To this we reply again: That this is not because of baptism, but alone through the mild election of grace, Eph. 1: 6; for it is grace and not merit, Rom. 11: 6.

In the third place they say, "That children should be baptized that they may the better be trained in the word of God and his commandments." To this we reply again: That we desire to know where such is expressed and written in the holy Scriptures. Give a discreet answer, we pray you, who assert infant baptism to be right, just and necessary, and who so lamentably slander and profane us on account of baptism, that we may no longer be deceived in our hearts; but that we may assuredly know by the word of God where to find this infant baptism. For however industriously we may search day and night, we yet find but one baptism in the water, pleasing to God, which is expressed and contained in his word, namely: Baptism on the confession of faith, commanded by Christ Jesus, taught and administered by his holy apostles, which is administered and received for the forgiveness and remission of sins in such a manner, as we have fully proven above by the words of Peter, Acts. 2: 38. But of this other baptism, that is, infant baptism, we find nothing.

Because this infant baptism is nowhere commanded nor implied in the divine word, therefore we take issue with you and all the world, that we regard it not only as vain, but we believe and proclaim it as idolatrous, useless, and unavailable, not only by words merely, but at the cost of our lives, as has been proven by events in many countries of Germany. The reason is this, because it is administered without the word and commandment of God; because righteousness is sought therein; and because the true baptism of the believing must be so lamentably rejected and trampled upon, by the whole world, as an heretical baptism, as far as the name of Christ is mentioned. Therefore, brethren, it is nothing but opinion and human righteousness, to teach, without the word of God, that infants should be baptized, that they may be the better trained in the word of God and his commandments; as we find to the contrary that, although these parents have their infants baptized, they yet, from youth on, are trained by these same parents in this Adamic nature, in all manner of pride, pomp, avarice, vanity, lying, cursing, swearing, dancing, singing, foolishness, artfulness, hatred, enmity, revengefulness and to the accursed life of this world, the same, as from the beginning the heathen have done who never confessed God.

What profits such baptism as they have received? Is it not merely folly, deceit, mockery and shame in the sight of God? Certainly. Beware. There can be no greater hypocrisy, mockery or blasphemy in his sight. Inasmuch as, perhaps, the secret awfulness which is hidden in infant baptism, is not yet rightly understood by you —therefore I will briefly present the matter, that you may the better distinguish between truth and falsehood. I will present to you that which for many centuries, as all men may have seen, has been of daily occurrence and which, alas, yet occurs daily.

In the first place, we will imagine an extremely corrupted, ungodly, carnal knave who is yet called a priest, pastor, vicar or prebendary by the world. This same unchaste man, full of all manner of roguery and deceit, covers his condemnable knavery with such a pleasant semblance that none suspicion him, as does the ravening wolf in sheeps clothing, Matt. 7 : 5. His head is frequently shaven, perhaps, as proof that he wants thus violently to shave off and destroy all lusts and desires of his wicked, sinful flesh; he desires to walk in long robes, as Christ says, Luke 20: 46, as if he were pious, holy and venerable; he daily reads his prayers with folded hands and uncovered head, as if he were very ardently inspired; he kneels and burns incense before stone and wooden blocks, which he calls Peter, Paul, Mary and the worthy crucifix of the Lord. I tell this verily without facetiousness, of which God is my witness. Judge now whether this is not the case.

Besides he buys a hundred wafers for a stiver, takes one at a time, consecrates it as he savs, and that mentally, without saying a word, nods to it, worships, implores and eats it; and this same thing he believes and teaches to be the true flesh and blood of our beloved Lord, Jesus Christ, the Son of the Almighty and living God. Besides he must be so pure and chaste in his walk that he is not allowed to have a legitimate or wedded consort, although the Holy Scriptures allow it, but the Pope has forbidden it. All these and other abominations he calls and teaches to be the holy worship, and the most holy, christian faith. Such fruits are begotten and produced by this evil tree, by the faith that is within him; and after he has orderly, sumptuously and well performed his carnal holiness, he proves his inward holiness, by seeking the best female company, wine and beer; drinks, sings, dances, laughs, shouts, scolds, fights, curses, swears, boasts, plays, courts and defiles himself with his female servant, his neighbors daughter, or wife whose husband perhaps is at sea, or some other place, trying to earn a livelihood by the labor of his hands. Thus he lives in shameful adultery until, by the fruits thereof, it can no longer be concealed, when the blame is cast upon some one else, and the fruit (understand what I write), is disposed of, and by falsehood and deception their shame and adultery are concealed.

Behold, brethren, they of whom such illegitimate children are born, have been baptized in their infancy, claiming thereby to be christians; they boast of Jesus Christ and of his precious blood. But we may see by their fruits what kind of christians they are, and what kind of faith they have.

Therefore I tell you these things, O kind reader, that you may know in the first place, what kind of christian parents these are, what kind of faith they have, of whom some children are born who are, notwithstanding all this, carried to the baptism and are baptized on the faith of their hypocritical parents, and are therefore called christians. O, abominable mockery!

In the second place, I find at many places, throughout the world, numbers of vain and abandoned characters, some of them sanctified, others not, some claiming nobility, in a worldly sense, some of large means, some of mediocrity, some poor, in short, of all classes, who, in the same manner, live in all manner of debauchery, vanity, inebriety and uncleanliness, according to their shameful, inordinate lusts and devilish desires, and in all manner of fornication and adultery. They seduce all they can, notwithstanding they are baptized. And when they, by their recklessness, have succeeded in accomplishing the ruin of such simple and uncircumspect souls who are also born of Adam, and who are, perhaps, deceived by false promises and gifts, and led thereto by their accursed actions, then yet, it must be considered by those of their class as a great honor and respectability, as the prophet says. Yet, notwithstanding all this, these same persons alike carry the children who are thus illegitimately born of such profaners, rogues and abandoned women, to the baptism, that they may be called christians and be trained up in the same works and fruits as their adulterous parents, in whom and by whom they are conceived, and begotten in accursed and damnable adultery. O, unbelief!

In the third place, I find almost universally, both among men and women of whatever class or condition they are, noble, rich, poor, citizen or yeoman, who were baptized in infancy, and on that account are called christians, yet they lead such sinful lives that we can form no idea thereof. Their pride, unchastity, avarice, fraud in buying and selling, quarreling, hatred, unrighteousness, unmercifulness towards the tenant and the poor, their cursing, swearing, lying, cheating, pomp, debauchery, drinking, vanity, foolery, blood-thirstiness, cruelty, hypocrisy, tyranny, transgressions, idolatry and all manner of wickedness know no bounds.

If there are some who are not guilty of all the beforementioned vices, on account of their natural indisposition thereto, it must be admitted that there is not one in a thousand who industriously seeks and desires to walk according to the commandments of God, or to live according to his blessed will. Nor do they ask for the right way to eternal life that they may be saved; yet they must be called the right, christian church. Thus has God, the righteous judge, obscured the understanding and natural intellect of those who reject his holy word, and who make and honor things of their own choice, as an idol.

Notwithstanding the heathenish life of both father and mother, yet their infants which are born of them must, without the word of God and merely out of their own choice, be conjured, blessed, rubbed with spittle, anointed, crucifixed and baptized, and after this has been done at the instance of their parents, although contrary to the commandment of God, they are called believing, christian people, no matter how ungodly, inhuman and devilish a life they lead; and are admitted and received into the church as full and proper members.

O, Lord, Father, how very broad, easy and pleasing to the flesh is the entrance into this miserable, carnal church; for it is all as said, no matter who, or what, or how he is, it is all right, if he has but been sworn before a fountain, and washed and baptized in it by an idolater. But how wonderfully narrow, O Lord, is thy way, and how very strait is the gate which leadeth into thy poor and holy church. Yea, so narrow that on its posts are stripped off gold and possessions, flesh and blood and all the lusts and inclinations of those who desire and sincerely seek to enter in at this narrow gate; and thus, by thy grace, to rest and remain forever in thy holy church, Matt. 7: 13.

Behold, kind readers, I have referred to this in this manner, first, that you may the better conceive and understand what kind of christians, those are, what kind of faith they have, and what kind of life they lead, to whom infant baptism has been administered and who now have it administered to their children, that the true, divine knowledge may multiply in you, that you may rightly comprehend, by the word of God, what abominable mockery and hypocrisy infant baptism is before the Almighty God; and that there is no other fruitful, pleasing and available baptism before God, than alone the baptism which is administered and received according to the command of Christ, Mark 16: 16; namely, the baptism upon the confession of faith, as has been frequently remarked. Secondly, I must refer you, in the same manner, to how wonderfully far the custom of the godfathers, who lift the child upon the basin and answer their confession of faith, is different from the Spirit, commandment and word of Christ, that by all these facts, falsehood, unbelief, abuse, and satanic imposture may appear to you and be demolished; and that, on the other hand, truth, faith, the right practice and the divine will may be made known and acted upon.

Inasmuch as Christ commanded that the baptized should first believe, Mark 16: 16, before baptism should be administered, Acts 8: 38, and as the world well knew that infants had no faith; and as they, notwithstanding this, would have unconscious infants baptized, as human righteousness ever has looked upon, profaned, persecuted, despised and rejected the righteousness of God as useless, imperfect and foolish; therefore the ninth or tenth pope, named Higinius, without any commandment of God, hit upon a happy idea, with which the world has hitherto been well satisfied, and by means of which they baptized their infants, and those who feared God more, and therefore understood the word of God better, were for the greater part thereby excommunicated as heretics. This means was this: That some should be chosen from the church, whom they called godfathers, who should lift the children up to the fountain, to be baptized, and who should care for and answer to the faith of the child. Most beloved reader, it is true this matter has a fine appearance and show, but is not in accordance with Christ's Spirit and meaning because the practice of godfathers is a human institution, as history plainly shows; therefore I am at a loss to know why it is that all the learned of the upper and eastern countries yet have this practice of godfathers, since they have so bravely and incessantly written, taught and battled with the word of God, against all human institutions and teachings; for nowhere in the divine word are we taught the practice of such godfathers, in any manner whatever; but every where in the Scriptures where baptism is spoken of, it is shown in very plain characters that the baptized must believe for themselves, must confess it verbally and by their works, and thus desire and receive baptism as a commandment of God, Mark 16: 16, Acts 2: 38; 8: 36; 10: 48; 16: 33; and other passages.

Again, if it were even so that the practice of godfathers was in accordance to the word of God or the commandment of Christ, which however is not so, O, how extensively and closely, and with what great care we would have to search, in city and country, for a suitable person to discharge the duties of such an office. For, How can one blind man lead another? How can one fool make another wise? How can one poor person be surety for another? Understand what I write. In the same manner one unbelieving person can be no surety for the faith of another; "For every man shall bear his own burden," Gal. 6: 5. Neither can he teach nor advocate the faith of another so long as he himself has no true, christian faith; for whatever I am to teach another I must understand myself; and prayer must be the prayer of faith, Jas. 5: 16, in Spirit and in truth, Jn. 4: 24.

As the unbelieving cannot be surety, before God, for the faith of another, nor teach him faith, nor advocate it, even if the practice of godfathers were founded on the ordinance of God, which however it is not, so it must be acknowledged and admitted, that the practice of godfathers in infant baptism is entirely vain, useless and unavailable. I will leave every intelligent christian to judge what faith there is in the godfathers.

I know that I will be asked if there are no right, believing godfathers, who with good consciences, hold the infants to the basin? To this I briefly answer: No. For, in the first place, it is human righteousness, contrary to the word of God, and without the ordinance of Christ; and therefore it can not be practiced with a good conscience. In the second place I admit that there are godfathers who are honorable and virtuous; but, truly, I do not know that they are truly believing; for if they were true believers it would be impossible that they could ever be led to practice such abominable shame with infants, without the word of Christ. For there is no word to be found in all the apostolic Scriptures which in any manner teaches and commands us such a thing; not to say any thing about the impurity, avarice, pomp, ignorance concerning divine matters, idolatry, foolishness, vanity, refractoriness against God and his blessed word, and of the accursed, carnal life of most of those who are called to this office by the church, that the faith of the parents and of the godfathers alike, upon which they baptize these infants and through which they are thought to acquire faith themselves, may go over on them; as we have too often seen that the one adulterous knave calls upon the other; one drunkard on the other; or one proud person upon the other. By their works they show plainly that it is not of God; but that it is deceit, devilish hypocrisy, human righteousness, blasphemy, mockery, destruction of the ordinances of Christ, and, in every respect contrary to the blessed word of God.

Behold, worthy brethren, in the course of time they have thus subtlely converted and changed the heavenly doctrine, and lovely ordinance of our beloved Lord Jesus Christ into such unclean mocking, abuse and shameful practice. O, Lord, Father of grace, that this fearful and abominable snare and imposture to our miserable souls, might once be destroyed, Amen.

In the third place, as we have first shown you the faith and life of the parents; second, the command, faith and life of the godfathers, we will now show you who those are whose office it is to baptize these infants and thus to make christian people out of them, and will point you, faithful reader, to your own pastor, vicar, prebendary or chaplain, as you call them. Yea to all the priests round about you; that you may closely scrutinize them according to the word of God, and see if there is one amongst all of them, I say *one*, however many there may be, who is called of an unblamable, christian church, who is moved by the Holy Spirit, and who is unblamable in both doctrine and life. O, brother, not one, no, not one, however far you may travel, and however industriously you may search. Their calling is of the dragon and of the beast. They have nothing which forces them to this office, but, solely, their lazy, greedy, avaricious, proud and gluttonous flesh. Their teaching for the greater part, is merely deceit; their worship is all idolatry, spiritual enchantment of the bottomless pit and a cause for shedding innocent blood. Besides, their daily walk is so shameful, unclean, sodomic, adulterous, lustful, greedy, avaricious, backbiting, envious, unmerciful, treacherous, ambitious, blind, ungodly, fearful and so abominable that all reasonable men, the angels of God and the heavens must be astounded and ashamed thereat.

Say, kind reader, is it not so? Have you, ever found greater pride, avarice, gluttony, adultery, fornication, spitefulness, hypocrisy, mockery and shame than is found amongst them? I am aware that they are not all alike unchaste and shameful in their daily walk; yet there is not one amongst them, however finely he appears before the world, but his worship and life is of the flesh—of the devil; contrary to God and his blessed word.

Worthy, beloved brethren, he who knoweth all things, knows that I do not write this with hatred or with bad intentions. Therefore, judge for yourselves all things according to the word of God, and according to your rational, natural understanding; as you may daily perceive these things amongst them. You will without doubt acknowledge that I have discovered and presented to you nothing but the truth, out of love for your salvation. Say, have I done wrong to discover and present unto you the wiles of a thief or murderer? Pluck from your eyes this accursed and abominable blindness, and look to the truth of your Lord; root all unbelief from your obscured hearts, and believe the word of God. Behold, the holy apostle Paul says, "Not to keep company, if any man that is called a brother, be a fornicator, or covetous, or an idolater, or a railer, or a drunkard, or an extortioner; with such a one no not to eat." A proof that, although they call themselves brethren or christians, they are not in the church of Christ on account of their disreputable life. For the church of Christ is holy, pure and unblamable. In another place he teaches that such shall not inherit the kingdom of God, Rom. 1: 32; 1 Cor. 5: 11; Gal. 5: 22; Eph. 5: 6.

Now if they are not in the church of Christ, and if they cannot inherit the kingdom of God, tell me what things divine, or christian can then be served or practiced by them in the house of the Lord, that is, in the church of Christ? Notwithstanding that we should not keep the company of such, nor eat with them, and notwithstanding they have not the promise of salvation according to Paul, on account of their unbelief and their terrible, wicked, beastly life, yet the world is so blinded by them and so estranged from God that they look upon, honor and accept them as true shepherds, teachers and pastors who have power from God to do anything they please while they only make their pretensions under the false cover of christianity and of the holy, christian church, as they call it. O, blindness!

These are they, O ye men, who yet this day are allowed to mislead the whole world by their false doctrine, and to uselessly bless, conjure and baptize infants, without the word or command of God, notwithstanding that the most holy gospel of Jesus Christ opposes and rebukes such things.

As these spiritual fathers or teachers are, so also are their children who are begotten of them, that is, those whom they teach and baptize as they plainly prove and verify by their fruits.

Behold, brethren, by no other means than by these beforementioned teachers and infant baptists, the church of Christ is converted into such a work of hypocrisy, shame, mockery, deceit, degeneration, knavery and prostitution. O, misery of misery!

Now you have presented to you, first, the parents of whom the children are born, with their unbelief and carnal life; secondly, the papal godfathers, together with their abuse, unbelief and evil fruits, who lift the children to the basin for baptism, and answer their confession. Thirdly, the teachers, or baptizers together with their sending, calling, doctrine, idolatry, unbelief, and ungodly works, who baptize the infants, and, as they call it, cleanse and wash them of their inherent sins; all of which parties, namely, parents, godfathers and baptizers, themselves feel in their hearts neither knowledge, faith, truth, love, fear of God, gospel, christian fruits, obedience, remission of sins, peace of mind, prayer, promise, God, Christ, Spirit, nor eternal life; but are only nominal christians. These deliberately claim to make a christian out of a child just taken from the mother's womb, which can neither stand, walk, hear, speak, nor comprehend; which for lack of understanding, is as the irrational animals; which cannot distinguish between good and evil; without the word and without faith—by no other means than by crucifixes, breathing, salt, oil, crisma, candles, clothing, useless questions and answers, blessings, conjuring, baptizing, offering, and such like abominations, and when this noisy, idolatrous hypocrisy has been practiced upon the infants, then they are christian people, as the nurses tell the mother after these things have been performed, saying, we have received from you a heathen but a christian we return and deliver to you again.

The next thing in order, is setting the table. Victuals and drink are prepared, the neighbors and friends partake thereof, and the parents are well satisfied with their baptized infant. And from that hour it is trained in all manner of foolishness, unbelief, vanity, sin, shame, wickedness, idolatry and all manner of carnal and devilish works; in a manner, that no knowledge, faith, fear, and love of God, evangelical truth and life can ever take root in it. And should anything occur that something christian-like would spring up in it, then it will have to suffer much and bear the cross of Christ. I repeat it, because of this baptism it is henceforth considered a christian person, no matter how it acts. Behold, beloved brethren, they call this the holy church of to-day, and in this manner one of these christians begets the other, until the world is full of them.

Honored reader, understand rightly what I have written unto you, for I have treated so extensively of this matter that you may be convinced of what a secret, hidden snare and what a terrible, fearful idol, infant baptism is against God; and how very useless and idolatrous it is to teach that infants should be baptized that they may be the better trained in the word and commandments of God. Thus human doctrine ever puts on a fine and holy air, but in fact it is, verily nothing but hypocrisy, falsehood and a deadly venom.

Those who do not depend on this antichristian, infant baptism, but practice the true, christian baptism which was commanded of Christ Jesus and taught and practiced by his holy apostles, take care of the salvation of their children. Therefore they train them in the fear of God by teaching, admonishing and chastising them, and with an example of an unblamable life, that when they become of mature years, they may hear, believe and accept the most holy gospel of Jesus Christ, and receive the holy, christian baptism, as Jesus and his holy apostles have taught all the believing of God, in divers places of the New Testament.

In the third place, Paul, also, teaches us so, saying, "Know ye not, that so many of us as were baptized into Jesus Christ, were baptized into his death? Therefore we are buried with him by baptism into death; that like as Christ was raised up from the dead by the glory of the Father, even so we also should walk in newness of life," Rom. 6: 3, 4.

Here the baptism of the believing is again undeniably confirmed, and infant baptism is made void. For as Christ Jesus commanded that we should baptize the believing, Mark 16: 16, so, also, it is evident from these words of Paul that baptism represents and signifies something which none can realize but those, alone, who are believing, namely, it represents death unto sin or a burying of the old life, and a resurrection into newness of life.

Since Paul says, This christian baptism is such a death unto sin, and a raising up into a new life, therefore they must confess and admit that none can die unto, and bury his shameful lusts and desires, his inordinate, carnal, ungodly life; and that none can raise up into a pious, unblamable, godly life but those, alone who, as obedient children of God, are taught and regenerated by the word of the Lord; which spiritual death, burial and resurrection are represented in holy baptism. At another place Paul calls it the spiritual circumcision, saying, "Ye are circumcised with the circumcision made without hands, in putting off the body of the sins of the flesh by the circumcision of Christ; buried with him in baptism, wherein also ye are risen with him through the faith of the operation of God, who hath raised him from the dead," Col. 2: 11, 12.

Inasmuch as it clearly appears that the believing alone die unto their sins, and bury them, and, with Christ, enter into, and are raised up into the new, godly life; and as little children cannot do this because they have no faith by which God operates in his children, therefore it must be acknowledged and admitted, whether they are willing or not, that infant baptism is not commanded by the Lord Jesus Christ, nor taught or implied in the apostolic doctrine.

Kind reader, it is sometimes alleged that other apostles also left Scripture behind them; which Scriptures Pope Gelasius has selected, and that perhaps infant baptism was expressed and implied in them.

Beloved reader, if our opponents build their cause upon the selected Scriptures of the apostles and have no certainty therefrom, but only presuming that infant baptism may have been expressed therein, we would discreetly answer, and ask, first, since they refer to the apostolic Scriptures which we do not have, we would like to know of them what these apostles have taught and commanded concerning infant baptism?

Secondly, as they seek to establish their doctrine by uncertain Scriptures which they do not have, and that only on presumption, they show thereby that they are unable to verify their doctrine at all by the apostolic Scriptures which we now have.

Thirdly, we say that we should not teach and practice the ceremonies of the Lord, namely: The holy baptism, upon presumption and adventure, but on certainties.

Fourthly, we say that the apostles have all written, taught and preached in one spirit. Inasmuch as Christ Jesus has commanded baptism on the confession of faith, Mark 16: 16, and as Peter, Paul and Philip taught and practiced, according to the commandment of Christ, the baptism of the believing, and not of infants, therefore you may surely deduce therefrom that it was not taught and practiced differently by the other apostles whose Scriptures we do not have; even if they had written and published six hundred volumes. For if infant baptism was an apostolic institution it would appear so in their Scriptures. Nor would Tertullian, who lived not long after the days of the apostles, have written, that among his ancestors, almost invariably adults were baptized, as has been said above. Also would Alexander, bishop of Alexandria, have baptized the infants of his church; and the ancients would not have disputed about it, as all those who feared God would act according to the Scriptures and not deviate therefrom; for what God-fearing person would dare to despise, oppose, or in any manner contradict an apostolic institution or practice?

Those who did not rightly confess Christ, but sought their righteousness and placed their trust in outward ceremonies, got the upper hand of the world; and therefore it was not necessary that this infant baptism should be confirmed by any papal decree or council, as it gradually and of its own accord stole its way into all classes, nations and tongues and took its full sway; for the whole church, after the demise of the apostles, through the ignorant teachings of the bishops, gradually degenerated from the trust in Jesus Christ to the trust in outward ceremonies, as may be plainly seen.

Again, brethren, however plain this passage of Paul, Rom. 6, applies to the believing, yet the learned of this barren world have inverted and explained it as confirming and asserting infant baptism, saying, *That infants should be baptized that they may become partakers of the death and holy blood of Christ Jesus; and that when they become of mature age, they may die unto sin and walk righteously before God.*

My beloved children in Christ Jesus, if it would do thus to bend, twist and garble, of our own choice, and carnal fancy, the plain truth and will of God and the most holy and glorious gospel of our beloved Lord Jesus Christ, then verily, I do not see why we could not so adorn and beautify almost any abomination or idolatry as to give it a good appearance in the sight of the ignorant. No, most beloved, no. The eternal, omnipotent, and saving word of God, must be taught, explained and understood according to the true meaning of the Holy Spirit. For they baptize before that which is represented by it (namely, faith,) is found in us. This is no more sensible than to place the cart before the horse, to sow before we have plowed, to build before we have the lumber at hand, or to seal the letter before it is written. Would this not be ridiculed by all the world as foolishness? Yes, certainly. Therefore the Holy Spirit of God did not *imply* infant baptism in this beforementioned Scripture of Paul. Yet they are partakers of the death and blood of Christ by the precious promise which was graciously given of God through Christ Jesus our Lord, and not through baptism, Luke 18:16. But this passage of Paul speaks and teaches of those who, in their baptism, through their new birth from above and through their fruitful, operating faith, have died unto and buried their old, sinful life, as Christ Jesus once died in his flesh and was buried. For whosoever thus died with Christ, is already justified of his sins, and is thus victoriously raised up, with Christ, from the power of sin, to the praise of the Lord, in a new, just, godly, and unblamable life, which is by no other means than through God's word alone, which is accepted and believed by them through faith, as has been alleged above, and is written "Ye are circumcised with the circumcision made without hands, in putting off the body of the sins of the flesh by the circumcision of Christ; buried with him in baptism, wherein also ye are risen with him through the faith of the operation of God, who hath raised him from the dead," Col. 2:11, 12.

O, beloved brethren, open the eyes of your hearts and understanding and take heed; for he who will not willfully battle against his God, or his holy word, certainly, can not mistake these plain words of Paul. Yet Henry Bullenger and many others, on the strength of this epistle to the Colossians, have taught baptism to have taken the literal place of the Israelitic circumcision, although without a good reason and without the Scriptures, yet not without a good deal of blasphemy and vituperation. For what reason they have done so, I do not know; perhaps because Paul has so closely placed together and so intimately connected both the spiritual circumcision and the baptism of the believing or upright christians.

O, Lord, thy divine, blessed word is ever garbled into a shelter for all manner of false doctrine, heresy and wrong doing, so that the Bible is called by some the book of heresy! Notwithstanding their opposition and subtle lying and philosophizing, the eternal truth of God shall obtain and triumph in the chosen children of God who sincerely desire and seek the same.

I repeat it that I am heartily ashamed to write or speak one single word against such highly renowned and learned men. But what will we do? It will never do to be robbed, by these learned men, of God's eternal truth which leads to eternal life, and which was so plainly taught us by Jesus Christ our Lord, and by his holy apostles. For, verily, I find nowhere that we should follow and obey such learned men rather than Christ and his holy apostles. If it should be said that they are wise and pious, I say that Christ is the most wise and pious; and if it be said that they are versed in many tongues and sciences, I rejoin, briefly, that the Spirit of the Lord Jesus Christ is not bound by tongues and science. Therefore the most holy and invincible truth of God must be defended and maintained by us, not only against them, but against all the gates of hell, by the most holy word of God, in so far as God has bestowed on us grace, mercy and knowledge.

For this reason I will refer all my readers to Col. 2: 12, and would humbly beseech them to judge impartially whether we find in this or any other divine Scriptures that the *circumcision of the Israelites was the prototype of infant baptism*. It is incontrovertible that Paul, in this passage and also in Rom. 2: 29, taught that the literal circumcision was a figure of the spiritual circumcision and not of infant baptism, which circumcision cannot be applied to any but the believing as may be plainly inferred from the figurative, literal practice; for the literal circumcision was to be performed with *stone knives on the foreskin,

---
*German translation of the Bible.

Josh. 5: 2, 3; Gen. 17: 23. This spiritual Rock is Jesus Christ, 1 Cor. 10: 4, the knife with which the believing are circumcised is his holy word. Brethren, understand it well. If we wish to remain with believing, circumcised Abraham in the covenant with God—into which covenant we are all graciously accepted, young and old, male and female, through Christ Jesus and not through any sign—then our earthly, carnal birth which is of the earthly, carnal Adam, must be circumcised with this same, stone knife, which is Christ Jesus and his holy word. Therefore examine the beforementioned words of Paul to the Colossians, and judge whether they are spoken in regard to the believing or to unconscious infants. Say, who is it that is circumcised by the circumcision of Christ? Is it not the believing? Who is it that has put off the body of sin by the circumcision of Christ? Is it not the believing? Who is it that is buried in baptism with Christ? Is it not the believing? Who is it that is raised up into a new life by the faith of the operation of God? Is it not the believing? Yea, they are those who hear the word of God and believe it; and not the little infants. Never.

Kind reader, since the infant baptizers seek to prove their cause by the circumcision of Abraham and by his promise, therefore observe and ponder how unreasonably they make this assertion; and observe and ponder also on that which will be briefly taught and presented by us, from Scriptural truth.

In the first place, as we said before, we are all accepted into the covenant with God, not by any signs but by grace, and have obtained the promise by it, if we accept them by faith and walk according to the will of the giver; as Abraham was accepted of God by grace, from amongst the nations, and was made glad with the promise of grace; for he accepted it by faith, and walked according to the will of him who had accepted him as the Scriptures say, He believed in the Lord, and it was counted to him for righteousness, Gen. 15: 6; Rom. 4: 3; Gal. 3: 6; Jas. 2: 23.

To all those who are thus, by faith, graciously accepted of God into the covenant of peace with Abraham, God has given his ceremonies and figurative signs. Not that they should thereby be justified (for if it were by the signs it would not be grace, Rom. 11: 6), but that they should be justified by faith; be children of God, children of the promise, &c., that they should show their obedience to the commandments of God who has graciously called, accepted and consoled them by his promise. For those that are obedient unto God, are his friends, Jn. 15.

Behold, brethren, this is one reason why God commanded his ceremonies, as is plainly shown in the case of Abraham; for Abraham was already in the covenant with God, before he was circumcised; as Paul shows, that his faith was already counted for righteousness when he was yet uncircumcised; and because he was in the covenant with God, justified by faith therefore God commanded him the circumcision, in itself a useless and dishonorable ceremony. First, it was in itself quite useless, because it did not benefit any neighbor. Secondly, dishonorable, for it is performed upon the most dishonorable member of the body. And it was commanded him that the believing father, Abraham, should deny himself and not live according to his own desires, but according to the will of him, alone, who, by grace, had accepted him and chosen him from among the nations; and thus he sealed, by this performance, which was dishonorable in itself, that his faith was true and fruitful before God. Why these ceremonies were again commanded, will be shown hereafter, if God please.

Behold, kind reader, in this manner Abraham was circumcised, and thus we are baptized; because it is thus commanded by God. Whosoever disobeys and opposes the voice of the Lord commanding these ceremonies, and despises the performance of them because of their uselessness and triflingness, not observing that it was commanded by God, excludes himself from the precious covenant of grace, by his disobedience; neither does he prove his faith to be fruitful and living, but on the contrary he proves that it is unfruitful and dead before God. For he hears not the voice of his Lord nor lives in accordance therewith, but despises it as powerless, vain and useless. Therefore observe and know that we are not accepted into the covenant by an outward sign, but alone by grace through Christ Jesus. And because we are in the covenant by grace, therefore he has given and commanded us his signs, that we shall perform them upon those on whom he has commanded them to be performed, namely, upon the faithful; for if it were possible that we could come into the covenant with God by any signs or ceremonies, then the merits of Christ were vain, and grace was ended. No, brethren, no. Abraham was already chosen, accepted and justified by God, through faith, before he was circumcised; and because he was faithful, and justified through faith, therefore the circumcision was commanded him of God that he should thereby seal his faith. Again, as Abraham and all his seed born of Isaac, together with others, were already included in the covenant with God, women as well as men, and as the promise was given to both sexes, yet it was not commanded that the females should be circumcised, but the males.

Observe well, beloved reader, had they obtained the covenant with God by the sign and not by grace, then the females must have been excluded and without the promise. Not so, it was by grace, it is by grace, and it ever will be by grace. If they had been disobedient to the word of God, and not circumcised their males on the appointed day; or if they had done differently from the commandment of God, and circumcised their females, then they would have had to bear the punishment of their disobedience in their children, Gen. 17: 14, excluded them from the covenant with the Lord, and not have obtained the gift of his grace. For God, the Almighty Father, whose voice, will and commandment all creatures, both in heaven and earth, should obey, will have the commanded ceremonies performed as it pleases him and as he has commanded them to be performed, for therefore he has commanded them. If we do not perform them or perform them differently, we have, by our disobedience, neither covenant nor promise. This is the right, scriptural meaning of Abraham's covenant, circumcision and promise. Whosoever teaches you differently deceives your soul; for he points you to merits and works, and not to Christ Jesus through whom alone are received the eternal covenant of peace and promise of grace, given of God.

O brethren, brethren, how long will you oppose the Holy Gnost! Give the word of God its due praise, and observe that little infants are not buried with Christ in baptism; nor are raised into newness of life; for if they did die, and were buried in baptism, then sin would be so destroyed in them that it would never more vanquish their spirit. Inasmuch as sin, after their baptism, so powerfully, and so abundantly flourishes in them as they begin to come to understanding, as may be plainly seen, therefore the infant baptizers must acknowledge and confess that they bury the children alive, which should not be; or else that they baptize them all without faith, and contrary to the ordinance of Christ, therefore useless and vain.

For this reason, learn once, beloved reader, that infant baptism is not of God nor through him. But whosoever rightly acknowledges the love of God for himself through Christ Jesus and is baptized upon his own faith through true love of God, according to the doctrine of Christ, Peter, Paul and Philip, is rightly circumcised in his heart with the circumcision of Christ, as Paul teaches; he is buried with Christ Jesus; he has died unto sin, and is again raised up by a fruitful faith with Jesus Christ in a new life, Rom. 6: 4; Col. 2: 12.

In opposition to this, the infant baptizers have still another point, saying, *Because Paul, in this passage, has not forbidden infant baptism, therefore it is right*. To this we reply by asking: Whether infant baptism is commanded in this or any other Scripture? They must own the truth and answer, no. If it is not commanded of God, then it is not his ordinance, and therefore it has no promise. Again, if it is not commanded of God, then it is not his ordinance; if it is not his ordinance, then it has no promise; and if it has no promise, it is doubtlessly useless and vain.

Again, we ask them, Where in the word of God it is expressly forbidden to baptize bells? They must own the truth and answer, *nowhere*. If it is, then, not expressly forbidden to baptize bells, is therefore bell-baptism just and right? Not at all.

Thirdly, Israel was not forbidden to circumcise the females. Now, would it have been right if they had circumcised their females? Far from it. For the Scriptures commanded that the males should be circumcised therefore they considered that it was forbidden to circumcise their females.

In the same manner Christ Jesus commands us to baptize the believing, and that which is represented by baptism is only found in the believing, as may be plainly seen from Peter and Paul, therefore we infer that infant baptism is sufficiently forbidden; for they have no faith and do not understand the representation of baptism which comes by faith.

I repeat it, If the infant baptists assert that by this Scripture of Paul, infant baptism is not forbidden, and that therefore it is right, that it is not expressly forbidden in the holy Scriptures to bless (as they call it), holy water, candles, palms, goblets and robes; to hold mass, and other ceremonies; yet we pointedly say that it is wrong. First, because trust is put in it. Secondly, because it is done without the ordinance of God, for he has not commanded us a word thereof; and there is no ordinance in which his holy, blessed word is not expressed and implied either in spirit or letter.

Since Christ Jesus has commanded baptism upon the confession of faith, Mark 16: 16; since the apostles have thus taught and practiced it, and as the meaning of baptism Rom. 6: 3; Col. 2: 12; Tit. 3: 5; Gal. 3: 27; 1 Cor. 12: 13; 1 Pet. 3: 21, cannot be applicable but to the believing, therefore it is sufficiently forbidden by this divine ordinance, to baptize infants; for there is no faith in them nor do they understand the meaning thereof; notwithstanding that infant baptism commenced soon after the time of the apostles, or perhaps yet in their time, and thus it has been practiced many centuries; for length of time can not prevail against the word of God, as we have sufficiently shown the pious, god-fearing reader, above.

Fourthly, Thus says the holy apostle Paul, "The kindness and love of God our Savior toward man appeared, not by works of righteousness which we have done, but according to his mercy he saved us, by the washing of regeneration, and renewing of the Holy Ghost," Tit. 3: 4, 5.

Most beloved brethren, if we rightly and thoroughly examine this passage of Paul, with spiritual eyes, and weigh it with the Scriptures, then the infant baptizers, by force of the Scriptures, must acknowledge that the christian baptism which is commanded by God, pertains alone to the believing, according to the commandment of Christ, Mark 16: 16, and not to those who are naturally unable to hear, speak and understand, namely, infants; for it is a washing of regeneration as holy Paul has taught and testified to by the above words.

My worthy, kind brethren, because the holy, christian baptism is a washing of regeneration, according to the doctrine of Paul, therefore none can be washed therewith, to the pleasure and will of God, but those alone who are regenerated through the word of God; for we are not regenerated because of baptism, as may be perceived in the infants who have been baptized; but we are baptized because we are regenerated by faith in God's word, as regeneration is not the result of baptism, but baptism the result of regeneration. This cannot well be controverted by any man, by force of the Scriptures. Therefore all should be shamed by this passage of Paul, let them be ever so learned; the learned, who so shamefully teach and make the unsuspecting populace believe that infants are regenerated by baptism. Beloved reader, such teaching and belief is, verily, nothing but fraud and deceit. For if the infants were regenerated, as the learned say, then their whole course would be humility, longsuffering, mercy, pure and chaste love, true faith, certain knowledge, sure hope, obedience to God, spiritual joy, inward peace, and an unblamable life; for these are the true and natural fruits of the new, heavenly birth; but what fruits are found in infants every intelligent reader may judge from every day experience.

Do you think, most beloved, that the new birth consists in nothing but in that which the miserable world hitherto has thought that it consists in, namely, baptism? or in the expression, I baptize thee in the name of the Father, and of the Son, and of the Holy Ghost? No, worthy brother, no. The new birth consists, verily, not in water nor in words; but it is the heavenly, living and quickening power of God in our hearts, which comes from God, and which, by the preaching of the divine word, if we accept it by faith, quickens, renews, pierces and converts our hearts, so that we are changed and converted from unbelief into faith, from unrighteousness into righteousness, from evil into good, from carnality into spirituality, from the earthly into the heavenly, from the wicked nature of Adam into the good nature of Jesus Christ; and of such Paul spoke in the alleged Scripture.

Behold, those who are of such a nature are the truly regenerated children of God; those are the beloved brethren and sisters of Jesus Christ, who are born with him from above of one Father, namely, of God, Jn. 1: 13; Heb. 2: 13. And these regenerated are those to whom, alone, he has taught and commanded the holy, christian baptism, as a seal of faith, Matt. 28: 19; Mark 16: 15, by which they receive remission of sin; Acts 2: 38, and not the unconscious infants, as has been frequently shown above, from the word of God. Therefore the holy apostle Paul teaches us by this Scripture that God sanctifies the regenerated by the baptism of regeneration; because they are regenerated by the word of God, they deny themselves by the power of their regeneration and have obediently taken upon themselves all that which God, the Almighty Father, in his holy word, has taught and commanded his chosen children, through his beloved Son, Jesus Christ our Lord, and through all his true servants and messengers. Therefore I repeat that the baptism by which God sanctifies us, belongs to the believing or regenerated, as Paul teaches. And in this manner: First, there must be the preaching of the gospel of Christ, Matt. 28: 19; Secondly, The hearing of the divine word, Rom. 10: 17; thirdly, faith, by hearing the word, Rom. 10: 17; fourthly, there must be the new birth, by faith; fifthly, baptism, by the new birth, Tit. 3: 5, in obedience to God's word, and, lastly, the promise follows.

If we do not desire willfully to oppose the

Holy Ghost and reject the grace of God, it is impossible to believe that a true faith can be without regeneration and obedience, and that this obedience can be without the promise. For the eternal truth, the blessed Jesus Christ, will never fail nor deceive us in his holy word; and it is he who taught this: First, to preach the holy gospel, saying, *Go ye into all the world, and preach the gospel to every creature;* therefrom follows faith, saying, *And whoever shall believe;* from faith follows baptism, saying, *And be baptized;* and from these follows the promise, saying, *Shall be saved*, Mark 16.

Inasmuch as the ordinance of Jesus Christ thus reads, and as the one follows from the other, therefore Paul here teaches us that God sanctifies us by the washing of regeneration and the renewing of the Holy Ghost; for in case true faith and obedience be separated from each other, as is sometimes the case, such as grieving the Holy Ghost and sinning against him, then such faith does not profit us; for it has no promise, on account of disobedience and is, besides, useless and dead before God, Jas. 2.

To all those, who, of their own choice, and contrary to the Scriptures, assert the regeneration of infants, because they were baptized, notwithstanding there are no fruits in them, as may be plainly seen, I reply: First, that he does not know what the new birth is. Secondly, with the same propriety and reasonability, bells are baptized. God in his word has no more commanded the one than the other, for according to their nature, there is as little faith and fruits in the one as there are in the other. O, Lord! when will this awful abomination once cease to be practiced. When will those who now call themselves christians be christians? Yea, when will the blessed Lord Jesus Christ be acknowledged as wise, true and perfect in his holy word? I fear, never. The false teaching, unbelief and opinion is esteemed and loved by these miserable, carnal men, far above the same doctrine of Jesus Christ and his holy apostles. Notwithstanding we say in Christ Jesus, let them baptize their infants as much as they will, let them teach it as long and as strong as they will, and let them assert it on the strength of the garbled Scriptures, of learned men, and of long usage—yet it is all vain and useless before God; for the regeneration of infants cannot be maintained by virtue of the word of God.

Chosen brethren, let them freely cry out against us, let them adduce all doctors, learned and famous men who have lived centuries ago, let them console themselves with long usage, even from the apostles' time; yet where there is no new birth there can be no baptism administered in accordance with the commandment of Jesus, for baptism is the washing of regeneration, Tit. 3; which regeneration none have but the believing, alone, as we have shown our readers before.

Therefore I would admonish all my beloved readers in the Lord, not to heed the philosophy of the learned, nor to look at the long usage, but to the plain and unmixed word of God, and you will surely find by this Scripture of Paul, and others, that, according to the commandment of Christ, the christian baptism should be administered to none but those who, by grace have become believing and regenerated through the word of God. As long as baptism is administered to infants, it is no washing of regeneration. For the new birth is of the word of God, as has been often said, which word infants cannot hear and understand; therefore they cannot be born again as long as they are minded as a child. All that which the Father has not planted should be plucked from the heart by the word of God, Matt. 15. God's word shall stand forever, and according to the divine word, every pious christian shall and must build the structure of his faith, if his work shall be pleasing before God; and should not build it according to his own pleasure. For God, the Almighty Father, who rules all things by his word, will not be honored by human doctrine and commandments, Matt. 15: 9; Mark 7: 7; Col. 2: 22; Jer. 29: 8.

In the fifth place holy Paul teaches us saying, For ye are all children of God by faith in Christ Jesus. "For as many of you as have been baptized into Christ, have put on Christ," Gal. 3: 27; Rom. 6: 3.

My beloved children in Christ Jesus, you

CHRISTIAN BAPTISM.

are aware that all the world, by their blind and foolish unbelief, have hitherto whored with outward works and ceremonies. Yet you should not do likewise. But you should know that the righteousness which avails before God, consists not in any ceremonies and outward works, but solely in a true, pious and fruitful faith and in nothing else, in this manner. For the faith which comes by the word of God cannot be without fruit only in those who sin against the Holy Ghost, as said above, but it leads into all manner of righteousness, it willingly submits itself in all obedience and it cheerfully complies not only with baptism, but with all the words and ceremonies which God, the gracious Father, through his blessed Son, has so clearly taught and commanded in his holy gospel.

Therefore true faith is the fullness of righteousness, Rom. 3 and 6; yea, it is the true begetter of all christian virtues; and by reason of this, the word of God ascribes to it righteousness, Rom. 3: 23, the blessing, salvation, and life everlasting, Jn. 3: 36; 17: 4, and does not ascribe these to ceremonies. If ceremonies *are* commanded by him, it is not because of these ceremonies, but it is because of the faith which compels us to observe these ceremonies for they are commanded of God. Therefore you should know, kind reader, that when the ceremonies in God's word are coupled with the promise, as the Israelitic offerings in the law, and baptism under the gospel, then it is not because of ceremonies, but it is by virtue of faith, which obediently and in love fulfills not alone the commanded ceremonies, but also all that which God has commanded, as has been said above.

For this reason holy Paul taught the Galatians that they were become the children of God through faith and not by baptism, saying, "Ye are all the children of God by faith in Christ Jesus." And again, because they were the children of God by faith, they showed obedience to his word, and therefore Paul said unto them, "As many of you as have been baptized into Christ, have put on Christ." Therefore the principal thing is in faith, and not in ceremonies. But this godly, fruitful faith, in which all consists, together with its christian fruits, is not known to many, and for that reason they ever seek their righteousness in outward ceremonies, yea, also in the most useless ceremonies of human invention which are neither taught nor commanded of God, as they have shown, these many centuries, in baptizing infants. Read what we told you above about the parents, godfathers and baptizers and you will see that all the world is led into a false trust by infant baptism; has become estranged from God, and is blinded in regard to all christian matters. And to give their false pretensions a beautiful, holy and divine appearance, they mutilate and twist the precious word of God to suit them, as they fully show in this case; for, by this Scripture of Paul, and other garbled Scriptures, they have fooled and deceived the poor, ignorant people these many years; teaching them that infants put on Christ in baptism, plainly showing by such doctrine that they do not know what regeneration is, nor what it is to put on Christ Jesus.

Most beloved brethren, verily it is the nature of all heretics to tear a fragment from the holy Scriptures and thereby to prove their chosen worship; never observing what is written before or after, by which we may ascertain the right meaning, as in this instance they have so plainly shown. For this sentence: "as many of you as are baptized have put on Christ," they pick out to give their infant baptism an appearance; but the foregoing sentence: "Ye are all the children of God because you believed on Christ Jesus," from which, as we have shown above, all the rest must follow, that they seem not to have noticed; and thus they seek merit in ceremonies and not through faith in Jesus Christ.

Besides, inasmuch as they are not clothed with Christ nor have put him on, either actively or passively, and have not tested his heavenly, spiritual nature and Spirit, because they are carnally minded—therefore they do not understand, however much they write and teach, what it means to put on Christ Jesus, I repeat, either actively or passively.

That we may convince all gainsayers of the word of the Lord, and that we may neither stumble nor err in these words, therefore I would refer all my readers to holy Paul. He shows who they are that put on Christ, and what fruits they manifest, by which we may know that they have put on Christ, thus saying, "If Christ be in you, the body is dead because of sin; but the spirit is life because of righteousness," Rom. 8: 10; 6: 5.

Kind reader, however dexterously the scribes and infant baptizers may controvert under a false semblance of the divine word, yet none can deny that Christ dwells in those who have put on Christ. Since the truly baptized put on Christ Jesus, he is in them; and if he is in them then the body is dead unto sin and the spirit is life because of righteousness; this being the case, I again call on all reasonable persons to judge impartially for themselves, whether it is found in truly believing persons, or in infants? If they say, in the believing, their judgment is right; for Christ Jesus dwells in the hearts of the believing, Eph. 3: 17. But if they say in infants, then I would again ask by what means we may find this out, inasmuch as in these infants the death unto sin and the spiritual life are not shown nor found? For all of them, from infancy, so long as they do not believe the word of God, notwithstanding their baptism, are not alone prone to evil, but also to disobedience, as daily experience openly shows in all those baptized of this world.

Therefore I conclude from this Scripture of Paul, and say, If the infant baptists remain constant in their opinion and belief, that by their baptism, infants put on Christ, that they must come to the conclusion by virtue of the word of God, that Christ Jesus is unbelieving, proud, ambitious, envious, vain, drunk, adulterous, refractory and disobedient to the word of God; for whosoever has put on Christ Jesus does not live himself, but Christ lives in him. If they, then, have put on Christ by their baptism, as they claim, and as, according to Paul, Christ lives in them and rules their actions, so it must follow that Christ is vain and useless in them, or that their accursed works are begotten of Christ, for they yet live in all manner of carnality and ungodliness, and it therefore follows that they have not put on Christ.

No, verily, no. For Christ Jesus cannot be without fruits; but whosoever has put on the humble, long-suffering, merciful, amiable, peaceable, sober, chaste and obedient Christ, in such an one the beforementioned accursed works are not found; for whosoever has put on Christ, is dead unto sin and lives in righteousness, Rom. 8; is led by the Holy Spirit, born with Jesus, from above, of the Father; and therefore he lives according to the will of the Father, and cannot sin because he is born of God, 1 Jn. 3: 9; 5: 18.

Inasmuch as all those who are baptized without faith, prove the contrary by their life and do not manifest the nature and virtues of Christ whom they have put on, as they falsely claim; but they manifest in their whole walk the nature and vices of the flesh and of Satan; therefore it proves clearly that they have not put on Christ who is from heaven; but that they have put on the devil, who is from hell; for it is he who actuates and leads them at will, as may be plainly seen; as all their thoughts and works of the flesh and of Satan are natural, inherent fruits which are found all over the world, in all men; no matter of what state, trade, condition, class or sect they are.

Beloved reader, you will acknowledge that every tree brings forth fruits after its own kind, and that by the fruit we may know the tree, Matt. 7: 20; 12: 33. Therefore it can not fail but that where Christ Jesus is, there are the good fruits of life everlasting; but where the devil is, there are the wicked fruits of eternal death. Yea, whosoever has put on Christ, in him the works of the devil are not found. On the contrary, where the devil is, there Christ is not; the one must give place to the other; for they are two princes so very different that it is impossible for them to dwell in one heart, or for the two to be conceived and included in one human heart, Matt. 6: 24; Eph. 2: 2.

For this reason I would admonish all God fearing christians in the Lord to ponder well upon these words of Paul, and to understand them according to the divine truth, and you will plainly see that Paul taught by this Scripture just what Christ had commanded, Mark 16: 16. The believing, alone, put on Christ Jesus in their baptism, and they alone bring forth true fruits, and not the infants, as we have here, and also in our first writings sufficiently proven to all the pious and true believers.

Most beloved brethren, let the infant baptizers, to their own condemnation, thus scornfully ridicule such plain Scriptures, and let them subtlely garble and twist them as much as they please, yet this Scripture will ever remain unbroken by them; it will remain so firm and binding that they will stumble thereon, be shamed thereby and will have to stand back, notwithstanding all their flattering. If they would but rightly look into the matter and then judge according to the word of God, what it means according to Paul, what it implies, to put on Christ, whether spoken in the active or in the passive (for all those who are not content with the active may apply the passive to Rom. 13, although it is in the active by Paul, according to the translation of Erasmus), they would soon perceive that it makes no difference in this matter whether it is used in the active or in the passive. But what will it benefit? If the learned have nothing wherewith to obscure the truth they garble things before the ignorant, simple populace, by strange tongues, false explanations, lies, and high-sounding philosophical reasons. O how justly Christ Jesus said unto the Pharisees, "Woe unto you, scribes and Pharisees, hypocrites! for ye shut up the kingdom of heaven against men; for ye neither go in yourselves, neither suffer ye them that are entering to go in," Matt. 23: 13.

In the sixth place, Paul teaches, saying, "For by one Spirit are we all baptized into one body, whether we be Jews or Gentiles, whether we be bond or free; and have been all made to drink into one Spirit," 1 Cor. 12: 13.

By these words of Paul the baptism of the beleiving is again plainly taught and confirmed, and, on the other hand, the anti-christian, infant baptism is rejected and made of none effect, because God, the merciful Father, in his holy gospel, points us to faith, alone, through Jesus Christ, and to the new birth. Because the believing or regenerated act rightly before God, and diligently seek and fulfill his holy will according to the grace they have received—therefore we must forcibly acknowledge that we cannot be led to this godly gift of faith and of regeneration, otherwise than by the word of God, through his Holy Spirit. All writing, reading, and teaching is in vain, when the Holy Spirit of God, the true Teacher of all righteousness, does not quicken, pierce and turn the hearts of the disciples or hearers, by the only means for this purpose given of God, which is his word.

Since we are baptized by one Spirit into one body, according to the teaching of Paul, and since this same Spirit must quicken and turn the hearts by the word of God— therefore it incontrovertibly follows that none should be baptized but those alone whose hearts are quickened and turned by this Spirit through the word of God.

All those, then, who hear the holy gospel of Jesus Christ and sincerely believe it and are thus inwardly quickened and pierced by the Holy Spirit (let them be of whatever nation or sex), are baptized by this quickening Spirit into one holy, spiritual body, of which Christ is the head, that is into the church. And thus Paul has taught by this Scripture in conformity to the command of Christ, Mark 16: 16.

Beloved reader, as those should be baptized who are urged by faith and forced by the Spirit, as Paul teaches, so I will again leave it to your judgment who they are that are led and impelled by this Spirit. Whether they are the believing or whether they are the infants? If you say the believing, your answer is right. For the believing die unto their flesh, lusts and desires, Gal. 5: 24; they put off the old man and all his works, Eph. 4: 23; seek Christ Jesus in purity of heart; bring forth the precious fruits of the Spirit which is in them, and show outwardly and inwardly in all their actions that they are taught, led and impelled by this Holy Spirit, Gal. 5: 18; Rom. 8: 14. But if you answer, *the infants*, then I would ask you, Where are their spiritual fruits? As nothing appears in a child but their childish actions, as we said above. Yet they are baptized and called christians, without doctrine, faith and commandment, from which follows that in all the baptized of the world nothing is found but abominable blindness, idolatry, hypocrisy, evil thoughts, vain words, madness against the truth, disobedience, blasphemy, trickery and a very wicked life contrary to God and his blessed word.

I am aware, brethren, that children have *spiritum vitalem*, that is, the *spirit by which they live*, which God breathed into Adam and into all flesh that they might live, Gen. 2: 7; Acts 17: 25. But they have not the *Spiritum justificantum, aut innovantem*, that is, the *spirit which sanctifies or regenerates*. For if the latter spirit was in them it would surely be manifested in the fruits, as it is impossible that the Holy Spirit of God, which of itself is awake, living and fruitful, and by which all true christians are justified, taught, led and urged, should be idle, dormant, and fruitless in those in whom it dwells. Let the infant baptists controvert this as much as they please, no matter whether they are old, learned, or of high renown, yet it will never be proven by the word of God, that the Holy Spirit of God is ever idle, useless and without fruits. I am aware that one may stumble, notwithstanding he has the Spirit of God, as is shown in the case of the pride, adultery, and manslaughter of David; the hypocrisy of Peter, and the quarrel of Paul and Barnabus; they will not long continue therein, but will be immediately admonished to repentance, either by the kind admonition of the brethren or by the Spirit. For it is impossible that those, in whom is the spirit of love and the fear of God, can long continue in a shameful sin and transgression. If the baptized infants, now, have the Holy Spirit, as the infant baptists affirm, then they must admit that it is a dead, unfruitful and powerless spirit which can beget neither faith, love, fear of God, obedience, nor any evangelical, divine righteousness, in these children.

Because they have, of their own choice, contrary to all scriptural truth, and by their own righteousness, taught infant baptism—therefore they subtlely seek to clothe and adorn it with a garbled form of the divine word, that the adulterous, enchanting wine which is in the goblet of the Babylonian whore, may be swallowed as a good and pure wine, Saying: "That infants should be baptized that they may be the better trained in the word and commandments of God; cleansed of their inherent sins; buried in the death of Christ; regenerated and put on Christ Jesus, yea, baptized into the body of Jesus Christ and thus become partakers of the Holy Spirit." Which teaching is, verily, nothing but open deceit, lies, garbling of the Scriptures and a deception of satan. For in all the baptized of the world we find the very contrary in their fruits, all through their lives, as every intelligent christian may plainly observe.

Most beloved brethren in the Lord, never let such shameful and abominable lies find place in your hearts, but examine all things rightly and according to the word of God, that you may rightly understand all evangelical truth. For thus to ornament infant baptism with the virtues which only belong to the baptism of the believing, is just as reasonable as it is to clothe an ape in purple and silk, as the common saying of the learned implies, which reads, *Simia semper manet simia, etiamsi induatur purpura;* which means: *an ape is an ape though he be clothed in purple*. In the same manner infant baptism will remain a stench and abomination before God, however finely it be ornamented with garbled Scriptures, by the learned; for an infant, so long as it is in its infancy, will remain ignorant, simple and of childish mind, notwithstanding it be baptized a hundred times and its baptism be still more subtlely asserted by six times a hundred garbled Scriptures; as it is plain to all intelligent persons that with infants are found neither doctrine, faith, spirit, fruits nor idea of God's commandment; and that therefore they should not be baptized; that is, if we believe that the word of God is true and will ever remain true, as we have abundantly proven in our first writings concerning baptism, as also in this.

O, kind reader! Verily, if it were not that this bitter, cancerous, lime spittle of false doctrine and long usage had so deeply eaten into the eyes of your hearts, you would acknowledge at once that this large church, in its young days, was not embodied into the pure, chaste, god-serving, and unblamable body of Jesus Christ, by the office of a clean and christian spirit, but rather into the adulterous, idolatrous and blamable body of anti-christ, by an unclean and anti-christian spirit.

For if it were the case that they were incorporated into the most holy body of Jesus Christ, as they persistently boast, they should prove by their works that they are serviceable, and fruitful members of that body into which they are incorporated. For we plainly see that there is no member of the human body created but for some use and purpose, be it ever so small and trifling; but it is in its way profitable and useful to the body to which it belongs. But how useful the beforementioned infants are to the body of Christ Jesus will be perceived by all those taught of the spirit.

From this it incontrovertibly follows, that if they are the body of Christ, as they claim, and that Christ is the head of his church, that Christ is the head of the unbelieving, the avaricious, perjurious, gamblers, drunkards, adulterers, fornicators, Sodomites, thieves, murderers, liars, idolaters, disobedient, blood-thirsty, traitors, tyrants, proud, and of all rogues and knaves. For where is there one in the whole church of those who were baptized in infancy, that walks unblamably in all the commandments of our beloved Lord Jesus Christ, and who, either inwardly or openly, is not guilty before God, in some or many of the beforementioned crimes. O no, kind reader, no. The most holy and glorious body of Jesus Christ is wonderfully far different from such a cruel, ungodly, refractory, disobedient, carnal, bloody and idolatrous body.

Most beloved brethren, since they plainly are such transgressors, blasphemers, and willful sinners, judge for yourselves from these and other scriptural reasons, what kind of a body they are; by whose doctrine, commandment and practice; by what Spirit they were and are yet daily incorporated into this very horrible body; yea, such a body that has neither gospel, faith, christian baptism, supper, nor christian life; and therefore neither God, prayer, promise nor eternal life; but only false doctrine, false faith, false sacraments, false promise, ungodly life and eternal death. O, Lord, save all thy beloved children from such an abominable, bloody body.

But in the most holy body of Jesus Christ is a true and orderly state of things according to the word of God, as the true doctrine, faith, baptism, supper, love, life, worship and true excommunication; and therefore also grace, favor, mercy, remission of sins, prayer, God's promise and eternal life. Behold, brethren, where these are, there also, is the true body of Jesus Christ, of which Christ Jesus is the head. They are the true brethren of Jesus Christ who with him are born of God the Father; the spiritual Mount Zion which will never be moved; the spiritual house of Israel which is wisely ruled by Christ Jesus our only King, according to the Spirit, with the unbroken scepter of his divine word; the spiritual Jerusalem in which the great King, the blessed Christ Jesus has placed the glorious, kingly throne of his honor; the spiritual temple of the Lord in which his holy name is sincerely glorified; the spiritual ark of the covenant with his heavenly bread; blooming, red and stone tables upon which the throne of mercy, the blessed Christ Jesus is found under the two cherubims of his testaments according to his promise. Yea, the lovely bride of Jesus Christ; flesh of his flesh, and bone of his bone, Eph. 5 : 30; which he placed in his chamber, Cant. 1: 4, and kissed with the mouth of his eternal peace, Col. 1; Eph. 1. Therefore no one can be a profitable member in this most holy, glorious and pure body of Christ, who is not believing, regenerated, converted, changed and renewed; who is not amiable, mild, meek, obedient, merciful, chaste, sober, humble, forbearing, peaceable, just, constant, and who are heavenly and spiritually minded with Christ; for it is impossible, according to Scripture, that Christ Jesus will or can be a Prince or head of those who do not conform themselves to him, that is, of those who do not sincerely seek, hear, believe and serve him; but rather trample upon, blaspheme and resist him.

But those who hear and believe the word of God, are, by the Holy Spirit which has taught, begotten and enlightened them, baptized into the body of Christ, on their own faith, according to the commandment of Christ; for these are regenerated of the word of God; bury their sins and are raised up with Christ into new life; have a good conscience; receive remission of sins; put on Christ Jesus; become true members of the most holy body of Jesus Christ, which are fruitful, useful and serviceable according to their strength, 1 Cor. 12: 13; Rom. 6: 5; 1 Pet. 3: 21; Acts 2: 38; Gal. 3: 27. On all such are the affectionate eyes of the Lord, the heavenly blessing, and the merciful mind, protection and solicitude of the eternal Father; because they have sincerely and fully denied themselves, and have obediently followed the will of God to live according to the will of him who has graciously called them, Christ Jesus. Beloved reader, since infants have not this mind, and as the Holy Spirit does not operate, nor show itself to be in them, and since they cannot serve in the body of Christ as is required by the word of God, since it is plain to all intelligent persons, they should not be baptized; for without the quickening Spirit of God, none should be baptized, as we have abundantly proven to all the pious children of God, from his word.

Therefore I conclude in regard to this matter of baptism, with these plain words: Inasmuch as Christ Jesus, the true Teacher, sent of the Father, has commanded us to baptize the believing, Mark 16: 16, and as the holy apostles have, in the above adduced Scriptures, so explained that which is represented by baptism as pertaining to none but the believing, and as infant baptism is no such baptism because it is evident that they have no faith nor its fruits, which faith and fruits are the true representation of baptism—therefore we are again necessarily forced by the word of the Lord, by faith and by the love of God, diligently to teach and receive the baptism of the believing, and to assert it to the praise of the Lord before lords, princes, and the whole world, at the risk of life and goods as true witnesses of Jesus Christ.

HOW THE HOLY APOSTLES PRACTICED BAPTISM IN THE WATER.

IN the third and last place we are forced to assert the christian baptism of the believing, even at the risk of life and blood for the reason, that the holy apostles of God baptized none but those alone who desired to be baptized, as Christ expressly and plainly commanded them, saying, "Go ye into all the world and preach the gospel to every creature; he that believeth and is baptized shall be saved," Mark 16: 15. This commandment the apostles received from the mouth of the Lord and have proclaimed the holy gospel, the glad tidings of grace, throughout the world, Rom. 10, and preached it to every creature which was under the heavens, Col. 1. They baptized all who accepted this gospel by faith, and no others as is shown and perceived in many Scriptures treating of the acts of the apostles; some of which Scriptures I shall place before the reader, by which all the rest of the Scriptures will be easily explained.

When Philip was led by the angel of the Lord, to the chariot of the eunuch, who was come from the land of Ethiopia, and read the gospel of Jesus Christ from Esaias the prophet, "Philip preached unto him Jesus and as they went on their way, they came unto a certain water; and the eunuch said, See here is water; what doth hinder me to be baptized? And Philip said, If thou believest with all thine heart thou mayest. And he answered and said, I believe that Jesus Christ is the Son of God," Acts 8: 35—37.

My chosen, beloved brethren, If all the earth were full of learned orators or highly renowned doctors, and these were, by sharp subtlety and human philosophy, exalted as high as the stars; yet, by the grace of God, the word will never be wrung from us, namely this: That where there is no faith, no baptism should be administered, according to the word of God; or else we must admit, first, that the command of Christ

CHRISTIAN BAPTISM.

Jesus is wrong. Secondly, that the holy apostles have taught wrongfully; thirdly, that the holy Philip here asked wrongfully; fourthly, that the eunuch was concerned about this matter more than all the rest of humanity.

No, kind reader, no. But as Peter and Paul, together with all the pious witnesses of Christ always had their eyes fixed upon the commandment of the Lord Jesus Christ and did not act in opposition thereto, so also, the holy Philip, the true servant of God who preached and taught with the same spirit, would not baptize until the illustrious and famous man had sincerely confessed his faith; for it was thus commanded him of Christ Jesus, his true Master, our Redeemer and Savior, Matt. 28: 19; Mark 16: 15.

As the holy apostles required of those that were to be baptized, first, to make a confession of their faith before baptism, so I ask you, beloved reader, How can we require a confession of faith of infants before they are baptized, and who shall confess for them? If you should say the godfathers, then I would reply, that the godfathers were first gotten up by pope Higinius, as we have shown above. Inasmuch as Higinius is the getter up of them, and as infant baptism has been practiced ever since the time of the apostles as Origen and Augustine write, and as I believe, because those who do not rightly confess Christ, ever seek their righteousness in wrought ceremonies, notwithstanding it is no divine command nor apostolic usage, as may be particularly proven by the holy Scriptures, and also by Tertullian and Ruffinus and others—therefore I verily do not see who, by the faith of infants, has answered for them in their baptism which were baptized during the period between the apostles and pope Higinius, inasmuch as the godfathers were first gotten up by Higinius who was either the ninth or tenth pope, and as the infants which were before him had as little doctrine, hearing, voice or understanding as the children of the present day, as they plainly prove by their fruits.

Observe, kind reader, that all their doings with children, such as catechism, godfathers, baptism, crisma, and such like things, is nothing but open hypocrisy, human righteousness, idolatry, useless fantasy and opinion.

Inasmuch as Christ Jesus has commanded but one baptism on the confession of faith, and as the apostles have taught and practiced it—therefore the infant baptists must consent and admit, by virtue of the word of God, that infant baptism is not by the commandment of Christ, not by the teaching and practice of the holy apostles, but by the doctrine of anti-christ and by the practice of his preachers.

I repeat that the holy apostles baptized none but those that desired it, or those who confessed the most holy faith either verbally or proved it by their walk, as did holy Peter; for although he was previously informed by a heavenly vision that he might go amongst the Gentiles to teach them the gospel, yet he refused to baptize the pious, noble and godly centurion and his consorts, so long as he did not see that the Holy Spirit was descended upon them, that they spoke with tongues, and glorified God. But when Peter plainly saw that they were truly believing and that the Spirit was descended on them, he said, "Can any man forbid water, that these should not be baptized which have received the Holy Ghost as well as we? And he commanded them to be baptized in the name of the Lord," Acts 10: 47, 48.

Behold, kind reader, here you are plainly taught that Peter commanded that those only should be baptized who had received the Holy Ghost; who spoke with tongues and glorified God, which only pertains to the believing and not the unconscious infants. Thus the practice of Peter was in accordance with the commandment of Christ, Mark 16: 16. Therefore Peter did not command infant baptism; for the Holy Ghost does not operate in them, as may be plainly seen. This may also be understood from a passage of Paul; for he says, "When they believed Philip preaching the things concerning the kingdom of God, and the name of Jesus Christ, they were baptized both men and women," Acts 8: 12. Observe, nothing is said of infants.

Paul, a preacher and apostle, also baptized upon the confession of faith and truth.

He required faith before baptism to such perfection that he regarded the baptism of the holy John the baptist, as useless and vain among the disciples at Ephesus, because they knew not the Holy Ghost, saying, "Unto what then were ye baptized? And they said Unto John's baptism. Then said Paul, John verily baptized with the baptism of repentance, saying unto the people, that they should believe on him which should come after him, that is, on Christ Jesus. When they heard this, they were baptized in the name of the Lord Jesus. And when Paul had laid his hands upon them, the Holy Ghost came on them, and they spake with tongues and prophesied; and all the men were about twelve," Acts 19: 3—7.

Hear, most beloved readers; for I would here present to you and to all the world three points, which you should impartially consider and judge according to the word of God. First, Was the baptism of John not of God? I know you will give an affirmative reply. If now the baptism of John is of God, as it is indeed, and if Paul yet considered this baptism which was from above, as insufficient and imperfect in these disciples because they did not acknowledge the Holy Ghost, and as he, after preaching to them Christ, again baptized them with the baptism of Jesus Christ, as is mentioned in Luke, for what purpose must we consider the baptism of children that are naturally unable to understand the divine word, and therefore they acknowledge neither Father, Son, nor Holy Ghost; neither can they distinguish between truth and lies, righteousness and sinfulness, good and evil, right and wrong? Does not this prove infant baptism to be useless, vain and unfruitful? and as administered and received without the ordinance of God? and if we acknowledge this by the word of God through faith, is it therefore not necessary to be baptized with the baptism of Jesus Christ? as Christ has commanded and as Paul has administered to these disciples? I say, verily, if we do not, there is, according to the word of God, neither faith, regeneration, obedience, nor Spirit in us, and therefore no eternal life, as we have frequently shown above.

Let all the learned garble this invincible Scripture and practice of Paul as subtlely as they please, yet it will never be asserted by virtue of the word of God but that these disciples, notwithstanding that they were baptized with the baptism of John, were again baptized, after they were taught by Paul, with the baptism of Jesus Christ; because they knew not that there was a Holy Ghost; that is, if baptism is to be baptism according to the word of God. But, brethren, the preaching of the cross is ever opposed because it is to them that perish, foolishness, 1 Cor. 1: 18.

Again, judge for yourselves kind readers, since Christ Jesus himself and also the holy apostles, Peter, Paul and Philip, have commanded and taught no other baptism in all the Scriptures of the New Testament, but upon the confession or proof of faith, and as the whole world in opposition thereto, teaches and practices a different baptism, which is founded neither in the command of Jesus nor in the teaching and practice of the holy apostles, namely, infant baptism, and asserts it not by the word of God, but solely by the opinion and long usage of the learned; and forces it upon the world by the cruel, bloody sword; therefore judge, I say, which of the two we should follow. The divine truth of Christ Jesus, or the lies of the ungodly world? If you answer, *Christ*, your judgment is right; but the consequence according to the flesh, is anxiety, being robbed, apprehension, banishment, poverty, water, fire, sword, the wheel, shame, cross, suffering and temporal death; yet in the end eternal life. But if you answer, the *world*, then you verily judge wrongfully; notwithstanding, on the contrary according to the flesh, the consequence is honor, peace, ease, liberty, temporal life and such perishable advantages; yet the end is eternal death.

Thirdly and lastly, judge rightly whether the ordinance of Jesus Christ which he commanded into his church, and which the holy apostles learned and administered from his blessed mouth, can ever be changed and broken by human wisdom or excellency. If you answer in the affirmative, you must prove it by the divine and evangelical Scriptures or else we should not believe it. But if you answer in the negative, as it should be, you must acknowledge that those, no matter who they are, whether they lived at the time of the apostles, and were even their disciples, who say that the apostles baptized infants, shamefully misrepresent the apostles and load falsehood upon them, yea, that they speak their own opinion and not the word of God, for the most holy apostles, the true witnesses of christian truth, never taught two different baptisms in the water; neither did they act contrary to the command and ordinance of Christ, nor administer it contrary to their own doctrine.

O, had the educated and learned men, Origen, Augustine, Jeronimus, Lactantius and others, not soared so high in their smartness and philosophy; and had they been satisfied with the clear, chaste, and plain doctrine of Jesus Christ and his apostles, and had they conformed their intelligence and subtle reasoning to the word of God, then the heavenly doctrine and unchangeable ordinance of our beloved Lord Jesus Christ would not have been subjected to such shame and change! And in particular has the great Origen, by his philosophy and self-conceit, so shamefully treated with the Holy Scripture that Martin Luther in his book called *Seruum Arbitrium*, calls him *Spercissimus scripturarum interpres*, that is: *The falsest explainer of the Scriptures*. And besides, it is annotated in the Lutheran New Testament, that this Origen is the great star which fell from heaven, burning like a lamp, and that his name is Wormwood, Rev. 8: 11. Therefore we will leave it to God who and what he is. Notwithstanding he has treated the word of God so shamefully and has erred so terribly, yet, because he pleases the world in regard to infant baptism—the holy doctrine of Christ Jesus and the apostles must stand back; and Origen is heeded, accepted and followed as a sure testimony to this idolatrous ceremony. O, abominable blindness! O, shameful foolishness! That we do not believe the sure word of our Lord Jesus Christ, the word of truth, and the true witnesses who were sent by him! but that we would rather follow, to the loss of our souls, those who teach to please us, notwithstanding it is plain from their writings that they have so often stumbled and erred, and been mistaken in regard to the truth of Almighty God!

Therefore I beseech you all, beloved brethren in the Lord, by the grace of God to open your understanding, that you may be no longer deceived, and that you may perceive, you who are made uneasy by the writings of the learned, that all the writers, both ancient and modern, have ever sought righteousness in wrought ceremonies, which we should only seek in Christ Jesus. And again, that, because they have not the word of God on their side they do not follow the same path in regard to this matter, do not speak of one accord nor write unanimously. For as their writings show, some seek the *washing* away of *inherent sin*. Others teach that they should be baptized on account of their *faith*. Again, to train them in the *word* and *commandments of God*. Still others, to have them included into the *covenant with God*; and, again, to baptize them into the *church of Christ*. Behold, kind readers, thus each of the beforementioned writers follows his own course, and does not follow the same way. If they were supported by the word of God, in regard to this matter, they would all be unanimous. But because they have not the word of God—each one follows his own inclination, thinking that he can, under a scriptural appearance, palm off pernicious falsehood as being the truth. Yea, he tickles his vision so long with garbled Scriptures, that his mind becomes so obscured that he can no more conceive that he teaches, follows and administers accursed falsehood for the blessed truth of God.

Thus, most beloved children, because the learned have ever sought and yet seek righteousness in infant baptism, you can easily surmise that these infant baptists have, by that means, made this innovation. For with the ancients it was not the common practice, I say common, as may be deduced from Tertullian, Ruffin and others; but as appears, just after the demise of the apostles or perhaps yet in their times, they commenced to abuse the true, christian baptism, which solely belongs to the believing. As some of the Corinthians already in the time of Paul suffered themselves to be baptized for the dead, 1 Cor. 15: 29, so, also, through the false doctrine and opinions of foolish bishops, the abominable serpent of infant baptism crept in, and was so confirmed by long usage that, at last, it was thought and accepted by all the world as an apostolic institution for the sake of righteousness which they all seek therein. Therefore you must acknowledge, beloved brethren, notwithstanding infant baptism is of old date, that it is still not by the command of Jesus Christ, and by the teaching and practice of the holy apostles; and is therefore idolatrous, useless and vain.

And because the true, christian baptism has such a great promise, namely, the remission of sins, and other promises, Acts 2: 38; Mark 16: 16; 1 Cor. 12: 13; 1 Pet. 3: 21; Eph. 4: 5, the pedo-baptists apply the same baptism to infants; never once observing that the beforementioned promises are solely to those who show obedience to the word of God; for Christ Jesus has so commanded it. Inasmuch as pedo-baptism is not commanded, therefore it is not required of children as obedience. For where there are no commandments there are no transgressions. Again, baptism is not commanded to infants, by God; and therefore they have no promise in their baptism, from which it follows that infant baptism is idolatrous, vain, useless and void, before God, as was said above; for God, the Lord, has no pleasure in the ceremonies, unless they are administered according to his divine and blessed word.

But the little children, and particularly those of christian seed, have a peculiar promise which was given them of God without any ceremony, but out of pure grace, through Christ Jesus our Lord, who says, "Suffer little children, and forbid them not, to come unto me; for of such is the kingdom of heaven," Matt. 19: 14; Mark 10: 14; Luke 18: 16. This promise makes glad and assures all the chosen saints of God, in regard to their children or infants; being assured that the true word of our beloved Lord Jesus Christ can never fail. Inasmuch as he has shown such great mercy towards the children that were brought to him, that he took them up in his arms, blessed them, laid his hands upon them, promised them the kingdom of heaven and has neither done nor commanded them any thing more; therefore they have in their hearts a sure and firm faith in the grace of God, concerning their beloved children, that they are children of the kingdom, of grace, of the promise and of eternal life through Christ Jesus our Lord, to whom alone be the glory; and not by any ceremony. Yea, by this same promise they are assured that their beloved children, so long as they are not of understanding years, are clean, holy, saved and pleasing unto God, be they alive or dead. Therefore they give thanks to the eternal Father through Jesus Christ our Lord, for his inexpressibly great love to their children, and train them in the love of God and in wisdom, by correcting, chastising, teaching and admonishing them, and by walking before them with an unblamable life until they may hear the word of God, believe it and fulfill it in their works. Then is the time, of whatever age they may be, that they should receive the christian baptism which Christ Jesus has commanded, in obedience to his word, to all christians; and which his apostles have thus practiced and taught.

Behold, brethren, if it should be said that we thus rob the children of the promise and of the grace of God, you will observe that they contradict us out of hatred and envy, and do not tell the truth. Say, who has the strongest ground and hope of the salvation of their children? Is it he who places his hopes upon an outward sign? or is it he who bases his hopes upon the promise of grace, given and promised of Christ Jesus? Still the evangelical truth must, in all respects, be blasphemed and belied by the ignorant and light minded. But, notwithstanding this, the just and impartial Judge, Christ Jesus, will some time pass the true sentence between them and us, although they do not fear it now. I am forced to think that then it will be acknowledged by many, too late, that they did not believe and follow the truth of Christ Jesus but the falsehood of anti-christ. Take heed and watch.

Again, it is sometimes, and very foolishly too, asserted by the pedo-baptists, "That the apostles baptized whole households, as the household of Cornelius, Acts 10: 48;

the household of Stephanus, 1 Cor. 1: 13; the household of Lydia, and of the jailer, Acts 16: 15, 33; from which, they say, it may be presumed that there were also small children among them." From this allegation, beloved brethren, they show, although not intentionally, that they can not produce Scriptures to prove infant baptism. For whenever we must follow (build on) presumption, there is evidently no proof of the assertion.

To such opponents I would reply, in plain language, thus: Three households, namely, of Cornelius, Stephanus and of the jailer, were all believing. Of the first household it is written, "There was a certain man in Cesarea, called Cornelius, a centurion of the band called the italian band; a devout man and one that feared God with all his house, which gave much alms to the people, and prayed to God always," Acts 10: 1, 2. If they all served and feared God, as Luke writes, then they were not baptized without faith, as is plainly shown in the same chapter; for Peter commanded that those should be baptized who had received the Holy Ghost, as they had who spoke with tongues and glorified God; which are all fruits of faith, as every intelligent person will admit.

Again, of the household of Stephanus it is written, "I beseech you, brethren (ye know the house of Stephanus, that it is the first fruits of Achaia, and that they have addicted themselves to the ministry of the saints); that ye submit yourselves unto such, and to every one that helpeth with us, and laboreth," 1 Cor. 16: 15, 16. I repeat it to serve the saints is a work of faith. Since the house of Stephanus served the saints, as Paul writes, therefore they showed by their fruits that they had faith.

Again, of the house of the jailer it is written that Paul and Silas spake unto him and said, "Believe on the Lord Jesus Christ, and thou shalt be saved and thy house; and they spake unto him the word of the Lord, and to all that were in his house. And he (the jailer) took them the same hour of the night, and washed their stripes; and was baptized, he and all his, straightway. And when he had brought them into his house, he set meat before them and rejoiced believing in God with all his house," Acts 16: 31—34; or as Erasmus says, "He has rejoiced because he believed in God with all his house." Beloved reader, observe first, that they spake unto him the word of the Lord, and to all that were in his house. Secondly, he rejoiced with all his house. To hear the word is something which pertains to those of understanding minds, and spiritual rejoicing is a fruit of the believing or of the spiritual, Gal. 5: 18. Inasmuch as they all heard the word and rejoiced in God, therefore it incontrovertibly follows that the holy apostles did not baptize them without faith.

In the fourth place, in regard to the house of Lydia, I reply: Because the world tries to establish their cause on presumption, therefore we would say first, that presumption ought not to establish faith; and if it were so that it could avail before God, then still the presumption in the case of the house of Lydia would not be in favor of the world but against it; because it is the custom in the Holy Scriptures and also with the world, that a house is named after the man and not after the woman, so long as the husband lives, because the husband is the lord of his wife and household. As in this case the house is named after the woman, and as there is no mention made of the man, therefore it follows that she, at the time, was not married. If she was a young woman or widow, as appears, then the presumption of the world is contradictory; and it is probable that she had no children and still more probable, that she had no infants, since she at that time had no husband.

Again, we would further say in reference to this Scripture, that if it were that Lydia had infants, they would not be counted among the baptized of the house. For Christ commanded that the believing should be baptized and the holy apostles taught and practiced such baptism; from which it may be safely deduced that when the holy Scriptures speak of houses being baptized, or houses being subverted that it has reference to those of understanding years, who may be taught or subverted, as Paul shows in another Scripture, that some "subvert whole houses, teaching things which they ought not, for filthy lucre's sake," Tit. 1: 11.

If you take the term *whole houses* as applying also to infants; and as whole houses were subverted, as Paul says, then it would follow that infants were subverted by false doctrine. No, beloved reader, no. An infant without understanding can be neither taught nor subverted; therefore they are not counted in the number of baptized, or those who were subverted, of which the Scriptures speak. But the Holy Scripture teaches and admonishes, both by words and sacraments, as they are called, those alone who have ears to hear and minds to understand, as we have frequently shown above.

If any one would like to have more information about the ceremony of baptism and about the objections made to it, let him read our first treatise on baptism which we published; and by the grace of the Lord, he will be enlightened upon the subject from the word of God.

Brethren, I conclude this treatise on baptism in the water in these words: Inasmuch as God, the merciful Father, has graciously sent into this miserable, blind and erring world his chosen, beloved Son, Christ Jesus, who has taught us the holy will of his Father, in great clearness; and as he has, in his great love, offered up his precious and most holy flesh and blood for us, and as to him the eternal Father has not only pointed us through his holy prophets, but also from high heaven, saying, "This is my beloved Son in whom I am well pleased; hear ye him," Matt. 17: 5; therefore we say and testify that we should hear this Christ Jesus; that we should believe in him and follow him in all things which he has taught and commanded us; and that we should also hear and follow his holy apostles who by his own divine command were sent out with the most precious word of grace, namely, with the holy gospel—or else we have neither God, promise, nor eternal life, as is plain and intelligible to all mankind, from the New Testament.

As this Christ Jesus has given us this express and incontrovertible command in this wise: First to teach the gospel and then to baptize those who believe, and those that are thus baptized shall be saved, Mark 16: 16; Matt. 28: 19; Acts 19: 5; 2: 38; 10: 48; 16: 33. And as the holy apostles have taught and used no other baptism than baptism on faith, according to the command of Christ, as shown and proven by many reasons from Acts 2; 8; 10; 16; 19; Rom. 6: 4; Col. 2; 1 Cor. 12: 13; Tit. 3: 5; 1 Pet. 3: 21; therefore we again declare before you, before all the world and before God, that we are prompted by nothing but by the fear of God, being so taught by his word, thus to teach this christian baptism, and thus to receive it upon the confession of faith, for the remission of sins, Acts 2: 38, as said before, and are thus baptized with the washing of water, by the word, Eph. 5: 26; and by a Holy Spirit which quickens our hearts, into one body, 1 Cor. 12: 13; of which body Christ Jesus is the head, Col. 1: 18; Eph 1: 22. Nor do we know of any other baptism, of which God is a witness, than this alone; of which, by the grace of God, we have so much taught and written.

I herewith beseech you, kind reader, not to do like the angry, blind and bloody world, who condemn everything from an envious, rebellious, refractory and raving heart before they have thoroughly perused and understood it; who reject all good, christian doctrine and usage; sometimes because of fashion, again, because of the cross, and sometimes because of the plainness of the person. Do not thus; but judge this and all our writings according to the Spirit and holy word of the Lord, and you will plainly see whether we have written and taught you truth or falsehood; whether we teach two baptisms or one; whether we seek to save your souls or destroy them; whether we seek the praise and honor of the Lord, or his dishonor. For I trust, by the grace of God, if you are desirous of your own salvation, and if you peruse what we have written and judge it with a spiritual judgment, that you will find nothing in it but the teaching which is of God; the eternal, heavenly, true and saving will of God, and the very strait way of truth which the ever blessed Jesus Christ and his apostles have, in the most holy gospel taught and shown all mankind.

Take heed, ye illustrious, noble and pious lords! Take heed ye judges and keepers of the law, against whom your cruel, bloody sword is sometimes sharpened and drawn. I tell you in Christ Jesus that we seek nothing but what we have here told you, as you may clearly see by many, namely, that there is not a false syllable nor deceitful word heard from their mouths or found in them, and these are forced and led by you to the sword, fire and water, as poor, innocent sheep to the slaughter. And if you should point me to the abominable actions of the corrupted sects, and say that you must therefore oppose baptism, by the sword, that such ungodly doings may be averted and hindered; then I would again reply, first: Christian baptism belongs not to corrupted sects; but it is the word of God. Secondly, the holy, christian baptism does not cause mutiny nor shameful actions; but it is caused by the false teachers and false prophets who boast themselves to be baptized christians, and yet, before God, are not such. Thirdly, there is nothing under heaven at which I am more alarmed than I am at the ungodly actions of the false, corrupted sects. They frighten me more than death; for I know that all men must once die, Heb. 9: 27. More than the tyrannical sword; for if they take my body, it is all they can do, Matt. 10: 28. More than Satan; for I have vanquished him through Christ. But in case the terrible doctrine of the corrupted sects adhered to me, then I would verily, be lost; eternal woe would be to my poor soul. Therefore I would rather die the temporal death (that he knows who knows all things) than to eat, drink, commune, greet or converse with such, if I knew that they would not be helped by my conversation or admonition; for it is forbidden in the word of Christ to keep the company of such, Matt. 7: 15; 1 Cor. 5: 11; 2 Thess. 3: 14; Phil. 3. And, by the grace of God, I know to a certainty, that they are not in the house of the Lord, in the church of the living God and in the body of Jesus Christ. Therefore I say, if you find in me or in my teachings, which is the word of God, or among those who are taught by me or by my brethren, any thieving, murdering, perjury, mutiny, rebellion or any other criminal acts, as were formerly, and are yet found among the corrupted sects—then punish all of us; as we would be culpable if this were the case. I repeat, if we are disobedient to God in religious matters, we are willing to be instructed and corrected by the word of God; for we mean diligently to do and fulfill his most holy will. Or if we are not obedient unto the emperor in matters belonging to him as he is called and ordained of God, I say in matters belonging to him, then we will willingly submit to such punishment as you may inflict upon us. But if we sincerely fear and seek our Lord and God, as I trust we do, and if we are obedient unto the emperor in temporal matters, as we should be according to the word of God, Matt. 22: 21; Rom. 13: 7; 1 Pet. 2: 13; Tit. 3: 1, and are yet to suffer and be persecuted and crucified for the sake of the truth of the Lord—then we should consider that "the disciple is not above his master nor the servant above his lord. * * If they have called the master of the house Beelzebub, how much more shall they call them of his household?" Matt. 10: 24, 25. Yet you should know and acknowledge, O ye beloved, noble, illustrious, pious lords, ye judges and keepers of the law, that as often as you take, condemn and put to the sword such people, that you put your tyrannical sword into the blessed flesh of the Lord Jesus Christ, and that you break the bones of his holy body; for they are flesh of his flesh and bone of his bone, Eph. 5: 30; they are his chosen, beloved brethren and sisters, who are with him, born from above, of one Father, Jn. 1: 13; they are his sincerely beloved children who are born of the seed of his holy word; they are his holy, spotless and pure bride whom he, in his great love has wedded as his consort. Why? Because they have, by the operation of their faith, and led by the Holy Spirit, cordially committed themselves to the service of our beloved Lord Jesus Christ, and do not live any more according to their lusts, but agreeably to the will of God, alone, according to the direction of his holy, blessed word. Yea, they would rather surrender every thing which they possess, and suffer envy, slander, scourging, persecution, anxiety, famine, thirst, nakedness, cold, heat, poverty, imprisonment, banishment, water, fire, sword or any other punishment than to forsake the gospel of grace and the confession of God and be separated from the love of Christ Jesus, Rom. 8: 35. But they will never accept the vain doctrine and commandments of men.

Therefore we pray you, as our beloved and gracious rulers according to the flesh, by the grace of God, to consider and realize, if there is any reasonableness about you, in what great anxiety and suspense we poor, miserable people are placed. For if we abandon Christ Jesus and his holy word, we fall into the wrath of God; and if we remain firm in his holy word, we are put to your cruel sword. O, Lord! if it were true that this large church were thy holy church, bride and body, as they boast it to be, then we might truthfully assert that thou art the prince, bridegroom and head of an abominable, detestable band of murderers, who thirst after the innocent blood of those who sincerely seek, fear, love and serve God. For the ignorant, blind people go about like a backsliding heifer, as the prophet says, seeking nothing but the persecution, imprisonment and destruction of God's saints and children.

All the priests and monks, who seek and fear nothing but their gluttonous, greedy belly, and their avaricious, pompous flesh, do nothing but upbraid, slander, lie and persecute; the judges and magistrates, who seek to live of the bloody labor of the miserable; take them and deliver them into the hands of the tyrants, that they may become favorites of the rulers, as the prophet says, Mic. 7; "The prince asketh and the judge asketh for a reward." The lords and keepers of the law, as a body, are after nothing but the favor and friendship of their prince to whom they are sworn; after authority, good wages and aggrandizement. They are those who torture, banish, confiscate and murder, as the prophet says, "Her princes within her are roaring lions; her judges are evening wolves; they gnaw not the bones till the morrow," Zeph. 3: 3. At another place, "Her princes in the midst thereof are like wolves, ravening the prey to shed blood, and to destroy souls, to get dishonest gain," Ezek. 22: 27. O, how just was the revelation of holy John, when he saw that the Babylonian woman was drunk with the blood of the saints and with the blood of the martyrs of Jesus, Rev. 17: 6.

O, beloved lords and judges of the land, observe once, how all the righteous, the prophets, Christ Jesus himself, together with his holy apostles and servants, have been treated from the beginning; and to-day *you* still treat those thus, who in purity of heart seek the truth and life eternal. Therefore we must run the risk; for in case you do not fear God, and do not sheathe your murderous sword against Christ Jesus and against his holy church, then we esteem it of less consequence to fall in the hands of worldly princes and judges, than to fall into the hands of God. I repeat it, take heed, awake, and be converted, that the innocent blood of the pious children of God, which calls for vengeance in heaven, may never more be found on your hands.

Take heed, also, ye wise and learned and ye common people! For such a people are they and such is their doctrine and faith whom you daily ridicule and mock as fools; whom you slander as heretics and deceivers; and whom you take and deliver, and murder in your hearts, as thieves, murderers and criminals. Yet, God's word shall never be broken, 1 Pet. 1: 24; Jas. 1: 10; Ps. 90: 6. O ye miserable people, what will become of you! that you are not ashamed daily to mock and ridicule the blessed Christ Jesus; to trample upon him and thus ravingly tear to pieces his most holy and glorious body, notwithstanding you boast of his divinity, word, death, grace, mercy and blood.

Say, beloved, if you are the church of Christ, why are you not obedient unto him? If you are the body of Christ why destroy its holy members? If you are the children of God why trample upon your brethren? If you are the servants of Christ, why not do the things he has commanded? If you are the bride of Christ why not hear his holy voice? If you are the truly regenerated where are, then, the fruits? If you are the true disciples of Christ, where is your love? If you are the true christians where are your christian ordinances of baptism, Supper, deacons, ban and life as commanded in his word? If you are the truly baptized ones of Christ where is your faith, your new birth, your death unto sin, your unblamable life, your good conscience, your christian body into which you were baptized, and your Christ whom you have put on?

O beloved brethren, error has been rampant long enough! Christ Jesus will be no longer mocked as a fool. I tell you as truly as the Lord lives, that so long as you are thus earthly, carnally and devilishly-minded; so long as you oppose God and his holy word; so long as you live without the fear of God, according to the lusts of your flesh, so long you are not the true church of Christ, even if it were that you were using the true sacraments, which, however is far from being so. Beloved brethren, First our hearts must be cleansed and afterward our outward actions will show; or else it is hypocrisy before the eyes of God. I repeat it, so long as you live thus ungodly, as you have done hitherto, Christ Jesus was, verily, born in vain, died in vain, arose and ascended in vain. He is no Lord, Deliverer or Savior of the willful, obdurate, unrepenting and disobedient sinners, but he is a Lord, Deliverer and Savior of those who willingly hear his divine word; who sincerely renounce evil, and walk diligently according to his holy commandments, all the days of their lives.

May God, the gracious Father, who lives in mercy forever, grant you all true knowledge to comprehend all divine truth; and a heart, mind and will to fulfill that which you now confess by faith from the word of God, through Christ Jesus our beloved Lord. To him be the honor, praise, kingdom, power and glory forever and ever, Amen.

Let the bride of Christ rejoice.

HEREIN, reader, you have most devoutly what the mode of God's baptism, which perished through the long degeneracy of the ages, in the church ought to be, being restored whole by the unspeakable gift of God. Therefore let the writers oppose as they please; let the learned oppose by their shrewdness as they know how; let all the world under the heavens oppose in every way in which they are able, this is the only mode of baptism which Christ Jesus himself instituted and the apostles taught and practiced.

The invincible truth will ever abide, although powerfully opposed by many. He who reads the teachings of christianity and considers well, will welcome this divine truth, of Christ, though for many ages lost, and now thus made to appear, because it is not without merit by its favor toward us.

May the reader give thanks to the infinitely great and good God.

Mayest thou be well, be humble, read, obtain, believe and live, and may the Lord be with thee.

A LETTER OF CAUTION ON DISCORD.

To the brethren in Groeningen, and the country thereabout, copied and sent by the faithful brother John Aertsen. Receive it in love.

Grace and Peace: Since, beloved brethren, it is known to all churches, that in the southern countries, great trouble exists in regard to the divinity of Christ, and the Holy Spirit, whereby much unbelief, discord and division have been caused in some bodies, to the great affliction of all the saints; and, since it sometimes happens that this one or that one, who comes from those countries, is affected thereby and causes trouble with some—therefore love has constrained me to write the following to the churches, and for these reasons:

First, that the unaffected and sound hearts may beware of such frightful disputations and incomprehensible murmurings, lest their hearts, to their eternal loss, drown in such bottomless profoundness, and become forever ashamed before their God.

Secondly, that all those who ignorantly and unwittingly err and are bound in their consciences, and yet fear God, and walk under the cross, may be saved and freed, through this our service and christian warning, to the eternal praise and glory of God, and to the joy of all the saints. I have written it to all my beloved brethren and fellows out of sincere love and compassion. If but one afflicted, wavering, doubting soul could be helped thereby, I would esteem it the dearest thing under heaven. My children, beware of all discord and division, that ye may thrive and multiply in Christ Jesus. Avoid all those who disturb you and excite you to disunion; all those who would institute something novel and peculiar whereby they might weaken and destroy the christian, evangelical love, peace and unity. O, my sincerely beloved brethren and sisters in the Lord! Consider diligently that which I write to you, that God the heavenly Father with his blessed Son Christ Jesus, and with his Holy Spirit, may retain their divine honor. Peace be with you.

Note. To write with my own hand such long writings and send them to each particular church, I can not do.

MENNO SIMON.

ANOTHER LETTER.

My very faithful brother in Christ, grace and peace with thee.

Chosen brethren in the Lord, I have nothing particular to write to you, but that I wish you would write to me how far the choosing of the brethren in Waterhorne and of Lebe Pieters has progressed. Not that I desire to impede the choosing of Lebe; but I would have been glad to have had a conversation with him, before his entering upon the office of bishop; for my soul is troubled about that which passed between us last year.

O, brother Rein, that I could speak with you half a day, and make known to you a little of my affliction, sorrow and sadness, and also of my great solicitude which I yet bear for the future of the church; what an ameliorating, pleasing application that would be to my sorrowful soul! As it is I must bear it all myself. If the omnipotent God had not preserved me last year, as well as now, I would already have been deprived of my mind; for there is nothing upon earth which my heart loves more than it does the church; and yet I must live to see this sad affliction upon her. I think much, yet I write and say but little. Help me pray that I may find refreshment, and may yet see a gracious result, with all afflicted souls.

Brethren, beware of discord; foster love and unity with sincerity; accompany the peaceful; make use of few words, and in every respect show yourselves to be children of God. O, chosen brethren! Come and unite your ardent prayers for me in my great affliction. I pray you for Jesus' sake, let my affliction be buried with you; but if you should speak about it to any one, then know with whom you speak. If all hearts were pure, all tongues seasoned with salt, and all the mistakes of last year were honestly and truly acknowledged, how soon would I be found a cheerful man. Now, now the Lord will be my Comforter. May the poor church be saved! O brethren, let us pray! I trust that you will not be offended at the writing in my last, to a private brother, concerning the sixty dollars annually. I took the liberty of so writing, for I do need it annually. The merciful Lord will send them to me. He knows where. Greet the pious with the peace of the Lord. My daughters greet you. The God of all grace be with you most beloved brother, and with all the pious, forever, Amen.

If something should be sent to my assistance, send it the first opportunity; for slaughtering time will soon be at hand and I have little wherewith to buy. O, brethren, do not think hard of it; it is necessity which compels me to do so.

Your unworthy and affectionate brother,

MENNO SIMON.

September 1st.

THE REASON

MENNO SIMON

DOES NOT CEASE

TEACHING AND WRITING.

WRITTEN BY HIMSELF.

"Preach the word; be instant in season, out of season; reprove, rebuke, exhort, with all longsuffering and doctrine," 2 Tim. 4 : 2.

"For other foundation can no man lay than that is laid, which is Jesus Christ," 1 Cor. 8 : 11.

ELKHART, INDIANA:
PUBLISHED BY JOHN F. FUNK AND BROTHER.
1871.

THE REASON WHY MENNO SIMON
DOES NOT CEASE TEACHING AND WRITING.

For Zion's sake will I not hold my peace, and for Jerusalem's sake I will not rest, until the righteousness thereof go forth as brightness, and the salvation thereof as a lamp that burneth; and the Gentiles shall see thy righteousness, and all kings thy glory," Isa. 62: 1, 2.

I am well aware, most beloved readers, that we are, on account of our teaching and writing, cursed, envied, hated, slandered, persecuted and condemned to death, by innumerable persons of both high and low stations in life. As roaring lions they gnash their teeth at us. Lords, princes, learned and ignorant people, no matter of what station in life, exercise their tyranny over us, as may at all times be seen; not solely upon us, but also upon all those who accept and fulfill, by their works, this our doctrine, with believing, faithful, obedient and resigned hearts. Not that we claim it to be our doctrine, understand, but it is the eternal, heavenly and unchangeable doctrine of our beloved Lord Jesus Christ, which he himself has carried from high heaven, from the bosom of his Father, to earth with his own blessed mouth which cannot lie; which he has taught, and proclaimed to the world by his faithful witnesses, the holy apostles, which he had chosen for that purpose. Whosoever does not believe that our doctrine is the pure, undefiled and saving doctrine of Jesus Christ, may piously examine the rest of the plain Scriptures of the New Testament and he will come to the conclusion and acknowledge that it is the pure doctrine, testimony and Spirit of Christ Jesus, however much his reluctant, lazy, rebellious, refractory, selfish and disobedient flesh may oppose, frighten, tremble and be awe-stricken thereat. Yet, however incontrovertible our cause appears, so much so that it can not be controverted or refuted by the Scriptures, still it must be persecuted by this ignorant, blind world as an abominable crime and treated as heresy. The prophet says, "I have written to him the great things of my law, but they were counted as a strange thing." Hosea 8: 12.

O, worthy, beloved reader, if you would consider and realize how earnestly the righteous God ever enforces his holy word, and how terribly his wrath has ever been enkindled against those who did not abide firm in his divine word, you would, without doubt, in case you are not within the word of God, tremble, and be frightened in your inmost soul before God, on account of your disobedience! Did you never read that the parents of all mankind, Adam and Eve, who were, by the power of the divine Word created by God himself and punished by him on account of their disobedience; banished from paradise; subjected to manual labor; that the earth was accursed in them, and that all their daughters must suffer and give birth to their children in perilous travail and excruciating pain; not to mention that they would be subject to eternal death, if the new Man of grace, the blessed Christ Jesus, had not, by grace, prevented this? Why was it? For no other reason than that they did not abide in the true word of the living God, but lived according to their lusts, contrary to the word of God, trusting in the deceit of the lying serpent rather than in the warning of the true God, who, by grace, had created them, wise, righteous and incorrupt, and placed them as lords of all creatures, Gen. 2: 26.

Again, do you not know that all the creatures under the heaven, both rational and irrational, were destroyed by water, through the righteous judgment of God, except those that were in the ark with Noah, because they became corrupt and lived according to their lusts, and in my opinion, because they did not acknowledge the Spirit of the Lord, as their judge? Gen. 6; 7; 8. O do consider these things, and doubtlessly, you will hereafter sincerely fear your God, and ever abide in his holy word!

Besides, you must have often heard, and perchance read for yourselves about Sodom and Gomorrah, Gen. 18; 20; 19: 4; Er and Onan, Gen. 38: 7—9; the idolaters, Ex. 32: 5; the man who gathered sticks upon the Sabbath day, Num. 15: 32—36; Korah, Dathan, and Abiram, Num. 16; about the murmurers, Num. 21: 5; Zimri and the other adulterers, Num. 25: 14, 15; Nadab and Abihu, Lev. 10: 2; those who hid the forbidden things, Joshua 7; King Saul, 1 Sam. 15: 17—22; Jeroboam, Manasseh and the other kings, priests and prophets who did not abide in the true worship and in obedience to the divine word, which was given through Moses, but taught and practiced either more or less or something quite different from the law of the Lord; how terribly and in how many different ways they and their followers were punished and smitten by God, who desires to have his will obeyed. Some suddenly died; some were pierced with the sword, Ex. 32: 27; Num. 25: 5; some were stoned to death, Num. 15: 36; Josh. 7: 25; some were swallowed up by the earth, Num. 16: 32; some were bitten by serpents; Num. 21: 6; some were hanged, Num. 25: 4; some were consumed by the fire, Lev. 10: 2; Saul's kingdom was taken from him, 1 Kings 15: 28; and put to death with the sword; the house of Jeroboam and Achab were taken from the earth; the eyes of Zedechias were put out; Manasseh was captured; and all Israel was in exile in foreign countries, as in Assyria, Babylonia, and Egypt as recorded in Chronicles, Kings, and the prophets. I repeat, why was it? Solely because they did not abide in the law of their God, but either by their own choice or else out of disrespect for the law, transgressed it, establishing without the command of God, images, temples and altars, in many countries and cities, Jer. 2; Hosea 10; in many mountains and under large trees, Hosea 4: 13; notwithstanding, as may be seen by the writings of many prophets, that Moses so strenuously commanded them as also was commanded their fathers, thus, "What thing soever I command you, observe to do it: thou shalt not add thereto nor diminish from it," Deut. 12: 32. At another place, that on all those who do not abide by the works of the covenant, which are written in the Book, all the plagues will come, and on the contrary, all the blessings will be to all those who abide thereby, Deut. 28: 58, 59. The children of Israel did not always abide by the express, commanding word of him who had, by his powerful hand, brought them out of the land of Egypt; but suffered themselves to be misled by ungodly princes and false prophets, and chose for themselves, without the divine commandment, places for divine worship; carved for themselves images and built themselves temples. All this by their own choice, and not by divine command; besides, they committed all manner of idolatry. This the Holy Spirit, in divers Scriptures, has called shameful whoredom, perjury, accursed idolatry and despising the Lord. The prophet says, "Woe unto them, for they have fled from me; destruction unto them! because they have transgressed against me; though I have redeemed them, yet they have spoken lies against me," Hosea 7: 13.

As Israel deviated from the law of their God, and committed themselves to the service of Baal, not being content with the law, doctrine and service which God had commanded them through Moses, which Baal with his altars they however erected to the service of the living God, as it appears; so God in his grace and paternal love which he bore to Israel for the sake of their fathers, again sent his faithful servants, the prophets, Isaiah, Jeremiah, Elias, Ezekiel, and others, who sharply reproved, in behalf of God, the degenerated princes, false prophets and the miserable, confused people; and again returned them to the true worship and ceremonies of the law which God had commanded, and which they had forsaken.

Besides, they prophesied famine, pestilence, failures, drought, war, conflagration, robbery, imprisonment and destruction, as plagues on account of their sins and disobedience. And also concerning the divine grace, salvation, deliverance, peace, mercy, and the eternal glory, which in the latter days will so gloriously appear unto all the world through Christ Jesus our Lord, who is the only promised prophet, Deut. 18: 15. The truly anointed of the Lord; the spiritual King David, Ezek. 37: 24; who establishes his kingdom by right and righteousness, Isa. 9: 7; the true Shepherd who leads us into the pastures of eternal life, Ezek. 34: 14; whose name is Emmanuel, that is, God with us, Isa. 7: 14; Matt. 1: 23: and the Lord who makes us righteous, who shall reign over the house of Jacob forever, Luke 1: 33; and this was the peculiar work of the holy prophets who were graciously sent of God the Lord, to the carnal Israel. But what did it avail, dear reader? They preached both mildly and harshly, punishment and grace, judgment and mercy; yet it was all in vain, as God plainly proclaimed by these same prophets, saying, "I have spread out my hands all the day unto a rebellious people, which walketh in a way that was not good, after their own thoughts," Isa. 65: 2.

Again, "Proclaim all these words in the cities of Judah and in the streets of Jerusalem, saying," "Obey my voice. Yet they obeyed not, nor inclined their ear, but walked every one in the imagination of their evil hearts; therefore I will bring upon them all the words of this covenant which I commanded them to do; but they did them not," Jer. 11: 6, 7, 8. Again, "O Ephraim, thou committest whoredom and Israel is defiled; they will not frame their doings to turn unto their God; for the spirit of whoredoms is in the midst of them, and they have not known the Lord," Hosea 5. Again, at another place, "The Lord has testified against Israel and against Judah, by all the prophets, and by all the seers, saying, Turn ye from your evil ways, and keep my commandments, and my statutes, according to all the law, which I commanded your fathers, and which I sent to you by my servants, the prophets. Notwithstanding they would not hear, but hardened their necks, like to the neck of their fathers, that did not believe in the Lord their God," 2 Kings 17: 13, 14. Again, "Thus speaketh the Lord of hosts, saying, Execute true judgment, and show mercy and compassions every man to his brother; and oppress not the widow, nor the fatherless, the stranger, nor the poor, and let none of you imagine evil against his brother, in your heart; but they refused to hearken, and pulled away the shoulder, and stopped their ears, that they should not hear. Yea, they made their hearts as an adamant stone, lest they should hear the law, and the words which the Lord of hosts hath sent in his Spirit by the former prophets; therefore came a great wrath from the Lord of hosts," Zech. 7: 9—12.

Yea, most beloved reader, they have so stopped their ears and so hardened their hearts that they would not only not hear, but all of them, as a general rule, and particularly most of the kings, princes, prophets and priests, wittingly thirsted after the innocent blood of the true witnesses of God, who, by an inextinguishable fire of love fraternally reproved them of their sins, called them to repent and turn to God, and they proclaimed and taught the way of the Lord in righteousness.

Thus the mad, blind world has thanked and rewarded the faithful servants of God, the true prophets and true teachers of the divine truth, who sincerely seek their salvation, by upbraiding, imprisoning, beating, banishing and slaying them. For the obdurate, ignorant, whoring, refractory people will not be reproved as may be read in the fourth chapter of Hosea, and of the men of Anathoth to Jeremiah, saying, "Prophesy not in the name of the Lord that thou die not by our hand," Jer. 11: 21; and "As for the word which thou hast spoken unto us in the name of the Lord, we will not hearken unto thee," Jer. 44: 13.

The selfish and lustful teachers will not suffer themselves to be reproved or admonished; they boast of their wisdom, and say, "We are supported by the Holy Scriptures; although all that the scribes say and teach is falsehood."

Above all, the proud, carnal, worldy, idolatrous and tyrannical princes, who do not acknowledge God, I speak of the evil princes, who do not want to be right in all their mandates, projects and undertakings, however much they may be at variance with God and his blessed word; as if the Almighty Father, the Creator of all things, who holds heaven and earth in his hands, who rules all things by the word of his power, had given them the privilege not only to command, rule and administer according to their will in temporal government, but also in the celestial kingdom of Jesus Christ. O no, beloved, no. This is not the intention of God; but it is an abomination in his blessed sight when mortal man substitutes himself in his stead. And when he raised up and sent his beloved servants, the prophets who, fraternally reproved and admonished all the princes, prophets, priests and common people from the mouth of God; the princes destroyed them as seditious persons, and the learned and common people as deceivers and heretics; as was the case with Zechariah, the son of Berechiah; with Isaiah, Jeremiah, Uriah, Kiriathaim and others, as may be read in history.

However ravenously the princes and the learned tyranized and opposed the law and its followers, yet the law and word of God remained immutable until Christ Jesus; so that every one who desired to be saved had to regulate and conform himself according to the law and his conscience, if he would see the dawn of day. For God is an eternal God and his will can never be changed and diverted by man. In this case neither prince nor learned man can avail. God alone, has dominion over man; he will keep them in all eternity.

Therefore all things which they instituted and practiced as holy worship without the command of God, or against it (notwithstanding it was in honor of the living God who had so gloriously led their fathers and them from the land of Egypt), was nothing less than open idolatry, spiritual whoredom, perfidy, degeneracy, blasphemy and an awful abomination, as we have above briefly shown the reader from the prophetic Scriptures. God is a God who does not need our aid and offerings, because he has made all things. Mine, he says, are the cattle, upon a thousand hills. What then can I offer? He will take no other sacrifices than those alone which are commanded in his holy word, as Samuel spake unto Saul, "Behold to obey is better than sacrifice." The Lord God of Israel spake through Jeremiah, saying, "Obey my voice, and do them, according to all which I commanded you, so shall ye be my people, and I will be your God," Jer. 11: 4; 2 Cor. 6: 17.

All those, beloved reader, who sought a different way of salvation than the one which God had commanded, either did not esteem God as wise enough to teach the right way; or else that he would deceive them by his word. They despised the commanding voice of their God; they honored and exalted their own opinions and deceiving wisdom far above the wisdom of God; and they transgressed the precious covenant which God, by mere grace and mercy, had entered into with them and their fathers; for the most shameful obduracy, and the worst disesteem of God, is not to abide by his divine word, as the Scriptures say, They transgress the covenant, as did Adam, and thereby they despise and abhor me.

O, had Israel acknowledged the most glorious promise of grace which was given them and their fathers in regard to the promise of the seed, land, kingdom and glory? And had they considered the beneficences of God, so abundantly shown to them and their fathers, in miraculously leading them from the land of Egypt, and letting them pass through the Red Sea, Ex. 14: 22; that "He went before them by day in a pillar of a cloud to lead them the way; and by night in a pillar of fire," Ex. 13: 21; that he gave them bread from heaven, Ex. 16: 4; that he gave them to drink from the rock, Ex. 17: 6; that their clothes nor their shoes did not wax old, Deut. 29: 5; that he scattered the giants from before them; that he led them into the promised land overflowing with milk and honey; that he gave to them the strongly fortified cities and well built houses full of gold and silver, which they had not built; that he gave them the vineyards they had not planted, Deut. 6: 11; that he gave them these not for their righteousness' sake, but by grace, and because he would fulfill his promise which he had sworn to Abraham, Isaac and Jacob. Yea he gave it as a permanent possession, if they should abide by his holy word and should walk in his divine commands, statutes and righteousness, as Moses the faithful servant had, in divers instances, taught and commanded. Besides, that he gave them corn, oil, wine, peace, freedom, religion, and fame above all the people round about; for there was no people under all the heavens which was like unto them, Deut. 4. He led them by the hand, as a young child; carried them in his blessed arms; and girded himself round about them as a lancer, as Jeremiah says; raising up among them his righteous men and prophets who spake unto them the words of the Lord, fraternally reproving all disobedient transgressors, and mildly consoling the pious hearts with the gracious promise of both temporal and eternal life.

O, had the children of Israel sincerely realized all these favors and many others, they would never have deviated so shamefully from the word, law, will and commandments of God their Savior and Deliverer, who in every respect treated them with such a paternal spirit. But because they did not acknowledge the gracious beneficences which the Lord showed unto them, and because they did not fear the righteous judgments against them, therefore the wicked, blind flesh and the adulterous spirit of idolatry has so misled them, so estranged them from God, and made them so drunk and mad that they acted worse than the Gentiles which were before them, whom God had, on account of their sinfulness, rejected and scattered, as the holy prophets in divers Scriptures show and proclaim.

O, fearful wrath of God! We can never escape it. If we do not desire grace, light, truth, righteousness, salvation, true religion, life, the kingdom, blessing and God himself, we must, by his righteous judgment, doubtlessly, inherit disgrace, darkness, falsehood, unrighteousness and idolatry, and hereafter eternal damnation, death, hell, malediction, and the devil himself.

Sincerely beloved readers, God knows that I love you with pure love in Christ Jesus. Inasmuch as I find in proof of many Scriptures how severely God has, from the beginning of the creation, ever punished all transgression of his divine word and disobedience thereto, as every intelligent reader may clearly understand from the history of Israel; and as I clearly see that the whole world, from east to west, from south to north, in the course of time, has been misled by ignorant teachers and preachers, who seek nothing but carnality, aided by unfaithful lords and princes, and that they have lost their faith in and knowledge of our beloved Lord Jesus Christ, the ever blessed Savior, his holy gospel and sacraments, true religion and the pious, unblamable life which is of God; and as they are falsely led, under the name of Christ, to put faith in a man of proud, unclean, idolatrous and ungodly flesh, in useless fables, doctrines and human commandments; in an idolatrous baptism and supper; in images, wood, stone, gold, silver, water, bread and wine; in a shameful idolatry; in mere vain, false and useless promises, so that it has gone so far among those who boast of the name of Christ, that there is nothing left them, neither in regard to faith, love, sacraments, nor in their life of which it can be truthfully said that it comports to the life and doctrine of Christ, judge for yourselves whether or not I speak the truth; and although some of them, to-day, boast of the holy gospel of Christ, yet there is nothing preached but that is useless and vain, and this no stronger than the temporal lords and princes allow them to do; and, as the princes are, so are the preachers; and, as the preachers are, so are the people; and as by this we are asked to abandon Christ and his holy apostles and humble them in their doctrine and believe and adhere to the princes and the learned, if we do not want to be tortured or burned, at their hands, or be murdered by some other tyrannical means; as if the preachers were sent by the princes, and not of Christ —therefore, for the sake of the chosen of Zion and of Jerusalem, I can no longer hold my tongue, but must tell the truth; that their righteousness may go forth as a light, and their salvation burn as a torch; and that thus all mankind may acknowledge the righteousness of the Lord, and all tongues, generations and people confess his glory; although I have sometimes, with Jeremiah, thought not to teach any more in the name of the Lord, because so many thirst after my blood. Yet, I can no longer hold my tongue; for I am, with the prophet, very much troubled at heart; my heart trembles in my bosom; all my joints shake and quake, with the idea that the whole world, lords, princes, learned and ignorant people, males and females, bond and free, are so widely estranged from Christ Jesus, from evangelical truth and from life eternal.

When I think to find a magistrate who fears God, rightly performs his office and uses his sword, I verily find, as a general thing, nothing but a winebibbing Lucifer, Antioch, or Nero; for they place themselves in Christ's stead so that their decrees must be respected above the word of God. Whosoever does not regulate himself according to their contents; does not serve Baal; maintains the ceremonies of Christ and fulfills the word of God in fruits, must be taken and suffer as a rogue, his property be confiscated, and the poor, innocent orphans who have now lost their faithful parents because of the testimony of the Lord, must be cast out and find their way begging through the land. But the idolaters, deceivers of souls, whoremongers, knaves, adulterers, fornicators, blasphemers, perjurers, drunkards and like transgressors, are not persecuted, but can live at liberty and peace, under their protection, I do not here speak of the good magistrates, who are few; but of the evil ones, which are numerous. Besides, we have their unseasonable pomp, pride, greed, uncleanness, lying, robbing, stealing, burning, hatred, envy, avarice and idolatry. Yet they want to be called christian princes and gracious lords. O, Lord! Of what little benefit will these hypocritical, lying titles and false boasting be to them before Christ, when he shall appear!

Again, when I think of finding true teachers, such as are sent of God, quickened by the Holy Spirit; who sincerely seek the salvation of their brethren; who are not earthly minded, but preach the saving, wholesome word of our beloved Lord Jesus Christ, in purity of heart, and who are quite unblamable in their doctrine and life, I find myself altogether mistaken. But instead, I find all over the world and among most of the sects, nothing but robbers of the glory of God, and murderers of souls; deceivers, blind watchmen, mute dogs, masters of sects who are carnally, earthly and devilishly minded; enemies of the cross; serving their bellies instead of serving God; false prophets, idolaters, vain talkers, liars, and wizards. If any person does not believe my words, let him prove their walk by the word of the Lord; let him compare their doctrine, sacraments, spirit, object, walk and life with the doctrine, sacraments, spirit, object, walk and life of Christ, and common sense will teach you, without, even the word of God, of whom they are sent; how, what and why they teach and what fruits their teachings bear.

In the third place, when I think of finding an unblamable church without spot and blemish, which serves the Lord with all its power and which conforms itself to his word —I verily find such an ungodly, abominable, corrupted and confused people; so carnal, idolatrous, whoring, cruel, ungodly, unbelieving, ignorant, blood-thirsty, unmerciful, drunken, pompous, luxurious, proud, avaricious, greedy, envious, adulterous, false, deceiving, sodomitic, refractory, disobedient, rebellious, vain, and so devilish, that a godfearing soul must stand dumbfounded and be ashamed thereat. Yet they claim to be the true bride, the believing church of Christ. O no, dear reader, no. Christ Jesus does not own such a bride or church. But his bride is flesh of his flesh and bone of his bone, Eph. 5: 30; she conforms to him, Rom. 8: 29; is created after his image, Col. 3: 10; partakes of his nature, 2 Pet. 1: 4; is minded as he is, Phil. 2: 5; seeks nothing but heavenly things where Christ Jesus is, sitting at the right hand of his Father, Col. 3: 1; yea in God's church nothing is heard, seen or found but the true doctrine of our beloved Lord Jesus Christ and his holy apostles, according to the Holy Scripture. But in the beforementioned churches it is mostly doctrines, flatterings, comments, councils and commandments of men. Here is faith, truth, obedience, baptism of the believing, according to the word of God, true fraternal love, and

MENNO'S REASONS FOR TEACHING AND WRITING.

the service of our neighbors; yonder is unbelief, falsehood, disobedience, infant baptism without God's word, hatred, envy, tyranny, cruelty, shedding blood, quarreling, lawsuits, backbiting, cheating, stealing, robbing and murdering; here is teaching, admonition, consolation, reproof in righteousness—there, mere corruption, heresy, upbraiding and slandering; here, blessing, praise and thanksgiving—there, cursing and swearing by the suffering of the Lord, by his wounds, sacraments, flesh, blood and judgment; here, longsuffering—there, inflammable temper; here, humility—there, pride; here, mercy—there, mercilessness; here, true religion—there, idolatry; here, spirit and spiritual wisdom—there, flesh and foolishness; here is prayer in spirit and in truth—there, mockery with many powerless words; here is prayer for the Lord's truth—there the righteousness of the Lord is persecuted; here is faith in Christ—there, idolatrous ceremonies; in short, here is Christ and God—there, anti-christ and the devil. Yea, most beloved brethren, the pure, chaste and spotless bride of our Lord Jesus Christ (judge for yourselves) is quite different from this carnal, unclean, adulterous and shameful cause.

Verily, they are not the true church of Christ who merely boast of his name. But those are the true church of Christ, who were converted, who are born from above of God, who are of a regenerated mind and by the operation of the Holy Spirit from the hearing of the divine word have become children of God; who obey him, and live, unblamably in his holy commandments and according to his holy will, all their days, or after their calling.

Inasmuch as the worldly church is no such amiable, obedient bride, but has left her lawful husband, Christ, and follows after strange adulteries, as may be plainly seen, and all this through blindness, ignorance and the deceit of their teachings—therefore I seek to accomplish nothing by my writing and teaching, according to the talent God was pleased to give me, but to reclaim this adulterous bride, the erring church, from her adulterous actions and again to return her to her first husband, Christ Jesus, to whom she was so unfaithful, notwithstanding he did her such great service, showing and declaring to all sects, nations and individuals who desire to read or hear our doctrine, writings and admonitions, not by flatterings and my own opinion, but by the express word of God, which alone avails, that there is no salvation on earth or in heaven otherwise than in Christ Jesus, that is, in his doctrine, faith, sacraments, obedience and walk. All doctrine which is contrary to his word or without his command, is vain, such as, in the papal church, purgatory, false promises, differences in places, in victuals and in days, pilgrimages, false sacrifices, &c. Again, in the German churches, the availibility of infant baptism. Again, with the corrupted sects, the third David; the carnal kingdom; that every thing is clean to the clean, such as to show to idols outward honor and reverence, to baptize infants, polygamy, shameful confession, to make indecent show of person, not to believe in angels or the devil; that a more perfect doctrine will be proclaimed than was taught by Christ Jesus, Paul and the other apostles, and more like abominations.

Again, all the sacraments not comprised in the word of God, as the idolatrous baptism of infants, the false supper in a church which neither seeks, knows, fears nor loves its God; which believes that the bread is actual flesh and the wine actual blood; also, the confirmation, the holy oil, as they call it; again, all the services which are neither taught nor commanded by Christ nor his apostles, such as holy water, altars, images, masses, vigils, absolution, the invocation of the departed, monkhood, pilgrimages and the like abominations. Again, the private and public life which does not comport with the Spirit and life of Jesus Christ; such as unclean, vulgar thoughts, evil desires, unbecoming, shameful words; uncleanness, adultery, fornication, drinking to excess, hatred, envy, the shedding of blood contrary to the ordinance of God, avarice, pride, lying, cheating, backbiting, jesting, theft, usury, murder, swearing and fighting. All these matters and articles, such as doctrines, sacraments, worship and life, which are here noted, and others which are not, every reader can easily understand by the inward unction of God, that they, not being comprised, expressed, nor commanded in his word and in the wholesome doctrine of our beloved Lord Jesus Christ, but most of them being diametrically contrary to the Word, therefore we deem them, according to the sentence of the Holy Scriptures, as nothing else than false doctrine, deceit and fantasy; as false and garbled, idolatrous sacraments, as abominable idolatry, spiritual whoredom, degeneracy, and as carnal, earthly and deadly life, of which the Holy Spirit of God has so abundantly testified through Paul and John that those who commit these things shall not inherit the kingdom of God, Rom. 1: 22; 1 Cor. 6: 8; Gal. 5: 21; Eph. 3: 5; Rev. 22: 5.

For if the literal Israel was so severely punished and crushed by God, because they did not abide by the law, commandments, statutes and righteousnesses of their God, and because they did not hear and receive the reproving, admonition and teachings of their faithful prophets who spoke to them through the inspiration of God, but stoned them, put them to the sword, killed, upbraided and blasphemed them; following a worship to suit their own taste, as has been shown above—O, what must we, then, expect from God, if we do not abide by the wholesome doctrine of grace, by the right holy sacraments, by the works of love which are pleasing to God and by the pious, unblamable life which no Moses, prophet, angel, nor creature has taught us, but which the eternal Son of God, the eternal wisdom and truth, the eternal love and mercy, the blessed Christ Jesus has taught us by his own blessed mouth, by the command of his Almighty Father, which command is eternal and immutable, whose love for us is ineffable, who has confirmed it by virtue of miracles and at last sealed it with his precious blood; and has proclaimed the same to all the world by his faithful testimony, his holy apostles, in incomprehensible power of the Spirit; which doctrine is nothing else, nor will it ever be any thing else, than the precious gospel of peace, the glad tidings of grace, the remission of sin, the victory over death, hell and the devil; besides, grace, peace, freedom and admission to the Father; and all this out of love and grace —not by works or merit of our own; but by means of Christ Jesus alone.

Again, these are the sacraments which Christ Jesus has instituted and taught: First, the holy baptism of the believing, in which we bury our sinful flesh and take unto ourselves a new life, seal and confess our faith, testify to the new birth and good conscience; and thus we enter into the obedience of Jesus Christ, who has taught and commanded us thus himself and also in his Holy Spirit through his disciples. Secondly, the Holy Supper, in which is represented the death of the Lord, who died for us in his great love; and in which is represented true, brotherly love; and also the righteous, unblamable, christian life which must be lived inwardly and outwardly in full measure of death unto sin and unfeigned love, conformable to the word of God.

Behold, worthy reader, since the whole world, yea, all tongues, tribes and people have become degenerated, according to the righteous sentence of God, in the doctrines, sacraments and life which is pleasing to God, for they prefer falsehood to truth, unrighteousness to righteousness; as they have committed themselves to all manner of false teachings, false ceremonies and carnal life, so that we may consider them rather as brutes than human beings, rather as devils than christians, as every reasonable being can easily, even without the word of God, comprehend and understand; and as the learned and preachers, who, we should reasonably expect to reprove such things, themselves are committed to such false doctrine, unbelief and abominable idolatry and lead, even, a more beastly and infernal life—yea, as these learned people diligently lead and force all mankind to such idolatry, unbelief, transgression and accursed life, both by their teaching and example, as most of the learned have done from the beginning, as they are ever earthly, carnally and devilishly minded, and as they ever reject the spiritual and heavenly wisdom and will of Jesus Christ which tempers the carnal lusts, as a displeasure and inconvenience, Col. 3 : 5; 1 Pet. 2 : 11; Rom. 13: 14; therefore, since I clearly see this awful disesteem of the holy word of God, and the condemnation of innumerable thousands of souls whom Christ Jesus has so dearly bought and ransomed by his precious blood, for outside of the obedience to the divine word there is no salvation, therefore I cannot be silent; for the honor and praise of my Lord and God are at stake, and it avails the salvation of a poor, erring brother—although, perchance, it may be at the risk of my life.

Who knows but that God, through me and through my beloved brethren who are and who shall be, has chosen and provided in his grace, that some of those who now unwittingly err, may yet acknowledge and confess the right way, doctrine, truth and life, and walk unblamably in Christ, before God and before all the world all the days of their lives. O, Lord, that it might be so, Amen.

Behold, most beloved reader, inasmuch as the Babylonian king, namely, the antichrist, has, through his servants, that is, through the false prophets and teachers, demolished the disobedient Jerusalem, the temple of the Lord, and has thus imprisoned Israel these many years—therefore I and my brethren in the Lord desire nothing but that we may, to the honor of God, so labor at his fallen city, temple and imprisoned people, according to the talent received of him, that we may rebuild that which is demolished, repair that which is damaged and free those who are imprisoned, with the word of God, by the power of the Holy Spirit, the same as it was before the fall, that is, in freedom of the Spirit, on the doctrines, sacraments, ceremonies, love and life of Jesus Christ and of his holy apostles.

For this reason I am not ashamed to write down, publish and loudly proclaim my faith, doctrine, seeking and desire, before all mankind who will hear, no matter who they are. Yea, I doubt not but if those could see my inmost heart who now assiduously seek my life, they would change their hatred against me and my brethren, into love for us.

In the first place we desire, according to the word of God, that no bishop, pastor or teacher shall be admitted into the church of the Lord, to teach and administer the sacraments of the Lord, other than those who are comprised in the doctrine, ordinance and life of our Lord Jesus Christ—unblamable in all things, 1 Tim. 3: 2; Tit. 1: 6; Lev. 21: 7; Ezek. 44: 21; for the word of the Lord is truth, Jn. 17: 17; it is Spirit and life, Jn. 6: 63; therefore they can not be administered by the carnal minded; by no children of death, nor by liars; but by the truthful, by the spiritual minded, and by those who rightly confess Christ Jesus; who surely feel the life eternal in their hearts, and who live unblamably before God and walk in Christ Jesus, so that they may truthfully say with Paul, "Be ye followers of me, even as I also am of Christ," 1 Cor. 11: 1.

In the second place we desire with ardent hearts, even at the cost of life and blood, that the holy gospel of Jesus Christ and his apostles, which alone is the true doctrine, and will remain so until Jesus Christ will reappear in the clouds, may be taught and preached through all the world, as the Lord Jesus Christ commanded his disciples at the last moments while he was on earth, Matt. 28: 19; Mark 16: 15.

In the third place we seek, teach and desire a true faith and christian life conformable to the doctrine of Jesus Christ and his apostles; for the doctrine of the preachers is all vain and useless if the word which is preached is not accepted by faith, Heb. 4: 2; and faith is vain, and dead before God when it does not work by love, Jas. 2: 20.

In the fourth place, we teach, seek and desire a right, christian baptism; first, with Spirit and fire, Luke 3: 16; afterward in the water, in obedience to faith; for thus has Christ Jesus commanded all the believing; and thus the holy apostles have taught and administered it, Matt. 28: 19; Mark 16: 15; Acts 2: 38; 9: 5; 16: 31; 10: 47.

In the fifth place, we teach, seek and desire such a Supper as Christ Jesus himself has instituted and administered, Matt. 26: 19; Mark 14: 22; Luke 22: 19; first, to a church which is outwardly without spot and blemish, that is, without any considerable transgression and wickedness; for the church can only judge as to the visible; but what is inwardly wicked and not outwardly apparent to the church, as the betraying of Judas, of that God is to judge, for he alone tries the hearts and reins, and not the church. Secondly, in both forms, namely, bread and wine; thirdly, to the remembrance of the Lord's death. Fourthly, as a renewal and proof of brotherly love, as this supper was also called amongst the ancients, a brotherly supper, as Tertullian writes.

In the sixth place we seek and desire that all strange ceremonies and manners of worship which are without the word of God, or instituted contrary thereto and tend to abominable idolatry, such as holy water, oral confession, infant baptism, masses, matins, vespers, images, altars, false promises and the like ceremonies, may be abolished, not by force of arms, but peaceably by the word of God, that the poor, ignorant populace may no longer be deceived by such vain works which are nothing short of idolatry; but that they may put their faith in the living God and in the merits of our ever blessed Lord Jesus Christ and that they may cordially walk in his divine commandments, not varying to the right or the left; for in him is life everlasting, Jn. 12:50, and in none other.

In the seventh place we seek, desire, teach and preach, that all magistrates, emperors, kings, dukes, counts, barons, mayors, knights and other officers may be so taught and trained by the Spirit and word of God, that they may sincerely seek, honor, fear and serve Christ Jesus, the true head of all lords and potentates; that they may rightly administer their office, and use the sword given them of God, in his fear and in brotherly love, to the praise of God, to the protection of the good and to the punishment of the evil, according to the intent of the word of God, Rom. 13:3; 1 Pet. 2:13; as did the men of God, as Moses, Joshua, David, Ezekiel, Josiah and others. Read also Deut. 17:2, 3, and you will clearly understand what God has commanded all magistrates to do.

Besides, we teach the true love and fear of God, the true love of our neighbor, to aid and assist all mankind and to injure none; to crucify the flesh and its lusts; to circumcise the heart, mouth and the whole body with the knife of the divine word, of all unclean thoughts, unbecoming words and actions. Now consider whether these things are not the will of God, the true doctrine of Jesus Christ, the true ministering of the sacraments and the true life which is of God; although all the gates of hell may willfully oppose them.

Behold, dear brethren, against these doctrines, sacraments and life no imperial decrees, no papal bulls, no councils of the learned, no long usage, no human philosophy, no Origen, Augustine, Luther, Bucer, prison, banishment or murder can prevail; for it is the eternal, imperishable word of God; it is, I repeat, the *eternal word of God*, and will remain immutable forever. *Etiamsi rumpantur illa codro.* Whosoever yet opposes and wars against these things, either at heart, verbally or by the sword, does not war against flesh and blood, that is, against man, but he wars against the Lamb, against him who has all power, and who by a word created heaven and earth and the fullness thereof. Nay, against him who lifts up his hand and says, "I live forever," Deut. 32:40.

As this is the true doctrine of Jesus Christ which alone leads to life eternal, and as there is no other true doctrine beside; therefore I might be asked by the reader why it is that so very few men sincerely believe and fulfill it in works? In my opinion there are four reasons for this. First, because all lords, preachers and common people are carnal and earthly minded; therefore they cannot admit the lovely doctrine of the Holy Ghost, the doctrine of eternal peace. Secondly, because they are drunk and full of the enchanting wine of the Babylonian whore, exceedingly rich and not in want of any thing, Rev. 17:2; 3:17. Thirdly, because they do not fear the awful judgment and fearful wrath of God against all disobedience and transgression, yea, so utterly disregard the word of God, as if the Holy Ghost was merely jesting, when threatening temporal or eternal punishment. Fourthly, because they do not acknowledge the great beneficence of God toward them in Christ Jesus; for in case they did acknowledge the works of divine love toward them, namely, that God has created heaven and earth and the fullness thereof for their benefit; that he formed them after his own image from the dust of earth; placed them at the head of all creation; gave them gold, silver, land, house and home and all the necessaries of life; gave them his divine word; first, the law of nature, then Moses and the prophets, and afterward his only begotten Son, his wisdom, his power, Christ Jesus, who has taught them the will of his Father in great clearness; opened heaven and closed hell; vanquished death, sin and the devil for them; fulfilled the cumbersome, threatening law on the cross, and acquired for them grace, favor, mercy, peace, freedom, deliverance, remission of sins and eternal life with the Father, if they in truth believe, seek and desire it, besides calling them daily to repentance, regeneration and the glory of the chosen children of God; desiring to draw them forth from the darkness of the world and deliver them into the kingdom of his beloved Son; not letting his righteous judgment come on them as it did on Sodom and Gomorrah; giving them day and night, sun and moon, rain and drought; again, blessing them with wisdom and understanding, wife, children, cattle and fruits; if they did cordially acknowledge these rich gifts of his abundant grace, then all the tyrants under heaven would not separate them from the doctrine, love, sacraments, life and confession of Jesus Christ even if it were possible that they could testify to and assert it by a thousand deaths. Yea, they would say with the apostle Paul, "Who shall separate us from the love of Christ? Shall tribulation, or distress, or persecution, or famine, or nakedness, or peril, or sword?" Rom. 8: 35.

But because they do not acknowledge the God of all grace in his divine word, judgments and beneficences; and do neither acknowledge the Spirit, power, will and life which was in Christ Jesus whom we should follow, according to the word of God; therefore they so wrongfully oppose and persecute the heavenly doctrine of Jesus Christ, and diligently follow, teach and protect all manner of falsehood, deceit, fraud and idolatry. Again I repeat, If they rightly acknowledged and believed the paternal heart, mind and love, protection, favor, will, solicitude and affection of the Almighty God in Christ Jesus, they would doubtlessly accept and cordially fulfill his blessed word and admonition; but as they do not rightly acknowledge Christ Jesus and his Father—the Savior said, "God so loved the world, that he gave his only begotten Son, that whosoever believeth in him should not perish, but have everlasting life. For God sent not his Son into the world to condemn the world; but that the world through him might be saved. He that believeth on him is not condemned; but he that believeth not, is condemned already, because he hath not believed in the name of the only begotten Son of God. And this is the condemnation, that light is come into the world and men loved darkness rather than light because their deeds were evil," Jn. 3: 16—19.

Take heed, O ye miserable, erring men! For here the eternal wisdom of the blessed Christ Jesus has expressed, why you do not believe his precious word, and do not fulfill his divine will, because you prefer the damnable darkness to the saving light. Yea, I repeat, that if you sincerely accepted and believed the divine goodness, mercy, and the ineffable love of our beloved Lord Jesus Christ toward you, namely, that by his ardent love he became an humble mortal man for you; came down from high heaven into these lower parts of the earth, taught and preached unto you the eternal kingdom of God, performed miracles, prayed, suffered tribulation, anxiety, apprehension and prison; that he was beaten, mocked, derided, spit upon, scourged, crowned with thorns, drenched with gall and vinegar, blasphemed, crucified and that he died and was buried for you; was again raised up, ascended to heaven, seated at the right hand of the Father; and that by his precious blood he became your faithful Servant, Reconciler, Deliverer, Mediator and Advocate; that by love he sent to you and the whole world, his faithful servants, the holy apostles, with the word of grace—if you believe all this, you would, doubtlessly, love *him* who has shown you such great love and grace without any merit on your part; and if you would return the love with which he has loved you and yet loves you, you would, verily, not tire of seeking and following him, so that you might live unblamably according to his blessed will, and walk all your life in his divine commandments, as he himself says, "He that hath my commandments, and keepeth them, he it is that loveth me," Jn. 14: 21.

Behold, most beloved reader, thus true faith or true knowledge begets love, and love begets obedience to the commandments of God. Therefore Christ Jesus says, "He that believeth on him is not condemned." Again at another place, "Verily, verily, I say unto you, he that heareth my word, and believeth on him that sent me, hath everlasting life, and shall not come into condemnation; but is passed from death into life," Jn. 5: 24. For true evangelical faith is of such a nature that it cannot lay dormant; but manifests itself in all righteousness and works of love; it dies unto flesh and blood; destroys all forbidden lusts and desires; cordially seeks, serves and fears God; clothes the naked; feeds the hungry; consoles the afflicted; shelters the miserable; aids and consoles all the oppressed; returns good for evil; serves those that injure it; prays for those that persecute it; teaches, admonishes and reproves with the Word of the Lord; seeks that which is lost; binds up that which is wounded; heals that which is diseased and saves that which is sound. The persecution, suffering and anxiety which befalls it for the sake of the truth of the Lord, is to it a glorious joy and consolation.

All those who have a faith as is here mentioned, namely, a faith that makes desirous to walk in the commandments of the Lord, to do the will of the Lord, and which shows itself in all righteousness, love and obedience, also acknowledge that the word and will of our beloved Lord Jesus Christ is true wisdom, truth and life, yea, unchangeable and immutable until Christ Jesus shall reappear in the clouds of heaven at the judgment day; they do not scoff at God's word as if it were a vapor, as do the ignorant world, saying, "What can water avail me?" but they will diligently try to obey the word of Jesus Christ in every particular, even at the risk of death according to the flesh.

Behold, beloved brethren, I speak frankly with a certain and sure conviction not by any revelation or heavenly inspiration, but by the express, definite word of the Lord, and from my inmost heart I am convinced that this doctrine is not our doctrine, but the doctrine of him who sent us, that is Christ Jesus. All those who are desirous of doing his will, will acknowledge that this doctrine is of God; and that we do not preach our own opinion, dreamings, and visions. But those who do not fear God; do not believe on Christ Jesus; who trample upon his word, and do not do his will; who love darkness rather than light; by those, all evangelical truth must be called damnable heresy and considered and treated as deadly treason. Notwithstanding all this, the word of God shall remain unbroken until the judgment day.

Woe unto such! For in them are lost the abundant gifts of grace, the heavenly word of peace, the mild admonitions, the hard and bitter labor, the precious treasure, which is the precious blood and bitter death of our Lord Jesus Christ. Again, woe, woe unto them! For it can never be that we can be saved without faith, love and obedience to our Lord Jesus Christ. I speak of those of understanding age. Paul says, "Without faith it is impossible to please him (God)," Heb. 11: 6. "He that believeth not is condemned," Jn. 3: 18.

As the literal law of Moses could not, at any time, be changed by the tyranny of princes, the accuteness of the learned, or by the madness of the common people; and as there could be nothing added to, nor taken from it, it had to remain unchanged until the coming of Christ. Yea, as all who did not abide by this law were the children of the wrath and of death; so, also, it is to-day. If all the deceased apostles should be raised up and should teach us differently from what they did at the time of their ministration; and besides these, Moses and the prophets, all the angels of heaven and as many eloquent and miraculous prophets as we have hairs on our heads; and if besides these, all the princes should roar like devouring lions and ravening wolves, and if every learned tongue should cut as a razor, it would yet be impossible that those could be saved who do not abide by the wholesome doctrine, sacraments, obedience and life of Jesus Christ. Yea they are the children of wrath, the curse and of death eternal, as Christ himself says, "Not every one that saith unto me, Lord, Lord, shall enter into the kingdom of heaven; but he that doeth the will of my Father which is in heaven," Matt. 7: 21. At another place he says, "If ye continue in my word then are ye my disciples indeed; and ye shall know the truth, and the truth shall make you free," Jn. 8: 31, 32. From this follows the opposite, beloved brethren, namely, that if we do not abide in Christ's word, we cannot be his disciples; that we do not acknowledge the truth; and if we do not acknowledge the truth how can we then be made free thereby? And if we are not freed by truth, woe unto us that we were ever born; for then we are yet in sin, under the curse, wrath, children of hell, of the devil and of eternal death. O, misery, misery! Fear with all your heart, faithful reader! For this will never be found otherwise.

If the bloodthirsty, tyrannical lords and princes had, from the beginning, acknowledged this, and would now acknowledge it, namely, that the word is eternal and will remain unchangeable and that it cannot be changed by the most exalted of men, never would they thus have opposed and murdered the professors of the divine word.

If the Roman bishop and his learned fellows had taken this matter to heart, he would never have taken from Italy her emperor, and from Christ Jesus the spiritual reign. But he would, doubtlessly, have bidden adieu to his worldly glory, pomp, luxury, idolatry, false doctrine, easy life, garbled sacraments, sodomitic uncleanness, councils, statutes and decrees and would have contented himself with the immutable, heavenly doctrine of the only, true Shepherd, Teacher and Bishop of our souls, Christ Jesus.

As the whole burden of our salvation is included and comprised in Christ Jesus and his holy word, and in no one else, nor in any other doctrine—therefore I warn every godfearing soul, by the word of God, through nothing but brotherly love, not to be shaken and misled, either by the exalted position of man, or by old age, learning, eloquence, finely gotten up ceremonies, dreams, prophesies, visions, signs and jugglery. For there can never be a wiser, truer, more diligent, more righteous, godpleasing, unblamable, powerful, perfect, higher or holier Prophet than the ever blessed Christ Jesus. Every thing, too, has testified this of him, both in heaven and upon earth. In the first place God testified this to Adam; afterward to Moses, David, Isaiah, Jeremiah, Ezekiel, Hosea, Zechariah, and to most of the prophets; to the angel Gabriel; to the angels at his birth; by the star of heaven; by the wise from the east; the learned at Jerusalem; John the Baptist. Again at his baptism by the Father and the Holy Ghost; afterward by the multitudes, the devils; by the healing, the raising up of the dead; by changing water into wine; commanding the storm to cease; by the loaves, fishes, fig-tree, and the children on palms-day; at his death; by the murderer; the firmament of heaven; the whole earth; the curtains of the temple; the stones; the deceased dead, and the centurion under the cross, Ps. 22: 7; Isa. 53: 5; Dan. 9: 25. Say, what is there that has not testified to Christ Jesus? Yea he is the one, as he himself says, who after his resurrection again ascended to heaven, to whom all power is given of the Father both in heaven and in earth, Matt. 28. Therefore it is just and right, yea it is absolutely required, if they do not want to be lost, that all magistrates bow themselves under his scepter; all reason and sagaciousness place themselves under his heavenly wisdom; all flesh lay at his blessed feet; and that every tongue confess that he is the Lord, to the honor and praise of his Father. Therefore I pray all godfearing readers in the Lord, by the merits of our blessed Lord Jesus Christ, to whom be the kingdom, the praise and honor; not to consider me any higher than a mere, humble servant of Jesus Christ and as a dispenser of his mysteries, according to the faith given me of him. I, miserable sinner that I am, on account of my unclean, greedy, proud, vain, idolatrous and carnal life which I formerly led, and on account of my yet often sinning and transgressing before my God, who am not worthy to be the least servant in the house of my Lord! Yet, by his grace I am that I am.

Brethren, I tell you the truth and lie not. I am no Enoch, no Elias, I have no visions, am no prophet, who can teach and prophesy differently from what it is written in the word of God and whosoever tries to teach something else will soon miss the right way and be deceived in his learning. I trust that the merciful Father will keep me in his word so that I shall write or speak nothing but that which I can prove by Moses, the prophets, the evangelists or by other apostolic Scriptures and doctrines, explained in their true sense, Spirit and intent of Christ. Judge ye that are spiritually minded. Again, I have no visions nor angelic inspirations, neither do I desire such, lest I be thereby deceived. The word of Christ, alone, is sufficient for me. If I do not follow his testimony, then, verily, all that I do is useless. And even if I had such visions and inspirations, which is not the case, even then it would have to be conformable to the word and Spirit of Christ, or else it would be mere fantasy, deceit and satanic temptation. For Paul says, "Let us prophesy according to the proportion of faith," Rom. 12: 6. Nor am I a third David, as some have falsely passed themselves and yet pass themselves for. There are but two Davids comprised in the word of God. The first, a literal and figurative, namely, the son of Jesse; and the second, the spiritual, the only begotten Son of God, Christ Jesus. Whosoever, now, passes himself for the third, is a falsifier and blasphemer. Let every soul take heed, lest he err in his faith.

According to my first birth I am nothing but unclean slime and dust of earth, conceived and born in sin from my mother's womb, and educated all my life in all manner of ignorance, sin and blindness, until the clear light of grace and knowledge appeared unto me from high heaven and which has given me such a heart, will and desire, that I willingly seek after that which is good, and strive, with holy Paul to "follow after, if that I may apprehend that for which also I am apprehended of Christ Jesus," Phil. 3: 12.

O, most beloved reader, I repeat that I have formerly acted shamefully against God and my neighbors; and yet I do, sometimes think, speak and act recklessly, of which however I sincerely repent. What am I that I should boast of, seek and teach any thing else than the ever blessed Christ Jesus alone, his word, sacraments, obedience and his god-pleasing, virtuous and unblamable life. He is the only one of whom it is written: That he was begotten of the Holy Ghost; that he knew no sin; that guile was not found in his mouth, that his doctrine, word, will, and commandments are life eternal, Matt. 1: 25; Luke 1: 31; 1 Pet. 2: 22; Isa. 53: 12.

Therefore take heed and save your soul. For thus every christian must be minded in regard to Christ Jesus, his Savior and in regard to his holy word; nor must he think himself more exalted, no matter what gifts he has received, if he would not rob Christ Jesus of his glory; and remain in a humble walk before God, in the right measure of his faith as becomes him in Christ. I advise all not to deceive themselves. Let spiritual pride, and vain boasting be far from you, "For God resisteth the proud, and giveth grace to the humble," 1 Pet. 5: 5.

Inasmuch as I daily see the perils which have surrounded us from the beginning; and as so many souls are deceived by false prophesies, smooth words, seeming holiness, lying, jugglery, boasting and false promises of the anti-christians and the false prophets who are ever intent upon their own honor, fame and gain, under a semblance of God's word, as was the case with the popes of Rome, with John of Leyden, the Munsterites, and others—therefore I deem it essential and well, sincerely to warn and admonish all beloved readers in the Lord, not to accept my doctrine as the gospel of Jesus Christ until they have weighed it in the balance with the Spirit and word of God, that they may not place their faith in me, nor in any teacher or writer, but, solely in Christ Jesus. For if they should accept it for my sake, and should not first compare it with the word of the Lord, and should, thus depend upon me or any other man, and not upon Christ Jesus, they would be like unto the culpable Corinthians, whom Paul severely reproved because there were dissensions among them; some were of Paul, some of Apollos, and not all of Christ Jesus, 1 Cor. 1. They would be like unto those of whom it is written, "Cursed be the man that trusteth in man, and maketh flesh his arm, and whose heart departeth from the Lord," Jer. 17: 5.

If I should, by my teaching, gain disciples for myself and not for Christ Jesus, seeking my own gain, praise and honor, then, indeed, woe unto my soul! No brethren, no. The Lord be blessed I seek not that which Judas, Gallio and Theudas sought. By the grace of God I am not minded like those who, in their imagination soar above the clouds and want to be like unto the Most High, Acts 5: 37. But I repeat it. I am a poor, miserable sinner, who must daily fight with my flesh, the world and the devil, and daily seek the mercy of the Lord; and who, with holy Paul boasts of nothing but of Christ Jesus alone; and that he was crucified for us.

My writing and preaching is for nothing but for the sake of Christ Jesus; for I seek and desire nothing (this the Lord knows) but that the most glorious name, the divine will, and the glory of our beloved Lord Jesus Christ may be acknowledged throughout the world. I desire and seek sincere teachers, true doctrines, true faith, true sacraments, true worship and an unblamable life; for which I must pay with much tribulation, trouble, uneasiness, labor, watching, fear, anxiety, sorrow, envy, shame, heat and cold, and perhaps, at last by torture, yea by my blood and death. For my reward, according to the flesh, must be that of him who, from the beginning, in his great love, has sought the salvation of the world. I say with holy John the Baptist; Christ Jesus must increase, but I must decrease, Jn. 3: 30; he lives forever and ever, but I shall again return to the dust from whence I came, as all the children of men.

Therefore I beseech you again, by the grace of God, and for the salvation of your souls, that you may weigh my doctrine and the doctrine of all mankind, who have been from the times of the apostles, are now, and shall yet be, with the gospel balance of Jesus Christ and the doctrine of his holy apostles, lest you be deceived by me or by any other man, no matter whether he be a prince, learned or unlearned, holy in appearance, or miraculous. If it be the word of God which I teach, accept it in the name of the Lord, if ye would not be lost. But if it be human doctrine, then let it be accursed of God. "For other foundation can no man lay than that is laid (by the apostles) which is Jesus Christ," 1 Cor. 3: 11.

No doctrine is profitable or serviceable to our salvation but the doctrine of Christ Jesus and his holy apostles, as he himself says, "Teach them to observe all things whatsoever I have commanded you," Matt. 28: 19.

All Scripture, both of the Old and New Testaments, rightly explained according to the intent of Christ Jesus and his holy apostles, is profitable for doctrine, for reproof, for correction, for instruction in righteousness, 2 Tim. 3: 16; but whatever is taught contrary to the Spirit and doctrine of Jesus is accursed of God, Gal. 1.

Inasmuch as there is but one corner stone laid of God, the Almighty Father, in the foundation of Zion, which is Christ Jesus, Isa. 28: 16; Rom. 9: 33; 1 Pet. 2: 6; upon whom alone we should build conformable to his word, and upon none other; and as the whole world, to the contrary, have built upon strange corner stones, such as popes, councils, doctors, doctrines and commandments of men; upon wrong practices of long standing, and still continue to build upon pretending prophets; and as they thus so shamefully reject the only, noble and finished corner stone, the ever blessed Christ Jesus—therefore I can not be restrained, but must warn all godfearing souls in the Lord, by my writings, wherever they shall be taken, read and heard, that from this moment they may awaken, if they desire to be saved (whether I live or die by so doing), and that they may without delay, enter upon the wholesome doctrine, sacraments, obedience and life of our beloved Lord Jesus Christ; for in him alone is life eternal, as has been frequently said above.

Beloved reader, verily, I can not but wonder at the obduracy, deafness and blindness of the world, inasmuch as they are not ashamed to bear the name of Christ, and to boast of his merits, blood and death, while nothing is found among them at all by which they prove the good will and nature of Christ Jesus. O ye vain boasters, if you are the true christians in whom God is pleased, as you pretend, where then, is your christian baptism in which you have buried your sins and put on the new life? Where is your true Supper in which you proclaim the death of the Lord and show your brotherly love? Where is your love and fear of God? your love of your neighbors? Your humility of heart? Your mercifulness towards the needful? Your obedience to the commandments of God? Your new birth from above, from which results a new life which should be unblamable before God, and before all the world? Jas. 1:27. Where is the living, holy and pleasing sacrifice of your own body, which you should ever be ready to present for the sake of the Lord's truth? We find nothing amongst you but unbelief and its evil fruits; an anti-christian baptism, idolatrous supper; unclean love of flesh, unmercifulness, pride, avarice, disobedience in all divine matters, carnal birth, earthly mindedness, and the old blamable life, led according to the will of him who, from the beginning, was a proud, false, deceitful, cruel and bloody murderer.

We find amongst you no worship but only a self-begotten set of rites which are pleasing to the flesh, such as, bells, organs, singing, celebration, ornamented churches, beautiful images, differences in victuals and in days, false purification and promises, reading many psalms and pater nosters with the mouth and not spiritually, adulteration of the sacraments, and a destruction and garbling of all that which Christ Jesus has taught and commanded in his holy gospel. All of which are, verily, no works of regenerated christians; but rather the works of Satan or of the foolish, blind and ignorant flesh. For by these works neither the word nor righteousness of God is taught; no flesh is crucified; no neighbors are served; and above all they are not pleasing to God. Therefore they can not be considered, according to Scripture, services of God, but rather an abominable, fearful and terrible service of idols. For by such means the ignorant, trusting populace is led away from the true faith and trust in Christ Jesus and is led into a false trust in ceremonies, yea, in such ceremonies as the eternal wisdom, the blessed Christ Jesus, has never commanded. By which ceremonies they plainly show that they believe at heart that Christ Jesus is imperfect, foolish, and unclean. For in case they believed him to be wise and perfect how could they thus shamefully adulterate, break, despise and garble his perfect, evangelical word and ordinances? And if they acknowledged him to be spotless why do they seek their salvation in such impure and strange means, and not in the only pure sacrifice, which is Christ Jesus?

But because true religion opposes your carnal mindedness, pride, avarice, uncleanness, vanity, ease and the lusts of your flesh, therefore you have chosen for yourselves a vain and strange religion by which you think to be saved, although you do not live according to the word and will of God. O, no, dear reader, no. I repeat it, if all creatures under the heavens were devouring swords, fire and water; if all men were cruel, horrible and bloody tyrants; and if the acuteness of the learned, ruled all the people, yet all would be vanity. If you would enter into life, you must be born again, Jn. 3:5, you must be regenerated and in malice you should be children, 1 Cor. 14:20; yea, you must keep the commandments which were taught and commanded of Jesus Christ, Matt. 18. Nothing can be devised as a substitute; for there will never be a way to salvation other than Christ Jesus.

It is too plain, and indiscreet blindness to think that we could be saved and at the same time be avaricious, spiteful, envious, proud, adulterous and idolatrous, as all the Scriptures too plainly show and teach that such shall not inherit the kingdom of God. Did you ever find falsehood with God? I think not. Holy Paul says that God is one "that can not lie," Tit. 1:2. Christ Jesus says, "Thy word is truth," Jn. 17:17. If he be, then, a God that can not lie; and if his holy word be truth; O, ye miserable, then all is lost with you. For his doctrine and truth is, that the unbelieving, refractory, disobedient, avaricious, vain, lying, whoring, greedy, obdurate, idolatrous, adulterous, ambitious, bloodthirsty and carnal man shall not enter into the kingdom of heaven; but his portion shall be "everlasting destruction," 1 Thess. 1: 9, eternal darkness and eternal death.

As you are such ungodly, obdurate and willful sinners, therefore you are, according to the word of Christ which can not lie, and according to the doctrine of the apostles who spoke in like Spirit, deprived of the glorious revelation of the children of God, and of the future life; and must remain forever, by the wrath of God, in the lake which burns with fire and brimstone, Rev. 21: 8.

And if you, notwithstanding this, trust to be saved while you do not sincerely repent of your old life, then, verily, your trust is vain. For by such trust you make God a liar, because you trust to acquire life contrary to his holy word.

What! Do ye think, O ye perverse, that we shall surprise, blind and bribe the Almighty, wise and just God? Do you think that the eternal truth shall become falsehood for your sake? No, beloved reader, no. Beware. The irrepressible sentence of God was passed, irrepealably more than fifteen hundred years ago, namely: "If ye live after the flesh, ye shall die," Rom. 8: 13. This word is sure and firm.

O world, world, that you thus despise as vain and useless, the calling and inviting voice of your God who is as faithful to you as a faithful Father to his beloved children! And that you speak in your hearts, with beautiful Tyrus, "I am of perfect beauty," Ezek. 27: 3; and with proud Babel, "I am, and none else besides me; I shall not sit as a widow, neither shall I know the loss of children," Isa. 47: 8. Yea, although you now say, as do the ignorant, It is peace and freedom; yet I tell you, as Ezekiel said unto Tyrus, Thou art nothing; nothing wilt thou be forever; and as Isaiah said unto Babel, Thou shalt fall and not rise again; and with Paul, "That the day of the Lord so cometh as a thief in the night," and, "as travail upon a woman with child; and they shall not escape," 1 Thess. 5: 2, 3; and although you may now, with Capernaum, be exalted unto heaven yet you will be brought down to hell, unlooked for, Matt. 11: 23. You eat, drink, dress, grab, hoard, and you act in all your transactions as if you would ever remain in this tabernacle of clay; and you never reflect that soon the word will be heard by all of us, "Give an account of thy stewardship; for thou mayest be no longer steward."

The precious word of grace and of eternal peace, which is the most holy gospel of Jesus Christ, you account for nothing more than a fable, nay, as accursed heresy; for you drown, burn, persecute, and murder those who teach, admonish and reprove you by this word, and who by a strong power of the Spirit are sent to you of God, by grace; just as the mad synagogue of the Jews did; so that they did not only persecute and destroy the chosen children of God, the holy prophets, but also the only begotten Son of God himself; who by the ineffable love of the merciful Father was sent to them for their own, eternal salvation. What did they say? "This is the heir; come, let us kill him, and let us seize on his inheritance," Matt. 21: 38.

How long will you continue in your damnable blindness, your refractory obduracy and your pernicious madness? Reflect upon the abundant, ineffable works of grace which Christ Jesus has shown you, and if his great love cannot move you to withdraw from your idolatry, disobedience and accursed life, then remember his rigid judgments which, from the beginning of the creation, came upon all those who did not abide in his blessed word and obedience, that you may by such fear, since you are not moved by his love, be drawn away from all evil.

Behold the weeping eyes, O, miserable world, and hear the tender voice of our beloved Lord Jesus Christ, how he wept for obdurate Jerusalem, and said unto them, "If thou hadst known, even thou, at least in this thy day, the things which belong unto thy peace! But now they are hid from thine eyes," Luke 19: 42. At another place, "Behold, I send unto you prophets and wise men and scribes; and some of them ye shall kill and crucify; and some of them ye shall scourge in your synagogues, and persecute them from city to city: That upon you may come all the righteous blood shed upon the earth; from the blood of righteous Abel unto the blood of Zacharias, son of Barachias, whom ye slew between the temple and the altar. Verily, I say unto you, All these things shall come upon this generation. O, Jerusalem, Jerusalem, thou that killest the prophets, and stonest them which are sent unto thee, how often would I have gathered thy children together, even as a hen gathereth her chickens under her wings, and ye would not! Behold, your house is left unto you desolate," Matt. 23: 34—38.

O, sincerely beloved readers, in case you would rightly take to heart these words of Christ, your bones would become dry by fear; they would shake and tremble; for it is with you, even as it was with Jerusalem and Judah. You willfully deny that Christ Jesus is your Lord. You do not desire the true knowledge of his ways. But you desire to do as all gentiles have done from the beginning, namely, worship wood, stone, gold, silver, bread, wine and the works of your own hands. Besides your earthly, carnal and corrupt life, which, so to speak, does not conform in the least to the word and will of him who, by grace, created you, to his honor.

Indeed, you have so entirely rejected Christ Jesus and cast him from you in mockery, that there is no doctrine, sacraments or any thing left you which conforms to his word; but you have instituted self-begotten doctrines, sacraments, ceremonies and commandments, as if Christ Jesus, the only begotten Son and Wisdom of the Almighty Father, were not the true Messenger. And all those who, about this damnable, deadly error, fraternally admonish and mildly reprove you and seek to return you to Christ Jesus and to his blessed word, must be taken and suffer as rebellious heretics, in all cities and countries.

Behold, kind reader, as you have ever been and yet are so unthankful for his paternal grace, God has shut out from you his mercy, and has brought his just judgment upon you so that there is neither right, godfearing truth, nor true teachers, **nor deacons, nor gospel, nor faith, nor christian baptism, nor christian Supper, nor christian life, nor knowledge, nor truth, nor spiritual wisdom, nor judgment, nor ban, nor love, nor piety left upon earth. Thus the house of which Christ Jesus has spoken, is entirely destroyed** and the well prepared vineyard of the Lord is without fruit, and is become useless, as the prophet says, "Now will I sing to my well beloved a song of my beloved touching his vineyard. My well beloved hath a vineyard in a very fruitful hill; and he fenced it and gathered out the stones thereof, and planted it with the choicest vine, and built a tower in the midst of it, and also made a wine-press therein; and he looked that it should bring forth grapes, and it brought forth wild grapes. And now, O inhabitants of Jerusalem, and men of Judah, judge, I pray you, betwixt me and my vineyard. What could have been done more to my vineyard, that I have not done in it? wherefore, when I looked that it should bring forth grapes, brought it forth wild grapes? And now, go to; I will tell you what I will do to my vineyard. I will take away the hedge thereof, and it shall be eaten up; and break down the wall thereof, and it shall be trodden down; and I will lay it waste; it shall not be pruned nor digged; but there shall come up briers and thorns: I will also command the clouds that they rain no rain upon it. For the vineyard of the Lord of hosts is the house of Israel, and the men of Judah his pleasant plant; and he looked for judgment, but behold oppression; for righteousness, but behold a cry," Isa. 5: 1—7.

Behold, dear brethren, as this judgment came first upon Israel, so it also has come upon us. For all flesh has corrupted his way, from the lowest to the highest. The heavens are iron, and earth is metal. There are found in the vineyard of the Lord no dew, no moisture nor ripe fruits; there is no digger, no pruner nor tender. Every where it is accursed; the walls and hedges are trampled down; it is laid waste to be trampled upon by all men; strangers have dominion thereof. The Gentiles have entered into the sanctuary, and have soiled the temple of the Lord. Our princes are to us devouring lions; our fathers are our betrayers; our pastors are our deceivers; our shepherds are our wolves; our watchmen are the thieves and murderers of our souls. We find nothing but thistles and thorns; it is all plundered and robbed; it is all torn up and broken down wherever we turn.

And all this on account of our sinfulness; this we must confess before our God.

Yea, dearest reader, compare our transgressions with those of Sodom and Gomorrah and the other cities which God has destroyed on account of their sinfulness, and see how far they stand above us yet. For if we will rightly look into the matter we can conceive of no sinfulness greater than that of our time; no matter how great a sin it is, as pride, avarice, fornication, adultery, idolatry, backbiting, hatred, envy, greediness, treason, murder, disobedience to God, refractoriness, lying, stealing, hypocrisy or any other ungodliness, as may be plainly seen.

Besides, flesh is accounted Spirit; falsehood, truth; sinfulness, righteousness; and Satan is accounted as Christ, by this miserable, blind, erring world. Anti-christ is seated in the temple of God. Pharaoh arms himself against Israel. The powerful miracles and the beseeching voice of the Lord are neither seen nor heeded. Thus has this abominable darkness covered the whole land of Egypt. I repeat, thus the fearful judgment of God is come upon us because of our sinfulness, as the prophet says, "Your iniquities have separated between you and your God, and your sins have hid his face from you, that he will not hear. For your hands are defiled with blood, and your fingers with iniquity; your lips have spoken lies, your tongue hath muttered perverseness. None calleth for justice, nor any pleadeth for truth; they trust in vanity and speak lies; they conceive mischief, and bring forth iniquity. They hatch cockatrice' eggs, and weave the spider's web: he that eateth of their eggs dieth, and that which is crushed breaketh out into a viper. Their webs shall not become garments, neither shall they cover themselves with their works; their works are works of iniquity, and the act of violence is in their hands. Their feet run to evil, and they make haste to shed innocent blood; their thoughts are thoughts of iniquity; wasting and destruction are in their paths. The way of peace they know not; and there is no judgment in their goings: they have made them crooked paths: whosoever goeth therein shall not know peace. Therefore is judgment far from us, neither doth justice overtake us. We wait for light, but behold obscurity; for brightness, but we walk in darkness. We grope for the wall like the blind, and we grope as if we had no eyes: we stumble at noon-day as in the night; we are in desolate places as dead men. We roar all like bears, and mourn sore like doves; we look for judgment but there is none; for salvation, but it is far off from us. For our transgressions are multiplied before thee, and our sins testify against us; for our transgressions are with us; and as for our iniquities, we know them: In transgressing and lying against the Lord, and departing away from our God, speaking oppression and revolt, conceiving and uttering from the heart words of falsehood. And judgment is turned away backward, and justice standeth afar off: for truth is fallen in the street, and equity can not enter. Yea, truth faileth; and he that departeth from evil, maketh himself a prey: and the Lord saw it, and it displeased him that there was no judgment. And he saw that there was no man, and wondered that there was no intercessor," Isa. 59: 2—16.

Most beloved, thus has God, the just judge, sent his fearful judgment into this wicked world, although you do not feel it. For inasmuch as you trample upon the Son of God, deem the blood of the New Testament as unclean, grieve the Holy Spirit of grace—therefore you are under the terrible judgment and have fallen into the hands of the living God, so that you prefer falsehood to truth, obscurity to light, death to life; and therefore God has sent you error, and deprived you of his holy word, faith, knowledge and truth, so that you have, in this world, neither light nor way, nor spiritual wisdom, nor prayer, nor God, nor Christ, nor promise, nor righteousness, nor peace, nor conscientious freedom, nor inward joy nor hope; notwithstanding you so highly boast of the name, mercy, merits, death and blood of the Lord. For since you say that you acknowledge God, and yet do not honor and thank him as God, therefore he has suffered you to be deceived by your sensual thoughts, and your foolish heart is become obscured, 1 Jn. 1: 6; Jn. 1: 10; Rev.

22: 15; Jn. 9: 31; Eph. 4: 18; Rom. 1: 18, 22. Besides, you deem it but mockery to acknowledge God, therefore God has delivered you to a perverse mind, to do the things you should not do; "Being filled with all unrighteousness, fornication, wickedness, covetousness, maliciousness; full of envy, murder, debate, deceit, malignity; whisperers; backbiters, haters of God, despiteful, proud, boasters, inventers of evil things, disobedient to parents, without understanding, covenant-breakers, without natural affection, implacable, unmerciful," Rom. 1: 29—31.

Behold, beloved reader, thus mysteriously God punishes by his righteous judgment. For God, the Mighty Lord visits this world in many different ways, on account of the sinfulness thereof. As with bondage, war, bloodshed, drought, famine, pestilence and many other diseases; at which plagues and chastisements the world is horror-stricken. But above all, the most terrible wrath of God is his depriving us of his divine word. For the first mentioned plagues, such as pestilence, famine, sword, &c., only punish us according to the flesh, and are chastisements for our correction, as the prophet says, which he inflicts that his children may learn wisdom; but when he deprives us of his word, then all is lost. For if we have not the word, we verily, have nothing but unbelief, blindness, error, disobedience, conceit, acrimony, an unclean, foolish and adulterous spirit, and eternal death. But how few, yea, how *very few* are horror-stricken at these plagues, however abundantly they have come upon them.

If we should desire to put out a man's eyes, cut off his ears, take his life or take from him the inheritance of his natural father, would not such an one use all his reason, wit and wisdom to prevent such pain, shame, danger, and damage? And to-day the whole world have eyes and see not, ears and hear not, life and yet are dead; and, above all, bereft of the eternal inheritance of the merciful Father, but do not mind it. O, if they acknowledged their own misfortune how diligently they would seek him who gives sight to the blind, hearing to the deaf, and true wisdom to the unlearned, which is Christ Jesus, Ps. 94: 9.

But the finely attired woman has so enchanted you, and the whoring spirit of the spiritual whoredom has so kept you under its wings, that I fear, indeed, that your abominable unbelief, obscurity, blindness, falsehood and madness will never more be taken from your hearts, but that the wrath of God will remain upon you to the end; so that in this earthly life you will err, without any piety, from one unclean thing to another until the time that we shall be placed before the just judge, where every one shall receive his reward according to his works. Then, when too late, your blind eyes will be opened amidst sighs and unavailing remorse, acknowledging that you have not walked in the ways of righteousness to life eternal, but in the dark ways to death eternal. O misery, where will you then hide yourselves from the wrath of God? Then you will cry in terror: Ye mountains fall upon us and ye hills cover us, Rev. 6: 16. For then there can not be found a place of prayer, of mercy, nor of repentance for the sinner. But the awful sentence of the just God against all the wicked, unbelieving, willful and disobedient sinners will then be pronounced, "Depart from me, ye cursed, into everlasting fire, prepared for the devil and his angels," Matt. 25: 41. O, how well it would be for such if they had never been born.

Therefore I will not cease, while I live, to teach and admonish both verbally and by writing, so far as God, the merciful Father, by his ineffable kindness, is giving me knowledge, spirit, grace and wisdom, to all those that seek the truth; that they may awaken while it is yet time and seek the Lord while he may yet be found, and call upon him while he is near, that their righteousness may go forth as a light and their salvation burn like a torch; which consists in nothing but casting off the works of darkness and putting on the armor of light, which is to renounce all false doctrine, sacraments, false religion and the unbecoming, dishonest, carnal life, and again to enter into the divine doctrine, the evangelical sacraments, the services and works of love and the sincere, christian life, as it was taught, instituted and practiced by Christ Jesus, our only Deliverer and Shepherd himself, according to the will of his Father, Isa. 55: 6; 62: 2; Rom. 13: 12.

Thus I labor and strive, according to the small talent given me of God, of which God is my witness, after nothing else than that the Day-star, the blessed Christ Jesus, the ever shining Light may arise in your hearts and enlighten you in all divine truth, knowledge, spiritual understanding and wisdom, unto life eternal. Amen, 2 Pet. 1: 19.

Most beloved reader, herewith I beseech you all, whether you be lord, prince, learned or unlearned, to peruse these and all my writings, with the fear of God in your hearts, and I have no doubt but you will clearly find that our doctrine, which is the doctrine of Jesus Christ and his holy apostles, does not tend to mutiny, discord, treason and rebellion; but rather, yea surely, to true, christian love, unity and peace. For Christ Jesus whom we preach, is the true Prince of eternal peace, and not of discord, Isa. 9. Say, whom have we curtailed? Whom have we injured? We sincerely seek nothing but that we may save all mankind. Not only at the cost of our chattels, shelter, gold, silver, and labor, but also (understand it in an spiritual sense) at the cost of our life-blood.

Verily, verily, I say, If all lords and princes and their subjects who boast of the name of Christ, would acknowledge the beforementioned doctrine of Jesus Christ as right and true, and were minded as the doctrine, life and Spirit of Christ require, then it would not be necessary to fortify cities and towns; to keep cavalry and infantry, nor to manufacture deadly weapons such as guns, swords and spears. I do not here speak of the sword of justice which is given as a punishment to the wicked and protection of the good. But it would be as the prophet says, "They shall beat their swords into plowshares and their spears into pruning-hooks; nation shall not lift up sword against nation, neither shall they learn war any more." "But they shall sit every man under his vine and under his fig tree," Isa. 2: 4; Micah 4: 3, 4. For it is impossible that those who have committed themselves to the doctrine, life, body and church of Jesus Christ and remain therein, should seek or desire any thing but divine love, peace and unity; to suppress all evil, and protect all good, as becomes us in Christ Jesus. But we do not abet the false prophets of the corrupted sects which in many actions transgress the doctrine, rule and measure of Christ.

Herewith we commend you to the Lord, O, faithful readers. And now judge for yourselves according to the word of the Lord, whether or not I have, by his grace pointed out to you the truth of our beloved Lord Jesus Christ. Grace, peace, mercy, true knowledge and life eternal be to all who, in truth, love Christ Jesus, Amen. Do not hide the praise of God. But let it be read, and heard by all who diligently seek and desire it.

Beloved brethren, do not deviate from the doctrine and life of Christ.

A FUNDAMENTAL AND CLEAR CONFESSION

OF THE

POOR AND DISTRESSED CHRISTIANS

CONCERNING

JUSTIFICATION, THE PREACHERS, BAPTISM, THE LORD'S SUPPER, AND THE SWEARING OF OATHS; ON ACCOUNT OF WHICH WE ARE SO MUCH HATED, SLANDERED, AND BELIED, FOUNDED UPON THE WORD OF GOD.

BY

MENNO SIMON.

A. D., 1552.

"Whosoever therefore shall confess me before men, him will I confess also before my Father which is in heaven; but whosoever shall deny me before men, him will I also deny before my Father which is in heaven," Matt. 10 : 32, 33.

"For other foundation can no man lay than that is laid, which is Jesus Christ," 1 Cor. 3 : 11.

ELKHART, INDIANA:
PUBLISHED BY JOHN F. FUNK AND BROTHER.
1871.

A TRUE knowledge of the divine word, a fruitful faith in Christ Jesus, unfeigned love, and a pious, penitent, unblamable life I sincerely wish to all those who shall see, read or hear this our confession, of God our heavenly Father through Christ Jesus our Lord, who has loved us and cleansed us of our sins with his blood. To him be the honor, praise, kingdom, power and glory, forever and ever, Amen.

Christ says, "Whosoever heareth these sayings of mine, and doeth them, I will liken him unto a wise man, which built his house upon a rock; and the rain descended, and the floods came, and the winds blew, and beat upon that house; and it fell not, for it was founded upon a rock. And every one that heareth these sayings of mine, and doeth them not, shall be likened unto a foolish man, which built his house upon the sand; and the rain descended, and the floods came, and the winds blew, and beat upon that house; and it fell; and great was the fall of it," Matt. 7: 24—27.

PREFACE.

Honored reader, the reason why we write is this: Because we and our ancestors, for many centuries, have sought the light in obscurity, the truth in falsehood, life in death, and the way among the deceivers; and have wandered about like a flock of sheep without a shepherd; and, alas, there was none who pointed us to the way of life and led us into the pasture of the Lord. The accursed doctrine of anti-christ had so drawn the shameful smoke of deceit from the bottomless pit; had so obscured the glorious dazzling of the divine word, nay, the just judgment of God was come upon this reckless world, on account of its sinfulness, so that, alas, there was neither true doctrine nor true knowledge of God and Christ, nor faith, baptism, Supper, ban in accordance with God's word, nor love, nor righteousness found among men, and of which very little is found as yet; for all over the world we find false teachers, hypocritical deceivers, and enemies of the cross, who diligently serve their own bellies, who by their tickling, erring doctrine proclaim peace to those who know of no peace, and thus strengthen the hands of the wicked so that none converts himself from his wickedness, as the prophet says.

Yea, they have carried on their wrangling, writing and preaching so far that they adjudge the Lord's express ordinances of baptism, Supper and ban, as commanded by him, and as taught, practiced and testified to by his holy apostles, not only as heretical, but also fiend-like, they upbraid and persecute those who keep them, as may be plainly seen; and have instituted a new baptism, which the Scripture knows not, which is more pleasing to the flesh than the baptism of Christ; a new Supper which is a false consolation to the ungodly; also a ban which serves for nothing but the destruction of the pious, and which is not founded on anything reasonable; for if they are not banished from city and country, they are sentenced to the stake or water; nor is it practiced sparingly upon the pious in many places.

In short, they have so led the common world from God, and so estranged them by their carnal doctrine and false sacraments, and led them into such unbelief and heathenish life, that all heaven must be afflicted and ashamed thereat. Say reasonable reader, who can enumerate the accursed, ungodly pride, pomp, adultery, fornication, idolatry, Roman and Spanish abominations, unfaithfulness, fraud, avarice, usury, unrighteousness, debauchery, luxury, hatred, envy, murder, thefts, robbery, incendiarism, treason, blood-shed, unmannerly, obscene words, the terrible lying, shameful diseases, lameness, suffering and wounds, which are found with this wicked, reckless world. Yet they claim to be the church of Christ. Yea, every thing is in such a condition that we may well say with the prophet Hosea, "There is no truth, nor mercy, nor knowledge of God in the land; but swearing, and lying, and killing, and stealing, and committing adultery; they break out, and blood toucheth blood," Hosea 4: 1, 2; with Jeremiah, that "A wonderful and horrible thing is committed in the land," Jer. 5: 30; with John, that "The whole world lieth in wickedness," Jn. 5: 19; and with John the divine that their "sins have reached unto heaven," Rev. 18: 5. O, faithful reader, it is worse than I can express. Whosoever is reasonably disposed may realize the truth.

Inasmuch as the brightness of the sun has not shone for so many years; as heaven and earth have been as copper and iron; as the brooks and springs have not run, nor the dew dropped from heaven; as the beautiful trees and verdant fields have been dry and barren (I mean spiritually); but, inasmuch as, in these latter days, the gracious, great Lord, by the rich treasures of his love, has again opened the windows of heaven, and let drop the dew of his divine word, so that the earth once more produces its green branches and plants of righteousness, as before, which bear fruit unto the Lord and glorify his adorable name; and inasmuch as the holy word and sacraments of the Lord again lift up their heads from the ashes, by means of which the blasphemous deceit and abominations of the learned are made manifest—therefore all the infernal gates are opened in opposition; foam and rave, and that with such subtle deceit, blasphemous falsehood and tyranny that if the strong God did not interpose with his gracious power, no man could be saved. But they will never wrest from him his chosen ones.

Inasmuch as they so fearfully teach and strive against the truth, weigh out dross for silver, and, besides, accuse us of all manner of shame, blasphemy, roguery and profanity, as they did from the beginning to all those who fear the Lord—therefore we are forced, and constrained by the true love of the divine word and the salvation of your souls, to explain briefly to you according to the word of the Lord, the sure, divine foundation, and the pure, immutable truth of Justification, of the Preachers, of Baptism, of the Supper, and of the swearing of oaths, on account of which we are so much hated and slanderously belied by every person, and especially of the learned, that you may thereby acknowledge what the Holy Scriptures clearly teach us in regard to these articles; and to show whether we are such useless, ungodly people, as the learned incessantly cry against us and tell the people. If you have ears to hear, then hear the word of the Lord; and if you have understanding hearts, take heed, and follow the truth.

A FUNDAMENTAL AND CLEAR

CONFESSION OF THE POOR, AFFLICTED CHRISTIANS.

Honored reader, it is plain and manifest that Adam and Eve, the father and mother of us all, were, in the beginning, created after the image of God by Christ, pure, good, without sin, righteous and incorrupt, as the Scripture teaches, Gen. 1: 27; 5: 1; 2: 7; Acts 17: 24; Eccl. 17: 9. And that they remained pure and righteous until they sinned against their Creator's word and commandment. For God had said unto them, "Of the tree of the knowledge of good and evil thou shalt not eat of it; for in the day that thou eatest thereof thou shalt surely die;" as also it happened. For as soon as Adam and Eve, deceived by the serpent, ate of the forbidden fruit they became impure, unrighteous, corrupt, of sinful nature, children of death and of the devil; and thus, by their disobedience they lost their being children of God, and the purity in which they were created; and must have forever remained, with all their descendants, in sin, under the curse and servitude of death and devil, if God, the merciful Father whose love endures forever, had not again comforted and raised them up by the promise of Christ whom he promised to send in the future to bruise the Serpent's head; for whose sake he would be gracious unto them, would forgive their transgression, would show them mercy and favor, so far as they should believe.

When Adam and Eve heard these glad tidings of grace, the gospel of peace, from the mouth of the Lord, they joyfully accepted and believed it as the immutable truth of God, anxiously cleaved to it, and consoled themselves therewith as a sure foundation of salvation. And thus Adam and Eve were again accepted of God through Christ Jesus, justified and delivered from the eternal death and curse; for they, according to the promise of God, believed and trusted in him and looked for him in latter days as the Conquerer, Savior and means of grace to eternal reconciliation.

But had they despised this means and not accepted it by faith, they would have suffered eternal death; this is incontrovertible, as Christ himself says, "He that believeth not, is condemned already;" again, John the Baptist says, "He that believeth on the Son, hath everlasting life; and he that believeth not the Son, shall not see life; but the wrath of God abideth on him," Jn. 3: 18, 36.

As Adam and Eve, then, were bitten and poisoned by the infernal serpent, and became of sinful nature, and would have been subject to eternal death if God had not again accepted them in grace through Christ Jesus, so we, their descendants, are also born of sinful nature of them, poisoned by the serpent, inclined to evil, and by inherent sin, children of hell, of the devil and everlasting death; and cannot be delivered therefrom (we speak of those who have come to years of understanding, and hence to sinful works) unless we accept Christ Jesus the only and eternal means of grace, by true and unfeigned faith, and thus conscientiously look upon the brazen serpent which is erected by God, our heavenly Father, as a sign of salvation; for without him there is no help for our souls, no reconciliation nor peace; but disgrace, wrath and eternal death can only be expected, as was said before. But those who accept this Christ by a true faith which, according to the doctrine of Paul, was given us of the Father for the purpose of wisdom, righteousness, sanctification and deliverance, are in grace for Christ's sake, and God is their Father; for by faith they are born of him; he forgives them all their sins; has compassion on all their human failings and weaknesses; turns them from the curse, wrath and eternal death; accepts them as his beloved children, and gives them Christ Jesus, together with all his merits, fastings, prayers, tears, sufferings, tribulation, cross, blood and death; besides, also, his Spirit, inheritance, kingdom, glory, joy and life; not, we say, by our own merits and works, but by grace through Christ Jesus, as Paul says, "God, who is rich in mercy, for his great love wherewith he loves us, even when we were dead in sins, hath quickened us together with Christ (by grace ye are saved); and hath raised us up together, and made us sit together in heavenly places in Christ Jesus; that in the ages to come he might show the exceeding riches of his grace, in his kindness toward us through Christ Jesus. For by grace are ye saved through faith; and that not of yourselves; it is the gift of God; not of works, lest any man should boast. For we are his workmanship, created in Christ Jesus unto good works which God hath before ordained that we should walk in them," Eph. 2: 4—10.

Behold, kind reader, thus we do not seek our salvation in works, words or sacraments, as do the learned, although they blame us therefor, but we seek them alone in Christ Jesus and in no other means in heaven or earth. In this only means we rejoice and in no other. We trust, by the grace of God, to abide therein unto death.

But that we abhor the carnal works and desire to suit ourselves to his word and commandment, according to our weakness, we do because he has so taught and commanded us. For, whosoever does not walk according to his doctrine, proves in fact, that he does not believe on him nor knows him, and that he is not in the communion of the saints, 1 Jn. 3: 10; 5: 10; 2 Jn. 1: 6.

All those, now, who accept this means of divine grace, Jesus Christ, with believing hearts, and enclose him in their consciences, believe and confess that their sins are forgiven through his sacrifice, death, and blood; that his wrath and damnation will not be upon them forever; that he accepts them as his beloved sons and daughters, and gives them life eternal. All such become of peaceable and joyous spirit, and give thanks to God, with renewed hearts; for the power of faith quickens and changes them into newness of life, and they walk thus, by the gift and grace of the Holy Spirit in the power of their new birth, according to the measure of their faith, in obedience to their God who has shown them such great love; they diligently watch lest they fall from the grace and favor of God by licentiousness and ungodliness. They acknowledge by the Scriptures that Adam and Eve, the antediluvian world, Sodom and Gomorrah, and the patriarchs in the wilderness were severely punished of God on account of their sins; that the wages of sin is death; and that, also, Christ Jesus, the innocent Lamb of God who knew no sin, was so deeply humiliated and tortured on account of our sinfulness, Gen. 3: 7; 19: 9, 10; Lev. 10: 1—4; Rom. 6: 23; 1 Pet. 1: 19.

Inasmuch as they believe the word of the Lord which says, that to be carnally minded is death—if thou livest according to the flesh thou shalt die—adulterers, fornicators, drunkards, the avaricious, proud, liars, &c., shall not inherit the kingdom of God—and besides, believe that God is truth; that none can be saved contrary to his word; that he will judge in accordance with his word, because he is truth and cannot lie, as the Scriptures testify, Rom. 8: 6, 13; 1 Cor. 5: 10; 6: 10; Gal. 5: 21; Eph. 5: 5; Rev. 22: 15; therefore it is that they sincerely fear the Lord, and by fear die unto their flesh, crucify their lusts and desires, and shun and abhor the unclean, ungodly works which are contrary to the word of the Lord.

Besides this they acknowledge the abundant grace, favor and love of God towards us, as shown in Christ Jesus, and therefore, in return they love their God, for he first loved us, and stand prepared by this love to obey, in their weakness, his holy word, will, commandments, advice, doctrine and ordinances, according to the talent received; and thus they show, in fact, that they believe, they are born of God, and are spiritually minded; they lead a pious, unblamable life before all men; suffer themselves to

JUSTIFICATION.

be baptized according to the commandment of the Lord, as proof that they bury their sins in the death of Christ, and are prepared to walk with him in newness of life; they break the bread of peace with their beloved brethren as proof and testimony that they are one in Christ and his holy church and that they have, or know no other means of grace and remission of their sins, neither in heaven nor in earth, than the innocent flesh and blood of our Lord Jesus Christ alone, which he once, by his eternal Spirit in obedience to the Father, sacrificed and shed upon the cross for us poor sinners; they walk in all love and mercy, and serve their neighbors. In short, they suit themselves, in their weakness, to all words, commandments, ordinances, Spirit, rule, example and measure of Christ, as the Scripture teaches; for they are in Christ and Christ is in them; and therefore they live no longer in the old life of sin after the first earthly Adam (weakness excepted), but in the new life of righteousness which comes by faith, after the second and heavenly Adam, Christ; Paul says, I do not now live, "But Christ liveth in me; and the life which I now live in the flesh, I live by the faith of the Son of God, who loved me, and gave himself for me," Gal. 2: 20. Christ says, "If ye love me, keep my commandments," Jn. 14: 15.

Think not beloved reader, that we boast of being perfect and without sins. Not at all. I for myself confess that often my prayer is mixed with sin and my righteousness with unrighteousness; for by the grace of God I feel, by the unction which is in me, when I compare my weak nature to Christ and his commandments, what kind of a flesh I inherited from Adam. Yea, if God should judge us according to our worthiness, righteousness, works and merits, and not according to his great goodness and mercy, then I confess with holy David that no man could stand before his judgment, Ps. 143: 2; 130: 3. Therefore it should be far from us that we should console ourselves with any thing but the grace of God through Christ Jesus; for it is he, alone, and none other, who has perfectly fulfilled the righteousness required by God. We are also aware, by the grace of God, that all saints, from the beginning, have lamented the corruption of their flesh, as may be seen by the writings of Moses, David, Job, Isaiah, Paul, James and John.

But for Christ's sake we are in grace; for his sake we are heard; and for his sake our failings and transgressions, which are committed involuntarily, are remitted. For it is he who stands between his Father and his imperfect children, with his perfect righteousness, and with his innocent blood and death; and intercedes for all those who believe on him and who strive by faith in the divine word, to turn from evil, follow that which is good and who sincerely desire, with Paul, that they may attain the perfection which is in Christ, Phil. 3: 12.

Mark, beloved reader, that we do not believe nor teach that we are to be saved by our merits and works, as the envious accuse us of without truth; but that we are to be saved solely by grace, through Christ Jesus, as has been said before. By grace man was created, through Christ Jesus, Gen. 1: 27.

By grace he was again accepted through Christ when he was lost. By grace Christ was sent to us of the Father, Jn. 3: 34. By grace he has sought the lost sheep, Luke 15: 4, taught them repentance and remission of sins. Died for us when we were yet ungodly, and enemies, Rom. 5: 6; by grace we receive faith. By grace the Holy Ghost was given us, in the name of Jesus, Jn. 14: 16. In short, by grace we receive eternal life through Christ Jesus, Rom. 6: 8.

Behold, kind reader, this is, concerning this article of our faith and confession, namely: That we can not obtain salvation, grace, reconciliation nor peace of the Father, otherwise than through Christ Jesus, as he himself says, "No man cometh unto the Father but by me," Jn. 14: 6. Peter also says, "There is none other name under heaven given among men, whereby we must be saved" than the name of Jesus; and that all those who accept this grace in Christ, preached by the gospel and accepted by a firm faith, and cordially adhered to by the power of the Holy Ghost through faith, and become new men, born of God; changed in their hearts, renewed and of a different mind; yea, transferred from Adam unto Christ; and thus walk in newness of life, as obedient children, in the grace which is manifested unto them; for they are renewed; have become humble minded, meek, merciful, compassionate, peaceable, patient, hungry and thirsty after righteousness; they strive firmly by good works after eternal life, for they are believing, born of God, are in Christ and Christ in them; they are partakers of his Spirit and nature, and thus live according to the word of the Lord by the power of Christ which is in them. And this is, according to Scripture, to be believing; to be a christian; and to be in Christ and Christ in us.

Again, that all those who disregard this preached grace and do not accept Christ Jesus by faith; who reject his holy word, will, commandments and ordinances, and hate and persecute them; who live according to their lusts and licentiously, are lost, and that it will avail them nothing before the Lord to boast of their faith, new creature, Christ's grace, death and blood; for they do not believe; they remain in their first birth, namely, unchanged in their earthly, corrupted nature, impenitent, carnally minded, nay, utterly without Spirit, Word and Christ; and therefore are children of death, as Scripture teaches; for they know not Christ in whom is life, as John says, "This is the record that God hath given to us eternal life, and that this life is in his Son. He that hath the Son hath life; and he that hath not the Son of God hath not life," 1 Jn. 5: 11, 12.

Behold, worthy reader, this now is our foundation and confession of justification, as you have here read. Judge for yourself whether the preachers act rightly in so slanderously belying us, saying that we expect to be saved by our merits and works; and that we boast to be without sin.

May the Lord forgive them that they so fiendishly belie us with such shameful lies. O, that these miserable men would once take to heart that the backbiters, slanderers and liars are of the devil and worthy of death; that God abhors all liars; that they shall have no part in his kingdom; and that a lying mouth killeth the soul, Jn. 8:44; Rom. 1: 32; Ps. 5: 7; Rev. 21: 27; 22: 15.

This, I say, is our foundation, and, by the grace of God, it will ever remain our foundation, for we truly know and confess that it is the invincible word and truth of the Lord; therefore we testify before you and before all the world that we do not agree with those who teach and institute a dead faith, which they gather from profane history: First, that without change, there can be Spirit, power and fruits. Secondly, that we can be saved by our own merits and works, for reasons above stated.

May the merciful, gracious Father, through his beloved Son Jesus Christ our Lord, grant us all the gift of his Holy Spirit, that we may sincerely believe and confess this beforementioned grace in and through Christ; and that we may walk and abide therein firmly and faithfully unto the end, to the eternal praise and glory of God, Amen.

HEARING THE PREACHERS.

It is a well known fact, kind reader, that, on account of this article, principally, we are so hated and persecuted by the learned, and that all the world cries against us and complains, That we will not hear God's word. Therefore we are necessarily impelled, inasmuch as it concerns the praise of God and the salvation of our souls, to assign the reason according to the word of God (which we would gladly omit if we were not required by Scripture), to assign the reason why we do not hear them, and conscientiously dare not listen to them; on account of which we have to suffer so much pain and tribulation. Jesus said to Nicodemus, "Verily, verily, I say unto thee, except a man be born again, he can not see the kingdom of God." Paul also says, "If any man have not the Spirit of Christ, he is none of his," and John says, "Whosoever transgresseth, and abideth not in the doctrine of Christ, hath not God," Jn. 3: 3; Rom. 8: 9; 1 Jn. 1: 9.

Honored reader, consider the word of the Lord. That the preachers of the world are not born again and have not the Spirit of Christ, and do not abide in his word, their fruits abundantly prove; for it is manifest that they pitiably adulterate the word of the Lord and walk according to the flesh, as will be clearly shown in the following:

First, I am convinced that you never saw that the preachers, who are one with their church, have ever converted an avaricious person from his avarice; a drunkard from his inebriety or a proud person from his pride and luxury, which are plainly works of the flesh, and, according to Scripture punishable with eternal death, if not repented of. Inasmuch as they convert none as it appears, therefore it is plain that their doctrine is nothing but vain prattle without power and fruit; which, alas, is clearly shown and proven by all the world by their unbecoming life.

Secondly, the reckless people are chained to and consoled in their unbelief and licentious, carnal life by their light minded doctrine, sacraments and easy life; for they preach and teach you, "There are none that can truly believe; we are all sinners—therefore none can rightly keep the commandments of God. In your baptism (they say) you became a regenerated christian and received the Holy Ghost. Although you could not understand the word; although you have no faith in Christ Jesus nor knowledge of good or evil, nor any change or renewing of heart, because you were an unconscious child, and like false consolations." You hear their absolutions, and receive their bread, as if that were sufficient; and never mind that you are yet an impenitent, avaricious, proud, drunken, unclean, envious and idolatrous man. We will leave you to judge whether these can be called preachers of peace who make arm cushions and pillows for the people and preach such things as are pleasing to them, Deut. 1: 39; Ezra 13: 18.

Inasmuch as none are made better by their doctrine and sacraments but are more and more comforted in unrighteousness— therefore it must be acknowledged that they strengthen you in your evil doing, shut unto you the kingdom of heaven, lead you into the ditch, and rob and murder your souls, Jer. 23; 14; Matt. 15: 14.

O, kind reader, they have so enchanted the ignorant people who so gladly walk upon the broad road, with their light minded doctrine that we may well exclaim with Jeremiah, that "No man repented him of his wickedness, saying, What have I done?" Jer. 8: 6; or who enquires after a pious, penitent or godly life? What is worse, they have carried it so far, that alas, those must be called *work-saints* and *heaven-stormers* who, with faithful hearts hear, believe, fear, love, and, according to the measure of their faith, obey the word of the Lord. Behold, thus entirely has the smoke of the pit darkened the sun and sky, Rev. 9: 2.

As to their sacraments, it is manifest that they do not have the sacraments of Christ; but self-begotten abominations and idols, only a semblance of the Lord's sacraments. For they baptize infants; of which Christ has not taught nor commanded a single word in the whole New Testament, and are therefore called christians, notwithstanding that such baptized persons generally, walk in perverse ways all their lives, and not only not confess Christ Jesus together with his holy word, but also hate him and oppose the word.

Again, their supper must be called the Lord's flesh and blood; while the Scripture, at many places testifies that he ascended up to heaven, Mark 16: 19; Luke 24: 51; Acts 1: 9; Eph. 4: 8; and is seated at the right hand of his Father, while common sense, besides the Scripture, teaches us that he cannot be chewed with teeth nor consumed by the stomach. Besides, it is administered by some as for the remission of sins. Behold they have so entirely forsaken the Lord who has purchased them with his blood, that they have changed his praise and honor into such a weak creature. If this cannot be called serving Baal and moulding calves you may judge according to Scripture.

Lastly, How they conform their lives according to the doctrine of Paul you may best deduce from their fruits and life. That they do not walk in humility of heart before the Lord, their looks and names prove. They suffer themselves to be greeted as lords and masters; notwithstanding it is forbidden by the mouth of the Lord. Say kind reader, did you ever hear or read that the holy apostles and prophets were covetous of such high, vain names as are the learned and the preachers of the world. It is true the word Rabbi or Master was applied to the ambitious Scribes and Pharisees, but not to the apostles and prophets. For we do not read of Doctor Isaiah, of Master Ezekiel and of Lords Paul and Peter. No, no. All those who have rightly taught the word of the Lord, were in their time not honored with such high-sounding names. This I write that you may know that such ambitious, proud spirits can never rightly teach you the humble word of the cross.

Besides, also, consider their avarice, and solicitude for their appetite; for they do not preach nor render services without pay, as if the office of a preacher and shepherd were a profession or trade. Jude says, They honor the persons for the sake of profits. Where there are no liens and rents there we find no preachers; but where liens and rents are abundant there is no want of preachers.

Again, they are in part usurers, in part fornicators or adulterers, greedy, liars, irascible, proud, hateful, lustful, vain, and lazy, envious, cruel, treacherous and rebellious toward all those who sincerely seek and fear God. In short, if you rightly confess the Lord and his word, then you must acknowledge that the best and most pious of them are yet far outside of Christ and his word in regard to doctrine, sacraments and also to their walk.

Inasmuch as all of them, in doctrine, sacraments and walk are so diametrically opposed to the Spirit, word and walk of the Lord, as appears, and inasmuch as Christ says, "Every tree is known by his own fruit," Luke 6: 44; therefore it is plainly proven that they see not the kingdom and glory of God; are not of the Lord, and have not God, as was said before.

If they see not the kingdom of God as Christ speaks, how, then, can they rightly preach it and teach it to others?

If they have not the Spirit of the Lord and are not of him (as appears), how then, can they be true ministers and servants of the spiritual office?

And if they have not God, how can they, then, rightly teach and point out his precious word unto righteousness? Inasmuch as it is well known to all theologians that they do not understand the kingdom of God and his glory; are not of the Lord, and have no God, as was said, therefore we conclude therefrom, and that truly, that their sending, calling, office and service is not of God and his word; but they are of the bottomless pit, and of the dragon and beast, Rev. 9: 2. By this we do not mean this one, or that one; but all preachers in general who do not act according to the word of God; no matter of which denomination or sect. We do not judge according to their boasting and appearance, but truthfully, according to doctrine, sacraments, fruits and life; for we are sure that the high and holy office, which should be filled in the power of the Spirit, can never be filled by the avaricious; neither by the proud and unrighteous, the carnal and earthly minded, nor by drunkards and the lustful who serve their appetites before their God, as Paul says; nor by slanderers nor by vain prattlers, nor liars, nor soothsayers, nor hirelings, nor by those who adulterate, hate and oppose the Spirit, will, word, ordinances and commandments of the Lord, and who are ignorant and blind in all spiritual and evangelical matters; for the Spirit and word of God do not know such shepherds and teachers, but the Scripture portrays them with many terrible names and calls them profane, blind watchmen and greedy dogs, blind leaders, consumers of souls, false daubers, fools who seek not the Lord, preachers of peace, of whom it is written, "The prophets prophesy lies in my name; I sent them not, neither have I commanded them, neither spake unto them; they prophesy unto you false vision and divination, and a thing of nought, and the deceit of their heart," Jer. 23: 11; Matt. 15: 14; Ezek. 13: 10; Jer. 10: 8; 14: 14. In short, they are the teachers against whom the word of the Lord has faithfully warned

HEARING THE PREACHERS.

us. Read here and there in the prophets, particularly Jer. 23:13; Matt. 7:15; 15:14; 16:12; 24:11; Mark 12:38; Luke 12:1; 20:45.

Say, kind reader, did you ever read in the Scriptures of any proud, avaricious, unclean, lying, inebriated and idolatrous prophets, apostles and shepherds who were pleasing unto the Lord? Or of such who, to please the world, have adulterated, changed and abused the word, ordinances and commandments of the Lord? Or, of such who said to cities, districts or towns, If you will care for our necessaries of life; or, if you will give us so much money or income, we will teach you the word of the Lord? O no, reader, no. It never was nor never will be the way of the holy prophets, apostles or servants of Christ. Of this we are sure.

The teachers and preachers who are sent of God are born of God, are of godly nature, and are prompted by the Spirit of the Lord; they acknowledge the kingdom of heaven; are forced into the vineyard of the Lord by pure, unfeigned love of God and of their neighbors; seek not the gifts of Balak, nor the tables of Jezebel; but they seek the praise of God and the salvation of your souls and commend their carnal cares to him, who, according to the word of his promise, furnishes the necessaries of life to all creatures upon earth, Matt. 13:25; Num. 22:28; 2 Pet. 2:16.

They teach the word of the law in the power of the Spirit, to the remission of sins and the denial of all flesh by the gospel of grace to the consolation, peace and joy of all the godfearing, pious hearts, who before disregarded the law and so greatly feared the wrath and judgment of the Lord.

They reprove and shun all false doctrine, deceit, abuse, idolatry and licentious reckless life, which is of the flesh and contrary to the word of the Lord; they use baptism, Supper, ban and all the ordinances of God as is commanded them by the word of the Lord, be it unto life or death; they admonish lords and princes, learned, unlearned, male and female, so far as they possibly can, if they are favored with a hearing; for the word of God excuses neither emperor nor king, doctor nor master, rich nor poor; all must follow the word of the Lord who wish to be saved, Matt. 28:19; Acts 2:38; 9:6.

They lead their lives in the fear of the Lord; they daily die, with holy Paul, for the sake of their brethren; they are pointed at by all the world; are slandered, persecuted and deemed the sap and substance of all knaves and rogues, notwithstanding they are ever ready to show their love and faithfulness to all, as was formerly the case with Jeremiah, Ezekiel, Zechariah the son of Berechiah, John the Baptist, the apostles and Christ himself; and how the pious are thanked and rewarded at the present time, for their love and services, the burning, the sword, the stake and the wheel show, 1 Cor. 15:32. Carefully observe and understand me, kind reader. Since the sending, calling, doctrine, sacraments and life of the preachers do not conform to this beforementioned rule, and are therefore not of God, as was said; for they, generally, do not enter but to destroy, steal and murder, as the Lord says; to adulterate and garble the precious word and the holy sacraments, to gratify their appetites; to exclude the word of God and institute their own; to kill the souls which would have eternal life; and promise life to those that will die the eternal death; and for the sake of a handful of barley and a mouthful of bread, as the prophet says; rule but do not serve; deceive but do not lead; corrupt but do not teach; weaken but do not cure; scatter but do not gather; shut the kingdom of heaven against man and freely lead all poor souls to hell. Behold, therefore it is that we do not hear them, neither can we conscientiously hear them; for the word of the Lord every where admonishes and commands us that we should be aware of them, flee and shun them, and not hear them, as was said before, Ezek. 13:14; 34:1; Jer. 5:26; Phil. 3:17; 1 Tim. 6:4; Tit. 3:8; 2 Jn. 1:8.

Judge now, kind reader, whether these reasons are not sufficient to shun the preachers. We have not here presented to you philosophical words, garbled flatterings, nor falsehood; but we have pointed you to such facts as you may daily observe and hear of among your preachers. This is what our much beloved brethren and sisters in Christ Jesus—fellow-partakers of the tribulation, kingdom and obedience of Christ, the faithful children of God, have for many long years, so frankly confessed, and so heroically asserted before this idolatrous, bloody world, in excessive measure of poverty, by preaching and writing, at the peril of life, property, blood, prison, banishment, water, fire, chains, gallows, wheels and the stake; but preachers remain preachers and the world remains the world. They, as appears, will never be converted. They, so firmly adhere to their idolatry, that they do not suffer themselves to be converted, Jer. 8.

Honored reader, we pray you for Christ's sake that you will rightly understand this our confession; do not think that we have written this out of bitter feelings or hatred, inasmuch as it so openly reproves, discovers and points out the shame of the preachers. O, no. We testify before you and before the Lord who has created us, that there is no hatred or bitterness in our hearts; for we know and confess that they are works of the flesh and will be rewarded by death. But we have written in purity of heart, as before him, who tries the hearts and reins, to the service of you and all mankind, no matter whether they be our opponents or not, learned or unlearned; to the service of all those who seek the truth; that we may so discover the judgment of the Babylonian whore, the covert wiles of the learned, by such expositions, that you and all godfearing hearts, by such exposition, may tire of the inhuman abominations, and so understand the word and truth of the Lord, and with all your hearts seek and obey the same, that you may be saved, Rom. 1:32; Gal. 5:21; 1 Cor. 6:10; Eph. 5:5; Rev. 17:1.

OF BAPTISM.

CONCERNING baptism we believe and confess that it is the institution, word, ordinance and command of the Lord; and therefore a holy, divine sacrament or sign by which faith and its powers, fruits and mysteries are gloriously represented and portrayed when rightly administered according to the ordinance of God and not after our own choice, namely: To the believing, and not to infants.

We teach and administer baptism upon the confession of faith, for these reasons: First, because Christ himself has commanded so, for he says, "Go ye into all the world and preach the gospel to every creature; he that believeth and is baptized, shall be saved," Mark 16:15; Matt. 28:19.

Secondly, because the holy apostles have taught and administered it upon the confession of faith, according to the commandment of God, and not to infants, Acts 2:38; 8:37; 10:47; 16:15; 18:8; 19:5. Thirdly, because the effect, or the signification, that is, that which is represented by baptism, is found with the believing and not with infants, Rom. 6:4; Col. 2:12; 1 Cor. 12:13; Eph. 4:4; 1 Pet. 3:21; Gal. 3:27.

Inasmuch as the Wisdom and Truth himself has commanded that we should baptize the believing; and as his faithful witnesses, the holy apostles, have not otherwise taught and administered it than according to the commandment of their Lord; and as the signification is only applicable to the believing and not to infants as remarked; and as, by the grace of the Lord, we acknowledge from the Scriptures that Moses and the prophets, yea, the Father himself, point us to Christ, that we shall hear him; and as, according to the doctrine of Paul, there can be laid no other foundation, nor other gospel preached but that preached to us by the apostles—behold—therefore it is that we teach, receive, assert and maintain baptism upon the confession of faith, at the cost of so much misery, even at the peril of property and life; for we truly confess, and that in accordance with the Scripture, which is the true light of our feet, that it is the institution, word, ordinance and command of the Lord, Jer. 23:33; Matt. 17:5; Mark 9:6; Luke 9:30; 1 Cor. 3:11; Ps. 119:105.

INFANT BAPTISM.

In regard to infant baptism we hold and confess, first, that it is a self-begotten rite and human righteousness; for in all the New Testament there is not a word said or commanded about baptizing infants, by Christ nor by the apostles.

Secondly, that it is a breaking and tearing to pieces of the ordinance of Christ; for he has commanded that the gospel should be preached and that those should be baptized who believe, Matt. 28:19; Mark 16:15. But here they baptize without divine command, without the preaching of the word, without knowledge, faith, repentance, new life, and without all consciousness and knowledge, yet it is called by the learned a holy, glorious work and a christian baptism and sacrament.

Thirdly, that it is a vain consolation and boasting of all the unrighteous; for, although they do not understand the word of God, do not know the truth and lead a licentious, carnal life, yet they boast themselves to be baptized christians.

Since infant baptism is such a pernicious superstition that it entirely destroys the Lord's baptism, and as the poor, blind world suffer themselves to be misled and consoled therewith, and as, besides, there is connected with it such fearful blasphemy, hypocrisy, adjuration, witchcraft and abuse of the glorious name of God that a godfearing heart may well be astounded thereat, therefore it is that we so strenuously oppose infant baptism, and openly confess that it is not of God or of his word but of anti-christ and of the bottomless pit.

Luther writes in a book on "Human doctrine" that that which is not commanded of God in religious matters of faith, is forbidden." Again, concerning the 12th chapter of Genesis he says, "That we should not accept any doctrines without certain reasons from the divine word."

Daniel writes, "Worship, without the word of God, is idolatry."

Philip Melancthon, in a book on the *Jurisdiction and authority of the church*, says, "That all worship which is not instituted of God by his express word, is false and wrong, let it be glozed over ever so much."

Here Luther and Melancthon have rightly expressed themselves according to the Scripture, although alas, they did not practice upon it. For if we read and well consider the Scriptures then we clearly find how pointedly God has commanded us that we shall not institute a religion of our own choice, but that we should do as he has commanded. On account of self-righteousness and self-chosen religion, Israel was severely visited and punished of the Lord.

Say not, beloved reader, as the ignorant do, that we thereby condemn our children because we do not suffer them to be baptized. O, no. For the Scripture does not connect the kingdom to words and water, but to the election and grace of the Father, in the merits of the death and blood of Christ.

Christ has promised the kingdom to small children, without baptism, Matt. 19:14; Mark 10:14; Luke 18:16. On account of this promise we are exceedingly rejoiced, and give thanks unto the Lord for the grace shown our children. Therfore, take heed, and mistake not; for to connect the election, grace, favor and kingdom of God to words, works, signs and the elements, is quite contrary to the merits, death, blood and word of the Lord; yea, open deceit, abomination and idolatry.

THE LORD'S HOLY SUPPER.

In the same manner we believe and confess concerning the Lord's Holy Supper, that it is a holy sacramental sign, instituted of the Lord himself, in the shape of bread and wine; and left to his own in remembrance of him, Matt. 26; Mark 14; Luke 22; 1 Cor. 11; which was also thus taught and administered by the apostles among the brethren, according to the commandment of the Lord, by which, first, the Lord's death is proclaimed, 1 Cor. 11; and also to remember how he offered his holy flesh and shed his precious blood for the remission of our sins, Matt. 26: 27; Mark 14: 24; Luke 22: 19.

Secondly, it is an emblem of christian love, of unity and of peace in the church of Christ. Paul says, "For we, being many, are one bread, and one body; for we are all partakers of that one bread," 1 Cor. 10: 17. For as a loaf being composed of many grains, is but one bread, so we, also, being composed of many members, are but one body in Christ; and as the members of a natural body are not disunited but are in every respect united and peaceable among themselves, so it is with all those who in Spirit and faith are true members of the body of Christ; and for this reason this same supper was called by Tertullian a brotherly meal, or supper of love.

Thirdly it is a communion of the flesh and blood of Christ, as Paul says, "The cup of blessing which we bless, is it not the communion of the blood of Christ? The bread which we break, is it not the communion of the body of Christ?" 1 Cor. 10: 16; which communion is, that Christ has accepted us in his great love and we are become partakers of him, as Paul says, "We are made partakers of Christ, if we hold the beginning of our confidence steadfast unto the end," Heb. 3: 14.

Inasmuch as it is a sign, which is left us of Christ, in such power that it is to represent and admonish us of his death, the love, peace and unity of the brethren and also the communion of his flesh and blood, as was said, therefore none can rightly partake of this Supper, according to Scripture, but he that is a disciple of Christ, flesh of his flesh, and bone of his bone, who seeks the reconciliation and remission of sins in no other means than, alone, in the merits, sacrifice, death and blood of Christ, who walks in unity, love and peace with his brethren, and who leads a pious unblamable life in Christ Jesus, according to the Scriptures.

Here you have the true Supper of our Lord Jesus Christ together with what it represents, briefly stated, which the mouth of the Lord has left and taught you by his holy word. If you would be a becoming guest at the Lord's table, and would rightly enjoy his bread and wine then you must also be his true disciple, that is, you must be an upright, pious and godly christian. Therefore, prove yourself according to the doctrine of Paul, 1 Cor. 11: 27, before you eat of this bread and drink of this cup; for before God no feigning avails. He did not institute this ceremony with the intention that God would be pleased in the mere eating of the bread or drinking of the wine. O, no. But he instituted it that thereby you should observe and faithfully conform yourself to that which is represented and admonished by this sacrament. For not the ceremony itself, but the meaning represented by it, rightly understood and fulfilled in actions, constitutes a sincere christian.

THE SUPPER OF THE PREACHERS.

In regard to the supper of the preachers we hold and confess, first, that it is a false and idolatrous consolation and sign of peace to all those who delight in walking upon the broad way, such as, greedy, covetous, avaricious, usurious, adulterous, lying, deceiving, proud, unrighteous persons. For, as it is represented to them, by their preachers, as being a means of the remission of their sins, they console themselves and think that if they partake of it they are the people of the Lord. O no. The ceremony makes no christian; for, so long as they do not convert themselves, and become new men, born of God, of spiritual mind, it is a vain baptism and a vain supper, even, if it were administered by either Peter or Paul. Paul says, "For in Jesus Christ neither circumcision availeth any thing, nor uncircumcision; but faith which worketh by love," Gal. 5:6, the new creature; and the keeping of the commandments of God, 1 Cor. 7:19; Matt. 18:4; Jn. 3:3—5; 2 Pet. 1:3.

Secondly, we assert that it is openly a feigned work, although it is acknowledged by few. For Christ instituted it in remembrance of his death, as a sign of christian peace, and as a communion of his flesh and blood; while the common world partake of the supper in semblance, as if they believed thus and were thus minded; and, yet, they seek the remission of their sins and their salvation in infant baptism, absolutions, and in bread and wine, as is manifest.

Besides, their fruits openly show that they are not the body of peace; for they make use of such tricks and perfidy amongst each other in buying and selling; some, also, commit adultery, lie and cheat; the one slanders, defames and robs the other, that it may be truly said of them that they do not acknowledge christian peace which is of God, and that they are not in the communion of Christ, but that they are in the communion of him, of whom John says, "Little children, let no man deceive you," "He that committeth sin, is of the devil; for the devil sinneth from the beginning," 1 Jn. 3:7, 8.

Thirdly, we say, that it is a horrible blasphemy, abomination and adultery, nay a new calf and Moaz; for the blind, reckless world sees plainly that it is a perishable fruit of earth which they have planted, cut, pressed and baked with their own hands, and which again returns to earth; that it must be taken care of by man lest the worms and age consume it—and yet it is called by many the imperishable precious flesh and blood of Christ, and worshipped and honored as the true Son of the living God, which we also with our ancestors have done these five hundred years, and which is yet done in many large kingdoms, principalities, cities and districts, as was in bygone times the case with Israel in the worship of the brazen serpent, which was afterwards broken in pieces by Hezekiah, king of Judah, 2 Kin. 18:4.

Behold, to such rude idolaters and deceivers has the apocalyptic Apollyon rendered the scribes of this world, that they have, by their own wisdom, doctrine and council, erected such a powerless, earthly cereal and fruit as being, or filling the place of the true Son of the Almighty and eternal God; behold, thus entirely has the noble Sun of righteousness lost its brightness and the Egyptian darkness covered the entire land, Rev. 9:2; Exod. 10:22.

Faithful reader, by this our exposition and confession of the preachers and their baptism, supper and envious hearts toward all the pious, learn the judgment of the finely attired woman, seated upon the scarlet colored beast, Rev. 17:3. Mark: The beast upon which the woman was seated, is full of names of blasphemy; understand the spiritual sense. The woman was arrayed in purple and scarlet color—in celebrations, churches, bells, choirs, organs, baptism and supper. The cup in her hand was of gold. They boast of the word of God—but are filled with abominations and filthiness of their fornication and have made all the world drunk therewith; and the name was written upon her forehead and may be read by all who have spiritual eyes, and is called, "MYSTERY, BABYLON THE GREAT, THE MOTHER OF HARLOTS AND ABOMINATIONS OF THE EARTH."

And although she is so finely arrayed that all kings commit fornication therewith, yet she is called a whore by the angel, and of such an inhuman and wolfish nature that she is "drunken with the blood of the saints, and with the blood of the martyrs of Jesus."

John, the holy man of God, saw this in the Spirit, and was astounded thereat. Yea, kind reader, whosoever rightly understands the abominable power, idolatrous array, spiritual enchantment and fornication, inhuman abominableness and fearful bloodthirstiness and tyranny of the woman may well be astounded thereat. Therefore, fear God and learn wisdom. We have, by the grace of God, thoroughly shown her, exposed her shame and diligently and in faithful love warned you against her.

THE SWEARING OF OATHS.

David says, who shall ascend into the hill of the Lord? or who shall stand in his holy place? he that hath clean hands, and a pure heart; who hath not lifted up his soul unto vanity, nor sworn deceitfully. He shall receive the blessing from the Lord, and righteousness from the God of his salvation," Ps. 24.

These words of David are full of spirit and wisdom, yet not regarded by the world. For every where we find guilty hands, unclean hearts, false doctrine, faithlessness and but little truth. Yea, it has come to this, among the children of men that the precious *yea* and *nay* which was commanded of the Lord himself can no longer be trusted. But nearly everything which is transacted before the magistracy, must be affirmed by an oath, although the Lord has so plainly forbidden the swearing of oaths to all christians, Matt. 5: 34.

The Scripture teaches that we should hear Christ, for he is the king in Jacob, Isa. 9: 7, the king of righteousness, the Teacher and Prophet promised of God, who hath taught us the word of the Father, and his word is truth, his commandment eternal life, Deut. 18: 15; Matt. 17: 5; Mark 9: 7; Isa. 9: 7; Jer. 23: 6; 33: 16; Deut. 18: 15; Acts 3: 26; Jn. 3: 17; 5: 46; 17: 17; 12: 50.

Inasmuch as we thus confess and cordially believe, and besides, confess that no emperor or king may rule or command contrary to his word, since he is the Head of all princes, Eph. 1: 21; Col. 2: 10; and is the King of all kings, Rev. 1: 5; 19: 16; and that unto him every knee shall bow which is in heaven, in earth or under the earth, Phil. 2; and as he has plainly forbidden us to swear, and pointed us to *yea* and *nay*, alone, therefore it is that we swear not, by the fear of God, nor dare swear, though we must hear and suffer so much on that account from the world.

Since throughout the world they act so fearlessly contrary to the word of God, in regard to this article; and as sometimes some of the godfearing are thereby put into difficulty, therefore I will, by the grace of God, show the kind hearted reader, from the word of God what the Holy Scriptures at different times teach and imply concerning the swearing of oaths.

First, the reader should observe that swearing was not always practiced uniformly among the people of the Lord. Before the law the holy fathers had a custom to lay their hands under the thighs, and thus swore to others, as may be read in the case of Abraham and his servant, Gen. 24: 3; and in the case of Jacob and his son Joseph, Gen. 47: 29—31. Joseph also swore by the life of Pharaoh, Gen. 42; and it seems that such swearing was customary among the Egyptians.

Secondly, the reader should observe, that Israel was bound by the law to swear by the name of the Lord and to keep their oath, as Moses says, "And ye shall not swear by my name falsely, neither shalt

THE SWEARING OF OATHS.

thou profane the name of thy God. I am the Lord, Lev. 19: 12; and this oath settled all dispute among Israel, Ex. 22: 11;" Heb. 6: 16. Thirdly, It should be observed, that Christ Jesus does not in the New Testament, point his disciples, in regard to swearing, to the law, as in the imperfect, which allowed swearing—but he points us now from the law to *yea* and *nay*, as in the perfect, and speaks thus, "Ye have heard that it hath been said by them of old time (that is, to the fathers under the law, by Moses), Thou shalt not foreswear thyself, but shalt perform unto the Lord thine oaths (that is, thou shalt swear truly and fulfill thine oath): but I (Christ) say unto you (my disciples), Swear not at all (that is, neither truly nor falsely); neither by heaven; for it is God's throne; nor by the earth; for it is his footstool; neither by Jerusalem; for it is the city of the great King. Neither shalt thou swear by thy head, because thou canst not make one hair white or black. But let your communication be, yea, yea; nay, nay: for whatsoever is more than these, cometh of evil." Here you have Christ's own doctrine and ordinance concerning swearing, Matt. 5: 35—37; Jas. 5: 12; Ex. 20: 7.

Behold, beloved reader, before these words of Christ all human laws and regulations concerning swearing must stand back and be abolished; such as *Juramentum Calumniae. Jerumentum de veritate dicenda, or Fede*; no matter how they be performed; be it by words, or by raising your hand, or holding your hands upon your breast, or upon a cross, or upon the New Testament, &c. And the truthful yea and nay, ordained of the Lord himself must be restituted, if the magistrates and subjects do not want licentiously to transgress the word of the Lord and reject it as vain; for, whatsoever is more than yea and nay (says Christ) cometh of evil. This same the holy James also teaches, "Above all things, my brethren, swear not, neither by heaven, neither by the earth, neither by any other oath: (understand, such as, *By God's word—By the Lord's cross—By the salvation of your soul*); but let your yea be yea, and your nay, nay (and not *So help me God, So help me God and all the saints*, as is alas, the custom in many places); lest ye fall into condemnation," Jas. 5: 12.

We are aware that the magistracy claim and say, *We are allowed to swear when justice is on our side.* This we simply answer with the word of the Lord. To swear truly was allowed to the Jews under the law; but the gospel forbids this to christians. As Christ does not allow us to swear, and as the magistracy, notwithstanding, proceed according to their rule, although contrary to the Scriptures, and as the Scriptures may not be set aside by man, what shall now the conscientious christian do? If he swear, he falls into the hands of the Lord; but if he does not swear he will have to bear the disfavor and punishment of the magistracy.

O, ye beloved lords! if we, now, had christian eyes and could see and sincerely acknowledge what it is, according to the justice of God, licentiously to despise and transgress the word of God, we would rather die than weaken or break the precious gospel of our Lord Jesus Christ, the ordinance of the eternal God, by temporal statutes and policies.

Nor would we, even, think of asking more than yea and nay, particularly of the pious, godfearing hearts, who, by the fear of their God, dare not speak anything but the truth; who esteem every word which comes from their mouths as an oath, and keep their yea and nay unto death; while, now, alas, they dare force them to swear to a trifle, as concerning some temporal goods or something of the kind, even with their fingers raised to heaven or with their hands upon the New Testament, by the God of heaven and by his living word.

O, ye beloved lords! how pitiably your teachers and leaders lead you upon the way which tends to damnation, who ever console you by saying that we should obey the magistracy (as is, also, becoming so far as is not contrary to God's word); as if the magistracy may act and rule against the Lord, at pleasure.

O, no, beloved lords, no! We warn you in faithful love. Repent, wake up and take heed. Your preachers deceive you. With God there is no respect of person. If you do not repent, are not born of God, become like unto children in malice, do not in love execute your office and service agreeably to the will of God, do not act justly to the poor and miserable, and do not walk obediently to the word of the Lord with godly, humble hearts, you will find your judge at the judgment day. Beloved lords, take to heart this saying, "Mighty men shall be mightily tormented," Wis. 6: 6.

Again, ye learned, you who by your flatterings and errors assert and maintain it, how dare you so flatly contradict the eternal wisdom and truth of God and say, Thou sayest: thou shalt not swear; but we say; *Thou mayest swear when the love, profit and need of thy neighbor require it.* We will leave it to your judgment whether that is not teaching contrary to Christ; as it is so plain that it was allowed to the Jews under the law, to swear sincerely; but to us, christians, it is forbidden and as it is very plain that, according to the New Testament, no love of neighbors nor kinsmen nor peril of life is any excuse to strain or break the word of the Lord, Matt. 10: 37; Mark 8: 38.

Therefore, worthy reader, if you fear the Lord and if it should happen that you are asked to swear, then pray the Most High for wisdom, courage and strength; do not listen to the flatterings of the learned, for they deceive you; do not look to numbers lest you follow in their evil ways, as Moses says, Respect no flesh in this matter, no difference who, what or where they be, but admonish them in a becoming manner and in love when they ask of you more than the Scriptures command; abide in the Lord's word which so plainly has forbidden you to swear; and let your yea and nay, be your oath, as was commanded, whether life or death be your lot, that you, by your courage and firm truthfulness, may admonish and reprove unto righteousness the useless, fruitless, vain world (who, in their faithlessness respect nothing less than the word of the Lord) by your truthful yea and nay; that some might yet be converted from their unrighteousness and thereby more deeply study the truth, and be saved, Matt. 5: 37; Phil. 2: 12.

It is better to incur the disfavor, scorn and slander of man and remain in the truth, than to be the favorite of man and sin against God. The good John Huss* confessed when he was asked to swear and said, *I am pressed on all sides. If I swear, I have eternal death; and if I do not swear, I will fall into your hands. But I would rather fall into your hands, without swearing than to sin in the face of God.* Thus considerately this worthy man weighed the oath.

Also read Hieronymus, Theophilact, Chrysostom, Erasmus of Rotterdam in their annotations; Philip Melancthon's Treatise on the fifth Chapter of Matthew. Heymon's Treatise on the Tenth Chapter of Revelations and also Origen, and you will find that in this article they agree with our foundation, faith, doctrine and confession. This is our foundation and understanding in regard to this article. Inasmuch as the Lord has forbidden us to swear at all (understand in temporal matters) neither sincerely nor falsely, as was said; and has commanded that our yea shall be yea and our nay, nay, Matt. 5: 37; as Paul and James, also, testify to this, 2 Cor. 1: 18; Jas. 5: 12; and as we know that no man, nor commandment of man may supersede God and his commandment, therefore it is that we, in temporal matters, dare not affirm to truth with more than yea or nay, as the case may be; for thus the word of the Lord teaches us.

Reader, mark. We say, *In temporal matters*, and for this reason: Because Christ sometimes in his teachings makes use of the word, *verily*, Matt. 18: 18; Jn. 3: 3, 5; 8: 34; 10: 1; and because Paul called upon the Lord as a witness of his soul. For this reason some think that swearing is allowable; not observing that Christ and Paul did not do this in speaking of temporal matters, as in a matter of flesh or blood, or money or property; but as an affirmation of the eternal truth, to the praise of God and to the salvation and edification of their brethren.

We hereby pray all lords and magistrates, for Jesus' sake, to fear the Lord sincerely, and to conform their policy, in this matter of swearing, to the word of the Lord,

---

*John Huss was condemned by the Papists, at their council, at Constance, to be burned, in 1415.

and to consider why they require the oath, namely: That that shall be fulfilled to which one swears. Inasmuch as we deem our yea and nay to be no less than an oath, why require any further affirmation at our hands than the word of the Lord teaches and allows; for, by the grace of God, we trust, inasmuch as we are partakers of the Lord, and adhere to the word in which yea is amen—that it will be found with us that it is yea where it should be yea, and nay where it should be nay; much more so than with the world under strong oaths. But in case that a man's yea and nay is not kept, let him be punished as a perjurer. That it is yea and amen with all true christians, is sufficiently proven by those who, in our Netherlands, are so tyrannically visited with imprisonment, confiscation and torture; besides, with fire, the stake and the sword; while with one word they could escape all these if they would but break their yea and nay; but as they are born of the truth, therefore they walk in the truth and testify to the truth unto death, as may be abundantly seen in Flanders, Braband, Holland, West Vriesland, and other places.

CONCLUSION.

It is manifest, honored reader, that the world is so degenerated that it esteems every thing wrong which God teaches, commands and desires, and hates it with envious hearts persecutes and destroys it. On the contrary, all that which God hates, accurses and esteems as an abomination, it looks upon as good, and diligently asserts and maintains; and yet they want to be the holy, christian church and the people of God, as if we could be such by the mere name; by baptizing children &c.; without faith, the new birth, and the Spirit and obedience of God. O, no, reader, no. Take heed. Your consolers deceive you and corrupt the way you should go, Isa. 3: 11.

Inasmuch as the world is so entirely degenerated, as was said, and as our opponents so shamefully lie and war against us, that we cannot answer for ourselves, as is manifest, therefore we have written this our confession, that every one who may read, hear or see it, may know why and whereby we seek to be saved—why we do not hear the preachers, and why we so strictly administer baptism to the believing and oppose infant baptism; what is represented by the Lord's Holy Supper and what abominations are implied in the baptism of the learned; and that it is not allowed to a true christian to swear in temporal matters, but only affirm by yea and nay. And by so doing we have compared truth with falsehood, light with darkness and white with black, as you will perceive. If you do not want to be willfully blind, you have here a good eye-salve. Yea, we have presented it so plainly and clearly that you must acknowledge it to be the truth; or else reject it in perverseness, and say, No, I do not want to believe it thus. What kind of a christian you are you may consider for yourself.

Kind reader, do not associate with those who say unto God, "Depart from us; for we desire not the knowledge of thy ways," Job 21: 14. Nor with those who are intent upon blood, for their reward will be death, Rom. 1: 32; Rev. 21: 27. Behold, this is our foundation, as you here have read. If, now, you are of a pious mind and not led by the blind spirit of the spiritual whoredom, then judge our cause according to the word and truth of the Lord. If you do not understand it then fear God and pray. All those who are born of God and inclined to the word of the Lord, must acknowledge that our doctrine is of God and that truth is on our side; whosoever accepts them and abides in them unto the end, has eternal life; but whosoever rejects them does not reject us, but Christ Jesus himself who has thus taught from the mouth of his Father and sealed it with his blood, Rev. 1: 5; 1 Pet. 1: 19; Acts 20: 28. The gracious Father, through his beloved Son, Jesus Christ our Lord, enlighten you and all hungry hearts by the gift of his Holy Spirit, and lead you by his strength into his eternal, saving truth, Amen.

To the praise of God and the service of all mankind.

MENNO SIMON.

A. D. 1552.

QUESTIONS AND ANSWERS.

QUESTION 1. Is separation a command or is it a counsel of God?

Answer. Let every one weigh the words of Christ and of Paul, referred to above, and he will discover whether it is a divine commandment or whether it is a counsel. Every thing which Paul says in regard to separation he generally speaks in the imperative mode; that is, in a commanding manner. *Expurgo*, that is, Purge, 1 Cor. 5: 7. *Profligo*, that is, drive out. *Sejungere*, that is, withdraw from, 1 Tim. 6: 5; *Fuge*, that is, flee, Tit. 3: 9. Again, "We command you, brethren, in the name of our Lord Jesus Christ," 2 Thess. 3: 6. I think, brethren, these Scriptures show that it is a command; and if it even were not a command but an advice of God, Should we not diligently follow such advice? If my spirit despise the counsel of the Holy Spirit, then I truly acknowledge that my spirit is not of God. And to what end many have come who did not follow God's Spirit, but their own, may be read in many passages of sacred history and may be seen in many instances, at the present time.

QUESTION 2. If any person should not maintain this ban and yet be pious otherwise, should such an one be banned on that account?

Answer. Whoever is pious will show his piety in obedience, and not knowingly or willfully despise and disregard the word, commandment, will, counsel, admonition and doctrine of God. For if any one willfully keeps *commercium* (intercourse, company) with such whose company is forbidden in Scripture, to be kept, then we must come to the conclusion that he despises the word of God, yea, is in open rebellion and refractoriness (I speak of those who well know and acknowledge, and yet do so). "For rebellion is as the sin of witchcraft and stubbornness is as iniquity and idolatry," 1 Sam. 15: 23.

Since the Scriptures admonishes and commands, That we shall not associate with such, nor eat with them, nor greet them, nor receive them into our houses, &c.; and yet if some body should say, I will associate with them, I will eat with them, I will greet them in the Lord and receive them into my house—he would plainly prove that he did not fear the commandment and admonition of the Lord, but that he despised it, rejected the Holy Spirit and that he trusted, honored and followed his own opinion rather than the word of God. Now judge for yourself what kind of a sin it is not to be willing to hear and obey God's word. Paul says, "Now we command you, brethren, in the name of our Lord Jesus Christ, that ye withdraw yourselves from every brother that walketh disorderly, and not after the tradition which ye received of us;" again, "And if any man obey not our word by this epistle, note that man, and have no company with him, that he may be ashamed," 2 Thess. 3: 6, 14. Inasmuch as the ban was so strictly commanded by the Lord, and practiced by the apostles, Matt. 18: 17; therefore we must also use it and obey it, since we are thus taught and enlightened by God, or else we should be shunned by the church of God. This must be acknowledged.

QUESTION 3. Should husband and wife shun each other on account of the ban—as also parents and children?

Answer. First, that the rule of the ban is a general rule, and excepts none; neither husband nor wife, nor parent nor child. For God's judgment judges all flesh with the same judgment and knows no respect of persons. Inasmuch as the rule of the ban is general, excepts none, and is no respecter of persons—therefore it is reasonable and necessary to hear and obey the word of the Lord in this respect; no matter whether it be husband or wife, parents or children, Rom. 2: 11; Gal. 6: 1; Eph. 6: 9; Col. 3: 25; Jas. 2: 4; 1 Pet. 1: 17.

Secondly we say, That separation must be made by the church; and therefore the husband must consent and vote with the church, in the separation of his wife; and the wife in the separation of her husband. If the pious consort must give his consent, then it is also becoming that he also shun her, with the church; for what use is there in the ban when the shunning and avoiding are not connected with it, 1 Cor. 5: 3.

Thirdly we say, That the ban was instituted to make ashamed unto reformation. Do not understand this shame as the world is ashamed; but understand as in the conscience, and therefore let it be done in all discretion, reasonableness and love. If, then the husband or wife, parent or child is judged in the church, in the name of Christ and by virtue of Christ, to be banned, it becomes us (inasmuch as the evangelical ban is unto reformation) according to the counsel of the Holy Spirit, to seek the reformation of our own body, namely, of our consort, and also of our nearest kinsfolk as parent or child; for spiritual love must be preferred to any thing else; aside from this I would care for them and provide the temporal necessaries of life, so far as it would be in my power.

Fourthly we say, That the ban was given, that we should not be leavened by the leaven of false doctrine or of unclean flesh, by the degenerated. And as it is plain that none can corrupt and leaven us more than our own consorts, parent, &c., therefore the Holy Spirit counsels us to shun them, lest they leaven our faith and thus make us ashamed before God. If we love husband or wife, parent or child more than Christ Jesus, we cannot possibly be the disciples of Christ, Matt. 10: 37; Luke 14: 26.

Some object to this, saying, that there is no divorce but by reason of adultery. This is just what we say; and therefore we do not speak of divorce; but of shunning, and that for the beforementioned reasons. To shunning Paul has decidedly consented, 1 Cor. 7: 10; although this is not always coupled with adultery; but not to divorce. For divorce is not allowed by the Scripture only by reason of adultery, Matt. 5: 32; Luke 6: 18; therefore we shall never consent to it for other reasons.

Therefore we understand it that the husband should shun his wife, the wife her husband, parents their children and the children their parents when they apostatize. For the rule of the ban is general. They must consent, with the church, to their sentence, they must seek their scriptural shame unto reformation and diligently watch, lest they be leavened by them, as said above.

Beloved in the Lord, I would here sincerely pray you that you would make a difference between commandment and commandment and not consider all commandments as equally hard. For adultery, idolatry, shedding blood, and the like shameful and abominable works of the flesh will be punished more severely than a misunderstanding in regard to the ban, and particularly when not committed willfully and perversely. Therefore beware, that in this matter of matrimony, you press none farther than he is taught of God, and that he in his conscience can bear, and thus seethe the kid in his mother's milk, Ex. 23: 19; 34: 26; Deut. 14: 21. On every hand the Scriptures teach that we should bear with the weak. Brethren, it is a delicate matter. I know too well what has been the result of pressing this matter too far by some in my time, Rom. 15: 1; Gal. 6: 4. Therefore I advise you to point all to the sure and certain ground. And those consciences that are through the Scripture, and the Holy Spirit, free and unencumbered, will freely, without the interference of any one, by the unction of the Holy Spirit and not by human encouragement, do that which he advises, teaches and commands in the Holy Scripture," if it should be that either consort should be banned. For verily I know that whoever obeys the Holy Spirit, with faithful heart will never be made ashamed.

QUESTION 4. Should we greet one that is banned, with the common, every day greeting, or return our respects at his greeting? Since John says, "If there come any unto you, and bring not this doctrine, receive him not into your house, neither bid him God speed; for he that biddeth him God speed is partaker of his evil deeds," 2 Jn. 10, 11.

Answer. Mildness, politeness, respectfulness and friendliness to all mankind becomes all christians. If, then, an apostate should greet me with the common greeting of *Good Morning*, or *Good Day* and I should be silent; if he should be respectful to me and I should turn my face from him, and bear myself austerely and unfriendly toward him, I might well be ashamed of myself, as Syrach says. For how can such an one be convinced, led to repentance, and be moved to do better, by such austerity? The ban is not given to destroy but to build up. If it should be said, That John has forbidden such greeting, I for myself would say, That, before my God, I can not understand that John said this in regard to the every day greeting. But that he says, That if some deceiver should come to us who has left the doctrine of Christ that we should not receive such an one into our houses, lest he deceive us; and that we should not greet him as a brother lest we have communion with him. But not so with the worldly greeting For if the worldly greeting have such power in itself that it causes the communion of the vain works of those whom I greet, then it must follow that I would have communion with the adultery, fornication, drunkenness, avarice, idolatry and blood shed of the world, whenever I should greet a worldly man with the common greeting or return his compliment. O no. But the greeting or kiss of peace signifies the communion. Yet if one should have conscientious scruples in this matter, with such an one I do not dispute about it. For it is not worth contending about. But I would much rather see all scruples in regard to this matter, removed, and have christian discretion, love, politeness and respectfulness practiced, to the building up, and not unbecoming stubbornness, unfriendliness, malice and unmercifulness to the destruction of our fellow man. Brethren, beware of discord. The Lord grant every godfearing person a wholesome understanding of his holy word, Amen.

QUESTION 5. Are we allowed to show the banned any charity, love and mercy?

Answer. Every one should consider, first, the exact meaning of the word *commercium* (intercourse, communion).

Secondly, for what reason and purpose the ban was ordained by the Holy Spirit, in the Scriptures.

Thirdly, how a true, regenerated christian is minded.

Fourthly, how the merciful Father himself acts with those who are already worthy of his judgment and wrath.

All those who can rightly see into these will doubtlessly not deny charity, love and mercy to the banned. For the word *commercium* does not forbid these, but it forbids daily company, conversation, society and business as was explained above. The ban is also a work of divine love and not of perverse, unmerciful, heathenish cruelty. A true christian will serve, aid and commiserate with every body; yea, even with his most bitter enemies. Austerity, cruelty, and unmercifulness he sincerely hates. He has a nature like his Father of whom he is born, "For he maketh his sun to rise on the evil and on the good, and sendeth rain on the just and on the unjust." If I, then, be of a different nature, I show that I am not his child.

Therefore I say with our faithful brother Dietrick Philip that we should not *practice* the ban to the destruction of mankind (as the Pharisees did their Sabbath) but to their improvement; and thus we desire to serve the bodies of the fallen, in love, reasonableness and humility, with our temporal goods when necessary, and their souls with the spiritual goods of the Holy Word; and should rather show mercy to the wounded, with the Samaritan, than to pass by him with the priest and Levite. James says, "For he shall have judgment without mercy, that hath showed no mercy, and mercy rejoiceth against judgment." "Be ye therefore merciful as your Father also is merciful." "Blessed are the merciful; for they shall obtain mercy," Jas. 2: 13; Luke 16: 36; Matt. 5: 7. In short, if we understand the true meaning of the word *commercium;* understand for what reason and purpose the ban was instituted; how a true christian is and should be minded; and conform ourselves to the example of Christ and of God, then the matter is clear. And if we have not this grace we will shamefully err in this ban and be cruel, unmerciful christians; from which error and abomination may the gracious

QUESTIONS AND ANSWERS.

Father eternally save all his beloved children.

Brethren, I tell the truth and lie not when I say that I sincerely hate such unmerciful and cruel mindedness. Nor do I wish to be considered a brother of such unmerciful, cruel brethren, if there should be such, unless they desist from such abomination, and discreetly follow, in love and mercy, the example of God and Christ. For my heart cannot consent to such unmerciful action which exceeds the cruelty of the heathen and Turks; and by the grace of God I will fight against it with the sword of the Lord unto death. For it is against the doctrine of the New Testament, and contrary to the Spirit, mind and nature of God and Christ, according to which all the Scriptures of the New Testament should be judged and understood. All those who do not understand it thus are already in great error.

But in case my necessary service, charity, love and mercy should become a *commercium*, or that my soul should thereby be led into corruption, then we confess (the Lord must be glorified), that our daily intercourse is forbidden in the Scripture, and that it is better to leave off our charity, love and mercy, than to ensnare our souls thereby and lead them into error. The unction of the Holy Spirit will teach us what we should best do in these premises.

QUESTION 6. Are we allowed to sell to, and buy of the apostates, inasmuch as Paul says that we should not have intercourse with them; and yet the disciples bought victuals in Sychar, and the Jews dealt with the Gentiles? Jn. 4:5.

Answer. That the apostles bought victuals in Sychar proves nothing at all; for many of the Samaritans were a remnant of the ten tribes, as we have sufficiently shown above, from the Holy Scripture. But we do not deny that the Jews dealt with the Gentiles, yet they shunned their *commercium*, that is, their daily association, company and conversation, and did not eat nor drink with them, as the writings of the evangelist sufficiently and plainly show in many scriptural passages.

And inasmuch as Christ points us to the Jewish ban or shunning, namely, That as they shunned the gentiles and sinners, so we should likewise shun an apostate christian; and as the Jews had dealings with them, although they shunned their daily intercourse in company, association and conversation; therefore we say that we can not maintain, either by the Jewish example to which Christ points or by any explicit Scripture, that we should not in any manner deal with the apostate, if no such daily intercourse arises therefrom. For such intercourse with the apostate is strictly prohibited by Scripture; and since it is prohibited, it is manifest that a pious, godfearing christian could have no apostate as a regular buyer or seller. For as I have daily to get my cloth, bread, corn, salt, &c., and exchange for it my grain, butter, &c., it can not fail but that intercourse will arise therefrom. But with a trading which is conducted without such intercourse this is not the case.

And because such merchandizing, which is carried on without intercourse can not be avoided by virtue of the Scripture, as was said, therefore we would pray all godfearing brethren and sisters in the Lord, for the sake of God and of love, to act in this matter, as in all others, as reasonable, good, discreet, wise and prudent christians, and not as vain, reckless, self-conceited, proud, obdurate and offensive boasters; for a true christian should always strive after that which is the best and the surest, and follow the pure, unfeigned love, lest he abuse the freedom which he seems to have, to the injury and hindrance of his own soul, to the affliction and destruction of his beloved brethren, to the scornful boasting of the perverse, and to the shameful blemishing of the Holy word and the afflicted church of Christ. Besides, I pray and desire in like manner, that none will thus in the least be offended at his brother and mistake and judge him by an unscriptural judgment; as he has in this case no reproving example among the Jews nor forbidding word [in the Scriptures.]

O my sincerely beloved brethren! let us sincerely pray for understanding and wisdom, that all misunderstanding, error, jealousy, offense, division and undue reports may once be exterminated, root and branch; that a wholesome understanding, doctrine, friendship, love, edification and opinion may be restituted and prevail. Let every one look with pure eyes and impartial hearts to the example to which Christ points, and to the wholesome, natural meaning of the holy apostles, and let true, christian love ever prevail, and he will know, by the grace of God, how he should act in this matter.

QUESTION 7. Are we allowed to be seated with an apostate in a ship or wagon, or to eat with them at the table of a tavern?

Answer. The first part of this question, namely, to be seated with an apostate in a ship or vehicle, when the captain or driver is no apostate, we deem childish and useless, since this so often happens without intercourse, and must needs happen. As to the second part, namely, to eat at the table with an apostate, while traveling, we can point the questioner to no surer ground and answer than this, namely, We advise, pray and admonish every pious christian, as he loves Christ and his word, to fear God sincerely, and follow the most certain way, that is, not to eat by or with him; for thereby none can be deceived; and if perchance some godfearing brother might do so, then let every one beware, lest he sin against his brother by an unscriptural judgment; for none may judge unless he have the judging word on his side.

Whosoever fears God, whosoever desires to follow after his holy word, with all his strength; loves his brother; seeks to avoid all offense and desires to walk in the house of God in all peace and unity, will act justly in all things and will not offend or afflict his brethren.

QUESTION 8. Who, according to Scripture, should be banned or excommunicated?

Answer. Christ says, Matt. 18: 15—17, If thy brother trespass against thee, &c., and will not hear thee nor the witnesses, nor the church, let him be unto thee as a heathen man and a publican. And Paul, "If any man that is called a brother, be a fornicator, or covetous, or an idolater, or a railer, or a drunkard, or an extortioner; with such an one no not to eat," 1 Cor. 5: 11; Jer. 16: 8. To this class also belong perjurers, thieves, violent persons, haters, fighters and all those who walk in open, well known, damnable works of the flesh, of which Paul enumerates a great many, Rom. 1: 29; Gal. 5: 19; 1 Cor. 6: 9; Eph. 5: 5. Again, disorderly persons, working not at all, but which are busy bodies; such as do not abide in the doctrine of Christ and his apostles and do not walk therein, but are disobedient, 2 Thess. 3: 11, 14. Again, masters of sects. Again, those who give offense, cause dispute and discord concerning the doctrine of Christ and of his apostles.

In short, all those who openly lead a shameful, carnal life, and those who are corrupted by a heretical, unclean doctrine, Tit. 3: 10, and who will not be overcome by the wine and oil of the Holy Spirit, but remain, after they have been admonished and sought to be regained in all love and reasonableness, obdurate in their corrupted walk and opinion. They should, at last, in the name of our Lord Jesus Christ, by the power of the Holy Spirit, that is, by the binding word of God, be reluctantly but unanimously separated from the church of Christ, and afterward, according to the Scriptures, be shunned in all divine obedience, until they repent, Rom. 16: 16; Gal. 5: 16; 1 Tim. 5: 24; 6: 3.

CONCLUSION.

MOST beloved brethren and sisters in the Lord, as we have hinted in the beginning of this admonition, and as you are all aware that for some years there have been much division and discord concerning the ban by which christian love has been and is yet much retarded; therefore I have endeavored (while I see that this is carried on without the foundation of the word, without reason and discretion, and without the nature of Christ Jesus and his holy gospel, both as to stringency or leniency, to the ensnarement of many consciences; as every one asserts and follows his own view as the best,

CONCLUSION.

to advise all my beloved brethren and sisters in the Lord who seek the amiable peace and unity, not to seek more nor less than the Scriptures teach, show and require), to write this explanation of the ban or separation, compiled with the greatest care from the Holy Scriptures and to the promotion of the peace of all the pious children of God; and trust, before God, that this will satisfy all humble, peaceable consciences; for, behold, I seek nothing, before God through Christ Jesus, but that these unscriptural proceedings and mournful disputations concerning the ban, both as to stringency and leniency, may be thereby ended, and that the noble, glorious peace and unity in Christ Jesus may remain unbroken and undamaged.

Although I have written this out of pure love and upheld the peace according to the true nature and direction of the Holy Word, as before my God who shall judge me at the last day; yet I know that by some I will not be thanked; for to some it will be too stringent, and too lenient to others; but I must bear with this, as I have done these fifteen years. Still, I would pray you, for the sake of the merits of the precious blood of my Lord Jesus Christ, that if any one should find fault with this my treatise, be it on account of mildness or stringency, not to do so otherwise than by authority of the Word, Spirit and life of the Lord, and not recklessly and without thought, lest he mistake. Whatsoever any person can advance and prove thereby I will gladly hear and be obedient thereunto; but I dare not go higher nor lower, more stringent nor lenient than the Scriptures and the Holy Spirit teach me; and that out of great fear and anxiety of my conscience, lest I again burden the godfearing hearts who now have renounced the commandments of men, with those commandments. Self-conceit and human opinions I hate, nor do I desire them; for I know what tribulation and affliction they have caused me for many years.

Sincerely beloved brethren and sisters in Christ Jesus! Understand my writings rightly, and faithfully follow this my advice, explanation, understanding and admonition, and you will doubtlessly find great peace and joy (so far as regards separation) among all the brethren; but whosoever rejects them, let him take heed, for he will one day meet his Judge.

In short, it is my inward and outward faith, foundation and confession of the separation which I never before wrote and published with such clearness and minuteness. But now necessity urges me; and with this my faith, foundation and confession, which I thus had from the beginning, I desire to die in Christ Jesus and to appear before the throne of God; for I am aware that it is the most important showing of the separation which can be explained and taught to the godfearing consciences, from the Holy Scriptures. Therefore I ask of all my brethren and sisters in the Lord to leave me at peace about this matter and not to trouble me further; for, by the grace of God, there will be nothing heard from my lips but that which my writings teach and imply.

Let every brother seek the wholesome understanding of the word of Christ and of his apostles, with a humble spirit, in brotherly love and in christian peace, and he will, doubtlessly, drive back all unscriptural dispute and discord and sincerely follow the true god-pleasing unity.

May the Almighty, merciful Father, through his blessd Son Christ Jesus, grant all brethren and sisters the heavenly gift of the Holy Spirit that there may become an end to this sad dispute and discord, and thus become a sound body with the perfect bond of unfeigned, christian love, bound together in becoming, steady peace in Christ Jesus, Amen.

Beloved brethren and sisters in the Lord, I pray you by the bloody wounds of my Lord Jesus Christ to beware of dispute and discord, and that you may receive this my labor with affectionate hearts, for in true christian love I have written it to your service, as before God in Christ Jesus.

MENNO SIMON.

A. D. 1550.

A THOROUGH ANSWER

TO THE

SLANDER, DEFAMATION, BACKBITING,

UNSEASONED AND BITTER WORDS OF

Zylis and Lemmekes,

CONCERNING

OUR FOUNDATION AND DOCTRINE, FULL OF INSTRUCTION AND ADMONITION, WHICH DOCTRINE IS (IN OUR OPINION) THE UNADULTERATED FOUNDATION AND DOCTRINE OF THE HOLY APOSTLES, CONCERNING THE

BAN, SEPARATION OR SHUNNING.

BY

MENNO SIMON.

"The man that is accustomed to opprobrious words will never be reformed all the days of his life," Eccl. 23 : 15.

"The dispostion of a liar is dishonorable, and his shame is ever with him," Eccl. 20 : 26.

"For other foundation can no man lay than that is laid, which is Jesus Christ," 1 Cor. 3 : 11.

ELKHART, INDIANA:
PUBLISHED BY JOHN F. FUNK AND BROTHER.
1871.

If thy brother, the son of thy mother, or thy son, or thy daughter, or the wife of thy bosom, or thy friend, which is as thine own soul, entice thee secretly, saying, Let us go and serve other gods, which thou hast not known, thou, nor thy fathers; Namely, of the gods of the people which are round about you, nigh unto thee, or far from thee, from the one end of the earth, even unto the other end of the earth, thou shalt not consent unto him, nor hearken unto him; neither shall thine eye pity him, neither shalt thou spare him, neither shalt thou conceal him; but thou shalt surely kill him; thine hand shall be first upon him to put him to death, and afterwards the hand of all the people. * * Because he hath sought to thrust thee away from the Lord thy God, which brought thee out of the land of Egypt, from the house of bondage. And all Israel shall hear, and fear, and shall do no more any such wickedness as this is among you." "Then his father and his mother that begat him, shall say unto him, Thou shalt not live; for thou speakest lies in the name of the Lord: And his father and his mother that begat him, shall thrust him through when he prophesieth," Deut. 13: 6—11; Zech. 13: 3.

THOROUGH ANSWER,

REPLETE WITH

Instruction and Admonition.

A true, pure and pious mind, unfeigned love of God and neighbor, a true and well seasoned tongue which speaks nothing else but the trnth, and a resigned, impartial and pious heart wherein the Holy Spirit dwells, together with the sure knowledge of Jesus Christ and of his holy word, I wish to Zylis and Lemmekes, to all righteousness, now and forever, from my inmost heart, Amen.

I HEAR and understand, dear friends, that you, alas, mistake yourselves against God and against myself, both by writing and speaking; using untrue, slanderous words and abominable, bitter backbiting, which are not becoming a christian; which I had not in the least expected from you; for I thought that you were so taught of the Lord that you would not thus enviously smite your poor brother who cannot now answer for himself; nor that you would, as is the case, defame your faithful friend, who, according to his small talent, has ever sincerely served you and all the pious in Christ, and thus thank him for his faithful service and love. But my good opinion of you, alas, has been a mistake in this case. For my case in regard to you is the same as that of the good Jeremiah, when his enviers counseled about him, and said, "Come, and let us smite him with the tongue, and let us not give heed to any of his words," Jer. 18:18. Yet the innocence of my hands, the true intention of my labors, the unfeigned love of my unction, together with the incontrovertible, sure foundation of the truth shall be my refuge, yea, my invincible shield and surety against all unreasonable upbraiders and defamers, now and at all times. By the grace of God I am sure of this.

Inasmuch as you prove yourselves quite unreasonable and devoid of love (as I am at such a great distance from you, yea, as if you never had heard a syllable of the word of the Lord), by which you do not only make me an abomination and stench (which I deem very little in you) in the sight of many of those who are not versed in this matter, but also make the holy word such, which, in my weakness, has been preached by me for some time, not altogether without fruit, and thus deter those of little understanding from the right way, and strengthen them in their blindness, and rob them of the true light and understanding of the true ban; therefore I am forced by a sense of duty to send you and your brethren (whom you deprive of the light, by your cunning), my humble, but true reply, as briefly and clearly as possible, in writing, as I can not attend personally, hoping that you may thereby take the matter to heart and henceforth sin no more, but truly repent of your great mistake, and yet find grace in that day before the Lord and his righteous judgment. Therefore I pray you earnestly to consider that to which I shall point you.

Understand, then, first, that I am blamed by Zylis of being a trifler. The reason is that (as he says) I should have published two small books which contradict each other. To which I thus answer, in my humility: It is well known to a great many that I have been combatted on all sides by many sharp spirits, for more than twenty-three years; and that I have had to withstand many a hard assault. Yet (glory to him who has saved me) I did not go, unsteadily, from one church to the other as both of you have done (do not think hard of my thus writing; for you urge me to it); but I remained firm and peaceable in the faith and doctrine with my beloved brethren until this day. And as I have borne testimony in the name of the Lord in such dark days, I trust, by the grace of God, to remain firm and peaceable, so long as I remain in this tabernacle. To which of us this name of trifler (if so it must be called) is now applicable, I will leave to the judgment of every intelligent reader. But as to the two publications of which you seem to think hard, this is my plain reply: Eighteen or nineteen years ago, when I wrote the first book, I was not well enough enlightened to understand all things thoroughly; and I freely and frankly admit, that until that time I included all sin in three admonitions. This I acknowledge verbally and in writing and do not deny it. But, as all well minded servants of God, who seek the crucified Christ and not their own honor or flesh, are ever ready to investigate the sure foundation of truth still further, thus I, the least of all servants (on account of many abominations which were, from time to time discovered in the church, and also on account of the miserable disputation and discord which crept in without my fault) came to a serious reflection concerning this matter and, at last, plainly saw that we men may not retain those whom God himself, by his Spirit and word excludes, or else the church of Christ must be divided. This is as clear as day.

Therefore it would be advisable for you to season your words a little better. For you do not thereby slander and despise me, but the Holy Spirit, which, according to the word of promise, has led me, his poor, weak servant and instrument into his truth and discovered unto me the true foundation in this matter.

Yea, dear men, if I, on that account, am to be called by you, a trifler because I was not perfectly enlightened from the beginning, nor claim to be perfectly enlightened at this hour, O Lord! what a trifler you would call the beloved Peter and others, if they were alive to-day, and if you loved him no more than you love me, as he, although taught by the Lord's mouth and enlightened by the Holy Spirit, was yet so unintelligent that he dared not preach the gospel to the heathen until he was admonished and told to do so by a heavenly vision or revelation from God, and thus first took the liberty to teach them.

Oh! oh! Terrible is the word, that slanderers, defamers and liars shall have no part in the kingdom of God. Behold, chosen Zylis and Lemmekes, let it be told you.

Secondly, I understand besides, that Zylis said I published a book from which nothing but hatred, murder and blasphemy could emanate.

To which I reply with Christ's own words, thus. "Think not that I am come to send peace on earth; I came not to send peace, but a sword," Matt. 10:34. At another place, "I am come to send fire on the earth; and what will I, if it be already kindled?" Luke 12:49. From which words and also from experience it is plain that the pure doctrine of Christ and of his holy apostles, truly taught and practiced upon, is of such a nature that it engenders, among the obdurate and unbelieving, hatred, envy, falsehood, slander, upbraiding, persecution, rebellion, murder, misery and tribulation. But should we not on this account teach and practice upon the pure doctrine and truth? If you answer in the affirmative, you judge that we should not suppress the truth on account of danger, if that should be the result, but that notwithstanding it should be taught and practiced upon. And what kind of a spirit it is that teaches you this pretense of hatred, murder, blasphemy, &c., by which you frighten the poor people from the truth, I will leave you to reflect upon in the fear of God. But if you answer in the negative you make yourselves merely men of blood, as you still continue in teaching, baptizing and the like, while you daily hear that many a pious child is, on that account, robbed, and even murdered. O, I pray you, learn to know the spirit of upbraiding. Say, beloved, is not the word of Christ called the word of the cross? You must answer in the affirmative. For here, in the kingdom and reign of Christ upon earth, the command to the believing, is nothing but to deny yourselves and take up the cross and follow him, Matt. 16: 24. If we love father, mother, husband, wife, children, property or ourselves better than Christ, we are not worthy of him. Yea, he says, if we do not hate all these we cannot be his disciples, Matt. 10: 37. Inasmuch as this is the case with the gospel of Christ, as has been heard; therefore your trifling darts and powerless thunderbolts of hatred, murder and blasphemy, cannot nor should not deter me in the least, so long as you do not convince me by the binding truth and power of the divine, Holy Scriptures, that I, in this matter of the ban or separation, have mistaken the word of the Lord, or in any manner not fulfilled the requirements thereof; but I am the more assured, by your slander, inasmuch as it is done altogether without truth or the Scripture, that the invincible foundation of truth and of the immutable word of the Lord is on our side. But as for the word slander or blasphemy, I would make this my brotherly reply: Learn to know with more fear of God what, according to the Scripture, is blasphemy or sinning against the Holy Spirit. For in my opinion it is this, that when the truth of God is imprinted and conceived into the heart of man, with such a power of the divine, Holy Scripture, by the Spirit and finger of his power, that we, convinced in spirit, must confess that it is the true foundation of truth, and can not be controverted by the Scriptures, yet, by reason of self-conceit or choice we are so audacious and stubborn as to persist in hating, upbraiding and slandering this inspired and truly known truth, or ascribing it to the devil, by our ambitious, partial, proud and obdurate flesh, as the obdurate Pharisees and Scribes ascribed the glorious miracles and power of Christ to Beelzebub. This the mouth of the Lord (if we persevere, as I understand it) calls blasphemy and sinning against the Holy Spirit. Of which they will not be forgiven in this world nor in the world to come. O, dear, take heed, Luke 12: 10.

Inasmuch as such slander and sin, is the true blasphemy and sin in the Holy Spirit, as was heard, and as God before whom we stand exposed with all our teachings and doings, knows that I have written the book which you slander, with a good, sealed and assured conscience and as all theologians must acknowledge that it is the truth and word of the Lord; and as you cannot disprove it by virtue of the Scriptures, and as you, notwithstanding all this are so obdurate and lost as to call this undisproven writing of mine, a book of fables, and heretical doctrine; therefore I will leave the impartial reader to judge with which of us this slander is to be found. O, that you would see!

Thirdly, I understand that you call our doctrine concerning the ban between husband and wife as heretical. To which I would reply: First, Paul says, "Knowing that he that is such (a heretic) is sebverted, and sinneth, being condemned of himself," Tit. 3: 11. Inasmuch as such a one is subverted and condemned of himself, as was shown, therefore I know by the grace of God, that I am not worthy of such heretical name; for he that knows and tries all hearts, also knows me. He knows that I never knew, and much less fostered any obduracy, licentiousness, partiality or perverseness in my heart contrary to his word and will. I am sure that the merciful Father (who alone is the true Father of my soul), will not thus condemn to hell his despised, weak servant, nor look at him as such an heretic, although I must hear the despicable slander, not from the world alone, but also from you. O, no, no. His name is, Our faithful God, Merciful Father, Deliverer, Emmanuel, &c. Therefore let all under heaven judge, upbraid and slander; his paternal word, conceived in my open and willing heart, together with the Holy Spirit of his love which leads all souls, hungering and thirsting after righteousness, to the bread of life and to the true fountain of his living waters, will doubtlessly refresh me in the ardor of such, and of all my tribulations, and extend unto me his hand of consolation. For where is he who thus sought him that did not find grace? and where is he who trusted in him that was not aided and protected? O, that you would once see the abomination of your perverse and unseasonable judgment!

Secondly, I answer: That according to the Scripture, heretics are self-conceited, disquiet, licentious and perverse sectarians, who choose, collect and establish for themselves a peculiar foundation, doctrine and church, contrary to the true foundation of truth in which the true church which avails before God, should be founded; by means of which they disturb the unity of the pious, extinguish love, destroy peace, and cause much disturbance, trouble, sorrow and tribulation among those who would gladly walk in the truth. O, I pray you, learn to know the heretic.

As such are really heretics, as has been heard, so necessity requires to show the division between us, and to explain it; that the intelligent reader and auditor may thereby understand and comprehend with which of us such perverseness and heretical foundation is to be found. Take heed. Judge not by words and semblance, but by God's Word.

So this, our first foundation and doctrine, is that all obedient children of God, without any respect of person, must withdraw from all brethren and sisters who walk disorderly and who are disobedient to the institution, ordinance and doctrine received from the apostles; because it is so commanded of the Holy Spirit in the name of Christ. But your foundation and doctrine is that this does not apply to husband and wife in case one or the other deviates from the truth. You have respect of person, of which the Holy Spirit of wisdom does not command nor imply a single word in all the Holy Writ. Mark our first difference, 2 Thess. 3: 14; Jas. 2: 9; Deut. 3: 6; Zech. 13: 3.

Our second foundation and doctrine is that the true apostolic ban and shunning has not reference alone to the spiritual communion, as Supper, hand and kiss and greeting of peace (as you think), but also to the carnal communion, as eating, dealing, to receive into one's house, &c., and that it is plainly forbidden. But your foundation and doctrine is (for your deeds show it, which in my opinion proves more than words and confession would do) that the shunning applies alone to the spiritual communion, and that it does not apply to natural association. For it is a well known fact that you allow the natural association between husband and wife; and that you eat with the separated, and deal with them, if you have not changed. Mark our second difference.

Our third foundation and doctrine is, that the second table, namely, the commandment concerning our neighbor, must give way to the first, which is, the commandment concerning God. But your foundation and doctrine is (for your action in regard to husband and wife testify it), that not the second table must give way to the first, but the first to the second. As if the Creator must do the will of the creature, and the creature not the will of the Creator. O! O!! Mark our third difference.

Our fourth foundation and doctrine is, that the Holy Spirit ever cares for his, and has therefore commanded us to shun the sectarian and offensive sinners, lest they leaven with the leaven of their unrighteousness, or by their intercourse or conversation (as is generally the case), the pious and draw them into their wicked works; and also, that the apostates may thereby be made ashamed before the Lord and his church, repent, and be converted. But your foundation and doctrine combats and disputes this so cruelly that you quite bitterly call us divorcers and heretics; because we, in this regard, through the zealous fear of God, follow the command of the holy apostles, and point every one, whose lot it becomes, to the surest way, according to Scripture. You pretend to the poor people that it is an abomination that, on account of the ban, a husband should shun his wife, or a wife her husband. The same as it is also an abomination to the world that we should baptize the believing and not hear the false preachers; and thus reprove the Holy Spirit of the love of Christ; accuse and abuse his holy apostles of a false doctrine, as if the leaven of corruption (against which they have faithfully warned us) could not leaven husband or wife; also, as if we were at liberty, according to the rule of the holy word, not to seek the reformation of our consorts, 2 Thess. 3: 14; Tit. 3: 10; 1 Cor. 5: 5; Gal. 5: 9; 1 Cor. 5: 3; 2 Tim. 2: 18, 21.

Our fifth foundation and doctrine is that the ban without the shunning is quite useless and dead, yea, as a mill without a millstone, and as a knife without a blade; for it is very clear that the apostolic ban, properly, has its power and effect in the outward shunning. For else the danger of corrupting others would not be in the least avoided, which, properly, is the first and main reason of the ban, as has been heard. Your actions openly show that you have and teach a ban without the shunning, and that the same is therefore without effect, since you first except husband and wife from the shunning, and second, eat, deal, &c., with those who are banned, while the Holy Scriptures plainly and pointedly forbid it, saying, With such ye shall not eat; with such do not keep company; but shun them. Have no dealings with them; do not greet them, nor take them into your houses. Mark our fifth division, 1 Cor. 5: 10; Rom. 16: 16; 2 Tim. 3: 5; Tit. 3: 10.

But if you should say, *That if the pious can abide in his faith, living with the impious*, that in such case there is no necessity of *shunning*, I would then answer: First, that by such acceptation of the matter you, in fact annul all the plain commandments of the Scriptures concerning the outward, bodily shunning; as not to eat, deal or take them into your houses. Yea, if some liberty should be taken, it would be more reasonable to give the whole church liberty to eat and deal with apostates than to allow it between husband and wife. For there would be less danger accompanied with it to the church than to husband and wife who are of necessity in continual intercourse; something which the church could easily avoid. This is too clear to be denied. O, men, take heed.

My second reply is, that none under heaven can abide in his faith, living with his degenerate consort. For, first, he would transgress all the explicit commandments of the Holy Spirit concerning the ban and shunning. Secondly, he would not seek the repentance of his consort in such a manner as the Scripture teaches. And, thirdly, he keeps company with one who should, according to the command of the word, be shunned by all pious persons. I will leave it to the consideration of all of you, if this can be called abiding in the faith. Therefore, I pray you again, take heed.

Behold, beloved, if you compare this division with the doctrine of the Scripture, and in the fear of God impartially weigh it in the balance of the holy word, you will clearly see that I and my beloved brethren have the immutable, incontrovertible word to sustain us; and that you only have a vain presumption and a self-conceived opinion; that we have a restoring ban, while you have one that is fruitless, vain and dead; that we have obedience, you, disobedience; that we cordially seek to save all afflicted souls from the inherent disease of corruption, according to the doctrine and command of the holy apostles, while you, contrary to all admonition, doctrine and the explicit commandment of the holy apostles leave them to corruption, without all aid, succor, consolation, assistance and earnest trial; not looking at what is pleasing to the spirit, but only at what is pleasing to the flesh. Therefore it shows that you are, alas, those who are covered with the abominable shame of heresy of which you undeservedly blame me. If you are intelligent, mark what is the meaning.

Fourthly, I understand that you call us divorcers, telling your followers that of such shunning of husband and wife there can not be found a single example in all the Scriptures. To which I answer, first, that Moses taught the Israelites that they should not excuse their own wives, sons, daughters and friends who were as precious to them as their own hearts, if they should want to lead them to strange gods; but that they should, without mercy, slay or stone them,

Deut. 13: 6—10. Say, beloved, who was the cause of this? Moses or God? Not Moses; but God who had thus commanded him. Thus it is with us also. We teach that the apostates and sectarians should be shunned, without respect of person. Yet not we, but God, who has thus commanded us to do, in his word, as has been sufficiently shown. O, mark this.

Again I reply by asking this question: If one of your number had a dishonest, wicked, thievish, sodomitic, murderous, incendiary wife or one that should try to take his life, and were aware of it, would he yet continue to live with her? If you answer in the affirmative, you must acknowledge and own that he is an abominable, fearful, murderous rogue, to be one flesh with her; something which would not well become a servant of Christ. But if you answer in the negative, you judge yourself that you, in this matter, without previous adultery or fornication, are no less divorcers than we are. I repeat, mark this also.

Again, I ask, If one of your number had such a consort that he would have to renounce his faith or could not abide therein, would he, or should he continue to live with such consort? Jer. 17: 5. If you answer in the affirmative you thereby plainly testify that such perverse and ungodly flesh avails you more than Christ Jesus himself, together with his kingdom, truth, word, promise, blood, and death, besides your faith, unction, love, and the salvation of your souls. If you answer in the negative, I again say, that you, in this matter, without previous adultery or fornication, are no less divorcers than we are. Mark this.

Thirdly, I answer, If this our doctrine must be called a divorce by you, then it is evident that holy Paul was no less a divorcer than we are, for he says "But and if she depart, let her remain unmarried (observe he openly admits separation), or be reconciled to her husband," 1 Cor. 7: 11. Paul also allows such separation when it is for their betterment if they remain unmarried, as is also our doctrine, and so you yourselves (if the above is your answer), are no less divorcers than we are, as shown in the above two articles; therefore I would have you to consider in the fear of God what kind of a spirit it is that prompts you to make use of such slanderous, cunning words as divorcers, book of fables, heresy, &c. Venom is deadly, and gall is bitter, but much more poisonous and bitter is the tongue which is charged and laden with partiality and hatred. O, mind this, Jas. 3: 5—10.

But as to the beforementioned example this is our answer, first: That all those who make such pretensions manifest thereby that they do not believe the Scriptures of the apostles concerning the ban and shunning, nor understand the reasons, utility and effects of the ban, and alas, have but little regard for the explicit commandments concerning the outward, bodily shunning.

Again we say, concerning the opinion that a doctrine without example cannot stand in the church of Christ, as seems to be your ground; that in such case we are all badly mistaken, both you and we; because we allow our women to approach the Lord's Supper, of which there is not a syllable to be found in the Scriptures. But if you should say, *That our women are believing; therefore they should be admitted to the Supper, along with the believing men*, I would answer in like manner: As the pious consort is believing, he should shun his apostate wife, according to the common rule of Scripture, together with all other believing ones without exception. Whosoever is intelligent will judge and consider the inference.

In the fifth place, I understand that Lemmekes has boasted that he is going to rebut more than half of the books. To which I briefly reply: To promise mountains of gold and not to have sandhills to give, is called boasting by the world; therefore, it would be well not to boast of more than we have Scripture and talent for. But whosoever will rebut it must first establish the following ten articles, by virtue of the Word.

First, that the first table of the commandments in Christ's Kingdom and reign must give way to the second. Mark.

Secondly, that the Scripture teaches two bans or shunnings. Mark.

Thirdly, that there can be a scriptural ban without the shunning. Mark.

Fourthly, that the deadly disease of

corruption cannot leaven or make unclean the husband and wife when they do not shun each other. Mark.

Fifthly, that it is not required at the hands of the pious spouse earnestly to seek the reformation and repentance of the impious spouse, according to the counsel, doctrine and commandments of the Holy Scripture. Mark.

Sixthly, that the pious spouse is not bound to agree to the separation of his impious consort. Mark.

Seventhly, that the carnal ban and love must be preferred to the spiritual ban and love. Mark.

Eighthly, that the marriage with Christ, in the Spirit, must give way to the marriage consummated in the human flesh. Mark.

Ninthly, that the Holy Spirit has taught exceptions or respect of persons concerning the ban or shunning, in the Scripture. Mark.

Tenthly, that the spouse is not subject to the explicit commandments concerning the outward or bodily shunning. Mark.

Behold, dear Lemmekes, whenever you or any of your followers dissolve or untie this knot by virtue of the Scriptures, then we will further consider the matter.

But as we know that no man, no matter who he be, can ever do so by virtue of the truth, of which, before the Lord, we are certain; therefore we let men slander and boast as much as they please. Firm and immutable the doctrine remains, namely, that all pious husbands and wives as also the church are bound to shun their impious spouses, according to the common rule, doctrine and command of the Holy Scriptures, as has been frequently shown, by virtue of the holy Word. Whosoever seeks and loves the truth, may ponder upon that which we say and consider the meaning of the Scriptures.

In the sixth place I understand that Lemmekes should have said, that if we were of one mind in regard to the article concerning husband and wife, that there would yet be three or four articles about which we could not agree. To which I would say this, that I would like to have him put in writing these articles and points of difference, and send them to me. If you have truth on your side, and we have not, then, by the grace of God, I for myself will say, yea with you. But still I would warn you not to call that which is right and pure, wrong and impure; nor that which is wrong and impure, right and pure; not to dissolve that which the Scripture binds, nor to bind that which it makes free, as some, alas, are in the habit of doing; so that not our self-chosen righteousness nor human propositions and holiness, but the word of God alone, be our guide and way. In love, take heed.

In the seventh place, I understand that Lemmekes also said, that I first came to the Franekers and their followers and agreed with them; but was afterward instructed by the brethren, and remained with them. To which I reply to you and all who believe your untrue story, with truth, thus: I fraternally asked the Franekers when I was in conversation with them, If they had any further doings with carnal transgressors after the third admonition? To this they answered, no. Then I said (after passing a few words concerning secret sins), If that is your doctrine we will not remain divided. Then they thanked the Lord, as if we were quite of one mind in regard to the matter. Observing this, I said, Not so, brethren, but I will also talk to the others, and see what grace the Lord will give. That this is true I can prove by our beloved brother, Nette Lippes, and is also known to the omniscient Lord whose hand and judgment I cannot escape if I lie and do not speak the truth.

Afterwards I came to them and conversed with them and got my full satisfaction (praise the Lord for his grace) concerning secret sinning, at which my heart was rejoiced more than I am able to write, not, now, doubting in the least but that the matter would come to a good result, until the time that the Franekers came and showed that they did not abide by their understanding concerning carnal works, as they had confessed to me. This caused in me sorrow, as bitter as death. In my affliction I knew not what to do; for there is nothing upon earth I love more than the Lord's church. But as it is, I see that the leavening spirit of the false parties has leavened many. Yea, had not the gracious breath of the Omnipotent saved me I would probably have had my mind wrecked. In short, the Franekers would not unite before they had first consulted Henry Naeldeman. In the course of time, Henry came to us, and in love, we informed him that we were not those who thus judge the offensive transgressors; but that, according to the word, we could not do the will of God by retaining those whom his Spirit and Word exclude. He was so startled that he openly said before us all, that he had never so taken the matter to heart, in his life, hoping to place the Franekers on a better footing. I then left the country. Not long afterward he again sent for me. He had studied the matter over; and all we had built before, with the Lord's word, was again broken, in the poor man. Yea, it is known to me and to the Lord how unstable and childish he proved himself once or twice, in a short time, concerning the matter of husband and wife. His own handwriting shall be my testimony of this assertion.

Behold, dear men, here you have the outline of our action in this matter of which you so quite partially dare to upbraid me, which I assert with a good conscience, before the eyes of the Lord. If you had acted the part of wisdom in this matter and had not inclined your ears to the backbiting of the unpeaceable of the sectarian parties, you would never have offended against me by such gross falsehood and slander. Justly did Paul say "That a little leaven leaveneth the whole lump," 1 Cor. 5: 6.

In the eighth place I understand that Lemmekes publishes that I should have said to him, the people build upon, and look to me so much that I am afraid that the Lord will yet cause me to stumble, so that they shall no more look to me or any other man. To which I reply first: If I should now or at any time say to Lemmekes or any one else—the people build upon and look to me; then my own mouth would convince me that I would be like unto a fool who is quick to praise himself. I trust that not only the word of the Lord but also common sense will teach me better. And as I have experienced more than once in my time that the spirit of Diotrephes is not yet dead, 3 Jn. 9, which generally clothes itself in a sheep skin, sighing and complaining—saying: Oh, oh! The people build upon and look too much to Menno, whereby the hearts are turned from love; therefore I have not said once, but perhaps ten times: If the unversed should thus build upon and look to me, then my desire is that the Lord would cause me to stumble, but not take his grace altogether from me, that they might learn to know not to build their foundation, hope and consolation upon me, but solely upon the living corner stone, Christ Jesus. Whosoever hath the bride, says John, is the bridegroom, and that is Christ Jesus, who, according to the will of his Father (to his honor), has called us in his eternal love, and married us by faith in his death and blood; and not Menno or Lemmekes. Oh, that they would not garble my words, and not tell any thing but the truth which stands before God.

Secondly I answer, If you thus turn to shame the word of my piety, whereby I only seek the praise and honor of my Redeemer, which I had not thus expected, then I desire that in love, you point out my error according to the truth; for although I am a poor sinner who, at times, is mastered by his flesh, I yet thank God for his grace that he has to this day saved his poor, weak servant, without any considerable offense, both in doctrine and in life. But if your sight is so weak and dim that you call it stumbling, namely, that I teach according to the Holy Scriptures that we should shun the offensive transgressors until they repent; or that the ban should be used without respect of person; or that I am ever prepared to accept a better instruction of God or admonition and doctrine of his Holy Spirit, as I have done in regard to the doctrine of carnal abominations—then I may well console myself that the holy apostles are, in this matter, no less stumblers than I am. For before God, I do not know but that I teach the essence of their word unadulterated and walk in the footsteps of their spirit, so far as I have received grace and strength from my God. O, how quite carnal, unintelligent, blind and perverse is the judgment of a person who, before his God, is led away by partiality and envy. If you fear God then heed what I tell you, Jas. 3: 2, 17; 1 Cor. 2: 4.

In the ninth place, I understand that you slander and upbraid our brethren in Friesland, not a little. To which I briefly reply: It is not necessary that I should be the brethren's advocate, since the merciful Lord has not denied them his grace, Spirit and gifts. Yet for myself I would say that the worldly privileges are, or imply that we should give both sides a hearing. We also read of Alexander the Great, that when one party or one side laid in a complaint to him without the presence of the other side or party, that he would shut up one ear to give the other side a hearing therewith. Since there was found such great decency among the gentiles; and as it is the common usage, in all matters and policies, not to judge until after a hearing has been granted; therefore you have acted very unscripturally and unreasonably not only to give the one party (and that the party which are separated from the church on account of their contention) a hearing, but besides, accept them as your beloved brethren, while the other party you reject, to the great shame of you and your counselors; and because you would not give them a verbal explanation and hearing, although they so frequently and brotherly desired it. At which unreasonableness, unwillingness and childish ignorance we can not sufficiently satisfy our astonishment. We are of the opinion that it was never heard of people who seemingly feared God. Yet you proceed on the strength of the sayings of the partizans with intolerable lying and misgivings, without any certainty about the matter, and by this violence and wrong doing you take from us that which, I fear, you can never restore to us. But if you had given both parties a reasonable and christian hearing you might have (if you had the gift) passed a just sentence between them, and thus have sought unity and peace between them, according to the intent of the holy word. But now you have manifested yourselves to all mankind, while you see that with your unscriptural ban, now used by you and your followers these many years, you cannot stand before the sharpness of the Holy Spirit of Christ and of his strong word; that you seek to assert and maintain as much as you can; not the desirable unity and peace, nor the unfaltering, abiding truth which is of God, but your own ignorant opinion and carnal intentions by wrong and violence, dissention, partiality, slander and defamation. You should, however, know that not such wrong and violence as you commit, is to be the judgment and decision in this matter but that the Holy Spirit and word of Christ Jesus are to decide it. In love, take heed.

In the tenth place, I understand that Lemmekes said, "That he would rather be banned by our elders than to agree with them." To which I answer: That one of two things is made true by his words; that he either does not know what the ban is in fact; or else that the elders are such abominable people that they are not worthy of the church. For all the world I would not pass such a sentence. If these elders were such evil people, even, as his words imply, why be so unreasonable (since it is his office) as not to show his brotherly love by pointing out to them, in accordance with the Scriptures their errors and abominations of which he shows such abhorrence, since it becomes him before God and his church to seek their salvation, in love. But I presume that you feared the sharpness of truth and that you, therefore, were afraid to face them. O, that you would hear the voice of the Lord and not harden your hearts while it is yet to-day.

I must also, lastly, remind you that you came to us in A. D. 1556, just before May, and that we had a conference of two days, in the fear of our God. Yea, such a conference that Lemmekes, the morning of his departure openly confessed before me, that he quite agreed with us although not quite satisfied in the matter of husband and wife, but as he had not confessed this before the brethren, he had come hither that he and they would come to us, and as he had now opened his heart before all, his word would thereafter avail but little. And he wished to further treat with you, on the way, Exod. 17: 2; Gal. 6: 2; Jn. 3: 29. Behold, such were his pretenses. Besides he said, If the Upperlanders will not agree, and Zylis and Henry will remain with them,

I will (he said) go over to the Netherlanders.

Again he said, There are some strangers at Weert who would gladly come under the Word of the Lord; and asked: To whom shall I take these? to Zylis or to the Netherlanders? Besides this he desired of me that when we would have the consent or dissent of Zylis, to send one or two faithful brethren to his assistance, that the ban and shunning might be thus introduced into his church. Dear friends, that he thus agreed with us he did not only confess before me, but also before our beloved brethren Herman of T. and John S. And what is become of all these words and promises? Were they not all vain wind and falsehood? You must answer in the affirmative. And yet you do not want it said at Cologne and thereabout that you had thus agreed with us. The most lamentable of all is that that which he then confessed to be good and right is now called by him heresy and deceit. Whether such an inconsistent person can not be justly called an apostate I will herewith leave to the judgment of all reasonable and intelligent readers. Zylis and Henry wanted to consider the matter and propose it to the Upperlanders; they sent a written message, but whether or not you showed it to the elders of your church, I do not know. But Lemmekes has written, Yes. And the brethren write, No; and it is said that Zylis said, No. Their answers are contradictory.

In short, at last we, after long delay and waiting, received an answer from you and the Upperlanders: That we should not push the ban to its utmost, for it would have to be broken, and that there were as many Scriptures concerning marriage as for the ban and shunning. Behold this was the instruction of scriptural argument, by which he puts aside all apostolic Scriptures concerning this matter, and rejects them as useless.

If I do not write the truth, I am willing to bear my punishment. In my opinion it is come so far with you that, before God, I do not know who could ever agree with you. For first you agreed with us; afterward dissented without our knowledge and joined the Upperlanders. Observe, Lemmekes agreed with us, but the same summer yet turned his back upon us and again agreed with them. Observe again: Those that were separated on account of their dissension and shamefulness you again accepted as your brethren.

Observe, thirdly: Our elders and church you despised, answered their prayer quite unfriendly and sneeringly, and said that you did not come on their account.

Fourthly, observe: The spirit of the disquiet partizans you believed behind our backs.

Fifthly, observe: You belie, upbraid, backbite, slander, and accuse me and my beloved brethren without any truth; while I for myself never said an unfriendly word about you, of which God is my witness, but have ever shown regard for your well being until this hour of your unbearable action.

Sixthly, mark: The plain word of the holy apostles as regards the ban and shunning, you reject. Seventhly, mark: You uphold many lightminded, carnal babblers. Eighthly, mark: You encourage many disquiet, unpeaceable dissenters and quarrelers.

Ninthly, mark: Many, yea, thousands of faithful hearts who sincerely seek God and his sure truth, you afflict. Tenthly, mark: Many pious children who would gladly obey the word of the Lord in this regard, and thus save their souls, you hinder.

Eleventhly, observe: You beget many defamers, liars, profaners and upbraiders. In short, you have brewed such beer that, if the Lord does not save you by his mercy, I fear you will yet stumble over the heaped pot. For beware, if you again renounce the Upperlanders and also those whom you, alas, have now given the hand of brotherhood they will not depict you in very pleasing colors.

And if you, even, remain with them, all intelligent persons must confess that you build your faith, in this matter, with a sectarian spirit, upon vain self-conceit, opinion, flesh and man, and not upon the firm rock and foundation of the divine word. If you change your doctrine which you have so long wrongly practiced and taught in your church, then you will have to hear that you are miserable teachers, that you have deceived many souls and that you do not know the light of truth.

But if you do not, you make it manifest that you do not seek and uphold the souls or the salvation of the church, nor the word of God, but your own honor and flesh, only.

If, too, you acknowledge that you have, through partizanism, wrongfully defamed me, a cry from the pious will issue against you, that you have defamed the reputation of your brethren, without cause, not as faithful servants of Christ, but rather as envious defamers.

If you do not acknowledge it, nor do such penance as can avail before God, then the just sentence of his immutable word will be upon you, that is, the defamers, backbiters, slanderers and liars have no portion in the kingdom of God and Christ. O, awful is the sentence. Woe unto those on whom it is inflicted! With fear, trembling and shaking reflect, I pray you, 2 Pet. 2: 18; Jude 1: 10; Rom. 1: 30.

Behold, dear, chosen men, how perilously you are sailing! Like a ship that is cast about between two rocks. If she avoid the one she will sail upon the other. Therefore, take heed. Take heed, that you may prevent the eternal shipwreck of your poor souls, and yet arrive in the haven of eternal peace with the Most High, Amen. Amen.

This, now, is the proper content, conclusion, intent and meaning of my writing to you, and yours, First, that you may behold the abomination of your actions in this clear mirror, turn from evil, come before the Lord with a contrite heart and sincerely pray for his grace. Secondly, that also, the simple, and those of little understanding who are, in this respect, imprisoned by you, may taste and see therefrom that you have fed and satiated them not with the bread of their heavenly Father, but with mere swill and chaff, and human self-conceit.

Thirdly, that you may know that I and the pious who are with me, dare not, by the fear of our God, be your brethren, so long as there are not found with you such doctrine, obedience, confession, reconciliation and repentance as to pacify the church of the Lord and to be pleasing unto him.

This is written in sorrow. If you fear God, then take heed, and reflect. The God of all grace and the Holy Spirit of peace and of the love of Christ grant you grace that you may read with impartial hearts, and that it may be to your service, Amen. Amen. Amen.

By Menno Simon, who loves you souls according to the truth.

January 23rd, 1559.

A HUMBLE AND CHRISTIAN JUSTIFICATION AND REPLICATION,

CONCERNING THE

BITTER, ENVIOUS LIES AND FALSE ACCUSATIONS OF OUR ENVIERS, ON WHOSE ACCOUNT WE ARE, WITHOUT ANY COMPASSION AND MERCY, SO LAMENTABLY HATED, BELIED, SLANDERED, UPBRAIDED AND PERSECUTED UNTO DEATH, AS MAY, ALAS, BE WITNESSED DAILY IN MANY CITIES AND COUNTRIES.

BY

MENNO SIMON.

"Blessed are ye, when men shall revile you, and persecute you, and shall say all manner of evil against you falsely, for my sake.

Rejoice and be exceeding glad; for great is your reward in heaven; for so persecuted they the prophets which were before you," Matt. 5 : 11, 12.

"For other foundation can no man lay than that is laid, which is Jesus Christ," 1 Cor. 3 : 11.

ELKHART, INDIANA:
PUBLISHED BY JOHN F. FUNK AND BROTHER.
1871.

TO THE READER.

May the blessing and Salvation be with the Christian Reader:

Inasmuch, christian reader, as we poor, despised strangers and pilgrims are rejected and despised by all the world; are accounted the off-scourings, and that because we diligently seek our salvation, so that the pious and godfearing heart must tremble and be astounded at the defamation which they unjustly heap upon the righteous, so that some who strive after the truth dare hardly join this ardent people; therefore, christian reader, this book, the band with which we shall tie the arrant liars and their slander, is translated, out of pure love, and to the profit and use of the reader from the eastern tongue, which is not used in this country, into the Holland language, that every godfearing person may stop the mouth of the slanderer. For it is said, *Jacula previsa minus feriunt*. Wherefore we pray you to accept in love this our labor, which we performed to your service. For our sincere desire, wish, striving and laboring is, that many may come to the true knowledge of the truth, and be saved. Fare ye well.

PREFACE.

ALL that we sincerely desire, reasonable reader (behold, before God we lie not), is, that by our writing, teaching, living, misery and confiscation of our goods we may once acquire so much mercy from the children of men that we shall be allowed a private discussion with our adversaries, before any number of pious, intelligent, and reasonable men who love and fear the Lord and who can distinguish between good and evil, if it cannot be allowed us in public; and that their lies and accusations shall not be believed, until teacher is confronted with teacher, and the accuser before the accused with equal rights and liberty, as the word of God, christian love and natural reason teach and imply, that thus the ungodly may no longer be protected in their ungodliness, the wicked in their evil doing and that the pious and righteous be no longer condemned and suppressed, that God's holy word, by which our souls must live, may be made manifest, the fearful lying cease and the unmerciful and cruel blood-shedding be stopped, which in itself is nothing but the manifest works of the infernal serpent, as Christ himself says; and which are, in appearance of true zeal and love of God, made use of without fear, reflection or mercy, by those who boast of the name, Spirit, word, death and blood of Christ, against those who with Asaph wash their hands in innocence. But we apprehend that it will not be allowed us. For in both sacred and profane history we read and find that the pure, wholesome truth, from the beginning of the world has generally been hated, belied and persecuted and that it has, as a general thing, only found shelter with a few in obscure nooks and corners, as a hateful, ungodly abomination. And that it can not be made manifest without tribulation and peril of life.

Because the good, pious Jeremiah reproved the Scribes for their false doctrine and wickedness; admonished the ignorant, confused and evil populace to repent, and threatened them with future plagues, he was called by them a heretic and deceiver, and by the princes a rebel and mutineer. He had to experience much misery although he was chosen of God, a prophet from his mother's womb, and spake from the mouth of the Lord; he had to hear, that on his account, they had to bear such sore plagues. Ahab, the blood-thirsty and idolatrous king, blamed the pious and spiritual man that it was he who seduced all Israel, 1 Kings 18: 18.

Again King Joram thought that Elisha had entailed the great famine in Samaria, 2 Kings 6.

John, a man sent from God, blessed in his mother's womb, the greatest born of woman, a burning, shining light, the messenger of the Lord, a voice crying in the wilderness, the second and spiritual Elias, was accused that he was possessed of devils, and was at last beheaded because of his reproving a shameful case of fornication, Luke 1 : 15; Matt. 11 : 11; Jn. 5 : 35; Mal. 3: 1; Mk. 1: 3; Matt. 11: 14.

Again, Jesus Christ, the eternal Light and Life himself, was called Beelzebub, a Samaritan, and possessed of a devil, a mover of insurrection, a transgressor of the law, a blasphemer, a glutton and wine-bibber, a friend of publicans and sinners; he was deemed worse than a murderer; and, at last, he was rewarded for all his glorious miracles, kindness and love shown to them, by putting on him a mock robe, a crown of thorns, scourging, cross and death, after they had derided and blasphemed him to their satisfaction.

How they treated Stephen, Peter, Paul, James and others, the Scriptures abundantly show, Acts 5, 6, 7, 12, 17, 18, 19, 21.

At the time or commencement of the primitive church, the christians were called swine by some; others called them robbers of God's glory, murderers, infanticides, abominable, unchaste persons, who committed all manner of abominations with their mothers and sisters; and that they in their worship, shed human blood and also offered their children to idols; that they were rebels, and that because of their separation from the priesthood of Balaam, and their occasional night-meetings to partake of the Lord's Supper.

Again, enemies of the human race; unfruitful, corrupted people, because they would not keep company with the winebibbers, liars, &c., but led a sober, godly, humble and circumcised life, in the love and fear of God.

Again, enemies of God, accursed melefactors, and rogues, because they kept aloof from the shameful idolatry, and suffered themselves to be exiled and freely gave their goods and life blood for the sake of the testimony of the Lord and true religion and honor of God.

Behold, thus the blind, ungrateful world has ever rewarded and treated those who sought and feared God, with all their hearts, with all their souls, and with all their power, as Cyprian, Tertullian and other historians testify. Darkness can not bear the light; nor falsehood, truth. God's word is an abomination to the ungodly, for it is a treasure of wisdom hidden from them. Christ says, "That light is come into the world, and men loved darkness rather than light, because their deeds were evil," Jn. 3: 19. The pious and godfearing are ever an offense and sting in their hearts and are a hurt in their sight. And this is the cause that the world, which in all its doings will ever live unrebuked and unhindered in idolatry, pride, pomp, licentiousness and lust, from the beginning, has so enviously hated, miserably belied and so tyrannically persecuted the pious and godfearing.

O kind reader, thus it is to-day as you can see on every hand. The whole world is saturated with all manner of wickedness. False doctrine, idolatry, unbelief, licentiousness, shame and blasphemy are in the ascendency; it will not be reproved nor admonished. It hates all who would, in pure love, at the cost of their goods and life, gladly deliver them from their wicked and inordinate life, point and lead them in the way of peace and save their souls, if possible.

The wise and learned, who ever have plagued and pestered the pious and righteous the most, as was said in our *Confessions*, heap one abominable lie upon another, lest their unreasonable and shameful gain and false boasting be destroyed. They pretend and cry that we are Munsterites; that we do not want to be subject to and obey the magistracy; that we mean to take cities and countries by force; that like the irrational creatures, we have our goods and women in common; that we say to each other, Sister, my spirit desires thee. Again, that we claim to be without sin, and that we mean to be saved by our own merits and works, and the like unfounded lies, that they may thus lead from truth, all mankind and particularly the lords, princes and magistrates which they have inebriated by their golden cup, that they may embitter and turn them against all the pious children of God. He is called and considered a fine, evangelical preacher and a competent teacher well lettered, who can only quarrel, upbraid, slander and lie sufficiently to move the magistracy, who perhaps, would be reasonable, kind and favorable enough if they were not spurred on and vexed by this unreasonable generation of vipers, to persecution, so that the innocent, belied sheep that would not injure a hair on any one, are, without a hearing, led captive, and mercilessly exiled from country, city and town, into misery and privation, and chased by the ravening wolves until they are consumed by over-exertion, heat, cold or rain. In this, I think, they fill the measure of their ancestors of whom Christ said, Oh Lord! oh, beloved Lord! how long will these inhuman tyrannies and fearful abominations continue?

Inasmuch as they have so embittered all lords, princes, regents, potentates and common people against us by their fearful cry of murder, and by their slanderous lying that we can not acquire sufficient mercy by all our prayers, beseechings and supplications, by all our innocence, tears, patience, misery, cross, goods and blood that we might be allowed a public conference and discussion with our enviers; and as according to justice and christianity it becomes the magistracy to allow us a fair hearing and trial, and that they do not usurp to themselves, in the judgment seat of the Most High God, to shed innocent blood; and as we are ever slandered by their unfounded lies, and as truth is thus smothered; therefore we are impelled by the urging of the word of God and the love of our neighbors, to publish in writing our excuse and answer with pure, christian truth, that by our defense in writing, since they are so enraged that we can not appear publicly to defend ourselves, the godfearing conscience which would not knowingly act contrary to the will of God, no matter whether he be a magistrate or citizen, learned or unlearned, may know that by the beforementioned abominations we are innocently slandered and belied by our opponents; or that God would grant that thus the word and truth of the Lord might become more known and manifest thereby, and that the deceit and feigned holiness of the learned and priests, must become discovered and manifest to all the world.

Honorable reader, we humbly beseech you for the Lord's sake, to consider impartially why we so often refer to the preachers, admonish and reprove them of many things which, alas, are not to their honor and reputation. For, as we clearly see that they are those who, for the sake of shameful gain and avarice, so falsely console, retain and bind the whole world in their unbelief, idolatry and impenitent, carnal life; so miserably break the truth and trample it under foot; so miserably murder the poor souls which are so dearly bought, not with perishable gold and silver, but with the precious blood of Christ; so enviously and scornfully hate, slander and belie the pious and godfearing and take their goods and even their lives, which is quite different from the Spirit of the Lord, that they may hold to their shameful gain, lustful, vain and fruitless life without reproof; and as they do not suffer themselves to be admonished, taught and warned by the word of God, by love, longsuffering, piety and the blood of the saints; therefore the glory of God and the salvation of your souls require us to do so. The Almighty Lord is our testimony, that we aim at nothing but that those who are reasonably minded and yet do not know the mystery of unrighteousness, as Paul calls it, 2 Thess. 2: 9 (as they are yet carnally minded, not born of God and kept back by the preachers), may learn to know the preachers and teachers by such clear and plain discoverings; further reflect upon it and thus become tired of their shameful deceit and seduction; and that all lords and magistrates who dare boast of the name of Christ may know what kind of people and teachers those are who slander us and to whom they give ear and faithfully protect by their arms.

A HUMBLE AND CHRISTIAN DEFENSE.

In the first place, they complain and accuse us of being Munsterites; and warn all people to beware of us and take an example from those of Munster.

Answer. We do not like to reprove and judge those who are already reproved and judged of God and man; yet, as we are wrongfully attacked and accused by our opponents, and that without truthfulness, therefore we would say in defense of us all that we consider the Munsterian doctrine and life, in regard to king, sword, rebellion, retaliation, revenge, polygamy and the temporal kingdom of Christ, as a new Jewism, and a misleading error, doctrine and abomination which is not at all in keeping with the Spirit, word and example of Christ. Behold, in Christ, we lie not.

Besides, I can fearlessly challenge any body, that none under the broad canopy of heaven can show and prove that I ever agreed with the Munsterites in regard to the beforementioned articles; for from the beginning until the present moment I have opposed them with diligence and earnestness, both privately and publicly, verbally and in writing, for over seventeen years, and ever since I confessed the word of the Lord and knew and sought his holy name according to my weakness.

I also, according to my small talent, have faithfully warned every body against their error and abomination, as I would that it should be done unto me. And in the mean time I have pointed and returned several of them to the true way, by the grace, assistance and power of the Lord.

I have never seen Munster nor have I ever been in their communion. And I trust that by the grace of the Lord, I shall never eat nor drink with such if there should yet be any, as the Scripture teaches me not to do; unless they sincerely acknowledge their abomination and truly repent, and follow the truth and the gospel in a becoming manner.

Behold, kind reader, this is my understanding and opinion of the Munsterites, as is also the opinion of all those who are known and accepted of us as brethren and sisters, that is, those of us who, on account of the false doctrine, unclean pedo-baptism and supper of the preachers, are visited with superabundance of misery, tribulation and anxiety, and who assert and testify unto death their pure doctrine of baptism and Supper, with an humble confession and a pious, unblamable life.

But all those who reject the cross of Christ, as did the Munsterites; turn their backs upon the Word of the Lord; again revert to carnality, idolatry and its communion; walk in all pomp, pride and inebriety; in short, all those who are on the broad road, although they may be baptized, we do not know nor accept as brethren and fellows, inasmuch as they do not abide in the word of the Lord. Behold, kind reader, this is the truth and it will ever be found so. The learned may upbraid and garble to their satisfaction, yet they should know that although they are now honored and respected on earth, as the Psalmist testifies, we shall at last appear before a Judge who has no respect of person and who will not judge according to the complaint, nor favor and partiality, but according to the truth.

But if they should say we are one church with the Munsterites, because they and we are baptized with one baptism, then we would reply that if outward baptism has the power to make all those who are thus baptized with one baptism, one church, and that it causes all those who are thus baptized to share in the unrighteousness, wickedness and corruption of every individual, then our adversaries may well consider what kind of a church or body theirs is, as it is evident and well known to every body that perjurers, murderers, highway-men, thieves, &c., have received the same baptism which they have. If we, then are

Munsterites because of our baptism, they must be perjurers, murderers, highwaymen, thieves, &c., on account of their baptism. This is incontrovertible.

O, no. The Scripture does not teach that we are baptized into one body by any mere sign, as water, but that we are baptized into one body by one Spirit, 1 Cor. 12: 13. The prophet says, "The Son shall not bear the iniquity of the father," but "The soul that sinneth, it shall die," Ezek. 18: 20. Paul says, "Every one shall bear his own burden." And if they, now, should say that the transgressors are punished by the magistracy according to the sentence of justice, we would reply, that we also thus judge and punish them with the sword of the Spirit, according to the ordinance and commandment of God, namely, according to the word of the Lord, that is, we separate from us all those who turn away from the truth by any unclean or false doctrine or by any licentious, carnal walk, as was said.

In short, we herewith, testify and confess before God, before you, and before the whole world, that we, from our inmost hearts detest the errors and abominations of the Munsterites, as also all evil sectarianism which are contrary to the Spirit, word and ordinance of the Lord; and that before God, in Christ Jesus, we neither seek nor desire anything more than that we may turn the whole world from its wickedness, to the right way, and that we may, by the word, grace and assistance of the Lord, deliver many souls from the kingdom of the devil, and gain them to the Kingdom of Christ; that we may lead a pious, humble and godly life in Christ Jesus, and that we may glorify his great and adorable name, forever. For we firmly believe and confess that all false doctrine, idolatry, ungodliness and sin are of the devil; and that the reward of sin is everlasting death. Therefore we labor so diligently and earnestly; and would, the Lord knows, be pious and fear God, notwithstanding we miserable men are so shamefully belied, hated and scandalized and often slain, on that account, Rom. 1: 26; 1 Cor. 6; Gal. 3; Eph. 5; 1 Pet. 3.

In the second place they say that we will not obey the magistracy.

Answer. The writings which we have published during several years past abundantly prove that this accusation against us is wrong and untrue. We now publicly confess that the office of a magistrate is ordained of God, as we ever have confessed since we serve, according to our small talent, the word of the Lord. And, in the meantime, we have ever obeyed them when not contrary to the word of God, and we intend to do so all our lives; for we are not so stupid as not to know what the Lord's word commands in this respect. We render unto Ceasar the things which are Ceasar's as Christ teaches, Matt. 17: 22; we pray for the imperial majesty, kings, lords, princes and all in authority, honor and obey them, 1 Tim. 2: 2; Rom. 13: 1. And yet they cry that we will not be subject to and obey the powers that be, that they may disturb the hearts of those that have authority and excite them to all unmercifulness, wrath and bitterness against us, and that, thus, by their continual cries the bloody sword may be unmercifully used against us and never be sheathed, as may be seen, Rom. 13: 7; Tit. 3: 2; 1 Pet. 2: 13.

Inasmuch as they ever excite the magistracy by such gross falsehood; besides, will say yea and amen to every thing the magistracy do, whether agreeable to the Scripture or not; and as they thus by their tickling doctrine lead these souls into condemnation, because they seek not their salvation, but their own enjoyment and gain; therefore love compels us respectfully and humbly to show all high in authority who would do right if they knew it, and had one to point it out to them (since it was concealed from the preachers), how, according to the word of the Lord, they should be minded; also, how they should rightfully execute their office to the praise and glory of the Lord.

Moses speaks thus, "And it shall be, when he (the king) setteth upon the throne of his kingdom, that he shall write him a copy of this law in a book out of that which is before the priests, the Levites. And it shall be with him and he shall read therein all the days of his life; that he may learn to fear the Lord his God, to keep all the words of this law and these statutes, to do

A HUMBLE AND CHRISTIAN DEFENSE.

them (dear lords, mark, it reads: *to do them*). That his heart be not lifted up above his brethren, and that he turn not aside from the commandments, to the right hand, or to the left." "He shall not multiply horses to himself;" "Neither shall he multiply wives to himself, nor silver and gold," Deut. 17: 16—20. Concerning rulers Jethro thus speaks to Moses, "Provide out of all the people able men, such as fear God, men of truth, hating covetousness, and place such over them, to be rulers," Ex. 18: 21.

Moses says, "And I charged your judges at that time, saying, Hear the causes between your brethren, and judge righteously between every man and his brother, and the stranger that is with him. Ye shall not respect persons in judgment; but ye shall hear the small as well as the great; ye shall not be afraid of the face of man; for the judgment is God's," Deut. 1: 16, 17.

Jehoshaphat, the king of Judah, said to the judges, "Take heed what ye do; for ye judge not for man, but for the Lord, who is with you in judgment." O, an important and heroic word. "Wherefore now let the fear of the Lord be upon you; take heed and do it; for there is no iniquity with the Lord our God, nor respect of person, nor taking of gifts," 2 Chron. 19: 6, 7.

Paul says, "Rulers are not a terrror to good works, but to evil (mark ye rulers). Wilt thou, then, not be afraid of the power? Do that which is good, and thou shalt have praise of the same. For he is the minister of God to thee for good. But if thou do that which is evil, be afraid: for he beareth not the sword in vain; for he is the minister of God, a revenger to execute wrath upon him that doeth evil," Rom. 13: 3, 4.

Behold, beloved rulers and judges, if you take to heart these cited Scriptures and diligently reflect upon them, you will observe, first, that your office is not your own but God's office and service, that you may bend your knees before his Majesty; fear his great and adorable Name and rightly and reasonably execute your ordained office; and that you may not thus freely usurp the kingdom, dominion and jurisdiction of Christ, and judge and punish by your iron swords that which belongs solely to the eternal Judgment of the Most High God, as in matters of faith, which also, Luther and others wrote in the beginning. But after they became more exalted they seem to have forgotten it all. Dear rulers, observe how very much Moses, Joshua, David, Ezekiel, Josiah, Zorobabel and others are praised in the Scriptures, because they feared the Lord and faithfully and diligently kept his commandments, counsel and word.

If you lift your hearts above all the mountains, and will not hear what the mouth of the Lord commands you, but only listen to the whisperings of your flesh; if you will not confess that you are the officers and servants of the Lord and that you have received of him country and people to rule, you cannot possibly avoid the punishment of him who has called you to be such exalted potentates, commanders, heads and regents.

Beloved, observe, and beware. Before him Crœsus and Irus are alike respected. Therefore sincerely fear and love your God; examine the Scriptures and take into consideration how the great Lord in his wrath has, on account of their tyranny, cruelty, pride, blasphemy, disobedience, and idolatry, mercilessly upset and destroyed the thrones of potentates; as of Pharaoh, Nebuchadnezzar, Sanherib, Antiochus, Saul, Jeroboam, Ahab and others, as may be clearly and plainly read in the Scriptures.

Secondly, you may understand from these Scriptures that you are called and ordained to your offices to punish the transgressors and protect the good; to judge rightly between man and his fellow; to do justice to the widows and orphans; to the poor, despised stranger and pilgrim; to protect them against violence and tyranny, rule cities and countries justly by a good policy and administration not contrary to God's word, to the peaceable and quiet enjoyment of the life of all, and that you should anxiously seek and love the holy word (by which the soul lives), name and glory of God, and promote, protect and maintain the same as much as possible, without bloodshed and uproar.

Behold, beloved lords and judges, this is the proper office to which you are called. Whether you fulfill these requirements piously and faithfully, I will leave to your own consideration. I think with holy Jeremiah that you have all broken the yoke and rent it in pieces; for you reject and detest, as a venomous serpent, the dear word which you should reasonably protect; the false teachers and prophets who deceive the whole world and whom, according to the word of God, we should shun, are by you kept in high esteem; and the poor, miserable sheep who, in their weakness, sincerely fear and obey the Lord and who speak not a harmful word of any one, because they dare not do aught against his word; who lead a penitent, pious life; make the right use of his sacraments according to the Scriptures; abhor all false doctrine, sectarianism and ungodliness; are exiled from city and country and are often adjudged to fire, water or the sword; their goods are confiscated; their children, who according to the words of the prophet, are not responsible for the transgressions of their fathers, if the fathers were, even, guilty, are sent to wander about naked; and thus the labor and sweat of their parents they must leave in the hands of these avaricious, greedy, unmerciful and bloodthirsty robbers.

O, ye beloved lords and judges, we will leave it to your own judgment whether this is to protect the good and punish the evil, to judge justly between man and man; to do justice to the widow, orphan and stranger, as the Scriptures teach and your office implies. O no, beloved rulers, no. Take heed, the matter is changed. The good are punished and the evil encouraged and protected. For the events of every day prove that it is as the prophets complained of. Perjurers, usurers, blasphemers, liars, deceivers, fornicators and adulterers are in no danger of death, but those that fear and love the Lord are the prey of all the world. The prophet says, "Behold, the princes of Israel, every one were in thee to their power to shed blood. In thee have they set light by father and mother; in the midst of thee have they dealt by oppression with the stranger: in thee have they vexed the fatherless and the widow," Ezek. 22: 6, 7. Read and diligently ponder upon the prophetic Scriptures, and you will find what terrible threats the holy and faithful men of God have ever prophesied of such evils and abuses. And if you do despise these our admonitions, they, nevertheless, are the firm truth; this you must acknowledge. For it is manifest and undeniable that in our Netherlands the lascivious, unchaste, and vain men whom they call pastors, ministers, masters and teachers, some of whom defile one maiden and woman after another, who openly live in all manner of licentiousness, ungodliness, idolatry, and drunkenness, and who do not rightly live in obedience to the word of God in any particular, rob, by their shameful treason, many godfearing people who, before God and his angels, seek nothing but to lead a righteous, unblamable life, according to the direction of the word of God, of their country, honor, possessions and, even, life; while they (the traitors) live at liberty and ease.

Inasmuch as the scale of justice is so very much out of balance; and as you are chosen and ordained of God to judge without respect of person and to deliver from the hands of the oppressor all the afflicted and oppressed strangers; therefore we pray you humbly, most beloved rulers and judges, for the sake of him who has called and chosen you to your offices, that you do not believe these cruel and envious men, who, according to Peter are born to corruption and torture; and who, ever publicly and privately, make us so obnoxious, by their cries, that we are not allowed a hearing and facing—so long as they, in our presence, do not prove (which, we are sure, they cannot do) against us that which they every day from their throne of pestilencies and mockery, so shamefully proclaim to the world, to the shame and injury of great numbers of pious and godfearing children. Beloved rulers, we beseech you for Christ's sake, to fear and love God sincerely. Believe his true word and act accordingly, Isa. 1: 23; Ps. 73: 6.

In the third place, you will also observe from the Scriptures, that, although you are chosen authority on earth, yet you dare not act according to your own option and opinion. But you are to love your Lord and God sincerely as your Creator, Deliverer and Savior, and to fear and obey him as your Head, King, Prince and Judge; ever diligently to follow the directions of his word; not to lift yourselves above your subjects and brethren; and, never to deviate from the ways and commandments of the Lord. Henceforth, beloved rulers, diligently observe that you be christians in actions, works and truth, inasmuch as you boast yourselves such. Water, bread, wine and name make none a christian; but those are christians who are born of God: are of divine nature, are of the same mind as Christ Jesus; led by the Spirit of God, who daily crucify their evil and corrupt flesh; walk not after the flesh, but after the Spirit; love nothing above God's word; love their neighbors as themselves; lead an unblamable, humble, pious life; who meekly walk in the footsteps of Christ and who are become new, changed and converted men and creatures in Christ. These the word of God calls christians, 2 Pet. 1: 4; Phil. 2: 5; Rom. 8: 14; Gal. 5: 24; Rom. 8: 2; Matt. 10: 37; 7: 12; 16: 24.

Beloved lords, observe that we do not read in the biblical Scriptures of proud, carnal, perjurious, adulterous, drunken, pompous, unrighteous, idolatrous and bloodthirsty christians. But that the portion of such shall be eternal weeping and gnashing of teeth, darkness, fire, hell, death and devil. Their portion will be in the lake which burneth with fire and brimstone, Rev. 21: 8; Rom. 1.

Dear lords, take heed, and be no longer deceived. For with God there is no respect of persons. This all the Scriptures teach. It is life everlasting, with the angels around the heavenly throne, or everlasting death with the devils in the bottomless pit; for it must all be judged according to the Spirit, example and word of God. "Therefore if any man be in Christ, he is a new creature," 1 Cor. 5: 17. "He that saith he abideth in him (Christ), ought himself also so to walk, even as he walked," 1 Jn. 2: 6. It matters not whether one be emperor or king.

Beloved lords, this is God's word. This is the price and measure after which you and we should strive. Whosoever does not strive after and conform himself to this measure, cannot be a christian. Therefore examine your teachers well; earnestly and diligently consider whether or not they point you to this narrow way. I presume that they preach peace to you; make your pillows soft and agreeable, and that they do not severely reprove your court-manners and practices, such as, dancing, drinking, fornication, gambling and debauchery in general. In short, that you build the wall, and they daub it with untempered mortar, Ezek. 13: 10.

Beloved rulers, we do not do so; but we teach and direct you in the right way which you should walk if you wish to be saved. We do not point you to the pope, or Luther, or Augustine, or Hieronymus, but according to Scripture, to Christ Jesus, to hear him, to believe and faithfully follow him. For he is the Prophet promised of God; the Teacher sent of God; the Light of the world; the true Shepherd of our souls. Whosoever shall hear, believe, and follow him has eternal life, Deut. 18: 18; Jn. 3: 2; 8: 12; 3: 15. He calls to emperor, king and to every one, "Except ye be converted, and become as little children, ye shall not enter into the kingdom of heaven;" "If any man will come after me (or whosoever will be a true christian), let him deny himself, and take up his cross, and follow me;" whosoever loves any thing more than he loves me cannot be my disciple; and is not worthy of me, and many other passages, Matt. 18: 3; 16: 24; Luke 14; Matt. 10: 38.

Rulers, awake, and learn to know him. He is the Son of the Most High God, the Lord of lords and the King of kings; the eternal power, word and wisdom of God. What kind of pomp, ease and comfort he enjoyed on earth, the Scriptures abundantly teach us. At his birth, there was no room for him in the inn, Luke 2: 8. In his preaching, he had not where to lay his head, Luke 9: 58. His entrance into Jerusalem was not accompanied with cavalry, guards and knights, but upon an ass. At his death he had neither water nor wine wherewith to quench his thirst. Why was it? Was it that we should live a lustful, pleasurable life? O, no. But, according to Peter, it was that we should die unto sin and live in righteousness, Matt. 21: 7; 1 Pet. 4: 3; Rom. 6: 7; 2 Tim. 2: 11; Col. 3: 5.

Behold, beloved rulers, behold! This is the court-practice which the heavenly Prince, Christ Jesus, has taught all his courtiers on earth, namely, all christians. O, the narrow way! The strait gate! How few find, and fewer still who walk therein! Matt. 7: 14; Luke 13: 24.

I write this admonition that the princes, regents and lords may take heed, and observe that they are miserably deceived by the preachers, since they preach such easy and sweet things, and point out such a broad way, while the word of God shows us such a strait way. I herewith humbly beseech you, lords, princes, kings and judges, one and all, for the sake of the precious blood of our Lord Jesus Christ, with which we are besprinkled, not to think hard of me, poor, miserable, and despised man, that I have thus faithfully shown my sincere love to you. For I would joyfully see that your poor souls were saved. My admonition is general, and I do not mention any particular name. Whosoever is guilty, let him repent; and whosoever is not guilty, let him take heed. God is my witness, that I desire nothing but that you all may be such indeed, that you may be praised and honored by all, by noble lords, and a christian magistracy, that you will stand impartially between us and our opponents, the learned, as becomes your office, that the enchanting, deceiving falsehood may once go down and be destroyed, and that the unadulterated truth which for centuries has been kept back, may be restituted. Beloved rulers, the word of God is truth. Love, embrace and kiss it; for its riches are immeasurable, its beauty exceeding, its fruits precious and its power is eternal life, Jn. 17.

In the third place, they say, That we are rebellious; that we would take cities and countries, if we had the power.

Answer. This prophecy is false and will ever remain so; and by the grace of God, time and experience will prove that those who thus prophesy, according to the word of Moses, are not of God. Faithful reader, understand what I write.

The Scriptures teach that there are two opposing princes and two opposite kingdoms. The one is the Prince of peace; the other the prince of rebellion. Each of the princes has his particular kingdom and as the prince is, so is also the kingdom. The Prince of peace is Christ Jesus; his kingdom is the kingdom of peace, which is his church; his messengers are the messengers of peace; his word is the word of peace; and his body is the body of peace; his children are the seed of peace; and his inheritance and reward are the inheritance and reward of peace, Heb. 7; Isa. 9; Dan. 2: 7; Luke 1; Isa. 52; Rom. 10; Jn. 14; Col. 3; Zech. 8. In short, with this King and in this kingdom and reign it is nothing but peace; every thing that is seen, heard and done is peace.

Inasmuch as we have heard the word of peace, namely, the consoling gospel of peace, from the mouth of his messengers; therefore we, by his grace, have thus believed and accepted it in peace, and have committed ourselves to the only, eternal and true Prince of peace, Christ Jesus, in his kingdom of peace and under his reign, and are thus, by the gift of his Holy Spirit, by means of faith, incorporated into his body, and henceforth we look with all the children of his peace for the promised inheritance and reward of peace, Rom. 10: 15; Isa. 52: 7; 9: 6; Luke 2: 7.

As such exceeding grace of God has appeared unto us poor, miserable sinners, that we, who were formerly no people at all, and who knew of no peace, are now called to be such a glorious people of God, to be a church, kingdom, inheritance, body and property of peace; therefore we desire not to break this peace, but, by his great power by which he has called us to this grace and portion, to walk in this grace and peace, unchangeably and unwaveringly unto death, 1 Pet. 2: 9.

Peter was commanded to sheathe his sword. All christians are commanded to love their enemies; to do good unto those who abuse and persecute them; if any man shall smite thee on thy right cheek, turn to him the other, and if he take away thy coat, let him have thy cloak also. Say, beloved, how can a christian, scripturally, retaliate, rebel, war, murder, slay, torture, steal, rob and burn cities and conquer countries? Matt. 26: 52; Jn. 18: 10; Matt. 5: 12, 39, 40.

The great Lord who has created you and us, who has placed our hearts in the midst of our bodies, knows, and he only, knows that our hearts and hands are clear of all rebellion and murderous mutiny; and by his grace, they will ever remain clear. For we truly confess, that all rebellion is of the flesh and of the devil, Rom. 1: 30; 1 Jn. 3: 8; Rev. 21: 8; 22: 15.

O, beloved reader, our weapons are not swords and spears, but patience, silence and hope, and the word of God. With these we must maintain our cause and defend it. Paul says, "The weapons of our warfare are not carnal; but mighty through God." With these we intend and desire to resist the kingdom of the devil; and not with swords, spears, cannons and coats of mail. For "he (God) esteemeth iron as straw, and brass as rotten wood;" that we may thus, with our Prince, Teacher and Example, Christ Jesus, raise the father against the son and the son against the father, and that we may cast down imaginations, and every high thing that exalteth itself against the knowledge of God, and bring into captivity every thought to the obedience of Christ, Isa. 30: 7; Eph. 6: 17; Heb. 4: 12; 2 Cor. 10: 4; Job 41: 27; Matt. 10: 21; Luke 12: 53; 2 Cor. 10: 5.

Behold, reader, such a rebellion we seek and cause; but never, a rebellion of carnality. Not if we were as numerous as the spears of grass and the sand upon the sea shore, which, however, will never be the case, inasmuch as all men have not faith. O, that the way is so narrow and the gate so strait, 2 Thess. 3: 3; Matt. 7: 13; Luke 13: 24.

True christians know not vengeance, no matter how they are maltreated; in patience they possess their souls, Luke 21: 18; and do not break their peace, even, if they should be tempted by bondage, torture, poverty, and, besides, by the sword and fire. They do not cry for vengeance as do the world; but, with Christ, they supplicate and pray: "Father, forgive them; for they know not what they do," Luke 23: 34; Acts 7: 60.

According to the declaration of the prophet, they have beaten their swords into plowshares and their spears into pruning-hooks. They shall sit every man under his vine, and under his fig-tree, Christ; neither shall they learn war any more, Isa. 2: 4; Mic. 4: 3.

They do not seek your money, goods, injury nor blood, but they seek the honor and praise of God and the salvation of your souls. They are the children of peace; their hearts overflow with it; their mouths speak it, and they walk in the way of peace; they are full of peace; they seek, desire and know nothing but peace; and are ever prepared to forsake country, goods, life and all, for its sake; for they are the kingdom, people, church, city, property and body of peace, as has been heard.

Beloved reader, I, poor, miserable man (do not think hard of it), in my weakness have been writing these seventeen years; have feared the word of the Lord, and served my neighbors, and, I have unwaveringly borne his scorn and cross, with much misery, anxiety, tribulation and peril; and, I trust by his grace I will to the end continue to testify with a good conscience, his holy, worthy word, will and ordinance, verbally, by writing and at the peril of life, as much as is in me; and should I then yet at heart be a disquiet, rebellious, vengeful and bloody murderer? May the Most High save his poor servant from that!

Again, in Brabant, Flanders, Friesland and Gelderland the godfearing, pious hearts are, daily led to the slaughter as innocent sheep, and are tyrannically and inhumanly martyrized! Their hearts are full of spirit and strength; their mouths flow like the rivulets; their fruits scent like holy spices; their doctrine is powerful and their life is unblamable. Neither emperor nor king, fire nor sword, life nor death can frighten or separate them from the word of the Lord! And should their hearts yet be ensnared by bitterness, rebellion, vengeance, robbery, hatred and bloodshed? If so, what vain suffering it would be!

O, no, reader, no. Learn to know what a true christian is, of whom he is born, how he is minded, what is, properly, his intention and seeking, and you shall find that they are not rebels, murderers, and robbers, as the learned accuse them of, but that they are a godfearing, pious, peaceable people, as the Scriptures teach.

The other prince is the prince of darkness, anti-christ, and Satan. This prince is a prince of all evil, as rebellion, bloodshed, uproar and murder, which agree with his proper nature, arts, and doings, Jn. 8: 44, his commandments and teachings and his kingdom, body and church are of the same nature, 1 Jn. 3. Here we need not much Scripture. Seeing, hearing and daily occurrences and experience prove the truth.

Our opponents charge that we are intent upon rebellion; something of which we never thought. But we say, and that truthfully, that they and their ancestors for more than a thousand years have been that of which they accuse us. If we search history we will be convinced of this assertion. All those who placed themselves in opposition to their shamefulness, dishonor and evil-doing, had to suffer for it. Even so today.

For what they have done these last few years by their writings, teachings and cries, cities and countries prove. How wily they have placed potentate in antagonism to potentate and said to them, *Since the sword is placed in your hands you may maintain the word of the Lord thereby*, until they prevailed on them, and have shed human blood like water, torn the hearts from each other's body and made innumerable fornicators, rogues, widows and orphans; have eaten up and plundered the innocent civilian, and destroyed and ruined cities and countries. In short, they have done as if neither prophet, nor Christ nor apostle nor the word of God had ever been upon earth. Notwithstanding, they wish to be called the holy, christian church and body. O, dear Lord, how lamentably is thy holy, worthy word mocked, and thy glorious works derided! as if thy divine and powerful doings in thy church were nothing but reading, crying, water, bread, wine and name; and as if all rebellion, warring, robbing, murder and devilish works were allowable. Beloved reader, behold, and observe and learn, once to know this kingdom and body. For, if they, with such actions and doings, were the kingdom and body of Christ, as the learned pretend, then Christ's holy, glorious kingdom, church and body would be an inhuman, cruel, rebellious, bloody, robbing, crying, unmerciful and unrighteous people; this is incontrovertible. O, damnable error! O, dark blindness!!

And, yet, it does not suffice that they, by their light minded, licentious doctrine, lead the whole world into corruption and misery, and rob their own members of their property, welfare, doctrine, life and soul; but, besides, in their madness, they must lay hands upon the innocent, peaceable and humble kingdom and body of Christ, which will do no harm to the least upon earth. They continually lie, blaspheme, upbraid, betray and rebel, that we may well say with holy Peter, that they are born to torture and corruption; for their hearts, mouths and hands drip and reek with blood.

O, how exactly the Holy Spirit has depicted them, saying, "I saw the woman drunken with the blood of the saints, and with the martyrs of Jesus;" "And in her was found the blood of the prophets, and of the saints, and of all that were slain upon the earth," Rev. 17: 6; 18: 20.

Behold, kind reader, thus you will observe that they fall by their own sword which they drew against us, as the prophet says. For we may with clear consciences appear before the world (eternal praise be to the Lord) and truthfully maintain that we, from the time of our confession until the present moment, have harmed no one, have desired none of the property of others, much less laid hands upon it; that we have not sought the destruction, or blood of any, either by word or deed; and which, by the grace of God, we never shall do. But what they have done by their rebellious upbraiding, lying, slander, crying, writing and treason we will commend to the judgment of the Lord.

The merciful and gracious Lord grant and give you and them wisdom, that you may learn to know of what spirit and kingdom you are the children, what you seek, what prince you serve, what doctrine you maintain, what sacraments you have, what fruits you produce, what life you lead, and in what kingdom, body and church you are incorporated. This is our sincere wish.

Kind reader, earnestly reflect upon this our brief treatise on the two princes and their kingdoms, and by the grace of God, it will give you no mean insight into the Scriptures.

In the fourth place, some of them charge that we have our property in common.

Answer. This charge is false and without truth. We do not teach and practice the doctrine of having goods in common. But we teach and maintain by the word of the Lord, that all truly believing christians are members of one body and are baptized by one Spirit into one body, 1 Cor. 12: 13; that they are partakers of one bread, 1 Cor. 10: 18; that they have one Lord and one God, Eph. 4: 5, 6.

Inasmuch as they are thus one, therefore it is christian and reasonable that they divinely love one another, and that the one member be solicitous for the welfare of the other, for thus both the Scripture and nature teach. The whole Scriptures speak of mercifulness and love; and it is the only sign whereby a true christian may be known, as the Lord says, "By this shall all men know that ye are my disciples (that is, that ye are christians), if ye have love one to another," Jn. 13: 35.

Beloved reader, it is not customary that an intelligent person clothes and cares for one part of his body and leaves the rest destitute and naked. O, no. The intelligent person is solicitous for all his members. Thus it should be with those who are the Lord's church and body. All those who are born of God, who are gifted with the Spirit of the Lord, and who, according to the Scriptures, are called into one body of love in Christ Jesus, are prepared by such love, to serve their neighbors, not only with money and goods, but also after the example of their Lord and Head, Jesus Christ, in an evangelical manner, with life and blood. They show mercy and love, as much as they can; suffer no beggars amongst them; take to heart the need of the saints; receive the miserable; take the stranger into their houses; console the afflicted; assist the needy; clothe the naked; feed the hungry; do not turn their face from the poor, and do not despise their own flesh, Isa. 58: 7, 8; Rom. 12: 13.

Behold such a community we teach. And not, that the one should take and possess the land and property of the other, as many falsely charge. Thus Moses says, "If there be among you a poor man, of one of thy brethren, within any of thy gates, in thy land which the Lord thy God giveth thee, thou shalt not harden thine heart, nor shut thine hand from thy poor brother." Tobias says, "Give of thy bread to the hungry, and of thy garments to them that are naked." Christ says, "Be ye therefore merciful, as your Father also is merciful." "Blessed are the merciful for they shall obtain mercy." Paul says, "Put on therefore, as the elect of God, holy and beloved, bowels of mercies," &c., "For he shall have judgment without mercy, that hath shewed no mercy; and mercy rejoiceth against judgment," Deut. 15: 7; Tobit 4: 16; Luke 6: 36; Matt. 3: 7; Col. 3: 12; Jas. 2: 13; Matt. 18: 33; 25: 36.

Again, this mercy, love and community we teach and practice and have taught and practiced them for seventeen years, so that, glory be to God, notwithstanding our property has to a great extent been taken from us, and is yet daily taken; many a pious father and mother are put to the sword or fire and we are not allowed the free enjoyment of our homes, as is manifest, and, besides, we have dear times and famine, yet none of the pious nor any of their children who commit themselves to us, have been forced to beg. If this is not christianity, then we may well abandon the whole gospel of our Lord Jesus Christ, his holy sacraments and christian name, and say that the love-like, merciful life of all saints is mere fantasy and dreams. O, no. "God is love; and he that dwelleth in love dwelleth in God and God in him," 1 Jn. 4: 16.

This I write to shame our backbiters, because of their envy; they are so blinded that they are not ashamed thus shamefully to slander us, and wickedly to convert good into evil. For although we, in accordance with all Scripture, teach mercy and love and serve the godfearing poor by the sweat of our brow, and would not let them suffer for want, yet we must hear *That we teach community of goods; that every person should beware of us; for that we would reach into the chests and pockets of others.* While they well know that it is written, "He shall have judgment without mercy, that has shewed no mercy," Jas. 2; and, "He that loveth not his brother, abideth in death," 1 Jn. 3: 14; and while they also plainly see that we daily, and freely sacrifice our goods for the testimony of Jesus Christ and our consciences.

O reader, it would be well for your souls that you would once take notice and learn to know your preachers. For how can they teach you that which is good, while they can hear no mercy?

Is it not terrible hypocrisy that these poor people boast of having the word of God, and of being the true, christian church, never remembering that they have entirely lost their sign of true christianity? For, although many of them have plenty of everything, go about in silk and velvet, gold and silver, and in all manner of pomp and splendor, ornament their houses with all manner of costly ornaments, have their coffers filled and live in voluptuousness — yet they suffer many of their poor, afflicted members (notwithstanding they are fellow-believers, have received one baptism and partaken of the same bread with them), to ask alms; and poor, hungry, suffering, old, lame, blind and sore people to beg their bread at their doors.

O, teachers, teachers! Yea, beloved teachers, where are the fruits of the gospel you preach? Where is the signification of the supper you administer? Where are the fruits of the spirit you have received? And where is the righteousness of your faith which you so beautifully adorn before the poor, ignorant people? Is it not all hypocrisy that you preach, maintain and assert? Be ashamed at the vain preaching and bread-breaking of your easy gospel which you have these many years practiced with your doctrine and sacraments which you have preached to your needy, miserable members of the streets, notwithstanding the Scripture plainly teaches and says, "Whoso hath this world's good, and seeth his brother have need, and shutteth up his bowels of compassion for him, how dwelleth the love of God in him?" Also Moses, There shall be no beggars among you, 1 Jn. 3: 17; Deut. 15: 8.

Behold, kind reader, thus his charge is false and wrong in fact, as are also their other charges. For although we know that the apostolic churches, from the beginning have practiced it, as may be seen by the acts of the apostles, yet we may observe from their epistles that it went down, in their times, and (perhaps not without cause) was not practiced. Since we do not find that it was continually practiced by the apostles as we said, therefore we also leave it behind and have never taught nor practiced community of goods. But we diligently and earnestly teach and admonish assistance, love and mercy, as the apostolic Scriptures abundantly teach us this. Behold, in Christ we tell you the truth and lie not.

And, even if we did teach and practice community of goods, as we are charged, we would but do that which the holy apostles, full of the Holy Spirit, did in the primitive church at Jerusalem, although afterward abolished, as was said.

But the reason why our opponents charge us with it may be easily immagined. For generally, their hearts are filled with avarice, as Peter says, and they know that their disciples are intent upon the lusts of the flesh, money and goods. They are all covetous, as the prophet says, and therefore they make the charge, that thus the precious gospel, the limpid truth of our Lord Jesus Christ, which now springs up in many places, may become a stench and abomination to all. Behold the arts and wiles of the serpent!

Reader, beware; let not such liars deceive you. Adam and Eve believed the deceiver, and thereby so wickedly sinned against their God. Israel was miserably deceived by the false prophets. And what good things they have done in the gospel times and yet do, their deeds and fruits openly show.

In the fifth place some of them falsely charge, That we believe in poligamy; that we have our women in common; that we say to each other, Sister, my spirit desires your flesh.

Answer. As to poligamy we would say, The Scriptures show that before the law, some of the patriarchs had many wives. Yet they did not take the same liberty under the law and before the law. For Abraham, who was before the law, had his own sister for wife, as he himself testifies before Abimeleck, the king, saying, "And yet she is my sister; she is the daughter of my father, but not the daughter of my mother," Gen. 20 : 12. Jacob had two sisters for wives, Leah and Rachel, the daughters of Laban, his mother's brother, Gen. 22. These liberties to marry their own sister and to marry two sisters at once, were afterwards strictly forbidden Israel under the law, Lev. 18.

As each period has had its particular liberty and usage according to the Scriptures; and as we now, under the New Testament, are not pointed by the Lord to the usage of the patriarchs before the law nor under the law, in the matter of marriage, but to the beginning of creation, to Adam and Eve (which word we sincerely desire to obey); therefore we teach, practice and consent to no other than the one which was in the beginning in Adam and Eve, namely, one husband and one wife, as the Lord's mouth has ordained, Matt. 19.

We say one husband and one wife, and not one husband and two, three, or four wives, and these counted as one, as many, alas, charge us without any truth. These two, one husband and one wife, are one flesh, and cannot be separated from each other, to marry again, otherwise than for adultery, as the Lord says, Matt. 5: 19; Mark 10; Luke 16.

Behold, this is our proper foundation, doctrine and practice concerning marriage, as we here confess by the Holy Scriptures, and by the grace of God, it will ever remain the foundation of all pious souls, no matter what false charges and slander may be preferred against us. For we know and confess truly, that it is the express ordinance, command, intent and unchangeable, plain word of Christ.

But as to the charge of the shameful licentiousness of having our wives in common, we reply with Solomon: "Answer not a fool according to his folly, lest thou also be like unto him. Answer a fool according to his folly, lest he be wise in his own conceit," Prov. 26: 4, 5.

Kind reader, I am heartily ashamed to touch upon such accursed charges of licentiousness and roguishness before the ears of blushing, pious persons. For they are not only in opposition to the Scriptures but also to all rationality, intelligence and virtue. But as they not only charge us hereby with shameful roguery and knavery, but also with the worst of doggery, and as the pious, virtuous hearts who, if possible, would rather die ten deaths than commit such abominations, may see how they are spit upon by some indiscreet slanderers; therefore it is no more than reasonable to do so for the purpose of defending our reputation in a christian manner to the praise of the Lord, and to ward off such slander from us, to the extent possible.

We hereby testify, now and forever, in this place, before God, that we, with the angel of the church of Ephesus, hate the words of the Nicolaitans, which, also, God hates, Rev. 2. We teach, as from the mouth of the Lord, "That whosoever looketh on a woman to lust after her, hath committed adultery with her already in his heart," Matt. 5: 28. And with Paul, That the adulterers and fornicators cannot inherit the kingdom of God, 1 Cor. 6.

As we are thus so plainly taught by the Scriptures, and as, by the grace of the Lord, we not only believe so, but also teach others so by virtue of the divine word, and besides, as we are in constant danger of apprehension, prison and death; are tied to the stake by threes and fours, by sixes and sevens; are tortured, burned or drowned, and thus unmercifully murdered, therefore judge whether we would yet practice such terrible abominations and shame, at which every reasonable person should stand astounded, and which, according to many Scriptures, are rewarded by everlasting death and eternal, unquenchable, hell fire. O, what miserable men we should be! It is shameful slander! No, no. We trust, that in our weakness, by the grace of the Lord we have reared our bodies and members for a temple and dwelling place of the Holy Spirit, according to our received gift. We trust, by the grace and assistance of the Lord, that we shall never commune with adulterers and fornicators, understand, if they do not repent, Rom. 1; 1 Cor. 6; Gal. 5; Eph. 5; Heb. 13; Rev. 21.

But how our slanderers and backbiters are minded; into what body they have incorporated their bodies and members, and by what kind of spirit they are urged, their intolerable lies and slander plainly show. Christ says, "Out of the abundance of the heart the mouth speaketh," Matt. 2:34. Every tree beareth fruit after its own kind. Seneca says, "As the man, so is his word." Yea, if these vain men were christians, and if they had but a little of the Lord's word and a spark of his Holy Spirit, as they boast of having, they would never think of such abominable slander against their neighbors who, as is plain, sincerely seek and fear the Lord, much less would they mock and deride them.

O, Ye indiscreet slanderers (I mean all those who are guilty of the shamefulness), Do you think that we are irrational creatures? and that there is no rationality left in us? Be ashamed of your inhuman lies and slander. This disreputable report and bad repute is saddled upon us who are innocent, by many who are guilty of this very thing. If my writing is wrong, then I am willing to bear the punishment. It is manifest and undeniable that many of your fellow-believers miserably defile their own members. For, by their deception, sleekness of tongue, promises and gifts, they seduce many a young maiden, who is, by one baptism, faith and supper incorporated into one body with them. In your brotherhood, many an honorable man's bed is defiled! many a shameful adulterer is found! many an unsuspecting soul is deceived! and many an illegitimate child is born! We will leave it to the judgment of all pious persons if that is not adultery, and a desire to have the women in common.

Beloved reader, judge aright and know the truth. Is not your church full of such debauchees, defilers, perjurers, and adulterers? are there not others that are keepers of houses of prostitution? Can we not hear and see unchaste women sing and drink, throng and act indecorous in allies and streets? Do they not live in city and country in open prostitution? Your answer must be, yes; for it cannot be denied. And all these are your fellows in faith, members of your body; grains of your bread. O, vain doctrine and faith! O, fruitless baptism and supper! O, unclean body and church!!

Behold, kind reader, if you are reasonably minded you must admit that our slanderers are guilty of the things with which they charge us. My friend, beware lest you commit violence against the godfearing, with these slanderers. Syrach says, Whosoever accustoms himself to evil saying and whoring will never reform. For as we hate all abominations which are contrary to the word of God, and not only reprove them by our teaching, but also at the risk of life, how much more, then, this abomination? For it is not alone contrary to God's word, but also contrary to reasonableness. O, dear Lord, thus are those slandered who sincerely glorify thy name, who walk in thy ways, and sacrifice property and life for the sake of thy holy word.

In the sixth place they falsely charge, That if one, after he has made confession and received baptism, again falls into his sins, we refuse such an one all penance and grace.

Answer. This charge, if true, would be a fine excuse for the licentious to persecute the truth. But, happily, it is false and wrong in fact, as are their other charges, and can never be substantiated.

Inasmuch as the charge is false, and as there might be some among the pious who are not acquainted in the matter, therefore I will present my foundation and confession, as taken from the word of the Lord, of the nature of different sins; which will be forgiven and which are unpardonable. And thus present it to the pious and godly reader, to ponder diligently upon it.

In my opinion the Scripture speaks of different kinds of sin. The first kind is the corrupt, sinful nature, namely, the lust or desire of our flesh, contrary to God's law, and contrary to the first righteousness, which is inherited at birth by all descendants and children of corrupt, sinful Adam; and is not inaptly called inherent sin. Of this sin, David says, "Behold, I was shapen in iniquity; and in sin did my mother conceive me." Again, the Lord said unto

Noah, "The imagination of man's heart is evil from his youth." Again, Paul says, "We were, by nature, children of wrath, even as others," Ps. 51: 5; Gen. 8: 21; Eph. 2: 3.

Yea, kind reader, as we are all stained by this evil, we would all have abided in death, if the righteousness, intercession, death and blood of Christ Jesus were not given us as a reconciliation to God our heavenly Father, Rom. 5: 8. But now, for Christ's sake, it is not accounted as sin, Rom. 3: 5, 6, 8.

The second kind are the fruits of the first sin, and are not inaptly called actual sins, by the learned. They are these: Adultery, fornication, avarice, debauchery, hatred, envy, lying, theft, murder and idolatry. These are also called works of the flesh, by Paul, Gal. 5; and that, because they have their origin in the flesh which is born of Adam, corrupt and sinful, Rom. 5; Eph. 5.

But if inherent sin which is the mother, and actual sin, which is the fruit, are connected together, there is no forgiveness nor promise of life; but there wrath and death abide, unless they are repented of, as the Scriptures teach.

If this inherent sin is to loose its effect, and actual sin be forgiven, then we must believe the word of the Lord, be regenerated by faith, and thus, by virtue of the new birth, by true repentance, resist the inherent sin, die unto actual sin, and be pious.

For, as the carnal birth which is of Adam, is unclean and sinful and begets all evil and unrighteousness unto death, at the instance of thh devil—thus, on the other hand the heavenly birth which is of God, is clean and pure, and begets all righteousness and piety unto life, according to the will of God, Rom. 5; 1 Jn. 3: 5.

The third kind are human frailties, errors and stumblings which are yet daily found among the saints and regenerated; such as untempered thoughts, careless words and rashness in our actions. These although they spring from those sins mentioned, as the sins of the unbelieving and impenitent, are yet not of the same kind; and have this difference: the unbelieving which are yet unchanged in their first birth, commit sin unrestrainedly and fearlessly, because of the blindness of their corrupt nature they do not realize the wickedness of their sins; and besides, they do not consider their actions sinful. For sin is not made manifest unto them by the law, because of their unbelief.

But those who are born from above are fearful of all sin; they know by the law that all which is contrary to the first, righteousness, is sin, be it inwardly or outwardly, important or trifling; and therefore they daily fight, in spirit and faith with their weak flesh; sigh and lament about their errors, which they, with Paul, sincerely abhor. For, they know them to be contrary to the first righteousness and God's law, and are, therefore, sins; they daily approach the throne of grace, with contrite hearts, and pray: Holy Father, forgive us our trespasses as we forgive those that trespass against us. And thus, they are not rejected by the Lord on account of such transgressions, which are not committed willfully and intentionally, but contrary to their will, out of mere thoughtlessness and frailty. Yea, even as Peter, although he thrice denied the Lord; for they are under grace, and not under the law, as Paul says. The seed of God, faith in Christ Jesus, the birth which is of God, and the unction of the Holy Spirit abide in them. They exercise themselves continually in warring against their flesh; die unto their lusts; watch and pray incessantly and, although they are such poor, weak children, the are rejoiced in the sure trust of the merits of Christ, and praise the Father for his grace, Heb. 4; Matt. 6; Luke 12; Rom. 6; 1 Jn. 3: 5; Job 7; Eph. 6; 2 Tim. 2; Gal. 5; 2 Cor. 6; 1 Pet. 5.

Behold this deficient and weak nature all the saints have ever lamented; and hence John says, "If we say that we have no sin, we deceive ourselves, and the truth is not in us; if we confess our sins he is faithful and just to forgive us our sins, and to cleanse us from all unrighteousness," 1 John 1: 8, 9.

The fourth kind is, that after one is enlightened in his heart by the heavenly lustre of the everlasting truth; has received the true knowledge of Christ and his holy word, has tasted the heavenly gifts, the kindness of the Lord, and the enjoyment of the future world, has partaken of the Holy Ghost and is born of God; he again, by stubbornness, malice and willfulness, contrary to his heart, mind and spirit which is in him, renounces all knowledge and grace; rejects the Spirit and word of God; ejects the sweet, new wine; hates and blasphemes all truth willfully with the Pharisees and scribes; ascribes it to the devil, notwithstanding his conscience convinces him that it is the will, word, power and work of God; returns to the broad way and says at heart with all evil disposed, I will not submit. What kind of sin this is, I will leave to the sentence of the word of the Lord, Num. 15; Matt. 12; Mark 3; Luke 12; 1 Jn. 5; Heb. 6.

Kind reader, understand me. I do not speak of such persons as are overtaken in a fault, even though their transgressions were as great as the fall of David (from which the great Lord save all his), who was so miserably deceived by the lusts of the flesh, but I speak of those who, out of mere petulance, willfully trample upon the Son of God, deem the blood of the New Testament unclean, and profane the Spirit of grace.

O reader, kind reader, take heed, and remember that it is written, "It is a fearful thing to fall into the hands of the living God," Heb. 10: 31.

And although such willful blasphemy and sin had no offering in Israel, Num. 15, and the sinning against the Holy Spirit has no forgiveness, as Christ says, Matt. 12; Mark 3; Luke 12; yet I would advise all the godfearing, as far as I am able, that if any should revert to the works of the flesh and of death, after his confession and baptism, wisely to consider the matter and not make a mistake in such a case by an unseasonable and undue sentence; for the Lord, to whom nothing is concealed, knows what sin he has committed; whether he has sinned against the Holy Ghost or not; but let them admonish such according to the word of the Lord. If he be converted, if he show true fruits of repentance according to the Scriptures; if he again receive a broken, contrite and penitent heart, and besides, a peaceable, joyful and cheerful mind, then it is manifest that he did not sin against the Holy Ghost. But if he remain unrepentant, continue in his perverseness, and this unto the end, willfully despise Christ and his word, then his work shows what sin he has committed, and that his end and reward will be death, Rom. 1: 8; 1 Cor. 6; Gal. 5; Eph. 5; 1 Jn. 3: 5; Rev. 21: 22.

Behold, kind reader, thus we believe that all sins, both outward and inward, have their reconciliation in the merit and power of the blood of the Lord, if truly repented of, according to the Scriptures.

Let every one take heed that he walk in the fear of the Lord and accept the grace, lest he be given to the wrong spirit, fall into the judgment of the Lord, and the penance, which avails before God, be refused him. For Christ says, "Whosoever committeth sin is the servant of sin." Peter says, "Of whom a man is overcome, of the same is he brought in bondage." Let therefore none be overcome of sin, else he will be the servant of sin. This is incontrovertible. Jn. 8: 34; 2 Pet. 2: 19.

I think that this our confession and also the ban or separation, which the Scripture teaches and which we practice, by which we seek the scriptural shame of the degenerated to their reformation, fully prove that we are villified by our opponents in this regard. Yea we testify before the Lord and before you that we desire nothing upon earth more ardently than that we may return a poor, erring sinner to the right way.

But this we say, That the promises of God of eternal salvation, as preached by the gospel, are not made to the unrepentant sinners, hypocrites, avaricious, earthly-minded, mockers, nor perverse; but they are made to those who, with all their heart, hear, truly believe the lovely word of our Lord Jesus Christ, and thereby become new men born of God; become dead unto this fearful world of ungodly pride, pomp, vanity and lustfulness. For the unrepentant would boast of the Scripture and console themselves thereby, while their life is contrary thereto, and is open blasphemy. Christ says, "If ye continue in my word, then are ye my disciples indeed," Jn. 8: 31. "Ye are my friends, if ye do whatsoever I command you," Jn. 15: 14; for the vine bears after its own kind.

In the seventh place they slander us and say, That we are vagabonds, sneak-thieves, deceivers, new monks and hypocrites; that we claim to be without sin, heaven-stormers and work-saints, who want to be saved by our own merits and works; that we are an ungodly sect and conspirators, murderers of the souls of infants, anabaptists, profaners of the sacraments and possessed of the devil.

Answer. These and like slanders, Christ Jesus, together with the holy apostles, prophets and saints of the primitive church, had to hear many times, as was said in the preface. "If they have called the master of the house Beelzebub, how much more they of his household?" "The disciple is not above his master, nor the servant above his lord." Yet we trust that it is known to all honorable, pious and reasonable men that all these slanders are spoken against us by our opponents without any truth, out of mere hatred and envy, that they may thus hinder and oppose the course of the word and afflict the innocent, Matt. 10:25,24.

Reply to the charge, Vagabonds. Vagabonds are rogues, evil-disposed and idle persons, and evil-doers, who on account of their criminality, wander from place to place without a home. But we are poor, miserable pilgrims, and, according to the flesh, strangers, who, not on account of any crime, but for the testimony of Jesus Christ and our consciences, must flee, with our wives and children from before the tyrannical, bloody sword, to save our lives, and thus we have to earn our bread in foreign lands, in anxiety and tribulation, hearing many scornful and abusive words, we who, agreeable to Scripture and reason, should be received in love, and provided for and protected, and not be so unmercifully rejected and slandered as we are, at present, on every hand, 1 Pet. 1; 1 Cor. 4; Ex. 22:24; Isa. 58:6; Jer. 7:5; Zech. 7; Matt. 25; Rom. 13; 1 Pet. 4; Heb. 13.

Reply to the charge, Sneak-thieves. Sneaks are thieves and murderers, who secretly enter houses for the purpose of taking the property or lives of others. Also perjurers, adulterers and fornicators who are intent upon defiling the houses of their neighbors. For such wait for the darkness, and say, "No eye shall see me; and distinguish his face. In the dark they dig through houses," Job 24:15, 16. But this is not the case with us. Yet it has gone so far by the lying, upbraiding and cries of the learned, that alas, one cannot publicly say anything about the word of the Lord, although it is the only bread whereby our souls must live; and as we learn and understand from the Scriptures that Moses and all Israel ate the passover at night, Ex. 12; that Christ admonished Nicodemus at night, Jn. 3:2; that the church assembled at night to pray, Acts 12:12; that Paul taught the word of the Lord all night, Acts 20; and that the primitive church assembled at night to break the bread of the Lord, as the Scriptures mention; therefore we confess that it is admissible to preach the word of the Lord at night as well as in day time, to the praise of the Lord; and thus we ofttimes assemble in the fear of God, without injury to any body (the Lord knows) at night in a christian manner, to teach the word of the Lord and to admonish and reprove in all godliness; also to pray and administer the sacraments in a manner as the word of the Lord teaches us.

Reply to the charge, Deceivers. Deceivers are those who call impenitent, carnal persons, christians, and console them in their blindness, avarice, pride, pomp, splendor, debauchery and idolatry, with water, absolutions, bread, wine and ceremonies; who so shamefully adulterate the word and sacraments of God and lead the poor, miserable souls into death for the sake of a meal of bread or a handful of barley, all of which, before the Lord, we are innocent, by his grace. For we teach the word of the Lord unadulterated and with a good conscience, without respect of person. We seek the salvation of every soul and not their favor and gifts. We administer the Lord's baptism and Supper according to the direction of his holy word. And although we are poor, weak, miserable, and of evil, unclean flesh, and diseased sinners, yet we would gladly, in our weakness, act rightly and be pious and live unblamably before the world.

We seek and desire, by the grace and assistance of the Lord, according to our small talent, to re-establish that which is fallen; make right that which is wrong; seek that which is lost; humble the high-minded; direct the hungry into the right pasture; lead the thirsty to the true fountain and the blind in the right way, that we may thereby sow the gospel of our Lord Jesus Christ in many hearts, to the praise of our God, and publish his great and adorable name, Ezek. 34; 2 Cor. 10.

Reply to the charge, New Monks. We would consider those to be new monks who formerly established churches, cloisters, human statutes, and the easy epicurean life, in the semblance of zeal, which they have abandoned and in its place accepted a more lustful, pompous and carnal life, without change of heart and remained in their sins, and these placed the firmness of their faith, hope and salvation, from the beginning upon human choice, opinion and flattery. It is the manner and custom of monks to follow human statutes, commands and institutions, and not the word of God. They have their abbots, priors and pursers or procurators, and are called by their founders and masters, Augustinians, Franciscans, Dominicans, Bernardinians and Jacobins.

Not so with us. But we trust, by the grace and mercy of the Lord, that we are children of God and disciples of Christ. We know of no other Abbot than him on whom all true christians call in spirit and truth, and say, "Abba Father," Rom. 8: 15; Gal. 4: 6. Our head or Prior is Christ Jesus, Col. 1; Eph. 1.

Our procurator or purser who distributes his gifts to every one, is the Holy Spirit, 1 Cor. 12: 11.

Our profession is, the sincere, frank and fearless confession of faith, Matt. 10; Rom. 10: 9, 10.

Our statutes and laws are the express commandments of the Lord, Matt. 19: 17.

Our cap and cloak are the garments of righteousness, with which we would gladly clothe ourselves, Matt. 22: 11.

Our cloisters are the assemblage of the saints, the city of the living God, the heavenly Jerusalem, Heb. 12: 22; Rev. 21: 2.

Our easy, monk-life and pleasure are daily expectation of prison and fetters, fire and water, and to be exiled with our wives and children, to suffer hunger, tribulation, anxiety and pain, for the testimony of Jesus.

Behold, kind reader, this is the monkhood which we confess and practice, and none other. By the grace and power of the Lord, we also hope to abide therein unchangeably, all our lives. O, indiscreet slanderers and blasphemers! Jn. 4: 23.

Reply to the charge, Hypocrites. According to the Scriptures, hypocrites are those who, for the outward world, put on a holy appearance by words and gestures, such as the Scribes and Pharisees, Matt. 23, and who are inwardly full of all unrighteousness, avarice, hatred and deceit, as our opponents are, who pretend to be christians, talk much about the word of the Lord, boast much of the gospel and christianity, claim that they practice the true doctrine of Christ and that they are his holy church; while at the same time, they adulterate the word of God, call the wholesome administering of the sacraments, heresy; hate all the pious, and practice the works of the flesh, openly, as may be seen. We will leave all intelligent persons to judge whether such are not the companions and fellows of the Scribes and Pharisees.

The reason why we are accused as hypocrites, and why we are thus belied that we claim to be without sins, is because we teach penitence according to the Scripture; because we testify with holy Paul, that perjurers, adulterers, idolaters, wine-bibbers, avaricious, liars and unrighteous shall not inherit the kingdom of God, 1 Cor. 6: 10; Gal. 5: 21; Eph. 5: 5; that those who are carnally-minded shall die, Rom. 8: 13. And with John, that those who sin (understand, willfully) are of the devil, 1 John 3: 8, and that we, therefore, in our weakness, abhor such works; although with Moses we have often confessed, verbally and in writing, as we ever will confess, that none is clear before God, on account of the inborn nature, Gen. 6: 5; 8: 21; with Isaiah, that we are all as the unclean; with David, that there is no living man righteous before God, Ps. 14: 3; with Paul, that nothing good dwells in our flesh, Rom. 7: 18; with John that if we say, we are without sin, we deceive ourselves and no truth is in us, 1 John 1: 8, and with James, that in many things we offend all, Jas. 3: 2.

Behold, kind reader, this is why the preachers call us hypocrites who claim to be without sin. Such abominable lies are told by those who pretend to preach the word of God!

Reply to the charge, Heaven-stormers. Henceforth, because we teach from the mouth of the Lord: That if we would enter into life we must keep the commandments, Matt. 19, 17; Mark 10: 19; Jn. 15: 10, that in Christ neither circumcision nor uncircumcision avail; but the keeping of the commandments of God, 1 Cor. 7: 19, and that the love of God is that we keep his commandments; and his commandments are not grievous, 1 Jn. 5: 3, therefore we are called by the preachers *heaven-stormers* and work-saints; and that we want to be saved by our own merits; although we always have confessed, and by the grace of God, ever will, that we cannot be saved by means of anything in heaven nor in earth other than by the merits, intercession, death and blood of Christ, as has been amply demonstrated above, Jn. 14: 3; Acts 4: 12; Phil. 2: 10.

Behold, thus the best of these perverse people have been changed to the very worst, and do not observe that the whole Scripture, condemns, all licentious, obstinate despisers and transgressors of the commandments of God, to death, who plainly prove by their deeds that they do not confess the saving grace of God; do not believe in Christ Jesus, and, according to Scripture, abide in damnation, wrath and death, Jn. 3: 36. For whoso doeth unrighteously, showeth by his works whose disciple he is.

Reply to the bitter slander, Ungodly Sects and Conspirators. So far as regards the bitter, envious slander and charge that we are a perverse, ungodly sect and conspirators we answer: If we were allowed an impartial hearing with our opponents before a tribunal of persons who understand the word of God, we would soon be cleared of the infamous charge and they would be found guilty. For what kind of conspirators they are, this Scripture testifies, "There is a conspiracy (mark, conspiracy) of her prophets in the midst thereof, like a roaring lion ravening the prey; they have devoured souls; they have taken the treasure and precious things; they have made her many widows in the midst thereof," Ezek. 22: 25.

All may find a place in their sect who will but keep their ceremonies and acknowledge them to be the true preachers and messengers no matter what kind of life they lead if they but steer clear of falling into the hands of the executioner. No drunkard, no avaricious or pompous person, no defiler of women, no cheat or liar, no thief, robber or shedder of blood (understand, by going to war), no curser or swearer so great and ungodly but he must be called a christian. If he but say, I am sorry. It is all ascribed to his weakness and he is admitted to their supper; for, say they, he is saved by grace and not by merits. He remains a member of their church notwithstanding he remains in all his doings an unrepentant, obdurate and ungodly heathen; to-day as yesterday; also, to-morrow as to-day notwithstanding the Scripture so plainly testifies that such shall not inherit the kingdom of God, Rom. 1: 32; 1 Cor. 6: 10; for they are of the devil, Jn. 8: 44; 1 Jn. 2: 11.

O, preachers, preachers! learn once to know your own sect and conspirators, we pray you for Christ's sake. You boast that you are the true, christian church, but we fear you are a new Sodom, Egypt and Babylon. Oh! oh!! For many years we have drank from the same goblet with you and walked in the same Spirit; we have received one crisma and anointment with you, we know very well; but we have received mercy, and spewed out the inhaled abomination and willingly entered into the lovely communion of his saints, into the house, kingdom and body of Christ; who hate all ungodliness and sinfulness, and with all their strength, strive after and desire righteousness and godliness. Although they are called by you and all the world an ungodly sect and conspirators, yet, they are peaceable and joyous in spirit, and are assured in their consciences that truth is on their side; and that they are not an ungodly sect and conspirators, but God's own peculiar people, church and body, 1 Cor. 12: 13; Eph. 1: 5; Col. 1: 18; 1 Pet. 2: 10. O Lord, how lamentably thy small flock is ever slandered! Rom. 12: 4; Eph. 1: 23; 5: 27.

Reply to the slander and false charge, Murderers of the souls of Infants. In the same manner we must often hear from these poor, blind people who seek the salvation of their children in the baptism of their preachers, that we murder the souls of our infants, because we believe the word of the Lord that the kingdom is promised them by grace, by the election of God our heavenly Father through the merits of Jesus Christ, as he says, "Suffer little children and forbid them not, to come unto me; for of such is the kingdom of heaven," Matt. 19:14; Mark 10:14; Luke 18:16; and that we therefore do not suffer to have them baptized with the baptism of anti-christ. For not the baptism of anti-christ but the promise of Jesus Christ assures us of the salvation of our little children if they die and depart from here. But if the good Father suffer them to grow up and grant them his grace, then we would educate them in the instruction and fear of the Lord as much as we are able. When they can understand God's word and believe it, the Scripture directs them to be baptized, Matt. 28:19; Mark 16:16. But those who practice such manifest hypocrisy and anti-christian works, banish the devil from the innocent vessels which are cleansed with the blood of the Lord; they conjure, salt, anoint, and consecrate them, baptize them on the faith of others, while they find not a single commandment to practice such flummery and mockery, in all the Scriptures.

The parents console themselves with the thought that they are now christians; and thus they are, from the cradle on, raised in all manner of blindness, pomp, splendor and idolatry, without the fear of God, so that when they become of understanding age they have no information of the word of God, and walk all their lives, trusting in infant baptism, upon a crooked and dark way, without confession, faith and new birth, without Spirit, word and Christ. What such do to the souls of their little children I will leave to their own consideration and to the sentence of the word of the Lord.

Reply to the base charge of being Anabaptists. We must also be called anabaptists by the learned, because we baptize at the confession of faith, as Christ commanded his disciples to do, and as the holy apostles taught and practiced, as did also the worthy martyr Cyprian, all of the African bishops; and besides, because we, with the Nicene Council, cannot accept the heretical baptism which is of anti-christ, as christian baptism; and because we are also informed by the Scriptures that St. Paul rebaptized some of those who were baptized with the baptism of John which was from heaven, because they did not acknowledge the Holy Ghost, Acts 19:3. Inasmuch as we but baptize according to the command of Christ and according to the teaching and practice of the holy apostles; nor do any more than Cyprian did, together with the council of Carthage and Nice, in this matter (although we acknowledge that we do not believe in all their doctrine); and, inasmuch as we rebaptize those who are not baptized with a divine baptism (as were those who were baptized of John), but with the baptism of anti-christ, and had at the time of their baptism no knowledge of divine matters, as both nature and the Scriptures teach, since they were yet unconscious infants, and as we are for this reason called anabaptists by the learned; therefore, indeed, Christ and his apostles, Cyprian and his bishops, the Nicene Council, the holy apostle Paul also must have been an anabaptist. This is incontrovertible.

Reply to the blind charge that we are profaners of the Sacraments. Again, some of the learned, also, call us profaners of the sacraments, because we do not believe that the bread and wine of their Supper is the actual, real flesh and blood of the Lord; or, as some have it, because we do not believe that we, through the wine and bread, actually partake of the flesh and blood of the Lord; notwithstanding that we reverentially administer the supper to the penitent (as far as man can judge), as a figurative or sacramental sign, with fear and trembling, also with thanksgiving and joy, according to the Scripture and according to the practice of the fathers, such as Gregory, Augustin, Chrisostom, Tertullian, Tyrill, Eusebius, &c., and, in our weakness, diligently strive rightly to commemorate and fulfill the holy, glorious mystery, the Lord's death, love, peace and the unity of his church and the communion of his holy flesh and blood which by this sign of bread and wine are symbolized to all true christians.

A HUMBLE AND CHRISTIAN DEFENSE.

The poor slanderers do not observe how fearfully they profane the sacraments of the Lord, if we call those sacraments, which they administer. Although they believe that they distribute the actual flesh and blood of the Lord, they yet esteem it so trifling that they distribute it to known drunkards, avaricious, liars, impenitent, &c., as if the Lord's Supper were to be partaken of by the penitent and impenitent alike. Whether this is not profaning the sacraments you may judge according to the Scriptures.

Reply to the pharisaic charge that we are possessed of the devil. We consider those of the devil who speak his words, who teach falsehood instead of truth, Gen. 3: 4, steal the glory from God and miserably deceive souls. But we trust, by the grace of the Lord (eternal glory be to God), that we hate the word of the devil from our inmost hearts; and that we are very desirous for the words of eternal truth, and of the fruits of the Spirit, according to the talent received, which is a decided proof that we are not of the spirit of the devil, but of the Lord. For if we were of the devil, as we are charged, we would walk upon a broader road and be befriended by the world, and not so resignedly offer our property and blood for the cause of the word of the Lord. Yet it is but just that the disciple be not above the master. The Father of the house himself had to hear that he was of the devil, Jn. 10: 20; 8: 48. The Pharisees and Scribes must manifest their nature and Spirit. For if they can not stand with their foolish wisdom before the power and truth of the Lord (for the spirit of Belial must ever give way to the Spirit of the Lord), they break forth in madness, heap falsehood upon falsehood, upbraid and lie with all their might, and ascribe it to the devil, although their consciences testify that it is the Spirit of the Lord. By what kind of a spirit such are urged their words and works sufficiently testify.

Behold, kind reader, here you have our reply to the principal slanderous charges with which we are greeted by our backbiters, opponents and persecutors. With such slander their writings are filled and their mouths overflow. We are pictured in such colors (the Lord forgive them) that we will quite likely be considered a perverse, ungodly people, by the great mass who walk upon the broad way, so long as the world shall stand. O, perverse nature! "O, generation of vipers (says Christ), how can ye, being evil, speak good things," Matt. 12: 34. I fear that they are members of the awful beast which arose from the sea, which was like unto a leopard, whose feet were as the feet of a bear and whose mouth as the mouth of a lion; and which opened his mouth to blaspheme the name of God and his tabernacle, and them that dwell in heaven, Rev. 13: 2, 6. For what is there which is holy and right according to the Scripture which they do not trample with their feet and blaspheme, with their mouth as an ungodly, accursed abomination? O, dear Lord, save all thy beloved children from this lying, deceiving generation, forever!

Eighthly and lastly, they say, Well, if truth is on their side, let them come before the public.

Answer. We would faithfully admonish the reader to consider well from what motive and with what intention they say so. For most of them say so from motives of mere envy and blood-thirstiness, we are sure, thinking that if we would do so it would soon be brought to an end. Others, perhaps, through simpleness and ignorance; thinking that we cannot defend it by virtue of the Scripture, since Christ and his apostles, as also the prophets, generally preached in public before the people, and were also sent for that purpose. To those that do so from motives of blood-thirstiness, we would say that they, with the Pharisees and Scribes, have burdened themselves with the blood of the innocent; and are counted as murderers, Matt. 23: 34; Jn. 10: 16; Luke 11: 49.

But to those who do so through ignorance (if there be such, which we hope there may be), we would say in all love, diligently to search all the Scriptures to see if they will find any passages to show that the apostles and prophets went forth publicly to preach when they were sure, beforehand, that it would cost them their lives, as we know to be the case if we would publicly go forth. No, no. If I mind aright, they ever avoided the places and cities which they were sure would seek their lives; or else they kept themselves concealed, as did Baruch and Jeremiah, when king Joachim had commanded that they should be taken, Jer. 36: 19.

They have all feared death and fled from it however much they were gifted with the Spirit of the Lord. "Moses cried unto the Lord, saying, What shall I do unto this people? they be almost ready to stone me," Exod. 17: 4.

Jeremiah says, "O my lord the king, let my supplication, I pray thee, be accepted before thee; that thou cause me not to return to the house of Jonathan the scribe, lest I die there," Jer. 37: 20.

David fled before Saul from one mountain to the other, and from one wilderness to another.

Urijah of Kirjath-jearim, a prophet of the Lord, fled from before the sword of the king of Judah, into the land of Egypt, Jer. 26: 20, 21.

Elijah, the spiritual man of God, fled to the wilderness, before the threats of Jezebel, 1 Kin. 19: 3. From fear of those of Nineveh, Jonah wanted to flee into Tarshish, Jonah 1.

When Paul knew that they were laying in wait for him he was let down by the wall in a basket, by night, Acts 9: 24, 25.

Behold, kind reader, thus the exalted men of God have feared and avoided death, and did not, generally, go where they feared violence, until they were admonished to do so by an oracle or by a revelation from angels.

So also Elijah appeared before king Ahab, after the long drought and famine, 1 Kin. 17. Thus the apostles freely spoke the word of the Lord in the temple, after they were led from prison, by an angel, Acts 5: 19; 12: 7; 26; 20.

Thus Paul preached at Corinth one year and a half after the Lord, in a vision, spake unto him, "Be not afraid, but speak, and hold not thy peace: For I am with thee, and no man shall set on thee to hurt thee: for I have much people in this city," Acts 18: 9, 10, and other like Scriptures. We are aware, beloved reader, that God has the power to save his own, if it be his will. For he smote the Syrians with blindness, who wanted to take Elisha. He sent Jonas through the turbulent waves, in a whale, to Nineveh. He took from the fire its power, and shut the lions' mouths. He delivered the apostles by the aid of angels. He is the Lord who lives unchangeable in his power and glory, 2 Kin. 6: 18; Jonah 1: 17; Dan. 3: 27; 6: 22; Acts 12: 11.

But as these are particular miracles of God which are not shown to every one, and as no Scriptures direct us to go there where we surely know that we shall die or be imprisoned for life, but as we are admonished in plain words to flee from the tyrants; and as the faithful men and servants of God, filled with the Holy Spirit, have done the same, as was said; therefore we simply say (and that with a good conscience) that we will not now, nor at any future time, publicly go forth unless it is proven to us in sincerity of heart, by Scripture (which we know, is impossible), that we should do so before we are urged as were the apostles and prophets by the power of the Lord, be it by a revelation from angels or by the urging of the Holy Spirit, as was heard. But in such a case we are at all times prepared to do the will of the Lord, and publicly to teach his holy word and administer his sacraments, at the peril of our lives, Matt. 10: 23; Jer. 1: 7; Matt. 2: 13; 4: 12.

It is also well known to the honorable reader, and to all who are acquainted with us, that we are called rebels and mutineers every where by the learned, notwithstanding that we are ever quiet and act justly with all mankind; and, if we now, should publicly teach the word of the Lord in the face of the upbraidings of the learned, of the mandates, of the rulers and of the mad cries of the populace, some of them would cry, rebels! rebels!! although we are, thank the Lord, clear of all rebellion and bloodshed, as has been heard.

Others would say, and not unjustly, that we killed ourselves by unlimited zeal, as we were well aware what was, in places, resolved against us, and we yet in the face of it publicly taught our doctrine.

We further desire the reasonable reader to take into consideration that a true teacher who preaches the word of the Lord unblamably cannot, at the present time, safely dwell in any kingdom, country or city under heaven, so far as our knowledge goes, if he be known. If he be not allowed to dwell safely, how can he safely preach and teach?

Besides, we plainly see that the innocent sheep must suffer and be led to the slaughter though they are no teachers, and should the teachers then, who are blamed for all, and who with Christ are hated above all evil-doers, yet go before the public in these mad, fearful times of all evil and tyranny? It would be foolishness; for to do so is not taught by common sense nor by the Scriptures.

And although we do not teach at public meetings where all classes assemble, yet the truth is not kept silent but is preached here and there both by day and by night, in cities and country, verbally and in writing, at the peril of life. This is testified to by judges, tormentors, prisons, fetters, water, fire, sword and stake.

Also must Flanders, Brabant, Holland, Gelderland, &c., confess at the last judgment that the word was preached to them, for they, on account of the word being preached, have shed innocent blood like water; it is so preached in these countries that we may well say with holy Paul, "If our gospel be hid, it is hid to them that are lost; in whom the god of this world hath blinded the minds of them which believe not," 2 Cor. 4: 3, 4.

Besides, I have, about the year 1545 or 1546, asked of the preachers of Bon a public meeting and discussion, under bishop Herman of Cologne, on condition of safe conduct.

I have also twice asked this in writing of those of Emden, and once of those of Wesel, on the same condition.

But, although those of Bon, and also those of Wesel had offered this to some of the brethren, still, when they found that I was willing to do so, it was, under a false pretense of necessity, refused by those of Bon as also by those of Emden.

Those of Wesel wished that the devil might treat with me.

Again, I have also offered to discuss with them for many years, in print; but it was not accepted.

Behold, kind reader, thus we have from the beginning of our service, been prepared and ready to give an account of our faith to every person who desired it in good faith, no matter whether he were ruler or citizen, learned or unlearned, rich or poor, man or woman. And we are to-day ready to do so as far as possible; we are not ashamed of the gospel of the glory of Christ. If one desire to hear from us, we are prepared to teach; if one desires to know our foundation, we sincerely desire to explain it clearly, if our writings do not suffice. If any one desires to discuss with us, no matter who he be (except those who have renounced us after scriptural exhortation was exhausted in their case), in sincerity of heart, the matter of our faith, without philosophy, flattery and garbling, and according to the unadulterated, evangelical doctrine and truth, the commandments, prohibitions, usage, Spirit and example of Christ and of his disciples, and that without any trickery, deceit or roguery, as did, in their time, Hilarius and Augustin and others, with some who were suspected in their doctrine; we will not, by the grace of the Lord, refuse to do so, if we possibly can before a public meeting or before twenty or more impartial, reasonable witnesses. For our most ardent desire is that the truth may be made manifest. But the bloody murder of anti-christ must be omitted; for it is devilish and unbecoming in a christian, Rev. 17: 18; Jn. 8: 44.

Inasmuch as our adversaries and opponents make our life and doctrine suspicious with many, by saying, that if truth be on our side we should come out in public (although they say so out of mere vindictiveness for they know very well that we can not do so, as there are tyrants and bloodshedders every where, as may be seen); therefore we give them this discreet answer.

Further, I would say, that if the truth be on the side of our opponents and not with us, as they claim, and, as they can freely go abroad before the whole world (understand each sect in its way) to preach their doctrine, faith and life; and, as we have to be subjected daily to suffering and torture they should, therefore, show enough of reason and love toward us, poor creatures, to obtain liberty for us from the magistracy whom they have, by their crying and slander against us, caused to be so bitterly opposed to us (something which does not become reasonable men, not to say christians), that we may thus, in their presence, before a public assembly or before twenty or more impartial, reasonable witnesses, as was said before, cause our foundation, doctrine and faith to be heard and explained according to the sure and true testimony of the Holy Scriptures. If they, then, have any thing to advance against our foundation, doctrine and faith, let them do so in the name of the Lord. Truth shall bear the crown. If not, let them lay their hands upon their mouths and keep silent and never more blaspheme that which is right and just.

Kind reader, if this could be accomplished many hard words would be saved; many miserable souls which are now kept by them in such accursed blindness, would be delivered from the snares of hell; and the noble, glorious truth, now so very much hated and despised by the world, would be made manifest in splendor and beauty. But so much discretion has not been found up to the present time.

As we are not allowed a public discussion, in a christian manner, as we have anxiously, and at different times asked of them, and as the ignorant and unversed yet cry, *If they be right why do they not come out publicly;* therefore we will leave it to the consideration and judgment of the intelligent reader, from what motives they thus cry; what kind of faith, love, gospel and truth they have, and by what kind of a spirit they are urged. For, whosoever has the truth will never come to shame; for truth is great, stronger than wine, kings and women.

CONCLUSION.

Here, dear reader, you have our defense and discreet reply to the bitter, envious falsehoods and slanders of our enviers by which we will live or die, and appear before our God at the judgment day, for which, perhaps, I shall not be thanked by many. Yet, since they, on every hand, by such inhuman falsehoods and slanders, rob us of our honor and reputation; so lamentably adulterate and suppress the precious, worthy word of our Lord Jesus Christ; maintain and uphold all the earth in their impenitent, ungodly being and cause so much misery to many a pious child; therefore we have written this in this emergency as a reasonable defense and christian reply of all pious and godfearing persons, that thereby all intelligent and reasonable readers, who cannot hear our verbal defense, may rightly judge between us and our opponents, may see the innocence of us all, and may learn to confess the poor, despised truth which is so lamentably stolen from them by their preachers; and we would herewith place in the hands of the Lord, this and all other shameful charges and accusations which are so enviously published against us, and leave them to his last judgment.

They may prove the nature of their father and fill the measure of their bloodthirstiness, for they will not do otherwise. We trust, by the grace of the Lord, to possess our souls in patience, and not turn our faces from the spies until the coming of him who shall come. Then shall they see him whom they have pierced, Rev. 1. And I would herewith sincerely pray the readers and auditors, be their station high or low, learned or unlearned, for Christ's sake to accept this my labor in love and to rightly interpret it; for I have performed it for no other purpose than to the praise of my God and to the service of all well-disposed persons; and with the intention that the rulers (I mean those who are reasonably minded, and would not willfully act contrary to the will of God) may be warned against pro-

CONCLUSION.

tecting this ungodly state of affairs and against heaping upon themselves the innocent [blood, that the preachers who err unwittingly may no longer serve and protect the kingdom of hell by their falsehood, slander, upbraiding, ungodly doctrine, sacraments and lives; that the common people may place their trust in the word of the Lord, seek the right way, fear the Lord, die unto their sins and reform their sinful life.

Cordially beloved reader, be not repulsed if it should taste bitter to your flesh. Behold, in Christ, it is the truth, to which we have here testified; nor will there ever be found any other foundation, doctrine, way, light and truth.

Therefore I desire that it be not kept hid from any reasonable persons; but that it may be read by or to every one, no matter who or where they be, if it might be of use to them, and they be not intent upon the corruption or blood of any one, that thereby the saving truth of Jesus Christ may be extended and the accursed falsehood of anti-christ be destroyed.

May the Almighty, eternal Father, the Creator of all things, the God of heaven and of earth, grant all my hearers and readers the heavenly gift and power of his Holy Spirit that they may hear and read this my humble treatise in the true fear of God, and with pure, impartial hearts, may wisely examine, well understand and accept it with true faith, and humbly fulfill it in willing obedience, to the praise of their God and the salvation of their souls, by his beloved Son Jesus Christ our Lord. To him be the honor, praise, kingdom, power and glory for ever and ever, Amen.

"Lying lips are abomination to the Lord: but they that deal truly are his delight," Prov. 12: 22; 6: 17.

"Devise not a lie against thy brother: neither do the like to thy friend. Use not to make any manner of lie: for the custom thereof is not good," Eccl. 7: 12, 13.

MENNO SIMON.

A BRIEF AND CLEAR CONFESSION

AND

SCRIPTURAL DEMONSTRATION,

FIRST,

OF THE INCARNATION OF OUR BELOVED LORD JESUS CHRIST.

SECONDLY,

HOW BOTH THE TEACHERS AND THE CHURCH OF CHRIST SHOULD BE MINDED ACCORDING TO THE SCRIPTURES.

WRITTEN TO

John A'Lasco and his Fellow-laborers at Emden.

A. D., 1544.

BY

MENNO SIMON.

"If ye continue in my word, then are ye my disciples indeed; and ye shall know the truth, and the truth shall make you free," Jn. 8 : 31, 32.

"For other foundation can no man lay than that is laid, which is Jesus Christ," 1 Cor. 3 : 11.

ELKHART, INDIANA:
PUBLISHED BY JOHN F. FUNK AND BROTHER.
1871.

PREFACE.

Menno Simon wishes the learned John A'Lasco and his fellows, and to all the people of East Friesland, of whatever class or condition in life they be, true faith, true light and knowledge, the Holy Spirit, the lovely fear and pure love of the Lord, an unblamable life and the eternal life of God our heavenly Father, through Jesus Christ, his beloved Son, our Lord, who has loved us and washed us in his blood. To him be the glory, honor, praise, kingdom, power and majesty for ever and ever, Amen.

BELOVED friends and brethren, as I, in the latter part of the first month of the year 1543, met you at Emden to discuss with you for three or four days, the disputed articles of our faith and religion, for which purpose I was invited to come, by writing; first, the incarnation of our beloved Lord Jesus Christ, to which, you well know, you forced me against my will; secondly, infant baptism. Not agreeing in this, you let me depart in peace at our separation, desiring however, that I should send to you, by U. L., the foundation of my faith, which I had compiled in writing, inside of a stipulated period, which was three months, so that you might thus show to your god-called rulers, our faith, diligence, desire, seeking and life (which, however, is very weak); upon what foundation, Scriptures and reasons our intended doctrine, faith and life was founded. I hope and trust, by the grace of the Lord, that you have desired and required this of me without any malice or bad intention.

Therefore I have promised to fulfill your kind bidding and desire, rejoiced in spirit; because also through U. L., our faith, doctrine and life could be best explained to those of high, social standing, to whose care the carnal sword was entrusted, and thus the suspicion be destroyed which is held against us by the pernicious uproar and shameful doctrine and practice of the false prophets, who, under a holy semblance, ever creep into society to the hindrance of the wise and intelligent; as before God, who knows our hearts, we are certainly clear of all their abominable doctrine, uproar, mutiny, bloodshed, polygamy and the like abominations. Yea, we hate, and with sincere affection fight against them as acknowledged heresy; as snares to the conscience; as deceit, seduction and fraud, and as pestilential doctrine, accursed by all divine Scripture. For how should the true brethren and sisters of Jesus Christ, the well-disposed children of God, who, with Christ Jesus, are born of God the Father, and the powerful seed of the divine word in Christ Jesus; regenerated by Christ, partake of his Spirit and nature, conform unto him, are christian and heavenly minded, teach rebellion of any kind? inasmuch as they are ever prepared, according to the measure of their faith, to do the will of the eternal Prince of peace, who has taught his disciples nothing but patience and eternal peace, saying, "Peace I leave with you, my peace I give unto you," Jn. 14 : 27. Again, "Peace be with you." For his kingdom is a kingdom of love, of unity, of peace, and of reformation; and not of hatred, rebellion, blood, disquiet and destruction. Again, In peace we are called of God; peace should rule in our hearts to him by whom we are called. Again, Blessed are the peace-makers. Paul says,

PREFACE.

"The God of hope fill you with all joy and peace in believing," Rom. 15 : 13. I am aware, kind reader, that the cited Scriptures have, for the most part, reference to the inward peace, which comes through Christ; yet, whoever has this inward, christian peace in his heart will nevermore be found guilty, before God and the world, of rebellion, treason, mutiny, murder, robbery or such unbecoming acts. For the Spirit of Christ which is in him seeks no evil, but good; no destruction, but healing; no corruption, but assistance; seeks to live everywhere in peace with all mankind, as far as possible. He follows "peace with all men, and holiness, without which no man can see the Lord," Heb. 12: 14; Jn. 14: 17; 21: 15; Rom. 14: 19; 1 Cor. 7: 15; Col. 3: 15; Matt. 5: 9; Rom. 15: 13.

Behold, beloved friends and brethren, by these and other Scriptures we are taught and warned not to take up the literal sword, nor ever to give our consent thereto, *Excepto ordinario potestatis gladio, indebitum usum verso*; but to take up the two-edged, powerful, sharp sword of the Spirit, which goes forth from the mouth of the Lord, namely, the word of God. By this we intend to destroy the kingdom of satan, constrain all the world to regeneration and salvation and bruise, crush and pierce all petrified and obdurate hearts. Desiring, I say, by the grace, Spirit and power of the Lord, therewith to circumcise all flesh, high, low, rich, poor, learned or unlearned, of all pride, vain show, pomp, avarice, usury, smuggling, lies, deceit, robbery, shedding of innocent blood, hatred, envy, adultery, fornication, unchastity, unnatural desires, gluttony, wine-bibbing, drunkenness, debauchery, cursing and swearing, blindness, vanity, and of the fearful, unbecoming idolatry; that all of them, no matter who they be, by the pure fear of the Lord, of whom comes the sure knowledge of the judgment of God, become first inwardly humble before him, and then, by the sure knowledge of his blessings, so abundantly shown to us, be refreshed and consoled by Christ Jesus, and thus willingly renounce, by the power of their faith, working by love, their own wisdom, intelligence, philosophy, sophistry, **unwillingness**, sloth, evil lusts, unbelief, disobedience and the very erroneous, carnal, mad life of this world, and enter into all divine wisdom, truth, love, zeal and soberness; the true sacraments and true religion, in full obedience to God and Christ and in all the christian fruits which flow from a pure heart, good conscience and unfeigned faith, Tit. 2: 7; 1 Pet. 1: 23; Eph. 6: 7; Heb. 4: 12; Rev. 1: 16; 19: 15.

Thus we do not contend with carnal, but with spiritual weapons, patience and with the word of the Lord, against all flesh, world and devil, trusting in Christ. Nor shall there ever be found other weapons with us. Therefore, be not afraid of us (behold, in Christ Jesus I lie not); for we do not desire your destruction, but your regeneration; not your condemnation, but your everlasting salvation; not your flesh and blood, but your spirit and soul; on account of which I have these seven years suffered and yet suffer slander and scorn, anxiety, suspension, persecution, and great peril of being imprisoned.

The more the word of the Lord is extended, by the grace of God, to the reformation of some persons, who, however, are few, the more hatred and bitterness increases against me; so that up to this hour I could not find, in all the country, where, alas, the mere boasting of the divine word is a great deal more plenty than the fear of God, a cabin, or hut (blessed be the Lord) in which my wife and little children can safely sojourn for a year or two. O, cruel, unmerciful christians! O, that all magistrates and princes, as also all the wise and learned knew the seeking, intention and desire of my heart, as also of my beloved brethren who, by the grace, Spirit and word of God, are converted into a new spirit or new birth! If they rightly understood our teaching how soon their hearts and minds would be changed into a different sense! But as all of them, with but few exceptions, are nothing but earth and flesh and not gifted with the Spirit of Christ; therefore, alas, we hear nothing from them but upbraiding and slander, can expect nothing from them (I mean the evil-disposed) but the stake, water, fire, wheel and sword, as a reward of gratitude, that we have sought and yet seek our conversion, salvation and eternal life, and that of the whole world, with such diligence, solicitude, pains and labor from our inmost heart. For I strive after nothing, of which God is my witness, but that the God of heaven and of earth, through his blessed Son, Jesus Christ may have the glory and praise of his blessed word; that all men may be saved; and that they may awaken in this convenient time of grace, from their profound sleep of sinfulness; that they may lay by all adhering sin and the damnable works of darkness; that they may put on the armor of light, that they may thus become, with us by true penance, faith, baptism, Supper, ban or separation, love, obedience and true life, one holy, christian church and body in Christ Jesus. Something which the whole world to-day yet opposes with all its strength with both shoulders and horns; not being willing that Christ Jesus, forever blessed, shall reign over them. Yea, they persecute, banish, burn, murder, and destroy all those who willingly teach and uphold the glory, praise, honor, will and commandments of the Lord. *De bis satis*, Heb. 12:15; Rom. 13:11; Heb. 12:2; Rom. 13:12; Luke 3:3; Matt. 3:1; 28:19; Mark 16:15; Acts 2; Matt. 18:17; 1 Cor. 5:5; 2 Thess. 3; 1 Tim. 1:20; Luke 19:47.

Inasmuch as I do your kind bidding in this matter by briefly compiling in writing my doctrine, faith and seeking, as I did before, verbally, which I am ever prepared to do to all mankind, according to the doctrine of Peter, as was said above, therefore I desire of you, so dear as Christ is to you, that you do not look upon this my confession, which is the word of God, with carnal, blind eyes, as the mad, unintelligent world do who want to have all things taught according to their own fancy and will, under the name of christianity; that you will not measure and judge according to the carnal way, as with logical questions and other like human wisdom; but that you will look at and judge it according to the word and truth of the Lord, as those would who understand spiritual matters, as unblamable, regenerated christians who are full of the knowledge, love and fear of God; are urged by the Holy Spirit, and do not seek human favor, praise and honor, self and carnal welfare, but alone the honor and glory of God, and the eternal salvation of their brethren. For such, alone, can judge of spiritual matters; and not the carnal minded, 1 Cor. 14:29. The Spirit of God teaches, judges and understands all things. Paul says, "What man knoweth the things of a man, save the spirit of man which is in him? even so the things of God knoweth no man but the Spirit of God," 1 Cor. 2:11. Therefore try your intention and the inmost of your hearts, as if before God who seeth all things. Search yourselves thoroughly and open your hearts before the Lord. In case you yet seek any carnal liberty, lusts, honor and profit, then, doubtlessly, your judgment in spiritual matters (especially as regards the mere confession) will be quite carnal, selfish, partial, unjust and false; you will also garble and pervert the plain testimony of the Holy Scriptures, by logic and false reasoning, to free yourselves and to please the world. Beware, lest you do so, and thus the terrible wrath of the Lord come upon you. I know why I write this. I am in doubt about your sincerity. Remember what I mean. And if your hearts be sincere, clean and pious before God, as I hope; and if you actually are desirous of the truth, then you will confess, by the grace of God, that our humble, plain doctrine, faith, sacraments, and the life of nearly all, particularly the outward, unblamable, christian, evangelical life, is conformable to the Spirit and word of God.

And if God, by his loving kindness, should grant that you sincerely acknowledge it in your inmost soul as being the unchangeable word and will of God, even as the Spirit and power of God; then I pray you by the precious blood of our Lord Jesus Christ to receive it in gladness and gratitude of heart and let it be examined by your ordained rulers and by all men and let them know what your heart, spirit or conscience testifies concerning our doctrine, faith, sacraments and lives. Fear not the exalted position of any man, nor despise his humbleness. Go upon the kingly highway speaking the truth to all mankind, with a clear conscience, lest you teach, judge or testify contrary to your inward understanding, judgment and conviction, to your everlasting condemnation. For you are certainly taught by the word of the Lord that whosoever speaketh against the Holy Ghost, it shall not be forgiven him, neither in this world, neither in the world to come, Matt. 12: 32; Luke 10: 12; Mark 3: 28. Therefore, most beloved, search your spirits. If you be spiritual then your judgment, doubtlessly, will be spiritual, just and right. If you be not, and judge spiritual matters according to your own will, woe unto you! I speak to you as to one whose soul I seek and love with all my strength. Although you are more learned than I am, yet I teach and admonish you to judge justly in all things, without carnality or partiality. For I am afraid that there were not a few, part of whom were also famous men, excelling in learning, who, in semblance of fearing God, for the sake of shameful gain, worldly honor and carnal lusts have shamefully written, judged and taught the blessed word of the Lord by garbling the Scriptures, against their own consciences, to the despising of the cross of Christ, in order to please those who are in authority.

Be this as it may, let every soul seek the pure, christian truth, in purity of heart; and strive after the same with all diligence, and he will be successful. Jesus says, "If ye continue in my word, then are ye my disciples indeed; and ye shall know the truth, and the truth shall make you free," again, those who trust in him, shall understand the truth, and the believing in love shall be agreeable unto him. Again, "The secret of the Lord is with them that fear him; and he will show them his covenant," Jn. 8 : 31, 32; Ps. 25 : 14.

May the Almighty Father, through his blessed son Jesus Christ, give you all, in all things, a true understanding and clear vision to judge rightly in all things, to distinguish rightly between that which is holy and that which is unholy; between good and evil; right and wrong, and between the clean and unclean, according to the evangelical truth; that all those of you who have renounced gain, honor and fame, for the sake of the gospel of Jesus Christ, may, henceforth, be taught by the sure and true confession of Scripture, be impelled by the Holy Ghost, and enter into all divine wisdom, truth, righteousness and obedience to him who has taught us by his powerful word, drawn us by his Spirit and bought and delivered us by his precious blood, that is, Christ Jesus, Amen.

Judge aright, and confess the truth.

A TRUE CONFESSION

AND

SCRIPTURAL DEMONSTRATION OF THE MOST HOLY INCARNATION OF OUR BELOVED LORD JESUS CHRIST. WRITTEN TO JOHN A'LASCO AND HIS FELLOW-LABORERS AT EMDEN.

BELOVED LORDS, friends and brethren, when this matter of the incarnation of our beloved Lord Jesus Christ was first mentioned by the brethren, on hearing it I was terrified at heart, lest I should err in the matter and be found, before God, in pernicious unbelief. On account of this article I was often so troubled at heart, after receiving baptism, that for many days I abstained from food and drink, by the over-anxiety of my soul, beseeching and praying God in extreme necessity that the kind Father by his mercy and grace would disclose unto me, poor sinner, who, although in extreme weakness, desired to do his blessed will and pleasure, the mystery of the incarnation of his blessed Son, to the extent necessary to the glorification of his holy name and to the consolation of my afflicted conscience.

Thus wandering about for days, weeks and months, I have frequently asked the opinion or belief of some of you in regard to this matter which bore so heavily upon my heart. Yet none could instruct me sufficiently to quiet my conscience. For gross misunderstanding of some Scriptures which they alleged as proof of their assertion, I found with them, not only according to my opinion, but according to the meaning of the Scriptures; so that, at last, after much fasting, weeping, praying, tribulation and anxiety, I became, by the grace of God, quiet and refreshed at heart, firmly acknowledging and believing, assured by the infallibly sure testimony of the Scriptures, understood in the Spirit, that Christ Jesus forever blessed, is the Lord from heaven, 1 Cor. 15: 47; the promised spiritual seed of the new and spiritual Eve, Gen. 3: 15, namely, the eternal Truth, Jn. 14 : 16; the powerful Conqueror of the serpent and his seed, Gen. 3 : 15; Luke 11 : 21; Jn. 16 : 33; Heb. 2: 14; which promised seed is the eternal Truth and word of God, and, in the fullness of time, was sent forth from the Almighty and merciful Father, Gal. 4: 4, in a pure virgin, Mary, Isa. 7: 14, conceived by the Holy Ghost and power of the Most High. She heard and believed the heavenly message and pleasure of the Father, that was brought to her by Gabriel, Luke 1: 28; this eternal Word of God is become flesh; it was in the beginning with God and was God, Jn. 1: 2. Conceived and begotten of the Holy Ghost, Matt. 1: 18; generated and nourished in Mary, as a natural child is by its mother; a true Son of God and a true son of man, born of her, truly flesh and blood, suffering, hungry, thirsty, passive, mortal according to the flesh; immortal according to the Spirit, like unto us in all things, yet without sin, Heb. 2 : 9; 4 : 15. Truly God and man, man and God. Not divided nor separated as being half heavenly and half earthly, half of the seed of man and half of God, as some express it; but an unmixed, whole Christ, namely, spirit, soul and body, as Paul says, all men are, "Who, being in the form of God, thought it not robbery to be equal with God. But made himself of no reputation, and took upon him the form of a servant, and was made in the likeness of men. And being found in fashion as a man, he humbled himself," (mark, *humbled himself*), Phil. 2: 6–8. He who was more exalted than the angels, is made a little lower than they are. For as he was subject to

CONFESSION OF THE INCARNATION OF JESUS CHRIST.

death, he became flesh and blood, Heb. 2: 9.

I believe and confess without a doubt that he was thus, according to the flesh, conceived and come of the Holy Ghost, born of the seed or lineage of David and of Abraham, and made of a woman, under the law, Gal. 4 : 4, circumcised the eighth day, obedient unto his parents, growing and waxing strong in Spirit, filled with wisdom; and the grace of God was upon him, Luke 2: 40.

This same man, Christ Jesus, preached, was crucified, died, was buried, arose, and ascended to heaven and is there seated at the right hand of his Almighty Father, according to the testimony of all the Scriptures, and from thence he will return to judge the sheep and the goats, the good and the evil, the quick and the dead, 2 Cor. 5: 10; 2 Tim. 4: 1.

Thus I believe and confess that the pure word of God, Christ Jesus, the Creator, Commander and accurser of Adam, instituted himself in Adam's stead, that is, in his wrath, death and curse, and has, by his great compassion, love and mercy, taken upon himself the accursed burden of his erring creatures; that he himself became like Adam in the flesh. And thus he has, by his death, again given life; and by humbling himself, by his righteousness and obedience, he has reunited and fulfilled the eternal righteousness of the righteous God, as he speaks through David, "I restored that which I took not away," Ps. 69: 4.

God has not reconciled the world unto himself by Adam's flesh, for by his righteousness it was subject to the wrath and curse. And what can be reconciled by wrath and curse? But he has done so by himself, by mere grace, by his eternal Word, that is, by his blessed Son, who became like unto the first Adam in all things except in unrighteousness, disobedience and sin, that all honor and praise should belong to God and not to us or to Adam. Yea, "Christ Jesus, who of God is made unto us wisdom and righteousness, and sanctification and redemption, that, according as it is written, He that glorieth let him glory in the Lord," 1 Cor. 1: 30, 31.

Behold, beloved lords, friends and brethren, thus I believe that God has sent "His own Son in the likeness of sinful flesh, and for sin (which he conquered, or for which he was offered), condemned sin in the flesh; that the righteousness of the law might be fulfilled in us, who walk not after the flesh, but after the Spirit," Rom. 8: 3, 4. Again, "He hath made him to be sin for us, who knew no sin; that we might be made the righteousness of God in him," 2 Cor. 5 : 21. And thus he is become our only offer and sacrifice, fulfillment and requisition, by whom God, the Father is reconciled, by whom his righteousness is fulfilled, the malediction removed, the devil, sin and everlasting death conquered and eternal life restored, yea, grace, favor, mercy, peace and eternal life. Paul says, "He that spared not his own Son, but delivered him up for us all, how shall he not with him also freely give us all things?" Rom. 8 : 32.

Thus I believe and confess that "God was made manifest in the flesh," 1 Tim. 3 : 16; "That God was in Christ reconciling the world unto himself," 2 Cor. 5 : 19; that he has blotted out our sins, and has again seated himself at the right hand of the Majesty on high; and all the angels of God worship him there, Heb. 1: 6. And with this doctrine of the conception and incarnation of Christ, all scriptural testimony and truth agree.

First, Paul says, "What is it but that he also descended first into the lower parts of the earth? He that descended is the same also that ascended up far above all heavens, that he might fill all things," Eph. 4 : 9, 10. Again, Christ himself says, "No man hath ascended up to heaven, but he that came down from heaven, even the Son of man which is in heaven." Again, "He that cometh from above, is above all; he that is of the earth, is earthly, and speaketh of the earth: he that cometh from heaven, is above all, and what he hath seen and heard, that he testifieth; and no man receiveth his testimony," Jn. 3 : 31, 32. Again, "I am the living bread which came down from heaven; if any man eat of this bread, he shall live forever; and the bread that I will give is my flesh, which I will give for the life of the world," "Doth this offend you? What and if ye shall see the Son of man ascend up where he was before?" Jn. 6 : 51, 61, 62. Again, "I came forth from the Father, and am come unto the world; again, I leave the world and go to the Father," Jn. 16:28. Again, "Father, I will that they also, whom thou hast given me, be with me where I am; that they may behold my glory, which thou hast given me, for thou lovedst me before the foundation of the world," Jn. 17:24. Again, "That which was from the beginning, which we have heard, which we have seen with our eyes, which we have looked upon and our hands have handled, of the word of Life (for the life was manifested)," 1 Jn. 1:1; and also many other Scriptures, particularly of John.

All those who, by the grace of God, clearly and intelligently see into and confess this doctrine of the incarnation of our beloved Lord Jesus Christ, will rightly confess and comprehend the unspeakable grace, favor, compassion, mercy, and the inexpressibly great love of God the Father expressed and manifested in Christ Jesus, as he himself says, "For God so loved the world that he gave his only begotten Son, that whosoever believeth in him should not perish but have everlasting life," Jn. 3:16. Again, "In this was manifested the love of God towards us, because that God sent his only begotten Son into the world, that we might live through him. Herein is love, not that we loved God, but that he loved us, and sent his Son to be the propitiation for our sins," 1 Jn. 4:9, 10. For how could God show greater paternal love to us than so to humble his eternal Wisdom and Truth, his pure, powerful Word, his blessed Son, by whom he created all things; who was like unto him in form, the image of his blessed being, that he became less than the angels, a poor, despised, passive, mortal man or servant, who alone had to bear the trouble, labor, transgression, curse and death of the whole world. He so humbled him that he became the most miserable of men, 1 Pet. 2:24; Isa. 53:6, "a worm, and no man; a reproach of men, and despised of the people," Ps. 22:6; and thus the innocent, the true, the wise, the righteous, the obedient and the pure Christ Jesus had to wash off, blot out, and satisfy the guilt, falsehood, foolishness, unrighteousness, disobedience and uncleanness of all men. Say, beloved, who ever heard of greater love?

Beloved, holy father and brother, this is, before God, my doctrine, faith and confession of the consoling incarnation of our beloved Lord Jesus Christ, which is, in my opinion, very strong and incontrovertible by the Holy Scriptures; nor can I, therefore, be convinced by any view of the matter, by any of your reasonings and writings hitherto advanced by you against our doctrine, faith and confession; as you turn and explain them according to a natural and carnal sense, and not to the true explanation and sense of the Holy Spirit; which, doubtlessly, should not be the case in this matter, since this glorious work of the incarnation of Christ is wrought and accomplished by God through his Holy Spirit, above all natural causes solely in faith, as the pleasure of God directs.

I repeat, this is my confession to those who desired to hear my belief and feeling in regard to this article. Yet, I never teach it so profoundly in my common admonitions to the brethren and friends; nor have I, heretofore, ever taught it thus profoundly, as I have told you verbally. But I simply teach that the blessed Christ Jesus is truly God and man, a Son of God, and a son of man, conceived of the Holy Ghost, born of the virgin Mary, a poor, despised man, like unto us in all things, except sin; that it is he who was promised in the law by the prophets, and is our true Messiah, Christ, King, David, Prophet, Bishop and Priest, the Deliverer, Savior, Sacrifice, Reconciliation, Fulfiller, Shepherd, Teacher, Example, Mediator, Advocate, Ruler, Commander, Bridegroom, Light of the world, the true Door to the fold, the eternal Wisdom, the image of God, the Father's Word, the right Way, Truth and Life, &c. For I know full well that there are few who can understand this particular matter, even after it is explained to them. Therefore, I say, I deem it unnecessary for me and for all teachers to teach this matter of the incarnation of Christ further than, simply, to the teaching of the regeneration of the church, to love, to consolation, to the sanctification and to live and act according to his holy doctrine and life. Would to God that we were all of such a mind. But in case one wants to search further and inquire into

CONFESSION OF THE INCARNATION OF JESUS CHRIST.

this matter, if meet to know and his understanding reaches far enough, it will not be hidden from him; if not it will be said unto him, *A litora te ne quaefieris*, Eccl. 3: 21.

Well, as this is our doctrine and understanding, not otherwise than according to the testimony of the Scriptures, as we can by the grace of God, best understand and comprehend it, we yet fear that our explanation from the word of God will not satisfy and convince you to unite with us in this matter, but that you will persevere in your adopted reasonings and arguments and try to explain it literally, naturally and humanlike; not observing that Isaiah, Matthew, Luke and John clearly testify that it was brought about by faith in Mary, by the power of the Holy Ghost, as was said above.

O, let us not humble the Almighty Father in his mercy! Let us not rob the blessed Son of God of his glory. Beloved brethren the Scripture remains eternal and unbroken. Take heed, lest you err. Thus speaks Isaiah, "Behold, a virgin shall conceive, and bear a Son," Isa. 7: 14. Again, the angel of the Lord said unto Joseph, "That which is conceived in her is of the Holy Ghost," Matt. 1: 20. Again, when Mary asked the angel the manner of the conception, how it shall be, he answered: "The Holy Ghost shall come upon thee, and the power of the Highest shall overshadow thee," Luke 1: 35. Again, this is the sure testimony of John the servant of God and of Christ, concerning the incarnation of Jesus Christ. "The word was made flesh," Jn. 1: 14. He does not say, *The word took unto itself flesh.*

Behold, dear brethren, however incontrovertible these reasons and Scriptures be by which we try to establish our assertion, yet I fear that we, on account of this article, will be judged and considered as being sectarian, heretical and deceitful, notwithstanding there may be many among us who fear the Lord from their inmost hearts, who never in their lives, heard a word spoken in regard to the mystery of this matter as previously expressed with great clearness; nor ever inquired into it, besides they neither knew nor understood anything about it; but they are satisfied with the Father's favor through Christ; obey his holy word, follow his example, love, doctrine and life, and are rejoiced, solely, at the remission of sins, freedom of the Spirit, grace, favor, promise, mercy and eternal life, which they have received through him. O, that all the wise and learned, even all the men of this world would satisfy themselves with the plain, humble teaching of Jesus Christ and his apostles, not climbing higher nor remaining lower; would seek God, with purity of heart—and firmly believe, fear, love and obey his blessed word. O, what precious talents and what glorious gain would then, by the grace of God, be gathered into the treasury of the Lord. But, as it is, there are many, alas, whose faith and knowledge is not in their hearts but solely upon their lips and tongues, *non loquor ad erubescentiam proborum*, who find pleasure in foolish and useless questions and in disputation; who are versed more in the wisdom of man than in the wisdom of God; who are of broken minds, who ever learn and never come to the true knowledge of the eternal truth; and who ever contradict and reprove them by the plain word of the holy gospel of Jesus Christ, out of mere brotherly love, is from that moment considered by them as being a shameful sectarian or a wicked perverse heretic; *Ipsi judicate, an ne verum sit quod dico?* notwithstanding that their own unbelieving hearts are quite earthly, carnal, and devilish and their whole life nothing but mere flesh, pride, vanity, laziness, unchristianlike avarice, hatred, cruelty, blood-thirstiness, drunkenness, flattery, in short, nothing but sin and shame. O, might it be that I lie and do not tell the truth!

Nevertheless let them slander and upbraid as much as they please; we will willingly bear it. We will all be judged by one Judge who will scrupulously try and reward their doctrine, faith, zeal, seeking and life, as well as ours. Then it will appear who have anxiously sought the everlasting truth of God, the praise and honor of the Lord, and the everlasting salvation of all mankind. Brethren, beware, lest you become like these fruitless disputers. Take heed, if you would save your souls, that you sincerely seek, desire, believe, receive, and live according to the saving truth of God, Amen.

OBJECTIONS.

As I have shown and confessed to you the firm foundation of the incarnation of the Lord, that he did not become flesh of Mary, but that he became flesh in Mary; and as I have also, in part, adduced the reasons and Scriptures by which we are forced to such belief therefore I will now briefly reply to your Scriptures and arguments, hitherto advanced, by which you teach and undertake to prove that he did not simply become flesh in Mary but of Mary.

First, you ask, "If he is not the seed of woman?" We answer, Yes, Gen. 3: 15.

From this you conclude that if he is the seed of woman, he is also man born of woman. We answer by asking, had not the deceiving serpent a body? You must answer, Yes. For God said, "Upon thy belly shalt thou go and dust shalt thou eat all the days of thy life." Again, Was not the deceived woman corporeal? Doubtlessly so. If the natural and corporeal seed of the deceived woman be bodily, then the seed of the serpent must also be a natural, bodily seed, of which God himself has spoken and testified in Genesis. Or else you must admit and confess that the one should be understood spiritually and the other literally. Not at all, beloved brethren. But the bodily serpent represents the spiritual serpent, namely Satan, Rev. 12: 14, and has his spiritual seed, which is falsehood, Jn. 8: 44. Thus also, the woman, who is the mother of all mankind, a like image of Adam, flesh of his flesh, and bone of his bone; subject to her husband, after she had sinned—the image of the new spiritual bride, namely, of the church of Christ, which is the image of Christ, Rom. 8: 29, flesh of Christ's flesh and bone of his bone, subject to Christ, Eph. 5: 30. If the bride be spiritual then the seed must be spiritual, namely, the eternal truth, which truth is Christ himself, Jn. 14: 6. Behold, most beloved, thus the serpent is spiritual and his seed is spiritual of which he begets all his children of accursed falsehood. On the contrary, the bride is spiritual and her seed is spiritual, of which she begets all her children of the saving truth. Between these is constant opposition, as may be plainly seen. Yet truth triumphs, and falsehood is vanquished, notwithstanding falsehood opposes with all its power. O, brethren, do understand the Scriptures aright, lest we, through misunderstanding or pernicious obduracy, deceive ourselves and with us many souls. If you be not satisfied with the clear explanation of these Scriptures, but still maintain that both the woman and the seed must be corporeal, then we know and confess that this same woman conceived in her womb the beforementioned seed, which is God's word, Jn. 1: 1; not from her body nor of her body, but of God, by the power of the Holy Ghost, Matt. 1: 18, through faith, Luke 1: 34.

Secondly, You ask, *If he is not called the seed of Abraham?* We answer: Yes, Gal. 3: 16. From this you conclude that he must, according to the flesh, be descended from the flesh and blood of Abraham. In confirmation you cite the saying of Paul, "For verily he took not on him the nature of angels; but he took on him the seed of Abraham; wherefore in all things it behooved him to be named like unto his brethren," Heb. 2: 16, 17. To this in the first place we reply, That your conclusion is according to the flesh and not with the word of God. John says, "The word was made flesh, and dwelt among us;" and it is of the Holy Ghost, Matt. 1: 25; therefore it was not Abraham's natural flesh and blood. But by grace it was promised the beloved father Abraham, that he, that is, the true blessing of all nations, should not come of the seed of his brethren, nor of the gentiles nor uncircumcised, but of his seed, that is, of his generation, as it is written, "In thee shall all families of the earth be blessed," Gen. 12: 3. Thus is Christ Jesus promised, to Abraham and born of his seed, according to the promise, as Christ himself says, that "salvation is of the Jews," Jn. 4: 22, and thus he is called the seed and son of Abraham, Gal. 3: 16; Matt. 1: 1. For he

CONFESSION OF THE INCARNATION OF JESUS CHRIST.

is, doubtlessly, according to his blessed flesh which is conceived of the Holy Ghost of Abraham's seed, come and born for the salvation of us all.

Again, the saying of Paul which you allege to sustain your cause was not taught and spoken by the Holy Ghost in such a sense as you claim; but Paul says, "Both he that sanctifieth and they who are sanctified are all of one (that is, you say, "of one Adam." But we say they are of one, that is, of one God), for which cause he (the Savior) is not ashamed to call them (the sanctified) brethren, saying, I will declare thy name unto my brethren; in the midst of the church will I sing praise unto thee," Heb. 2: 11, 12. For as Christ Jesus was born from above of the Father and is therefore called God's child or Son, having God as Father, thus, also, all who receive Christ "to them gave he power to become the sons of God," Jn. 1: 12. Such also have God as their Father. As the regenerated are born, together with Christ Jesus, of one God, and have one Father, therefore he calls the sanctified who, with him, are born of God, his brethren, not because of the flesh but because of the new birth. If it were otherwise you would have to consent and admit that all wicked, unbelieving and perverse men and women were brethren and sisters of Christ Jesus as well as the believing, sincere and pious ones. Not so, for Christ Jesus says, "Whosoever shall do the will of my Father which is in heaven, the same is my brother and sister, and mother, Matt. 12: 50. Read and understand it rightly. Further, Paul says, "Behold I and the children which God hath given me," Heb. 2: 13. Forasmuch then as the children are partakers of flesh and blood, he also himself partook of the same (that is, mortal, as a consequence); that through death he might destroy him that had the power of death, that is, the devil, and deliver them who through fear of death were all their lifetime subject to bondage, which was the seed and generation of Abraham, and, by the terrible threat, subject to the heavy burden and intolerable yoke of the law of Moses. For verily he took not on him the nature of angels; if you understand it as meaning the good, then you should know that they did not sin; but if you take it as meaning the evil ones, then you should know that he rejected them and keeps them in the bondage of eternal darkness unto the great judgment day. Therefore Paul says, "For verily he took not on him the nature of angels; but he took on him the seed of Abraham. Wherefore in all things it behooved him to be made like unto his brethren (to wit: weak and mortal), that he might be a merciful and faithful High Priest in things pertaining to God, to make reconciliation for the sins of the people. For in that he himself hath suffered being tempted, he is able to succor them that are tempted," Heb. 2: 16—18. Now, judge for yourselves whether this is not the right meaning of this Scripture of Paul. In the third place you declare and say thus: *Paul plainly teaches that Christ Jesus is born of the seed of David according to the flesh, and is proven to be the Son of God, with power; according to the spirit of sanctification.* Therefore he is, you conclude, according to the flesh, of the seed or loins of David, and according to the Spirit, alone, born of God.

To which we reply: It is true that it would follow in the common course of nature that Christ was born of the seed or loins of David; but it is not in accordance with the testimony of Scripture. The reason is this: Because the Scripture teaches that the "Word was made flesh," and that it came forth from the Holy Ghost, Jn. 1: 14; Matt. 1: 20; Rom. 1: 2. Therefore, beloved brethren this is the true meaning of Paul in regard to this and like Scriptures; the consoling promise of the future Savior was given to Abraham; that he should be born of his seed or generation. Abraham's offspring were, Ishmael, Isaac, and the children of Keturah. The promise of the patriarch was again given to Isaac, and not to the others. Isaac begat Esau and Jacob. Not Esau, but Jacob again received the promise given to his father Abraham and Isaac. Jacob multiplied into twelve tribes; and, that the promised Savior might not be looked for from the tribe of Reuben, Dan, Gad, or any of the eleven tribes, therefore the Holy Ghost points to Judah and not to any of the other tribes, Gen. 49: 10. Judah, multiplying into many branches, the promise is renewed in David, 2 Kin. 7: 12. Thus the merciful Father has ever testified and shown beforehand, from one patriarch to another and from one generation to another, that all men might know from which patriarchs and generations the promised Savior and Deliverer of all mankind should be born, according to the flesh, as the Jews well knew by such showing of Scripture, saying, "Hath not the Scripture said that Christ cometh of the seed of David, and out of the town of Bethlehem," Jn. 7: 42. "He came unto his own and his own received him not." He is come of the seed or generation of David, according to the promise; but they did not receive him. Yea, the appointed hour is come. Gabriel was sent of God to a virgin named Mary who was promised to a man. Mary believed the word of the Lord; the Holy Ghost overshadowed her, &c. The Word, in her, became flesh, Jn. 1: 14. It is conceived and brought forth of the Holy Ghost, Matt. 1: 20; and according to this same flesh, or with this same flesh, which was conceived of and brought forth of the Holy Ghost, he is born of Mary, the pure virgin, who was of the seed and generation of David; David was of Judah; Judah of Jacob; Jacob of Isaac; Isaac of Abraham; and thus the divine promise was fulfilled, which God through grace alone had promised and given to the abovementioned patriarchs; and thus was born, according to the flesh, as was said above, of the seed or generation of David; and by his saving Spirit is proven to be the living Son of God, Rom. 1: 4. For if he were to prove or declare himself to be the Son of God, it must, without doubt, be according to his sanctifying Spirit, inasmuch as he could not be such according to the flesh, as he had humbled himself, and was forsaken of the Father, was weak, despised, hungry, thirsty, passive, mortal, and like unto us in all things, yet without sin. Beloved brethren, take heed. The alleged Scripture of Paul is very clear, and has every where a scruple, Rom. 1: 13.

In the fourth place, you say, Christ is called a fruit of the loins of David. Therefore he must be the natural and pleasing seed of David.

Answer. These words, according to the letter were spoken of Solomon and not of Christ; which Solomon was naturally born of the loins of David. Thus Nathan spoke unto David, "And when thy days be fulfilled, and thou shalt sleep with thy fathers, I will set up thy seed after thee, which shall proceed out of thy bowels, and I will establish thy kingdom. He shall build a house for my name, and I will stablish the throne of his kingdom forever. I will be his father, and he shall be my son (now note of whom it is spoken). If he commit iniquity, I will chasten him with the rod of men, and with the stripes of the children of men," 2 Sam. 7: 12—14. Now, Christ never committed iniquity; for he knew not sin; neither was guile found in his mouth, 1 Pet. 2: 22. Again, in the Psalms, "The Lord hath sworn in truth unto David; he will not turn from it; of the fruit of thy body will I set up on thy throne. If thy children will keep my covenant, and my testimony that I shall teach them, their children shall also sit upon thy throne for ever more," Ps. 132: 11, 12. That this is literally spoken of Solomon, he himself testifies in plain words, 1 Kin. 3: 6; 8: 20; which Solomon, without doubt, represented in figure, Christ Jesus, as in his glory, wisdom, building of the temple, &c. Behold, most beloved, thus we should not take the letter for the spirit and the spirit for the letter. But that the promise according to the Spirit had reference to Christ, is incontrovertible; for this the holy prophets of God plainly show; and particularly, Isa. 9: 6; Jer. 23: 5; 33: 15.

In the fifth place you ask, If he is not a fruit of the womb of Mary?

Answer. Yes, Luke 1: 38. From this you conclude,

If he be a fruit of the womb of Mary then he is also brought forth of her flesh and blood by the power of the Holy Ghost. For if he were not of her flesh and blood then he could not be called a fruit of her womb. But because he is of her flesh he is called the fruit of her body, as an apple is called the fruit of a tree, because it grows upon the tree, and partakes of its nature, through the strength of the earth.

Answer. According to the course of nature your conclusion is in part right, but according to scriptural testimony quite wrong. For the Scriptures say, that Mary, the pure virgin, by faith, conceived the eternal word of God which in the beginning was with God, and was God, that it became

CONFESSION OF THE INCARNATION OF JESUS CHRIST.

flesh, Jn. 1: 14; conceived and brought forth of the Holy Spirit, Matt. 1: 20; that it was human and natural-like; nourished in her; and was in due time born as a natural child is born of its mother. Thus Christ Jesus remains the precious, blessed fruit of the womb of Mary, according to the words of Elizabeth, which was conceived not *of* her womb but *in* her womb wrought by the Holy Spirit through faith, of God the omnipotent Father, from high heaven, as we have frequently shown.

You allege a natural reason concerning the tree and its fruits in proof of your assertion. Inasmuch as you do so, I will reply to your reasoning according to nature, namely, I have a well prepared field, well pulverized and manured, bearing abundance of wheat, corn, or rye. I say, ah, that is a beautiful crop, which fruit this field could not produce of itself, however well-tilled and rich the same was, and however much it was induced to do so by the heat of the sun and the moisture of the atmosphere, until the seed was sown in by the sower. Being sown, and grown up it is called the fruit of the field, notwithstanding it was first sown thereon. An apple is called the fruit of the tree, although it is produced and grown by the soil on which the tree is grown.

In the same manner the heavenly seed, namely, the word of God, was sown in Mary, and by her faith, being conceived in her by the Holy Ghost, became flesh; and thus it is called the fruit of her womb, the same as a natural fruit or offspring is called the fruit of its natural mother, Jn. 1: 14. For Christ Jesus, of his origin, is no earthly man, that is, a fruit of the flesh and blood of Adam; but he is a heavenly fruit or man. For his beginning or origin is of the Father, Jn. 16: 28, like unto the first Adam, yet without sin. Given to Adam and his children, in case they hear and receive him in his holy word, to their everlasting salvation and deliverance, of God the merciful Father alone through grace and mercy; without price and without any previous mention on our part.

In the sixth place you say, God could not suffer. If Christ's flesh were not of earth or of Adam, but from heaven, then he could not have been passive, and consequently he could not have died.

Answer. Be impartial and judge rightly. Your meaning is, that Christ Jesus according to the Spirit alone, is of the Father, in which Spirit he was impassive and immortal, as you say, but that he was not of the Father according to the flesh. But according to the flesh, in which he suffered and died, you teach that he is of earth, that thus the law (wherewith earthly man was cursed on account of his disobedience) concerning the earthly man, namely Christ, might be fulfilled, that he by obedience might save, and we in him, by the communion of his human nature and blood, whereby he has fulfilled the righteousness of the Father in our flesh. This foundation is implied in your Latin syllogisms. We will not controvert this by subtle syllogisms nor by acute human cavilings, for we do not have them; but we controvert it by the plain testimony of the word alone, which cannot be turned by flatterings, nor broken by human reason.

First, we confess and consent before all the world that God, the Almighty, eternal Father is quite impassive and immortal; for with him there is no change, Jas. 1: 17. *Ego Deus, inquit Propheta, &c., non mutor.* But God, the Son, the eternal Word is humbled, has denied himself, became less than the angels, miserable, mortal flesh or man, Jn. 1: 14.

You say, God cannot suffer; but the Scripture says otherwise, that God, the Son, has suffered, for he himself says, I am the first and the last, I am he that liveth and was dead, and behold I am alive for evermore, Rev. 1: 18; 22: 13. Adam's flesh was not the first and the last; but he who was before every creature, by whom all things were created, Eph. 3: 9. Whose goings forth were from the beginning and from eternity. This is the first and the last; this same one is become flesh; he has suffered, he died, he again became living and shall live forever. Take heed, lest you willfully oppose the Scriptures. Christ can not be divided into two parts, as you think.

I repeat, the Father is impassive, immortal and unchangeable; but for our sakes the Son is humbled, became passive and mortal, according to the testimony of the Scriptures, Phil. 2: 7; Heb. 2: 14; 1 Pet. 1: 19, and many other Scriptures. Therefore he prayed his beloved Father that he might again acquire the glory that he had with the Father, which he had lost in becoming man, Jn. 17:5. If he remained unchanged in his divine form, and if he suffered in that which he took of earth, as you say, then tell me, beloved, what he had lost that he desired again to acquire of his Father? Examine the Scriptures rightly and pray, and by the grace of God, your eyes will be opened to behold the truth of Christ.

Again, in the second place we answer, that the whole Christ Jesus went forth from his Father, Jn. 1:14; 3:31; 6:27; 8:42; 14:24; 16:28; 17:8; that the word of God became flesh in Mary, the Lord himself from heaven, 1 Cor. 15:47; and that he was afflicted and oppressed in the flesh, soul and Spirit, according to the testimony of the Scriptures. In the flesh, because he was crucified. In his soul, because he himself says, My soul is exceeding sorrowful, even unto death. In the Spirit, as he said Jn. 13:21, *Turbatus est Jesus Spiritu*, "He was troubled in spirit." Which Christ Jesus (that he might be an offering unto God), suffered the judgment of the unrighteous; died according to the flesh, but was made alive according to the Spirit.

Again, in the third place we reply to your syllogisms, thus: The commandment was not given to the heavenly Christ, but to the earthly Adam and his seed, through Christ, that is, through the word. Adam, transgressing, was condemned to death through the Word Christ, Gen. 3:19. As the righteousness of God is unchangeable and eternal, as you yourselves say, therefore disobedient Adam must die according to the immutable righteousness of God. As Adam was earthly and of earth, and was cursed by the word on account of his disobedience and had to die, therefore nothing could be expected nor taken from earth but earth, from curse nothing but curse, and from death nothing but death, as Paul plainly shows, Rom. 5:12. Adam, being disobedient to the word which created him, in not giving heed to it, and eating what it had forbidden, had to die involuntarily the death, with his seed, which the word had promised him. Because it was for righteousness' sake that Adam and his descendants had to die, he having sinned and not having wherewith to requite; therefore it is solely grace, mercy and love that he should live. But how? Through the righteousness of Adam's flesh? Not at all; but the word which had made Adam a living being, which gave him the commandment and promised him death, if he should commit iniquity, as was said above. This same word (as death had to be the consequence, according to righteousness, as truth had spoken) which God again promised to Adam, was to become flesh; that, as he was deceived by the liar, and therefore, according to the justice of God, had to die, he might again be delivered by the promised truth, and thus by grace and mercy alone, inherit life eternal. Adam believed it and was consoled, and as a sign of the truth of the promised favor and love, God made unto Adam and unto his consort, coats of skins and clothed them, Gen. 3:21.

Thus has not the earthly, guilty, transgressing, accursed and mortal flesh of Adam requited the righteousness, and appeased his wrath, as you claim, but only the heavenly, innocent, obedient, blessed and quickening flesh of Christ, as the Scriptures testify; that he bare our sins, 1 Pet. 2:24; Isa. 53:8; by his wounds are we healed. For the promised Word, Christ Jesus, is become man and has fulfilled the righteousness required by the law, as Paul says, "For what the law could not do, in that it was weak through the flesh, God sending his own Son in the likeness of sinful flesh, and for sin, condemned sin in the flesh. That the righteousness of the law might be fulfilled in us, who walk not after the flesh, but after the Spirit," Rom. 8:3, 4.

Hence it follows that all those who are born of Adam, and remain his in not receiving by faith the promised seed (I am speaking of those of understanding age), must, by the immutable righteousness of God, inherit the curse of Adam, that is, death, as a reward of sin. Christ himself says, "He that believeth not shall be damned," Mark 16:16. Again, Paul says, "The wages of sin is death," Rom. 6:23. For they have no communion of the most holy flesh and blood of Christ Jesus; nor can they ever enjoy his deliverance, kindness, merits and blessing unless they be truly converted from the shameful darkness of unbelief and sin, to the eternal, clear, heavenly light, Christ Jesus, 1 Jn. 1: 7. But those who, with Adam, truly receive the promised seed and thus become renewed and consoled in God, who are born anew by this same seed; who are changed or converted from the disobedient nature of Adam, into the obedient nature of the Word, Christ Jesus, these he calls flesh of his flesh and bone of his bone; he gives these unto himself, by mere grace, and makes them partakers of his righteousness, merits, cross, blood and bitter death, yea, his whole life, love and Spirit; for they are one body and one Spirit with him; so that they willingly fulfill, by this spirit of love which they have received of him, for God is love, all that which the merciful Father, by his saving truth, Christ Jesus has commanded as John testifies, saying, "And whatsoever we ask, we receive of him, because we keep his commandments, and do those things that are pleasing in his sight," 1 Jn. 3: 22. Again, Paul says, "Love is the fulfilling of the law," Rom. 13: 10. Again, Christ says, "He that hath my commandments, and keepeth them, he it is that loveth me," Jn. 14: 21.

Besides you say, What is born of the spirit is spirit. Just brethren, we do not say Christ is born of the Spirit, but we do say with the Scripture that he is incarnate and conceived by the Spirit. Now it is different as you know, to be born of the Spirit and to be incarnate and conceived by the Spirit. Who doubts, moreover, but that to be born of the Spirit is regeneration! I beseech you therefore, through the Lord as not being led rightly by the Scriptures, if you hold these things, you are ready to defend your cause. Herewith, beloved lords, friends and brethren, I conclude this my confession of the incarnation of our beloved Lord Jesus Christ. I write you this in accordance to your desire, and place it before you in all clearness, as one who is not ashamed of his faith; although I do not thus deeply go into the matter in my admonitions to the brethren; but, alone, in an apostolic manner admonish them to regeneration and love. I desire, by the grace of the Lord, that you will rightly see into all things and rightly observe who have sinned. On the contrary, who has requited sin, that we may put on Adam and his descendants, their unrighteousness, darkness, sin and shame; and give to Christ Jesus his righteousness, brightness, praise and honor. Praying you, I say, not to follow in this and other matters, human wisdom, but the wisdom of God; not intelligence, but Scripture; not flesh, but Spirit; not the writings and opinions of the learned, but alone the testimony of Christ and his apostles, fearing God in purity of heart from your inmost souls, as I should, also myself, that we may not be like unto them who are ever learning and never come to the knowledge of the truth. Observe well that you do not otherwise ask, hear and answer, but by sincere zeal. Before God, faith and works avail. In all things be prepared to do the will of God and not the will of your idle, vain unwilling flesh.

I know there are many who are disposed to nothing but to search, inquire and dispute, and have never once confessed and received the most necessary things, without which none can be saved, namely, the piercing, regenerating and sanctifying faith, the urging fear of the Lord, and the burning love of God and their brethren. Be not like unto them. But, beloved brethren, seek and strive after true wisdom; open unto her; she stands before your door; behold her beauty; taste of her fruits; search her strength, and you will love, embrace and gladly receive her; your flesh will go under and the Spirit arise, and go before you in the word and truth of the Lord, until Adam dieth in you and Christ prevail. May God give us all his divine grace, Amen.

"Take ye heed, watch and pray," Mark 13: 33.

AN ADMONISHING CONFESSION

AND CLEAR DEMONSTRATION

TO THE LEARNED JOHN A'LASCO, ARCH-BISHOP AT EMDEN, EAST FRIESLAND, ALSO TO HIS BRETHREN. HOW THE PREACHERS OF THE DIVINE WORD AND THE CHURCH OF CHRIST SHOULD BE MINDED, ACCORDING TO THE TESTIMONY OF THE SCRIPTURES.

BELOVED sirs, friends and brethren, as I have disclosed unto you, at your own request, the foundation of my faith and feelings concerning the very consoling incarnation of our beloved Lord Jesus Christ, although I do not teach the same so deeply before the church, therefore I will now briefly point out my foundation and feeling how the teachers and church, who can rightly be called christians, should be affected and minded before God and before all the world, according to the showing of the Scriptures, so far as we can, by the grace of God, comprehend and understand it from his word; yet I will not dwell upon this matter long, lest I become tedious.

First, I would say in regard to the preachers and adduce this Scripture, "As my Father hath sent me, even so send I you," Jn. 20: 21. Ever remain unchangeable in the church of God, thus: As all true teachers and preachers are sent of Christ Jesus, as he is sent of his Father, therefore we should rightly consider how and who this Christ Jesus was, how and what he taught when the Father sent him. He is doubtlessly the Son and image of God, the Teacher of righteousness who has taught and testified nothing but the truth, namely, the word of his Father. He taught it in the power of the Spirit and was urged by the Holy Ghost through an unquenchable fire of love to the service of all mankind. Besides, he was the burning, shining light of the world, the true pattern of all virtue who could truly say, "Learn of me, for I am meek and lowly of heart." Again, "For I have given you an example," &c., and therefore he gloried by the true testimony of his Holy Spirit, saying, "I am the good Shepherd," Jn. 18: 37; 7: 16; 1: 9; 3: 19; 8: 12; 12: 36; Matt. 11: 29; Jn. 13: 15; 10: 11.

This Christ Jesus, the Bishop of bishops, and the Shepherd of shepherds, who was faithful in all things unto which he was sent of his heavenly Father, never sends any other bishops, teachers, shepherds and laborers in his vineyard, to his members, children and sheep to care for them, to pasture and protect them, than those who are of one body, Spirit and mind with him, as he is one with his Father, who, by the divine Word, which is Christ, in him and in his heavenly nature, are so renewed, converted and changed that he may truly say of them, Behold, these are the children which God hath given me. Whosoever shall hear you shall hear me, as the Father testified of Christ, saying, "This is my beloved Son in whom I am well pleased, hear ye him," Matt. 17: 5. Again, those who are of one spirit with Christ Jesus are members of his holy body, full of the love of God and of their brethren, who with Christ Jesus, their Bishop, seek nothing but the eternal gain, honor, glory and praise of God, and the inward conversion, regeneration and eternal salvation of those whose brotherly care is entrusted and commended to them of God. Yea, he sends such as are unblamable both in doctrine and life; as are urged by the Holy Spirit; who sincerely lament, with

Christ, about those who do not acknowledge the gracious time of their temptation, who are rejoiced, with all the angls of God, at the conversion of a sinner, who so thirst after the salvation of all mankind as a hungry person hungers after bread; who so apply the word and truth of the Lord that they dare not teach or practice a word otherwise than Christ Jesus himself has taught, practiced and commanded, namely, the pure, unadulterated, biblical word in the true sense and meaning of Christ and of his holy apostles; who practice the sacramental signs conformable to the gospel of Christ, namely, the baptism of the believing (and not of infants), and the Supper under both forms, in such church as is flesh of Christ's flesh and bone of his bone; such as are outwardly unblamable and inwardly of one heart, spirit, soul and body in Christ Jesus. Yea, he sends such whose doctrine is a salt; whose life is as a shining light, long suffering, meek, lowly, merciful, hospitable, not avaricious or selfish, not desirous of shameful gain, not puffed up, of good report among those of the world, ruling well his own house, having a well-minded consort, if they have the gift of cleanliness and obedient children. Yea, in all things chaste, sober, unblamable, having the Spirit, fear and love of God. Again, so minded in all things that they can truly say with Paul, to their entrusted sheep, "Be ye followers of me, even as I am of Christ." "Be thou an example of the believers in word, in conversation, in charity, in Spirit, in faith, in purity," Heb. 3:2; Jn. 17:11; Heb. 2:13; Matt. 28:19; Mark 16:15; Eph. 5:30; Matt. 5:14; 1 Tim. 3:2; Tit. 1:6; 1 Cor. 4:2; 11:1; 1 Tim. 4:12; Phil. 2:17.

Behold, most beloved, thus the teachers should be minded who shall serve the Lord's church, that they may not hear from the obdurate and refractory: "Why do you teach others and not yourselves?" Nor can they otherwise teach to the glory of God; for the service of the New Testament is a service of the Spirit and not of the letter, 2 Cor. 3:6. Therefore Christ never chooses as laborers in his vineyard, as servants and builders, such as are avaricious, drunkards and idlers, that the kingdom of God, which is spiritual, may be taught in purity of heart, pasturing the sheep of Christ, not by force, but willingly, not being intent on shameful gain but on affection, not as those who seek dominion over others, but as examples to the flock of Christ, not serving for a certain benefice, pension, or stipulated salary as do your teachers, but, solely, for the gain of the souls which Christ Jesus has so dearly bought with his precious blood. Entrusting and commending to the God, who, by his grace, created, delivered, regenerated and sent them to his ministration, to the care of their temporal necessaries of life, diligently feeding themselves, by the grace of the Lord, from their own or their rented lands, or from the labor of their hands, so far as is possible; that they do not sell the free word of God, given them without price, and thus live on shameful gain, robbery and theft. Let all sincere and pious servants of Christ beware of this, and whatever they cannot obtain by due prudence and diligence will doubtlessly be provided for them by the begotten brethren who fear the Lord, for whom they sow spiritual things; and not by inconvertible heathen, drunkards, usurers, whoremongers and such like. For such teachers are the oxen which tread out the corn, which should not be muzzled, 1 Cor. 9:9; 1 Tim. 5:18; Deut. 25:4; they are those who are worthy of double honor, with whom all things should be shared, and who shall live by the gospel according to the Lord's own ordinance, as the priests under the law, lived by the altar; these are the true laborers worthy of their reward as Christ says; such teachers we shall acknowledge, honor, maintain in love, and for their labors' sake keep peace with them, as Paul teaches, "For they watch for your souls as they that must give account," Heb. 13:17.

Behold most beloved sirs, friends and brethren, thus has God, the merciful Father, sent his blessed Son, who was in his own form, and minded like him in all things, namely, Christ Jesus, who has sent such as were of one spirit, soul and body with him, without a staff, purse, shoes, scabbard, money, gold and silver, that is, without all solicitude and avarice. The apostles ordained, at all places where they had begotten churches, such bishops and teachers as were unblamable both in doctrine and in life, and have never mentioned annual incomes, benefices or rents. For they were men of God, servants of Christ, full of the love of God and their beloved brethren, who labored, taught, sought, pastured and watched through mere love, urged by the Spirit, not only for one, two or three hours a week, in the synagogue, but at all hours and places, in synagogues, streets, houses, mountains and fields. And, as they had received the knowledge of the kingdom of God, the truth, love and Spirit of God, without price, so they were, again, prepared to dispense it diligently and teach it without price, to their needy brethren; and, as for the temporal necessaries of life, the begotten church was sufficiently urged by love, through the Spirit and word of God to give unto such faithful servants of Christ, and watchers of their souls, all the necessaries of life, to assist them and provide for them all such things they could not obtain themselves. O, brethren, flee from avarice!

Again, those teachers did not go about offering their services, as these do, but they were called of God, as were Aaron, Jeremiah, Isaiah, Zechariah, Paul and others. Others, born of the unblamable church of Christ, were chosen by lot, as was Matthias Acts 1: 26. Being called, they were constrained by the Spirit, to teach, to admonish, to console, to reprove and to serve and protect their poor brethren and sisters according to God's holy word, with all their strength. As they were thus called, and felt in them an urging spirit and moved by love, as was said above, so they reasonably filled their office with all solicitude and diligence, watching night and day for the eternal salvation of their sheep, working diligently in the vineyard of the Lord, ruling the people of God with the rod of the Lord; they did not doubt, made use of no flattery; but in a good conscience they reproved the great as well as the small, the rich as well as the poor, the learned as well as those that were not learned; the word was proclaimed in their church, wholesome and unadulterated, at all times and in all places, as was said above, according to the measure of their faith and Spirit which God, by his grace, had given to every one of them. Most beloved, do not excuse yourselves because all who boasted themselves as being teachers of the church of Christ, even in the times of Paul, were not sincere, pious, and urged by love, as appears from Phil. 1: 15; 2: 21; 3: 2. Verily, I say unto you, they boasted of being such, but in truth, before God they were not. For it is not hidden from you what kind of fruits they produced and how Paul regarded them. As you are aware that it is not the intention and will of God, nor ever shall be, that his holy word should be proclaimed to the erring world unto salvation, either by drunkards, whoremongers, avaricious, idolaters, despisers of the Scripture, gluttons, proud, thieves, bloodthirsty, vain talkers, enemies of the cross of Christ, by those whose belly is their God, by those who are already condemned by the word of God, or by the carnal or earthly-minded. But only, by the truly regenerated christian, unblamable men who sincerely seek God from their inmost souls, urged by the Holy Ghost and constrained by love, as Christ said thrice unto Peter, "Lovest thou me? Yea, Lord (answered Peter); thou knowest all things and knowest that I love thee. Jesus saith unto him, Feed my lambs," Jn. 21: 15.

O, most beloved, take heed what spirit urges you, what love constrains you, what church calls you and what things you seek. Follow the good and not the evil. I tell you in Christ Jesus that my soul is troubled for your sakes. I pray you, beloved brethren, receive it with a will. I must frankly speak my mind; for as much as I can deduce and understand from my past actions and from your apparent fruits, you are all, none of your teachers excepted, urged by your flesh and belly, and are therefore all hirelings and not shepherds, Jn. 10: 12. Or, at best, are such shepherds as seek the wool, milk and flesh and do not care for the Lord's sheep. For wherever the fattest are, there are also the best sheep. O brethren, consider what the Lord's prophets have so often threatened on such. Yea, how many are found among you who, for the sake of an earthen house, or for ten guilders, move from one place to another, as if they were not all bought equally dear at one price? I fear that you would all do it.

AN ADMONITION TO THE PREACHERS.

O brethren, if you confess this to be true then judge for yourselves what is your seeking, and if you will not verbally confess it, *superbia five pertinacia impediente*, it can yet not be denied by the intelligent. God has been mocked long enough. Brethren, be converted!

As the teachers are serving their bellies. avaricious, desirous of shameful gain, earthly-minded, as Paul says, not to say proud, lazy, vain, drunken, spiteful and envious, so are also minded, all those who are taught and begotten of them, as may be plainly seen, inasmuch as both teacher and church live and walk so shamefully that all heaven must be ashamed and astounded thereat. For their avarice, unchastity, pride, pomp, greed, drunkenness, hatred, envy, fornication, adultery, blood-thirstiness, usury, fraud, vanity, and all manner of shame have no limits or bonds. Moreover, we find open fencing-schools, gambling houses, houses of ill-fame and drinking houses. For as the teachers are, so are also their doctrine, sacraments and church, as is said, *Qualis Papa, tale Evangelium and omnia*. Verily, I say, believe it if you choose, Christ does not send such avaricious, selfish and carnal teachers, nor does he acknowledge such a self-conceited, carnal and blamable church. But those who are sent of Christ Jesus have his Spirit, crucify the lusts and desires of their flesh, that they, preaching to others may not be found shameful, seeking alone, the praise of God and the salvation of their beloved brethren, refusing all shameful gain, presents and gifts, so long as they have wherewith to maintain themselves, honoring none for the sake of gain, living unblamably, teaching the word wholesomely and using the sacraments according to the commandments of the Lord, excluding all degenerated sisters and brethren, again proclaiming grace to those that are converted, having eternal vigilance and care for those whose care is entrusted to them of the Lord's church.

As you are not such as the Scriptures require you to be, but are as yet in opposition to the true doctrine, and also, blamable in life, as is apparent, therefore I admonish you in all earnestness and fraternal love, to become first sincere christians before you undertake to impress and teach Christ unto others. Let us examine ourselves, that we may learn to know our own ailings, and knowing them, die unto them. For before God, neither smooth words nor semblance will avail. Brethren, I must tell you the plain truth which may be galling and bitter to you because there is found neither Spirit nor power, nor trust in Christ, nor fear of God, nor love of the brethren with your teachers, but only a vain calling of words for the sake of a stipulated salary, without any show of christian fruits. Therefore all your calling is nothing but to sow on the shore to reap the wind; for the pure word of God and the teaching of the Holy Spirit cannot be pointed out and taught by servants who are unclean and carnal. To this all intelligent persons must, doubtlessly, consent.

As you then, I say, are blamable both in doctrine and in life, and as your doctrine, such as you have, is hired for a salary and without spiritual fruit, and as no unblamable church is begotten of you, and as the signs of the Word are abused by you; therefore it is apparent that you are not the true messengers of God, but you run your own course, urged by the flesh and not by the Spirit; not sincerely seeking the salvation of the church, but rather the temporal profits and rents, and that with such rapacity that you are not ashamed to receive them as a reward and price of your preaching, which were in ancient times, by feigned words and fraudulent commerce, as Peter says, nay, by nothing but theft and sly robbery, taken from the true and legal heirs.

Thus you sell, first, the precious, free word of God which, by grace, was given us of God, without price. And secondly, it is paid for by that which was stolen. Here lies hidden more than I will disclose. *Qui de furto vivit and rapina non dubium est, quim fur est and raptor*. Do look at the matter in a christian light. Behold, feel and taste your manifest error, unworthiness and plain avarice. I here speak of all your preachers; for they all enjoy such gain. Your teachings, benefices, pensions and rents are such an abomination before my eyes, that brethren, verily I would rather be beheaded, burned, drowned or torn into quarters by four horses than to receive, on account of my preaching, such benefices, pensions or rents. Yea, when giving salaries to preachers was established, there surely crept into the church of Christ a very fearful, corrupting pestilence; which has corrupted so that, alas, there are scarcely any left who have retained the breath of Christ in them. To this you must all consent. What other reason is there than this that the preachers have sought the temporal gain of their own bellies more than the eternal gain of the souls of Christ? As you freely accept and enjoy the beforementioned shameful gain, and what is still worse, as you diligently seek and desire the same, how can you defend yourselves and say that you are not desirous of the filthy lucre? 1 Tim. 3: 3, and that you do not honor the person for filthy lucre's sake? O, brethren, I wish you would awaken, to consider the matter, and that you were all of one mind with us in this matter; for it would doubtlessly be profitable to both the praise and truth of God, and to your poor souls, that we would without pay, dispense the precious word of God, the word of eternal salvation and heavenly grace, which can be merited by no works nor requited by money, as we, by grace only, received it of God without price, that we again would dispense it without pay, and solely by brotherly love would teach it to the hungering consciences, God surely would not forsake us, but would in every emergency paternally care for us and protect us. But it can not thus be with you because you are devoid of faith and love.

As you are all buried to your ears in filthy lucre; earthly and carnally minded in all things; not yet dead unto the flesh by the power of regeneration, not yet received Christ Jesus in all his words, and on that account, are not yet wholesome in doctrine, do not conform the ministration of the signs to the word of God; are blamable in doctrine, as is plain, and as there is found with you no power, no fruit of the Spirit, no true fear of God and no brotherly love; but rather heresy, upbraiding, blasphemy and profaning of the teachings and lives of the pious saints and children of God, who for the testimony of their consciences, confirmed by the word of God, have fled from their country and kindred, and for the sake of the testimony are prepared for water, fire and sword if God so will. Besides, your doctrine being quite powerless and fruitless, the church which you beget being quite earthy, carnal and contrary to the testimony and fruits of the holy word of the Lord; therefore, we repeat it that you are not the true messengers of Jesus Christ. Be not angry with me, most beloved.

It is for the beforementioned reasons that we will not hear nor attend your preaching, nor partake of your supper. For we shall never desire to enter into your church and to become one body with you until you sincerely repent and embrace a free, christian doctrine, not hired nor sold out, but solely urged by the Holy Spirit through brotherly love, a true use of the sacramental signs, according to the command, doctrine and usage of Christ and his apostles, and an unblamable life and walk, led in the love and fear of the Lord. If we do so before these are found with you, we are sure that we sin against God and his holy word, from which may the kind, merciful Father save us. For before God, it does not become us to commit ourselves to such doctrine, admonition and church, who first, err in doctrine, and secondly, do not in the least show by their lives that they are the truly regenerated children of God, or the true church of Jesus Christ. But most beloved, it behooves you, as you have not the unblamable doctrine and walk of Jesus Christ, to renounce your doctrine and life and voluntarily bid adieu to all the lusts of the flesh, to seek the kingdom of God in sincerity of heart, to enter with us, into all obedience to our beloved Lord Jesus Christ with all your strength, if you do not desire to err willfully, that we together, may become the holy, christian and unblamable church, godly, holy, clean, obedient unto God, serving all mankind, powerful in truth, shining forth in righteousness, dead unto sin, living by the Spirit, nay, in all things christian, heavenly and unblamable in Christ Jesus.

Do receive my admonishing confession,

AN ADMONITION TO THE PREACHERS.

in good faith, and do not understand it as too far-reaching, namely, such words as, *clean, unblamable*, and the like. For they are spoken of Christ Jesus himself, and of his holy apostles to the church of the Lord, Jn. 13: 10; Phil. 2: 15. Do not understand it, most beloved, that we deem ourselves so clean and unblamable as being without sin. Not at all, dear brethren; for I know full well that holy John teaches, saying, "If we say that we have no sin, we deceive ourselves, and the truth is not in us," 1 Jn. 1: 8. Again, James says, *In multis enim labimur omnes.* "In many things we offend all," Jas. 3: 2. Yea, beloved brethren, with Paul, I find the disposition to commit sin, at all times, so strong in my flesh, that I often think recklessly, speak inconsiderately and "the evil which I would not, that I do," Rom. 7: 8, 19.

But the abominable, shameful sins and offenses, such as adultery, fornication, hatred, envy, inebriety, pomp, splendor, cursing, swearing, gambling, desire of filthy lucre, abuse of the ordinances of Christ and fraud I verily, detest from the inmost of my heart, and they should never, by the grace of the Lord, be practiced by any sincere, godfearing christians, inasmuch as they hate and oppose them; for the spirit which is in them is a deadly enemy to all ungodliness, wickedness and sin (in the mean while we often find that we are born of Adam). Besides, their spirit strives and hungers after the truth, righteousness, will and commandments of God, yet in great weakness; for they are very much retarded in the works, fruits, and fulfillment by the heavy burden of the sinful flesh. Nevertheless, because the good Spirit of God abides in them, they do not cease to fight their tardy flesh. For the life of true christians is nothing but a continual combat upon earth. Whosoever shall valiantly battle and overcome, will be clothed in white raiments, and fed with the heavenly bread of the tree of life, Rev. 2: 17.

Behold, most beloved, inasmuch as you and your church have never triumphed in this battle (I judge from what I hear, and from your actions which I see), but still serve the world, the flesh and the devil carelessly; therefore we deem, according to the testimony of the Scripture, that you vainly and wrongfully boast of the name, grace, deliverance, merits, death, blood, and promises of Christ; as you have not his word, and by the word, his faith, Spirit, fear and love, and consequently do not follow them.

Therefore, I pray you by the mercy of the Lord, to consider once, what kind of teachers you are, what kind of spirit urges you, what kind of love prompts you, with what intentions and by what motives you teach, what kind of fruits you produce, what kind of ordinances you use, and unto what kind of a church you teach and minister. Judge all things according to the divine testimony, without self-love, flesh and partiality. I doubt not but if you examine the matter rightly, you will not be surprised that we will not hear your doctrine, nor use your sacraments, and refuse unto death to become members of your church. For this remains incontrovertible, eternally unchangeable; that as Christ Jesus is of one mind with the Father, and sent of him, so all teachers should be of one mind with Christ Jesus who can be considered as sent of him. Those who are one with Christ in Spirit, love and life; who teach that which was commanded by Christ, such as repentance and the peaceable gospel of grace, which he himself received of God, and taught to the world, all those who hear, believe, keep and fulfill the same in true fear, are the church of Christ, the truly believing, christian church, the body and bride of Christ, the ark of the Lord, the mount and paradise, the house, people, city and temple of God, the spiritual Eve, flesh of Christ's flesh and bone of his bone, children of God, the chosen generation, the spiritual seed of Abraham, children of the promise, branches and trees of righteousness, sheep of the heavenly pasture, kings and priests, a holy begotten people which is God's own. Besides, they are chosen to proclaim the power of him who has called them from darkness into his marvelous light, Col. 1: 14; 1 Cor. 12: 27; Heb. 12: 22; Matt. 5: 14; 2 Cor. 6: 16; 11: 5; Eph. 5: 30; 1 Pet. 2: 9; Rom. 9: 8; Isa. 61: 3; Ps. 95: 7; 79: 13; Rev. 1: 6; 1 Pet. 2: 9.

All those who have not the Spirit, love and life of Christ, nor sincerely desire them, have no share in the glorious Jerusalem of God, that is, in Christ's church; no matter whether they be teacher or disciple, prince or subject, man or woman; besides they have neither prayer, nor God, nor Christ, nor promise, nor remission of sins, nor any sure consolation in eternal life, so long as they do not sincerely repent, receive God's word, and fulfill it in the true fear, as Christ himself says, "He that believeth not is already condemned," Jn. 3: 18.

Dear brethren, you may contradict this as much as you will, yet this foundation shall stand forever, and will never be changed. The words of Paul shall never be broken, "If any man have not the Spirit of Christ, he is none of his," Rom. 8: 9; and where the Spirit is there shall also be the fruits of the Spirit, as it is infallible that if the Spirit is in man, the evil one as well as the good, it will manifest itself by its fruits, Gal. 5: 16; Matt. 7: 17.

Lastly, most beloved, if you want to be the true church of Christ and boast of the truth, grace, word, Spirit, and blood of the Lord, then separate, first, all your preachers who are urged by the unclean spirit and flesh, who, therefore are not of the church of Christ, namely, all those who are desirous of filthy lucre, as was said above. Again, also, all drunkards, wranglers, flatterers, proud, envious and avaricious; for all these testify by their fruits that they have not the Spirit of Christ. And if they have not the Spirit of Christ, how can these poor, miserable men, then, teach and impress the Spirit, power and will of God, the word of grace, and the word of eternal life, which they do not confess? Yea, brethren, it is impossible for me to teach the things which I do not know myself, and how shall I serve in the house of the Lord while I myself am a castaway? Judge for yourselves.

Secondly, cleanse your church, also. Exclude, according to the word of God, all adulterers and fornicators, drunkards, slanderers, swearers, those who lead a shameful and inordinate life, the proud, avaricious, idolatrous, disobedient unto God, whoremongers and the like, that you may become the holy, christian church which is without spot or blemish, which is as a city built upon a rock. In case these are truly observed and found with you, and, besides, a free, christian doctrine, the true ministration of the sacraments of Christ, not according to the opinion of men or of the learned, but according to the true doctrine of Christ and his apostles—again, the fear and love of God, and an unblamable life, according to God's word, then you will ever have us as your brethren; for it is such we seek. But if you remain as you are, then I say publicly, Better to die than to enter into your doctrine, sacraments, life, and church, as was said above.

Beloved brethren, it is no use to allege the Scripture of the Pharisees sitting in the seat of Moses, Matt. 23: 2; nor that Herod sent the wise of the east; nor that some say, If the devil should preach the word of God, why not hear it? Christ Jesus did not send the Pharisees, the servants of the letter, to preach the word of the Spirit and of life; Herod did not send the wise, with good intentions; nor has the devil ever sincerely given praise to God; nor does God want the praise of the devil, for Christ says, "Hold thy peace, and come out of him," Luke 4: 35; therefore it is useless to adduce such reasons, inasmuch as God, by his mercy and grace, has so opened the eyes of our mind that we surely know that the spiritual service of the New Testament can be administered by none but by servants of the Spirit impelled in love by the power of the Holy Ghost; for it is and remains a service of the Spirit and not of the letter, 2 Cor. 3: 6. Enough has been adduced on this.

In short, deny yourselves, be prepared to do the will of God, seek nothing but his honor and praise, and the eternal salvation of your brethren, and hunger and thirst after the righteousness of God. Believe and receive Christ Jesus rightly in his blessed word, and you will undoubtedly understand and comprehend the true way, the truth, and life eternal, to the praise of God, and to your own salvation. May God, the kind and merciful Father, grant us all this, Amen, Matt. 5: 6; Jer. 31: 25.

As I, dear brethren, have diligently reproved the preachers, on account of the receiving of filthy lucre, in this my admonishing confession, according to the word of God, therefore I do not doubt but that there are some who will bitterly contradict me in this matter, and say, "Beloved Menno, you can not deprive us of the privileges Christ Jesus has given us; as you have alleged from Paul, that those who serve the gospel shall live by the gospel. Say why seek you to take away that of which we have the privilege?" To those who contradict me thus, I would first reply by asking, If the teachers, to whom this privilege is given of Christ by the gospel, are not sent of Christ Jesus? They must answer in the affirmative. Then I say again, as *they* are sent of Christ, who enjoyed this privilege given of Christ, therefore those have not this privilege, who run their own course and are not sent of Christ.

Again, I ask if these teachers to whom this privilege is given by the Scriptures, were not men of the Spirit of love and of truth? Doubtlessly so. Then I reply: If they are men of Spirit, of love and of truth, to whom this privilege is granted by the gospel, those who do not teach and serve by the Spirit, love and truth, may not appropriate and make use of this privilege; for they are not the teachers to whom it was given and promised by the word of God.

Thirdly, I ask, if the teachers which are sent of Christ Jesus, who, according to the Scriptures may enjoy this privilege, led a shameful life after their being called? and if they led a shameful life, and were found corrupt before God and his church, if they could longer remain as teachers in the unblamable church of Christ? They must doubtlessly answer, No. Then, if they answer, no, as it is in truth, that those whose life and walk in the church of Christ, are no more pure and useful than the filthy carrion by the roadside, are no teachers in the church of the Lord; such as drunkards, perjurers, those filled with all unrighteousness, fornication, wickedness, covetousness, maliciousness; full of envy, murder, deceit, debate and malignity. For if the salt have lost his savor, says Christ, it is thenceforth good for nothing, but to be cast out, and to be trodden under foot of men, Matt. 5: 13; 1 Cor. 5: 10; 2 Cor. 6: 10; Rom. 1: 29. And if the church is to be unblamable, and without spot or blemish, how much more so the teachers, as Christ himself teaches, saying, Ye are the light of the world. Ye are the salt of the earth, Eph. 5: 30; Matt 5: 13. Inasmuch as the beforementioned, carnal teachers are already excluded from, and deprived of the christian office of teacher, by God's own ordinance and word, as they do not live up to the doctrine, and by their apparent unbelief and inordinacy are not in the church of Christ; therefore they can not enjoy that privilege; for Christ Jesus has promised and given sincere, pious, spiritual, meek, true, unblamable teachers, sent of God, and not inordinate, lazy, vain, idle, drunken, shameful, lying, pompous, gluttonous, avaricious and carnal rogues, Rom. 10: 16; Isa. 51: 7; 62: 6.

Fourthly, I ask, whether the men of God, the prophets, apostles, and teachers sent of God, were also hired or bought at a stipulated, annual salary, to teach and proclaim the free word of grace? I know that the answer must be, no. For they did not teach but by the urging of the Spirit and love. I say again, Inasmuch as your preachers are hired and bought at a stipulated salary or rents, and do not preach unless they are hired, they must acknowledge that they are hirelings, and not teachers that are sent; for they do not teach by the urging of the Spirit and love, but are enticed and drawn on as was Balaam by the promised salary, benefices and rents. *Qui id negat, Solem in die splendere minus concedet.*

Fifthly, I ask, if the teachers, sent of God, men of the Spirit, of love and of truth, enlightening both in doctrine and in life, lived of a stipulated salary, benefice or rents; or whether they did not live by the services or assistance of the brethren, so far as they could not obtain it of themselves? They must confess that it was by the assistance of the brethren, and not of certain benefices, pensions or rents. This I teach, seek and sincerely desire. Therefore this is my brief conclusion and christian admonition to all preachers and teachers. Brethren, humble yourselves and become unblamable disciples, that you may hereafter become called teachers. Try your Spirit, love and life before you commence to pasture and to teach. Run not your own course, but wait until you are called of the Lord's church; I say,

Lord's church, of the Spirit of God, and are constrained by urging love. If this is the case, brethren, then pasture diligently, preach and teach valiantly, cast from you all filthy lucre and booty; rent lands, milk cows, learn a trade, if possible, do manual labor, as did Paul, and all that which you then fall short of will doubtlessly be given and provided you by the pious brethren, by the grace of God. Understand it not as 'superfluously,' but as 'necessarily.'

Such privileges the holy gospel grants to the unblamable preachers which are sent of Christ Jesus, and nothing further. But the preachers who run their own course, are earthly and carnally minded, are blamable in doctrine and in life, "serve not our Lord Jesus Christ, but their own bellies," who, on account of their lazy, gluttonous, easy flesh, teach and serve to please the world, as hired servants, at certain wages, the Scriptures do not know. Therefore I say for once and for all time, If they will not do differently, but always say in their hearts—*Erret quilibet homo ad libitum, nihil ad nos, modo ventri nostro provisum fuerit*—then I will leave them in the hands of him who shall judge them and us according to his most holy word and to his pleasure.

Brethren, decide the more wisely, and living in the great God through all things, refuse not to bid adieu to your carnal bodies.

CONCLUSION.

HERE you have, beloved sirs, friends, and brethren, our plain confession of the incarnation of our beloved Lord Jesus Christ, which I thus sincerely confess and believe; for you requested me to do so, and, I trust, with a good intention. Therefore I have not hidden my faith. Now, judge the matter rightly, if you be spiritually minded, and if I should, as you think I do, err as is natural to man, which I trust I do not, then do not think that I do so out of obduracy, or partiality, but before God, my Creator, it is because I know no better but that it is the firm, immutable foundation of God's word and truth. Brethren, do not look at me as one who seeks something contrary to the will of God. Not at all. The eternal truth, word and will of God, I am prepared to do, at the risk of all that his paternal kindness may inflict upon me. This I say in sincerity of heart, and have no doubt. Therefore I say to you, that if you have any plainer Scriptures in support of this article of the incarnation of Christ; if you have a clearer foundation, truth, or clearer proof than we have, then assist us. I will, by the grace of the Lord, change my heart in regard to this matter, and follow your doctrine. But, above all, brethren, I want you to understand that I will not accept nor listen to human doctrines, nor cleverness, nor garbling of the Scriptures, nor flatterings, nor presumption, in regard to this but solely to the plain Scriptures, truth and immutable testimony; as we have presented to you, in this matter of our confession, nothing but scriptural truth and immutable testimony. But if you cannot advance such, then give heed, keep your peace and leave us our faith in peace; for, most beloved brethren, before God, I seek nothing but the pure, unadulterated word of God and its testimony.

Besides, I have here presented to you, how and in what manner I admonish and teach the open hearted brethren; with which doctrine no godfearing consciences can be afflicted, nor christian souls be deceived. I pray and desire you to do likewise, that you may build and not break. Brethren, if you do not then take heed how and what you teach, I can beseech and admonish you in love, but it behooves me not to force you, even if I could. Every person shall have to render an account of his teaching and doing, before God and not before men.

In the third place you have my admonishing confession how both teacher and church should be minded according to the Scriptures. Again, I pray and desire by the

AN ADMONITION TO THE PREACHERS.

mercy of the Lord, that you will not accept this scriptural truth in bitterness; for that which I have written is the unchangeable word and will of God, and will remain so forever. Therefore take heed that you do not be angry with me on account of my writing, because it is contrary to your flesh. It verily is not mine, but the doctrine of Christ; not my will, but the will of Christ. If you be angry, you are not angry with me, but with Christ, who has thus taught and instructed us in his holy gospel or word. And in case you fear God, you will doubtlessly love me the more, because I, by the grace, Spirit and word of God, as far as he bestows on me, open unto you the kingdom of heaven, and show you the right way. Yea, because I, fearlessly, and in true brotherly love, of which God is my witness, speak unto you and point you to the eternal, immutable truth; because I cut the cankering flesh from your wounds, and do not flatter you; for I seek not your carnal, but your spiritual friendship; not *your* praise, but the praise of God; not your goods and gifts, but your salvation and souls. For these reasons I tell you the pure truth of God, and do not spare you. O, brethren, receive it in gladness of heart. It is the only word and will of Christ. If you reject it, you do not reject me, but Christ Jesus who has so dearly bought us all. Therefore take heed to awaken yet to-day, and no longer wander and proceed in darkness and deadly blindness. And let the poor, ignorant people, the poor, innocent souls, no longer err under your name and cover. The whole, wide world depends upon you learned. As you pipe, so they dance; as you teach, so they believe; and as you proceed, so they follow. Therefore, woe unto you if you teach wrongly; if you destroy and do not gather; if you deceive and do not pasture; if you corrupt and do not convert.

Receive eyes of wisdom, that you may rightly teach and lead others, according to the will of God; and that the word which Christ spoke be not applicable to you, "If the blind lead the blind, both shall fall into the ditch," Matt. 15: 14. Lastly, I shall soon send you, if God please, my treatise on the baptism of the believing, with other doctrines, from which you may clearly learn my foundation, doctrine, seeking and intentions; why I labor, after what I strive, and by what Scriptures and for what reasons we assert the baptism of the believing; and for what reasons we deem and consider infant baptism as vain, idolatrous and contrary to the word.

Read it all in sincerity of heart, ponder upon it, follow alone the true sense of the divine Spirit and truth. Let opinions go, let flesh and adroitness be destroyed. Many have been deceived thereby. This our doctrine concerning the preachers, concerning the unblamableness of the church, concerning the baptism of the believing, concerning the Supper of an unblamable assembly, and concerning the separation of the penitent, is, doubtlessly, the eternal, immutable word, will and ordinance of God; therefore, by the grace of the Lord, we will never be reasoned out of it by human wisdom, cleverness, threats nor tyranny. Yea, at all times I am prepared to testify and assert this doctrine before God and my brethren, with the sure testimony of my conscience, at the cost of all anxiety, persecution, blood and death. Let the merciful, kind Father treat me and all those who sincerely seek and fear him, according to his divine, blessed will. Read it discreetly and judge it in a christian way.

This is briefly my foundation and conviction of the articles of the christian church; that before God neither baptism, nor Supper, nor any other outward ordinances avail if partaken without Spirit and the new creature. But before God, only faith, love, Spirit, the new creature or regeneration avail, as Paul plainly shows, Gal. 5: 6. All those who, by the grace of God receive these from above, suffer themselves to be baptized according to the commandment of the Lord, and rightly partake of his Supper, Acts 2: 38; 9: 19; 8: 38; Matt. 28: 19.

Yea, they with ardent desire commit themselves to the ordinance and doctrine of Jesus Christ, and shall nevermore willfully oppose the holy will, and plain testimony of God. For this reason I amicably beseech you, most beloved, from my inmost heart, not to dispute with me, nor any other person concerning any outward articles and literal ordinances; but first conquer and subject yourselves; that is, your unbelieving, miserable, refractory, obdurate flesh which yet keeps and hinders you from the truth, faith, knowledge, righteousness and obedience of God. Yea, doubtlessly, if that is rightly vanquished, you will see into all of the ordinances of God, confess and practice them. But as long as it lives in you and has its sway, you will dispute and oppose, and nevermore comprehend, understand and follow the immutable foundation of eternal truth. Beware.

No more at present. But rightly compare Christ with yourselves; his love and Spirit, with your love and spirit; his seeking, doctrine, sacraments and life, with your seeking, doctrine, sacraments and life; and you will, no doubt, find wherein you fall short.

May God, the merciful Father, grant unto you and to us all, true wisdom, understanding, faith, knowledge and true judgment; an ardent heart, true fear, love, doctrine, life, sacraments and ordinances, through Christ Jesus, our Savior and eternal Deliverer of the world, Amen.

"Enter ye in at the strait gate," Matt. 7: 13.

Amara est veritas, and qui eam prædicant repletus amaritudine, dicit Hieronymus.

A
VERY PLAIN AND POINTED REPLY

TO THE

Anti-Christian Doctrine

AND

FALSE ACCOUNT BY MARTIN MICRON CONCERNING THE DISCUSSION BETWEEN HIM AND MYSELF, BEFORE MANY WITNESSES, HELD A. D., 1553, CONCERNING THE INCARNATION OF OUR LORD JESUS CHRIST, ACCORDING TO THE TRUTH AND POWER OF THE HOLY SCRIPTURES, TOGETHER WITH A SINCERE EPISTLE OR ADMONITION TO HIM, TO LEARN TO KNOW HIMSELF, TO REPENT AND BE SAVED.

BY

MENNO SIMON.

WRITTEN A. D., 1556.

"This is life eternal, that they might know thee, the only true God and Jesus Christ, whom thou hast sent," Jn. 17:3.

"For other foundation can no man lay than that is laid, which is Jesus Christ," 1 Cor. 3:11.

ELKHART, INDIANA:
PUBLISHED BY JOHN F. FUNK AND BROTHER.
1871.

PREFACE.

To the well-disposed Reader:

It is manifest, honorable reader, that as Satan, the envier of the divine honor and of our salvation, in the beginnning of creation, used the serpent as an instrument to lead Adam and Eve off the way of life, and thus to lead them into death, as he actually did, Gen. 3: 19, he now uses his false authors and preachers to do so, some of whom he clothes with an angelic appearance of innocence, by using many garbled Scriptures, philosophy, sophistry, words of human wisdom, and by leading a reasonable, private life, whereby he detains and ensnares the poor, bound souls in their great blindness and abominations, and robs them by his many wiles of their only means of salvation, which is Jesus Christ.

For the serpent said unto Eve, "Ye shall not surely die." Thus, now, our opponents say, *Should Christ be the Son of God? No, he is not. The man Christ has no father*, and like expressions. For from the beginning, the devil neither did nor could confess the true faith in Christ Jesus, namely, that we should acknowledge him to be the true Son of God, as may be plainly understood from 1 Jn. 2: 22; 4: 3; 2 Jn. 7. "Whosoever shall confess that Jesus is the Son of God, God dwelleth in him, and he in God," 1 Jn. 4: 15. In short he has life everlasting. Such destroy the dominion of the devil and the kingdom of falsehood. Yea Christ himself had to suffer death because he confessed himself to be the Son of God, Matt. 26: 64; Mark 14: 62, Jn. 5: 18; 19: 7.

If Satan, then, did not confess such faith, in the beginning, as was heard, how shall he now suffer, as by the righteous judgment of God, he is arisen, through anti-christ and his servants, to full dominion, for the sake of sin, and has bound all earth by his deceitful doctrine, explanations, flatterings, statutes, commandments, idolatry, tyranny and violence?

We see clearly, since Christ Jesus, by his grace, has shown himself through the clouds so that we, with Peter, and with all the Scriptures confess him in power and truth to be the Son of the true and living God, and submissively seal this faith with the sign of the holy baptism, as did the Ethiopian, Acts 8: 36, according to his command, because we would, in our weakness, walk according to his commandments and be saved by his grace; how terribly we are upbraided, slandered, belied, accursed, persecuted and murdered by this wicked, perverse, blind, and carnal generation, on that account. For Satan, never, from the beginning confessed true faith in Christ Jesus, nor submissively sealed it by true baptism. Nor will he ever do so, unto the end.

The apocalyptical Apollyon has so corrupted things by the locusts of the bottomless pit, that but little truth remains with man; for it is manifest that not only the Turks and the Papists are inimical to the clearness of the most holy birth of Jesus Christ in which consists true faith, to the nature, power, fruit, impression and sealing of faith, but also those of whom we should expect better things, as may be seen by the writings of our opponents.

Oh! oh! how very little these poor children have and know of the kingdom of God, and of the power of his holy word, although they may think, perhaps, that they understand a great deal. For it is very clear that an earthly, carnal minded heart, an ambitious, proud mind, a spiteful, envious person, and an untrue and false tongue is not of the good, but of the evil one, 1 Jn. 3: 8; that the writings of our opponents were prompted by an earthly, carnal, hateful and false heart; that they did not seek the glory, name and honor of God, but their own; and that they are partial and untruthful, can be easily deduced from the fact that from begnining to end they do not speak a kind word about me nor our beloved brethren; that they are quite silent upon the favor, faithfully rendered them in need; nor once mention that they were so often silenced and could not present any excuses, something which I do not mention to our honor, but to the praise of the Lord; also, that they did not at all in their writings touch upon their confession which they made before us all, that woman has no seed, * * * whereby, in fact, his whole cause was already lost. Again, that there were two persons in Christ; and that the crucified one was not the Son of God; something which does not become an impartial writer who does not seek his own honor, but sincerely seeks the honor of God; also, that they call me quite ignorant, yea, as a cuckoo (as he also calls me) which always sings the same song, and passes himself for a spiritual master, versed in Scripture, while, before God and his angels and before all present, it was actually found to be quite different, as, by the grace of God, will be found and clearly seen from my following writings, if judged according to the divine truth. Very little, alas, have they meditated upon the Scripture of Paul, saying, that we should not be desirous of vain glory, Gal. 5: 26. Inasmuch as they give such an untrue account of the discussion, and as they have so lamentably profaned the Father and his Son, and their precious, dear, powerful and true word and all their confessors as also, our beloved brethren who daily, piously suffer and die for the sake of the Lord's word, and who are slandered as if their whole life and death were but madness, and their forsaking possessions and kindred, were but heresy; therefore I am impelled, as in duty bound, and for the love of my Lord and Savior Jesus Christ and his holy church (not urged by wrath; for this I leave to him who in due time shall judge us all without respect of person), faithfully and truthfully to annotate all that which Micron has willfully suppressed, to the dishonor of Christ and his holy word. Besides also, how slanderously he has blasphemed the Father and the Son, the Word and its confessors, and how wrongfully he opposes our faith and doctrine concerning the incarnation of Christ, which is taught and testified to throughout the Scriptures in incontrovertible power and clearness.

I therefore beseech all readers, for the Lord's sake, to peruse this my explanation, with impartial hearts, to consider well the foundation and to pray the Lord for grace and understanding. I trust to be able to show and explain it, by the aid of God, with such power and clearness of the holy Scriptures, that it will be plainly seen that anti-christian deceit is on the side of our opponents and that the clear ground of truth is on our side. Therefore I would have the judicial term, *Alteram partem audito*, that is, hear also the other party, applied, and to compare my writings with theirs and not be mistaken through prejudice as do the partial.

I also beseech you not to think hard of my having to use such terms as, seed of man, seed of woman, &c.; God knows how unwillingly I do so; but necessity forces me to make use of such terms, that the glory of Christ Jesus may not be obscured with many, and that the heavenly brightness of his most holy birth may not remain obscured by the anti-christian flattering and sophisty of the breath of Micron.

I can not sufficiently wonder at the man's heart and mind that he dares publish such absurd fables to the world, and that he dares show himself so ambitious and proud (something which, before God, I must deduce from his writings), as it will doubtlessly be read by many an intelligent person; for what else does he do all through his writings, but exalt himself, and trample me in the dust as is the nature of all the ambitious, something which I would not have written if it only touched me, and not the honor of God, while so many godfearing, pious men were present who heard the discussion from beginning to end. Yet besides, it is well known, perhaps, to thousands, as I presume, to whom it is known through my printed writings which are daily read here and there, that I have frequently solicited a public discussion, at the risk of being burned if I could not maintain my faith and doctrine by virtue of the Scriptures; but which, alas, has never been accepted.

If I, now, were so entirely ignorant, as must be understood from his writing, it would be very curious why such a discussion should have been so long denied me, as he might thereby have gained many a soul, might have redeemed many a child, if we were wrong; and as he might have won such a fame and reputation, if he had been successful, among those of high standing and also among the whole world. But Micron has not yet forgotten how they were situated with us, notwithstanding he wrote thus sneeringly. If Micron and Herman had feared God as they pretend by their sheep's clothing, they would not have acted so foolishly as they have done by their writings. But I presume that the one who urged Pharaoh to persecute Israel (notwithstanding he had seen such miracles in Egypt by the hands of Moses and Aaron), and found his punishment in the Red Sea, Ex. 7: 25; 8: 2; 9: 6; 10: 14; 11 : 5; 14 : 28; who urged Antiochus to turn Jerusalem into a death-pit, and on his way met the punisher; that this same one has urged Micron and Herman to write thus, that their covert hypocrisy, their many gross falsehoods, ambitious partiality (I call it as I judge them before the Lord), ingratitude, slander, adulteration and willful garbling of the holy, divine word, their corrupting flatterings, sophistical philosophy, miserable deceit of the poor, despised souls, abominable, anti-christian doctrine, blasphemy of both the Father and his blessed Son, palpable blindness, and their vain, carnal hearts, may once be made manifest through this our explanation; and that thus the hearts which are bound by their snares through the falsehoods which they publish against us, by the fine appearance they put on, and by the garbled Scriptures which they teach by smooth, flattering words, may be unbound and delivered, to the glory of the Lord.

I do not know what else to say or think of the matter. For, more than two years ago I warned him by a man of considerable name and one of his fellow-believers, that if he would put it in print (for I was told that he intended to do so), and would not tell the tale just as it truthfully happened, for I observed that he did not spare falsehood, I should reply to him, if I lived and the Lord granted it. But he was aware that if he did not tell it differently from what it was, he would have acquired but little fame and honor with the world; for it would have sounded: *Micron lost it all;* something that conceited, proud flesh does not like to hear.

Yet, I would never, in my life, have thought that he was of such extremely ambitious, partial, untrue, infamous, and shameless mind, if I had not been convinced thereof in our discussion and by this writing of his. I thought that his intellect would have told him, even without the warning of any one, that if he should do as he did, while I am yet living, that it would produce him nothing but shame and dishonor with all reasonable readers and auditors. But Micron had to speak, as his heart was full.

But perhaps, he hoped or thought that I might, in the mean time, die, and that he might thus acquire fame and honor, unrebuked, with the world. He was also aware that he could not offend the world, who gladly accept and hear false consolations and slanders, by abusing me; for whosoever can best belie, defame, upbraid, and depict me and my brethren in evil colors, is, with them, a great prophet, and a pleasing preacher. Let them run their course until hindered by the Lord! John says, "They are of the world, and therefore they speak of the world, and the world hear them," 1 Jn. 4: 5. If possible, the beloved Lord grant them grace. Let the reader take due notice of the following reply, that he may learn to know Christ, do right, and be saved.

A VERY PLAIN AND DISCREET

ANSWER TO MARTIN MICRON'S

ANTI-CHRISTIAN DOCTRINE, AND UNTRUE ACCOUNT OF THE DISCUSSION OF 1553, ACCORDING TO THE TRUTH AND POWER OF THE HOLY, DIVINE SCRIPTURES.

How and when the so called English came to us, and what faithful love our brethren showed them.

In the year 1553, a little before midwinter, it happened that it was told the brethren that a ship-load of people had arrived from Denmark, who, on account of their faith, were driven from England, and that they lay a short distance from the shore, frozen up in the ice.

When the brethren heard of this, they were moved by christian mercy on their account, as was proper. They counseled together and concluded to lend them their assistance to help them out of the ice and properly escort them to the city, without any commotion, as they also did; although they conjectured that it might cause trouble with their governments, as was also the fact.

They met them with wheat bread and wine, so that if there should be any sick among them, they might refresh and stimulate them therewith. And after they had escorted them into the city they made a collection of twenty-four thalers out of their poverty, and presented that sum to the leading ones of them, to be distributed among the needy if such there should be among them. They refused the money, and said they had enough; but would like that labor might be procured for some of their number; in which our brethren assisted them as much as they could.

One of our number offered to take the children of John A'Lasco into his house, and to do the best he could for them. To which Herman Backereel answered: No, this can not be granted; for John A'Lasco is a man who has dealings with lords, princes and other high personages. It might (oh! reader observe) injure his reputation if his children should sojourn with such people. On hearing this, I observed that we had not met with the true, plain and humble pilgrims of Jesus Christ.

Behold, thus was their arrival and reception by us; and such faithful love have our brethren shown them, which was, not long afterward, taken quite amiss by ungrateful Herman; and as appears, is not touched upon in Micron's account, merely out of hatred of the truth and out of disfavor to the brethren, lest piety should be ascribed to them.

HOW THE ENGLISH CAME INTO DISCUSSION WITH US.

After they had been a few days in the city, Herman and his followers called some of us together and desired a discussion with them, and after many broad assertions he said unto them, "I am a teacher, and would like to have a teacher put against me; for I have heard that Menno was to be in the city. Therefore I would have him or some other teacher to discuss with me. For I have had discussions with hundreds of yours, and when they would be vanquished they would invariably appeal to their teachers." Behold, thus he spoke! I might here write a good deal about his false pretensions and ambitious expressions; also about his infamous talk behind my back, and seeking if he could not find a splinter about me to magnify into a beam and to tie this upon my back as a sign of shame. Also, how he inquired of an unconscious child about my secret shelter, &c. But, as it can not be serviceable to the reader, therefore I will commend it to the Lord, and leave the shame of Herman untouched, that the reader may not think that I wish to retaliate evil with evil, from which may the Lord forever save me. Yet it is my heart's desire that he would be more truthful, and more impartial of heart, and that he would fear the Lord, his God, more.

The discussion was agreed upon with Herman and his fellows upon this condition: That they were to tell none where the discussion took place (as I was a poor, weak man, hated of all the world). Upon which they, on their part, gave our brethren their hands that they would never tell it. But how they kept their word their deeds have shown. For it was but a short time until it was known in the streets of Emden where Menno lived, and that Micron and his fellows had a discussion with him. And besides, they have published it in print, to all the world. If honorable, pious persons are not bound to respect their word and pledge (which is considered the same as an oath by all reasonable people) better than this, I will leave to the judgment of all readers, both those for and against me. But there are many who think that they cannot misuse us.

In the same manner they have been ungrateful to the city which showed more mercy to them than all Eastland and Denmark, when in midwinter they knew not where to find shelter; as they, with their unsalted, partial writings, have made the city suspicioned by lords, princes and other cities, that the city maintained us; while the city knew no more of my sojourning than they knew of the hour of their death.

Lastly, they registered the names of some good persons who had not merited such treatment, that they might be known in all countries to which they might move. A reward of thousands has been offered for the apprehension of one and his little children, who have rendered them such great services if the Lord, by his grace, do not prevent it. If they had now, in all this considered the unfeigned, pure love (which wishes harm to none, much less does it), common honesty, and their word and honor, since such a course instructs none upon the earth, nor makes them better in God, and appears more like the work of a traitor, than of a pious man; then, according to my opinion, the evangelical, christian character, spirit, discipline and reasonableness would have been more uniform than it now is. The Lord's word is true: The fruit shows what the tree is, Matt. 12:33. Behold, thus have they acted who pretend to be christians and say that we are heretics; who call upon God as their witness and judge that they have faithfully described the discussion, while they are well aware that the first sentence they wrote was a falsehood. And how quite untrue it is, will, by the grace of the Lord, be shown by self-evident truths from my following explanation of the discussion between Herman and myself.

DISCUSSION BETWEEN HERMAN AND MYSELF.

It happened when we met for the purpose of a discussion, that I briefly admonished them in regard to the suffering, oppression, tribulation, persecution and cross of the true christians. To which he immediately answered: "That I wished to make his doctrine suspected." Something of which I had not thought of in the least. I then quit, and said, Well Herman, I presume you would rather discuss the question of the incarnation? He answered in the affirmative. Then, I said, confess your faith. When he had made his confession, I said, Beloved Herman, take heed of your words. For behold, all these inconsistencies follow from your belief. And enumerated eight of them.

And behold, when I had finished my discourse there was one among them (J. M. whose name is frequently referred to in Micron's writings), who asked me if I could prove that to be the fact, according to Scripture? thinking that I had thus spoken in regard to my own faith. I told him that he might ask Herman, as it was his faith and doctrine. On hearing this he dropped his head and was silent. I told him thrice, successsively, to get Herman to prove it to him, according to the Scriptures. I have yet to receive his answer.

When I observed such partiality, I was very sorry. I said, Great God, are we thus to treat the word of the Lord. O shame! When you thought that it was my doctrine you wanted Scripture; but since you find that it is the doctrine of Herman, now you have Scripture enough! O, friend, I said, repent and be ashamed before God; for you do not treat his word, as becomes a true christian. And this is one of the principal, impartial witnesses, as Micron wrongfully boasts.

Afterward Herman replied and said, "I will scatter these inconsistencies as the wind scatters the dust." Dear Herman, I said, do not speak so boldly, it does not become a christian. I know you can not do it. And, praise to the Lord for his grace, it is verified to the present time as I can plainly see by Micron's Appendix, notwithstanding they have revolved the matter in their heads for more than two years.

The inconsistencies remained unreplied to, and it was mostly *granting* that could be heard from him. So at last I said, My dear sir, show me, where do you find it written that he took on him our flesh or our human nature, as you claim? He then answered: Paul teaches us that Christ "took on him the form of a servant," Phil. 2: 7.

When he had finished his discourse I asked him whether or not he agreed with John A'Lasco, in doctrine? He answered in the affirmative. I replied: Well, A'Lasco has made an antithesis of this Scripture of Paul "In the form of God," and, "the form of a servant." That as he was in a divine form and thereby truly *was* God, he has thus, also, taken upon himself our sinful form and was thereby, truly, made man, "but" (he says), "the sins, on account of which we are called servants in Scripture, he did not have."

From which antithesis one of two things must be true. Either, if he had the sinful form and not the sin, that he then, by virtue of the antithesis, also, must have had the divine form; but he did not have the divine form. Or if he had, and therewith the divinity also, that he, also, must have had the sinful form, and therewith sin; else the antithesis is false and can not stand, in fact. In this view of the matter one of two things is true, that Christ Jesus was either a sinner, or else he was not God. And how such doctrine agrees with the Scriptures, I will leave to your own judgment.

Then he replied: "The Scriptures testify that he was without sin." It is true, I said. Therefore it is manifest that this antithesis of A'Lasco is false, and that you can not maintain your doctrine by this Scripture. But if the Scripture is to remain unbroken, then this is the true antithesis; as Christ was in the godly form, and was thereby truly God, as he humbled himself and did not take on himself the form of a potentate, emperor, or king, whom we should serve, but the form of a poor servant, because he wanted to serve; for as he has been truly God in God, and with God his Father, from eternity; thus he became our true servant, in due time, Isa. 7: 15; 9: 5; 40: 28; Jer. 23: 5; 33: 15; Jn. 1: 2; Rom. 9: 26; 1 Jn. 5: 5; Matt. 12: 18; 20: 28.

He then abandoned that Scripture, and said, "There is another one much plainer, which has it that," "He has taken on him the seed of Abraham," Heb. 2: 16. Not so Herman, I said. We should not thus adulterate the Scriptures. For it does not read that *he has taken* on him the seed of Abraham, but it reads that *he took* it on himself. Which taking on shall last unto the end.

He then took the words of the same chapter and said, "That Christ had taken upon himself the children's flesh and blood, and is thus, on account of the flesh, called our brother."

On hearing this I replied: That that was again an adulteration of the Scriptures; for it is written that he took upon himself *flesh and blood;* but not the flesh and blood of children. Therefore let us get at the meaning of these words at the start, lest we adulterate the Scriptures. Thus Paul says, "He that sanctifieth, and they who are sanctified, are of one." Now I ask, to whom has it reference? To God or to Adam? He replied: "To Adam." Then it follows, I said, incontrovertibly, that all ungodly children of the devil, such as thieves, murderers, drunkards, haters, idolaters, whores and rogues, are Christ's brethren and sisters. He frankly admitted this to be the case.

It would further follow, if we were Christ's brethren and sisters on account of the flesh, then also we would be his children on account of the flesh; for Paul says, "Behold, I and my children," &c. From which it would surely follow that the one brother had generated the other, and the children their father, according to the flesh. And I will leave you to study out how such a generation could be, according to the Scriptures, and according to the ordinance of God.

After passing some other words concerning *the partaking of*, I asked him if Adam had not partaken of flesh and blood? He answered in the affirmative. Well, said I, of whose flesh and blood did he partake, if we are to understand *participation* as you do? Therefore beloved Herman, take heed. Your learned ones deceive you. Thus Paul says, "He that threshes in hope, should be partaker of his hope," that is, that he may obtain that for which he hopes. Again, in the same chapter: "If others be partakers of this power over you, are not we rather?" 1 Cor. 9: 10, 12, that is, if others have this power. Again, "We are made partakers of Christ, if we hold the beginning of our confidence steadfast unto the end," Heb. 3: 14. Not that we partake partly but wholly.

Therefore, beloved Herman, I warn you, let the Scripture remain Scripture and do not garble it to suit your opinion. For Paul does not say that the unsanctified, such as, liars, haters, proud, adulterers, and the children of the devil are one with Christ, our Savior, but that the sanctified are of one with him, that is, those who, with him are born of one God. On account of which birth of God, and not of Adam, we are his brethren; for the regenerated with him, have one Father, as he is the first begotten Son of God, thus he is also the firstborn among many brethren, Heb. 1: 6; Rom. 8: 29.

As holy Paul, then, teaches us that he is thus the first-begotten among the brethren; therefore it is very plain that he is not our brother of Adam, but of God; for he was not the first-begotten of Adam, therefore Adam's children must, through regeneration by faith, also become the children of God, Jn. 1: 12, and thus be Christ's brethren, Matt. 12: 50; Mark 3: 35; Luke 8: 21; Heb. 2: 11.

Behold, he is not ashamed to call his brethren, such regenerated and sanctified ones who, with him, have one Father (no whores, rogues and children of the devil), saying, Thy name (he means his Father's name and not Adam's) I will promulgate to my brethren. Again, I will trust in him (namely, in the Father, and not in Adam). Again, behold, "I and the children which God (not Adam) hath given me." Inasmuch as it is very plain that his children are not the carnal, but the spiritual children (for he had no carnal children) then his brethren must be spiritual brethren; or else one Scripture must be understood spiritually and the other carnally, then, also sister Mary must have generated her brother Christ, in the flesh. This is incontrovertible.

Although now such regenerated, the sanctified, are his brethren and sisters they yet have, contrary to their own will, communion with flesh and blood, through the inherent sinful nature; they frequently sin, stumble and transgress, and are thus through the beforementioned communion, conscious of guilt according to the law which requires perfect righteousness. And behold, therefore he is their Savior, first-begotten Brother, and Father Christ, who in like manner, has partaken of flesh and blood, not of the children, for it does not read so, and in that case he must have been one of two sons, one of whom was of heaven, eternal and immortal, the other of earth and mortal, but the Word itself (I add some words for explanation) is become flesh, that is, a truly passive, mortal man, in Mary, as John says, "The word is become flesh," like unto his sanctified brethren in all things, except sin, that he might fulfill the law in his innocent flesh and not by our guilty flesh; that he might take away the deserved death by his innocent death; destroy the devil who had the power of death; bruise the Serpent's head; sanctify us unto God, his Father, by virtue of his precious blood; and assist us in all our temptations and besetting sins which result from our wicked flesh and the inspirations of Satan. Behold, this is the proper explanation of Heb. 2 : 14. And by such explanation Christ remains the undivided Son of God, the Scripture remains unbroken, Christ remains the Sanctifier and we are the sanctified. Brethren and children, there is not a single Scripture which contradicts this, while Herman's confession and faith are very inconsistent as has been heard.

When I again touched upon the inconsistencies, he asked me to confess my faith, as he had done his; and he was going to show, he said, more inconsistencies (although he had not yet heard it) in my faith than I had shown in his. And when I had made my confession, he said, "This is too long for me; I can not *reply to* it." I then made a brief statement. Yet I was shown no inconsistency.

Behold, worthy reader, these are the principal points and Scriptures which Herman and I discussed concerning the incarnation of Christ. I say the principal ones; for to repeat all the words which passed between us, is impossible.

After meal time we came to the discussion of pedo-baptism, which he tried to make right by the assertion, that the children, as he said, are accounted as believing, by the Scriptures, and that Zaccheus (he insisted upon Zaccheus, notwithstanding I told him that it was not Zaccheus), and his whole house were baptized.

Kind reader, if I were to give an account of the discussion as it happened it would seem to some readers as if I were partial; again, to others, who know me, that it was very foolish of him to challenge us while he did not know more of Scripture. I told him twice, dear Herman, you are too young; you will have to learn a great deal before you ought to try to defend your cause. What is become of all your bold assertions which you made at the start? Yet, Micron writes that some of their weak brethren were very much strengthened by Herman during the discussion. I will leave the matter here. Thus they hoodwink the reader that he may not observe that Herman acted so childish, to their shame.

I know to a certainty that Micron was written to immediately after the discussion, as his own writing implies. For their brethren who were with us were in great need, inwardly and outwardly. What he means by 'inwardly' I will leave the reader to judge.

HOW PARTIALLY MICRON NARRATED OUR FIRST DISCUSSION; HOW SILENT HE IS ON THE PRINCIPAL POINTS; HOW HE GARBLES MY WORDS AND HOW HE ADORNS HIS OWN.

WHEN we were met for the discussion, I said to Micron, I hear that your name is Martin Micron. You are unknown to me, and I have never heard of you before you came here. But I understand that you have made quite a reputation at London, England, that you have published writings, as I hear. Therefore my fraternal admonition to you is, that if you hear more powerful truths and firmer foundation in this our discussion, than you have heard or learned before this, that you seek not your own fame and honor, but the praise and honor of God. To which he replied: "Menno, this is also my admonition to you." I said, I am here for that very purpose; and I have suffered for many years because I would gladly have the truth and follow it.

This brotherly admonition, given him in faithfulness of heart, he has lamentably disregarded in the latter part of the discussion, as he was every time conquered in his false, anti-christian doctrine, and he said it before my face that I had blamed him with seeking his own praise and honor by his writing, in London. Something which I had, then, never thought of; for I was not acquainted with him.

He called upon his own as witnesses, which poor, enchanted children all agreed with him, at which I was very sorry, and said, Is the fear of God, then, not before you? There are now ten of you, all of whom answer to suit him. If there were ten thousand more besides you, you would not tell the truth in this matter. For how could it be possible that I should at the first start run up to a man with whom I was not acquainted, and of whom I had heard nothing but a good report, and say, that he had sought his own honor with his writings.

Also, all of our brethren contradicted him, and said, "Good Micron, you are mistaken; for so and so has Menno admonished you, and thus you have answered him." Yet it was of no avail. These unkind, bitter, lying, and defaming words must, alas, be published in his book. What kind of a spirit this is; how he follows the unadulterated, christian truth, piety and love; and how faithfully he narrates the matter, I will let all impartial, reasonable readers judge by his dishonest adulteration of my words which I spoke to him with such good intentions. We then discussed some articles with which my writings are replete; and to which it is useless to reply. Lastly, we came to the discussion of the incarnation, for the sake of which we are called such abominable heretics and deceivers by them, namely, because we confess with God, the Father, with Christ, with the angel Gabriel, with Peter, and with all the Scriptures that Jesus Christ is the Son of God, Matt. 3:17; 17:5; Mark 1:11; 9:7; Luke 1:31; 3:22; Jn. 1:45; 5:22; 6:35; 7:21; 8:23; 9:37; 10:36.

His proper confession and foundation was, *That there are two Sons in Christ. The one eternal and impassive; the other temporal and passive; and that the one which was crucified for us, was not the Son of God.* Which confession he did not make thoughtlessly and by mistake, but with premeditation and a sober mind, before us all; and he has repeated it, at least four or five times. Yet he calls on the judgment and name of the Lord, that they frequently confessed, with us, that the Son of God died for us. Syrach truly says, "Many would rather do the worst than to lose their honor; and do it for the sake of the ungodly," Syr. 20:24.*

I proposed the inconsistencies of his belief and after many long and broad assertions I let him read undisturbedly an hour or an hour and a half from the Bible, about the seed of woman, the seed of Abraham, and of David; and about the fruit of the loins of David. When he had finished reading, I asked, what he wanted to assert thereby? "I assert thereby, he said, that the man Christ is of the fathers, and that the word did not become flesh, as you say." This was the amount of his words.

I replied, I cordially acknowledge and confess all these Scriptures to be right and good; for they teach us, and testify that such a Savior should come. But now we will find out from the Scriptures of whom the human fruit comes; whether it comes of the father or of the mother. On hearing this, he said, "Are you going to find that out?" I answered in the affirmative; for I trust, by the grace of God, to be able to prove by virtue of the holy, divine Scriptures, that the origin of the child is of the father, and not of the mother, but through the mother. This, I think, was something new to him; for he said, "Sir, let us hear it." I pointed him to 1 Cor. 11:8, where Paul says, "Man is not of the woman, but the woman of the man." On hearing this he interrupted me and said, "This is spoken of Adam and Eve."

---

*German Bible.

Hold, said I; but it further reads: "Even so is the, man also by the woman." Was Adam, then, by Eve? He was then silent, as one who is beaten. I showed him many plain Scriptures, as Gen. 15:4; 17:6; 19:32; Rom. 9:7; Heb. 7:10; 11:12. I also referred him to the genealogy, Matt. 1, that Christ, according to his foundation, must also have been a Syrian, Canaanite, Moabite and an Ammonite. I also made some natural illustrations, as of the sower, his seed and soil; from which he tries to make it appear to the reader that I made use of my intellect and not of the Scripture, against him. But, as the saying is, Micron's little finger knows full well that the seed of the land and the seed of man are called by the same name, in the Scriptures; and that also Abraham cast his seed, that is, sowed it, Heb. 11:11, although he garbles it in his writings and would apply the casting to Sarah. What we are to judge of such willful adulterers of the holy, divine word, I will leave to the impartial reader. It is the same means of which the serpent made use when he led Adam and Eve into death, Gen. 3:1. Kind reader, as the Scriptures, together with daily occurrences, openly testify to us by the ordinance of God, that there are sowers, and also that there is seed, which is sown, there must also be a fit soil to be sown; for neither in the unplowed land, nor upon houses, trees and rocks do we sow, as may be seen. And whether or not my comparison of the husbandman, of his seed, and of his field can stand according to the Scriptures, I will not leave to the calumniating Micron and Herman, but to the reasonable reader.

When I had finished my argument I said, Behold, Martin, this natural comparison which I have proposed, you may take into consideration, at your leisure, but let us have a reply to my Scriptures. Then he appeared as one who is in doubt, and said, "Away with this pilosophy of the seed of woman." On hearing this, I replied: I have proposed to you the plain Scriptures whereby I have proved that the child is originally of the father, and not of the mother; and you want it to be of the mother, without the Scriptures. Say, kind sir, which of us two makes use of philosophy? You or I? He made no reply at all. But he now writes as if he had then said, thus, "The words of Paul, 1 Cor. 11:7, should be understood as having reference to Adam and Eve; for Paul wanted to humble the men that they should not exalt themselves above woman, on account of their glory," which in one sense is right, yet not according to the sense of Paul in this instance. For Micron desires to apply it to Adam and Eve, and Paul spoke it in reference to all who are born of Adam and Eve. For he says, "For as the woman is of the man, even so is the man also by the woman." Mark, he says, *By the woman.* If Onan had done as he did, Gen. 38:9, a thousand times; and besides, all men with him, who were from the beginning, no human fruit would be born therefrom. For the seed must have a proper soil to produce fruit and to generate according to the word and ordinance of the Lord, and therefore Paul says, "Neither is the man without the woman, neither the woman without the man, in the Lord," 1 Cor. 11:11. I trust that such plain Scriptures can be understood.

Again, concerning the Scripture, Wis. 7:2, Micron says, "It does not read of man's seed alone." To which I reply: Micron must be a man who esteems the judgment of the Almighty God too little, that he is not afraid to adulterate such plain words, or to obscure them by the breath of the abyss, as it is so plain that the Holy Spirit in plain words here ascribes to the father that which belongs to the father, according to the ordinance of God, and to the mother what belongs to the mother. * * I repeat it, that such plain words of the Scriptures are easily understood.

Again, to my pointing him how Sarah conceived of Abraham, and Rebecca of Isaac, Heb. 11:11; Rom. 9:7, he replies thus, but in the discussion he did not refer to it, the reason why Abraham and Isaac are called the origin of their descendants, he says, is to exclude other men, and also, because woman has lost her privilege through sin. This is such glozing as if both the Scripture and that were lost. Therefore this is my brief reply: God does not require of any one that which he has not given, nor does he envy any one for that which is given him; for he is a God of the truth and not of a mere name. And if the Lord had done so, for the reason given by Micron, then God would have had pleasure in the name, and not in truth. He would also have given more to those patriarchs than truthfully belonged to them, and taken from woman what belonged to her. Mark what kind of a God the sophistry of Micron teaches.

As for the privilege, of which he writes, I would in all love ask him what kind of a privilege this was, which woman has lost through sin? If she is no more woman, and if she is become unfit to fulfill her maternal calling and office to which she was ordained of God? That she is woman still, and necessary to fill her place in the world, is too clear to need arguing. Therefore I do not know what the privilege might be, as the Scriptures say no more than, "I will greatly multiply thy sorrow, and thy conception; in sorrow thou shalt bring forth children: and thy desire shall be to thy husband and he shall rule over thee," Gen. 3: 16. But thus something must be done to deceive the humble reader, when flattery will not give it a scriptural appearance.

Oh! oh!! If we poor children were to treat the Scriptures the twentieth part as they do (something from which may the Lord save us), and would vail the eyes of the ignorant as does Micron by his flatterings, great God! how they would be offended. They would also have full right to do so. Nevertheless, however they teach and do, it is a welcome gospel to the poor, deceived world, as was commonly the case from the beginning with all false prophets and their followers. He is allowed to break the bones of the passover, and to cut off Samson's hair, Ex. 12: 46; Num. 9: 12, until the time comes that it is ended with him and he has to give an account of his deceit before the Lord.

After some passing remarks, we came to the inconsistency that they had an impure Christ; and I asked him if he confessed Mary to be of the impure and sinful seed of Adam? He answered, "Yes." But he said she was pure, because the angel said unto her, "Blessed art thou among women," Luke 1: 28. To this I replied: The Lord said unto Abraham, "I shall bless thee;" "and I will bless them that bless thee," Gen. 12. Again, he promised to the obedient parents under the law: "Blessed shall be the fruit of thy body," Deut. 28: 4. Were, thereby, Abraham, together with all those that bless him, and all those who are born of such pious parents, pure and without sin?

He said, "Christ was pure and without sin, and that because he was not of human seed." I replied: From such explanation the greatest inconsistencies would follow.

He then replied: "God was the cause that the nature of Adam was corrupted." I noticed that he was unable to reply, and that he knew not what to say. I asked him, Why? Because, said he, "God said," "In the day that thou eatest thereof thou shalt surely die." So I hear, I said, that God was the cause of the transgression of Adam? together with some other remarks. "No," he said, "I do not say so." Oh, Micron! I said, Consider what inconsistencies you advance and what a weak, unscriptural foundation it is which you would assert and maintain! He did not reply again, yet he claims in his writing that he asserted and maintained the purity of Christ, against us. If that is not seeking one's own honor and to give an untrue account of the discussion, I will leave the reader to judge. And how the assertions which he now makes in his writings, will stand according to the Scriptures, we will show by the Scripture. Thus he writes: "We can conclude nothing under sin, but that which the Scriptures conclude under it." In this he is right, yet contrary to himself. For the Scriptures conclude Adam and all his seed under sin. Therefore it must be so with Adam and all his seed; this cannot be denied, 1 Cor. 15: 21; Rom. 5: 18; Gal. 3: 22; Eph. 2: 1. He further writes: That which the Scriptures make free, we also should consider free. Again he is right; but contrary to himself, for the Scripture makes Christ free, and therefore we also consider him as free, because he is from above, of God who is pure, and not from below of impure Adam; which Adam, I repeat, according to the Scriptures, is concluded under sin, with all his seed, and the Scriptures do not contradict themselves.

He further writes that the apostles and prophets had no need of saying so much about the holiness of Christ, if he were from above, and not of Adam. This is so simple, that it looks surprising. For, if Christ were such a pure man of impure Adam, as our opponents say, then the Scriptures would contradict themselves; or else Adam must have had two seeds of which one was corrupt and the other remained pure, which is not thus taught by holy writ. Observe what blind arguments he advances.

Lastly, he writes: "That which God testifies to be holy; man can not make common or unholy," and adduces, Acts 10: 15. Here the most holy holiness of the flesh of Jesus Christ is compared, by him, to the flesh of the animals, which, under the law, were forbidden Israel to eat, Lev. 11; Deut. 14: 7, and which are now, under the gospel, allowed as clean, Matt. 15: 11; Mark 7: 15; Acts 10: 15; Rom. 14: 20; Tit. 1: 15, as if Adam, thus, by one word (as the animals under the law), was made unclean; and now, again, by one word (as also these animals), was made clean, in this his seed (of which, according to him, Christ should be generated); by which he blasphemes the most holy holiness of Christ's flesh. O, abominable flattery!

Behold, dear reader, this is the best foundation upon which Micron can build his assertion of the purity of the flesh of Christ, after a study of two years of which he, at the time of the discussion did not advance a single word. You may consider for yourselves whether he does not make his doctrine suspected by such flattery.

And when he was defeated in his assertion about the seed of woman, by virtue of the Scripture, and could find nothing to solve the inconsistency, and was hedged in on all sides, he proposed the following question, as if he was so confused that he knew not what to say and yet wanted to say something, that it might not be said that he was silenced: "Do you believe that Mary was a human being?" For God's sake, hear what he has proposed!

On hearing this, I became recklessly excited, and answered thoughtlessly: She certainly was no brute. What is this for a base question? Behold thus the brute came into play; upon the cause of which he is silent; and which he adduces quite strangely, and little to my honor.

I confess before him and before all readers that I did not answer him respectfully; and I am sorry for it; for it would have been proper to have given him a considerate answer; and not to return foolishness with foolishness. But to which of us the greatest blame should be attributed, to Micron with his surprisingly indiscreet question, or to myself with my unseasoned answer, I would gladly leave to his own consideration if he were impartial.

After this had taken place I had but very little desire to discuss with him at that time, as I saw that he so quite partially placed himself against the truth although he had nothing to advance whereby he could defend his foundation, so that I was forced to say, Good Martin, do not take it amiss; it would be well if you would learn to know yourself better, for you are yet too much of a novice in the Scriptures to defend the foundation of your doctrine in regard to this matter.

"Attend," he said then, "I will tell you something else." But as it had no foundation at all, and was nothing but nonsense; and as he went from one thing to another, I recklessly answered: Away with your talk. All you adduce is nothing but anathema.

He then became very angry and cried out thrice: "The pope has taught you this." No, I answered with the same words, thrice, Not the pope, but Paul has taught me this, Gal. 1: 8. For it is a strange gospel, your philosophy about Christ, which is not taught us by the apostles nor by the Scriptures; and I did not say a word about 1 Cor. 16: 22, although he, without any truth, said and wrote so, the like of which alas, he often does to defame me, out of malice.

I again acknowledge that I might have borne with him more patiently than I did. Yet the Son of God has not lost his son-ship and rights, by my inconsiderate answer; nor was Micron's anti-christian doctrine thereby rendered the christian doctrine. I became very tired of answering his foolish questions; for I began to observe by what kind of a spirit he was prompted.

Besides, he has quite reversed the narration of the discussion; has enlarged his ten words into very many, to flatter his cause; has abreviated mine in many instances, to weaken our cause, and has written many things which were never thought of; and such by which he was quite stunned, he has not mentioned at all. Yet this audacious man dares call on God as his witness that he has given a true narration. O Lord!

Well, every one will have to give an account of himself before his God, let him adorn his falsehoods and seal them as much as he pleases. By the grace of God, I shall affirm my humble truth with yea, and nay, as Scripture teaches. Whosoever will, may therewith believe my writings; and if he will not I can not help it. I will call on nothing higher. I have suffered much pain and trouble for about twenty-one years for the sake of truth, yea and nay, and have borne it submissively; nor shall I by the merciful assistance of the Lord leave it in my old age, on account of Micron and all anti-christians' false doctrine, however Satan may portray me by his authors and servants.

HOW AND WHAT MICRON CONFESSED DURING OUR SECOND DISCUSSION, AND HOW UNFAITHFULLY HE HAS NARRATED IT.

* * * *

In the second place, I asked him if he admitted the confession which he had made, concerning the two Sons in Christ, at the time of our first discussion? He answered, "Yes." Then I desired Andrew whom he calls Cananeus, to write it down, which he did in Micron's presence, and reads thus: "Two sons in Christ. The first, God's eternal Son, born of him before time was, without mother, and impassive. The second, Mary's son, or the son of man, born of her in due time, without father, and passive. In which passive son of Mary, the impassive Son of God, dwelt. So that the man Christ who died for us, was not the Son of God; for he had no father." Behold, this was his confession which we all heard from his own mouth, and which was written down in his presence.

When Andrew had written it down, Micron said, "Read it to me." After it was read I asked him if he had not written it down right. He replied "Yes." And now this untruthful man comes and writes that they frequently confessed that the Son of God died for us; while it did not happen otherwise than it is here narrated; and comes now again in his writing and says that he had no father. For on the thirty-second page he writes: "As to the real origin of the human substance (which he called before us, the second son), he had, according to the testimony of the Holy Scriptures, no father; and refers to Matt. 1: 2, 3. And thus the pure, Holy Scriptures (because they call Mary a virgin), must be the cover of his abominably false doctrine; notwithstanding it clearly testifies in many places that God is his Father; and that he is the Son of God, Luke 1: 31; 9: 35; Matt. 3: 17; 14: 33; 16: 16; 17: 5; Mark 3: 11; 9: 6; 15: 39; Jn. 1: 45; 3: 16; 6: 69; 7: 28; 8: 23; 9: 37; 10: 36; 11: 27. Behold this is the man who, according to his own writing, has so cleverly discussed and so powerfully asserted the foundation of his doctrine, as he falsely makes his followers believe; and who has, to his own everlasting shame, placed such a bright crown upon his head, as he claims in his book. The proverb, "That honor shames those that seek it," is true.

In the third place, I asked him, since he says that the man Christ had no father, whether he did not call him the Son of God? He answered, "Yes." I asked him again, for what reason he called him so; whether it was on account of his birth, or of regeneration, or of his creation, or of the acceptation? For if he should be truly called such it must be because of one of these four reasons; or else one would speak a falsehood as often as he would call him such. I received this answer: "On account of none of these four reasons." This is all the answer he gave me; but he sought another retreat, that he might not be caught in the net of truth. This question (then left unanswered) he now adduces quite garbled, and says, page 173, "That he is called the Son of God, on account of the union of the two sons" (which he artfully calls two natures that it may not sound too strange), of which union we can find not a letter in all the Scriptures, whereby he confesses publicly that the crucified Christ Jesus who has borne the sins of all the world and reconciled it unto God his Father, was merely *called* the Son of God; and that God is therefore but a God in name, and not a God in truth. Surely, this is too much of blasphemy, that the Almighty, great God and his blessed, beloved Son must hear of such a man.

In the fourth place, I asked him if he knew that Gellius Faber had issued a publication against us, and if he had read it? He answered, "Yes." Well, said I, how do you like it? "It is a very fine thing," he said, "I have also let our brethren read it."

Ah, Martin! said I, do you endorse that ungodly homily which is so replete with falsehood, by which the word and ordinances of the Lord are so lamentably broken, and wherein the most holy flesh of Christ is called a *boose-geld** and ransom? If the Lord will help me he will be replied to, for when this happened mine was almost in print. Behold, I tell the truth. Then Micron said, "I have spoken to Gellius about the *boose-geld*; and he claims that it is a mistake of the printer, and that it should be *loose-geld* (a ransom). Then one of ours said, *loose* means, in this sense, false or frivolous." Should Christ's flesh, then, have been a false or frivolous money? &c.

On hearing this, I said: I have often thought to myself how is it possible that a man could thus write? It must be a mistake. Reflecting upon the matter, I said, I remembered that John A'Lasco and he were unanimous in this doctrine; and that A'Lasco wrote: "If Christ be holy why was he then condemned by the judgment of the Father, on account of sin?" Again, "Christ partook of no other flesh but that of sin, that he might be tempted, and subject to death." Inasmuch as they agreed, I thought, and as these sayings of A'Lasco openly testify, that he (Christ) was not holy, but that he was of a sinful flesh, guilty of death, therefore it might, in the same manner, be called by the learned, a *boose-geld* and ransom. Behold, thus I answered, and not otherwise.

When I told it thus, Micron desired to read the sayings of A'Lasco, and said at last, after having studied about them: "It is very obscure." Yes, certainly, I said, Not obscure but ungodly. And this discreet reply of mine he has not only suppressed, but lamentably garbled, to my disadvantage. Besides, he has left the writings of A'Lasco out of the narrative and thus he blames me of what others are guilty. I will leave it to the all-seeing God and to his own mind whether he has written it with the Spirit of truth, which is quite impartial, and with true, christian love, as if standing before God.

Inasmuch as I have thus found it printed in his book, and as the sayings of A'Lasco imply that Christ's flesh was guilty of death; as has been heard, which may rightfully be called a *boose-geld* and ransom, as he deems it to be sinful, then say, beloved, what have I said about which to make such an ado? and, as he perhaps thinks, on account of which he has so mortally wounded me; besides, according to truth it is their foundation and the unmistakable result of their doctrine. But thus he must render Gellius a favor at my expense, although he once spoke quite differently to some preachers at Emden, about Gellius' book.

We then came to the inconsistency of concluding two persons in Christ. To which Micron answered: "We do not assert that there are two persons in Christ; but we say there is but one. For although the Word, from eternity, was one person, yet when it was conceived in Mary it was no person." Beloved, mark, what indiscreetness he uses.

---

*Boose in Dutch means wicked.

He further said: "Although every man is a person, and although the man Christ was a man as any other man, yet the man Christ, for himself alone, was no person." Is it not a shame that one has to repeat such ignorant words before intelligent persons? Paul truly asks: "Where is the disputer of this world?" 1 Cor. 1:20. When we had finished our arguments in regard to this matter, I said, I understand that some of you say, "Menno said sometime ago that the whole Christ was God's Son; but he did not prove it by the Scripture." Therefore I desire to do so now; and I will read the Scriptures of the New Testament to you, which testify that the whole Christ Jesus, from head to foot, visible and invisible, is God's own, only and first-begotten, true Son, if you will patiently attend, as I did when you were reading. "Do so," he said.

I read about twenty-four or twenty-five strong, plain Scriptures, to some of which I shall here refer. The first was, "The Holy Ghost shall come upon thee and the power of the Highest shall overshadow thee; therefore also that holy thing which shall be born of thee shall be called the Son of God," Luke 1:35. Here the angel of the Lord testifies that Christ Jesus should be the Son of God, and you, Micron, say that he was not.

The Father himself says, "This is my beloved Son in whom I am well pleased," Matt. 3:17; 17:5; Mark 9:7; Luke 3:22; 9:35. And you, Micron, boldly contradict it, and say that he is not. Again, Christ said unto the blind man, "Dost thou believe on the Son of God? He answered and said, Who is he, Lord, that I may believe on him? And Jesus said unto him, Thou hast both seen him, and it is he that speaketh with thee," Jn. 9:35, 36. Here the visible, speaking Christ confesses himself to be the Son of God. And you, Micron, say he is not.

Christ says, "What and if ye shall see the son of man ascend up where he was before?" Jn. 6:62. Here Christ testifies that the Son of man was from above, and that he would again return thither. And you, Micron, say that the son of man is not of heaven, but of earth.

Peter answered Christ to the question: "Whom say ye that I am?" "Thou art the Christ, the Son of the living God," Matt. 16:16; and Christ blessed him for it. And you, Micron, say that the man Christ is not the Son of God.

The centurion confessed him to be such; at the cross. He said, "Truly this man was the Son of God," Mark 15:39. And you, Micron, controvert it, and say that he was not.

All the apostles confessed Christ to be the Son of God, Matt. 14:33; also, John, the Baptist; Nathaniel and Martha, Jn. 1:45; 11:27. And you, Micron, are not ashamed to say that he is not.

John says, "These are written, that ye might believe that Jesus is the Christ, the Son of God; and that believing ye might have life through his name," Jn. 20:31. Beloved Micron, take heed. At another place it reads, "He that believeth not God, hath made him a liar; because he believeth not the record that God gave of his Son," 1 Jn. 5:10. "He is anti-christ that denieth the Father and the Son," 1 Jn. 2:22. Behold, Micron, what kind of spirits you are we will let you judge by this Scripture of John. What is your answer to all those plain Scriptures, which I have read?

He was again puzzled as before, during the first discussion when he was overcome on the subject of woman's seed. Both he and Herman became pale (as the brethren told me, for I did not notice it), and Micron said, "Most of these Scriptures I confess to be right and just." Not all? I asked. I have not added a single word; but merely read from the Bible. Tell me which are *not* right.

I received no answer at all. But again he asked a strange question three or four times, which I refused to answer, desiring an answer to the Scriptures which I had read. At last he spoke, but merely deceitfully, that he might lead me off my Scriptures which he could not answer because they were too powerful and plain, and also because he yet wanted to make a show: "They shall be answered," he said. Then ask on, said I. "Do you believe," he said, "that Christ was born of the Father, and seated with the Father, from eternity?" I let him ask the question again.

Martin, said I, you do not act as becomes a true and pious man. Is that an answer to my Scriptures? Immediately he began to boast that I could not answer his question. I was sorry that I had commenced to discuss with such a perverse man; for I saw clearly that he was not prompted by the spirit of truth. I further said, that I have never read of such a birth, in the Scriptures, as the one which he enquired about, which implied a seat with God from eternity. If you read of it, I said, then show me where to find it.

"No," he said, "We want to find it out by you." Martin, said I, be ashamed. When I want to see the Scriptures you are not willing to show them. He again said, "He wanted to find it out by me." Man, man, I said, By this you show what kind of a spirit there is in you. What indiscreet perverseness, to require of me to show that which is not to be found in the Scriptures. Heaven and earth have not yet stood six thousand years, and the Scriptures say that heaven is God's throne, and earth his footstool, and that God is an eternal God who has neither beginning nor end. If I should ask, now, what were God's throne and footstool before heaven and earth were created, would you be obliged to answer me, while the Scriptures say nothing about it? I again received the answer: "We want to find out by you." Mark with what kind of a spirit this man discussed with me.

Observing that the bait which he threw out was to get something peculiar from me, I said to him: Micron, since you can not stand before the truth, I can see what your object is. Therefore understand me, that you may give a true account of me. Whatever the Scripture testifies concerning the eternal, divine form of Christ, I sincerely believe, although I may not thoroughly commprehend it, as that his goings forth have been from of old, from everlasting, Micah 5: 2; that he is the Alpha and Omega, Rev. 1: 8; 2: 8; the eternal Word of the Father, his Wisdom and Son, by whom all things were created, Gen. 1: 1; Ps. 33: 6; Prov. 8: 22; Jn. 1: 3; Eph. 3: 9; Col. 1: 16; Heb. 1: 2; the firstborn of every creature, Col. 1: 15, who is before Abraham was, Jn. 8: 58, and other like Scriptures I do not comprehend. But that there was a birth from everlasting, as you say, I can not find in the Scriptures.

Inasmuch as I can not find this in the Scriptures, and, as I am prepared to obey them unto death, therefore I ask you to show me (as you ask it of me) where it is written, and, by the grace of God, I will not in the least controvert it; for I was certain that he could not show it. He answered again: "No, we want to find out by you." Now judge of the spirit of the discussion.

I will now leave this to the judgment of all impartial, reasonable readers whether Micron has met us in discussion as a godly, humble, kind and pious christian, to teach me and all of us, or to be taught of us in the matters pertaining to Christ Jesus, by the Spirit and word of the Lord; or, whether he met us as an ungodly, proud, cruel and infamous pharisee.

A more abominable discussion I never heard of. In the first place, because he wanted to find out by us something which is not in the Scriptures. And in the second place, because I desired him to show it to me, and he would not do it for the sake of truth and love. But Micron knew that he could not find it in the Scriptures, yet, by such trickery, after he had lost this foundation, he tried to make a show among his followers who understood so little about the Scriptures. But he was caught in the net he set for us, as you may clearly see from the following account. For, when I observed that he had lost all christian reasonableness; that no Scriptures would avail anything in his case, and that he strove for nothing else but to catch me at some expression or other, which he might, by falsely adding to it, himself, fasten upon us, to our disadvantage, I desired of him to explain his question a little better, namely, whether he believed that Christ, from everlasting, was born of the Father, or that he was from eternity seated with the Father, and separated from him? Three or four times, he said, "Born."

Born? I said, I do not contradict it; for you have heard my confession, clear enough, but explain your question. It was again, "Born."

Then I said to Herman, Do tell, what is

your faith? He spoke in his usual, thoughtless manner and frankly said, "That he was seated, separate from the Father."

Well, Micron, I said, is that your faith also? He again answered, Born. For the fox was afraid that he should be caught in his den.

Micron, said I, say yes or no. We have heard enough of your, Born. Then he said, "Yes!" Well, I said, give attention!

I presume, I said, that you have read that there was a sect in ancient times which was called *Triticole* or *Tritoites* (Tritheists),* because they worshipped three Gods. If you have the same faith concerning the Holy Ghost, that you have concerning the Father, and the Son, then it is plain that you are Tritheists; for you so divide them, as being seated separate, one from the other, as was seen. He made no reply to this, at all.

In the second place, I said, You are aware that Arius was deemed a heretic, because he said that Christ had a beginning! He answered, "Yes." This is right, I said. But reflect. If Christ was from eternity with the Father, separated from him, as you say, having neither beginning nor end, then he is not the Father's Son; for in such case he is not born of the Father; and if he be born in such a manner, that he was divided from the Father, and separated from him, as you have it, then he must have had a beginning; for that the begetter must be before the begotten, in a natural sense as you assume, is as clear as day. And if you, then, are not Arians, I will leave to your own judgment. I am yet to be answered.

In the third place I said, Some ancient authors have compared the eternal, divine Being to the Sun, that is, they have compared the body to the Father, the Word or Son to the brightness, and the Holy Ghost to the heat. For as these three, the body, the brightness and the heat are one sun, thus the Father, his Word, and his Holy Ghost are one God.

And, as the brightness cannot be separated from the sun and yet remain brightness, thus the Word can not be separated from God and still remain the Word. Yet the Word is not the Father, nor is the Father the Word. And therefore you daily sing in your temples, *Lumen de lumine*, that is, *a Light of lights*. Also says Paul, "He is the brightness of the glory of God," Heb. 1:3.

Behold, dear Micron, this the beforementioned writers have confessed concerning the eternal, divine Being, and you confess thus. I will leave it to your own judgment whether you did not forsake their faith and whether you did not make them false writers, by your confession. He did not reply at all to this.

In the fourth place I said, You surely confess that Christ Jesus from everlasting, was the Almighty word, wisdom and power of God? He replied, "Yes." Well, I said, if such a birth, then, took place, as you say, that he was seated, divided and separated from the Father, then the Father must have been seated without wisdom, word and power from eternity, inasmuch as they were separated, as you claim. This is too plain to be controverted, Jn. 1:1; Gen. 1:1; Isa. 40:8; Bar. 3:5. Dear Micron, consider how you blaspheme God. Not a word did he reply to this.

But now he comes and says that Christ, from eternity was born of the Father, although yet remaining in the Father. Mark, what a double tongue and unsteady spirit it is. At the time of the discussion, Christ was, from everlasting, seated, divided and separated from the Father; and now, he remained in the Father. In such a short space of time he has changed his mind on five points concerning the incarnation of Christ, as is shown in the "Admonition" written to him, and now he comes to cast upon me the base stains of his own unsteadiness; while the merciful Lord has, by his grace and power, for about twenty-one years, kept me steady in one sense and foundation of the doctrine, notwithstanding the many artifices devised against me by so very many crafty spirits, as all must testify who have impartially read my books and heard my admonitions.

Here I would faithfully admonish all readers, in love, and would humbly pray them, for God's sake, that none will say or

---

*Tritheist, One who believes that the three persons in the Trinity are three distinct Gods.

think that I, by these four answers to his proposed and explained question, would change or forsake my doctrine concerning the birth of Christ, the eternal Word, before every creature. Not at all. For, with all those who, with holy Paul, in truth, confess Christ Jesus to be the first-born of every creature, and that without the intermixture of any human philosophy, with these I hereby confess to be unanimous, now and forever.

I declare that if Micron had asked, in accordance with the Scriptures, if I confessed Christ, according to his divine form, to be the first-born of every creature, then I would immediately have answered him in the affirmative. It would, then also have prevented his irrelevant questions. But as his questions were the result of reason and not of the Scriptures, and as he would thus make of the word a separate person, from everlasting, of which not a single word is found in the Scriptures, before his ascension, therefore, he was immediately defeated by the four inconsistencies concerning the eternal, divine Being, from which he could not extricate himself at all, as was heard.

Mark also, that he has reflected upon the foolishness of his wisdom which he, without any Scripture, used against me, so that he is now ashamed of his own confession and words; for he says, "If I received the correct news, that he never talked about" "being seated." If this is true, then, alas, it is too gross a falsehood. He also writes now that he is born of the Father, from everlasting, but, that he yet abided in him as is also the doctrine of the Nicene council, Athanasius, Erasmus of Rotterdam, Luther, Pomeranius, Melanchthon, Bullinger and of the most learned persons, as can be easily deduced from their comparison of the sun, as also from the writings of some of them.

He again makes use of philosophy and not of the Scriptures, as he did in his first which he has now eaten up. For the spirit of wisdom has not left us a single word concerning the ineffable, incomprehensible mystery of the eternal birth, at all; whether he became separate from the fatherly Being at his birth, before all creatures, or whether he remained ineffably one therewith. For God is a Spirit, Jn. 4:24, and that Spirit is ineffable.

As he again makes use of philosophy and not of the Scriptures, the searching, curious philosopher might again ask him in regard to the word, *born*: How can one be born and yet remain in the begetter? I do not know where Micron can find a direct answer, wherewith he could stand before the disputer. Therefore I would that the ineffable mystery was left with God. For all who want to follow their own intellect in this ineffable mystery, and maintain their opinion thereby, are immediately caught in the snare of the disputer. No matter how he manage.

Inasmuch as we clearly find and know that the Holy Ghost has hidden this mystery in the Scriptures, and that he has not, in any manner, revealed it unto us, neither by prophet, apostle nor by the Son himself; and, inasmuch as it is manifest that it can not be explained by intellect how short or how long; how near or how far he was to the Father; or whether at birth, he became separate from the Father or not; as he is a Spirit; besides, as we learn from history, and find in our own time how many piercing eyes are dazzled by this impenetrable brightness; therefore I warn all pious hearts that would walk with a good conscience before their God, not to speculate about this ineffable and indescribable majesty of the immeasurable, eternal Godhead and not to conclude, assert, teach or maintain any thing more than the Holy Ghost has revealed and taught, lest they, by their fancies, make themselves a god which is not revealed unto them, by the Scriptures. For it is sufficient for all godly souls that they have such faith in God, as his word directs and points out, that Christ Jesus is from everlasting; the ineffable, eternal word, wisdom and power of the Father, and firstborn of every creature, an eternal, true, perfect, divine substance or being in, by, and with God, and that this same, by the power of the Almighty, eternal Spirit, according to the promise, became, in due time, a true, passive, mortal man, in Mary, as the Scriptures teach.

For, if we should have needed more knowledge and understanding of this ineffable birth, the Holy Spirit which rightly teaches his unto all godliness, would undoubtedly not have hidden it from us, but would have revealed or explained it to us by some of his holy apostles, or prophets, or by the Son himself.

I hereby pray all pious hearts, for Jesus' sake, to submit their intellect to the word of the Lord, to feel and believe of God as the Scriptures command and teach, not to ascend higher nor descend lower, and to walk before God and his church with a patient, humble, contrite heart, and he shall find peace therein. Whosoever feareth God, let him reflect upon what I write.

When he was again met in his question, and unable to reply, he broke forth with a disturbed mind, as it appeared, and said, "Do you also believe that Christ was nourished by Mary?" Yes, I said, I sincerely believe so. "Fy!" he said then, "what an impure Christ; for if he was nourished by her, then he must also have become impure." He knew not, as I thought, what to say, for surprise.

Dear Micron, I said, control your heart and tongue. We speak of his origin and not of his nourishment. And if nourishment could make him impure, which is contrary to Christ's own word, Matt. 15: 11; Mark 7: 15, how much more the substance taken from such body of which the fruit should have come as you say and teach, and that Mary was born of the impure, sinful seed of Adam, of which you say the flesh or humanity of Christ came; this you admitted yourself; nor could you produce a single Scripture by which you could prove her spotlessness, as I mentioned sufficiently plain in the narration of the first discussion.

Behold, honorable reader, here you have the principal foundation of that which Micron and Herman have suppressed in their narration. It is easy to guess for what purpose and with what intention they have done so.

Inasmuch as it did not happen otherwise than we have here told, and as it is well know to the all-seeing God, to Micron and Herman, as also to their own witnesses and all of us who were present, that he was quite outdone in the argumentation in regard to the question under discussion and on which their whole foundation rests, whereby the cause was already lost, had he not again admitted it, as also, that there were two sons in Christ, and that the crucified one was not God's Son, whereby he had already forsaken the Son of God; and as he could not prove by the Scriptures the spotlessness of the flesh of Christ, according to his view of the matter; nor that there were two persons in the one Christ, as he professes to believe, nor did he know how he could show the fatherless Christ (as he makes him) to be the Son of God; and as he could not reply a single word to all the plain Scriptures which I produced to prove that the visible, palpable, speaking and crucified Christ Jesus was God's own Son; and, lastly, as he was so inextricably caught in his unscriptural, strange question; and as he is silent on all these, not even touching them, and yet calls upon the name and judgment of the Lord, and upon my own conscience, that he has faithfully narrated the matter in discussion; therefore I will leave it to the judgment of all reasonable, impartial readers whether he has written as a true writer or as a false one; whether he gained the discussion or lost it; whether he has done justice to truth and to us, or whether he has done wrong; whether he sought the honor and glory of God, or his own honor and fame; and also, whether he should be deemed a pious, praiseworthy, honorable, unblamable, true teacher, or an impious, unfaithful, ungodly, blamable and lying deceiver and calumniator; as he wrote through envious partiality and carnality, without truth, and yet, to affirm his falsehood, so highly seals it, alas! as was heard.

When I had answered his last question, they left me, and went to the front part of the building. What was said there I can not say to a certainty; for I was not there myself. But I was told by the brethren that he was still arguing there, notwithstanding the weapons were knocked out of his hands by force of the Scriptures. Also some of their members about the doors next the street were too noisy in their talk. For which reason some of the brethren said they would better go, and asked them to help us all out of the gates. Of which he so unworthily has made, *thrust out*, that he might thereby make a greater stench and hatred for the pious and true, and make them a bad name.

Justly has the Holy Spirit likened this generation unto the fearful apocalyptic locusts whose shapes were like unto horses prepared unto battle, who have crowns on their heads, like gold; which however are not gold; of which Micron and Herman have placed one on each others head, by their writings; their teeth are as the teeth of lions, and they have tails like unto scorpions, and there are stings in their tails, Rev. 9. Consider what the Holy Spirit means, as also that the serpent should bruise the heel of the seed of woman, Gen. 3: 15. I think they have not stung a little by this writing of theirs. The Lord forgive them and grant that they may yet sometime find his merciful grace, if possible.

Had they now been people of contrite hearts, as they should reasonably be expected to be, insignificant in their own sight, born of truth, and gifted with the power of the word, they would have thought: What is the use to write. Our cause is lost. And if we now defame them we do so out of partiality, and not with truthfulness; for it is manifest that they do not hate us, because they have shown us such faithfulness and love, in time of need. But, alas, there was not so much prudence, honorableness, reasonableness, reflection and love found with them.

As we have truthfully and plainly shown all that which Micron has artfully suppressed in his narration, to the dishonor of God and of his holy church, as was heard, thus we shall now, by the grace of God, briefly show to the reader how far we differ with them in regard to this matter, that, thereby, truth may be the more clearly distinguished from falsehood, and light from darkness.

THIRTY-ONE ARTICLES AHD DIFFERENCES, PRESENTED TO THE READER, TO SHOW THAT MICRON SAYS THIS, WITHOUT THE SCRIPTURES, AND WE THAT, ACCORDING TO SCRIPTURE.

First. Micron and Herman have clearly and publicly confessed before us all, "That Christ Jesus was so born of the Father, from everlasting, that he was separated from the Father, and seated separate from him, from eternity," Mark that this being *seated* separate from the Father, is without the Scriptures.

We confess, and that according to the Scriptures, that Christ Jesus was from eternity the Father's wisdom, Prov. 8: 12. His eternal Word, Jn. 1: 1, by which all things are created, Gen. 1: 1; Ps. 23: 6; Jn. 1: 3; Eph. 3: 9; Col. 1: 16; Heb. 1: 2; that his goings forth were from the beginning and from the days of eternity, Micah 5: 2; that he was before Abraham was born, Jn. 8: 58; that he was before John the Baptist, and came after him, John 1: 3; the first and last, Rev. 1: 8; 2: 8; the firstborn of every creature, Col. 1: 15. But of such a birth which implies a separate seat, from everlasting, as Micron and Herman confessed before us, we do not read in the Scriptures. Consider whether this our confession is not in accordance with the Scriptures.

Secondly. The doctrine and belief of our opponents is, "That this separate Son of God, in due time, became a real son, body and soul, of the flesh and blood of Mary." Mark, *two* Sons, and a *divided* Christ.

Our doctrine and belief is that this same Word, Wisdom, or Firstborn, as we have confessed, in due time descended from heaven, and that he became a true, passive, mortal man, by the power of the Most High and his Holy Spirit; not of Mary, but in Mary, above all human comprehension, as John says, "The word is made flesh." Observe if this our confession is not in accordance with the Scriptures.

Thirdly. Micron and Herman frequently

confessed before us all, "That there were two Sons in Christ; the one, the eternal Son of God, the other the temporal son of Mary." Mark, again, *two* sons, and a *divided* Christ. We confessed, as said before, that he who was the Word, Wisdom and first-born from everlasting, became the son of man, in due time, an only, undivided Son, whose Father was God, from everlasting, and whose mother was Mary temporally, Luke 1: 31; Matt. 1; Jn. 1: 49. Observe if this our confession is not according to the Scriptures.

Fourthly. Micron and Herman frequently, have plainly confessed before us all, and do so in their narration many times, that the son of man had no father, sometimes they say, no near father, which is the same as no father. Mark, how they blaspheme both the Father and the Son, Christ. We confess with the angel Gabriel, Luke 1: 28; with the heavenly Father, Matt. 4: 17; 17: 5; Mark 1: 11; 9: 7; Luke 3: 22; 9: 20; with Christ himself, Jn. 3: 16; 5: 22; 6: 69; 7: 28; 8: 23; with all the apostles, Matt. 14: 33; with Peter, Matt. 16: 16; with John, the baptist, with Nathaniel, Jn. 1: 49; with Martha, Jn. 11: 27; and with all the Scriptures, that God is his Father, Jn. 1: 14; 9: 38. Observe whether this confession is not right according to the Scriptures.

Fifthly. Micron and Herman have frequently confessed before us all, and yet do so in their narration, "That the crucified Jesus, who died for us, was not the Son of God and is one with the other." Observe if this is not forsaking the Lord who has purchased them, as Peter says. We confess according to the Scriptures, that the crucified Christ Jesus is God's first and only begotten, own true Son, whom he has not spared, for our sake, Rom. 8: 32; but sent him to be the propitiation for our sins, by his paternal, divine love, 1 Jn. 4: 10, by whose blood we are cleansed and bought, 1 Cor. 6: 20; 7: 23; who also, in the last extremity confessed God the Father to be his Father, crying, "Father, into thy hands I commend my Spirit," Luke 23: 46. Mark, whether our confession is not right according to the Scriptures.

Sixthly. Micron makes use of a parable that as body and soul are an undivided man, thus the Son of God and the son of Mary are an undivided person. Mark, in the third place, *two* Sons, and a *divided* Christ.

We call one what the Holy Scriptures, and all the world call one, that which is one; and that which they call two, are two. If there are two sons in Christ which generated at different times, the one from eternity, the other in due time, of different persons, namely, of God and of Mary, in different forms, the one invisible and impassive, and the other visible and passive, as is the doctrine of our opponents, then there must also be two persons in him; or else the Word was no real Son of God, or the son of Mary no real son of man, or else the one must be taken away by the other and absorbed thereby. Of this, we can not, by the grace of God, be convinced by human reasoning, without the Scriptures.

Nor is such a parable of body and soul, in regard to this matter, known to the Scriptures; nor such a Savior and Christ, who was changed from one Son into two sons, from one person into two persons, from earthly into heavenly, from holy into sinful, from good into evil, from pure into impure, from blessed into cursed, and who was changed from man into Jesus Christ.

Seventhly. The foundation and doctrine of our opponents is, "That as the man Christ was born of Mary, he was, therefore, also of her flesh and seed;" and refer to Matt. 1: 16. Mark, fourthly, *two* Sons, and a *divided* Christ.

We say, Obed is also born of Ruth, and Solomon of Bathsheba; nevertheless Boaz and David were their fathers, who begat Obed of Ruth, and Solomon of Bathsheba, thus, also, the man Christ was born of Mary; yet, God the heavenly Father, was his Father, Matt. 1: 20; Gen. 17: 6; 19: 32; 35: 11; Wis. 7: 2; Rom. 9: 5; Heb. 11: 11. Observe whether I do not rightly teach you according to the Scriptures.

* * * *

Ninthly. The foundation and doctrine of our opponents is, "That the man Christ is of the natural seed of David," because the Scriptures say, "Of the fruit of thy body will I set upon thy throne," Ps. 132: 11;

89: 4. Mark, fifthly, *two* sons, and a *divided* Christ.

We say, according to the foundation and doctrine of the Holy Scriptures, that he is David's supernatural, promised and given son; for if he were David's natural son, as our opponents have it, then he must have been of Joseph's natural seed (for the evangelists count to Joseph), and the Word did not become flesh. Observe whether we do not teach according to the Scriptures.

Tenthly. Again, the foundation and doctrine of our opponents is, "That the man Christ was of David's seed, and refer to Rom. 1: 3; 9: 5." Mark, sixthly, *two* sons, and a *divided* Christ.

We say that the foundation and doctrine of the Holy Scriptures are, that the same who was God's Almighty, eternal Word, from eternity, in due time, according to the promise, became man by his Almighty power, in the virgin Mary, who was promised to a man of the generation of David, called Joseph, to which Joseph, the evangelists count, Matt. 1: 16; Luke 3: 23; Matt. 1: 18; Jn. 1: 14, and was thus, in due time, born according to the flesh of the same generation of which he was incarnated, as the Lord had promised unto David. And thus Christ is born of the seed of David, that is, of the generation of David; but did not become flesh of the seed of David, as our opponents claim, by garbling this Scripture. Observe whether we do not teach rightly according to the Scriptures.

Eleventhly. The foundation and doctrine of our opponents is, "That the man Christ is flesh of our flesh, and bone of our bone, and that our flesh is seated at the right hand of the Father." This he advocates in his book on "The Doctrine of the Church of God." Mark, seventhly, *two* sons, and a *divided* Christ.

We say that the foundation and doctrine of the Holy Scriptures are, That the regenerated church of Christ is flesh of his flesh, and bone of his bone, as Adam testifies of his Eve that she was flesh of his flesh and bone of his bone, Gen. 2: 23, but Eve was not thus of Adam. Thus Christ also testifies of his church which he has begotten by virtue of his holy word in the sprinkling of his most holy blood, by faith, that she is flesh of his flesh, and bone of his bone; but the church can not thus testify of Christ, Eph. 5: 30. See if we do not rightly teach you according to the Scriptures.

Twelfthly. The foundation and doctrine of our opponents is, "That the man Christ, and we, are of one Adam, and are thus brethren by virtue of the flesh." The foundation of this assertion is that Paul says, "He that sanctifieth and they who are sanctified are all of one," that is, of "one Adam," they say. Mark, in the eighth place, *two* sons, and a *divided* Christ.

We say that the foundation and doctrine of the Holy Scriptures are, that Christ and his regenerated church are of one God, Jn. 1: 12, that is, those who hear and obey his word, Mark 3: 35; Luke 8: 21, and therefore he calls them his brethren, and says, "I will declare thy name unto my brethren;" for as he is God's firstborn Son, Heb. 1: 6, thus he is also the firstborn, of the brethren, Rom. 8: 9. If he were our brother in Adam, as is the doctrine of our opponents, then he must, also, have been Adam's first-begotten son, as he is the first-begotten of the brethren, as was heard. Then, also, all the ungodly of the whole world, who have the devil as their father, Jn. 8: 44, must be Christ's brethren and sisters, as well as the regenerated who have God as their Father. See if we do not teach you rightly according to the Scriptures.

Thirteenthly. The foundation and doctrine of our opponents is, "That Christ has partaken of the flesh and blood of his children; which can not be explained or understood otherwise than that he has received his flesh and blood of the children." Mark, in the ninth place, *two* sons, and a *divided* Christ.

We say that they thereby deny the word of the Lord and the ordinance of creation. For the Scriptures say, only, that he partook of flesh and blood. If they should say that the children are spiritual children (as is also the case, because Christ had no carnal children), and, if then the brethren should yet be carnal brethren, then they first break the Scripture, in explaining the one word, which is so closely connected to the other, as being understood in a spiritual, and the other in a carnal sense. And, secondly, they assert an inconsistency. Consider whether they teach according to the Scriptures.

Fourteenthly. Micron frequently writes that Christ has taken unto himself the seed of Abraham, and refers to Heb. 2: 16. In the tenth place, mark, *two* sons, and a *divided* Christ.

We say, and that truthfully, that Micron lamentably adulterates the text; for Paul does not say, *has taken*, but he says, *takes* unto himself the seed of Abraham, that is, the children and descendants of Abraham. Mark, how he deals with the Scriptures.

* * * *

Eighteenthly. Micron confessed before us all, "That although Mary was of the impure, sinful flesh of Adam, she was, nevertheless, pure and holy, because the angel said unto her, 'Blessed art thou among women,'" Luke 1: 28. See whether such doctrine can stand the test of the Scriptures.

We confess, and that according to the Scriptures, that as Mary was of the sinful seed of Adam, as we are, she, therefore, was concluded under sin, the same as we; for the Scriptures except none of Adam's seed, Rom. 5: 12; 1 Cor. 15: 21; Gal. 3: 22; Eph. 2: 3. For if she would have been pure on account of such, as Micron says, "Then God might have cleansed the whole world by such a word; and it would have been vain to have sent his beloved Son into this wicked world, in such an humble form." Oh no. It required another who must requite the debt, fulfill the law and be the pleasing sin-offering for Mary, no less than for us, if we were to be saved. Observe and see if we do not rightly teach you in accordance with the Scriptures.

* * * *

Twentieth. Now Micron writes, "That we should free from sin whatever the Scripture frees therefrom; and that man should not declare common or unholy that which God testifies to be holy," and refers to Acts 10: 15.

We confess and say, and that in accordance with the Lord's word, that the Scripture frees none from sin but him that is free indeed, namely, Christ Jesus, Isa. 53: 12; 2 Cor. 2: 15; 1 Pet. 2: 22; 1 Jn. 3: 5; whereby it is plainly shown that he is not of Mary's flesh, which was also concluded under sin; but that the Father's most glorious word, which knew not sin, became flesh, Jn. 1: 14. For he is holy, and that in truth, and shall ever remain holy. Therefore, in my opinion, it is blasphemy against the most holy flesh of Christ, which is the true food for our souls, the living bread, given in such great love, to the reconciliation of the sins of all the world, thus to compare it to the flesh of irrational animals which were forbidden as food, under the law, and were, therefore, deemed unclean; and which are now again, under the gospel allowed as clean and free, as was once heard. See if we do not teach in accordance with Scripture, Jn. 6: 51; Lev. 11: 4; Deut. 14: 7; Rom. 14: 20; Matt. 15: 11; Mark 7: 15; Acts 10: 15; Tit. 1: 15.

Twenty-first. The doctrine of our opponents is, "That the Son of God has fulfilled the law in our flesh." In the fourteenth place, mark, *two* sons, and a *divided* Christ.

We say, that it is the doctrine of the Holy Scripture that none born of the accursed and sinful flesh of Adam, could fulfill the law which was spiritual; for the seed of Adam was too much corrupted, and was also, by the righteous judgment of God, subject to the curse, Deut. 27: 26. Inasmuch, then, as it is become so quite impotent and weak in Adam, and as the law accused us before God, therefore he, in his great love, took pity upon Adam and all his seed, and did not spare his own Son, but he sent him in the form of sinful flesh, Rom. 8: 3, 32, who fulfilled the law for us, Matt. 5: 17; Eph. 2: 13, who innocently died for us guilty sinners that through him we might live, 1 Pet. 2: 24; and thus he became our holy, innocent and spotless High Priest, Mediator, Advocate and Reconciler, with God, his Father, Heb. 5: 1; 6: 20; 7: 26; 8: 1; 9: 14; 10: 12; 13: 12; 1 Tim. 2: 5; 1 Jn. 1: 2. And thus the glory is to God our Almighty Father, by his blessed Word or Son, alone, as the Scriptures teach; and not by the accursed, sinful flesh of Adam, as our opponents teach, Rom. 7: 14. Observe whether we do not teach you in accordance with the Scriptures.

Twenty-second. The distinct doctrine of our opponents is, "That the man Christ who died for us, was not of heaven, but of earth." In the fifteenth place, mark, *two* sons, and a *divided* Christ.

Our foundation and doctrine is, according to the Scriptures, that he was of heaven and not of earth, as he himself says, "I am the living bread which came down from heaven;" "and the bread that I will give, is my flesh," Jn. 6: 51. Again in verse 62, "What and if ye shall see the son of man (mark he says, The *son of man*, who Micron says, was of earth) ascend up where he was before?" Again, "I am from above; ye are of this world," Jn. 8: 23. Again, "He that cometh from above, is above all," Jn. 3: 31. Christ says, "I came forth from the Father, and am come into the world; again, I leave the world, and go to the Father," Jn. 16: 28. Paul also says, "The first man is of the earth, earthy; the second man is the Lord from heaven," 1 Cor. 15: 47, and many other similar Scriptures. By the grace of God, we will, at the proper time plainly show what kind of spirits those are who deny these plain Scriptures and point the poor, ignorant people to a divided, earthly, impure and sinful creature and Christ, as also what abominations they commit by their false doctrine. Observe whether we do not rightly teach in accordance with the Scriptures.

Twenty-third. Micron writes: "They testify sufficiently that the name without truth and works is vain; and, that none can be saved by the name, unless he have, above all, the reality of the being; for the name cometh of the truth." Mark how he here judges himself.

We say, that he is right, that the name without the reality avails nothing; and yet he confesses in different parts of his writings that the man Christ (as he calls him), had no father, still he calls him the Son of God; he calls him of heaven, yet he says that he is of earth; he calls him pure, yet confesses that he is of the impure seed of Adam, and says other like things. Whether or not Micron proves thereby that he calls vain names and does not speak the truth—for according to his doctrine the Son of God is the son of man, and the man Christ, the son of God. I will let himself and all intelligent persons judge according to his own word.

Twenty-fourth. Micron writes: "As, then, the same human nature (he means, the whole man of Mary's flesh) in which he suffered, was his own flesh and body, and was none other; therefore it can not be concluded therefrom that God's Son did not suffer for us." Mark how, here, the mere name, and not the reality, must avail with him, contrary to his own doctrine.

We say that Micron manages it so with his flatterings that they may not be too much alarmed; for at different places he says that Christ, according to his human substance and nature, had no Father, and that he suffered in this same human substance and nature, which had no father; and here he says that this was God's Son, and that he suffered for us. What kind of a flatterer and writer Micron is, and what one should think of his foundation and doctrine, I will let each one judge for himself, from his own writings. This is not simply truthful declaiming, as he writes. I know not what greater shame one could think of.

Twenty-fifth. Micron writes that the Scriptures say, "That the Son of God suffered and died for us. This he writes for two particular reasons. First, to prove the inseparable union of both the divine and human natures, in one person, Christ. Secondly, to show that Christ's suffering, in his body and flesh, could not conduce to man's salvation otherwise than by such inseparable union of both the divine and human natures in one person, Jesus Christ." In the seventeenth place, mark, *two* sons, and a *divided* Christ.

We say, Micron generally sings the same tune about the union of both natures all through his appendix, of which not a single word can be found in all the Scriptures. We ask nothing more than that he shall show us where the Scripture says, "This is the divine nature in Christ," or, "that is the human nature in Christ," although I confess both natures to be in Christ; but not as the doctrine and teaching of our opponents have it. Or else, that he show us where the Scriptures say this is the union of the two natures in one person, as he generally writes; or that he show us where the perfect Son of God is called only of divine nature, or the perfect man, body and soul, only of human nature, as he would make the reader believe, that we may reflect upon it. If it is no Scripture, it is anathema, Gal. 1: 8, and if it is Scripture, let it be shown us, and we will yield. O, God! what abominable deceit which they falsely teach the poor, ignorant people under semblance of the Scriptures!

I would further say, that if it were such inseparable union, and that the same made his suffering have the power unto salvation, as he says, then it is manifest that also the divine nature suffered. For that which is inseparable cannot be separated, and in other places he says that the divine nature did not suffer; whereby he makes the natures separable. Thus he contradicts himself, and deceit remains deceit however he garbles the Scriptures by his flatterings. See if we do not rightly teach you according to the Scriptures.

Twenty-sixth. Micron writes, "Those speak very unintelligently of this great and holy mystery of our salvation, who say that Mary's flesh was crucified for us, when the man Christ was born of her, for they do not consider that Christ was not only man, but also God." Mark, *two* sons and a *divided* Christ.

We say that Micron makes his glozings worse and worse, so that it must be apparent that he advocates the cause of antichrist. I leave it to the judgment of all the world if the man Christ (mark what he means by saying the man Christ) were of the seed of Mary, born of her, as the wine is of the vine, and the blossom and fruit are of the tree, if he was not, then, Mary's flesh and blood who was crucified for us? Although one could not say when Absalom hung upon the tree, there hangs David, as he writes, yet one could have truthfully said, There hangs David's flesh and blood; neither do we say, that Mary was crucified, but Mary's flesh and blood (mind, I speak this in the manner of Micron) was crucified; that is, if he were born of the flesh and blood of Mary; or else the whole Scriptures must be wrong, which say that we are the seed, children, flesh and blood of Adam, on account of our carnal birth. Mark whether we do not rightly teach you in accordance with the Scriptures.

Twenty-seventh. Micron says, "That David confessed Christ to be his Lord, according to his divinity, and to be his son, according to his humanity," Ps. 110: 1; Matt. 22 : 42. Mark again, *two* sons, and a *divided* Christ.

We say that the prophets call him, without any distinction as to his divinity or humanity, our "Immanuel," Isa. 7: 14, "The mighty God" and "everlasting Father," Isa. 9: 6, "The Lord Our Righteousness," Jer. 23: 6; 33 : 16. Paul calls him our Lord, 1 Cor. 8: 6; 12: 3. Thomas called him, "my Lord and my God," Jn. 20: 28. Christ says, "All power is given unto me in heaven and in earth," Matt. 28: 18. Paul says, "That at the name of Jesus, every knee should bow, of things in heaven, and things in earth, and things under the earth; and that every tongue should confess that Jesus Christ is Lord," Phil. 2: 10, 11. As also, that all things are put under his feet; and that the Father gave him to be the head over all things to the church; "and set him at his own right hand in the heavenly places, far above all principality, and power, and might, and dominion, and every name that is named, not only in this world, but also in that which is to come," Eph. 1: 21; that he is the Lord both of the dead and living; and if he is thus not also David's Immanuel, the Powerful, God, Father, Jehovah, Lord, Head, and Judge, all those may reflect upon in the fear of the Lord, who rightly confess the Lord and his word. Consider whether we do not rightly teach you according to the Scriptures.

Twenty-eighth. Micron writes, "If the flesh of Christ were of the substance of the heavenly Father, as Menno dreams, then the heavenly Father must also have flesh and blood; or else Christ could have no flesh and blood; but would only be a Spirit, as God is a Spirit." Behold what blind reason, and no faith.

We testify and confess before God and all our readers, and that in accordance with the word of the Lord, that the eternal, ineffable word is of the eternal, ineffable substance of the Father, and must be, if it be God. For what can be God, with God and in God which is not of his substance or being? And, also, that this same word came down, in due time, and that it became truly man in Mary, by the Almighty power of God, Jn. 1: 14. Behold, thus the Holy Scriptures teach, and thus we believe, notwithstanding Micron dares call it "dreaming."

The holy angel Gabriel, and the dear evangelist, together with John the Baptist, Peter, and all the apostles, nay, Christ himself certainly knew as well as Micron and the learned do, that God the Father was a Spirit, and that he was not of flesh and blood; yet they confessed before all the world that the visible, palpable, eating, drinking, speaking, sleeping, waking, walking, teaching, sighing, weeping, dying and resurrecting Christ Jesus was the invisible, eternal and living Son of God, as may be plainly seen by the general tenor of the whole New Testament. O God, what abominable snares to catch the poor souls and to drag them to the pit of destruction.

Twenty-ninth. The foundation and doctrine of our opponents is, "That the word was God from the beginning, and could therefore not suffer." They refer to Jn. 1: 1. "It was flesh, and could, therefore, not become flesh." Mark, it is reason, and not faith.

We say and confess, and that by the strength of the Scriptures that this same Word, which was, in the beginning with God, and was God, in due time became man, and dwelt among us, Jn. 1: 14. For "God so loved the world," says Christ himself, "that he gave his only begotten Son." He spared not his own Son, says Paul, but delivered him up for us all, Rom. 8: 32; and John says, "He sent his Son to be the propitiation for our sins," 1 Jn. 4: 10.

All those who controvert this, deny first, the eternal love of God who so loved us that he gave his only begotten Son, Jn. 3: 16; 1 Jn. 4: 10.

Secondly, they deny the promise of truth whereby God promised that the Messiah should be our Immanuel, Isa. 7: 4, our God, Isa. 40: 10, and the Lord Our Righteousness, Jer. 23: 6; 33: 16.

Thirdly, they deny the Almighty power of God, by which he can do whatsoever he will. They make Gabriel a false messenger, as he said that nothing was impossible with God, Luke 1: 37.

Fourthly, they are in opposition to all the Scriptures which testify, without any separation, that Christ Jesus is the own, only and first-begotten Son of God, Jn. 1: 14; 3: 16; 1 Jn. 4: 9; Heb. 1: 5; Rom. 8: 32.

Fifthly, they make the Father a liar; for they do not believe the testimony which he has given of his Son, 1 Jn. 5: 10.

Sixthly, they have neither Father nor Son; for they deny the Son, 1 Jn. 2: 22.

Seventhly, they remain under the wrath of God; for they believe not in the name of the only, begotten Son of God, Jn. 3: 36.

Eighthly, they attach to Christ all the gross inconsistencies which neither Micron nor any other man can explain away, as may be clearly seen by his writings, if one has spiritual eyes. Consider whether we do not rightly teach you in accordance with the Scriptures.   *   *   *

Thirtieth. Micron and Herman say, "That if the Word became flesh, and did not take on himself the flesh of Mary, there must have been a new creation in Mary. Mark, how diametrically they oppose the foundation of truth.

We say (note it) that if all miracles and powers of God, by which many things were changed into different beings or forms from what they were before, were to be called a new creation, then we would find many such new creations in the Scriptures, as when water was changed into wine, Jn. 2: 9, it was turned into blood, Ex. 7: 20. Lot's wife was changed into a pillar of salt, Gen. 19: 26. All the dust of Egypt was changed into lice, Ex. 8: 17; and many other miracles. The omnipotence of God was thereby acknowledged; yet it is not called a new creation in the Scriptures.

But we will let the polite, impartial reader judge according to the Scriptures, if there would not have taken place a new creation in the case of Christ being born of Mary, as was in the beginning the case with Eve being made of Adam's rib, if our opponent's foundation were true. Consider whether we do not rightly teach in accordance with the Scriptures.

Thirty-first. Micron writes "That we place in the stead of the true Christ, a new, unknown Christ whom neither the patriarchs, prophets, apostles, nor the many thousands of martyrs, &c., ever confessed."

We say that Micron, as also all the false prophets, thereby lamentably slander the pious patriarchs, prophets, apostles, and witnesses of Christ; and that he thereby denies their sure, true testimony, left in the Holy Scriptures, concerning Christ Jesus the Son of God. For it is manifest that the prophets confessed him to be their Immanuel; and that he was to be the son of a virgin, who was to conceive of the Holy Ghost, Isa. 7: 14, for God himself was to be his Father, Luke 1: 31—35. They confess him to be their mighty God, and everlasting Father, Isa. 9: 6, their Jehovah who would make them and us righteous, Jer. 23: 6; 33: 16; that his goings forth were from everlasting, who was to be Lord and Prince of Israel; that he was the wisdom of God, and was to show himself on earth and dwell among men. David confessed him to be his Lord, Ps. 110: 2, he was to be the Lord, strong and mighty, and to be the Lord Sabaoth, Ps. 24 : 8, which no man of Adam could be. Also, all the holy apostles, Matt. 14: 33, the angel of God, Luke 1: 28, the Father, Matt. 3: 17; 17: 16; Mark 1: 11; 9: 7; Luke 3: 22; 9: 35, and Christ himself, Jn. 9: 35, John the Baptist, Jn. 1: 34; 3: 28. Nathaniel, Jn. 1: 49, and Martha, Jn. 11: 27, confessed him to be the true Son of the true and living God, nay, to be his only, and first-born, inseparable Son, all through the New Testament. I say *inseparable;* for, that the son of man was God's Son, and that the Son of God was the son of man, Peter plainly confessed, upon which, also, salvation was promised him of Christ; that the church would be built thereupon, and that flesh and blood had not revealed it unto him, but the Father which is in heaven, Matt. 16: 17.

And now these thoughtless people come and divide Christ, without Scripture for it; he must not be the Son of God, on account of the flesh; but is only called so for the sake of their garbled union; rob us of both Father and Son, make false and untrue all the Scriptures, together with all the apostles and prophets, nay, also, the Father and the Son, and take the innocent apostles, patriarchs, and prophets, with whom we agree in all particulars, as a mere cover for their falsehood; they point us from the firm foundation of truth to the quick-sands of criticism, garbled Scriptures and glozing; build their church upon a man and creature of the impure, sinful seed and flesh of Adam, without father. And although they, poor children, are quite earthly and carnal, as may be seen by their writings and works, yet they boast that they rightly teach Christ; which none can do but by the revelation of the Father through the Holy Ghost, as Christ himself says, "No man knoweth the Son, but the Father; neither knoweth any man the Father, save the Son, and he to whomsoever the Son will reveal him," Matt. 11: 27.

Observe whether we teach a Christ to whom the prophets and apostles have not pointed us, as these unfaithful people falsely accuse us of, before all the world.

Oh! That they meant God! that they sought the glory of God and the salvation of their neighbors, and not their own vain honor and glory! How gladly would they confess that we had the pure, saving truth, and they the impure, accursed falsehood. But as it is, it is hid from them by their earthly, carnal vision.

Behold, honorable reader, here you have distinctly presented to view the principal differences between us and our opponents, concerning this article. And I will now faithfully show you, for further explanation, their unscriptural confessions, garblings and adulterations of the Scriptures, together with their principal glozings of which they make use without the Scriptures, or with a false and garbled understanding of them, whereby they quite obscure the brightness of Jesus Christ the Son of God, break the foundation of truth, ensnare the simple reader, deprive him of the Father and Son, and thus detain him in the curse, sin and death, as has been heard.

FORTY-FIVE UNSCRIPTURAL CONFESSIONS,

EXPLANATIONS, FALSE GLOZINGS, ADULTERATED AND GARBLED SCRIPTURES, PRESENTED TO THE READER FOR THE EXPLANATION OF THE MATTER.

First. We do not read in the Scriptures, that Mary, who was a natural daughter of the impure and sinful flesh of Adam, was without sin and pure, as Micron confessed before us all, at the discussion, or:

Secondly. That such pure, innocent, spotless and blessed fruit, as was Christ Jesus, was born of such impure, sinful flesh, guilty of death, as was the flesh of Mary, since she was a daughter of the impure seed of Adam, as Micron says, or:

Thirdly. That Adam had two seeds, of which the one was holy and pure, as was Christ, and the other sinful and impure, as we are; as must be concluded from the doctrine of Micron, or:

Fourthly. That Christ was born of the Father, from eternity, that he was seated separate from the Father, and outside of the Father, from eternity, as Micron and Herman confessed before us all, or:

* * * *

Eleventhly. That the Word, or the eternal Son of God, without mother (I write it according to their foundation), thus united himself with a son of man, without father; that he accepted, or took on the same, that he dwelt therein, and thus became one person and son, as is the foundation and doctrine of our opponents, or:

Twelfthly. That there were two sons in Christ, as was heard, of which one was visible, passive, and earthly—the other invisible, impassive, and heavenly, as is the foundation and doctrine of our opponents, or:

Thirteenthly. That the divine nature thus united itself with the human nature (whereby he means, two perfect sons) into one person, which he so often repeats, or:

Fourteenthly. That such a union of God's Son and Mary's son, as Micron says, should be compared to the union of the body and soul of man, or:

Fifteenthly. That such a divided, double, earthly and heavenly, righteous and unrighteous, pure and impure Christ was promised by the prophets, and preached by the apostles, as Micron says, without any truth, or:

Sixteenthly. That Christ was God and man in such a sense as Micron teaches, or:

* * * *

Eighteenthly. That the Son of God is called the son of man, and the son of man is called the Son of God, by reason of such union, as our opponents assert, without any Scripture, or:

* * * *

Twentieth. That the flesh of Christ was sinful, and guilty of death, as John A'Lasco (with whom Micron agrees) blasphemously teaches, or:

Twenty-first. That the word, which from the beginning was God, thus took its tabernacle, tent, or dwelling in our flesh, as John A'Lasco philosophizes, or:

Twenty-second. That the Son of God thus covered his divinity with humanity, so long as he was upon earth, as John A'Lasco writes, or:

Twenty-third. That the one who had transgressed, also, had to requite it in his nature, as is the foundation of our opponents, or:

Twenty-fourth. That the Son of God fulfilled the law and reconciled the Father in our flesh, as is the foundation of our opponents, or:

Twenty-fifth. That we could not have partaken, unto salvation, of his heavenly and spiritual attributes, such as his life, holiness, righteousness, merits, &c., if Christ had not had our human nature, form and substance, as Micron writes, or:

Twenty-sixth. That the son of man, who is confessed to be the Son of God by Peter, by John the Baptist, by the angel and by all the Scriptures, said in any part of Scripture: No, I am not the Son of God, but he that dwelleth in me whom you do not see, is the Son of God, and for his sake

I am called his Son, as is the doctrine of our opponents, or:

Twenty-seventh. That the angel Gabriel told Mary that such a divided son would be conceived in her, Luke 2: 28, as Micron garbles it, or:

Twenty-eighth. That Christ Jesus was not God's Son, according to his most holy humanity, as well as according to his eternal divinity, as our opponents teach, or:

Twenty-ninth. That the man Christ was of earth and was called heavenly, only, on account of some honorable attributes as Micron writes, or:

Thirtieth. That the flesh and blood of the seed of Adam, as our opponents say, that the flesh of Christ is the true bread of life, on account of some divine attributes as they garble the word of Christ, Jn. 6: 51, or:

Thirty-first. That Abraham and Isaac were called the *autores* or origin, in the Scriptures, that it should not be attributed to strange men, as Micron says, without the Scriptures, or:

Thirty-second. That Christ took on him our sinful form as John A'Lasco says, Phil. 2: 7, or:

Thirty-third. That Christ took on him the seed of Abraham, as Micron garbles the text of Heb. 2: 16, or:

Thirty-fourth. That Christ partook of the flesh and blood of the children by generation, as our opponents garble or falsely explain the text, Heb. 2: 14, or:

Thirty-fifth. That God was manifested in our flesh, as our opponents explain the Scripture of Paul, 2 Tim. 3: 5, or:

Thirty-sixth. That Christ dwelt in our flesh by generation, as our opponents explain, 1 Jn. 2: 4, or:

Thirty-seventh. That we are to compare to purity the most holy flesh of Christ with the cleanness of the animals which were declared clean, as Micron compared Acts 10: 15, or:

Thirty-eighth. That the most holy flesh of Christ Jesus was flesh of our impure, sinful flesh, as our opponents make the poor people believe, or:

Thirty-ninth. That Christ would be the Immanuel in our flesh as our opponents claim, or:

Fortieth. That Christ and we, are brethren on account of the flesh, as Micron teaches the unrepentant, ignorant world, without the truth, or:

Forty-first. That the children of the devil, such as liars, haters, murderers, adulterers of the Scriptures, blasphemers, &c., are Christ's brethren and sisters as well as the children of God, as we must conclude from the teachings of our opponents, or:

Forty-second. That the Son of God united himself with human nature, that is, with a man of the flesh of Mary, and that he ascended with such flesh, as Micron unscripturally garbles Eph. 4: 10, or:

Forty-third. That our flesh is seated at the right hand of the Father, as is the doctrine of our opponents, or:

Forty-fourth. That Christ is our Head, and we, his body, members and brethren, on account of the flesh, as we must understand it from the teachings and foundation of our opponents, or:

Forty-fifth. That a man of the impure, sinful seed of Adam is our Advocate, Mediator, Reconciler and High Priest with God the Father; and, that with him we should worship, honor and serve him as the true and living God, as our opponents teach.

CONCLUSION.

HERE, observe, kind reader, that the whole foundation and belief of our opponents concerning this article is built upon mere carnal wisdom, philosophy, explanation, glozings, adulteration and garbled Scriptures whereby they make it appear as if their anti-christian doctrine was the doctrine of the Son of God, and whereby they cause themselves to be called the true teachers, and us the deceivers, by the world who, alas, are little versed in divine matters. But how they will stand at the coming of

Christ, before his impartial judgment seat, I fear most of them will find out too late.

I will now point out to you, by the grace of the Lord, the inconsistencies that must follow from their doctrine and faith, in such clearness that you can see that their doctrine is not of the Fountain of the eternal Wisdom, as Micron dares boast, without any truth, but that it is exhaled from the abyss by the locusts of Apollyon. Take heed.

FOURTEEN INCONSISTENCIES, WHICH MUST RESULT AND FOLLOW FROM THE FOUNDATION AND DOCTRINE OF OUR OPPONENTS.

First, it follows incontrovertibly from their doctrine and faith that there are two sons in Christ, of which one was the impassive, eternal Son of God, without mother, and the other the son of Mary or the son of man, without father. And whether or not such doctrine and faith is not an inconsistency, I will leave you to judge according to the Scriptures.

Secondly, it follows incontrovertibly that there are two persons in Christ; for where there are two actual sons there must be two persons. Or else the one must have taken unto him the other, and by the fictitious union quite absorbed the other. If this can not be called an inconsistency you may judge according to the Scriptures.

Thirdly, it follows incontrovertibly that the eating, drinking, sighing, weeping, passive, dying and crucified Christ Jesus was not the Son of God, notwithstanding he is confessed by all the Scriptures to be the first and only begotten, own Son of God; for, they say that he had no Father. You may judge by the Scriptures whether this may not be called a blasphemous inconsistency and denial of the Son of God.

Fourthly, it follows incontrovertibly that they utter a falsehood as often as they call the man Christ, the Son of God; for how can he be a Son of God according to their doctrine? for they publicly write and verbally confess that he was not of God but of Mary. You may judge according to the Scriptures whether this is not a blasphemous inconsistency, which is not conformable to the true God who deals according to truth, and does not use idle names.

Fifthly, it follows incontrovertibly that it is a divided Christ, who became a Savior, and Jesus Christ, of God and man, of the heavenly and earthly, of the pure and impure, of the righteous and unrighteous, of the good and evil, and of the blessed and accursed, as was once heard above. You may judge by the Scriptures whether this may not, also, rightly be called an inconsistency.

Sixthly, it follows incontrovertibly that the eternal expiatory offering, once offered for all the world, is not the spotless lamb which the Scriptures confess him to be, but an impure, sinful, and accursed man of the impure, sinful and accursed flesh and seed of Adam. You may judge by the Scriptures whether this is not an abominable, blasphemous inconsistency.

Seventhly, it incontrovertibly follows that, as the holy apostle Thomas confessed the crucified, visible Christ to be his Lord and God, and, as all Scripture testifies that he is our Reconciler, Mediator, Advocate, High Priest, Savior, and Deliverer, and if he were a man of Adam's impure seed, as our opponents assert, then it is manifest that an earthly, impure, sinful and accursed creature, of the earthly, impure, sinful and accursed flesh of Adam is our Reconciler, Mediator, Advocate, High Priest, Savior, Deliverer, Lord and God. You may judge by the Scriptures whether this may not, also, be called a blasphemous inconsistency and anti-christian abomination.

* * * *

Tenthly, it incontrovertibly follows that if the man Christ were of the unclean, sinful flesh of Adam, as is the foundation of our opponents, that one of two things must be true, either that the Scriptures do not rightly teach us, or that all are idolaters who worship, honor, thank and serve such an earthly, sinful and accursed Christ, as our opponents teach and advocate without the Scriptures; for they say, "Thou shalt worship the Lord thy God, and him only shalt thou serve," Matt. 4: 10; Deut. 6: 13. The prophet, also says, I will give my praise to none other. And it is clear that one does not worship our Savior Christ any less than he does the Father himself. You may judge according to the Scriptures whether this is not also an idolatrous inconsistency and an infamous blasphemy.

* * * *

Twelfthly, it incontrovertibly follows, if I understand the writing of Micron, that the eternal Word became the Spirit of man, and that it only took on itself a tabernacle of Mary's flesh. For, as I think, he alleges Peter for such a purpose, and says he was put to death in the flesh, but quickened by the Spirit, 1 Pet. 3: 18.

If he understands the Spirit of Christ as being the Spirit which he commended to the Father, as also, being the immortal Son of God with which, according to his doctrine, he was united, then Peter did not write enough by merely saying "quickened by the Spirit," and not, "as also by the immortal Son of God with which he was united." Mark what I say.

And if he understand it as solely having reference to the Spirit of Christ, and not, also, to the immortal Son, as he confesses him to be, then the Son of God must have become, according to his doctrine, a spirit of man; or else I do not know for what purpose he adduces this Scripture. You may judge by it whether this is not an abominable inconsistency, and blind-folding of the poor, ignorant world.

Thirteenthly, it incontrovertibly follows, if the doctrine of the learned is right, that the Almighty Word, whereby heaven and earth were replenished, must have united itself with such a small body of the flesh of Mary, and thus sighed, wept, ate, drank, suffered and died with it and lay dead in the grave; or else it must have merely sheltered in Christ's Spirit, and thus, at death, departed therewith, and at the resurrection again united therewith, the second time, Wis. 18: 15. You may judge by the Scriptures, whether this may not rightfully be called a wonderful inconsistency.

Fourteenthly, it incontrovertibly follows that if the word or the eternal Son of God thus took on him such a man of Mary's flesh and blood, and united himself therewith into one person and son, as our opponents, by their philosophy pretend, then, God the Father, was not the true Father of Christ, Mary not the true mother, Christ not a true Son; and all the Scriptures are thereby denied, which confess Christ to be the first and only begotten, true Son of God, without any distinction between divine or human, between spirit and flesh, invisible and visible, immortal and mortal, as we have clearly explained above and shall still further explain below, by virtue of the word of the Lord. You may, in the fear of God, judge by the Scriptures whether this can not be rightfully called a blasphemous inconsistency, and a direct denial of both Father and Son.

Behold, chosen readers, it is such an unscriptural, divided, unclean, sinful and earthly Savior and Christ which our opponents teach and point to by their anti christian, covert, garbled, mysterious and obscure reasonings of human wisdom. I place before you, in plain and clear words the mirror of their deceit. If you will, you may clearly see how lamentably you are deceived by them.

Inasmuch, then, as their doctrine and faith is nothing in fact but anti-christian deceit, and the temptation of the old serpent, for it is all *taking unto, uniting two into one, divine* and *human nature, honorable virtues* and the like whatever we read or hear from them, of which we find nothing in Scripture; and as they make these assertions and adorn them with many broken Scriptures, glozings and false explanations; therefore I say, first, in Micron's own language, that all they philosophize and teach avails us nothing, since it is not according to Scripture. And secondly, in the language of holy Paul, it is anathema, since it is a strange gospel of which not a single word is taught in the Scriptures, neither by the prophets, nor by Christ, nor by any of his apostles, in such a sense as our opponents teach it. Take heed.

We will now, by the grace of the Lord, present to view, in the first place, the foundation of the confession and doctrine of our opponents, concerning this article, together with its proper contents, fruits, end, and promise, and, in the second place, the foundation of our confession together with its proper contents, fruits, end, and promise, that you may, by such comparison in black and white, the more readily guard against the deceit of the old serpent, and find the sure and firm foundation of truth, and believe and follow it, with a sure conscience, without any fear.

THE FOUNDATION AND FAITH

OF OUR OPPONENTS CONCERNING CHRIST JESUS, TOGETHER WITH THEIR PROPER CONTENTS, FRUITS, ENDS, AND PROMISE.

HONORABLE reader, take heed. The following is the whole contents, conclusion, sense, explanation, foundation and meaning of the faith and doctrine of our opponents, concerning the incarnation of our Lord, whereby they, by their human wisdom and the cunning of the old serpent, proclaim that all the glorious promises concerning Christ, the Son of God, contained in Moses and the prophets, such as, of grace, mercy, remission of our sins, peace of conscience, reconciliation, and life eternal, are concluded, in the unclean, sinful flesh of Adam, which they call clean although they confess that it is of him without any Scripture.

They confess publicly (witness their own confession), that there are two Sons in Christ; of which the one is the Son of God, from everlasting, without mother, and impassive; and the other, the son of Mary, or the son of man, without father, and passive. Which two sons, they say (but without Scripture), are united into one; so that the man, Christ, who visibly walked, ate, drank, sighed, wept, and hung on the cross, and who cried to his Father: "Father into thy hands I commend my Spirit," and who lay in the tomb three days, was not the Son of God.

They make the Holy of holies, the ever blessed Christ Jesus, a sinful and accursed man; [one of their number asks publicly: If Christ were holy, why was he adjudged unto death by the judgment of the Father, on account of sin?] and say that he partook of sinful flesh, that he might be tempted and be subject to, or guilty of death. They place their salvation in an earthly, sinful creature of the unclean, sinful seed of Adam, and make Christ Jesus not alone of the sinful and accursed flesh of Adam, Abraham and David, but also, a gentile of the gentiles, namely, a Syrian of the daughters of Bethuel and Laban, Gen. 24; 29: 18, a Canaanite of Rahab, a Moabite of Ruth, Matt. 1: 5, and an Ammonite of the mother of Rehoboam, of the son of Solomon, 1 Kin. 14: 21.

They make a creature of the unclean, sinful flesh and seed of Adam, their seat of grace, and sin-offering, their High Priest, Mediator, Advocate, Intercessor, and Reconciler, and falsely call him the Son of God. I say falsely; for they publicly confess that he had no father. Call them their Lord and God, still, they say and write that he is of earth, and not of heaven. They worship, honor and serve him as they do the Father himself. Oh, abomination!

They garble and break the Scriptures, because they do not believe the testimony of John, that the Word was made flesh. They adulterate the plain confession of the angel of God, concerning the Father and the Son himself, of John the Baptist, of Peter and of all the apostles, of Paul, and of all the Scriptures, which unanimously testify that the conceived, born, suffering, whole Christ, outwardly and inwardly, visible and invisible is inseperable, the first and only begotten Son of God.

They break and contradict the whole gospel and the precious epistle of John in which he testifies more than sixty times that Christ confessed himself to be the Son of God and confessed God to be his Father. Also, frequently, that he went forth from the Father, that he was sent and came from heaven.

They garble and profane the Holy Scriptures quite lamentably, heap one abominable flattery and fictitious explanation upon another. Christ, say they, has taken on himself our human nature of Mary; then, there are two sons and natures combined into one person and Son. Now the Son of God has put on the flesh and blood of Mary, dwelt therein, placed his tabernacle or tent therein.

One of their learned writes, "That the Son of God has brought all his attributes to the son of man." Another writes, "That the man Christ was God's *adoptivus filius*, that is, the adopted and well-pleasing Son of God." Still another, "That the one nature in Christ was quite divine, and the other half divine and half human." Some write, "That the divine nature also suffered." Others write and say, "That he only suffered in his human nature and not in his divine nature. Micron says, "That Mary's blood became in her, our flesh; that Christ's flesh is of our flesh, and that, notwithstanding he is of earth, and of Adam's seed, he is still called heavenly, on account of certain virtues," and other like anathematic words and self-conceited glozings and abominations, of which not a word is found in the Scriptures.

Is it not a pity, nay, a horrible thing, to wade in such pure, limpid waters, with such filthy feet, and thus to obscure the precious and bright sun of righteousness with such infernal exhalations of the anti-christian doctrine? Rev. 9: 2. And that for no other reason than that they do not trust the testimony of John and of the angel; do not believe the Almighty power of the Father, judge every thing according to nature and not according to the Scriptures, and attribute more to Mary than belongs to a true mother, according to the ordinance and word of the Lord.

From which it incontrovertibly follows, and is manifest, according to the doctrine and testimony of John, that they, alas, have neither the Father, nor the Son; "Whosoever denieth the Son, the same hath not the Father," 1 Jn. 2: 23, that the wrath of God abides on them, and that they shall not see life; for they do not believe in the name of the only begotten Son of God; that they must die in their sins; for they do not believe that it is he, Jn. 8: 24; that they do not vanquish the world, that they are not in God, nor God in them; for they do not confess that Jesus is the Son of God, 1 Jn. 4: 3. Oh! how well it would be if these poor people would take heed, rightly confess Christ, the Son of God, and give him his due praise and honor.

OUR DOCTRINE AND FAITH IN JESUS CHRIST,

THE SON OF GOD, TOGETHER WITH THEIR PROPER CONTENTS, FRUITS, END, AND PROMISE.

Our foundation and faith is, and that, according to the Scriptures, in power and truth, that the whole Christ Jesus, visible and invisible, outwardly and inwardly, mortal and immortal, is the first and only begotten Son of God, Heb. 1: 6; Jn. 1: 14; 3: 18; 1 Jn. 4: 10, as the angel, John the Baptist, the apostles and all the Scriptures confess him to be; that he is the ineffable, eternal word, by which all things are created, ineffably come from heaven, and that, by the power of the Holy Ghost he became man in Mary, the virgin, who was promised to a man of the house and generation of David, named Joseph, above all human understanding, and that, according to this flesh he was generated in her, and in due time born of her, an only, undivided person, Son, and Christ, God's true and natural Son, by virtue of his origin; and Mary's supernatural son, by virtue of his conception, I say, supernatural; for it was not brought about by the will of man; who was promised that he should be born of the generation of Abraham, Isaac, Jacob, Judah and David; as it also happened; that he is, also, by reason of his mother, Joseph's wife, called in the Scriptures the righteous branch of David, a rod out of the stem of Jesse, the fruit of the loins of David, represented by the literal Solomon; that he is the Wonderful, Counsellor, The Mighty God, The everlasting Father, our Immanuel, our God, The Lord Our Righteousness, The Wisdom of God, the Lord of David, the Strong and Mighty God, who in the beginning founded the earth, and made the heavens; our new and spiritual Solomon, seated upon the new spiritual throne in the new and spiritual kingdom and reign of David; God's true Son, I say, by reason of his Father; Abraham and David's son, by reason of his mother; an only, undivided Son of God and Mary, gone forth from the Father, come down from heaven; conceived in Mary, born of her, a true man, like unto us, poor children of Adam, in all things except sin; that he hungered and ate, thirsted and drank, tired and rested; that he was made in the likeness of men; that he has fulfilled the law for us; that he sought the lost sheep; taught the kingdom of God, and that he confirmed his sending by miracles; and that he, at last died the bitter death, innocently, for us who were guilty (when we were yet ungodly and enemies); that he has thus purchased, sanctified and cleansed us by his own blood, and not by the blood of another; that he has reconciled us with God, our Father, nay, made us kings and priests; that he was delivered and resurrected from the bonds of death, and ascended to his Father, where he was before, and that, by his precious innocent blood, he became our only and eternal High Priest, Intercessor, Mediator, Advocate and Reconciler, with God his Father; that he is our Lord and God, whom we, in our weakness, should honor and praise because of his ineffable love and merits, even as we honor the Father himself, Gen. 1: 1; Ps. 33: 6; Jn. 1: 3; 3: 13; 8: 23; 16: 28; 1 Cor. 15: 47; Eph. 4: 10; Matt. 1: 20; Luke 1: 23; Jn. 1: 14; Rom. 1: 3; Gal. 4: 4; Luke 1: 30; Gen. 12: 3; 18: 18; 22: 18; 26: 4; 28: 14; 49: 10; 2 Sam. 7: 12; Rom. 1: 3; 9: 5; Matt. 1: 18; Luke 2: 7; 3: 23; 2 Tim. 2: 8; Jer. 23: 6; 33: 16; Isa. 11: 1; 1 Kin. 5: 5; Ps. 89: 37; Matt. 1: 16; Luke 3: 23; Acts 2: 30; Isa. 9: 6; 7: 14; Matt. 1: 23; Isa. 40: 3; Jer. 23: 6; 33: 16; Prov. 8: 12; Bar. 3: 36; Ps. 110: 1; 24: 8; Heb. 1: 10; Isa. 9: 5; Luke 1: 28; Jn. 16: 28; 6: 32; Eph. 4: 10; Matt. 1: 18; Luke 1: 31; Jn. 1: 14; Luke 2: 7; Gal. 4: 4; Heb. 2: 14; 4: 15; Jn. 4: 6; Phil. 2: 7; Matt. 5: 17; Rom. 8: 3; Eph. 2: 13; Col. 2: 13; Ezek. 34: 23; Matt. 18: 11; 4: 17; Jn. 2: 11; Rom. 5: 8; 1 Jn. 1: 7; 1 Pet. 1: 19; Heb. 9: 12; Eph. 2: 15; Col. 1: 20; 1 Pet. 2: 9; Rev. 1: 6; 5: 10; Matt. 28: 6; Mark 16: 6; Luke 24: 6; Jn. 20; Eph. 1: 20; Mark 16: 19; Acts 1; Jn. 6: 62; Rom. 3: 25; Heb. 3: 1; 5: 1; 6: 20; 7: 24; 8: 1; 9: 11; 10: 11; Rom. 8: 27; Heb. 7: 25; 1 Tim. 2: 5; 1 Jn. 2: 1; Heb. 9: 11; 12: 24; Jn. 20: 28; 5: 22.

We confess and believe that, as the Almighty, eternal Father, through mere grace and love, has, in the beginning, created Adam and Eve by Christ, his Almighty, eternal word, Gen. 1: 27. He, also, now by pure love and grace, has again raised them and all their seed (since they fell) by the same word, now incarnated by his Almighty power, and that he has again accepted them as his children, Jn. 1: 14, that we may give the eternal honor and praise to God, for his grace, by his Word or Son, and not to the sinful flesh of Adam, of which they are.

And behold, such a confession concerning this matter leaves the whole Scriptures unbroken and unchanged. Not an inconsistent flattery, nor an adulterated Scripture is found, as is, alas, the case with the confession of our opponents.

The Almighty, eternal God alone, retains his glory and honor, by his Word or Son. The Father remains the true Father of the whole Christ, the mother the true mother, and the Son the true Son of both his Father and his mother, which Son is from above and not from beneath, who is from heaven and not of earth; pure of the pure God, an only Son and person, the Potentate and Lord of heaven and of earth, the Savior of all the world, in whom all the present and future promises are fulfilled, and by whom they are given and received. Eternal praise be to his adorable, glorious, and exalted name, Amen.

All those who can thus firmly believe this miraculously high work of the ineffable, great love of God, and who can confess, with Peter and all the Scriptures, that Christ Jesus is the true Son of the true and living God, they have both the Father and the Son, 1 Jn. 2: 23; they vanquish the world; they are in God, and God is in them, 1 Jn. 4: 15; they are freed from the wrath of God, and have eternal life; they acknowledge the severe justice and the merited curse which came upon Adam and all his descendants through Adam's disobedience. They, therefore, fear God, bury their sins, and turn from evil. They also acknowledge the inexpressible love of God, so richly shown us in Christ Jesus; they enter into newness of life with Christ, Rom. 6: 4; they believe in the name of the only begotten Son of God, Jn. 3: 18.

Honorable reader, take heed. I warn you in sincere and faithful love; for it avails eternal life, or eternal death. If you be not quite blinded you must observe the deceit of Micron by these "Thirty-one differences," "Forty-five unscriptural confessions, explanations, fictitious glozings, adulterated and garbled Scriptures," and by these "Fourteen insolvable, blasphemous inconsistencies;" and you must observe that his inconsistencies, together with the foundation of their confessions concerning this matter, which I have faithfully and plainly set forth, are nothing but anti-christian deceit of the old serpent; and that our foundation and faith, on account of which we must, alas, hear and suffer so much, are the firm, immutable, invincible rock and stone of the eternal truth which the holy apostles and prophets, together with all the pious witnesses of God in the primitive, incorrupted church, before the man of sin entered into, and was seated in the temple of God, who cannot bear this foundation, as may be seen, 1 Jn. 2: 22; 4: 3; 2 Jn. 1: 7, confessed with us.

Not a single Scripture is adulterated or broken by us. We make use of no glozing. No inconsistency is the result. It is the plain Scripture and its foundation which we present to the reader, as you may feel and see.

* * * *

OF GEN. 3: 15, "I WILL PUT ENMITY BETWEEN THEE AND THE WOMAN, AND BETWEEN THY SEED AND HER SEED."

MICRON, in his writing, reports that I said that we should not understand the seed of woman, Gen. 3: 15, in a carnal, but in a spiritual sense only. To this I reply unreservedly, that the assertion is without foundation. For never in my life was it my intention that I would exclude Christ from this promise. For, as deceived Eve was a literal woman, thus also, was the deceitful serpent a literal serpent, through which the devil deceived her. For the Lord said, "Upon thy belly shalt thou go, and dust shalt thou eat all the days of thy life," Gen. 3: 14, something which the devil, who is a spirit, could not do. If we, now, are to understand the seed of woman as a generative seed, as does Micron, then also, the seed of the serpent must be understood as being a generative seed, between which two the enmity would exist, solely; for the one seed must be after its own kind, for the reason that it is of one name. In that sense the literal serpent, only, was vanquished by Christ. Understand rightly what I write.

On the other hand, if the serpent be a spiritual serpent (as it indeed is) represented by the deceitful serpent, then the woman must also be a spiritual woman, represented by the deceived woman, and thus, again, the seed be after its own kind; for as the serpent is spiritual, so also, is her seed spiritual, which is falsehood, Jn. 8: 44, of which alas, she begets such children as write such deceiving, lying, infamous, and partial books as Micron and Herman have done in this instance.

In the same manner, as the woman is spiritual, Eph. 5 : 25; Rev. 12 : 6; 19 : 7, thus, also, is her seed spiritual, that is, the truth of which (eternal glory be to God for his grace), she begets such children as walk in the truth, sincerely speak the truth, and for the sake of the truth, willingly submit to death with yea, and nay.

And behold, between these two, the children of truth, and the children of falsehood, there is an eternal enmity. The seed of woman vanquishes, and that by sincere, firm faith, in christian patience by the Spirit and word of the Lord; yet it receives many stings in the heel from the vanquished seed of the serpent. For their name is slandered, their doctrine is ridiculed, their life is hated unto death, their effects are stolen, their flesh is burned, and they are drowned, and must expect to be daily bitten by the venomous, bloodguilty seed, as I, in my weakness, have experienced for more than twenty years.

Behold, if we understand it in such a sense as we have here shown, the spiritual things remain spiritual, carnal things, carnal, and the Scriptures remain unbroken. But the Lord save me from hereby excluding Christ from the promise. For I am aware, by the grace of the Lord, that Christ is the power, the beginning, means and end of the whole promise, and that he will remain such forever. For he is the spiritual husband of this spiritual woman, Jn. 3: 6; Rev. 19: 7; Eph. 5: 25. His Word is the seed of woman, which Word he is himself, as he says, "Even the same that I said unto you from the beginning," Jn. 8: 25. He spoke and taught the truth and he is the truth, Jn. 14: 6. He spoke and taught love, and he is love, 1 Jn. 4: 8. In short, he spoke of wisdom, righteousness, holiness, and deliverance, and he is himself Wisdom, Righteousness, Sanctification and Redemption, 1 Cor. 1: 30.

He alone is the victorious Prince, and triumphant Conqueror who was promised by those words, who has bruised the serpent's head for us, and also, we in him, by him, as Paul says, "In all these things we are more than conquerors, through him that loved us," Rom. 8: 37. And "I can do all things through Christ which strengtheneth me," Phil. 4: 13, and, "Who is he that overcometh the world, but he that believeth that Jesus is the Son of God?" 1 Jn. 5: 5.

Inasmuch as it is manifest from all this, that Christ and his Spirit, word, wisdom, truth, righteousness, sanctification, peace, deliverance, and all other attributes can never be separated in power and truth; and as it is manifest that where the one is the other must be also, therefore I will not leave it to the judgment of Micron and Herman, but to the judgment of the impartial reader, whether I exclude the man Christ, in whom our salvation is, from this promise, and say that it should only be understood spiritually, notwithstanding the allegory is spiritual in him, as Micron reports.

It has always been my understanding that he was hereby promised unto us of a woman, and have so stated it in some of my books; yet he must thus misquote my writings, as alas, he often does. I would not know for what reason I should contradict it, as he is not here promised of a man, but of a woman, Isa. 7: 14, of a virgin; from which we must deduce that he was not to be the impure seed of mortal man, but the Son of the Most High.

* * * *

Behold, here you have our incontrovertible reply, founded on the Scriptures, to all the unfounded, wordy, sophistic and powerless arguments which Micron and Herman adduce in their writing about the seed of woman.

I do not see why the godly women, of which he writes and to whom he complains, should not submit to this, as I allow their husbands and lords, whose honor, all virtuous and honorable wives should gladly maintain, and to themselves each in her sphere, according to the measure of eternal truth, that which their God the Lord, has allowed them himself, by his word, by the works of his creation, according to his divine pleasure.

I will not say anything about what shame Micron commits against all honorable women by his unseasoned writing; I do not delight in chiding and upbraiding. It suffices me to assert the foundation of our doctrine, to the praise of the Lord. He must once in a while maliciously pierce me, that

MICRON'S CONFESSION, IN HIS NARRATIVE, THAT CHRIST IS THE SON OF GOD AND OF MAN.

Micron writes: Jesus Christ is called the Son of God on account of his eternal and ineffable generation of God the Father, according to his divine form. Thus he is also called the son of man on account of his being born in the fullness of time, of a human being, of Mary, according to the flesh or human nature, Matt. 1. HAC ILLE.

Answer. I would here faithfully admonish the kind reader earnestly to consider my reply to Micron's confession, and to judge it with a frank, impartial heart. I trust, by the grace of God, that if he do so he will discover the adulteration and deceit of our opponents in great clearness; and he will see, on the other hand, that the truth is with us.

In the first place, if we compare the verbal confession which he made to us, with his confession in writing, he appears to be as slippery as an eel. For at the time of the discussion he confessed repeatedly before us all, that the crucified Christ Jesus had no father or near father; and says so yet at different places in his writing. Nevertheless he now comes and writes, but without the truth, that they repeatedly confessed before us, that the Son of God died for us. He repeats the same song, but he sings it to the unintelligent, and to a little better tune.

It would sound too much out of tune thus bluntly to forsake the crucified Christ Jesus, and say, that he had no Father, as he did before us.

In fact, I do not know what to say or to think of this man. Now the man Christ is the Son of God, then again he is not; now God is his Father, then again, he had no father. For he writes pointedly that the man Christ, who died for us was generated not of God, but of the seed of Mary, and that he had no father. If he then, be of her seed, and not generated of God, and if he had no father, as he says, then it is plainly falsehood, lies and deceit, to say that the Son of God died for us. If we take the best view as to his meaning he can be no more than an adopted, or a nominal Son, without truth, let him gloze the matter over as much as he can. I will leave the impartial reader to consider whether this is a simple and plain reasoning according to the truth, or an equivocal and dark argument of falsehood.

Now observe, first, his equivocation together with the unconformable, wavering, lightminded foundation of his doctrine, and his intolerable error, to teach that the crucified Christ Jesus was not God's own true Son, but merely a nominal Son, as was heard. I do not see what greater blasphemy one could commit. Yet he is a good teacher and writer, and that for the reason that he has so finely, but falsely, portrayed the old heretic, Menno.

* * * *

Thirdly, so long as they do not prove to us by the Scriptures that the Son of God is called the son of man, and the son of man, the Son of God for the reason that there was a union of the two as they frequently assert without the Scripture, so long, they mistake the truth as often as they call the Son of God the son of man, and the son of man the Son of God; for the name is given, as Micron himself confesses, in truth and in fact. And how this assertion of his agrees therewith, the reader may consider. To mock man is disreputable; but to mock God is too abominable and blasphemous.

Fourthly, so long as they do not prove to us by the Scriptures, that such union took place, as they assert, so long it is the lies and deceit of the old serpent, as it is not according to Scripture. For it is manifest that it is no union, as they call it, but a fearful division of the most holy and undivided person of Christ, whereby he manifestly makes two persons and sons in Christ, which are born of two different persons, at two different times, in two different forms; that he robs the crucified Christ Jesus of his beloved Father, and the Father of his only begotten, beloved Son; that he makes the greater part of the most holy flesh of Christ of gentile origin; that he esteems the man Christ no higher than an adopted or nominal Son of God; that he points us to an unholy, sinful, accursed offering, to an impure seat of justice, High Priest, Savior, Mediator, Advocate, and Christ, of the unholy, sinful, accursed and created flesh of Adam; that in fact, he makes Mary both the father and mother of Christ; that he breaks and disputes the whole Scriptures, together with the ordinances of God concerning generation; and that he includes so many abominable inconsistencies in Christ that a feeling heart is pained thereat, when the matter is earnestly considered.

Behold, upon such a foundation has Micron built his false doctrine of the union of the Son of God, which he teaches all through his book, in so many smooth sentences and garbled Scriptures. It is easily perceived what kind of an abomination, Babylon, the mother of whoredom, pours from her golden cup, by her messengers and servants. Woe unto those that drink thereof; for she will so enchant them that they will become drunk, and fall.

HOW CHRIST, THE SON OF GOD, IS ALSO THE SON OF ABRAHAM AND DAVID, ACCORDING TO THE SCRIPTURES.

IF we would have the true understanding of Christ being also the son of Abraham and David, and not break or go beyond the Scriptures, then we must keep in view the ordinances of God, and as it is manifest that Christ Jesus is not in truth confessed to be the Son of Joseph, but the Son of God, by the Scriptures, therefore it may be easily discerned how or in what manner Christ is also the Son of Abraham, and of David, and why he is thus called in Scripture, because of his human birth, as Paul says, "To Abraham and his seed (that is, his sons), were the promises made. He saith not, And to seeds, as of many; but as of one, and to thy seed, which is Christ," Gal. 3: 16; Rom. 1: 3; 9: 5; 2 Tim. 2: 8.

In the same manner we should consider also that both the evangelists, Matthew and Luke, count the genealogy up to Joseph, and not to Mary. Luke makes no mention at all of Mary, but says, "Being (as was supposed), the son of Joseph, which was the son of Heli," &c., Luke 3: 23. Mark what the evangelists mean. From this it is plain that they do but show the generation of which, according to the promise, is born he who is forever the Jehovah, Immanuel, Savior, and Lord of the world.

For, if such a man as was Christ, should have been begotten of human seed, as our opponents say he is, who was to be the Deliverer of the whole world, as is Christ Jesus, then the Scriptures would point to the one of whom he was generated and originally came, and not to the one of whom he was not. For the Holy Ghost is a Spirit of truth, which teaches and instructs rightly. According to the foundation of the learned, our salvation would not be attached to the Scriptures, but to an uncertain meaning. For it is manifest that there is not a word found in them, which shows that Mary was of David's generation. Luke says that she was a cousin to Elisabeth who was a daughter of Aaron, Luke 1: 5, 36.

* * * *

Kind reader, understand me. I do not mean that Mary was not a daughter of David, but I say that the Scripture does not say so. But, inasmuch as our opponents found their whole structure upon the ground that the man Christ was to be a natural seed and son of David, and that by Mary, therefore they must have the sure testimony of the Holy Scriptures whereby they can prove it to be as they assert, before one can accept such an important thing concerning the salvation of all the chosen. Since it is founded on mere presumption and not on the Scriptures, it may be that she was a daughter of David, and again, it may be that she was not, inasmuch as they did not follow one rule in regard to marriage, as may be seen by sacred history, and whereas it has nothing to do with the matter, and was, according to the evangelists sufficient that she was the wife of a son of David, that the promise might be fulfilled in the generation to which it was promised, as was frequently said, therefore I do not contradict it in the least that she was a daughter of David. But a sure testimony of the Holy Scriptures, on which the foundation of eternal salvation should be built, they can not adduce, to prove their doctrine.

* * * *

If they should say that it was to be a virgin, according to the word of the prophet, and that therefore, it could not be of the seed of man, then I would answer in plain words that they thereby pronounce their own sentence that Christ was not the natural seed and son of Abraham and David, but their supernatural and promised seed. For he was not of one of Abraham and David's sons, but of one of their daughters, who was a virgin, and knew no man, but was promised to one of David's sons, begotten of the ineffable, eternal word of the Almighty, great God, which she conceived by faith, Jn. 1:14. Being the first and only begotten, true Son of God, on account of his eternal Father, and the promised, given, and born son of Abraham, Judah and David, on account of his mother, who was a daughter of Abraham, and the wife of Joseph, the son of David, as heard, Heb. 1:2; Jn. 1:14; 3:16; 1 Jn. 4:16.

I will now conclude all the passages of the Holy Scriptures which treat about the seed, fruit and branch of Abraham and David, with the following remarks. Inasmuch as the Savior, King, Prince, Conqueror, and Prophet, graciously promised to Abraham, Isaac, Jacob, Judah and David, Gen. 12:3; 18:18; 22:18; 26:4; 28:14; 49:20; 2 Sam. 7:12, was, in due time, born a true man of one of their daughters, according to the promise, Luke 2:7, to whom the kingdom and throne of David was promised beforehand by Isaiah, and again at his conception, when it was already fulfilled in the letter by the angel, that he was to reign forever therein, Isa. 9:6; Luke 1:29, which kingdom and throne he did not receive literally, but spiritually, for it was then already fulfilled; his kingdom is eternal, Luke 19; and shall not be left to other people, Dan. 2:44; and as he is acknowledged all through the Scriptures as the first and only begotten Son of God, which he could not be if he were generated of impure human seed, as our opponents say, and not of God; and as his house or temple which he builds, is not a literal house, of literal wood, stone, metal, gold, and silver, as was the perishable house of Solomon; but as it is built of living precious stones, of the imperishable gold and silver, 1 Cor. 3:12, upon the immutable foundation of the holy apostles and prophets, put together by the Holy Ghost, Eph. 2:19; 1 Pet. 2:4, 19, therefore it is thereby manifest that the promise made to David, should be understood in the old, literal form, as fulfilled in Solomon, and in the new spiritual being, Christ, 1 Kin. 5:5; Ps. 89:37; 132:11; for if we measure the genealogy of his blessed flesh the most minutely, in the line of David, then we find that he was no more than the son of the daughter of David, while there is not a word in all the Scriptures to prove that she actually was one of David's daughters.

Behold, such a foundation has the strong argument of Micron, as he boasts, that the gates of hell will not prevail against it, something which they, doubtlessly, will not; for they would rather strengthen and aid him in such a cause; it is the strongest fortification and shield of hell, as may be clearly seen by John. But it takes a heavenly gate to prevail against it, the strong Spirit and word of the Lord, against which neither the gates of hell, nor the devil can prevail.

Whosoever desires to have more information upon this subject may examine our reply to John A'Lasco, impartially, and by the grace of God, he will find the true foundation and meaning thereof.

And behold, thus our foundation and doctrine remain firm and invincible; that

Jesus Christ is the only, first-born, and undivided Son of God, Heb. 1: 6; Jn. 1: 49; 3: 16; 1 Jn. 4: 9; Rom. 8: 32, by whom he has created heaven and earth, and the sea with their fullness, Gen. 1: 1; Ps. 33: 9; Jn. 1: 1; Eph. 3: 9; Col. 1: 16; and that he is not the impure, sinful, accursed, earthly seed of Abraham and David, as our opponents philosophize it.

Truly, he is the new Melchisedec, the King of perfect righteousness and of eternal peace, whose Father, mother, and generation, according to the true foundation of the Holy Scriptures are unknown to the whole world, the glorious Prince and wise Lord, the peaceful Solomon, who is seated upon the spiritual throne of his father David, prepared for him by his eternal Father, in eternal glory, and shall reign forever over the house and kingdom of Jacob, Isa. 9: 6, 7; Luke 1: 29. Consider whether we do not rightly teach you in accordance with the Scriptures.

CONCERNING THE TWO NATURES IN CHRIST, HOW IT SHOULD BE RIGHTLY UNDERSTOOD ACCORDING TO THE SCRIPTURES.

MICRON criticises my sixth point, and remarks concerning my saying, That God's Son did not die for us according to their doctrine, is caused by a misconception on my part, that I do not, or will not understand the union of the two natures, the divine and the human, into one person, Christ; and says, That in both discussions they have repeatedly stated that God's Son died for us.

To which I reply thus: First, that they can not truthfully say that they once stated, during the discussion, that the Son of God died for us. For they have distinctly asserted, all the time, that the man Christ had no father, or as Micron sometimes said, that he had no near father, and repeats it in different places in his book, as any one may read and see.

O, dear Lord, what a terrible abomination that mortal man and an earthly creature dares so boldly lie against his own conscience, that he dares so lamentably belittle the King of all honor, so unrestrainedly deceive the poor souls, and commit such great deceit and shame against the word of the Lord! O, that they could see what they are doing!

Secondly, I reply as I did before him, that there can not be a word found in all the Scriptures about this union of the two sons, of God's Son and the son of man, in one person, Christ, which he, generally, artfully calls two natures, and which he compares to the union of the body and soul of man.

That the body and soul of a living man are one person, is as clear as the light of the sun.

But, that such a man, body and soul, which is a perfect person, was thus united into one with the Son of God who is eternal; or, that the eternal Son of God thus united himself with the son of man (which two sons they call two natures, without Scripture), may be read in the flatterings of Micron, but we do not find it written in the Scriptures. You may further consider what kind of a Christ they teach you, by comparing this criticism of ours with the Scriptures.

Thirdly, I say that if Micron desired to deal with the readers as a faithful teacher, he would not make use of such equivocal and dark reasoning, but would express and explain his foundation and meaning without any duplicity, and say that the eternal, immortal Son of God put on a temporal, mortal son, body and soul, of the flesh and blood of Mary, and that he has thereby delivered us; for this is, in this matter, the proper meaning, sense and understanding of all their writing, flattering, and teaching, as their public confession, before us all, clearly testified and implied, as was heard.

But now he deals unfaithfully; for he means two actual sons, of which one was divine and the other human and calls them but two natures, that the unsuspicious reader may not be offended at the harshness; which nature is but a property of him who possesses it, and which is not the one himself who possesses it. For, if one sees a man, he does not say that is a human nature, but that is a man; for the property is not the being itself, but the being possesses the property. And if Christ had but the properties, namely, the natures, and if he had not the being itself, which are the substances, then he was neither God nor man; for the natures are not the being itself, but the being possesses the nature. Therefore it would be becoming in Micron to deal unequivocally, and not to deceive his readers and hearers by such incomprehensible, strange words, that they might comprehend the foundation of his doctrine, and understand what he means. For we teach in such a manner that it may be understood.

But it would offend the thoughtful reader thus boldly to confess and teach that there are two Sons in Christ, and say, that the crucified Son was not God's Son, but a sinful, acccursed man, of the sinful, accursed flesh or seed of Adam. And therefore they must fix it so as to retain their honor and name with the world, and enjoy their salaries and liens at ease.

Behold, thus we must, by virtue of the Scriptures, lift the fine cloak of the Babylonian whore, which Micron and the preachers would keep down by their glozings, wrong explanations and adulterated Scriptures, since they live off her table, that you may rightly observe and see their infamy, loathsome diseases, lumps, and deadly leprosy, understand it spiritualy, and that you may, in the fear of your God beware thereof.

I cordially admit, however, that Christ had two natures; but not in such a sense as Micron believes, but in a scriptural sense; in this manner Peter writes to the church of God, and says, Ye are partakers of the divine nature, 2 Pet. 1: 4; whereby he clearly testifies that there are two natures in a christian; the one, the human nature with which he is born of Adam, and the other, the divine nature of which he partakes by faith, in the birth which is of God, by the Holy Ghost.

If there are, then, two natures in one christian, as there are in truth, why then not in Christ? For, as he is the only and true Son of God, having no other origin but of God, then he must also have the nature of the one of whom he is, this is too plain to be controverted. That he had the divine nature he has proven by these manifest, apparent attrributes of a true, divine nature; as by his perfect righteousness, truth, holiness, love, and miracles.

As he had the divine nature, I say, on account of his divine origin, thus he also had the unblemished, pure, human nature (like unto the nature of Adam, before the fall), and that by reason of his true humanity. For as truly as he was the Father's Almighty Word from everlasting, so truly also, he, in the fullness of time, became a true, passive, mortal man, Jn. 1: 14; 1 Jn. 1: 1. And as he thus became a true man he must also have had the property of a true man, which is a true, human nature (though not corrupted), or else he would not have been a true man; this is incontrovertible.

Although the Scriptures say nothing about the two natures in Christ, yet I admit it with the above understanding; for I am sure that one can not separate the nature from any thing any more than he can separate the light from the sun, the heat from the fire and humidity from water.

That he had the true, human nature as well as the divine, he has shown by the apparent fruits of the real, human nature, as by hungering, thirsting, being weary, sighing, weeping, suffering and death.

Behold, thus I plainly confess according to the style and ordinance of the holy, divine Scriptures, that there were two natures in the only, undivided person and Son of God, Christ; and not as Micron does, who makes one Son of two sons, and one person of two persons, without the Scriptures, which he calls two natures, and according to his glozings, were born at two different times, of two different persons, in two different forms, and which several natures remained distinct, and were incomprehensibly united into one person, Christ, according to his writing, without the Scriptures. Observe which of us points you to the Scriptures.

REPLY TO MARTIN MICRON.

It is hardly necessary to reply to some Scriptures which he adduces, whereby he tries to prove that not the Son of God, but the son of man, suffered. Of these Scriptures, in my opinion, the strongest is, that Peter says, Christ was "put to death in the flesh, but quickened in the Spirit," 1 Pet. 3: 18. For who ever suffered but in the flesh? Also, "Forasmuch then as Christ hath suffered for us in the flesh, arm yourselves likewise with the same mind: for he that hath suffered in the flesh hath ceased from sin," 1 Pet, 4: 1. Mark, Christians also suffer in the flesh, as Christ himself did, yet they are not one son, composed of two sons, as Micron says that Christ is.

Nobody can suffer otherwise than in the flesh, for Christ himself says, "Fear not them that kill the body, but are not able to kill the soul," Matt. 10: 28; Luke 12: 4. Again, to the murderer, "To-day thou shalt be with me in paradise," Luke 23: 43. His flesh hung upon the cross, and was afterward buried, from which it is very plain that it was said in regard to his immortal Spirit.

Again, Christ said, "Father, into thy hands I commend my Spirit." He did not cry, Father, into thy hands I commend thy Son with whom I have been united into one person, and which was my Spirit. For one of three conclusions must be drawn from Micron's writing. Either the indwelling Son of God whom he generally calls the divine nature, and the son of Mary, whom he generally calls the human nature, together, must have had one Spirit or soul, and this Spirit he must have commended into the hands of the Father; or that the two remained alive at the death of Christ. First, the immortal, eternal Son of God, which had dwelt in him. Secondly, the Spirit or soul which he had received of Mary, or else the eternal Son of God must have become the Spirit of a mortal man, which had put on a dwelling place or tabernacle of Mary, which he offered for us, as was said in treating about the inconsistencies.

From which it follows that it is mere quicksand upon which they build their doctrine of the two natures, or two sons in Christ, according to their manner; and that it can stand no better before the power of the divine word, than the stubble can stand before the fire. And thus we firmly hold our ground that Jesus Christ is the only, undivided, and true Son of God; and that he is not one Son composed of two different sons, as is the anti-christian, false foundation and doctrine of our opponents.

THAT GOD THE FATHER IS THE TRUE FATHER OF THE WHOLE CHRIST, HIS SON; AND THAT THE WHOLE CHRIST IS A TRUE SON OF GOD, HIS FATHER, WHICH MICRON CONTRADICTS IN MANY PLACES, AND SAYS THAT IT IS NOT SO.

Micron writes at some places, "That the son of man had no father, or near father." He often said so at the time of the discussion, too. Something which is so diametrically opposed to all Scripture that one must be astounded and ashamed thereat.

Since he so indiscreetly denies the Father of Christ Jesus, according to his humanity—therefore, I trust I will show to the reader, who is the Father of Christ, by a number of scriptural references and by their power that he must say, if he be not entirely given up, that Micron and the learned, by their writings, have lamentably deceived him, and that they have taught nothing but an anti-christian foundation.

Thus spake the angel of the Most High to Mary, when she wondered how this should be, as she knew not a man: "The Holy Ghost shall come upon thee, and the power of the Highest shall overshadow thee; therefore also that holy thing which shall be born of thee shall be called the Son of God," Luke 1: 35.

Which plain Scripture Micron has obscured by his infernal smoke, saying, "The angel meant to say to Mary, that her child should not be man, only (he means of her flesh), but also truly God, and his Son, according to his eternal, divine being." Not a single word did the angel say to that effect; nor did he make such a division in Christ, as does Micron. But the angel merely made it known that she should conceive, and that the fruit should be the Son of God, and that God should be the Father of the child. Behold, thus Micron breaks the testimony of the holy angel, which he, at God's command, bore to Mary from high heaven, that the holy thing which should be born of her, should be the Son of God.

Again, the heavenly Father himself testifies of Christ Jesus, saying, "This is my beloved Son in whom I am well pleased. Hear ye him," Matt. 17: 5; Mark 9: 7; Luke 9: 35. Here the Father proclaims him to be his beloved Son, without any division. And Micron says that he is not.

Again, Christ said unto the blind man, "Dost thou believe on the Son of God? He answered and said, who is he, Lord, that I might believe on him? And Jesus said unto him, Thou hast both seen him, and it is he that talketh with thee," Jn. 9: 35. Here the palpable, visible Christ, who, according to the foundation of Micron, was only the son of man, confesses himself to be the Son of God, without any division; and Micron says that he is not. Again, at another place Christ says, "What and if ye shall see the son of man (mark, he says the son of man) ascend up where he was before?" Jn. 6: 62. Here Christ himself confesses that the son of man was from heaven; and Micron says that he was of earth, and that he is called heavenly, on account of some virtues, as if Christ was a nominal Christ and not a Christ in truth.

Again, when Christ asked his disciples, saying, "Whom do men say that I, the son of man, am?" (mark, he asks about the son of man). Then Peter said, "Thou art the Christ (without a division), the Son of the living God," Matt. 16: 16, &c.; and Micron says that the son of man was not the Son of God.

Again, John the Baptist says, "He that sent me to baptize with water, the same said unto me, Upon whom thou shalt see the Spirit descending, and remaining on him, the same is he which baptizeth with the Holy Ghost. And I saw and bare record that this is the Son of God," Jn. 1: 33. Here John confesses the visible Christ (who, according to our opponent's foundation, was only the son of man), to be the Son of God; and Micron writes that he is not.

Again, the centurion, on Golgotha said, "Truly, this man (mark, he says, this man) was the Son of God," Mark 15: 39; and Micron says, he is not. Paul says, "God sent forth his Son, made of a woman," Gal. 4: 4; and Micron writes, God sent forth his Son, who came of a woman. At another place, Paul writes, "He that spared not his own Son," Rom. 8: 32. Mark, he says, *His own Son*, and we are reconciled to God by the death of his Son. Rom. 5: 10. John says, "The blood of Jesus Christ his Son cleanseth us from all sin," 1 Jn. 1: 7. At another place, "He (God) sent his Son to be the propitiation for our sins," 1 Jn. 4: 10, which reconciliation, according to Micron's false doctrine, is not brought about by the blood of the Son of God, as John and Paul teach, but by the blood of the son of man, who, according to Micron, had no father, as has often been heard.

Kind reader, if you closely observe it you will find more than sixty instances in the New Testament where Christ Jesus confesses God the heavenly Father to be his Father, and himself to be his Son. And from the beginning to the end, you will not find anything about such a division and union as our opponents teach, neither in Christ's words, nor in those of any of the holy apostles or evangelists.

Micron writes at more than one place, "If God, the Father, is the Father of the man Christ, then he must have also had flesh and blood." From which it is manifest, first, that he does not allow the crucified Christ a Father. Whereby the angel of God, the Father, and the Son, themselves, also John the Baptist, Peter, John, Paul, Nathaniel, Martha, and the whole Scriptures are made bare-faced liars and false witnesses, by him, Luke 1: 31; Matt. 17: 5; Jn. 9: 36; 1: 33; 3: 16; Matt. 16: 16. For they have repeatedly confessed him to be the true Son of the true and living God.

Secondly, it is manifest that all such writing is not of the living Fount of the

Holy Ghost; nor of an enlightened, firm, believing heart which, without all wavering, trusts, with Joshua and Caleb, in the power and true promise of the Almighty God; but that it is solely of human wisdom and an unbelieving, carnal heart, which can not judge but according to nature; and yet, through excessive blindness, destroys the ordinances of this same nature, which God established in the first creation.

Kind reader, take heed! The Almighty power of God, the ineffable miracle of his divine love, and the undeceiving, sure word of his eternal truth should avail more than the blind intellect of our corrupted nature, if we would rightly learn to know Christ, and follow and obey his holy word.

The dead body of Adam, created of the dust, by the breath of God, became a living soul, Gen. 1: 27, and the water gushed forth from the rock, Ex. 17: 6. Yet the earth, from which the living Adam was made, was no living soul, neither was the rock from which the water flowed for Israel to drink, the ingredients of water. If they should now say that this was done by the power of God, by supernatural means, as is the case, too, then I would reply again: Thus was also brought about the miraculous incarnation of Jesus Christ, in Mary, by the omnipotence of God by which he can do any thing he pleases, as the angel says, "The power of the Highest shall overshadow thee;" for with God nothing is impossible, Luke 1: 35.

I entertain the opinion that all those who believe, in power and in truth, that God was able, in the beginning, to create heaven, earth and sea, and the fullness thereof, by his mighty word, and now, by the same word, rules, disposes and maintains all this; and who believe that he is able to raise Adam and all his descendants, at the end, by the same power, from the dust, and reclaim them from the undermost parts of the earth and the depths of the sea, and place them before the sight of his majesty, will also believe that this same God had the power to send his ineffable, eternal word from heaven and to let it become, by the power of his Holy Spirit, a true, passive, mortal man, in Mary, as John says, "The Word was made flesh," Jn. 1: 14.

I repeat it, in Mary, for in the Father, or in heaven, before he was conceived, he was not flesh. This I have often confessed in plain language, and thoroughly proved by the Scriptures. Notwithstanding this he is not ashamed so to garble my words as if I should have said that the Word was flesh in the Father, or in heaven. Something which I can say with a good conscience never to have thought of in all my life.

I do not see what difference there can be between the spirit of our opponents and the spirit of the Pharisees and of the false prophets. For as *they* always garbled the words of the pious prophets and of the Lord Christ, and were always intent upon making them disreputable, and thus, out of mere hatred and envy of the truth, make way with them by violence, falsehood and wrong; thus *these*, out of mere hatred and envy of the truth, deal with me, old, afflicted man; for, alas, they have portrayed me all through their book, in such colors, that I do not see how they could have depicted Behemoth and Beelzebub in more unpleasant colors than they have depicted me; notwithstanding that, I have never in my life, wished them any harm and much less done them any; but have shown them all christian faithfulness and discretion by giving them good counsel in their need, as the love which is of God teaches all true christians to do. Yet, however, they have written this lying, infamous and slanderous falsehood against me, undeservedly, as thanks for my faithfulness, whereby they cause me to be tenfold more obnoxious in all countries than I was before. And this for no other reason in fact, than that we confess Christ Jesus to be the true Son of the true and living God, with the angel Gabriel, with the Father, with Christ himself, with John the Baptist, with Peter, and with all the Scriptures, and that we, in our weakness, would gladly hear and follow his word, commandments, prohibitions, ordinances and unblamable example, that we might thus be saved by his grace, which our opponents utterly hate and oppose. For they publicly avow that the son of man, whom we confess to be the Son of God, according to the Scriptures, was not the Son of God. They contradict his express ordinance of baptism, which he taught and commanded us with his own mouth, whereby all the regenerated, believing children of God submissively testify before Christ and his church that they are prepared and willing to follow his holy word and divine will, unto death.

Beloved, do observe what abomination and poisonous draught it is which they pour out for you from the Babylonian cup! True and immutable remains the testimony of the Father: "This is my beloved Son in whom I am well pleased," Matt. 3: 17; 17: 5; Mark 1: 11; 9: 7; Luke 9: 35; 2 Pet. 1: 17.

HOW THE DIVINE WORD, IN THE FULLNESS OF TIME, ACCORDING TO THE SCRIPTURES, WAS MADE FLESH.

* * * *

You have heard that God, the Father, is a true Father of the whole Christ, and that the whole Christ is the true Son of God, his Father. We will now show you, by the grace of the Lord, by virtue of the holy, divine Scriptures, what kind of divine substance, matter, seed, or being it was of which this same Son of God and Mary was brought forth, that you may confess and see the clearness of the human birth of Jesus Christ, according to the Scriptures, through the smoke of the bottomless pit, cleared away by the power of the strong word and scattered by the breeze of the Holy Ghost.

Thus John teaches us, saying, "In the beginning was the Word, and the Word was with God, and the Word was God. The same was in the beginning with God. All things were made by him; and without him was not any thing made that was made. In him was life, and the life was the light of men." "And the Word (which was in the beginning) was made flesh, and dwelt among us (and we beheld his glory, the glory as of the only begotten of the Father), full of grace and truth," Jn. 1.

Behold, dear reader, here John shows us as a true witness of the truth, the divine being of the man Christ, the ineffable, eternal Word.

If you would have an immutable, true and firm foundation of faith, and the true sense of these words of John, and not be deceived by the lying seed of the old serpent, nor be robbed of your Savior by the subtle deceit of anti-christ, you must well observe and hold to these facts.

First, that God the Father is confessed to be the true Father of his Son Christ, by the Scriptures, Matt. 3: 17; 16: 16; 17: 5; Luke 1: 31; Jn. 1: 45; 3: 16; 5: 22.

Secondly, that Christ Jesus is confessed to be the true Son of God, his Father, by all the Scriptures, Matt. 3: 17; 14: 33; 16: 16; 17: 5; Mark 1: 11; 9: 7: 15: 39; Luke 2: 48; Jn. 9: 37.

As it is plain that God the heavenly Father is a true Father of Christ, his Son, and that Christ is a true Son of God, his Father, as is testified all through the Scriptures; therefore it is sure and manifest that we should leave the testimony of John unglozed and unbroken, where he says, "The word was made flesh." For since Christ is God's true Son, and God the Father, Christ's true Father, the Father must also have had his ineffable Word, by which all things were made that are made, as was heard.

If our opponents should say, "That the Word was Spirit from the beginning, and could therefore not become flesh," then you may answer, first, If the Word could not become flesh, as you say, the power of the Father is made less and his arm is shortened, by which he can do anything he pleases; and the angel bore a false testimony to Mary, when he said that there is nothing impossible with God, Luke 1: 37.

Secondly, you may answer: If the Word was not made flesh, as you say, then all the Scriptures deceive us, which testify and teach, without any division, union, or exception as to nature, sons or persons, that Christ Jesus is God's Son, and that God is his Father, as was said.

Thirdly, you may answer: If the Word

was not made flesh, as you say, then the Holy Scriptures testify falsely, that he is of heaven and not of earth, Jn. 3: 31; 8: 23; Eph. 4: 10, that he came forth from the Father, Jn. 16: 28, that he is the bread and Lord from heaven, Jn. 6: 35; 1 Cor. 15: 47, that he is the Alpha and Omega, Rev. 1: 8; 22: 13, and other like Scriptures.

Fourthly, you may answer: If the Word could not become flesh, as you say, then one or the other of you must be wrong. Either you who say that he could not become flesh, or John, who says that he was made flesh, as was heard.

If they should further say, that the Word put on, by generation, of Mary's seed, as they actually do, you may answer then thus: First, Then we desire that you show to us where this is written in the Scriptures or else we say, that it is the flattering and falsehood of the old serpent, and not the Lord's truth.

Secondly, you answer: By such acceptation you rob the Father of his Son, and the Son of his Father. You divide Christ into two parts, into good and evil, into righteous and unrighteous, into heavenly and earthly. You point us to a sinful creature and an impure offering. You idolize the earthly and sinful flesh of Adam. You make all the pious witnesses of Christ, such as John the Baptist, Peter, &c., false and lying, and yourselves anti-christ; and make the Scriptures contradictory.

Thirdly, you may answer: Becoming is *becoming*, and putting on is *putting* on; nor will it be found otherwise in the Scriptures. Thus when Christ became twelve years of age, he did become twelve years of age, counting from the time of his human birth. Christ became a curse, Gal. 3: 13. He became such, so as to be hung between two murderers, on the cross, Matt. 27: 38; Mark 15: 27; Luke 23: 32. Water was made wine, and it was made, John 2: 9; Lot's wife became a pillar of salt, and she did become one, Gen. 19: 26. For becoming I say, is becoming, and cannot be explained in any part of the Scriptures as meaning *putting on*.

If they would still follow their intellect and say, "If the Word is become flesh, it has lost its first being by the change," you might answer, first: John has taught us that it was made flesh, and he has not said a word further, as to how or to what extent it was changed; something that you, inquisitive ones, want to know and hear of us, without any Scripture.

Secondly, you might answer: Adam was made a living soul, 1 Cor. 15: 45; yet he remained dust, for the Lord said unto him, "Dust thou art, and unto dust shalt thou return, Gen. 3: 19.

Thirdly, you might reply: We ought to believe sincerely, and not intellectually comprehend. For Paul says, that "Faith is the substance of things hoped for, the evidence of things not seen," Heb. 11: 1.

Fourthly, you might reply: Paul says, That he is God, and Christ says that he is a Spirit. Zophar the Naamathite says, "It is as high as heaven; deeper than hell; longer than the earth; and broader than the sea," Job 11: 8, 9. And the prophet says, that he comprehended the dust of the earth in a measure, Isa. 40: 12; also, "saith the Lord, The heaven is my throne, and the earth is my footstool," Isa. 66: 1. There is no man born of Adam who is so intellectual and wise that he can measure this God and Spirit, or comprehend his being, therefore it would be well for them to abandon their high, soaring intellect to search such ineffable profundity, to humbly bow themselves under the word of the Lord, and to ponder on the saying of Solomon, "It is not good to eat much honey; so for men to search their own glory is not glory," Prov. 25: 27. Read also Syrach 3: 21.

Kind reader, if intellect were to avail in this ineffable, deep matter, and not the Scriptures, then I would ask them an intellectual question concerning their faith, of which they could scarcely extricate themselves. It would be this: Whether or not they believe that the Almighty, ineffable Word, of which heaven and earth are full, Wis. 18: 15, and which is also, the eternal wisdom and power of the Almighty, eternal Father, has placed itself out and out in such *concreto sanguine*, as Micron calls it at one place, as is his doctrine now? I presume they will leave the question unanswered. For if they say that it was therein, out and out, then they make a Father who has separated his word, wisdom and power from himself, and placed it outside of himself. And if they say that it was not all therein, then they make their own foundation untrue and false; for they say and teach that the Son of God (which is God's eternal Word, wisdom and power) has put on the son of man or of Mary, and that he has united himself therewith into one person.

Therefore I repeat that it would be well for them to leave such ineffable profundity unsearched, to stay under the clouds, and not to soar above heaven, with their earthly, ignorant intellect; for, I presume that when they have measured the height of the heavens and the depth of the abyss, have weighed the mountains and enumerated the drops of rain, then they will give me an intelligent answer, and explain how this thing is, about which I asked concerning their faith, foundation and doctrine. And therefore I say that I do not at all charge my mind with this incomprehensible miracle, but adduce the word of the Lord, whereby I am plainly taught that Mary, the Lord's mother, conceived the Almighty, eternal Word of the Father (by which all things were made that are made), by faith, Luke 1: 31, and that the same, by the great power and operation of his Almighty, eternal Spirit, became a true, visible, palpable, passive, mortal, pure and holy man, not of her, but in her, above the comprehension of all mankind. And thus he who was already the first-born of every creature, and, also, according to his human form, the first and only begotten, true Son of God, was supernaturally born unto God, his Father, of Mary, according to the flesh, as Isaac was naturally born unto Abraham, by Sarah; Solomon unto David, by Bath-sheba, and John the Baptist unto Zacharias, by Elisabeth, Gen. 21; 2 Sam. 12: 24; Luke 1: 12; which first and only begotten, true Son of God became also, according to the promise, a son of Abraham, Isaac, Jacob, Judah, and David on account of his mother (but in the genealogy of Christ, Joseph's son, Matt. 1: 16; Luke 3: 23), who graciously fulfilled the spiritual law which no flesh of Adam could fulfill, for all of the descendants of Adam, in perfect righteousness, Rom. 8: 2; and who innocently trod the wine press of bitter death, Isa. 63: 3; Rev. 19: 15, to whom the law and all the prophets point, and in whom all the glorious promises of the inexpressibly great grace and love of God are fulfilled. And thus, after he had done the service of his divine love he again ascended up where he was before, Jn. 6: 62. He has all power in heaven and upon earth, Matt. 28: 18, and is, through faith in his blood, our only and eternal Propitiator, Reconciler, High Priest, Mediator, Advocate, and Peace-maker with God, his Father, Rom. 3: 25; Jn. 4: 25; 1 Tim. 2: 5; 1 Jn. 2: 1.

Behold, thus the most high, most gracious, and most merciful God and Father retains his glory, praise and honor through his blessed, eternal Word and Son; and not through the unclean, sinful flesh of Adam, as our opponents teach and pretend.

Mark, now, beloved reader, how our opponents are deceived in this matter by their earthly, carnal intellect which would explain this miracle, not according to the Scriptures, but according to the laws of nature, and therefore, do not believe that the Almighty God had the power to let his eternal Word become flesh, and a true man; for which reason they have depicted me in such unbecoming colors, although these poor souls are doubly what they would make us to be, namely, false teachers, and perverse heretics. For they say and teach without any Scriptures, that the man Christ who died for us, was not the Son of God, and that he had no Father; and we say that he is God's Son, and that God is his Father, according to all Scripture.

They say and teach, without any Scripture, "That the Word has put on a whole man of Mary's flesh and seed;" and we say and teach, according to the plain testimony of John, That the Word was made flesh, not of Mary, but in Mary.

They teach, "That there are two different persons and sons, one divine, the other human, in the one Christ," without Scripture; and we say that there is but one undivided person and Son, according to the Scriptures.

They say and teach, "That the visible Christ was earthly, of the earth," without the Scriptures; and we say and teach that he is heavenly, of heaven, according to the Scriptures.

They say and teach, "That he is pure of impure Adam," without Scripture; and we say and teach that he is pure of the pure God, according to the Scriptures.

They point us to an "accursed, sinful offering," without Scripture; and we point to a spotless, innocent offering, according to the Scriptures.

They worship an Adamitic flesh, contrary to all Scripture; and we, the Almighty, eternal Word which became man by the infinite power of God, according to the Scriptures.

In short, they place their whole salvation in the unclean, sinful seed of Adam, that is, in a man, who, according to their fabulous writing, and contrary to the word and ordinance of God, was generated from the seed or blood of Mary, without father; and we, in the Almighty, eternal Word, which became man in the fullness of time, by which all things are made, ruled, and have their being, forever, which was from everlasting the eternal wisdom, power and glory of God, his Father, one with God, his eternal Father and the eternal Holy Ghost, blessed forever, Amen.

Invincible and firm remains the word: "The word was made flesh," Jn. 1: 14; 1 Jn. 1: 1. O, merciful, gracious Lord, enlighten the eyes of all the blind, that they may see thy heavenly brightness and rightly confess the majesty of thy honor, Amen. Dear Lord, Amen.

CONCLUSION.

HONORABLE reader, here you have our fundamental explanation and plain reply to the untrue, and partial narration, and anti-christian, false doctrine concerning Jesus Christ the Son of God by Micron and Herman, wherewith I am now and at all times willing and ready to appear before God and his angels, before friend and foe, and before the whole world, unto water, fire, sword, and before the coming judgment.

I would pray you all, reasonable readers, through Jesus, as if before God, to reflect earnestly what kind of spirits and people they are who have written the "Narration" and its appendix and articles concerning us, as they have kept quite silent about the beneficence so faithfully shown them in their need; nor said anything about the distinct confessions which they made, as above stated, whereby they had already lost the whole point in discussion, as also, that they were frequently so puzzled that they knew not what to say, and as they have not written a single, discreet word about me in their whole book; and from the beginning of the discussion to the end of their writing, they have only studied and aimed how they might most expertly defame me, and thus make our doctrine, which is the pure doctrine of Christ, a stench to many.

In several instances they have lamentably garbled and misinterpreted my words; have added to, or subtracted therefrom, and changed the meaning of their own. The order of the discussion they have changed, made many unscriptural glozings, adulterated the Holy Scriptures, made false witnesses of the Father himself and his blessed Son, of the angel of the Lord, of John the Baptist, of all the evangelists, apostles and of all the Scriptures, as may be seen.

However, they fill the measure of their predecessors, the false prophets, who, from the beginning, have praised and taught falsehood by hypocrisy, have hated the truth, and upbraided the faithful servants of God, and defamed them; who have taken amiss the faithful service of their love, accused them before lords and princes, have hindered them in the doctrine and true religion, and at last, have taken their lives and confiscated their goods. It is but little to me, that they have thus trampled upon me, and caused me to be a stench to many; for I am aware that I am unworthy of honor, since I am born of Adam, of impure seed, an unworthy sinner; as all those have complained, from the beginning, who were rightly overshadowed by the glory of the Lord. But, the Lord forbid that I am such an unsteady falsifier, and artful rogue, as I am depicted to be by our opponents through the infamous, false, indiscreet and bitter spirit of envy. Many pious people of both the Old and the New Testament had to hear this same thing, with me. Christ promises us a great reward in heaven; for it is done for his name's sake, Matt. 5: 11; Luke 6: 22. But it pierces my soul night and day that they so lamentably blaspheme the Son of God, adulterate the Scriptures, and so falsely console the poor, unenlightened souls by such open falsehood, and thus encourage and keep them in their accursed blindness. For which reason I was urged to write this reply, to the praise of the Lord, and to your service.

I would, therefore, that you would earnestly consider what a pure, clear and unadulterated foundation of truth we have pointed out to you and to all the world, concerning Christ. And, on the other hand, also, how plainly and convincingly we have discovered and manifested unto you and all reasonable readers the anti-christian foundation and doctrine of our opponents. Whosoever has but half sight may see where the deceit is hidden.

We now and at all times willingly offer, that if they can prove to us by the unbroken and unadulterated Scriptures, that Adam had two kinds of seed, of which one was pure and the other impure, or, that the Scriptures any where call that holy, pure, and heavenly which is unholy, impure and earthly in itself, or, that two sons can be one Son, or, that the Scriptures any where mention such a union, as our opponents falsely pretend, or, that ever any one was the true son of another without his being generated of his substance or seed, or, that God is a God of falsehood, so that he would call the man Christ his Son, without his actually being such, then we will gratefully and diligently reconsider the matter, in all love. Behold, before God, it is the truth that I write. And, in case they cannot do so (something which they surely never can), then our opponents, if they be reasonable men, should acknowledge that they have the impure, deceitful doctrine of antichrist, and we the wholesome doctrine of Christ; notwithstanding we must hear and suffer so exceedingly much.

Dear reader, if we consider the Scriptures of John the evangelist, we clearly find that the spirit and doctrine of our opponents already existed in his time. For, at that time they denied that Jesus Christ was the Son of God, and that he was made flesh; something which these, also, often did in their writings and verbal discussion which they had with us. From which it is manifest that it is the roguery and deceit of the old serpent.

I would, therefore, humbly beseech all the godly, pious hearts who sincerely and diligently seek Christ and eternal life, for the Lord's sake, first, to pray for all of our opponents, both of high and low station in life, learned or unlearned, rich or poor, who ignorantly err, and who are encouraged and consoled in their impenitent, reckless life, by such false teachers and writers as are our opponents, that the merciful, gracious Lord may give them eyes to see his glorious, exalted origin, and rightly confess his truth, that *that* may not be lost with which they are so dearly bought.

And secondly, pray that the Lord may grant me, and all our fellow laborers of the house of God, together with the whole church, the Spirit of his wisdom; grant that we, by his grace, may remain wholesome in doctrine; steady in faith; ardent in love; quickened in hope; unremittent in the work of the Lord; unblamable in life, and patient in all oppression and tribulation; of which alas, we do not experience a little by the infamous crying and writing of our opponents; that we may set a living example to the world; that many may see our new, christian walk in the truth and examine it, repent, and thus be eternally saved.

I beseech you in the same manner not to leave these our writings idle and hidden, but to send them east, west, north and south, into the hands of all men, and to let many read them, that the bright sun of righteousness which, alas, has been obscured for so many centuries by the smoke of the bottomless pit of the anti-christian, false doctrine, may shine forth with the power of truth, and that our glorious and holy Savior, the first and only begotten, true Son of the Almighty, living God, the ever blessed Jesus Christ, may be rightly confessed by many, in his glory.

To this only and eternal Savior, together with his heavenly Father and Holy Ghost be the praise forever, Amen.

MENNO SIMON.

October 5.

A LETTER.

From Menno Simon to Margaret, wife of Rein Edes.

CHOSEN beloved sister in Christ Jesus, Mercy, grace and peace be to thee! Most beloved sister whom I sincerely love in Christ. From your beloved husband's letter I understand, that during all the winter you have been a sick and afflicted child, which I very much regret to hear. But we pray daily: Father, thy will be done. By which we commit ourselves to the Father to treat with us as is pleasing in his blessed sight. Therefore bear with your affliction resignedly. For all this is his paternal will for your own good; that you may put your trust in the eternal living God alone, and not in any perishable things. Be consoled in Christ Jesus; for after the cold of winter, comes summer; and after death, comes life. O, sister! rejoice that you are a true daughter of your beloved Father. Soon will the inheritance of his glorious promise be due; a little while yet, says the word of the Lord, and he who is coming shall come and his reward will be with him. May the Almighty, merciful God and Lord, before whom you have bent your knees, to his honor, and whom, according to your weakness you have sought, grant you a strong and patient heart, a sufferable pain, a lovely refreshment, a gracious cure or godly dissolution, through Christ Jesus whom we daily expect with you, my beloved sister and child in Christ Jesus.

Secondly, I understand that your conscience is troubled because you have not and do not now walk in such perfection as the Scriptures direct us; on which account I write the following to my faithful sister, as a fraternal consolation, from the true word and eternal truth of the Lord: The Scripture, says Paul, hath concluded all under sin. There is no man on earth, says Solomon, who does righteously and sinneth not, Eccl. 7. At another place, "A just man falleth seven times, and riseth up again," Prov. 24: 16. Moses says, "The Lord, the Lord God, merciful and gracious, longsuffering, and abundant in goodness and truth; keeping mercy for thousands, forgiving iniquity and transgression and sin, and that will by no means clear the guilty," Ex. 34: 6, 7. O, dear sister! Observe, he says, None are guiltless before God. Again, David says, "Lord, enter not into judgment with thy servant; for in thy sight shall no man living be justified;" "If they sin against thee (for there is no man who sinneth not);" "We are all as an unclean thing, and all our righteousness are as filthy rags;" Christ, also, says, "There is none good but one, that is, God;" "The evil which I would not, that I do;" "In many things we offend all;" "If we say that we have no sin, we deceive ourselves, and the truth is not in us," Ps. 143: 2; 1 Kin. 8: 46; Isa. 64: 6; Matt. 19: 17; Mark 10: 18; Rom. 7: 19; 1 Jn. 1: 8.

As it is plain from all these Scriptures that we must all acknowledge ourselves to be sinners, as we, also, are in fact; and as no one has perfectly fulfilled the righteousness required of God but Christ Jesus alone; therefore none can approach God, obtain grace and be saved except by the perfect righteousness, reconciliation and advocacy of Jesus Christ; however godly, righteous, holy and unblamable he is. We must all acknowledge, whosoever we are, that we are sinners in thoughts, words and works. Yea, if we had not before us the righteous

Christ Jesus, no prophet nor apostle could be saved. Therefore, be of good cheer and be consoled in the Lord. You can expect no greater righteousness in yourself than all the chosen of God had in them from the beginning. In and by yourself you are a poor sinner; and by the eternal righteousness, banished, accursed and adjudged to eternal death; but in and through Christ you are justified and pleasing unto God, and accepted of him in eternal grace as a daughter and child. In this all saints have consoled themselves, trusted in Christ, esteemed their own righteousness as unclean, weak and imperfect, with contrite hearts approached the throne of grace, in the name of Christ, and with firm faith prayed the Father: O, Father, forgive us our trespasses as we forgive those that trespass against us, Matt. 6; Luke 11.

It is a very precious word which Paul speaks, "When we were yet without strength, in due time Christ died for the ungodly;" yea, when we were yet ungodly, and thereby he manifests his love toward us. "For if, when we were enemies, we were reconciled to God by the death of his Son much more, being reconciled, we shall be saved by his life, Rom. 5: 6, 10. Behold, my chosen, beloved child and sister in the Lord, this I write from the sure foundation of eternal truth. I herewith pray you, and desire that you will wholly commend all your doings outward and inward unto Christ Jesus and his merits; believing and confessing that his precious blood, alone, is your cleansing; his righteousness your piety; his death your life; and his resurrection your justification; for he is the forgiveness of all your sins; his bloody wounds are your reconciliation; and his invincible strength the staff and consolation of your weakness, as we have, in former days, according to our small gift, often shown you from the Scriptures. Yea, most beloved child and sister, so long as you find and feel such a spirit in yourself which is desirous of following that which is good, and abhorring that which is evil, notwithstanding the remnant of sin is not entirely dead in you, as also all the saints complained of from the beginning, so long you may rest assured that you are a child of God, and that you will inherit the kingdom of grace in eternal joy, with all the saints. "Hereby know we that we dwell in him, and he in us, because he hath given us of his Spirit," Jn. 4: 13. I sincerely pray that you may, by faith, rightly understand this ground to the refreshment, strengthening and consolation of your conscience and soul, and remain firm unto the end. I commend you, most beloved child and sister, to the faithful, merciful and gracious God, in Christ Jesus, now and forever. Let him do with you and with all of us according to his blessed will. Either in the flesh, yet to remain a little while with your beloved husband and children; or out of the flesh, to the honor of his name and to the salvation of your soul. You before, and we after, or we before and you afterward. Separation must once come. In the city of God, in the new Jerusalem there we will wait on each other, before the throne of God and of the Lamb; there sing hallelujah! and praise his name in perfect joy. Your husband and children I commend to him who has given them to you, and he will do with them justly. The saving power of the most holy blood of Christ be with my most beloved child and sister, now and forever, Amen.

Your brother, who sincerely loves you in Christ.

MENNO SIMON.

A VERY SINCERE EPISTLE

TO

MARTIN MICRON

AS

A NECESSARY REPLY TO HIS INDISCREET FALSEHOOD, ABUSE, AND FALSE ACCUSATIONS, CONCERNING THE MAGISTRACY, SWEARING OF OATHS, &C., WHICH HE HAS PRESENTED FOR THE PERUSAL OF THE WHOLE WORLD, TO THE DISGRACE OF THE HOLY, DIVINE WORD AND OF HIS (THE LORD'S) CHURCH; AS ALSO SERVING AS A MIRROR TO HIS ERRING SOUL, THAT HE MAY LEARN TO KNOW HIMSELF, AND MAY KNOW, TOGETHER WITH THE READERS OF BOTH OUR WRITINGS, HOW WICKEDLY HE HAS ACTED AGAINST GOD AND MAN, THAT HE MAY MAKE CONFESSION, REPENT, AND BE SAVED.

BY

MENNO SIMON.

"For other foundation can no man lay than that is laid, which is Jesus Christ," 1 Cor. 3:11.

ELKHART, INDIANA:
PUBLISHED BY JOHN F. FUNK AND BROTHER.
1871.

THE pure, true knowledge of Jesus Christ, the Son of God in truth; a new, regenerated, and understanding heart; a new, impartial, true hand and tongue; a new, godly, unblamable life in the fear and love of God; together with the unadulterated, pure, and good disposition, nature, fruits and unction of the Holy Ghost, I wish to Martin Micron from the inmost of my heart, to the enlightenment of his soul, from him who is the Giver of every good and perfect gift, through Jesus Christ, his beloved, chosen Son, our Lord and eternal Savior, Amen.

A VERY SINCERE EPISTLE TO MARTIN MICRON.

All Scriptures teach and enjoin, honorable Martin, that we should love the Lord, our God, with all our heart, and with all our soul, and with all our strength, and our neighbors as ourselves. On these two commandments, says Christ, hang all the law and the prophets, Matt. 22: 37—40; Mark 12: 29; Luke 10: 27; Deut. 6: 5.

All that Scripture teaches is *love*. "Every one that loveth," says John, "is born of God, and knoweth God. He that loveth not, knoweth not God; for God is love," And, "He that dwelleth in love, dwelleth in God, and God in him," 1 Jn. 4 : 7, 8, 16. Without this love, it is all vain, whatever we may know, judge, speak, do or write, 1 Cor. 13: 1. The property and fruit of love is meekness, kindness, not envious, not crafty, not deceitful, not puffed up, nor selfish. In short, where love is, there is a christian, also.

Since we are pointed to love by the Scriptures, and cannot be christians without love, and as you do not only call yourself a common layman, but also an exemplary teacher; therefore you have done quite wrong not to have taken into consideration the commandment of love, in the fear of God, before you published your false, infamous, ambitious, anti-christian "Narration" and book.

You have manifested yourself before God and man in such a manner as though you had, never in your life, felt and confessed the least particle of the pure, unadulterated nature of love, as I shall show and explain, by the grace of the Lord, in an impartial, sincere conscience, by this my admonition, out of love of the divine honor and the holy word; as also, out of love for your poor soul, that you (if there is yet a spark of life and a faint light left in you), by such showing, written for your own good, may be induced to see your ulcers and deadly wounds, and yet be cured by the heavenly medicine of the Lord's Spirit and word by sincere repentance, to the praise of the Lord and the salvation of your soul. If there be yet any reason left in you, reflect upon what what I tell you.

First, it is manifest, and cannot be successfully denied by you nor by any person else that you have by your writing made a liar of the Almighty, great God, the God of heaven and of earth, the Father of our Lord Jesus Christ, who can neither lie nor deceive; for he testifies of Christ, and says, "This is my beloved Son in whom I am well pleased," Matt. 3 : 17; 17 : 5; Mark 1: 11; 9: 7; Luke 3: 22; 9: 35; 2 Pet. 1: 16; and you say that he is not; for you have verbally confessed to us, and you write so yet at different places, that the man Christ (which you call the human nature in Christ) had no Father.

Observe, whether you are not one of the spirits, of whom John says, "He that believeth not God has made him a liar; because he believeth not the record that God gave of his Son," 1 Jn. 5: 10. Beloved Micron, reflect, and see if I do not write the truth.

Secondly, it is manifest that you have also made a liar of Christ, who is the eternal truth, by your writing; for he confesses more than sixty or seventy times, in John, that he is the Son of God, and that God is his Father; that he came from heaven, and that he was gone forth from the Father; that he is the only begotten Son, &c., and you boldly proclaim to the public, that he is not; that he had no father, according to his humanity; that he is of the flesh and seed of Mary, of earth, and the natural son or seed of Abraham and David.

Observe and see if you are not one of the false teachers and prophets who forsake the Lord who bought them, 2 Pet. 2: 1. Dear Micron, reflect and see if it is not the truth that I write.

Thirdly, it is manifest that by your writing you make false witnesses of the heavenly messenger, the angel of the Most High, Luke 1: 31; of the humble, plain Nathaniel in whom was no guile, Jn. 1: 47; of John the Baptist, the holiest born of woman, Matt. 11: 11; of Martha, the hostess and servant of the Lord, Luke 10: 38; of Peter the faithful shepherd, Jn. 21: 6; John the apostle whom Jesus loved, Jn. 13: 23; 21: 20; and of Paul the chosen vessel, Acts 9: 15. For they all unanimously testify, and that without any division whatever as to humanity and divinity that Christ Jesus is the Son of God; and you publicly proclaim that he is not according to his humanity.

Observe, and see whether you are not a servant of the abominable beast which opened his mouth in blasphemy against God, to blaspheme his name and his tabernacle, and them that dwell in heaven, Rev. 13: 6. Dear Micron reflect, and see if I do not write the truth.

Fourthly, it is manifest that you have made such witnesses of your own brethren who were present at the discussion (and, who, alas, did not know much about the matter), as those were who testified against Christ, Stephen, and Naboth (that is, if your brethren agree with your unjust, partial charges; which I hope they do not); for as those testified, out of hatred of the truth, against the righteous, to please Jezebel and the Scribes, thus these, out of hatred of the truth, testify against me, to please you and those of your faith (I speak of the guilty ones), to defame me thus, notwithstanding that they heard your confession concerning the seed of woman, on which foundation your whole doctrine is built; also, concerning the two Sons in Christ, that the crucified one should have had no father; again, that you could not successfully maintain the purity of your Christ; that you could make no reply to the Scriptures we have read; that you tried to shelter behind an unscriptural question, which we answered in such a manner, that all your refuge was cut off, and that you had to turn from one thing to another. One would reasonably suppose, if they were people of common self-respect who sought the honor of God, and your salvation, as we supposed them to be at first meeting them, that they must charge you before all men that you have, out of mere hatred and envy, spoken partial, devilish falsehoods, and not the impartial, godly truth, to defame your neighbors, and that you have done so to your own eternal shame. But it is an old proverb: "As the shepherd goes, the sheep follow." Christ truly says, "If the blind lead the blind, both shall fall into the ditch," Matt. 15: 14. Dear Micron reflect, and see if I do not speak the truth.

Fifthly, it is manifest that you lamentably deceive all your readers and hearers who believe your writing, and that you kill their poor souls. For it is known to the Lord, who has eyes as a flame of fire, to yourself, and to us all who were present, that in fact your cause was lost; yet you console them with devised lies, as is the way with all false prophets, whereby you rob them, according to John, of both the Father and the Son, 1 Jn. 2: 23; keep them under the wrath and curse, Jn. 3: 36; whereby you keep them out of God, and God out of them, 1 Jn. 4: 15, so that they do not overcome the world, 1 Jn. 5: 4; for they do not believe that Jesus is the Son of God.

Observe and see if you are not one of those who shut up the kingdom of heaven against men, as the Lord says, Matt. 23: 13. Dear Micron reflect, and see whether it is not the truth I write.

Sixthly, it is manifest that you have, with your writing acted toward some of us, and also toward myself personally, not as an honest, virtuous, godly, pious christian, but rather as a dishonest, shameless, indiscreet and blood-thirsty *Corycæus*, or informer. For it is a fact that you have, without the truth, registered a poor, innocent man (whom you well knew), as a teacher, who is no teacher, nor apt ever to become one, whereby you will, perhaps, deprive him or his poor children of their whole welfare, nay, of thousands, if the Lord in his providence does not prevent it. The Spirit of the Lord does not enjoin you thus to act toward the innocent.

Dear Micron, if you would have had a single drop of pious blood in your veins you would have had mercy on the poor, innocent, unworthy servant; whom you thus, alas, repay before the whole world, for his faithful services of love willingly shown you and yours with sincere, christian intentions.

In the same manner you have acted toward the others who furnished you with a dwelling place, victuals and drink, who solicitously led yours into the city, furnished them situations, and showed them all manner of kindness, in pure love. Let the christian reflect and judge according to the Lord's Spirit and word, whether this is the work of unadulterated, christian love, which wishes harm to none, much less does it.

Besides, you have also, nearly pointed out my place of abode which I had enjoyed until that time (of which Herman, also, had to deprive a poor child), while you are well aware that every where they try innocently to take my life, out of mere hatred of the truth. By which doings you surely can not teach unto righteousness, nor instruct the ignorant. And the work in itself does not prove to be the reasonableness and love of a regenerated christian, but it rather shows an unmerciful, cruel, envious, hateful, ravenous, blood-thirsty heart, and the bitter mind of an informer, as all the reading world must judge and say.

Whether you have done this by the merciful, compassionate, faithful, unadulterated and pure Spirit of Christ, as a pious, virtuous man, or by the unmerciful, tyrannical, faithless, false and unclean spirit of anti-christ, as an ungodly and shameless spy, to cause me, an old, afflicted man, some trouble, I will leave to the consideration of your own soul, as before God who tries the hearts and reins, in Christ Jesus.

Observe and see if you are not one of those, who say in their hearts, It is hard for us to see him; for his life does not conform to ours. Dear Micron, reflect and see if it is not the truth I write.

Seventhly, it is also manifest that you encourage and strengthen the rulers in their impenitent lives, not a little, by your writing, who are, as a general thing, quite obdurate, proud, ambitious, puffed up, self-conceited, pompous, selfish, earthly, carnal, and in part, blood-thirsty. And, that you may the more gain their favor and praise, I, miserable man, must be your blind and imprisoned Samson whom you make to play and dance before the princes of the Philistine, as a mockery and derision, although I never, in my life, spoke an indiscreet word against the rulers, or against their office and service.

I have, from the beginning of my ministration, fraternally warned them in my writings in faithful, unadulterated truth, from my soul, against the corruption of their souls; admonished them to a godly, penitent, christian life; pointed them with the Scriptures to the unblamable Spirit, word, commandments, prohibitions, ordinances and example of Christ; and, when you proposed your Pharisaical, Herodian question concerning the Magistracy, I said nothing more to you than that it would hardly become a true, christian ruler to shed blood, for this reason: If the transgressor should truly repent before his God, and be born of him, he would then also be a chosen saint and child of God, a fellow-partaker of grace, a spiritual member of the Lord's body, sprinkled with his precious blood, and anointed with his Holy Ghost, a living grain of the bread of Christ, and an heir to eternal life, and for such an one to be hanged on the gallows, put on the wheel, placed upon the funeral-pile, or in any manner be harmed by another christian, who is of one heart, spirit and soul with him, would look somewhat strange and unbecoming, according to the compassionate, merciful, kind nature, disposition, Spirit and example of Christ, the meek Lamb, which example he has commanded all his chosen children to follow.

Again, If he remain impenitent, and his life be taken, one would do nothing else but unmercifully rob him of the time of repentance, of which, in case his life were spared, he might yet avail himself; do nothing but tyrannically offer his poor soul, which was purchased with such a precious treasure, unto the devil of hell, under the intolerable judgment, punishment and wrath of God, so that he would forever have to suffer and bear the tortures of the unquenchable burning, the consuming fire, eternal pain, woe and death. Never taking into consideration that the son of man, who says, "Learn of me," Matt. 11: 28, I have given you an example, Jn. 13: 15, follow me, Matt. 16: 24, is not come to corrupt souls, but to save them, Matt. 18: 11; Luke 19: 10.

Behold, this was the foundation of my innocent words which I at that time spoke to you in sincerity of heart, according to the style and Spirit of the gospel of Christ, to which words you give this hateful color, before all men, saying, "That I make many pious rulers, murderers of men; that I protect and encourage the rogues in their wickedness." I will leave it to your own judgment what kind of a spirit prompted you thus enviously to write about my plain words. O, Micron, you carry this thing too far. For what else do you do by your writing, but upbraid and blaspheme Christ Jesus himself, whose example I follow in this matter, for pointing to the adulterous woman, who was already adjudged by the law of Moses, to repentance, and letting her go unpunished, Lev. 20: 10; Deut. 22: 22; Jn. 8: 11; as also, faithful Paul, who did no further punish the Corinthian, who, according to the Mosaic and human law, was deserving of death, than with separation, whereby he won him unto God; something which he could not have done had he been killed. Dear Micron, reflect, and see if I do not write correctly.

I do not doubt in the least but that all reasonable men who shall read my writings, if they have any scriptural knowledge at all, will say that I have not spoken unreasonably, but truly and christianly, although I have to hear from you such a base greeting.

Profane history shows that the Lacedæmonians, who were gentiles, did not practice capital punishment; but they imprisoned them and put them at labor. There are instances that when some of them showed natural piety and found them to be wise in counsel, honorable, and master of their passions, were called to high offices. They were not urged by the blood-thirsty spirit of murder, as is the case with some of the preachers and writers who dare boast of the crucified Christ and his office or service, who do not only imprison and take the life of those who are guilty according to the justice of the world, such as thieves, murderers, wizards, &c., but also the sincere, faithful children of God who sincerely seek Christ Jesus and his holy truth, and walk unblamably before the world, to deliver them without mercy into the hands of the blood-stained beadle to be tortured, drowned, burned, or put to the sword, out of mere hatred of the truth, because they shun their deceiving doctrine and false religion, according to the word of God. O Lord!

That I write the truth in regard to this matter, is shown to you and all the world, not only by the Papist and Lutheran writers, but also by the books of your highly esteemed predecessors and brethren, John Calvin, Theodore Weselin Beza, and John A'Lasco, which were prepared to be printed; but by the contradiction of some people, were again recalled.

Beloved Micron, if you and they were born of God, and urged by the Spirit of the Lord; if you had tasted the sweet word of God, and the fruits of the future world, you would never have thus troubled the pious, as you have done by your untrue, false writing; nor would you encourage any body in their bloody doings; but point them to the meek Lamb, and let the dead bury the dead. Ponder upon what I mean.

I cordially agree with you that the office of the magistrates is of God, and that it is an ordinance of God; but I deny that one is, or can be a christian and not follow his Prince, Head, and Predecessor, Christ, but ornaments and decks his unrighteousness, boldness, pomp, splendor, avarice, robbery and tyranny with the name magistrate; for whosoever would be a christian, must follow the Spirit, word, and example of Christ, no matter whether he be emperor, king or anything else, Matt. 22: 21; Rom. 13: 1; 1 Tim. 2: 1; Tit. 3: 1. For these following admonitions apply to all alike: "Let this mind be in you, which was also in Christ Jesus," Phil. 2: 5. "He that saith he abideth in him, ought himself also so to walk, even as he walked," 1 Jn. 2: 6.

Behold, you show by actual facts that you speak and teach to tickle their ears, and the lusts of their hearts, inasmuch as you again point them to the vengeance of the Mosaic law, and not to the longsuffering of Christ, and thus you encourage them in their vain, proud, pompous, and unmerciful, carnal life which is so little in keeping with the life of an innocent, contrite, humble, merciful, compassionate, pious and regenerated christian whose conversation is in heaven, Phil. 3: 20. It is manifest that you are a deadly enemy to their poor souls and do not deal by them as becomes the service of a true messenger of God. For they build the wall, and you daub it with untempered mortar, Ezek. 13: 10. You cry peace, peace, while there is no peace, Jer. 8: 11. Beloved Micron, reflect if it is not the truth I write.

Your unscriptural adulations concerning the oath show that I write the truth. For Christ says, "Ye have heard that it hath bren said by them of old time, Thou shalt not forswear thyself, but shalt perform unto the Lord thine oaths; But I say unto you, Swear not at all; neither by heaven; for it is God's throne: Nor by the earth; for it is his footstool, &c., Matt. 5: 33—35. And you, Micron, say that nothing but lightminded, false oaths are hereby prohibited, as if Moses allowed Israel to swear light-mindedly and falsely; and that Christ, under the New Testament only forbade it; notwithstanding that all intelligent readers know that it was not merely *allowed* Israel to swear truly, but also commanded them to do so, Lev. 19: 12; Deut. 10: 20.

If the Israelites, then, had the same liberty in this matter that we have, as you have it, and if it be such a glorious thing and honor to God rightly to swear by the name of God, as you dare boldly lie against your God, then tell me why the wisdom did not say, You have heard that it hath been said to them of old, thou shalt not forswear thyself, thus I say, Thou shalt do likewise? while he says, Moses commanded not to forswear thyself, but I say unto you, Thou shalt not swear at all. O God, what pity that such plain words of the Son of God are thus lamentably adulterated and daubed over with the foul mortar of serpentile flattery, merely to suit the rulers who are but of dust; as Musculus and you have done! How little you have pondered upon the Scriptures which say, "We ought to obey God rather than men," Acts 5: 29.

Inasmuch as it is very plain that Christ Jesus, the teacher of righteousness, forbids us the oath of Moses, which was also an oath of truth, and sworn by the name of the Lord, which you use and highly recommend to the reader, and commands us to the true, yea and nay; and as I know to a certainty that his word is the truth, and his commandment life eternal; therefore I am sincerely frank and bold thus to teach it, truly believing that he will not deceive us by his doctrine, Jn. 17: 17; 12: 50.

I cordially rejoice that such faithful children in truth are found, who are prepared to seal the holy commandments and testimony of the Lord with their possessions and blood, notwithstanding I have to hear so much on that account, at your hands. Nor am I in the least doubtful but that they, at the day of Christ, will have a part in my crown; for they, for a testimony against you and all the world, suffer for reproving your deceiving, lying hearts and tongues, in faithful love, that you may be brought to reflect; notwithstanding that they, alas, are called such detestable people, by you.

If they were no more faithful to truth than Herman and you have shown yourselves to be towards me, then they would not so valiantly adhere to their true yea and nay, unto death. Of this we are convinced.

As it is manifest that they so faithfully adhere to their undeceiving yea and nay, which Christ has commanded us, Matt. 5: 37; Jas. 5: 12, that they would rather forsake their possessions and life than to transgress this commandment; and their whole mind and life ever conform to this yea and nay, always spoken truthfully, before God and man; and, as these same people are now troubled on that account; therefore I will herewith leave it to the consideration of all impartial, reasonable readers as also to yourselves, whether I and our beloved brethren are deserving of such innocent bloodshed because we lead them by the assistance and power of the Lord, by virtue of the word in the Holy Spirit, from falsehood unto truth, from unrighteousness unto righteousness, from darkness unto light and from the old, sinful life of ungodliness unto the penitent, new life of godliness, to which Moses and Christ, together with all the prophets, apostles, sacrifices, commandments, prohibitions, ceremonies and sacraments unanimously point; or, whether those are deserving of being called deceivers by you, and your like, tickling, and blood-thirsty preachers and writers, who teach the powerful doctrine as taught from the lips of the Lord; and whether all such valiant witnesses and saints of Christ who would rather die than willfully transgress the word of the Lord, or confirm aught further than by yea or nay, are deserving of such treatment, whereby you open the doors wide, to the rapacious rulers to rob such pious souls, and to the bloodthirsty, to murder them.

Dear Micron, if you were one of the true messengers and servants of Christ, as alas, you boldly boast, you would reasonably be expected to point the magistracy who have, as a general thing, high and proud minds and are quite carnal in their life, to the true, sincere repentance which avails before God; and to teach them the Spirit, mind, nature, and word of the Lord; for then the unction itself would teach them, without, even the counsel of man, how they should conduct themselves in regard to the delicate matters of bloodshed, the oath and other matters. But now, alas, things are inverted, that there may be something invented wherewith to charge us before the blind world, and cry that we are unfit to live. O, Martin, your scorpion's sting and lion's teeth are too sharp and envious; for your venomous, deadly stings and bites are, alas, too numerous!

Say, who is wronged because we can not conscientiously swear? because the Lord has forbidden it, if we testify to the truth when required, and make use of no deceit?

The oath is required for no other purpose but that we shall truthfully testify. Can the truth not be told without being sworn? Do all testify to the truth, even, when under oath? To the first question you must answer in the affirmative, and to the last in the negative.

As the oath is not the truth itself to which one testifies, or as the truth is not established by the one that takes the oath, why can not the magistracy, then, accept the testimony confirmed by yea and nay, as commanded of God, instead of that confirmed by that which is forbidden? For they can punish those who are found false in their yea and nay, as well as those who commit perjury by forswearing themselves.

I trust that no person is so confused but he knows that the ordinances of God, which are of heaven, should not give way to the ordinances of men, which are of earth, but that the earthly ordinances of men should give way to God's ordinances, if they would be christians and do according to the truth.

Therefore it would be well for you to observe, first, that you by your writing concerning *the oath* make ignorant or false teachers of Christ, the Son of God, and of his holy apostle James. For Christ's foundation and doctrine is, that Moses had commanded not to forswear thyself; but that under the New Testament one should not swear at all. James says, That we should not swear "neither by heaven, neither by the earth, neither by any other oath," Jas. 5: 12 (mark, he says, neither by *any other oath*), and you gloze it, by the infatuation of the serpent, that it is not so, but that we may swear to the truth, &c. And thus the eternal Wisdom himself, and his holy witness James, alas, must be your disciples and servants.

Secondly, that you condemn the innocent, and clear the ungodly, both of which are an abomination in the sight of the Lord, Prov. 17: 15, whereby you strengthen the hands of the evil-doers, and daub the wall with untempered mortar, Jer. 23: 14; Ezek. 13: 10, as was once said. Beloved, reflect, and see if you are not one of those whose mouths speak great swelling words, having men's persons in admiration because of advantage, Jude 16.

Thirdly, that you cause great tribulation to the pious hearts who are born of the truth and faithfully walk and seal it with yea and nay, with their possessions and blood, and thus load the innocent blood upon yourselves, Rev. 17: 3.

John saw the finely attired whore upon the scarlet colored beast, drunk with the blood of the saints, and with the blood of the witnesses of Jesus. And whether or not you, in your heart, have drank or do drink such a draught of blood with her, I will leave to the omniscient Judge, and to yourself. Dear Micron, reflect, and see if I do not rightly point out your sores.

As you did not fear, but diligently exerted yourself, to adulterate, obscure, and break the Lord's express word, for the purpose of pleasing the magistracy; thus you, also have, alas, exerted yourself to garble my words, as if I had cited the words of David (who does not delight in false doctrine neither has sworn deceitfully, Ps. 24: 4), in my article concerning *swearing*, for the purpose of proving that under the New Testament we should not swear; while I adduced these words for no other purpose, as my words plainly imply, than to show that but little attention was alas, given to the piety implied in the words of said psalm, as is plainly shown by your false, defaming tongue and hand, toward me, poor man, who, alas, has or finds but little consolation from the children of men.

Besides, I had written a note in the margin of the page, in plain words, that it was spoken by David in a spiritual sense; and that under the New Testament we were to use yea and nay, instead. You have spared nothing to make me ridiculous and obnoxious to the reader.

In the same manner, you have not avoided to call me inconsistent, because I wrote that we should not swear at all in regard to temporal matters, because Christ did not use the word *verily*, in worldly matters, but merely in his doctrine, &c. I know of nothing that I wrote which you did not wrongly explain and garble. I wish that you would once consider, in the fear of God, what kind of a spirit it is that thus taught you. My saying that one should not swear at all in worldly dealings, was taught me, not by the flattery of the old serpent, but by the word of the Lord, Matt. 5: 37; Jas. 5: 12.

But that I made an exception in regard to the doctrine, I did it to aid the reader, for the purpose of showing that Paul and Christ did not make use of the terms, *Verily*, and, *God is my witness* (which the learned would construe into an oath for the purpose of making a foundation for their doings), in treating of temporal matters, but in their teachings only.

If this matter is to be strictly weighed in the balance of the holy, divine word, in such a manner as to keep unanimity between all the Scriptures, then it should be observed that the oath and some affirmations are not of the same form, in the Scriptures. For it is manifest, that an oath was always sworn by God, or by something else, and is so sworn yet, which is not the case with an affirmation, as Paul and Christ used in their teaching. Abraham said unto his servant, "Put, I pray thee, thy hand under my thigh; and I will make thee swear (mark) by the Lord, the God of heaven, and the God of the earth," Gen. 24: 2.

Again: "By the life of Pharaoh (mark) ye shall not go forth hence, except your youngest brother come hither," Gen. 42: 15.

Again: "Thou shalt fear the Lord thy God; him shalt thou serve, and to him shalt thou cleave, and swear by his name" (mark), Deut. 10: 20.

Again, Christ says, Neither by heaven, nor by earth, neither by Jerusalem, neither by thy head, Matt. 5: 34, nor by the temple, nor by the altar, Matt. 23: 16, 18. Read also Jas. 5: 12. Again, neither with the world, nor by God, nor by the gospel, nor by a cross, &c.

Behold, thus an oath is always sworn *by* something. But this is not the case with an affirmation which is made without an oath.

An affirmation may be made without an oath; but an oath cannot be made without an affirmation. And thus Christ and Paul often affirmed their words with strong testimony, but did not swear to them. For nowhere did they say, "This we swear or affirm by the truth," or, "By God," or, "By our soul, but solely, *verily*, or, *God is my witness*, and other like affirming words.

As I thus humbly, plainly and strictly abide by the holy word, commandments, and prohibitions of the Lord; and, as I point my neighbors, who would do things in the fear of God, honestly to yea, and nay, as the mouth of Truth has commanded me and all true christians to do; and as I sincerely strive to instruct, according to my small talent, the poor, blind world in the true, divine knowledge, through Jesus Christ without any respect of person, and to point out the falsehood of anti-christ and the old serpent, according to the truth, thus to lead them to eternal peace, by his grace; and as the doctrine shows its fruit in many, as may be seen; therefore it is that they are so enraged at me, that neither Turk nor Tartar, neither tyrant nor fiend under the whole heavens, no matter how ungodly he be, is so hated as I, persecuted man, am hated of the world through this defaming, false, blood-thirsty writing and crying of the learned, who, for the sake of their bellies, teach the broad, easy way, with all the false prophets. He who created me knows what love I bear to you and all my enemies and slanderers. If I could serve you with my life, unto righteousness, I would at all times be willing and prepared to do so, by the grace of God. This I write with a good conscience, as if before God, in Christ Jesus.

Dear Micron, do consider how you, out of mere hatred of the truth, treat me, old, infirm man, quite contrary to all truth, as also contrary to the virtuous, pious nature of the divine, christian love which would curtail nor harm none, to the dishonor of the Almighty, great God. But what will it benefit? The innocent, defenseless Lamb must be hated and murdered in his members.

I will let you teach and counsel (as you will not be convinced) your church, the world, to fight and retaliate as did Moses and the patriarchs, according to your manner; teach them to punish, scatter, imprison and destroy their enemies; to adjudge the criminals, no matter whether they repent or not, as you write. Teach them also to swear and be sworn, after the manner that Moses commanded the Israelites. But I shall and will, by the grace of God, faithfully teach and counsel all truly regenerated children of God, and followers of Christ, both rulers and subjects, according to the sure word of the holy gospel, to use no other sword than the one Christ Jesus and his holy apostles used, to be merciful unto the penitent sinners, as Christ is merciful unto us; mercifully to punish the impenitent, and to admonish them in love, as Christ admonished us; and scrupulously to stand by their yea and nay, as the true Teacher and Executor of the New Testament, the ever blessed Christ Jesus himself, has distinctly commanded and taught us with his guileless mouth; no matter what the consequences to my person may be. Dear Micron, reflect and see if I have not rightly pointed to the Scriptures; and consider, also, by what Spirit you have slandered me. True is the wise man's word: "Who is able to stand before envy?" Prov. 27: 4.

Eighthly, it is manifest that throughout your book you have labored with all your might to make the truth of Christ, taught by us to the measure of our talent, obnoxious and hateful to the reader and hearer, by my person, and to make the falsehood of anti-christ, taught by you, pleasing and taking, by your own person. You have so presented the matter, but alas, not with God's Spirit, that if I had been a tyro in the church for three or four months, I would probably have done about as I now did, according to your untrue, partial writing.

But thus the righteous Lord makes manifest unto the unsuspecting and innocent, the impure Spirit, heart, bitterness, ambition, hatred, envy, falsehood, and infamy, as also their false doctrine of all such people who so cover up their ravenous heart with a sheepskin, as you do, that they can scarcely perceive it. The venomous, deadly arrows and lies directed against me, show to the whole world what kind of a spirit is in you. Now it is Menno's inconstancy, anon, his ignorance, or deceitful intellect, or artful roguery, Menno's lies, &c., and you also say that I should have changed my doctrine. In short, I do not know what you wrote that was not written to the dishonor of God, of the saints, of the truth, of the church and of myself.

I thank my God, with joyful heart, that by his grace he has kept me these twenty-one years in one doctrine and foundation of faith without any change, notwithstanding that I was unworthily called to my hard service, in such perilous, dark, erring times, as all those will admit who have walked with me in Christ Jesus during the time of my pilgrimage; who have from the beginning read my humble works and books, and heard my admonitions.

It may be that I am an ignorant, coarse and unintelligent man, but I have never in my life boasted of great intellectuality, learning, arts and science; but I do boast that I, in my weakness, seek the praise of the Lord, and the salvation of my soul, and that I have learned so much in the school of God, by his grace, that I know that the whole, undivided Christ is God's first and only begotten, and true Son, and that those who contradict this are the spirits of antichrist; that all blasphemers against God, profaners against the saints, adulterers of the Scriptures, willful liars, public defamers, enviers of the pious, ambitious, blood-thirsty men, are ungodly persons, and not christians. Again, that all those who hear and follow Christ, and submissively, obediently and conscientiously follow his word, ordinances and unblamable example in faith, by virtue of the new birth, are the children of God, and that they shall forever inherit the kingdom of honor. I trust that I shall stand before the throne of High Majesty in his grace, with this my gross ignorance, which is wisdom in the sight of God, but hidden from the world, while all high minded and bold hearted, who are so wise in their own sight, shall hear: "I never knew you; Depart from me, ye that work iniquity, Matt. 7: 22. My dear friend Micron, take heed.

Again, I trust that I shall be found innocent before the Lord and his judgment of the charge, *artful roguery*, which you prefer against me; for I have dealt with you with no more artful and roguish heart than those do who, daily for the sake of the testimony of Christ and of their consciences, are, with a glad and joyous mind, martyrized; notwithstanding this I have to hear from you this unkind, false charge made before all the world. But the Lord will be our judge.

Again, as to the charge of falsehood, which you prefer against me, this is my plain answer: I am also concluded in the word, "All men are liars," Ps. 116: 11; Rom. 3: 4. I trust that I would submit to be killed before I should willfully lie, be it slightly or grossly. I hate falsehood. I hated falsehood, even before I knew of whose seed it was. I shall also, in my old age, by the grace of the Lord, avoid it, so far as possible, since I know its origin or father.

O, Micron, Micron, how pecisely do you treat me, as the false prophets and stiff-necked Jews, out of mere hatred of the truth, treated the good Jeremiah, saying, "Come, and let us devise devices against Jeremiah," and not pay attention to his words, Jer. 18: 18. John the Baptist had to hear from the Pharisees and Scribes that he was possessed of the devil; and Christ Jesus was called by them a wine-bibber and glutton, Matt. 11: 19, that he cast out devils in the name of Beelzebub, as they said, Luke 11: 15, that they might by these means lead the ignorant, reckless people from the truth, and keep them in their leaven and vain, false doctrine. Just so you treat me, infirm man, out of mere hatred of the truth. For if you could but daub me with so much filthy falsehood, that they would be affrighted at me, then you would think that the cause of Christ was already lost. Thus blind is poor, foolish flesh which is not overshadowed by the brightness of the Lord.

You may fulfill the measure of your fathers, so long as the hand of God does not intercede, yet I am assured in my heart, by the grace of the Lord, that as Jeremiah, John and Christ remained Jeremiah, John and Christ however much they were belied by their enviers, and persecuted by them, out of hatred against the truth, I also, by the merciful grace and power of God, will remain the same Menno Simon in Christ which I was, in my weakness, for more than twenty years, however infamously you may belie me, and depict or portray me, out of hatred against the truth; as also, that as the false prophets, scribes, and Pharisees were inimical to truth, and were blood-thirsty men, and therefore died without God, you also are without God and his grace, and that you, together with all false hypocrites, will receive your reward, unless you sincerely repent; something of which there is but a very faint hope, because you so willfully suppress the truth in regard to our discussion, tell so many falsehoods, so wittingly adulterate the Scriptures, and act so deceitfully against your neighbor in his absence; something which no regenerated christian will or can do. For the word stands firm. Reflect, and see if I do not truly point out your errors.

Ninthly, it is manifest that you have committed against yourself and your soul which was purchased at such a precious price, the grossest kind of shame and injury; for these reasons, first, because by your writing you have made yourself an open accuser, reprover, nay, teacher and instructor of God the Father, of Christ the Son, of Gabriel the angel, and of all the apostles and saints of the New Testament. The Father confesses Christ Jesus to be his beloved Son, without any division; Christ confesses the Father to be his Father; and the angel and the apostles, together with all the other witnesses unanimously testify the same, in regard to the visible, palpable, dying, and resurrected Christ; and you boldly say and write, that he is not. I will leave you to consider, in the fear of God, whether you are not such an one as I have here written.

Secondly, you prove yourself to be an open corrupter of the Holy Scriptures. For you write, "That Christ is of David's seed, Rom. 1:3; that he is of a woman;" whilst all the unadulterated texts have it: Born of the seed (that is, of the generation) of David. Born of a woman, as may be seen by the Lutheran and Zurian translations.

Thirdly, you write, "That Christ has partaken of the flesh and blood of the children," Heb. 2:14; and the text says nothing more than "flesh and blood" without the addition of, "of the children;" if we accept of the Scriptural meaning of the pronoun, *eorundem*, that is, of the same.

Fourthly, you write at different places, "That Christ has taken on him Abraham's seed" (in *præterito*, that is, in the past tense), while the text says, He *takes on him* (in *præsenti*, that is, in the present tense). Whosoever does not believe it may read the text, Heb. 2:16.

* * * *

Since it is manifest that you have premeditatedly adulterated the holy, divine Scriptures and made yourself a translation and Scripture (as Tatian made himself a gospel, as you write) of your own, that you may the better maintain your anti-christian doctrine before the unsuspicious and ignorant, therefore I will leave it to the judgment of all the impartial, reasonable readers of all the world what kind of a teacher and writer you are.

O, dear Micron, consider to what you have already come. It appears as if you had nearly lost both the Scriptures and common sense by the deadly disease of your ambitious and envious partiality. If you should thus defame his imperial majesty, and his son Philip, as you have defamed the heavenly Father and his blessed Son Christ, in your writing, and should plainly say, No, king Philip is not the son of the emperor; but he is the son of another person, and is only *called* the son of the emperor; if you should, besides, adulterate their public mandates, sentences, and commandments, as you have done the adduced Scriptures, and the plain ordinances, word, and commandments of Christ concerning baptism, and the oath; and moreover, should deride, upbraid, scorn, and belie their sworn courtiers, and faithful servants, because they honored and respected the emperor as the true father of Philip, and Philip as the true son of the emperor, and because they faithfully respected and obeyed their mandates, sentences and policies, O, Lord, what ado there would be made about you, and what blood-songs there would be sung. But of what reward you are now deserving, and must expect in due time from God the Lord, because you so lamentably blaspheme the Emperor of all emperors, the God of heaven and of earth, and his blessed Son Christ Jesus, because you adulterate and break their heavenly mandates, ordinances, and explicit and plain commandments, and because you so lamentably slander, upbraid, belie, hate, and persecute their faithful servants by your indiscreet writing, I will leave to Almighty God and his judgment. Dear friend, ponder upon what is here said.

First, you have made yourself to be an open, perfidious falsifier; for you call on God as a witness (which in my opinion is the same as an oath), that you have given a true narration of the discussion; and the first thing you wrote in your book is an untruth. For you write: "A true Narration." And how quite untrue it is, God knows, as also you yourself, and we. We have also partly touched on this, above, in the description of the discussion.

Secondly, you have quoted in your book my first words and very brotherly admonition: "If you now hear more powerful truths and surer foundation from us than you have heard hitherto, then you ought not to seek your own praise and honor; but you ought cordially to seek the honor and praise of the Lord, &c.," and have coupled a gross falsehood therewith, and rendered it as if I should have said, that you had sought your own honor and praise by your writing, in England. Something which, at that time, I had never thought about; for I knew no more about you than I would have known had you never been in the world. Yet, you garble my words to make it appear so. I will leave yourself to judge whether it was the Spirit of truth and of godly, faithful love, or the spirit of impure falsehood and faithless envy which inspired you thus to write.

Thirdly, you write, "That Herman Backereel had already proved to me that Mary was a daughter of David." It seems that you are not at all ashamed to tell a falsehood, if it can but make your cause apparently true. He who can prove to me, by virtue of the Scriptures that Mary was a daughter of David, must have a Bible and Scripture different from ours; for it can not be found in our Bibles and Scriptures. I asked no proof of you nor of Herman, as it was irrelevant. And now you make it falsely appear that I should have said that she was not, and that Herman proved to me that she was. This is certainly a falsehood.

Fourthly, you write, "That you frequently confessed to us that the Son of God died for us;" while I dare say and testify with a good conscience that you never touched upon it during the whole discussion. But when I asked you at the last discussion, whether you did not still call the man Christ (who you said had no Father) the Son of God? you answered, *yes*. When I asked again, why you called him so, what kind of an answer I received to that question, was related above. Yet you dare falsely write down, "That you frequently confessed it to us," as has been heard.

Though you were not ashamed of telling gross falsehoods against us before men, because you are aware that you can not sufficiently abuse us, in the sight of the world, which is your church; yet one would reasonably expect that you would be ashamed to do so before your God who tries the hearts and reins; and that you would remember that it is written, that "A thief is not so bad as a man accustomed to lies;" "for he can never attain to honor," Eccl. 20: 27, 28; that the lying mouth killeth the soul, Wis. 1: 11; that God will destroy the liars, Ps. 5: 6, and that their part will be in the lake which burns with fire and brimstone, Rev. 21: 8.

Fifthly, you write, "That you maintained the purity of your Christ against us;" while, before the Lord, before you, and before us all, it did not occur otherwise than I related in the narration of the first discussion, concerning the inconsistency that you had an impure Christ.

* * * *

I was also surprised at the fact that there was not sufficient common sense left in you to consider that you might have made it so by your partial writing and gross falsehoods, that many of the readers, and particularly of those present at the discussion, might suspect you of writing falsehoods out of mere partiality, and might thereby leave your church. But the spirit of wisdom, alas, has not kissed the dwelling-place of your soul, nor greeted it with the friendly lips of its truth.

Fourthly, you have also made yourself a very unsteady, wavering and inconstant person, whom one can not overtake on one foundation and doctrine. For, at the time of the discussion you confessed, "That

Christ, from everlasting, was born of the Father; that he was, also, from everlasting, seated, divided, and separated from the Father. Now you have changed yourself, and you write, that he remained in the Father. Mark your first change.

Secondly, you confessed two Sons in Christ; and now you say there is but one; yet, in fact two, if we impartially consider your doctrine.

Thirdly, you confessed that the crucified Christ who died for us, was not God's Son; and now you write that you frequently confessed that he was. Mark your second, and third changes; and yet you write that he had no Father. Whether this is, *Simplex veritates oratio*, the word of truth is plain, as you write, I will leave yourself to consider. It must be admitted that if one can not see lightminded unsteadiness and false duplicity in this, he must be quite unintelligent and blind.

Fourthly, you confessed, "That Christ should not be worshipped according to his human nature;" and now you say, "That he should be." Mark your fourth change; yet you confess that he was an earthly man, of earth, who was born of Adam's seed. If this be not idolatry we may truly say that the Scriptures deceive us.

Whether so many confessions and recallings are consistent with a sincere, pious, constant, and wellfounded teacher and writer (as you want to be), who, out of ambition falsely denies it all, I will herewith leave all impartial readers to judge.

Fifthly, you have made yourself, before all intelligent persons, a very proud, self-conceited, bold and ambitious boaster, because you sing such great triumphs and glory in your book, while it is manifest to God, to yourself and to all who were present that you had already lost the whole point in discussion. It would also be manifest to the whole world, if you had but impartially told it as it happened; for you confessed two Sons in Christ, and that the crucified one was not God's Son, as you, in fact, do yet; whereby you had already finished the discussion. You could not answer a word to all the Scriptures I read, whereby I testified unto you, that the Son of man, the visible, palpable, eating, drinking, suffering, dying, and arisen Christ, was also God's own, true Son, nor could you reply a word to my four convincing answers, with which I overcame your unscriptural question concerning the birth from everlasting, separation, &c., all of which you have left out of your "Narration."

Neither did you say anything about the union of the two sons, which you generally called two natures, in our discussion, which is now your strongest Scripture, although, in fact, it is not found in the whole Bible. For if you had made mention of it at the time of the discussion, you would, by the assistance of the Lord, have received an answer. And, besides, having told such abominable falsehoods, you have changed the order of the discussion, garbled my words, misinterpreted them, abbreviated or added to them, at pleasure, and changed your own, whereby it is manifest before God and man that your discussion with us, and particularly the account thereof, was not prompted by an humble, converted, and contrite heart; not by the Spirit and love of Christ, but by an ambitious, self-conceited, proud, obdurate flesh and mind. I will leave it to the all-knowing God, and to yourself (to whom are best known your seeking) as also, to the pious reader, who walks in the truth, whether this is not the truth. O, friend, teach yourself before you undertake to teach others. Behold yourself, inwardly and outwardly, in the clear mirror of Christ and his holy word, that you may realize what an ignorant teacher and unfit christian you are before God.

Sixthly, you have also made of yourself a false prophet and teacher, a deceiver of men, an apparent hypocrite and ravening wolf in sheep's clothing. Do not take it amiss that I call you such, and tell the truth. For how can you teach a more false doctrine than to teach that God the Father, is not the true Father of the whole Christ; and that the whole Christ is not the true Son of God; to make the angel of God, John the Baptist and all the apostles of God, false witnesses; to make Christ, the eternal truth, a false teacher; for he says, that we shall not swear at all, Matt. 5: 34, and you say that we are allowed to swear to the truth; to make the baptism, which was commanded by Christ, and taught and practiced by his holy apostles, a false baptism; and to want to teach a different doctrine and practice, of which not a word is found in all the Scriptures.

Dear Micron, if you would follow good counsel, you would at once quit your writing. For make it as you will, it is certain that you by your strongest arguments and best points do nothing, in fact, but supersede and teach the eternal wisdom, Christ Jesus, the Son of God, and his Holy Ghost, together with the apostles of Christ; nothing but change their words, doctrine, commandments, institutions, ordinances and practices, as if they in themselves were not essential and right, yea, powerless, vain, and useless, and thereby show that you are their teacher and master. Beloved Micron, take heed. The more you write the more manifest you make your own shame and false doctrine, and the greater you make the guilt of your deceit. My friend, let yourself be warned.

You console the poor, blind people with falsehood, deprive them of both Father and Son, 1 Jn. 2: 22, lamentably adulterate the word of the Lord; from which it is very plain, that you forsake the Lord who has purchased us, 2 Pet. 2: 1, that you are prompted by the Spirit of anti-christ, 1 Jn. 4: 3; that it is anathema, Gal. 1: 8. You teach us a gospel which was not taught us by the apostles of Christ. It shows that you rob God of his honor, and are a murderer of souls, Jn. 10: 1, which Christ Jesus has purchased at such a great price, 1 Pet. 1: 8, a messenger of darkness who transforms himself into an angel of light, 2 Cor. 11: 14.

Do not take it amiss, that I write the truth. I repeat, a ravening wolf in sheep's clothing, Matt. 7: 15, who devours the souls of men by a false explanation of the Scripture, under a fictitious semblance of truth, robs them of the truth, and thus offers and sacrifices them to the prince of hell, for the sake of a woolen rag and a piece of bread. Not to mention that you cause so much trouble to many a chosen saint of God, deprive him of possession, and even of life, by your false doctrine, because you falsely charge, slander, defame, and trample under foot the doctrine, which is the clear, pure, unadulterated, powerful, saving and regenerating doctrine of Christ, as being heresy and deceit, and the faithful children which are thereby converted from unrighteousness unto righteousness, and from the dumb idols unto the living God, as being deceitful, sectarian people, before the erring, blind, and carnal world of blasphemers, blood-preachers, messengers of the devil, blood-thirsty tyrants and covetous robbers.

O, Micron, friend, how good it would be for your poor soul (if you do not sincerely repent) if you had never been born. What have you, miserable man, suffered your ambitious, proud, evil flesh to do, that you, for the sake of a little breeze of vain honor, which you can enjoy but a short time in this confused evil world, have committed such abominable blasphemy against the Almighty, eternal, and great God; have so lamentably defamed his holy apostles and faithful witnesses; so grossly profaned the Lord's word; so deadly deceived the people; so unmercifully caused trouble to the godly and pious, and that you have heaped such great guilt and sin upon your own, poor soul, by your writing. Surely your whole book is nothing but a plain declaration and manifestation of your own shame and anti-christian doctrine, both for the present and future world, which discovers, proclaims, and publishes your abominably great abuse and error unto all men who seek the Lord. Friend Micron, reflect, and see if I do not rightly point out your very dangerous wounds and deadly sores, according to the Scriptures.

Lastly, you have made yourself a shame and dishonor to all the rest of the preachers, who are your fellows in doctrine and service, in the sight of all the pious of the world. For, as you migrated from Flanders to England; from England to Friesland, for the sake of the gospel, as is said; and as you do much writing and disputing, lead a reasonable, civil life before the world; are not particularly considered as an adulterer, wine-bibber or coxcomb; in short, as you are finely clothed in sheep's clothing, &c.; therefore you are probably looked upon and considered as an exemplary person, head, light, or at least, as one of the principal of them. And you are yet in truth found to be, before God and all intelligent persons, such an one as we have partly shown you to be in this epistle, by your own writings, therefore we will let the reader consider in the fear of God, what we should think of the others who are not thus covered with sheep's clothing, but who grasp, eat, drink, and lead a pompous, ostentatious, careless, easy and carnal life, who fear neither God nor devil, who sell the souls of men for a trifle, who gladly accept liens and easy times, and still are in the same doctrine, vocation and service, with you. And what we should do in regard to attending the preaching of both you and them (on which account they would bite their own tongues for madness), I will let every one judge who cordially seeks God, according to the word of the Lord, Matt. 7: 15; 15: 13; 16: 6; Jn. 10: 1; Rom. 16: 16; Gal. 5: 8; 1 Tim. 6: 3; 2 Tim. 2: 3; Tit. 3: 9; 2 Jn. 1: 7; 2 Cor. 6: 14; Rev. 18: 4.

I am very much surprised that the other preachers, part of whom (though they do not want to be upon the narrow path with Christ and his chosen ones), are naturally intelligent, do not reprove you and stop your slanderous writing, as it is a shame to them as well as to yourself; for never was your anti-christian foundation and doctrine concerning Christ, the Son of God, made so manifest, as it was by your bold assertions and blindness, and by my necessary reply thereto. All those that have eyes may see what fearful unbelief and abominable foundation and doctrine you have. Still, you will remain good teachers in the sight of the world; for it is such they seek and desire. John truly says, "They are of the world; therefore speak they of the world, and the world heareth them," 1 Jn. 4: 5.

Behold, dear Micron, I have placed the clear mirror of truth before the eyes of your conscience, and properly dissected the invisible members of your soul. Now open your eyes, and you shall see what kind of a man you are, and how greatly you are spiritually diseased; from which, spring all these obnoxious exhalations, such as upbraiding, lying, defaming, false explanations, adulteration of the Scriptures and flatterings. "For by the law, is the knowledge of sin," Rom. 3: 20, thus this epistle will discover unto you how deadly you are stung by the serpent, and how he has corrupted you, before God, by the accursed venom of his evil nature, and poisoned your whole life.

If the merciful Lord, by his loving kindness, should make you feel and know your abominable shame which you have committed against God and man by your slanderous writing, which, I fear, you have until now, by your great blindness, hatred, ambition, and self-love, but little noticed, then be not dilatory (if you would not die in your ungodliness) in coming before the throne of grace, the ever blessed Christ Jesus, with a broken, contrite, repentant spirit, in an adulterated faith, with a changed, penitent, and new heart; for he is the spiritual, brazen serpent, raised unto all of Adam's children (who are poisoned in Adam) as a wholesome sign. He is the man who can cure you of all the deep wounds of your diseased soul. He is the Physician in Israel. With him alone, is found the ointment and medicine of eternal life. And if you would commit yourself to him and follow his advice, that you may find help and health for your diseased soul, you must give yourself up to him; obey his word, will, commandments and prohibitions; deny your selfish, ambitious, false, partial, envious, vain, wrathful flesh which leads you to this abominably false writing; become little in your own sight; lay a better and christian foundation in your heart; quit your flattering, adulteration of the Scriptures, idolatrous sacraments and all hypocrisy; truly seek and fear the Lord and his holy word, with sincerity of heart; reconcile your neighbors whom you have wronged through pernicious falsehood, with tears, in sincere brotherly love, and by other writings publish to the world that through mere hatred against the truth, you have causelessly still more defamed their name, which was already hated too much for truth's sake; something which, I fear, you will hardly do unless you become a more godly, penitent and pious Micron than you, alas, have been hitherto.

So long as you do not do as here pointed out, it is manifest that you without cause hate your neighbor, and are inimical to him, out of hatred of the truth; and are therefore separate from Christ, with the murderers. O, friend, reflect and repent. Take heed, lest you forever destroy your precious soul for the sake of a little temporary and vain praise! But a short time, and Micron is no more! O, the sentence, Depart from me, ye cursed, into the everlasting fire! Oh, oh, what a sentence!

Friend Micron, in faithful love I warn you. Take heed, I pray you. I have known several persons who were prompted by a like spirit of bitter zeal against the Lamb and his chosen ones, who were adjudged and punished by the Lord, who does justly, and properly rewards the unjust, before the eyes of men.

It is about eighteen or nineteen years since that highly esteemed man, who was much respected by the world (whose name and country I will not mention), wickedly advised that they should destroy me together with the pious. His words and ungodly thoughts were hardly finished until the avenging hand of the Lord was laid upon him. He dropped at the table; and thus in a moment his blood-thirsty, impenitent, ungodly life was ended in a terrible way. O, fearful judgment!

About the same time it happened to another man, who thought that he would so set his trap that I could not escape, that he at the same meal he was eating while speaking these words, was suddenly struck by an arrow from the Lord, stricken with a severe disease, and thus had to give an account before the Lord. He was buried within eight days from the time he spoke these words.

Another who was to become an officer to the emperor at a certain place, thought that he would destroy this people, if there was any virtue in the imperial army. He came to the place where he was to be situated and serve in his capacity; and four or five days thereafter the bell was tolled and the requiem sung over him. Behold, thus God, the Lord, annihilates the designs of the ungodly who storm this holy mount, and destroys those who hate his truth and are inimical thereto.

In the year 1554 three of our brethren were at Wisburg, in Gotland, for the purpose of earning a livelihood. A preacher of the city, named Lawrence, who was of the spirit of his father (the devil), cried after them in the street, hooted at them, and said "That they should not there practice their religion, if it were to cost him all that was surrounded by his clothes," meaning, his body and soul. A few days afterwards he conversed with one of these brethren in the presence of another preacher who was not unreasonably minded. He behaved outrageously. The great Lord, in the presence of both of them, smote him so that he, at once, lost his voice; and within twenty-four hours he was a corpse. O, terrible punishment and judgment of God!

A case almost similar happened the same year at Wismer. They had accepted a crier, named Doctor Smedesteet, who said, "That he would rather have a hat full of our blood than a hat full of our gold." He persuaded the magistracy, who glady hear such makers of pillows, "To proclaim, just before cold winter, to the poor children to clear the place before St. Martin's day; or else they would be put where they would not like to go." Smedesteet was very joyous that he had accomplished the fulfillment of his heart's desire, but to his sorrow; for the same day the Almighty, great Lord laid the hands of his wrath upon him, and within seven days the Lord took him away by a severe illness; yet the blind, obdurate world does not observe these things.

In the year 1555 in the same city there was a preacher named Vincent, who lives there yet, who was never tired of upbraiding and slandering. On the day they call the Lord's ascension-day, he read the Scripture, "He that believeth, and is baptized, shall be saved," Mark 16: 16. He said, "He would upbraid and slander us so long as his mouth would open." The same hour the strong Lord closed it, and bound his tongue. He fell down in the pulpit, and was carried by some of those present as a punished one into his house, a dumb man. Behold, thus he may punish those who would touch the apple of his eye and harm it. If I were to relate all the incidents which in my time befell the enemies of the saints, it would require a separate volume. Therefore I advise you in sincerity of heart, no longer to oppose such a strong and avenging God and Lord. I tell you in Christ that it will be too hard, yes, too hard for you to kick against the pricks, Acts 9: 5. For his name is Sovereign Lord, Mighty Prince, Isa. 9: 6. "Who is like thee, glorious in holiness, fearful in praises, doing wonders?" Ex. 15: 11. His arrows never miss, and when he calls we must appear. None can escape from him, and avoid his wrath. O, Micron, take heed.

Good friend, if your battle was against me, as you perhaps think it is, you would already have won it. For the whole world, in this matter, is on your side, nay, the serpent himself, and against me; for this foundation is the only weapon, according to the doctrine of John, which is to conquer his kingdom, the world. But the battle is not against me, but against the truth itself, against the Father and his blessed Son, against the whole Scriptures, and against those who dwell in heaven. Therefore take heed. For, although the reckless, rough world may say amen to your cause, yet it will not be the case with the Most High, whose glory, honor, truth and testimony I, according to my small talent, uphold, by his grace and assistance.

And if you do even deprive me of my honor, reputation, body and life, which I have already long deemed of little consequence, for Christ's sake, in the sight of the world, which are not concluded under Christ's prayer, Jn. 17: 9, though, thank God, I have never harmed you, nor wished you any harm. Still, God the Father will remain the true Father of Christ, and Christ the true Son of God; and you will have to turn from your impure, anti-christian doctrine to the unadulterated, pure doctrine of Christ, or else you will be one of those of whom it is written: "He that believeth not is condemned already, because he hath not believed in the name of the only begotten Son of God," Jn. 3: 18. Neither partizanism nor disputing will prevail against God and his word. He is the one who will have the praise, and his word is the doctrine which will remain the truth. If you do not believe that Jesus Christ is the Son of God, that his testimony and word are true, and that his ordinances are the true ordinances; if you be not born of God; do not become of divine disposition and nature; are not urged by and possessed of the Holy Ghost; do not sincerely repent; if you be not in Christ, nor Christ in you, then, according to the doctrine of John, you are one of those who have no God, 1 Jn. 2: 22.

But if you have Christ, if you actually believe that he is the true Son of God, then you have both the Father and the Son, 1 Jn. 2: 24; and you will walk as he walked, you will not willfully tell a falsehood; for you are born of the truth; you will not hate; you will not defame; you will not inform against your neighbors; and you will wrong no person. You will seek the salvation of others, and not their corruption; you will reprove their sins; you will rightly teach, and not deceive them, for the spirit of love which does justly by God and man will dwell in you and prompt you.

If you have Christ, in truth, you will walk in the light, Jn. 3: 21; 8: 12; you will follow the true shepherd, and will enter in at the right door, Jn. 10: 2; you will walk upon the true road; remain in the truth, in the right vineyard, Jn. 15: 1; build upon the true rock, Eph. 2: 20; 1 Pet. 2: 5; you will not adulterate the word of God; for your spirit is one with the Spirit of Christ; your faith will be one with his word, and your life, though in weakness, one with his life.

You will seek the praise and honor of the Lord, and not your own; you will confess Christ as your Savior, at the risk of life or death by all the world; all your pleasure will be in the law of the Lord, and your whole life in his fear; your thoughts will be pure, and all your words well-seasoned; your daily combat will be against the world, the devil, and your own evil flesh; and you will, by your honest, virtuous life, set an example to all the world; the cross, taken upon yourself for the sake of the Lord's word and testimony, you will patiently bear; and, if you should thoughtlessly think, say or do any thing wrong, you will sincerely lament it. In short, you

AN EPISTLE TO MARTIN MICRON.

will prove by all your actions that you are a chosen child of God, born of the heavenly seed of the holy Word, and that you are become a live member of the body of the Lord.

Behold, dear Micron, such penitence and and reformation I sincerely wish you; and I would like to see it truly manifest in you, in power and truth, and that I then, for the sake of the testimony of Jesus, together with you, would have to make a sacrifice of my blood, to the praise of the Lord, and to the edification of our neighbors. I repeat it, repent, that the precious treasure, given for us, be not lost in your case.

I would herewith commend you to Almighty God. He will bestow upon you according to his great grace, as I would like to see you receive. No more hereafter, however much you may cry and write, unless you be converted into a better mind, and I constrained and urged to do so by the godfearing.

Nor shall I hereafter solicit a public discussion with any person, and that for this reason, first: Because I have these many years, desired it by numerous written and verbal requests, and have never been granted it. From which it is manifest that they care but little about the glory of God, and the souls of men.

Secondly, because your principal teachers and exemplary men, as John A'Lasco, Calvin, and Theodore Beza, whom you confess to be your most worthy and most beloved brethren, are men of blood. That this is the case is testified to by their own books, as also by old Seructus of Geneva, and Joris of Paris, who was burned in England.

Thirdly, because your brethren, the Welsh church, as they are called, at Frankfort have, in their publications, sworn against us; which two things we did not so positively know heretofore as we do now.

Inasmuch as I plainly see that there is but deceit, faithlessness, blood-thirstiness and perverseness found among the children of men wherever one may turn himself; and as nothing does, nor can avail on earth but the praise of Christ and the salvation of souls; therefore I will let Babylon, with its false preachers, impure doctrine, idolatrous baptism and supper, together with its false religion, and impenitent, vain, easy life, be Babylon, and will, with the holy prophet Habakkuk, stand upon my watch, and set me upon the tower, and thus clearly sound the trumpet of the holy, divine word from the walls and gates of Jerusalem, according to my small talent and faithfully awaken the citizens of the eternal peace, joyfully to sing the lovely Hallelujah through the streets, with grateful, joyous hearts, to the honor of God, Heb. 2: 1; to attire themselves, before God and the world, in the shining, white raiment of the saints, in sincerity of heart and purity of doctrine. I will faithfully admonish them with careful, pious Esdras and say, My people, hear my word, and prepare yourselves for the battle, and evil things, &c., 4 Esdras 16: 41. With holy Paul, "Take unto you the whole armor of God, that you may be able to withstand in the evil day," Eph, 6: 13. And with Christ himself: Watch and pray, Matt. 24: 42; Mark 13: 33; Luke 21: 36; 1 Pet. 4: 7. For the prince of darkness with his whole force and kingdom, besieges the city of God, storms by night and day, uses many means, with flesh and blood, as falsehood and false doctrine, lusts of the eye, imprisonment, banishment, confiscation, bloodshed, tyranny and violence. Whosoever does not constantly pray, and fear the Lord, can not stand.

I will let Babylon be Babylon. Those who are piously inclined will leave off their ungodliness and wed themselves to Christ; for truth is revealed, and the repast is prepared. Blessed is he who enters in with sincerity of heart, and saves his wedding garment. I would sincerely warn all the chosen children of God, the sincere faithful brethren and sisters of Christ, with beloved John, our most beloved brother and fellow in tribulation, in the kingdom and in the patience of Jesus Christ, and say, children, "Love not the world, neither the things that are in the world. If any man love the world, the love of the Father is not in him. For all that is in the world, the lust of the flesh, and the lust of the eyes, and the pride of life, is not of the Father, but is of the world; and the world passeth away, and the lust thereof; but he that doeth the will of God, abideth forever," 2 Jn. 2: 15—17. Friend Micron, again be warned; repent, pray to God for grace, and earnestly reflect upon that which I have written. And be not angry because I have thus sharply reproved you. I have done so truthfully, and to the honor of God, and to the benefit of the reader, as I reprove the whole world, without respect of person, that you may rightly learn the brightness of Christ, see and feel your foul sores, be healed by the Lord's medicine, sincerely repent, and be eternally saved. I herewith commend you to the gracious, merciful God and Father, for the enlightenment of your blind soul, and the reformation of your sinful life, by his blessed, first-born, and only true Son, Christ Jesus, by the manifestation of his eternal Holy Ghost unto more righteousness. "Open rebuke is better than secret love. Faithful are the wounds of a friend; but the kisses of an enemy are deceitful," Prov. 27: 5, 6.

MENNO SIMON.

October 16th.

A HUMBLE PRAYER TO THE READER.

IT is an old proverb, dear reader, that "Many men have many minds." Every person, generally judges according to his own ideas, whereby many an unjust and wicked sentence is rendered, especially where blind partiality has its sway.

Since I find that our opponents, with their false doctrine cannot stand before the power of the holy, divine word, and since they diligently try so to defame and calumniate us, and so garble our words, that we, with truth on our side, are rejected by the world, and they, with falsehood on their side, are honored by the world; therefore I pray all impartial readers not to be offended at their saying, "Menno has not truthfully written this or that."

In accordance with the doctrine of Christ, I rejoice in being called a liar by the liars. I trust that those who are born of the truth shall not charge me with falsehood; for I have chosen truth for a mother, more than twenty-one years, since. I also desire, in my weakness, to walk in her ways as an obedient, faithful child, without looking back and without offense, so long as I remain on earth. Of this my hand and mouth, my humble life, together with my tribulation, poverty, privation, misery, cross and death shall be witness against my enemies, at the judgment of Christ. Take heed.

I deem it impossible literally to describe those parts of the discussion which Micron has suppressed or misinterpreted, just as it happened. Nor have the holy apostles and evangelists who described the actions and doctrine of Christ, by the inspiration of the Holy Ghost, done so. For the one describes the same occurrence this way, and the other that way. It sufficed them to show the foundation of truth; so it does me. I do not desire to wrangle about a word. I only care about showing to the the reader that the crucified Christ Jesus is God's first-born and only begotten, true Son; and to show that Micron has given quite an untrue account of the discussion, and that he has deceived his readers by open falsehood.

Secondly, I pray them not to take it amiss that I also referred to John A'Lasco. It was not done through hatred nor dis-favor; but zeal for the glory of God and of Christ his Son, and for the honor of eternal truth, and for the sincerely desired salvation of your souls, have urged me to do so; because Micron says, "That they are of one mind in doctrine," and I do not see that one could believe, teach, write, speak, hold, or feel more abominably concerning the crucified Christ than he does in his defense against me. Besides, I hear that he, also, is become a man guilty of blood, notwithstanding he verbally confessed to me that none should be harmed on account of the faith.

But now, as I hear, it is claimed that it was not on account of faith, but on account of disobedience. As the foundation is quicksand so are their assertions. Let the rulers command things in keeping with the gospel of Christ and neighborly love; and if we refuse to obey them, then we are culpable. I will leave it to the judgment of all reasonable rulers, as before God in Christ, whether it is in accordance with, or contrary to the Scriptures, to expatriate the poor souls because they fear God; confess the crucified Christ to be God's Son; receive the holy baptism according to the commandment of the Lord and the doctrine of the apostles; affirm their testimony by yea or nay, in accordance with Christ's command, and because they lead a penitent, pious life in righteousness, &c.

I am aware that there are many unsuspecting hearts who look more to John A'Lasco and to the learned than they do to Christ and his apostles; therefore I have also referred to his errors in regard to this matter that all godfearing readers may see what kind of writers and teachers *they* are who are so highly esteemed and whose names are considered so worthy.

Thirdly, I pray that none will accept my saying that I will no longer solicit a public discussion, in such a sense as meaning that I have no courage to do so. This is not the meaning I wish to impart. But I do not desire, to discuss publicly nor privately with such people as those to whom I referred in my epistle; nor with such as dishonestly adulterate, change, break and misinterpret my words and testimony, and slander us as did Micron from the beginning to the end of his writing. For I generally find myself deceived by them on all hands, as it is the nature which would lead an easy life and not take up the cross of the Lord.

But if any rulers should be troubled at heart concerning the Scriptures and be suspicious of their preachers and teachers, and would ask me to a public discussion for the sake of finding out the truth, it would be as glad a tiding to me as I could hear on earth; nor would I, I trust, be dissuaded nor prevented by the godfearing, to whose hands and counsel I always willingly commend myself. For we are sure that we have the Scriptures and truth on our side.

Fourthly, I pray them not to take it as upbraiding and slandering that I sometimes handle Micron roughly, according to the truth. It was done for no other purpose than that he and his followers may acknowledge their deceiving, lying spirit, through such earnest admonitions which are in keeping with the foundation of Scripture, that they may take a dislike to their abominable doings, and thus renounce their evil ways; as, also, that all the unsuspecting, good hearts which are bound by their snares of unrighteousness, may be delivered to the praise of the Lord.

It was done in the same spirit which actuated the holy apostles and prophets, which actuated Christ himself, in their several reproaches. If any one now should reprove me of pithiness, they must first reprove Christ and his messengers. For it is they who have, in the Holy Scriptures, thus taught me and all teachers who follow and uphold the right.

All those who have a scriptural understanding, know that where we find mention made in the Scriptures of the despising of, and blasphemy against God we also find added the sentence and sharp rebuke of the Holy Ghost.

Inasmuch as it is manifest that Micron is not ashamed to fasten one falsehood upon another, to make a translation to suit himself; to deny the testimony of God, the Father of Christ Jesus, his blessed Son, of the angel Gabriel, together with that of all the other witnesses of the New Testament; to flatter the rulers; to seek the favor of men, and to deceive the poor souls for which the Lord's blood was shed; therefore it surely is not wrong to call him by such names as are applied to him in the Scriptures by the Holy Ghost. The truth must have its course, and does not respect emperor nor king; much less a false prophet or teacher, who advocates the cause of the serpent; perverts the testimony of God into falsehood; and, for the sake of vain honor, and of his lusts, strengthens the ungodly, and troubles the saints. Whosoever has sound judgment and knows the way of the Holy Ghost in the Scriptures, must say that I am right.

Fifthly, I pray that no person will think that I thus write to retaliate Micron's writing. O, no. I leave wrath to him who is judge of all the world. I have done so to the service of Micron and all the erring, that they may be converted, and give becoming praise and honor to Christ, the Son of God, Deut. 32: 35; Heb. 10: 39; 1 Pet. 2: 3, 23; 3: 9. The truth is presented to them, by the grace of God, in such power and clearness that no man can disannul it by virtue of the Scriptures, nor contradict it by virtue of intellect. Therefore it would be well if our opponents would behold it more clearly, that they may, with all the saints, flee from the future judgment, and that they may, in the day of his appearance, stand before the throne of his Majesty in eternal joy.

If they do not, but refuse, remain obdurate and partial; if they repay good with evil, and love with hatred; if they seek assistance from the worldly powers, since they are too weak in the Scriptures, and thus watch for the corruption and misfortune of the pious, by falsehood and ornamented inventions, as has, alas, been the case hitherto, with many, then we must leave them to the Lord, possess our souls in patience, and remember the saying of Christ: "For so persecuted they the prophets which were before you," Matt. 5: 12.

Lastly, I would faithfully warn all my readers and hearers, both great and small, rich and poor, favorable and unfavorable, as before God, and sincerely pray them in Christ Jesus, to read impartially this our incontrovertible, thorough answer and explanation; and rightly to weigh it in the balance of the holy, divine word, and to compare it with the fictitious foundation and doctrine of our opponents, that they, enlightened by the truth, may find the true way to life.

Let none believe me; but believe the truth which I have, according to my small talent, placed before you in invincible power and clearness, according to the pure doctrine of the holy apostles, evangelists, prophets, and of Christ himself. In Christ, be warned. Your poor souls are lamentably deceived by the doctrine of our opponents; for it is the smoke from the bottomless pit, Rev. 9: 2, which obscures the bright Sun, Christ Jesus, and the air of his holy word; it is the falsehood of the old serpent; its egg and brood; he that eateth it dieth, and that which is crushed breaketh out into a viper, Isa. 59: 5; it is the spiritual dung with which Ezekiel had to bake his bread, Ezek. 4: 12. In short, it is the horrible, abominable draught of the golden cup of the Babylonian whore, drunken with the blood of the saints, with which she has made drunk all who dwell in the earth, Rev. 17: 4.

Their doctrine and confession stand clear and manifest, that the crucified Christ Jesus, was not the true Son of God; for they say he had no Father, and is only called so on account of their fictitious union; they reject the baptism of Christ; they rage and blaspheme against it, and institute a different baptism which is neither taught nor commanded them by the Scriptures. The difference between the oath of Christ and Moses they deny, and say, we are allowed to swear to the truth, that it is a holy thing, &c., Matt. 5: 34. Let him who is intelligent, understand what we have explained in both our book and epistle.

John says, "The Word was made flesh," Jn. 1: 14. Paul says, "Great is the mystery of godliness. God was manifest in the flesh, justified in the Spirit, seen of angels, preached unto the gentiles, believed on in the world, received up into glory," 1 Tim. 3: 16. Because we sincerely confess this testimony, as also all others which confess the visible, palpable, crucified Christ to be the Son of God, to be true and just; therefore we must, alas, be called by the world, sectarians and heretics. It is time to beware. Kind reader take heed. God grant you his grace, Amen. Read attentively and judge impartially, Amen.

A PLAIN

AND

CONVINCING PROOF,

FROM THE SCRIPTURES,

THAT

JESUS CHRIST IS THE TRUE, PROMISED, SPIRITUAL DAVID, THE KING OF KINGS, THE LORD OF LORDS, AND THE TRUE, SPIRITUAL KING OF SPIRITUAL ISRAEL, THAT IS, OF HIS CHURCH WHICH HE HAS BEGOTTEN AND BOUGHT WITH HIS OWN BLOOD. FORMERLY WRITTEN TO ALL THE TRUE BRETHREN AND FELLOW-CHRISTIANS, SCATTERED HITHER AND THITHER, AGAINST THE ABOMINABLE AND TERRIBLE BLASPHEMY OF JOHN VAN LEYDEN, WHO PASSED HIMSELF FOR THE JOYOUS KING OF ALL, AND AS HAVING BECOME THE JOY OF THE MISERABLE; HE PLACED HIMSELF IN THE STEAD OF GOD.

BY

MENNO SIMON.

"For other foundation can no man lay than that is laid, which is Jesus Christ," 1 Cor. 3:11.

ELKHART, INDIANA:
PUBLISHED BY JOHN F. FUNK AND BROTHER.
1871.

TESTIMONY AGAINST JOHN VAN LEYDEN.

Grace, peace, and mercy, from God the Father, through Jesus Christ, be with all true brethren and fellows scattered hither and thither.

THE eternal, merciful God, who has called us from darkness into his marvelous light, nay, who has led us into the kingdom of his beloved Son, Jesus Christ, must keep us upon the right way, that Satan by his wiles does not deceive us, and that no root of bitterness spring up among us to make confusion, and many be thereby made unclean, as is, alas, now the case to some extent. And thus it must be that sects will arise amongst us that the tried may be made manifest, 1 Pet. 2: 9; Col. 1: 13; Heb. 11: 15; Deut. 29: 18; 1 Cor. 1: 18.

Let none be offended thereat. But let all give heed to the word of God, and abide by it, that they may be delivered from the strange woman, as Solomon says (by which woman we should understand all the false teachers), "Even from the stranger which flattereth with her words; which forsaketh the guide of her youth, and forgetteth the covenant of her God," Prov. 2: 16; 4: 6, 7. This is the true nature of all false teachers.

First, they forget the pure doctrine of Christ, and choose a strange doctrine. They enchant others so that they can not believe the truth, and use smooth talk, as Paul says, "By good words and fair speeches they deceive the hearts of the simple," Rom. 16: 18.

Secondly, they leave their Master, Christ, whom alone, they should hear, as the Father testifies of him, saying, "This is my beloved Son in whom I am well pleased. Hear ye him," Matt. 17: 5; Mark 9: 7; Luke 9: 35. But this voice from the Father, all false teachers forget, and they leave their only Master, Christ Jesus; for as they are not of his sheep they hear not his voice, Matt. 23: 9; Jn. 10: 26.

Thirdly, the false teachers forget the covenant of God; and that to which we should give most heed, they pay no attention, as Christ reprovingly said unto the Pharisees, "Ye pay tithe of mint, and anise, and cummin, and have omitted the weightier matters of the law, judgment, mercy, and faith: these ought ye to have done, and not to leave the other undone. Ye blind guides! which strain at a gnat and swallow a camel," Matt. 23: 23, 34; and as Paul said, "The end of the commandment is charity, out of a pure heart, and of a good conscience, and of faith unfeigned; from which some having swerved, have turned aside unto vain jangling; desiring to be teachers of the law; understanding neither what they say nor whereof they affirm," 1 Tim. 1: 5—7. Thus all false teachers forget the covenant of God whereby they are bound to him, as is, alas, the case with many at present, who have forgotten all upon which they were baptized, namely, the cross, and would recommend and make use of the sword. May the Almighty God save all true christians from this, and may he give them wisdom and intelligence to keep the covenant of God, and to be always mindful of what kind of a spirit Christ wants his disciples to be, Luke 9: 55.

Grant that they may be aware of this strange woman; for her house is inclined to death, and her ways to corruption. All those who enter in unto her, will not come out again, nor do they get on the way of life. And this strange woman now reigns extensively, and as she deceives many, as did and yet does the prophetess Jezebel, and as the serpent deceived Eve; therefore we will, by the grace of God, discover some things, that those who are yet blind may become seeing, and that when they acknowledge anti-christ to be an abomination standing in the holy place, they may see all deceit, Rev. 2: 20; Gen. 3: 13; Matt. 24: 15;

Mark 13: 14; Luke 21: 7; Dan. 9: 17; Rev. 17: 18. And that, as they will not drink of the cup of the Babylonian whore, they may beware of the venom of the serpent, and that if they be bitten by the serpent, they may become aware of it and get rid of the venom by looking on the true serpent, and be thus cured. All of which God must give us, Num. 21: 6; Jn. 3: 14.

We should not have written, but it becomes necessary; partly because we can not tolerate the shameful deceit and blasphemy against God, that a man be placed in Christ's stead; partly, because we are not allowed a verbal, scriptural defense against such deceit and abominable heresy concerning the promised David, and other articles. But it is the nature of all impostors and erring spirits to flee from the word of God, as Christ says, "For every one that doeth evil, hateth the light, neither cometh to the light, lest his deeds should be reproved. But he that doeth truth cometh to the light, that his deeds may be made manifest that they are wrought in God," Jn. 3: 20, 21. Therefore, he that flees from the light, that is, from the word of God, manifests that his deeds are not wrought in God.

But if there are some who can not yet see this they need the eyesalve which is spoken of in the revelation of John, Rev. 3: 18. O, God, what perilous times these are! How the prophet Baal conspires with the Moabite king, against the Israel of God! Num. 24; 25.

The Egyptian sorcerers, how they stand against the true Moses! Ex. 6.

The lying Pashur, how he is heeded, because he prophecies prosperity, of which nothing is realized! Jer. 20; 2 Tim. 3.

How the false Hananiah deceives the pious children of Israel, and makes them trust in falsehood! Jer. 28.

The Almighty God shall raise a Jeremiah to reprove the deceiver of the people, who shall speak nothing but that which God commands him to speak, and the Lord will place his word in the mouth of this Jeremiah, as a fire, and all false teachers as stubble, that truth may prevail, Jer. 1: 17.

And if ever so many prophets of Baal be raised, yet the Lord will leave behind a Micron who shall promulgate the true word of the Lord. But sufficient of this. We shall commence the matter to the honor of God, and to the edification of the church.

In the first place. It is incontrovertible that Almighty God has made his Son, Christ Jesus our Lord, King of all the earth and of his faithful church. That Christ is the King of all the earth is abundantly testified to by the Scriptures; particularly the prophet David, who says, "The Lord most high is terrible; He is a great king over all the earth," Ps. 47: 2; and, "God is gone up with a shout, the Lord with the sound of a trumpet. Sing praises to God, sing praises, sing praises unto our King, sing praises. For God is the King of all the earth: sing ye praises with understanding. God reigneth over the heathen; God sitteth upon the throne of his holiness," Ps. 47: 2, 5—8.

Therefore, as true as Christ is God, so true he is King of all the earth.

Paul testifies this to the Ephesians, saying, that God, the Father, "raised him from the dead, and set him at his own right hand in the heavenly places, far above all principality, and power, and might and dominion, and every name that is named, not only in this world, but also in that which is to come. And he hath put all things under his feet, and gave him to be head over all things to the church," Eph. 1: 20—22.

Christ testifies of himself that he is a mighty King, saying, "All power is given unto me in heaven and in earth," Matt. 28: 18. Paul says that Christ is the express image of God, upholding all things by the word of his power, Heb. 1: 3.

Thus Christ is the king of all the earth notwithstanding the wicked may deny it. Therefore the prophet says, "The Lord reigneth; let the people tremble; he sitteth between the cherubim; let the earth be moved," Ps. 99: 1. Still they can do nothing more than the Lord allows them to do, Jn. 19: 11; and none can withstand him. The mountains melt as wax before the Lord, the ruler of all the earth, Ps. 97: 5.

Further, that Christ is king of his believing church is clearly testified to by the Scriptures. Thus speaks Isaiah, "Unto us a child is born, unto us a Son is given, and the government shall be upon his shoulder and his name shall be called Wonderful, Counselor, The Mighty God, The everlasting Father, The Prince of peace. Of the increase of his government and peace there shall be no end," Isa. 9: 6.

The house of Jacob is the believing church as is generally understood. Of this, Christ is king, as the angel clearly testified; and as Jeremiah says concerning Christ, that he would be a king who should reign and prosper, Jer. 23:5. Also Isaiah says, "Behold, a king shall reign in righteousness, and princes shall rule in judgment," Isa. 32: 1.

As Christ is king, both of all the earth and of his believing church, as we have shown by the plain Scriptures, according to the grace received of God, how can John Van Leyden, now, call himself a joyous king of all, who is become the joy of the miserable?

If he would be our king, our Lord, then Paul and Isaiah must stand back. Paul says, "For though there be that are called gods, whether in heaven or in earth (as there be gods many, and lords many), but to us there is but one God, the Father, of whom are all things, and we in him; and one Lord Jesus Christ, by whom are all things, and we by him," 1 Cor. 8: 5. Isaiah says, "The Lord is our judge, the Lord is our law-giver, the Lord is our king," Isa. 33: 22.

Behold, as true as Christ is our judge, and as sure as he is our law-giver, so sure is he our king. Where, now, is John Van Leyden? O, abominable blasphemy against God, that a man should call himself the joyous king of all! while it is written, O Lord, Lord God, Creator of all things, who art fearful, and strong, and righteous, and merciful, and the only and gracious King," 2 Mac. 1: 24; who alone art good, who alone art a mighty king, who alone art righteous, omnipotent, and eternal, who deliverest Israel of all evil. Paul says, "I give thee charge in the sight of God, who quickeneth all things, and before Christ Jesus, who before Pontius Pilate witnessed a good confession: that thou keep this commandment without spot, unrebukable, until the appearing of our Lord Jesus Christ; which in his time he shall show, who is the blessed and only Potentate, the King of kings, and Lord of lords," 1 Tim. 6: 13—15. Again, it is the greatest blasphemy a man can speak, that John Van Leyden asserts that he is become the joy of the miserable.

Christ became our joy at his birth, according to the testimony of the angel to the shepherds, saying, "Behold, I bring you good tidings of great joy, which shall be to all people. For unto you is born this day, in the city of David, a Savior, which is Christ the Lord," Luke 2: 10, 11; with this the words of David accord, "Light is sown for the righteous, and gladness for the upright in heart. Rejoice in the Lord, ye righteous; and give thanks at the remembrance of his holiness," Ps. 97 : 11, 12. "Make a joyful noise unto the Lord, all ye lands. Serve the Lord with gladness; come before his presence with singing, know ye that the Lord he is God: it is he that hath made us, and not we ourselves: we are his people, and the sheep of his pasture," Ps. 100: 1—3. "Rejoice in the Lord alway: and again I say, rejoice," Phil. 4: 4. Thus all the Scriptures admonish us that we shall rejoice in Christ, our Lord; for it is he of whom the patriarch Jacob prophesied that he would be the expected one of the people, that is, the one for whom the people of God should look with great desire, as Christ also testifies, "Your father Abraham rejoiced to see my day; and he saw it, and was glad," Jn. 8: 56.

Christ is the true Melchisedec, king of Salem, that is, the king of peace; who has made peace between God, the Father and the human race, Heb. 7: 1. He is the pious Isaac who by his sacrifice has reconciled us with his heavenly Father; and his sacrifice remains worthy forever, Heb. 10: 10; 9: 12. He is the true David, who has slain the great Goliath, and has taken away the blasphemer of Israel, 1 Sam. 17: 49; Eccl. 47: 4. Yea he has caused great rejoicing, as it is written, "The Spirit of the Lord God is upon me (says Christ), because the Lord hath anointed me to preach good tidings unto the meek; he hath sent me to bind up the broken hearted, to proclaim liberty to the captives, and the opening of the prison to them that are bound; to proclaim the acceptable year of the Lord, and the day of vengeance of our God; to comfort all that mourn; to appoint unto them that mourn in Zion, to give unto them beauty for ashes, the oil of joy for mourning, the garment of praise for the Spirit of heaviness," Isa. 61: 1—3; Luke 4: 18, 19. Behold, how clearly it is shown here that Christ is become the joy of the miserable, in whom all pious christians rejoice, saying, Rejoicing we will rejoice in the Lord; our souls shall be rejoiced in the Lord; for he has clothed us in raiments of righteousness, and surrounded us with the mantle of righteousness, as a bride ornamented with bracelets. To this the prophet Zechariah admonishes us, saying, "Rejoice greatly O daughter of Zion; shout, O daughter of Jerusalem; behold, thy King cometh unto thee; he is just, and having salvation; lowly, and riding upon an ass, and upon a colt, the foal of an ass," Zech. 9: 9; Matt. 21: 2. And the king's prophet David, says, "Sing unto the Lord a new song, and his praise in the congregation of saints. Let Israel rejoice in him that made him: let the children of Zion be joyful in their king. Let them praise his name in the dance; let them sing praises unto him with the timbrel and harp," Ps. 149: 1—3.

Thus did all the saints of God, as did David, who says, "Our soul waiteth for the Lord; he is our help and our shield. For our heart shall rejoice in him; because we have trusted in his holy name," Ps. 33: 20, 21. And, "Lo, this is our God; we have waited for him, and he will save us; this is the Lord; we have waited for him, we will be glad and rejoice in his salvation," Isa. 25: 9. By this we may see how all the saints have rejoiced in God. And how can we rejoice in man, as it is written, "Put not your trust in princes, nor in the son of man, in whom there is no help. His breath goeth forth, he returneth to his earth; in that very day his thoughts perish. Happy is he that hath the God of Jacob for his help, whose hope is in the Lord his God," Ps. 146: 3—5; who helps the miserable, and raises up the crushed. "He is their mighty protection and strong stay, a defense from heat, and a cover from the sun at noon, a preservation from stumbling and an help from falling. He raiseth up the soul, and lighteneth the eyes, he giveth health, life, and blessing," Eccl. 34: 16, 17.

As Christ is become our joy, so every one may judge for himself what an abomination it is in the sight of God, that a man would be that which our Savior, Christ is. Is it not an abominination standing in the holy place? And what is worse yet, this John Van Leyden is not satisfied with passing himself for the joyous king of all, who is become the joy of the miserable; but he also claims to be the promised David of whom all the prophets testify; and does not admit that Christ is he who was promised.

Of such a mind are all false prophets and anti-christs. That they have on their heads names of blasphemy, and crowns like unto gold, by which is meant pride, as may be seen by the Babylonian whore who was arrayed in scarlet color, having a golden cup in her hand, full of abominations and filthiness of her fornication; for she saith in her heart, I sit a queen, and shall see no sorrow, Rev. 17: 4; 18: 7. But the Lord can not tolerate it, and says, "Babylon, the glory of kingdoms, the beauty of the chaldees' excellency, shall be as when God overthrew Sodom and Gomorrah," Isa. 13: 19. Therefore, shall her plagues come in one day, Rev. 18: 7. And not Babylon alone, but also all anti-christs, together with their deceit and false writings, shall be destroyed, as Christ says, "Every plant which my heavenly Father hath not planted, shall be rooted up," Matt. 15: 13.

And greater anti-christ than he is who passes himself for the promised David, can not make his appearance, which promised David is Christ, as the Scriptures abundantly testify. He that hath ears to hear let him hear.

First, the prophet Hosea says, "For the children of Israel shall abide many days without a king, and without a prince, and without a sacrifice, and without an image, and without and ephod, and without a teraphim; afterward shall the children of Israel return and seek the Lord their God, and David their king, and shall fear the

Lord, and his goodness in the latter days," Hosea 3: 4, 5.

It is incontrovertible that this king David can be none other than Christ Jesus, whom all must seek who want to be saved, as it is written, Seek the Lord and ye shall live, Amos 5: 4. Isaiah says, "Seek ye the Lord while he may be found, call ye upon him while he is near," Isa. 55: 6. For this reason David says, "I sought the Lord and he heard me, and delivered me from all my fears," Ps. 34: 5. And Christ, the wisdom of God says, He that findeth me findeth the life, and shall have the pleasure of the Lord. And what other king should the children of Israel have than Christ Jesus, the true Melchisedec, king of Salem, which is, King of peace? Heb. 7: 1; of whom the whole number of disciples have testified thus: "Blessed be the King that cometh in the name of the Lord; peace in heaven, and glory in the highest," Luke 19: 28; 2: 14.

The Jews despised this King, Christ, and therefore they were blinded, yet they shall return and come to Christ, their King David, as Paul testifies, saying, "That blindness in part is happened to Israel, until the fullness of the gentiles be come in. And so all Israel shall be saved: as it is written, There shall come out of Zion the Deliverer, and shall turn away ungodliness from Jacob. For this is my covenant unto them, when I shall take away their sins," Rom. 11: 26; Isa. 59: 20. As Israel is yet to be converted unto Christ, it follows incontrovertibly that the King David, whom Israel shall seek, can be no other than Christ.

Therefore every righteous person will understand in what terrible error those are who do not believe that by David, we should understand Christ, but another man. And of such, Christ says, "I am come in my Father's name, and ye receive me not; if another shall come in his own name, him ye will receive," Jn. 5: 43. But those who with Jerusalem, will not receive Christ, will also be destroyed with it; and those who, with the Pharisees, oppose Christ, and yet think that they are enlightened, should also be blinded with the Pharisees. Let all pray to God for wisdom, and they shall understand that Christ is the true David, Luke 19: 7: Isa. 6: 10; Jn. 9: 12.

Again, Jeremiah says, "It shall come to pass in that day, saith the Lord of hosts, that I will break his yoke from off thy neck, and will burst thy bonds, and strangers shall no more serve themselves of him: But they shall serve the Lord their God, and David their king, whom I will raise up unto them," Jer. 30: 8, 9.

Now the commandment of the Lord is, "Thou shalt worship the Lord thy God, and him only shalt thou serve," Matt. 4: 10. Therefore this king David is none but Christ, which the Father has raised unto us, saying, Yet have I set my king upon my holy hill of Zion. And the christian church acknowledges no other king, no other Lord but Christ. Therefore all the saints say, "The Lord is our defense; and the Holy One of Israel is our King," Ps. 89: 18. Now who is the Holy One but he of whom Isaiah testifies, saying, "For thus saith the high and lofty One that inhabiteth eternity, whose name is Holy," Isa. 57: 16. And "These things saith he that is holy, ... he that hath the key of David," Rev. 3: 7. Thus speaks Jeremiah concerning Babylon, "Recompense her according to her work; according to all that she hath done, do unto her; for she hath been proud against the Lord, against the Holy One of Israel," Jer. 50: 29.

Thus the Holy One of Israel is none but the true God and Lord, Christ Jesus; therefore none can be the King of his believing church, but Christ, as the Spirit of God testifies through the prophet Micah, saying, "The Lord shall reign over them in mount Zion, from henceforth, even forever," Micah 4: 7; who else is this Shepherd but Christ, of whom was prophesied, "Behold, the Lord God will come with strong hand, and his arm shall rule for him; behold, his reward is with him, and his work before him. He shall feed his flock like a shepherd; he shall gather the lambs with his arm, and carry them in his bosom, and shall gently lead those that are with young," Isa. 40: 10, 11.

Christ testifies of himself that he is this shepherd, for he says, "I am the good shepherd; the good shepherd giveth his life for the sheep," Jn. 10: 11. Christ truly pastures his sheep; he is the door to the sheep-fold; all who enter into the fold through him, shall be saved; he shall go in and out, and find good pasture. Therefore David says, "The Lord is my shepherd; I shall not want. He maketh me to lie down in green pastures: He leadeth me beside the still waters," Ps. 23: 1, 2; and the apostle Peter says, "For ye were as sheep going astray, but are now returned unto the Shepherd and Bishop of your souls," 1 Pet. 2: 25. Further, the Lord God says, My servant David shall be a Prince among them. Let none be offended at God the Father, calling his Son Christ, servant, saying, "Behold my servant, whom I uphold, mine elect, in whom my soul delighteth," Isa. 42: 1; and at another place: "Behold my servant, whom I have chosen; my beloved, in whom my soul is well pleased," Matt. 12: 18; at still another place, the Father speaks concerning Christ, "By his knowledge shall my righteous servant justify many," Isa. 53: 11.

Therefore this servant David is Christ; and he is the Prince of the christians. And who else should be a prince of the church of Christ, but Christ, as Paul testifies that he alone is the Prince; and as the prophet says, "Thou Bethlehem Ephratah, though thou be not the least among the thousands of Judah, yet out of thee shall he come forth unto me that is to be ruler in Israel; whose goings forth have been from of old, from everlasting," Micah 5: 2.

The Lord further speaks through the same prophet, "So shall they be my people and I will be their God, and David my servant shall be King over them; and they all shall have one Shepherd," Ezek. 37: 24. We have heretofore clearly proven by the Scriptures that God the Father has placed no other king over Zion, than his Son Jesus Christ, and that he gave him an eternal kingdom, therefore it is needless to go over this again; and that God the Lord says, "David my servant shall be King over them, and they all shall have one shepherd," is also understood to be said in regard to Christ; for no man can be our only shepherd; and although God gives "some, apostles; and some, prophets; and some, evangelists; and some, pastors and teachers," Eph. 4: 11; yet the only Shepherd is Christ, and nobody else, as may be plainly understood from the words of Christ, "Other sheep I have, which are not of this fold; them also I must bring, and they shall hear my voice; and there shall be one fold and one shepherd," Jn. 10: 16.

All the believing are the sheep of Christ and there is but one fold, of which Christ is the Shepherd. From this it must follow that Christ is the only Shepherd, and that no one else can be the only Shepherd. For this reason Peter calls Christ, the chief Shepherd; and Paul says, "Now the God of peace, that brought again from the dead our Lord Jesus, that great Shepherd of the sheep through the blood of the everlasting covenant, make you perfect in every good work to do his will," Heb. 13: 20; 1 Pet. 5: 4.

Thus Christ is the only Shepherd; for all the believing must hear his voice and the voice of no other. From this it follows incontrovertibly, that he is also the promised David, according to the words of the Lord, "David my servant shall be King over them; and they all shall have one Shepherd." Besides this God says, "My servant David shall be their Prince forever." I trust that none are so ignorant (unless he be mad, and accursed), as to understand these words as having reference to some man, that a man shall be our eternal Prince. For it is written that God alone is eternal, and alone immortal, and that he dwells in a light to which none can come. No man can be our eternal Prince; but Christ is our eternal Prince, and his kingdom is an eternal kingdom, as it is written, "Thy throne, O God, is forever," Ps. 45: 6; Heb. 1: 8. Paul and Peter say that Christ's kingdom is eternal; and the angel said to Mary, "The Lord God shall give him the throne of his father David, and he shall reign over the house of Jacob, forever, and of his kingdom there shall be no end," Luke 1: 33. Again the prophet says, "His seed shall endure forever, and his throne as the sun before me. It shall be established forever as the moon, and as a faithful witness in heaven," Ps. 89: 36, 37. From this all must be convinced that our eternal Prince is none but Christ, therefore our promised **David** is none but Christ.

Fourthly, it reads thus in one of the Psalms, "Then thou spakest in vision to thy Holy One, and saidst, I have laid help upon one that is mighty; I have exalted one chosen out of the people. I have found David my servant; with my holy oil have I anointed him," Ps. 89: 19, 20. Who is this mighty one on whom God laid help, but Christ Jesus who has all power in heaven and on earth, to whom God has submitted all things and to whom are committed all things pertaining to the church? Matt. 28: 18; Heb. 2: 8; Eph. 1: 22.

On this Christ, the Almighty God has laid help; for we are helped and saved by him as Christ says, "If the Son therefore shall make you free, ye shall be free indeed," Jn. 8: 36; and Paul says, "For what the law could not do, in that it was weak through the flesh, God sending his own Son in the likeness of sinful flesh, and for sin, condemned sin in the flesh," Rom. 8: 3.

Christ is the strong Samson who broke the jaw bones of the lion; he is the pious David who slew the great Philistine with whom none of the Israelites dared fight; he is the chosen one, whom the Father has chosen as his own Son, saying, "Behold, my servant whom I have chosen," Matt. 12: 18. This chosen one the Father has exalted from out the people, inasmuch as he has placed him as King of his holy mount Zion, as the Prince who shall rule his people; for this reason the church acknowledges him to be their head, and to be the most exalted of men on earth, saying, "As the apple tree among the trees of the wood, so is my beloved among the sons. I sat down under his shadow with great delight, and his fruit was sweet to my taste," Cant. 2: 3. Further the Lord says, "I have found my servant David; with my holy oil have I anointed him," Ps. 89: 20.

This anointed David is Christ; for he is the truly anointed of the Lord to whom God the Father speaks, "Thy throne, O God, is forever; a sceptre of righteousness is the sceptre of thy kingdom; thou hast loved righteousness, and hated iniquity; therefore God, even thy God, hath anointed thee with the oil of gladness above thy fellows;" Christ says, "The Spirit of the Lord is upon me, because he hath anointed me." Peter also says, "God anointed Jesus of Nazareth with the Holy Ghost and with power," Heb. 1: 8, 9; Ps. 45: 6, 7; Luke 4: 18; Acts 10: 38.

If any one should yet be in doubts (something which is impossible, in view of such plain Scripture), then let him consider the following words, "He shall cry unto me, Thou art my Father, my God, and the Rock of my salvation. Also I will make him my first-born, higher than the kings of the earth," Ps. 89: 26, 27. Christ is the first-begotten Son of God, as Paul says, God the Father has predestinated us to be conformed to the image of his Son, that he might be the first-born among many brethren. And to the Hebrews, "When he bringeth in the first-begotten into the world, he saith, And let all the angels of God worship him," Heb. 1: 6; Rom. 8: 29.

Therefore, as true as Christ is the first-begotten Son of God, so true he is the servant David whom the Father anointed with the holy oil, that is, with his Holy Ghost.

Again, the Lord says concerning his servant David, "My mercy will I keep for him forevermore, and my covenant shall stand fast with him. His seed also will I make to endure forever, and his throne as the days of heaven," Ps. 89: 28, 29. This seed is the children; for it further reads: If his children forsake my law. Now it is manifest that this should not be understood as having reference to the carnal children of the figurative David; for they committed themselves to idolatry, and quite forsook the law of God. For this they were often punished, and, at last, cut from the olive tree as unfruitful branches, Rom. 11: 21.

Nor did the worldly kingdom of David remain unbroken; but it was destroyed; as the holy patriarch Jacob, and other prophets prophesied. And to understand it as having reference to the carnal children of David, is contrary to the epistle of Paul to the Romans, as he there says, "For they are not all Israel, which are of Israel. Neither, because they are the seed of Abraham, are they all children: but, in Isaac shall thy seed be called. That is, they which are the children of the flesh, these are not the children of God; but the children of the promise are counted for the seed," Rom. 9: 6—8;

therefore we should not understand this seed as having reference to the carnal children, but to the spiritual seed, of which it is written: When my servant shall have given his life as a sacrifice then he shall have seed and live long. This seed are all the true children of God, which are born again, "not of corruptible seed, but of incorruptible, by the word of God," 1 Pet. 1:23.

Christ says, "Behold I and the children which God hath given me," Heb. 2:13; and these children of God abide in eternity, eternal joy and peace shall be upon them: they shall always reign with Christ, and Christ their King has an eternal kingdom, and his throne shall be as the days of heaven. This psalm quite agrees with the words of the prophet Nathan, which he spoke unto David promising him Solomon. As we must not understand the words of the prophet Nathan as referring to Solomon alone, but rather as referring to Christ (although the words in a literal sense are spoken in reference to Solomon), thus we should not understand the words of the psalm as referring to carnal David alone, but rather to the true David, Christ Jesus. And this the following text strongly implies, which speaks of the peace of Christ. This is our confession of the promised David.

We might, by the grace of God, write a great deal more to show that Christ is our promised David; but we presume that sufficient has been written for the intelligent. We do not serve the contentious. Let them cry. Let them make unto themselves a different king, yet Christ will remain the eternal King reigning in his believing church. He is the Lord. He will not give his glory to another. He will have incense which shall be sanctified unto him. And whosoever shall make such incense unto himself, his soul shall be rooted out from Israel, Ex. 5.

None shall succeed in exalting himself to Christ and opposing truth. They may make a disturbance, but Moses and Aaron will gain the victory. Jannes and Jambres must give way and be shamed, 2 Tim. 3:8. Korah, Dathan and Abiram may rise against Moses, but they shall perish with their confederates, Num. 16:32.

A proud Uzziah may rise and appropriate the glory which is not due him, but he will be smitten of God, 2 Chron. 26:16.

Hophni and Phinehas may for a time make the people transgress, and turn them from the true religion, but they shall obtain their reward, 1 Sam. 2:12; 4:11. Let every one take heed and remain in Christ. Sufficient of this.

By the grace of God we will also write a little about warfare, that christians are not allowed to fight with the sword, that we may unanimously leave the armor of David to the carnal Israelites; and the sword of Zerubbabel to those who build the temple of Zerubbabel in Jerusalem, which was a figure of them and a shadow of things coming. For the body itself is in Christ as Paul says, Col. 2:9.

Now we should not understand that the figure of the Old Testament is so applied to the truth of the New Testament, that flesh is understood as referring to flesh; but the figure must answer the truth; the image, the being, and the letter, the Spirit.

If we take this view of it we shall easily understand with what kind of arms christians should fight, namely, with the word of God, which is a two edged sword, of which we will, by the assistance of God, say a few words, Heb. 4:12; Eph. 6:17.

Whereas the eternal God has raised his Son Christ, a Prophet unto us whom we shall hear; and whereas Christ testifies of himself that he is our only Master, therefore it is incontrovertible that we dare not accept any other doctrine but the doctrine of Christ. No *strange* doctrine, which is contrary to the doctrine of Christ and that which the apostles by the Holy Ghost have written and taught unto us, I say, we dare accept, Deut. 18:15; Acts 3:22; 7:37; Matt. 23:9. For there may be no strange fire offered unto God. Christ will not tolerate the leaven of the Pharisees, Lev. 10:1; Matt. 16:8.

Moses had to make the cherubims of pure gold, Ex. 25:18. "The words of the Lord are pure words; as silver tried in a furnace of earth, purified seven times," Ps. 12:6.

The Lord does not suffer his doctrine to be adulterated; he punishes all false doctrine, as he spoke about Jerusalem, "Thy silver is become dross, thy wine mixed with water," "and I will turn my hand upon thee and purely purge away thy dross," Isa. 1: 22, 25; thus God hates all false doctrine; and therefore the apostles admonish us that we shall abide in God's word alone, as John says, "Let that therefore abide in you which ye have heard from the beginning. If that which ye have heard from the beginning shall remain in you, ye also shall continue in the Son, and in the Father," 1. Jn. 2: 24. Paul says that we should beware of those who raise contentions and are offended at the doctrine which he preached, that they should be separated. Yea, so strongly does Paul urge his doctrine that he says, "If any man preach any other gospel unto you than that ye have received, let him be accursed," Gal. 1: 8. Thus Paul teaches in all his epistles to beware of a strange gospel, and to abide in the doctrine which is not his, but of the Holy Ghost, according to the words of Christ, "For it is not ye that speak, but the Spirit of your Father which speaketh in you." Now the Spirit of God speaks thus through Paul, "My brethren, be strong in the Lord, and in the power of his might. Put on the whole armor of God, that ye may be able to stand against the wiles of the devil. For we wrestle not against flesh and blood, but against principalities, against powers, against the rulers of the darkness of this world, against spiritual wickedness in high places. Wherefore take unto you the whole armor of God, that ye may be able to withstand in the evil day, and, having done all, to stand. Stand, therefore, having your loins girt about with truth, and having on the breastplate of righteousness; and your feet shod with the preparation of the gospel of peace. Above all, taking the shield of faith, wherewith ye shall be able to quench all the fiery darts of the wicked; and take the helmet of salvation, and the sword of the Spirit, which is the word of God," Eph. 6: 10—17; 1 Thess. 5: 8. At another place: "For the weapons of our warfare are not carnal, but mighty through God to the pulling down of strongholds; casting down imaginations, and every high thing that exalteth itself against the knowledge of God, and bringing into captivity every thought to the obedience of Christ. And having in a readiness to revenge all disobedience, when your obedience is fulfilled," 2 Cor. 10: 4—6. He that is not blind will understand with what weapons the christian is to fight, namely, with the word of God; with this they should be well armored. For thus speaks the holy church: "Behold, his bed which is Solomon's; threescore valiant men are about it, of the valiant of Israel; they all hold swords, being expert in war; every man hath his sword upon his thigh because of fear in the night," Cant. 3: 7, 8; that is, each one is armed with the sword of the Spirit against all the wiles of the devil, against all false doctrine. Concerning Christ it is written, "Gird thy sword upon thy thigh, O most Mighty, with thy glory and thy majesty. And in thy majesty ride prosperously, because of truth and meekness, and righteousness; and thy right hand shall teach thee terrible things. Thine arrows are sharp in the heart of the king's enemies; whereby the people fall under thee," Ps. 45: 3—5.

Here the Scriptures say that Christ shall have a sword. What sword now shall Christ have? This he himself tells in the "Revelation," in these words, "Repent; or else I will come unto thee quickly, and will fight against them with the sword of my mouth," Rev. 2: 16.

If Christ fights his enemies with the sword of his mouth, if he smites the earth with the rod of his mouth, and slay the wicked with the breath of his lips; and if we are to be conformed unto his image, how can we, then, fight our enemies with any other sword? Does not the apostle Peter say, "For even hereunto were ye called, because Christ also suffered for us, leaving us an example, that ye should follow his steps: who did not sin, neither was guile found in his mouth: who, when he was reviled, reviled not again; when he suffered he threatened not; but committed himself to him that judgeth righteously?" 1 Pet. 2: 21—23; Matt. 16: 24. This accords with the words of John who says, That he that abides in Christ, walks as Christ walked. Christ himself says, "Whosoever will come after me, let him deny himself, and take up his cross, and follow me," Mark 8: 34; Luke 9: 23. Again, "My sheep hear my voice ....and they follow me," Jn. 10 27. And this is the voice of Christ, "Ye have heard that it hath been said, "An eye for an eye, and a tooth for a tooth: But I say unto you, that ye resist not evil: but whosoever shall smite thee on thy right cheek, turn to him the other also."

Again, "Ye have heard that it was said, Thou shalt love thy neighbor, and hate thine enemy: But I say unto you, Love your enemies, bless them that curse you, do good to them that hate you, and pray for them which despitefully use you, and persecute you; That ye may be the children of your Father which is in heaven, for he maketh his sun to rise on the evil and on the good, and sendeth rain on the just and on the unjust. For if ye love them which love you what reward have ye? Do not even the publicans the same? And if ye salute your brethren only, what do you more than others? Do not even the publicans so? Be ye therefore perfect, even as your Father which is in heaven is perfect," Matt. 5: 39, 43—47; Rom. 12: 20; 1 Pet. 3: 9; Luke 6: 34; 1 Pet. 1: 15. Behold this is the voice of Christ. All those now who are his sheep will hear his voice. But those who are not his sheep will not hear his voice, as Christ said unto the Pharisees, "Ye believe not because ye are not of my sheep." The Pharisees thought they had Moses and the prophets, they also had a semblance of holiness; but they did not hear the voice of Christ, therefore it was all in vain. Thus it is with all those who do not submit themselves to the commandments of Christ.

It is not in the leaves of the tree, but in the fruit. And which is the right kind of fruit, Paul clearly testifies, saying, "The fruit of the Spirit is love, joy, peace, long-suffering, gentleness, goodness, faith, meekness, temperance," Gal. 5: 22, 23. Here we are not taught to take up the carnal sword, or to repay evil with evil. But rather as Paul says at another place, "Recompense to no man evil for evil. Provide things honest in the sight of all men. If it be possible, as much as lieth in you, live peaceably with all men. Dearly beloved, avenge not yourselves; but rather give place unto wrath: For it is written, Vengeance is mine; I will repay, saith the Lord. Therefore if thine enemy hunger, feed him; if he thirst, give him drink; for in so doing thou shalt heap coals of fire on his head. Be not overcome of evil, but overcome evil with good," Rom. 12: 17—21. And how can christians fight with the implements of war? Paul plainly says, "Let this mind be in you, which was also in Christ Jesus," Phil. 2: 5. Now, Christ Jesus was minded to suffer; thus, all christians must be so minded.

Christ did not suffer Peter to defend him with the sword; how can a christian, then, defend himself with the sword? Christ would drink the cup which the Father had given him; how then, can a christian refuse to drink it? Matt. 26: 51; Luke 22: 50; Mark 14: 47; Jn. 18: 11.

Or does any person expect to be saved by other means than those which Christ has taught us? Is not Christ the way, the truth, and the life? Is he not the door to the fold, so that none can enter into the fold but by him? Jn. 10: 9; 14: 6.

Is he not the Shepherd of his sheep, whom the sheep should follow? Is not he our Lord and Prince? And who is it that would be above his Master but he that would not suffer, as he has suffered. Who is it that would be above his master but he that is not satisfied with his Master's doctrine? Let every one take heed. It is forbidden us to take up arms, Matt. 10: 24; Jn. 13: 16; 15: 20.

Paul says, "Put them in mind to be subject to principalities and powers, to obey magistrates, to be ready to every good work, to speak evil of no man, to be no brawlers, but gentle, shewing all meekness unto all men," Titus 3: 1, 2. And the holy apostle James says, "Be patient, therefore brethren unto the coming of the Lord. Behold the husbandman waiteth for the precious fruit of the earth, and hath long patience for it, until he receive the early and latter rain. Be ye also patient; stablish your heart; for the coming of the Lord draweth nigh. ...... Take, my brethren, the prophets, who have spoken in the name of the Lord, for an example of suffering, affliction, and of patience. Behold, we count them happy which endure. Ye have heard of the patience of Job, and have seen the end of the Lord; that the Lord is very pitiful, and of tender mercy," Jas. 5: 7—11. If we are to be longsuffering until the coming of the Lord, then it is, surely, forbidden to fight inasmuch as the Lord is not yet come.

And if we are to take the prophets as an example to bear with persecution, then we must put on the apostolic armor, and the armor of David must be left behind. How would it comport with the word of God, that one who boasts of being a christian, should lay aside the spiritual weapons and take up the carnal ones, for Paul says, "The servant of the Lord must not strive; but be gentle unto all men, apt to teach, patient; in meekness instructing those that oppose themselves; if God peradventure will give them repentance to the acknowledging of the truth. And that they may recover themselves out of the snare of the devil, who are taken captive by him at his will," 2 Tim. 2: 24—26.

All of you who would fight with the sword of David, and be the servants of the Lord, consider these words, which show how a servant should be minded. If he is not to strive, how can he war? If he is to be gentle to all men, how can he then hate them and do evil unto them? If he is to be apt to teach, how can he lay aside the apostolic weapons? If he is to teach he will need them. If he is to instruct in meekness those that oppose, how can he destroy them?

If he is to instruct in meekness those that oppose truth, how can he angrily punish those that do not yet acknowledge the truth? Paul says, if God peradventure will give them repentance. But some will not wait for that, and if they even do it with good intention, still they with Uzzah lay their hands on the ark of God. Therefore I fear that it will not be left unpunished. And if they with Saul, even saved the best beasts of the Amalekites, for sacrifices unto God, yet it will not please the Lord; for it is contrary to his word. He has pleasure in obedience and not in sacrifices.

But now some say, the Lord wants to punish Babylon, and that by his christians; they must be his instruments. O, God! It would be well if we would leave the Lord to do his works, and remember the words of Ecclesiasticus: "Seek not out the things that are too hard for thee, neither search the things that are above thy strength. But what is commanded thee, think thereupon with reverence; for it is not needful for thee to see with thine eyes the things that are in secret. Be not curious in unnecessary matters," Eccl. 3: 21—23.

For many things are shown men above their understanding, and presumption has caused many to fall, and held their understanding in vanity. It would also be well for those who ask, with the disciples of the Lord, when the kingdom of Israel is to be restored, to observe the answer of the Lord: "It is not for you to know the times or the seasons, which the Father hath put in his own power," Acts 1: 6. But this they forget, and cry: God will shortly punish and destroy Babylon. To do this the christians must be his instruments; and this they make the simple believe; for which reason we will adduce some Scriptures. It is true that God will punish Babylon, but not by his christians; for thus speaks Jeremiah: "The Lord hath raised up the spirits of the kings of the Medes; for his device is against Babylon to destroy it; because it is the vengeance of the Lord, the vengeance of his temple." Again: "Prepare against her the nations, with the kings of the Medes, the captains thereof, and all the rulers thereof, and all the land of his dominion. And the land shall tremble and sorrow: for every purpose of the Lord shall be performed against Babylon, to make the land of Babylon a desolation without an inhabitant," Jer. 51: 11, 28, 29.

I am aware that this was fulfilled against Babylon, in the Chaldee country, though the Roman Babylon shall not escape the same plague; but I have adduced this for the service of the advocates of the sword who want to prove by this Scripture of Jeremiah, that the christians shall punish Babylon, while the prophet clearly testifies that God has done this by heathen hands, and that it is his will that it shall be done by such, as is shown by Rev. 17: 16: "The ten horns which thou sawest upon the beast, these shall hate the whore, and shall make her desolate and naked, and shall eat her flesh, and burn her with fire. For God hath put in their hearts to fulfill his will, and to agree and give their kingdom unto the beast, until the words of God shall be fulfilled."

Thus it may be plainly understood from these words that the Babylonian whore shall be destroyed, not by christians; as also, that christians should not destroy. A Theudas may rise up and cause a disturbance, but he shall not succeed, Acts 5: 36. There may rise up a Judas Galilee and cause a riot, but he shall perish, and all his followers shall perish and be scattered. Let every person beware and diligently observe the Scriptures, and he shall see that the Lord himself will destroy, at his coming again, and punish all his enemies who will not submit to him. For Luke says, "It came to pass, that when he was returned, having received the kingdom, then he commanded these servants to be called unto him, to whom he had given the money, that he might know how much every man had gained by trading;" and when his servants had given an account, he said, "But those mine enemies which would not that I should reign over them, bring hither, and slay them before me," Luke 19: 15, 27.

This Scripture clearly testifies that the Lord Christ, must first come again, before all his enemies are punished. And how Christ will come again he himself testifies, saying, "For the son of man shall come in the glory of his Father, with his angels; and then he shall reward every man according to his works," Matt. 16: 27. Again, "For as the lightening cometh out of the east, and shineth even unto the west; so shall also the coming of the son of man be." "And then shall appear the sign of the son of man in heaven: and then shall all the tribes of the earth mourn, and they shall see the son of man coming in the clouds of heaven, with power and great glory," Matt. 24: 27, 30; Mark 13: 26; Luke 17: 24. The two angels also testified how Christ would come again, saying, "Ye men of Galilee, why stand ye gazing up into heaven? This same Jesus, which is taken up from you into heaven, shall so come in like manner as ye have seen him go into heaven," Acts 1: 11. From this it is plain to everybody how Christ shall come; therefore, when ye shall see Christ come in this manner then you may rest assured that all the enemies of God will be punished; and do not suppose that it shall be so before his coming again, for you will find yourselves mistaken; or else God's word must be false, which is impossible. Luke also says, that the Lord had received the kingdom.

Of this Daniel says, "I saw in the night visions, and behold, one like the son of man came with the clouds of heaven, and came to the Ancient of days, and they brought him near before him. And there was given him dominion, and glory, and a kingdom, that all people, nations, and languages, should serve him: his dominion is an everlasting dominion, which shall not pass away, and his kingdom, that which shall not be destroyed," Dan. 7: 13, 14. Here observe of whom Christ receives this kingdom, that you may see what abominable deceit it is that some say that John Van Leyden would take the kingdom, and that he who has taken it will give it unto Christ, as David gave the kingdom unto Solomon.

Further, the evangelist says, That Christ will take account with his servants, which will not be until the day of judgment; Paul says, "We must all appear before the judgment seat of Christ; that every one may receive the things done in his body, according to that he hath done, whether it be good or bad," 2 Cor. 5: 10. Jesus says, "That every idle word that men shall speak, they shall give account thereof in the day of judgment," Matt. 12: 36. Then the faithful servants shall enter into the kingdom of their Lord; then shall the wicked be punished, and all whose names are not found written in the book of life will be cast into the lake of fire; for they would not confess Christ to be their king, but worshipped the beast and his image, Rev. 20: 15; 13: 8.

This parable some adulterate, and say, "The enemies of God must be destroyed before the coming of Christ, and therefore we will be the instruments to do so." But they must come to shame; "For thus saith the Lord God, the Holy One of Israel; In returning and rest shall ye be saved; in quietness and in confidence shall be your strength: and ye would not. But ye said,

No; for we will flee upon horses; therefore shall ye flee; and we will ride upon the swift; therefore shall they that pursue you be swift," Isa. 30: 15. O, that the advocates of the sword would observe these words! Yea, those who would be angels to root up the tares! while Christ told the parable with a different understanding, saying, "The good seed are the children of the kingdom; but the tares are the children of the wicked one; the enemy that sowed them is the devil, the harvest is the end of the world; and the reapers are the angels," Matt. 13: 38, 39. Inasmuch as the christians are the good seed, how then can they be the angels or reapers; or if they be the reapers, how can they be the seed? These two are quite different things, the seed and the reapers; its plainness is incontrovertible.

It is true that the christians are sometimes called angels. But we cannot always understand it, when reading of angels, as meaning the believing. There are also other angels of which it is written: "Who maketh his angels spirits; his ministers a flaming fire," Ps. 104: 4; 103: 20; Heb. 1: 7. With these angels Christ will come, as Paul says, "The Lord Jesus shall be revealed from heaven with his mighty angels, in flaming fire, taking vengeance on them that know not God, and that obey not the gospel of our Lord Jesus Christ," 2 Thess. 1: 7, 8. These angels will be the reapers who, at the end of the world, that is, in the day of judgment, will root up all tares and cast them into the lake of fire. Until that time the tares will be left among the good seed; let none think that we should root up the tares now, or that we should now separate the goats from the sheep. "When the son of man shall come in his glory, and all the holy angels with him, then shall he sit upon the throne of his glory: And before him shall be gathered all nations; and he shall separate them one from another, as a shepherd divideth his sheep from the goats: and he shall set the sheep on his right hand, but the goats on the left," Matt. 25: 31—33.

These words are as clear as the sun, yet some do not understand them, so that we may well say unto them, "O foolish Galations, who hath bewitched you, that ye should not obey the truth, before whose eyes Jesus Christ hath been evidently set forth, crucified among you? This only would I learn of you." Whether you are baptized on the sword or on the cross? "Are ye so foolish? having begun in the Spirit, are ye now made perfect by the flesh? Have ye suffered so many things in vain? if it be yet in vain," Gal. 3: 1—4.

What avails it that you have left Egypt if you again look back to Egypt, that is, to darkness, and leave the true light, yea, are desirous after the flesh of Egypt, that is, human doctrine, and are not satisfied with the bread from heaven? Ex. 14: 11; Num. 14: 2.

What does it avail that you are gone away from Pharaoh, if you are slain by Amalek on account of your disobedience; that is, because you fight against the will of the Lord? What does it profit that you have gone through the Red Sea with the children of Israel, if you do not enter with Joshua and Caleb, into the promised land, by firm faith in God's word? And how we are to enter into the promised land, in the eternal kingdom of God, is testified to by Paul and Barnabas, who taught the churches that they had to enter into the kingdom through many tribulations.

Christ has not taken his kingdom with the sword, but he entered it through much suffering. Yet they mean to take it by the sword! O, blindness of man! But thus it must be, that those who will not confess Christ to be their only Shepherd, that they may be pastured by him, will have to eat of the pastures which are trampled upon; and that those who will not draw the clear, crystal water from the fount of the Savior, will have to drink the impure water which the false shepherds have made impure with their feet. And that for the reason, because they have done double evil to the children of Israel. They have forsaken the Lord, the living fountain, and have made fountains of their own which appear beautiful, but they afford no water. Therefore I admonish all beloved brethren, yea, I pray you by the mercy of God our Lord Jesus Christ, to give heed to the word of God, and do not forsake it; for you have seen your Master Christ, with the eye of faith, and you have heard his voice, saying, This is the true way, walk upon it, go neither to the right hand nor to the left.

Let every one of you guard against all strange doctrine, of the sword, of opposition and of other like things, which is nothing short of a fine cover, under which lies hidden an evil serpent which has blown its venom into many. Let every one beware of it!

Let every one behave himself in accordance with the example of the divine word, which he has received from the apostles, by faith and love. Let every one remember that Christ was taught to him in no other way but through tribulation. Abide in it.

For in Christ is an upright being; he is the light of the world; he who follows him shall not walk in darkness, but have the light of life, Ps. 67: 1. God, the Father of our Lord Jesus Christ, be gracious unto us, and enlighten us that we on earth may acknowledge his way, and his salvation among the Gentiles.

All you who have tasted the kindness of the Lord, love him. The Lord upholds the upright. Be of good cheer, and doubt not; for the Lord will strengthen your souls, who patiently wait for his coming. "The Lord reigneth; let the people tremble; he sitteth between the cherubim; let the earth be moved," Ps. 99: 1. This King the Jews scorned, and they became blind.

A KIND ADMONITION OR INSTRUCTION

FROM THE WORD OF GOD,

HOW A CHRISTIAN SHOULD BE DISPOSED; AND CONCERNING THE SHUNNING AND SEPARATION OF THE UNFAITHFUL BRETHREN AND SISTERS, EITHER DECEIVED BY HERETICAL DOCTRINE, OR LEADING A CARNAL, SHAMEFUL LIFE.

BY

MENNO SIMON.

"For other foundation can no man lay than that is laid, which is Jesus Christ," 1 Cor. 3 : 11.

ELKHART, INDIANA:
PUBLISHED BY JOHN F. FUNK AND BROTHER.
1871.

A KIND ADMONITION.

Menno Simon wishes all true brethren and sisters in Jesus Christ the grace and peace of God our heavenly Father, through Jesus Christ his Son, our Lord, who loved us, and cleansed us of our sins by his blood. To him be glory, now and forever, Amen.

Hear, believe, and fulfill God's word, and you shall have everlasting life. Do not judge until you have perused and well understood this.

SINCERELY beloved children in Christ Jesus, you are aware with what diligence, nay, how sincerely I have of late admonished most of you, according to the word of the Lord, by many Scriptures, flowing from a loving, inclined and moved Spirit, as you yourselves have witnessed, I, who seek nothing (of which God is my witness) but alone the salvation of your souls; teaching nothing, desiring nothing, admonishing you to nothing but alone that your most holy faith and works may be powerful and fruitful before God; and that your life and walk may be found before God, before his angels, and before all the world, holy, pure, sober, chaste, temperate, humble, gentle, kind, mild, merciful, righteous, unblamable, in conformity with, and obedient to the gospel of Christ, a shining light, that in all your doings you may express Christ Jesus whom you have put on, if you have rightly put him on, as I trust; and thus show in your life his divine and heavenly image after which you are created, Col. 3; Eph. 4.

You know that I do not desire your money, silver, and carnal gifts, although I may be blamed of it by the infamous, lying world. I beseech all of you, and would with much solicitation, anxiety, tribulation, sighing, weeping, and pains, teach you such faith, love, spirit, conscience and walk that you can stand before the righteous judgment of God, and that in Christ Jesus.

I do not doubt, most beloved brethren, that you well know (if you be born with Christ, of God the Father of the heavenly seed of the divine word), that you must be conformed unto Christ in mind, spirit, courage and will, both in doctrine and life, as Christ Jesus is conformed unto the nature and image of his blessed, heavenly Father, to which he was so conformed that he did nothing but that his Father did, Jn. 5; that he taught nothing but the word of his Father, Jn. 7. In the same manner with those who are begotten of the living, saving word of our beloved Lord Jesus Christ; they are, by virtue of their new birth, so conformed unto Christ, so like unto him, so really implanted into him, so converted into his heavenly nature, that they do not teach nor believe any doctrine but that which conforms unto the doctrine of Christ; do not make use of any religious ceremonies but Christ's ceremonies, which he has taught and commanded in his holy gospel; for how can the natural branches bear fruit different from that of the vine itself of which they budded forth? Jn. 15.

As there is nothing found in Christ Jesus but solely the holiness, wisdom, brightness, righteousness, power, love, peace, mercy, and truth of the Almighty Father, thus you have in the same manner partaken of his being and goodness, because you with him are regenerated and renewed of the same Father.

Behold, brethren, such regenerated and godly minded, live unblamably, even according to the measure of the rule of the holy gospel of Jesus Christ and his apostles. Therefore he kisses them as his beloved, chosen ones, with the mouth of his peace, Cant. 1, and calls them his church, his bride, flesh of his flesh, and bone of his bone, of which he begets, with inexpressible pleasure, by his powerful seed, his holy word, the children of God, the children of the promise, the children of righteousness, the children of truth, and the children of life eternal. But of the Babylonian, Sodomitic, whoring, adulterous, idolatrous, bloody, unbelieving, blind and unclean whore with which they have, for centuries, lived in adultery by the use of wood, stone, gold, silver, bread, wine, false doctrine, and of the very vain, accursed works of their own hands, contrary to Jesus Christ and his holy word, he will never beget them, Rev. 17; 18.

Therefore I admonish all our beloved brethren and sisters in the Lord, so precious as is Christ Jesus to you, never to let it go out of your mind, but ever to remember for what purpose you are called, taught, and baptized. Remember the covenant of the most high God, that into which you voluntarily entered; into which you have voluntarily desired and accepted, being taught by the word of God, and operated upon by the Holy Spirit; and remember that according to the doctrine of Paul, you have voluntarily buried in baptism, all your avarice, uncleanness, pride, hatred, envy, abuse of the sacramental signs, idolatry, gluttony, drunkenness, sensuality, falsehood, deceit, &c., and that you are arisen with Christ Jesus, into newness of life, Rom. 6, if you are rightly arisen with him; which new life is nothing else but righteousness, unblamableness, love, mercifulness, humility, long-suffering, peace, truth, yea, the whole, gentle life which is taught by the gospel, and was found in Christ Jesus.

O, brethren, how far are some of us, alas, yet distant from the evangelical life which is of God! Notwithstanding that they stay out of the other churches, and are outwardly baptized in water, they yet are carnal and devilish minded in all things, thinking perhaps, that christianity consists of outward baptism and the non-attendance of the church. No, beloved, no! I tell you, as truly as the Lord lives, before God avails no outward baptism, nor staying away from the churches, nor supper, nor being persecuted, if we do not obey the commandments of God, 1 Cor. 7; if our faith does not manifest itself in love, and the new creature, as also Christ Jesus says, "Verily, verily, I say unto you, except a man be born again, he can not see the kingdom of God," Jn. 3: 3. At another place he says, "Verily, I say unto you, Except ye be converted and become as little children, ye shall not enter into the kingdom of heaven," Matt. 18: 3. But the regenerated and converted, that is the believing, are rightly baptized in accordance with God's word; for they bury their sins in baptism, and arise with Christ into newness of life, Rom. 6; they are spiritually circumcised with the circumcision of Christ, Col. 2; they put on Christ Jesus; they show by the washing of regeneration that they are born again; for it is a washing of the new birth, Tit. 3.

These regenerated ones use the true Supper; for they proclaim the death of Christ until his coming again, 1 Cor. 11; their pleasure is in the church of the righteous, their works are nothing but brotherly love, one heart, one soul, one spirit. Yea, one undivided body, fruitful, serving, and common in Christ Jesus, which are symbolized by the outward cup, and the outward bread, 1 Cor. 10.

These regenerated ones shun all false doctrine, all idolatry, all improper usage of the sacramental signs in the church or out of the church; they seek only the true teachers who are unblamable both in doctrine and in life; the true religion, as taught and expressed in Christ's word, namely, the dying unto the flesh, Rom. 12; Gal. 5; the service of the afflicted, Matt. 15; the visiting of the widows and orphans; as James says, They seek to keep themselves unblemished and unspotted from the world, Jas. 1. These regenerated ones bear the cross of Christ with gladness of heart, so established in Christ Jesus that they can not be separated from the eternal truth and love of God, by false doctrine, nor by horrible torments, ever remembering their Lord's word, where he says, "Whosoever therefore shall confess me before men, him will I confess also before my Father which is in heaven," Matt. 10: 32.

All their thoughts are chaste, gentle, peaceful, heavenly and of the Holy Spirit; all their words are wisdom, truth, doctrine, admonition in grace, well seasoned, the words of God and words spoken at the right time. They are spirit, and they are life. In short, all their works are love, mercifulness, righteousness, piety, and are done in the fear of the Lord.

Behold, brethren, this is the true nature and mind of the children of God, who are by grace converted in their hearts and with Christ born of God the Father. Therefore I beseech you as my sincerely beloved brethren, by the grace of God, nay I command you with holy Paul, by the Lord Jesus Christ, who at his coming will judge the living and the dead, diligently to observe each other unto salvation, in all becoming ways teaching, instructing, admonishing, reproving, threatening and consoling each other as occasion requires, not otherwise than in accordance with the word of God, and in unfeigned love, that we may all grow up in God, and become united in faith and in the knowledge of the Son of God, into one perfect man, and according to the measure of the gift of Jesus Christ, Eph. 4: 7.

Therefore take heed. If you see your brother sin, then pass not by him, as one that does not prize his soul; but if his fall be curable, from that moment endeavor to raise him up by gentle admonition and brotherly instruction, before you eat, drink, sleep or do any thing else, as one who ardently desires his salvation, lest your poor, erring brother harden and corrupt in his fall, and perish in his sin.

Do not act so unfaithfully as you have hitherto done, as not to make the transgressions of your dying brother or sister known to those within the church before those without; but rather exhort them, and seek by prayer, by words, and by actions to convert him from the error of his way, to save his soul and thus to stop the multiplying of his transgressions, Jas. 5. Take heed, brethren, take heed! that you allow no defamer among you, as Moses taught, Lev. 19, no double, lying, roguish, nor backbiting tongue; and do not consent, lest you fall into the wrath of God. Let every one take heed, how, where, when and what he speaks, lest his tongue blaspheme his God and his neighbor; but always remember the words of Ecclesiasticus, "Honor and shame is in talk, and the tongue of man is his fall," Eccl. 5: 13.

But brethren, if those of years of understanding who were with us, by the urging of the Spirit, baptized in the most holy body of Jesus Christ, which is the church, again withdraw themselves from the body or church of Christ, actuated either by false doctrine or vain, carnal life, no matter whether it be father or mother, sister or brother, husband or wife, son or daughter, or any one else, for God's word applies to all flesh, without respect of person, Acts 10: 34; Rom. 2: 11; Gal. 2; Eph. 6; Col. 3, if he or she do not heed the admonitions of the brethren, which is given with sorrow, tears and a compassionate spirit of love, but continue in their Jewish doctrine, namely, of sword, kingdom, polygamy or the like deceit; again, in the doctrine of the infamous confession, of shamelessness in exposing their persons, and the like unnatural, inhuman actions; again in the doctrine which is opposed to the cross of Christ, such as that uncleanness is pure to the pure, and thus having communion in fruitless works, as the hearing of the preachers of the world, infant baptism, the worldly supper, and the like abominations. Again, continue in drunkenness, avarice, adultery, fornication, unbecoming words, &c., with such have nothing to do, nor eat with them, as Paul has taught and commanded us in plain words, 1 Cor. 5.

But if he affectionately receive the admonitions of his faithful brethren, if he confess his fall, if he be sorry, promise reformation, show signs of penitence, and acknowledge his transgression, then, no matter how he has transgressed, receive him as a returning, beloved brother or sister, but beware, lest he mock his God; for the acceptation of brethren does not avail if we be not accepted of God. Beware, I say, lest his hearing the admonitions, his sorrow, his promise of reformation, and his penitence be not sincere before God; for he searches the hearts and reins, and he knows all inward feignedness and thoughts of men, Jer. 17; Jn. 2; Rom. 8.

If his hearing the admonitions, his sorrow, promise and penitence are not sincere and from his heart, but merely indifferent, feigned, spiritless, hypocritical, just because he does not want to be outwardly thrown out of the communion of the brethren, he is still cut off by Christ, and is a hypocrite in the sight of God. Nor will he be looked upon nor judged by God as being any thing else. For God the righteous Judge does not judge according to the outward appearance, but solely according to the inward intentions of the heart.

Say, beloved, inasmuch as this is the

case, what does it avail to go by the mere name of a christian brother if he have not the inward, evangelical faith, love, and unblamable life of a true brother of Jesus Christ?

Or what does it avail to partake of the Holy Supper of our Lord Jesus Christ with the brethren if we have not the true symbolized fruits of this Supper, namely, the love of the brethren, and the peaceable unity of faith in Christ Jesus? Or does it avail anything outwardly to converse in the communion of the brethren, if we are not inwardly in the communion of our beloved Lord Jesus Christ?

Therefore, brethren, none is cut off by us, or ejected from the communion of the brethren (judge rightly) but those who have already ejected themselves either by false doctrine, or by a blamable life, from Christ and his communion. For we do not wish to eject any, but to accept them; not to cut them off, but to restore them; not to reject, but to win them back; not to afflict, but to console them; not to condemn, but to save them. For this is the true nature of a christian brother. Whosoever renounces evil, be it false doctrine or vain life, and conforms himself to the gospel of Jesus Christ, unto which he is baptized neither shall nor can be ejected or cut off by any of the brethren.

But those whom we cannot raise up and admonish unto repentance by tears, threatening, reproving, or by any other christian services and divine means, we should reluctantly separate from us, sincerely deploring the fall and damnation of such erring brethren, lest we also be deceived and led astray by such false doctrine which eats about itself like a cancer, 2 Tim. 2; lest we corrupt our flesh which is inclined to evil, by the contagion; and that we may thus obey the word of God which commands us to do so; and that thus the separated brother or sister, whom we can not convert by gentle services, may, by means of the separation, be shamed unto repentance, 2 Thess. 2, and acknowledge to what he has come and from what he is fallen. Thus the ban is a great work of love, notwithstanding it is looked upon by the unintelligent as an act of hatred.

Brethren and sisters this separation or ban, so earnestly taught and commanded in the Scriptures by Christ Jesus and his holy apostles was instituted to be practiced for these causes and reasons, first: For false doctrine, Matt. 7; 16; Rom. 16; 2 Tim. 2; 1 Tim. 6; Tit. 3; Phil. 3; 2 Jn. 1; again, for sinful, carnal life, Matt. 18; 1 Cor. 5; 2 Thess. 3; 2 Tim. 3; again, that we should admonish them (understand, those that will be admonished), Matt. 18; Tit. 3. Therefore take heed, and watch your own soul, lest you despise the word of God in this necessary matter of separation, and transgress his ordinances; but that you in every respect practice upon and uphold it with divine wisdom, discretion, gentleness and prudence, in the case of those who have gone aside from the evangelical doctrine or life; not with austerity, nor with cruelty, but rather with gentleness, reluctance, and with sorrow and pity for the diseased members who are not cured, in whose case pains and labor avail nothing, who should be cut off with the knife of the divine word, lest the others be corrupted, and lest the abominable scurvy is imparted to the other sheep. Yea it should be done in such a manner that the erring sister or brother may be made ashamed at heart, and thus be won, as was said above. And in case there be any moving of the Spirit, any spark of life, or any fear of God in such sister or brother, their heart will surely quake and tremble; for by the admonition of the word of God, and by the testimony of his own conscience he will acknowledge that he has cut himself off from the communion of Jesus Christ, by his vain, carnal life, and that he has again entered into the communion of the devil; and that therefore his lot and part shall not be with the blessed souls in heaven, but with the damned in hell unto eternity, unless he convert himself.

May God, the merciful Father, save all his chosen children who have entered into his holy covenant and communion, from such a fearful fall, obduracy, and separation, Amen.

All the apostate sisters and brethren who are offended at and angry with us on account of this open doctrine and practice of the christian ban or separation, will be of-

A KIND ADMONITION.

fended more and more; for whosoever is impure will be rendered still more impure, as the Holy Spirit of the prophecies teaches, Rev. 22. For the word of God is unto the reformation, righteousness, and life of the pious and godly; but unto the lost it is unto offense, unrighteousness and death. What! be angry with us because we obey Scripture in this respect? Let them rather be angry with themselves; for they dare teach and live contrary to the commandment of God. If they want to renounce their heresy, and reform their ungodly life, the heavenly doctrine of our beloved Lord Jesus Christ will not offend them nor make them worse, but rather urge, affright and convert them.

If they, by their apostatic, refractory and carnal hatred, are so deprived of grace and the knowledge of God, and become worse and worse, so that they see death in the eternal life, and darkness in the heavenly light of divine truth, then we can claim to be clear before God and his holy angels, from their sins, obduracy, and eternal death if we do toward them that which the Lord's word has commanded us in regard to this matter. Therefore we desire not to have communion with them, nor lot nor part, unto eternity, so long as they do not sincerely renounce their false doctrine and reform their miserable, accursed, earthly, carnal, and devilish life, to the praise of the Lord. But in case true penitence is found in them, in good faith, as before God who sees all things, then we say, welcome beloved brethren, welcome, beloved sisters, and we sincerely rejoice at the sincere conversion of such brethren and sisters. Yea, we rejoice as one is rejoiced at the restoration of an only Son who was dangerously ill as at the restoration of a lost sheep or penny; and as at the reappearance of a son who was given up as lost, Matt. 18; Luke 15.

Behold, brethren, therefore I will leave every apostate brother to consider why, and wherefore, with what kind of spirit, and with what intention this separation or ban was so diligently practiced, first by Christ Jesus and his apostles and afterward by us who are again placed in their doctrine and practice of all christian doings, as may be easily deduced from the alleged Scriptures.

Well, dear brethren in the Lord, you who are baptized by one Spirit into one body, and have voluntarily entered into the communion of Jesus Christ, and also you who are of a good mind, inasmuch as you must shun the apostatic in accordance with the word of God, therefore, take heed, that while you shun them as diseased, foul and useless members, unfit for the body of Christ, you yourselves may be found to be sound, fit, and fruitful members in Christ Jesus; and that while you shun them as children of darkness and of death, you yourselves may be children of the light and of eternal life, that the righteous sentence of God may not be pronounced against you; take heed, lest you who shun others on account of their evil doing, secretly commit worse things in the sight of God. Take heed, lest you adjudge others of what you yourselves are guilty, Rom. 2. Behold, brethren, thus the ban or separation should be practiced in the house of the Lord, that is, in God's church; nor have they any other weapon unto eternity. Of this I would have written more but defer it to some other time, if it please God.

Now, beloved brethren, take heed, take heed, brethren, this I advise you that there may never be any thoughts in your hearts otherwise than such as are pure, holy, chaste, heavenly, and of the Holy Spirit. "Blessed are the pure in heart; for they shall see God," Matt. 5: 8. "The mouth of the righteous speaketh wisdom and his tongue talketh of judgment," Ps. 37: 30. Let all thy words be as a sworn oath before God and before the world, Matt. 5; Jas. 5. Let all your actions be wrought of God by God, and in God, Jn. 3. Measure all your thoughts, words and actions by the rule of the divine word, that the ungodly defamer who so diligently watches all your words and actions may find nothing which he can truly cast up to you, whereby he can accuse or blame you, as Paul taught and requested the church, in some instances, Eph. 4; 1 Tim. 3; Tit. 2.

It is also the nature of those who are in God, not to sin, as John says, "Whosoever abideth in him (God) sinneth not: whosoever sinneth hath not seen him, neither known him. Little children, let no man deceive you: he that doeth righteousness, is righteous, even as he is righteous. He that committeth sin is of the devil; for the devil sinneth from the beginning. For this purpose the Son of God was manifested, that he might destroy the works of the devil. Whosoever is born of God doth not commit sin: for his seed remaineth in him: and he cannot sin, because he is of God, 1 Jn. 3: 6—9. Therefore I implore and pray you to consider well the nature of the new birth, and examine what it is in reality, namely, the divine nature, and the divine image; of whom it is, that it is of God; from whence it is—from heaven; and what is obtained by it—life eternal. For without the new birth it is merely the nature of earthly Adam, sin, evil, blindness, transgression, devil and eternal death (I speak in regard to those of mature years), whatever we do; but in whomsoever the new birth is, there is also everything godly, wisdom, goodness, light, righteousness, truth, peace, Spirit, Christ, God and life eternal. Therefore the eternal Truth, Christ Jesus, says in plain words, that we must repent and be born again, if we would enter into the kingdom of heaven, Matt. 18; Jn. 3. For the first birth is of the earth, earthly, and inclined to the earth; but the second birth is of heaven, and is heavenly, and inclined to heaven, Jn. 3, that is to say, the birth of earth makes earthly minded and the birth of heaven makes heavenly minded.

If this good and perfect gift of the new birth be given us of the Father of light, by grace, then we become the chosen children of God, Jn. 1; Eph. 1; then we are the true sisters and brethren of Christ, Luke 8; then we are conformed unto Christ, Rom. 8; then we are created after the image of God, Col. 3; Eph. 4; then we have the sign Tau on our foreheads; then the kingdom of God is ours, Luke 18; then we are the bride of Christ, Jn. 3, the church of Christ, Eph. 5, the body of Christ, 1 Cor. 12; Eph. 1. Col. 1; then Christ dwells in our hearts, Eph. 3; then we are led by the Holy Ghost, Rom. 8; we are the chosen generation, the royal priesthood, the holy, begotten people, which is God's own, 1 Pet. 2; then we are the temple of the Lord, 1 Cor. 3; 6; 2 Cor. 6; the spiritual Mount Zion, and the new heavenly Jerusalem, Heb. 12; the spiritual Israel of God, Gal. 6; we are of divine mind and nature; we are delivered from the sentence of the law, Isa. 9; Gal. 5; 1 Tim. 3; yea from hell, sin, devil, and eternal death, Eph. 2; then we have Christ Jesus forever blessed; his word, life, flesh, blood, cross, suffering, bitter death, burial, resurrection, ascension, kingdom and eternal joy, with him, received as a gift from God the Father, Rom. 8. But in case we be not born again (understand, those of understanding age), then we have not such promises.

Therefore, sincerely beloved brethren, partakers of the heavenly calling through Christ Jesus; "Humble yourselves therefore under the mighty hand of God," 1 Pet. 5: 6, and sincerely deny yourselves. Fear God in all your thoughts, words and works, love and serve God and your neighbor; love God above all things created, and your neighbor as yourselves, Matt. 22. Let all your meditations be in the law of the Lord, Ps. 1. Keep God's word; I repeat it, brethren, keep the word of God which has been so often taught you in love, both verbally and in writing.

Let your ardent prayer at all times go up to God, for all men; for emperors, kings, lords, princes, judges, and for all those that are placed in authority, that God may so direct their hearts that we, if it be his blessed will, may lead a peaceable and godly life, 1 Tim. 2: 2.

Be not envious in your hearts and not inconsiderate in your talking about others, whether he be a slanderer, traitor, persecutor, priest or monk, no matter who he be; for they shall receive their reward from God. But ever remember the longsuffering of our beloved Lord Jesus Christ, as also, that we were all foolish and unbelieving, erring, serving divers lusts and desires; we were also naturally, children of the wrath, the same as they are. Willingly obey all human ordinances if they be not against the ordinances of God, 1 Pet. 2. Be liberal in rendering assistance to all the children of God. Receive each other without murmuring, 1 Pet. 4. Let each one work with his own hands, and eat his own bread, if possible, 2 Thess. 3. Shun all manner of idleness and worldly pomp. Take faithful care of each other by admonitions, Heb. 10, as I have verbally admonished you to do before, and now again in this epistle.

Wash the feet of your beloved brethren and sisters who are come to you from a distance, tired. Be not ashamed to do the work of the Lord, but humble yourselves with Christ, before your brethren's feet, that all humility, according to the divine nature, may be found in you, Jn. 13; 1 Tim. 5.

Above all pray for your poor humble servant, whose life is sought with all diligence, that God, the gracious Father, may strengthen him with his Holy Spirit, and save him from the hands of those who so unjustly seek his life, if it be his fatherly will, and if it be not his will, that he may then give him in all tribulation, torture, oppression and death, such heart, mind, wisdom and strength, that he may steadily fulfill the glorious work of God, which is begun in us, by the Holy Ghost, to the praise of the Lord.

O, beloved brethren, fulfill my desire, and finish, as obedient children of God that which I have faithfully taught, admonished and written unto you from the word of God, to your eternal salvation, that you may also be partakers of the glorious crown, hope and joy, in the day of the coming of Christ, 1 Thess. 2. "Not slothful in business; fervent in spirit," Rom. 12:11. Bless God in all his works toward us, and pray him to guide your way, and let all your counsel be in him, Tob. 4. Walk fearlessly in the commandments of the Lord. Go not in any manner beyond the gospel of Christ, Gal. 1. Be firm in the way of the Lord. Overcome the world, the flesh, and the devil by the most holy faith which is in you, 1 Jn. 5. Joyfully serve each other, "In patience possess ye your souls," Luke 21:19. "Be patient in tribulation," Rom. 12:12. Prepare your hearts for the cross of Christ, so that when it comes you may not be terrified with the cowardly.

No more at present, but watch closely all the days of your lives, the unexpected coming of our beloved Lord Jesus Christ, who has made us such dear creatures, bought us with his precious blood, graciously called, enlightened and regenerated us, and who will crown us with the crown of glory, array us in the garment of unblamableness, and give us the gift of eternal life. To him be eternal praise and glory, now and forever, Amen.

Ponder, holy brethren, upon every word which I have written unto you; read it attentively; reflect upon it diligently, understand it rightly, judge spiritually, and live up to it divinely. O, brethren, then my admonition and writing, and your perusal and hearing shall be fruitful.

I pray you with holy Paul, by the grace of God, not to suppress this admonition, nor to lay it away, but to read it to all faithful brethren and sisters in the Lord; as also to all the apostates who are not entirely given up, that they may be won back. Yea, not alone to these, but to all men in or out of the church, who may desire to hear it. The grace of our beloved Lord Jesus Christ be with all true brethren and sisters, Amen.

Again, pray for me and for all your servants in the Lord.

Beware of all doctrine and works which are not conformable to the gospel of Christ. Beware.

May grace and peace remain with all the true children of God, and fellow-laborers of the promise, in the kingdom of Christ.

MENNO SIMON.

A LETTER.

Most beloved in Christ Jesus. Grace and peace. Dear, faithful sister in the Lord. My inmost soul is grieved in your behalf. More so than I can write; for I understand from our beloved brethren, that you can hardly acquiesce in the desire and prayer of the afflicted and pastorless church in regard to your beloved husband. I cannot severely reprove you for your action if I look at it in a carnal, and not in a spiritual light. I also understand from the words of Lenart and Helmicht, that you hoped that Lenart would be excused from serving, by me. Most beloved sister in Christ Jesus, I trust that I, by the grace of God, sincerely love you with divine love in God; and that I am prepared to serve you and all pious people, even, with my blood if so required. But, beloved sister, who am I that I should resist the Holy Spirit? You are aware that not I, but the church, has called him to this service, unknown to me. As the church so imploringly desires him; and as he perhaps can not conscientiously deny them, how could I then oppose it? as I can find nothing in Lenart for which I could scripturally oppose his being called. Dear sister, I am sorry that I can not aid you in this matter; for the sorrow and fear of your flesh pierces my heart as often as I think of it; but above all, we must act in love to God and our brethren. You are called of the Lord, and by the operation of your faith you have committed yourself to the service of Jesus Christ and of your brethren as long as you live; and I trust that you will willingly fulfill it even at the risk of money, possessions and life. You certainly comprehend how needful it is. Therefore, be mindful of the days of your enlightenment, and obediently and resignedly fulfill that which, willingly and without constraint, you have promised the Most High.

O, beloved sister, look at the abandonment and misery of your beloved brethren. The spiritual fathers are become betrayers of souls; the watchmen, blind leaders, and the shepherds, wolves. The walls of Jerusalem are laid waste; the stones of the sanctuary are trampled upon at the corners of every street. Great is the plague of Israel. With Jeremiah and Ezra we may well bitterly sigh and weep, and let our tears flow over our cheeks, nay, our inmost soul must be grieved at the need of our beloved brethren, when we take to heart the very great hungering and thirsting of many pious hearts, the accursed deceiving of evil spirits, and dissensions, sects and all like evils. Inasmuch, then, as the merciful Lord has gifted our beloved brother with his divine knowledge, has enlightened him with his Holy Spirit and gifted him with speech and wisdom, so that the brethren are pleased with him, sincerely love him and desire his talent; and if you, for the sake of your flesh and blood should oppose this and not acquiesce therein, would seem to me as being nothing else than that if you should see your brethren in imminent danger of life, should see them in fire or water, suffering, want and misery, you would not assist them at your own peril. Dear sister, love your brethren as Christ Jesus has loved us. If, for the sake of your brethren, you should be deprived of your property, remember that Christ has, for a time, left the glory of his Almighty Father and the company of angels, that we might obtain an eternal inheritance in heaven. So long as we live we shall have enough of the necessaries of life, if we fear God, depart from evil and do righteously.

Yea, sister, be of good cheer. The eternal Truth has promised us salvation if we seek the kingdom of God and his righteousness. The necessaries of life will be provided for us. If then you are solicitous for your husband's flesh, remember and believe that our life is measured by spans; that life and death are in the hands of the Lord; that not a hair falls from our heads without the will of our Father. He protects us as the apple of his eye.

Elias, David, Daniel, Shadrach, Meshach and Abednego, Peter and Paul, have all evaded the hands of the tyrant, and none could injure a single hair of their heads so long as the appointed day and hour was not come. For so long as the Lord has more pleasure in our life than in our death, they cannot injure us; but when our death is more pleasing to the Lord than our life, we can not escape from their hands. O, beloved sister, if our beloved brother should not serve our brethren, yet he has years ago, already committed himself to danger of death, tribulation, misery, scorn, persecution, anxiety, robbery, water, fire and sword; and if he had not committed himself to the cross by baptism, nay, if he could pass through all cities, countries, and nations unmolested, you know not at what moment he would have to put off the tabernacle of clay and appear before his God. Therefore, beloved, faithful sister, be strong in the Lord; be of good cheer; commend yourself to the Most high God, who holds heaven and earth in his hand; who has given you and your husband body and soul; who has called you in the word of his grace; who has purchased and delivered you with the blood of his blessed Son; who has washed, sanctified and cleansed you with his Holy Spirit. His mercy is above all his works; he knows your going out and coming in; your setting down and rising up. Yea, you were before him before you were formed in your mother's womb; he it is who searches the hearts and reins; he knows what our brethren seek. Beloved sister strengthen your husband, and do not weaken him; for it is required of us that if we love God we should also love our brethren. In short, prove yourself to be to your neighbor what Christ has proven to be to you; for by this only, sure and immutable rule must all christian actions be measured and judged. Behold, worthy, faithful sister, as the church calls our beloved brother to the office and service, I cannot conscientiously interfere; or else I should love flesh, your flesh, more than Christ Jesus my Lord and Savior, and my sincerely beloved brethren.

May the Almighty, merciful Father act in this measure according to his divine pleasure, and guide the heart of my beloved sister so as to be resigned to his holy will. I sincerely thank my beloved sister for the gift of your love you have sent me. The Lord repay you the heavenly riches of eternal glory. My consort greets you with the peace of the Lord. The Lord Jesus Christ be forever with my most beloved friend and sister, Amen.

Your brother in the Lord,
MENNO SIMON.
A. D. 1553.

PROVIDENTIAL DELIVERANCES OF MENNO SIMON.

THE following is an extract from *Book 16 of the Ondergangh der Tyrannen, en Jaerlycksche Geschiedenisse* (Downfall of the Tyrants, and Annual Events) by Peter Jansz Twisck, Pages 1074 and 1075, in which it is shown how wonderfully the Lord preserved Menno Simon, from the cunning artifices of his opponents, as in his divine zeal for the truth, he exhorted all men to true repentance and regeneration.

The daughter of Menno Simon, a praiseworthy woman, in our presence related the following incident: A certain traitor had agreed, without fail for a certain sum of money, to deliver the person of Menno or his head into the hands of his enemies, expecting to apprehend him in one of their meetings; but it so happened that he was not able to accomplish his object, for whenever he arrived at the place where he sought to spy him out, Menno in a providential manner escaped.

At another time this same traitor, in company with an officer or police, as they were in search of Menno, unexpectedly met him as he was going along on the canal, in a small boat. The traitor kept silent until Menno had passed them some distance, and had leaped ashore in order to escape with less peril. Then the traitor cried out, "Behold, the bird has escaped!" The officer chastized him—called him a villian, and demanded why he did not tell of it in time; to which the traitor replied, "I could not speak; for my tongue was bound." The lords were so displeased at this that the traitor, according to his promise, had to forfeit his own head. It is worthy of consideration, how wonderfully God, in this and in other like instances preserves his people, and especially how fearfully he punishes the tyrants.

Menno had to suffer so many dangers, perils and so much misery, that in the memory of the oldest persons it is almost indescribable, and afterwards died a natural death; notwithstanding he often with great zeal and resolution preached, conversed, disputed with, and reproved the priests of Baal, and opposed his opponents openly in their presence, so that a number of his fellow-laborers did not remain faithful under these severe persecutions.

Among other incidents it happened (which I have received as creditable), that Menno came into the priest's church in Eenigenburgh, a village in the north of Holland, after the pastor had performed his services, and conversed with him in Latin about different papistic superstitions, with great boldness, fluency and profoundness, upon which the priest or pastor was greatly surprised, and after he was through with his papal services, he had a long conversation with Menno. Menno often conversed with the priests, and at one time with no little boldness, unknown, entered a cloister, conversed with the Superior, pointed him to repentance, showed him his great folly and such like things.

Although his name, and a description of his clothing, person, &c., was nailed to the church doors, with the certain promise of a hundred, or several hundred guilders to any one who should discover to or deliver him into the hands of his enemies, yet God preserved him from all the designs and cunning devices of his enemies, so that it truly is as he wrote in a letter to the wife of Leonard Bouwensz in which he says, "If you regard the life of your husband, think and believe, that our lives are but as a hand breadth; that both life and death are in the hands of the Lord; that not a hair shall fall from our heads without our heavenly Father's notice; he preserves us as the apple of his eye. Elias, Elisha, David, Daniel, Shadrach, Meshach, and Abednego, Peter and Paul, all escaped the hands of the tyrants, and no one could injure a hair of them, as long as their day and hour had not come, for as long as the merciful Lord has more pleasure in our lives than in our death they shall not be permitted to injure us, but when the Lord shall be more pleased to remove us, then we will not escape their hands."

NOTE 1.—*It is due to the reader, at the conclusion of this work, to say that in the translation of the writings of Menno Simon upon the "Incarnation of Christ," the publishers have taken the liberty to condense and abridge some parts thereof and also, here and there, to leave out such parts as they considered of no importance in the illustration and explanation of the subject, and which were not edifying to the reader. But in no case have they perverted the meaning or purpose of the author. Throughout the entire work they have labored, with the translator and reviewer, conscientiously to give the true sentiments of the writer, that they might be able to present to the reader, as true and faithful a translation as possible, and they hope that the blessing of God may rest upon their efforts, and that a generous public will throw the mantle of charity upon any errors that in any way may have crept into the wrok.* THE PUBLISHERS.

NOTE 2.—*I have carefully read and compared with the original Holland, the entire works of Menno Simon, herewith presented to the public, and do hereby bear testimony that this is a true and faithful translation of the same.* JOSEPH SUMMERS.

INDEX, TO PART II.

A

	PAGE.
Accusations against Menno,	94
A very humble supplication of the poor, despised christians,	107
A letter of consolation to an afflicted widow,	113
A complaint or apology of the despised christians and exiled strangers,	115
A scriptural explanation of Excommunication,	123
Associate not with an apostate after separation,	136
An incontrovertible confession founded on the Holy Scriptures,	139
A confession of the Triune, Eternal and true God, Father, Son, and Holy Ghost,	179, 183
An explanation of christian baptism in the water,	189
Apostles teach baptism as Christ taught it,	210
A letter of caution on discord,	231
A clear confession, concerning Justification, Preachers, Baptism, &c.,	257
A christian, in some cases may deal with an apostate,	279
———Can have no apostate as a regular customer,	ib
A thorough answer to Zylis and Lemmekes concerning Excommunication,	283
A humble and christian Justification, replication, &c.,	297
A scriptural demonstration of the Incarnation of Jesus Christ,	325
An admonition to the Preachers and how they should be minded,	340
A plain and pointed reply to the antichristian doctrine of Martin Micron,	351
Articles, thirty-one presented to the reader,	371
An epistle to Martin Micron,	403
Affirmation,	411
A humble prayer to the reader,	422
A convincing proof, that Jesus Christ is the true, spiritual David, &c.,	425
A kind admonition, concerning shunning and separation,	441
A Letter,	450

B

	PAGE.
Baptism, concerning,	39
———Rhenanus, Cyprian, Erasmus, Zuinglius, Bucer, Oecolampadius, Luther, and others, on infant,	49
Ban, Excommunication or Separation,	69
Baptism,	189, 268
———In the water,	200
———No remission of sins through,	201
———Degenerated in early days,	203
———But one in the water pleasing to God,	204
———How the apostles practiced it in the water,	222
———Applied only to the believing,	227
———Infant,	269
Ban, should husband and wife shun each other on account of,	276
Banned, should we greet one that is?,	277
———Are we allowed to show any charity, love and mercy to the?,	278
———Are we allowed to deal with the?,	279
———Are we allowed to travel with the?,	280
———Who should be,	ib
Ban, a work of love,	446

C

Calling, Preachers,	17
Concerning Baptism,	39
Church of Christ and anti-christ, how to distinguish,	77
———Six signs by which both churches may be known,	81, 83
Concerning some accusations against us,	94
Confession of the learned concerning Christ,	97
Conclusion,	105
Complaint or apology,	117
Confession of the Incarnation,	147
Confutation, reply to the points of defense of John A'Lasco, on the Incarnation,	154
Confession of the Triune God,	179, 183

INDEX, TO PART II.

	PAGE.
Christian Baptism,	195
Children, Little, have a peculiar promise,	226
Confession of Justification, &c.,	261
Conclusion to Justification, Baptism, &c.,	275
——To questions and answers,	280
——To a humble defense,	322
——To admonition to preachers,	348
——To unscriptural confessions,	380
Confession, Micron's,	388
Concerning the two natures in Christ,	391
Conclusion to reply to Martin Micron,	399
Christ is King of kings, convincing proof,	425

D

Doctrine of the church of Christ and anti-christ,	83
Description of a true preacher,	120
Difference between willful sin, and error,	277
Discussion, How the English came into with us,	355
——Between Herman and Myself,	356
——Partial narration of, by Micron,	359
——Micron's confession during our second,	364
Deliverances of Menno Simon,	451

E

Excommunication, Ban or Separation,	69
——Scriptural explanation of,	123
——Not to shun before,	136
——Questions and answers,	276
Error, difference between willful sin and,	277

F

Fourteen inconsistencies which must result and follow from the foundation and doctrine of our opponents,	381
Foundation and faith of our opponents concerning Christ Jesus, &c.,	383
Faith and doctrine in Jesus Christ,	384

G

Gellius Faber, Reply to,	1
Genesis 3: 15,	386
God the Father is the true Father of the whole Christ his Son,	393

H

How to distinguish between the church of Christ, and anti-christ,	77
Hearing the Preachers,	264
Holy Supper, The Lord's,	270
Husband and wife, should they shun each other on account of the ban,	276
How the English came into discussion with us,	355
Herman, Discussion with,	356
How and what Micron confessed during our second discussion,	364
How Christ is the Son of God, is also the son of Abraham and David, &c.,	389
How the divine word, in the fullness of time according to the Scriptures, was made flesh,	396

I

Incarnation, Menno's confession of,	147
——Scriptural references upon,	168
——Conclusion of,	177
Israelites received their remission of sins through the promise,	201
Incarnation, Confession of,	330
——Thirty-one Articles on,	371
——Forty-five Unscriptural confessions, of	379
Inconsistencies, Fourteen,	381

J

John A'Lasco, Reply to concerning the Incarnation,	143
Justification,	261
John Van Leyden, Testimony against,	427

L

Letter addressed to an afflicted widow,	113
——Of Caution on discord,	231
——Another,	232
——From Menno Simon to Margaret, wife of Rein Edes,	401
Leyden, John Van, Testimony against,	427
Letter,	450

M

Menno Simon's confession of the Incarnation,	147
——Salutation,	190
——Reasons for teaching and writing,	233
Martin Micron, Reply to,	355
——Confession, in his narrative, that Christ is the Son of God and man,	388
——An epistle to,	403
Menno Simon, Summary punishment to those who would injure him,	419
——Willing to enter into discussion,	423
——Providential deliverances of,	

O

Our confession,	147
Oaths,	272, 409

P

Preface, Reply to Gellius Faber,	3
Preachers, Their Calling,	17
——Description of a true,	120
Preface to the reply to John A'Lasco,	141
——To the Triune God,	181
——To Menno Simon's Salutation,	191
——To Justification, Baptism, &c.,	259
Preachers, Hearing the,	264

	PAGE.		PAGE.
Preface to Justification, &c.,	298	Salutation, Menno Simon's,	190
——To the Incarnation,	326	Supper of the preachers,	271
——To reply to Martin Micron,	352	Swearing, Oaths,	272, 409
Punishment to those who would injure Menno,	419	Shunning, Is it a command?	276
Prayer to the reader,	422	Shunning and separation,	441

Q

Questions and answers on Shunning, ...276

T

The Lord's Supper, ...64
The Confutation, ...154

R

Reply to Gellius Faber, ...1
——To John A'Lasco, on the Incarnation, ...138
——To Zylis and Lemmekes, ...283
——To Martin Micron, ...351

Teachings of the holy apostles concerning baptism in the water, ...200
The reason Menno Simon does not cease teaching and writing, ...233
The Lord's Holy Supper, ...270
The Supper of the preachers, ...271
The Swearing of Oaths, ...272
To the reader, ...298
Thirty-one articles presented to the reader, &c., ...371
The foundation and faith of our opponents concerning Christ Jesus, ...383
Testimony against John Van Leyden, ...427

S

Supper, The Lord's, ...64
Separation, Ban or Excommunication, ...69
Signs, six by which the church of Christ and anti-christ may be known, ...81, 83
Shunning does not apply to necessary dealings, ...135
Separation, Not to shun before, ...136
Scriptures, A clear confession of, ...143
Scriptural references upon the Incarnation, ...168

W

Warfare, ...434

Z

Zylis and Lemmekes, reply to, ...283